# ITALIAN·ENGLISH ENGLISH·ITALIAN DICTIONARY

# DIZIONARIO ITALIANO·INGLESE INGLESE·ITALIANO

COLLINS
GEM
DICTIONARY

# ITALIAN·ENGLISH
# ENGLISH·ITALIAN

# ITALIANO·INGLESE
# INGLESE·ITALIANO

**Catherine E. Love**

*new edition*
*nuova edizione*

**Collins**
*London and Glasgow*

**Mondadori**          **Harper & Row**
*Milano*                    *New York*

*first published in this edition 1982*
*revised edition 1989*

© William Collins Sons & Co. Ltd. 1982, 1989

**latest reprint 1990**

ISBN 0 00 458546 1

---

*contributors/hanno collaborato*
Paolo L. Rossi, Davina M. Chaplin,
Fernando Villa, Ennio Bilucaglia,
Michela Clari

*editorial staff/segreteria di redazione*
Elspeth Anderson, Angela Campbell,
Susan Dunsmore, Vivian Marr

*The first edition of this book was prepared for*
*Collins Publishers by*
LEXUS

---

*Printed in Great Britain*
**Collins Clear-Type Press**

| INTRODUZIONE | | INTRODUCTION |
|---|---|---|

Questo dizionario offre a chi deve leggere e comprendere l'inglese una nomenclatura dettagliata e aggiornata, con vocaboli e locuzioni idiomatiche parlate e scritte della lingua inglese contemporanea. Vi figurano anche, in ordine alfabetico, le principali forme irregolari, con un rimando alla forma di base dove si trova la traduzione, così come i più comuni nomi di luogo, le sigle e le abbreviazioni.

The user whose aim is to read and understand Italian will find in this dictionary a comprehensive and up-to-date wordlist including numerous phrases in current use. He will also find listed alphabetically the main irregular forms with a cross-reference to the basic form where a translation is given, as well as some of the most common abbreviations, acronyms and geographical names.

A loro volta, quanti hanno la necessità di esprimersi in inglese trovano in questo dizionario una trattazione chiara ed essenziale di tutti i vocaboli di base, con numerose indicazioni per una esatta traduzione e un uso corretto ed appropriato.

The user who wishes to communicate and to express himself in Italian will find clear and detailed treatment of all the basic words, with numerous indications pointing to the appropriate translation, and helping him to use it correctly.

# ABBREVIAZIONI                    ABBREVIATIONS

| | | |
|---|---|---|
| aggettivo | a | adjective |
| abbreviazione | abbr | abbreviation |
| avverbio | ad | adverb |
| amministrazione | ADMIN | administration |
| aeronautica, viaggi aerei | AER | flying, air travel |
| aggettivo | ag | adjective |
| agricoltura | AGR | agriculture |
| amministrazione | AMM | administration |
| anatomia | ANAT | anatomy |
| architettura | ARCHIT | architecture |
| astronomia, astrologia | ASTR | astronomy, astrology |
| l'automobile | AUT | the motor car and motoring |
| avverbio | av | adverb |
| aeronautica, viaggi aerei | AVIAT | flying, air travel |
| biologia | BIOL | biology |
| botanica | BOT | botany |
| inglese della Gran Bretagna | Brit | British English |
| consonante | C | consonant |
| chimica | CHIM, CHEM | chemistry |
| congiunzione | cj | conjunction |
| familiare (! da evitare) | col(!) | colloquial usage (! particularly offensive) |
| commercio, finanza, banca | COMM | commerce, finance, banking |
| informatica | COMPUT | computers |
| congiunzione | cong | conjunction |
| edilizia | CONSTR | building |
| sostantivo usato come aggettivo, non può essere usato né come attributo, né dopo il sostantivo qualificato | cpd | compound element: noun used as adjective and which cannot follow the noun it qualifies |
| cucina | CUC, CULIN | cookery |
| davanti a | dav | before |
| determinativo: articolo, aggettivo dimostrativo o indefinito etc | det | determiner: article, demonstrative etc |
| diritto | DIR | law |
| economia | ECON | economics |
| edilizia | EDIL | building |
| elettricità, elettronica | ELETTR, ELEC | electricity, electronics |
| esclamazione | escl, excl | exclamation |
| femminile | f | feminine |
| familiare (! da evitare) | fam(!) | colloquial usage (! particularly offensive) |

vi

| ABBREVIAZIONI | | ABBREVIATIONS |
|---|---|---|
| ferrovia | FERR | railways |
| figurato | fig | figurative use |
| fisiologia | FISIOL | physiology |
| fotografia | FOT | photography |
| (verbo inglese) la cui particella è inseparabile dal verbo | fus | (phrasal verb) where the particle cannot be separated from main verb |
| nella maggior parte dei sensi; generalmente | gen | in most or all senses; generally |
| geografia, geologia | GEO | geography, geology |
| geometria | GEOM | geometry |
| impersonale | impers | impersonal |
| informatica | INFORM | computers |
| insegnamento, sistema scolastico e universitario | INS | schooling, schools and universities |
| invariabile | inv | invariable |
| irregolare | irg | irregular |
| grammatica, linguistica | LING | grammar, linguistics |
| maschile | m | masculine |
| matematica | MAT(H) | mathematics |
| termine medico, medicina | MED | medical term, medicine |
| il tempo, meteorologia | METEOR | the weather, meteorology |
| maschile o femminile, secondo il sesso | m/f | either masculine or feminine depending on sex |
| esercito, lingua militare | MIL | military matters |
| musica | MUS | music |
| sostantivo | n | noun |
| nautica | NAUT | sailing, navigation |
| numerale (aggettivo, sostantivo) | num | numeral adjective or noun |
| | o.s. | oneself |
| peggiorativo | peg, pej | derogatory, pejorative |
| fotografia | PHOT | photography |
| fisiologia | PHYSIOL | physiology |
| plurale | pl | plural |
| politica | POL | politics |
| participio passato | pp | past participle |
| preposizione | prep | preposition |
| psicologia, psichiatria | PSIC, PSYCH | psychology, psychiatry |
| tempo passato | pt | past tense |
| sostantivo che non si usa al plurale | q | uncountable noun: not used in the plural |
| qualcosa | qc | |
| qualcuno | qn | |
| religione, liturgia | REL | religions, church service |

vii

# ABBREVIAZIONI

# ABBREVIATIONS

| | | |
|---|---|---|
| sostantivo | s | noun |
| | sb | somebody |
| insegnamento, sistema scolastico e universitario | SCOL | schooling, schools and universities |
| singolare | sg | singular |
| soggetto (grammaticale) | sog | (grammatical) subject |
| | sth | something |
| congiuntivo | sub | subjunctive |
| soggetto (grammaticale) | subj | (grammatical) subject |
| termine tecnico, tecnologia | TECN, TECH | technical term, technology |
| telecomunicazioni | TEL | telecommunications |
| tipografia | TIP | typography, printing |
| televisione | TV | television |
| tipografia | TYP | typography, printing |
| inglese degli Stati Uniti | US | American English |
| vocale | V | vowel |
| verbo | vb | verb |
| verbo o gruppo verbale con funzione intransitiva | vi | verb or phrasal verb used intransitively |
| verbo riflessivo | vr | reflexive verb |
| verbo o gruppo verbale con funzione transitiva | vt | verb or phrasal verb used transitively |
| zoologia | ZOOL | zoology |
| marchio registrato | ® | registered trademark |
| introduce un'equivalenza culturale | ≈ | introduces a cultural equivalent |

viii

# TRASCRIZIONE FONETICA

# PHONETIC TRANSCRIPTION

## CONSONANTS  CONSONANTI

NB The pairing of some vowel sounds only indicates approximate equivalence/La messa in equivalenza di certi suoni indica solo una rassomiglianza approssimativa.

| | | |
|---|---|---|
| *puppy* | p | *padre* |
| *baby* | b | *bambino* |
| *tent* | t | *tutto* |
| *daddy* | d | *dado* |
| cork kiss *chord* | k | *cane che* |
| *gag guess* | g | *gola ghiro* |
| *so rice kiss* | s | *sano* |
| cousin *buzz* | z | *svago esame* |
| *sheep sugar* | ʃ | *scena* |
| pleasure bei*ge* | ʒ | |
| *church* | tʃ | *pece lanciare* |
| *judge general* | dʒ | *giro gioco* |
| *farm raffle* | f | *afa faro* |
| *very rev* | v | *vero bravo* |
| *thin maths* | θ | |
| *that other* | ð | |
| *little ball* | l | *letto ala* |
| | ʎ | *gli* |
| rat brat | r | *rete arco* |
| *mummy comb* | m | *ramo madre* |
| *no ran* | n | *no fumante* |
| | ɲ | *gnomo* |
| *singing bank* | ŋ | |
| *hat reheat* | h | |
| *yet* | j | *buio piacere* |
| *wall bewail* | w | *uomo guaio* |
| *loch* | x | |

## MISCELLANEOUS

* per l'inglese: la "r" finale viene pronunciata se seguita da una vocale.

' precede la sillaba accentata.

## VOWELS  VOCALI

NB p, b, t, d, k, g are not aspirated in Italian/sono seguiti da un'aspirazione in inglese.

| | | |
|---|---|---|
| *heel bead* | iː i | *vino idea* |
| *hit pity* | ɪ | |
| | e | *stella edera* |
| *set tent* | ɛ | *epoca eccetto* |
| *apple bat* | æ a | *mamma amore* |
| after car *calm* | ɑː | |
| *fun cousin* | ʌ | |
| over ab*ove* | ə | |
| *urn fern work* | əː | |
| *wash pot* | ɔ | *rosa occhio* |
| *born cork* | ɔː | |
| | o | *ponte ognuno* |
| *full soot* | u | *utile zucca* |
| *boon lewd* | uː | |

## DIPHTHONGS  DITTONGHI

| | | |
|---|---|---|
| | ɪə | *beer tier* |
| | ɛə | *tear fair there* |
| | eɪ | *date plaice day* |
| | aɪ | *life buy cry* |
| | au | *owl foul now* |
| | əu | *low no* |
| | ɔɪ | *boil boy oily* |
| | uə | *poor tour* |

## VARIE

ix

# ITALIAN PRONUNCIATION

## VOWELS

Where the vowel e or the vowel o appears in a stressed syllable it can be either open [ɛ], [ɔ] or closed [e], [o]. As the open or closed pronunciation of these vowels is subject to regional variation, the distinction is of little importance to the user of this dictionary. Phonetic transcription for headwords containing these vowels will therefore only appear where other pronunciation difficulties are present.

## CONSONANTS

c before "e" or "i" is pronounced *tch*.

ch is pronounced like the "k" in "kit".

g before "e" or "i" is pronounced like the "j" in "jet".

gh is pronounced like the "g" in "get".

gl before "e" or "i" is normally pronounced like the "lli" in "million", and in a few cases only like the "gl" in "glove".

gn is pronounced like the "ny" in "canyon".

sc before "e" or "i" is pronounced *sh*.

z is pronounced like the "ts" in "stetson", or like the "d's" in "bird's-eye".

Headwords containing the above consonants and consonant groups have been given full phonetic transcription in this dictionary.

NB All double written consonants in Italian are fully sounded: eg. the *tt* in "tutto" is pronounced as in "ha*t* trick".

# ITALIANO - INGLESE
# ITALIAN - ENGLISH
## A

---
*PAROLA CHIAVE*

---

**a** *prep* (*a* + *il* = **al**, *a* + *lo* = **allo**, *a* + *l'* = **all'**, *a* + *la* = **alla**, *a* + *i* = **ai**, *a* + *gli* = **agli**, *a* + *le* = **alle**) **1** (*stato in luogo*) at; (: *in*) in; essere alla stazione to be at the station; essere ~ casa/~ scuola/~ Roma to be at home/at school/in Rome; è ~ 10 km da qui it's 10 km from here, it's 10 km away

**2** (*moto a luogo*) to); andare ~ casa/~ scuola to go home/to school

**3** (*tempo*) at; (*epoca, stagione*) in; alle cinque at five (o'clock); ~ mezzanotte/Natale at midnight/ Christmas; **al mattino** in the morning; ~ **maggio/primavera** in May/ spring; ~ **cinquant'anni** at fifty (years of age); ~ **domani!** see you tomorrow!

**4** (*complemento di termine*) to); dare qc ~ qn to give sth to sb

**5** (*mezzo, modo*) with, by; ~ **piedi/ cavallo** on foot/horseback; **fatto** ~ **mano** made by hand, handmade; **una barca** ~ **motore** a motorboat; ~ **uno** ~ **uno** one by one; **all'italiana** the Italian way, in the Italian fashion

**6** (*rapporto* **a**, per; (: *con prezzi*) at; prendo 500.000 lire al mese I get 500,000 lire a per month; pagato ~ ore paid by the hour; vendere qc ~ 500 lire il chilo to sell sth at 500 lire a o per kilo.

**a'bate** *sm* abbot.

**abbacchi'ato, a** [abbak'kjato] *ag* downhearted, in low spirits.

**abbagli'ante** [abbaʎ'ʎante] *ag* dazzling; **accendere gli** ~**i** to put one's headlights on full (*Brit*) o high (*US*)

beam.

**abbagli'are** [abbaʎ'ʎare] *vt* to dazzle; (*illudere*) to delude; (*fig*) *sm* blunder; **prendere un abbaglio** to blunder, make a blunder.

**abbai'are** *vi* to bark.

**abba'ino** *sm* dormer window; (*soffitta*) attic room.

**abbando'nare** *vt* to leave, abandon, desert; (*trascurare*) to neglect; (*rinunciare a*) to abandon, give up; ~**rsi** *vr* to let o.s. go; ~**rsi a** (*ricordi, vizio*) to give o.s. up to; **abban'dono** *sm* abandoning; neglecting; (*stato*) abandonment; neglect; (*SPORT*) withdrawal; (*fig*) abandon; **in abbandono** (*edificio, giardino*) neglected.

**abbas'sare** *vt* to lower; (*radio*) to turn down; ~**rsi** *vr* (*chinarsi*) to stoop; (*livello, sole*) to go down; (*fig: umiliarsi*) to demean o.s.; ~ **i fari** (*AUT*) to dip o dim (*US*) one's lights.

**ab'basso** *escl:* ~ **il re!** down with the king!

**abbas'tanza** [abbas'tantsa] *av* (*a sufficienza*) enough; (*alquanto*) quite, rather, fairly; **non è** ~ **furbo** he's not shrewd enough; **un vino** ~ **dolce** quite a sweet wine, a fairly sweet wine; **averne** ~ **di qn/qc** to have had enough of sb/sth.

**ab'battere** *vt* (*muro, casa*) to pull down; (*ostacolo*) to knock down; (*albero*) to fell; (: *sog: vento*) to bring down; (*bestie da macello*) to slaughter; (*cane, cavallo*) to destroy, put down; (*selvaggina, aereo*) to shoot down; (*fig: sog: malattia, disgrazia*) to lay low; ~**rsi** *vr* (*avvilirsi*) to lose heart; **abbat'tuto, a** *ag* (*fig*) despondent, depressed.

**abba'zia** [abbat'tsia] *sf* abbey.

**abbece'dario** [abbetʃe'darjo] *sm* primer.

**abbel'lire** *vt* to make beautiful; (*ornare*) to embellish.

**abbeve'rare** *vt* to water; ~rsi *vr* to drink.

**'abbi, 'abbia, abbi'amo, 'abbiano, abbi'ate** *forme del vb* avere.

**abbicci** [abbit'tʃi] *sm inv* alphabet; (*sillabario*) primer; (*fig*) rudiments *pl*.

**abbi'ente** *ag* well-to-do, well-off.

**abbi'etto, a** *ag* = **abietto**.

**abbiglia'mento** [abbiʎʎa'mento] *sm* dress *q*; (*indumenti*) clothes *pl*; (*industria*) clothing industry.

**abbigli'are** [abbiʎ'ʎare] *vt* to dress up.

**abbi'nare** *vt*: ~ (a) to combine (with).

**abbindo'lare** *vt* (*fig*) to cheat, trick.

**abbocca'mento** *sm* talks *pl*, meeting.

**abboc'care** *vt* (*tubi, canali*) to connect, join up // *vi* (*pesce*) to bite; (*tubi*) to join; ~ (all'amo) (*fig*) to swallow the bait.

**abboc'cato, a** *ag* (*vino*) sweetish.

**abbona'mento** *sm* subscription; (*alle ferrovie etc*) season ticket; **fare l'~** to take out a subscription (*o* season ticket).

**abbo'narsi** *vr*: ~ **a un giornale** to take out a subscription to a newspaper; ~ **al teatro/ai ferrovie** to take out a season ticket for the theatre/the train; **abbo'nato, a** *smf* subscriber; season-ticket holder.

**abbon'dante** *ag* abundant, plentiful; (*giacca*) roomy.

**abbon'danza** [abbon'dantsa] *sf* abundance; plenty.

**abbon'dare** *vi* to abound, be plentiful; ~ **in** *o* **di** to be full of, abound in.

**abbor'dabile** *ag* (*persona*) approachable; (*prezzo*) reasonable.

**abbor'dare** *vt* (*nave*) to board;

(*persona*) to approach; (*argomento*) to tackle; ~ **una curva** to take a bend.

**abbotto'nare** *vt* to button up, do up.

**abboz'zare** [abbot'tsare] *vt* to sketch, outline; (*SCULTURA*) to rough-hew; ~ **un sorriso** to give a hint of a smile; **ab'bozzo** *sm* sketch, outline; (*DIR*) draft.

**abbracci'are** [abbrat'tʃare] *vt* to embrace; (*persona*) to hug, embrace; (*professione*) to take up; (*contenere*) to include; ~rsi *vr* to hug *o* embrace (one another); **ab'braccio** *sm* hug, embrace.

**abbreviazi'one** [abbrevjat'tsjone] *sf* abbreviation.

**abbron'zante** [abbron'dzante] *ag* tanning, sun *cpd*.

**abbron'zare** [abbron'dzare] *vt* (*pelle*) to tan; (*metalli*) to bronze; ~rsi *vr* to tan, get a tan; **abbronza'tura** *sf* tan, suntan.

**abbrusto'lire** *vt* (*pane*) to toast; (*caffè*) to roast.

**abbru'tire** *vt* to exhaust; to degrade.

**abbu'ono** *sm* (*COMM*) allowance, discount; (*SPORT*) handicap.

**abdi'care** *vi* to abdicate; ~ **a** to give up, renounce.

**aberrazi'one** [aberrat'tsjone] *sf* aberration.

**a'bete** *sm* fir (tree); ~ **rosso** spruce.

**abi'etto, a** *ag* despicable, abject.

**'abile** *ag* (*idoneo*): ~ (a qc/a fare qc) fit (for sth/to do sth); (*capace*) able; (*astuto*) clever; (*accorto*) skilful; ~ **al servizio militare** fit for military service; **abilità** *sf inv* ability; cleverness; skill.

**abili'tato, a** *ag* qualified; (*TEL*) which has an outside line; **abilitazi'one** *sf* qualification.

**a'bisso** *sm* abyss, gulf.

**abi'tacolo** *sm* (*AER*) cockpit; (*AUT*) inside; (*: di camion*) cab.

**abi'tante** *smf* inhabitant.

**abi'tare** *vt* to live in, dwell in // *vi*:

~ **in campagna/a Roma** to live in the country/in Rome; **abi'tato, a** *ag* inhabited; lived in // *sm* (*anche*: **centro abitato**) built-up area; **abitazi'one** *sf* residence; house.

'**abito** *sm* dress *q*; (*da uomo*) suit; (*da donna*) dress; (*abitudine, disposizione, REL*) habit; ~**i** *smpl* clothes; **in** ~ **da sera** in evening dress.

**abitu'ale** *ag* usual, habitual; (*cliente*) regular.

**abitu'are** *vt*: ~ **qn** a to get sb used *o* accustomed to; ~**rsi** a to get used to, accustom o.s. to.

**abitudi'nario, a** *ag* of fixed habits // *smf* regular customer.

**abi'tudine** *sf* habit; **aver l'**~ **di fare qc** to be in the habit of doing sth; **d'**~ usually; **per** ~ from *o* out of habit.

**abo'lire** *vt* to abolish; (*DIR*) to repeal.

**abomi'nevole** *ag* abominable.

**abo'rigeno** [abo'ridʒeno] *sm* aborigine.

**abor'rire** *vt* to abhor, detest.

**abor'tire** *vi* (*MED*: *accidentalmente*) to miscarry, have a miscarriage; (: *deliberatamente*) to have an abortion; (*fig*) to miscarry, fail; **a'borto** *sm* miscarriage; abortion; (*fig*) freak.

**abrasi'one** *sf* abrasion; **abra'sivo, a** *ag*, *sm* abrasive.

**abro'gare** *vt* to repeal, abrogate.

**A'bruzzo** *sm*: **l'**~, **gli** ~**i** the Abruzzi.

'**abside** *sf* apse.

**a'bulico, a, ci, che** *ag* lacking in will power.

**abu'sare** *vi*: ~ **di** to abuse, misuse; (*alcool*) to take to excess; (*approfittare, violare*) to take advantage of; **a'buso** *sm* abuse, misuse; excessive use.

**a.C.** *ad abbr* (= *avanti Cristo*) B.C.

'**acca** *sf* letter H; **non capire un'**~ not to understand a thing.

**acca'demia** *sf* (*società*) learned

society; (*scuola*: *d'arte, militare*) academy; **acca'demico, a, ci, che** *ag* academic // *sm* academician.

**acca'dere** *vb impers* to happen, occur; **acca'duto** *sm*: **raccontare l'accaduto** to describe what has happened.

**accalappi'are** *vt* to catch; (*fig*) to trick, dupe.

**accal'care** *vt* to crowd, throng.

**accal'darsi** *vr* to grow hot.

**accalo'rarsi** *vr* (*fig*) to get excited.

**accampa'mento** *sm* camp.

**accam'pare** *vt* to encamp; (*fig*) to put forward, advance; ~**rsi** *vr* to camp.

**accani'mento** *sm* fury; (*tenacia*) tenacity, perseverance.

**acca'nirsi** *vr* (*inferire*) to rage; (*ostinarsi*) to persist; **acca'nito, a** *ag* (*odio, gelosia*) fierce, bitter; (*lavoratore*) assiduous, dogged; (*fumatore*) inveterate.

**ac'canto** *av* near, nearby; ~ **a** *prep* near, beside, close to.

**accanto'nare** *vt* (*problema*) to shelve; (*somma*) to set aside.

**accapar'rare** *vt* (*COMM*) to corner, buy up; (*versare una caparra*) to pay a deposit on; ~**rsi qc** (*fig*: *simpatia, voti*) to secure sth (for o.s.).

**accapigli'arsi** [akkapiʎ'ʎarsi] *vr* to come to blows; (*fig*) to quarrel.

**accap'patoio** *sm* bathrobe.

**accappo'nare** *vi*: **far** ~ **la pelle a qn** (*fig*) to bring sb out in goosepimples.

**accarez'zare** [akkaret'tsare] *vt* to caress, stroke, fondle; (*fig*) to toy with.

**acca'sarsi** *vr* to set up house; to get married.

**accasci'arsi** [akkaʃ'ʃarsi] *vr* to collapse; (*fig*) to lose heart.

**accat'tone, a** *smf* beggar.

**accaval'lare** *vt* (*gambe*) to cross; ~**rsi** *vr* (*sovrapporsi*) to overlap; (*addensarsi*) to gather.

**acce'care** [attʃe'kare] *vt* to blind // *vi* to go blind.

**ac'cedere** [at'tʃedere] vi: ~ a to enter; (richiesta) to grant, accede to.

**accele'rare** [attʃele'rare] vt to speed up // vi (AUT) to accelerate; ~ **il passo** to quicken one's pace; **accele'rato** sm (FERR) slow train; **accelera'tore** sm (AUT) accelerator; **accelerazi'one** sf acceleration.

**ac'cendere** [at'tʃendere] vt (fuoco, sigaretta) to light; (luce, televisione) to put o switch o turn on; (AUT: motore) to switch on; (COMM: conto) to open; (fig: suscitare) to inflame, stir up; ~**rsi** vr (luce) to come o go on; (legna) to catch fire, ignite; **accen'dino** sm, **accendi'sigaro** sm (cigarette) lighter.

**accen'nare** [attʃen'nare] vt to indicate, point out; (MUS) to pick out the notes of; to hum // vi: ~ a (fig: alludere a) to hint at; (: far atto di) to make as if; ~ **un saluto** (con la mano) to make as if to wave; (col capo) to half nod; **accenna a piovere** it looks as if it's going to rain.

**ac'cenno** [at'tʃenno] sm (cenno) sign; nod; (allusione) hint.

**accensi'one** [attʃen'sjone] sf (vedi accendere) lighting; switching on; opening; (AUT) ignition.

**accen'tare** [attʃen'tare] vt (parlando) to stress; (scrivendo) to accent.

**ac'cento** [at'tʃento] sm accent; (FONETICA, fig) stress; (inflessione) tone (of voice).

**accen'trare** [attʃen'trare] vt to centralize.

**accentu'are** [attʃentu'are] vt to stress, emphasize; ~**rsi** vr to become more noticeable.

**accerchi'are** [attʃer'kjare] vt to surround, encircle.

**accerta'mento** [attʃerta'mento] sm check; assessment.

**accer'tare** [attʃer'tare] vt to ascertain; (verificare) to check;

(reddito) to assess; ~**rsi** vr: ~**rsi (di)** to make sure (of).

**ac'ceso, a** [at'tʃeso] pp di **accendere** // ag lit; on; open; (colore) bright.

**acces'sibile** [attʃes'sibile] ag (luogo) accessible; (persona) approachable; (prezzo) reasonable; (idea): ~ **a qn** within the reach of sb.

**ac'cesso** [at'tʃɛsso] sm (anche IN-FORM) access; (MED) attack, fit; (impulso violento) fit, outburst.

**acces'sorio, a** [attʃes'sɔrjo] ag secondary, of secondary importance; ~**i** smpl accessories.

**ac'cetta** [at'tʃetta] sf hatchet.

**accet'tabile** [attʃet'tabile] ag acceptable.

**accet'tare** [attʃet'tare] vt to accept; ~ **di fare** qc to agree to do sth; **accettazi'one** sf acceptance; (locale di servizio pubblico) reception; **accettazione bagagli** (AER) check-in (desk).

**ac'cetto, a** [at'tʃetto] ag: (ben) ~ welcome; (persona) well-liked.

**accezi'one** [attʃet'tsjone] sf meaning.

**acchiap'pare** [akkjap'pare] vt to catch.

**acci'acco, chi** [at'tʃakko] sm ailment.

**acciaie'ria** [attʃaje'ria] sf steelworks sg.

**acci'aio** [at'tʃajo] sm steel.

**acciden'tale** [attʃiden'tale] ag accidental.

**acciden'tato, a** [attʃiden'tato] ag (terreno etc) uneven.

**acci'dente** [attʃi'dɛnte] sm (caso imprevisto) accident; (disgrazia) mishap; **non si capisce un** ~ it's as clear as mud; ~**!** (fam: per rabbia) damn (it)!; (: per meraviglia) good heavens!

**accigli'ato, a** [attʃiʎ'ʎato] ag frowning.

**ac'cingersi** [at'tʃindʒersi] vr: ~ **a fare** to be about to do.

**acciuf'fare** [attʃuf'fare] vt to seize,

catch.

**acci'uga, ghe** [at'tʃuga] *sf* anchovy.

**accla'mare** *vt* (*applaudire*) to applaud; (*eleggere*) to acclaim; **acclamazi'one** *sf* applause; acclamation.

**acclima'tare** *vt* to acclimatize; ~rsi *vr* to become acclimatized.

**ac'cludere** *vt* to enclose; **ac'cluso, a** *pp di* **accludere** // *ag* enclosed.

**accocco'larsi** *vr* to crouch.

**accogli'ente** [akkoʎ'ʎɛnte] *ag* welcoming, friendly; **accogli'enza** *sf* reception; welcome.

**ac'cogliere** [ak'kɔʎʎere] *vt* (*ricevere*) to receive; (*dare il benvenuto*) to welcome; (*approvare*) to agree to, accept; (*contenere*) to hold, accommodate.

**accol'lato, a** *ag* (*vestito*) highnecked.

**accoltel'lare** *vt* to knife, stab.

**ac'colto, a** *pp di* **accogliere**.

**accoman'dita** *sf* (*DIR*) limited partnership.

**accomia'tare** *vt* to dismiss; ~rsi *vr*: ~rsi (da) to take one's leave (of).

**accomoda'mento** *sm* agreement, settlement.

**accomo'dante** *ag* accommodating.

**accomo'dare** *vt* (*aggiustare*) to repair, mend; (*riordinare*) to tidy; (*conciliare*) to settle; ~rsi *vr* (*sedersi*) to sit down; s'accomodi! (*venga avanti*) come in!; (*si sieda*) take a seat!

**accompagna'mento** [akkompaɲ-ɲa'mento] *sm* (*MUS*) accompaniment.

**accompa'gnare** [akkompaɲ'ɲare] *vt* to accompany, come *o* go with; (*MUS*) to accompany; (*unire*) to couple; ~ la porta to close the door gently.

**accomu'nare** *vt* to pool, share; (*avvicinare*) to unite.

**acconcia'tura** [akkontʃa'tura] *sf* hairstyle.

**accondi'scendere** [akkondiʃ-

'ʃendere] *vi*: ~ a to agree *o* consent to; **accondi'sceso, a** *pp di* **accondiscendere**.

**acconsen'tire** *vi*: ~ (a) to agree *o* consent (to).

**acconten'tare** *vt* to satisfy; ~rsi di to be satisfied with, content o.s. with.

**ac'conto** *sm* part payment; pagare una somma in ~ to pay a sum of money as a deposit.

**accoppia'mento** *sm* coupling, pairing off; mating; (*TECN*) coupling.

**accoppi'are** *vt* to couple, pair off; (*BIOL*) to mate; ~rsi *vr* to pair off; to mate.

**accorci'are** [akkor'tʃare] *vt* to shorten; ~rsi *vr* to become shorter.

**accor'dare** *vt* to reconcile; (*colori*) to match; (*MUS*) to tune; (*LING*): ~ qc con qc to make sth agree with sth; (*DIR*) to grant; ~rsi *vr* to agree, come to an agreement; (*colori*) to match.

**ac'cordo** *sm* agreement; (*armonia*) harmony; (*MUS*) chord; essere d'~ to agree; andare d'~ to get on well together; d'~! all right!, agreed!

**ac'corgersi** [ak'kɔrdʒersi] *vr*: ~ di to notice; (*fig*) to realize; **accorgi'mento** *sm* shrewdness *q*; (*espediente*) trick, device.

**ac'correre** *vi* to run up.

**ac'corto, a** *pp di* **accorgersi** // *ag* shrewd; stare ~ to be on one's guard.

**accos'tare** *vt* (*avvicinare*): ~ qc a to bring sth near to, put sth near to; (*avvicinarsi a*) to approach; (*socchiudere: imposte*) to half-close; (: *porta*) to leave ajar // *vi* (*NAUT*) to come alongside; ~rsi a to draw near, approach; (*fig*) to support.

**accovacci'arsi** [akkovat'tʃarsi] *vr* to crouch.

**accoz'zaglia** [akkot'tsaʎʎa] *sf* (*peg: di idee, oggetti*) jumble, hotchpotch; (: *di persone*) odd assortment.

**accredi'tare** *vt* (*notizia*) to confirm the truth of; (*COMM*) to credit;

(*diplomatico*) to accredit; ~**rsi** *vr* (*fig*) to gain credit.

ac'crescere [ak'kreʃʃere] *vt* to increase; ~**rsi** *vr* to increase, grow; accresci'tivo, a *ag*, *sm* (*LING*) augmentative; accresci'uto, a *pp di* accrescere.

accucci'arsi [akkut'tʃarsi] *vr* (*cane*) to lie down.

accu'dire *vt* (*anche*: *vi*: ~ a) to attend to.

accumu'lare *vt* to accumulate.

accura'tezza [akkura'tettsa] *sf* care; accuracy.

accu'rato, a *ag* (*diligente*) careful; (*preciso*) accurate.

ac'cusa *sf* accusation; (*DIR*) charge; la pubblica ~ the prosecution.

accu'sare *vt*: ~ qn di qc to accuse sb of sth; (*DIR*) to charge sb with sth; ~ ricevuta di (*COMM*) to acknowledge receipt of.

accu'sato, a *smf* accused; defendant.

accusa'tore, 'trice *smf* accuser // *sm* (*DIR*) prosecutor.

a'cerbo, a [a'tʃɛrbo] *ag* bitter; (*frutta*) sour, unripe; (*persona*) immature.

'acero ['atʃero] *sm* maple.

a'cerrimo, a [a'tʃɛrrimo] *ag* very fierce.

a'ceto [a'tʃeto] *sm* vinegar.

ace'tone [atʃe'tone] *sm* nail varnish remover.

A.C.I. ['atʃi] *sigla m* (= Automobile Club d'Italia) ≈ A.A.

'acido, a ['atʃido] *ag* (*sapore*) acid, sour; (*CHIM*) acid // *sm* (*CHIM*) acid.

'acino ['atʃino] *sm* berry; ~ d'uva grape.

'acne *sf* acne.

'acqua *sf* water; (*pioggia*) rain; ~e *sfpl* waters; fare ~ (*NAUT*) to leak, take in water; ~ in bocca! mum's the word!; ~ corrente running water; ~ dolce fresh water; ~ minerale mineral water; ~ potabile drinking water; ~ salata salt water; ~ tonica tonic water.

acqua'forte, *pl* acque'forti *sf* etching.

a'cquaio *sm* sink.

acqua'ragia [akkwa'radʒa] *sf* turpentine.

a'cquario *sm* aquarium; (*dello zodiaco*): A~ Aquarius.

acqua'santa *sf* holy water.

ac'quatico, a, ci, che *ag* aquatic; (*sport, sci*) water *cpd*.

acqua'vite *sf* brandy.

acquaz'zone [akkwat'tsone] *sm* cloudburst, heavy shower.

acque'dotto *sm* aqueduct; waterworks *pl*, water system.

'acqueo, a *ag*: vapore ~ water vapour.

acque'rello *sm* watercolour.

acquie'tare *vt* to appease; (*dolore*) to ease; ~**rsi** *vr* to calm down.

acqui'rente *smf* purchaser, buyer.

acqui'sire *vt* to acquire.

acquis'tare *vt* to purchase, buy; (*fig*) to gain; a'cquisto *sm* purchase; fare acquisti to go shopping.

acqui'trino *sm* bog, marsh.

acquo'lina *sf*: far venire l'~ in bocca a qn to make sb's mouth water.

ac'quoso, a *ag* watery.

'acre *ag* acrid, pungent; (*fig*) harsh, biting.

a'crobata, i, e *smf* acrobat.

acu'ire *vt* to sharpen.

a'culeo *sm* (*ZOOL*) sting; (*BOT*) prickle.

a'cume *sm* acumen, perspicacity.

a'custica *sf* (*scienza*) acoustics *sg*; (*di una sala*) acoustics *pl*.

a'cuto, a *ag* (*appuntito*) sharp, pointed; (*suono, voce*) shrill, piercing; (*MAT, LING, MED*) acute; (*MUS*) high-pitched; (*fig*: *dolore, desiderio*) intense; (: *perspicace*) acute, keen.

ad *prep* (*dav V*) = a.

adagi'are [ada'dʒare] *vt* to lay o set down carefully; ~**rsi** *vr* to lie down, stretch out.

**a'dagio** [a'dadʒo] av slowly // sm (MUS) adagio; (proverbio) adage, saying.

**adatta'mento** sm adaptation.

**adat'tare** vt to adapt; (sistemare) to fit; ~rsi (a) (ambiente, tempi) to adapt (to); (essere adatto) to be suitable (for).

**a'datto, a** ag: ~ (a) suitable (for), right (for).

**addebi'tare** vt: ~ qc a qn to debit sb with sth; (fig: incolpare) to blame sb for sth.

**ad'debito** sm (COMM) debit.

**adden'sare** vt to thicken; ~rsi vr to thicken; (nuvole) to gather.

**adden'tare** vt to bite into.

**adden'trarsi** vr: ~ in to penetrate, go into.

**ad'dentro** av (fig): essere molto ~ in qc to be well-versed in sth.

**addestra'mento** sm training.

**addes'trare** vt, ~rsi vr to train; ~rsi in qc to practise (Brit) o practice (US) sth.

**ad'detto, a** ag: ~ a (persona) assigned to; (oggetto) intended for // sm employee; (funzionario) attaché; ~ commerciale/stampa commercial/press attaché; gli ~i ai lavori authorized personnel; (fig) those in the know.

**addì** av (AMM): ~ 3 luglio 1978 on the 3rd of July 1978 (Brit), on July 3rd 1978 (US).

**addi'accio** [ad'djattʃo] sm (MIL) bivouac; **dormire all'**~ to sleep in the open.

**addi'etro** av (indietro) behind; (nel passato, prima) before, ago.

**ad'dio** sm, escl goodbye, farewell.

**addirit'tura** av (veramente) really, absolutely; (perfino) even; (direttamente) directly, right away.

**ad'dirsi** vr: ~ a to suit, be suitable for.

**addi'tare** vt to point out; (fig) to expose.

**addi'tivo** sm additive.

**addizio'nare** [addittsjo'nare] vt (MAT) to add (up); **addizi'one** sf addition.

**addob'bare** vt to decorate; **ad'dobbo** sm decoration.

**addol'cire** [addol'tʃire] vt (caffè etc) to sweeten; (acqua, fig: carattere) to soften; ~rsi vr (fig) to mellow, soften.

**addolo'rare** vt to pain, grieve; ~rsi (per) to be distressed (by).

**ad'dome** sm abdomen.

**addomesti'care** vt to tame.

**addormen'tare** vt to put to sleep; ~rsi vr to fall asleep, go to sleep.

**addos'sare** vt (appoggiare): ~ qc a qc to lean sth against sth; (fig): ~ la colpa a qn to lay the blame on sb; ~rsi qc (responsabilità etc) to shoulder sth.

**ad'dosso** av (sulla persona) on; mettersi ~ il cappotto to put one's coat on; **non ho soldi** ~ I don't have any money on me; ~ a prep (sopra) on; (molto vicino) right next to; **stare** ~ a qn (fig) to breathe down sb's neck; **dare** ~ a qn (fig) to attack sb.

**ad'durre** vt (DIR) to produce; (citare) to cite.

**adegu'are** vt: ~ qc a to adjust o relate sth to; ~rsi vr to adapt; **adegu'ato, a** ag adequate; (conveniente) suitable; (equo) fair.

**a'dempiere, adem'pire** vt to fulfil, carry out.

**ade'rente** ag adhesive; (vestito) close-fitting // smf follower; **ade'renza** sf adhesion; **aderenze** sfpl (fig) connections, contacts.

**ade'rire** vi (stare attaccato) to adhere, stick; ~ a to adhere to, stick to; (fig: società, partito) to join; (: opinione) to support; (richiesta) to agree to.

**ades'care** vt to lure, entice.

**adesi'one** sf adhesion; (fig) agreement, acceptance; **ade'sivo, a** ag, sm adhesive.

**a'desso** av (ora) now; (or ora, poco

*fa)* just now; *(tra poco)* any moment now.

**adia'cente** [adja'tʃɛnte] *ag* adjacent.

**adi'bire** *vt (usare):* ~ qc a to turn sth into.

**adi'rarsi** *vr:* ~ (con *o* contro qn per qc) to get angry (with sb over sth).

**a'dire** *vt (DIR):* ~ le vie legali to take legal proceedings.

**'adito** *sm:* dare ~ a to give rise to.

**adocchi'are** [adok'kjare] *vt (scorgere)* to catch sight of; *(occhieggiare)* to eye.

**adole'scente** [adoleʃ'ʃɛnte] *ag, sm/f* adolescent; **adole'scenza** *sf* adolescence.

**adope'rare** *vt* to use; **~rsi** *vr* to strive; **~rsi per qn/qc** to do one's best for sb/sth.

**ado'rare** *vt* to adore; *(REL)* to adore, worship.

**adot'tare** *vt* to adopt; *(decisione, provvedimenti)* to pass; **adot'tivo, a** *ag (genitori)* adoptive; *(figlio, patria)* adopted; **adozi'one** *sf* adoption.

**adri'atico, a, ci, che** *ag* Adriatic // *sm:* l'A~, il mare A~ the Adriatic, the Adriatic Sea.

**adu'lare** *vt* to adulate, flatter.

**adulte'rare** *vt* to adulterate.

**adul'terio** *sm* adultery.

**a'dulto, a** *ag* adult; *(fig)* mature // *sm* adult, grown-up.

**adu'nanza** [adu'nantsa] *sf* assembly, meeting.

**adu'nare** *vt,* **~rsi** *vr* to assemble, gather; **adu'nata** *sf (MIL)* parade, muster.

**a'dunco, a, chi, che** *ag* hooked.

**a'ereo, a** *ag* air cpd; *(radice)* aerial // *sm* aerial; *(aeroplano)* plane; ~ a **reazione** jet (plane); **ae'robica** *sf* aerobics *sg;* **aerodi'namico, a, ci, che** *ag* aerodynamic; *(affusolato)* streamlined // *sf* aerodynamics *sg;* **aero'nautica** *sf (scienza)* aeronautics *sg;* **aeronautica militare** air force; **aero'plano** *sm* (aero)plane *(Brit)*, (air)plane *(US);* **aero'porto**

*sm* airport; **aero'sol** *sm inv* aerosol.

**'afa** *sf* sultriness.

**af'fabile** *ag* affable.

**affaccen'darsi** [affattʃen'darsi] *vr:* ~ **intorno a** qc to busy o.s. with sth.

**affacci'arsi** [affat'tʃarsi] *vr:* ~ (a) to appear (at).

**affa'mato, a** *ag* starving; *(fig):* ~ **(di)** eager (for).

**affan'nare** *vt* to leave breathless; *(fig)* to worry; **~rsi** *vr:* **~rsi per** qn/qc to worry about sb/sth; **af'fanno** *sm* breathlessness; *(fig)* anxiety, worry; **affan'noso, a** *ag (respiro)* difficult; *(fig)* troubled, anxious.

**af'fare** *sm (faccenda)* matter, affair; *(COMM)* piece of business, (business) deal; *(occasione)* bargain; *(DIR)* case; *(fam: cosa)* thing; **~i smpl** *(COMM)* business; **A~i esteri** Foreign Secretary *(Brit)*, Secretary of State *(US);* **affa'rista, i** *sm* profiteer, unscrupulous business-man.

**affasci'nante** [affaʃʃi'nante] *ag* fascinating.

**affasci'nare** [affaʃʃi'nare] *vt* to bewitch; *(fig)* to charm, fascinate.

**affati'care** *vt* to tire; **~rsi** *vr (durar fatica)* to tire o.s. out.

**af'fatto** *av* completely; **non** ... ~ not ... at all; **niente** ~ not at all.

**affer'mare** *vt (dichiarare)* to main-tain, affirm; **~rsi** *vr* to assert o.s., make one's name known; **affermazi'one** *sf* affirmation, asser-tion; *(successo)* achievement.

**affer'rare** *vt* to seize, grasp; *(fig: idea)* to grasp; **~rsi** *vr:* **~rsi a** to cling to.

**affet'tare** *vt (tagliare a fette)* to slice; *(ostentare)* to affect; **affet'tato, a** *ag* sliced; affected // *sm* sliced cold meat.

**affet'tivo, a** *ag* emotional, affective.

**af'fetto** *sm* affection; **affettu'oso, a** *ag* affectionate.

**affezio'narsi** [affettsjo'narsi] *vr:* ~ a to grow fond of.

**affezi'one** *sf* (*affetto*) affection; (*MED*) ailment, disorder.

**affian'care** *vt* to place side by side; (*MIL*) to flank; (*fig*) to support; ~ qc a qc to place sth next to o beside sth; ~rsi a qn to stand beside sb.

**affia'tarsi** *vr* to get on well together.

**affibbi'are** *vt* (*fig: dare*) to give.

**affida'mento** *sm* (*DIR: di bambino*) custody; (*fiducia*): **fare ~ su** qn to rely on sb; **non dà nessun ~** he's not to be trusted.

**affi'dare** *vt*: ~ qc o qn a qn to entrust sth *o* sb to sb; ~**rsi** *vr*: ~**rsi a** to place one's trust in.

**affievo'lirsi** *vr* to grow weak.

**af'figgere** [af'fiddʒere] *vt* to stick up, post up.

**affi'lare** *vt* to sharpen.

**affili'are** *vt* to affiliate; ~**rsi** *vr*: ~**rsi a** to become affiliated to.

**affi'nare** *vt* to sharpen.

**affinché** [affin'ke] *cong* in order that, so that.

**af'fine** *ag* similar; **affinità** *sf inv* affinity.

**affio'rare** *vi* to emerge.

**affissi'one** *sf* billposting.

**af'fisso, a** *pp di* **affiggere** // *sm* bill, poster; (*LING*) affix.

**affit'tare** *vt* (*dare in affitto*) to let, rent (out); (*prendere in affitto*) to rent; **af'fitto** *sm* rent; (*contratto*) lease.

**af'fliggere** [af'fliddʒere] *vt* to torment; ~**rsi** (*di*) to grieve; **af'flitto, a** *pp di* **affliggere**; **afflizi'one** *sf* distress, torment.

**afflosci'arsi** [affloʃ'farsi] *vr* to go limp; (*frutta*) to go soft.

**afflu'ente** *sm* tributary; **afflu'enza** *sf* flow; (*di persone*) crowd.

**afflu'ire** *vi* to flow; (*fig: merci, persone*) to pour in; **af'flusso** *sm* influx.

**affo'gare** *vt, vi* to drown; ~**rsi** *vr* to drown; (*deliberatamente*) to drown o.s.

**affol'lare** *vt*, ~**rsi** *vr* to crowd; **affol'lato, a** *ag* crowded.

**affon'dare** *vt* to sink.

**affran'care** *vt* to free, liberate; (*AMM*) to redeem; (*lettera*) to stamp; (: *meccanicamente*) to frank (*Brit*), meter (*US*); ~**rsi** *vr* to free o.s.; **affranca'tura** *sf* (*di francobollo*) stamping; franking (*Brit*), metering (*US*); (*tassa di spedizione*) postage.

**af'franto, a** *ag* (*esausto*) worn out; (*abbattuto*) overcome.

**af'fresco, schi** *sm* fresco.

**affret'tare** *vt* to quicken, speed up; ~**rsi** *vr* to hurry; ~**rsi a fare** qc to hurry *o* hasten to do sth.

**affron'tare** *vt* (*pericolo etc*) to face; (*assalire: nemico*) to confront; ~**rsi** *vr* (*reciproco*) to come to blows.

**af'fronto** *sm* affront, insult.

**affumi'care** *vt* to fill with smoke; to blacken with smoke; (*alimenti*) to smoke.

**affuso'lato, a** *ag* tapering.

**a'foso, a** *ag* sultry, close.

**'Africa** *sf*: **l'~** Africa; **afri'cano, a** *ag, sm/f* African.

**afrodi'siaco, a, ci, che** *ag, sm* aphrodisiac.

**a'genda** [a'dʒenda] *sf* diary.

**a'gente** [a'dʒente] *sm* agent; ~ **di cambio** stockbroker; ~ **di polizia** police officer; **agen'zia** *sf* agency; (*succursale*) branch; **agenzia di collocamento** employment agency; **agenzia immobiliare** estate agent's (office) (*Brit*), real estate office (*US*); **agenzia pubblicitaria/viaggi** advertising/travel agency.

**agevo'lare** [adʒevo'lare] *vt* to facilitate, make easy.

**a'gevole** [a'dʒevole] *ag* easy; (*strada*) smooth.

**agganci'are** [aggan'tʃare] *vt* to hook up; (*FERR*) to couple.

**ag'geggio** [ad'dʒeddʒo] *sm* gadget, contraption.

**agget'tivo** [addʒet'tivo] *sm* adjective.

**agghiacci'ante** [aggjat'tʃante] *ag* (*fig*) chilling.

**agghin'darsi** [aggin'darsi] $vr$ to deck o.s. out.

**aggior'nare** [addʒor'nare] $vt$ (opera, manuale) to bring up-to-date; (seduta etc) to postpone; **~rsi** $vr$ to bring (o keep) o.s. up-to-date; **aggior'nato, a** $ag$ up-to-date.

**aggi'rare** [addʒi'rare] $vt$ to go round; (fig: ingannare) to trick; **~rsi** $vr$ to wander about; **il prezzo s'aggira sul milione** the price is around the million mark.

**aggiudi'care** [addʒudi'kare] $vt$ to award; (all'asta) to knock down; **~rsi** $qc$ to win sth.

**ag'giungere** [ad'dʒundʒere] $vt$ to add; **aggi'unto, a** $pp$ $di$ **aggiungere** // (assistente) $cpd$ // $sm$ assistant // $sf$ addition; **sindaco aggiunto** deputy mayor.

**aggius'tare** [addʒus'tare] $vt$ (accomodare) to mend, repair; (riassettare) to adjust; (fig: lite) to settle; **~rsi** $vr$ (arrangiarsi) to make do; (con senso reciproco) to come to an agreement.

**agglome'rato** $sm$ (di rocce) conglomerate; (di legno) chipboard; **~ urbano** built-up area.

**aggrap'parsi** $vr$: **~ a** to cling to.

**aggra'vare** $vt$ (aumentare) to increase; (appesantire: anche fig) to weigh down, make heavy; (fig: pena) to make worse; **~rsi** $vr$ (fig) to worsen, become worse.

**aggrazi'ato, a** [aggrat'tsjato] $ag$ graceful.

**aggre'dire** $vt$ to attack, assault.

**aggre'gare** $vt$: **~ qn a qc** to admit sb to sth; **~rsi** $vr$ to join; **~rsi a** to join, become a member of; **aggre'gato, a** $ag$ associated // $sm$ aggregate; **aggregato urbano** built-up area.

**aggressi'one** $sf$ aggression; (atto) attack, assault.

**aggres'sivo, a** $ag$ aggressive.

**aggrot'tare** $vt$: **~ le sopracciglia** to frown.

**aggrovigli'are** [aggroviʎ'ʎare] $vt$ to

tangle; **~rsi** $vr$ (fig) to become complicated.

**agguan'tare** $vt$ to catch, seize.

**aggu'ato** $sm$ trap; (imboscata) ambush; **tendere un ~ a qn** to set a trap for sb.

**agguer'rito, a** $ag$ fierce.

**agi'ato, a** [a'dʒato] $ag$ (vita) easy; (persona) well-off, well-to-do.

**'agile** ['adʒile] $ag$ agile, nimble; **agilità** $sf$ agility, nimbleness.

**'agio** ['adʒo] $sm$ ease, comfort; **~i** $smpl$ comforts; **mettersi a proprio ~** to make o.s. at home o comfortable.

**a'gire** [a'dʒire] $vi$ to act; (esercitare un'azione) to take effect; (TECN) to work, function; **~ contro qn** (DIR) to take action against sb.

**agi'tare** [adʒi'tare] $vt$ (bottiglia) to shake; (mano, fazzoletto) to wave; (fig: turbare) to disturb; (: incitare) to stir (up); (: dibattere) to discuss; **~rsi** $vr$ (mare) to be rough; (malato, dormitore) to toss and turn; (bambino) to fidget; (emozionarsi) to get upset; (POL) to agitate; **agi'tato, a** $ag$ rough; restless; fidgety; upset, perturbed; **agitazi'one** $sf$ agitation; (POL) unrest, agitation; **mettere in agitazione qn** to upset o distress sb.

**'agli** ['aʎʎi] prep + det vedi **a**.

**'aglio** ['aʎʎo] $sm$ garlic.

**a'gnello** [aɲ'ɲello] $sm$ lamb.

**'ago, pl aghi** $sm$ needle.

**ago'nia** $sf$ agony.

**ago'nistico, a, ci, che** $ag$ athletic; (fig) competitive.

**agoniz'zare** [agonid'dzare] $vi$ to be dying.

**agopun'tura** $sf$ acupuncture.

**a'gosto** $sm$ August.

**a'grario, a** $ag$ agrarian, agricultural; (riforma) land $cpd$ // $sf$ agriculture.

**a'gricolo, a** $ag$ agricultural, farm $cpd$; **agricol'tore** $sm$ farmer; **agricol'tura** $sf$ agriculture, farming.

**agri'foglio** [agri'fɔʎʎo] $sm$ holly.

**agrimen'sore** sm land surveyor.

**agritu'rismo** sm farm holidays pl.

**'agro,** a ag sour, sharp; **~dolce** ag bittersweet; (salsa) sweet and sour.

**a'grume** sm (spesso al pl: pianta) citrus; (: frutto) citrus fruit.

**aguz'zare** [agut'tsare] vt to sharpen; ~ gli orecchi to prick up one's ears.

**a'guzzo, a** [a'guttso] ag sharp.

**'ai** prep + det vedi **a**.

**'Aia** sf: l'~ the Hague.

**'aia** sf threshing-floor.

**ai'rone** sm heron.

**aiu'ola** sf flower bed.

**aiu'tante** smif assistant // sm (MIL) adjutant; (NAUT) master-at-arms; ~ di campo aide-de-camp.

**aiu'tare** vt to help; ~ qn a (fare) to help sb (to do).

**ai'uto** sm help, assistance, aid; (aiutante) assistant; venire in ~ di qn to come to sb's aid; ~ chirurgo assistant surgeon.

**aiz'zare** [ait'tsare] vt to incite; ~ i cani contro qn to set the dogs on sb.

**al** prep + det vedi **a**.

**'ala,** pl **'ali** sf wing; fare ~ to fall back, make way; ~ destra/sinistra (SPORT) right/left wing.

**a'lacre** ag quick, brisk.

**a'lano** sm Great Dane.

**a'lare** ag wing cpd.

**'alba** sf dawn.

**Alba'nia** sf: l'~ Albania.

**al'batro** sm albatross.

**albeggi'are** [albed'dʒare] vi, vb impers to dawn.

**albera'tura** sf (NAUT) masts pl.

**alberghi'ero, a** [alber'gjero] ag hotel cpd.

**al'bergo, ghi** sm hotel; ~ della gioventù youth hostel.

**'albero** sm tree; (NAUT) mast; (TECN) shaft; ~ genealogico family tree; ~ a gomiti crankshaft; ~ di Natale Christmas tree; ~ maestro mainmast; ~ di trasmissione transmission shaft.

**albi'cocca, che** sf apricot; **albi'cocco, chi** sm apricot tree.

**'albo** sm (registro) register, roll; (AMM) notice board.

**'album** sm album; ~ da disegno sketch book.

**al'bume** sm albumen.

**'alce** [altʃe] sm elk.

**al'colico, a, ci, che** ag alcoholic // sm alcoholic drink.

**alcoliz'zato, a** [alcolid'dzato] smif alcoholic.

**'alcool** sm alcohol; **alco'olico** etc vedi **alcolico** etc.

**al'cuno, a** det (dav sm: **alcun** + C, V, **alcuno** + s impura, gn, pn, ps, x, z; dav sf: **alcuna** + C, **alcun'** + V) (nessuno): **non** ... ~ no, not any; **~i(e)** det pl, pronome pl some, a few; **non c'è ~a fretta** there's no hurry, there isn't any hurry; **senza alcun riguardo** without any consideration.

**aldilà** sm: l'~ the after-life.

**a'letta** sf (TECN) fin; tab.

**alfa'beto** sm alphabet.

**alfi'ere** sm standard-bearer; (MIL) ensign; (SCACCHI) bishop.

**al'fine** av finally, in the end.

**'alga, ghe** sf seaweed q, alga.

**'algebra** ['aldʒebra] sf algebra.

**Alge'ria** [aldʒe'ria] sf: l'~ Algeria.

**ali'ante** sm (AER) glider.

**'alibi** sm inv alibi.

**a'lice** [a'litʃe] sf anchovy.

**alie'nare** vt (DIR) to alienate, transfer; (rendere ostile) to alienate; **~rsi qn** to alienate sb; **alie'nato, a** ag alienated; transferred; (fuor di senno) insane // sm lunatic, insane person; **alienazi'one** sf alienation; transfer; insanity.

**ali'eno, a** ag (avverso): ~ **(da)** opposed (to), averse (to) // smif alien.

**alimen'tare** vt to feed; to supply; (fig) to sustain // ag food cpd; **~i** smpl foodstuffs; (anche: **negozio di ~i**) grocer's shop; **alimentazi'one** sf feeding; supplying; sustaining; (gli alimenti) diet.

**ali'mento** *sm* food; ~**i** *smpl* food *sg*; (*DIR*) alimony.

**a'liquota** *sf* share; (*d'imposta*) rate.

**alis'cafo** *sm* hydrofoil.

**'alito** *sm* breath.

**all.** *abbr* (= *allegato*) encl.

**'alla** *prep* + *det vedi* **a**.

**allacci'are** [allat'tʃare] *vt* (*scarpe*) to tie, lace (up); (*cintura*) to do up, fasten; (*due località*) to link; (*luce, gas*) to connect; (*amicizia*) to form.

**alla'gare** *vt, ~rsi vr* to flood.

**allar'gare** *vt* to widen; (*vestito*) to let out; (*aprire*) to open; (*fig: dilatare*) to extend.

**allar'mare** *vt* to alarm.

**al'larme** *sm* alarm; ~ **aereo** air-raid warning.

**allar'mismo** *sm* scaremongering.

**allat'tare** *vt* to feed.

**'alle** *prep* + *det vedi* **a**.

**alle'anza** [alle'antsa] *sf* alliance.

**alle'arsi** *vr* to form an alliance; **alle'ato, a** *ag* allied // *sm/f* ally.

**alle'gare** *vt* (*accludere*) to enclose; (*DIR: citare*) to cite, adduce; (*denti*) to set on edge; **alle'gato, a** *ag* enclosed // *sm* enclosure; **in allegato** enclosed.

**allegge'rire** [alleddʒe'rire] *vt* to lighten, make lighter; (*fig: sofferenza*) to alleviate, lessen; (: *lavoro, tasse*) to reduce.

**alle'gria** *sf* gaiety, cheerfulness.

**al'legro, a** *ag* cheerful, merry; (*un po' brillo*) merry, tipsy; (*vivace: colore*) bright // *sm* (*MUS*) allegro.

**allena'mento** *sm* training.

**alle'nare** *vt, ~rsi vr* to train; **allena'tore** *sm* (*SPORT*) trainer, coach.

**allen'tare** *vt* to slacken; (*disciplina*) to relax; ~**rsi** *vr* to become slack; (*ingranaggio*) to work loose.

**aller'gia** [aller'dʒia] *sf* allergy; **al'lergico, a, ci, che** *ag* allergic.

**alles'tire** *vt* (*cena*) to prepare; (*esercito, nave*) to equip, fit out; (*spettacolo*) to stage.

**allet'tare** *vt* to lure, entice.

**alleva'mento** *sm* breeding, rearing; (*luogo*) stock farm.

**alle'vare** *vt* (*animale*) to breed, rear; (*bambino*) to bring up.

**allevi'are** *vt* to alleviate.

**alli'bire** *vi* to be astounded.

**allibra'tore** *sm* bookmaker.

**allie'tare** *vt* to cheer up, gladden.

**alli'evo** *sm* pupil; (*apprendista*) apprentice; (*MIL*) cadet.

**alliga'tore** *sm* alligator.

**alline'are** *vt* (*persone, cose*) to line up; (*TIP*) to align; (*fig: economia, salari*) to adjust, align; ~**rsi** *vr* to line up; (*fig: a idee*): ~**rsi a** to come into line with.

**'allo** *prep* + *det vedi* **a**.

**al'locco, a, chi, che** *sm* tawny owl // *sm/f* oaf.

**allocuzi'one** [allokut'tsjone] *sf* address, solemn speech.

**a'lodola** *sf* (sky)lark.

**allogi'are** [allod'dʒare] *vt* to accommodate // *vi* to live; **al'loggio** *sm* lodging, accommodation (*Brit*), accommodations (*US*); (*appartamento*) flat (*Brit*), apartment (*US*).

**allontana'mento** *sm* removal; dismissal.

**allonta'nare** *vt* to send away, send off; (*impiegato*) to dismiss; (*pericolo*) to avert, remove; (*estraniare*) to alienate; ~**rsi** *vr* ~**rsi (da)** to go away (from); (*estraniarsi*) to become estranged (from).

**al'lora** *av* (*in quel momento*) then // *cong* (*in questo caso*) well then; (*dunque*) well then, so; **la gente d'~** people then *o* in those days; **da ~ in poi** from then on.

**allor'ché** [allor'ke] *cong* (*formale*) when, as soon as.

**al'loro** *sm* laurel.

**al'luce** [al'lutʃe] *sm* big toe.

**alluci'nante** [allutʃi'nante] *ag* awful; (*fam*) amazing.

**allucinazi'one** [allutʃinat'tsjone] *sf* hallucination.

**al'ludere** *vi*: ~ **a** to allude to, hint

at.

**allu'minio** *sm* aluminium (*Brit*), aluminum (*US*).

**allun'gare** *vt* to lengthen; (*distendere*) to prolong, extend; (*diluire*) to water down; ~**rsi** *vr* to lengthen; (*ragazzo*) to stretch, grow taller; (*sdraiarsi*) to lie down, stretch out.

**allusi'one** *sf* hint, allusion.

**alluvi'one** *sf* flood.

**al'meno** *av* at least // *cong:* (**se**) ~ if only; (**se**) ~ **piovesse!** if only it would rain!

**a'lone** *sm* halo.

**'Alpi** *sfpl:* **le** ~ the Alps.

**alpi'nismo** *sm* mountaineering, climbing; **alpi'nista, i, e** *sm/f* mountaineer, climber.

**al'pino, a** *ag* Alpine; mountain *cpd*.

**al'quanto** *av* rather, a little; ~, **a** *det* a certain amount of, some // *pronome* a certain amount; some; ~**i(e)** *det pl*, *pronome pl* several, quite a few.

**alt** *escl* halt!, stop! // *sm:* **dare l'**~ to call a halt.

**alta'lena** *sf* (*a funi*) swing; (*in bilico, anche fig*) seesaw.

**al'tare** *sm* altar.

**alte'rare** *vt* to alter, change; (*cibo*) to adulterate; (*registro*) to falsify; (*persona*) to irritate; ~**rsi** *vr* to alter; (*cibo*) to go bad; (*persona*) to lose one's temper.

**al'terco, chi** *sm* altercation, wrangle.

**alter'nare** *vt*, ~**rsi** *vr* to alternate; **alterna'tivo, a** *ag* alternative // *sf* alternative; **alter'nato, a** *ag* alternate; (*ELETTR*) alternating; **alterna'tore** *sm* alternator.

**al'terno, a** *ag* alternate; **a giorni** ~**i** on alternate days, every other day.

**al'tezza** [al'tettsa] *sf* height; width, breadth; depth; pitch; (*GEO*) latitude; (*titolo*) highness; (*fig: nobiltà*) greatness; **essere all'**~ **di** to be on a level with; (*fig*) to be up to o equal to; **altez'zoso, a** *ag*

haughty.

**al'ticcio, a, ci, ce** [al'tittʃo] *ag* tipsy.

**altipi'ano** *sm* = **altopiano**.

**alti'tudine** *sf* altitude.

**'alto, a** *ag* high; (*persona*) tall; (*tessuto*) wide, broad; (*sonno, acqua*) deep; (*suono*) high(-pitched); (*GEO*) upper; (*: settentrionale*) northern // *sm* top (part) // *av* high; (*parlare*) aloud, loudly; **il palazzo è** ~ **20 metri** the building is 20 metres high; **il tessuto è** ~ **70 cm** the material is 70 cm wide; **ad** ~**a voce** aloud; **a notte** ~**a** in the dead of night; **in** ~ up, upwards; at the top; **dall'**~ **in** o **al basso** up and down; **degli** ~**i e bassi** (*fig*) ups and downs; ~**a fedeltà** high fidelity, hi-fi; ~**a moda** haute couture.

**alto'forno** *sm* blast furnace.

**altolo'cato, a** *ag* of high rank, highly placed.

**altopar'lante** *sm* loudspeaker.

**altopi'ano** *sm*, *pl* **altipiani** plateau, upland plain.

**altret'tanto, a** *ag*, *pronome* as much; (*pl*) as many // *av* equally; **tanti auguri!** — **grazie,** ~ all the best! — thank you, the same to you.

**'altri** *pronome inv* (*qualcuno*) somebody; (*: in espressioni negative*) anybody; (*un'altra persona*) another (person).

**altri'menti** *av* otherwise.

┌─────────────────┐
│ *PAROLA CHIAVE* │
└─────────────────┘

**'altro, a** ◆ *det* **1** (*diverso*) other, different; **questa è un'**~**a cosa** that's another o a different thing

**2** (*supplementare*) other; **prendi un** ~ **cioccolatino** have another chocolate; **hai avuto** ~**e notizie?** have you had any more o any other news?

**3** (*nel tempo*): **l'**~ **giorno** the other day; **l'altr'anno** last year; **l'**~ **ieri** the day before yesterday; **domani l'**~ the day after tomorrow; **quest'**~ **mese** next month

**4: d'~a parte** on the other hand
◆ *pronome* **1** (*persona, cosa diversa o supplementare*): **un ~, un'~a** another (one); **lo farà un ~** someone else will do it; **~i(e)** others; **gli ~i** (*la gente*) others, other people; **l'uno e l'~** both (of them); others **l'un l'~** to help one another; **da un giorno all'~** from day to day; (*nel giro di 24 ore*) from one day to the next; (*da un momento all'altro*) any day now

**2** (*sostantivato: solo maschile*) something else; (*: in espressioni interrogative*) anything else; **non ho ~ da dire** I have nothing else o I don't have anything else to say; **più che ~** above all; **se non ~** at least; **tra l'~** among other things; **ci mancherebbe ~!** that's all we need!; **non faccio ~ che lavorare** I do nothing but work; **contento? — ~ che!** are you pleased? — and how!; *vedi* **senza, noialtri, voialtri, tutto.**

**al'tronde** *av*: **d'~** on the other hand.

**al'trove** *av* elsewhere, somewhere else.

**al'trui** *ag inv* other people's // *sm*: **l'~** other people's belongings *pl*.

**altru'ista, i, e** *ag* altruistic.

**al'tura** *sf* (*rialto*) height, high ground; (*alto mare*) open sea; **pesca d'~** deep-sea fishing.

**a'lunno, a** *sm/f* pupil.

**alve'are** *sm* hive.

**'alveo** *sm* riverbed.

**al'zare** [al'tsare] *vt* to raise, lift; (*issare*) to hoist; (*costruire*) to build, erect; **~rsi** *vr* to rise; (*dal letto*) to get up; (*crescere*) to grow tall (*o* taller); **~ le spalle** to shrug one's shoulders; **~rsi in piedi** to stand up, get to one's feet; **al'zata** *sf* lifting, raising; **un'alzata di spalle** a shrug.

**a'mabile** *ag* lovable; (*vino*) sweet.

**a'maca, che** *sf* hammock.

**amalga'mare** *vt*, **~rsi** *vr* to

amalgamate.

**a'mante** *ag*: **~ di** (*musica etc*) fond of // *sm/f* lover/mistress.

**a'mare** *vt* to love; (*amico, musica, sport*) to like.

**amareggi'ato, a** [amared'dʒato] *ag* upset, saddened.

**ama'rena** *sf* sour black cherry.

**ama'rezza** [ama'rettsa] *sf* bitterness.

**a'maro, a** *ag* bitter // *sm* bitterness; (*liquore*) bitters *pl*.

**ambasci'ata** [ambaʃ'fata] *sf* embassy; (*messaggio*) message; **ambascia'tore, 'trice** *sm/f* ambassador/ambassadress.

**ambe'due** *ag inv*: **~ i ragazzi** both boys // *pronome inv* both.

**ambien'tare** *vt* to acclimatize; (*romanzo, film*) to set; **~rsi** *vr* to get used to one's surroundings.

**ambi'ente** *sm* environment; (*fig: in sieme di persone*) milieu; (*stanza*) room.

**am'biguo, a** *ag* ambiguous; (*persona*) shady.

**am'bire** *vt* (*anche: vi*: **~ a**) to aspire to.

**'ambito** *sm* sphere, field.

**ambizi'one** [ambit'tsjone] *sf* ambition; **ambizi'oso, a** *ag* ambitious.

**'ambo** *ag inv* both.

**'ambra** *sf* amber; **~ grigia** ambergris.

**ambu'lante** *ag* travelling, itinerant.

**ambu'lanza** [ambu'lantsa] *sf* ambulance.

**ambula'torio** *sm* (*studio medico*) surgery.

**amenità** *sf inv* pleasantness *q*.

**a'meno, a** *ag* pleasant; (*strano*) funny, strange; (*spiritoso*) amusing.

**A'merica** *sf*: **l'~** America; **l'~ latina** Latin America; **ameri'cano, a** *ag, sm/f* American.

**ami'anto** *sm* asbestos.

**a'mica** *sf vedi* **amico.**

**ami'chevole** [ami'kevole] *ag* friendly.

**ami'cizia** [ami'tʃittsja] *sf* friendship; **~e** *sfpl* (*amici*) friends.

a'mico, a, ci, che *sm/f* friend; (*amante*) boyfriend/girlfriend; ~ del cuore *o* intimo bosom friend.

'amido *sm* starch.

ammac'care *vt* (*pentola*) to dent; (*persona*) to bruise; ~rsi *vr* to bruise.

ammaes'trare *vt* (*animale*) to train; (*persona*) to teach.

ammai'nare *vt* to lower, haul down.

amma'larsi *vr* to fall ill; amma'lato, a *ag* ill, sick // *sm/f* sick person; (*paziente*) patient.

ammali'are *vt* (*fig*) to enchant, charm.

am'manco, chi *sm* (ECON) deficit.

ammanet'tare *vt* to handcuff.

ammas'sare *vt* (*ammucchiare*) to amass; (*raccogliere*) to gather together; ~rsi *vr* to pile up; to gather; am'masso *sm* mass; (*mucchio*) pile, heap; (ECON) stockpile.

ammat'tire *vi* to go mad.

ammaz'zare [ammat'tsare] *vt* to kill; ~rsi *vr* (*uccidersi*) to kill o.s.; (*rimanere ucciso*) to be killed; ~rsi di lavoro to work o.s. to death.

am'menda *sf* amends *pl*; (DIR, SPORT) fine; fare ~ di qc to make amends for sth.

am'messo, a *pp di* ammettere // *cong*: ~ che supposing that.

am'mettere *vt* to admit; (*riconoscere: fatto*) to acknowledge, admit; (*permettere*) to allow, accept; (*supporre*) to suppose.

ammez'zato [ammed'dzato] *sm* (*anche: piano* ~) mezzanine, entresol.

ammic'care *vi*: ~ (a) to wink (at).

amminis'trare *vt* to run, manage; (REL, DIR) to administer; amministra'tivo, a *ag* administrative; amminis'tratore *sm* administrator; (*di condominio*) flats manager; amministratore delegato managing director; amministrazi'one *sf* management; administration.

ammiragli'ato [ammira'ʎʎato] *sm* admiralty.

ammi'raglio [ammi'raʎʎo] *sm* admiral.

ammi'rare *vt* to admire; ammira'tore, 'trice *sm/f* admirer; ammirazi'one *sf* admiration.

ammis'sibile *ag* admissible, acceptable.

ammissi'one *sf* admission; (*approvazione*) acknowledgment.

ammobili'are *vt* to furnish.

am'modo, a 'modo *a* properly // *ag inv* respectable, nice.

am'mollo *sm*: lasciare in ~ to leave to soak.

ammo'niaca *sf* ammonia.

ammoni'mento *sm* warning; admonishment.

ammo'nire *vt* (*avvertire*) to warn; (*rimproverare*) to admonish; (DIR) to caution.

ammon'tare *vi*: ~ a to amount to // *sm* (total) amount.

ammorbi'dente *sm* fabric conditioner.

ammorbi'dire *vt* to soften.

ammortiz'zare [ammortid'dzare] *vt* (ECON) to pay off, amortize; (: *spese d'impianto*) to write off; (AUT, TECN) to absorb, deaden; ammortizza'tore *sm* (AUT, TECN) shock-absorber.

ammucchi'are [ammuk'kjare] *vt*, ~rsi *vr* to pile up, accumulate.

ammuf'fire *vi* to go mouldy (*Brit*) *o* moldy (US).

ammutina'mento *sm* mutiny.

ammuti'narsi *vr* to mutiny.

ammuto'lire *vi* to be struck dumb.

amnis'tia *sf* amnesty.

'amo *sm* (PESCA) hook; (*fig*) bait.

a'more *sm* love; ~i *smpl* love affairs; il tuo bambino è un ~ your baby's a darling; fare l'~ *o* all'~ to make love; per ~ *o* per forza by hook or by crook; amor proprio self-esteem, pride; amo'revole *ag* loving, affectionate.

a'morfo, a *ag* amorphous; (*fig*: *persona*) lifeless.

**amo'roso, a** *ag* (*affettuoso*) loving, affectionate; (*d'amore: sguardo*) amorous; (: *poesia, relazione*) love *cpd.*

**ampi'ezza** [am'pjettsa] *sf* width, breadth; spaciousness; (*fig: importanza*) scale, size.

**'ampio, a** *ag* wide, broad; (*spazioso*) spacious; (*abbondante: vestito*) loose; (: *gonna*) full; (: *spiegazione*) ample, full.

**am'plesso** *sm* (*eufemismo*) embrace.

**ampli'are** *vt* (*ingrandire*) to enlarge; (*allargare*) to widen.

**amplifi'care** *vt* to amplify; (*magnificare*) to extol; **am'plifica'tore** *sm* (*TECN, MUS*) amplifier.

**am'polla** *sf* (*vasetto*) cruet.

**ampu'tare** *vt* (*MED*) to amputate.

**anabbagli'ante** [anabbaλ'λante] *ag* (*AUT*) dipped (*Brit*), dimmed (*US*); **~i** *smpl* dipped (*Brit*) o dimmed (*US*) headlights.

**a'nagrafe** *sf* (*registro*) register of births, marriages and deaths; (*ufficio*) registration office.

**analfa'beta, a, i, e** *ag, sm/f* illiterate.

**anal'gesico, a, ci, che** [anal'dʒɛziko] *ag, sm* analgesic.

**a'nalisi** *sf inv* analysis; (*MED: esame*) test; ~ **grammaticale** parsing; **ana'lista, i, e** *sm/f* analyst; (*PSIC*) (psycho)analyst.

**analiz'zare** [analid'dzare] *vt* to analyse; (*MED*) to test.

**analo'gia, 'gie** [analo'dʒia] *sf* analogy.

**a'nalogo, a, ghi, ghe** *ag* analogous.

**'ananas** *sm inv* pineapple.

**anar'chia** [anar'kia] *sf* anarchy; **a'narchico, a, ci, che** *ag* anarchic(al) // *sm/f* anarchist.

**'ANAS** *sigla f* (= *Azienda Nazionale Autonoma delle Strade*) national roads department.

**anato'mia** *sf* anatomy; **ana'tomico, a, ci, che** *ag*

anatomical; (*sedile*) contoured.

**'anatra** *sf* duck.

**'anca, che** *sf* (*ANAT*) hip; (*ZOOL*) haunch.

**'anche** ['anke] *cong* (*inoltre, pure*) also, too; (*perfino*) even; **vengo anch'io** I'm coming too; ~ **se** even if.

**an'cora** *av* still; (*di nuovo*) again; (*di più*) some more; (*persino*): ~ **più forte** even stronger; **non** ~ not yet; ~ **una volta** once more, once again; ~ **un po'** a little more; (*di tempo*) a little longer.

**'ancora** *sf* anchor; **gettare/levare l'**~ to cast/weigh anchor; **anco'raggio** *sm* anchorage; **anco'rare** *vt*, **ancorarsi** *vr* to anchor.

**anda'mento** *sm* progress, movement; course; state.

**an'dante** *ag* (*corrente*) current; (*di poco pregio*) cheap, second-rate // *sm* (*MUS*) andante.

**an'dare** *sm*: **a lungo** ~ in the long run // *vi* to go; (*essere adatto*): ~ **a** to suit; (*piacere*): **il suo comportamento non mi va** I don't like the way he behaves; **ti va di andare al cinema?** do you feel like going to the cinema?; **andarsene** to go away; **questa camicia va lavata** this shirt needs a wash o should be washed; ~ **a cavallo** to ride; ~ **in macchina/aereo** to go by car/plane; ~ **a fare qc** to go and do sth; ~ **a pescare/sciare** to go fishing/skiing; ~ **a male** to go bad; **come va?** (*lavoro, progetto*) how are things?; **come va?** — **bene, grazie!** how are you? — fine, thanks!; **va fatto entro oggi** it's got to be done today; **ne va della nostra vita** our lives are at stake; **an'data** *sf* going; (*viaggio*) outward journey; **biglietto di sola andata** single (*Brit*) o one-way ticket; **biglietto di andata e ritorno** return (*Brit*) o round-trip (*US*) ticket; **anda'tura** *sf* (*modo di andare*) walk, gait; (SPORT) pace; (NAUT) tack.

an'dazzo [an'dattso] sm (peg): prendere un brutto ~ to take a turn for the worse.

andirivi'eni sm inv coming and going.

'andito sm corridor, passage.

an'drone sm entrance hall.

a'neddoto sm anecdote.

ane'lare vi: ~ a (fig) to long for, yearn for.

a'nelito sm (fig): ~ di longing o yearning for.

a'nello sm ring; (di catena) link.

a'nemico, a, ci, che ag anaemic.

a'nemone sm anemone.

aneste'sia sf anaesthesia; anes'tetico, a, ci, che ag, sm anaesthetic.

anfite'atro sm amphitheatre.

an'fratto sm ravine.

an'gelico, a, ci, che [an'dʒɛliko] ag angelic(al).

'angelo ['andʒelo] sm angel; ~ custode guardian angel.

anghe'ria [ange'ria] sf vexation.

an'gina sf tonsillitis; ~ pectoris angina.

angli'cano, a ag Anglican.

angli'cismo [angli'tʃizmo] sm anglicism.

anglo'sassone ag Anglo-Saxon.

ango'lare ag angular.

angolazi'one [angolat'tsjone] sf (FOT etc, fig) angle.

'angolo sm corner; (MAT) angle.

an'goscia, sce [an'gɔʃʃa] sf deep anxiety, anguish q; angosci'oso, a ag (d'angoscia) anguished; (che dà angoscia) distressing, painful.

angu'illa sf eel.

an'guria sf watermelon.

an'gustia sf (ansia) anguish, distress; (povertà) poverty, want.

angusti'are vt to distress; ~rsi vr: ~rsi (per) to worry (about).

an'gusto, a ag (stretto) narrow; (fig) mean, petty.

'anice ['anitʃe] sm (CUC) aniseed;

(BOT) anise.

a'nidride sf (CHIM): ~ carbonica/ solforosa carbon/sulphur dioxide.

'anima sf soul; (abitante) inhabitant; non c'era ~ viva there wasn't a living soul.

ani'male sm, ag animal.

ani'mare vt to give life to, liven up; (incoraggiare) to encourage; ~rsi vr to become animated, come to life; ani'mato, a ag animate; (vivace) lively, animated; (: strada) busy; anima'tore, 'trice sm/f guiding spirit; (CINEMA) animator; (di festa) life and soul; animazi'one sf liveliness; (di strada) bustle; (CINEMA) animation; animazione teatrale amateur dramatics.

'animo sm (mente) mind; (cuore) heart; (coraggio) courage; (disposizione) character, disposition; avere in ~ di fare qc to intend o have a mind to do sth; perdersi d'~ to lose heart.

'anitra sf = anatra.

anna'cquare vt to water down, dilute.

annaffi'are vt to water; annaffia'toio sm watering can.

an'nali smpl annals.

annas'pare vi to flounder.

an'nata sf year; (importo annuo) annual amount; vino d'~ vintage wine.

annebbi'are vt (fig) to cloud; ~rsi vr to become foggy; (vista) to become dim.

annega'mento sm drowning.

anne'gare vt, vi to drown; ~rsi vr (accidentalmente) to drown; (deliberatamente) to drown o.s.

anne'rire vt to blacken // vi to become black.

an'nesso, a pp di annettere // ag attached; (POL) annexed; ... e tutti gli ~i e connessi ... and so on and so forth.

an'nettere vt (POL) to annex; (accludere) to attach.

annichi'lare, annichi'lire

[anniki'lare, anniki'lire] *vt* to annihilate.

**anni'darsi** *vr* to nest.

**annienta'mento** *sm* annihilation, destruction.

**annien'tare** *vt* to annihilate, destroy.

**anniver'sario** *sm* anniversary.

**'anno** *sm* year.

**anno'dare** *vt* to knot, tie; (*fig*: *rapporto*) to form.

**annoi'are** *vt* to bore; (*seccare*) to annoy; ~**rsi** *vr* to be bored; to be annoyed.

**anno'tare** *vt* (*registrare*) to note, note down; (*commentare*) to annotate; **annotazi'one** *sf* note; annotation.

**annove'rare** *vt* to number.

**annu'ale** *ag* annual.

**annu'ario** *sm* yearbook.

**annu'ire** *vi* to nod; (*acconsentire*) to agree.

**annul'lare** *vt* to annihilate, destroy; (*contratto, francobollo*) to cancel; (*matrimonio*) to annul; (*sentenza*) to quash; (*risultati*) to declare void.

**annunci'are** [annun'tʃare] *vt* to announce; (*dar segni rivelatori*) to herald; **annuncia'tore, 'trice** *sm/f* (*RADIO, TV*) announcer; **l'Annunciazi'one** *sf* the Annunciation.

**an'nuncio** [an'nuntʃo] *sm* announcement; (*fig*) sign; ~ **pubblicitario** advertisement; ~**i economici** classified advertisements, small ads.

**'annuo, a** *ag* annual, yearly.

**annu'sare** *vt* to sniff, smell; ~ **tabacco** to take snuff.

**'ano** *sm* anus.

**anoma'lia** *sf* anomaly.

**a'nomalo, a** *ag* anomalous.

**a'nonimo, a** *ag* anonymous // *sm* (*autore*) anonymous writer (*o painter etc*); **società** ~**a** (*COMM*) joint stock company.

**anor'male** *ag* abnormal // *sm/f* subnormal person; (*eufemismo*) homosexual.

**ANSA** *sigla f* (= *Agenzia Nazionale Stampa Associata*) press agency.

**'ansa** *sf* (*manico*) handle; (*di fiume*) bend, loop.

**'ansia, ansietà** *sf* anxiety.

**ansi'mare** *vi* to pant.

**ansi'oso, a** *ag* anxious.

**'anta** *sf* (*di finestra*) shutter; (*di armadio*) door.

**antago'nismo** *sm* antagonism.

**an'tartico, a, ci, che** *ag* Antarctic // *sm*: **l'A~** the Antarctic.

**antece'dente** [antetʃe'dɛnte] *ag* preceding, previous.

**ante'fatto** *sm* previous events *pl*; previous history.

**antegu'erra** *sm* pre-war period.

**ante'nato** *sm* ancestor, forefather.

**an'tenna** *sf* (*RADIO, TV*) aerial; (*ZOOL*) antenna, feeler; (*NAUT*) yard.

**ante'prima** *sf* preview.

**anteri'ore** *ag* (*ruota, zampa*) front; (*fatti*) previous, preceding.

**antia'ereo, a** *ag* anti-aircraft.

**antia'tomico, a, ci, che** *ag* antinuclear; **rifugio** ~ fallout shelter.

**antibi'otico, a, ci, che** *ag, sm* antibiotic.

**anti'camera** *sf* anteroom; **fare** ~ to wait (for an audience).

**antichità** [antiki'ta] *sf inv* antiquity; (*oggetto*) antique.

**antici'pare** [antitʃi'pare] *vt* (*consegna, visita*) to bring forward, anticipate; (*somma di denaro*) to pay in advance; (*notizia*) to disclose // *vi* to be ahead of time; **anticipazi'one** *sf* anticipation; (*di notizia*) advance information; (*somma di denaro*) advance; **an'ticipo** *sm* anticipation; (*di denaro*) advance; **in anticipo** early, in advance.

**an'tico, a, chi, che** *ag* (*quadro, mobili*) antique; (*dell'antichità*) ancient; **all'**~**a** old-fashioned.

**anticoncezio'nale** [antikontʃetsjo'nale] *sm* contraceptive.

**anticonfor'mista, i, e** *ag, sm/f* nonconformist.

**anti'corpo** sm antibody.

**anti'furto** sm (anche: sistema ~) anti-theft device.

**An'tille** sfpl: le ~ the West Indies.

**antin'cendio** [antin't∫endjo] ag inv fire cpd.

**antio'rario** [antio'rarjo] ag: in senso ~ anticlockwise.

**anti'pasto** sm hors d'œuvre.

**antipa'tia** sf antipathy, dislike; **anti'patico, a, ci, che** ag unpleasant, disagreeable.

**antiquari'ato** sm antique trade; un oggetto d'~ an antique.

**anti'quario** sm antique dealer.

**anti'quato, a** ag antiquated, old-fashioned.

**antise'mita, i, e** ag anti-Semitic.

**anti'settico, a, ci, che** ag, sm antiseptic.

**antista'minico, a, ci, che** ag, sm antihistamine.

**antolo'gia, 'gie** [antolo'dʒia] sf anthology.

**anu'lare** ag ring cpd // sm third finger.

**'anzi** ['antsi] av (invece) on the contrary; (o meglio) or rather, or better still.

**anzianità** [antsjani'ta] sf old age; (AMM) seniority.

**anzi'ano, a** [an'tsjano] ag old; (AMM) senior // smf old person; senior member.

**anziché** [antsi'ke] cong rather than.

**anzi'tutto** [antsi'tutto] av first of all.

**apa'tia** sf apathy, indifference.

**'ape** sf bee.

**aperi'tivo** sm aperitif.

**a'perto, a** pp di aprire // ag open; all'~ in the open (air).

**aper'tura** sf opening; (ampiezza) width, spread; (POL) approach; (FOT) aperture; ~ alare wing span.

**'apice** ['apit∫e] sm apex; (fig) height.

**apicol'tore** sm beekeeper.

**ap'nea** sf: immergersi in ~ to dive without breathing apparatus.

**a'polide** ag stateless.

**apoples'sia** sf (MED) apoplexy.

**a'postolo** sm apostle.

**a'postrofo** sm apostrophe.

**appa'gare** vt to satisfy; ~rsi vr: ~rsi di to be satisfied with.

**ap'palto** sm (COMM) contract; dare/prendere in ~ un lavoro to let out/undertake a job on contract.

**appan'nare** vt (vetro) to mist; (metallo) to tarnish; (vista) to dim; ~rsi vr to mist over; to tarnish; to grow dim.

**appa'rato** sm equipment, machinery; (ANAT) apparatus; ~ scenico (TEATRO) props pl.

**apparecchi'are** [apparek'kjare] vt to prepare; (tavola) to set // vi to set the table; **apparecchia'tura** sf equipment; (macchina) machine, device.

**appa'recchio** [appa'rekkjo] sm piece of apparatus, device; (aeroplano) aircraft inv; ~ televisivo/ telefonico television set/telephone.

**appa'rente** ag apparent; **appa'renza** sf appearance; in o all'apparenza apparently, to all appearances.

**appa'rire** vi to appear; (sembrare) to seem, appear; **appari'scente** ag (colore) garish, gaudy; (bellezza) striking.

**apparta'mento** sm flat (Brit), apartment (US).

**appar'tarsi** vr to withdraw; **appar'tato, a** ag (luogo) secluded.

**apparte'nere** vi: ~ a to belong to.

**appassio'nare** vt to thrill; (commuovere) to move; ~rsi a qc to take a great interest in sth; to be deeply moved by sth; **appassio'nato, a** ag passionate; (entusiasta): appassionato (di) keen (on).

**appas'sire** vi to wither.

**appel'larsi** vr (ricorrere): ~ a to appeal to; (DIR): ~ contro to appeal against; **ap'pello** sm roll-call; (implorazione, DIR) appeal; fare appello to a appeal to.

**ap'pena** av (a stento) hardly,

scarcely; (*solamente, da poco*) just // *cong* as soon as; (**non**) ~ **furono arrivati** ... as soon as they had arrived ...; ~ ... **che** o **quando** no sooner ... than.

**ap'pendere** *vt* to hang (up).

**appen'dice** [appen'ditʃe] *sf* appendix; **romanzo d'**~ popular serial.

**appendi'cite** [appendi'tʃite] *sf* appendicitis.

**Appen'nini** *smpl*: **gli** ~ the Apennines.

**appesan'tire** *vt* to make heavy; ~**rsi** *vr* to grow stout.

**ap'peso, a** *pp di* **appendere**.

**appe'tito** *sm* appetite; **appeti'toso, a** *ag* appetising; (*fig*) attractive, desirable.

**appia'nare** *vt* to level; (*fig*) to smooth away, iron out.

**appiat'tire** *vt* to flatten; ~**rsi** *vr* to become flatter; (*farsi piatto*) to flatten o.s.; ~**rsi al suolo** to lie flat on the ground.

**appic'care** *vt*: ~ **il fuoco a** to set fire to, set on fire.

**appicci'care** [appittʃi'kare] *vt* to stick; (*fig*): ~ **qc a qn** to palm sth off on sb; ~**rsi** *vr* to stick; (*fig: persona*) to cling.

**appi'eno** *av* fully.

**appigli'arsi** [appiʎ'ʎarsi] *vr*: ~ **a** (*afferrarsi*) to take hold of; (*fig*) to cling to; **ap'piglio** *sm* hold; (*fig*) pretext.

**appiso'larsi** *vr* to doze off.

**applau'dire** *vt, vi* to applaud; **ap'plauso** *sm* applause.

**appli'care** *vt* to apply; (*regolamento*) to enforce; ~**rsi** *vr* to apply o.s.; **applicazi'one** *sf* application; enforcement.

**appoggi'are** [appod'dʒare] *vt* (*mettere contro*): ~ **qc a qc** to lean o rest sth against sth; (*fig: sostenere*) to support; ~**rsi** *vr*: ~**rsi a** to lean against; (*fig*) to rely upon; **ap'poggio** *sm* support.

**appollai'arsi** *vr* (*anche fig*) to

perch.

**ap'porre** *vt* to affix.

**appor'tare** *vt* to bring.

**apposita'mente** *av* specially; (*apposta*) on purpose.

**ap'posito, a** *ag* appropriate.

**ap'posta** *av* on purpose, deliberately.

**appos'tare** *vt* to lie in wait for; ~**rsi** *vr* to lie in wait.

**ap'prendere** *vt* (*imparare*) to learn; (*comprendere*) to grasp.

**appren'dista, i, e** *sm/f* apprentice.

**apprensi'one** *sf* apprehension; **appren'sivo, a** *ag* apprehensive.

**ap'presso** *av* (*accanto, vicino*) close by, near; (*dietro*) behind; (*dopo, più tardi*) after, later // *ag inv* (*dopo*): **il giorno** ~ the next day; ~ **a** *prep* (*vicino a*) near, close to.

**appres'tare** *vt* to prepare, get ready; ~**rsi** *vr*: ~**rsi a fare qc** to prepare o get ready to do sth.

**ap'pretto** *sm* starch.

**apprez'zabile** [appret'tsabile] *ag* noteworthy, significant.

**apprezza'mento** [apprettsa'mento] *sm* appreciation; (*giudizio*) opinion.

**apprez'zare** [appret'tsare] *vt* to appreciate.

**ap'proccio** [ap'prɔttʃo] *sm* approach.

**appro'dare** *vi* (*NAUT*) to land; (*fig*): **non** ~ **a nulla** to come to nothing; **ap'prodo** *sm* landing; (*luogo*) landing-place.

**approfit'tare** *vi*: ~ **di** to make the most of, profit by.

**approfon'dire** *vt* to deepen; (*fig*) to study in depth.

**appropri'ato, a** *ag* appropriate.

**approssi'marsi** *vr*: ~ **a** to approach.

**approssima'tivo, a** *ag* approximate, rough; (*impreciso*) inexact, imprecise.

**appro'vare** *vt* (*condotta, azione*) to approve of; (*candidato*) to pass; (*progetto di legge*) to approve; **approvazi'one** *sf* approval.

approvvigio'nare [approvvi-dʒo'nare] vt to supply; ~rsi vr to lay in provisions, stock up; ~ qn di qc to supply sb with sth.

appunta'mento sm appointment; (amoroso) date; darsi ~ to arrange to meet (one another).

appun'tato sm (CARABINIERI) corporal.

ap'punto sm note; (rimprovero) reproach // av (proprio) exactly, just; per l'~!, ~! exactly!

appu'rare vt to check, verify.

apribot'tiglie [apribot'tiʎʎe] sm inv bottleopener.

a'prile sm April.

a'prire vt to open; (via, cadavere) to open up; (gas, luce, acqua) to turn on // vi to open; ~rsi vr to open; ~rsi a qn to confide in sb, open one's heart to sb.

apris'catole sm inv tin (Brit) o can opener.

a'quario sm = acquario.

'aquila sf (ZOOL) eagle; (fig) genius.

aqui'lone sm (giocattolo) kite; (vento) North wind.

A'rabia 'Saudita sf: l'~ Saudi Arabia.

'arabo, a ag, sm/f Arab // sm (LING) Arabic.

a'rachide [a'rakide] sf peanut.

ara'gosta sf crayfish; lobster.

a'raldica sf heraldry.

a'rancia, ce [a'rantʃa] sf orange; aranci'ata sf orangeade; a'rancio sm (BOT) orange tree; (colore) orange // ag inv (colore) orange; aranci'one ag inv: (color) arancione bright orange.

a'rare vt to plough (Brit), plow (US).

a'ratro sm plough (Brit), plow (US).

a'razzo [a'rattso] sm tapestry.

arbi'trare vt (SPORT) to referee; to umpire; (DIR) to arbitrate.

arbi'trario, a ag arbitrary.

ar'bitrio sm will; (abuso, sopruso) arbitrary act.

'arbitro sm arbiter, judge; (DIR)

arbitrator; (SPORT) referee; (: TENNIS, CRICKET) umpire.

ar'busto sm shrub.

'arca, che sf (sarcofago) sarcophagus; l'~ di Noè Noah's ark.

ar'cangelo [ar'kandʒelo] sm archangel.

ar'cano, a ag arcane, mysterious.

ar'cata sf (ARCHIT, ANAT) arch; (ordine di archi) arcade.

archeolo'gia [arkeolo'dʒia] sf arch(a)eology; arche'ologo, a, gi, ghe sm/f arch(a)eologist.

ar'chetto [ar'ketto] sm (MUS) bow.

archi'tetto [arki'tetto] sm architect; architet'tura sf architecture.

ar'chivio [ar'kivjo] sm archives pl; (INFORM) file.

arci'ere [ar'tʃɛre] sm archer.

ar'cigno, a [ar'tʃiɲo] ag grim, severe.

arci'vescovo [artʃi'veskovo] sm archbishop.

'arco sm (arma, MUS) bow; (ARCHIT) arch; (MAT) arc.

arcoba'leno sm rainbow.

arcu'ato, a ag curved, bent; dalle gambe ~e bow-legged.

ar'dente ag burning; (fig) burning, ardent.

'ardere vt, vi to burn.

ar'desia sf slate.

ar'dire vi to dare // sm daring; ar'dito, a ag brave, daring, bold; (sfacciato) bold.

ar'dore sm blazing heat; (fig) ardour, fervour.

'arduo, a ag arduous, difficult.

'area sf area; (EDIL) land, ground.

a'rena sf arena; (per corride) bullring; (sabbia) sand.

are'narsi vr to run aground.

areo'plano sm = aeroplano.

'argano sm winch.

argente'ria [ardʒente'ria] sf silverware, silver.

argenti'ere [ardʒen'tjere] sm silversmith.

Argen'tina [ardʒen'tina] sf: l'~ Argentina; argen'tino, a ag, sm/f

Argentinian.

**ar'gento** [ar'dʒɛnto] *sm* silver; ~ vivo quicksilver.

**ar'gilla** [ar'dʒilla] *sf* clay.

**'argine** ['ardʒine] *sm* embankment, bank; (*diga*) dyke, dike.

**argomen'tare** *vi* to argue.

**argo'mento** *sm* argument; (*motivo*) motive; (*materia, tema*) subject.

**argu'ire** *vt* to deduce.

**ar'guto, a** *ag* sharp, quick-witted; **ar'guzia** *sf* wit; (*battuta*) witty remark.

**'aria** *sf* air; (*espressione, aspetto*) air, look; (*MUS: melodia*) tune; (: *di opera*) aria; **mandare all'~ qc** to ruin o upset sth; **all'~ aperta** in the open (air).

**'arido, a** *ag* arid.

**arieggi'are** [arjed'dʒare] *vt* (*cambiare aria*) to air; (*imitare*) to imitate.

**ari'ete** *sm* ram; (*MIL*) battering ram; (*dello zodiaco*): **A~** Aries.

**a'ringa, ghe** *sf* herring *inv*.

**'arista** *sf* (*CUC*) chine of pork.

**aristo'cratico, a, ci, che** *ag* aristocratic.

**arit'metica** *sf* arithmetic.

**arlec'chino** [arlek'kino] *sm* harlequin.

**'arma, i** *sf* weapon, arm; (*parte dell'esercito*) arm; **chiamare alle ~i** to call up (*Brit*), draft (*US*); **sotto le ~i** in the army (*o* forces); **alle ~i!** to arms!; **~ da fuoco** firearm.

**ar'madio** *sm* cupboard; (*per abiti*) wardrobe.

**armamen'tario** *sm* equipment, instruments *pl*.

**arma'mento** *sm* (*MIL*) armament; (: *materiale*) arms *pl*, weapons *pl*; (*NAUT*) fitting out; manning.

**ar'mare** *vt* to arm; (*arma da fuoco*) to cock; (*NAUT: nave*) to rig, fit out; to man; (*EDIL: volta, galleria*) to prop up, shore up; **~rsi** *vr* to arm o.s.; (*MIL*) to take up arms;

**ar'mata** *sf* (*MIL*) army; (*NAUT*) fleet; **arma'tore** *sm* shipowner; **arma'tura** *sf* (*struttura di sostegno*) framework; (*impalcatura*) scaffolding; (*STORIA*) armour *q*, suit of armour.

**armeggi'are** [armed'dʒare] *vi*: ~ (**intorno a qc**) to mess about (with sth).

**armis'tizio** [armis'tittsjo] *sm* armistice.

**armo'nia** *sf* harmony; **ar'monico, a, ci, che** *ag* harmonic; (*fig*) harmonious // *sf* (*MUS*) harmonica.

**armoni'oso, a** *ag* harmonious.

**armoniz'zare** [armonid'dzare] *vt* to harmonize; (*colori, abiti*) to match // *vi* to be in harmony; to match.

**ar'nese** *sm* tool, implement; (*oggetto indeterminato*) thing, contraption; **male in ~** (*malvestito*) badly dressed; (*di salute malferma*) in poor health; (*di condizioni economiche*) down-at heel.

**'arnia** *sf* hive.

**a'roma, i** *sm* aroma; fragrance; ~i *smpl* herbs and spices; **aro'matico, a, ci, che** *ag* aromatic; (*cibo*) spicy.

**'arpa** *sf* (*MUS*) harp.

**ar'peggio** [ar'peddʒo] *sm* (*MUS*) arpeggio.

**ar'pia** *sf* (*anche fig*) harpy.

**arpi'one** *sm* (*gancio*) hook; (*cardine*) hinge; (*PESCA*) harpoon.

**arrabat'tarsi** *vr* to do all one can, strive.

**arrabbi'are** *vi* (*cane*) to be affected with rabies; ~**rsi** *vr* (*essere preso dall'ira*) to get angry, fly into a rage; **arrabbi'ato, a** *ag* rabid, with rabies; furious, angry.

**arraf'fare** *vt* to snatch, seize; (*sottrarre*) to pinch.

**arrampi'carsi** *vr* to climb (up).

**arran'care** *vi* to limp, hobble.

**arran'giare** [arran'dʒare] *vt* to arrange; ~**rsi** *vr* to manage, do the best one can.

**arre'care** *vt* to bring; (*causare*) to cause.

**arreda'mento** sm (studio) interior design; (mobili etc) furnishings pl.

**arre'dare** vt to furnish; **arreda'tore, 'trice** smf interior designer; **ar'redo** sm fittings pl, furnishings pl.

**ar'rendersi** vr to surrender.

**arres'tare** vt (fermare) to stop, halt; (catturare) to arrest; ~**rsi** vr (fermarsi) to stop; **ar'resto** sm (cessazione) stopping; (fermata) stop; (cattura, MED) arrest; **subire un arresto** to come to a stop o standstill; **mettere agli arresti** to place under arrest; **arresti domiciliari** house arrest sg.

**arre'trare** vt, vi to withdraw; **arre'trato, a** ag (lavoro) behind schedule; (paese, bambino) backward; (numero di giornale) back cpd; **arretrati** smpl arrears.

**arric'chire** [arrik'kire] vt to enrich; ~**rsi** vr to become rich.

**arricci'are** [arrit'tʃare] vt to curl; ~ **il naso** to turn up one's nose.

**ar'ringa, ghe** sf harangue; (DIR) address by counsel.

**arrischi'are** [arris'kjare] vt to risk; ~**rsi** vr to venture, dare; **arri-schi'ato, a** ag risky; (temerario) reckless, rash.

**arri'vare** vi to arrive; (accadere) to happen, occur; ~ **a** (livello, grado etc) to reach; **lui arriva a Roma alle 7** he gets to o arrives at Rome at 7; **non ci arrivo** I can't reach it; (fig: non capisco) I can't understand it.

**arrive'derci** [arrive'dertʃi] escl goodbye!

**arrive'derla** escl (forma di cortesia) goodbye!

**arri'vista, i, e** smf go-getter.

**ar'rivo** sm arrival; (SPORT) finish, finishing line.

**arro'gante** ag arrogant.

**arro'lare** vb = **arruolare**.

**arros'sire** vi (per vergogna, timidezza) to blush, flush; (per gioia, rabbia) to flush.

**arros'tire** vt to roast; (pane) to toast; (ai ferri) to grill.

**ar'rosto** sm, ag inv roast.

**arro'tare** vt to sharpen; (investire con un veicolo) to run over.

**arroto'lare** vt to roll up.

**arroton'dare** vt (forma, oggetto) to round; (stipendio) to add to; (somma) to round off.

**arrovel'larsi** vr: ~ (il cervello) to rack one's brains.

**arruf'fare** vt to ruffle; (fili) to tangle; (fig: questione) to confuse.

**arruggi'nire** [arruddʒi'nire] vt to rust; ~**rsi** vr to rust; (fig) to become rusty.

**arruo'lare** (MIL) vt to enlist; ~**rsi** vr to enlist, join up.

**arse'nale** sm (MIL) arsenal; (cantiere navale) dockyard.

**'arso, a** pp di **ardere** // ag (bruciato) burnt; (arido) dry; **ar'sura** sf (calore opprimente) burning heat; (siccità) drought.

**'arte** sf art; (abilità) skill.

**arte'fatto, a** ag (cibo) adulterated; (fig: modi) artificial.

**ar'tefice** [ar'tefitʃe] smf craftsman/woman; (autore) author.

**ar'teria** sf artery.

**'artico, a, ci, che** ag Arctic.

**artico'lare** ag (ANAT) of the joints, articular // vt to articulate; (suddividere) to divide, split up; **articolazi'one** sf articulation; (ANAT, TECN) joint.

**ar'ticolo** sm article; ~ **di fondo** (STAMPA) leader, leading article.

**'Artide** sm: **l'**~ the Arctic.

**artifici'ale** [artifi'tʃale] ag artificial.

**arti'ficio** [arti'fitʃo] sm (espediente) trick, artifice; (ricerca di effetto) artificiality.

**artigia'nato** sm craftsmanship; craftsmen pl.

**artigi'ano, a** [arti'dʒano] sm craftsman/woman.

**artiglie'ria** [artiʎʎe'ria] sf artillery.

**ar'tiglio** [ar'tiʎʎo] sm claw; (di rapaci) talon.

**ar'tista, i,** e *smf* artist; **ar'tistico, a, ci, che** *ag* artistic.

**'arto** *sm* (ANAT) limb.

**ar'trite** *sf* (MED) arthritis.

**ar'trosi** *sf* osteoarthritis.

**ar'zillo, a** [ar'dzillo] *ag* lively, sprightly.

**a'scella** [aʃʃella] *sf* (ANAT) armpit.

**ascen'dente** [aʃʃen'dɛnte] *sm* ancestor; (fig) ascendancy; (ASTR) ascendant.

**ascensi'one** [aʃʃen'sjone] *sf* (ALPINISMO) ascent; (REL): **l'A~** the Ascension.

**ascen'sore** [aʃʃen'sore] *sm* lift.

**a'scesa** [aʃ'ʃesa] *sf* ascent; (al trono) accession.

**a'scesso** [aʃ'ʃɛsso] *sm* (MED) abscess.

**'ascia,** pl **'asce** ['aʃʃa] *sf* axe.

**asciugaca'pelli** [aʃʃugaka'pelli] *sm* hair-drier.

**asciuga'mano** [aʃʃuga'mano] *sm* towel.

**asciu'gare** [aʃʃu'gare] *vt* to dry; ~rsi *vr* to dry o.s.; (diventare asciutto) to dry.

**asci'utto, a** [aʃ'ʃutto] *ag* dry; (fig: magro) lean; (: burbero) curt; **restare a bocca ~a** (fig) to be disappointed.

**ascol'tare** *vt* to listen to; **ascolta'tore, 'trice** *smf* listener; **as'colto** *sm*: **essere** o **stare in ascolto** to be listening; **dare** o **prestare ascolto (a)** to pay attention (to).

**as'falto** *sm* asphalt.

**asfissi'are** *vt* to suffocate, asphyxiate; (fig) to bore to tears.

**'Asia** *sf*: **l'~** Asia; **asi'atico, a, ci, che** *ag, smf* Asiatic, Asian.

**a'silo** *sm* refuge, sanctuary; ~ **(d'infanzia)** nursery(-school); ~ **nido** crèche; ~ **politico** political asylum.

**'asino** *sm* donkey, ass.

**'asma** *sf* asthma.

**'asola** *sf* buttonhole.

**as'parago** [pl *gi* asparagus *q.*

**aspet'tare** *vt* to wait for; (anche COMM) to await; (aspettarsi) to expect // *vi* to wait; ~rsi *vr* to expect; ~ **un bambino** to be expecting (a baby); **questo non me l'aspettavo** I wasn't expecting this; **aspetta'tiva** *sf* wait; expectation; **inferiore all'aspettativa** worse than expected; **essere in aspettativa** (AMM) to be on leave of absence.

**as'petto** *sm* (apparenza) aspect, appearance, look; (punto di vista) point of view; **di bell'~** good-looking.

**aspi'rante** *ag* (attore etc) aspiring // *smf* candidate, applicant.

**aspira'polvere** *sm* *inv* vacuum cleaner.

**aspi'rare** *vt* (respirare) to breathe in, inhale; (sog: apparecchi) to suck (up) // *vi*: ~ **a** to aspire to; **aspira'tore** *sm* extractor fan.

**aspi'rina** *sf* aspirin.

**aspor'tare** *vt* (anche MED) to remove, take away.

**'aspro, a** *ag* (sapore) sour, tart; (odore) acrid, pungent; (voce, clima, fig) harsh; (superficie) rough; (paesaggio) rugged.

**assaggi'are** [assad'dʒare] *vt* to taste.

**as'sai** *av* (molto) a lot, much; (: con ag) very; (a sufficienza) enough // *ag* *inv* (quantità) a lot of, much; (numero) a lot of, many; ~ **contento** very pleased.

**assa'lire** *vt* to attack, assail.

**as'salto** *sm* attack, assault.

**assassi'nare** *vt* to murder; to assassinate; (fig) to ruin; **assas'sinio** *sm* murder; assassination; **assas'sino, a** *ag* murderous // *smf* murderer; assassin.

**'asse** *sm* (TECN) axle; (MAT) axis // *sf* board; ~ **f da stiro** ironing board.

**assedi'are** *vt* to besiege; **as'sedio** *sm* siege.

**asse'gnare** [asseɲ'ɲare] *vt* to assign, allot; (premio) to award.

**as'segno** [as'seɲɲo] *sm* allowance; (anche: ~ **bancario**) cheque (Brit), check (US); **contro** ~ cash on delivery; ~ **circolare** bank draft; ~ **sbarrato** crossed cheque; ~ **di viaggio** traveller's cheque; ~ **a vuoto** dud cheque; **~i familiari** ~ child benefit $q$.

**assem'blea** *sf* assembly.

**assen'nato, a** *ag* sensible.

**as'senso** *sm* assent, consent.

**as'sente** *ag* absent; *(fig)* faraway, vacant; **as'senza** *sf* absence.

**asses'sore** *sm (POL)* councillor.

**assesta'mento** *sm (sistemazione)* arrangement; *(EDIL, GEOL)* settlement.

**asses'tare** *vt (mettere in ordine)* to put in order, arrange; **~rsi** *vr* to settle in; ~ **un colpo a qn** to deal sb a blow.

**asse'tato, a** *ag* thirsty, parched.

**as'setto** *sm* order, arrangement; *(NAUT, AER)* trim; **in ~ di guerra** on a war footing.

**assicu'rare** *vt (accertare)* to ensure; *(infondere certezza)* to assure; *(fermare, legare)* to make fast, secure; *(fare un contratto di assicurazione)* to insure; **~rsi** *vr (accertarsi)*: **~rsi (di)** to make sure (of); *(contro il furto etc)*: **~rsi (contro)** to insure o.s. (against); **assicu'rato, a** *ag* insured // *sf (anche: lettera assicurata)* registered letter; **assicurazi'one** *sf* assurance; insurance.

**assidera'mento** *sm* exposure.

**assi'eme** *av (insieme)* together; ~ **a** *prep* (together) with.

**assil'lare** *vt* to pester, torment.

**as'sillo** *sm (fig)* worrying thought.

**as'sise** *sfpl (DIR)* assizes; **Corte d'A~** Court of Assizes, ≈ Crown Court *(Brit)*.

**assis'tente** *smlf* assistant; ~ **sociale** social worker; ~ **di volo** *(AER)* steward/stewardess.

**assis'tenza** [assis'tɛntsa] *sf* assistance; ~ **ospedaliera** free hospital treatment; ~ **sanitaria** health service; ~ **sociale** welfare services *pl*.

**as'sistere** *vt (aiutare)* to assist, help; *(curare)* to treat // *vi*: ~ **(a qc)** *(essere presente)* to be present (at sth), to attend (sth).

**'asso** *sm* ace; **piantare qn in ~** to leave sb in the lurch.

**associ'are** [asso't'fare] *vt* to associate; *(rendere partecipe)*: ~ **qn a** *(affari)* to take sb into partnership in; *(partito)* to make sb a member of; **~rsi** *vr* to enter into partnership; **~rsi a** to become a member of, join; *(dolori, gioie)* to share in; ~ **qn alle carceri** to take sb to prison.

**associazi'one** [assot'fat'tsjone] *sf* association; *(COMM)* association, society; ~ **a o per delinquere** *(DIR)* criminal association.

**asso'dato, a** *ag* well-founded.

**assogget'tare** [assoddʒet'tare] *vt* to subject, subjugate.

**asso'lato, a** *ag* sunny.

**assol'dare** *vt* to recruit.

**as'solto, a** *pp di* **assolvere**.

**assoluta'mente** *av* absolutely.

**asso'luto, a** *ag* absolute.

**assoluzi'one** [assolut'tsjone] *sf (DIR)* acquittal; *(REL)* absolution.

**as'solvere** *vt (DIR)* to acquit; *(REL)* to absolve; *(adempiere)* to carry out, perform.

**assomigli'are** [assomiʎ'ʎare] *vi*: ~ **a** to resemble, look like.

**asson'nato, a** *ag* sleepy.

**asso'pirsi** *vr* to doze off.

**assor'bente** *ag* absorbent // *sm*: ~ **igienico** sanitary towel; ~ **interno** tampon.

**assor'bire** *vt* to absorb; *(fig: far proprio)* to assimilate.

**assor'dare** *vt* to deafen.

**assorti'mento** *sm* assortment.

**assor'tito, a** *ag* assorted; matched, matching.

**as'sorto, a** *ag* absorbed, engrossed.

**assottigli'are** [assotti'ʎʎare] *vt* to make thin, to thin; *(aguzzare)* to sharpen; *(ridurre)* to reduce; **~rsi** *vr* to grow thin; *(fig: ridursi)* to be reduced.

**assue'fare** *vt* to accustom; ~**rsi** *a* to get used to, accustom o.s. to.

**as'sumere** *vt* (*impiegato*) to take on, engage; (*responsabilità*) to assume, take upon o.s.; (*contegno, espressione*) to assume, put on; (*droga*) to consume; **as'sunto, a** *pp di* **assumere** // *sm* (*tesi*) proposition.

**assurdità** *sf inv* absurdity; **dire delle** ~ to talk nonsense.

**as'surdo, a** *ag* absurd.

**'asta** *sf* pole; (*modo di vendita*) auction.

**astan'te'ria** *sf* casualty department.

**aste'nersi** *vr*: ~ (**da**) to abstain (from), refrain (from); (*POL*) to abstain (from).

**aste'risco, schi** *sm* asterisk.

**astice** ['astitʃe] *sm* lobster.

**asti'nenza** [asti'nɛntsa] *sf* abstinence; **essere in crisi di** ~ to suffer from withdrawal symptoms.

**'astio** *sm* rancour, resentment.

**as'tratto, a** *ag* abstract.

**'astro** *sm* star.

**'astro...** *prefisso*: **astrolo'gia** [astrolo'dʒia] *sf* astrology; **as'trologo, a, ghi, ghe** *smf* astrologer; **astro'nauta, i, e** *smf* astronaut; **astro'nave** *sf* space ship; **astrono'mia** *sf* astronomy; **astro'nomico, a, ci, che** *ag* astronomic(al).

**as'tuccio** [as'tuttʃo] *sm* case, box, holder.

**as'tuto, a** *ag* astute, cunning, shrewd; **as'tuzia** *sf* astuteness, shrewdness; (*azione*) trick.

**A'tene** *sf* Athens.

**ate'neo** *sm* university.

**'ateo, a** *ag, smf* atheist.

**at'lante** *sm* atlas.

**at'lantico, a, ci, che** *ag* Atlantic // *sm*: **l'A~, l'Oceano A~** the Atlantic, the Atlantic Ocean.

**at'leta, i, e** *smf* athlete; **at'letica** *sf* athletics *sg*; **atletica leggera** track and field events *pl*; **atletica pesante** weightlifting and wrestling.

**atmos'fera** *sf* atmosphere.

a'tomico, a, ci, che *ag* atomic; (*nucleare*) atomic, atom *cpd*, nuclear.

**'atomo** *sm* atom.

**'atrio** *sm* entrance hall, lobby.

**a'troce** [a'trotʃe] *ag* (*che provoca orrore*) dreadful; (*terribile*) atrocious.

**attacca'mento** *sm* (*fig*) attachment, affection.

**attacca'panni** *sm* hook, peg; (*mobile*) hall stand.

**attac'care** *vt* (*unire*) to attach; (*cucendo*) to sew on; (*far aderire*) to stick (on); (*appendere*) to hang (up); (*assalire: anche fig*) to attack; (*iniziare*) to begin, start; (*fig: contagiare*) to pass on // *vi* to stick, adhere; ~**rsi** *vr* to stick, adhere; (*trasmettersi per contagio*) to be contagious; (*afferrarsi*): ~**rsi** (**a**) to cling (to); (*fig: affezionarsi*): ~**rsi** (**a**) to become attached (to); ~ **discorso** to start a conversation; **at'tacco, chi** *sm* (*azione offensiva: anche fig*) attack; (*MED*) attack, fit; (*SCI*) binding; (*ELETTR*) socket.

**atteggia'mento** [atteddʒa'mento] *sm* attitude.

**atteggi'arsi** [atted'dʒarsi] *vr*: ~ **a** to pose as.

**attem'pato, a** *ag* elderly.

**at'tendere** *vt* to wait for, await // *vi*: ~ **a** to attend to.

**atten'dibile** *ag* (*storia*) credible; (*testimone*) reliable.

**atte'nersi** *vr*: ~ **a** to keep *o* stick to.

**atten'tare** *vi*: ~ **a** to make an attempt on; **atten'tato** *sm* attack; **attentato alla vita di qn** attempt on sb's life.

**at'tento, a** *ag* attentive; (*accurato*) careful, thorough; **stare** ~ **a qc** to pay attention to sth // *escl* be careful!

**attenu'ante** *sf* (*DIR*) extenuating circumstance.

**attenu'are** *vt* to attenuate; (*dolore, rumore*) to lessen, deaden; (*pena, tasse*) to alleviate; ~**rsi** *vr* to ease, abate.

**attenzi'one** [atten'tsjone] *sf* attention // *escl* watch out!, be careful!

**atter'raggio** [atter'raddʒo] *sm* landing.

**atter'rare** *vt* to bring down // *vi* to land.

**atter'rire** *vt* to terrify.

**at'teso, a** *pp di* **attendere** // *sf* waiting; (*tempo trascorso aspettando*) wait; **essere in attesa di qc** to be waiting for sth.

**attes'tato** *sm* certificate.

**'attico, ci** *sm* attic.

**at'tiguo, a** *ag* adjacent, adjoining.

**attil'lato, a** *ag* (*vestito*) close-fitting, tight; (*persona*) dressed up.

**'attimo** *sm* moment; **in un** ~ in a moment.

**atti'nente** *ag*: ~ **a** relating to, concerning.

**atti'rare** *vt* to attract.

**atti'tudine** *sf* (*disposizione*) aptitude; (*atteggiamento*) attitude.

**atti'vare** *vt* to activate; (*far funzionare*) to set going, start.

**attività** *sf inv* activity; (*COMM*) assets *pl.*

**at'tivo, a** *ag* active; (*COMM*) profit-making, credit *cpd* // *sm* (*COMM*) assets *pl*; **in** ~ in credit.

**attiz'zare** [attit'tsare] *vt* (*fuoco*) to poke.

**'atto** *sm* act; (*azione, gesto*) action, act, deed; (*DIR: documento*) deed, document; ~**i** *smpl* (*di congressi etc*) proceedings; **mettere in** ~ to put into action; **fare** ~ **di fare qc** to make as if to do sth.

**at'tonito, a** *ag* dumbfounded, astonished.

**attorcigli'are** [attortʃiʎ'ʎare] *vt*, ~**rsi** *vr* to twist.

**at'tore, 'trice** *sm/f* actor/actress.

**at'torno** *av*, ~ **a** *prep* round, around, about.

**at'tracco, chi** *sm* (*NAUT*) docking *q*; berth.

**attra'ente** *ag* attractive.

**at'trarre** *vt* to attract; **attrat'tiva** *sf*

(*fig: fascino*) attraction, charm; **at'tratto, a** *pp di* **attrarre**.

**attraversa'mento** *sm*: ~ **pedonale** pedestrian crossing.

**attraver'sare** *vt* to cross; (*città, bosco, fig: periodo*) to go through; (*sog: fiume*) to run through.

**attra'verso** *prep* through; (*da una parte all'altra*) across.

**attrazi'one** [attrat'tsjone] *sf* attraction.

**attrez'zare** [attret'tsare] *vt* to equip; (*NAUT*) to rig; **attrezza'tura** *sf* equipment *q*; rigging; **at'trezzo** *sm* tool, instrument; (*SPORT*) piece of equipment.

**attribu'ire** *vt*: ~ **qc a qn** (*assegnare*) to give *o* award sth to sb; (*quadro etc*) to attribute sth to sb; **attri'buto** *sm* attribute.

**at'trice** [at'tritʃe] *sf vedi* **attore**.

**at'trito** *sm* (*anche fig*) friction.

**attu'ale** *ag* (*presente*) present; (*di attualità*) topical; (*che è in atto*) actual; **attualità** *sf inv* topicality; (*avvenimento*) current event; **attual'mente** *av* at the moment, at present.

**attu'are** *vt* to carry out; ~**rsi** *vr* to be realized.

**attu'tire** *vt* to deaden, reduce.

**au'dace** [au'datʃe] *ag* audacious, daring, bold; (*provocante*) provocative; (*sfacciato*) impudent, bold; **au'dacia** *sf* audacity, daring; boldness; provocativeness; impudence.

**audiovi'sivo, a** *ag* audiovisual.

**audizi'one** [audit'tsjone] *sf* hearing; (*MUS*) audition.

**'auge** [audʒe] *sf*: **in** ~ popular.

**augu'rare** *vt* to wish; ~**rsi qc** to hope for sth.

**au'gurio** *sm* (*presagio*) omen; (*voto di benessere etc*) (good) wish; **essere di buon/cattivo** ~ to be of good omen/be ominous; **fare gli** ~**i a qn** to give sb one's best wishes; **tanti** ~**i!** all the best!

**'aula** *sf* (*scolastica*) classroom; (*universitaria*) lecture theatre; (*di* *edificio pubblico*) hall.

**aumen'tare** *vt*, *vi* to increase; **au'mento** *sm* increase.

**au'reola** *sf* halo.

**au'rora** *sf* dawn.

**ausili'are** *ag*, *sm*, *sm/f* auxiliary.

**aus'picio** [aus'pitʃo] *sm* omen; (*protezione*) patronage; **sotto gli ~i di** under the auspices of.

**aus'tero, a** *ag* austere.

**Aus'tralia** *sf*: **l'~** Australia; **au- strali'ano, a** *ag*, *sm/f* Australian.

**'Austria** *sf*: **l'~** Austria; **aus'triaco, a, ci, che** *ag*, *sm/f* Austrian.

**au'tentico, a, ci, che** *ag* (*quadro*, *firma*) authentic, genuine; (*fatto*) true, genuine.

**au'tista, i** *sm* driver.

**'auto** *sf inv* car.

**autoade'sivo, a** *ag* self-adhesive // *sm* sticker.

**autobiogra'fia** *sf* autobiography.

**auto'botte** *sf* tanker.

**'autobus** *sm inv* bus.

**auto'carro** *sm* lorry (*Brit*), truck.

**autocorri'era** *sf* coach, bus.

**au'tografo, a** *ag*, *sm* autograph.

**auto'linea** *sf* bus company.

**au'toma, i** *sm* automaton.

**auto'matico, a, ci, che** *ag* automatic // *sm* (*bottone*) snap fastener; (*fucile*) automatic.

**automazi'one** [automat'tsjone] *sf* automation.

**auto'mezzo** [auto'mɛddzo] *sm* motor vehicle.

**auto'mobile** *sf* (motor) car.

**autono'mia** *sf* autonomy; (*di volo*) range.

**au'tonomo, a** *ag* autonomous, independent.

**autop'sia** *sf* post-mortem (examination), autopsy.

**auto'radio** *sf inv* (*apparecchio*) car radio; (*autoveicolo*) radio car.

**au'tore, 'trice** *sm/f* author; **l'~ del furto** the person who committed the robbery.

**auto'revole** *ag* authoritative;

(*persona*) influential.

**autori'messa** *sf* garage.

**autorità** *sf inv* authority.

**autoriz'zare** [autorid'dzare] *vt* (*permettere*) to authorize; (*giustificare*) to allow, sanction; **autorizzazi'one** *sf* authorization.

**autoscu'ola** *sf* driving school.

**autos'top** *sm* hitchhiking; **auto- stop'pista, i, e** *sm/f* hitchhiker.

**autos'trada** *sf* motorway (*Brit*), highway (*US*).

**auto'treno** *sm* articulated lorry (*Brit*), semi (trailer) (*US*).

**autove'icolo** *sm* motor vehicle.

**autovet'tura** *sf* (motor) car.

**au'tunno** *sm* autumn.

**avam'braccio**, *pl(f)* **cia** [avam- 'brattʃo] *sm* forearm.

**avangu'ardia** *sf* vanguard.

**a'vanti** *av* (*stato in luogo*) in front; (*moto: andare, venire*) forward; (*tempo: prima*) before // *prep* (*luogo*): **~ a** before, in front of; (*tempo*): **~ Cristo** before Christ // *escl* (*entrate*) come (o go) in!; (*MIL*) forward!; (*coraggio*) come on! // *sm inv* (*SPORT*) forward; **~ e indietro** backwards and forwards; **andare ~** to go forward; (*continuare*) to go on; (*precedere*) to go (on) ahead; (*orologio*) to be fast; **essere ~ negli studi** to be well advanced with one's studies.

**avanza'mento** [avantsa'mento] *sm* progress; promotion.

**avan'zare** [avan'tsare] *vt* (*spostare in avanti*) to move forward, advance; (*domanda*) to put forward; (*promuovere*) to promote; (*essere creditore*): **~ qc da qn** to be owed sth by sb // *vi* (*andare avanti*) to move forward, advance; (*fig: progredire*) to make progress; (*essere d'avanzo*) to be left, remain; **avan'zata** *sf* (*MIL*) advance; **a'vanzo** *sm* (*residuo*) remains *pl*, left-overs *pl*; (*MAT*) remainder; (*COMM*) surplus; **averne d'avanzo di qc** to have more than enough of sth; **avanzo di galera** (fig) jailbird.

**ava'ria** sf (guasto) damage; (: meccanico) breakdown.

**a'varo, a** ag avaricious, miserly // sm miser.

**a'vena** sf oats pl.

---

PAROLA CHIAVE

---

**a'vere** ◆ sm (COMM) credit; **gli ~i** (ricchezze) wealth sg

◆ vt 1 (possedere) to have; **ha due bambini/una bella casa** she has (got) two children/a lovely house; **ha i capelli lunghi** he has (got) long hair; **non ho da mangiare/bere** I've (got) nothing to eat/drink, I don't have anything to eat/drink

2 (indossare) to wear, have on; **aveva una maglietta rossa** he was wearing o he had on a red tee-shirt; **ha gli occhiali** he wears o has glasses

3 (ricevere) to get; **hai avuto l'assegno?** did you get o have you had the cheque?

4 (età, dimensione) to be; **ha 9 anni** he is 9 (years old); **la stanza ha 3 metri di lunghezza** the room is 3 metres in length; vedi **fame, paura** etc

5 (tempo): **quanti ne abbiamo oggi?** what's the date today?; **ne hai per molto?** will you be long?

6 (fraseologia): **avercela con qn** to be angry with sb; **cos'hai?** what's wrong o what's the matter (with you)?; **non ha niente a che vedere** o **fare con me** it's got nothing to do with me

◆ vb ausiliare 1 to have; **aver bevuto/mangiato** to have drunk/eaten

2 (+ da + infinito): **~ da fare qc** to have to do sth; **non hai che da chiederlo** you only have to ask him.

'**avi** smpl ancestors, forefathers.

**avia'tore, 'trice** sm/f aviator, pilot.

**aviazi'one** [avjat'tsjone] sf aviation; (MIL) air force.

**avidità** sf eagerness; greed.

'**avido, a** ag eager; (peg) greedy.

**avo'cado** sm avocado.

**a'vorio** sm ivory.

**Avv.** abbr = **avvocato**.

**avvalla'mento** sm sinking q; (effetto) depression.

**avvalo'rare** vt to confirm.

**avvam'pare** vi (incendio) to flare up.

**avvantaggi'are** [avvantad'dʒare] vt to favour; **~rsi** vr: **~rsi negli affari/sui concorrenti** to get ahead in business/of one's competitors.

**avvele'nare** vt to poison.

**avve'nente** ag attractive, charming.

**avveni'mento** sm event.

**avve'nire** vi, vb impers to happen, occur // sm future.

**avven'tarsi** vr: **~ su** o **contro qn/qc** to hurl o.s. o rush at sb/sth.

**avven'tato, a** ag rash, reckless.

**avven'tizio, a** [avven'tittsjo] ag (impiegato) temporary; (guadagno) casual.

**av'vento** sm advent, coming; (REL): **l'A~** Advent.

**avven'tore** sm (regular) customer.

**avven'tura** sf adventure; (amorosa) affair.

**avventu'rarsi** vr to venture.

**avventu'roso, a** ag adventurous.

**avve'rarsi** vr to come true.

**av'verbio** sm adverb.

**avver'sario, a** ag opposing // sm opponent, adversary.

**av'verso, a** ag (contrario) contrary; (sfavorevole) unfavourable.

**avver'tenza** [avver'tentsa] sf (ammonimento) warning; (cautela) care; (premessa) foreword; **~e** sfpl (istruzioni per l'uso) instructions.

**avverti'mento** sm warning.

**avver'tire** vt (avvisare) to warn; (rendere consapevole) to inform, notify; (percepire) to feel.

**av'vezzo, a** [av'vettso] ag: **~ a** used to.

**avvia'mento** sm (atto) starting; (effetto) start; (AUT) starting; (:

*dispositivo*) starter; (*COMM*) goodwill.

**avvi'are** *vt* (*mettere sul cammino*) to direct; (*impresa, trattative*) to begin, start; (*motore*) to start; ~**rsi** *vr* to set off, set out.

**avvicen'darsi** [avvitʃen'darsi] *vr* to alternate.

**avvici'nare** [avvitʃi'nare] *vt* to bring near; (*trattare con: persona*) to approach; ~**rsi** *vr*: ~**rsi** (**a qn/qc**) to approach (sb/sth), draw near (to sb/sth).

**avvi'lire** *vt* (*umiliare*) to humiliate; (*degradare*) to disgrace; (*scoraggiare*) to dishearten, discourage; ~**rsi** *vr* (*abbattersi*) to lose heart.

**avvilup'pare** *vt* (*avvolgere*) to wrap up; (*ingarbugliare*) to entangle.

**avvinaz'zato, a** [avvinat'tsato] *ag* drunk.

**av'vincere** [av'vintʃere] *vt* to charm, enthral.

**avvinghi'are** [avvin'gjare] *vt* to clasp; ~**rsi** *vr*: ~**rsi a** to cling to.

**avvi'sare** *vt* (*far sapere*) to inform; (*mettere in guardia*) to warn; **av'viso** *sm* warning; (*annuncio*) announcement; (: *affisso*) notice; (*inserzione pubblicitaria*) advertisement; **a mio avviso** in my opinion.

**avvis'tare** *vt* to sight.

**avvi'tare** *vt* to screw down (o in).

**avviz'zire** [avvit'tsire] *vi* to wither.

**avvo'cato, 'essa** *smf* (*DIR*) barrister (*Brit*), lawyer; (*fig*) defender, advocate.

**av'volgere** [av'voldʒere] *vt* to roll up; (*avviluppare*) to wrap up; ~**rsi** *vr* (*avvilupparsi*) to wrap o.s. up; **avvol'gibile** *sm* roller blind (*Brit*), blind.

**avvol'toio** *sm* vulture.

**azi'enda** [ad'dzjɛnda] *sf* business, firm, concern; ~ **agricola** farm.

**azio'nare** [attsjo'nare] *vt* to activate.

**azi'one** [at'tsjone] *sf* action; (*COMM*) share; **azio'nista, i, e** *smf* (*COMM*) shareholder.

**a'zoto** [ad'dzɔto] *sm* nitrogen.

**azzan'nare** [attsan'nare] *vt* to sink one's teeth into.

**azzar'darsi** [addzar'darsi] *vr*: ~ **a fare** to dare (to) do; **azzar'dato, a** *ag* (*impresa*) risky; (*risposta*) rash.

**az'zardo** [ad'dzardo] *sm* risk.

**azzec'care** [attsek'kare] *vt* (*risposta etc*) to get right.

**azzuf'farsi** [attsuf'farsi] *vr* to come to blows.

**az'zurro, a** [ad'dzurro] *ag* blue // *sm* (*colore*) blue; **gli ~i** (*SPORT*) the Italian national team.

# B

**bab'beo** *sm* simpleton.

**'babbo** *sm* (*fam*) dad, daddy; **B~ natale** Father Christmas.

**bab'buccia, ce** [bab'buttʃa] *sf* slipper; (*per neonati*) bootee.

**ba'bordo** *sm* (*NAUT*) port side.

**ba'cato, a** *ag* worm-eaten, rotten.

**'bacca, che** *sf* berry.

**baccalà** *sm* dried salted cod; (*fig peg*) dummy.

**bac'cano** *sm* din, clamour.

**bac'cello** [bat'tʃello] *sm* pod.

**bac'chetta** [bak'ketta] *sf* (*verga*) stick, rod; (*di direttore d'orchestra*) baton; (*di tamburo*) drumstick; ~ **magica** magic wand.

**baci'are** [ba'tʃare] *vt* to kiss; ~**rsi** *vr* to kiss (one another).

**baci'nella** [batʃi'nɛlla] *sf* basin.

**ba'cino** [ba'tʃino] *sm* basin; (*MINERALOGIA*) field, bed; (*ANAT*) pelvis; (*NAUT*) dock.

**'bacio** [bat'ʃo] *sm* kiss.

**'baco, chi** *sm* worm; ~ **da seta** silkworm.

**ba'dare** *vi* (*fare attenzione*) to take care, be careful; (*occuparsi di*): ~ **a** to look after, take care of; (*dar ascolto*): ~ **a** to pay attention to; **bada ai fatti tuoi!** mind your own business!

**ba'dia** *sf* abbey.

**ba'dile** *sm* shovel.

'**baffi** *smpl* moustache *sg*; (*di animale*) whiskers; **ridere sotto i ~** to laugh up one's sleeve; **leccarsi i ~** to lick one's lips.

**bagagli'aio** [bagaʎ'ʎajo] *sm* luggage van (*Brit*) *o* car (*US*); (*AUT*) boot (*Brit*), trunk (*US*).

**ba'gagli** [ba'gaʎʎi] *smpl* luggage *sg*.

**bagli'ore** [baʎ'ʎore] *sm* flash, dazzling light; **un ~ di speranza** a ray of hope.

**ba'gnante** [baɲ'ɲante] *sm/f* bather.

**ba'gnare** [baɲ'ɲare] *vt* to wet; (*inzuppare*) to soak; (*innaffiare*) to water; (*sog: fiume*) to flow through; (*: mare*) to wash, bathe; **~rsi** *vr* (*al mare*) to go swimming *o* bathing; (*in vasca*) to have a bath.

**ba'gnato, a** [baɲ'ɲato] *ag* wet.

**ba'gnino** [baɲ'ɲino] *sm* lifeguard.

'**bagno** ['baɲɲo] *sm* bath; (*locale*) bathroom; **~i** *smpl* (*stabilimento*) baths; **fare il ~** to have a bath; (*nel mare*) to go swimming *o* bathing; **fare il ~ a qn** to give sb a bath; **mettere a ~** to soak; **~ schiuma** bubble bath.

**bagnoma'ria** [baɲɲoma'ria] *sm*: **cuocere a ~** to cook in a double saucepan.

'**baia** *sf* bay.

**baio'netta** *sf* bayonet.

**balaus'trata** *sf* balustrade.

**balbet'tare** *vi* to stutter, stammer; (*bimbo*) to babble // *vt* to stammer out.

**balbuzi'ente** [balbut'tsjɛnte] *ag* stuttering, stammering.

**bal'cone** *sm* balcony.

**baldac'chino** [baldak'kino] *sm* canopy.

**bal'danza** [bal'dantsa] *sf* self-confidence, boldness.

'**baldo, a** *ag* bold, daring.

**bal'doria** *sf*: **fare ~** to have a riotous time.

**ba'lena** *sf* whale.

**bale'nare** *vb impers*: **balena** there's lightning // *vi* to flash; **mi balenò un'idea** an idea flashed through my mind; **ba'leno** *sm* flash of lightning; **in un baleno** in a flash.

**ba'lestra** *sf* crossbow.

**ba'lia** *sf*: **in ~ di** at the mercy of.

'**balla** *sf* (*di merci*) bale; (*fandonia*) (tall) story.

**bal'lare** *vt*, *vi* to dance; **bal'lata** *sf* ballad.

**balle'rina** *sf* dancer; ballet dancer; (*scarpa*) ballet shoe.

**balle'rino** *sm* dancer; ballet dancer.

**bal'letto** *sm* ballet.

'**ballo** *sm* dance; (*azione*) dancing *q*; **essere in ~** (*fig: persona*) to be involved; (*: cosa*) to be at stake.

**ballot'taggio** [ballot'taddʒo] *sm* (*POL*) second ballot.

**balne'are** *ag* seaside *cpd*; (*stagione*) bathing.

**ba'locco, chi** *sm* toy.

**ba'lordo, a** *ag* stupid, senseless.

'**balsamo** *sm* (*aroma*) balsam; (*lenimento, fig*) balm.

'**Baltico** *sm*: **il (mar) ~** the Baltic (Sea).

**balu'ardo** *sm* bulwark.

'**balza** ['baltsa] *sf* (*dirupo*) crag; (*di stoffa*) frill.

**bal'zare** [bal'tsare] *vi* to bounce; (*lanciarsi*) to jump, leap; '**balzo** *sm* bounce; jump, leap; (*del terreno*) crag.

**bam'bagia** [bam'badʒa] *sf* (*ovatta*) cotton wool (*Brit*), absorbent cotton (*US*); (*cascame*) cotton waste.

**bam'bina** *ag*, *sf vedi* **bambino**.

**bambi'naia** *sf* nanny, nurse(maid).

**bam'bino, a** *sm/f* child.

**bam'boccio** [bam'bɔttʃo] *sm* plump child; (*pupazzo*) rag doll.

'**bambola** *sf* doll.

**bambù** *sm* bamboo.

**ba'nale** *ag* banal, commonplace.

**ba'nana** *sf* banana; **ba'nano** *sm* banana tree.

'**banca, che** *sf* bank; **~ dei dati** data bank.

**banca'rella** *sf* stall.

**ban'cario, a** *ag* banking, bank *cpd* // *sm* bank clerk.

**banca'rotta** sf bankruptcy; **fare ~** to go bankrupt.

**ban'chetto** [ban'ketto] sm banquet.

**banchi'ere** [ban'kjɛre] sm banker.

**ban'china** [ban'kina] sf (di porto) quay; (per pedoni, ciclisti) path; (di stazione) platform; **~ cedevole** (AUT) soft verge (Brit) o shoulder (US).

'**banco, chi** sm bench; (di negozio) counter; (di mercato) stall; (di officina) (work-)bench; (GEO, banca) bank; **~ di corallo** coral reef; **~ degli imputati** dock; **~ di prova** (fig) testing ground; **~ dei testimoni** witness box.

'**Bancomat** sm inv ® automated banking; (tessera) cash card.

**banco'nota** sf banknote.

'**banda** sf band; (di stoffa) band, stripe; (lato, parte) side; **~ perforata** punch tape.

**banderu'ola** sf (METEOR) weathercock, weathervane.

**bandi'era** sf flag, banner.

**ban'dire** vt to proclaim; (esiliare) to exile; (fig) to dispense with.

**ban'dito** sm outlaw, bandit.

**bandi'tore** sm (di aste) auctioneer.

'**bando** sm proclamation; (esilio) exile, banishment; **~ alle chiacchiere!** that's enough talk!

'**bandolo** sm: **il ~ della matassa** (fig) the key to the problem.

**bar** sm inv bar.

'**bara** sf coffin.

**ba'racca, che** sf shed, hut; (peg) hovel; **mandare avanti la ~** to keep things going.

**bara'onda** sf hubbub, bustle.

**ba'rare** vi to cheat.

'**baratro** sm abyss.

**barat'tare** vt: **~ qc con** to barter sth for, swap sth for; **ba'ratto** sm barter.

**ba'rattolo** sm (di latta) tin; (di vetro) jar; (di coccio) pot.

'**barba** sf beard; **farsi la ~** to shave; **farla in ~ a qn** (fig) to do sth to sb's face; **che ~!** what a bore!

**barbabi'etola** sf beetroot (Brit), beet (US); **~ da zucchero** sugar beet.

**bar'barico, a, ci, che** ag barbarian; barbaric.

'**barbaro, a** ag barbarous; **~i** smpl barbarians.

**barbi'ere** sm barber.

**bar'bone** sm (cane) poodle; (vagabondo) tramp.

**bar'buto, a** ag bearded.

'**barca, che** sf boat; **~ a remi** rowing boat; **barcai'olo** sm boatman.

**barcol'lare** vi to stagger.

**bar'cone** sm (per ponti di barche) pontoon.

**ba'rella** sf (lettiga) stretcher.

**ba'rile** sm barrel, cask.

**ba'rista, i, e** sm/f barman/maid; bar owner.

**ba'ritono** sm baritone.

**bar'lume** sm glimmer, gleam.

**ba'rocco, a, chi, che** ag, sm baroque.

**ba'rometro** sm barometer.

**ba'rone** sm baron; **baro'nessa** sf baroness.

'**barra** sf bar; (NAUT) helm; (linea grafica) line, stroke.

**barri'care** vt to barricade; **barri'cata** sf barricade.

**barri'era** sf barrier; (GEO) reef.

**ba'ruffa** sf scuffle.

**barzel'letta** [bardzel'letta] sf joke, funny story.

**ba'sare** vt to base, found; **~rsi** vr: **~rsi su** (sog: fatti, prove) to be based o founded on; (: persona) to base one's arguments on.

'**basco, a, schi, sche** ag Basque // sm (copricapo) beret.

'**base** sf base; (fig: fondamento) basis; (POL) rank and file; **di ~** basic; **in ~ a** on the basis of, according to; **a ~ di caffè** coffee-based.

**ba'setta** sf sideburn.

**ba'silica, che** sf basilica.

**ba'silico** sm basil.

**bassi'fondi** smpl (fig) dregs.

'**basso, a** *ag* low; (*di statura*) short; (*meridionale*) southern // *sm* bottom, lower part; (*MUS*) bass; **la** ~**a Italia** southern Italy.

**bassorili'evo** *sm* bas-relief.

'**basta** *escl* (that's) enough!, that will do!

**bas'tardo, a** *ag* (*animale, pianta*) hybrid, crossbreed; (*persona*) illegitimate, bastard (*peg*) // *sm/f* illegitimate child, bastard (*peg*).

**bas'tare** *vi, vb impers* to be enough, be sufficient; ~ **a qn** to be enough for sb; **basta chiedere** *o* **che chieda a un vigile** you have only to *o* need only ask a policeman.

**basti'mento** *sm* ship, vessel.

**basto'nare** *vt* to beat, thrash.

**baston'cino** [baston'tʃino] *sm* (*SCI*) ski pole.

**bas'tone** *sm* stick; ~ **da passeggio** walking stick.

**bat'taglia** [bat'taʎʎa] *sf* battle; fight.

**bat'taglio** [bat'taʎʎo] *sm* (*di campana*) clapper; (*di porta*) knocker.

**battagli'one** [battaʎ'ʎone] *sm* battalion.

**bat'tello** *sm* boat.

**bat'tente** *sm* (*imposta: di porta*) wing, flap; (*: di finestra*) shutter; (*batacchio: di porta*) knocker; (*: di orologio*) hammer; **chiudere i** ~**i** (*fig*) to shut up shop.

'**battere** *vt* to beat; (*grano*) to thresh; (*percorrere*) to scour // *vi* (*bussare*) to knock; (*urtare*): ~ **contro** to hit *o* strike against; (*pioggia, sole*) to beat down; (*cuore*) to beat; (*TENNIS*) to serve; ~**rsi** *vr* to fight; ~ **le mani** to clap; ~ **i piedi** to stamp one's feet; ~ **le ore** to strike the hours; ~ **su un argomento** to hammer home an argument; ~ **a macchina** to type; ~ **bandiera italiana** to fly the Italian flag; ~ **in testa** (*AUT*) to knock; **in un batter d'occhio** in the twinkling of an eye.

**bat'teri** *smpl* bacteria.

**batte'ria** *sf* battery; (*MUS*) drums *pl.*

**bat'tesimo** *sm* baptism; christening.

**battez'zare** [batted'dzare] *vt* to baptize; to christen.

**batticu'ore** *sm* palpitations *pl;* **avere il** ~ to be frightened to death.

**batti'mano** *sm* applause.

**batti'panni** *sm inv* carpet-beater.

**battis'tero** *sm* baptistry.

**battis'trada** *sm inv* (*di pneumatico*) tread; (*di gara*) pacemaker.

**battitap'peto** *sm* upright vacuum cleaner.

'**battito** *sm* beat, throb; ~ **cardiaco** heartbeat; ~ **della pioggia/ dell'orologio** beating of the rain/ ticking of the clock.

**bat'tuta** *sf* blow; (*di macchina da scrivere*) stroke; (*MUS*) bar; beat; (*TEATRO*) cue; (*frase spiritosa*) witty remark; (*di caccia*) beating; (*POLIZIA*) combing, scouring; (*TENNIS*) service.

**ba'ule** *sm* trunk; (*AUT*) boot (*Brit*), trunk (*US*).

'**bava** *sf* (*di animale*) slaver, slobber; (*di lumaca*) slime; (*di vento*) breath.

**bava'glino** [bavaʎ'ʎino] *sm* bib.

**ba'vaglio** [ba'vaʎʎo] *sm* gag.

'**bavero** *sm* collar.

**ba'zar** [bad'dzar] *sm inv* bazaar.

**baz'zecola** [bad'dzekola] *sf* trifle.

**bazzi'care** [battsi'kare] *vt* to frequent // *vi:* ~ **in/con** to frequent.

**be'ato, a** *ag* blessed; (*fig*) happy; ~ **te!** lucky you!

**bec'caccia, ce** [bek'kattʃa] *sf* woodcock.

**bec'care** *vt* to peck; (*fig: raffreddore*) to pick up, catch; ~**rsi** *vr* (*fig*) to squabble.

**becchegi'are** [bekked'dʒare] *vi* to pitch.

**bec'chino** [bek'kino] *sm* gravedigger.

'**becco, chi** *sm* beak, bill; (*di caffettiera ecc*) spout; lip.

**Be'fana** *sf* old woman who, according to legend, brings children their presents at the Epiphany; (*Epifania*) Epiphany; (*donna brutta*): b~ hag, witch.

'**beffa** *sf* practical joke; **farsi ~e di qn** to make a fool of sb; **bef'fardo, a** *ag* scornful, mocking; **bef'fare** *vt* (*anche*: **beffarsi di**) to make a fool of, mock.

'**bega, ghe** *sf* quarrel.

'**begli** ['beʎʎi], '**bei, bel** *ag vedi* **bello**.

**be'lare** *vi* to bleat.

'**belga, gi, ghe** *ag, sm/f* Belgian.

'**Belgio** ['bɛldʒo] *sm*: **il ~** Belgium.

**bel'lezza** [bel'lettsa] *sf* beauty.

'**bello, a** *ag* (*dav sm* **bel** + *C*, **bell'** + *V*, **bello** + *s impura, gn, pn, ps, x, z, pl* **bei** + *C*, **begli** + *s impura etc o V*) beautiful, fine, lovely; (*uomo*) handsome // *sm* (*bellezza*) beauty; (*tempo*) fine weather // *sf* (*SPORT*) decider // *av*: **fa ~** the weather is fine, it's fine; **una ~a cifra** a considerable sum of money; **un bel niente** absolutely nothing; **è una truffa ~a e buona!** it's a real fraud!; **è bell'e finito** it's already finished; **adesso viene il ~** now comes the best bit; **sul più ~ at** the crucial point; **cosa fai di ~?** are you doing anything interesting?; **belle arti** fine arts.

'**belva** *sf* wild animal.

**belve'dere** *sm inv* panoramic viewpoint.

**benché** [ben'ke] *cong* although.

'**benda** *sf* bandage; (*per gli occhi*) blindfold; **ben'dare** *vt* to bandage; to blindfold.

'**bene** *av* well; (*completamente, affatto*): **è ben difficile** it's very difficult // *ag inv*: **gente ~** well-to-do people // *sm* good; **~i** *smpl* (*averi*) property *sg*, estate *sg*; **io sto ~/poco ~** I'm well/not very well; **va ~** all right; **volere un ~ dell'anima a qn** to love sb very much; **un uomo per ~** a respectable man; **fare ~** to do the right thing; **fare ~ a** (*salute*) to be good for; **fare del ~ a qn** to do

sb a good turn; **~i di consumo** consumer goods.

**bene'detto, a** *pp di* **benedire** // *ag* blessed, holy.

**bene'dire** *vt* to bless; to consecrate; **benedizi'one** *sf* blessing.

**benedu'cato, a** *ag* well-mannered.

**benefi'cenza** [benefi'tʃɛntsa] *sf* charity.

**bene'ficio** [bene'fitʃo] *sm* benefit; **con ~ d'inventario** (*fig*) with reservations.

**be'nefico, a, ci, che** *ag* beneficial; charitable.

**beneme'renza** [beneme'rɛntsa] *sf* merit.

**bene'merito, a** *ag* meritorious.

**be'nessere** *sm* well-being.

**benes'tante** *ag* well-to-do.

**benes'tare** *sm* consent, approval.

**be'nevolo, a** *ag* benevolent.

**be'nigno, a** [be'niɲɲo] *ag* kind, kindly; (*critica etc*) favourable; (*MED*) benign.

**benin'teso** *av* of course.

**bensì** *cong* but (rather).

**benve'nuto, a** *ag, sm* welcome; **dare il ~ a qn** to welcome sb.

**ben'zina** [ben'dzina] *sf* petrol (*Brit*), gas (*US*); **fare ~** to get petrol (*Brit*) o gas (*US*); **benzi'naio** *sm* petrol (*Brit*) o gas (*US*) pump attendant.

'**bere** *vt* to drink; **darla a ~ a qn** (*fig*) to fool sb.

**ber'lina** *sf* (*AUT*) saloon (car) (*Brit*), sedan (*US*).

**Ber'lino** *sm* Berlin.

**ber'noccolo** *sm* bump; (*inclinazione*) flair.

**ber'retto** *sm* cap.

**bersagli'are** [bersaʎ'ʎare] *vt* to shoot at; (*colpire ripetutamente, fig*) to bombard; **bersagliato dalla sfortuna** dogged by ill fortune.

**ber'saglio** [ber'saʎʎo] *sm* target.

**bes'temmia** *sf* curse; (*REL*) blasphemy.

**bestemmi'are** *vi* to curse, swear; to blaspheme // *vt* to curse, swear at; to blaspheme.

'**bestia** *sf* animal; andare in ~ *(fig)* to fly into a rage; **besti'ale** *ag* beastly; animal *cpd*; *(fam)*: fa un freddo bestiale it's bitterly cold; **besti'ame** *sm* livestock; *(bovino)* cattle *pl.*

'**bettola** *sf (peg)* dive.

be'**tulla** *sf* birch.

be'**vanda** *sf* drink, beverage.

bevi'**tore**, '**trice** *sm/f* drinker.

be'**vuto**, a *pp di* **bere** // *sf* drink.

bi'**ada** *sf* fodder.

bianche'**ria** [bjanke'ria] *sf* linen; ~ intima underwear; ~ da donna ladies' underwear, lingerie.

bi'**anco**, a, chi, che *ag* white; *(non scritto)* blank // *sm* white; *(intonaco)* whitewash // *sm/f* white, white man/woman; in ~ *(foglio, assegno)* blank; *(notte)* sleepless; in ~ e nero *(TV, FOT)* black and white; mangiare in ~ to follow a bland diet; pesce in ~ boiled fish; andare in ~ *(non riuscire)* to fail; ~ dell'uovo egg-white.

biasi'**mare** *vt* to disapprove of, censure; **bi'asimo** *sm* disapproval, censure.

'**bibbia** *sf* bible.

bibe'**ron** *sm inv* feeding bottle.

'**bibita** *sf* (soft) drink.

biblio'**teca**, **che** *sf* library; *(mobile)* bookcase; **bibliote'cario, a** *sm/f* librarian.

bicarbo'**nato** *sm*: ~ (di sodio) bicarbonate (of soda).

bicchi'**ere** [bik'kjɛre] *sm* glass.

bici'**cletta** [bitʃi'kletta] *sf* bicycle; andare in ~ to cycle.

**bidé** *sm inv* bidet.

bi'**dello, a** *sm/f (INS)* janitor.

bi'**done** *sm* drum, can; *(anche: ~ dell'immondizia)* (dust)bin; *(fam: truffa)* swindle; fare un ~ a qn *(fam)* to let sb down; to cheat sb.

bien'**nale** *ag* biennial.

bi'**ennio** *sm* period of two years.

bi'**etola** *sf* beet.

bifor'**carsi** *vr* to fork; **biforcazi'one** *sf* fork.

bighello'**nare** [bigello'nare] *vi* to loaf (about).

bigiotte'**ria** [bidʒotte'ria] *sf* costume jewellery; *(negozio)* jeweller's *(selling only costume jewellery)*.

bigli'**ardo** *sm* = biliardo.

bigliette'**ria** [biʎʎette'ria] *sf (di stazione)* ticket office; booking office; *(di teatro)* box office.

bigli'**etto** [biʎ'ʎetto] *sm (per viaggi, spettacoli etc)* ticket; *(cartoncino)* card; *(anche:* ~ di banca) (bank)note; ~ d'auguri/da visita greetings/visiting card; ~ d'andata e ritorno return (ticket), round-trip ticket *(US)*.

bignè [bin'nɛ] *sm inv* cream puff.

bigo'**dino** *sm* roller, curler.

bi'**gotto, a** *ag* over-pious // *sm/f* church fiend.

bi'**lancia, ce** [bi'lantʃa] *sf (pesa)* scales *pl*; *(: di precisione)* balance; *(dello zodiaco)*: B~ Libra; ~ commerciale/dei pagamenti balance of trade/payments; **bilanci'are** *vt (pesare)* to weigh; *(: fig)* to weigh up; *(pareggiare)* to balance.

bi'**lancio** [bi'lantʃo] *sm (COMM)* balance(-sheet); *(statale)* budget; fare il ~ di *(fig)* to assess; ~ consuntivo *(final)* balance; ~ preventivo budget.

'**bile** *sf* bile; *(fig)* rage, anger.

bili'**ardo** *sm* billiards *sg*; billiard table.

bi'**lico, chi** *sm*: essere in ~ to be balanced; *(fig)* to be undecided; tenere qn in ~ to keep sb in suspense.

bi'**lingue** *ag* bilingual.

bili'**one** *sm (mille milioni)* thousand million; *(milione di milioni)* billion *(Brit)*, trillion *(US)*.

'**bimbo, a** *sm/f* little boy/girl.

bimen'**sile** *ag* fortnightly.

bimes'**trale** *ag* two-monthly, bimonthly.

bi'**nario, a** *ag (sistema)* binary // *sm*

(railway) track o line; (piattaforma) platform; ~ morto dead-end track.
bi'nocolo sm binoculars pl.
bio... prefisso: bio'chimica [bio'kimika] sf biochemistry; biode-gra'dabile ag biodegradable; bio-gra'fia sf biography; bio'logia sf biology; bio'logico, a, ci, che ag biological.
bi'ondo, a ag blond, fair.
bir'bante sm rogue, rascal.
biri'chino, a [biri'kino] ag mischievous // smf scamp, little rascal.
bi'rillo sm skittle (Brit), pin (US); ~i smpl (gioco) skittles sg (Brit), bowling (US).
'biro sf inv ® biro ®.
'birra sf beer; a tutta ~ (fig) at top speed; birre'ria sf = bierkeller.
bis escl, sm inv encore.
bis'betico, a, ci, che ag ill-tempered, crabby.
bisbigli'are [bisbiʎ'ʎare] vt, vi to whisper.
'bisca, sche sf gambling-house.
'biscia, sce ['biʃʃa] sf snake; ~ d'acqua grass snake.
bis'cotto sm biscuit.
bises'tile ag: anno ~ leap year.
bis'lungo, a, ghi, ghe ag oblong.
bis'nonno, a smf great grandfather/grandmother.
biso'gnare [bizoɲ'ɲare] vb impers: bisogna che tu parta/lo faccia you'll have to go/do it; bisogna parlargli we'll (o I'll) have to talk to him.
bi'sogno [bi'zoɲo] sm need; ~i smpl: fare i propri ~i to relieve o.s.; avere ~ di qc/di fare qc to need sth/to do sth; al ~, in caso di ~ if need be; biso'gnoso, a ag needy, poor; bisognoso di in need of, needing.
bis'tecca, che sf steak, beefsteak.
bisticci'are [bistit'tʃare] vi, ~rsi vr to quarrel, bicker; bis'ticcio sm quarrel, squabble; (gioco di parole) pun.
'bisturi sm scalpel.

bi'sunto, a ag very greasy.
'bitter sm inv bitters pl.
bi'vacco, chi sm bivouac.
'bivio sm fork; (fig) dilemma.
'bizza ['biddza] sf tantrum; fare le ~e (bambino) to be naughty.
biz'zarro, a [bid'dzarro] ag bizarre, strange.
biz'zeffe [bid'dzeffe]: a ~ av in plenty, galore.
blan'dire vt to soothe; to flatter.
'blando, a ag mild, gentle.
bla'sone sm coat of arms.
blate'rare vi to chatter, blether.
blin'dato, a ag armoured.
bloc'care vt to block; (isolare) to isolate, cut off; (porto) to blockade; (prezzi, beni) to freeze; (meccanismo) to jam; ~rsi vr (motore) to stall; (freni, porta) to jam, stick; (ascensore) to get stuck.
'blocco, chi sm block; (MIL) blockade; (dei fitti) restriction; (quadernetto) pad; (fig: unione) coalition; (il bloccare) blocking; isolating; cutting-off; blockading; freezing; jamming; in ~ (nell'insieme) as a whole; (COMM) in bulk; ~ cardiaco cardiac arrest.
blu ag inv, sm dark blue.
'blusa sf (camiciotto) smock; (camicetta) blouse.
'boa sm inv (ZOOL) boa constrictor; (sciarpa) feather boa // sf buoy.
bo'ato sm rumble, roar.
bo'bina sf reel, spool; (di pellicola) spool; (di film) reel; (ELETTR) coil.
'bocca, che sf mouth; in ~ al lupo! good luck!
boc'caccia, ce [bok'kattʃa] sf (malalingua) gossip; fare le ~ce to pull faces.
boc'cale sm jug; ~ da birra tankard.
boc'cetta [bot'tʃetta] sf small bottle.
boccheggi'are [bokked'dʒare] vi to gasp.
boc'chino [bok'kino] sm (di sigaretta, sigaro: cannella) cigarette

holder; cigar-holder; (*di pipa, strumenti musicali*) mouthpiece.

'**boccia, ce** ['bɔttʃa] *sf* bottle; (*da vino*) decanter, carafe; (*palla*) bowl; **gioco delle** ~ce bowls *sg*.

**bocci'are** [bot'tʃare] *vt* (*proposta, progetto*) to reject; (*INS*) to fail; (*BOCCE*) to hit; **boccia'tura** *sf* failure.

**bocci'olo** [bot'tʃɔlo] *sm* bud.

**boc'cone** *sm* mouthful, morsel.

**boc'coni** *av* face downwards.

'**boia** *sm inv* executioner; hangman.

**boi'ata** *sf* botch.

**boicot'tare** *vt* to boycott.

'**bolide** *sm* meteor; **come un** ~ like a flash, at top speed.

'**bolla** *sf* bubble; (*MED*) blister; ~ **papale** papal bull; ~ **di consegna** (*COMM*) delivery note.

**bol'lare** *vt* to stamp; (*fig*) to brand.

**bol'lente** *ag* boiling; boiling hot.

**bol'letta** *sf* bill; (*ricevuta*) receipt; **essere in** ~ to be hard up.

**bollet'tino** *sm* bulletin; (*COMM*) note; ~ **di spedizione** consignment note.

**bol'lire** *vt, vi* to boil; **bol'lito** *sm* (*CUC*) boiled meat.

**bolli'tore** *sm* (*CUC*) kettle; (*per riscaldamento*) boiler.

'**bollo** *sm* stamp.

'**bomba** *sf* bomb; **tornare a** ~ (*fig*) to get back to the point; ~ **atomica** atom bomb.

**bombarda'mento** *sm* bombardment; bombing.

**bombar'dare** *vt* to bombard; (*da aereo*) to bomb.

**bombardi'ere** *sm* bomber.

**bom'betta** *sf* bowler (hat).

'**bombola** *sf* cylinder.

**bo'naccia, ce** [bo'nattʃa] *sf* dead calm.

**bo'nario, a** *ag* good-natured, kind.

**bo'nifica, che** *sf* reclamation; reclaimed land.

**bo'nifico, ci** *sm* (*riduzione, abbuono*) discount; (*versamento a terzi*) credit transfer.

**bontà** *sf* goodness; (*cortesia*) kindness; **aver la** ~ **di fare qc** to be good *o* kind enough to do sth.

**borbot'tare** *vi* to mumble; (*stomaco*) to rumble.

'**borchia** ['borkja] *sf* stud.

**borda'tura** *sf* (*SARTORIA*) border, trim.

'**bordo** *sm* (*NAUT*) ship's side; (*orlo*) edge; (*striscia di guarnizione*) border, trim; **a** ~ **di** (*nave, aereo*) aboard, on board; (*macchina*) in.

**bor'gata** *sf* hamlet.

**bor'ghese** [bor'geze] *ag* (*spesso peg*) middle-class; bourgeois; **abito** ~ civilian dress; **borghe'sia** *sf* middle classes *pl*; bourgeoisie.

'**borgo, ghi** *sm* (*paesino*) village; (*quartiere*) district; (*sobborgo*) suburb.

'**boria** *sf* self-conceit, arrogance.

**boro'talco** *sm* talcum powder.

**bor'raccia, ce** [bor'rattʃa] *sf* canteen, water-bottle.

'**borsa** *sf* bag; (*anche:* ~ **da signora**) handbag; (*ECON*): **la B**~ (*valori*) the Stock Exchange; ~ **nera** black market; ~ **della spesa** shopping bag; ~ **di studio** grant; **borsai'olo** *sm* pickpocket; **borsel'lino** *sm* purse; **bor'setta** *sf* handbag; **bor'sista, i, e** *smf* (*ECON*) speculator; (*INS*) grant-holder.

**bos'caglia** [bos'kaʎʎa] *sf* woodlands *pl*.

**boscai'olo** *sm* woodcutter; forester.

'**bosco, schi** *sm* wood; **bos'coso, a** *ag* wooded.

'**bossolo** *sm* cartridge-case.

**bo'tanico, a, ci, che** *ag* botanical // *sm* botanist // *sf* botany.

**botola** *sf* trap door.

'**botta** *sf* blow; (*rumore*) bang.

'**botte** *sf* barrel, cask.

**bot'tega, ghe** *sf* shop; (*officina*) workshop; **botte'gaio, a** *smf* shopkeeper; **botte'ghino** *sm* ticket office; (*del lotto*) public lottery office.

**bot'tiglia** [bot'tiʎʎa] *sf* bottle; **botti-**

**glie'ria** sf wine shop.

**bot'tino** sm (di guerra) booty; (di rapina, furto) loot.

**'botto** sm bang; crash; **di ~** suddenly.

**bot'tone** sm button; **attaccare ~ a qn** (fig) to buttonhole sb.

**bo'vino, a** ag bovine; **~i** smpl cattle.

**boxe** [bɔks] sf boxing.

**'bozza** ['bɔttsa] sf draft; sketch; (TIP) proof; **boz'zetto** sm sketch.

**'bozzolo** ['bɔttsolo] sm cocoon.

**BR** sigla fpl = **Brigate Rosse**.

**brac'care** vt to hunt.

**brac'cetto** [brat'tʃetto] sm: **a ~** arm in arm.

**bracci'ale** [brat'tʃale] sm bracelet; (distintivo) armband; **braccia'letto** sm bracelet, bangle.

**bracci'ante** [brat'tʃante] sm (AGR) day labourer.

**bracci'ata** [brat'tʃata] sf (nel nuoto) stroke.

**'braccio** ['brattʃo] sm (pl(f) **braccia**; ANAT) arm; (pl(m) **bracci**: di gru, fiume) arm; (: di edificio) wing; **~ di mare** sound; **bracci'olo** sm (appoggio) arm.

**'bracco, chi** sm hound.

**bracconi'ere** sm poacher.

**'brace** ['bratʃe] sf embers pl; **braci'ere** sm brazier.

**braci'ola** [bra'tʃɔla] sf (CUC) chop.

**bra'mare** vt: **~ qc/di fare** to long for sth/to do.

**'branca, che** sf branch.

**'branchia** ['brankja] sf (ZOOL) gill.

**'branco, chi** sm (di cani, lupi) pack; (di uccelli, pecore) flock; (peg: di persone) gang, pack.

**branco'lare** vi to grope, feel one's way.

**'branda** sf camp bed.

**bran'dello** sm scrap, shred; **a ~i** in tatters, in rags.

**bran'dire** vt to brandish.

**'brano** sm piece; (di libro) passage.

**bra'sato** sm braised beef.

**Bra'sile** sm: **il ~** Brazil;

**brasili'ano, a** ag, sm/f Brazilian.

**'bravo, a** ag (abile) clever, capable, skilful; (buono) good, honest; (: bambino) good; (coraggioso) brave; **~!** well done!; (al teatro) bravo!

**bra'vura** sf cleverness, skill.

**'breccia, ce** ['brettʃa] sf breach.

**bre'tella** sf (AUT) link; **~e** sfpl braces.

**'breve** ag brief, short; **in ~** in short.

**brevet'tare** vt to patent.

**bre'vetto** sm patent; **~ di pilotaggio** pilot's licence (Brit) o license (US).

**'brezza** ['breddza] sf breeze.

**'bricco, chi** sm jug; **~ del caffè** coffeepot.

**bric'cone, a** sm/f rogue, rascal.

**'briciola** ['britʃola] sf crumb.

**'briciolo** ['britʃolo] sm (specie fig) bit.

**'briga, ghe** sf (fastidio) trouble, bother; **pigliarsi la ~ di fare qc** to take the trouble to do sth.

**brigadi'ere** sm (dei carabinieri etc) ≈ sergeant.

**bri'gante** sm bandit.

**bri'gata** sf (MIL) brigade; (gruppo) group, party.

**'briglia** ['briʎʎa] sf rein; **a ~ sciolta** at full gallop; (fig) at full speed.

**bril'lante** ag bright; (anche fig) brilliant; (che luccica) shining // sm diamond.

**bril'lare** vi to shine; (mina) to blow up // vt (mina) to set off.

**'brillo** ag merry, tipsy.

**'brina** sf hoarfrost.

**brin'dare** vi: **~ a qn/qc** to drink to o toast sb/sth.

**'brindisi** sm inv toast.

**'brio** sm liveliness, go; **bri'oso, a** ag lively.

**bri'tannico, a, ci, che** ag British.

**'brivido** sm shiver; (di ribrezzo) shudder; (fig) thrill.

**brizzo'lato, a** ag [brittso'lato] (persona) going grey; (barba, capelli) greying.

**'brocca, che** sf jug.

**broc'cato** sm brocade.

**'broccolo** sm broccoli sg.

**'brodo** sm broth; (per cucinare) stock; ~ ristretto consommé.

**brogli'accio** [broʎˈʎattʃo] sm scribbling pad.

**'broglio** ['brɔʎʎo] sm: ~ elettorale gerrymandering.

**bron'chite** [bronˈkite] sf (MED) bronchitis.

**'broncio** ['brontʃo] sm sulky expression; tenere il ~ to sulk.

**'bronco, chi** sm bronchial tube.

**bronto'lare** vi to grumble; (tuono, stomaco) to rumble.

**'bronzo** ['brondzo] sm bronze.

**bru'care** vt to browse on, nibble at.

**brucia'pelo** [brutʃaˈpelo]: a ~ av point-blank.

**bruci'are** [bruˈtʃare] vt to burn; (scottare) to scald // vi to burn; **brucia'tore** sm burner; **brucia'tura** sf (atto) burning q; (segno) burn; (scottatura) scald; **bruci'ore** sm burning o smarting sensation.

**'bruco, chi** sm caterpillar; grub.

**brughi'era** [bruˈgjɛra] sf heath, moor.

**bruli'care** vi to swarm.

**'brullo, a** ag bare, bleak.

**'bruma** sf mist.

**'bruno, a** ag brown, dark; (persona) dark(-haired).

**'brusco, a, schi, sche** ag (sapore) sharp; (modi, persona) brusque, abrupt; (movimento) abrupt, sudden.

**bru'sio** sm buzz, buzzing.

**bru'tale** ag brutal.

**'bruto, a** ag (forza) brute cpd // sm brute.

**brut'tezza** [brutˈtettsa] sf ugliness.

**'brutto, a** ag ugly; (cattivo) bad; (malattia, strada, affare) nasty, bad; ~ tempo bad weather; **brut'tura** sf (cosa brutta) ugly thing; (sudiciume) filth; (azione meschina) mean action.

**Bru'xelles** [bryˈsɛl] sf Brussels.

**'buca, che** sf hole; (avvallamento) hollow; ~ delle lettere letterbox.

**buca'neve** sm inv snowdrop.

**bu'care** vt (forare) to make a hole (o holes) in; (pungere) to pierce; (biglietto) to punch; ~rsi vr (con eroina) to mainline; ~ una gomma to have a puncture.

**bu'cato** sm (operazione) washing; (panni) wash, washing.

**'buccia, ce** ['buttʃa] sf skin, peel; (corteccia) bark.

**bucherel'lare** [bukerelˈlare] vt to riddle with holes.

**'buco, chi** sm hole.

**bu'dello** sm intestine; (fig: tubo) tube; (vicolo) alley; ~a sfpl bowels, guts.

**bu'dino** sm pudding.

**'bue** sm ox; (anche: carne di ~) beef.

**'bufalo** sm buffalo.

**bu'fera** sf storm.

**'buffo, a** ag funny; (TEATRO) comic.

**bu'gia, 'gie** [buˈdʒia] sf lie; (candeliere) candleholder; **bugi'ardo, a** ag lying, deceitful // sm/f liar.

**bugi'gattolo** [budʒiˈgattolo] sm poky little room.

**'buio, a** ag dark // sm dark, darkness; fa ~ pesto it's pitch-dark.

**'bulbo** sm (BOT) bulb; ~ oculare eyeball.

**Bulga'ria** sf: la ~ Bulgaria.

**bul'lone** sm bolt.

**buona'notte** escl good night! // sf: dare la ~ a to say good night to.

**buona'sera** escl good evening!

**buon gi'orno** [bwonˈdʒorno] escl good morning (o afternoon)!

**buongus'taio, a** sm/f gourmet.

**buon'gusto** sm good taste.

**bu'ono, a** ag dark // sm buon + C o V, buono + s impura, gn, pn, ps, x, z; dav sf buon' + V) good; (benevolo): ~ (con) good (to), kind (to); (adatto): ~ a/da fit for/to // sm good; (COMM) voucher, coupon; alla buona ag simple // av in a simple way, without any fuss; **buona fortuna** good luck; **buon com-**

**pleanno** happy birthday; **buon divertimento** have a nice time; **a buon mercato** cheap; **di buon'ora** early; ~ **di cassa** cash voucher; ~ **di consegna** delivery note; ~ **fruttifero** bond bearing interest; ~ **a nulla** good-for-nothing; ~ **del tesoro** Treasury bill; **buon riposo** sleep well; **buon senso** common sense; **buon viaggio** bon voyage, have a good trip.

**buontem'pone, a** *sm/f* jovial person.

**burat'tino** *sm* puppet.

'**burbero, a** *ag* surly, gruff.

'**burla** *sf* prank, trick; **bur'lare** *vt*: burlarsi qc/qn, burlarsi di qc/qn to make fun of sth/sb.

**burocra'zia** [burokrat'tsia] *sf* bureaucracy.

**bur'rasca, sche** *sf* storm; **burras'coso, a** *ag* stormy.

'**burro** *sm* butter.

**bur'rone** *sm* ravine.

**bus'care** *vt* (*anche*: ~**rsi**: raffreddore) to get, catch; buscarle (*fam*) to get a hiding.

**bus'sare** *vi* to knock.

'**bussola** *sf* compass; perdere la ~ (*fig*) to lose one's bearings.

'**busta** *sf* (*da lettera*) envelope; (*astuccio*) case; in ~ aperta/chiusa in an unsealed/sealed envelope; ~ paga pay packet.

**busta'rella** *sf* bribe, backhander.

'**busto** *sm* bust; (*indumento*) corset, girdle; **a mezzo** ~ (*foto*) half-length.

**but'tare** *vt* to throw; (*anche*: ~ **via**) to throw away; ~ **giù** (*scritto*) to scribble down, dash off; (*cibo*) to gulp down; (*edificio*) to pull down, demolish; (*pasta, verdura*) to put into boiling water; ~**rsi dalla finestra** to jump *o* throw o.s. out of the window.

# C

**ca'bina** *sf* (*di nave*) cabin; (*da spiaggia*) beach hut; (*di autocarro, treno*) cab; (*di aereo*) cockpit; (*di ascensore*) cage; ~ **telefonica** call *o* (tele)phone box.

**ca'cao** *sm* cocoa.

'**caccia** ['kattʃa] *sf* hunting; (*con fucile*) shooting; (*inseguimento*) chase; (*cacciagione*) game // *sm inv* (*aereo*) fighter; (*nave*) destroyer; ~ **grossa** big-game hunting; ~ **all'uomo** manhunt.

**cacciabombardi'ere** [kattʃabombar'djere] *sm* fighter-bomber.

**cacciagi'one** [kattʃa'dʒone] *sf* game.

**cacci'are** [kat'tʃare] *vt* to hunt; (*mandar via*) to chase away; (*ficcare*) to shove, stick // *vi* to hunt; ~**rsi** *vr* (*fam*: *mettersi*): ~**rsi tra la folla** to plunge into the crowd; dove s'è cacciata la mia borsa? where has my bag got to?; ~**rsi nei guai** to get into trouble; ~ **fuori** qc to whip *o* pull sth out; ~ **un urlo** to let out a yell; **caccia'tore** *sm* hunter; **cacciatore di frodo** poacher.

**caccia'vite** [kattʃa'vite] *sm inv* screwdriver.

'**cactus** *sm inv* cactus.

**ca'davere** *sm* (dead) body, corpse.

**ca'dente** *ag* falling; (*casa*) tumbledown.

**ca'denza** [ka'dɛntsa] *sf* cadence; (*andamento ritmico*) rhythm; (MUS) cadenza.

**ca'dere** *vi* to fall; (*denti, capelli*) to fall out; (*tetto*) to fall in; **questa gonna cade bene** this skirt hangs well; **lasciar** ~ (*anche fig*) to drop; ~ **dal sonno** to be falling asleep on one's feet; ~ **dalle nuvole** (*fig*) to be taken aback.

**ca'detto, a** *ag* younger; (*squadra*) junior *cpd* // *sm* cadet.

**ca'duta** *sf* fall; **la ~ dei capelli** hair loss.

**caffè** *sm inv* coffee; (*locale*) café; **~ macchiato** coffee with a dash of milk; **~ macinato** ground coffee.

**caffel'latte** *sm inv* white coffee.

**caffetti'era** *sf* coffeepot.

**cagio'nare** [kadʒo'nare] *vt* to cause, be the cause of.

**cagio'nevole** [kadʒo'nevole] *ag* delicate, weak.

**cagli'are** [kaʎ'ʎare] *vi* to curdle.

**'cagna** ['kaɲɲa] *sf* (*ZOOL*, *peg*) bitch.

**ca'gnesco, a, schi, sche** [kaɲ'nesko] *ag* (*fig*): **guardare qn in ~** to scowl at sb.

**cala'brone** *sm* hornet.

**cala'maio** *sm* inkpot; inkwell.

**cala'maro** *sm* squid.

**cala'mita** *sf* magnet.

**calamità** *sf inv* calamity, disaster.

**ca'lare** *vt* (*far discendere*) to lower; (*MAGLIA*) to decrease // *vi* (*discendere*) to go (o come) down; (*tramontare*) to set, go down; **~ di peso** to lose weight.

**'calca** *sf* throng, press.

**cal'cagno** [kal'kaɲɲo] *sm* heel.

**cal'care** *sm* limestone // *vt* (*premere coi piedi*) to tread, press down; (*premere con forza*) to press down; (*mettere in rilievo*) to stress; **~ la mano** to overdo it, exaggerate.

**'calce** ['kaltʃe] *sm*: **in ~ at** the foot of the page // *sf* lime; **~ viva** quicklime.

**calces'truzzo** [kaltʃes'truttso] *sm* concrete.

**calci'are** [kal'tʃare] *vt*, *vi* to kick; **calcia'tore** *sm* footballer.

**cal'cina** [kal'tʃina] *sf* (*lime*) mortar.

**'calcio** ['kaltʃo] *sm* (*pedata*) kick; (*sport*) football, soccer; (*di pistola, fucile*) butt; (*CHIM*) calcium; **~ d'angolo** (*SPORT*) corner kick; **~ di punizione** (*SPORT*) free kick.

**'calco, chi** *sm* (*ARTE*) casting, moulding; cast, mould.

**calco'lare** *vt* to calculate, work out,

reckon; (*ponderare*) to weigh (up);

**calcola'tore, 'trice** *ag* calculating // *sm* calculator; (*fig*) calculating person // *sf* (*anche*: **macchina calcolatrice**) calculator; **calcolatore elettronico** computer.

**'calcolo** *sm* (*anche MAT*) calculation; (*infinitesimale etc*) calculus; (*MED*) stone; **fare i propri ~i** (*fig*) to weigh the pros and cons; **per ~** out of self-interest.

**cal'daia** *sf* boiler.

**caldeggi'are** [kalded'dʒare] *vt* to support.

**'caldo, a** *ag* warm; (*molto ~*) hot; (*fig: appassionato*) keen; hearty // *sm* heat; **ho ~** I'm warm; I'm hot; **fa ~** it's warm; it's hot.

**calen'dario** *sm* calendar.

**'calibro** *sm* (*di arma*) calibre, bore; (*TECN*) callipers *pl*; (*fig*) calibre; **di grosso ~** (*fig*) prominent.

**'calice** ['kalitʃe] *sm* goblet; (*REL*) chalice.

**ca'ligine** [ka'lidʒine] *sf* fog; (*mista con fumo*) smog.

**'callo** *sm* callus; (*ai piedi*) corn.

**'calma** *sf* calm.

**cal'mante** *sm* sedative, tranquillizer.

**cal'mare** *vt* to calm; (*lenire*) to soothe; **~rsi** *vr* to grow calm, calm down; (*vento*) to abate; (*dolori*) to ease.

**calmi'ere** *sm* controlled price.

**'calmo, a** *ag* calm, quiet.

**'calo** *sm* (*COMM: di prezzi*) fall; (: *di volume*) shrinkage; (: *di peso*) loss.

**ca'lore** *sm* warmth; heat; **in ~** (*ZOOL*) on heat.

**calo'ria** *sf* calorie.

**calo'roso, a** *ag* warm.

**calpes'tare** *vt* to tread on, trample on; **"è vietato ~ l'erba"** "keep off the grass".

**ca'lunnia** *sf* slander; (*scritta*) libel.

**cal'varo** *sm* (*fig*) affliction, cross.

**cal'vizie** [kal'vittsje] *sf* baldness.

**'calvo, a** *ag* bald.

'calza ['kaltsa] sf (da donna) stocking; (da uomo) sock; fare la ~ to knit; ~e di nailon nylons, (nylon) stockings.

cal'zare [kal'tsare] vt (scarpe, guanti: mettersi) to put on; (: portare) to wear // vi to fit; calza'tura sf footwear.

calzet'tone [kaltset'tone] sm heavy knee-length sock.

cal'zino [kal'tsino] sm sock.

calzo'laio [kaltso'lajo] sm shoemaker; (che ripara scarpe) cobbler; calzole'ria sf (negozio) shoe shop.

calzon'cini [kaltson'tʃini] smpl shorts.

cal'zone [kal'tsone] sm trouser leg; (CUC) savoury turnover made with pizza dough; ~i smpl trousers (Brit), pants (US).

cambi'ale sf bill (of exchange); (pagherò cambiario) promissory note.

cambia'mento sm change.

cambi'are vt to change; (modificare) to alter, change; (barattare): ~ (qc con qn/qc) to exchange (sth with sb/for sth) // vi to change, alter; ~rsi vr (variare abito) to change; ~ casa to move (house); ~ idea to change one's mind; ~ treno to change trains.

'cambio sm change; (modifica) alteration, change; (scambio, COMM) exchange; (corso dei cambi) rate of exchange; (TECN, AUT) gears pl; in ~ di in exchange for; dare il ~ a qn to take over from sb.

'camera sf room; (anche: ~ da letto) bedroom; (POL) chamber, house; ~ ardente mortuary chapel; ~ d'aria inner tube; (di pallone) bladder; C~ di Commercio Chamber of Commerce; C~ dei Deputati Chamber of Deputies, ≈ House of Commons (Brit), ≈ House of Representatives (US); ~ a gas gas chamber; ~ a un letto/a due letti/matrimoniale single/twin-bedded/double room; ~ oscura

(FOT) dark room.

came'rata, i, e sm/f companion, mate // sf dormitory.

cameri'era sf (domestica) maid; (che serve a tavola) waitress; (che fa le camere) chambermaid.

cameri'ere sm (man)servant; (di ristorante) waiter.

came'rino sm (TEATRO) dressing room.

'camice ['kamitʃe] sm (REL) alb; (per medici etc) white coat.

cami'cetta [kami'tʃetta] sf blouse.

ca'micia, cie [ka'mitʃa] sf (da uomo) shirt; (da donna) blouse; ~ di forza straitjacket; camici'otto sm casual shirt; (per operai) smock.

cami'netto sm hearth, fireplace.

ca'mino sm chimney; (focolare) fireplace, hearth.

'camion sm inv lorry (Brit), truck (US); camion'cino sm van.

cam'mello sm (ZOOL) camel; (tessuto) camel hair.

cammi'nare vi to walk; (funzionare) to work, go.

cam'mino sm walk; (sentiero) path; (itinerario, direzione, tragitto) way; mettersi in ~ to set o start off.

camo'milla sf camomile; (infuso) camomile tea.

ca'morra sf camorra; racket.

ca'moscio [ka'moʃʃo] sm chamois.

cam'pagna [kam'paɲɲa] sf country, countryside; (POL, COMM, MIL) campaign; in ~ in the country; andare in ~ to go to the country; fare una ~ to campaign; campa'gnolo, a ag country cpd // sf (AUT) cross-country vehicle.

cam'pale ag field cpd; (fig): una giornata ~ a hard day.

cam'pana sf bell; (anche: ~ di vetro) bell jar; campa'nella sf small bell; (di tenda) curtain ring; campa'nello sm (all'uscio, da tavola) bell.

campa'nile sm bell tower, belfry; campani'lismo sm parochialism.

cam'pare *vi* to live; *(tirare avanti)* to get by, manage.

cam'pato, a *ag*: ~ in aria unsound, unfounded.

campeggi'are [kamped'dʒare] *vi* to camp; *(risaltare)* to stand out; campeggia'tore, 'trice *sm/f* camper; cam'peggio *sm* camping; *(terreno)* camp site; fare (del) campeggio to go camping.

cam'pestre *ag* country *cpd*, rural.

campio'nario, a *ag*: fiera ~a trade fair // *sm* collection of samples.

campio'nato *sm* championship.

campi'one, 'essa *sm/f* (SPORT) champion // *sm* (COMM) sample.

'campo *sm* field; (MIL) field; *(: accampamento)* camp; *(spazio delimitato: sportivo etc)* ground; field; *(di quadro)* background; i ~i *(campagna)* the countryside; ~ da aviazione airfield; ~ di concentramento concentration camp; ~ di golf golf course; ~ da tennis tennis court; ~ visivo field of vision.

campo'santo, *pl* campisanti *sm* cemetery.

camuf'fare *vt* to disguise.

'Canada *sm*: il ~ Canada; cana'dese *ag*, *sm/f* Canadian // *sf* *(anche:* tenda canadese) ridge tent.

ca'naglia [ka'naʎʎa] *sf* rabble, mob; *(persona)* scoundrel, rogue.

ca'nale *sm* *(anche fig)* channel; *(artificiale)* canal.

'canapa *sf* hemp.

cana'rino *sm* canary.

cancel'lare [kantʃel'lare] *vt* (con la gomma) to rub out, erase; *(con la penna)* to strike out; *(annullare)* to annul, cancel; *(disdire)* to cancel.

cancelle'ria [kantʃelle'ria] *sf* chancery; *(quanto necessario per scrivere)* stationery.

cancelli'ere [kantʃel'ljere] *sm* chancellor; *(di tribunale)* clerk of the court.

can'cello [kan'tʃello] *sm* gate.

can'crena [kan'krɛna] *sf* gangrene.

'cancro *sm* (MED) cancer; *(dello* zodiaco) C~ Cancer.

can'dela *sf* candle; ~ (di accensione) (AUT) spark(ing) plug.

cande'labro *sm* candelabra.

candeli'ere *sm* candlestick.

candi'dato, a *sm/f* candidate; *(aspirante a una carica)* applicant.

'candido, a *ag* white as snow; *(puro)* pure; *(sincero)* sincere, candid.

can'dito, a *ag* candied.

can'dore *sm* brilliant white; purity; sincerity, candour.

'cane *sm* dog; *(di pistola, fucile)* cock; fa un freddo ~ it's bitterly cold; non c'era un ~ there wasn't a soul; ~ da caccia/guardia hunting/guard dog; ~ lupo alsatian.

ca'nestro *sm* basket.

cangi'ante [kan'dʒante] *ag* iridescent.

can'guro *sm* kangaroo.

ca'nile *sm* kennel; *(di allevamento)* kennels *pl*; ~ municipale dog pound.

ca'nino, a *ag*, *sm* canine.

'canna *sf* *(pianta)* reed; *(: indica, da zucchero)* cane; *(bastone)* stick, cane; *(di fucile)* barrel; *(di organo)* pipe; ~ fumaria chimney flue; ~ da pesca (fishing) rod; ~ da zucchero sugar cane.

can'nella *sf* (CUC) cinnamon.

cannel'loni *smpl* pasta tubes stuffed with sauce and baked.

cannocchi'ale [kannok'kjale] *sm* telescope.

can'none *sm* (MIL) gun; *(: STORIA)* cannon; *(tubo)* pipe, tube; *(piega)* box pleat; *(fig)* ace.

can'nuccia, ce [kan'nuttʃa] *sf* (drinking) straw.

ca'noa *sf* canoe.

ca'none *sm* canon, criterion; *(mensile, annuo)* rent; fee.

ca'nonico, ci *sm* (REL) canon.

ca'noro, a *ag* *(uccello)* singing, song *cpd*.

canot'taggio [kanot'taddʒo] *sm* rowing.

**canotti'era** *sf* vest.

**ca'notto** *sm* small boat, dinghy; canoe.

**cano'vaccio** [kano'vattʃo] *sm* (*tela*) canvas; (*strofinaccio*) duster; (*trama*) plot.

**can'tante** *sm/f* singer.

**can'tare** *vt, vi* to sing; **cantau'tore, 'trice** *sm/f* singer-composer.

**canti'ere** *sm* (*EDIL*) (building) site; (*anche*: ~ **navale**) shipyard.

**canti'lena** *sf* (*filastrocca*) lullaby; (*fig*) sing-song voice.

**can'tina** *sf* (*locale*) cellar; (*bottega*) wine shop.

**'canto** *sm* song; (*arte*) singing; (*REL*) chant; chanting; (*poesia*) poem, lyric; (*parte di una poesia*) canto; (*parte, lato*): **da un ~** on the one hand; **d'altro ~** on the other hand.

**canto'nata** *sf* corner; **prendere una ~** (*fig*) to blunder.

**can'tone** *sm* (*in Svizzera*) canton.

**can'tuccio** [kan'tuttʃo] *sm* corner, nook.

**canzo'nare** [kantso'nare] *vt* to tease.

**can'zone** [kan'tsone] *sf* song; (*POESIA*) canzone; **canzoni'ere** *sm* (*MUS*) songbook; (*LETTERATURA*) collection of poems.

**'caos** *sm inv* chaos; **ca'otico, a, ci, che** *ag* chaotic.

**C.A.P.** *sigla m* = **codice di avviamento postale**.

**ca'pace** [ka'patʃe] *ag* able, capable; (*ampio, vasto*) large, capacious; **sei ~ di farlo?** can you *o* are you able to do it?; **capacità** *sf inv* ability; (*DIR, di recipiente*) capacity; **capaci'tarsi** *vr*: **capacitarsi di** to make out, understand.

**ca'panna** *sf* hut.

**capan'none** *sm* (*AGR*) barn; (*fabbricato industriale*) (factory) shed.

**ca'parbio, a** *ag* stubborn.

**ca'parra** *sf* deposit, down payment.

**ca'pello** *sm* hair; **~i** *smpl* (*capigliatura*) hair *sg*.

**capez'zale** [kapet'tsale] *sm* bolster;

(*fig*) bedside.

**ca'pezzolo** [ka'pettsolo] *sm* nipple.

**capi'enza** [ka'pjɛntsa] *sf* capacity.

**capiglia'tura** [kapiʎʎa'tura] *sf* hair.

**ca'pire** *vt* to understand.

**capi'tale** *ag* (*mortale*) capital; (*fondamentale*) main, chief // *sf* (*città*) capital // *sm* (*ECON*) capital; **capita'lismo** *sm* capitalism; **capita'lista, i, e** *ag, sm/f* capitalist.

**capi'tano** *sm* captain.

**capi'tare** *vi* (*giungere casualmente*) to happen to go, find *o.s.*; (*accadere*) to happen; (*presentarsi: cosa*) to turn up, present itself // *vb impers* to happen; **mi è capitato un guaio** I've had a spot of trouble.

**capi'tello** *sm* (*ARCHIT*) capital.

**ca'pitolo** *sm* chapter.

**capi'tombolo** *sm* headlong fall, tumble.

**'capo** *sm* head; (*persona*) head, leader; (: *in ufficio*) head, boss; (: *in tribù*) chief; (*di oggetti*) head; top; end; (*GEO*) cape; **andare a ~** to start a new paragraph; **da ~** over again; **~ di bestiame** head *inv* of cattle; **~ di vestiario** item of clothing.

**'capo...** *prefisso*: **capocu'oco, chi** *sm* head cook; **Capo'danno** *sm* New Year; **capo'fitto**: **a capofitto** *av* headfirst, headlong; **capo'giro** *sm* dizziness *q*; **capola'voro, i** *sm* masterpiece; **capo'linea, pl capi'linea** *sm* terminus; **capo'lino** *sm*: **fare capolino** to peep out (*o in etc*); **capolu'ogo, pl capilu'oghi** *sm* chief town, administrative centre.

**capo'rale** *sm* (*MIL*) lance corporal (*Brit*), private first class (*US*).

**'capo...** *prefisso*: **capostazi'one, pl capistazi'one** *sm* station master; **capo'treno, pl capi'treno** *o* **capo'treni** *sm* guard.

**capo'volgere** [kapo'voldʒere] *vt* to overturn; (*fig*) to reverse; **~rsi** *vr* to overturn; (*barca*) to capsize; (*fig*) to be reversed; **capo'volto, a** *pp di* capovolgere.

'cappa sf (mantello) cape, cloak; (del camino) hood.

cap'pella sf (REL) chapel; cappel'lano sm chaplain.

cap'pello sm hat.

'cappero sm caper.

cap'pone sm capon.

cap'potto sm (over)coat.

cappuc'cino [kapput'tʃino] sm (frate) Capuchin monk; (bevanda) frothy white coffee.

cap'puccio [kap'puttʃo] sm (copricapo) hood; (della biro) cap.

'capra sf (she-)goat; ca'pretto sm kid.

ca'priccio [ka'prittʃo] sm caprice, whim; (bizza) tantrum; fare i ~i to be very naughty; capric'cioso, a ag capricious, whimsical; naughty.

Capri'corno sm Capricorn.

capri'ola sf somersault.

capri'olo sm roe deer.

'capro sm billy-goat; ~ espiatorio (fig) scapegoat.

'capsula sf capsule; (di arma, per bottiglie) cap.

cap'tare vt (RADIO, TV) to pick up; (cattivarsi) to gain, win.

cara'bina sf rifle.

carabini'ere sm member of Italian military police force.

ca'raffa sf carafe.

cara'mella sf sweet.

ca'rattere sm character; (caratteristica) characteristic, trait; avere un buon ~ to be good-natured; caratte'ristico, a, ca, che ag characteristic // sf characteristic, trait, peculiarity; caratteriz'zare vt to characterize, distinguish.

car'bone sm coal.

carbu'rante sm (motor) fuel.

carbura'tore sm carburettor.

car'cassa sf carcass; (fig: peg: macchina etc) (old) wreck.

carce'rato, a [kartʃe'rato] sm/f prisoner.

'carcere ['kartʃere] sm prison; (pena) imprisonment.

car'ciofo [kar'tʃɔfo] sm artichoke.

car'diaco, a, ci, che ag cardiac, heart cpd.

cardi'nale ag, sm cardinal.

'cardine sm hinge.

'cardo sm thistle.

ca'renza [ka'rentsa] sf lack, scarcity; (vitaminica) deficiency.

cares'tia sf famine; (penuria) scarcity, dearth.

ca'rezza [ka'rettsa] sf caress; carez'zare vt to caress, stroke, fondle.

'carica sf vedi carico.

cari'care vt to load; (aggravare: anche fig) to weigh down; (orologio) to wind up; (batteria, MIL) to charge.

'carico, a, chi, che ag (che porta un peso); ~ di loaded o laden with; (fucile) loaded; (orologio) wound up; (batteria) charged; (colore) deep; (caffè, tè) strong // sm (il caricare) loading; (ciò che si carica) load; (fig: peso) burden, weight // sf (mansione ufficiale) office, position; (MIL, TECN, ELETTR) charge; persona a ~ dependent; essere a ~ di qn (spese etc) to be charged to sb; ha una forte ~a di simpatia he's very likeable.

'carie sf (dentaria) decay.

ca'rino, a ag lovely, pretty, nice; (simpatico) nice.

carità sf charity; per ~! (escl di rifiuto) good heavens, no!

carnagi'one [karna'dʒone] sf complexion.

car'nale ag (amore) carnal; (fratello) blood cpd.

'carne sf flesh; (bovina, ovina etc) meat; ~ di manzo/maiale/pecora beef/pork/mutton; ~ tritata mince (Brit), hamburger meat (US), minced (Brit) o ground (US) meat.

car'nefice [kar'nefitʃe] sm executioner; hangman.

carne'vale sm carnival.

car'noso, a ag fleshy.

'caro, a ag (amato) dear; (costoso)

dear, expensive.

**ca'rogna** [ka'roɲɲa] sf carrion; (fig: fam) swine.

**caro'sello** sm merry-go-round.

**ca'rota** sf carrot.

**caro'vana** sf caravan.

**caro'vita** sm high cost of living.

**carpenti'ere** sm carpenter.

**car'pire** vt: ~ qc a qn (segreto etc) to get sth out of sb.

**car'poni** av on all fours.

**car'rabile** ag suitable for vehicles; "passo ~" "keep clear".

**car'raio, a** ag: "passo ~" vehicle entrance.

**carreggi'ata** [karred'dʒata] sf carriageway (Brit), (road)way.

**car'rello** sm trolley; (AER) undercarriage; (CINEMA) dolly; (di macchina da scrivere) carriage.

**carri'era** sf career; fare ~ to get on; a gran ~ at full speed.

**carri'ola** sf wheelbarrow.

**'carro** sm cart, wagon; ~ armato tank.

**car'rozza** [kar'rɔttsa] sf carriage, coach.

**carrozze'ria** [karrottse'ria] sf body, coachwork (Brit); (officina) coachbuilder's workshop (Brit), body shop.

**carroz'zina** [karrot'tsina] sf pram (Brit), baby carriage (US).

**'carta** sf paper; (al ristorante) menu; (GEO) map; plan; (documento, da gioco) card; (costituzione) charter; ~e sfpl (documenti) papers, documents; alla ~ (al ristorante) à la carte; ~ assegni bank card; ~ assorbente blotting paper; ~ bollata o da bollo official stamped paper; ~ di credito credit card; ~ (geografica) map; ~ d'identità identity card; ~ igienica toilet paper; ~ d'imbarco (AER, NAUT) boarding card; ~ da lettere writing paper; ~ libera (AMM) unstamped paper; ~ da parati wallpaper; ~ verde (AUT) green card; ~ vetrata sandpaper; ~ da visita visiting card.

**cartac'cone**, pl **cartecar'bone** sf carbon paper.

**car'taccia, ce** [kar'tattʃa] sf waste paper.

**cartamo'neta** sf paper money.

**carta'pecora** sf parchment.

**carta'pesta** sf papier-mâché.

**car'teggio** [kar'teddʒo] sm correspondence.

**car'tella** sf (scheda) card; (custodia: di cartone) folder; (: di uomo d'affari etc) briefcase; (: di scolaro) schoolbag, satchel; ~ clinica (MED) case sheet.

**car'tello** sm sign; (pubblicitario) poster; (stradale) sign, signpost; (ECON) cartel; (in dimostrazioni) placard; **cartel'lone** sm (pubblicitario) advertising poster; (della tombola) scoring frame; (TEATRO) playbill; tenere il **cartellone** (spettacolo) to have a long run.

**carti'era** sf paper mill.

**car'tina** sf (AUT, GEO) map.

**car'toccio** [kar'tɔttʃo] sm paper bag.

**cartole'ria** sf stationer's (shop).

**carto'lina** sf postcard.

**car'tone** sm cardboard; (ARTE) cartoon; ~i animati smpl (CINEMA) cartoons.

**car'tuccia, ce** [kar'tuttʃa] sf cartridge.

**'casa** sf house; (specialmente la propria casa) home; (COMM) firm, house; essere a ~ to be at home; vado a ~ mia/tua I'm going home/ to your house; ~ di cura nursing home; ~ dello studente student hostel; ~e popolari ≈ council houses (o flats) (Brit), ≈ public housing units (US).

**ca'sacca, che** sf military coat; (di fantino) blouse.

**casalingo, a, ghi, ghe** ag household, domestic; (fatto a casa) homemade; (semplice) homely; (amante della casa) home-loving // ~i sf housewife; ~ghi smpl household articles; cucina ~a plain home cooking.

**cas'care** vi to fall; **cas'cata** sf fall;

(d'acqua) cascade, waterfall.

'casco, schi sm helmet; (del parrucchiere) hair-drier; (di banane) bunch.

casei'ficio [kazei'fitʃo] sm creamery.

ca'sella sf pigeon-hole; ~ postale (C.P.) post office box (P.O. box).

casel'lario sm filing cabinet; ~ giudiziale court records pl.

ca'sello sm (di autostrada) toll-house.

ca'serma sf barracks pl.

ca'sino sm (confusione) row, racket; (casa di prostituzione) brothel.

casinò sm inv casino.

'caso sm chance; (fatto, vicenda) event, incident; (possibilità) possibility; (MED, LING) case; a ~ at random; per ~ by chance, by accident; in ogni ~, in tutti i ~i in any case, at any rate; al ~ should the opportunity arise; nel ~ che in case; ~ mai if by chance; ~ limite borderline case.

'cassa sf case, crate, box; (bara) coffin; (mobile) chest; (involucro: di orologio etc) case; (macchina) cash register; (luogo di pagamento) checkout (counter); (fondo) fund; (istituto bancario) bank; ~ automatica prelievi automatic telling machine, cash dispenser; ~ continua night safe; ~ integrazione: mettere in ~ integrazione ≈ to lay off; ~ mutua o malattia health insurance scheme; ~ di risparmio savings bank; ~ toracica (ANAT) chest.

cassa'forte, pl casseforti sf safe.

cassa'panca, pl cassapanche o cassepanche sf settle.

casseru'ola, casse'rola sf saucepan.

cas'setta sf box; (per registratore) cassette; (CINEMA, TEATRO) box-office takings pl; film di ~ box-office draw; ~ di sicurezza strongbox; ~ delle lettere letterbox.

cas'setto sm drawer; casset'tone sm chest of drawers.

cassi'ere, a smf cashier; (di banca) teller.

'casta sf caste.

cas'tagna [kas'taɲɲa] sf chestnut.

cas'tagno [kas'taɲɲo] sm chestnut (tree).

cas'tano, a ag chestnut (brown).

cas'tello sm castle; (TECN) scaffolding.

casti'gare vt to punish; cas'tigo, ghi sm punishment.

castità sf chastity.

cas'toro sm beaver.

cas'trare vt to castrate; to geld; to doctor (Brit), fix (US).

casu'ale ag chance cpd.

cata'comba sf catacomb.

ca'talogo, ghi sm catalogue.

catarifran'gente [catarifran'dʒɛnte] sm (AUT) reflector.

ca'tarro sm catarrh.

ca'tasta sf stack, pile.

ca'tasto sm land register; land registry office.

ca'tastrofe sf catastrophe, disaster.

catego'ria sf category.

ca'tena sf chain; ~ di montaggio assembly line; ~e da neve (AUT) snow chains; cate'naccio sm bolt.

cate'ratta sf cataract; (chiusa) sluice-gate.

cati'nella sf: piovere a ~e to pour, rain cats and dogs.

ca'tino sm basin.

ca'trame sm tar.

'cattedra sf teacher's desk; (di università) chair.

catte'drale sf cathedral.

catti'veria sf malice, spite; naughtiness; (atto) spiteful act; (parole) malicious o spiteful remark.

cattività sf captivity.

cat'tivo, a ag bad; (malvagio) bad, wicked; (turbolento: bambino) bad, naughty; (: mare) rough; (odore, sapore) nasty, bad.

cat'tolico, a, ci, che ag, smf (Roman) Catholic.

cat'tura sf capture.

cattu'rare vt to capture.

**cauccià** [kaut'tʃu] *sm* rubber.
**'causa** *sf* cause; (*DIR*) lawsuit, case, action; a ~ di, per ~ di because of; fare o muovere ~ a qn to take legal action against sb.
**cau'sare** *vt* to cause.
**cau'tela** *sf* caution, prudence.
**caute'lare** *vt* to protect; ~rsi *vr*: ~rsi (da) to take precautions (against).
**'cauto, a** *ag* cautious, prudent.
**cauzi'one** [kaut'tsjone] *sf* security; (*DIR*) bail.
**cav.** *abbr* = **cavaliere**.
**'cava** *sf* quarry.
**caval'care** *vt* (*cavallo*) to ride; (*muro*) to sit astride; (*sog: ponte*) to span; **caval'cata** *sf* ride; (*gruppo di persone*) riding party.
**cavalca'via** *sm inv* flyover.
**cavalcioni** [kaval'tʃoni]: **a ~ di** *prep* astride.
**cavali'ere** *sm* rider; (*feudale, titolo*) knight; (*soldato*) cavalryman; (*al ballo*) partner; **cavalle'resco, a, schi, sche** *ag* chivalrous; **cavalle'ria** *sf* chivalry; (*milizia a cavallo*) cavalry.
**cavalle'rizzo, a** [kavalle'rittso] *smf* riding instructor; circus rider.
**caval'letta** *sf* grasshopper.
**caval'letto** *sm* (*FOT*) tripod; (*da pittore*) easel.
**ca'vallo** *sm* horse; (*SCACCHI*) knight; (*AUT: anche*: ~ **vapore**) horsepower; (*dei pantaloni*) crotch; a ~ on horseback; a ~ di astride, straddling; ~ di battaglia (*fig*) hobby-horse; ~ **da corsa** racehorse.
**ca'vare** *vt* (*togliere*) to draw out, extract, take out; (: *giacca, scarpe*) to take off; (: *fame, sete, voglia*) to satisfy; **cavarsela** to get away with it; to manage, get on all right.
**cava'tappi** *sm inv* corkscrew.
**ca'verna** *sf* cave.
**'cavia** *sf* guinea pig.
**cavi'ale** *sm* caviar.
**ca'viglia** [ka'viʎʎa] *sf* ankle.
**ca'villo** *sm* quibble.

**'cavo, a** *ag* hollow // *sm* (*ANAT*) cavity; (*grossa corda*) rope, cable; (*ELETTR, TEL*) cable.
**cavolfi'ore** *sm* cauliflower.
**'cavolo** *sm* cabbage; (*fam*): **non m'importa un** ~ I don't give a damn; ~ **di Bruxelles** Brussels sprout.
**cazzu'ola** [kat'tswɔla] *sf* trowel.
**c/c** *abbr* = **conto corrente**.
**ce** [tʃe] *pronome*, *av vedi* **ci**.
**cece** [tʃetʃe] *sm* chickpea.
**cecità** [tʃetʃi'ta] *sf* blindness.
**Cecoslo'vacchia** [tʃekoslo'vakkja] *sf*: **la** ~ Czechoslovakia; **ceco-slo'vacco, a, chi, che** *ag*, *smf* Czechoslovakian.
**'cedere** [tʃedere] *vt* (*concedere: posto*) to give up; (*DIR*) to transfer, make over // *vi* (*cadere*) to give way, subside; ~ (**a**) to surrender (to), yield (to), give in (to); **ce'devole** *ag* (*terreno*) soft; (*fig*) yielding.
**'cedola** [tʃedola] *sf* (*COMM*) coupon; voucher.
**'cedro** [tʃedro] *sm* cedar; (*albero da frutto, frutto*) citron.
**C.E.E.** [tʃee] *sigla f* = **Comunità Economica Europea**.
**'ceffo** [tʃeffo] *sm* (*peg*) ugly mug.
**cef'fone** [tʃef'fone] *sm* slap, smack.
**ce'larsi** [tʃe'larsi] *vr* to hide.
**cele'brare** [tʃele'brare] *vt* to celebrate; **celebrazi'one** *sf* celebration.
**'celebre** [tʃelebre] *ag* famous, celebrated; **celebrità** *sf inv* fame; (*persona*) celebrity.
**'celere** [tʃelere] *ag* fast, swift; (*corso*) crash *cpd*.
**ce'leste** [tʃe'leste] *ag* celestial; heavenly; (*colore*) sky-blue.
**'celibe** [tʃelibe] *ag* single, unmarried // *sm* bachelor.
**'cella** [tʃella] *sf* cell.
**'cellula** [tʃellula] *sf* (*BIOL, ELETTR, POL*) cell.
**cemen'tare** [tʃemen'tare] *vt* (*anche fig*) to cement.
**ce'mento** [tʃe'mento] *sm* cement; ~

armato reinforced concrete.

'cena ['tʃena] sf dinner; (leggera) supper.

ce'nare [tʃe'nare] vi to dine, have dinner.

'cencio ['tʃentʃo] sm piece of cloth, rag; (per spolverare) duster.

'cenere ['tʃenere] sf ash.

'cenno ['tʃenno] sm (segno) sign, signal; (gesto) gesture; (col capo) nod; (con la mano) wave; (allusione) hint, mention; (breve esposizione) short account; far ~ di sì/no to nod (one's head)/shake one's head.

censi'mento [tʃensi'mento] sm census.

cen'sore [tʃen'sore] sm censor.

cen'sura [tʃen'sura] sf censorship; censor's office; (fig) censure.

cente'nario, a [tʃente'narjo] ag (che ha cento anni) hundred-year-old; (che ricorre ogni cento anni) centennial, centenary cpd // smlf centenarian // sm centenary.

cen'tesimo, a [tʃen'tezimo] ag, sm hundredth.

cen'tigrado, a [tʃen'tigrado] ag centigrade; 20 gradi ~i 20 degrees centigrade.

cen'timetro [tʃen'timetro] sm centimetre.

centi'naio, pl(f) aia [tʃenti'najo] sm: un ~ (di) a hundred; about a hundred.

'cento ['tʃento] num a hundred, one hundred.

cen'trale [tʃen'trale] ag central // sf: ~ telefonica (telephone) exchange; ~ elettrica electric power station; centra'lista smlf operator; cen'tralino sm (telephone) exchange; (di albergo etc) switchboard.

cen'trare [tʃen'trare] vt to hit the centre of; (TECN) to centre.

cen'trifuga [tʃen'trifuga] sf spindrier.

'centro ['tʃentro] sm centre; ~ commerciale shopping centre; (città) commercial centre.

'ceppo ['tʃeppo] sm (di albero) stump; (pezzo di legno) log.

'cera ['tʃera] sf wax; (aspetto) appearance, look.

ce'ramica, che [tʃe'ramika] sf ceramic; (ARTE) ceramics sg.

cerbi'atto [tʃer'bjatto] sm (ZOOL) fawn.

'cerca ['tʃerka] sf: in o alla ~ di in search of.

cer'care [tʃer'kare] vt to look for, search for // vi: ~ di fare qc to try to do sth.

'cerchia ['tʃerkja] sf circle.

'cerchio ['tʃerkjo] sm circle; (giocattolo, di botte) hoop.

cere'ale [tʃere'ale] sm cereal.

ceri'monia [tʃeri'monja] sf ceremony; cerimoni'oso, a ag formal, ceremonious.

ce'rino [tʃe'rino] sm wax match.

'cernia ['tʃernja] sf (ZOOL) stone bass.

cerni'era [tʃer'njera] sf hinge; ~ lampo zip (fastener) (Brit), zipper (US).

'cernita ['tʃernita] sf selection.

'cero ['tʃero] sm (church) candle.

ce'rotto [tʃe'rotto] sm sticking plaster.

certa'mente [tʃerta'mente] av certainly, surely.

cer'tezza [tʃer'tettsa] sf certainty.

certifi'cato sm certificate; ~ medico/di nascita medical/birth certificate.

PAROLA CHIAVE

'certo, a ['tʃerto] ♦ ag (sicuro): ~ (di/che) certain o sure (of/that)

♦ det 1 (tale) certain; un ~ signor Smith a (certain) Mr Smith

2 (qualche; con valore intensivo) some; dopo un ~ tempo after some time; un fatto di una ~a importanza a matter of some importance; di una ~a età past one's prime, not so young

♦ pronome: ~i(e) pl some

♦ av (certamente) certainly; (senz'altro) of course; di ~

certainly; **no (di)** ~!, ~ **che no!** certainly not!; **sì** ~ yes indeed, certainly.

**cer'tuni** [tʃer'tuni] *pronome pl* some (people).

**cer'vello**, *pl* i (*anche: pl(f)* a o e) [tʃer'vɛllo] *sm* brain.

'**cervo, a** ['tʃɛrvo] *sm/f* stag/doe // *sm* deer; ~ **volante** stag beetle.

**ce'sello** [tʃe'zɛllo] *sm* chisel.

**ce'soie** [tʃe'zoje] *sfpl* shears.

**ces'puglio** [tʃes'puʎʎo] *sm* bush.

**ces'sare** [tʃes'sare] *vi, vt* to stop, cease; ~ **di fare qc** to stop doing sth; **cessate il fuoco** *sm* ceasefire.

'**cesso** ['tʃɛsso] *sm (fam: gabinetto)* bog.

'**cesta** ['tʃɛsta] *sf* (large) basket.

**ces'tino** [tʃes'tino] *sm* basket; (*per la carta straccia*) wastepaper basket; ~ **da viaggio** (FERR) packed lunch (o dinner).

'**cesto** ['tʃɛsto] *sm* basket.

'**ceto** ['tʃɛto] *sm* (social) class.

**cetrio'lino** [tʃetrio'lino] *sm* gherkin.

**cetri'olo** [tʃetri'ɔlo] *sm* cucumber.

**cfr.** *abbr* (= *confronta*) cf.

**CGIL** *sigla f* (= *Confederazione Generale Italiana del Lavoro*) trades union organization.

**che** [ke] ◆ *pronome* **1** (*relativo: persona: soggetto*) who; (: *oggetto*) whom, that; (: *cosa, animale*) which, that; **il ragazzo** ~ **è venuto** the boy who came; **l'uomo** ~ **io vedo** the man (whom) I see; **il libro** ~ **è sul tavolo** the book which *o* that is on the table; **il libro** ~ **vedi** the book (which *o* that) you see; **la sera** ~ **ti ho visto** the evening I saw you

**2** (*interrogativo, esclamativo*) what; ~ (**cosa**) **fai?** what are you doing?; **a** ~ (**cosa**) **pensi?** what are you thinking about?; **non sa** ~ (**cosa**) **fare** he doesn't know what to do; **ma** ~ **dici!** what are you saying!

**3** (*indefinito*): **quell'uomo ha un** ~

**di losco** there's something suspicious about that man; **un certo non so** ~ an indefinable something

◆ **det 1** (*interrogativo: tra tanti*) what; (: *tra pochi*) which; ~ **tipo di film preferisci?** what sort of film do you prefer?; ~ **vestito ti vuoi mettere?** what (*o* which) dress do you want to put on?

**2** (*esclamativo: seguito da aggettivo*) how; (: *seguito da sostantivo*) what; ~ **buono!** how delicious!; ~ **bel vestito!** what a lovely dress!

◆ *cong* **1** (*con proposizioni subordinate*) that; **credo** ~ **verrà** I think he'll come; **voglio** ~ **tu studi** I want you to study; **so** ~ **tu c'eri** I know (that) you were there; **non** ~: **non** ~ **sia sbagliato, ma** ... not that it's wrong, but ...

**2** (*finale*) so that; **vieni qua,** ~ **ti veda** come here, so (that) I can see you

**3** (*temporale*): **arrivai** ~ **eri già partito** you had already left when I arrived; **sono anni** ~ **non lo vedo** I haven't seen him for years, it's years since I saw him

**4** (*in frasi imperative, concessive*): ~ **venga pure!** let him come by all means!; ~ **tu sia benedetto!** may God bless you!

**5** (*comparativo: con più, meno*) than; *vedi anche* **più, meno, così** *etc.*

**cheti'chella** [keti'kɛlla]: **alla** ~ *av* stealthily, unobtrusively.

'**cheto, a** ['keto] *ag* quiet, silent.

**chi** [ki] *pronome* **1** (*interrogativo: soggetto*) who; (: *oggetto*) who, whom; ~ **è?** who is it?; **di** ~ **è questo libro?** whose book is this?, whose is this book?; **con** ~ **parli?** who are you talking to?; **a** ~ **pensi?** who are you thinking about?; ~ **di voi?** which of you?; **non so a** ~ **rivolgermi** I don't know who to ask

**2** (relativo) whoever, anyone who; dillo a ~ vuoi tell whoever you like **3** (indefinito): ~ ... ~ ... some ... others ...; ~ dice una cosa, ~ dice un'altra some say one thing, others say another.

**chiacchie'rare** [kjakkje'rare] vi to chat; (discorrere futilmente) to chatter; (far pettegolezzi) to gossip; **chiacchie'rata** sf chat; **chi'acchiere** sfpl: fare due o quattro chiacchiere to have a chat; **chiacchie'rone, a** ag talkative, chatty; gossipy // smf chatterbox; gossip.

**chia'mare** [kja'mare] vt to call; (rivolgersi a qn) to call (in), send for; ~rsi vr (aver nome) to be called; mi chiamo Paolo my name is Paolo, I'm called Paolo; ~ alle armi to call up; ~ in giudizio to summon; **chia'mata** sf (TEL) call; (MIL) call-up.

**chia'rezza** [kja'rettsa] sf clearness; clarity.

**chia'rire** [kja'rire] vt to make clear; (fig: spiegare) to clear up, explain; ~rsi vr to become clear.

**chia'ro, a** [kj'aro] ag clear; (luminoso) clear, bright; (colore) pale, light.

**chiaroveg'gente** [kjaroved'dʒɛnte] smf clairvoyant.

**chi'asso** [kj'asso] sm uproar, row; **chias'soso, a** ag noisy, rowdy; (vistoso) showy, gaudy.

**chi'ave** [kj'ave] sf key // ag inv key cpd; ~ d'accensione (AUT) ignition key; ~ inglese monkey wrench; ~ di volta (anche fig) keystone; **chiavis'tello** sm bolt.

**chi'azza** [kj'attsa] sf stain; splash. **'chicco, chi** [kikko] sm (di cereale, riso) grain; (di caffè) bean; ~ d'uva grape.

**chi'edere** [kj'edere] vt (per sapere) to ask; (per avere) to ask for // vi: ~ di qn to ask after sb; (al telefono) to ask for o want sb; ~ qc a qn to ask

sb sth; to ask sb for sth.

**chi'erico, ci** [kj'eriko] sm cleric; altar boy.

**chi'esa** [kj'eza] sf church.

**chi'esto, a** pp di chiedere.

**'chiglia** [kiʎʎa] sf keel.

**'chilo** [kilo] sm kilo; **chilo'grammo** sm kilogram(me); **chi'lometro** sm kilometre.

**'chimico, a, ci, che** [kimiko] ag chemical // smf chemist // sf chemistry.

**'china** [kina] sf (pendio) slope, descent; (BOT) cinchona; (inchiostro di) ~ Indian ink.

**chi'nare** [ki'nare] vt to lower, bend; ~rsi vr to stoop, bend.

**chi'nino** [ki'nino] sm quinine.

**chi'occia, ce** [kj'ɔttʃa] sf brooding hen.

**chi'occiola** [kj'ɔttʃola] sf snail; scala a ~ spiral staircase.

**chi'odo** [kj'ɔdo] sm nail; (fig) obsession.

**chi'oma** [kj'ɔma] sf (capelli) head of hair; (di albero) foliage.

**chi'osco, schi** [kj'ɔsko] sm kiosk, stall.

**chi'ostro** [kj'ɔstro] sm cloister.

**chiro'mante** [kiro'mante] smf palmist.

**chirur'gia** [kirur'dʒia] sf surgery; **chi'rurgo, ghi** o gi sm surgeon.

**chissà** [kis'sa] av who knows, I wonder.

**chi'tarra** [ki'tarra] sf guitar.

**chi'udere** [kj'udere] vt to close, shut; (luce, acqua) to put off, turn off; (definitivamente: fabbrica) to close down, shut down; (strada) to close; (recingere) to enclose; (porre termine) to end // vi to close, shut; to close down, shut down; to end; ~rsi vr to shut, close; (ritirarsi: anche fig) to shut o.s. away; (ferita) to close up.

**chi'unque** [ki'unkwe] pronome (relativo) whoever; (indefinito) anyone, anybody; ~ sia whoever it is.

**chi'uso, a** [kj'uso] pp di chiudere //

*sf (di corso d'acqua)* sluice; lock; *(recinto)* enclosure; *(di discorso etc)* conclusion; ending; **chiu'sura** *sf* closing; shutting; closing *o* shutting down; enclosing; putting *o* turning off; ending; *(dispositivo)* catch; fastening; fastener.

**PAROLA CHIAVE**

**ci** [tʃi] *(dav lo, la, li, le, ne diventa* **ce**) ♦ *pronome* 1 *(personale: complemento oggetto)* us; *(: a noi: complemento di termine)* (to) us; *(: riflessivo)* ourselves; *(: reciproco)* each other, one another; *(impersonale)*: ~ **si veste** we get dressed; ~ **ha visti** he's seen us; **non** ~ **ha dato niente** he gave us nothing; ~ **vestiamo** we get dressed; ~ **amiamo** we love one another *o* each other

2 *(dimostrativo: di ciò, su ciò, in ciò etc)* about *(o* on *o* of) it; **non so cosa far**~ I don't know what to do about it; ~ **puoi contare** you can depend on it; **che c'entro io?** what have I got to do with it?

♦ *av (qui)* here; *(lì)* there; *(moto attraverso luogo)*: ~ **passa sopra un ponte** a bridge passes over it; **non** ~ **passa più nessuno** nobody comes this way any more; **esser**~ *vedi* **essere**.

**C.ia** *abbr* (= *compagnia*) Co.
**cia'batta** [tʃa'batta] *sf* mule, slipper.
**ci'alda** [tʃi'alda] *sf* (*CUC*) wafer.
**ciam'bella** [tʃam'bella] *sf* (*CUC*) ring-shaped cake; *(salvagente)* rubber ring.
**ci'ao** [tʃao] *escl (all'arrivo)* hello!; *(alla partenza)* cheerio! (*Brit*), bye!
**ciarla'tano** [tʃarla'tano] *sm* charlatan.
**cias'cuno, a** [tʃas'kuno] *(dav sm:* **ciascun** + *C, V,* **ciascuno** + *s impura, gn, pn, ps, x, z; dav sf:* **ciascuna** + *C,* **ciascun'** + *V*) *det, pronome* each.
**'cibo** [tʃibo] *sm* food.

**ci'cala** [tʃi'kala] *sf* cicada.
**cica'trice** [tʃika'tritʃe] *sf* scar.
**'cicca** [tʃikka] *sf* cigarette end.
**'ciccia** [tʃittʃa] *sf (fam: carne)* meat; *(: grasso umano)* fat, flesh.
**cice'rone** [tʃitʃe'rone] *sm* guide.
**ci'clismo** [tʃi'klizmo] *sm* cycling; **ci'clista, i, e** *smf* cyclist.
**'ciclo** [tʃiklo] *sm* cycle; *(di malattia)* course.
**ciclomo'tore** [tʃiklomo'tore] *sm* moped.
**ci'clone** [tʃi'klone] *sm* cyclone.
**ci'cogna** [tʃi'koɲɲa] *sf* stork.
**ci'coria** [tʃi'kɔrja] *sf* chicory.
**ci'eco, a, chi, che** [tʃɛko] *ag* blind // *smf* blind man/woman.
**ci'elo** [tʃɛlo] *sm* sky; *(REL)* heaven.
**'cifra** [tʃifra] *sf (numero)* figure; numeral; *(somma di denaro)* sum, figure; *(monogramma)* monogram, initials *pl; (codice)* code, cipher.
**'ciglio** [tʃiʎʎo] *sm (margine)* edge, verge; *(pl(f)* **ciglia**: *delle palpebre)* (eye)lash; (eye)lid; *(sopracciglio)* eyebrow.
**'cigno** [tʃiɲɲo] *sm* swan.
**cigo'lare** [tʃigo'lare] *vi* to squeak, creak.
**'Cile** [tʃile] *sm:* **il** ~ Chile.
**ci'lecca** [tʃi'lekka] *sf:* **far** ~ to fail.
**cili'egia, gie** *o* **ge** [tʃi'ljɛdʒa] *sf* cherry; **cili'egio** *sm* cherry tree.
**cilin'drata** [tʃilin'drata] *sf (AUT)* (cubic) capacity; **una macchina di grossa** ~ a big-engined car.
**ci'lindro** [tʃi'lindro] *sm* cylinder; *(cappello)* top hat.
**'cima** [tʃima] *sf (sommità)* top; *(di monte)* top, summit; *(estremità)* end; **in** ~ **a** at the top of; **da** ~ **a fondo** from top to bottom; *(fig)* from beginning to end.
**'cimice** [tʃimitʃe] *sf (ZOOL)* bug; *(puntina)* drawing pin (*Brit*), thumbtack (*US*).
**cimini'era** [tʃimi'njɛra] *sf* chimney; *(di nave)* funnel.
**cimi'tero** [tʃimi'tɛro] *sm* cemetery.
**ci'murro** [tʃi'murro] *sm (di cani)* dis-

temper.

'**Cina** ['tʃina] *sf*: la ~ China.

**cin'cin, cin cin** [tʃin'tʃin] *escl* cheers!

'**cinema** ['tʃinema] *sm inv* cinema; **cine'presa** *sf* cine-camera.

**ci'nese** [tʃi'nese] *ag, sm/f, sm* Chinese *inv*.

**ci'netico, a, ci, che** [tʃi'netiko] *ag* kinetic.

'**cingere** ['tʃindʒere] *vt (attorniare)* to surround, encircle; ~ **la vita con una cintura** to put a belt round one's waist.

'**cinghia** ['tʃingja] *sf* strap; *(cintura, TECN)* belt.

**cinghi'ale** [tʃin'gjale] *sm* wild boar.

**cinguet'tare** [tʃingwet'tare] *vi* to twitter.

'**cinico, a, ci, che** ['tʃiniko] *ag* cynical // *sm/f* cynic; **ci'nismo** *sm* cynicism.

**cin'quanta** [tʃin'kwanta] *num* fifty; **cinquan'tesimo, a** *num* fiftieth.

**cinquan'tina** [tʃinkwan'tina] *sf (serie)*: **una ~ (di)** about fifty; *(età)*: **essere sulla ~** to be about fifty.

'**cinque** ['tʃinkwe] *num* five; **avere ~ anni** to be five (years old); **il ~ dicembre 1988** the fifth of December 1988; **alle ~** *(ora)* at five (o'clock).

**cinque'cento** [tʃinkwe'tʃento] *num* five hundred // *sm*: **il C~** the sixteenth century.

'**cinto, a** ['tʃinto] *pp di* cingere.

**cin'tura** [tʃin'tura] *sf* belt; ~ **di salvataggio** lifebelt *(Brit)*, life preserver *(US)*; ~ **di sicurezza** *(AUT, AER)* safety *o* seat belt.

**ciò** [tʃɔ] *pronome* this; that; ~ **che** what; ~ **nonostante** *o* **nondimeno** nevertheless, in spite of that.

**ci'occa, che** ['tʃɔkka] *sf (di capelli)* lock.

**ciocco'lata** [tʃokko'lata] *sf* chocolate; *(bevanda)* (hot) chocolate; **cioccola'tino** *sm* chocolate; **ciocco'lato** *sm* chocolate.

**cioè** [tʃo'ɛ] *av* that is (to say).

**ciondo'lare** [tʃondo'lare] *vi* to

dangle; *(fig)* to loaf (about); **ci'ondolo** *sm* pendant.

**ci'otola** ['tʃɔtola] *sf* bowl.

**ci'ottolo** ['tʃɔttolo] *sm* pebble; *(di strada)* cobble(stone).

**ci'polla** [tʃi'polla] *sf* onion; *(di tulipano etc)* bulb.

**ci'presso** [tʃi'prɛsso] *sm* cypress (tree).

'**cipria** ['tʃiprja] *sf* (face) powder.

'**Cipro** ['tʃipro] *sm* Cyprus.

'**circa** ['tʃirka] *av* about, roughly // *prep* about, concerning; a **mezzogiorno** ~ about midday.

'**circo, chi** ['tʃirko] *sm* circus.

**circo'lare** [tʃirko'lare] *vi* to circulate; *(AUT)* to drive (along), move (along) // *ag* circular // *sf (AMM)* circular; *(di autobus)* circle (line); **circolazi'one** *sf* circulation; *(AUT)*: **la circolazione** *(del)* traffic.

'**circolo** ['tʃirkolo] *sm* circle.

**circon'dare** [tʃirkon'dare] *vt* to surround.

**circonfe'renza** [tʃirkonfe'rɛntsa] *sf* circumference.

**circonvallazi'one** [tʃirkonvallat- 'tsjone] *sf* ring road *(Brit)*, beltway *(US)*; *(per evitare una città)* by-pass.

**circos'critto, a** [tʃirkos'kritto] *pp di* circoscrivere.

**circos'crivere** [tʃirkos'krivere] *vt* to circumscribe; *(fig)* to limit, restrict; **circoscrizi'one** *sf (AMM)* district, area; **circoscrizione elettorale** constituency.

**circos'petto, a** [tʃirkos'petto] *ag* circumspect, cautious.

**circos'tante** [tʃirkos'tante] *ag* surrounding, neighbouring.

**circos'tanza** [tʃirkos'tantsa] *sf* circumstance; *(occasione)* occasion.

**cir'cuito** [tʃir'kuito] *sm* circuit.

**CISL** *sigla f* = *Confederazione Italiana Sindacati Lavoratori) trades union organization.*

'**ciste** ['tʃiste] *sf* = **cisti**.

**cis'terna** [tʃis'tɛrna] *sf* tank, cistern.

'**cisti** ['tʃisti] *sf* cyst.

**C.I.T.** [tʃit] *sigla f* = *Compagnia*

*Italiana Turismo.*

**ci'tare** [tʃi'tare] *vt (DIR)* to summon; *(autore)* to quote; *(a esempio, modello)* to cite; **citazi'one** *sf* summons *sg;* quotation; *(di persona)* mention.

**ci'tofono** [tʃi'tɔfono] *sm* entry phone; *(in uffici)* intercom.

**città** [tʃit'ta] *sf inv* town; *(importante)* city; ~ **universitaria** university campus.

**cittadi'nanza** [tʃittadi'nantsa] *sf* citizens *pl,* inhabitants *pl* of a town *(o* city); *(DIR)* citizenship.

**citta'dino, a** [tʃitta'dino] *ag* town *cpd;* city *cpd // sm/f (di uno Stato)* citizen; *(abitante di città)* townsman, city dweller.

**ci'uco, a, chi, che** ['tʃuko] *sm/f* ass, donkey.

**ci'uffo** ['tʃuffo] *sm* tuft.

**ci'vetta** [tʃi'vetta] *sf (ZOOL)* owl; *(fig: donna)* coquette, flirt // *ag inv:* auto/nave ~ decoy car/ship.

**'civico, a, ci, che** ['tʃiviko] *ag* civic; *(museo)* municipal, town *cpd;* municipal, city *cpd.*

**ci'vile** [tʃi'vile] *ag* civil; *(non militare)* civilian; *(nazione)* civilized // *sm* civilian.

**civilizzazi'one** [tʃivilidzdzat'tsjone] *sf* civilization.

**civiltà** [tʃivil'ta] *sf* civilization; *(cortesia)* civility.

**'clacson** *sm inv (AUT)* horn.

**cla'more** *sm (frastuono)* din, uproar, clamour; *(fig)* outcry; **clamo'roso, a** *ag* noisy; *(fig)* sensational.

**clandes'tino, a** *ag* clandestine; *(POL)* underground, clandestine // *sm/f* stowaway.

**clari'netto** *sm* clarinet.

**'classe** *sf* class; **di** ~ *(fig)* with class; of excellent quality.

**'classico, a, ci, che** *ag* classical; *(tradizionale: moda)* classic(al) // *sm* classic; classical author.

**clas'sifica** *sf* classification; *(SPORT)* placings *pl.*

**classifi'care** *vt* to classify;

*(candidato, compito)* to grade; ~**rsi** *vr* to be placed.

**'clausola** *sf (DIR)* clause.

**'clava** *sf* club.

**clavi'cembalo** [klavi'tʃembalo] *sm* harpsichord.

**cla'vicola** *sf (ANAT)* collar bone.

**cle'mente** *ag* merciful; *(clima)* mild; **cle'menza** *sf* mercy, clemency; mildness.

**'clero** *sm* clergy.

**cli'ente** *sm/f* customer, client; **clien'tela** *sf* customers *pl,* clientèle.

**'clima** *sm* climate; **cli'matico, a, ci, che** *ag* climatic; **stazione climatica** health resort; **climatizzazi'one** *sf (TECN)* air conditioning.

**'clinico, a, ci, che** *ag* clinical // *sm (medico)* clinician // *sf (scienza)* clinical medicine; *(casa di cura)* clinic, nursing home; *(settore d'ospedale)* clinic.

**clo'aca, che** *sf* sewer.

**'cloro** *sm* chlorine.

**cloro'formio** *sm* chloroform.

**club** *sm inv* club.

**c.m.** *abbr* = **corrente mese.**

**coabi'tare** *vi* to live together, live under the same roof.

**coagu'lare** *vt* to coagulate // *vi,* ~**rsi** *vr* to coagulate; *(latte)* to curdle.

**coalizi'one** [koalit'tsjone] *sf* coalition.

**co'atto, a** *ag (DIR)* compulsory, forced.

**'COBAS** *sigla mpl (= Comitati di base)* independent trades unions.

**coca'ina** *sf* cocaine.

**cocci'nella** [kottʃi'nella] *sf* ladybird *(Brit),* ladybug *(US).*

**'coccio** ['kɔttʃo] *sm* earthenware; *(vaso)* earthenware pot; ~**i** *smpl* fragments (of pottery).

**cocci'uto, a** [kot'tʃuto] *ag* stubborn, pigheaded.

**'cocco, chi** *sm (pianta)* coconut palm; *(frutto):* **noce di** ~ coconut // *sm/f (fam)* darling.

**cocco'drillo** *sm* crocodile.

**cocco'lare** *vt* to cuddle, fondle.

**co'cente** [ko'tʃɛnte] *ag* (*anche fig*) burning.

**co'comero** *sm* watermelon.

**co'cuzzolo** [ko'kuttsolo] *sm* top; (*di capo, cappello*) crown.

**'coda** *sf* tail; (*fila di persone, auto*) queue (*Brit*), line (*US*); (*di abiti*) train; **con la ~ dell'occhio** out of the corner of one's eye; **mettersi in ~** to queue (up) (*Brit*), line up (*US*); to join the queue (*Brit*) o line (*US*); **~ di cavallo** (*acconciatura*) pony-tail.

**co'dardo, a** *ag* cowardly // *smf* coward.

**'codice** ['koditʃe] *sm* code; **~ di avviamento postale (C.A.P.)** postcode (*Brit*), zip code (*US*); **~ fiscale** tax code; **~ della strada** highway code.

**coe'rente** *ag* coherent; **coe'renza** *sf* coherence.

**coe'taneo, a** *ag, smf* contemporary.

**'cofano** *sm* (*AUT*) bonnet (*Brit*), hood (*US*); (*forziere*) chest.

**'cogli** ['koʎʎi] *prep + det* vedi **con**.

**'cogliere** ['kɔʎʎere] *vt* (*fiore, frutto*) to pick, gather; (*sorprendere*) to catch, surprise; (*bersaglio*) to hit; (*fig: momento opportuno etc*) to grasp, seize, take; (*: capire*) to grasp; **~ qn in flagrante o in fallo** to catch sb red-handed.

**co'gnato, a** [koɲ'ɲato] *smf* brother-/sister-in-law.

**cognizi'one** [koɲɲit'tsjone] *sf* knowledge.

**co'gnome** [koɲ'ɲome] *sm* surname.

**'coi** *prep + det* vedi **con**.

**coinci'denza** [kointʃi'dɛntsa] *sf* coincidence; (*FERR, AER, di autobus*) connection.

**coin'cidere** [koin'tʃidere] *vi* to coincide; **coin'ciso, a** *pp di* **coincidere**.

**coin'volgere** [koin'vɔldʒere] *vt*: **~ in** to involve in; **coin'volto, a** *pp di* **coinvolgere**.

**col** *prep + det* vedi **con**.

**cola'brodo** *sm inv* strainer.

**cola'pasta** *sm inv* colander.

**co'lare** *vt* (*liquido*) to strain; (*pasta*) to drain; (*oro fuso*) to pour // *vi* (*sudore*) to drip; (*botte*) to leak; (*cera*) to melt; **~ a picco** *vt, vi* (*nave*) to sink.

**co'lata** *sf* (*di lava*) flow; (*FONDE-RIA*) casting.

**colazi'one** [kolat'tsjone] *sf* (*anche*: **prima ~**) breakfast; (*anche*: **seconda ~**) lunch; **fare ~** to have breakfast (o lunch).

**co'lei** *pronome* vedi **colui**.

**co'lera** *sm* (*MED*) cholera.

**'colica** *sf* (*MED*) colic.

**'colla** *prep + det* vedi **con** // *sf* glue; (*di farina*) paste.

**collabo'rare** *vi* to collaborate; **~ a** to collaborate on; (*giornale*) to contribute to; **collabora'tore, 'trice** *smf* collaborator; contributor.

**col'lana** *sf* necklace; (*collezione*) collection, series.

**col'lant** [kɔ'lã] *sm inv* tights *pl*.

**col'lare** *sm* collar.

**col'lasso** *sm* (*MED*) collapse.

**collau'dare** *vt* to test, try out; **col'laudo** *sm* testing o; test.

**'colle** *sm* hill.

**col'lega, ghi, ghe** *sm/f* colleague.

**collega'mento** *sm* connection; (*MIL*) liaison.

**colle'gare** *vt* to connect, join, link; **~rsi** *vr* (*RADIO, TV*) to link up; **~rsi con** (*TEL*) to get through to.

**col'legio** [kol'lɛdʒo] *sm* college; (*convitto*) boarding school; **~ elettorale** (*POL*) constituency.

**'collera** *sf* anger.

**col'lerico, a, ci, che** *ag* quick-tempered, irascible.

**col'letta** *sf* collection.

**collettività** *sf* community.

**collet'tivo, a** *ag* collective; (*interesse*) general, everybody's; (*biglietto, visita etc*) group *cpd* // *sm* (*POL*) (political) group.

**col'letto** *sm* collar.

**collezio'nare** [kollettsjo'nare] *vt* to collect.

**collezi'one** [kollet'tsjone] *sf* collection.

**colli'mare** *vi* to correspond, coincide.

**col'lina** *sf* hill.

**col'lirio** *sm* eyewash.

**collisi'one** *sf* collision.

'**collo** *sm* neck; (*di abito*) neck, collar; (*pacco*) parcel; ~ **del piede** instep.

**colloca'mento** *sm* (*impiego*) employment; (*disposizione*) placing, arrangement.

**collo'care** *vt* (*libri, mobili*) to place; (*persona: trovare un lavoro per*) to find a job for, place; (*COMM: merce*) to find a market for.

**col'loquio** *sm* conversation, talk; (*ufficiale, per un lavoro*) interview; (*INS*) preliminary oral exam.

**col'mare** *vt*: ~ **di** (*anche fig*) to fill with; (*dare in abbondanza*) to load o overwhelm with; '**colmo, a** *ag*: **colmo (di)** full (of) // *sm* summit, top; (*fig*) height; **al colmo della disperazione** in the depths of despair; **è il colmo!** it's the last straw!

**co'lombo, a** *smf* dove; pigeon.

**co'lonia** *sf* colony; (*per bambini*) holiday camp; (**acqua di**) ~ (eau de) cologne; **coloni'ale** *ag* colonial // *smf* colonist, settler.

**co'lonna** *sf* column; ~ **vertebrale** spine, spinal column.

**colon'nello** *sm* colonel.

**co'lono** *sm* (*coltivatore*) tenant farmer.

**colo'rante** *sm* colouring.

**colo'rare** *vt* to colour; (*disegno*) to colour in.

**co'lore** *sm* colour; **a ~i** in colour, colour *cpd*; **farne di tutti i ~i** to get up to all sorts of mischief.

**colo'rito, a** *ag* coloured; (*viso*) rosy, pink; (*linguaggio*) colourful // *sm* (*tinta*) colour; (*carnagione*) complexion.

**co'loro** *pronome pl vedi* **colui**.

'**colosso** *sm* colossus.

'**colpa** *sf* fault; (*biasimo*) blame; (*colpevolezza*) guilt; (*azione colpevole*) offence; (*peccato*) sin; **di chi è la ~?** whose fault is it? ~ **sua** it's his fault; **per ~ di** through, owing to; **col'pevole** *ag* guilty.

**col'pire** *vt* to hit, strike; (*fig*) to strike; **rimanere colpito da qc** to be amazed o struck by sth.

'**colpo** *sm* (*urto*) knock; (: *affettivo*) blow, shock; (: *aggressivo*) blow; (*di pistola*) shot; (*MED*) stroke; (*rapina*) raid; **di ~** suddenly; **fare ~** to make a strong impression; ~ **di grazia** coup de grâce; ~ **di sole** sunstroke; ~ **di Stato** coup d'état; ~ **di telefono** phone call; ~ **di testa** (sudden) impulse o whim; ~ **di vento** gust (of wind).

**coltel'lata** *sf* stab.

**col'tello** *sm* knife; ~ **a serramanico** clasp knife.

**colti'vare** *vt* to cultivate; (*verdura*) to grow, cultivate; **coltiva'tore** *sm* farmer; **coltivazi'one** *sf* cultivation; growing.

'**colto, a** *pp di* **cogliere** // *ag* (*istruito*) cultured, educated.

'**coltre** *sf* blanket.

**col'tura** *sf* cultivation.

**co'lui, co'lei**, *pl* **co'loro** *pronome* the one; ~ **che parla** the one o the man o the person who is speaking; **colei che amo** the one o the woman o the person (whom) I love.

'**coma** *sm inv* coma.

**comanda'mento** *sm* (*REL*) commandment.

**coman'dante** *sm* (*MIL*) commander, commandant; (*di reggimento*) commanding officer; (*NAUT, AER*) captain.

**coman'dare** *vi* to be in command // *vt* to command; (*imporre*) to order, command; ~ **a qn di fare** to order sb to do; **co'mando** *sm* (*ingiunzione*) order, command; (*autorità*) command; (*TECN*) control.

**co'mare** *sf* (*madrina*) godmother.

**combaci'are** [kombaˈtʃare] *vi* to meet; (*fig: coincidere*) to coincide, correspond.

**com'battere** *vt* to fight; (*fig*) to combat, fight against // *vi* to fight; **combatti'mento** *sm* fight; fighting *q*; (*di pugilato*) match.

**combi'nare** *vt* to combine; (*organizzare*) to arrange; (*fam: fare*) to make, cause; **combinazi'one** *sf* combination; (*caso fortuito*) coincidence; **per combinazione** by chance.

**combus'tibile** *ag* combustible // *sm* fuel.

**com'butta** *sf* (*peg*): **in ~ in** league.

*PAROLA CHIAVE*

**'come** ♦ *av* **1** (*alla maniera di*) like; **ti comporti ~ lui** you behave like him *o* like he does; **bianco ~ la neve** (as) white as snow; **~ se** as if, as though

**2** (*in qualità di*) as a; **lavora ~ autista** he works as a driver

**3** (*interrogativo*) how; **~ ti chiami?** what's your name?; **~ sta?** how are you?; **com'è il tuo amico?** what is your friend like?; **~?** (*prego?*) pardon?, sorry?; **~ mai?** how come?; **~ mai non ci hai avvertiti?** why on earth didn't you warn us?

**4** (*esclamativo*): **~ sei bravo!** how clever you are!; **~ mi dispiace!** I'm terribly sorry!

♦ *cong* **1** (*in che modo*) how; **mi ha spiegato ~ l'ha conosciuto** he told me how he met him

**2** (*correlativo*): as; (*con comparativi di maggioranza*) than; **non è bravo ~** pensavo he isn't as clever as I thought; **è meglio di ~ pensassi** it's better than I thought

**3** (*appena che, quando*) as soon as; **~ arrivò, iniziò a lavorare** as soon as he arrived, he set to work; *vedi* **così, tanto.**

**'comico, a, ci, che** *ag* (*TEATRO*) comic; (*buffo*) comical // *sm* (*attore*) comedian, comic actor; (*comicità*) comic spirit, comedy.

**co'mignolo** [koˈmiɲɲolo] *sm* chimney top.

**cominci'are** [komin'tʃare] *vt, vi* to begin, start; **~ a fare/col fare** to begin to do/by doing.

**comi'tato** *sm* committee.

**comi'tiva** *sf* party, group.

**co'mizio** [koˈmittsjo] *sm* (*POL*) meeting, assembly.

**com'mando** *sm inv* commando (squad).

**com'media** *sf* comedy; (*opera teatrale*) play; (: *che fa ridere*) comedy; (*fig*) playacting *q*; **commedi'ante** *smf* (*peg*) third-rate actor/actress; (: *fig*) sham.

**commemo'rare** *vt* to commemorate.

**commenda'tore** *sm* official title awarded for services to one's country.

**commen'tare** *vt* to comment on; (*testo*) to annotate; (*RADIO, TV*) to give a commentary on; **commenta'tore, 'trice** *smf* commentator; **com'mento** *sm* comment; (*a un testo, RADIO, TV*) commentary.

**commerci'ale** [kommer'tʃale] *ag* commercial, trading; (*peg*) commercial.

**commerci'ante** [kommer'tʃante] *smf* trader, dealer; (*negoziante*) shopkeeper.

**commerci'are** [kommer'tʃare] *vt, vi*: **~ in** to deal *o* trade in.

**com'mercio** [kom'mertʃo] *sm* trade, commerce; **essere in ~** (*prodotto*) to be on the market *o* on sale; **essere nel ~** (*persona*) to be in business; **~ all'ingrosso/al minuto** wholesale/retail trade.

**com'messo, a** *pp di* **commettere** // *smf* shop assistant (*Brit*), sales clerk (*US*) // *sm* (*impiegato*) clerk // *sf* (*COMM*) order; **~ viaggiatore** commercial traveller.

**commes'tibile** *ag* edible; ∼**i** *smpl* foodstuffs.

**com'mettere** *vt* to commit.

**com'miato** *sm* leave-taking.

**commi'nare** *vt* (*DIR*) to threaten; to inflict.

**commissari'ato** *sm* (*AMM*) commissionership; (: *sede*) commissioner's office; (: *di polizia*) police station.

**commis'sario** *sm* commissioner; (*di pubblica sicurezza*) ≈ (police) superintendent (*Brit*), (police) captain (*US*); (*SPORT*) steward; (*membro di commissione*) member of a committee *o* board.

**commissio'nario** *sm* (*COMM*) agent, broker.

**commissi'one** *sf* (*incarico*) errand; (*comitato, percentuale*) commission; (*COMM: ordinazione*) order; ∼**i** *sfpl* (*acquisti*) shopping *sg.*

**commit'tente** *smf* (*COMM*) purchaser, customer.

**com'mosso, a** *pp di* **commuovere**

**commo'vente** *ag* moving.

**commozi'one** [kommot'tsjone] *sf* emotion, deep feeling; ∼ **cerebrale** (*MED*) concussion.

**commu'overe** *vt* to move, affect; ∼**rsi** *vr* to be moved.

**commu'tare** *vt* (*pena*) to commute; (*ELETTR*) to change *o* switch over.

**comò** *sm inv* chest of drawers.

**como'dino** *sm* bedside table.

**comodità** *sf inv* comfort; convenience.

**'comodo, a** *ag* comfortable; (*facile*) easy; (*conveniente*) convenient; (*utile*) useful, handy // *sm* comfort; convenience; **con** ∼ at one's convenience *o* leisure; **fare il proprio** ∼ to do as one pleases; **far** ∼ to be useful *o* handy.

**compae'sano, a** *smf* fellow countryman; person from the same town.

**com'pagine** [kom'padʒine] *sf* (*squadra*) team.

**compa'gnia** [kompaɲ'ɲia] *sf* company; (*gruppo*) gathering.

**com'pagno, a** [kom'paɲɲo] *smf* (*di classe, gioco*) companion; (*POL*) comrade; ∼ **di lavoro** workmate.

**compa'rare** *vt* to compare.

**compara'tivo, a** *ag, sm* comparative.

**compa'rire** *vi* to appear; **com'parso, a** *pp di* **comparire** // *sf* appearance; (*TEATRO*) walk-on; (*CINEMA*) extra.

**compartecipazi'one** [kompartetʃi-pat'tsjone] *sf* sharing; (*quota*) share; ∼ **agli utili** profit-sharing.

**comparti'mento** *sm* compartment; (*AMM*) district.

**compas'sato, a** *ag* (*persona*) composed.

**compassi'one** *sf* compassion, pity; **avere** ∼ **di** qn to feel sorry for sb, to pity sb.

**com'passo** *sm* (pair of) compasses *pl*; callipers *pl.*

**compa'tibile** *ag* (*scusabile*) excusable; (*conciliabile, INFORM*) compatible.

**compa'tire** *vt* (*aver compassione di*) to sympathize with, feel sorry for; (*scusare*) to make allowances for.

**com'patto, a** *ag* compact; (*roccia*) solid; (*folla*) dense; (*fig: gruppo, partito*) united, close-knit.

**com'pendio** *sm* summary; (*libro*) compendium.

**compen'sare** *vt* (*equilibrare*) to compensate for, make up for; ∼ **qn di** (*rimunerare*) to pay *o* remunerate sb for; (*risarcire*) to pay compensation to sb for; (*fig: fatiche, dolori*) to reward sb for; **com'penso** *sm* compensation; payment, remuneration; reward; **in compenso** (*d'altra parte*) on the other hand.

**'compera** *sf* (*acquisto*) purchase; **fare le** ∼**e** to do the shopping.

**compe'rare** *vt* = **comprare.**

**compe'tente** *ag* competent; (*mancia*) apt, suitable; **compe'tenza** *sf* competence;

competenze *sfpl* (*onorari*) fees.

com'petere *vi* to compete, vie; (*DIR: spettare*): ~ a to lie within the competence of; **competizi'one** *sf* competition.

compia'cente [kompja'tʃɛnte] *ag* courteous, obliging; **compia'cenza** *sf* courtesy.

compia'cere [kompja'tʃere] *vi:* ~ a to gratify, please // *vt* to please; ~rsi *vr* (*provare soddisfazione*): ~rsi di o per qc to be delighted at sth; (*rallegrarsi*): ~rsi con qn to congratulate sb; (*degnarsi*): ~rsi di fare to be so good as to do; **compiaci'uto, a** *pp di* compiacere.

compi'angere [kom'pjandʒere] *vt* to sympathize with, feel sorry for; **compi'anto, a** *pp di* compiangere.

'compiere *vt* (*concludere*) to finish, complete; (*adempiere*) to carry out, fulfil; ~rsi *vr* (*avverarsi*) to be fulfilled, come true; ~ gli anni to have one's birthday.

compi'tare *vt* = compiere.

'compito *sm* (*incarico*) task, duty; (*dovere*) duty; (*INS*) exercise; (: *a casa*) piece of homework; fare i ~i to do one's homework.

com'pito, a *ag* well-mannered, polite.

comple'anno *sm* birthday.

complemen'tare *ag* complementary; (*INS: materia*) subsidiary.

comple'mento *sm* complement; (*MIL*) reserve (troops); ~ oggetto (*LING*) direct object.

complessità *sf* complexity.

comples'sivo, a *ag* (*globale*) comprehensive, overall; (*totale: cifra*) total.

com'plesso, a *ag* complex // *sm* (*PSIC, EDIL*) complex; (*MUS: corale*) ensemble; (: *di musica pop*) group; in o nel ~ on the whole.

comple'tare *vt* to complete.

com'pleto, a *ag* complete; (*teatro,*

*autobus*) full // *sm* suit; al ~ full; (*tutti presenti*) all present.

compli'care *vt* to complicate; ~rsi *vr* to become complicated; **complicazi'one** *sf* complication.

'complice ['komplitʃe] *smlf* accomplice.

complimen'tarsi *vr:* ~ con to congratulate.

compli'mento *sm* compliment; ~i (*cortesia eccessiva*) ceremony *sg*; (*ossequi*) regards, compliments; ~i! congratulations!; senza ~i! don't stand on ceremony!; make yourself at home!; help yourself!

com'plotto *sm* plot, conspiracy.

compo'nente *smlf* member // *sm* component.

componi'mento *sm* (*DIR*) settlement; (*INS*) composition; (*poetico, teatrale*) work.

com'porre *vt* (*musica, testo*) to compose; (*mettere in ordine*) to arrange; (*DIR: lite*) to settle; (*TIP*) to set; (*TEL*) to dial.

comporta'mento *sm* behaviour.

compor'tare *vt* (*implicare*) to involve; (*consentire*) to permit, allow (of); ~rsi *vr* (*condursi*) to behave.

composi'tore, 'trice *smlf* composer; (*TIP*) compositor, typesetter.

composizi'one [kompozit'tsjone] *sf* composition; (*DIR*) settlement.

com'posta *sf vedi* composto.

compos'tezza [kompos'tettsa] *sf* composure; decorum.

com'posto, a *pp di* comporre // *ag* (*persona*) composed, self-possessed; (: *decoroso*) dignified; (*formato da più elementi*) compound *cpd* // *sm* compound // *sf* (*CUC*) stewed fruit *q*; (*AGR*) compost.

'compra *sf* = compera.

com'prare *vt* to buy; **compra'tore, 'trice** *smlf* buyer, purchaser.

com'prendere *vt* (*contenere*) to comprise, consist of; (*capire*) to understand.

comprensi'one *sf* understanding.

**compren'sivo, a** *ag (prezzo)*: ~ **di** inclusive of; *(indulgente)* understanding.

**com'preso, a** *pp di* **comprendere** // *ag (incluso)* included.

**com'pressa** *sf vedi* **compresso**.

**compressi'one** *sf* compression.

**com'presso, a** *pp di* **comprimere** // *ag (vedi comprimere)* pressed; compressed; repressed // *sf (MED: garza)* compress; (: *pastiglia)* tablet.

**com'primere** *vt (premere)* to press; *(FISICA)* to compress; *(fig)* to repress.

**compro'messo, a** *pp di* **compromettere** // *sm* compromise.

**compro'mettere** *vt* to compromise.

**compro'vare** *vt* to confirm.

**com'punto, a** *ag* contrite.

**compu'tare** *vt* to calculate; *(addebitare)*: ~ **qc a qn** to debit sb with sth.

**com'puter** *sm inv* computer.

**computiste'ria** *sf* accounting, book-keeping.

**'computo** *sm* calculation.

**comu'nale** *ag* municipal, town *cpd*, ≈ borough *cpd*.

**co'mune** *ag* common; *(consueto)* common, everyday; *(di livello medio)* average; *(ordinario)* ordinary // *sm (AMM)* town council; (: *sede)* town hall // *sf (di persone)* commune; **fuori del** ~ out of the ordinary; **avere in** ~ to have in common, share; **mettere in** ~ to share.

**comuni'care** *vt (notizia)* to pass on, convey; *(malattia)* to pass on; *(ansia etc)* to communicate; *(trasmettere: calore etc)* to transmit, communicate; *(REL)* to administer communion to // *vi* to communicate; ~**rsi** *vr (propagarsi)*: ~**rsi a** to spread to; *(REL)* to receive communion.

**comuni'cato** *sm* communiqué; ~ **stampa** press release.

**comunicazi'one** [komunikat'tsjone] *sf* communication; *(annuncio)*

announcement; *(TEL)*: ~ **(telefonica) (telephone)** call; **dare la** ~ **a qn** to put sb through; **ottenere la** ~ to get through.

**comuni'one** *sf* communion; ~ **di beni** *(DIR)* joint ownership of property.

**comu'nismo** *sm* communism; **comu'nista, i, e** *ag, sm/f* communist.

**comunità** *sf inv* community; C~ **Economica Europea (C.E.E.)** European Economic Community (EEC).

**co'munque** *cong* however, no matter how // *av (in ogni modo)* in any case; *(tuttavia)* however, nevertheless.

**con** *prep (nei seguenti casi con può fondersi con l'articolo definito:* **con** + **il** = **col**, **con** + **gli** = **cogli**, **con** + **i** = **coi**) with; **partire col treno** to leave by train; ~ **mio grande stupore** to my great astonishment; ~ **tutto ciò** for all that.

**co'nato** *sm*: ~ **di vomito** retching.

**'conca, che** *sf (GEO)* valley.

**con'cedere** [kon'tʃedere] *vt (accordare)* to grant; *(ammettere)* to admit, concede; ~**rsi qc** to treat o.s. to sth, to allow o.s. sth.

**concentra'mento** [kontʃentra'mento] *sm* concentration.

**concen'trare** [kontʃen'trare] *vt*, ~**rsi** *vr* to concentrate; **concentrazi'one** *sf* concentration.

**conce'pire** [kontʃe'pire] *vt (bambino)* to conceive; *(progetto, idea)* to conceive (of); *(metodo, piano)* to devise.

**con'cernere** [kon'tʃernere] *vt* to concern.

**concer'tare** [kontʃer'tare] *vt (MUS)* to harmonize; *(ordire)* to devise, plan; ~**rsi** *vr* to agree.

**con'certo** [kon'tʃerto] *sm (MUS)* concert; (: *componimento)* concerto.

**concessio'nario** [kontʃessjo'narjo] *sm (COMM)* agent, dealer.

**con'cesso, a** [kon'tʃesso] *pp di*

**concedere**.

**con'cetto** [kon'tʃɛtto] sm (pensiero, idea) concept; (opinione) opinion.

**concezi'one** [kontʃet'tsjone] sf conception.

**con'chiglia** [kon'kiʎʎa] sf shell.

**'concia** ['kontʃa] sf (di pelle) tanning; (di tabacco) curing; (sostanza) tannin.

**conci'are** [kon'tʃare] vt (pelli) to tan; (tabacco) to cure; (fig: ridurre in cattivo stato) to beat up; ~rsi vr (sporcarsi) to get in a mess; (vestirsi male) to dress badly.

**concili'are** [kontʃi'ljare] vt to reconcile; (contravvenzione) to pay on the spot; (favorire: sonno) to be conducive to, induce; (procurare: simpatia) to gain; ~rsi qc to gain o win sth (for o.s.); ~rsi qn to win sb over; ~rsi con to be reconciled with; **conciliazi'one** sf reconciliation; (DIR) settlement.

**con'cilio** [kon'tʃiljo] sm (REL) council.

**con'cime** [kon'tʃime] sm manure; (chimico) fertilizer.

**con'ciso, a** [kon'tʃizo] ag concise, succinct.

**conci'tato, a** [kontʃi'tato] ag excited, emotional.

**concitta'dino, a** [kontʃitta'dino] sm/f fellow citizen.

**con'cludere** vt to conclude; (portare a compimento) to conclude, finish, bring to an end; (operare positivamente) to achieve // vi (essere convincente) to be conclusive; ~rsi vr to come to an end, close; **conclusi'one** sf conclusion; (risultato) result; **conclu'sivo, a** ag conclusive; (finale) final; **con'cluso, a** pp di **concludere**.

**concor'danza** [konkor'dantsa] sf (anche LING) agreement.

**concor'dare** vt (tregua, prezzo) to agree on; (LING) to make agree // vi to agree; **concor'dato** sm agreement; (REL) concordat.

**con'corde** ag (d'accordo) in agree-

ment; (simultaneo) simultaneous.

**concor'rente** sm/f competitor; (INS) candidate; **concor'renza** sf competition.

**con'correre** vi: ~ (in) (MAT) to converge o meet (in); ~ (a) (competere) to compete (for); (: INS: a una cattedra) to apply (for); (partecipare: a un'impresa) to take part (in), contribute (to); **con'corso, a** pp di **concorrere** // sm competition; (INS) competitive examination; **concorso di colpa** (DIR) contributory negligence.

**con'creto, a** ag concrete.

**concussi'one** sf (DIR) extortion.

**con'danna** sf sentence; conviction; condemnation.

**condan'nare** vt (DIR): ~ a to sentence to; ~ **per** to convict of; (disapprovare) to condemn; **condan'nato, a** sm/f convict.

**conden'sare** vt, ~rsi vr to condense; **condensazi'one** sf condensation.

**condi'mento** sm seasoning; dressing.

**con'dire** vt to season; (insalata) to dress.

**condi'videre** vt to share; **condi'viso, a** pp di **condividere**.

**condizio'nale** [kondittsjo'nale] ag conditional // sm (LING) conditional // sf (DIR) suspended sentence.

**condizio'nare** [konditsjo'nare] vt to condition; **ad aria condizionata** air-conditioned.

**condizi'one** [kondit'tsjone] sf condition; ~i sfpl (di pagamento etc) terms, conditions; a ~ che on condition that, provided that.

**condogli'anze** [kondoʎ'ʎantse] sfpl condolences.

**con'dominio** sm joint ownership; (edificio) jointly-owned building.

**condo'nare** vt (DIR) to remit; **con'dono** sm remission; **condono fiscale** conditional amnesty for people evading tax.

**con'dotta** sf vedi **condotto**.

**con'dotto, a** pp di **condurre** // ag:
**medico** ~ local authority doctor (in
country district) // sm (canale, tubo)
pipe, conduit; (ANAT) duct // sf
(modo di comportarsi) conduct,
behaviour; (di un affare etc) handling; (di acqua) piping; (incarico
sanitario) country medical practice
controlled by a local authority.

**condu'cente** [kondu'tʃente] sm
driver.

**con'durre** vt to conduct; (azienda)
to manage; (accompagnare:
bambino) to take; (automobile) to
drive; (trasportare: acqua, gas) to
convey, conduct; (fig) to lead // vi to
lead; **condursi** vr to behave, conduct
o.s.

**condut'tore** ag: filo ~ (fig) thread
// sm (di mezzi pubblici) driver;
(FISICA) conductor.

**con'farsi** vr: ~ a to suit, agree
with.

**confederazi'one** [konfederat'tsjone]
sf confederation.

**confe'renza** [konfe'rentsa] sf (discorso) lecture; (riunione) conference; ~ **stampa** press conference;
**conferenzi'ere, a** smf lecturer.

**confe'rire** vt: ~ qc a qn to give sth
to sb, bestow sth on sb // vi to confer.

**con'ferma** sf confirmation.

**confer'mare** vt to confirm.

**confes'sare** vt, ~**rsi** vr to confess;
andare a ~**rsi** (REL) to go to confession; **confessio'nale** ag, sm con-
fessional; **confessi'one** sf confession; (setta religiosa) denomination;
**confes'sore** sm confessor.

**con'fetto** sm sugared almond;
(MED) pill.

**confezio'nare** [konfettsjo'nare] vt
(vestito) to make (up); (merci,
pacchi) to package.

**confezi'one** [konfet'tsjone] sf (di
abiti: da uomo) tailoring; (: da
donna) dressmaking; (imballaggio)
packaging; ~**i** sfpl garments,
clothes; ~ **regalo** gift pack.

**confic'care** vt: ~ qc in to hammer

o drive sth into; ~**rsi** vr to stick.

**confi'dare** vi: ~ **in** to confide in,
rely on // vt to confide; ~**rsi con qn**
to confide in sb; **confi'dente** smf
(persona amica) confidant/confidante;
(informatore) informer; **confi'denza** sf (familiarità) intimacy, familiarity; (fiducia) trust, confidence;
(rivelazione) confidence; **confiden-
zi'ale** ag familiar, friendly; (segreto) confidential.

**configu'rarsi** vr: ~ a to assume the
shape o form of.

**confi'nare** vi: ~ **con** to border on //
vt (POL) to intern; (fig) to confine;
~**rsi** vr (isolarsi): ~**rsi in** to shut
o.s. up in.

**Confin'dustria** sigla f (= Confede-
razione Generale dell'Industria
Italiana) employers' association, ≈
CBI (Brit).

**con'fine** sm boundary; (di paese)
border, frontier.

**con'fino** sm internment.

**confis'care** vt to confiscate.

**con'flitto** sm conflict.

**conflu'enza** [konflu'entsa] sf (di
fiumi) confluence; (di strade) junction.

**conflu'ire** vi (fiumi) to flow into
each other, meet; (strade) to meet.

**con'fondere** vt to mix up, confuse;
(imbarazzare) to embarrass; ~**rsi** vr
(mescolarsi) to mingle; (turbarsi) to
be confused; (sbagliare) to get mixed
up; ~ **le idee a qn** to mix sb up,
confuse sb.

**confor'mare** vt (adeguare): ~ **a** to
adapt o conform to; ~**rsi** vr: ~**rsi**
(a) to conform (to).

**conforme'mente** av accordingly;
~ **a** in accordance with.

**confor'tare** vt to comfort, console;
**confor'tevole** ag (consolante)
comforting; (comodo) comfortable;
**con'forto** sm comfort, consolation;
comfort.

**confron'tare** vt to compare.

**con'fronto** sm comparison; **in** o **a**
~ **di** in comparison with, compared

to; **nei miei** (o **tuoi** etc) ~**i** towards me (o you etc).

**confusi'one** sf confusion; (chiasso) racket, noise; (imbarazzo) embarrassment.

**con'fuso, a** pp di **confondere** // ag (vedi confondere) confused; embarrassed.

**confu'tare** vt to refute.

**conge'dare** [kondʒe'dare] vt to dismiss; (MIL) to demobilize; ~**rsi** vr to take one's leave; **con'gedo** sm (anche MIL) leave; **prendere congedo da qn** to take one's leave of sb; **congedo assoluto** (MIL) discharge.

**conge'gnare** [kondʒeɲ'ɲare] vt to construct, put together; **con'gegno** sm device, mechanism.

**conge'lare** [kondʒe'lare] vt, ~**rsi** vr to freeze; **congela'tore** sm freezer.

**congesti'onare** [kondʒestjo'nare] vt to congest.

**congesti'one** [kondʒes'tjone] sf congestion.

**conget'tura** [kondʒet'tura] sf conjecture, supposition.

**con'giungere** [kon'dʒundʒere] vt, ~**rsi** vr to join (together).

**congiunti'vite** [kondʒunti'vite] sf conjunctivitis.

**congiun'tivo** [kondʒun'tivo] sm (LING) subjunctive.

**congi'unto, a** [kon'dʒunto] pp di **congiungere** // ag (unito) joined // smf relative.

**congiun'tura** [kondʒun'tura] sf (giuntura) junction, join; (ANAT) joint; (circostanza) juncture; (ECON) economic situation.

**congiunzi'one** [kondʒun'tsjone] sf (LING) conjunction.

**congi'ura** [kon'dʒura] sf conspiracy; **congiu'rare** vi to conspire.

**conglome'rato** sm (GEO) conglomerate; (fig) conglomeration; (EDIL) concrete.

**congratu'larsi** vr: ~ **con qn per qc** to congratulate sb on sth.

**congratulazi'oni** [kongratulat'tsjoni] sfpl congratulations.

**congrega, ghe** sf band, bunch.

**con'gresso** sm congress.

**congu'aglio** [kon'gwaʎʎo] sm balancing, adjusting; (somma di denaro) balance.

**coni'are** vt to mint, coin; (fig) to coin.

**co'niglio** [ko'niʎʎo] sm rabbit.

**coniu'gare** vt (LING) to conjugate; ~**rsi** vr to get married; **coniu'gato, a** ag (sposato) married; **coniugazi'one** sf (LING) conjugation.

**'coniuge** ['kɔnjudʒe] smf spouse.

**connazio'nale** [konnattsjo'nale] smf fellow-countryman/woman.

**connessi'one** sf connection.

**con'nesso, a** pp di **connettere**.

**con'nettere** vt to connect, join // vi (fig) to think straight.

**conni'vente** ag conniving.

**conno'tati** smpl distinguishing marks.

**'cono** sm cone; ~ **gelato** ice-cream cone.

**cono'scente** [konoʃ'ʃente] smf acquaintance.

**cono'scenza** [konoʃ'ʃentsa] sf (il sapere) knowledge q; (persona) acquaintance; (facoltà sensoriale) consciousness q; **perdere** ~ to lose consciousness.

**co'noscere** [ko'noʃʃere] vt to know; **ci siamo conosciuti a Firenze** we (first) met in Florence; **cono-sci'tore, 'trice** smf knower; **conosci'uto, a** pp di **conoscere** // ag well-known.

**con'quista** sf conquest.

**conqui'stare** vt to conquer; (fig) to gain, win.

**consa'crare** vt (REL) to consecrate; (: sacerdote) to ordain; (dedicare) to dedicate; (fig: uso etc) to sanction; ~**rsi a** to dedicate o.s. to.

**consangu'ineo, a** smf blood relation.

**consa'pevole** ag: ~ **di** aware o

conscious of; **consapevo'lezza** sf awareness, consciousness.

'**conscio, a, sci, sce** ['kɔnʃo] ag: ~ **di** aware o conscious of.

**consecu'tivo, a** ag consecutive; (successivo: giorno) following, next.

**con'segna** [kon'seɲɲa] sf delivery; (merce consegnata) consignment; (custodia) care, custody; (MIL: ordine) orders pl: (: punizione) confinement to barracks; **pagamento alla** ~ cash on delivery; **dare qc in** ~ **a qn** to entrust sth to sb.

**conse'gnare** [konseɲ'ɲare] vt to deliver; (affidare) to entrust, hand over; (MIL) to confine to barracks.

**consegu'enza** [konse'gwentsa] sf consequence; **per** o **di** ~ consequently.

**consegu'ire** vt to achieve // vi to follow, result.

**con'senso** sm approval, consent.

**consen'tire** vi: ~ **a** to consent o agree to // vt to allow, permit.

**con'serva** sf (CUC) preserve; ~ **di frutta** jam; ~ **di pomodoro** tomato purée.

**conser'vare** vt (CUC) to preserve; (custodire) to keep; (: dalla distruzione etc) to preserve, conserve; ~**rsi** vr to keep.

**conserva'tore, 'trice** sm/f (POL) conservative.

**conservazi'one** [konservat'tsjone] sf preservation; conservation.

**conside'rare** vt to consider; (reputare) to consider, regard; ~ **molto qn** to think highly of sb; **considerazi'one** sf consideration; (stima) regard, esteem; **prendere in considerazione** to take into consideration; **conside'revole** ag considerable.

**consigli'are** [konsiʎ'ʎare] vt (persona) to advise; (metodo, azione) to recommend, advise, suggest; ~**rsi** vr: ~**rsi con qn** to ask sb for advice; **consigli'ere, a** sm/f adviser // sm: **consigliere d'amministrazione** board member; **consi-**

**gliere comunale** town councillor; **con'siglio** sm (suggerimento) advice q, piece of advice; (assemblea) council; **consiglio d'amministrazione** board; **il Consiglio dei Ministri** (POL) ≈ the Cabinet.

**consis'tente** ag thick; solid; (fig) sound, valid; **consis'tenza** sf consistency, thickness; solidity; validity.

**con'sistere** vi: ~ **in** to consist of; **consis'tito, a** pp di **consistere**.

**conso'lare** ag consular // vt (confortare) to console, comfort; (rallegrare) to cheer up; ~**rsi** vr to be comforted; to cheer up.

**conso'lato** sm consulate.

**consolazi'one** [konsolat'tsjone] sf consolation, comfort.

'**console** sm consul // [kon'sɔl] sf (quadro di comando) console.

**conso'nante** sf consonant.

'**consono, a** ag: ~ **a** consistent with, consonant with.

**con'sorte** sm/f consort.

**con'sorzio** [kon'sɔrtsjo] sm consortium.

**con'stare** vi: ~ **di** to consist of // vb impers: **mi consta che** it has come to my knowledge that, it appears that.

**consta'tare** vt to establish, verify; **constatazi'one** sf observation; **constatazione amichevole** jointly-agreed statement for insurance purposes.

**consu'eto, a** ag habitual, usual; **consue'tudine** sf habit, custom; (usanza) custom.

**consu'lente** sm/f consultant; **consu'lenza** sf consultancy.

**consul'tare** vt to consult; ~**rsi** vr: ~**rsi con qn** to seek the advice of sb; **consultazi'one** sf consultation; **consultazioni** sfpl (POL) talks, consultations.

**consu'mare** vt (logorare: abiti, scarpe) to wear out; (usare) to consume, use up; (mangiare, bere) to consume; (DIR) to consummate;

~**rsi** *vr* to wear out; to be used up; (*anche fig*) to be consumed; (*combustibile*) to burn out;

**consuma'tore** *sm* consumer; **consumazi'one** *sf* (*bibita*) drink; (*spuntino*) snack; (*DIR*) consummation; (*DIR*) consummation; **con'sumo** *sm* consumption; wear; use.

**consun'tivo** *sm* (*ECON*) final balance.

**con'tabile** *ag* accounts *cpd*, accounting // *smf* accountant; **contabilità** *sf* (*attività, tecnica*) accounting, accountancy; (*insieme dei libri etc*) books *pl*, accounts *pl*; (*ufficio*) accounts department.

**conta'dino** *sm* countryman/woman; farm worker; (*peg*) peasant.

**contagi'are** [konta'dʒare] *vt* to infect.

**con'tagio** [kon'tadʒo] *sm* infection; (*per contatto diretto*) contagion; (*epidemia*) epidemic; **contagi'oso, a** *ag* infectious; contagious.

**conta'gocce** [konta'gottʃe] *sm inv* (*MED*) dropper.

**contami'nare** *vt* to contaminate.

**con'tante** *sm* cash; **pagare in** ~**i** to pay cash.

**con'tare** *vt* to count; (*considerare*) to consider // *vi* to count, be of importance; ~ **su qn** to count o rely on sb; ~ **di fare qc** to intend to do sth; **conta'tore** *sm* meter.

**contat'tare** *vt* to contact.

**con'tatto** *sm* contact.

**'conte** *sm* count.

**conteggi'are** [konted'dʒare] *vt* to charge, put on the bill; **con'teggio** *sm* calculation.

**con'tegno** [kon'teɲɲo] *sm* (*comportamento*) behaviour; (*atteggiamento*) attitude; **darsi un** ~ to act nonchalant; to pull o.s. together.

**contem'plare** *vt* to contemplate, gaze at; (*DIR*) to make provision for.

**contemporanea'mente** *av* simultaneously; at the same time.

**contempo'raneo, a** *ag, smf* con-

temporary.

**conten'dente** *smf* opponent, adversary.

**con'tendere** *vi* (*competere*) to compete; (*litigare*) to quarrel // *vt*: ~ **qc a qn** to contend with o be in competition with sb for sth.

**conte'nere** *vt* to contain; **conteni'tore** *sm* container.

**conten'tare** *vt* to please, satisfy; ~**rsi di** to be satisfied with, content o.s. with.

**conten'tezza** [konten'tettsa] *sf* contentment.

**con'tento, a** *ag* pleased, glad; ~ **di** pleased with.

**conte'nuto** *sm* contents *pl*; (*argomento*) content.

**con'teso, a** *pp di* **contendere** // *sf* dispute, argument.

**con'tessa** *sf* countess.

**contes'tare** *vt* (*DIR*) to notify; (*fig*) to dispute; **contestazi'one** *sf* (*DIR*) notification; dispute; (*protesta*) protest.

**con'testo** *sm* context.

**con'tiguo, a** *ag*: ~ **(a)** adjacent (to).

**continen'tale** *ag, smf* continental.

**conti'nente** *ag* continent // *sm* (*GEO*) continent; (*: terra ferma*) mainland; **conti'nenza** *sf* continence.

**contin'gente** [kontin'dʒɛnte] *ag* contingent // *sm* (*COMM*) quota; (*MIL*) contingent; **contin'genza** *sf* circumstance; (*ECON*): (**indennità di**) **contingenza** cost-of-living allowance.

**continu'are** *vt* to continue (with), go on with // *vi* to continue, go on; ~ **a fare qc** to go on o continue doing sth; **continuazi'one** *sf* continuation.

**con'tinuo, a** *ag* (*numerazione*) continuous; (*pioggia*) continual, constant; (*ELETTR*): **corrente** ~**a** direct current; **di** ~ continually.

**'conto** *sm* (*calcolo*) calculation; (*COMM, ECON*) account; (*di ristorante, albergo*) bill; (*fig: stima*) consideration, esteem; **fare** i ~i **con qn** to settle one's account with sb; **fare** ~ **su qn/qc** to count o rely on sb; **rendere** ~ **a qn di qc** to be accountable to sb for sth; **tener** ~ **di qn/qc** to take sb/sth into account; **per** ~ **di** on behalf of; **per** ~ **mio** as far as I'm concerned; **a** ~**i fatti, in fin dei** ~**i** all things considered; ~ **corrente** current account; ~ **alla rovescia** countdown.

**con'torcere** [kon'tortʃere] vt to twist; (panni) to wring (out); ~**rsi** vr to twist, writhe.

**contor'nare** vt to surround.

**con'torno** sm (linea) outline, contour; (ornamento) border; (CUC) vegetables pl.

**con'torto, a** pp di **contorcere.**

**contrabbandi'ere, a** sm/f smuggler.

**contrab'bando** sm smuggling, contraband; **merce di** ~ contraband, smuggled goods pl.

**contrab'basso** sm (MUS) (double) bass.

**contraccambi'are** vt (favore etc) to return.

**contrac'ettivo, a** [kontratt'ʃet'tivo] ag, sm contraceptive.

**contrac'colpo** sm rebound; (di arma da fuoco) recoil; (fig) repercussion.

**con'trada** sf street; district.

**contrad'detto, a** pp di **contraddire.**

**contrad'dire** vt to contradict; **contraddit'torio, a** ag contradictory; (sentimenti) conflicting // sm (DIR) cross-examination; **contraddizi'one** sf contradiction.

**contraf'fare** vt (persona) to mimic; (alterare: voce) to disguise; (firma) to forge, counterfeit; **contraf'fatto, a** pp di **contraffare** // ag counterfeit; **contraffazi'one** sf mimicking q; disguising q; forging q; (cosa contraffatta) forgery.

**contrap'peso** sm counterbalance, counterweight.

**contrap'porre** vt: ~ **qc a qc** to counter sth with sth; (paragonare) to compare sth with sth; **contrap'posto, a** pp di **contrapporre.**

**contraria'mente** av: ~ **a** contrary to.

**contrari'are** vt (contrastare) to thwart, oppose; (irritare) to annoy, bother; ~**rsi** vr to get annoyed.

**contrarietà** sf adversity; (fig) aversion.

**con'trario, a** ag opposite; (sfavorevole) unfavourable // sm opposite; **essere** ~ **a qc** (persona) to be against sth; **in caso** ~ otherwise; **avere qc in** ~ to have some objection; **al** ~ on the contrary.

**con'trarre** vt, **contrarsi** vr to contract.

**contrasse'gnare** [kontrassen'nare] vt to mark; **contras'segno** sm (distintivo) distinguishing mark; **spedire in contrassegno** to send C.O.D.

**contras'tare** vt (avversare) to oppose; (impedire) to bar; (negare: diritto) to contest, dispute // vi: ~ (**con**) (essere in disaccordo) to contrast (with); (lottare) to struggle (with); **con'trasto** sm contrast; (conflitto) conflict; (litigio) dispute.

**contrat'tacco** sm counterattack.

**contrat'tare** vt, vi to negotiate.

**contrat'tempo** sm hitch.

**con'tratto, a** pp di **contrarre** // sm contract; **contrattu'ale** ag contractual.

**contravvenzi'one** [kontravven-'tsjone] sf contravention; (ammenda) fine.

**contrazi'one** [kontrat'tsjone] sf contraction; (di prezzi etc) reduction.

**contribu'ente** sm/f taxpayer; ratepayer (Brit), property tax payer (US).

**contribu'ire** vi to contribute; **con-tri'buto** sm contribution; (tassa) tax.

**'contro** prep against; ~ **di me/lui** against me/him; **pastiglie** ~ **la**

tosse throat lozenges; ~ **pagamento** (COMM) on payment // *prefisso:* **contro'battere** vt (fig: a parole) to answer back; (: confutare) to refute; **controfi'gura** sf (CINEMA) double; **controfir'mare** vt to countersign.

**control'lare** vt (accertare) to check; (sorvegliare) to watch, control; (tenere nel proprio potere, fig: dominare) to control; **con'trollo** sm check; watch; control; **controllo delle nascite** birth control; **control'lore** sm (FERR, AUTOBUS) (ticket) inspector.

**controprodu'cente** [kontroprodu-'tʃɛnte] ag counterproductive.

**contro'senso** sm (contraddizione) contradiction in terms; (assurdità) nonsense.

**controspio'naggio** [kontrospio-'naddʒo] sm counterespionage.

**contro'versia** sf controversy; (DIR) dispute.

**contro'verso, a** ag controversial.

**contro'voglia** [kontro'vɔʎʎa] av unwillingly.

**contu'macia** [kontu'matʃa] sf (DIR) default.

**contur'bare** vt to disturb, upset.

**contusi'one** sf (MED) bruise.

**convale'scente** [konvaleʃʃɛnte] ag, sm/f convalescent; **convale'scenza** sf convalescence.

**convali'dare** vt (AMM) to validate; (fig: sospetto, dubbio) to confirm.

**con'vegno** [kon'veɲɲo] sm (incontro) meeting; (congresso) convention, congress; (luogo) meeting place.

**conve'nevoli** smpl civilities.

**conveni'ente** ag suitable; (vantaggioso) profitable; (: prezzo) cheap; **conveni'enza** sf suitability; advantage; cheapness; **le convenienze** sfpl social conventions.

**conve'nire** vi (riunirsi) to gather, assemble; (concordare) to agree; (tornare utile) to be worthwhile // vb impers: **conviene fare questo** it is

advisable to do this; **conviene andarsene** we should go; **ne convengo** I agree.

**con'vento** sm (di frati) monastery; (di suore) convent.

**convenzio'nale** [konventsjo'nale] ag conventional.

**convenzi'one** [konven'tsjone] sf (DIR) agreement; (nella società) convention; **le** ~**i** sfpl social conventions.

**conver'sare** vi to have a conversation, converse.

**conversazi'one** [konversat'tsjone] sf conversation; **fare** ~ to chat, have a chat.

**conversi'one** sf conversion; ~ **ad U** (AUT) U-turn.

**conver'tire** vt (trasformare) to change; (POL, REL) to convert; ~**rsi** vr: ~**rsi (a)** to be converted (to); **conver'tito, a** sm/f convert.

**con'vesso, a** ag convex.

**con'vincere** [kon'vintʃere] vt to convince; ~ **qn di qc** to convince sb of sth; ~ **qn a fare qc** to persuade sb to do sth; **con'vinto, a** pp di convincere; **convinzi'one** sf conviction, firm belief.

**convis'suto, a** pp di convivere.

**con'vitto** sm (INS) boarding school.

**con'vivere** vi to live together.

**convo'care** vt to call, convene; (DIR) to summon; **convocazi'one** sf meeting; summons sg.

**convogli'are** [konvoʎ'ʎare] vt to convey; (dirigere) to direct, send; **con'voglio** sm (di veicoli) convoy; (FERR) train.

**con'vulso, a** ag (pianto) violent, convulsive; (attività) feverish.

**coope'rare** vi: ~ **(a)** to cooperate (in); **coopera'tiva** sf cooperative; **cooperazi'one** sf cooperation.

**coordi'nare** vt to coordinate; **coordi'nate** sfpl (MAT, GEO) coordinates; **coordi'nati** smpl (MODA) coordinates.

**co'perchio** [ko'perkjo] sm cover; (di pentola) lid.

**co'perta** *sf* cover; (*di lana*) blanket; (*da viaggio*) rug; (*AUT*) deck.

**coper'tina** *sf* (*STAMPA*) cover, jacket.

**co'perto, a** *pp di* **coprire** // *ag* covered; (*cielo*) overcast // *sm* place setting; (*posto a tavola*) place; (*al ristorante*) cover charge; ~ **di** covered in o with.

**coper'tone** *sm* (*telo impermeabile*) tarpaulin; (*AUT*) rubber tyre.

**coper'tura** *sf* (*anche ECON, MIL*) cover; (*di edificio*) roofing.

**'copia** *sf* copy; **brutta/bella** ~ rough/final copy.

**copi'are** *vt* to copy; **copia'trice** *sf* copier, copying machine.

**copi'one** *sm* (*CINEMA, TEATRO*) script.

**'coppa** *sf* (*bicchiere*) goblet; (*per frutta, gelato*) dish; (*trofeo*) cup, trophy; ~ **dell'olio** oil sump (*Brit*) o pan (*US*).

**'coppia** *sf* (*di persone*) couple; (*di animali, SPORT*) pair.

**coprifu'oco, chi** *sm* curfew.

**copri'letto** *sm* bedspread.

**co'prire** *vt* to cover; (*occupare: carica, posto*) to hold; ~**rsi** *vr* (*cielo*) to cloud over; (*vestirsi*) to wrap up, cover up; (*ECON*) to cover o.s.; ~**rsi di** (*macchie, muffa*) to become covered in.

**co'raggio** [ko'raddʒo] *sm* courage, bravery; ~! (*forza!*) come on!; (*animo!*) cheer up!; **coraggi'oso, a** *ag* courageous, brave.

**co'rallo** *sm* coral.

**co'rano** *sm* (*REL*) Koran.

**co'razza** [ko'rattsa] *sf* armour; (*di animali*) carapace, shell; (*MIL*) armour(-plating); **coraz'zata** *sf* battleship.

**corbelle'ria** *sf* stupid remark; ~**e** *sfpl* nonsense *q.*

**'corda** *sf* cord; (*fune*) rope; (*spago, MUS*) string; **dare** ~ **a** *qn* to let sb have his (*o* her) way; **tenere sulla** ~ *qn* to keep sb on tenterhooks; **tagliare la** ~ to slip away, sneak off;

~**e vocali** vocal cords.

**cordi'ale** *ag* cordial, warm // *sm* (*bevanda*) cordial.

**cor'doglio** [kor'dɔʎʎo] *sm* grief; (*lutto*) mourning.

**cor'done** *sm* cord, string; (*linea: di polizia*) cordon; ~ **ombelicale** umbilical cord.

**Co'rea** *sf*: **la** ~ Korea.

**coreogra'fia** *sf* choreography.

**cori'andolo** *sm* (*BOT*) coriander; ~**i** *smpl* confetti *sg.*

**cori'care** *vt* to put to bed; ~**rsi** *vr* to go to bed.

**'corna** *sfpl vedi* **corno**.

**cor'nacchia** [kor'nakkja] *sf* crow.

**corna'musa** *sf* bagpipes *pl.*

**cor'netta** *sf* (*MUS*) cornet; (*TEL*) receiver.

**cor'netto** *sm* (*CUC*) croissant; ~ **acustico** ear trumpet.

**cor'nice** [kor'nitʃe] *sf* frame; (*fig*) setting, background.

**'corno** *sm* (*ZOOL*: *pl(f)* ~**a**, *MUS*) horn; **fare le** ~**a a** *qn* to be unfaithful to sb; **cor'nuto, a** *ag* (*con corna*) horned; (*fam!*: *marito*) cuckolded // *sm* (*fam!*) cuckold; (: *insulto*) bastard (*!*).

**Corno'vaglia** [korno'vaʎʎa] *sf*: **la** ~ Cornwall.

**'coro** *sm* chorus; (*REL*) choir.

**co'rona** *sf* crown; (*di fiori*) wreath; **coro'nare** *vt* to crown.

**'corpo** *sm* body; (*cadavere*) (dead) body; (*militare, diplomatico*) corps *inv*; (*di opere*) corpus; **prendere** ~ to take shape; **a** ~ **a** ~ hand-to-hand; ~ **di ballo** corps de ballet; ~ **di guardia** guardroom; ~ **insegnante** teaching staff.

**corpo'rale** *ag* bodily; (*punizione*) corporal.

**corpora'tura** *sf* build, physique.

**corporazi'one** [korporat'tsjone] *sf* corporation.

**corpu'lento, a** *ag* stout.

**corre'dare** *vt*: ~ **di** to provide o furnish with; **cor'redo** *sm* equipment; (*di sposa*) trousseau.

**cor'reggere** [kor'rɛddʒere] *vt* to correct; (*compiti*) to correct, mark.

**cor'rente** *ag* (*fiume*) flowing; (*acqua del rubinetto*) running; (*moneta, prezzo*) current; (*comune*) everyday // *sm*: essere al ~ (di) to be well-informed (about); mettere al ~ (di) to inform (of) // *sf* (*movimento di liquido*) current, stream; (*spiffero*) draught; (*ELETTR*, *METEOR*) current; (*fig*) trend, tendency; la vostra lettera del 5 ~ mese (*COMM*) your letter of the 5th of this month; **corrente'mente** *av* commonly; parlare una lingua correntemente to speak a language fluently.

**'correre** *vi* to run; (*precipitarsi*) to rush; (*partecipare a una gara*) to race, run; (*fig: diffondersi*) to go round // *vt* (*SPORT: gara*) to compete in; (*rischio*) to run; (*pericolo*) to face; ~ dietro a qn to run after sb; corre voce che ... it is rumoured that ....

**cor'retto, a** *pp di* **correggere** // *ag* (*comportamento*) correct, proper; caffè ~ al cognac coffee laced with brandy.

**correzi'one** [korret'tsjone] *sf* correction; marking; ~ di bozze proof-reading.

**corri'doio** *sm* corridor.

**corri'dore** *sm* (*SPORT*) runner; (: *su veicolo*) racer.

**corri'era** *sf* coach (*Brit*), bus.

**corri'ere** *sm* (*diplomatico, di guerra*) courier; (*posta*) mail, post; (*COMM*) carrier.

**corrispet'tivo** *sm* (*somma*) amount due.

**corrispon'dente** *ag* corresponding // *sm/f* correspondent.

**corrispon'denza** [korrispon'dentsa] *sf* correspondence.

**corris'pondere** *vi* (*equivalere*): ~ (a) to correspond (to); (*per lettera*): ~ con to correspond with // *vt* (*stipendio*) to pay; (*fig: amore*) to return; **corris'posto, a** *pp di* **corrispondere**.

**corrobo'rare** *vt* to strengthen, fortify; (*fig*) to corroborate, bear out.

**cor'rodere** *vt*, ~rsi *vr* to corrode.

**cor'rompere** *vt* to corrupt; (*comprare*) to bribe.

**corrosi'one** *sf* corrosion.

**cor'roso, a** *pp di* **corrodere**.

**cor'rotto, a** *pp di* **corrompere** // *ag* corrupt.

**corrucci'arsi** [korrut'tʃarsi] *vr* to grow angry *o* vexed.

**corru'gare** *vt* to wrinkle; ~ la fronte to knit one's brows.

**corruzi'one** [korrut'tsjone] *sf* corruption; bribery.

**'corsa** *sf* running *q*; (*gara*) race; (*di autobus, taxi*) journey, trip; fare una ~ to run, dash; (*SPORT*) to run a race.

**cor'sia** *sf* (*AUT*, *SPORT*) lane; (*di ospedale*) ward.

**cor'sivo** *sm* cursive (writing); (*TIP*) italics *pl*.

**'corso, a** *pp di* **correre** // *sm* course; (*strada cittadina*) main street; (*di unità monetaria*) circulation; (*di titoli, valori*) rate, price; dar libero ~ a to give free expression to; in ~ in progress, under way; (*annata*) current; ~ d'acqua river, stream; (*artificiale*) waterway; ~ serale evening class.

**'corte** *sf* (court)yard; (*DIR, regale*) court; fare la ~ a qn to court sb; ~ marziale court-martial.

**cor'teccia, e** [kor'tettʃa] *sf* bark.

**corteggi'are** [korted'dʒare] *vt* to court.

**cor'teo** *sm* procession.

**cor'tese** *ag* courteous; **corte'sia** *sf* courtesy; per cortesia ... excuse me, please ....

**cortigi'ano, a** [korti'dʒano] *sm/f* courtier // *sf* courtesan.

**cor'tile** *sm* (court)yard.

**cor'tina** *sf* curtain; (*anche fig*) screen.

**'corto, a** *ag* short; essere a ~ di qc to be short of sth; ~ circuito short-circuit.

'**corvo** sm raven.

'**cosa** sf thing; (faccenda) affair, matter, business q; (che) ~? what?; (che) **cos'è**? what is it?; **a** ~ **pensi**? what are you thinking about?; **a** ~**e fatte** when it's all over.

'**coscia, sce** ['kɔʃʃa] sf thigh; ~ **di pollo** (CUC) chicken leg.

**cosci'ente** [koʃ'ʃɛnte] ag conscious; ~ **di** conscious o aware of; **co·sci'enza** sf conscience; (consapevolezza) consciousness; **co·scienzi'oso, a** ag conscientious.

**cosci'otto** [koʃ'ʃɔtto] sm (CUC) leg.

**cos'critto** sm (MIL) conscript.

PAROLA CHIAVE

**così** ◆ av **1** (in questo modo) like this, (in this way; (in tal modo) so; **le cose stanno** ~ this is the way things stand; **non ho detto** ~! I didn't say that!; **come stai**? — (**e**) ~ **how are you**? — so-so; **e** ~ **via** and so on; **per** ~ **dire** so to speak

**2** (tanto) so; ~ **lontano** so far away; **un ragazzo** ~ **intelligente** such an intelligent boy

◆ ag inv (tale): **non ho mai visto un film** ~ I've never seen such a film

◆ cong **1** (perciò) so, therefore **2**: ~ ... **come** as ... as; **non è** ~ **bravo come te** he's not as good as you; ~ ... **che** so ... that.

**cosid'detto, a** ag so-called.

**cos'metico, a, ci, che** ag, sm cosmetic.

**cos'pargere** [kos'pardʒere] vt: ~ **di** to sprinkle with; **cos'parso, a** pp di **cospargere**.

**cos'petto** sm: **al** ~ **di** in front of; in the presence of.

**cos'picuo, a** ag considerable, large.

**cospi'rare** vi to conspire; **co·spirazi'one** sf conspiracy.

'**costa** sf (tra terra e mare) coast(line); (litorale) shore; (ANAT) rib; **la C~ Azzurra** the French Riviera.

**costà** av there.

**cos'tante** ag constant; (persona) steadfast // sf constant.

**cos'tare** vi, vt to cost; ~ **caro** to be expensive, cost a lot.

**cos'tata** sf (CUC) large chop.

**cos'tato** sm (ANAT) ribs pl.

**costeggi'are** [kosted'dʒare] vt to be close to; to run alongside.

**cos'tei** pronome vedi **costui**.

**costernazi'one** [kosternat'tsjone] sf dismay, consternation.

**costi'ero, a** ag coastal, coast cpd // sf stretch of coast.

**costitu'ire** vt (comitato, gruppo) to set up, form; (collezione) to put together, build up; (sog: elementi, parti: comporre) to make up, constitute; (rappresentare) to constitute; (DIR) to appoint; ~**rsi alla polizia** to give o.s. up to the police.

**costituzio'nale** [kostitutsjo'nale] ag constitutional.

**costituzi'one** [kostitut'tsjone] sf setting up; building up; constitution.

'**costo** sm cost; **a ogni** o **qualunque** ~, **a tutti i** ~**i** at all costs.

'**costola** sf (ANAT) rib.

**costo'letta** sf (CUC) cutlet.

**cos'toro** pronome pl vedi **costui**.

**cos'toso, a** ag expensive, costly.

**cos'tretto, a** pp di **costringere**.

**cos'tringere** [kos'trindʒere] vt: ~ **qn a fare qc** to force sb to do sth; **cos'trizi'one** sf coercion.

**costru'ire** vt to construct, build; **co·struzi'one** sf construction, building.

**cos'tui, cos'tei,** pl **cos'toro** pronome (soggetto) he/she; pl they; (complemento) him/her; pl them; **si può sapere chi è** ~? (peg) just who is that fellow?

**cos'tume** sm (uso) custom; (foggia di vestire, indumento) costume; ~**i** smpl morals, morality sg; **il buon** ~ public morality; ~ **da bagno** bathing o swimming costume (Brit), swimsuit; (da uomo) bathing o swimming trunks pl.

co'tenna *sf* bacon rind.

co'togna [ko'toɲɲa] *sf* quince.

coto'letta *sf* (*di maiale, montone*) chop; (*di vitello, agnello*) cutlet.

co'tone *sm* cotton; ~ **idrofilo** cotton wool (*Brit*), absorbent cotton (*US*).

'cotta *sf* (*fam: innamoramento*) crush.

'cottimo *sm*: **lavorare a** ~ to do piecework.

'cotto, **a** *pp* di **cuocere** // *ag* cooked; (*fam: innamorato*) head-over-heels in love.

cot'tura *sf* cooking; (*in forno*) baking; (*in umido*) stewing.

co'vare *vt* to hatch; (*fig: malattia*) to be sickening for; (*: odio, rancore*) to nurse // *vi* (*fuoco, fig*) to smoulder.

'covo *sm* den.

co'vone *sm* sheaf.

'cozza ['kɔttsa] *sf* mussel.

coz'zare [kot'tsare] *vi*: ~ **contro** to bang into, collide with.

**C.P.** *abbr* = **casella postale**.

'crampo *sm* cramp.

'cranio *sm* skull.

cra'vatta *sf* tie.

cre'anza [kre'antsa] *sf* manners *pl*.

cre'are *vt* to create; **cre'ato** *sm* creation; **crea'tore, 'trice** *ag* creative // *sm* creator; **crea'tura** *sf* creature; (*bimbo*) baby, infant; **creazi'one** *sf* creation; (*fondazione*) foundation, establishment.

cre'dente *sm/f* (*REL*) believer.

cre'denza [kre'dɛntsa] *sf* belief; (*armadio*) sideboard.

credenzi'ali [kreden'tsjali] *sfpl* credentials.

'credere *vt* to believe // *vi*: ~ **in**, ~ **a** to believe in; ~ **qn** onesto to believe sb (to be) honest; ~ **che** to believe *o* think that; ~**rsi furbo** to think one is clever.

'credito *sm* (*anche COMM*) credit; (*reputazione*) esteem, repute; **comprare a** ~ to buy on credit.

'credo *sm inv* creed.

'crema *sf* cream; (*con uova, zucchero etc*) custard; ~ **solare** sun cream.

cre'mare *vt* to cremate.

Crem'lino *sm*: **il** ~ the Kremlin.

'crepa *sf* crack.

cre'paccio [kre'pattʃo] *sm* large crack, fissure; (*di ghiacciaio*) crevasse.

crepacu'ore *sm* broken heart.

cre'pare *vi* (*fam: morire*) to snuff it, kick the bucket; ~ **dalle risa** to split one's sides laughing.

crepi'tare *vi* (*fuoco*) to crackle; (*pioggia*) to patter.

cre'puscolo *sm* twilight, dusk.

'crescere ['kreʃʃere] *vi* to grow // *vt* (*figli*) to raise; 'crescita *sf* growth; cresci'uto, a *pp* di **crescere**.

cresima *sf* (*REL*) confirmation.

'crespo, **a** *ag* (*capelli*) frizzy; (*tessuto*) puckered // *sm* crêpe.

'cresta *sf* crest; (*di polli, uccelli*) crest, comb.

'creta *sf* chalk; clay.

cre'tino, **a** *ag* stupid // *sm/f* idiot, fool.

cric *sm inv* (*TECN*) jack.

'cricca, **che** *sf* clique.

'cricco, **chi** *sm* = **cric**.

crimi'nale *ag, sm/f* criminal.

'crimine *sm* (*DIR*) crime.

crine *sm* horsehair; crini'era *sf* mane.

crisan'temo *sm* chrysanthemum.

'crisi *sf inv* crisis; (*MED*) attack, fit; ~ **di nervi** attack *o* fit of nerves.

cristalliz'zare [kristalid'dzare] *vi*, ~**rsi** *vr* to crystallize; (*fig*) to become fossilized.

cris'tallo *sm* crystal.

cristia'nesimo *sm* Christianity.

cristi'ano, **a** *ag, sm/f* Christian.

'Cristo *sm* Christ.

cri'terio *sm* criterion; (*buon senso*) (common) sense.

'critica, **che** *sf vedi* **critico**.

criti'care *vt* to criticize.

'critico, **a**, **ci**, **che** *ag* critical // *sm* critic // *sf* criticism; **la** ~**a** (*attività*) criticism; (*persone*) the critics *pl*.

cri'vello *sm* riddle.

'croce ['krotʃe] sf cross; in ~ (di traverso) crosswise; (fig) on tenterhooks; la C~ Rossa the Red Cross.

croce'figgere [krotʃe'fiddʒere] etc = crocifiggere etc.

croce'via [krotʃe'via] sm inv crossroads sg.

croci'ata [kro'tʃata] sf crusade.

cro'cicchio [kro'tʃikkjo] sm crossroads sg.

croci'era [kro'tʃera] sf (viaggio) cruise; (ARCHIT) transept.

croci'figgere [krotʃi'fiddʒere] vt to crucify; crocifissi'one sf crucifixion; croci'fisso, a pp di crocifiggere.

crogi'olo, crogi'uolo [kro'dʒɔlo] sm (fig) melting pot.

crol'lare vi to collapse; 'crollo sm collapse; (di prezzi) slump, sudden fall.

cro'mato, a ag chromium-plated.

'cromo sm chrome, chromium.

cromo'soma, i sm chromosome.

'cronaca, che [kro'nakke] sf chronicle; (STAMPA) news sg; (: rubrica) column; (TV, RADIO) commentary; fatto o episodio di ~ news item; ~ nera crime news sg; crime column.

'cronico, a, ci, che ag chronic.

cro'nista, i sm (STAMPA) reporter, columnist.

cronolo'gia [kronolo'dʒia] sf chronology.

cro'nometro sm chronometer; (a scatto) stopwatch.

'crosta sf crust.

cros'tacei [kros'tatʃei] smpl shellfish.

cros'tata sf (CUC) tart.

cros'tino sm (CUC) croûton; (: da antipasto) canapé.

'cruccio ['kruttʃo] sm worry, torment.

cruci'verba sm inv crossword (puzzle).

cru'dele ag cruel; crudeltà sf cruelty.

'crudo, a ag (non cotto) raw; (aspro) harsh, severe.

cru'miro sm (peg) blackleg (Brit),

scab.

'crusca sf bran.

crus'cotto sm (AUT) dashboard.

'Cuba sf Cuba.

'cubico, a, ci, che ag cubic.

'cubo, a ag cubic // sm cube; elevare al ~ (MAT) to cube.

cuc'cagna [kuk'kaɲɲa] sf: paese della ~ land of plenty; albero della ~ greasy pole (fig).

cuc'cetta [kut'tʃetta] sf (FERR) couchette; (NAUT) berth.

cucchiai'ata [kukja'jata] sf spoonful.

cucchia'ino [kukkja'ino] sm teaspoon; coffee spoon.

cucchi'aio [kuk'kjajo] sm spoon.

'cuccia, ce ['kuttʃa] sf dog's bed; a ~! down!

'cucciolo ['kuttʃolo] sm cub; (di cane) puppy.

cu'cina [ku'tʃina] sf (locale) kitchen; (arte culinaria) cooking, cookery; (le vivande) food, cooking; (apparecchio) cooker; ~ componibile fitted kitchen; cuci'nare vt to cook.

cu'cire [ku'tʃire] vt to sew, stitch; cuci'trice sf stapler; cuci'tura sf sewing, stitching; (costura) seam.

cucù sm inv, cu'culo sm cuckoo.

'cuffia sf bonnet, cap; (da infermiera) cap; (da bagno) (bathing) cap; (per ascoltare) headphones pl, headset.

cu'gino, a [ku'dʒino] sm/f cousin.

---

| PAROLA CHIAVE |
|---|

'cui pronome 1 (nei complementi indiretti: persona) whom; (: oggetto, animale) which; la persona/le persone a ~ accennavi the person/ people you were referring to o to whom you were referring; i libri di ~ parlavo the books I was talking about o about which I was talking; il quartiere in ~ abito the district where I live; la ragione per ~ the reason why
2 (inserito tra articolo e sostantivo) whose; la donna i ~ figli sono scomparsi the woman whose chil-

dren have disappeared; **il signore, dal ~ figlio** ho avuto il libro the man from whose son I got the book.

**culi'naria** *sf* cookery.

**'culla** *sf* cradle.

**cul'lare** *vt* to rock.

**culmi'nare** *vi*: ~ **in** *o* **con** to culminate in.

**'culmine** *sm* top, summit.

**'culo** *sm* (*fam!*) arse (*Brit!*), ass (*US!*); (: *fig: fortuna*): **aver ~** to have the luck of the devil.

**'culto** *sm* (*religione*) religion; (*adorazione*) worship, adoration; (*venerazione: anche fig*) cult.

**cul'tura** *sf* culture; education, learning; **cultu'rale** *ag* cultural.

**cumula'tivo,** *a ag* cumulative; (*prezzo*) inclusive; (*biglietto*) group *cpd.*

**'cumulo** *sm* (*mucchio*) pile, heap; (*METEOR*) cumulus.

**'cuneo** *sm* wedge.

**cu'oca** *sf vedi* **cuoco.**

**cu'ocere** ['kwɔtʃere] *vt* (*alimenti*) to cook; (*mattoni etc*) to fire // *vi* to cook; ~ **al forno** (*pane*) to bake; (*arrosto*) to roast; **cu'oco, a, chi, che** *sm/f* cook; (*di ristorante*) chef.

**cu'oio** *sm* leather; ~ **capelluto** scalp.

**cu'ore** *sm* heart; ~**i** *smpl* (*CARTE*) hearts; **avere buon** ~ to be kind-hearted; **stare a ~ a qn** to be important to sb.

**cupi'digia** [kupi'didʒa] *sf* greed, covetousness.

**'cupo, a** *ag* dark; (*suono*) dull; (*fig*) gloomy, dismal.

**'cupola** *sf* dome; cupola.

**'cura** *sf* care; (*MED: trattamento*) (course of) treatment; **aver ~ di** (*occuparsi di*) to look after; **a ~ di** (*libro*) edited by; ~ **dimagrante** diet.

**cu'rare** *vt* (*malato, malattia*) to treat; (: *guarire*) to cure; (*aver cura di*) to take care of; (*testo*) to edit; ~**rsi** *vr* to take care of o.s.; (*MED*)

to follow a course of treatment; ~**rsi di** to pay attention to.

**cu'rato** *sm* parish priest; (*protestante*) vicar, minister.

**cura'tore, 'trice** *smf* (*DIR*) trustee; (*di antologia etc*) editor.

**curio'sare** *vi* to look round, wander round; (*tra libri*) to browse; ~ **nei negozi** to look *o* wander round the shops.

**curiosità** *sf inv* curiosity; (*cosa rara*) curio, curiosity.

**curi'oso, a** *ag* (*che vuol sapere*) curious, inquiring; (*ficcanaso*) curious, inquisitive; (*bizzarro*) strange, curious; **essere ~ di** to be curious about.

**cur'sore** *sm* (*INFORM*) cursor.

**'curva** *sf* curve; (*stradale*) bend, curve.

**cur'vare** *vt* to bend // *vi* (*veicolo*) to take a bend; (*strada*) to bend, curve; ~**rsi** *vr* to bend; (*legno*) to warp.

**'curvo, a** *ag* curved; (*piegato*) bent.

**cusci'netto** [kuʃʃi'netto] *sm* pad; (*TECN*) bearing // *ag inv*: **stato ~** buffer state; ~ **a sfere** ball bearing.

**cu'scino** [kuʃ'ʃino] *sm* cushion; (*guanciale*) pillow.

**'cuspide** *sf* (*ARCHIT*) spire.

**cus'tode** *smf* keeper, custodian.

**cus'todia** *sf* care; (*DIR*) custody; (*astuccio*) case, holder.

**custo'dire** *vt* (*conservare*) to keep; (*assistere*) to look after, take care of; (*fare la guardia*) to guard.

**'cute** *sf* (*ANAT*) skin.

**cu'ticola** *sf* cuticle.

**C.V.** *abbr* (= *cavallo vapore*) h.p.

# D

PAROLA CHIAVE

**da** *prep* (*da* + *il* = **dal**, *da* + *lo* = **dallo**, *da* + *l'* = **dall'**, *da* + *la* = **dalla**, *da* + *i* = **dai**, *da* + *gli* = **dagli**, *da* + *le* = **dalle**) **1** (*agente*) by; **dipinto ~ un grande artista**

painted by a great artist

**2** (*causa*) with; **tremare dalla paura** to tremble with fear

**3** (*stato in luogo*) at; **abito ~ lui** I'm living at his house *o* with him; **sono dal giornalaio/~ Francesco** I'm at the newsagent's/Francesco's (house)

**4** (*moto a luogo*) to; (*moto per luogo*) through; **vado ~ Pietro/dal giornalaio** I'm going to Pietro's (house)/to the newsagent's; **sono passati dalla finestra** they came in through the window

**5** (*provenienza, allontanamento*) from; **arrivare/partire ~ Milano** to arrive/depart from Milan; **scendere dal treno/dalla macchina** to get off the train/out of the car; **si trova a 5 km ~ qui** it's 5 km from here

**6** (*tempo: durata*) for; (*: a partire da: nel passato*) since; (*: nel futuro*) from; **vivo qui ~ un anno** I've been living here for a year; **la date 3 che ti aspetto** I've been waiting for you since 3 (o'clock); **~ oggi in poi** from today onwards; **~ bambino** as a child, when I (*o* he *etc*) was a child

**7** (*modo, maniera*) like; **comportarsi ~ uomo** to behave like a man; **l'ho fatto ~ me** I did it (by) myself

**8** (*descrittivo*): **una macchina ~ corsa** a racing car; **una ragazza dai capelli biondi** a girl with blonde hair; **un vestito ~ 100.000 lire** a 100,000 lire dress; **sordo ~ un orecchio** deaf in one ear.

**dab'bene** *ag inv* honest, decent.

**dac'capo, da 'capo** *av* (*di nuovo*) (once) again; (*dal principio*) all over again, from the beginning.

**dacché** [dak'ke] *cong* since.

**dado** *sm* (*a gioco*) dice *o* die (*pl* dice); (*CUC*) stock (*Brit*) *o* bouillon (*US*) cube; (*TECN*) (screw)nut; **~i** *smpl* (game of) dice.

**daf'fare, da 'fare** *sm* work, toil.

**dagli** ['daʎʎi], **'dai** *prep* + *det vedi*

da.

**'daino** *sm* (fallow) deer *inv*; (*pelle*) buckskin.

**dal, dall', 'dalla, 'dalle, 'dallo** *prep* + *det vedi* **da**.

**dal'tonico, a, ci, che** *ag* colourblind.

**'dama** *sf* lady; (*nei balli*) partner; (*gioco*) draughts *sg* (*Brit*), checkers *sg* (*US*).

**damigi'ana**     [dami'dʒana]     *sf* demijohn.

**da'naro** *sm* = **denaro.**

**da'nese** *ag* Danish // *sm/f* Dane // *sm* (*LING*) Danish.

**Dani'marca** *sf*: **la ~** Denmark.

**dan'nare** *vt* (*REL*) to damn; **~rsi** *vr* (*fig: tormentarsi*) to be worried to death; **far ~ qn** to drive sb mad; **dannazi'one** *sf* damnation.

**danneggi'are** [danned'dʒare] *vt* to damage; (*rovinare*) to spoil; (*nuocere*) to harm.

**'danno** *sm* damage; (*a persona*) harm, injury; **~i** *smpl* (*DIR*) damages; **dan'noso, a** *ag*: **dannoso (a, per)** harmful (to), bad (for).

**Da'nubio** *sm*: **il ~** the Danube.

**'danza** ['dantsa] *sf*: **la ~** dancing; **una ~** a dance.

**dan'zare** [dan'tsare] *vt, vi* to dance.

**dapper'tutto** *av* everywhere.

**dap'poco** *ag inv* inept, worthless.

**dap'prima** *av* at first.

**'dardo** *sm* dart.

**'dare** *vt* (*COMM*) debit // *vt* to give; (*produrre: frutti, suono*) to produce // *vi* (*guardare*): **~ su** to look (out) onto; **~rsi** *vr*: **~rsi a** to dedicate o.s. to; **~rsi al commercio** to go into business; **~rsi al bere** to take to drink; **~ da mangiare a qn** to give sb sth to eat; **~ per certo qc** to consider sth certain; **~ per morto qn** to give sb up for dead; **~rsi per vinto** to give in.

**'darsena** *sf* dock; dockyard.

**'data** *sf* date; **~ di nascita** date of birth.

**da'tare** *vt* to date // *vi*: **~ da** to date

from.

'**dato, a** *ag* (*stabilito*) given // *sm* datum; ~**i** *smpl* data *pl*; ~ **che** given that; **un** ~ **di fatto** a fact.

'**dattero** *sm* date.

**dattilogra'fare** *vt* to type; **dattilogra'fia** *sf* typing; **datti'lografo, a** *sm/f* typist.

**da'vanti** *av* in front; (*dirimpetto*) opposite // *ag inv* front // *sm* front; ~ **a** *prep* in front of; facing, opposite; (*in presenza di*) before, in front of.

**davan'zale** [davan'tsale] *sm* windowsill.

**da'vanzo, d'a'vanzo** [da'vantso] *av* more than enough.

**dav'vero** *av* really, indeed.

'**dazio** [dattsjo] *sm* (*somma*) duty; (*luogo*) customs *pl*.

**DC** *sigla f = Democrazia Cristiana*.

**d. C.** *ad abbr* (= *dopo Cristo*) A.D.

'**dea** *sf* goddess.

'**debito, a** *ag* due, proper // *sm* debt; (*COMM: dare*) debit; **a tempo** ~ at the right time; **debi'tore, 'trice** *sm/f* debtor.

'**debole** *ag* weak, feeble; (*suono*) faint; (*luce*) dim // *sm* weakness; **debo'lezza** *sf* weakness.

**debut'tare** *vi* to make one's début; **de'butto, a** *sm* début.

**deca'denza** [deka'dɛntsa] *sf* decline; (*DIR*) loss, forfeiture.

**decaffei'nato, a** *ag* decaffeinated.

**decappot'tabile** *ag, sf* convertible.

**dece'duto, a** [detʃe'duto] *ag* deceased.

**de'cennio** [de'tʃɛnnjo] *sm* decade.

**de'cente** [de'tʃɛnte] *ag* decent, respectable, proper; (*accettabile*) satisfactory, decent.

**de'cesso** [de'tʃɛsso] *sm* death; **atto di** ~ death certificate.

**de'cidere** [de'tʃidere] *vt*: ~ **qc** to decide on sth; (*questione, lite*) to settle sth; ~ **di fare/che** to decide to do/that; ~ **di qc** (*sog: cosa*) to determine sth; ~**rsi** (**a fare**) to decide (to do), make up one's mind (to do).

**deci'frare** [detʃi'frare] *vt* to decode; (*fig*) to decipher, make out.

**deci'male** [detʃi'male] *ag* decimal.

'**decimo, a** [detʃimo] *num* tenth.

**de'cina** [de'tʃina] *sf* ten; (*circa dieci*): **una** ~ (**di**) about ten.

**decisi'one** [detʃi'zjone] *sf* decision; **prendere una** ~ to make a decision.

**de'ciso, a** *pp di* **decidere**.

**declas'sare** *vt* to downgrade; to lower in status.

**decli'nare** *vi* (*pendio*) to slope down; (*fig: diminuire*) to decline; (*tramontare*) to set, go down // *vt* to decline; **declinazi'one** *sf* (*LING*) declension; **de'clino** *sm* decline.

**decol'lare** *vi* (*AER*) to take off; **de'collo** *sm* take-off.

**decolo'rare** *vt* to bleach.

**decom'porre** *vt*, **decomporsi** *vr* to decompose; **decom'posto, a** *pp di* **decomporre**.

**deconge'lare** [dekondʒe'lare] *vt* to defrost.

**deco'rare** *vt* to decorate; **decora'tore, 'trice** *sm/f* (*interior*) decorator; **decorazi'one** *sf* decoration.

**de'coro** *sm* decorum; **deco'roso, a** *ag* decorous, dignified.

**de'correre** *vi* to pass, elapse; (*avere effetto*) to run, have effect; **de'corso, a** *pp di* **decorrere**; (*evoluzione: anche MED*) course.

**de'crescere** [de'krɛʃʃere] *vi* (*diminuire*) to decrease, diminish; (*acque*) to subside, go down; (*prezzi*) to go down; **decresci'uto, a** *pp di* **decrescere**.

**de'creto** *sm* decree; ~ **legge** decree with the force of law.

'**dedalo** *sm* maze, labyrinth.

'**dedica, che** *sf* dedication.

**dedi'care** *vt* to dedicate.

'**dedito, a** *ag*: ~ **a** (*studio etc*) dedicated *o* devoted to; (*vizio*) addicted to.

**de'dotto, a** *pp di* **dedurre**.

**de'durre** *vt* (*concludere*) to deduce; (*defalcare*) to deduct; **deduzi'one**

*sf* deduction.

**defal'care** *vt* to deduct.

**defe'rente** *ag* respectful, deferential.

**defe'rire** *vt*: ~ a (DIR) to refer to.

**defezi'one** [defet'tsjone] *sf* defection, desertion.

**defici'ente** [defit'ʃɛnte] *ag* (mancante): ~ di deficient in; (insufficiente) insufficient // *smf* mental defective; (peg: cretino) idiot.

**'deficit** ['dɛfitʃit] *sm inv* (ECON) deficit.

**defi'nire** *vt* to define; (risolvere) to settle; **defini'tivo, a** *ag* definitive, final; **definizi'one** *sf* definition, settlement.

**deflet'tore** *sm* (AUT) quarter-light.

**de'flusso** *sm* (della marea) ebb.

**defor'mare** *vt* (alterare) to put out of shape; (corpo) to deform; (pensiero, fatto) to distort; ~rsi *vr* to lose its shape.

**de'forme** *ag* deformed; disfigured; **deformità** *sf inv* deformity.

**defrau'dare** *vt*: ~ qn di qc to defraud sb of sth, cheat sb out of sth.

**de'funto, a** *ag* late *cpd* // *smf* deceased.

**degene'rare** [dedʒene'rare] *vi* to degenerate; **de'genere** *ag* degenerate.

**de'gente** [de'dʒɛnte] *smf* bedridden person; (ricoverato in ospedale) inpatient.

**'degli** ['deʎʎi] *prep* + *det vedi* **di**.

**de'gnarsi** [deɲ'narsi] *vr*: ~ di fare to deign o condescend to do.

**'degno, a** *ag* dignified; ~ di worthy of; ~ di lode praiseworthy.

**degra'dare** *vt* (MIL) to demote; (privare della dignità) to degrade; ~rsi *vr* to demean o.s.

**degustazi'one** [degustat'tsjone] *sf* sampling, tasting.

**'dei, del** *prep* + *det vedi* **di**.

**dela'tore, 'trice** *smf* police informer.

**'delega, ghe** *sf* (procura) proxy.

**dele'gare** *vt* to delegate; **dele'gato** *sm* delegate.

**del'fino** *sm* (ZOOL) dolphin; (STORIA) dauphin; (fig) probable successor.

**delibe'rare** *vt* to come to a decision on // *vi* (DIR): ~ (su qc) to rule (on sth).

**delica'tezza** [delika'tettsa] *sf* (anche CUC) delicacy; frailty; thoughtfulness; tactfulness.

**deli'cato, a** *ag* delicate; (salute) delicate, frail; (fig: gentile) thoughtful, considerate; (: che dimostra tatto) tactful.

**deline'are** *vt* to outline; ~rsi *vr* to be outlined; (fig) to emerge.

**delin'quente** *sm* criminal, delinquent; **delin'quenza** *sf* criminality, delinquency; **delinquenza minorile** juvenile delinquency.

**deli'rare** *vi* to be delirious, rave; (fig) to rave.

**de'lirio** *sm* delirium; (ragionamento insensato) raving; (fig): **andare/mandare in** ~ to go/send into a frenzy.

**de'litto** *sm* crime.

**de'lizia** [de'littsja] *sf* delight; **delizi'oso, a** *ag* delightful; (cibi) delicious.

**dell', 'della, 'delle, 'dello** *prep* + *det vedi* **di**.

**delta'plano** *sm* hang-glider; **volo col** ~ hang-gliding.

**de'ludere** *vt* to disappoint; **delusi'one** *sf* disappointment; **de'luso, a** *pp* di **deludere**.

**de'manio** *sm* state property.

**de'menza** [de'mentsa] *sf* dementia; (stupidità) foolishness.

**demo'cratico, a, ci, che** *ag* democratic.

**democra'zia** [demokrat'tsia] *sf* democracy.

**democristi'ano, a** *ag, smf* Christian Democrat.

**demo'lire** *vt* to demolish.

**'demone** *sm* demon.

**de'monio** *sm* demon; devil; **il D~**

the Devil.

**de'naro** sm money.

**denomi'nare** vt to name; **~rsi** vr to be named o called; **denomina-zi'one** sf name; denomination.

**densità** sf inv density.

**'denso, a** ag thick, dense.

**den'tale** ag dental.

**'dente** sm tooth; (di forchetta) prong; (GEO: cima) jagged peak; **al ~** (CUC: pasta) cooked so as to be firm when eaten; **~i del giudizio** wisdom teeth; **denti'era** sf (set of) false teeth pl.

**denti'fricio** [denti'fritʃo] sm tooth-paste.

**den'tista, i, e** sm/f dentist.

**'dentro** av inside; (in casa) indoors; (fig: nell'intimo) inwardly // prep: **~** (a) in; **piegato in ~** folded over; **qui/là ~** in here/there; **~ di sé** (pensare, brontolare) to oneself.

**de'nuncia, ce** o **cie** [de'nuntʃa], **de'nunzia** [de'nuntsja] sf denuncia-tion; declaration; **~ dei redditi** (in-come) tax return.

**denunci'are** [denun'tʃare], **denunzi'are** [denun'tsjare] vt to denounce; (dichiarare) to declare.

**denutrizi'one** [denutrit'tsjone] sf malnutrition.

**deodo'rante** sm deodorant.

**depe'rire** vi to waste away.

**depila'torio, a** ag hair-removing cpd, depilatory.

**dépli'ant** [depli'ã] sm inv leaflet; (opuscolo) brochure.

**deplo'revole** ag deplorable.

**de'porre** vt (depositare) to put down; (rimuovere: da una carica) to remove; (: re) to depose; (DIR) to testify.

**depor'tare** vt to deport.

**deposi'tare** vt (gen, GEO, ECON) to deposit; (lasciare) to leave; (merci) to store.

**de'posito** sm deposit; (luogo) ware-house; depot; (: MIL) depot; **~ bagagli** left-luggage office.

**deposizi'one** [depozit'tsjone] sf

deposition; (da una carica) removal.

**de'posto, a** pp di **deporre**.

**depra'vato, a** ag depraved // sm/f degenerate.

**depre'dare** vt to rob, plunder.

**depressi'one** sf depression.

**de'presso, a** pp di **deprimere** // ag depressed.

**deprez'zare** [depret'tsare] vt (ECON) to depreciate.

**de'primere** vt to depress.

**depu'rare** vt to purify.

**depu'tato, a** o **'essa** sm/f (POL) deputy, ≈ Member of Parliament (Brit), ≈ Member of Congress (US); **deputazi'one** sf deputation; (POL) position of deputy, ≈ parliamentary seat (Brit), ≈ seat in Congress (US).

**deragli'are** [deraʎ'ʎare] vi to be de-railed; **far ~** to derail.

**dere'litto, a** ag derelict.

**dere'tano** sm (fam) bottom, buttocks pl.

**de'ridere** vt to mock, deride;

**de'riso, a** pp di **deridere**.

**de'riva** sf (NAUT, AER) drift; **andare alla ~** (anche fig) to drift.

**deri'vare** vi: **~ da** to derive from // vt to derive; (corso d'acqua) to divert; **derivazi'one** sf derivation; diversion.

**derma'tologo, a, gi, ghe** sm/f dermatologist.

**der'rate** sfpl commodities; **~ alimentari** foodstuffs.

**deru'bare** vt to rob.

**des'critto, a** pp di **descrivere**.

**des'crivere** vt to describe; **descri-zi'one** sf description.

**de'serto, a** ag deserted // sm (GEO) desert; **isola ~a** desert island.

**deside'rare** vt to want, wish for; (sessualmente) to desire; **~ fare/che qn faccia** to want o wish to do/sb to do; **desidera fare una passeggiata?** would you like to go for a walk?

**desi'derio** sm wish; (più intenso, carnale) desire.

**deside'roso, a** ag: **~ di** longing o

eager for.

**desi'nenza** [dezi'nɛntsa] *sf* (*LING*) ending, inflexion.

**de'sistere** *vi*: ~ **da** to give up, desist from; **desis'tito, a** *pp di* **desistere**.

**deso'lato, a** *ag* (*paesaggio*) desolate; (*persona: spiacente*) sorry.

**des'tare** *vt* to wake (up); (*fig*) to awaken, arouse; **~rsi** *vr* to wake (up).

**desti'nare** *vt* to destine; (*assegnare*) to appoint, assign; (*indirizzare*) to address; ~ **qc a qu** to intend to give sth to sb, intend sb to have sth; **destina'tario, a** *sm/f* (*di lettera*) addressee.

**destinazi'one** [destinat'tsjone] *sf* destination; (*uso*) purpose.

**des'tino** *sm* destiny, fate.

**destitu'ire** *vt* to dismiss, remove.

**'desto, a** *ag* (wide) awake.

**'destra** *sf vedi* **destro**.

**destreggi'arsi** [destred'dʒarsi] *vr* to manoeuvre (*Brit*), maneuver (*US*).

**des'trezza** [des'trettsa] *sf* skill, dexterity.

**'destro, a** *ag* right, right-hand; (*abile*) skilful, adroit // *sf* (*mano*) right hand; (*parte*) right (side); (*POL*): **la** ~a the Right; **a** ~a (*essere*) on the right; (*andare*) to the right.

**dete'nere** *vt* (*incarico, primato*) to hold; (*proprietà*) to have, possess; (*in prigione*) to detain, hold; **dete'nuto, a** *sm/f* prisoner; **detenzi'one** *sf* holding; possession; detention.

**deter'gente** [deter'dʒɛnte] *ag* detergent; (*crema, latte*) cleansing // *sm* detergent.

**deterio'rare** *vt* to damage; **~rsi** *vr* to deteriorate.

**determi'nare** *vt* to determine; **determinazi'one** *sf* determination; (*decisione*) decision.

**deter'sivo** *sm* detergent.

**detes'tare** *vt* to detest, hate.

**de'trarre** *vt*: ~ **(da)** to deduct

(from), take away (from); **de'tratto, a** *pp di* **detrarre**; **detrazi'one** *sf* deduction; **detrazione d'imposta** tax allowance.

**detri'mento** *sm* detriment, harm; **a** ~ **di** to the detriment of.

**de'trito** *sm* (*GEO*) detritus.

**dettagli'are** [dettaʎ'ʎare] *vt* to detail, give full details of.

**det'taglio** [det'taʎʎo] *sm* detail; (*COMM*): **il** ~ retail; **al** ~ (*COMM*) retail; separately.

**det'tare** *vt* to dictate; ~ **legge** (*fig*) to lay down the law; **det'tato** *sm* dictation; **detta'tura** *sf* dictation.

**'detto, a** *pp di* **dire** // *ag* (*soprannominato*) called, known as; (*già nominato*) above-mentioned // *sm* saying; ~ **fatto** no sooner said than done.

**detur'pare** *vt* to disfigure; (*moralmente*) to sully.

**devas'tare** *vt* to devastate; (*fig*) to ravage.

**devi'are** *vi*: ~ **(da)** to turn off (from) // *vt* to divert; **deviazi'one** *sf* (*anche AUT*) diversion.

**devo'luto, a** *pp di* **devolvere**.

**devoluzi'one** [devolut'tsjone] *sf* (*DIR*) devolution, transfer.

**de'volvere** *vt* (*DIR*) to transfer, devolve.

**de'voto, a** *ag* (*REL*) devout, pious; (*affezionato*) devoted.

**devozi'one** [devot'tsjone] *sf* devoutness; (*anche REL*) devotion.

*PAROLA CHIAVE*

**di** *prep* (*di* + *il* = **del**, *di* + *lo* = **dello**, *di* + *l'* = **dell'**, *di* + *la* = **della**, *di* + *i* = **dei**, *di* + *gli* = **degli**, *di* + *le* = **delle**) **1** (*possesso, specificazione*) of; (*composto da, scritto da*) by; **la macchina** ~ **Paolo/mio fratello** Paolo's/my brother's car; **un amico** ~ **mio fratello** a friend of my brother's, one of my brother's friends; **un quadro** ~ **Botticelli** a painting by Botticelli **2** (*caratterizzazione, misura*) of; **una**

casa ~ **mattoni** a brick house, a house made of bricks; **un orologio d'oro** a gold watch; **un bimbo** ~ **3 anni** a child of 3, a 3-year-old child
**3** (*causa, mezzo, modo*) with; **tremare** ~ **paura** to tremble with fear; **morire** ~ **cancro** to die of cancer; **spalmare** ~ **burro** to spread with butter
**4** (*argomento*) about, of; **discutere** ~ **sport** to talk about sport
**5** (*luogo: provenienza*) from; out of; **essere** ~ **Roma** to be from Rome; **uscire** ~ **casa** to come out of *o* leave the house
**6** (*tempo*) in; **d'estate/d'inverno** in (the) summer/winter; ~ **notte** by night, at night; ~ **mattina/sera** in the morning/evening; ~ **domenica** on Sundays
◆ *det* (*una certa quantità di*) some; (: *negativo*) any; (: *interrogativo*) any, some; **del pane** (some) bread; **delle caramelle** (some) sweets; **gli amici miei** some friends of mine; **vuoi del vino?** do you want some *o* any wine?

**dia'bete** *sm* diabetes *sg*.
**di'acono** *sm* (*REL*) deacon.
**dia'dema, i** *sm* diadem; (*di donna*) tiara.
**dia'framma, i** *sm* (*divisione*) screen; (*ANAT, FOT, contraccettivo*) diaphragm.
**di'agnosi** *sf* diagnosis *sg*.
**diago'nale** *ag, sf* diagonal.
**dia'gramma, i** *sm* diagram.
**dia'letto** *sm* dialect.
**di'alogo, ghi** *sm* dialogue.
**dia'mante** *sm* diamond.
**di'ametro** *sm* diameter.
**di'amine** *escl*: **che** ~ ...? what on earth ...?
**diaposi'tiva** *sf* transparency, slide.
**di'ario** *sm* diary; ~ **degli esami** (*SCOL*) exam timetable.
**diar'rea** *sf* diarrhoea.
**di'avolo** *sm* devil.
**di'battere** *vt* to debate, discuss;

~**rsi** *vr* to struggle; **di'battito** *sm* debate, discussion.
**di'cembre** [di'tʃɛmbre] *sm* December.
**dicas'tero** *sm* ministry.
**dice'ria** [ditʃe'ria] *sf* rumour, piece of gossip.
**dichia'rare** [dikja'rare] *vt* to declare; **dichiarazi'one** *sf* declaration.
**dician'nove** [ditʃan'nɔve] *num* nineteen.
**dicias'sette** [ditʃas'sɛtte] *num* seventeen.
**dici'otto** [di'tʃɔtto] *num* eighteen.
**dici'tura** [ditʃi'tura] *sf* words *pl*, wording.
**di'eci** [d]etʃi] *num* ten; **die'cina** *sf* = **decina**.
**'diesel** ['dizəl] *sm inv* diesel engine.
**di'eta** *sf* diet; **essere a** ~ to be on a diet.
**di'etro** *av* behind; (*in fondo*) at the back // *prep* behind; (*tempo: dopo*) after // *sm* back, rear // *ag inv* back *cpd*; **le zampe di** ~ the hind legs; ~ **richiesta** on demand; (*scritta*) on application.
**di'fatti** *cong* in fact, as a matter of fact.
**di'fendere** *vt* to defend; **difen'sivo, a** *ag* defensive // *sf*: **stare sulla difensiva** (*anche fig*) to be on the defensive; **difen'sore, a** *sm/f* defender; **avvocato difensore** counsel for the defence; **di'feso, a** *pp di* **difendere** // *sf* defence.
**difet'tare** *vi* to be defective; ~ **di** to be lacking in, lack; **difet'tivo, a** *ag* defective.
**di'fetto** *sm* (*mancanza*): ~ **di** lack of; shortage of; (*di fabbricazione*) fault, flaw, defect; (*morale*) fault, failing, defect; (*fisico*) defect; **far** ~ to be lacking; **in** ~ at fault; in the wrong; **difet'toso, a** *ag* defective, faulty.
**diffa'mare** *vt* to slander; to libel.
**diffe'rente** *ag* different.
**diffe'renza** [diffe'rɛntsa] *sf* difference; **a** ~ **di** unlike.

**differenzi'are** [differen'tsjare] *vt* to differentiate; **~rsi da** to differentiate o.s. from; to differ from.

**diffe'rire** *vt* to postpone, defer // *vi* to be different.

**dif'ficile** [dif'fitʃile] *ag* difficult; (*persona*) hard to please, difficult (to please); (*poco probabile*): **è ~ che sia libero** it is unlikely that he'll be free // *sm* difficult part; difficulty; **difficoltà** *sf inv* difficulty.

**dif'fida** *sf* (*DIR*) warning, notice.

**diffi'dare** *vi*: **~ di** to be suspicious o distrustful of // *vt* (*DIR*) to warn; **~ qn dal fare qc** to warn sb not to do sth, caution sb against doing sth; **diffi'dente** *ag* suspicious, distrustful; **diffi'denza** *sf* suspicion, distrust.

**dif'fondere** *vt* (*luce, calore*) to diffuse; (*notizie*) to spread, circulate; **~rsi** *vr* to spread; **diffusi'one** *sf* diffusion; spread; (*anche di giornale*) circulation; (*FISICA*) scattering; **dif'fuso, a** *pp di* **diffondere** // *ag* (*malattia, fenomeno*) widespread.

**difi'lato** *av* (*direttamente*) straight, directly; (*subito*) straight away.

**difte'rite** *sf* (*MED*) diphtheria.

**'diga, ghe** *sf* dam; (*portuale*) breakwater.

**dige'rente** [didʒe'rɛnte] *ag* (*apparato*) digestive.

**dige'rire** [didʒe'rire] *vt* to digest; **digesti'one** *sf* digestion; **diges'tivo, a** *ag* digestive // *sm* (*after-dinner*) liqueur.

**digi'tale** [didʒi'tale] *ag* digital; (*delle dita*) finger *cpd*, digital // *sf* (*BOT*) foxglove.

**digi'tare** [didʒi'tare] *vt, vi* (*INFORM*) to key (in).

**digiu'nare** [didʒu'nare] *vi* to starve o.s.; (*REL*) to fast; **digi'uno, a** *ag*: **essere digiuno** not to have eaten // *sm* fast; **a digiuno** on an empty stomach.

**dignità** [diɲɲi'ta] *sf inv* dignity; **di-gni'toso, a** *ag* dignified.

**'DIGOS** ['digɔs] *sigla f* (= *Divisione*

*Investigazioni Generali e Operazioni Speciali*) police department dealing with political security.

**digri'gnare** [digriɲ'nare] *vt*: **~ i denti** to grind one's teeth.

**dila'gare** *vi* to flood; (*fig*) to spread.

**dilani'are** *vt* (*preda*) to tear to pieces.

**dilapi'dare** *vt* to squander, waste.

**dila'tare** *vt* to dilate; (*gas*) to cause to expand; (*passaggio, cavità*) to open (up); **~rsi** *vr* to dilate; (*FISICA*) to expand.

**dilazio'nare** [dilattsjo'nare] *vt* to delay, defer; **dilazi'one** *sf* delay; (*COMM: di pagamento etc*) extension; (*rinvio*) postponement.

**dileggi'are** [diled'dʒare] *vt* to mock, deride.

**dilegu'are** *vi*, **~rsi** *vr* to vanish, disappear.

**di'lemma, i** *sm* dilemma.

**dilet'tante** *sm/f* dilettante; (*anche SPORT*) amateur.

**dilet'tare** *vt* to give pleasure to, delight; **~rsi** *vr*: **~rsi di** to take pleasure in, enjoy.

**di'letto, a** *ag* dear, beloved // *sm* pleasure, delight.

**dili'gente** [dili'dʒɛnte] *ag* (*scrupoloso*) diligent; (*accurato*) careful, accurate; **dili'genza** *sf* diligence; care; (*carrozza*) stagecoach.

**dilu'ire** *vt* to dilute.

**dilun'garsi** *vr* (*fig*): **~ su** to talk at length on o about.

**diluvi'are** *vb impers* to pour (down).

**di'luvio** *sm* downpour; (*inondazione, fig*) flood.

**dima'grire** *vi* to get thinner, lose weight.

**dime'nare** *vt* to wave, shake; **~rsi** *vr* to toss and turn; (*fig*) to struggle; **~ la coda** (*sog: cane*) to wag its tail.

**dimensi'one** *sf* dimension; (*grandezza*) size.

**dimenti'canza** [dimenti'kantsa] *sf* forgetfulness; (*errore*) oversight, slip; per ~ inadvertently.

**dimenti'care** vt to forget; ~rsi di qc to forget sth.

**di'messo, a** pp di **dimettere** // ag (voce) subdued; (uomo, abito) modest, humble.

**dimesti'chezza** [dimesti'kettsa] sf familiarity.

**di'mettere** vt: ~ qn da to dismiss sb from; (dall'ospedale) to discharge sb from; ~rsi (da) to resign (from).

**dimez'zare** [dimed'dzare] vt to halve.

**diminu'ire** vt to reduce, diminish; (prezzi) to bring down, reduce // vi to decrease, diminish; (rumore) to die down, die away; (prezzi) to fall, go down; **diminuzi'one** sf decreasing, diminishing.

**dimissi'oni** sfpl resignation sg; dare o presentare le ~ to resign, hand in one's resignation.

**di'mora** sf residence.

**dimo'rare** vi to reside.

**dimos'trare** vt to demonstrate, show; (provare) to prove, demonstrate; ~rsi vr: ~rsi molto abile to show o.s. o prove to be very clever; dimostra 30 anni he looks about 30 (years old); **dimo-strazi'one** sf demonstration; proof.

**di'namico, a, ci, che** ag dynamic // sf dynamics sg.

**dina'mite** sf dynamite.

**'dinamo** sf inv dynamo.

**di'nanzi** [di'nantsi]: ~ a prep in front of.

**dini'ego, ghi** sm refusal; denial.

**dinocco'lato, a** ag lanky; camminare ~ to walk with a slouch.

**din'torno** av round, (round) about; ~i smpl outskirts; nei ~i di in the vicinity o neighbourhood of.

**'dio, pl 'dei** sm god; D~ God; gli dei the gods; D~ mio! my goodness!, my God!

**di'ocesi** [di'ɔtʃɛzi] sf inv diocese.

**dipa'nare** vt (lana) to wind into a ball; (fig) to disentangle, sort out.

**diparti'mento** sm department.

**dipen'dente** ag dependent // sm/f employee; **dipen'denza** sf dependence; essere alle dipendenze di qn to be employed by sb o in sb's employ.

**di'pendere** vi: ~ da to depend on; (finanziariamente) to be dependent on; (derivare) to come from, be due to; di'peso, a pp di dipendere.

**di'pingere** [di'pindʒere] vt to paint; **di'pinto, a** pp di **dipingere** // sm painting.

**di'ploma, i** sm diploma.

**diplo'mare** vt to award a diploma to, graduate (US) // vi to obtain a diploma, graduate (US).

**diplo'matico, a, ci, che** ag diplomatic // sm diplomat.

**diploma'zia** [diplomat'tsia] sf diplomacy.

**di'porto** sm: imbarcazione f da ~ pleasure craft.

**dira'dare** vt to thin (out); (visite) to reduce, make less frequent; ~rsi vr to disperse; (nebbia) to clear (up).

**dira'mare** vt to issue // vi, ~rsi vr (strade) to branch.

**'dire** vt to say; (segreto, fatto) to tell; ~ qc a qn to tell sb sth; ~ a qn di fare qc to tell sb to do sth; ~ di sì/no to say yes/no; si dice che ... they say that ...; si direbbe che ... it looks (o sounds) as though ...; dica, signora? (in un negozio) yes, Madam, can I help you?

**diret'tissimo** sm (FERR) fast (through) train.

**di'retto, a** pp di **dirigere** // ag direct // sm (FERR) through train.

**diret'tore, 'trice** sm/f (di azienda) director; manager/ess; (di scuola elementare) head (teacher) (Brit), principal (US); ~ d'orchestra conductor.

**direzi'one** [diret'tsjone] sf board of directors; management; (senso di movimento) direction; in ~ di in the direction of, towards.

**diri'gente** [diri'dʒɛnte] sm/f executive; (*POL*) leader // *ag*: **classe** ~ ruling class.

**di'rigere** [di'ridʒere] *vt* to direct; (*impresa*) to run, manage; (*MUS*) to conduct; ~**rsi** *vr*: ~**rsi verso** *o* **a** to make *o* head for.

**dirim'petto** *av* opposite; ~ **a** *prep* opposite, facing.

**di'ritto, a** *ag* straight; (*onesto*) straight, upright // *av* straight, directly; **andare** ~ to go straight *o* // *sm* right side; (*TENNIS*) forehand; (*MAGLIA*) plain stitch; (*prerogativa*) right; (*leggi, scienza*): **il** ~ law; ~**i** *smpl* (*tasse*) duty *sg*; **stare** ~ to stand up straight; **aver** ~ **a qc** to be entitled to sth; ~**i d'autore** royalties.

**dirit'tura** *sf* (*SPORT*) straight; (*fig*) rectitude.

**diroc'cato, a** *ag* tumbledown, in ruins.

**dirot'tare** *vt* (*nave, aereo*) to change the course of; (*aereo*: *sotto minaccia*) to hijack; (*traffico*) to divert // *vi* (*nave, aereo*) to change course; **dirotta'tore, 'trice** *sm/f* hijacker.

**di'rotto, a** *ag* (*pioggia*) torrential; (*pianto*) unrestrained; **piovere a** ~ to pour, rain cats and dogs; **piangere a** ~ to cry one's heart out.

**di'rupo** *sm* crag, precipice.

**disabi'tato, a** *ag* uninhabited.

**disabitu'arsi** *vr*: ~ **a** to get out of the habit of.

**disac'cordo** *sm* disagreement.

**disadat'tato, a** *ag* (*PSIC*) maladjusted.

**disa'dorno, a** *ag* plain, unadorned.

**disagi'ato, a** [diza'dʒato] *ag* poor, needy; (*vita*) hard.

**di'sagio** [di'zadʒo] *sm* discomfort; (*disturbo*) inconvenience; (*fig*: *imbarazzo*) embarrassment; ~**i** *smpl* hardship *sg*, poverty *sg*; **essere a** ~ to be ill at ease.

**disappro'vare** *vt* to disapprove of; **disapprovazi'one** *sf* disapproval.

**disap'punto** *sm* disappointment.

**disar'mare** *vt, vi* to disarm; **di'sarmo** *sm* (*MIL*) disarmament.

**di'sastro** *sm* disaster.

**disat'tento, a** *ag* inattentive; **disattenzi'one** *sf* carelessness, lack of attention.

**disa'vanzo** [diza'vantso] *sm* (*ECON*) deficit.

**disavven'tura** *sf* misadventure, mishap.

**dis'brigo, ghi** *sm* (prompt) clearing up *o* settlement.

**dis'capito** *sm*: **a** ~ **di** to the detriment of.

**dis'carica, che** *sf* (*di rifiuti*) rubbish tip *o* dump.

**discen'dente** [diffen'dɛnte] *ag* descending // *sm/f* descendant.

**di'scendere** [diʃ'ʃɛndere] *vt* to go (*o* come) down // *vi* to go (*o* come) down; (*strada*) to go down; (*smontare*) to get off; ~ **da** (*famiglia*) to be descended from; ~ **dalla macchina/dal treno** to get out of the car/out of *o* off the train; ~ **da cavallo** to dismount, get off one's horse.

**di'scepolo, a** [diʃ'ʃepolo] *sm/f* disciple.

**di'scernere** [diʃ'ʃɛrnere] *vt* to discern.

**di'sceso, a** [diʃ'ʃeso] *pp di* **di'scendere** // *sf* descent; (*pendio*) slope; **in** ~**a** (*strada*) downhill *cpd*, sloping; ~**a libera** (*SCI*) downhill (race).

**disci'ogliere** [diʃ'ʃɔʎʎere] *vt*, ~**rsi** *vr* to dissolve; (*fondere*) to melt; **disci'olto, a** *pp di* **disciogliere**.

**disci'plina** [diʃʃi'plina] *sf* discipline; **discipli'nare** *ag* disciplinary // *vt* to discipline.

**'disco, schi** *sm* disc; (*SPORT*) discus; (*fonografico*) record; (*INFORM*) disk; ~ **orario** (*AUT*) parking disc; ~ **rigido** (*INFORM*) hard disk; ~ **volante** flying saucer.

**discol'pare** *vt* to clear of blame.

**disco'noscere** [disko'noʃʃere] *vt* (*figlio*) to disown; (*meriti*) to ignore,

**disregard; disconosci'uto, a** *pp di* **disconoscere**.

**dis'corde** *ag* conflicting, clashing; **dis'cordia** *sf* discord; (*dissidio*) disagreement, clash.

**dis'correre** *vi*: ~ **(di)** to talk (about).

**dis'corso, a** *pp di* **discorrere** // *sm* speech; (*conversazione*) conversation, talk.

**dis'costo, a** *ag* faraway, distant // *av* far away; ~ **da** *prep* far from.

**disco'teca, che** *sf* (*raccolta*) record library; (*luogo di ballo*) disco(thèque).

**discre'panza** [diskre'pantsa] *sf* disagreement.

**dis'creto, a** *ag* discreet; (*abbastanza buono*) reasonable, fair; **discrezi'one** *sf* discretion; (*giudizio*) judgment, discernment; a **discrezione di** at the discretion of.

**discriminazi'one** [diskriminat'tsjone] *sf* discrimination.

**discussi'one** *sf* discussion; (*litigio*) argument.

**dis'cusso, a** *pp di* **discutere**.

**dis'cutere** *vt* to discuss, debate; (*contestare*) to question // *vi* (*conversare*): ~ **(di)** to discuss; (*litigare*) to argue.

**disde'gnare** [disdeɲ'ɲare] *vt* to scorn.

**dis'detto, a** *pp di* **disdire** // *sf* cancellation; (*sfortuna*) bad luck.

**dis'dire** *vt* (*prenotazione*) to cancel; (*DIR*): ~ **un contratto d'affitto** to give notice (to quit).

**dise'gnare** [diseɲ'ɲare] *vt* to draw; (*progettare*) to design; (*fig*) to outline; **disegna'tore, 'trice** *sm/f* designer.

**di'segno** [di'seɲɲo] *sm* drawing; design; outline.

**diser'bante** *sm* weed-killer.

**diser'tare** *vt, vi* to desert; **diser'tore** *sm* (*MIL*) deserter.

**dis'fare** *vt* to undo; (*valigie*) to unpack; (*meccanismo*) to take to pieces; (*lavoro, paese*) to destroy;

(*neve*) to melt; ~**rsi** *vr* to come undone; (*neve*) to melt; ~ **il letto** to strip the bed; ~**rsi di qn** (*liberarsi*) to get rid of sb; **dis'fatto, a** *pp di* **disfare** // *sf* (*sconfitta*) rout.

**dis'gelo** [diz'dʒelo] *sm* thaw.

**dis'grazia** [diz'grattsja] *sf* (*ventura*) misfortune; (*incidente*) accident, mishap; **disgrazi'ato, a** *ag* unfortunate // *smf* wretch.

**disgre'gare** *vt*, ~**rsi** *vr* to break up.

**disgu'ido** *sm*: ~ **postale** error in postal delivery.

**disgus'tare** *vt* to disgust; ~**rsi** *vr*: ~**rsi di** to be disgusted by.

**dis'gusto** *sm* disgust; **disgus'toso, a** *ag* disgusting.

**disidra'tare** *vt* to dehydrate.

**disil'ludere** *vt* to disillusion, disenchant.

**disimpa'rare** *vt* to forget.

**disimpe'gnare** [dizimpeɲ'ɲare] *vt* (*persona: da obblighi*): ~ **da** to release from; (*oggetto dato in pegno*) to redeem, get out of pawn; ~**rsi** *vr*: ~**rsi da** (*obblighi*) to release o.s. from, free o.s. from.

**disinfet'tante** *ag, sm* disinfectant.

**disinfet'tare** *vt* to disinfect.

**disini'bito, a** *ag* uninhibited.

**disinte'grare** *vt, vi* to disintegrate.

**disinteres'sarsi** *vr*: ~ **di** to take no interest in.

**disinte'resse** *sm* indifference; (*generosità*) unselfishness.

**disintossi'care** *vt* (*alcolizzato, drogato*) to treat for alcoholism (*o* drug addiction); ~ **l'organismo** to clear out one's system.

**disin'volto, a** *ag* casual, free and easy; **disinvol'tura** *sf* casualness, ease.

**disles'sia** *sf* dyslexia.

**dislo'care** *vt* to station, position.

**dismi'sura** *sf* excess; a ~ to excess, excessively.

**disobbe'dire** *etc* = **disubbidire** *etc*.

**disoccu'pato, a** *ag* unemployed // *smf* unemployed person;

**disoccupazi'one** sf unemployment.
**diso'nesto, a** ag dishonest.
**diso'nore** sm dishonour, disgrace.
**di'sopra** av (con contatto) on top; (senza contatto) above; (al piano superiore) upstairs // ag inv (superiore) upper // sm inv top, upper part.
**disordi'nato, a** ag untidy; (privo di misura) irregular, wild.
**di'sordine** sm (confusione) disorder, confusion; (sregolatezza) debauchery.
**disorien'tare** vt to disorientate; ~rsi vr (fig) to get confused, lose one's bearings.
**di'sotto** av below, underneath; (in fondo) at the bottom; (al piano inferiore) downstairs // ag inv (inferiore) lower; bottom cpd // sm inv (parte inferiore) lower part; bottom.
**dis'paccio** [dis'pattʃo] sm dispatch.
**'dispari** ag inv odd, uneven.
**dis'parte:** in ~ av (a lato) aside, apart; tenersi o starsene in ~ to keep to o.s., hold aloof.
**dispendi'oso, a** ag expensive.
**dis'pensa** sf pantry, larder; (mobile) sideboard; (DIR) exemption; (REL) dispensation; (fascicolo) number, issue.
**dispen'sare** vt (elemosine, favori) to distribute; (esonerare) to exempt.
**dispe'rare** vi: ~ (di) to despair (of); ~rsi vr to despair; **dispe'rato, a** ag (persona) in despair; (caso, tentativo) desperate; **disperazi'one** sf despair.
**dis'perdere** vt (disseminare) to disperse; (MIL) to scatter, rout; (fig: consumare) to waste, squander; ~rsi vr to disperse; to scatter; **dis'perso, a** pp di **disperdere** // sm/f missing person.
**dis'petto** sm spite q, spitefulness q; fare un ~ a qn to play a (nasty) trick on sb; a ~ di in spite of; **dis'pettoso, a** ag spiteful.
**dispia'cere** [dispja'tʃere] sm (rammarico) regret, sorrow; (dolore)

grief; ~i smpl troubles, worries // vi: ~ a to displease // vb impers: mi dispiace (che) I am sorry (that); se non le dispiace, me ne vado adesso if you don't mind, I'll go now; **dispiaci'uto, a** pp di **dispiacere** // ag sorry.
**dispo'nibile** ag available.
**dis'porre** vt (sistemare) to arrange; (preparare) to prepare; (DIR) to order; (persuadere): ~ qn a to incline o dispose sb towards // vi (decidere) to decide; (usufruire): ~ di to use, have at one's disposal; (essere dotato): ~ di to have; disporsi vr (ordinarsi) to place o.s., arrange o.s.; disporsi a fare to get ready to do.
**disposi'tivo** sm (meccanismo) device.
**disposizi'one** sf arrangement, layout; (stato d'animo) mood; (tendenza) bent, inclination; (comando) order; (DIR) provision, regulation; a ~ di qn at sb's disposal.
**dis'posto, a** pp di **disporre.**
**disprez'zare** [dispret'tsare] vt to despise.
**dis'prezzo** [dis'prettso] sm contempt.
**'disputa** sf dispute, quarrel.
**dispu'tare** vt (contendere) to dispute, contest; (gara) to take part in // vi to quarrel; ~ di to discuss; ~rsi qc to fight for sth.
**dissan'guare** vt (fig: persona) to bleed white; (: patrimonio) to suck dry; ~rsi vr (MED) to lose blood; (fig: rovinarsi) to ruin o.s.
**dissec'care** vt, ~rsi vr to dry up.
**dissemi'nare** vt to scatter; (fig: notizie) to spread.
**dis'senso** sm dissent; (disapprovazione) disapproval.
**dissente'ria** sf dysentery.
**dissen'tire** vi: ~ (da) to disagree (with).
**dissertazi'one** [dissertat'tsjone] sf dissertation.

**disser'vizio** [disser'vittsjo] *sm* inefficiency.

**disses'tare** *vt* (*ECON*) to ruin; **dis'sesto** *sm* (financial) ruin.

**disse'tante** *ag* refreshing.

**dis'sidio** *sm* disagreement.

**dis'simile** *ag* different, dissimilar.

**dissimu'lare** *vt* (*fingere*) to dissemble; (*nascondere*) to conceal.

**dissi'pare** *vt* to dissipate; (*scialacquare*) to squander, waste.

**dis'solto, a** *pp di* **dissolvere**

**disso'lubile** *ag* soluble.

**disso'luto, a** *pp di* **dissolvere** // *ag* dissolute, licentious.

**dis'solvere** *vt* to dissolve; (*neve*) to melt; (*fumo*) to disperse; **~rsi** *vr* to dissolve; to melt; to disperse.

**dissu'adere** *vt*: ~ **qn da** to dissuade sb from; **dissu'aso, a** *pp di* **dissuadere**

**distac'care** *vt* to detach, separate; (*SPORT*) to leave behind; **~rsi** *vr* to be detached; (*fig*) to stand out; **~rsi da** (*fig*: *allontanarsi*) to grow away from.

**dis'tacco, chi** *sm* (*separazione*) separation; (*fig*: *indifferenza*) detachment; (*SPORT*: **vincere con un ~ di ...** to win by a distance of ....

**dis'tante** *av* far away // *ag*: ~ **(da)** distant (from), far away (from).

**dis'tanza** [dis'tantsa] *sf* distance.

**distanzi'are** [distan'tsjare] *vt* to space out, place at intervals; (*SPORT*) to outdistance; (*fig*: *superare*) to outstrip, surpass.

**dis'tare** *vi*: **distiamo pochi chilometri da Roma** we are only a few kilometres (away) from Rome.

**dis'tendere** (*coperta*) to spread out; (*gambe*) to stretch (out); (*mettere a giacere*) to lay; (*rilassare: muscoli, nervi*) to relax; **~rsi** *vr* (*rilassarsi*) to relax; (*sdraiarsi*) to lie down; **di-stensi'one** *sf* stretching; relaxation; (*POL*) détente.

**dis'teso, a** *pp di* **distendere** // *sf* expanse, stretch.

**distil'lare** *vt* to distil.

**distille'ria** *sf* distillery.

**dis'tinguere** *vt* to distinguish.

**dis'tinta** *sf* (*nota*) note; (*elenco*) list.

**distin'tivo, a** *ag* distinctive; distinguishing // *sm* badge.

**dis'tinto, a** *pp di* **distinguere** // *ag* (*dignitoso ed elegante*) distinguished; **~i saluti** (*in lettera*) yours faithfully.

**distin'zione** [distin'tsjone] *sf* distinction.

**dis'togliere** [dis'tɔʎʎere] *vt*: ~ **da** to take away from; (*fig*) to dissuade from; **dis'tolto, a** *pp di* **distogliere**.

**distorsi'one** *sf* (*MED*) sprain; (*FISICA, OTTICA*) distortion.

**dis'trarre** *vt* to distract; (*divertire*) to entertain, amuse; **distrarsi** *vr* (*non fare attenzione*) to be distracted, let one's mind wander; (*svagarsi*) to amuse o enjoy o.s.; **dis'tratto, a** *pp di* **distrarre** // *ag* absent-minded; (*disattento*) inattentive; **distrazi'one** *sf* absent-mindedness; inattention; (*svago*) distraction, entertainment.

**dis'tretto** *sm* district.

**distribu'ire** *vt* to distribute; (*CARTE*) to deal (out); (*consegnare: posta*) to deliver; (*lavoro*) to allocate, assign; (*ripartire*) to share out; **distribu'tore** *sm* (*di benzina*) petrol (*Brit*) o gas (*US*) pump; (*AUT, ELETTR*) distributor; (*automatico*) vending machine; **di-stribuzi'one** *sf* distribution; delivery.

**distri'care** *vt* to disentangle, unravel.

**dis'truggere** [dis'truddʒere] *vt* to destroy; **dis'trutto, a** *pp di* **distruggere**; **distruzi'one** *sf* destruction.

**distur'bare** *vt* to disturb, trouble; (*sonno, lezioni*) to disturb, interrupt; **~rsi** *vr* to put o.s. out.

**dis'turbo** *sm* trouble, bother, inconvenience; (*indisposizione*) (slight) disorder, ailment; **~i** *smpl* (*RADIO, TV*) static *sg*.

**disubbidi'ente** *ag* disobedient; **disubbidi'enza** *sf* disobedience.

**disubbi'dire** *vi*: **~** (a qn) to disobey (sb).

**disugu'ale** *ag* unequal; (*diverso*) different; (*irregolare*) uneven.

**disu'mano, a** *ag* inhuman.

**di'suso** *sm*: andare *o* cadere in **~** to fall into disuse.

**'dita** *fpl di* dito.

**di'tale** *sm* thimble.

**'dito,** *pl*(*f*) **'dita** *sm* finger; (*misura*) finger, finger's breadth; **~** (del piede) toe.

**'ditta** *sf* firm, business.

**ditta'tore** *sm* dictator.

**ditta'tura** *sf* dictatorship.

**dit'tongo, ghi** *sm* diphthong.

**di'urno, a** *ag* day *cpd*, daytime *cpd* // *sm* (*anche:* albergo **~**) public toilets with washing and shaving facilities etc.

**'diva** *sf vedi* divo.

**diva'gare** *vi* to digress.

**divam'pare** *vi* to flare up, blaze up.

**di'vano** *sm* sofa; divan.

**divari'care** *vt* to open wide.

**di'vario** *sm* difference.

**dive'nire** *vi* = **diventare**; **dive'nuto, a** *pp di* divenire.

**diven'tare** *vi* to become; **~** famoso/professore to become famous/a teacher.

**di'verbio** *sm* altercation.

**di'vergere** [di'vɛrdʒere] *vi* to diverge.

**diversifi'care** *vt* to diversify, vary; to differentiate.

**diversi'one** *sf* diversion.

**diversità** *sf inv* difference, diversity; (*varietà*) variety.

**diver'sivo** *sm* diversion, distraction.

**di'verso, a** *ag* (*differente*): **~** (da) different (from); (*pl*) several, various; (*COMM*) sundry // *pronome pl* several (people), many (people).

**diver'tente** *ag* amusing.

**diverti'mento** *sm* amusement, pleasure; (*passatempo*) pastime, recreation.

**diver'tire** *vt* to amuse, entertain; **~rsi** *vr* to amuse *o* enjoy o.s.

**divi'dendo** *sm* dividend.

**di'videre** *vt* (*anche MAT*) to divide; (*distribuire, ripartire*) to divide (up), split (up); **~rsi** *vr* (*separarsi*) to separate; (*strade*) to fork.

**divi'eto** *sm* prohibition; "**~** di sosta" (*AUT*) "no parking".

**divinco'larsi** *vr* to wriggle, writhe.

**divinità** *sf inv* divinity.

**di'vino, a** *ag* divine.

**di'visa** *sf* (*MIL etc*) uniform; (*COMM*) foreign currency.

**divisi'one** *sf* division.

**di'viso, a** *pp di* dividere.

**'divo, a** *sm/f* star.

**divo'rare** *vt* to devour.

**divorzi'are** [divor'tsjare] *vi*: **~** (da qn) to divorce (sb); **divorzi'ato, a** *sm/f* divorcee.

**di'vorzio** [di'vɔrtsjo] *sm* divorce.

**divul'gare** *vt* to divulge, disclose; (*rendere comprensibile*) to popularize; **~rsi** *vr* to become widespread.

**dizio'nario** [ditsjo'narjo] *sm* dictionary.

**dizi'one** [dit'tsjone] *sf* diction; pronunciation.

**do** *sm* (*MUS*) C; (*: solfeggiando la scala*) do(h).

**DOC** [dɔk] *abbr* (= denominazione di origine controllata) label guaranteeing the quality of wine.

**'doccia, ce** ['dɔttʃa] *sf* (*bagno*) shower; (*condotto*) pipe; fare la **~** to have a shower.

**do'cente** [do'tʃɛnte] *ag* teaching // *sm/f* teacher; (*di università*) lecturer; **do'cenza** *sf* university teaching *o* lecturing.

**'docile** ['dɔtʃile] *ag* docile.

**documen'tare** *vt* to document; **~rsi** *vr*: **~rsi** (su) to gather information *o* material (about).

**documen'tario** *sm* documentary.

**docu'mento** *sm* document; **~i** *smpl*

(d'identità etc) papers.

'**dodici** ['doditʃi] num twelve.

do'**gana** sf (ufficio) customs pl; (tassa) (customs) duty; **passare la ~** to go through customs; **doga'nale** ag customs cpd; **dogani'ere** sm customs officer.

'**doglie** ['dɔʎʎe] sfpl (MED) labour sg, labour pains.

'**dolce** ['doltʃe] ag sweet; (colore) soft; (carattere, persona) gentle, mild; (fig: mite: clima) mild; (non ripido: pendio) gentle // sm (sapore dolce) sweetness, sweet taste; (CUC: portata) sweet, dessert; (: torta) cake; **dol'cezza** sf sweetness; softness; mildness; gentleness; **dolci'umi** smpl sweets.

do'**lente** ag sorrowful, sad.

do'**lere** vi to be sore, hurt, ache; **~rsi** vr to complain; (essere spiacente): **~rsi** di to be sorry for; **mi duole la testa** my head aches, I've got a headache.

'**dollaro** sm dollar.

'**dolo** sm (DIR) malice.

**Dolo'miti** sfpl: **le ~** the Dolomites.

do'**lore** sm (fisico) pain; (morale) sorrow, grief; **dolo'roso, a** ag painful; sorrowful, sad.

do'**loso, a** ag (DIR) malicious.

do'**manda** sf (interrogazione) question; (richiesta) demand; (: cortese) request; (DIR: richiesta scritta) application; (ECON): **la ~** demand; **fare una ~ a qn** to ask sb a question; **fare ~** (per un lavoro) to apply (for a job).

doman'**dare** vt (per avere) to ask for; (per sapere) to ask; (esigere) to demand; **~rsi** vr to wonder; to ask o.s.; **~ qc a qn** to ask sb for sth; to ask sb sth.

do'**mani** av tomorrow // sm: **il ~** (il futuro) the future; (il giorno successivo) the next day; **~ l'altro** the day after tomorrow.

do'**mare** vt to tame.

domat'**tina** av tomorrow morning.

do'**menica, che** sf Sunday; **di** o **la**

**~ on** Sundays; **domeni'cale** ag Sunday cpd.

do'**mestica, che** sf vedi **domestico**.

do'**mestico, a, ci, che** ag domestic // sm/f servant, domestic.

domi'**cilio** [domi'tʃiljo] sm (DIR) domicile, place of residence.

domi'**nare** vt to dominate; (fig: sentimenti) to control, master // vi to be in the dominant position; **~rsi** vr (controllarsi) to control o.s.; **~ su** (fig) to surpass, outclass; **dominazi'one** sf domination.

do'**minio** sm dominion; (fig: campo) field, domain.

do'**nare** vt to give, present; (per beneficenza etc) to donate // vi (fig): **~ a** to suit, become; **~ sangue** to give blood; **dona'tore, 'trice** sm/f donor; **donatore di sangue/di organi** blood/organ donor.

dondo'**lare** vt (cullare) to rock; **~rsi** vr to swing, sway; '**dondolo** sm: **sedia/cavallo a dondolo** rocking chair/horse.

'**donna** sf woman; **~ di casa** housewife; home-loving woman; **~ di servizio** maid.

donnai'**olo** sm ladykiller.

don'**nesco, a, schi, sche** ag women's, woman's.

'**donnola** sf weasel.

'**dono** sm gift.

'**dopo** av (tempo) afterwards; (: più tardi) later; (luogo) after, next // prep after // cong (temporale): **~ aver studiato** after having studied; **~ mangiato** va a dormire after having eaten o after a meal he goes for a sleep // ag inv: **il giorno ~** the following day; **un anno ~** a year later; **~ di me/lui** after me/him.

dopo'**barba** sm inv after-shave.

dopodo'**mani** av the day after tomorrow.

dopogu'**erra** sm postwar years pl.

dopo'**pranzo** [dopo'prandzo] av after lunch (o dinner).

doposcì [dopoʃ'ʃi] sm inv après-ski

outfit.

**doposcu'ola** sm inv school club offering extra tuition and recreational facilities.

**dopo'tutto** av (tutto considerato) after all.

**doppi'aggio** [dop'pjadd30] sm (CINEMA) dubbing.

**doppi'are** vt (NAUT) to round; (SPORT) to lap; (CINEMA) to dub.

**'doppio, a** ag double; (fig: falso) double-dealing, deceitful // sm (quantità): il ~ (di) twice as much (o many), double the amount (o number) of; (SPORT) doubles pl // av double.

**doppio'petto** sm double-breasted jacket.

**do'rare** vt to gild; (CUC) to brown; **do'rato, a** ag golden; (ricoperto d'oro) gilt, gilded; **dora'tura** sf gilding.

**dormicchi'are** [dormik'kjare] vi to doze.

**dormigli'one, a** [dormiʎ'ʎone] sm/f sleepyhead.

**dor'mire** vt, vi to sleep; **dor'mita** sf: farsi una dormita to have a good sleep.

**dormi'torio** sm dormitory.

**dormi'veglia** [dormi'veʎʎa] sm drowsiness.

**'dorso** sm back; (di montagna) ridge, crest; (di libro) spine; a ~ di cavallo on horseback.

**do'sare** vt to measure out; (MED) to dose.

**'dose** sf quantity, amount; (MED) dose.

**'dosso** sm (rilievo) rise; (di strada) bump; (dorso): levarsi di ~ i vestiti to take one's clothes off.

**do'tare** vt: ~ di to endow o supply with; (fig) to endow o supply with; **dotazi'one** sf (insieme di beni) endowment; (di macchine etc) equipment.

**'dote** sf (di sposa) dowry; (assegnata a un ente) endowment;

(fig) gift, talent.

**Dott.** abbr (= dottore) Dr.

**'dotto, a** ag (colto) learned // sm (sapiente) scholar; (ANAT) duct.

**dotto'rato** sm degree; ~ **di ricerca** doctorate, doctor's degree.

**dot'tore, essa** sm/f doctor.

**dot'trina** sf doctrine.

**Dott.ssa** abbr (= dottoressa) Dr.

---

**PAROLA CHIAVE**

**'dove** av (gen) where; (in cui) where, in which; (dovunque) wherever; ~ **sei?/vai?** where are you?/are you going?; **dimmi dov'è** tell me where it is; **di** ~ **sei?** where are you from?; **per** ~ **si passa?** which way should we go?; **la città** ~ **abito** the town where o in which I live; **siediti** ~ **vuoi** sit wherever you like

♦ cong (mentre, laddove) whereas.

---

**do'vere** sm (obbligo) duty // vt (essere debitore): ~ **qc (a qn)** to owe (sb) sth // vi (seguito dall'infinito: obbligo) to have to; **rivolgersi a chi di** ~ to apply to the appropriate authority o person; **lui deve farlo** he has to do it, he must do it; **è dovuto partire** he had to leave; **ha dovuto pagare** he had to pay; (: intenzione): **devo partire domani** I'm (due) to leave tomorrow; (: probabilità) **dev'essere tardi** it must be late; **come si deve** (lavorare, comportarsi) properly; **una persona come si deve** a respectable person.

**dove'roso, a** ag (right and) proper.

**do'vunque** av (in qualunque luogo) wherever; (dappertutto) everywhere; ~ **io vada** wherever I go.

**do'vuto, a** ag (causato): ~ a due to.

**doz'zina** [dod'dzina] sf dozen; **una** ~ **di uova** a dozen eggs.

**dozzi'nale** [doddzi'nale] ag cheap, second-rate.

**dra'gare** vt to dredge.

**'drago, ghi** sm dragon.

'**dramma, i** *sm* drama; **dram'matico, a, ci, che** *ag* dramatic; **drammatiz'zare** *vt* to dramatize; **dramma'turgo, ghi** *sm* playwright, dramatist.

**drappeggi'are** [draped'dʒare] *vt* to drape.

**drap'pello** *sm* (MIL) squad; (*gruppo*) band, group.

'**drastico, a, ci, che** *ag* drastic.

**dre'naggio** [dre'naddʒo] *sm* drainage.

**dre'nare** *vt* to drain.

'**dritto, a** *ag, av* = **diritto**.

**driz'zare** [drit'tsare] *vt* (*far tornare diritto*) to straighten; (*volgere: sguardo, occhi*) to turn, direct; (*innalzare: antenna, muro*) to erect; ~**rsi** *vr*: ~**rsi (in piedi)** to stand up; ~ **le orecchie** to prick up one's ears.

'**droga, ghe** *sf* (*sostanza aromatica*) spice; (*stupefacente*) drug; **dro'gare** *vt* to season, spice; to drug, dope; **drogarsi** *vr* to take drugs; **dro'gato, a** *sm/f* drug addict.

**droghe'ria** [droge'ria] *sf* grocer's shop (*Brit*), grocery (store) (*US*).

'**dubbio, a** *ag* (*incerto*) doubtful, dubious; (*ambiguo*) dubious // *sm* (*incertezza*) doubt; **avere il** ~ **che** to be afraid that, suspect that; **mettere in** ~ **qc** to question sth; **dubbi'oso, a** *ag* doubtful, dubious.

**dubi'tare** *vi*: ~ **di** to doubt; (*risultato*) to be doubtful of.

**Dub'lino** *sf* Dublin.

'**duca, chi** *sm* duke.

**du'chessa** [du'kessa] *sf* duchess.

'**due** *num* two.

**due'cento** [due'tʃento] *num* two hundred // *sm*: **il D~** the thirteenth century.

**due'pezzi** [due'pettsi] *sm* (*costume da bagno*) two-piece swimsuit; (*abito femminile*) two-piece suit.

**du'etto** *sm* duet.

'**dunque** *cong* (*perciò*) so, therefore; (*riprendendo il discorso*) well (then) // *sm inv*: **venire al** ~ to come to

the point.

**du'omo** *sm* cathedral.

'**duplex** *sm inv* (TEL) party line.

**dupli'cato** *sm* duplicate.

'**duplice** ['dupliʧe] *ag* double, twofold; **in** ~ **copia** in duplicate.

**du'rante** *prep* during.

**du'rare** *vi* to last; ~ **fatica a** to have difficulty in; **du'rata** *sf* length (of time); duration; **dura'turo, a** *ag,* **du'revole** *ag* lasting.

**du'rezza** [du'rettsa] *sf* hardness; stubbornness; harshness; toughness.

'**duro, a** *ag* (*pietra, lavoro, materasso, problema*) hard; (*persona: ostinato*) stubborn, obstinate; (: *severo*) harsh, hard; (*voce*) harsh; (*carne*) tough // *sm* hardness; (*difficoltà*) hard part; (*persona*) tough guy; **tener** ~ to stand firm, hold out; ~ **d'orecchi** hard of hearing.

**du'rone** *sm* hard skin.

# E

**e, ed** *dav V spesso* **ed** *cong* and; ~ **lui?** what about him?; ~ **compralo!** well buy it then!

**E.** *abbr* (= *est*) E.

**è** *vb vedi* **essere**.

'**ebano** *sm* ebony.

**eb'bene** *cong* well (then).

**eb'brezza** [eb'brettsa] *sf* intoxication.

'**ebbro, a** *ag* drunk; ~ **di** (*gioia etc*) beside o.s. o wild with.

'**ebete** *ag* stupid, idiotic.

**ebolli'zione** [ebollit'tsjone] *sf* boiling; **punto di** ~ boiling point.

**e'braico, a, ci, che** *ag* Hebrew, Hebraic // *sm* (LING) Hebrew.

**e'breo, a** *ag* Jewish // *sm/f* Jew/ Jewess.

'**Ebridi** *sfpl*: **le (isole)** ~ the Hebrides.

**ecc** *av abbr* (= *eccetera*) etc.

**ecce'denza** [ettʃe'dentsa] *sf* excess, surplus.

**ec'cedere** [et'tʃedere] *vt* to exceed // *vi* to go too far; ~ **nel bere/ mangiare** to indulge in drink/food to excess.

**eccel'lente** [ettʃel'lɛnte] *ag* excellent; **eccel'lenza** *sf* excellence; *(titolo)* Excellency.

**ec'cellere** [et'tʃellere] *vi*: ~ **(in)** to excel (at); **ec'celso, a** *pp* di **eccellere**.

**ec'centrico, a, ci, che** [et'tʃentriko] *ag* eccentric.

**ecces'sivo, a** [ettʃes'sivo] *ag* excessive.

**ec'cesso** [et'tʃɛsso] *sm* excess; **all'~** *(gentile, generoso)* to excess, excessively; ~ **di velocità** *(AUT)* speeding.

**ec'cetera** [et'tʃetera] *av* et cetera, and so on.

**ec'cetto** [et'tʃetto] *prep* except, with the exception of; ~ **che** *(cong* except, other than; ~ **che (non)** unless.

**eccettu'are** [ettʃettu'are] *vt* to except.

**eccezio'nale** [ettʃetsjo'nale] *ag* exceptional.

**eccezi'one** [ettʃet'tsjone] *sf* exception; *(DIR)* objection; **a** ~ **di** with the exception of, except for; **d'~** exceptional.

**ec'cidio** [et'tʃidio] *sm* massacre.

**ecci'tare** [ettʃi'tare] *vt (curiosità, interesse)* to excite, arouse; *(folla)* to incite; ~**rsi** *vr* to get excited; *(sessualmente)* to become aroused; **eccitazi'one** *sf* excitement.

**'ecco** *av (per dimostrare)*: ~ **il treno!** here's o here comes the train!; *(dav pronome)*: ~**mi!** here I am!; ~**ne uno!** here's one (of them)!; *(dav pp)*: ~ **fatto!** there, that's it done!

**echeggi'are** [eked'dʒare] *vi* to echo.

**e'clissi** *sf* eclipse.

**'eco,** *pl(m)* **'echi** *sm* o *f* echo.

**ecolo'gia** [ekolo'dʒia] *sf* ecology.

**econo'mia** *sf* economy; *(scienza)* economics *sg*; *(risparmio: azione)* saving; **fare** ~ to economize, make economies; **eco'nomico, a, ci, che**

*ag* economic; *(poco costoso)* economical; **econo'mista, i** *sm* economist; **economiz'zare** *vt, vi* to save; **e'conomo, a** *ag* thrifty // *sm/f (INS)* bursar.

**ed** *cong vedi* **e**.

**'edera** *sf* ivy.

**e'dicola** *sf* newspaper kiosk o stand *(US)*.

**edifi'care** *vt* to build; *(fig: teoria, azienda)* to establish; *(indurre al bene)* to edify.

**edi'ficio** [edi'fitʃo] *sm* building; *(fig)* structure.

**e'dile** *ag* building *cpd*; **edi'lizio, a** *ag* building *cpd* // *sf* building, building trade.

**Edim'burgo** *sf* Edinburgh.

**edi'tore, 'trice** *ag* publishing *cpd* // *sm/f* publisher; *(curatore)* editor; **edito'ria** *sf* publishing; **editori'ale** *ag* publishing *cpd* // *sm* editorial, leader.

**edizi'one** [edit'tsjone] *sf* edition; *(tiratura)* printing; *(di manifestazioni, feste etc)* production.

**edu'care** *vt* to educate; *(gusto, mente)* to train; ~ **qn a fare** to train sb to do; **edu'cato, a** *ag* polite, well-mannered; **educazi'one** *sf* education; *(familiare)* upbringing; *(comportamento)* (good) manners *pl*; **educazione fisica** *(INS)* physical training o education.

**effemi'nato, a** *ag* effeminate.

**effet'tivo, a** *ag (reale)* real, actual; *(impiegato, professore)* permanent; *(MIL)* regular // *sm (MIL)* strength; *(di patrimonio etc)* sum total.

**ef'fetto** *sm (anche: COMM: cambiale)* bill; *(fig: impressione)* impression; **in** ~**i** in fact, actually; **effettu'are** *vt* to effect, carry out.

**effi'cace** [effi'katʃe] *ag* effective.

**effi'ciente** [effi'tʃɛnte] *ag* efficient; **effi'cienza** *sf* efficiency.

**ef'fimero, a** *ag* ephemeral.

**E'geo** [e'dʒɛo] *sm*: **l'~, il mare** o **il mare ~** the Aegean (Sea).

**E'gitto** [e'dʒitto] *sm*: **l'~** Egypt.

egizi'ano, a [edʒit'tsjano] ag, sm/f Egyptian.

'egli ['eʎʎi] pronome he; ~ stesso he himself.

ego'ismo sm selfishness, egoism; ego'ista, i, e ag selfish, egoistic // sm/f egoist.

egr. abbr = egregio.

e'gregio, a, gi, gie [e'gredʒo] ag distinguished; (nelle lettere): E~ Signore Dear Sir.

eguagli'anza [egwaʎ'ʎantsa] etc vedi uguaglianza etc.

E.I. abbr = Esercito Italiano.

elabo'rare vt (progetto) to work out, elaborate; (dati) to process; (digerire) to digest; elabora'tore sm (INFORM): elaboratore elettronico computer; elaborazi'one sf elaborazione; digestion; elaborazione dei dati data processing.

e'lastico, a, ci, che ag elastic; (fig: andatura) springy; (: decisione, vedute) flexible // sm (gommino) rubber band; (per il cucito) elastic q.

ele'fante sm elephant.

ele'gante ag elegant.

e'leggere [e'leddʒere] vt to elect.

elemen'tare ag elementary; le (scuole) ~i sfpl primary (Brit) o grade (US) school.

ele'mento sm element; (parte componente) element, component, part; ~i smpl (della scienza etc) elements, rudiments.

ele'mosina sf charity, alms pl; chiedere l'~ to beg.

elen'care vt to list.

e'lenco, chi sm list; ~ telefonico telephone directory.

e'letto, a pp di eleggere // sm/f (nominato) elected member; eletto'rale ag electoral, election cpd; eletto'rato sm electorate; elet'tore, 'trice sm/f voter, elector.

elet'trauto sm inv workshop for car electrical repairs; (tecnico) car electrician.

elettri'cista, i [elettri'tʃista] sm electrician.

elettricità [elettritʃi'ta] sf electricity.

e'lettrico, a, ci, che ag electric(al).

elettriz'zare [elettrid'dzare] vt to electrify.

e'lettro... prefisso: elettrocardio'gramma, i sm electrocardiogram; elettrodo'mestico, a, ci, che ag: apparecchi elettrodomestici domestic (electrical) appliances; elet'trone sm electron; elet'tronico, a, ci, che ag electronic // sf electronics sg.

ele'vare vt to raise; (edificio) to erect; (multa) to impose.

elezi'one [elet'sjone] sf election; ~i sfpl (POL) election(s).

'elica, che sf propeller.

eli'cottero sm helicopter.

elimi'nare vt to eliminate; elimina'toria sf eliminating round.

'elio sm helium.

'ella pronome she; (forma di cortesia) you; ~ stessa she herself; you yourself.

el'metto sm helmet.

e'logio [e'lɔdʒo] sm (discorso, scritto) eulogy; (lode) praise (di solito q).

elo'quente ag eloquent.

e'ludere vt to evade; elu'sivo, a ag evasive.

ema'nare vt to send out, give off; (fig: leggi, decreti) to issue // vi: ~ da to come from.

emanci'pare [emantʃi'pare] vt to emancipate; ~rsi vr (fig) to become liberated o emancipated.

embri'one sm embryo.

emenda'mento sm amendment.

emen'dare vt to amend.

emer'genza [emer'dʒentsa] sf emergency; in caso di ~ in an emergency.

e'mergere [e'mɛrdʒere] vi to emerge; (sommergibile) to surface; (fig: distinguersi) to stand out; e'merso, a pp di emergere.

e'messo, a pp di emettere.

e'mettere vt (suono, luce) to give

out, emit; (onde radio) to send out; (assegno, francobollo, ordine) to issue; (fig: giudizio) to express, voice.

emi'crania sf migraine.

emi'grare vi to emigrate; emigrazi'one f emigration.

emi'nente ag eminent, distinguished.

emis'fero sm hemisphere; ~ boreale/australe northern/southern hemisphere.

emissi'one sf (vedi emettere) emission; sending out; issue; (RADIO) broadcast.

emit'tente ag (banca) issuing; (RADIO) broadcasting, transmitting // sf (RADIO) transmitter.

emorra'gia, 'gie [emorra'dʒia] sf haemorrhage.

emo'tivo, a ag emotional.

emozio'nante [emottsjo'nante] ag exciting, thrilling.

emozio'nare [emottsjo'nare] vt (appassionare) to thrill, excite; (commuovere) to move; (innervosire) to upset; ~rsi vr to be excited; to be moved; to be upset.

emozi'one [emot'tsjone] sf emotion; (agitazione) excitement.

'empio, a ag (sacrilego) impious; (spietato) cruel, pitiless; (malvagio) wicked, evil.

emulsi'one sf emulsion.

enciclope'dia [entʃiklope'dia] sf encyclopaedia.

endove'noso, a ag (MED) intravenous.

'ENEL ['enel] sigla m (= Ente Nazionale per l'Energia Elettrica) = C.E.G.B. (= Central Electricity Generating Board).

ener'gia, 'gie [ener'dʒia] sf (FISICA) energy; (fig) energy, strength, vigour; e'nergico, a, ci, che ag energetic, vigorous.

'enfasi sf emphasis; (peg) bombast, pomposity; en'fatico, a, ci, che ag emphatic; pompous.

'ENIT ['enit] sigla m = Ente

Nazionale Italiano per il Turismo.

en'nesimo, a ag (MAT, fig) nth; per l'~a volta for the umpteenth time.

e'norme ag enormous, huge; enormità sf inv enormity, huge size; (assurdità) absurdity; non dire enormità! don't talk nonsense!

'ente sm (istituzione) body, board, corporation; (FILOSOFIA) being.

en'trambi, e pronome pl both (of them) // ag pl: ~ i ragazzi both boys, both of the boys.

en'trare vi to enter, go (o come) in; ~ in (luogo) to enter, go (o come) into; (trovar posto, poter stare) to fit into; (essere ammesso a: club etc) to join, become a member of; ~ in automobile to get into the car; far ~ qn (visitatore etc) to show sb in; questo non c'entra (fig) that's got nothing to do with it; en'trata sf entrance, entry; entrate sfpl (COMM) receipts, takings; (ECON) income sg.

'entro prep (temporale) within.

entusias'mare vt to excite, fill with enthusiasm; ~rsi (per qc/qn) to become enthusiastic (about sth/sb); entusi'asmo sm enthusiasm; entusi'asta, i, e ag enthusiastic // sm/f enthusiast; entusi'astico, a, ci, che ag enthusiastic.

enunci'are [enun'tʃare] vt (teoria) to enunciate, set out.

'epico, a ci, che ag epic.

epide'mia sf epidemic.

epi'dermide sf skin, epidermis.

Epifa'nia f Epiphany.

epiles'sia sf epilepsy.

e'pilogo, ghi sm conclusion.

epi'sodio sm episode.

e'piteto sm epithet.

'epoca, che sf (periodo storico) age, era; (tempo) time; (GEO) age.

ep'pure cong and yet, nevertheless.

epu'rare vt (POL) to purge.

equa'tore sm equator.

equazi'one [ekwat'tsjone] sf (MAT) equation.

e'questre ag equestrian.

**equi'latero, a** *ag* equilateral.

**equili'brare** *vt* to balance; **equi'librio** *sm* balance, equilibrium; perdere l'~ to lose one's balance.

**e'quino, a** *ag* horse *cpd*, equine.

**equipaggi'are** [ekwipad'dʒare] *vt (di persone)* to man; *(di mezzi)* to equip; **equi'paggio** *sm* crew.

**equipa'rare** *vt* to make equal.

**equità** *sf* equity, fairness.

**equitazi'one** [ekwitat'tsjone] *sf (horse-)riding.

**equiva'lente** *ag, sm* equivalent; **equiva'lenza** *sf* equivalence.

**equivo'care** *vi* to misunderstand; **e'quivoco, a, ci, che** *ag* equivocal, ambiguous; *(sospetto)* dubious // *sm* misunderstanding; **a scanso di equivoci** to avoid any misunderstanding; **giocare sull'equivoco** to equivocate.

**'equo, a** *ag* fair, just.

**'era** *sf* era.

**'erba** *sf* grass; *(aromatica, medicinale)* herb; in ~ *(fig)* budding; **er'baccia, ce** *sf* weed.

**e'rede** *sm/f* heir; **eredità** *sf (DIR)* inheritance; *(BIOL)* heredity; lasciare qc in eredità a qn to leave o bequeath sth to sb; **eredi'tare** *vt* to inherit; **eredi'tario, a** *ag* hereditary.

**ere'mita, i** *sm* hermit.

**ere'sia** *sf* heresy; **e'retico, a, ci, che** *ag* heretical // *sm/f* heretic.

**e'retto, a** *pp di* **erigere** // *ag* erect, upright; **erezi'one** *sf (FISIOL)* erection.

**er'gastolo** *sm (DIR: pena)* life imprisonment.

**'erica** *sf* heather.

**e'rigere** [e'ridʒere] *vt* to erect, raise; *(fig: fondare)* to found.

**ermel'lino** *sm* ermine.

**er'metico, a, ci, che** *ag* hermetic.

**'ernia** *sf (MED)* hernia.

**e'roe** *sm* hero.

**ero'gare** *vt (somme)* to distribute; (: *per beneficenza)* to donate; *(gas, servizi)* to supply.

**e'roico, a, ci, che** *ag* heroic.

**ero'ina** *sf* heroine; *(droga)* heroin.

**ero'ismo** *sm* heroism.

**erosi'one** *sf* erosion.

**e'rotico, a, ci, che** *ag* erotic.

**er'rare** *vi (vagare)* to wander, roam; *(sbagliare)* to be mistaken.

**er'rore** *sm* error, mistake; *(morale)* error; per ~ by mistake.

**'erta** *sf* steep slope; stare all'~ to be on the alert.

**erut'tare** *vt (sog: vulcano)* to throw out, belch.

**eruzi'one** [erut'tsjone] *sf* eruption.

**esacer'bare** [ezatʃer'bare] *vt* to exacerbate.

**esage'rare** *vt* to exaggerate // *vi* to exaggerate; *(eccedere)* to go too far; **esagerazi'one** *sf* exaggeration.

**e'sagono** *sm* hexagon.

**esal'tare** *vt* to exalt; *(entusiasmare)* to excite, stir; **esal'tato, a** *sm/f* fanatic.

**e'same** *sm* examination; *(INS)* exam, examination; fare o dare un ~ to sit o take an exam; ~ **del sangue** blood test.

**esami'nare** *vt* to examine.

**e'sanime** *ag* lifeless.

**esaspe'rare** *vt* to exasperate; to exacerbate; ~**rsi** *vr* to become annoyed o exasperated; **esasperazi'one** *sf* exasperation.

**esatta'mente** *av* exactly; accurately, precisely.

**esat'tezza** [ezat'tettsa] *sf* exactitude, accuracy, precision.

**e'satto, a** *pp di* **esigere** // *ag (calcolo, ora)* correct, right, exact; *(preciso)* accurate, precise; *(puntuale)* punctual.

**esat'tore** *sm (di imposte etc)* collector.

**esau'dire** *vt* to grant, fulfil.

**esauri'ente** *ag* exhaustive.

**esauri'mento** *sm* exhaustion; ~ **nervoso** nervous breakdown.

**esau'rire** *vt (stancare)* to exhaust, wear out; *(provviste, miniera)* to exhaust; ~rsi *vr* to exhaust o.s., wear o.s. out; (*provviste*) to run out; esau'rito, a *ag* exhausted; (*merci*) sold out; (*libri*) out of print; registrare il tutto esaurito (*TEATRO*) to have a full house; e'sausto, a *ag* exhausted.

'esca, *pl* esche *sf* bait.

escande'scenza [eskande∫'∫εntsa] *sf*: dare in ~e to lose one's temper, fly into a rage.

'esce, 'esci ['ε∫e,'ε∫i] *vb vedi* uscire.

eschi'mese [eski'mese] *ag, sm/f* Eskimo.

escla'mare *vi* to exclaim, cry out; esclamazi'one *sf* exclamation.

es'cludere *vt* to exclude.

esclu'sivo, a *ag* exclusive // *sf* (*DIR, COMM*) exclusive o sole rights *pl*.

es'cluso, a *pp di* escludere.

'esco, 'escono *vb vedi* uscire.

escursi'one *sf* (*gita*) excursion, trip; (: *a piedi*) hike, walk; (*METEOR*) range.

ese'crare *vt* to loathe, abhor.

esecu'tivo, a *ag, sm* executive.

esecu'tore, 'trice *sm/f* (*MUS*) performer; (*DIR*) executor.

esecuzi'one [ezekut'tsjone] *sf* execution, carrying out; (*MUS*) performance; ~ capitale execution.

esegu'ire *vt* to carry out, execute; (*MUS*) to perform, execute.

e'sempio *sm* example; per ~ for example, for instance; fare un ~ to give an example; esem'plare *ag* exemplary // *sm* example; (*copia*) copy; esemplifi'care *vt* to exemplify.

esen'tare *vt*: ~ qn/qc da to exempt sb/sth from.

e'sente *ag*: ~ da (*dispensato da*) exempt from; (*privo di*) free from; esenzi'one *sf* exemption.

e'sequie *sfpl* funeral rites; funeral service *sg*.

eser'cente [ezer't∫εnte] *sm/f* trader, dealer; shopkeeper.

eserci'tare [ezert∫i'tare] *vt* (*professione*) to practise (*Brit*), practice (*US*); (*allenare: corpo, mente*) to exercise, train; (*diritto*) to exercise; (*influenza, pressione*) to exert; ~rsi *vr* to practise; ~rsi alla lotta to practise fighting; esercitazi'one *sf* (*scolastica, militare*) exercise.

e'sercito [e'zεrt∫ito] *sm* army.

eser'cizio [ezer't∫ittsjo] *sm* practice; exercising; (*fisico, di matematica*) exercise; (*ECON*) financial year; (*azienda*) business, concern; in ~ (*medico etc*) practising.

esi'bire *vt* to exhibit, display; (*documenti*) to produce, present; ~rsi *vr* (*attore*) to perform; (*fig*) to show off; esibizi'one *sf* exhibition; (*di documento*) presentation; (*spettacolo*) show, performance.

esi'gente [ezi'dʒεnte] *ag* demanding; esi'genza *sf* demand, requirement.

e'sigere [e'zidʒere] *vt* (*pretendere*) to demand; (*richiedere*) to demand, require; (*imposte*) to collect.

e'siguo, a *ag* small, slight.

e'sile *ag* (*persona*) slender, slim; (*stelo*) thin; (*voce*) faint.

esili'are *vt* to exile; e'silio *sm* exile.

e'simere *vt*: ~ qn/qc da to exempt sb/sth from; ~rsi *vr*: ~rsi da to get out of.

esis'tenza [ezis'tεntsa] *sf* existence.

e'sistere *vi* to exist.

esis'tito, a *pp di* esistere.

esi'tare *vi* to hesitate; esitazi'one *sf* hesitation.

'esito *sm* result, outcome.

'esodo *sm* exodus.

esone'rare *vt*: ~ qn da to exempt sb from.

e'sordio *sm* début.

esor'tare *vt*: ~ qn a fare to urge sb to do.

e'sotico, a, ci, che *ag* exotic.

es'pandere *vt* to expand; (*confini*) to extend; (*influenza*) to extend, spread; ~rsi *vr* to expand; espansi'one *sf* expansion;

**espan'sivo, a** *ag* expansive, communicative.

**espatri'are** *vi* to leave one's country.

**espedi'ente** *sm* expedient.

**es'pellere** *vt* to expel.

**esperi'enza** [espe'rjɛntsa] *sf* experience; (*SCIENZA: prova*) experiment.

**esperi'mento** *sm* experiment.

**es'perto, a** *ag*, *sm* expert.

**espi'are** *vt* to atone for.

**espi'rare** *vt*, *vi* to breathe out.

**espli'care** *vt* (*attività*) to carry out, perform.

**es'plicito, a** [es'plitʃito] *ag* explicit.

**es'plodere** *vi* (*anche fig*) to explode // *vt* to fire.

**esplo'rare** *vt* to explore; **es-plora'tore** *sm* explorer; (*anche: giovane esploratore*) (boy) scout; (*NAUT*) scout (ship).

**esplosi'one** *sf* explosion; **esplo-'sivo, a** *ag*, *sm* explosive; **es'ploso, a** *pp di* **esplodere.**

**espo'nente** *smf* (*rappresentante*) representative.

**es'porre** *vt* (*merci*) to display; (*quadro*) to exhibit, show; (*fatti, idee*) to explain, set out; (*porre in pericolo, FOT*) to expose.

**espor'tare** *vt* to export; **esportazi'one** *sf* exportation; export.

**esposizi'one** [espozit'tsjone] *sf* displaying; exhibiting; setting out; (*anche FOT*) exposure; (*mostra*) exhibition; (*narrazione*) explanation, exposition.

**es'posto, a** *pp di* **esporre** // *ag*: ~ a nord facing north // *sm* (*AMM*) statement, account; (: *petizione*) petition.

**espressi'one** *sf* expression.

**espres'sivo, a** *ag* expressive.

**es'presso, a** *pp di* **esprimere** // *ag* express // *sm* (*lettera*) express letter; (*anche*: **treno** ~) express train; (*anche*: **caffè** ~) espresso.

**es'primere** *vt* to express; ~**rsi** *vr* to

express o.s.

**espulsi'one** *sf* expulsion; **es'pulso, a** *pp di* **espellere.**

**'essa** *pronome f*, **'esse** *pronome fpl vedi* **esso.**

**es'senza** [es'sɛntsa] *sf* essence; **essenzi'ale** *ag* essential; **l'essenziale** the main *o* most important thing.

| PAROLA CHIAVE |

**'essere** ♦ *sm* being; ~ **umano** human being

♦ *vb copulativo* **1** (*con attributo, sostantivo*) to be; **sei giovane/simpatico** you are *o* you're young/nice; **è medico** he is *o* he's a doctor

**2** (+ *di: appartenere*) to be; **di chi è la penna?** whose pen is it?; **è di Carla** it is *o* it's Carla's, it belongs to Carla

**3** (+ *di: provenire*) to be; **è di Venezia** he is *o* he's from Venice

**4** (*data, ora*): **è il 15 agosto/lunedì** it is *o* it's the 15th of August/Monday; **che ora è, che ore sono?** what time is it?; **è l'una** it is *o* it's one o'clock; **sono le due** it is *o* it's two o'clock

**5** (*costare*): **quant'è?** how much is it?; **sono 20.000 lire** it's 20,000 lire

♦ *vb ausiliare* **1** (*attivo*): **arrivato/venuto** to have arrived/come; **è già partita** she has already left

**2** (*passivo*): **è ~ fatto da** to be made by; **è stata uccisa** she has been killed

**3** (*riflessivo*): **si sono lavati** they washed, they got washed

**4** (+ *da* + *infinito*): **è da farsi subito** it must be *o* is to be done immediately

♦ *vi* **1** (*esistere, trovarsi*) to be; **sono a casa** I'm at home; ~ **in piedi/seduto** to be standing/sitting

**2**: **esserci**: **c'è** there is; **ci sono** there are; **che c'è?** what's the matter?, what is it?; **ci sono!** (*fig*: ho capito) I get it!; *vedi anche* **ci**

◆ *vb impers*: è tardi/Pasqua it's late/Easter; è possibile che venga he may come; è così that's the way it is.

**'esso, a** *pronome* it; *(riferito a persona: soggetto)* he/she; *(: complemento)* him/her; **~i, e** *pronome pl* they; *(complemento)* them.

**est** *sm* east.

**'estasi** *sf* ecstasy.

**es'tate** *sf* summer.

**es'tatico, a, ci, che** *ag* ecstatic.

**es'tendere** *vt* to extend; **~rsi** *vr (diffondersi)* to spread; *(territorio, confini)* to extend; **estensi'one** *sf* extension; *(di superficie)* expanse; *(di voce)* range.

**esteri'ore** *ag* outward, external.

**es'terno, a** *ag* *(porta, muro)* outer, outside; *(scala)* outside; *(alunno, impressione)* external // *sm* outside, exterior // *sm* *(allievo)* day pupil; **per uso** ~ for external use only.

**'estero, a** *ag* foreign // *sm*: **all'**~ abroad.

**es'teso, a** *pp di* **estendere** // *ag* extensive, large; **scrivere per** ~ to write in full.

**es'tetico, a, ci, che** *ag* aesthetic // *sf* *(disciplina)* aesthetics *sg*; *(bellezza)* attractiveness; **este'tista, i, e** *smf* beautician.

**'estimo** *sm* valuation; *(disciplina)* surveying.

**es'tinguere** *vt* to extinguish, put out; *(debito)* to pay off; **~rsi** *vr* to go out; *(specie)* to become extinct; **es'tinto, a** *pp di* **estinguere**; **estin'tore** *sm* (fire) extinguisher; **estinzi'one** *sf* putting out; *(di specie)* extinction.

**estir'pare** *vt* *(pianta)* to uproot, pull up; *(fig: vizio)* to eradicate.

**es'tivo, a** *ag* summer *cpd*.

**es'torcere** [es'tɔrtʃere] *vt*: ~ **qc (a qn)** to extort sth (from sb); **es'torto, a** *pp di* **estorcere**.

**estradizi'one** [estradit'tsjone] *sf* extradition.

**es'traneo, a** *ag* foreign; *(discorso)* extraneous, unrelated // *smf* stranger; **rimanere ~ a qc** to take no part in sth.

**es'trarre** *vt* to extract; *(minerali)* to mine; *(sorteggiare)* to draw; **es'tratto, a** *pp di* **estrarre** // *sm* extract; *(di documento)* abstract; **estratto di nascita** birth certificate; **estratto conto** statement of account; **estratto di nascita** birth certificate; **estrazi'one** *sf* extraction; mining; drawing *q*; draw.

**estremità** *sf inv* extremity, end // *sfpl* *(ANAT)* extremities.

**es'tremo, a** *ag* extreme; *(ultimo: ora, tentativo)* final, last // *sm* extreme; *(di pazienza, forze)* limit, end; **~i** *smpl* *(AMM: dati essenziali)* details, particulars; **l'~ Oriente** the Far East.

**'estro** *sm* *(capriccio)* whim, fancy; *(ispirazione creativa)* inspiration; **es'troso, a** *ag* whimsical, capricious; inspired.

**estro'verso, a** *ag* extrovert.

**'esule** *smf* exile.

**età** *sf inv* age; **all'**~ **di 8 anni** at the age of 8, at 8 years of age; **ha la mia** ~ he (o she) is the same age as me o as I am; **raggiungere la maggiore** ~ to come of age; **essere in** ~ **minore** to be under age.

**'etere** *sm* ether; **e'tereo, a** *ag* ethereal.

**eternità** *sf* eternity.

**e'terno, a** *ag* eternal.

**etero'geneo, a** [etero'dʒɛneo] *ag* heterogeneous.

**'etica** *sf vedi* **etico**.

**eti'chetta** [eti'ketta] *sf* label; *(cerimoniale)*: **l'~** etiquette.

**'etico, a, ci, che** *ag* ethical // *sf* ethics *sg*.

**etimolo'gia, 'gie** [etimolo'dʒia] *sf* etymology.

**Eti'opia** *sf*: **l'~** Ethiopia.

**'Etna** *sm*: **l'~** Etna.

**'etnico, a, ci, che** *ag* ethnic.

**e'trusco, a, schi, sche** *ag, sm*

Etruscan.

**'ettaro** sm hectare (= 10,000 $m^2$).

**'etto** sm abbr di **ettogrammo**.

**etto'grammo** sm hectogram(me) (= 100 grams).

**Eucaris'tia** sf: l'~ the Eucharist.

**Eu'ropa** sf: l'~ Europe; **euro'peo, a** ag, sm/f European.

**evacu'are** vt to evacuate.

**e'vadere** vi (fuggire): ~ **da** to escape from // vt (sbrigare) to deal with, dispatch; (tasse) to evade.

**evan'gelico, a, ci, che** [evan-'dʒɛliko] ag evangelical.

**evapo'rare** vi to evaporate; **evaporazi'one** sf evaporation.

**evasi'one** sf (vedi evadere) escape; dispatch; ~ **fiscale** tax evasion.

**eva'sivo, a** ag evasive.

**e'vaso, a** pp di **evadere** // sm escapee.

**eveni'enza** [eve'njɛntsa] sf: **pronto(a) per ogni** ~ ready for any eventuality.

**e'vento** sm event.

**eventu'ale** ag possible.

**evi'dente** ag evident, obvious; **evi'denza** sf obviousness; **mettere in evidenza** to point out, highlight.

**evi'tare** vt to avoid; ~ **di fare** to avoid doing; ~ **qc a qn** to spare sb sth.

**'evo** sm age, epoch.

**evo'care** vt to evoke.

**evo'luto, a** pp di **evolvere** // ag (civiltà) (highly) developed, advanced; (persona) independent.

**evoluzi'one** [evolut'tsjone] sf evolution.

**e'volversi** vr to evolve.

**ev'viva** escl hurrah!; ~ **il re!** long live the king!, hurrah for the king!

**ex** prefisso ex, former.

**'extra** ag inv first-rate; top-quality // sm inv extra; **extraconiu'gale** ag extramarital.

# F

**fa** vb vedi **fare** // sm inv (MUS) F; (: solfeggiando la scala) fa // av: **10 anni** ~ 10 years ago.

**fabbi'sogno** [fabbi'zoɲɲo] sm needs pl, requirements pl.

**'fabbrica** sf factory; **fabbri'cante** sm manufacturer, maker; **fabbri'care** vt to build; (produrre) to manufacture, make; (fig) to fabricate, invent.

**'fabbro** sm (black)smith.

**fac'cenda** [fat'tʃɛnda] sf matter, affair; (cosa da fare) task, chore.

**fac'chino** [fak'kino] sm porter.

**'faccia, ce** ['fattʃa] sf face; (di moneta, medaglia) side; ~ **a** ~ face to face.

**facci'ata** [fat'tʃata] sf façade; (di pagina) side.

**'faccio** ['fattʃo] vb vedi **fare**.

**fa'ceto, a** [fa'tʃeto] ag witty, humorous.

**'facile** ['fatʃile] ag easy; (affabile) easy-going; (disposto): ~ **a** inclined to, prone to; (probabile): **è** ~ **che piova** it's likely to rain; **facilità** sf easiness; (disposizione, dono) aptitude; **facili'tare** vt to make easier.

**facino'roso, a** [fatʃino'roso] ag violent.

**facoltà** sf inv faculty; (CHIMICA) property; (autorità) power.

**facolta'tivo, a** ag optional; (fermata d'autobus) request cpd.

**fac'simile** sm facsimile.

**'faggio** ['faddʒo] sm beech.

**fagi'ano** [fa'dʒano] sm pheasant.

**fagio'lino** [fadʒo'lino] sm French (Brit) o string bean.

**fagi'olo** [fa'dʒɔlo] sm bean.

**fa'gotto** sm bundle; (MUS) bassoon; **far** ~ (fig) to pack up and go.

**'fai** vb vedi **fare**.

**'falce** ['faltʃe] sf scythe; **fal'cetto** sm sickle; **falci'are** vt to cut; (fig) to mow down.

'**falco, chi** sm hawk.

**fal'cone** sm falcon.

'**falda** sf layer, stratum; (di cappello) brim; (di cappotto) tails pl; (di monte) lower slope; (di tetto) pitch; **nevica a larghe** ~e the snow is falling in large flakes; **abito a** ~e tails pl.

**fale'gname** [faleɲˈɲame] sm joiner.

**fal'lace** [falˈlatʃe] ag misleading, deceptive.

**falli'mento** sm failure; bankruptcy.

**fal'lire** vi (non riuscire): ~ (**in**) to fail (in); (DIR) to go bankrupt // vt (colpo, bersaglio) to miss; **fal'lito, a** ag unsuccessful; bankrupt // sm/f bankrupt.

'**fallo** sm error, mistake; (imperfezione) defect, flaw; (SPORT) foul; fault; **senza** ~ without fail.

**falò** sm inv bonfire.

**fal'sare** vt to distort, misrepresent; **fal'sario** sm forger; counterfeiter; **falsifi'care** vt to forge; (monete) to forge, counterfeit.

'**falso, a** ag false; (errato) wrong; (falsificato) forged; fake; (: oro, gioielli) imitation cpd // sm forgery; **giurare il** ~ to commit perjury.

'**fama** sf fame; (reputazione) reputation, name.

'**fame** sf hunger; **aver** ~ to be hungry; **fa'melico, a, ci, che** ag ravenous.

**fa'miglia** [faˈmiʎʎa] sf family.

**famili'are** ag (della famiglia) family cpd; (ben noto) familiar; (rapporti, atmosfera) friendly; (LING) informal, colloquial // sm/f relative, relation; **familiarità** sf familiarity; friendliness; informality.

**fa'moso, a** ag famous, well-known.

**fa'nale** sm (AUT) light, lamp (Brit); (luce stradale, NAUT) light; (di faro) beacon.

**fa'natico, a, ci, che** ag fanatical; (del tuatro, calcio etc): ~ **di** o **per** mad o crazy about // sm/f fanatic; (tifoso) fan.

**fanci'ullo, a** [fanˈtʃullo] sm/f child.

**fan'donia** sf tall story; ~e sfpl nonsense sg.

**fan'fara** sf brass band; (musica) fanfare.

'**fango, ghi** sm mud; **fan'goso, a** ag muddy.

'**fanno** vb vedi **fare**.

**fannul'lone, a** sm/f idler, loafer.

**fantasci'enza** [fantaʃˈʃɛntsa] sf science fiction.

**fanta'sia** sf fantasy, imagination; (capriccio) whim, caprice // ag inv: **vestito** ~ patterned dress.

**fan'tasma, i** sm ghost, phantom.

**fan'tastico, a, ci, che** ag fantastic; (potenza, ingegno) imaginative.

'**fante** sm infantryman; (CARTE) jack, knave (Brit); **fante'ria** sf infantry.

**fan'toccio** [fanˈtɔttʃo] sm puppet.

**fara'butto** sm crook.

**far'dello** sm bundle; (fig) burden.

'**fare ◆** sm 1 (modo di fare): **con** ~ **distratto** absent-mindedly; **ha un** ~ **simpatico** he has a pleasant manner 2: **sul far del giorno/della notte** at daybreak/nightfall

◆ vt 1 (fabbricare, creare) to make; (: casa) to build; (: assegno) to make out; ~ **un pasto/una promessa/un film** to make a meal/a promise/a film; ~ **rumore** to make a noise

2 (effettuare: lavoro, attività, studi) to do; (: sport) to play; **cosa fa?** (adesso) what are you doing?; (di professione) what do you do?; ~ **psicologia/italiano** (INS) to do psychology/Italian; ~ **un viaggio** to go on a trip o journey; ~ **una passeggiata** to go for a walk; ~ **la spesa** to do the shopping

3 (funzione) to be; (TEATRO) to play, be; ~ **il medico** to be a doctor; ~ **il malato** (fingere) to act the invalid

4 (suscitare: sentimenti): ~ **paura**

a qn to frighten sb; **mi fa rabbia** it makes me angry; **(non) fa niente** *(non importa)* it doesn't matter

**5** *(ammontare)*: **3 più 3 fa 6** 3 and 3 are o make 6; **fanno 6.000 lire** that's 6,000 lire; **Roma fa 2.000.000 di abitanti** Rome has 2,000,000 inhabitants; **che ora fai?** what time do you make it?

**6** (+ *infinito*): **far ~ qc a qn** *(obbligare)* to make sb do sth; *(permettere)* to let sb do sth; **fammi vedere** let me see; **far partire il motore** to start (up) the engine; **far riparare la macchina/costruire una casa** to get o have the car repaired/a house built

**7**: **~rsi**: **~rsi una gonna** to make o.s. a skirt; **~rsi un nome** to make a name for o.s.; **~rsi la permanente** to get a perm; **~rsi tagliare i capelli** to get one's hair cut; **~rsi operare** to have an operation; **si è fatto lavare la macchina** he got somebody to wash the car

**8** *(fraseologia)*: **farcela** to succeed, manage; **non ce la faccio più** I can't go on; **ce la faremo** we'll make it; **me l'hanno fatta!** *(imbrogliare)* I've been done!; **lo facevo più giovane** I thought he was younger; **fare sì/no con la testa** to nod/shake one's head

♦ *vi* **1** *(agire)* to act, do; **fate come volete** do as you like; **~ presto** to be quick; **~ da** to act as; **non c'è niente da ~** it's no use; **saperci ~ con qn/qc** to know how to deal with sb/sth; **faccia pure!** go ahead!

**2** *(dire)* to say; **"davvero?" fece** "really?" he said

**3**: **~ per** *(essere adatto)* to be suitable for; **~ per ~ qc** to be about to do sth; **fece per andarsene** he made as if to leave

**4**: **~rsi**: **si fa così** you do it like this, this is the way it's done; **non si fa così!** *(rimprovero)* that's no way to behave!; **la festa non si fa** the party is off

**5**: **~ a gara con qn** to compete o vie with sb; **~ a pugni** to come to blows; **~ in tempo a ~** to be in time to do

♦ *vb impers*: **fa bel tempo** the weather is fine; **fa caldo/freddo** it's hot/cold; **fa notte** it's getting dark

♦ *vr*: **~rsi 1** *(diventare)* to become; **~rsi prete** to become a priest; **~rsi grande/vecchio** to grow tall/old

**2** *(spostarsi)*: **~rsi avanti/indietro** to move forward/back

**3** *(fam: drogarsi)* to be a junkie.

**far'falla** *sf* butterfly.

**fa'rina** *sf* flour.

**farma'cia, 'cie** [farma'tʃia] *sf* pharmacy; *(negozio)* chemist's (shop) *(Brit)*, pharmacy; **farma'cista, i, e** *sm/f* chemist *(Brit)*, pharmacist.

**'farmaco, ci** o **chi** *sm* drug, medicine.

**'faro** *sm* *(NAUT)* lighthouse; *(AER)* beacon; *(AUT)* headlight.

**'farsa** *sf* farce.

**'fascia, sce** ['faʃʃa] *sf* band, strip; *(MED)* bandage; *(di sindaco, ufficiale)* sash; *(parte di territorio)* strip, belt; *(di contribuenti etc)* group, band; **essere in ~sce** *(anche fig)* to be in one's infancy; **~ oraria** time band.

**fasci'are** [faʃʃare] *vt* to bind; *(MED)* to bandage; *(bambino)* to put a nappy *(Brit)* o diaper *(US)* on.

**fa'scicolo** [faʃʃikolo] *sm* *(di documenti)* file, dossier; *(di rivista)* issue, number; *(opuscolo)* booklet, pamphlet.

**'fascino** ['faʃʃino] *sm* charm, fascination.

**'fascio** ['faʃʃo] *sm* bundle, sheaf; *(di fiori)* bunch; *(di luce)* beam; *(POL)*: **il F~** the Fascist Party.

**fa'scismo** [faʃʃizmo] *sm* fascism.

**'fase** *sf* phase; *(TECN)* stroke; **fuori ~** *(motore)* rough.

**fas'tidio** *sm* bother, trouble; **dare ~**

a **qn** to bother o annoy sb; **sento ~ allo stomaco** my stomach's upset; **avere ~i con la polizia** to have trouble o bother with the police; **fastidi'oso, a** ag annoying, tiresome; (schifiltoso) fastidious.

'**fasto** sm pomp, splendour.

'**fata** sf fairy.

**fa'tale** ag fatal; (inevitabile) inevitable; (fig) irresistible; **fatalità** sf inv inevitability; (avversità) misfortune; (fato) fate, destiny.

**fa'tica, che** sf hard work, toil; (sforzo) effort; (di metalli) fatigue; **a ~ with difficulty; fare ~ a fare qc** to have a job doing sth; **fati'care** vi to toil; **faticare a fare qc** to have difficulty doing sth; **fati'coso, a** ag tiring, exhausting; (lavoro) laborious.

'**fato** sm fate, destiny.

'**fatto, a** pp di **fare** // ag: **un uomo ~ a grown man; ~ a mano/in casa** hand-/home-made // sm fact; (azione) deed; (avvenimento) event, occurrence; (di romanzo, film) action, story; **cogliere qn sul ~** to catch sb red-handed; **il ~ sta o è che** the fact remains o is that; **in ~ di** as for, as far as ... is concerned.

**fat'tore** sm (AGR) farm manager; (MAT, elemento costitutivo) factor.

**fatto'ria** sf farm; farmhouse.

**fatto'rino** sm errand-boy; (di ufficio) office-boy; (d'albergo) porter.

**fat'tura** sf (COMM) invoice; (di abito) tailoring; (malia) spell.

**fattu'rare** vt (COMM) to invoice; (prodotto) to produce; (vino) to adulterate.

'**fatuo, a** ag vain, fatuous.

'**fauna** sf fauna.

**fau'tore, trice** smif advocate, supporter.

**fa'vella** sf speech.

**fa'villa** sf spark.

'**favola** sf (fiaba) fairy tale; (d'intento morale) fable; (fandonia) yarn; **favo'loso, a** ag fabulous; (incredibile) incredible.

**fa'vore** sm favour; **per ~ please;**

**fare un ~ a qn** to do sb a favour; **favo'revole** ag favourable.

**favo'rire** vt to favour; (il commercio, l'industria, le arti) to promote, encourage; **vuole ~?** won't you help yourself?; **favorisca in salotto** please come into the sitting room; **favo'rito, a** ag, smif favourite.

**fazzo'letto** [fattso'letto] sm handkerchief; (per la testa) (head)scarf.

**feb'braio** sm February.

**'febbre** sf fever; **aver la ~** to have a high temperature; **~ da fieno** hay fever; **feb'brile** ag (anche fig) feverish.

**'feccia** [fettʃa] sf dregs pl.

**'fecola** sf potato flour.

**fecondazi'one** [fekondat'tsjone] sf fertilization; **~ artificiale** artificial insemination.

**fe'condo, a** ag fertile.

**'fede** sf (credenza) belief, faith; (REL) faith; (fiducia) faith, trust; (fedeltà) loyalty; (anello) wedding ring; (attestato) certificate; **aver ~ in qn** to have faith in sb; **in buona/cattiva ~** in good/bad faith; **"in ~"** (DIR) "in witness whereof"; **fe'dele** ag: **fedele (a)** faithful (to) // smif follower; **i fedeli** (REL) the faithful; **fedeltà** sf faithfulness; (coniugale) fidelity; **alta fedeltà** (RADIO) high fidelity.

**'federa** sf pillowslip, pillowcase.

**fede'rale** ag federal.

**'fegato** sm liver; (fig) guts pl, nerve.

**'felce** [fɛltʃe] sf fern.

**fe'lice** [fe'litʃe] ag happy; (fortunato) lucky; **felicità** sf happiness.

**felici'tarsi** [felitʃi'tarsi] vr (congratularsi): **~ con qn per qc** to congratulate sb on sth.

**fe'lino, a** ag, sm feline.

**'feltro** sm felt.

**'femmina** sf (ZOOL, TECN) female; (figlia) girl, daughter; (spesso peg) woman; **femmi'nile** ag feminine; (sesso) female; (lavoro, giornale, *moda*) woman's // *sm* (*LING*) feminine; **femmi'nismo** *sm* feminism.

**'fendere** *vt* to cut through; **fendi'nebbia** *sm inv* (*AUT*) fog lamp.

**fe'nomeno** *sm* phenomenon.

**'feretro** *sm* coffin.

**feri'ale** *ag* working *cpd*, work *cpd*, week *cpd*; **giorno ~** weekday.

**'ferie** *sfpl* holidays (*Brit*), vacation *sg* (*US*); **andare in ~** to go on holiday *o* vacation.

**fe'rire** *vt* to injure; (*deliberatamente*: *MIL etc*) to wound; (*colpire*) to hurt; **fe'rito, a** *sm/f* wounded *o* injured man/woman // *sf* injury; wound.

**'ferma** *sf* (*MIL*) (period of) service; (*CACCIA*): **cane da ~** pointer.

**fer'maglio** [fer'maʎʎo] *sm* clasp; (*gioiello*) brooch; (*per documenti*) clip.

**fer'mare** *vt* to stop, halt; (*POLIZIA*) to detain, hold; (*bottone etc*) to fasten, fix // *vi* to stop; **~rsi** *vr* to stop, halt; **~rsi a fare qc** to stop to do sth.

**fer'mata** *sf* stop; **~ dell'autobus** bus stop.

**fer'mento** *sm* (*anche fig*) ferment; (*lievito*) yeast.

**fer'mezza** [fer'mettsa] *sf* (*fig*) firmness, steadfastness.

**'fermo, a** *ag* still, motionless; (*veicolo*) stationary; (*orologio*) not working; (*saldo*: *anche fig*) firm; (*voce, mano*) steady // *escl* stop!; keep still! // *sm* (*chiusura*) catch, lock; (*DIR*): **~ di polizia** police detention.

**'fermo 'posta** *av, sm inv* poste restante (*Brit*), general delivery (*US*).

**fe'roce** [fe'rotʃe] *ag* (*animale*) wild, fierce, ferocious; (*persona*) cruel, fierce; (*fame, dolore*) raging.

**ferra'gosto** *sm* (*festa*) feast of the Assumption; (*periodo*) August holidays *pl*.

**ferra'menta** *sfpl* ironmongery *sg*

(*Brit*), hardware *sg*; **negozio di ~** ironmonger's (*Brit*), hardware shop *o* store (*US*).

**fer'rato, a** *ag* (*FERR*): **strada ~a** railway (*Brit*) *o* railroad (*US*) line; (*fig*): **essere ~ in** to be well up in.

**'ferreo, a** *ag* iron *cpd*.

**'ferro** *sm* iron; **una bistecca ai ~i** a grilled steak; **~ battuto** wrought iron; **~ da calza** knitting needle; **~ di cavallo** horseshoe; **~ da stiro** iron.

**ferro'via** *sf* railway (*Brit*), railroad (*US*); **ferrovi'ario, a** *ag* railway *cpd* (*Brit*), railroad *cpd* (*US*); **ferrovi'ere** *sm* railwayman (*Brit*), railroad man (*US*).

**'fertile** *ag* fertile; **fertiliz'zante** *sm* fertilizer.

**'fervido, a** *ag* fervent.

**fer'vore** *sm* fervour, ardour; (*punto culminante*) height.

**'fesso** *ag pp di* **fendere** // *ag* (*fam*: *sciocco*) crazy, cracked.

**fes'sura** *sf* crack, split; (*per gettone, moneta*) slot.

**'festa** *sf* (*religiosa*) feast; (*pubblica*) holiday; (*compleanno*) birthday; (*onomastico*) name day; (*ricevimento*) celebration, party; **far ~ a qn** to welcome sb; (*ricevimento*) celebration, party; **far ~ a** to give sb a warm welcome.

**festeggi'are** [fested'dʒare] *vt* to celebrate; (*persona*) to have a celebration for.

**fes'tino** *sm* party; (*con balli*) ball.

**fes'tivo, a** *ag* (*atmosfera*) festive; **giorno ~** holiday.

**fes'toso, a** *ag* merry, joyful.

**fe'ticcio** [fe'tittʃo] *sm* fetish.

**'feto** *sm* foetus (*Brit*), fetus (*US*).

**'fetta** *sf* slice.

**fettuc'cine** [fettut'tʃine] *sfpl* (*CUC*) ribbon-shaped pasta.

**FF.SS.** *abbr* = **Ferrovie dello Stato.**

**fi'aba** *sf* fairy tale.

**fi'acca** *sf* weariness; (*svogliatezza*) listlessness.

**fiac'care** *vt* to weaken.

**fi'acco, a, chi, che** ag (stanco) tired, weary; (svogliato) listless; (debole) weak; (mercato) slack.

**fi'accola** sf torch.

**fi'ala** sf phial.

**fi'amma** sf flame.

**fiam'mante** ag (colore) flaming; **nuovo** ~ brand new.

**fiammeggi'are** [fjammed'dʒare] vi to blaze.

**fiam'mifero** sm match.

**fiam'mingo, a, ghi, ghe** ag Flemish // sm/f Fleming // sm (LING) Flemish; (ZOOL) flamingo; **i F~ghi** the Flemish.

**fiancheggi'are** [fjanked'dʒare] vt to border; (fig) to support, back (up); (MIL) to flank.

**fi'anco, chi** sm side; (MIL) flank; **di** ~ sideways, from the side; **a** ~ **a** ~ side by side.

**fi'asco, schi** sm flask; (fig) fiasco; **fare** ~ to be a fiasco.

**fi'ato** sm breath; (resistenza) stamina; **avere il** ~ **grosso** to be out of breath; **prendere** ~ to catch one's breath; ~**i** smpl (MUS) wind instruments; **strumento a** ~ wind instrument.

**'fibbia** sf buckle.

**'fibra** sf fibre; (fig) constitution.

**fic'care** vt to push, thrust, drive; ~**rsi** vr (andare a finire) to get to.

**'fico, chi** sm (pianta) fig tree; (frutto) fig; ~ **d'India** prickly pear; ~ **secco** dried fig.

**fidanza'mento** [fidantsa'mento] sm engagement.

**fidan'zarsi** [fidan'tsarsi] vr to get engaged; **fidan'zato, a** sm/f fiancé/ fiancée.

**fi'darsi** vr: ~ **di** to trust; **fi'dato, a** ag reliable, trustworthy.

**'fido, a** ag faithful, loyal // sm (COMM) credit.

**fi'ducia** [fi'dutʃa] sf confidence, trust; **incarico di** ~ position of trust, responsible position; **persona di** ~ reliable person.

**fi'ele** sm (MED) bile; (fig) bitterness.

**fie'nile** sm barn; hayloft.

**fi'eno** sm hay.

**fi'era** sf fair.

**fie'rezza** [fje'rettsa] sf pride.

**fi'ero, a** ag proud; (crudele) fierce, cruel; (audace) bold.

**'fifa** sf (fam): **aver** ~ to have the jitters.

**'figlia** ['fiʎʎa] sf daughter.

**figli'astro, a** [fiʎ'ʎastro] sm/f stepson/daughter.

**'figlio** ['fiʎʎo] sm son; (senza distinzione di sesso) child; ~ **di papà** spoilt, wealthy young man; ~ **unico** only child; **figli'occio, a, ci, ce** sm/f godchild, godson/daughter.

**fi'gura** sf figure; (forma, aspetto esterno) form, shape; (illustrazione) picture, illustration; **far** ~ to look smart; **fare una brutta** ~ to make a bad impression.

**figu'rare** vi to appear // vt: ~**rsi qc** to imagine sth; ~**rsi** vr: **figurati!** imagine that!; **ti do noia?** — **ma figurati!** am I disturbing you? — not at all!

**figura'tivo, a** ag figurative.

**figu'rina** sf figurine; (cartoncino) picture card.

**'fila** sf row, line; (coda) queue; (serie) series, string; **di** ~ in succession; **fare la** ~ to queue; **in** ~ **indiana** in single file.

**filantro'pia** sf philanthropy.

**fi'lare** vt to spin // vi (baco, ragno) to spin; (formaggio fuso) to go stringy; (discorso) to hang together; (fam: amoreggiare) to go steady; (muoversi a forte velocità) to go at full speed; (: andarsene lestamente) to make o.s. scarce; ~ **diritto** (fig) to toe the line.

**filas'trocca, che** sf nursery rhyme.

**filate'lia** sf philately, stamp collecting.

**fi'lato, a** ag spun // sm yarn; **3 giorni** ~**i** 3 days running o on end; **fila'tura** sf spinning; (luogo) spinning mill.

**fi'letto** sm (di vite) thread; (di

*carne*) fillet.

**fili'ale** *ag* filial // *sf* (*di impresa*) branch.

**fili'grana** *sf* (*in oreficeria*) filigree; (*su carta*) watermark.

**film** *sm inv* film; **fil'mare** *vt* to film.

**'filo** *sm* (*anche fig*) thread; (*filato*) yarn; (*metallico*) wire; (*di lana, rasoio*) edge; **per ~ e per segno** in detail; ~ **d'erba** blade of grass; ~ **di perle** string of pearls; ~ **spinato** barbed wire; **con un ~ di voce** in a whisper.

**'filobus** *sm inv* trolley bus.

**filon'cino** [filon'tʃino] *sm* ≈ French stick.

**fi'lone** *sm* (*di minerali*) seam, vein; (*pane*) ≈ Vienna loaf; (*fig*) trend.

**filoso'fia** *sf* philosophy; **fi'losofo, a** *sm/f* philosopher.

**fil'trare** *vt, vi* to filter.

**'filtro** *sm* filter; ~ **dell'olio** (*AUT*) oil filter.

**'filza** ['filtsa] *sf* (*anche fig*) string.

**fin** *av, prep* = **fino.**

**fi'nale** *ag* final // *sm* (*di opera*) end, ending; (: *MUS*) finale // *sf* (*SPORT*) final; **finalità** *sf* (*scopo*) aim, purpose; **final'mente** *av* finally, at last.

**fi'nanza** [fi'nantsa] *sf* finance; ~**e** *sfpl* (*di individuo, Stato*) finances; **finanzi'ario, a** *ag* financial; **finanzi'ere** *sm* financier; (*guardia di finanza: doganale*) customs officer; (: *tributaria*) inland revenue official.

**finché** [fin'ke] *cong* (*per tutto il tempo che*) as long as; (*fino al momento in cui*) until; **aspetta ~ io (non) sia ritornato** wait until I get back.

**'fine** *ag* (*lamina, carta*) thin; (*capelli, polvere*) fine; (*vista, udito*) keen, sharp; (*persona: raffinata*) refined, distinguished; (*osservazione*) subtle // *sf* end // *sm* aim, purpose; (*esito*) result, outcome; **secondo ~** ulterior motive; **in ~ alla ~** in the end, finally; ~ **settimana** *sm o f inv* weekend.

**fi'nestra** *sf* window; **fines'trino** *sm* (*di treno, auto*) window.

**'fingere** ['findʒere] *vt* to feign; (*supporre*) to imagine, suppose; ~**rsi** *vr:* ~**rsi ubriaco/pazzo** to pretend to be drunk/mad; ~ **di fare** to pretend to do.

**fini'mondo** *sm* pandemonium.

**fi'nire** *vt* (*lavoro*) // *vi* to finish, end; ~ **di fare** (*compiere*) to finish doing; (*smettere*) to stop doing; ~ **in galera** to end up o finish up in prison; **fini'tura** *sf* finish.

**finlan'dese** *ag, sm* (*LING*) Finnish // *sm/f* Finn.

**Fin'landia** *sf:* **la** ~ Finland.

**'fino, a** *ag* (*capelli, seta*) fine; (*oro*) pure; (*fig: acuto*) shrewd // *av* (*spesso troncato in* **fin**: pure, anche even // *prep* (*spesso troncato in* **fin:** tempo)) **fin quando?** till when?; (: *luogo*) **fin qui** as far as here; ~ **a** (*tempo*) until, till; (*luogo*) as far as, (up) to; **fin da domani** from tomorrow onwards; **fin da ieri** since yesterday; **fin dalla nascita** from o since birth.

**fi'nocchio** [fi'nɔkkjo] *sm* fennel; (*fam peg: pederasta*) queer.

**fi'nora** *av* up till now.

**'finto, a** *pp di* **fingere** // *ag* false; artificial // *sf* pretence, sham; (*SPORT*) feint; **far ~a (di fare)** to pretend (to do).

**finzi'one** [fin'tsjone] *sf* pretence, sham.

**fi'occo, chi** *sm* (*di nastro*) bow; (*di stoffa, lana*) flock; (*di neve*) flake; (*NAUT*) jib; **coi ~chi** (*fig*) first-rate; **~chi di granoturco** cornflakes.

**fi'ocina** ['fjɔtʃina] *sf* harpoon.

**fi'oco, a, chi, che** *ag* faint, dim.

**fi'onda** *sf* catapult.

**fio'raio, a** *sm/f* florist.

**fi'ore** *sm* flower; ~**i** *smpl* (*CARTE*) clubs; **a fior d'acqua** on the surface of the water; **avere i nervi a fior di pelle** to be on edge.

**fioren'tino, a** *ag* Florentine.

**fio'retto** *sm* (*SCHERMA*) foil.

**fio'rire** vi (rosa) to flower; (albero) to blossom; (fig) to flourish.

**Fi'renze** [fi'rɛntse] sf Florence.

**'firma** sf signature; (reputazione) name.

**fir'mare** vt to sign.

**fisar'monica, che** sf accordion.

**fis'cale** ag fiscal, tax cpd; **medico ~** doctor employed by Social Security to verify cases of sick leave.

**fischi'are** [fis'kjare] vi to whistle // vt to whistle; (attore) to boo, hiss.

**'fischio** ['fiskjo] sm whistle.

**'fisco** sm tax authorities pl, ≈ Inland Revenue (Brit), ≈ Internal Revenue Service (US).

**'fisico, a, ci, che** ag physical // sm/f physicist // sm physique // sf physics sg.

**fisiolo'gia** [fizjolo'dʒia] sf physiology.

**fisiono'mia** sf face, physiognomy.

**fisiotera'pia** sf physiotherapy.

**fis'sare** vt to fix, fasten; (guardare intensamente) to stare at; (data, condizioni) to fix, establish, set; (prenotare) to book; **~rsi su** (sog: sguardo, attenzione) to focus on; (fig: idea) to become obsessed with; **fissazi'one** sf (PSIC) fixation.

**'fisso, a** ag fixed; (stipendio, impiego) regular // av: **guardare ~** qc/qn to stare at sth/sb.

**'fitta, a** vedi **fitto**.

**fit'tizio, a** ag fictitious, imaginary.

**'fitto, a** ag thick, dense; (pioggia) heavy // sm depths pl, middle; (affitto, pigione) rent // sf sharp pain.

**fi'ume** sm river.

**fiu'tare** vt to smell, sniff; (sog: animale) to scent; (fig: inganno) to get wind of, smell; **~ tabacco/cocaina** to take snuff/cocaine; **fi'uto** sm (sense of) smell; (fig) nose.

**fla'gello** [fla'dʒɛllo] sm scourge.

**fla'grante** ag flagrant; **cogliere qn in ~** to catch sb red-handed.

**fla'nella** sf flannel.

**flash** [flaʃ] sm inv (FOT) flash; (giornalistico) newsflash.

**'flauto** sm flute.

**'flebile** ag faint, feeble.

**'flemma** sf (calma) coolness, phlegm; (MED) phlegm.

**fles'sibile** ag pliable; (fig: che si adatta) flexible.

**'flesso, a** pp di **flettere**.

**flessu'oso, a** ag supple, lithe; (andatura) flowing, graceful.

**'flettere** vt to bend.

**F.lli** abbr (= fratelli) Bros.

**'flora** sf flora.

**'florido, a** ag flourishing; (fig) glowing with health.

**'floscio, a, sci, sce** ['flɔʃʃo] ag (cappello) floppy, soft; (muscoli) flabby.

**'flotta** sf fleet.

**'fluido, a** ag, sm fluid.

**flu'ire** vi to flow.

**flu'oro** sm fluorine.

**fluo'ruro** sm fluoride.

**'flusso** sm flow; (FISICA, MED) flux; **~ e riflusso** ebb and flow.

**fluttu'are** vi to rise and fall; (ECON) to fluctuate.

**fluvi'ale** ag river cpd, fluvial.

**'foca, che** sf (ZOOL) seal.

**fo'caccia, ce** [fo'kattʃa] sf kind of pizza; (dolce) bun.

**'foce** ['fotʃe] sf (GEO) mouth.

**foco'laio** sm (MED) centre of infection; (fig) hotbed.

**foco'lare** sm hearth, fireside; (TECN) furnace.

**'fodera** sf (di vestito) lining; (di libro, poltrona) cover; **fode'rare** vt to line; to cover.

**'fodero** sm (di spada) scabbard; (di pugnale) sheath; (di pistola) holster.

**'foga** sf enthusiasm, ardour.

**'foggia, ge** ['fɔddʒa] sf (maniera) style; (aspetto) form, shape; (moda) fashion, style.

**'foglia** sf leaf; **~ d'argento/d'oro** silver/gold leaf; **fogli'ame** sm foliage, leaves pl.

**'foglio** ['fɔʎʎo] sm (di carta) sheet (of paper); (di metallo) sheet; (documento) document; (banconota) (bank)note; ~ **rosa** (AUT) provisional licence; ~ **di via** (DIR) expulsion order; ~ **volante** pamphlet.

'**fogna** ['foɲɲa] sf drain, sewer; **fogna'tura** sf drainage, sewerage.

**folgo'rare** vt (sog: fulmine) to strike down; (: alta tensione) to electrocute.

'**folla** sf crowd, throng.

'**folle** ag mad, insane; (TECN) idle; **in** ~ (AUT) in neutral.

**fol'lia** sf folly, foolishness; foolish act; (pazzia) madness, lunacy.

'**folto, a** ag thick.

**fomen'tare** vt to stir up, foment.

**fondamen'tale** ag fundamental, basic.

**fonda'mento** sm foundation; ~**a** sfpl (EDIL) foundations.

**fon'dare** vt to found; (fig: dar base): ~ **qc su** to base sth on; **fondazi'one** sf foundation.

'**fondere** vt (neve) to melt; (metallo) to fuse, melt; (fig: colori) to merge, blend; (: insieme, gruppi to merge // vi to melt; ~**rsi** vr to melt; (fig: partiti, correnti) to unite, merge; **fonde'ria** sf foundry.

'**fondo, a** ag deep // sm (di recipiente, pozzo) bottom; (di stanza) back; (quantità di liquido che resta, deposito) dregs pl; (sfondo) background; (unità immobiliare) property, estate; (somma di denaro) fund; (SPORT) long-distance race; ~**i** smpl (denaro) funds; **a notte** ~**a** at dead of night; **in** ~ **a** at the bottom of; at the back of; (strada) at the end of; **andare a** ~ (nave) to sink; **conoscere a** ~ to know inside out; **dar** ~ **a** (fig: provviste, soldi) to use up; **in** ~ (fig) after all, all things considered; **andare fino in** ~ **a** (fig) to examine thoroughly; **a** ~ **perduto** (COMM) without security; ~**i di caffè** coffee grounds; ~**i di magazzino** old o unsold stock sg.

**fo'netica** sf phonetics sg.

**fon'tana** sf fountain.

'**fonte** sf spring, source; (fig) source

// sm: ~ **battesimale** (REL) font.

**fo'raggio** [fo'raddʒo] sm fodder, forage.

**fo'rare** vt to pierce, make a hole in; (pallone) to burst; (biglietto) to punch; ~ **una gomma** to burst a tyre (Brit) o tire (US).

'**forbici** ['fɔrbitʃi] sfpl scissors.

'**forca, che** sf (AGR) fork, pitchfork; (patibolo) gallows sg.

**for'cella** [for'tʃella] sf (TECN) fork; (di monte) pass.

**for'chetta** [for'ketta] sf fork.

**for'cina** [for'tʃina] sf hairpin.

'**forcipe** ['fɔrtʃipe] sm forceps pl.

**fo'resta** sf forest.

**foresti'ero, a** ag foreign // sm/f foreigner.

'**forfora** sf dandruff.

'**forgia, ge** ['fɔrdʒa] sf forge; **forgi'are** vt to forge.

'**forma** sf form; (aspetto esteriore) form, shape; (DIR: procedura) procedure; (per calzature) last; (stampo da cucina) mould; ~**e** sfpl (del corpo) figure, shape; **le** ~**e** (convenzioni) appearances; **essere in** ~ to be in good shape.

**formag'gino** [formad'dʒino] sm processed cheese.

**for'maggio** [for'maddʒo] sm cheese.

**for'male** ag formal; **formalità** sf inv formality.

**for'mare** vt to form, shape, make; (numero di telefono) to dial; (fig: carattere) to form, mould; ~**rsi** vr to form, take shape; **for'mato** sm format, size; **formazi'one** sf formation; (fig: educazione) training.

**for'mica, che** sf ant; **formi'caio** sm anthill.

**formico'lare** vi (gamba, braccio) to tingle; (brulicare: anche fig): ~ **di** to be swarming with; **mi formicola la gamba** I've got pins and needles in my leg, my leg's tingling; **formico'lio** sm pins and needles pl; swarming.

**formi'dabile** ag powerful, formidable; (straordinario) remarkable.

'**formula** sf formula; ~ **di cortesia** courtesy form.

**formu'lare** vt to formulate; to express.

for'nace [for'natʃe] sf (per laterizi etc) kiln; (per metalli) furnace.

for'naio sm baker.

for'nello sm (elettrico, a gas) ring; (di pipa) bowl.

for'nire vt: ~ qn di qc, ~ qc a qn to provide o supply sb with sth, to supply sth to sb.

'**forno** sm (di cucina) oven; (panetteria) bakery; (TECN: per calce etc) kiln; (: per metalli) furnace.

'**foro** sm (buco) hole; (STORIA) forum; (tribunale) (law) court.

'**forse** av perhaps, maybe; (circa) about; essere in ~ to be in doubt.

forsen'nato, a ag mad, insane.

'**forte** ag strong; (suono) loud; (spesa) considerable, great; (passione, dolore) great, deep // av strongly; (velocemente) fast; (a voce alta) loud(ly); (violentemente) hard // sm (edificio) fort; (specialità) forte, strong point; essere ~ in qc to be good at sth.

for'tezza [for'tettsa] sf (morale) strength; (luogo fortificato) fortress.

for'tuito, a ag fortuitous, chance.

for'tuna sf (destino) fortune, luck; (buona sorte) success, fortune; (eredità, averi) fortune; per ~ luckily, fortunately; di ~ makeshift, improvised: atterraggio di ~ emergency landing; fortu'nato, a ag lucky, fortunate; (coronato da successo) successful.

forvi'are vt, vi = fuorviare.

'**forza** ['fɔrtsa] sf strength; (potere) power; (FISICA) force; ~e sfpl (fisiche) strength sg; (MIL) forces // escl come on!; per ~ against one's will; (naturalmente) of course; a viva ~ by force; a ~ di by dint of; ~ maggiore circumstances beyond one's control; la ~ pubblica the police pl; le ~e armate the armed

forces.

for'zare [for'tsare] vt to force; ~ qn a fare qc to force sb to do; for'zato, a ag forced // sm (DIR) prisoner sentenced to hard labour.

fos'chia [fos'kia] sf mist, haze.

'**fosco, a, schi, sche** ag dark, gloomy.

'**fosforo** sm phosphorous.

'**fossa** sf pit; (di cimitero) grave; ~ biologica septic tank.

fos'sato sm ditch; (di fortezza) moat.

fos'setta sf dimple.

'**fossile** ag, sm fossil.

'**fosso** sm ditch; (MIL) trench.

'**foto** sf photo // prefisso: foto'copia sf photocopy; fotocopi'are vt to photocopy; fotogra'fare vt to photograph; fotogra'fia sf (procedimento) photography; (immagine) photograph; fare una fotografia to take a photograph; una fotografia a colori/in bianco e nero a colour/black and white photograph; fo'tografo, a smf photographer; fotoro'manzo sm romantic picture story.

fra prep = tra.

fracas'sare vt to shatter, smash; ~rsi vr to shatter, smash; (veicolo) to crash; fra'casso sm smash; crash; (baccano) din, racket.

'**fradicio, a, ci, ce** ['fraditʃo] ag (molto bagnato) soaking (wet); ubriaco ~ blind drunk.

'**fragile** ['fradʒile] ag fragile; (fig: salute) delicate.

'**fragola** sf strawberry.

fra'gore sm roar; (di tuono) rumble. frago'roso, a ag deafening.

fra'grante ag fragrant.

frain'tendere vt to misunderstand; frain'teso, a pp di fraintendere.

fram'mento sm fragment.

'**frana** sf landslide; (fig: persona): essere una ~ to be useless; fra'nare vi to slip, slide down.

fran'cese [fran'tʃeze] ag French // smf Frenchman/woman // sm (LING)

French; **i F~i** the French.

**fran'chezza** [fran'kettsa] *sf* frankness, openness.

'**Francia** ['frantʃa] *sf*: **la ~** France.

'**franco, a, chi, che** *ag* (COMM) free; (*sincero*) frank, open, sincere // *sm* (*moneta*) franc; **farla ~a** (*fig*) to get off scot-free; **~ di dogana** duty-free; **~ a domicilio** delivered free of charge; **prezzo ~ fabbrica** ex-works price; **~ tiratore** *sm* sniper.

**franco'bollo** *sm* (postage) stamp.

**fran'gente** [fran'dʒɛnte] *sm* (*onda*) breaker; (*scoglio emergente*) reef; (*circostanza*) situation, circumstance.

'**frangia, ge** ['frandʒa] *sf* fringe.

**frantu'mare** *vt*, **~rsi** *vr* to break into pieces, shatter.

**frap'pé** *sm* milk shake.

'**frasca, sche** *sf* (leafy) branch.

'**frase** *sf* (LING) sentence; (*locuzione, espressione, MUS*) phrase; **~ fatta** set phrase.

'**frassino** *sm* ash (tree).

**frastagli'ato, a** [frastaʎ'ʎato] *ag* (*costa*) indented, jagged.

**frastor'nare** *vt* to daze; to befuddle.

**frastu'ono** *sm* hubbub, din.

'**frate** *sm* friar, monk.

**fratel'lanza** [fratel'lantsa] *sf* brotherhood; (*associazione*) fraternity.

**fratel'lastro** *sm* stepbrother.

**fra'tello** *sm* brother; **~i** *smpl* brothers; (*nel senso di fratelli e sorelle*) brothers and sisters.

**fra'terno, a** *ag* fraternal, brotherly.

**frat'tanto** *av* in the meantime, meanwhile.

**frat'tempo** *sm*: **nel ~** in the meantime, meanwhile.

**frat'tura** *sf* fracture; (*fig*) split, break.

**frazi'one** [frat'tsjone] *sf* fraction; (*borgata*): **~ di comune** hamlet.

'**freccia, ce** ['frettʃa] *sf* arrow; **~ di direzione** (AUT) indicator.

**fred'dare** *vt* to shoot dead.

**fred'dezza** [fred'dettsa] *sf* coldness.

'**freddo, a** *ag, sm* cold; **fa ~** it's cold; **aver ~** to be cold; **a ~** (*fig*)

deliberately; **freddo'loso, a** *ag* sensitive to the cold.

**fred'dura** *sf* pun.

**fre'gare** *vt* to rub; (*fam: truffare*) to take in, cheat; (: *rubare*) to swipe, pinch; **fregarsene** (*fam!*): **chi se ne frega?** who gives a damn (about it)?

**fre'gata** *sf* rub; (*fam*) swindle; (NAUT) frigate.

'**fregio** ['frɛdʒo] *sm* (ARCHIT) frieze; (*ornamento*) decoration.

'**fremere** *vi*: **~ di** to tremble o quiver with; '**fremito** *sm* tremor, quiver.

**fre'nare** *vt* (*veicolo*) to slow down; (*cavallo*) to rein in; (*lacrime*) to restrain, hold back // *vi* to brake; **~rsi** *vr* (*fig*) to restrain o.s., control o.s.; **fre'nata** *sf*: **fare una frenata** to brake.

**frene'sia** *sf* frenzy.

'**freno** *sm* brake; (*morso*) bit; **~ a disco** disc brake; **~ a mano** handbrake; **tenere a ~** to restrain.

**frequen'tare** *vt* (*scuola, corso*) to attend; (*locale, bar*) to go to, frequent; (*persone*) to see (often).

**fre'quente** *ag* frequent; **di ~** frequently; **fre'quenza** *sf* frequency; (INS) attendance.

**fres'chezza** [fres'kettsa] *sf* freshness.

'**fresco, a, schi, sche** *ag* fresh; (*temperatura*) cool; (*notizia*) recent, fresh // *sm*: **godere il ~** to enjoy the cool air; **stare ~** (*fig*) to be in for it; **mettere al ~** to put in a cool place.

'**fretta** *sf* hurry, haste; **in ~** a hurry; **in ~ e furia** in a mad rush; **aver ~** to be in a hurry; **fretto'loso, a** *ag* (*persona*) in a hurry; (*lavoro etc*) hurried, rushed.

**fri'abile** *ag* (*terreno*) friable; (*pasta*) crumbly.

**friggere** ['friddʒere] *vt* to fry // *vi* (*olio etc*) to sizzle.

'**frigido, a** ['fridʒido] *ag* (MED) frigid.

'**frigo** *sm* fridge.

**frigo'rifero, a** *ag* refrigerating // *sm*

refrigerator.

**fringu'ello** *sm* chaffinch.

**frit'tata** *sf* omelette; **fare una ~** *(fig)* to make a mess of things.

**frit'tella** *sf (CUC)* pancake; (: *ripiena)* fritter.

**'fritto, a** *pp di* **friggere** // *ag* fried // *sm* fried food; **~ misto** mixed fry.

**frit'tura** *sf (CUC)*: **~ di pesce** mixed fried fish.

**'frivolo, a** *ag* frivolous.

**frizi'one** [frit'tsjone] *sf* friction; (*di pelle)* rub, rub-down; *(AUT)* clutch.

**friz'zante** [frid'dzante] *ag (anche fig)* sparkling.

**'frizzo** ['friddzo] *sm* witticism.

**fro'dare** *vt* to defraud, cheat.

**'frode** *sf* fraud; **~ fiscale** tax evasion.

**'frollo, a** *ag (carne)* tender; (: *di selvaggina)* high; *(fig: persona)* soft; **pasta ~a** short(crust) pastry.

**'fronda** *sf* (leafy) branch; *(di partito politico)* internal opposition; **~e** *sfpl* foliage *sg*.

**fron'tale** *ag* frontal; *(scontro)* head-on.

**'fronte** *sf (ANAT)* forehead; *(di edificio)* front, façade // *sm (MIL, POL, METEOR)* front; **a ~, di ~** facing, opposite; **di ~ a** *(posizione)* opposite, facing, in front of; *(a paragone di)* compared with.

**fronteggi'are** [fronted'dʒare] *vt (avversari, difficoltà)* to face, stand up to; *(spese)* to cope with.

**fronti'era** *sf* border, frontier.

**'fronzolo** ['frondzolo] *sm* frill.

**'frottola** *sf* fib; **~e** *sfpl* nonsense *sg*.

**fru'gare** *vi* to rummage // *vt* to search.

**frul'lare** *vt (CUC)* to whisk // *vi (uccelli)* to flutter; **frul'lato** *sm* milk shake; fruit drink; **frulla'tore** *sm* electric mixer; **frul'lino** *sm* whisk.

**fru'mento** *sm* wheat.

**fru'scio** [fruʃʃio] *sm* rustle; rustling; *(di acque)* murmur.

**'frusta** *sf* whip; *(CUC)* whisk.

**frus'tare** *vt* to whip.

**frus'tino** *sm* riding crop.

**frus'trare** *vt* to frustrate.

**'frutta** *sf* fruit; *(portata)* dessert; **~ candita/secca** candied/dried fruit.

**frut'tare** *vi* to bear dividends, give a return.

**frut'teto** *sm* orchard.

**frutti'vendolo, a** *sm/f* greengrocer *(Brit)*, produce dealer *(US)*.

**'frutto** *sm* fruit; *(fig: risultato)* result(s); *(ECON: interesse)* interest; (: *reddito)* income; **~i di mare** seafood *sg*.

**FS** *abbr = Ferrovie dello Stato.*

**fu** *vb vedi* **essere** // *ag inv*: **il ~ Paolo Bianchi** the late Paolo Bianchi.

**fuci'lare** [futʃi'lare] *vt* to shoot; **fuci'lata** *sf* rifle shot.

**fu'cile** [fu'tʃile] *sm* rifle, gun; *(da caccia)* shotgun, gun.

**fu'cina** [fu'tʃina] *sf* forge.

**'fuga** *sf* escape, flight; *(di gas, liquidi)* leak; *(MUS)* fugue; **~ di cervelli** brain drain.

**fu'gace** [fu'gatʃe] *ag* fleeting, transient.

**fug'gevole** [fud'dʒevole] *ag* fleeting.

**fuggi'asco, a, schi, sche** [fudd'ʒasko] *ag, sm/f* fugitive.

**fuggi'fuggi** [fuddʒi'fuddʒi] *sm* scramble, stampede.

**fug'gire** [fud'dʒire] *vi* to flee, run away; *(fig: passar veloce)* to fly // *vt* to avoid; **fuggi'tivo, a** *sm/f* fugitive, runaway.

**ful'gore** *sm* brilliance, splendour.

**fu'liggine** [fu'liddʒine] *sf* soot.

**fulmi'nare** *vt (sog: fulmine)* to strike; (: *elettricità)* to electrocute; *(con arma da fuoco)* to shoot dead; *(fig: con lo sguardo)* to look daggers at.

**'fulmine** *sm* thunderbolt; lightning *q.*

**fumai'olo** *sm (di nave)* funnel; *(di fabbrica)* chimney.

**fu'mare** *vi* to smoke; *(emettere vapore)* to steam // *vt* to smoke; **fu'mata** *sf (segnale)* smoke signal;

farsi una **fumata** to have a smoke; **fuma'tore, 'trice** sm/f smoker.

**fu'metto** sm comic strip; **~i** smpl comics.

**'fumo** sm smoke; (vapore) steam; (il fumare tabacco) smoking; **~i** smpl fumes; **i ~i dell'alcool** the after-effects of drink; **vendere ~** to deceive, cheat; **fu'moso, a** ag smoky; (fig) muddled.

**fu'nambolo, a** sm/f tightrope walker.

**'fune** sf rope, cord; (più grossa) cable.

**'funebre** ag (rito) funeral; (aspetto) gloomy, funereal.

**fune'rale** sm funeral.

**'fungere** ['fundʒere] vi: **~ da** to act as.

**'fungo, ghi** sm fungus; (commestibile) mushroom; **~ velenoso** toadstool.

**funico'lare** sf funicular railway.

**funi'via** sf cable railway.

**funzio'nare** [funtsjo'nare] vi to work, function; (fungere): **~ da** to act as.

**funzio'nario** [funtsjo'narjo] sm official.

**funzi'one** [fun'tsjone] sf function; (carica) post, position; (REL) service; **in ~** (meccanismo) in operation; **in ~ di** (come) as; **fare la ~ di qn** (farne le veci) to take sb's place.

**fu'oco, chi** sm fire; (fornello) ring; (FOT, FISICA) focus; **dare ~ a qc** to set fire to sth; **far ~** (sparare) to fire; **~ d'artificio** firework.

**fuorché** [fwor'ke] cong, prep except.

**fu'ori** av outside; (all'aperto) outdoors, outside; (fuori di casa, SPORT) out; (esclamativo) get out! // prep: **~** (di) out of, outside // sm outside; **lasciar ~ qc/qn** to leave sth/sb out; **far ~ qn** (fam) to kill sb, do sb in; **essere ~ di sé** to be beside o.s.; **~ luogo** (inopportuno) out of place, uncalled for; **~ mano** out of the way, remote; **~ pericolo** out of danger; **~ uso** old-fashioned; obsolete.

**fu'ori... prefisso: fuori'bordo** sm inv speedboat (with outboard motor); outboard motor; **fuori'classe** sm/f inv (undisputed) champion; **fuorigi'oco** sm offside; **fuori'legge** sm/f inv outlaw; **fuori'serie** ag inv (auto etc) custom-built // sf custom-built car; **fuori'strada** sm (AUT) cross-country vehicle; **fuoru'scito, a, fuoriu'scito, a** sm/f exile; **fuorvi'are** vt to mislead; (fig) to lead astray // vi to go astray.

**'furbo, a** ag clever, smart; (peg) cunning.

**fu'rente** ag: **~ (contro)** furious (with).

**fur'fante** sm rascal, scoundrel.

**fur'gone** sm van.

**'furia** sf (ira) fury, rage; (fig: impeto) fury, violence; (fretta) rush; **a ~ di** by dint of; **andare su tutte le ~e** to get into a towering rage; **furi'oso, a** ag furious; (mare, vento) raging.

**fu'rore** sm fury; (esaltazione) frenzy; **far ~** to be all the rage.

**fur'tivo, a** ag furtive.

**'furto** sm theft; **~ con scasso** burglary.

**'fusa** sfpl: **fare le ~** to purr.

**fu'sibile** sm (ELETTR) fuse.

**fusi'one** sf (di metalli) fusion, melting; (colata) casting; (COMM) merger; (fig) merging.

**'fuso, a** pp di **fondere** // sm (FILATURA) spindle; **~ orario** time zone.

**fu'stagno** [fus'taɲɲo] sm corduroy.

**fus'tino** sm (di detersivo) tub.

**'fusto** sm stem; (ANAT, di albero) trunk; (recipiente) drum, can.

**fu'turo, a** ag, sm future.

# G

**gab'bare** *vt* to take in, dupe; ~**rsi** *vr*: ~**rsi di qn** to make fun of sb.

**'gabbia** *sf* cage; (*DIR*) dock; (*da imballaggio*) crate; ~ **dell'ascensore lift** (*Brit*) o elevator (*US*) shaft; ~ **toracica** (*ANAT*) rib cage.

**gabbi'ano** *sm* (sea)gull.

**gabi'netto** *sm* (*MED etc*) consulting room; (*POL*) ministry; (*di decenza*) toilet, lavatory; (*INS: di fisica etc*) laboratory.

**'gaffe** [gaf] *sf inv* blunder.

**gagli'ardo, a** [gaʎ'ʎardo] *ag* strong, vigorous.

**'gaio, a** *ag* cheerful, gay.

**'gala** *sf* (*sfarzo*) pomp; (*festa*) gala.

**ga'lante** *ag* gallant, courteous; (*avventura*) amorous; **galante'ria** *sf* gallantry.

**galantu'omo,** *pl* **galantu'omini** *sm* gentleman.

**ga'lassia** *sf* galaxy.

**gala'teo** *sm* (good) manners *pl*.

**gale'otto** *sm* (*rematore*) galley slave; (*carcerato*) convict.

**ga'lera** *sf* (*NAUT*) galley; (*prigione*) prison.

**'galla** *sf*: **a ~** afloat; **venire a ~** to surface, come to the surface; (*fig: verità*) to come out.

**galleggi'ante** [galled'dʒante] *ag* floating // *sm* (*natante*) barge; (*di pescatore, lenza, TECN*) float.

**galleggi'are** [galled'dʒare] *vi* to float.

**galle'ria** *sf* (*traforo*) tunnel; (*ARCHIT, d'arte*) gallery; (*TEATRO*) circle; (*strada coperta con negozi*) arcade.

**'Galles** *sm*: **il ~** Wales; **gal'lese** *ag, sm* (*LING*) Welsh // *sm/f* Welshman/woman.

**gal'letta** *sf* cracker.

**gal'lina** *sf* hen.

**'gallo** *sm* cock.

**gal'lone** *sm* piece of braid; (*MIL*) stripe; (*unità di misura*) gallon.

**galop'pare** *vi* to gallop.

**ga'loppo** *sm* gallop; **al** *o* **di ~** at a gallop.

**'gamba** *sf* leg; (*asta: di lettera*) stem; **in ~** (*in buona salute*) well; (*bravo, sveglio*) bright, smart; **prendere qc sotto ~** (*fig*) to treat sth too lightly.

**gambe'retto** *sm* shrimp.

**'gambero** *sm* (*di acqua dolce*) crayfish; (*di mare*) prawn.

**'gambo** *sm* stem; (*di frutta*) stalk.

**'gamma** *sf* (*MUS*) scale; (*di colori, fig*) range.

**ga'nascia, sce** [ga'naʃʃa] *sf* jaw; ~**sce del freno** (*AUT*) brake shoes.

**'gancio** ['gantʃo] *sm* hook.

**'gangheri** ['gangeri] *smpl*: **uscire dai ~** (*fig*) to fly into a temper.

**'gara** *sf* competition; (*SPORT*) competition; contest; match; (*: corsa*) race; **fare a ~** to compete, vie.

**ga'rage** [ga'raʒ] *sm inv* garage.

**garan'tire** *vt* to guarantee; (*debito*) to stand surety for; (*dare per certo*) to assure.

**garan'zia** [garan'tsia] *sf* guarantee; (*pegno*) security.

**gar'bato, a** *ag* courteous, polite.

**'garbo** *sm* (*buone maniere*) politeness, courtesy; (*di vestito etc*) grace, style.

**gareggi'are** [gared'dʒare] *vi* to compete.

**garga'rismo** *sm* gargle; **fare i ~i** to gargle.

**ga'rofano** *sm* carnation; **chiodo di ~** clove.

**'garza** ['gardza] *sf* (*per bende*) gauze.

**gar'zone** [gar'dzone] *sm* (*di negozio*) boy.

**gas** *sm inv* gas; **a tutto ~** at full speed; **dare ~** (*AUT*) to accelerate.

**ga'solio** *sm* diesel (oil).

**ga's(s)ato, a** *ag* (*bibita*) aerated, fizzy.

**gas'soso, a** *ag* gaseous; gassy // *sf* fizzy drink.

**gastrono'mia** *sf* gastronomy.

**gat'tino** *sm* kitten.

**'gatto, a** *sm/f* cat, tomcat/she-cat; ~ selvatico wildcat; ~ delle nevi (*AUT, SCI*) snowcat.

**gatto'pardo** *sm*: ~ africano serval; ~ americano ocelot.

**'gaudio** *sm* joy, happiness.

**ga'vetta** *sf* (*MIL*) mess tin; venire dalla ~ (*MIL, fig*) to rise from the ranks.

**'gazza** ['gaddza] *sf* magpie.

**gaz'zella** [gad'dzɛlla] *sf* gazelle; (*dei carabinieri*) (high-speed) police car.

**gaz'zetta** [gad'dzetta] *sf* news sheet; G~ Ufficiale official publication containing details of new laws.

**gel** [dʒɛl] *sm inv* gel.

**ge'lare** [dʒe'lare] *vt, vi, vb impers* to freeze; **ge'lata** *sf* frost.

**gelate'ria** [dʒelate'ria] *sf* ice-cream shop.

**gela'tina** [dʒela'tina] *sf* gelatine; ~ esplosiva dynamite; ~ di frutta fruit jelly.

**ge'lato, a** [dʒe'lato] *ag* frozen // *sm* ice cream.

**'gelido, a** ['dʒɛlido] *ag* icy, ice-cold.

**'gelo** ['dʒɛlo] *sm* (*temperatura*) intense cold; (*brina*) frost; (*fig*) chill; **ge'lone** *sm* chilblain.

**gelo'sia** [dʒelo'sia] *sf* jealousy.

**ge'loso, a** [dʒe'loso] *ag* jealous.

**'gelso** ['dʒɛlso] *sm* mulberry (tree).

**gelso'mino** [dʒelso'mino] *sm* jasmine.

**ge'mello, a** [dʒe'mɛllo] *ag, sm/f* twin; ~i *smpl* (*di camicia*) cufflinks; (*dello zodiaco*): G~i Gemini *sg*.

**'gemere** ['dʒɛmere] *vi* to moan, groan; (*cigolare*) to creak; (*gocciolare*) to drip, ooze; **'gemito** *sm* moan, groan.

**'gemma** ['dʒɛmma] *sf* (*BOT*) bud; (*pietra preziosa*) gem.

**gene'rale** [dʒene'rale] *ag, sm* general; in ~ (*per sommi capi*) in general terms; (*di solito*) usually, in general; a ~ richiesta by popular request; **generalità** *sfpl* (*dati*

d'identità) particulars; **generaliz'zare** *vt, vi* to generalize; **general'mente** *av* generally.

**gene'rare** [dʒene'rare] *vt* (*dar vita*) to give birth to; (*produrre*) to produce; (*causare*) to arouse; (*TECN*) to produce, generate; **genera'tore** *sm* (*TECN*) generator; **generazi'one** *sf* generation.

**'genere** ['dʒɛnere] *sm* kind, type, sort; (*BIOL*) genus; (*merce*) article, product; (*LING*) gender; (*ARTE, LETTERATURA*) genre; in ~ generally, as a rule; il ~ umano mankind; ~i alimentari foodstuffs.

**ge'nerico, a, ci, che** [dʒe'nɛriko] *ag* generic; (*vago*) vague, imprecise.

**'genero** ['dʒɛnero] *sm* son-in-law.

**generosità** [dʒenerosi'ta] *sf* generosity.

**gene'roso, a** [dʒene'roso] *ag* generous.

**ge'netico, a, ci, che** [dʒe'nɛtiko] *ag* genetic // *sf* genetics *sg*.

**gen'giva** [dʒen'dʒiva] *sf* (*ANAT*) gum.

**geni'ale** [dʒen'jale] *ag* (*persona*) of genius; (*idea*) ingenious, brilliant.

**'genio** ['dʒɛnjo] *sm* genius; andare a ~ a qn to be to sb's liking, appeal to sb.

**geni'tale** [dʒeni'tale] *ag* genital; ~i *smpl* genitals.

**geni'tore** [dʒeni'tore] *sm* parent, father *o* mother; ~i *smpl* parents.

**gen'naio** [dʒen'najo] *sm* January.

**'Genova** ['dʒɛnova] *sf* Genoa.

**gen'taglia** [dʒen'taʎʎa] *sf* (*peg*) rabble.

**'gente** ['dʒɛnte] *sf* people *pl*.

**gen'tile** [dʒen'tile] *ag* (*persona, atto*) kind; (*garbato*) courteous, polite; (*nelle lettere*): G~ Signore Dear Sir; (*: sulla busta*): G~ Signor Fernando Villa Mr Fernando Villa; **genti'lezza** *sf* kindness; courtesy, politeness; per gentilezza (*per favore*) please.

**gentilu'omo, pl gentilu'omini** [dʒenti'lwɔmo] *sm* gentleman.

**genu'ino, a** [dʒenu'ino] *ag* (*prodotto*) natural; (*persona, sentimento*) genuine, sincere.

**geogra'fia** [dʒeogra'fia] *sf* geography.

**geolo'gia** [dʒeolo'dʒia] *sf* geology.

**ge'ometra, i, e** [dʒe'ɔmetra] *sm/f* (*professionista*) surveyor.

**geome'tria** [dʒome'tria] *sf* geometry; **geo'metrico, a, ci, che** *ag* geometric(al).

**ge'ranio** [dʒe'ranjo] *sm* geranium.

**gerar'chia** [dʒerar'kia] *sf* hierarchy.

**ge'rente** [dʒe'rɛnte] *sm/f* manager/manageress.

**'gergo, ghi** ['dʒergo] *sm* jargon; slang.

**geria'tria** [dʒerja'tria] *sf* geriatrics *sg*.

**Ger'mania** [dʒer'manja] *sf*: **la ~ Germany**; **la ~ occidentale/orientale** West/East Germany.

**'germe** ['dʒerme] *sm* germ; (*fig*) seed.

**germogli'are** [dʒermoʎ'ʎare] *vi* to sprout; to germinate; **ger'moglio** *sm* shoot; bud.

**gero'glifico, ci** [dʒero'glifiko] *sm* hieroglyphic.

**'gesso** ['dʒesso] *sm* chalk; (*SCULTURA, MED, EDIL*) plaster; (*statua*) plaster figure; (*minerale*) gypsum.

**gesti'one** [dʒes'tjone] *sf* management.

**ges'tire** [dʒes'tire] *vt* to run, manage.

**'gesto** ['dʒesto] *sm* gesture.

**ges'tore** [dʒes'tore] *sm* manager.

**Gesù** [dʒe'zu] *sm* Jesus.

**gesu'ita, i** [dʒezu'ita] *sm* Jesuit.

**get'tare** [dʒet'tare] *vt* to throw; (*anche*: **~ via**) to throw away *o* out; (*SCULTURA*) to cast; (*EDIL*) to lay; (*acqua*) to spout; (*grido*) to utter; **~rsi** *vr*: **~rsi in** (*sog: fiume*) to flow into; **~ uno sguardo su** to take a quick look at; **get'tata** *sf* (*di cemento, gesso, metalli*) cast; (*diga*) jetty.

**'getto** ['dʒetto] *sm* (*di gas, liquido,*

*AER*) jet; **a ~ continuo** uninterruptedly; **di ~** (*fig*) straight off, in one go.

**get'tone** [dʒet'tone] *sm* token; (*per giochi*) counter; (: *roulette etc*) chip; **~ telefonico** telephone token.

**ghiacci'aio** [gjat'tʃajo] *sm* glacier.

**ghiacci'are** [gjat'tʃare] *vt* to freeze; (*fig*): **~ qn** to make sb's blood run cold // *vi* to freeze, ice over; **ghiacci'ato, a** *ag* frozen; (*bevanda*) ice-cold.

**ghi'accio** ['gjattʃo] *sm* ice.

**ghiacci'olo** [gjat'tʃɔlo] *sm* icicle; (*tipo di gelato*) ice lolly (*Brit*), popsicle (*US*).

**ghi'aia** ['gjaja] *sf* gravel.

**ghi'anda** ['gjanda] *sf* (*BOT*) acorn.

**ghi'andola** ['gjandola] *sf* gland.

**ghigliot'tina** [giʎʎot'tina] *sf* guillotine.

**ghi'gnare** [giɲ'ɲare] *vi* to sneer.

**ghi'otto, a** ['gjotto] *ag* greedy; (*cibo*) delicious, appetizing; **ghiot'tone, a** *sm/f* glutton.

**ghiri'bizzo** [giri'biddzo] *sm* whim.

**ghiri'goro** [giri'gɔro] *sm* scribble, squiggle.

**ghir'landa** [gir'landa] *sf* garland, wreath.

**'ghiro** ['giro] *sm* dormouse.

**'ghisa** ['giza] *sf* cast iron.

**già** [dʒa] *av* already; (*ex, in precedenza*) formerly // *escl* of course!, yes indeed!

**gi'acca, che** ['dʒakka] *sf* jacket; **~ a vento** windcheater (*Brit*), windbreaker (*US*).

**giacché** [dʒak'ke] *cong* since, as.

**giac'chetta** [dʒak'ketta] *sf* (*light*) jacket.

**gia'cenza** [dʒa'tʃɛntsa] *sf*: **merce in ~ goods** in stock; **capitale in ~ uninvested** capital; **~e di magazzino** unsold stock.

**gia'cere** [dʒa'tʃere] *vi* to lie; **giaci'mento** *sm* deposit.

**gia'cinto** [dʒa'tʃinto] *sm* hyacinth.

**gi'ada** ['dʒada] *sf* jade.

**giaggi'olo** [dʒad'dʒɔlo] *sm* iris.

**giagu'aro** [dʒa'gwaro] sm jaguar.

**gi'allo** ['dʒallo] ag yellow; (carnagione) sallow // sm yellow; (anche: romanzo ~) detective novel; (anche: film ~) detective film; ~ dell'uovo yolk.

**giam'mai** [dʒam'mai] av never.

**Giap'pone** [dʒap'pone] sm Japan; **giappo'nese** ag, sm/f, sm Japanese inv.

**gi'ara** ['dʒara] sf jar.

**giardi'naggio** [dʒardi'naddʒo] sm gardening.

**giardi'netta** [dʒardi'netta] sf estate car (Brit), station wagon (US).

**giardini'ere, a** [dʒardi'njere] sm/f gardener // sf (misto di sottaceti) mixed pickles pl; (automobile) = **giardinetta.**

**giar'dino** [dʒar'dino] sm garden; ~ d'infanzia nursery school; ~ pubblico public gardens pl, (public) park; ~ zoologico zoo.

**giarretti'era** [dʒarret'tjera] sf garter.

**giavel'lotto** [dʒavel'lɔtto] sm javelin.

**gi'gante, 'essa** [dʒi'gante] sm/f giant // ag giant, gigantic; (COMM) giant-size; **gigan'tesco, a, schi, sche** ag gigantic.

**'giglio** ['dʒiʎʎo] sm lily.

**gilè** [dʒi'lɛ] sm inv waistcoat.

**gin** [dʒin] sm inv gin.

**gine'cologo, a, gi, ghe** [dʒine-'kɔlogo] sm/f gynaecologist.

**gi'nepro** [dʒi'nepro] sm juniper.

**gi'nestra** [dʒi'nɛstra] sf (BOT) broom.

**Gi'nevra** [dʒi'nevra] sf Geneva.

**gingil'larsi** [dʒindʒil'larsi] vr to fritter away one's time; (giocare): ~ con to fiddle with.

**gin'gillo** [dʒin'dʒillo] sm plaything.

**gin'nasio** [dʒin'nazjo] sm the 4th and 5th year of secondary school in Italy.

**gin'nasta, i, e** [dʒin'nasta] sm/f gymnast; **gin'nastica** sf gymnastics sg; (esercizio fisico) keep-fit exercises; (INS) physical education.

**gi'nocchio** [dʒi'nɔkkjo], pl(m)

**gi'nocchi** o pl(f) **gi'nocchia** sm knee; stare in ~ to kneel, be on one's knees; **mettersi in** ~ to kneel (down); **ginocchi'oni** av on one's knees.

**gio'care** [dʒo'kare] vt to play; (scommettere) to stake, wager, bet; (ingannare) to take in // vi to play; (a roulette etc) to gamble; (fig) to play a part, be important; (TECN: meccanismo) to be loose; ~ a (gioco, sport) to play; (cavalli) to bet on; ~rsi la carriera to put one's career at risk; **gioca'tore, 'trice** sm/f player; gambler.

**gio'cattolo** [dʒo'kattolo] sm toy.

**gio'chetto** [dʒo'ketto] sm (tranello) trick; (fig): è un ~ it's child's play.

**gi'oco, chi** ['dʒɔko] sm game; (divertimento, TECN) play; (al casinò) gambling; (CARTE) hand; (insieme di pezzi etc necessari per un gioco) set; per ~ for fun; fare il doppio ~ con qn to double-cross sb; ~ d'azzardo game of chance; ~ della palla football; ~ degli scacchi chess set; i **Giochi Olimpici** the Olympic Games.

**giocoli'ere** [dʒoko'ljere] sm juggler.

**gio'coso, a** [dʒo'koso] ag playful, jesting.

**gi'ogo, ghi** ['dʒɔgo] sm yoke.

**gi'oia** ['dʒɔja] sf joy, delight; (pietra preziosa) jewel, precious stone.

**gioiel'leria** [dʒojelle'ria] sf jeweller's craft; jeweller's (shop).

**gioielli'ere, a** [dʒojel'ljere] sm/f jeweller.

**gioi'ello** [dʒo'jello] sm jewel, piece of jewellery; ~i smpl jewellery sg.

**gioi'oso, a** [dʒo'joso] ag joyful.

**Gior'dania** [dʒor'danja] sf: la ~ Jordan.

**giorna'laio, a** [dʒorna'lajo] sm/f newsagent (Brit), newsdealer (US).

**gior'nale** [dʒor'nale] sm (news)paper; (diario) journal, diary; (COMM) journal; ~ di bordo log; ~ radio radio news sg.

**giornali'ero, a** [dʒorna'ljero] ag

daily; (*che varia: umore*) changeable // *sm* day labourer.

**giorna'lismo** [dʒorna'lizmo] *sm* journalism.

**giorna'lista, i, e** [dʒorna'lista] *sm/f* journalist.

**gior'nata** [dʒor'nata] *sf* day; ~ **lavorativa** working day.

**gi'orno** [dʒorno] *sm* day; (*opposto alla notte*) day, daytime; (*luce del* ~) daylight; **al** ~ per day; **di** ~ by day; **al** ~ **d'oggi** nowadays.

**gi'ostra** [dʒɔstra] *sf* (*per bimbi*) merry-go-round; (*torneo storico*) joust.

**gi'ovane** ['dʒovane] *ag* young; (*aspetto*) youthful // *sm/f* youth/girl, young man/woman; **i** ~**i** young people; **giova'nile** *ag* youthful; (*scritti*) early; (*errore*) of youth; **giova'notto** *sm* young man.

**gio'vare** [dʒo'vare] *vi*: ~ **a** (*essere utile*) to be useful to; (*far bene*) to be good for // *vb impers* (*essere bene, utile*) to be useful; ~**rsi di qc** to make use of sth.

**giovedì** [dʒove'di] *sm inv* Thursday; **di** *o* **il** ~ on Thursdays.

**gioventù** [dʒoven'tu] *sf* (*periodo*) youth; (*i giovani*) young people *pl*, youth.

**giovi'ale** [dʒo'vjale] *ag* jovial, jolly.

**giovi'nezza** [dʒovi'nettsa] *sf* youth.

**gira'dischi** [dʒira'diski] *sm inv* record player.

**gi'raffa** [dʒi'raffa] *sf* giraffe.

**gi'randola** [dʒi'randola] *sf* (*fuoco d'artificio*) Catherine wheel; (*giocattolo*) toy windmill; (*banderuola*) weather vane, weathercock.

**gi'rare** [dʒi'rare] *vt* (*far ruotare*) to turn; (*percorrere, visitare*) to go round; (*CINEMA*) to shoot; to make; (*COMM*) to endorse // *vi* to turn; (*più veloce*) to spin; (*andare in giro*) to wander, go around; ~**rsi** *vr* to turn; ~ **attorno a** to go round; to revolve round; **far** ~ **la testa a qn** to make sb dizzy; (*fig*) to turn sb's head.

**girar'rosto** [dʒirar'rɔsto] *sm* (*CUC*)

spit.

**gira'sole** [dʒira'sole] *sm* sunflower.

**gi'rata** [dʒi'rata] *sf* (*passeggiata*) stroll; (*con veicolo*) drive; (*COMM*) endorsement.

**gira'volta** [dʒira'vɔlta] *sf* twirl, turn; (*curva*) sharp bend; (*fig*) about-turn.

**gi'revole** [dʒi'revole] *ag* revolving, turning.

**gi'rino** [dʒi'rino] *sm* tadpole.

**'giro** [dʒiro] *sm* (*circuito, cerchio*) circle; (*di chiave, manovella*) turn; (*viaggio*) tour, excursion; (*passeggiata*) stroll, walk; (*in macchina*) drive; (*in bicicletta*) ride; (*SPORT: della pista*) lap; (*di denaro*) circulation; (*CARTE*) hand; (*TECN*) revolution; **prendere in** ~ **qn** (*fig*) to pull sb's leg; **fare un** ~ to go for a walk (*o* a drive *o* a ride); **andare in** ~ to go about, walk around; **a stretto** ~ **di posta** by return of post; **nel** ~ **di un mese** in a month's time; **essere nel** ~ (*fig*) to belong to a circle (of friends); ~ **d'affari** [dʒiraf'fari] turnover; ~ **di parole** circumlocution; ~ **di prova** (*AUT*) test drive; ~ **turistico** sightseeing tour; **giro'collo** *sm*: **a girocollo** crew-neck *cpd*.

**gironzo'lare** [dʒirondzo'lare] *vi* to stroll about.

**'gita** [dʒita] *sf* excursion, trip; **fare una** ~ to go for a trip, go on an outing.

**gi'tano, a** [dʒi'tano] *sm/f* gipsy.

**giù** [dʒu] *av* down; (*dabbasso*) downstairs; **in** ~ downwards, down; ~ **di lì** (*pressappoco*) thereabouts; **bambini dai 6 anni in** ~ children aged 6 and under; ~ **per: cadere** ~ **per le scale** to fall down the stairs; **essere** ~ (*fig: di salute*) to be run down; (: *di spirito*) to be depressed.

**giub'botto** [dʒub'bɔtto] *sm* jerkin; ~ **antiproiettile** bulletproof vest.

**gi'ubilo** [dʒubilo] *sm* rejoicing.

**giudi'care** [dʒudi'kare] *vt* to judge; (*accusato*) to try; (*lite*) to arbitrate in; ~ **qn/qc bello** to consider sb/sth (to be) beautiful.

**gi'udice** ['dʒuditʃe] sm judge; ~ conciliatore justice of the peace; ~ popolare member of a jury.

**giu'dizio** [dʒu'dittsjo] sm judgment; (opinione) opinion; (DIR) judgment, sentence; (: processo) trial; (: verdetto) verdict; aver ~ to be wise o prudent; citare in ~ to summons; giudizi'oso, a ag prudent, judicious.

**gi'ugno** ['dʒuɲɲo] sm June.

**giul'lare** [dʒul'lare] sm jester.

**giu'menta** [dʒu'menta] sf mare.

**gi'unco, chi** ['dʒunko] sm rush.

**gi'ungere** ['dʒundʒere] vi to arrive o vt (mani etc) to join; ~ a to arrive at, reach.

**gi'ungla** ['dʒungla] sf jungle.

**gi'unto, a** ['dʒunto] pp di giungere // sm (TECN) coupling, joint // sf addition; (organo esecutivo, amministrativo) council, board; per ~a into the bargain, in addition; ~a militare military junta; giun'tura sf joint.

**giuo'care** [dʒwo'kare] vt, vi = giocare; giu'oco sm = gioco.

**giura'mento** [dʒura'mento] sm oath; ~ falso perjury.

**giu'rare** [dʒu'rare] vt to swear // vi to swear, take an oath; giu'rato, a ag: nemico giurato sworn enemy // sm/f juror, juryman/woman.

**giu'ria** [dʒu'ria] sf jury.

**giu'ridico, a, ci, che** [dʒu'ridiko] ag legal.

**giustifi'care** [dʒustifi'kare] vt to justify; giustificazi'one sf justification; (INS) (note of) excuse.

**gius'tizia** [dʒus'tittsja] sf justice; giustizi'are vt to execute, put to death; giustizi'ere sm executioner.

**gi'usto, a** ['dʒusto] ag (equo) fair, just; (vero) true, correct; (adatto) right, suitable; (preciso) exact, correct // av (esattamente) exactly, precisely; (per l'appunto, appena) just; arrivare ~ to arrive just in time; ho ~ bisogno di te you're just the person I need.

**glaci'ale** [gla'tʃale] ag glacial.

**'glandola** sf = ghiandola.

**gli** [ʎi] det mpl (dav V, s impura, gn, pn, ps, x, z) the // pronome (a lui) to him; (a esso) to it; (in coppia con lo, la, li, le, ne: a lui, a lei, a loro etc): gliele do I'm giving them to him (o her o them).

**gli'ela** ['ʎela] etc vedi gli.

**glo'bale** ag overall.

**'globo** sm globe.

**'globulo** sm (ANAT): ~ rosso/bianco red/white corpuscle.

**'gloria** sf glory; glori'oso, a ag glorious.

**glos'sario** sm glossary.

**'gnocchi** ['ɲɔkki] smpl (CUC) small dumplings made of semolina pasta o potato.

**'gobba** sf (ANAT) hump; (protuberanza) bump.

**'gobbo, a** ag hunchbacked; (ricurvo) round-shouldered // sm/f hunchback.

**'goccia, ce** ['gottʃa] sf drop; goccio'lare vi, vt to drip.

**go'dere** vi (compiacersi): ~ (di) to be delighted (at), rejoice (at); (trarre vantaggio): ~ di to enjoy, benefit from // vt to enjoy; ~rsi la vita to enjoy life; ~sela to have a good time, enjoy o.s.; godi'mento sm enjoyment.

**'goffo, a** ag clumsy, awkward.

**'gola** sf (ANAT) throat; (golosità) gluttony, greed; (di camino) flue; (di monte) gorge; fare ~ (anche fig) to tempt.

**golf** sm inv (SPORT) golf; (maglia) cardigan.

**'golfo** sm gulf.

**go'loso, a** ag greedy.

**'gomito** sm elbow; (di strada etc) sharp bend.

**go'mitolo** sm ball.

**'gomma** sf rubber; (colla) gum; (per cancellare) rubber, eraser; (di veicolo) tyre (Brit), tire (US); ~ a terra flat tyre (Brit) o tire (US); gommapi'uma sf ® foam rubber.

**'gondola** sf gondola; **gondoli'ere** sm gondolier.

**gonfa'lone** sm banner.

**gonfi'are** vt (pallone) to blow up, inflate; (dilatare, ingrossare) to swell; (fig: notizia) to exaggerate; ~rsi vr to swell; (fiume) to rise; **'gonfio, a** ag swollen; (stomaco) bloated; (vela) full; **gonfi'ore** sm swelling.

**gongo'lare** vi to look pleased with o.s.; ~ **di gioia** to be overjoyed.

**'gonna** sf skirt; ~ **pantalone** culottes pl.

**'gonzo** ['gondzo] sm simpleton, fool.

**gorgheggi'are** [gorged'dʒare] vi to warble; to trill.

**'gorgo, ghi** sm whirlpool.

**gorgogli'are** [gorgoʎ'ʎare] vi to gurgle.

**go'rilla** sm inv gorilla; (guardia del corpo) bodyguard.

**'gotta** sf gout.

**gover'nante** sm/f ruler // sf (di bambini) governess; (donna di servizio) housekeeper.

**gover'nare** vt (stato) to govern, rule; (pilotare, guidare) to steer; (bestiame) to tend, look after; **governa'tivo, a** ag government cpd; **governa'tore** sm governor.

**go'verno** sm government.

**gozzovigli'are** [gottsoviʎ'ʎare] vi to make merry, carouse.

**gracchi'are** [grak'kjare] vi to caw.

**graci'dare** [gratʃi'dare] vi to croak.

**'gracile** ['gratʃile] ag frail, delicate.

**gra'dasso** sm boaster.

**gradazi'one** [gradat'tsjone] sf (sfumatura) gradation; ~ **alcolica** alcoholic content, strength.

**gra'devole** ag pleasant, agreeable.

**gradi'mento** sm pleasure, satisfaction; **è di suo** ~? is it to your liking?

**gradi'nata** sf flight of steps; (in teatro, stadio) tiers pl.

**gra'dino** sm step; (ALPINISMO) foothold.

**gra'dire** vt (accettare con piacere) to accept; (desiderare) to wish, like;

gradisce una tazza di tè? would you like a cup of tea?; **gra'dito, a** ag pleasing; welcome.

**'grado** sm (MAT, FISICA etc) degree; (stadio) degree, level; (MIL, sociale) rank; **essere in** ~ **di fare** to be in a position to do.

**gradu'ale** ag gradual.

**gradu'are** vt to grade; **gradu'ato, a** ag (esercizi) graded; (scala, termometro) graduated // sm (MIL) non-commissioned officer.

**'graffa** sf (gancio) clip; (segno grafico) brace.

**graffi'are** vt to scratch.

**'graffio** sm scratch.

**gra'fia** sf spelling; (scrittura) handwriting.

**'grafico, a, ci, che** ag graphic // sm graph; (persona) graphic designer // sf graphic arts pl.

**gra'migna** [gra'miɲɲa] sf weed; couch grass.

**gram'matica, che** sf grammar; **grammati'cale** ag grammatical.

**'grammo** sm gram(me).

**gran** ag vedi **grande**.

**'grana** sf (granello, di minerali, corpi spezzati) grain; (fam: seccatura) trouble; (: soldi) cash // sm inv Parmesan (cheese).

**gra'naio** sm granary, barn.

**gra'nata** sf (frutto) pomegranate; (pietra preziosa) garnet; (proiettile) grenade.

**Gran Bre'tagna** [granbre'taɲɲa] sf: **la** ~ Great Britain.

**'granchio** ['grankjo] sm crab; (fig) blunder; **prendere un** ~ (fig) to blunder.

**grandango'lare** sm wide-angle lens sg.

**'grande, qualche volta gran** + C, **grand'** + V ag (grosso, largo, vasto) big, large; (alto) tall; (lungo) long; (in sensi astratti) great // smf (persona adulta) adult, grown-up; (chi ha ingegno e potenza) great man/woman; **fare le cose in** ~ to do things in style; **una gran bella**

**donna** a very beautiful woman; **non è una gran cosa** o **un gran che** it's nothing special; **non ne so gran che** I don't know very much about it.

**grandeggi'are** [granded'dʒare] *vi* (*emergere per grandezza*): ~ **su** to tower over; (*darsi arie*) to put on airs.

**gran'dezza** [gran'dettsa] *sf* (*dimensione*) size; magnitude; (*fig*) greatness; in ~ **naturale** lifesize.

**grandi'nare** *vb impers* to hail.

**grandine** *sf* hail.

**gran'duca, chi** *sm* grand duke.

**gra'nello** *sm* (*di cereali, uva*) seed; (*di frutta*) pip; (*di sabbia, sale etc*) grain.

**gra'nita** *sf* kind of water ice.

**gra'nito** *sm* granite.

**'grano** *sm* (*in quasi tutti i sensi*) grain; (*frumento*) wheat; (*di rosario, collana*) bead; ~ **di pepe** peppercorn.

**gran'turco** *sm* maize.

**'granulo** *sm* granule; (*MED*) pellet.

**'grappa** *sf* rough, strong brandy.

**'grappolo** *sm* bunch, cluster.

**gras'setto** *sm* (*TIP*) bold (type).

**'grasso, a** *ag* fat; (*cibo*) fatty; (*pelle*) greasy; (*terreno*) rich; (*fig: guadagno, annata*) plentiful; (: *volgare*) coarse, lewd // *sm* (*di persona, animale*) fat; (*sostanza che unge*) grease; **gras'soccio, a, ci, ce** *ag* plump.

**'grata** *sf* grating.

**gra'ticola** *sf* grill.

**gra'tifica, che** *sf* bonus.

**'gratis** *av* free, for nothing.

**grati'tudine** *sf* gratitude.

**'grato, a** *ag* grateful; (*gradito*) pleasant, agreeable.

**gratta'capo** *sm* worry, headache.

**grattaci'elo** [gratta'tʃɛlo] *sm* skyscraper.

**grat'tare** *vt* (*pelle*) to scratch; (*raschiare*) to scrape; (*pane, formaggio, carote*) to grate; (*fam: rubare*) to pinch // *vi* (*stridere*) to grate; (*AUT*) to grind; **~rsi** *vr* to

scratch o.s.

**grat'tugia, gie** [grat'tudʒa] *sf* grater; **grattugi'are** *vt* to grate; **pane grattugiato** breadcrumbs *pl*.

**gra'tuito, a** *ag* free; (*fig*) gratuitous.

**gra'vame** *sm* tax; (*fig*) burden, weight.

**gra'vare** *vt* to burden // *vi*: ~ **su** to weigh on.

**'grave** *ag* (*danno, pericolo, peccato etc*) grave, serious; (*responsabilità*) heavy, grave; (*contegno*) grave, solemn; (*voce, suono*) deep, low-pitched; (*LING*): **accento** ~ grave accent; **un malato** ~ a person who is seriously ill.

**gravi'danza** [gravi'dantsa] *sf* pregnancy.

**'gravido, a** *ag* pregnant.

**gravità** *sf* seriousness; (*anche FISICA*) gravity.

**gra'voso, a** *ag* heavy, onerous.

**'grazia** ['grattsja] *sf* grace; (*favore*) favour; (*DIR*) pardon; **grazi'are** *vt* (*DIR*) to pardon.

**'grazie** ['grattsje] *escl* thank you!; ~ **mille!** o **tante!** o **infinite!** thank you very much!; ~ **a** thanks to.

**grazi'oso, a** [grat'tsjoso] *ag* charming, delightful; (*gentile*) gracious.

**'Grecia** ['grɛtʃa] *sf*: **la** ~ Greece; **'greco, a, ci, che** *ag, sm/f, sm* Greek.

**'gregge,** *pl(f)* **i** [greddʒe] *sm* flock.

**'greggio, a, gi, ge** ['greddʒo] *ag* raw, unrefined; (*diamante*) rough, uncut; (*tessuto*) unbleached // *sm* (*anche*: **petrolio** ~) crude (oil).

**grembi'ule** *sm* apron; (*sopravveste*) overall.

**'grembo** *sm* lap; (*ventre della madre*) womb.

**gre'mito, a** *ag*: ~ (**di**) packed o crowded (with).

**'gretto, a** *ag* mean, stingy; (*fig*) narrow-minded.

**'greve** *ag* heavy.

**'grezzo, a** ['greddzo] *ag* = **greggio**.

**gri'dare** *vi* (*per chiamare*) to shout,

cry (out); (*strillare*) to scream, yell // *vt* to shout (out), yell (out); ~ aiuto to cry o shout for help.

'grido, *pl(m)* i o *pl(f)* a *sm* shout, cry; scream, yell; (*di animale*) cry; di ~ famous.

'grigio, a, gi, gie ['grid3o] *ag, sm* grey.

'griglia ['griʎʎa] *sf* (*per arrostire*) grill; (*ELETTR*) grid; (*inferriata*) grating; alla ~ (*CUC*) grilled; gri-gli'ata *sf* (*CUC*) grill.

gril'letto *sm* trigger.

'grillo *sm* (*ZOOL*) cricket; (*fig*) whim.

grimal'dello *sm* picklock.

'grinta *sf* grim expression; (*SPORT*) fighting spirit.

'grinza ['grintsa] *sf* crease, wrinkle; (*ruga*) wrinkle; non fare una ~ (*fig: ragionamento*) to be faultless; grin'zoso, a *ag* creased; wrinkled.

grip'pare *vi* (*TECN*) to seize.

gris'sino *sm* bread-stick.

'gronda *sf* eaves *pl*.

gron'daia *sf* gutter.

gron'dare *vi* to pour; (*essere bagnato*): ~ di to be dripping with // *vt* to drip with.

'groppa *sf* (*di animale*) back, rump; (*fam: dell'uomo*) back, shoulders *pl*.

'groppo *sm* tangle; avere un ~ alla gola (*fig*) to have a lump in one's throat.

gros'sezza [gros'settsa] *sf* size; thickness.

gros'sista, i, e *sm/f* (*COMM*) wholesaler.

'grosso, a *ag* big, large; (*di spessore*) thick; (*grossolano: anche fig*) coarse; (*grave, insopportabile*) serious, great; (*tempo, mare*) rough // *sm*: il ~ di the bulk of; un pezzo ~ (*fig*) a VIP, a bigwig; farla ~a to do something very stupid; dirle ~ to tell tall stories; sbagliarsi di ~ to be completely wrong.

grosso'lano, a *ag* rough, coarse; (*fig*) coarse, crude; (: *errore*) stupid.

grosso'modo *av* roughly.

'grotta *sf* cave; grotto.

grot'tesco, a, schi, sche *ag* grotesque.

grovi'era *sm o f* gruyère (cheese).

gro'viglio [gro'viʎʎo] *sm* tangle; (*fig*) muddle.

gru *sf inv* crane.

'gruccia, ce ['gruttʃa] *sf* (*per camminare*) crutch; (*per abiti*) coat-hanger.

gru'gnire [grup'nire] *vi* to grunt; gru'gnito *sm* grunt.

'grugno ['gruɲɲo] *sm* snout; (*fam: faccia*) mug.

'grullo, a *ag* silly, stupid.

'grumo *sm* (*di sangue*) clot; (*di fa-rina etc*) lump.

'gruppo *sm* group; ~ sanguigno blood group.

gruvi'era *sm o f* = groviera.

guada'gnare [gwadaɲ'ɲare] *vt* (*ottenere*) to gain; (*soldi, stipendio*) to earn; (*vincere*) to win; (*raggiungere*) to reach.

gua'dagno [gwa'daɲɲo] *sm* earnings *pl*; (*COMM*) profit; (*vantaggio, utile*) advantage, gain; ~ lordo/netto gross/net earnings *pl*.

gu'ado *sm* ford; passare a ~ to ford.

gu'ai *escl*: ~ a te (*o lui etc*)! woe betide you (*o him etc*)!

gua'ina *sf* (*fodero*) sheath; (*in-dumento per donna*) girdle.

gu'aio *sm* trouble, mishap; (*in-conveniente*) trouble, snag.

gua'ire *vi* to whine, yelp.

gu'ancia, ce ['gwantʃa] *sf* cheek.

guanci'ale [gwan'tʃale] *sm* pillow.

gu'anto *sm* glove.

gu'arda... *prefisso*: ~'boschi *sm inv* forester; ~'caccia *sm inv* game-keeper; ~'coste *sm inv* coastguard; (*nave*) coastguard patrol vessel; ~'linee *sm inv* (*SPORT*) linesman.

guar'dare *vt* (*con lo sguardo: osservare*) to look at; (*film, tele-visione*) to watch; (*custodire*) to look after, take care of // *vi* to look; (*badare*): ~ a to pay attention to;

(*luoghi*: *esser orientato*): ~ a to face; ~**rsi** *vr* to look at o.s.; ~**rsi da** (*astenersi*) to refrain from; (*stare in guardia*) to beware of; ~**rsi da fare** to take care not to do; **guarda di non sbagliare** try not to make a mistake; ~ **a vista** qn to keep a close watch on sb.

**guarda'roba** *sm inv* wardrobe; (*locale*) cloakroom; **guardarobi'ere, a** *sm/f* cloakroom attendant.

**gu'ardia** *sf* (*individuo, corpo*) guard; (*sorveglianza*) watch; **fare la ~ a** qc/qn to guard sth/sb; **stare in ~** (*fig*) to be on one's guard; **di ~** (*medico*) on call; ~ **carceraria** (*prison*) warder; ~ **del corpo** bodyguard; ~ **di finanza** (*corpo*) customs *pl*; (*persona*) customs officer; ~ **medica** emergency doctor service.

**guardi'ano, a** *sm/f* (*di carcere*) warder; (*di villa etc*) caretaker; (*di museo*) custodian; (*di zoo*) keeper; ~ **notturno** night watchman.

**guar'dingo, a, ghi, ghe** *ag* wary, cautious.

**guardi'ola** *sf* porter's lodge; (*MIL*) look-out tower.

**guarigi'one** [gwari'dʒone] *sf* recovery.

**gua'rire** (*persona, malattia*) to cure; (*ferita*) to heal // *vi* to recover, be cured; to heal (up).

**guarnigi'one** [gwarni'dʒone] *sf* garrison.

**guar'nire** *vt* (*ornare: abiti*) to trim; (*CUC*) to garnish; **guarnizi'one** *sf* trimming; garnish; (*TECN*) gasket.

**guasta'feste** *sm/f inv* spoilsport.

**guas'tare** *vt* to spoil, ruin; (*meccanismo*) to break; ~**rsi** *vr* (*cibo*) to go bad; (*meccanismo*) to break down; (*tempo*) to change for the worse; (*amici*) to quarrel, fall out.

**gu'asto, a** *ag* (*non funzionante*) broken; (: *telefono etc*) out of order; (*andato a male*) bad, rotten; (: *dente*) decayed, bad; (*fig: corrotto*) depraved // *sm* breakdown; (*avaria*)

failure; ~ **al motore** engine failure.

**guazza'buglio** [gwattsa'buʎʎo] *sm* muddle.

**gu'ercio, a, ci, ce** ['gwertʃo] *ag* cross-eyed.

**gu'erra** *sf* (*tecnica: atomica, chimica etc*) warfare; **fare la ~** (a) to wage war (against); ~ **mondiale** world war; **guerreggi'are** *vi* to wage war; **guerri'ero, a** *ag* warlike // *sm* warrior; **guer'riglia** *sf* guerrilla warfare; **guerrigli'ero** *sm* guerrilla.

**'gufo** *sm* owl.

**gu'ida** *sf* guide; (*comando, direzione*) guidance, direction; (*AUT*) driving; (: *sterzo*) steering; (*tappeto, di tenda, cassetto*) runner; ~ **a destra/sinistra** (*AUT*) right-/left-hand drive; ~ **telefonica** telephone directory.

**gui'dare** *vt* to guide; (*condurre a capo*) to lead; (*auto*) to drive; (*aereo, nave*) to pilot; **sai** ~? can you drive?; **guida'tore, trice** *sm/f* (*conducente*) driver.

**guin'zaglio** [gwin'tsaʎʎo] *sm* leash, lead.

**gu'isa** *sf*: **a ~ di** like, in the manner of.

**guiz'zare** [gwit'tsare] *vi* to dart; to flicker; to leap; ~ **via** (*fuggire*) to slip away.

**'guscio** ['guʃʃo] *sm* shell.

**gus'tare** *vt* (*cibi*) to taste; (: *assaporare con piacere*) to enjoy, savour; (*fig*) to enjoy, appreciate // *vi*: ~ **a** to please; **non mi gusta affatto** I don't like it at all.

**'gusto** *sm* taste; (*sapore*) flavour; (*godimento*) enjoyment; **al ~ di fragola** strawberry-flavoured; **mangiare di** ~ to eat heartily; **prenderci** ~: **ci ha preso** ~ he's acquired a taste for it, he's got to like it; **gus'toso, a** *ag* tasty; (*fig*) agreeable.

# H

**h** *abbr* = **ora, altezza**.

**ha, 'hai** [a, ai] *vb vedi* **avere**.

**hall** [hɔl] *sf inv* hall, foyer.

**'handicap** ['handikap] *sm inv* handicap; **handicap'pato**, **a** *ag* handicapped // *smf* handicapped person, disabled person.

**'hanno** ['anno] *vb vedi* **avere**.

**hascisc** ['haʃiʃ] *sm* hashish.

**'herpes** ['ɛrpes] *sm* (*MED*) herpes *sg*; ~ **zoster** shingles *sg*.

**ho** [ɔ] *vb vedi* **avere**.

**'hobby** ['hɔbi] *sm inv* hobby.

**'hockey** ['hɔki] *sm* hockey; ~ **su ghiaccio** ice hockey.

**'hostess** ['houstis] *sf inv* air hostess (*Brit*) *o* stewardess.

**ho'tel** *sm inv* hotel.

# I

**i** *det mpl* the.

**i'ato** *sm* hiatus.

**ibernazi'one** [ibernat'tsjone] *sf* hibernation.

**'ibrido, a** *ag, sm* hybrid.

**Id'dio** *sm* God.

**i'dea** *sf* idea; (*opinione*) opinion, view; (*ideale*) ideal; **dare l'~ di** to seem, look like; ~ **fissa** obsession; **neanche** *o* **neppure per** ~! certainly not!

**ide'ale** *ag, sm* ideal.

**ide'are** *vt* (*immaginare*) to think up, conceive; (*progettare*) to plan.

**i'dentico, a, ci, che** *ag* identical.

**identifi'care** *vt* to identify; **identificazi'one** *sf* identification.

**identità** *sf inv* identity.

**idi'oma, i** *sm* idiom, language; **idio'matico, a, ci, che** *ag* idiomatic; **frase idiomatica** idiom.

**idi'ota, i, e** *ag* idiotic // *smf* idiot.

**idola'trare** *vt* to worship; (*fig*) to idolize.

**'idolo** *sm* idol.

**idoneità** *sf* suitability.

**i'doneo, a** *ag*: ~ **a** suitable for, fit for; (*MIL*) fit for; (*qualificato*) qualified for.

**i'drante** *sm* hydrant.

**i'draulico, a, ci, che** *ag* hydraulic // *sm* plumber // *sf* hydraulics *sg*.

**idroe'lettrico, a, ci, che** *ag* hydroelectric.

**i'drofilo, a** *ag vedi* **cotone**.

**idrofo'bia** *sf* rabies *sg*.

**i'drogeno** [i'drɔdʒeno] *sm* hydrogen.

**idros'calo** *sm* seaplane base.

**idrovo'lante** *sm* seaplane.

**i'ena** *sf* hyena.

**i'eri** *av*, yesterday; **il giornale di** ~ yesterday's paper; ~ **l'altro** the day before yesterday; ~ **sera** yesterday evening.

**igi'ene** [i'dʒene] *sf* hygiene; ~ **pubblica** public health; **igi'enico, a, ci, che** *ag* hygienic; (*salubre*) healthy.

**i'gnaro, a** [iɲ'ɲaro] *ag*: ~ **di** unaware of, ignorant of.

**i'gnobile** [iɲ'ɲɔbile] *ag* despicable, vile.

**igno'rante** [iɲɲo'rante] *ag* ignorant.

**igno'rare** [iɲɲo'rare] *vt* (*non sapere, conoscere*) to be ignorant *o* unaware of, not to know; (*fingere di non vedere, sentire*) to ignore.

**i'gnoto, a** [iɲ'ɲɔto] *ag* unknown.

---

*PAROLA CHIAVE*

**il** *det m* (*pl* **i**); **i** *diventa* **lo** (*pl* **gli**) *davanti a s impura, gn, pn, ps, x, z*; **i'** (*pl* **le**) **1** the; ~ **libro/lo studente/l'acqua** the book/the student/the water; **gli scolari** the pupils

**2** (*astrazione*): ~ **coraggio/l'amore/la giovinezza** courage/love/youth

**3** (*tempo*): ~ **mattino/la sera** in the morning/evening; ~ **venerdì** etc (*abitualmente*) on Fridays etc; (*quel giorno*) on (the) Friday etc; **la settimana prossima** next week

**4** (*distributivo*) a, an; **2.500 lire** ~

chilo/paio 2,500 lire a o per kilo/pair; 110 km l'ora 110 km an o per hour
**5** (*partitivo*) some, any; hai messo lo zucchero? have you added sugar?; hai comprato ~ latte? did you buy (some o any) milk?
**6** (*possesso*): aprire gli occhi to open one's eyes; rompersi la gamba to break one's leg; avere i capelli neri/~ naso rosso to have dark hair/a red nose; mettiti le scarpe put your shoes on
**7** (*con nomi propri*): ~ Petrarca Petrarch; ~ Presidente Reagan President Reagan; dov'è la Francesca? where's Francesca?
**8** (*con nomi geografici*): ~ Tevere the Tiber; l'Italia Italy; ~ Regno Unito the United Kingdom; l'Everest Everest; le Alpi the Alps.

**'ilare** *ag* cheerful; **ilarità** *sf* hilarity, mirth.

**illangui'dire** *vi* to grow weak o feeble.

**illazi'one** [illat'tsjone] *sf* inference, deduction.

**ille'gale** *ag* illegal.

**illeg'gibile** [illed'dʒibile] *ag* illegible.

**ille'gittimo, a** [ille'dʒittimo] *ag* illegitimate.

**il'leso, a** *ag* unhurt, unharmed.

**illette'rato, a** *ag* illiterate.

**illi'bato, a** *ag*: donna ~a virgin.

**illimi'tato, a** *ag* boundless; unlimited.

**ill.mo** *abbr* = **illustrissimo**.

**il'ludere** *vt* to deceive, delude; ~rsi *vr* to deceive o.s., delude o.s.

**illumi'nare** *vt* to light up, illuminate; (*fig*) to enlighten; ~rsi *vr* to light up; ~ a giorno to floodlight; **illuminazi'one** *sf* lighting; illumination; floodlighting; (*fig*) flash of inspiration.

**illusi'one** *sf* illusion; farsi delle ~i to delude o.s.

**illusio'nismo** *sm* conjuring.

**il'luso, a** *pp di* illudere.

**illus'trare** *vt* to illustrate; illu-

stra'tivo, a** *ag* illustrative; **illustrazi'one** *sf* illustration.

**il'lustre** *ag* eminent, renowned; **illus'trissimo, a** *ag* (*negli indirizzi*) very revered.

**imbacuc'care** *vt*, ~rsi *vr* to wrap up.

**imbal'laggio** [imbal'laddʒo] *sm* packing o.

**imbal'lare** *vt* to pack; (*AUT*) to race; ~rsi *vr* (*AUT*) to race.

**imbalsa'mare** *vt* to embalm.

**imbambo'lato, a** *ag* (*sguardo*) vacant, blank.

**imban'dire** *vt*: ~ un pranzo to prepare a lavish meal.

**imbaraz'zare** [imbarat'tsare] *vt* (*mettere a disagio*) to embarrass; (*ostacolare: movimenti*) to hamper; (: *stomaco*) to lie heavily on.

**imba'razzo** [imba'rattso] *sm* (*disagio*) embarrassment; (*perplessità*) puzzlement, bewilderment; ~ di stomaco indigestion.

**imbarca'dero** *sm* landing stage.

**imbar'care** *vt* (*passeggeri*) to embark; (*merci*) to load; ~rsi *vr*: ~rsi su to board; ~rsi per l'America to sail for America; ~rsi in (*fig*: *affare etc*) to embark on.

**imbarcazi'one** [imbarkat'tsjone] *sf* (*small boat, small*) craft *inv*; ~ di salvataggio lifeboat.

**im'barco, chi** *sm* embarkation; loading; boarding; (*banchina*) landing stage.

**imbas'tire** *vt* (*cucire*) to tack; (*fig*: *abbozzare*) to sketch, outline.

**im'battersi** *vr*: ~ in (*incontrare*) to bump o run into.

**imbat'tibile** *ag* unbeatable, invincible.

**imbavagli'are** [imbavaʎ'ʎare] *vt* to gag.

**imbec'cata** *sf* (*TEATRO*) prompt.

**imbe'cille** [imbe'tʃille] *ag* idiotic // *sm/f* idiot; (*MED*) imbecile.

**imbel'lire** *vt* to adorn, embellish // *vi* to grow more beautiful.

**im'berbe** *ag* beardless.

**im'bevere** *vt* to soak; ~**rsi** *vr*: ~**rsi di** to soak up, absorb.

**imbian'care** *vt* to whiten; (*muro*) to whitewash // *vi* to become *o* turn white.

**imbian'chino** [imbjan'kino] *sm* (house) painter, painter and decorator.

**imboc'care** *vt* (*bambino*) to feed; (*entrare: strada*) to enter, turn into // *vi*: ~ **in** (*sog: strada*) to lead into; (: *fiume*) to flow into.

**imbocca'tura** *sf* mouth; (*di strada, porto*) entrance; (*MUS, del morso*) mouthpiece.

**im'bocco, chi** *sm* entrance.

**imbos'care** *vt* to hide; ~**rsi** *vr* (*MIL*) to evade military service.

**imbos'cata** *sf* ambush.

**imbottigli'are** [imbotti'ʎʎare] *vt* to bottle; (*NAUT*) to blockade; (*MIL*) to hem in; ~**rsi** *vr* to be stuck in a traffic jam.

**imbot'tire** *vt* to stuff; (*giacca*) to pad; **imbot'tita** *sf* quilt; **imbot'tura** *sf* stuffing; padding.

**imbrat'tare** *vt* to dirty, smear, daub.

**imbrigli'are** [imbriʎ'ʎare] *vt* to bridle.

**imbroc'care** *vt* (*fig*) to guess correctly.

**imbrogli'are** [imbroʎ'ʎare] *vt* to mix up; (*fig: raggirare*) to deceive, cheat; (: *confondere*) to confuse, mix up; ~**rsi** *vr* to get tangled; (*fig*) to become confused; **im'broglio** *sm* (*groviglio*) tangle; (*situazione confusa*) mess; (*truffa*) swindle, trick; **imbrogli'one, a** *smlf* cheat, swindler.

**imbronci'are** [imbron'tʃare] *vi* (*anche*: ~**rsi**) to sulk; **im-bronci'ato, a** *ag* sulky.

**imbru'nire** *vi, vb impers* to grow dark; **all'~ at** dusk.

**imbrut'tire** *vt* to make ugly // *vi* to become ugly.

**imbu'care** *vt* to post.

**imbur'rare** *vt* to butter.

**im'buto** *sm* funnel.

**imi'tare** *vt* to imitate; (*riprodurre*) to copy; (*assomigliare*) to look like; **imitazi'one** *sf* imitation.

**immaco'lato, a** *ag* spotless; immaculate.

**immagazzi'nare** [immagaddzi'nare] *vt* to store.

**immagi'nare** [immadʒi'nare] *vt* to imagine; (*supporre*) to suppose; (*inventare*) to invent; **s'immagini!** don't mention it!, not at all!; **immagi'nario, a** *ag* imaginary; **immaginazi'one** *sf* imagination; (*cosa immaginata*) fancy.

**im'magine** [im'madʒine] *sf* image; (*rappresentazione grafica, mentale*) picture.

**imman'cabile** *ag* certain; unfailing.

**immangi'abile** [imman'dʒabile] *ag* inedible.

**immatrico'lare** *vt* to register; ~**rsi** *vr* (*INS*) to matriculate, enrol; **immatricolazi'one** *sf* registration; matriculation, enrolment.

**imma'turo, a** *ag* (*frutto*) unripe; (*persona*) immature; (*prematuro*) premature.

**immedesi'marsi** *vr*: ~ **in** to identify with.

**immediata'mente** *av* immediately, at once.

**immedi'ato, a** *ag* immediate.

**im'memore** *ag*: ~ **di** forgetful of.

**im'menso, a** *ag* immense.

**im'mergere** [im'merdʒere] *vt* to immerse, plunge; ~**rsi** *vr* to plunge; (*sommergibile*) to dive, submerge; (*dedicarsi a*): ~**rsi in** to immerse o.s. in.

**immeri'tato, a** *ag* undeserved.

**immeri'tevole** *ag* undeserving, unworthy.

**immersi'one** *sf* immersion; (*di sommergibile*) submersion, dive; (*di palombaro*) dive.

**im'merso, a** *pp di* **immergere**.

**im'mettere** *vt*: ~ **in** to introduce (into); ~ **dati in un computer** to enter data on a computer.

**immi'grato, a** *sm/f* immigrant; **immigrazi'one** *sf* immigration.

**immi'nente** *ag* imminent.

**immischi'are** [immis'kjare] *vt*: ~ **qn in** to involve sb in; ~**rsi in** to interfere o meddle in.

**immissi'one** *sf* (*di aria, gas*) intake; ~ **di dati** (*INFORM*) data entry.

**im'mobile** *ag* motionless, still; **(beni)** ~**i** *smpl* real estate *sg*; **immobili'are** *ag* (*DIR*) property *cpd*; **immobilità** *sf* stillness; immobility.

**immo'desto, a** *ag* immodest.

**immo'lare** *vt* to sacrifice, immolate.

**immon'dizia** [immon'dittsja] *sf* dirt, filth; (*spesso al pl: spazzatura, rifiuti*) rubbish *q*, refuse *q*.

**im'mondo, a** *ag* filthy, foul.

**immo'rale** *ag* immoral.

**immor'tale** *ag* immortal.

**im'mune** *ag* (*esente*) exempt; (*MED, DIR*) immune; **immunità** *sf* immunity; **immunità parlamentare** parliamentary privilege.

**immu'tabile** *ag* immutable; unchanging.

**impacchet'tare** [impakket'tare] *vt* to pack up.

**impacci'are** [impat'tʃare] *vt* to hinder, hamper; **impacci'ato, a** *ag* awkward, clumsy; (*imbarazzato*) embarrassed; **im'paccio** *sm* obstacle; (*imbarazzo*) embarrassment; (*situazione imbarazzante*) awkward situation.

**im'pacco, chi** *sm* (*MED*) compress.

**impadro'nirsi** *vr*: ~ **di** to seize, take possession of; (*fig: apprendere a fondo*) to master.

**impa'gabile** *ag* priceless.

**impagi'nare** [impadʒi'nare] *vt* (*TIP*) to paginate, page (up).

**impagli'are** [impaʎ'ʎare] *vt* to stuff (with straw).

**impa'lato, a** *ag* (*fig*) stiff as a board.

**impalca'tura** *sf* scaffolding.

**impalli'dire** *vi* to turn pale; (*fig*) to fade.

**impa'nare** *vt* (*CUC*) to dip in breadcrumbs.

**impanta'narsi** *vr* to sink (in the mud); (*fig*) to get bogged down.

**impappi'narsi** *vr* to stammer, falter.

**impa'rare** *vt* to learn.

**impareggi'abile** [impared'dʒabile] *ag* incomparable.

**imparen'tarsi** *vr*: ~ **con** to marry into.

**'impari** *ag inv* (*disuguale*) unequal; (*dispari*) odd.

**impar'tire** *vt* to bestow, give.

**imparzi'ale** [impar'tsjale] *ag* impartial, unbiased.

**impas'sibile** *ag* impassive.

**impas'tare** *vt* (*pasta*) to knead; (*colori*) to mix.

**im'pasto** *sm* (*l'impastare: di pane*) kneading; (: *di cemento*) mixing; (*pasta*) dough; (*anche fig*) mixture.

**im'patto** *sm* impact.

**impau'rire** *vt* to scare, frighten // *vi* (*anche*: ~**rsi**) to become scared o frightened.

**impazi'ente** [impat'tsjɛnte] *ag* impatient; **impazi'enza** *sf* impatience.

**impaz'zata** [impat'tsata] *sf*: **all'**~ (*precipitosamente*) at breakneck speed.

**impaz'zire** [impat'tsire] *vi* to go mad; ~ **per qn/qc** to be crazy about sb/sth.

**impec'cabile** *ag* impeccable.

**impedi'mento** *sm* obstacle, hindrance.

**impe'dire** *vt* (*vietare*): ~ **a qn di fare** to prevent sb from doing; (*ostruire*) to obstruct; (*impacciare*) to hamper, hinder.

**impe'gnare** [impeɲ'ɲare] *vt* (*dare in pegno*) to pawn; (*onore etc*) to pledge; (*prenotare*) to book, reserve; (*obbligare*) to oblige; (*occupare*) to keep busy; (*MIL: nemico*) to engage; ~**rsi** *vr* (*vincolarsi*): ~**rsi a fare** to undertake to do; (*mettersi*

*risolutamente*): ~**rsi** in qc to devote o.s. to sth; ~**rsi con qn** (*accordarsi*) to come to an agreement with sb;
**impegna'tivo, a** *ag* binding; (*lavoro*) demanding, exacting;
**impe'gnato, a** *ag* (*occupato*) busy; (*fig: romanzo, autore*) committed, engagé.
**im'pegno** [im'peɲɲo] *sm* (*obbligo*) obligation; (*promessa*) promise, pledge; (*zelo*) diligence, zeal; (*compito, d'autore*) commitment.
**impel'lente** *ag* pressing, urgent.
**impene'trabile** *ag* impenetrable.
**impen'narsi** *vr* (*cavallo*) to rear up; (*AER*) to nose up; (*fig*) to bridle.
**impen'sato, a** *ag* unforeseen, unexpected.
**impensie'rire** *vt,* ~**rsi** *vr* to worry.
**impe'rare** *vi* (*anche fig*) to reign, rule.
**impera'tivo, a** *ag, sm* imperative.
**impera'tore, 'trice** *sm/f* emperor/ empress.
**imperdo'nabile** *ag* unforgivable, unpardonable.
**imper'fetto, a** *ag* imperfect // *sm* (*LING*) imperfect (tense);
**imperfezi'one** *sf* imperfection.
**imperi'ale** *ag* imperial.
**imperi'oso, a** *ag* (*persona*) imperious; (*motivo, esigenza*) urgent, pressing.
**impe'rizia** [impe'rittsja] *sf* lack of experience.
**imperma'lirsi** *vr* to take offence.
**imperme'abile** *ag* waterproof // *sm* raincoat.
**imperni'are** *vt*: ~ qc su to hinge sth on; (*fig*) to base sth on; ~**rsi** *vr* (*fig*): ~**rsi su** to be based on.
**im'pero** *sm* empire; (*forza, autorità*) rule, control.
**imperscru'tabile** *ag* inscrutable.
**imperso'nale** *ag* impersonal.
**imperso'nare** *vt* to personify; (*TEATRO*) to play, act (the part of).
**imperter'rito, a** *ag* fearless, undaunted; impassive.
**imperti'nente** *ag* impertinent.

**imper'sare** *vi* to rage.
**im'peto** *sm* (*moto, forza*) force, impetus; (*assalto*) onslaught; (*fig: impulso*) impulse; (: *slancio*) transport; **con** ~ energetically; vehemently.
**impet'tito, a** *ag* stiff, erect.
**impetu'oso, a** *ag* (*vento*) strong, raging; (*persona*) impetuous.
**impian'tare** *vt* (*motore*) to install; (*azienda, discussione*) to establish, start.
**impi'anto** *sm* (*installazione*) installation; (*apparecchiature*) plant; (*sistema*) system; ~ **elettrico** wiring; ~ **sportivo** sports complex; ~**i di risalita** (*SCI*) ski lifts.
**impias'trare, impiastricci'are** [impjastrit'tʃare] *vt* to smear, dirty.
**impi'astro** *sm* poultice.
**impic'care** *vt* to hang; ~**rsi** *vr* to hang o.s.
**impicci'are** [impit'tʃare] *vt* to hinder, hamper; ~**rsi** *vr* to meddle, interfere; **im'piccio** *sm* (*ostacolo*) hindrance; (*seccatura*) trouble, bother; (*affare imbrogliato*) mess; **essere d'impiccio** to be in the way.
**impie'gare** *vt* (*usare*) to use, employ; (*assumere*) to employ, take on; (*spendere: denaro, tempo*) to spend; (*investire*) to invest; ~**rsi** *vr* to get a job, obtain employment;
**impie'gato, a** *sm/f* employee.
**impi'ego, ghi** *sm* (*uso*) use; (*occupazione*) employment; (*posto di lavoro*) (regular) job, post; (*ECON*) investment.
**impieto'sire** *vt* to move to pity; ~**rsi** *vr* to be moved to pity.
**impie'trire** *vt* (*fig*) to petrify.
**impigli'are** [impiʎ'ʎare] *vt* to catch, entangle; ~**rsi** *vr* to get caught up o entangled.
**impi'grire** *vt* to make lazy // *vi* (*anche:* ~**rsi**) to grow lazy.
**impli'care** *vt* to imply; (*coinvolgere*) to involve; ~**rsi** *vr:* ~**rsi** (**in**) to become involved (in);
**implicazi'one** *sf* implication.

im'plicito, a [im'plit∫ito] ag implicit.

impolve'rare vt to cover with dust; ~rsi vr to get dusty.

impo'nente ag imposing, impressive.

impo'nibile ag taxable // sm taxable income.

impopo'lare ag unpopular.

im'porre vt to impose; (costringere) to force, make; (far valere) to impose, enforce; imporsi vr (persona) to assert o.s.; (cosa: rendersi necessario) to become necessary; (aver successo: moda, attore) to become popular; ~ a qn di fare to force sb to do, make sb do.

impor'tante ag important; impor'tanza sf importance; dare importanza a qc to attach importance to sth; darsi importanza to give o.s. airs.

impor'tare vt (introdurre dall'estero) to import // vi to matter, be important // vb impers (essere necessario) to be necessary; (interessare) to matter; non importa! it doesn't matter!; non me ne importa! I don't care!; importazi'one sf importation; (merci importate) imports pl.

im'porto sm (total) amount.

importu'nare vt to bother.

impor'tuno, a ag irksome, annoying.

imposizi'one [impozit'tsjone] sf imposition; order, command; (onere, imposta) tax.

imposses'sarsi vr: ~ di to seize, take possession of.

impos'sibile ag impossible; fare l'~ to do one's utmost, do all one can; impossibilità sf impossibility; essere nell'impossibilità di fare qc to be unable to do sth.

im'posta sf (di finestra) shutter; (tassa) tax; ~ sul reddito income tax; ~ sul valore aggiunto (I.V.A.) value added tax (VAT) (Brit), sales tax (US).

impos'tare vt (imbucare) to post; (preparare) to plan, set out; (avviare) to begin, start off; (voce) to pitch.

im'posto, a pp di imporre.

impo'tente ag weak, powerless; (anche MED) impotent.

impove'rire vt to impoverish // vi (anche: ~rsi) to become poor.

imprati'cabile ag (strada) impassable; (campo da gioco) unplayable.

imprati'chire [imprati'kire] vt to train; ~rsi in qc to practise (Brit) o practice (US) sth.

impre'gnare [impren'nare] vt: ~ (di) (imbevere) to soak o impregnate (with); (riempire: anche fig) to fill (with).

imprendi'tore sm (industriale) entrepreneur; (appaltatore) contractor; piccolo ~ small businessman.

im'presa sf (iniziativa) enterprise; (azione) exploit; (azienda) firm, concern.

impre'sario sm (TEATRO) manager, impresario; ~ di pompe funebri funeral director.

imprescin'dibile [impre∫∫in'dibile] ag not to be ignored.

impressio'nante ag impressive; upsetting.

impressio'nare vt to impress; (turbare) to upset; (FOT) to expose; ~rsi vr to be easily upset.

impressi'one sf impression; (fig: sensazione) sensation, feeling; (stampa) printing; fare ~ (colpire) to impress; (turbare) to frighten, upset; fare buona/cattiva ~ a to make a good/bad impression on.

im'presso, a pp di imprimere.

impres'tare vt: ~ qc a qn to lend sth to sb.

impreve'dibile ag unforeseeable; (persona) unpredictable.

imprevi'dente ag lacking in foresight.

impre'visto, a ag unexpected, unforeseen // sm unforeseen event; salvo ~i unless anything unexpected happens.

**imprigio'nare** [impridʒo'nare] *vt* to imprison.

**im'primere** *vt* (*anche fig*) to impress, stamp; (*comunicare*: *movimento*) to transmit, give.

**impro'babile** *ag* improbable, unlikely.

**im'pronta** *sf* imprint, impression, sign; (*di piede, mano*) print; (*fig*) mark, stamp; ~ **digitale** fingerprint.

**impro'perio** *sm* insult; ~**i** *smpl* abuse *sg*.

**im'proprio, a** *ag* improper; **arma** ~**a** offensive weapon.

**improvvisa'mente** *av* suddenly; unexpectedly.

**improvvi'sare** *vt* to improvise; ~**rsi** *vr*: ~**rsi cuoco** to (decide to) act as cook; **improvvi'sata** *sf* (pleasant) surprise.

**improv'viso, a** *ag* (*imprevisto*) unexpected; (*subitaneo*) sudden; **all'**~ unexpectedly; suddenly.

**impru'dente** *ag* unwise, rash.

**impu'dente** *ag* impudent.

**impu'dico, a, chi, che** *ag* immodest.

**impu'gnare** [impuɲ'ɲare] *vt* to grasp, grip; (*DIR*) to contest; **impu-gna'tura** *sf* grip, grasp; (*manico*) handle; (*: di spada*) hilt.

**impul'sivo, a** *ag* impulsive.

**im'pulso** *sm* impulse.

**impun'tarsi** *vr* to stop dead, refuse to budge; (*fig*) to be obstinate.

**impu'tare** *vt* (*ascrivere*): ~ **qc a** to attribute sth to; (*DIR*: *accusare*): ~ **qn di** to charge sb with, accuse sb of; **impu'tato, a** *smf* (*DIR*) accused, defendant; **imputazi'one** *sf* (*DIR*) charge.

**imputri'dire** *vi* to rot.

---

PAROLA CHIAVE

**in** (*in* + *il* = **nel**, *in* + *lo* = **nello**, *in* + *l'* = **nell'**, *in* + *la* = **nella**, *in* + *i* = **nei**, *in* + *gli* = **negli**, *in* + *le* = **nelle**) *prep* 1 (*stato in luogo*) in; **vivere** ~ **Italia/città** to live in Italy/town; **essere** ~ **casa/ufficio** to be at home/the office; **se fossi** ~ **te** if I were you

2 (*moto a luogo*) to; (*: dentro*) into; **andare** ~ **Germania/città** to go to Germany/town; **andare** ~ **ufficio** to go to the office; **entrare** ~ **macchina/casa** to get into the car/go into the house

3 (*tempo*) in; **nel 1989** in 1989; ~ **giugno/estate** in June/summer

4 (*modo, maniera*) in; ~ **silenzio** in silence; ~ **abito da sera** in evening dress; ~ **guerra** at war; ~ **vacanza** on holiday; **Maria Bianchi** ~ **Rossi** Maria Rossi née Bianchi

5 (*mezzo*) by; **viaggiare** ~ **autobus/treno** to travel by bus/train

6 (*materia*) made of; ~ **marmo** made of marble, marble *cpd*; **una collana** ~ **oro** a gold necklace

7 (*misura*) in; **siamo** ~ **quattro** there are four of us; ~ **tutto in all**

8 (*fine*): **dare** ~ **dono** to give as a gift; **spende tutto** ~ **alcool** he spends all his money on drink; ~ **onore di** in honour of.

---

**i'nabile** *ag*: ~ **a** incapable of; (*fisicamente, MIL*) unfit for; **inabilità** *sf* incapacity.

**inabi'tabile** *ag* uninhabitable.

**inacces'sibile** [inattʃes'sibile] *ag* (*luogo*) inaccessible; (*persona*) unapproachable; (*mistero*) unfathomable.

**inaccet'tabile** [inattʃet'tabile] *ag* unacceptable.

**ina'datto, a** *ag*: ~ **(a)** unsuitable *o* unfit (for).

**inadegu'ato, a** *ag* inadequate.

**inadempi'enza** [inadem'pjentsa] *sf*: ~ **(a)** non-fulfilment (of).

**inaffer'rabile** *ag* elusive; (*concetto, senso*) difficult to grasp.

**ina'lare** *vt* to inhale.

**inalbe'rare** *vt* (*NAUT*) to hoist, raise; ~**rsi** *vr* (*fig*) to flare up, fly off the handle.

**inalte'rabile** *ag* unchangeable;

(*colore*) fast, permanent; (*affetto*) constant.

**inalte'rato, a** *ag* unchanged.

**inami'dato, a** *ag* starched.

**inani'mato, a** *ag* inanimate; (*senza vita: corpo*) lifeless.

**inappa'gabile** *ag* insatiable.

**inappel'labile** *ag* (*decisione*) final, irrevocable; (*DIR*) final, not open to appeal.

**inappe'tenza** [inappe'tɛntsa] *sf* (*MED*) lack of appetite.

**inappun'tabile** *ag* irreproachable, flawless.

**inar'care** *vt* (*schiena*) to arch; (*sopracciglia*) to raise; ~**rsi** *vr* to arch.

**inari'dire** *vt* to make arid, dry up // *vi* (*anche*: ~**rsi**) to dry up, become arid.

**inaspet'tato, a** *ag* unexpected.

**inas'prire** *vt* (*disciplina*) to tighten up, make harsher; (*carattere*) to embitter; ~**rsi** *vr* to become harsher; to become bitter; to become worse.

**inattac'cabile** *ag* (*anche fig*) unassailable; (*alibi*) cast-iron.

**inatten'dibile** *ag* unreliable.

**inat'teso, a** *ag* unexpected.

**inattu'abile** *ag* impracticable.

**inau'dito, a** *ag* unheard of.

**inaugu'rare** *vt* to inaugurate, open; (*monumento*) to unveil.

**inavve'duto, a** *ag* careless, inadvertent.

**inavver'tenza** [inavver'tɛntsa] *sf* carelessness, inadvertence.

**incagli'are** [inka'ʎʎare] *vi* (*NAUT: anche*: ~**rsi**) to run aground.

**incal'lito, a** *ag* calloused; (*fig*) hardened, inveterate; (: *insensibile*) hard.

**incal'zare** [inkal'tsare] *vt* to follow o pursue closely; (*fig*) to press // *vi* (*urgere*) to be pressing; (*essere imminente*) to be imminent.

**incame'rare** *vt* (*DIR*) to expropriate.

**incammi'nare** *vt* (*fig: avviare*) to start up; ~**rsi** *vr* to set off.

**incande'scente** [inkandeʃ'ʃɛnte] *ag* incandescent, white-hot.

**incan'tare** *vt* to enchant, bewitch; ~**rsi** *vr* (*rimanere intontito*) to be spellbound; to be in a daze; (*meccanismo: bloccarsi*) to jam; **incanta'tore, 'trice** *ag* enchanting, bewitching // *smf* enchanter/ enchantress; **incan'tesimo** *sm* spell, charm; **incan'tevole** *ag* charming, enchanting.

**in'canto** *sm* spell, charm, enchantment; (*asta*) auction; **come per** ~ as if by magic; **mettere all'**~ to put up for auction.

**incanu'tire** *vi* to go white.

**inca'pace** [inka'patʃe] *ag* incapable; **incapacità** *sf* inability; (*DIR*) incapacity.

**incapo'nirsi** *vr* to be stubborn, be determined.

**incap'pare** *vi*: ~ **in qc/qn** (*anche fig*) to run into sth/sb.

**incapricci'arsi** [inkapritʃ'tarsi] *vr*: ~ **di** to take a fancy to o for.

**incapsu'lare** *vt* (*dente*) to crown.

**incarce'rare** [inkartʃe'rare] *vt* to imprison.

**incari'care** *vt*: ~ **qn di fare** to give sb the responsibility of doing; ~**rsi** *vr* **di** to take care o charge of; **incari'cato, a** *ag*: **incaricato (di)** in charge (of), responsible (for) // *smf* delegate, representative; **professore incaricato** *teacher with a temporary appointment*; **incari'cato d'affari** (*POL*) chargé d'affaires.

**in'carico, chi** *sm* task, job.

**incar'nare** *vt* to embody; ~**rsi** *vr* to be embodied; (*REL*) to become incarnate.

**incarta'mento** *sm* dossier, file.

**incar'tare** *vt* to wrap (in paper).

**incas'sare** *vt* (*merce*) to pack (in cases); (*gemma: incastonare*) to set; (*ECON: riscuotere*) to collect; (*PUGILATO: colpi*) to take, stand up to; **in'casso** *sm* cashing, encashment; (*introito*) takings *pl*.

**incasto'nare** vt to set; **incastona'tura** sf setting.

**incas'trare** vt to fit in, insert; (fig: intrappolare) to catch; ~rsi vr (combaciare) to fit together; (restare bloccato) to become stuck; **in'castro** sm slot, groove; (punto di unione) joint.

**incate'nare** vt to chain up.

**incatra'mare** vt to tar.

**incatti'vire** vt to make wicked; ~rsi vr to turn nasty.

**in'cauto, a** ag imprudent, rash.

**inca'vare** vt to hollow out; **inca'vato, a** ag hollow; (occhi) sunken; **in'cavo** sm hollow; (solco) groove.

**incendi'are** [intʃen'djare] vt to set fire to; ~rsi vr to catch fire, burst into flames.

**incendi'ario, a** [intʃen'djarjo] ag incendiary // sm/f arsonist.

**in'cendio** [in'tʃendjo] sm fire.

**incene'rire** [intʃene'rire] vt to burn to ashes, incinerate; (cadavere) to cremate; ~rsi vr to be burnt to ashes.

**in'censo** [in'tʃenso] sm incense.

**incensu'rato, a** [intʃensu'rato] ag (DIR): **essere** ~ to have a clean record.

**incen'tivo** [intʃen'tivo] sm incentive.

**incep'pare** [intʃep'pare] vt to obstruct, hamper; ~rsi vr to jam.

**ince'rata** [intʃe'rata] sf (tela) tarpaulin; (impermeabile) oilskins pl.

**incer'tezza** [intʃer'tettsa] sf uncertainty.

**in'certo, a** [in'tʃerto] ag uncertain; (irresoluto) undecided, hesitating // sm uncertainty.

**in'cetta** [in'tʃetta] sf buying up; **fare** ~ **di** qc to buy up sth.

**inchi'esta** [in'kjesta] sf investigation, inquiry.

**inchi'nare** [inki'nare] vt to bow; ~rsi vr to bend down; (per riverenza) to bow; (: donna) to curtsy; **in'chino** sm bow; curtsy.

**inchio'dare** [inkjo'dare] vt to nail

(down); ~ **la macchina** (AUT) to jam on the brakes.

**inchi'ostro** [in'kjɔstro] sm ink; ~ **simpatico** invisible ink.

**inciam'pare** [intʃam'pare] vi to trip, stumble.

**inci'ampo** [in'tʃampo] sm obstacle; **essere d'~** a qn (fig) to be in sb's way.

**inciden'tale** [intʃiden'tale] ag incidental.

**inci'dente** [intʃi'dɛnte] sm accident; ~ **d'auto** car accident.

**inci'denza** [intʃi'dɛntsa] sf incidence; **avere una forte** ~ **su** qc to affect sth greatly.

**in'cidere** [in'tʃidere] vi: ~ **su** to bear upon, affect // vt (tagliare incavando) to cut into; (ARTE) to engrave; to etch; (canzone) to record.

**in'cinta** [in'tʃinta] ag f pregnant.

**incipri'are** [intʃi'prjare] vt to powder.

**in'circa** [in'tʃirka] av: **all'**~ more or less, very nearly.

**incisi'one** [intʃi'zjone] sf cut; (disegno) engraving; etching; (registrazione) recording; (MED) incision.

**in'ciso, a** [in'tʃizo] pp di **incidere** // sm: **per** ~ incidentally, by the way.

**inci'vile** [intʃi'vile] ag uncivilized; (villano) impolite.

**incivi'lire** [intʃivi'lire] vt to civilize.

**incl.** abbr (= incluso) encl.

**incli'nare** vt to tilt // vi (fig): ~ **a** qc/a fare to incline towards sth/doing; to tend towards sth/to do; ~rsi vr (barca) to list; (aereo) to bank; **incli'nato, a** ag sloping; **inclinazi'one** sf slope; (fig) inclination, tendency; **in'cline** ag: incline **a** inclined to.

**in'cludere** vt to include; (accludere) to enclose; **inclu'sivo, a** ag inclusive di inclusive of; **in'cluso, a** pp di **includere** // ag included; enclosed.

**incoe'rente** ag incoherent; (contraddittorio) inconsistent.

**in'cognito, a** [in'koɲɲito] ag unknown // *sm*: **in** ~ incognito // *sf* (*MAT, fig*) unknown quantity.

**incol'lare** *vt* to glue, gum; (*unire con colla*) to stick together.

**incolon'nare** *vt* to draw up in columns.

**inco'lore** *ag* colourless.

**incol'pare** *vt*: ~ **qn di** to charge sb with.

**in'colto, a** *ag* (*terreno*) uncultivated; (*trascurato: capelli*) neglected; (*persona*) uneducated.

**in'colume** *ag* safe and sound, unhurt.

**in'combere** *vi* (*sovrastare minacciando*): ~ **su** to threaten, hang over.

**incominci'are** [inkomin'tʃare] *vi, vt* to begin, start.

**in'comodo, a** *ag* uncomfortable; (*inopportuno*) inconvenient // *sm* inconvenience, bother.

**incompe'tente** *ag* incompetent.

**incompi'uto, a** *ag* unfinished, incomplete.

**incom'pleto, a** *ag* incomplete.

**incompren'sibile** *ag* incomprehensible.

**incom'preso, a** *ag* not understood; misunderstood.

**inconce'pibile** [inkontʃe'pibile] *ag* inconceivable.

**inconcili'abile** [inkontʃi'ljabile] *ag* irreconcilable.

**inconclu'dente** *ag* inconclusive; (*persona*) ineffectual.

**incondizio'nato, a** [inkondittsjo'nato] *ag* unconditional.

**inconfu'tabile** *ag* irrefutable.

**incongru'ente** *ag* inconsistent.

**in'congruo, a** *ag* incongruous.

**inconsa'pevole** *ag*: ~ **di** unaware of, ignorant of.

**in'conscio, a, sci, sce** [in'konʃo] *ag* unconscious // *sm* (*PSIC*): **l'**~ the unconscious.

**inconsis'tente** *ag* insubstantial; unfounded.

**inconsu'eto, a** *ag* unusual.

**incon'sulto, a** *ag* rash.

**incon'trare** *vt* to meet; (*difficoltà*) to meet with; ~**rsi** *vr* to meet.

**incontras'tabile** *ag* incontrovertible, indisputable.

**in'contro** *av*: ~ **a** (*verso*) towards // *sm* meeting; (*SPORT*) match; meeting; ~ **di calcio** football match.

**inconveni'ente** *sm* drawback, snag.

**incoraggia'mento** [inkoraddʒa'mento] *sm* encouragement.

**incoraggi'are** [inkorad'dʒare] *vt* to encourage.

**incornici'are** [inkorni'tʃare] *vt* to frame.

**incoro'nare** *vt* to crown; **incoronazi'one** *sf* coronation.

**incorpo'rare** *vt* to incorporate; (*fig: annettere*) to annex.

**in'correre** *vi*: ~ **in** to meet with, run into.

**incosci'ente** [inkoʃ'ʃente] *ag* (*inconscio*) unconscious; (*irresponsabile*) reckless, thoughtless; **incosci'enza** *sf* unconsciousness; recklessness, thoughtlessness.

**incre'dibile** *ag* incredible, unbelievable.

**in'credulo, a** *ag* incredulous, disbelieving.

**incremen'tare** *vt* to increase; (*dar sviluppo a*) to promote.

**incre'mento** *sm* (*sviluppo*) development; (*aumento numerico*) increase, growth.

**incres'parsi** *vr* (*acqua*) to ripple; (*capelli*) to go frizzy; (*pelle, tessuto*) to wrinkle.

**incrimi'nare** *vt* (*DIR*) to charge.

**incri'nare** *vt* to crack; (*fig: rapporti, amicizia*) to cause to deteriorate; ~**rsi** *vr* to crack; to deteriorate; **in crina'tura** *sf* crack; (*fig*) rift.

**incroci'are** [inkro'tʃare] *vt* to cross; (*incontrare*) to meet // *vi* (*NAUT, AER*) to cruise; ~**rsi** *vr* (*strade*) to cross, intersect; (*persone, veicoli*) to pass each other; ~ **le braccia/le gambe** to fold one's arms/cross one's legs; **incrocia'tore** *sm* cruiser.

**in'crocio** [in'krotʃo] sm (anche FERR) crossing; (di strade) crossroads.

**incros'tare** vt to encrust.

**incuba'trice** [inkuba'tritʃe] sf incubator.

**'incubo** sm nightmare.

**in'cudine** sf anvil.

**incu'rante** ag: ~ **(di)** heedless (of), careless (of).

**incurio'sire** vt to make curious; ~rsi vr to become curious.

**incursi'one** sf raid.

**incur'vare** vt, ~rsi vr to bend, curve.

**in'cusso, a** pp di **incutere** .

**incusto'dito, a** ag unguarded, unattended.

**in'cutere** vt to arouse; ~ **timore/rispetto a qn** to strike fear into sb/command sb's respect.

**'indaco** sm indigo.

**indaffa'rato, a** ag busy.

**inda'gare** vt to investigate.

**in'dagine** [in'dadʒine] sf investigation, inquiry; (ricerca) research, study.

**indebi'tarsi** vr to run o get into debt.

**in'debito, a** ag undue; undeserved.

**indebo'lire** vt, vi (anche: ~rsi) to weaken.

**inde'cente** [inde'tʃɛnte] ag indecent; **inde'cenza** sf indecency.

**inde'ciso, a** [inde'tʃizo] ag indecisive; (irresoluto) undecided.

**inde'fesso, a** ag untiring, indefatigable.

**indefi'nito, a** ag (anche LING) indefinite; (impreciso, non determinato) undefined.

**in'degno, a** [in'deɲɲo] ag (atto) shameful; (persona) unworthy.

**indelica'tezza** [indelika'tettsa] sf tactlessness.

**indemoni'ato, a** ag possessed (by the devil).

**in'denne** ag unhurt, undamaged; **indennità** sf inv (rimborso: di spese) allowance; (: di perdita)

compensation, indemnity; **indennità di contingenza** cost-of-living allowance; **indennità di trasferta** travel expenses pl.

**indenniz'zare** [indennid'dzare] vt to compensate; **inden'nizzo** sm (somma) compensation, indemnity.

**indero'gabile** ag binding.

**'India** sf: **l'~** India; **indi'ano, a** ag Indian // smf (d'India) Indian; (d'America) Red Indian.

**indiavo'lato, a** ag possessed (by the devil); (: col dito) to point to, point out; (consigliare) to suggest, recommend; **indica'tivo, a** ag indicative // sm (LING) indicative (mood); **indica'tore** sm (elenco) guide; (TECN) gauge; indicator; **cartello indicatore** sign; **indicatore di velocità** (AUT) speedometer; **indicatore della benzina** fuel gauge; **indicazi'one** sf indication; (informazione) piece of information; **indicazioni per l'uso** instructions for use.

**indi'care** vt (mostrare) to show, indicate; (far vedere)...

**'indice** ['inditʃe] sm (ANAT: dito) index finger, forefinger; (lancetta) needle, pointer; (fig: indizio) sign; (TECN, MAT, nei libri) index; ~ **di gradimento** (RADIO, TV) popularity rating.

**indi'cibile** [indi'tʃibile] ag inexpressible.

**indietreggi'are** [indietred'dʒare] vi to draw back, retreat.

**indi'etro** av back; (guardare) behind, back; (andare, cadere: anche: **all'~**) backwards; **rimanere** ~ to be left behind; **essere** ~ (col lavoro) to be behind; (orologio) to be slow; **rimandare qc** ~ to send sth back.

**indi'feso, a** ag (città etc) undefended; (persona) defenceless.

**indiffe'rente** ag indifferent; **indiffe'renza** sf indifference.

**in'digeno, a** [in'didʒeno] ag indigenous, native // smf native.

**indi'gente** [indi'dʒɛnte] *ag* poverty-stricken, destitute; **indi'genza** *sf* extreme poverty.

**indigesti'one** [indidʒes'tjone] *sf* indigestion.

**indi'gesto, a** [indi'dʒɛsto] *ag* indigestible.

**indi'gnare** [indiɲ'ɲare] *vt* to fill with indignation; ~**rsi** *vr* to be (o get) indignant.

**indimenti'cabile** *ag* unforgettable.

**indipen'dente** *ag* independent; **indipen'denza** *sf* independence.

**in'dire** *vt* (*concorso*) to announce; (*elezioni*) to call.

**indi'retto, a** *ag* indirect.

**indiriz'zare** [indirit'tsare] *vt* (*dirigere*) to direct; (*mandare*) to send; (*lettera*) to address.

**indi'rizzo** [indi'rittso] *sm* address; (*direzione*) direction; (*avvio*) trend, course.

**indis'creto, a** *ag* indiscreet.

**indis'cusso, a** *ag* unquestioned.

**indispen'sabile** *ag* indispensable, essential.

**indispet'tire** *vt* to irritate, annoy // *vi* (*anche:* ~**rsi**) to get irritated o annoyed.

**in'divia** *sf* endive.

**individu'ale** *ag* individual; **individualità** *sf* individuality.

**individu'are** *vt* (*dar forma distinta a*) to characterize; (*determinare*) to locate; (*riconoscere*) to single out.

**indi'viduo** *sm* individual.

**indizi'are** [indit'tsjare] *vt*: ~ **qn di qc** to cast suspicion on sb for sth; **indizi'ato, a** *ag* suspected // *smf* suspect.

**in'dizio** [in'dittsjo] *sm* (*segno*) sign, indication; (*POLIZIA*) clue; (*DIR*) piece of evidence.

**'indole** *sf* nature, character.

**indolen'zito, a** [indolen'tsito] *ag* stiff, aching; (*intorpidito*) numb.

**indo'lore** *ag* painless.

**indo'mani** *sm*: l'~ the next day, the following day.

**Indo'nesia** *sf*: l'~ Indonesia.

**indos'sare** *vt* (*mettere indosso*) to put on; (*avere indosso*) to have on; **indossa'tore, 'trice** *smf* model.

**in'dotto, a** *pp di* **indurre**.

**indottri'nare** *vt* to indoctrinate.

**indovi'nare** *vt* (*scoprire*) to guess; (*immaginare*) to imagine, guess; (*il futuro*) to foretell; **indovi'nato, a** *ag* successful; (*scelta*) inspired; **indovi'nello** *sm* riddle; **indo'vino, a** *smf* fortuneteller.

**indubbia'mente** *av* undoubtedly.

**in'dubbio, a** *ag* certain, undoubted.

**indugi'are** [indu'dʒare] *vi* to take one's time, delay.

**in'dugio** [in'dudʒo] *sm* (*ritardo*) delay; **senza** ~ without delay.

**indul'gente** [indul'dʒɛnte] *ag* indulgent; (*giudice*) lenient; **indul'genza** *sf* indulgence; leniency.

**in'dulgere** [in'duldʒere] *vi*: ~ **a** (*accondiscendere*) to comply with; (*abbandonarsi*) to indulge in; **in'dulto, a** *pp di* **indulgere** // *sm* (*DIR*) pardon.

**indu'mento** *sm* article of clothing, garment; ~**i** *smpl* clothes.

**indu'rire** *vt* to harden // *vi* (*anche:* ~**rsi**) to harden, become hard.

**in'durre** *vt*: ~ **qn a fare qc** to induce o persuade sb to do sth; ~ **qn in errore** to mislead sb.

**in'dustria** *sf* industry; **industri'ale** *ag* industrial // *sm* industrialist.

**industri'arsi** *vr* to do one's best, try hard.

**industri'oso, a** *ag* industrious, hard-working.

**induzi'one** [indut'tsjone] *sf* induction.

**inebe'tito, a** *ag* dazed, stunned.

**inebri'are** *vt* (*anche fig*) to intoxicate; ~**rsi** *vr* to become intoxicated.

**inecce'pibile** [inettʃe'pibile] *ag* unexceptionable.

**i'nedia** *sf* starvation.

**i'nedito, a** *ag* unpublished.

**ineffi'cace** [ineffi'katʃe] *ag* ineffective.

**ineffici'ente** [ineffi'tʃɛnte] *ag* inefficient.

**inegu'ale** *ag* unequal; *(irregolare)* uneven.

**ine'rente** *ag*: ~ a concerning, regarding.

**i'nerme** *ag* unarmed; defenceless.

**inerpi'carsi** *vr*: ~ (su) to clamber (up).

**i'nerte** *ag* inert; *(inattivo)* indolent, sluggish; **i'nerzia** *sf* inertia; indolence, sluggishness.

**ine'satto, a** *ag (impreciso)* inexact; *(erroneo)* incorrect; *(AMM: non riscosso)* uncollected.

**inesis'tente** *ag* non-existent.

**inesperi'enza** [inespe'rjentsa] *sf* inexperience.

**ines'perto, a** *ag* inexperienced.

**i'netto, a** *ag (incapace)* inept; *(che non ha attitudine)*: ~ (a) unsuited (to).

**ine'vaso, a** *ag (ordine, corrispondenza)* outstanding.

**inevi'tabile** *ag* inevitable.

**i'nezia** [i'nettsja] *sf* trifle, thing of no importance.

**infagot'tare** *vt* to bundle up, wrap up; ~rsi *vr* to wrap up.

**infal'libile** *ag* infallible.

**infa'mare** *vt* to defame.

**in'fame** *ag* infamous; *(fig: cosa, compito)* awful, dreadful.

**infan'tile** *ag* child *cpd*; childlike; *(adulto, azione)* childish; **letteratura** ~ children's books *pl*.

**in'fanzia** [in'fantsja] *sf* childhood; *(bambini)* children *pl*; **prima** ~ babyhood, infancy.

**infari'nare** *vt* to cover with (*o* sprinkle with *o* dip in) flour; ~ **di** zucchero to sprinkle with sugar; **infarina'tura** *sf (fig)* smattering.

**in'farto** *sm (MED)*: ~ **(cardiaco)** coronary.

**infasti'dire** *vt* to annoy, irritate; ~rsi *vr* to get annoyed *o* irritated.

**infati'cabile** *ag* tireless, untiring.

**in'fatti** *cong* as a matter of fact, in fact, actually.

**infatu'arsi** *vr*: ~ **di** *o* **per** to become infatuated with, fall for; **infatuazi'one** *sf* infatuation.

**in'fausto, a** *ag* unpropitious, unfavourable.

**infe'condo, a** *ag* infertile.

**infe'dele** *ag* unfaithful; **infedeltà** *sf* infidelity.

**infe'lice** [infe'litʃe] *ag* unhappy; *(sfortunato)* unlucky, unfortunate; *(inopportuno)* inopportune, ill-timed; *(mal riuscito: lavoro)* bad, poor; **infelicità** *sf* unhappiness.

**inferi'ore** *ag* lower; *(per intelligenza, qualità)* inferior // *smf* inferior; ~ a *(numero, quantità)* less *o* smaller than; *(meno buono)* inferior to; ~ **alla media** below average; **inferiorità** *sf* inferiority.

**inferme'ria** *sf* infirmary; *(di scuola, nave)* sick bay.

**infermi'ere, a** *smf* nurse.

**infermità** *sf inv* illness; infirmity.

**in'fermo, a** *ag (ammalato)* ill; *(debole)* infirm.

**infer'nale** *ag* infernal; *(proposito, complotto)* diabolical.

**in'ferno** *sm* hell.

**inferri'ata** *sf* grating.

**infervo'rare** *vt* to arouse enthusiasm in; ~rsi *vr* to get excited, get carried away.

**infet'tare** *vt* to infect; ~rsi *vr* to become infected; **infet'tivo, a** *ag* infectious; **in'fetto, a** *ag* infected; *(acque)* polluted, contaminated; **infezi'one** *sf* infection.

**infiac'chire** [infjak'kire] *vt* to weaken // *vi (anche:* ~rsi) to grow weak.

**infiam'mabile** *ag* inflammable.

**infiam'mare** *vt* to set alight; *(fig, MED)* to inflame; ~rsi *vr* to catch fire; *(MED)* to become inflamed; *(fig)*: ~rsi **di** to be fired with; **infiammazi'one** *sf (MED)* inflammation.

**in'fido, a** *ag* unreliable, treacherous.

**infie'rire** *vi*: ~ **su** *(fisicamente)* to attack furiously; *(verbalmente)* to rage at; *(epidemia)* to rage over.

in'figgere [in'fiddʒere] vt: ~ qc in to thrust o drive sth into.

infi'lare vt (ago) to thread; (mettere: chiave) to insert; (: anello, vestito) to slip o put on; (strada) to turn into, take; ~rsi vr: ~rsi in to slip into; (indossare) to slip on; ~ l'uscio to slip into o nip out.

infil'trarsi vr to penetrate, seep through; (MIL) to infiltrate; infil-trazi'one sf infiltration.

infil'zare [infil'tsare] vt (infilare) to string together; (trafiggere) to pierce.

'infimo, a ag lowest.

in'fine av finally; (insomma) in short.

infinità sf infinity; (in quantità): un'~ di an infinite number of.

infi'nito, a ag infinite; (LING) infinitive // sm infinity; (LING) infinitive; all'~ (senza fine) endlessly.

infinocchi'are [infinok'kjare] vt (fam) to hoodwink.

infischi'arsi [infis'kjarsi] vr: ~ di not to care about.

in'fisso, a pp di infiggere // sm fixture; (di porta, finestra) frame.

infit'tire vt, vi (anche: ~rsi) to thicken.

inflazi'one [inflat'tsjone] sf inflation.

in'fliggere [in'fliddʒere] vt to inflict; in'flitto, a pp di infliggere.

influ'ente ag influential; influ'enza sf influence; (MED) influenza, flu.

influ'ire vi: ~ su to influence.

in'flusso sm influence.

infol'tire vt, vi to thicken.

infon'dato, a ag unfounded, ground-less.

in'fondere vt: ~ qc in qn to instill sth in sb.

infor'care vt to fork (up); (bicicletta, cavallo) to get on; (occhiali) to put on.

infor'mare vt to inform, tell; ~rsi vr: ~rsi (di o su) to inquire (about).

infor'matica sf computer science.

informa'tivo, a ag informative.

informa'tore sm informer.

informazi'one [informat'tsjone] sf piece of information; ~i sfpl in-formation sg; chiedere un'~ to ask for (some) information.

in'forme ag shapeless.

informico'larsi, informico'lirsi vr to have pins and needles.

infor'tunio sm accident; ~ sul lavoro industrial accident, accident at work.

infos'sarsi vr (terreno) to sink; (guance) to become hollow; infos'sato, a ag hollow; (occhi) deep-set; (: per malattia) sunken.

in'frangere [in'frandʒere] vt to smash; (fig: legge, patti) to break; ~rsi vr to smash, break; in-fran'gibile ag unbreakable; in'franto, a pp di infrangere // ag broken.

infrazi'one [infrat'tsjone] sf: ~ a breaking of, violation of.

infredda'tura sf slight cold.

infreddo'lito, a ag cold, chilled.

infruttu'oso, a ag fruitless.

infu'ori av out; all'~ outwards; all'~ di (eccetto) except, with the exception of.

infuri'are vi to rage; ~rsi vr to fly into a rage.

infusi'one sf infusion.

in'fuso, a pp di infondere // sm in-fusion; ~ di camomilla camomile tea.

Ing. abbr = ingegnere.

ingabbi'are vt to cage.

ingaggi'are [ingad'dʒare] vt (assumere con compenso) to take on, hire; (SPORT) to sign on; (MIL) to engage; in'gaggio sm hiring; sign-ing on.

ingan'nare vt to deceive; (coniuge) to be unfaithful to; (fisco) to cheat; (eludere) to dodge, elude; (fig: tempo) to while away // vi (apparenza) to be deceptive; ~rsi vr to be mistaken, be wrong; ingan'nevole ag deceptive.

in'ganno sm deceit, deception,

(*azione*) trick; (*menzogna, frode*) cheat, swindle; (*illusione*) illusion.

**ingarbugli'are** [ingarbuʎˈʎare] *vt* to tangle; (*fig*) to confuse, muddle; **~rsi** *vr* to become confused *o* muddled.

**inge'gnarsi** [indʒeɲˈnarsi] *vr* to do one's best, try hard; ~ **per vivere** to live by one's wits.

**inge'gnere** [indʒeɲˈnɛre] *sm* engineer; ~ **civile/navale** civil/naval engineer; **ingegne'ria** *sf* engineering.

**in'gegno** [inˈdʒeɲɲo] *sm* (*intelligenza*) intelligence, brains *pl*; (*capacità creativa*) ingenuity; (*disposizione*) talent; **inge'gnoso, a** *ag* ingenious, clever.

**ingelo'sire** [indʒeloˈzire] *vt* to make jealous // *vi* (*anche:* **~rsi**) to become jealous.

**in'gente** [inˈdʒɛnte] *ag* huge, enormous.

**ingenuità** [indʒenuiˈta] *sf* ingenuousness.

**in'genuo, a** [inˈdʒɛnuo] *ag* ingenuous, naïve.

**inges'sare** [indʒesˈsare] *vt* (*MED*) to put in plaster; **ingessa'tura** *sf* plaster.

**Inghil'terra** [ingilˈtɛrra] *sf*: **l'~** England.

**inghiot'tire** [ingjotˈtire] *vt* to swallow.

**ingial'lire** [indʒalˈlire] *vi* to go yellow.

**ingigan'tire** [indʒiganˈtire] *vt* to enlarge, magnify // *vi* to become gigantic *o* enormous.

**inginocchi'arsi** [indʒinokˈkjarsi] *vr* to kneel (down).

**ingiù** [inˈdʒu] *av* down, downwards.

**ingi'uria** [inˈdʒurja] *sf* insult; (*fig: danno*) damage; **ingiuri'are** *vt* to insult, abuse; **ingiuri'oso, a** *ag* insulting, abusive.

**ingius'tizia** [indʒusˈtittsja] *sf* injustice.

**ingi'usto, a** [inˈdʒusto] *ag* unjust, unfair.

**in'glese** *ag* English // *sm/f* Englishman/woman // *sm* (*LING*) English; **gli I~i** the English; **andarsene** *o* **filare all'~** to take French leave.

**ingoi'are** *vt* to gulp (down); (*fig*) to swallow (up).

**ingol'fare** *vt*, **~rsi** *vr* (*motore*) to flood.

**ingom'brare** *vt* (*strada*) to block; (*stanza*) to clutter up; **in'gombro, a** *ag* (*strada, passaggio*) blocked // *sm* obstacle; **essere d'ingombro** to be in the way.

**in'gordo, a** *ag*: ~ **di** greedy for; (*fig*) greedy *o* avid for.

**ingor'gare** *vt* to be blocked up, be choked up.

**in'gorgo, ghi** *sm* blockage, obstruction; (*anche:* ~ **stradale**) traffic jam.

**ingoz'zare** [ingotˈtsare] *vt* (*animali*) to fatten; (*fig: persona*) to stuff; **~rsi** *vr*: **~rsi (di)** to stuff o.s. (with).

**ingra'naggio** [ingraˈnaddʒo] *sm* (*TECN*) gear; (*di orologio*) mechanism; **gli ~i della burocrazia** the bureaucratic machinery.

**ingra'nare** *vi* to mesh, engage // *vt* to engage; ~ **la marcia** to get into gear.

**ingrandi'mento** *sm* enlargement; extension.

**ingran'dire** *vt* (*anche FOT*) to enlarge; (*estendere*) to extend; (*OTTICA, fig*) to magnify // *vi* (*anche:* **~rsi**) to become larger *o* bigger; (*aumentare*) to grow, increase; (*espandersi*) to expand.

**ingras'sare** *vt* to make fat; (*animali*) to fatten; (*AGR: terreno*) to manure; (*lubrificare*) to oil, lubricate // *vi* (*anche:* **~rsi**) to get fat, put on weight.

**in'grato, a** *ag* ungrateful; (*lavoro*) thankless, unrewarding.

**ingrazi'are** [ingratˈtsjare] *vt*: **~rsi qn** to ingratiate o.s. with sb.

**ingredi'ente** *sm* ingredient.

**in'gresso** sm (porta) entrance; (atrio) hall; (l'entrare) entrance, entry; (facoltà di entrare) admission; "~ libero" "admission free".

**ingros'sare** vt to increase; (folla, livello) to swell // vi (anche: ~rsi) to increase; to swell.

**in'grosso** av: all'~ (COMM) wholesale; (all'incirca) roughly, about.

**igual'cibile** [ingwal'tʃibile] ag crease-resistant.

**ingua'ribile** ag incurable.

**'inguine** sm (ANAT) groin.

**ini'bire** vt to forbid, prohibit; (PSIC) to inhibit; **inibizi'one** sf prohibition, inhibition.

**iniet'tare** vt to inject; ~rsi vr: ~rsi di sangue (occhi) to become bloodshot; **iniezi'one** sf injection.

**inimi'carsi** vr: ~ con qn to fall out with sb.

**inimi'cizia** [inimi'tʃittsja] sf animosity.

**ininter'rotto, a** ag unbroken; uninterrupted.

**iniquità** sf inv iniquity; (atto) wicked action.

**inizi'ale** [init'tsjale] ag, sf initial.

**inizi'are** [init'tsjare] vi, vt to begin, start; ~ qn a to initiate sb into; (pittura etc) to introduce sb to; ~ a fare qc to start doing sth.

**inizia'tiva** [inittsja'tiva] sf initiative; ~ privata private enterprise.

**i'nizio** [i'nittsjo] sm beginning; all'~ at the beginning, at the start; dare ~ a qc to start sth, get sth going.

**innaffi'are** etc = annaffiare etc.

**innal'zare** [innal'tsare] vt (sollevare, alzare) to raise; (rizzare) to erect; ~rsi vr to rise.

**innamo'rare** vt to enchant, charm; ~rsi vr: ~rsi (di qn) to fall in love (with sb); **innamo'rato, a** ag (che nutre amore): **innamorato (di)** in love (with); (appassionato): **innamorato di** very fond of // sm/f lover; sweetheart.

**in'nanzi** [in'nantsi] av (stato in luogo) in front, ahead; (moto a luogo) forward, on; (tempo: prima) before // prep (prima) before; ~ a in front of.

**in'nato, a** ag innate.

**innatu'rale** ag unnatural.

**inne'gabile** ag undeniable.

**innervo'sire** vt: ~ qn to get on sb's nerves; ~rsi vr to get irritated o upset.

**innes'care** vt to prime; **in'nesco, schi** sm primer.

**innes'tare** vt (BOT, MED) to graft; (TECN) to engage; (inserire: presa) to insert; **in'nesto** sm graft; grafting q; (TECN) clutch; (ELETTR) connection.

**'inno** sm hymn; ~ **nazionale** national anthem.

**inno'cente** [inno'tʃɛnte] ag innocent; **inno'cenza** sf innocence.

**in'nocuo, a** ag innocuous, harmless.

**inno'vare** vt to change, make innovations in.

**innume'revole** ag innumerable.

**ino'doro, a** ag odourless.

**inol'trare** vt (AMM) to pass on, forward; ~rsi vr (addentrarsi) to advance, go forward.

**i'noltre** av besides, moreover.

**inon'dare** vt to flood; **inondazi'one** sf flooding q; (flood).

**inope'roso, a** ag inactive, idle.

**inoppor'tuno, a** ag untimely, illtimed; inappropriate; (momento) opportune.

**inorgo'glire** [inorgoʎ'ʎire] vt to make proud // vi (anche: ~rsi) to become proud; ~rsi di qc to pride o.s. on sth.

**inorri'dire** vt to horrify // vi to be horrified.

**inospi'tale** ag inhospitable.

**inosser'vato, a** ag (non notato) unobserved; (non rispettato) not observed, not kept.

**inossi'dabile** ag stainless.

**inqua'drare** vt (foto, immagine) to frame; (fig) to situate, set.

**inquie'tare** vt (turbare) to disturb, worry; ~rsi vr to worry, become anxious; (impazientirsi) to get upset.

**inqui'eto, a** ag restless; (pre-occupato) worried, anxious; **inquie-'tudine** sf anxiety, worry.

**inqui'lino, a** sm/f tenant.

**inquina'mento** sm pollution.

**inqui'nare** vt to pollute.

**inqui'sire** vt, vi to investigate; **inquisi'tore, 'trice** ag (sguardo) inquiring; **inquisizi'one** sf (STORIA) inquisition.

**insabbi'are** vt (fig: pratica) to shelve; ~rsi vr (arenarsi: barca) to run aground; (fig: pratica) to be shelved.

**insac'cati** smpl (CUC) sausages.

**insa'lata** sf salad; ~ **mista** mixed salad; **insalati'era** sf salad bowl.

**insa'lubre** ag unhealthy.

**insa'nabile** ag (piaga) which cannot be healed; (situazione) irremediable; (odio) implacable.

**insangui'nare** vt to stain with blood.

**insa'puta** sf: all'~ **di qn** without sb knowing.

**insce'nare** [inʃe'nare] vt (TEATRO) to stage, put on; (fig) to stage.

**insedi'are** vt to install; ~rsi vr to take up office; (popolo, colonia) to settle.

**in'segna** [in'seɲɲa] sf sign; (emblema) sign, emblem; (bandiera) flag, banner; ~e sfpl (decorazioni) insignia pl.

**insegna'mento** [inseɲɲa'mento] sm teaching.

**inse'gnante** [inse'ɲɲante] ag teaching // sm/f teacher.

**inse'gnare** [inse'ɲɲare] vt, vi to teach; ~ **a qn qc** to teach sb sth; ~ **a qn a fare qc** to teach sb (how) to do sth.

**insegui'mento** sm pursuit, chase.

**insegu'ire** vt to pursue, chase.

**inselvati'chire** [inselvati'kire] vi (anche: ~rsi) to grow wild.

**insena'tura** sf inlet, creek.

**insen'sato, a** ag senseless, stupid.

**insen'sibile** ag (nervo) insensible;

(persona) indifferent.

**inse'rire** vt to insert; (ELETTR) to connect; (allegare) to enclose; (annuncio) to put in, place; ~rsi vr (fig): ~rsi in to become part of; **in'serto** sm (pubblicazione) insert.

**inservi'ente** sm/f attendant.

**inserzi'one** [inser'tsjone] sf insertion; (avviso) advertisement; **fare un'~ sul giornale** to put an advertisement in the paper.

**insetti'cida, i** [insetti'tʃida] sm insecticide.

**in'setto** sm insect.

**in'sidia** sf snare, trap; (pericolo) hidden danger; **insidi'are** vt: ~ **la vita di qn** to make an attempt on sb's life.

**insi'eme** av together // prep: ~ **a o con** together with // sm whole; (MAT, servizio, assortimento) set; (MODA) ensemble, outfit; **tutti** ~ all together; **tutto** ~ all together; (in una volta) at one go; **nell'~** on the whole; **d'~** (veduta etc) overall.

**insignifi'cante** [insiɲɲifi'kante] ag insignificant.

**insi'gnire** [insiɲ'ɲire] vt: ~ **qn di** to honour o decorate sb with.

**insin'cero, a** [insin'tʃero] ag insincere.

**insinda'cabile** ag unquestionable.

**insinu'are** vt (introdurre): ~ **qc** in to slip o slide sth into; (fig) to insinuate, imply; ~rsi vr: ~rsi in to seep into; (fig) to creep into; to worm one's way into.

**insi'stente** ag insistent; persistent.

**in'sistere** vi: ~ **su qc** to insist on sth; ~ **in qc/a fare** (perseverare) to persist in sth/in doing; **insis'tito, a** pp di **insistere**.

**insoddis'fatto, a** ag dissatisfied.

**insoffe'rente** ag intolerant.

**insolazi'one** [insolat'tsjone] sf (MED) sunstroke.

**inso'lente** ag insolent; **insolen'tire** vi to grow insolent // vt to insult, be rude to.

**in'solito, a** ag unusual, out of the

ordinary.

**inso'luto, a** _ag_ (_non risolto_) unsolved; (_non pagato_) unpaid, understanding.

**insol'vibile** _ag_ insolvent.

**in'somma** _av_ (_in breve, in conclusione_) in short; (_dunque_) well // _escl_ for heaven's sake!

**in'sonne** _ag_ sleepless; **in'sonnia** _sf_ insomnia, sleeplessness.

**insonno'lito, a** _ag_ sleepy, drowsy.

**insoppor'tabile** _ag_ unbearable.

**in'sorgere** [in'sordʒere] _vi_ (_ribellarsi_) to rise up, rebel; (_apparire_) to come up, arise.

**in'sorto, a** _pp di_ **insorgere** // _smf_ rebel, insurgent.

**insospet'tire** _vt_ to make suspicious // _vi_ (_anche:_ ~**rsi**) to become suspicious.

**inspi'rare** _vt_ to breathe in, inhale.

**in'stabile** _ag_ (_carico, indole_) unstable; (_tempo_) unsettled; (_equilibrio_) unsteady.

**instal'lare** _vt_ to install; ~**rsi** _vr_ (_sistemarsi_): ~**rsi** in to settle in; **installazi'one** _sf_ installation.

**instan'cabile** _ag_ untiring, indefatigable.

**instau'rare** _vt_ to introduce, institute.

**instra'dare** _vt_: ~ (**verso**) to direct (towards).

**insuc'cesso** [insut'tʃesso] _sm_ failure, flop.

**insudici'are** [insudi'tʃare] _vt_ to dirty; ~**rsi** _vr_ to get dirty.

**insuffici'ente** [insuffi'tʃɛnte] _ag_ insufficient; (_compito, allievo_) inadequate; **insuffici'enza** _sf_ insufficiency; inadequacy; (_INS_) fail.

**insu'lare** _ag_ insular.

**insu'lina** _sf_ insulin.

**in'sulso, a** _ag_ (_sciocco_) inane, silly; (_persona_) dull, insipid.

**insul'tare** _vt_ to insult, affront.

**in'sulto** _sm_ insult, affront.

**insussis'tente** _ag_ non-existent.

**intac'care** _vt_ (_fare tacche_) to cut into; (_corrodere_) to corrode; (_fig: cominciare ad usare: risparmi_) to

break into; (_: ledere_) to damage.

**intagli'are** [intaʎ'ʎare] _vt_ to carve; **in'taglio** _sm_ carving.

**intan'gibile** [intan'dʒibile] _ag_ untouchable; inviolable.

**in'tanto** _av_ (_nel frattempo_) meanwhile; in the meantime; (_per cominciare_) just to begin with; ~ che _cong_ while.

**in'tarsio** _sm_ inlaying _q_, marquetry _q_; inlay.

**inta'sare** _vt_ to choke (up), block (up); (_AUT_) to obstruct, block; ~**rsi** _vr_ to become choked _o_ blocked.

**intas'care** _vt_ to pocket.

**in'tatto, a** _ag_ intact; (_puro_) unsullied.

**intavo'lare** _vt_ to start, enter into.

**inte'grale** _ag_ complete; (_pane, farina_) wholemeal (_Brit_), whole-wheat (_US_); (_MAT_): **calcolo** ~ integral calculus.

**inte'grante** _ag_: **parte** ~ integral part.

**inte'grare** _vt_ to complete; (_MAT_) to integrate; ~**rsi** _vr_ (_persona_) to become integrated.

**integrità** _sf_ integrity.

**'integro, a** _ag_ (_intatto, intero_) complete, whole; (_retto_) upright.

**intelaia'tura** _sf_ frame; (_fig_) structure, framework.

**intel'letto** _sm_ intellect; **intellet tu'ale** _ag, smf_ intellectual.

**intelli'gente** [intelli'dʒɛnte] _ag_ intelligent; **intelli'genza** _sf_ intelligence.

**intem'perie** _sfpl_ bad weather _sg_.

**intempes'tivo, a** _ag_ untimely.

**inten'dente** _sm_: ~ **di Finanza** inland (_Brit_) _o_ internal (_US_) revenue officer; **inten'denza** _sf_: **intendenza di Finanza** inland (_Brit_) _o_ internal (_US_) revenue office.

**in'tendere** _vt_ (_avere intenzione_): ~ **fare** qc to intend _o_ mean to do sth; (_comprendere_) to understand; (_udire_) to hear; (_significare_) to mean; ~**rsi** _vr_ (_conoscere_): ~**rsi di** to know a lot about, be a connoisseur

of; (*accordarsi*) to get on (well);
**intendersela con qn** (*avere una relazione amorosa*) to have an affair
with sb; **intendi'mento** *sm* (*intelligenza*) understanding; (*proposito*) intention; **intendi'tore, 'trice**
*sm/f* connoisseur, expert.

**intene'rire** *vt* (*fig*) to move (to
pity); ~**rsi** *vr* (*fig*) to be moved.

**inten'sivo, a** *ag* intensive.

**in'tenso, a** *ag* intense.

**in'tento, a** *ag* (*teso, assorto*): ~
(a) intent (on), absorbed (in) // *sm*
aim, purpose.

**intenzio'nale** [intentsjo'nale] *ag* intentional.

**intenzi'one** [intentsjone] *sf* intention; (*DIR*) intent; avere ~ **di fare**
**qc** to intend to do sth, have the intention of doing sth.

**interca'lare** *sm* pet phrase, stock
phrase // *vt* to insert.

**interca'pedine** *sf* gap, cavity.

**intercet'tare** [intertʃet'tare] *vt* to
intercept.

**inter'detto, a** *pp di* **interdire** // *ag*
forbidden, prohibited; (*sconcertato*)
dumbfounded // *sm* (*REL*) interdict.

**inter'dire** *vt* to forbid, prohibit, ban;
(*REL*) to interdict; (*DIR*) to deprive
of civil rights; **interdizi'one** *sf*
prohibition, ban.

**interessa'mento** *sm* interest.

**interes'sante** *ag* interesting;
**essere in stato** ~ to be expecting (a
baby).

**interes'sare** *vt* to interest; (*concernere*) to concern, be of interest to;
(*far intervenire*): ~ **qn a** to draw
sb's attention to // *vi*: ~ **a** to interest,
matter to; ~**rsi** *vr* (*mostrare interesse*): ~**rsi a** to take an interest in,
be interested in; (*occuparsi*): ~**rsi**
**di** to take care of.

**inte'resse** *sm* (*anche COMM*) interest.

**inter'faccia, ce** [inter'fattʃa] *sf* (*INFORM*) interface.

**interfe'renza** [interfe'rɛntsa] *sf*
interference.

**interfe'rire** *vi* to interfere.

**interiezi'one** [interjet'tsjone] *sf*
exclamation, interjection.

**interi'ora** *sfpl* entrails.

**interi'ore** *ag* interior, inner, inside,
internal; (*fig*) inner.

**inter'ludio** *sm* (*MUS*) interlude.

**inter'medio, a** *ag* intermediate.

**inter'mezzo** [inter'mɛddzo] *sm*
(*intervallo*) interval; (*breve spettacolo*) intermezzo.

**inter'nare** *vt* (*arrestare*) to intern;
(*MED*) to commit (to a mental institution).

**internazio'nale** [internatsjo'nale]
*ag* international.

**in'terno, a** *ag* (*di dentro*) internal,
interior, inner; (*: mare*) inland;
(*nazionale*) domestic; (*allievo*)
boarding // *sm* inside, interior; (*di
paese*) interior; (*fodera*) lining; (*di
appartamento*) flat (number); (*TEL*)
extension // *sm/f* (*INS*) boarder; ~**i**
*smpl* (*CINEMA*) interior shots; **all'**~
inside; **Ministero degli I~i** Ministry
of the Interior, ≈ Home Office (*Brit*),
Department of the Interior (*US*).

**in'tero, a** *ag* (*integro, intatto*)
whole, entire; (*completo, totale*)
complete; (*numero*) whole; (*non
ridotto: biglietto*) full.

**interpel'lare** *vt* to consult.

**inter'porre** *vt* (*ostacolo*): ~ **qc a**
**qc** to put sth in the way of sth; (*influenza*) to use; ~ **appello** (*DIR*) to
appeal; **interporsi** *vr* to intervene;
**interporsi fra** (*mettersi in mezzo*)
to come between; **inter'posto, a** *pp*
*di* **interporre**.

**interpre'tare** *vt* to interpret;
**in'terprete** *sm/f* interpreter; (*TEATRO*) actor/actress, performer;
(*MUS*) performer.

**interro'gare** *vt* to question; (*INS*) to
test; **interroga'tivo, a** *ag* (*occhi,
sguardo*) questioning, inquiring;
(*LING*) interrogative // *sm* question;
(*fig*) mystery; **interroga'torio, a**
*ag* interrogatory, questioning // *sm*
(*DIR*) questioning *q*; **interroga-**

zi'one *sf* questioning *q*; (*INS*) oral test.

inter'rompere *vt* to interrupt; (*studi, trattative*) to break off, interrupt; ~rsi *vr* to break off, stop; inter'rotto, a *pp di* interrompere.

interrut'tore *sm* switch.

interruzi'one [interrut'tsjone] *sf* interruption; break.

interse'care *vt*, ~rsi *vr* to intersect.

inter'stizio [inter'stittsjo] *sm* interstice, crack.

interur'bano, a *ag* inter-city; (*TEL: chiamata*) trunk *cpd*, long-distance; (: *telefono*) long-distance // *sf* trunk call, long-distance call.

inter'vallo *sm* interval; (*spazio*) space, gap.

interve'nire *vi* (*partecipare*): ~ a to take part in; (*intromettersi: anche POL*) to intervene; (*MED: operare*) to operate; inter'vento *sm* participation; (*intromissione*) intervention; (*MED*) operation; fare un intervento nel corso di (*dibattito, programma*) to take part in.

inter'vista *sf* interview; intervi'stare *vt* to interview.

in'teso, a *pp di* intendere // *ag* agreed // *sf* understanding; (*accordo*) agreement, understanding; non darsi per ~ di qc to take no notice of sth.

intes'tare *vt* (*lettera*) to address; (*proprietà*): ~ a to register in the name of; ~ un assegno a qn to make out a cheque to sb; intestazi'one *sf* heading; (*su carta da lettere*) letterhead; (*registrazione*) registration.

intes'tino, a *ag* (*lotte*) internal, civil // *sm* (*ANAT*) intestine.

inti'mare *vt* to order, command; intimazi'one *sf* order, command.

intimi'dire *vt* to intimidate // *vi* (*anche:* ~rsi) to grow shy.

intimità *sf* intimacy; privacy; (*familiarità*) familiarity.

'intimo, a *ag* intimate; (*affetti,

*vita*) private; (*fig: profondo*) inmost // *sm* (*persona*) intimate *o* close friend; (*dell'animo*) bottom, depths *pl*; parti ~e (*ANAT*) private parts.

intimo'rire *vt* to frighten; ~rsi *vr* to become frightened.

in'tingolo *sm* sauce; (*pietanza*) stew.

intiriz'zire [intirid'dzire] *vt* to numb // *vi* (*anche:* ~rsi) to go numb.

intito'lare *vt* to give a title to; (*dedicare*) to dedicate.

intolle'rabile *ag* intolerable.

intolle'rante *ag* intolerant.

in'tonaco *o chi sm* plaster.

into'nare *vt* (*canto*) to start to sing; (*armonizzare*) to match; ~rsi *vr* (*colori*) to go together; ~rsi a (*carnagione*) to suit; (*abito*) to go with, match.

inton'tire *vt* to stun, daze // *vi*, ~rsi *vr* to be stunned *o* dazed.

in'toppo *sm* stumbling block, obstacle.

in'torno *av* around; ~ a *prep* (*attorno a*) around; (*riguardo, circa*) about.

intorpi'dire *vt* to numb; (*fig*) to make sluggish // *vi* (*anche:* ~rsi) to grow numb; (*fig*) to become sluggish.

intossi'care *vt* to poison; intossicazi'one *sf* poisoning.

intralci'are [intral'tʃare] *vt* to hamper, hold up.

intransi'tivo, a *ag, sm* intransitive.

intrapren'dente *ag* enterprising, go-ahead.

intra'prendere *vt* to undertake.

intrat'tabile *ag* intractable.

intratte'nere *vt* to entertain; to engage in conversation; ~rsi *vr* to linger; ~rsi su qc to dwell on sth.

intrave'dere *vt* to catch a glimpse of; (*fig*) to foresee.

intrecci'are [intret'tʃare] *vt* (*capelli*) to plait, braid; (*intessere: anche fig*) to weave, interweave, intertwine; ~rsi *vr* to intertwine, become interwoven; ~ le mani to clasp one's hands; in'treccio *sm* (*fig: trama*) plot, story.

**intri'gare** *vi* to manoeuvre (Brit), maneuver (US), scheme; **in'trigo, ghi** *sm* plot, intrigue.

**in'trinseco, a, ci, che** *ag* intrinsic.

**in'triso, a** *ag*: ~ **(di)** soaked (in).

**intro'durre** *vt* to introduce; (chiave etc): ~ **qc in** to insert sth into; (persone: far entrare) to show in; **introdursi** *vr* (moda, tecniche) to be introduced; **introdursi in** (persona: penetrare) to enter; (: entrare furtivamente) to steal o slip into; **introduzi'one** *sf* introduction.

**in'troito** *sm* income, revenue.

**intro'mettersi** *vr* to interfere, meddle; (interporsi) to intervene.

**in'truglio** [in'truʎʎo] *sm* concoction.

**intrusi'one** *sf* intrusion; interference.

**in'truso, a** *sm/f* intruder.

**intu'ire** *vt* to perceive by intuition; (rendersi conto) to realize; **intu'ito** *sm* intuition; (perspicacia) perspicacity; **intuizi'one** *sf* intuition.

**inu'mano, a** *ag* inhuman.

**inumi'dire** *vt* to dampen, moisten; ~rsi *vr* to become damp o wet.

**i'nutile** *ag* useless; (superfluo) pointless, unnecessary; **inutilità** *sf* uselessness; pointlessness.

**inva'dente** *ag* (fig) interfering, nosey.

**in'vadere** *vt* to invade; (affollare) to swarm into, overrun; (sog: acque) to flood; **invadi'trice** *ag vedi* **invasore**.

**inva'ghirsi** [inva'girsi] *vr*: ~ **di** to take a fancy to.

**invalidità** *sf* infirmity; disability; (DIR) invalidity.

**in'valido, a** *ag* (infermo) infirm, invalid; (al lavoro) disabled; (DIR: nullo) invalid // *sm/f* invalid; disabled person.

**in'vano** *av* in vain.

**invasi'one** *sf* invasion.

**in'vaso, a** *pp* di **invadere**.

**inva'sore, invadi'trice** [invadi-'tritʃe] *ag* invading // *sm* invader.

**invecchi'are** [invek'kjare] *vi* (persona) to grow old; (vino, popolazione) to age; (moda) to become dated // *vt* to age; (far apparire più vecchio) to make look older.

**in'vece** [in'vetʃe] *av* instead; (al contrario) on the contrary; ~ **di** *prep* instead of.

**inve'ire** *vi*: ~ **contro** to rail against.

**inven'tare** *vt* to invent; (pericoli, pettegolezzi) to make up, invent.

**inven'tario** *sm* inventory; (COMM) stocktaking q.

**inven'tivo, a** *ag* inventive // *sf* inventiveness.

**inven'tore** *sm* inventor.

**invenzi'one** [inven'tsjone] *sf* invention; (bugia) lie, story.

**inver'nale** *ag* winter *cpd*; (simile all'inverno) wintry.

**in'verno** *sm* winter.

**invero'simile** *ag* unlikely.

**inversi'one** *sf* inversion; reversal; "divieto d'~" (AUT) "no U-turns".

**in'verso, a** *ag* opposite; (MAT) inverse // *sm* contrary, opposite; **in senso** ~ in the opposite direction; **in ordine** ~ in reverse order.

**inver'tire** *vt* to invert, reverse; ~ **la marcia** (AUT) to do a U-turn; **inver'tito, a** *sm/f* homosexual.

**investi'gare** *vt, vi* to investigate; **investiga'tore, trice** *sm/f* investigator, detective; **investigazi'one** *sf* investigation, inquiry.

**investi'mento** *sm* (ECON) investment; (scontro, urto) crash, collision; (incidente stradale) road accident.

**inves'tire** *vt* (denaro) to invest; (sog: veicolo: pedone) to knock down; (: altro veicolo) to crash into; (apostrofare) to assail; (incaricare): ~ **qn di** to invest sb with.

**invi'are** *vt* to send; **invi'ato, a** *sm/f* envoy; (STAMPA) correspondent.

**in'vidia** *sf* envy; **invidi'are** *vt*: ~ **qn (per qc)** to envy sb for sth; ~ **qc a qn** to envy sb sth; **invidi'oso,**

**a** ag envious.

**in'vio, 'vii** sm sending; (insieme di merci) consignment.

**invipe'rito, a** ag furious.

**invischi'are** [invis'kjare] vt (fig): ~ qn in to involve sb in; ~rsi vr: ~rsi (con qn/in qc) to get mixed up o involved (with sb/in sth).

**invi'sibile** ag invisible.

**invi'tare** vt to invite; ~ qn a fare to invite sb to do; **invi'tato, a** sm/f guest; **in'vito** sm invitation.

**invo'care** vt (chiedere: aiuto, pace) to cry out for; (appellarsi: la legge, Dio) to appeal to, invoke.

**invogli'are** [invoʎ'ʎare] vt: ~ qn a fare to tempt sb to do, induce sb to do.

**involon'tario, a** ag (errore) unintentional; (gesto) involuntary.

**invol'tino** sm (CUC) roulade.

**in'volto** sm (pacco) parcel; (fagotto) bundle.

**in'volucro** sm cover, wrapping.

**involuzi'one** [involut'tsjone] sf (di stile) convolutedness; (regresso): subire un'~ to regress.

**inzacche'rare** [intsakke'rare] vt to spatter with mud.

**inzup'pare** [intsup'pare] vt to soak; ~rsi vr to get soaked.

**'io** pronome I // sm inv: l'~ the ego, the self; ~ stesso(a) I myself.

**i'odio** sm iodine.

**i'ogurt** sm inv = **yoghurt**.

**i'onio** sm: lo ~, il mar ~ the Ionian (Sea).

**iperme'cato** sm hypermarket.

**ipertensi'one** sf high blood pressure, hypertension.

**ip'nosi** sf hypnosis; **ipno'tismo** sm hypnotism; **ipnotiz'zare** vt to hypnotize.

**ipocri'sia** sf hypocrisy.

**i'pocrita, i, e** ag hypocritical // sm/f hypocrite.

**ipo'teca, che** sf mortgage; **ipote'care** vt to mortgage.

**i'potesi** sf inv hypothesis; **ipo'tetico, a, ci, che** ag hypothetical.

**'ippico, a, ci, che** ag horse cpd // sf horseracing.

**ippocas'tano** sm horse chestnut.

**ip'podromo** sm racecourse.

**ippo'potamo** sm hippopotamus.

**'ira** sf anger, wrath.

**I'ran** sm: l'~ Iran.

**I'raq** sm: l'~ Iraq.

**'iride** sf (arcobaleno) rainbow; (ANAT, BOT) iris.

**Ir'landa** sf: l'~ Ireland; l'~ del Nord Northern Ireland, Ulster; la Repubblica d'~ Eire, the Republic of Ireland; **irlan'dese** ag Irish // sm/f Irishman/woman; **gli Irlandesi** the Irish.

**iro'nia** sf irony; **i'ronico, a, ci, che** ag ironic(al).

**irradi'are** vt to radiate; (sog: raggi di luce: illuminare) to shine on // vi (diffondersi: anche: ~rsi) to radiate; **irradiazi'one** sf radiation.

**irragio'nevole** [irradʒo'nevole] ag irrational; unreasonable.

**irrazio'nale** [irrattsjo'nale] ag irrational.

**irre'ale** ag unreal.

**irrecupe'rabile** ag irretrievable; (fig: person) irredeemable.

**irrecu'sabile** ag (offerta) not to be refused; (prova) irrefutable.

**irrego'lare** ag irregular; (terreno) uneven.

**irremo'vibile** ag (fig) unshakeable, unyielding.

**irrepa'rabile** ag irreparable; (fig) inevitable.

**irrepe'ribile** ag nowhere to be found.

**irrequi'eto, a** ag restless.

**irresis'tibile** ag irresistible.

**irrespon'sabile** ag irresponsible.

**irridu'cibile** [irridu'tʃibile] ag irreducible; (fig) indomitable.

**irri'gare** vt (annaffiare) to irrigate; (sog: fiume etc) to flow through; **irrigazi'one** sf irrigation.

**irrigi'dire** [irridʒi'dire] vt, ~rsi vr to stiffen.

**irri'sorio, a** ag derisory.

**irri'tare** vt (mettere di malumore) to

irritate, annoy; (MED) to irritate; ~**rsi** vr (stizzirsi) to become irritated o annoyed; (MED) to become irritated; **irritazi'one** sf irritation; annoyance.

**ir'rompere** vi: ~ **in** to burst into.

**irro'rare** vt to sprinkle; (AGR) to spray.

**irru'ente** ag (fig) impetuous, violent.

**irruzi'one** [irrut'tsjone] sf: **fare** ~ **in** to burst into; (sog: polizia) to raid.

'**irto, a** ag bristly; ~ **di** bristling with.

**is'critto, a** pp di **iscrivere** // smf member; **per o in** ~ in writing.

**is'crivere** vt to register, enter; (persona): ~ (a) to register (in), enrol (in); ~**rsi** vr: ~**rsi** (a) (club, partito) to join; (università) to register o enrol (at); (esame, concorso) to register o enter (for); **iscrizi'one** sf (epigrafe etc) inscription; (a scuola, società) enrolment, registration; (registrazione) registration.

**Is'lam** sm: **l'**~ Islam.

**Is'landa** sf: **l'**~ Iceland.

'**isola** sf island; ~ **pedonale** (AUT) pedestrian precinct.

**isola'mento** sm isolation; (TECN) insulation.

**iso'lante** ag insulating // sm insulator.

**iso'lare** vt to isolate; (TECN) to insulate; (: acusticamente) to soundproof; **iso'lato, a** ag isolated; insulated // sm (edificio) block.

**ispetto'rato** sm inspectorate.

**ispet'tore** sm inspector.

**ispezio'nare** [ispettsjo'nare] vt to inspect.

**ispezi'one** [ispet'tsjone] sf inspection.

'**ispido, a** ag bristly, shaggy.

**ispi'rare** vt to inspire; ~**rsi** vr: ~**rsi a** to draw one's inspiration from.

**Isra'ele** sm: **l'**~ Israel; **israeli'ano, a** ag, smf Israeli.

**is'sare** vt to hoist.

**istan'taneo, a** ag instantaneous // sf (FOT) snapshot.

**is'tante** sm instant, moment; **all'**~, **sull'**~ instantly, immediately.

**is'tanza** [is'tantsa] sf petition, request.

**is'terico, a, ci, che** ag hysterical.

**iste'rismo** sm hysteria.

**isti'gare** vt to incite; **istigazi'one** sf incitement; **istigazione a delinquere** (DIR) incitement to crime.

**is'tinto** sm instinct.

**istitu'ire** vt (fondare) to institute, found; (porre: confronto) to establish; (intraprendere: inchiesta) to set up.

**isti'tuto** sm institute; (di università) department; (ente, DIR) institution; ~ **di bellezza** beauty salon.

**istituzi'one** [istitut'tsjone] sf institution.

'**istmo** sm (GEO) isthmus.

**istra'dare** vt = **instradare**.

'**istrice** ['istritfe] sm porcupine.

**istri'one** sm (peg) ham actor.

**istru'ire** vt (insegnare) to teach; (ammaestrare) to train; (informare) to instruct, inform; (DIR) to prepare; **istrut'tore, 'trice** smf instructor // ag: **giudice istruttore** examining (Brit) o committing (US) magistrate; **istrut'toria** sf (DIR) (preliminary) investigation and hearing; **istruzi'one** sf education; training; (direttiva) instruction; (DIR) ~ **istruttoria; istruzioni per l'uso** instructions (for use).

**I'talia** sf: **l'**~ Italy.

**itali'ano, a** ag Italian // smf Italian // sm (LING) Italian; **gli I**~**i** the Italians.

**itine'rario** sm itinerary.

**itte'rizia** [itte'rittsja] sf (MED) jaundice.

'**ittico, a, ci, che** ag fish cpd; fishing cpd.

**lugos'lavia** sf = Jugoslavia.

**iugos'lavo, a** ag, smf = **jugoslavo, a**.

**i'uta** sf jute.

**I.V.A.** ['iva] sigla f = **imposta sul**

valore aggiunto.

# J

**jazz** [dʒaz] sm jazz.

**jeans** [dʒinz] smpl jeans.

**Jugos'lavia** [jugoz'lavja] sf: la ~ Yugoslavia; **jugos'lavo, a** ag, smf Yugoslav(ian).

**'juta** ['juta] sf = iuta.

# K

**K** abbr (INFORM) K.

**k** abbr (= kilo) k.

**karatè** sm karate.

**Kg** abbr (= chilogrammo) kg.

**'killer** sm inv gunman, hired gun.

**km** abbr (= chilometro) km.

**'krapfen** sm inv (CUC) doughnut.

# L

**l'** det vedi la, lo.

**la** det f (dav V l') the // pronome (dav V l') (oggetto: persona) her; (: cosa) it; (: forma di cortesia) you // sm inv (MUS) A; (: solfeggiando la scala) la.

**là** av there; **di ~** (da quel luogo) from there; (in quel luogo) in there; (dall'altra parte) over there; **di ~ di** beyond; **per di ~** that way; **più in ~** further on; (tempo) later on; **fatti in ~** move up; **~ dentro/sopra/sotto** in/up (o on)/under there; vedi quello.

**'labbro** sm (pl(f): labbra: solo nel senso ANAT) lip.

**labi'rinto** sm labyrinth, maze.

**labora'torio** sm (di ricerca) laboratory; (di arti, mestieri) workshop; **~ linguistico** language laboratory.

**labori'oso, a** ag (faticoso) laborious; (attivo) hard-working.

**labu'rista, i, e** ag Labour (Brit) cpd // smf Labour Party member

(Brit).

**'lacca, che** sf lacquer.

**'laccio** ['lattʃo] sm noose; (legaccio, tirante) lasso; (di scarpa) lace; **~ emostatico** tourniquet.

**lace'rare** [latʃe'rare] vt to tear to shreds, lacerate; **~rsi** vr to tear; **'lacero, a** ag (logoro) torn, tattered; (MED) lacerated.

**'lacrima** sf tear; **in ~e** in tears; **lacri'mare** vi to water; **lacri'mogeno, a** ag: gas lacrimogeno tear gas.

**la'cuna** sf (fig) gap.

**'ladro** sm thief; **ladro'cinio** sm theft, larceny.

**laggiù** [lad'dʒu] av down there; (di là) over there.

**la'gnarsi** [laɲ'narsi] vr: **~ (di)** to complain (about).

**'lago, ghi** sm lake.

**'lagrima** etc = lacrima etc.

**la'guna** sf lagoon.

**'laico, a, ci, che** ag (apostolato) lay; (vita) secular; (scuola) non-denominational // smf layman/woman // sm lay brother.

**'lama** sf blade // sm inv (ZOOL) llama; (REL) lama.

**lambic'care** vt to distil; **~rsi** il cervello to rack one's brains.

**lam'bire** vt to lick; to lap.

**la'mella** sf (di metallo etc) thin sheet, thin strip; (di fungo) gill.

**lamen'tare** vt to lament; **~rsi** vr (emettere lamenti) to moan, groan; (rammaricarsi): **~rsi (di)** to complain (about); **lamen'tela** sf complaining q; **lamen'tevole** ag (voce) complaining, plaintive; (destino) pitiful; **la'mento** sm moan, groan; wail; **lamen'toso, a** ag plaintive.

**la'metta** sf razor blade.

**lami'era** sf sheet metal.

**'lamina** sf (lastra sottile) thin sheet (o layer o plate); **~ d'oro** gold leaf; gold foil; **lami'nare** vt to laminate; **lami'nato, a** ag laminated; (tessuto) lamé // sm laminate.

**'lampada** sf lamp; ~ a gas gas lamp; ~ a spirito blow lamp (Brit), blow torch (US); ~ da tavolo table lamp.

**lampa'dario** sm chandelier.

**lampa'dina** sf light bulb; ~ tascabile pocket torch (Brit) o flashlight (US).

**lam'pante** ag (fig: evidente) crystal clear, evident.

**lampeggi'are** [lamped'dʒare] vi (luce, fari) to flash // vb impers: **lampeggia** there's lightning; **lampeggia'tore** sm (AUT) indicator.

**lampi'one** sm street light o lamp (Brit).

**'lampo** sm (METEOR) flash of lightning; (di luce, fig) flash; ~i smpl lightning ◊ // ag inv: cerniera ~ zip (fastener) (Brit), zipper (US); guerra ~ blitzkrieg.

**lam'pone** sm raspberry.

**'lana** sf wool; ~ d'acciaio steel wool; pura ~ vergine pure new wool; ~ di vetro glass wool.

**lan'cetta** [lan'tʃetta] sf (indice) pointer, needle; (di orologio) hand.

**'lancia** ['lantʃa] sf (arma) lance; (: picca) spear; (di pompa antincendio) nozzle; (imbarcazione) launch.

**lanciafi'amme** [lantʃa'fjamme] sm inv flamethrower.

**lanci'are** [lan'tʃare] vt to throw, hurl, fling; (SPORT) to throw; (far partire: automobile) to get up to full speed; (bombe) to drop; (razzo, prodotto, moda) to launch; ~rsi vr: ~rsi contro/su to throw o hurl o fling o.s. against/on; ~rsi in (fig) to embark on.

**lanci'nante** [lantʃi'nante] ag (dolore) shooting, throbbing; (grido) piercing.

**'lancio** ['lantʃo] sm throwing o; throw; dropping q; drop; launching q; launch; ~ del peso putting the shot.

**'landa** sf (GEO) moor.

**languido, a** ag (fiacco) languid, weak; (tenero, malinconico) lan-

guishing.

**langu'ore** sm weakness, languor.

**lani'ficio** [lani'fitʃo] sm woollen mill.

**la'noso, a** ag woolly.

**lan'terna** sf lantern; (faro) lighthouse.

**la'nugine** [la'nudʒine] sf down.

**lapi'dare** vt to stone.

**lapi'dario, a** ag (fig) terse.

**'lapide** sf (di sepolcro) tombstone; (commemorativa) plaque.

**'lapis** sm inv pencil.

**Lap'ponia** sf Lapland.

**'lapsus** sm inv slip.

**'lardo** sm bacon fat, lard.

**lar'ghezza** [lar'gettsa] sf width; breadth; looseness; generosity; ~ di vedute broad-mindedness.

**'largo, a, ghi, ghe** ag wide; broad; (maniche) wide; (abito: troppo ampio) loose; (fig) generous // sm width; breadth; (mare aperto): il ~ the open sea // sf: stare o tenersi alla ~a (da qn/qc) to keep one's distance (from sb/sth), keep away (from sb/sth); ~ due metri two metres wide; ~ di spalle broadshouldered; di ~ghe vedute broadminded; su ~a scala on a large scale; di manica ~a generous, open-handed; al ~ di Genova off (the coast of) Genoa; farsi ~ tra la folla to push one's way through the crowd.

**'larice** ['laritʃe] sm (BOT) larch.

**larin'gite** [larin'dʒite] sf laryngitis.

**'larva** sf larva; (fig) shadow.

**la'sagne** [la'zaɲe] sfpl lasagna sg.

**lasci'are** [laʃ'ʃare] vt to leave; (abbandonare) to leave, abandon, give up; (cessare di tenere) to let go of // vb ausiliare: ~ fare qn to let sb do // vi: ~ di fare (smettere) to stop doing; ~rsi andare/truffare to let o.s. go/be cheated; ~ andare o correre o perdere to let things go their own way; ~ stare qc/qn to leave sth/sb alone.

**'lascito** ['laʃʃito] sm (DIR) legacy.

**'laser** ['lazer] ag, sm inv: (raggio) ~

laser (beam).

**lassa'tivo, a** *ag, sm* laxative.

**'lasso** *sm*: ~ **di tempo** interval, lapse of time.

**lassù** *av* up there.

**'lastra** *sf* (*di pietra*) slab; (*di metallo, FOT*) plate; (*di ghiaccio, vetro*) sheet; (*radiografica*) X-ray (plate).

**lastri'care** *vt* to pave; **lastri'cato** *sm*, **'lastrico, ci** *o* **chi** *sm* paving.

**late'rale** *ag* lateral, side *cpd*; (*uscita, ingresso etc*) side *cpd* // *sm* (*CALCIO*) half-back.

**late'rizio** [late'rittsjo] *sm* (perforated) brick.

**lati'fondo** *sm* large estate.

**la'tino, a** *ag, sm* Latin; ~-**ameri'cano a** *ag* Latin-American.

**lati'tante** *smf* fugitive (from justice).

**lati'tudine** *sf* latitude.

**'lato, a** *ag* (*fig*) wide, broad // *sm* side; (*fig*) aspect, point of view; **in senso** ~ broadly speaking.

**la'trare** *vi* to bark.

**latro'cinio** [latro'tʃinjo] *sm* = **la-drocinio**.

**'latta** *sf* tin (plate); (*recipiente*) tin, can.

**lat'taio, a** *smf* milkman/woman; dairyman/woman.

**lat'tante** *ag* unweaned.

**'latte** *sm* milk; ~ **detergente** cleansing milk *o* lotion; ~ **secco** *o* **in polvere** dried *o* powdered milk; ~ **scremato** skimmed milk; **'latteo, a** *ag* milky; (*dieta, prodotto*) milk *cpd*; **latte'ria** *sf* dairy; **latti'cini** *smpl* dairy products.

**lat'tina** *sf* (*di birra etc*) can.

**lat'tuga, ghe** *sf* lettuce.

**'laurea** *sf* degree; **laure'ando, a** *smf* final-year student; **laure'are** *vt* to confer a degree on; **laurearsi** *vr* to graduate; **laure'ato, a** *ag, smf* graduate.

**'lauro** *sm* laurel.

**'lauto, a** *ag* (*pranzo, mancia*) lavish.

**'lava** *sf* lava.

**la'vabo** *sm* washbasin.

**la'vaggio** [la'vaddʒo] *sm* washing *q*; ~ **del cervello** brainwashing *q*.

**la'vagna** [la'vaɲɲa] *sf* (*GEO*) slate; (*di scuola*) blackboard.

**la'vanda** *sf* (*anche MED*) wash; (*BOT*) lavender; **lavan'daia** *sf* washerwoman; **lavande'ria** *sf* laundry; **lavanderia automatica** launderette; **lavanderia a secco** dry-cleaner's; **lavan'dino** *sm* sink.

**lavapi'atti** *smf* dishwasher.

**la'vare** *vt* to wash; ~**rsi** *vr* to wash, have a wash; ~ **a secco** to dry-clean; ~**rsi le mani/i denti** to wash one's hands/clean one's teeth.

**lava'secco** *sm o f inv* dry-cleaner's.

**lavasto'viglie** [lavasto'viʎʎe] *sm o f inv* (*macchina*) dishwasher.

**lava'toio** *sm* (public) washhouse.

**lava'trice** [lava'tritʃe] *sf* washing machine.

**lava'tura** *sf* washing *q*; ~ **di piatti** dishwater.

**lavo'rante** *smf* worker.

**lavo'rare** *vi* to work; (*fig: bar, studio etc*) to do good business // *vt* to work; ~**rsi qn** (*persuaderlo*) to work on sb; ~ **a** to work on; ~ **a maglia** to knit; **lavora'tivo, a** *ag* working; **lavora'tore, 'trice** *smf* worker // *ag* working; **lavorazi'one** *sf* (*gen*) working; (*di legno, pietra*) carving; (*di film*) making; (*di prodotto*) manufacture; (*modo di esecuzione*) workmanship; **lavo'rio** *sm* intense activity.

**la'voro** *sm* work; (*occupazione*) job, work *q*; (*opera*) piece of work, job; (*ECON*) labour; ~**i forzati** hard labour *sg*; ~**i pubblici** public works.

**le** *det fpl* the // *pronome* (*oggetto*) them; (: *a lei, a essa*) (to) her; (: *forma di cortesia*) (to) you.

**le'ale** *ag* loyal; (*sincero*) sincere; (*onesto*) fair; **lealtà** *sf* loyalty; sincerity; fairness.

**'lebbra** *sf* leprosy.

**'lecca 'lecca** *sm inv* lollipop.

**leccapi'edi** *smf inv* (*peg*) toady,

bootlicker.

**lec'care** *vt* to lick; (*sog: gatto: latte etc*) to lick *o* lap up; (*fig*) to flatter; **~rsi i baffi** to lick one's lips; **lec'cata** *sf* lick.

**'leccio** ['lettʃo] *sm* holm oak, ilex.

**leccor'nia** *sf* titbit, delicacy.

**'lecito, a** ['lɛtʃito] *ag* permitted, allowed.

**'ledere** *vt* to damage, injure.

**'lega, ghe** *sf* league: (*di metalli*) alloy.

**le'gaccio** [le'gattʃo] *sm* string, lace.

**le'gale** *ag* legal // *sm* lawyer; **legaliz'zare** *vt* to authenticate; (*regolarizzare*) to legalize.

**le'game** *sm* (*corda, fig: affettivo*) tie, bond; (*nesso logico*) link, connection.

**le'gare** *vt* (*prigioniero, capelli, cane*) to tie (up); (*libro*) to bind; (*CHIM*) to alloy; (*fig: collegare*) to bind, join // *vi* (*far lega*) to unite; (*fig*) to get on well.

**lega'tario, a** *sm/f* (*DIR*) legatee.

**le'gato** *sm* (*REL*) legate; (*DIR*) legacy, bequest.

**lega'tura** *sf* (*di libro*) binding; (*MUS*) ligature.

**le'genda** [le'dʒɛnda] *sf* (*di carta geografica etc*) = **leggenda**.

**'legge** ['leddʒe] *sf* law.

**leg'genda** [led'dʒɛnda] *sf* (*narrazione*) legend; (*di carta geografica etc*) key, legend.

**'leggere** ['leddʒere] *vt, vi* to read.

**legge'rezza** [leddʒe'rettsa] *sf* lightness; thoughtlessness; fickleness.

**leg'gero, a** [led'dʒero] *ag* light; (*agile, snello*) nimble, agile, light; (*tè, caffè*) weak; (*fig: non grave, piccolo*) slight; (: *spensierato*) thoughtless; (: *incostante*) fickle; free and easy; **alla ~a** thoughtlessly.

**leggi'adro, a** [led'dʒadro] *ag* pretty, lovely; (*movimenti*) graceful.

**leg'gio, 'gii** [led'dʒio] *sm* lectern; (*MUS*) music stand.

**legisla'tura** [ledʒizla'tura] *sf* legislature.

**legislazi'one** [ledʒizlat'tsjone] *sf* legislation.

**le'gittimo, a** [le'dʒittimo] *ag* legitimate; (*fig: giustificato, lecito*) justified, legitimate; **~a difesa** (*DIR*) self-defence.

**'legna** ['leɲɲa] *sf* firewood; **le'gname** *sm* wood, timber.

**'legno** ['leɲɲo] *sm* wood; (*pezzo di ~*) piece of wood; **di ~** wooden; **~** compensato plywood; **le'gnoso, a** *ag* wooden; woody; (*carne*) tough.

**le'gumi** *smpl* (*BOT*) pulses.

**'lei** *pronome* (*soggetto*) she; (*oggetto: per dare rilievo, con preposizione*) her; (*forma di cortesia: anche:* **L~**) you // *sm*: **dare del ~** a qn to address sb as "lei"; **~** stessa she herself; you yourself.

**'lembo** *sm* (*di abito, strada*) edge; (*striscia sottile: di terra*) strip.

**'lemma, i** *sm* headword.

**'lemme 'lemme** *av* (very) very slowly.

**'lena** *sf* (*fig*) energy, stamina.

**le'nire** *vt* to soothe.

**'lente** *sf* (*OTTICA*) lens *sg*; **~ d'ingrandimento** magnifying glass; **~i a contatto** *o* **corneali** contact lenses.

**len'tezza** [len'tettsa] *sf* slowness.

**len'ticchia** [len'tikkja] *sf* (*BOT*) lentil.

**len'tiggine** [len'tiddʒine] *sf* freckle.

**'lento, a** *ag* slow; (*molle: fune*) slack; (*non stretto: vite, abito*) loose // *sm* (*ballo*) slow dance.

**'lenza** ['lentsa] *sf* fishing-line.

**lenzu'olo** [len'tswɔlo] *sm* sheet; **~a** *sfpl* pair of sheets.

**le'one** *sm* lion; (*dello zodiaco:* **L~**) Leo.

**lepo'rino, a** *ag*: **labbro ~** harelip.

**'lepre** *sf* hare.

**'lercio, a, ci, cie** ['lɛrtʃo] *ag* filthy.

**'lesbica, che** *sf* lesbian.

**lesi'nare** *vt* to be stingy with // *vi*: **~** (**su**) to skimp (on), be stingy (with).

**lesi'one** *sf* (*MED*) lesion; (*in injury, damage*; (*EDIL*) crack.

**'leso, a** pp di **ledere** // ag (offeso) injured; **parte** ~a (DIR) injured party.

**les'sare** vt (CUC) to boil.

**'lessico, ci** sm vocabulary; lexicon.

**'lesso, a** ag boiled // sm boiled meat.

**'lesto, a** ag quick; (agile) nimble; ~ **di mano** (per rubare) light-fingered; (per picchiare) free with one's fists.

**le'tale** ag lethal; fatal.

**leta'maio** sm dunghill.

**le'tame** sm manure, dung.

**le'targo, ghi** sm lethargy; (ZOOL) hibernation.

**le'tizia** [le'tittsja] sf joy, happiness.

**'lettera** sf letter; ~e sfpl (letteratura) literature sg; (studi umanistici) arts (subjects); **alla** ~ literally; in ~e in words, in full; **lette'rale** ag literal.

**lette'rario, a** ag literary.

**lette'rato, a** ag well-read, scholarly.

**lettera'tura** sf literature.

**let'tiga, ghe** sf (portantina) litter; (barella) stretcher.

**let'tino** sm cot (Brit), crib (US).

**'letto, a** pp di **leggere** // sm bed; andare a ~ to go to bed; ~ a castello bunk beds pl; ~ a una piazza/a due piazze o matrimoniale single/double bed.

**let'tore, 'trice** sm/f reader; (INS) (foreign language) assistant (Brit), (foreign) teaching assistant (US) // sm (TECN): ~ ottico optical character reader.

**let'tura** sf reading.

**leuce'mia** [leutʃe'mia] sf leukaemia.

**'leva** sf lever; (MIL) conscription; far ~ su qn to work on sb; ~ del cambio (AUT) gear lever.

**le'vante** sm east; (vento) East wind; il L~ the Levant.

**le'vare** vt (occhi, braccio) to raise; (sollevare, togliere: tassa, divieto) to lift; (indumenti) to take off, remove; (rimuovere) to take away; (: dal di sopra) to take off; (: dal di dentro) to take out; ~rsi vr to get up; (sole) to rise; **le'vata** sf (di posta) collec-

tion.

**leva'toio, a** ag: **ponte** ~ drawbridge.

**leva'tura** sf intelligence, mental capacity.

**levi'gare** vt to smooth; (con carta vetrata) to sand.

**levri'ere** sm greyhound.

**lezi'one** [let'tsjone] sf lesson; (all'università, sgridata) lecture; **fare** ~ to teach; to lecture.

**lezi'oso, a** [let'tsjoso] ag affected; simpering.

**'lezzo** ['leddzo] sm stench, stink.

**li** pronome pl (oggetto) them.

**lì** av there; **di** o **da** ~ from there; **per di** ~ that way; **di** ~ **a pochi giorni** a few days later; ~ **per** ~ there and then; at first; **essere** ~ (~) **per fare** to be on the point of doing, be about to do; ~ **dentro** in there; ~ **sotto** under there; ~ **sopra** on there; up there; vedi **quello**.

**liba'nese** ag, sm/f Lebanese inv.

**Li'bano** sm: il ~ the Lebanon.

**'libbra** sf (peso) pound.

**li'beccio** [li'bettʃo] sm south-west wind.

**li'bello** sm libel.

**li'bellula** sf dragonfly.

**libe'rale** ag, sm/f liberal.

**liberaliz'zare** [liberalid'dzare] vt to liberalize.

**libe'rare** vt (rendere libero: prigioniero) to release; (: popolo) to free, liberate; (sgombrare: passaggio) to clear; (: stanza) to vacate; (produrre: energia) to release; ~rsi vr: ~rsi di qc/qn to get rid of sth/sb; **libera'tore, 'trice** ag liberating // sm/f liberator; **liberazi'one** sf liberation, freeing; release; rescuing.

**'libero, a** ag free; (strada) clear; (non occupato: posto etc) vacant; not taken; empty; not engaged; ~ **di fare** qc free to do sth; ~ **da** free from; ~ **arbitrio** free will; ~ **professionista** self-employed professional person; ~ **scambio** free trade; **libertà** sf inv freedom; (tempo disponi-

*bile*) free time // *sfpl* (*licenza*) liberties; **in libertà provvisoria/vigilata** released without bail/on probation; **libertà di riunione** right to hold meetings.

'**Libia** *sf*: **la ~** Libya; '**libico, a, ci, che** *ag*, *sm/f* Libyan.

li'**bidine** *sf* lust.

li'**braio** *sm* bookseller.

li'**brario, a** *ag* book *cpd*.

li'**brarsi** *vr* to hover.

libre'**ria** *sf* (*bottega*) bookshop; (*stanza*) library; (*mobile*) bookcase.

li'**bretto** *sm* booklet; (*taccuino*) notebook; (*MUS*) libretto; **~ degli assegni** cheque book; **~ di circolazione** (*AUT*) logbook; **~ di risparmio** (*savings*) bank-book, passbook; **~ universitario** student's report book.

'**libro** *sm* book; **~ bianco** (*POL*) white paper; **~ di cassa** cash book; **~ mastro** ledger; **~ paga** payroll.

li'**cenza** [li'tʃɛntsa] *sf* (*permesso*) permission, leave; (*di pesca, caccia, circolazione*) permit, licence; (*MIL*) leave; (*INS*) school leaving certificate; (*libertà*) liberty; licence; licentiousness; **andare in ~** (*MIL*) to go on leave.

licenzia'**mento** [litʃentsja'mento] *sm* dismissal.

licenzi'**are** [litʃen'tsjare] *vt* (*impiegato*) to dismiss; (*INS*) to award a certificate to; **~rsi** *vr* (*impiegato*) to resign, hand in one's notice; (*INS*) to obtain one's school-leaving certificate.

li'**ceo** [li'tʃɛo] *sm* (*INS*) secondary (*Brit*) o high (*US*) school (*for 14- to 19-year-olds*).

'**lido** *sm* beach, shore.

li'**eto, a** *ag* happy, glad; "**molto ~**" (*nelle presentazioni*) "pleased to meet you".

li'**eve** *ag* light; (*di poco conto*) slight; (*sommesso: voce*) faint, soft.

lievi'**tare** *vi* (*anche fig*) to rise // *vt* to leaven.

li'**evito** *sm* yeast; **~ di birra** brewer's yeast.

'**ligio, a, gi, gie** ['lidʒo] *ag* faithful, loyal.

'**lilla, lillà** *sm inv* lilac.

'**lima** *sf* file.

limacci'**oso, a** [limat'tʃoso] *ag* slimy; muddy.

li'**mare** *vt* to file (down); (*fig*) to polish.

'**limbo** *sm* (*REL*) limbo.

li'**metta** *sf* nail file.

limi'**tare** *vt* to limit, restrict; (*circoscrivere*) to bound, surround; **limita'tivo, a** *ag* limiting, restricting; **limi'tato, a** *ag* limited, restricted.

'**limite** *sm* limit; (*confine*) bound, boundary; **~ di velocità** speed limit.

li'**mitrofo, a** *ag* neighbouring.

limo'**nata** *sf* lemonade (*Brit*), (lemon) soda (*US*); lemon squash (*Brit*), lemonade (*US*).

li'**mone** *sm* (*pianta*) lemon tree; (*frutto*) lemon.

'**limpido, a** *ag* clear; (*acqua*) limpid, clear.

'**lince** ['lintʃe] *sf* lynx.

linci'**are** *vt* to lynch.

'**lindo, a** *ag* tidy, spick and span; (*biancheria*) clean.

'**linea** *sf* line; (*di mezzi pubblici di trasporto: itinerario*) route; (: *servizio*) service; **a grandi ~e** in outline; **mantenere la ~** to look after one's figure; **di ~: aereo di ~** airliner; **nave di ~** liner; **volo di ~** scheduled flight; **~ aerea** airline; **~ di partenza/d'arrivo** (*SPORT*) starting/finishing line; **~ di tiro** line of fire.

linea'**menti** *smpl* features, (*fig*) outlines.

line'**are** *ag* linear; (*fig*) coherent, logical.

line'**etta** *sf* (*trattino*) dash; (*d'unione*) hyphen.

lin'**gotto** *sm* ingot, bar.

'**lingua** *sf* (*ANAT, CUC*) tongue; (*idioma*) language; **mostrare la ~** to stick out one's tongue; **di ~ italiana** Italian-speaking; **~ madre** mother tongue; **una ~ di terra** a spit of land.

**lingu'aggio** [lin'gwaddʒo] *sm* language.

**lingu'etta** *sf (di strumento)* reed; *(di scarpa, TECN)* tongue; *(di busta)* flap.

**lingu'istica** *sf* linguistics *sg*.

**'lino** *sm (pianta)* flax; *(tessuto)* linen.

**li'noleum** *sm inv* linoleum, lino.

**lique'fare** *vt (render liquido)* to liquefy; *(fondere)* to melt; ~**rsi** *vr* to liquefy; to melt.

**liqui'dare** *vt (società, beni; persona; uccidere)* to liquidate; *(persona; sbarazzarsene)* to get rid of; *(conto, problema)* to settle; *(COMM: merce)* to sell off, clear; **liquidazi'one** *sf* liquidation; settlement; clearance sale.

**liquidità** *sf* liquidity.

**'liquido, a** *ag, sm* liquid; ~ **per freni** brake fluid.

**liqui'rizia** [likwi'rittsja] *sf* liquorice.

**li'quore** *sm* liqueur.

**'lira** *sf (unità monetaria)* lira; *(MUS)* lyre; ~ **sterlina** pound sterling.

**'lirico, a, ci, che** *ag* lyric(al); *(MUS)* lyric // *sf (poesia)* lyric poetry; *(componimento poetico)* lyric; *(MUS)* opera; **cantante/teatro** ~ opera singer/house.

**'lisca, sche** *sf (di pesce)* fishbone.

**lisci'are** [liʃ'ʃare] *vt* to smooth; *(fig)* to flatter.

**'liscio, a, sci, sce** ['liʃʃo] *ag* smooth; *(capelli)* straight; *(mobile)* plain; *(bevanda alcolica)* neat; *(fig)* straightforward, simple // *av:* andare ~ to go smoothly; **passarla** ~**a** to get away with it.

**'liso, a** *ag* worn out, threadbare.

**'lista** *sf (striscia)* strip; *(elenco)* list; ~ **elettorale** electoral roll; ~ **delle vivande** menu.

**lis'tino** *sm* list; ~ **dei cambi** (foreign) exchange rate; ~ **dei prezzi** price list.

**'lite** *sf* quarrel, argument; *(DIR)* lawsuit.

**liti'gare** *vi* to quarrel; *(DIR)* to litigate.

**li'tigio** [li'tidʒo] *sm* quarrel; **litigi'oso, a** *ag* quarrelsome; *(DIR)* litigious.

**litogra'fia** *sf (sistema)* lithography; *(stampa)* lithograph.

**lito'rale** *ag* coastal, coast *cpd* // *sm* coast.

**'litro** *sm* litre.

**livel'lare** *vt* to level, make level; ~**rsi** *vr* to become level; *(fig)* to level out, balance out.

**li'vello** *sm* level; *(fig)* level, standard; **ad alto** ~ *ag* ~ *(fig)* high-level; ~ **del mare** sea level.

**'livido, a** *ag* livid; *(per percosse)* bruised, black and blue; *(cielo)* leaden // *sm* bruise.

**li'vore** *sm* malice, spite.

**Li'vorno** *sf* Livorno, Leghorn.

**li'vrea** *sf* livery.

**'lizza** ['littsa] *sf* lists *pl*; **scendere in** ~ *(anche fig)* to enter the lists.

**lo** *det m (dav s impura, gn, pn, ps, x, z; dav V I')* the // *pronome (dav V I')* *(oggetto: persona)* him; (: *cosa)* it; ~ **sapevo** I knew it; ~ **so** I know; **sii buono, anche se lui non** ~ **è** be good, even if he isn't.

**lo'cale** *ag* local // *sm* room; *(luogo pubblico)* premises *pl*; ~ **notturno** nightclub; **località** *sf inv* locality; **localiz'zare** *vt (circoscrivere)* to confine, localize; *(accertare)* to locate, place.

**lo'canda** *sf* inn; **locandi'ere, a** *sm/f* innkeeper.

**loca'tario, a** *sm/f* tenant.

**loca'tore, 'trice** *sm/f* landlord/lady.

**locazi'one** [lokat'tsjone] *sf (da parte del locatario)* renting *q*; *(da parte del locatore)* renting out *q*, letting *q*; **(contratto di)** ~ lease; **(canone di)** ~ rent; **dare in** ~ to rent out, let.

**locomo'tiva** *sf* locomotive.

**locomo'tore** *sm* electric locomotive.

**locomozi'one** [lokomot'tsjone] *sf*

locomotion; **mezzi di** ~ vehicles, means of transport.

**lo'custa** $sf$ locust.

**locuzi'one** [lokut'tsjone] $sf$ phrase, expression.

**lo'dare** $vt$ to praise.

**lode** $sf$ praise; (INS): **laurearsi con 110 e** ~ ≈ to graduate with a first-class honours degree (Brit), graduate summa cum laude (US).

**'loden** $sm$ $inv$ (stoffa) loden; (cappotto) loden overcoat.

**lo'devole** $ag$ praiseworthy.

**loga'ritmo** $sm$ logarithm.

**'loggia, ge** ['lɔddʒa] $sf$ (ARCHIT) loggia; (circolo massonico) lodge; **loggi'one** $sm$ (di teatro): **il loggione** the Gods $sg$.

**'logico, a, ci, che** ['lɔdʒiko] $ag$ logical // $sf$ logic.

**logo'rare** $vt$ to wear out; (sciupare) to waste; ~**rsi** $vr$ to wear out; (fig) to wear o.s. out.

**logo'rio** $sm$ wear and tear; (fig) strain.

**'logoro, a** $ag$ (stoffa) worn out, threadbare; (persona) worn out.

**lom'baggine** [lom'baddʒine] $sf$ lumbago.

**Lombar'dia** $sf$: **la** ~ Lombardy.

**lom'bata** $sf$ (taglio di carne) loin.

**'lombo** $sm$ (ANAT) loin.

**lom'brico, chi** $sm$ earthworm.

**londi'nese** $ag$ London $cpd$ // $smlf$ Londoner.

**'Londra** $sf$ London.

**lon'gevo, a** [lon'dʒevo] $ag$ long-lived.

**longi'tudine** [londʒi'tudine] $sf$ longitude.

**lonta'nanza** [lonta'nantsa] $sf$ distance; absence.

**lon'tano, a** $ag$ (distante) distant, faraway; (assente) absent; (vago: sospetto) slight, remote; (tempo: remoto) far-off, distant; (parente) distant, remote // $av$ far; **è** ~**a la casa?** is it far to the house?, is the house far from here?; **è** ~ **un chilometro** it's a kilometre away $o$ a

kilometre from here; **più** ~ farther; **da** $o$ **di** ~ from a distance; ~ **da a** long way from; **alla** ~**a** slightly, vaguely.

**'lontra** $sf$ otter.

**lo'quace** [lo'kwatʃe] $ag$ talkative, loquacious; (fig: gesto etc) eloquent.

**'lordo, a** $ag$ dirty, filthy; (peso, stipendio) gross.

**'loro** pronome pl (oggetto, con preposizione) them; (complemento di termine) to them; (soggetto) they; (forma di cortesia: anche: **L**~) you; to you; **il(la)** ~, **i(le)** ~ det their; (forma di cortesia: anche: **L**~) your // pronome theirs; (forma di cortesia: anche: **L**~) yours; ~ **stessi(e)** they themselves; you yourselves.

**'losco, a, schi, sche** $ag$ (fig) shady, suspicious.

**'lotta** $sf$ struggle, fight; (SPORT) wrestling; ~ **libera** all-in wrestling; **lot'tare** $vi$ to fight, struggle; to wrestle; **lotta'tore, trice** $smlf$ wrestler.

**lotte'ria** $sf$ lottery; (di gara ippica) sweepstake.

**'lotto** $sm$ (gioco) (state) lottery; (parte) lot; (EDIL) site.

**lozi'one** [lot'tsjone] $sf$ lotion.

**lubrifi'cante** $sm$ lubricant.

**lubrifi'care** $vt$ to lubricate.

**luc'chetto** [luk'ketto] $sm$ padlock.

**lucci'care** [luttʃi'kare] $vi$ to sparkle, glitter, twinkle.

**'luccio** ['luttʃo] $sm$ (ZOOL) pike.

**'lucciola** ['luttʃola] $sf$ (ZOOL) firefly; glowworm.

**'luce** ['lutʃe] $sf$ light; (finestra) window; **alla** ~ **di** by the light of; **fare** ~ **su qc** (fig) to shed $o$ throw light on sth; ~ **del sole/della luna** sun/moonlight; **lu'cente** $ag$ shining.

**lu'cerna** [lu'tʃerna] $sf$ oil-lamp.

**lucer'nario** [lutʃer'narjo] $sm$ skylight.

**lu'certola** [lu'tʃertola] $sf$ lizard.

**luci'dare** [lutʃi'dare] $vt$ to polish; (ricalcare) to trace.

**lucida'trice** [lutʃida'tritʃe] $sf$ floor

polisher.

'lucido, a ['lutʃido] ag shining, bright; (lucidato) polished; (fig) lucid // sm shine, lustre; (per scarpe etc) polish; (disegno) tracing.

'lucro sm profit, gain; lu'croso, a ag lucrative, profitable.

lu'dibrio sm mockery q; (oggetto di scherno) laughing-stock.

'luglio ['luʎʎo] sm July.

lu'gubre ag gloomy.

'lui pronome (soggetto) he; (oggetto: per dare rilievo, con preposizione) him; ~ stesso he himself.

lu'maca, che (e slug; (chiocciola) snail.

'lume sm light; (lampada) lamp; (fig): chiedere ~i a qn to ask sb for advice; a ~ di naso (fig) by rule of thumb.

lumi'naria sf (per feste) illuminations pl.

lumi'noso, a ag (che emette luce) luminous; (cielo, colore, stanza) bright; (sorgente) of light, light cpd; (fig: sorriso) bright, radiant.

'luna sf moon; ~ nuova/piena new/ full moon; ~ di miele honeymoon.

'luna park sm inv amusement park, funfair.

lu'nare ag lunar, moon cpd.

lu'nario sm almanac; sbarcare il ~ to make ends meet.

lu'natico, a, ci, che ag whimsical, temperamental.

lunedì sm inv Monday; di o il ~ on Mondays.

lun'gaggine [lun'gaddʒine] sf slowness; ~i della burocrazia red tape.

lun'ghezza [lun'gettsa] sf length; ~ d'onda (FISICA) wavelength.

'lungi ['lundʒi]: ~ da prep far from.

'lungo, a, ghi, ghe ag long; (lento: persona) slow; (diluito: caffè, brodo) weak, watery, thin // sm length // prep along; ~ 3 metri 3 metres long; a ~ for a long time; a ~ andare in the long run; di gran ~a (molto) by far; andare in ~ o per le lunghe to drag on; saperla

~a to know what's what; in ~ e in largo far and wide, all over; ~ il corso dei secoli throughout the centuries.

lungo'mare sm promenade.

lu'notto sm (AUT) rear o back window.

lu'ogo, ghi sm place; (posto: di incidente etc) scene, site; (punto, passo di libro) passage; in ~ di instead of; in primo ~ in the first place; aver ~ to take place; dar ~ a to give rise to; ~ comune commonplace; ~ di nascita birthplace; (AMM) place of birth; ~ di provenienza place of origin.

luogote'nente sm (MIL) lieutenant.

lu'para sf sawn-off shotgun.

'lupo, a sm/f wolf.

'luppolo sm (BOT) hop.

'lurido, a ag filthy.

lu'singa, ghe sf (spesso al pl) flattery q.

lusin'gare vt to flatter; lusin-ghi'ero, a ag flattering, gratifying.

lus'sare vt (MED) to dislocate.

Lussem'burgo sm (stato): il ~ Luxembourg // sf (città) Luxembourg.

'lusso sm luxury; di ~ luxury cpd; lussu'oso, a ag luxurious.

lussureggi'are [lussured3are] vi to be luxuriant.

lus'suria sf lust.

lus'trare vt to polish, shine.

lustra'scarpe sm/f inv shoeshine.

lus'trino sm sequin.

'lustro, a ag shiny; (pelliccia) glossy // sm shine, gloss; (fig) prestige, glory; (quinquennio) five-year period.

'lutto sm mourning; essere in/ portare il ~ to be in/wear mourning; luttu'oso, a ag mournful, sad.

# M

**ma** *cong* but; ~ **insomma!** for goodness sake!; ~ **no!** of course not!

**'macabro, a** *ag* gruesome, macabre.

**macché** [mak'ke] *escl* not at all!, certainly not!

**macche'roni** [makke'roni] *smpl* macaroni *sg*.

**'macchia** ['makkja] *sf* stain, spot; (*chiazza di diverso colore*) spot; splash, patch; (*tipo di boscaglia*) scrub; **alla ~** (*fig*) in hiding; **macchiarsi** *vr* (*persona*) to get o.s. dirty; (*stoffa*) to stain; to get stained *o* marked.

**'macchina** ['makkina] *sf* machine; (*motore, locomotiva*) engine; (*automobile*) car; (*fig: meccanismo*) machinery; **andare in ~** (*AUT*) to go by car; (*STAMPA*) to go to press; **~ da cucire** sewing machine; **~ fotografica** camera; **~ da presa** cine *o* movie camera; **~ da scrivere** typewriter; **~ a vapore** steam engine.

**macchi'nare** [makki'nare] *vt* to plot.

**macchi'nario** [makki'narjo] *sm* machinery.

**macchi'netta** [makki'netta] *sf* (*fam: caffettiera*) percolator; (: *accendino*) lighter.

**macchi'nista, i** [makki'nista] *sm* (*di treno*) engine-driver; (*di nave*) engineer; (*TEATRO, TV*) stagehand.

**macchi'noso, a** [makki'noso] *ag* complex, complicated.

**mace'donia** [matfe'donja] *sf* fruit salad.

**macel'laio** [matfel'lajo] *sm* butcher.

**macel'lare** [matfel'lare] *vt* to slaughter, butcher; **macelle'ria** *sf* butcher's (shop); **ma'cello** *sm* (*mattatoio*) slaughterhouse, abattoir (*Brit*), (*fig*) slaughter, massacre; (: *disastro*) shambles *sg*.

**mace'rare** [matfe'rare] *vt* to macerate; (*CUC*) to marinate; **~rsi** *vr* (*fig*): **~rsi** in to be consumed with.

**ma'cerie** [ma'tferje] *sfpl* rubble *sg*, debris *sg*.

**ma'cigno** [ma'tfippo] *sm* (*masso*) rock, boulder.

**maci'lento, a** [matfi'lɛnto] *ag* emaciated.

**'macina** ['matfina] *sf* (*pietra*) millstone; (*macchina*) grinder; **macinacaffè** *sm inv* coffee grinder; **macina'pepe** *sm inv* peppermill.

**maci'nare** [matfi'nare] *vt* to grind; (*carne*) to mince (*Brit*), grind (*US*); **maci'nato** *sm* meal, flour; (*carne*) minced (*Brit*) *o* ground (*US*) meat.

**maci'nino** [matfi'nino] *sm* coffee grinder; peppermill.

**'madido, a** *ag*: ~ (**di**) wet *o* moist (with).

**Ma'donna** *sf* (*REL*) Our Lady.

**mador'nale** *ag* enormous, huge.

**'madre** *sf* mother; (*matrice di bolletta*) counterfoil // *ag inv* mother *cpd*; **ragazza ~** unmarried mother; **scena ~** (*TEATRO*) principal scene; (*fig*) terrible scene.

**madre'lingua** *sf* mother tongue, native language.

**madre'perla** *sf* mother-of-pearl.

**ma'drina** *sf* godmother.

**maestà** *sf inv* majesty; **maes'toso, a** *ag* majestic.

**ma'estra** *sf vedi* **maestro**.

**maes'trale** *sm* north-west wind, mistral.

**maes'tranze** [maes'trantse] *sfpl* workforce *sg*.

**maes'tria** *sf* mastery, skill.

**ma'estro, a** *smf* (*INS: anche*: ~ **di scuola** *o* **elementare**) primary (*Brit*) *o* grade school (*US*) teacher; (*esperto*) expert // *sm* (*artigiano, fig: guida*) master; (*MUS*) maestro // *ag* (*principale*) main; (*di grande abilità*) masterly, skilful; **~a d'asilo** nursery teacher; **~ di cerimonie** master of ceremonies.

**'mafia** *sf* Mafia; **mafi'oso** *sm*

member of the Mafia.

**'maga** *sf* sorceress.

**ma'gagna** [ma'gaɲɲa] *sf* defect, flaw, blemish; (*noia, guaio*) problem.

**ma'gari** *escl* (*esprime desiderio*): ~ fosse vero! if only it were true!; **ti piacerebbe andare in Scozia?** — ~! would you like to go to Scotland? — and how! // *av* (*anche*) even; (*forse*) perhaps.

**magaz'zino** [magad'dzino] *sm* warehouse; **grande** ~ department store.

**'maggio** ['maddʒo] *sm* May.

**maggio'rana** [maddʒo'rana] *sf* (*BOT*) (sweet) marjoram.

**maggio'ranza** [maddʒo'rantsa] *sf* majority.

**maggio'rare** [maddʒo'rare] *vt* to increase, raise.

**maggior'domo** [maddʒor'dɔmo] *sm* butler.

**maggi'ore** [mad'dʒore] *ag* (*comparativo: più grande*) bigger, larger; taller; greater; (: *più vecchio: sorella, fratello*) older, elder; (: *di grado superiore*) senior; (: *più importante, MIL, MUS*) major; (*superlativo*) biggest, largest; tallest; greatest; oldest, eldest // *sm* (*di grado*) superior; (*di età*) elder; (*MIL*) major; (: *AER*) squadron leader; **la maggior parte** the majority; **andare per la** ~ (*cantante etc*) to be very popular; **maggio'renne** *ag* of age // *sm/f* person who has come of age; **maggior'mente** *av* much more; (*con senso superlativo*) most.

**ma'gia** [ma'dʒia] *sf* magic; **'magico, a, ci, che** *ag* magic; (*fig*) fascinating, charming, magical.

**'magio** [madʒo] *sm* (*REL*): **i re** Magi the Magi, the Three Wise Men.

**magis'tero** [madʒis'tero] *sm* teaching; (*fig: maestria*) skill; (*INS*): **facoltà di M~** ≈ teachers' training college; **magis'trale** *ag* primary (*Brit*) *o* grade school (*US*) teachers', primary (*Brit*) *o* grade school (*US*) teaching *cpd*; skilful.

**magis'trato** [madʒis'trato] *sm* magistrate;. **magistra'tura** *sf* magistrature; (*magistrati*): **la magistratura** the Bench.

**'maglia** ['maʎʎa] *sf* stitch; (*lavoro ai ferri*) knitting *q*; (*tessuto, SPORT*) jersey; (*maglione*) jersey, sweater; (*di catena*) link; (*di rete*) mesh; ~ **diritta/rovescia** plain/purl; **maglie'ria** *sf* knitwear; (*negozio*) knitwear shop; **magli'etta** *sf* (*canottiera*) vest; (*tipo camicia*) T-shirt; **magli'ficio** *sm* knitwear factory.

**'maglio** ['maʎʎo] *sm* mallet; (*macchina*) power hammer.

**ma'gnete** [maɲ'nɛte] *sm* magnet; **ma'gnetico, a, ci, che** *ag* magnetic.

**magne'tofono** [maɲɲe'tɔfono] *sm* tape recorder.

**ma'gnifico, a, ci, che** [maɲ'nifiko] *ag* magnificent, splendid; (*ospite*) generous.

**'magno, a** ['maɲno] *ag*: **aula** ~**a** main hall.

**ma'gnolia** [maɲ'nɔlja] *sf* magnolia.

**'mago, ghi** *sm* (*stregone*) magician, wizard; (*illusionista*) magician.

**ma'grezza** [ma'grettsa] *sf* thinness.

**'magro, a** *ag* (very) thin, skinny; (*carne*) lean; (*formaggio*) low-fat; (*fig: scarso, misero*) meagre, poor; (: *meschino: scusa*) poor, lame; **mangiare di** ~ not to eat meat.

**'mai** *av* (*nessuna volta*) never; (*talvolta*) ever; **non** ... ~ never; ~ **più** never again; **come** ~? **why** (*o* how) on earth?; **chi/dove/quando** ~? whoever/wherever/whenever?

**mai'ale** *sm* (*ZOOL*) pig; (*carne*) pork.

**maio'nese** *sf* mayonnaise.

**'mais** *sm inv* maize.

**mai'uscolo, a** *ag* (*lettera*) capital; (*fig*) enormous, huge // *sf* capital letter.

**mal** *av, sm vedi* **male**.

**malac'corto, a** *ag* rash, careless.

**mala'fede** *sf* bad faith.

**mala'mente** av badly; dangerously.

**malan'dato, a** ag (persona: di salute) in poor health; (: di condizioni finanziarie) badly off; (trascurato) shabby.

**ma'lanno** sm (disgrazia) misfortune; (malattia) ailment.

**mala'pena** sf: a ~ hardly, scarcely.

**ma'laria** sf (MED) malaria.

**mala'sorte** sf bad luck.

**mala'ticcio, a** [mala'tittʃo] ag sickly.

**ma'lato, a** ag ill, sick; (gamba) bad; (pianta) diseased // sm/f sick person; (in ospedale) patient;

**malat'tia** sf (infettiva etc) illness, disease; (cattiva salute) illness, sickness; (di pianta) disease.

**malau'gurio** sm bad o ill omen.

**mala'vita** sf underworld.

**mala'voglia** [mala'vɔʎʎa] sf: di ~ unwillingly, reluctantly.

**mal'concio, a, ci, ce** [mal'kontʃo] ag in a sorry state.

**malcon'tento** sm discontent.

**malcos'tume** sm immorality.

**mal'destro, a** ag (inabile) inexpert, inexperienced; (goffo) awkward.

**maldi'cenza** [maldi'tʃentsa] sf malicious gossip.

**maldis'posto, a** ag: ~ (verso) ill-disposed (towards).

'**male** av badly // sm (ciò che è ingiusto, disonesto) evil; (danno, svantaggio) harm; (sventura) misfortune; (dolore fisico, morale) pain, ache; **di ~ in peggio** from bad to worse; **sentirsi ~** to feel ill; **far ~** (dolere) to hurt; **far ~ alla salute** to be bad for one's health; **far del ~ a qn** to hurt o harm sb; **restare** o **rimanere ~** to be sorry; to be disappointed; to be hurt; **andare a ~** to go bad; **come va? — non c'è ~** how are you? — not bad; **mal di mare** seasickness; **avere mal di gola/testa** to have a sore throat/a headache; **aver ~ ai piedi** to have sore feet.

**male'detto, a** pp di **maledire** // ag

cursed, damned; (fig: fam) damned, blasted.

**male'dire** vt to curse; **maledizi'one** sf curse; **maledizione!** damn it!

**maledu'cato, a** ag rude, ill-mannered.

**male'fatta** sf misdeed.

**male'ficio** [male'fitʃo] sm witchcraft.

**ma'lefico, a, ci, che** ag (aria, cibo) harmful, bad; (influsso, azione) evil.

**ma'lessere** sm indisposition, slight illness; (fig) uneasiness.

**ma'levolo, a** ag malevolent.

**malfa'mato, a** ag notorious.

**mal'fatto, a** ag (persona) deformed; (oggetto) badly made; (lavoro) badly done.

**malfat'tore, 'trice** sm/f wrongdoer.

**mal'fermo, a** ag unsteady, shaky; (salute) poor, delicate.

**malformazi'one** [malformat'tsjone] sf malformation.

**malgo'verno** sm maladministration.

**mal'grado** prep in spite of, despite // cong although; **mio** (o **tuo** etc) ~ against my (o your etc) will.

**ma'lia** sf spell; (fig: fascino) charm.

**mali'gnare** [malin'ɲare] vi: ~ su to malign, speak ill of.

**ma'ligno, a** [ma'liɲɲo] ag (malvagio) malicious, malignant; (MED) malignant.

**malinco'nia** sf melancholy, gloom; **malin'conico, a, ci, che** ag melancholy.

**malincu'ore: a ~** av reluctantly, unwillingly.

**malintenzio'nato, a** [malintentsjo'nato] ag ill-intentioned.

**malin'teso, a** ag misunderstood; (riguardo, senso del dovere) mistaken, wrong // sm misunderstanding.

**ma'lizia** [ma'littsja] sf (malignità) malice; (furbizia) cunning; (espediente) trick; **malizi'oso, a** ag malicious; cunning; (vivace, birichino) mischievous.

**malme'nare** *vt* to beat up; *(fig)* to ill-treat.

**mal'messo, a** *ag* shabby.

**malnu'trito, a** *ag* undernourished; **malnutrizi'one** *sf* malnutrition.

**ma'locchio** [ma'lɔkkjo] *sm* evil eye.

**ma'lora** *sf*: andare in ~ to go to the dogs.

**ma'lore** *sm* (sudden) illness.

**mal'sano, a** *ag* unhealthy.

**malsi'curo, a** *ag* unsafe.

**'Malta** *sf*: la ~ Malta.

**'malta** *sf* (EDIL) mortar.

**mal'tempo** *sm* bad weather.

**'malto** *sm* malt.

**maltrat'tare** *vt* to ill-treat.

**malu'more** *sm* bad mood; *(irritabilità)* bad temper; *(discordia)* ill feeling; di ~ in a bad mood.

**mal'vagio, a, gi, gie** [mal'vadʒo] *ag* wicked, evil.

**malversazi'one** [malversat'tsjone] *sf* (DIR) embezzlement.

**mal'visto, a** *ag*: ~ (da) disliked (by), unpopular (with).

**malvi'vente** *sm* criminal.

**malvolenti'eri** *av* unwillingly, reluctantly.

**'mamma** *sf* mummy, mum; ~ **mia!** my goodness!

**mam'mella** *sf* (ANAT) breast; *(di vacca, capra etc)* udder.

**mam'mifero** *sm* mammal.

**'mammola** *sf* (BOT) violet.

**ma'nata** *sf* *(colpo)* slap; *(quantità)* handful.

**'manca** *sf* left (hand); a destra e a ~ left, right and centre, on all sides.

**man'canza** [man'kantsa] *sf* lack; *(carenza)* shortage, scarcity; *(colpa)* fault; *(imperfezione)* failing, shortcoming; **per** ~ **di tempo** through lack of time; **in** ~ **di meglio** for lack of anything better.

**man'care** *vi* (essere insufficiente) to be lacking; *(venir meno)* to fail; *(sbagliare)* to be wrong, make a mistake; *(non esserci)* to be missing, not to be there; *(essere lontano)*: ~ **(da)** to be away (from) // *vt* to miss; ~ **di**

to lack; ~ **a** *(promessa)* to fail to keep; **tu mi manchi** I miss you; **mancò poco che morisse** he very nearly died; **mancano ancora 10 sterline** we're still £10 short; **manca un quarto alle 6** it's a quarter to 6; **man'cato, a** *ag* *(tentativo)* unsuccessful; *(artista)* failed.

**'mancia, ce** ['mantʃa] *sf* tip; ~ **competente** reward.

**manci'ata** [man'tʃata] *sf* handful.

**man'cino, a** [man'tʃino] *ag* *(braccio)* left; *(persona)* left-handed; *(fig)* underhand.

**'manco** *av* (nemmeno): ~ **per sogno** *o* **per idea!** not on your life!

**man'dare** *vt* to send; *(far funzionare: macchina)* to drive; *(emettere)* to send out; *(: grido)* to give, utter, let out; ~ **a chiamare qn** to send for sb; ~ **avanti** *(fig: famiglia)* to provide for; *(: fabbrica)* to run, look after; ~ **giù** to send down; *(anche fig)* to swallow; ~ **via** to send away; *(licenziare)* to fire.

**manda'rino** *sm* mandarin (orange); *(cinese)* mandarin.

**man'data** *sf* *(quantità)* lot, batch; *(di chiave)* turn; **chiudere a doppia** ~ to double-lock.

**manda'tario** *sm* (DIR) representative, agent.

**man'dato** *sm* *(incarico)* commission; *(DIR: provvedimento)* warrant; *(di deputato etc)* mandate; *(ordine di pagamento)* money order; ~ **d'arresto** warrant for arrest.

**man'dibola** *sf* mandible, jaw.

**'mandorla** *sf* almond; **'mandorlo** *sm* almond tree.

**'mandria** *sf* herd.

**maneggi'are** [maned'dʒare] *vt* *(creta, cera)* to mould, work, fashion; *(arnesi, utensili)* to handle; *(: adoperare)* to use; *(fig: persone, denaro)* to handle, deal with; **ma'neggio** *sm* moulding; handling; use; *(intrigo)* plot, scheme; *(per cavalli)* riding school.

**ma'nesco, a, schi, sche** *ag* free

with one's fists.

**ma'nette** sf/pl handcuffs.

**manga'nello** sm club.

**manga'nese** sm manganese.

**mange'reccio, a, ci, ce** [mandʒe'rettʃo] ag edible.

**mangia'dischi** [mandʒa'diski] sm inv record player.

**mangi'are** [man'dʒare] vt to eat; (intaccare) to eat into o away; (CARTE, SCACCHI etc) to take // vi to eat // sm eating; (cibo) food; (cucina) cooking; ~rsi le parole to mumble; ~rsi le unghie to bite one's nails; **mangia'toia** sf feedingtrough.

**man'gime** [man'dʒime] sm fodder.

**'mango, ghi** sm mango.

**ma'nia** sf (PSIC) mania; (fig) obsession, craze; **ma'niaco, a, ci, che** ag suffering from a mania; **maniaco (di)** obsessed (by), crazy (about).

**'manica** sf sleeve; (fig: gruppo) gang, bunch; (GEO): **la M~, il Canale della M~** the (English) Channel; **essere di ~ larga/stretta** to be easy-going/strict; **~ a vento** (AER) wind sock.

**mani'chino** [mani'kino] sm (di sarto, vetrina) dummy.

**'manico, ci** sm handle; (MUS) neck.

**mani'comio** sm mental hospital; (fig) madhouse.

**mani'cotto** sm muff; (TECN) coupling; sleeve.

**mani'cure** sm o f inv manicure // sf inv manicurist.

**mani'era** sf way, manner; (stile) style, manner; **~e** sf/pl manners; **in ~ che** so that; **in ~ da** so as to; **in tutte le ~e** at all costs.

**manie'rato, a** ag affected.

**manifat'tura** sf (lavorazione) manufacture; (stabilimento) factory.

**manifes'tare** vt to show, display; (esprimere) to express; (rivelare) to reveal, disclose // vi to demonstrate; **~rsi** vr to show o.s.; **~rsi amico** to prove o.s. (to be) a friend; **manifestazi'one** sf show, display; expres-

sion; (sintomo) sign, symptom; (dimostrazione pubblica) demonstration; (cerimonia) event.

**mani'festo, a** ag obvious, evident // sm poster, bill; (scritto ideologico) manifesto.

**ma'niglia** [ma'niʎʎa] sf handle; (sostegno: negli autobus etc) strap.

**manipo'lare** vt to manipulate; (alterare: vino) to adulterate; **manipolazi'one** sf manipulation; adulteration.

**manis'calco, chi** sm blacksmith.

**'manna** sf (REL) manna.

**man'naia** sf (del boia) (executioner's) axe; (per carni) cleaver.

**man'naro**: **lupo ~** sm werewolf.

**'mano, i** sf hand; (strato: di vernice etc) coat; **di prima ~** (notizia) first-hand; **di seconda ~** secondhand; **man ~** little by little, gradually; **man ~ che** as; **darsi o stringersi la ~** to shake hands; **mettere le ~i avanti** (fig) to safeguard o.s.; **restare a ~i vuote** to be left empty-handed; **venire alle ~i** to come to blows; **a ~ by hand; ~i in alto!** hands up!

**mano'dopera** sf labour.

**mano'messo, a** pp di **manomettere**.

**ma'nometro** sm gauge, manometer.

**mano'mettere** vt (alterare) to tamper with; (aprire indebitamente) to break open illegally.

**ma'nopola** sf (dell'armatura) gauntlet; (guanto) mitt; (di impugnatura) hand-grip; (pomello) knob.

**manos'critto, a** ag handwritten // sm manuscript.

**mano'vale** sm labourer.

**mano'vella** sf handle; (TECN) crank.

**ma'novra** sf manoeuvre (Brit), maneuver (US); (FERR) shunting; **mano'vrare** vt (veicolo) to manoeuvre (Brit), maneuver (US); (macchina, congegno) to operate;

(*fig: persona*) to manipulate // *vi* to manoeuvre.

**manro'vescio** [manro'veʃʃo] *sm* slap (*with back of hand*).

**man'sarda** *sf* attic.

**mansi'one** *sf* task, duty, job.

**mansu'eto, a** *ag* gentle, docile.

**man'tello** *sm* cloak; (*fig: di neve etc*) blanket, mantle; (*TECN: involucro*) casing, shell; (*ZOOL*) coat.

**mante'nere** *vt* to maintain; (*adempiere: promesse*) to keep, abide by; (*provvedere a*) to support, maintain; **~rsi** *vr*: **~rsi calmo/ giovane** to stay calm/young; **manteni'mento** *sm* maintenance.

**'mantice** ['mantitʃe] *sm* bellows *pl*; (*di carrozza, automobile*) hood.

**'manto** *sm* cloak; **~ stradale** road surface.

**manu'ale** *ag* manual // *sm* (*testo*) manual, handbook.

**ma'nubrio** *sm* handle; (*di bicicletta etc*) handlebars *pl*; (*SPORT*) dumbbell.

**manu'fatto** *sm* manufactured article.

**manutenzi'one** [manuten'tsjone] *sf* maintenance, upkeep; (*d'impianti*) maintenance, servicing.

**'manzo** ['mandzo] *sm* (*ZOOL*) steer; (*carne*) beef.

**'mappa** *sf* (*GEO*) map; **mappa'mondo** *sm* map of the world; (*globo girevole*) globe.

**ma'rasma, i** *sm* (*fig*) decay, decline.

**mara'tona** *sf* marathon.

**'marca, che** *sf* mark; (*bollo*) stamp; (*COMM: di prodotti*) brand; (*contrassegno, scontrino*) ticket, check; **prodotto di ~** (*di buona qualità*) high-class product; **~ da bollo** official stamp.

**mar'care** *vt* (*munire di contrassegno*) to mark; (*a fuoco*) to brand; (*SPORT: gol*) to score; (: *avversario*) to mark; (*accentuare*) to stress; **~ visita** (*MIL*) to report sick.

**'Marche** ['marke] *sfpl*: **le ~** the

Marches (*region of central Italy*).

**mar'chese, a** [mar'keze] *sm/f* marquis *o* marquess/marchioness.

**marchi'are** [mar'kjare] *vt* to brand; **'marchio** (*di bestiame*, *COMM*, *fig*) brand; **marchio depositato** registered trademark; **marchio di fabbrica** trademark.

**'marcia, ce** ['martʃa] *sf* (*anche MUS, MIL*) march; (*funzionamento*) running; (*il camminare*) walking; (*AUT*) gear; **mettere in ~** to start; **mettersi in ~** to get moving; **far ~ indietro** (*AUT*) to reverse; (*fig*) to back-pedal.

**marciapi'ede** [martʃa'pjede] *sm* (*di strada*) pavement (*Brit*), sidewalk (*US*); (*FERR*) platform.

**marci'are** [mar'tʃare] *vi* to march; (*andare: treno, macchina*) to go; (*funzionare*) to run, work.

**'marcio, a, ci, ce** ['martʃo] *ag* (*frutta, legno*) rotten, bad; (*MED*) festering; (*fig*) corrupt, rotten.

**mar'cire** [mar'tʃire] *vi* (*andare a male*) to go bad, rot; (*suppurare*) to fester; (*fig*) to rot, waste away.

**'marco, chi** *sm* (*unità monetaria*) mark.

**'mare** *sm* sea; **in ~** at sea; **andare al ~** (*in vacanza etc*) to go to the seaside; **il M~ del Nord** the North Sea.

**ma'rea** *sf* tide; **alta/bassa ~** high/ low tide.

**mareggi'ata** [mared'dʒata] *sf* heavy sea.

**ma'remma** *sf* (*GEO*) maremma, swampy coastal area.

**mare'moto** *sm* seaquake.

**maresci'allo** [mareʃ'ʃallo] *sm* (*MIL*) marshal; (: *sottufficiale*) warrant officer.

**marga'rina** *sf* margarine.

**marghe'rita** [marge'rita] *sf* (ox-eye) daisy, marguerite; (*di stampante*) daisy wheel; **margheri'tina** *sf* daisy.

**'margine** ['mardʒine] *sm* margin; (*di bosco, via*) edge, border.

**ma'rina** *sf* navy; (*costa*) coast; (*quadro*) seascape; ~ **militare/ mercantile** navy/merchant navy (*Brit*) *o* marine (*US*).

**mari'naio** *sm* sailor.

**mari'nare** *vt* (*CUC*) to marinate; ~ **la scuola** to play truant; **mari'nata** *sf* marinade.

**ma'rino, a** *ag* sea *cpd*, marine.

**mario'netta** *sf* puppet.

**mari'tare** *vt* to marry; **~rsi** *vr*: **~rsi a** *o* **con qn** to marry sb, get married to sb.

**ma'rito** *sm* husband.

**ma'rittimo, a** *ag* maritime, sea *cpd*.

**mar'maglia** [mar'maʎʎa] *sf* mob, riff-raff.

**marmel'lata** *sf* jam; (*di agrumi*) marmalade.

**mar'mitta** *sf* (*recipiente*) pot; (*AUT*) silencer.

**'marmo** *sm* marble.

**mar'mocchio** [mar'mɔkkjo] *sm* (*fam*) tot, kid.

**mar'motta** *sf* (*ZOOL*) marmot.

**Ma'rocco** *sm*: **il** ~ Morocco.

**ma'roso** *sm* breaker.

**mar'rone** *ag inv* brown // *sm* (*BOT*) chestnut.

**mar'sala** *sm inv* (*vino*) Marsala.

**mar'sina** *sf* tails *pl*, tail coat.

**marte'dì** *sm inv* Tuesday; **di** *o* **il** ~ on Tuesdays; ~ **grasso** Shrove Tuesday.

**martel'lare** *vt* to hammer // *vi* (*pulsare*) to throb; (: *cuore*) to thump.

**mar'tello** *sm* hammer; (*di uscio*) knocker.

**marti'netto** *sm* (*TECN*) jack.

**'martire** *sm/f* martyr; **mar'tirio** *sm* martyrdom; (*fig*) agony, torture.

**'martora** *sf* marten.

**martori'are** *vt* to torment, torture.

**mar'xista, i, e** *ag, sm/f* Marxist.

**marza'pane** [martsa'pane] *sm* marzipan.

**'marzo** [martso] *sm* March.

**mascal'zone** [maskal'tsone] *sm* rascal, scoundrel.

**ma'scella** [maʃ'ʃella] *sf* (*ANAT*) jaw.

**'maschera** ['maskera] *sf* mask; (*travestimento*) disguise; (: *per un ballo etc*) fancy dress; (*TEATRO, CINEMA*) usher/usherette; (*personaggio del teatro*) stock character; **masche'rare** *vt* to mask; (*travestire*) to disguise; to dress up; (*fig*: *celare*) to hide, conceal; (*MIL*) to camouflage; **~rsi da** to disguise o.s. as; to dress up as; (*fig*) to masquerade as.

**mas'chile** [mas'kile] *ag* masculine; (*sesso, popolazione*) male; (*abiti*) men's; (*per ragazzi*: *scuola*) boys'.

**'maschio, a** ['maskjo] *ag* (*BIOL*) male; (*virile*) manly // *sm* (*anche ZOOL, TECN*) male; (*uomo*) man; (*ragazzo*) boy; (*figlio*) son.

**masco'lino, a** *ag* masculine.

**'massa** *sf* mass; (*di errori etc*): **una** ~ **di** heaps of, masses of; (*di gente*) mass, multitude; (*ELETTR*) earth; **in** ~ (*COMM*) in bulk; (*tutti insieme*) en masse; **adunata in** ~ mass meeting; **di** ~ (*cultura, manifestazione*) mass *cpd*; **la** ~ **del popolo** the masses *pl*.

**mas'sacro** *sm* massacre, slaughter; (*fig*) mess, disaster.

**mas'saggio** [mas'saddʒo] *sm* massage.

**mas'saia** *sf* housewife.

**masse'rizie** [masse'rittsje] *sfpl* (household) furnishings.

**mas'siccio, a, ci, ce** [mas'sittʃo] *ag* (*oro, legno*) solid; (*palazzo*) massive; (*corporatura*) stout // *sm* (*GEO*) massif.

**'massima** *sf vedi* **massimo**.

**massi'male** *sm* maximum.

**'massimo, a** *ag, sm* maximum // *sf* (*sentenza, regola*) maxim; (*METEOR*) maximum temperature; **al** ~ **at** (the) most; **in linea di** ~a generally speaking.

**'masso** *sm* rock, boulder.

**mas'sone** *sm* freemason; **massone'ria** *sf* freemasonry.

**masti'care** vt to chew.

'**mastice** ['mastitʃe] sm mastic; (per vetri) putty.

**mas'tino** sm mastiff.

**ma'tassa** sf skein.

**mate'matico, a, ci, che** ag mathematical // sm/f mathematician // sf mathematics sg.

**mate'rasso** sm mattress; ~ a **molle** spring o interior-sprung mattress.

**ma'teria** sf (FISICA) matter; (TECN, COMM) material, matter q; (disciplina) subject; (argomento) subject matter, material; ~e **prime** raw materials; **in** ~ **di** (per quanto concerne) on the subject of; **materi'ale** ag material; (fig: grossolano) rough, rude // sm material; (insieme di strumenti etc) equipment q, materials pl.

**maternità** sf motherhood, maternity; (clinica) maternity hospital.

**ma'terno, a** ag (amore, cura etc) maternal, motherly; (nonno) maternal; (lingua, terra) mother cpd.

**ma'tita** sf pencil.

**ma'trice** [ma'tritʃe] sf matrix; (COMM) counterfoil; (fig: origine) background.

**ma'tricola** sf (registro) register; (numero) registration number; (nell'università) freshman, fresher.

**ma'trigna** [ma'trinɲa] sf stepmother.

**matrimoni'ale** ag matrimonial, marriage cpd.

**matri'monio** sm marriage, matrimony; (durata) marriage, married life; (cerimonia) wedding.

**ma'trona** sf (fig) matronly woman.

**mat'tina** sf morning; **matti'nata** sf morning; (spettacolo) matinée, afternoon performance; **mattini'ero, a** ag: essere mattiniero to be an early riser; **mat'tino** sm morning.

'**matto, a** ag mad, crazy; (fig: falso) false, imitation; (: opaco) matt, dull // sm/f madman/woman;

avere una voglia ~a di qc to be dying for sth.

**mat'tone** sm brick; (fig): **questo libro/film è un** ~ this book/film is heavy going.

**matto'nella** sf tile.

**matu'rare** vi (anche: ~rsi) (frutta, grano) to ripen; (ascesso) to come to a head; (fig: persona, idea, ECON) to mature // vt to ripen; to (make) mature.

**maturità** sf maturity; (di frutta) ripeness, maturity; (INS) school-leaving examination, ≈ GCE A-levels (Brit).

**ma'turo, a** ag mature; (frutto) ripe, mature.

'**mazza** ['mattsa] sf (bastone) club; (martello) sledge-hammer; (SPORT: da golf) club; (: da baseball, cricket) bat.

**maz'zata** [mat'tsata] sf (anche fig) heavy blow.

'**mazzo** ['mattso] sm (di fiori, chiavi etc) bunch; (di carte da gioco) pack.

**me** pronome me; ~ **stesso(a)** myself; **sei bravo quanto** ~ you are as clever as I (am) o as me.

**me'andro** sm meander.

**M.E.C.** [mɛk] sigla m (= Mercato Comune Europeo) EEC.

**mec'canico, a, ci, che** ag mechanical // sm mechanic // sf mechanics sg; (attività tecnologica) mechanical engineering; (meccanismo) mechanism.

**mecca'nismo** sm mechanism.

**me'daglia** [me'daʎʎa] sf medal; **medagli'one** sm (ARCHIT) medallion; (gioiello) locket.

**me'desimo, a** ag same; (in persona): **io** ~ I myself.

'**media** sf vedi medio.

**medi'ano, a** ag median; (valore) mean // sm (CALCIO) half-back.

**medi'ante** prep by means of.

**medi'are** vt (fare da mediatore) to act as mediator in; (MAT) to average.

**media'tore, 'trice** sm/f mediator;

(*COMM*) middle man, agent.

**medica'mento** *sm* medicine, drug.

**medi'care** *vt* to treat; (*ferita*) to dress; **medicazi'one** *sf* treatment, medication; dressing.

**medi'cina** [medi'tʃina] *sf* medicine; ~ legale forensic medicine; **medici'nale** *ag* medicinal // *sm* drug, medicine.

'**medico, a, ci, che** *ag* medical // *sm* doctor; ~ **generico** general practitioner, GP.

**medie'vale** *ag* medieval.

'**medio, a** *ag* average; (*punto, ceto*) middle; (*altezza, statura*) medium // *sm* (*dito*) middle finger // *sf* average; (*MAT*) mean; (*INS: voto*) end-of-term average; in ~a on average; licenza ~a *a leaving certificate awarded at the end of 3 years of secondary education*; scuola ~a *first 3 years of secondary school*.

**medi'ocre** *ag* mediocre, poor.

**medioe'vale** *ag* = **medievale**.

**medio'evo** *sm* Middle Ages *pl*.

**medi'tare** *vt* to ponder over, meditate on; (*progettare*) to plan, think out // *vi* to meditate.

**mediter'raneo, a** *ag* Mediterranean; **il (mare) M**~ the Mediterranean (Sea).

**me'dusa** *sf* (*ZOOL*) jellyfish.

**me'gafono** *sm* megaphone.

'**meglio** ['mɛʎʎo] *av, ag inv* better; (*con senso superlativo*) best // *sm* (*la cosa migliore*): il ~ the best (thing); faresti ~ ad andartene you had better leave; alla ~ as best one can; andar di bene in ~ to get better and better; fare del proprio ~ to do one's best; per il ~ for the best; aver la ~ su qn to get the better of sb.

'**mela** *sf* apple; ~ **cotogna** quince.

**mela'grana** *sf* pomegranate.

**melan'zana** [melan'dzana] *sf* aubergine (*Brit*), eggplant (*US*).

**me'lassa** *sf* molasses *sg*, treacle.

**me'lenso, a** *ag* dull, stupid.

**mel'lifluo, a** *ag* (*peg*) sugary,

honeyed.

'**melma** *sf* mud, mire.

'**melo** *sm* apple tree.

**melo'dia** *sf* melody.

**me'lone** *sm* (*musk*)melon.

'**membra** *sfpl vedi* membro.

'**membro** *sm* member; (*pl(f)* ~a: *arto*) limb.

**memo'randum** *sm inv* memorandum.

**me'moria** *sf* memory; ~e *sfpl* (*opera autobiografica*) memoirs; a ~ (*imparare, sapere*) by heart; a ~ d'uomo within living memory; **memori'ale** *sm* (*raccolta di memorie*) memoirs *pl*; (*DIR*) memorial.

**mena'dito**: a ~ *av* perfectly, thoroughly; sapere qc a ~ to have sth at one's fingertips.

**me'nare** *vt* to lead; (*picchiare*) to hit, beat; (*dare: colpi*) to deal; ~ la coda (*cane*) to wag its tail.

**mendi'cante** *sm/f* beggar.

**mendi'care** *vt* to beg for // *vi* to beg.

---

*PAROLA CHIAVE*

'**meno** ♦ *av* **1** (*in minore misura*) less; dovresti mangiare ~ you should eat less, you shouldn't eat so much

**2** (*comparativo*): ~ ... di not so ... as, less ... than; sono ~ alto di te I'm not as tall as you (are), I'm less tall than you (are); ~ ... che not as ... as, less ... than; ~ che mai less than ever; è ~ intelligente che ricco he's more rich than intelligent; ~ fumo più mangio the less I smoke the more I eat

**3** (*superlativo*) least; **il ~ dotato degli studenti** the least gifted of the students; è quello che compro ~ spesso it's the one I buy least often

**4** (*MAT*) minus; 8 ~ 5 8 minus 5, 8 take away 5; sono le 8 ~ un quarto it's a quarter to 8; ~ 5 gradi 5 degrees below zero, minus 5 degrees; mille lire in ~ a thousand lire less

**5** (*fraseologia*): quanto ~ poteva telefonare he could at least have

phoned; **non so se accettare** o ~ I
don't know whether to accept or not;
**fare a ~ di** qc/qn to do without sth/
sb; **non potevo fare a ~ di ridere**
I couldn't help laughing; ~ **male!**
thank goodness!; ~ **male che sei**
**arrivato** it's a good job that you've
come

◆ *ag inv* (*tempo, denaro*) less;
(*errori, persone*) fewer; **ha fatto ~**
**errori di tutti** he made fewer mistakes than anyone, he made the few-
est mistakes of all

◆ *sm inv* **1**: **il ~** (*il minimo*) the
least; **parlare del più e del ~** to
talk about this and that
**2** (*MAT*) minus

◆ *prep* (*eccetto*) except (for), apart
from; **a ~ che, a ~ di** unless; **a ~**
**che non piova** unless it rains; **non**
**posso, a ~ di prendere ferie** I
can't, unless I take some leave.

**meno'mare** *vt* (*danneggiare*) to
maim, disable.

**meno'pausa** *sf* menopause.

'**mensa** *sf* (*locale*) canteen; (: *MIL*)
mess; (: *nelle università*) refectory.

**men'sile** *ag* monthly // *sm* (*perio-*
*dico*) monthly (magazine);
(*stipendio*) monthly salary.

'**mensola** *sf* bracket; (*ripiano*)
shelf; (*ARCHIT*) corbel.

'**menta** *sf* mint; (*anche*: ~ **pipe-**
**rita**) peppermint; (*bibita*)
peppermint cordial; (*caramella*)
mint, peppermint.

**men'tale** *ag* mental; **mentalità** *sf*
*inv* mentality.

'**mente** *sf* mind; **imparare/sapere**
qc **a ~** to learn/know sth by heart;
**avere in ~ qc** to have sth in mind;
**passare di ~ a** qn to slip sb's mind.

**men'tire** *vi* to lie.

'**mento** *sm* chin.

**men'tolo** *sm* menthol.

'**mentre** *cong* (*temporale*) while;
(*avversativo*) whereas.

**menzio'nare** [mentsjo'nare] *vt* to
mention.

**menzi'one** [men'tsjone] *sf* mention;
**fare ~ di** to mention.

**men'zogna** [men'tsɔɲɲa] *sf* lie.

**mera'viglia** [mera'viʎʎa] *sf* amazement, wonder; (*persona, cosa*)
marvel, wonder; **a ~** perfectly,
wonderfully; **meravigli'are** *vt* to
amaze, astonish; **meravigliarsi (di)**
to marvel (at); (*stupirsi*) to be
amazed (at), be astonished (at);
**meravigli'oso, a** *ag* wonderful,
marvellous.

**mer'cante** *sm* merchant; ~ **d'arte**
art dealer; ~ **di cavalli** horse
dealer; **mercanteggi'are** *vt* (*onore,*
*voto*) to sell // *vi* to bargain, haggle;
**mercan'tile** *ag* commercial,
mercantile; (*nave, marina*) merchant
*cpd* // *sm* (*nave*) merchantman;
**mercan'zia** *sf* merchandise, goods
*pl.*

**mer'cato** *sm* market; ~ **dei cambi**
exchange market; **M~ Comune**
**(Europeo)** (European) Common
Market; ~ **nero** black market.

'**merce** ['mertʃe] *sf* goods *pl,*
merchandise; ~ **deperibile** perish-
able goods *pl.*

**mercé** [mer'tʃe] *sf* mercy.

**merce'nario, a** [mertʃe'narjo] *ag,*
*sm* mercenary.

**merce'ria** [mertʃe'ria] *sf* (*articoli*)
haberdashery (Brit); notions *pl* (US);
(*bottega*) haberdasher's shop (Brit),
notions store (US).

**mercoledì** *sm inv* Wednesday; **di** o
**il ~** on Wednesdays; ~ **delle Ceneri**
Ash Wednesday.

**mer'curio** *sm* mercury.

'**merda** *sf* (*fam!*) shit (!).

**me'renda** *sf* afternoon snack.

**meridi'ano, a** *ag* midday
*cpd*, noonday // *sm* meridian // *sf*
(*orologio*) sundial.

**meridio'nale** *ag* southern // *sm/f*
southerner.

**meridi'one** *sm* south.

**me'ringa, ghe** *sf* (*CUC*) meringue.

**meri'tare** *vt* to deserve, merit // *vb*
*impers*: **merita andare** it's worth

going.

**meri'tevole** *ag* worthy.

**'merito** *sm* merit; (*valore*) worth; in ~ a as regards, with regard to; dare ~ a qn di to give sb credit for; finire a pari ~ to finish joint first (*o* second *etc*); to tie; **meri'torio**, **a** *ag* praiseworthy.

**mer'letto** *sm* lace.

**'merlo** *sm* (*ZOOL*) blackbird; (*ARCHIT*) battlement.

**mer'luzzo** [mer'luttso] *sm* (*ZOOL*) cod.

**mes'chino**, **a** [mes'kino] *ag* wretched; (*scarso*) scanty, poor; (*persona: gretta*) mean; (: *limitata*) narrow-minded, petty.

**mesco'lanza** [mesko'lantsa] *sf* mixture.

**mesco'lare** *vt* to mix; (*vini, colori*) to blend; (*mettere in disordine*) to mix up, muddle up; (*carte*) to shuffle; ~rsi *vr* to mix; to blend; to get mixed up; (*fig*): ~rsi in to get mixed up in, meddle in.

**'mese** *sm* month.

**'messa** *sf* (*REL*) mass; (*il mettere*): ~ in moto starting; ~ in piega set; ~ a punto (*TECN*) adjustment; (*AUT*) tuning; (*fig*) clarification; ~ in scena = **messinscena**.

**messag'gero** [messad'dʒero] *sm* messenger.

**mes'saggio** [mes'saddʒo] *sm* message.

**mes'sale** *sm* (*REL*) missal.

**'messe** *sf* harvest.

**Mes'sia** *sm inv* (*REL*): il ~ the Messiah.

**'Messico** *sm*: il ~ Mexico.

**messin'scena** [messin'ʃena] *sf* (*TEATRO*) production.

**'messo**, **a** *pp di* **mettere** // *sm* messenger.

**mesti'ere** *sm* (*professione*) job; (: *manuale*) trade; (: *artigianale*) craft; (*fig: abilità nel lavoro*) skill, technique; essere del ~ to know the tricks of the trade.

**'mesto**, **a** *ag* sad, melancholy.

**'mestola** *sf* (*CUC*) ladle; (*EDIL*) trowel.

**'mestolo** *sm* (*CUC*) ladle.

**mestruazi'one** [mestruat'tsjone] *sf* menstruation.

**'meta** *sf* destination; (*fig*) aim, goal.

**metà** *sf inv* half; (*punto di mezzo*) middle; dividere qc a *o* per ~ to divide sth in half, halve sth; fare a ~ (di qc con qn) to go halves (with sb in sth); a ~ prezzo at half price; a ~ strada halfway.

**me'tafora** *sf* metaphor.

**me'tallico**, **a**, **ci**, **che** *ag* (*di metallo*) metal cpd; (*splendore, rumore etc*) metallic.

**me'tallo** *sm* metal.

**metalmec'canico**, **a**, **ci**, **che** *ag* engineering cpd // *sm* engineering worker.

**me'tano** *sm* methane.

**meteorolo'gia** [meteorolo'dʒia] *sf* meteorology; **meteoro'logico**, **a**, **ci**, **che** *ag* meteorological, weather cpd.

**me'ticcio**, **a**, **ci**, **ce** [me'tittʃo] *sm/f* half-caste, half-breed.

**me'todico**, **a**, **ci**, **che** *ag* methodical.

**'metodo** *sm* method; (*manuale*) tutor (*Brit*), manual.

**'metrico**, **a**, **ci**, **che** *ag* metric; (*POESIA*) metrical // *sf* metrics *sg*.

**'metro** *sm* metre; (*nastro*) tape measure; (*asta*) (metre) rule.

**metropoli'tano**, **a** *ag* metropolitan // *sf* underground, subway.

**'mettere** *vt* to put; (*abito*) to put on; (: *portare*) to wear; (*installare: telefono*) to put in; (*fig: provocare*): ~ fame/allegria a qn to make sb hungry/happy; (*supporre*): mettiamo che ... let's suppose *o* say that ... ; ~rsi *vr* (*persona*) to put o.s.; (*oggetto*) to go; (*disporsi: faccenda*) to turn out; ~rsi a sedere to sit down; ~rsi a letto to get into bed; (*per malattia*) to take to one's bed; ~rsi il cappello to put on one's hat; ~rsi a (*cominciare*) to begin to, start to; ~rsi al lavoro to set to work; ~rsi con qn (in società) to team up with sb; (in coppia) to start going out with sb; ~rci: ~rci molta cura/molto tempo to take a lot of care/a lot of time; ci ho messo 3 ore per venire it's taken me 3 hours to get here; ~rcela tutta to do one's best; ~ a tacere qn/qc to keep sb/ sth quiet; ~ su casa to set up house; ~ su un negozio to start a shop; ~ via to put away.

mez'zadro ['medʒdzadro] sm (AGR) sharecropper.

mezza'luna [meddza'luna] sf half-moon; (dell'islamismo) crescent; (coltello) (semicircular) chopping knife.

mezza'nino [meddza'nino] sm mezzanine (floor).

mez'zano, a [med'dzano] ag (medio) average, medium; (figlio) middle cpd // smf (intermediario) go-between; (ruffiano) pimp.

mezza'notte [meddza'nɔtte] sf midnight.

'mezzo, a ['mɛddzo] ag half; un ~ litro/panino half a litre/roll // av half-; ~ morto half-dead // sm (metà) half; (parte centrale: di strada etc) middle; (per raggiungere un fine) means sg; (veicolo) vehicle; (nell'indicare l'ora): le nove e ~ half past nine; mezzogiorno e ~ half past twelve // sf: la ~a half-past twelve (in the afternoon); ~i smpl (possibilità economiche) means; di ~a età middle-aged; un soprabito di ~a stagione a spring (o autumn) coat; di ~ middle, in the middle; andarci di ~ (patir danno) to suffer; levarsi o togliersi di ~ to get out of the way; in ~ a in the middle of; per o a ~ di by means of; ~i di comunicazione di massa mass media pl; ~i pubblici public transport sg; ~i di trasporto means of transport.

mezzogi'orno [meddzo'dʒorno] sm midday, noon; (GEO) south; a ~ at

12 (o'clock) o midday o noon; il ~ d'Italia southern Italy.

mez'z'ora, mez'zora [med'dzora] sf half-hour, half an hour.

mi pronome (dav lo, la, li, le, ne diventa me) (oggetto) me; (complemento di termine) to me; (riflessivo) myself // sm (MUS) E; (: solfeggiando la scala) mi.

'mia vedi mio.

miago'lare vi to miaow, mew.

'mica sf (CHIM) mica // av (fam): non ... ~ not ... at all; non sono ~ stanco I'm not a bit tired; non sarà ~ partito? he wouldn't have left, would he?; ~ male not bad.

'miccia, ce ['mittʃa] sf fuse.

micidi'ale [mitʃi'djale] ag fatal; (dannosissimo) deadly.

mi'crofono sm microphone.

micros'copio sm microscope.

mi'dollo [mi'dɔllo] (pl(f) ~a sm (ANAT) marrow.

'mie, mi'ei vedi mio.

mi'ele sm honey.

mi'etere vt (AGR) to reap, harvest; (fig: vite) to take, claim.

migli'aio [miʎ'ʎajo], pl(f) ~a sm thousand; un ~ (di) about a thousand; a ~a by the thousand, in thousands.

'miglio ['miʎʎo] sm (BOT) millet; (pl(f) ~a: unità di misura) mile; ~ marino o nautico nautical mile.

migliora'mento [miʎʎora'mento] sm improvement.

miglio'rare [miʎʎo'rare] vt, vi to improve.

migli'ore [miʎ'ʎore] ag (comparativo) better; (superlativo) best // sm: il ~ the best (thing) // smf: il(la) ~ the best (person); il miglior vino di questa regione the best wine in this area.

'mignolo ['miɲɲolo] sm (ANAT) little finger, pinkie; (: dito del piede) little toe.

mi'grare vi to migrate.

'mila pl di mille.

Mi'lano sf Milan.

**miliar'dario, a** *sm/f* millionaire.

**mili'ardo** *sm* thousand million, billion (US).

**mili'are** *ag*: pietra ~ milestone.

**mili'one** *sm* million; **un ~ di lire** a million lire.

**mili'tante** *ag, sm/f* militant.

**mili'tare** *vi* (MIL) to be a soldier, serve; (*fig*: *in un partito*) to be a militant // *ag* military // *sm* serviceman; **fare il ~** to do one's military service.

**'milite** *sm* soldier.

**millanta'tore, 'trice** *sm/f* boaster.

**'mille** *num* (*pl* **mila**) a *o* one thousand; **dieci mila** ten thousand.

**mille'foglie** [mille'fɔʎʎe] *sm inv* (CUC) cream *o* vanilla slice.

**mil'lennio** *sm* millennium.

**millepi'edi** *sm inv* centipede.

**mil'lesimo, a** *ag, sm* thousandth.

**milli'grammo** *sm* milligram(me).

**mil'limetro** *sm* millimetre.

**'milza** ['miltsa] *sf* (ANAT) spleen.

**mimetiz'zare** [mimetid'dzare] *vt* to camouflage; **~rsi** *vr* to camouflage o.s.

**'mimica** *sf* (*arte*) mime.

**'mimo** *sm* (*attore, componimento*) mime.

**mi'mosa** *sf* mimosa.

**'mina** *sf* (*esplosiva*) mine; (*di matita*) lead.

**mi'naccia, ce** [mi'nattʃa] *sf* threat; **minacci'are** *vt* to threaten; **minacciare qn di morte** to threaten to kill sb; **minacciare di fare qc** to threaten to do sth; **minacci'oso, a** *ag* threatening.

**mi'nare** *vt* (MIL) to mine; (*fig*) to undermine.

**mina'tore** *sm* miner.

**mina'torio, a** *ag* threatening.

**mine'rale** *ag, sm* mineral.

**mine'rario, a** *ag* (*delle miniere*) mining; (*dei minerali*) ore // *sm*.

**mi'nestra** *sf* soup; **~ in brodo/di verdure** noodle/vegetable soup; **mines'trone** *sm* thick vegetable and pasta soup.

**mingher'lino, a** [minger'lino] *ag* thin, slender.

**'mini** *ag inv* mini // *sf inv* miniskirt.

**minia'tura** *sf* miniature.

**mini'era** *sf* mine.

**mini'gonna** *sf* miniskirt.

**'minimo, a** *ag* minimum, least, slightest; (*piccolissimo*) very small, slight; (*il più basso*) lowest, minimum // *sm* minimum; **al ~** at least; **girare al ~** (AUT) to idle.

**minis'tero** *sm* (POL, REL) ministry; (*governo*) government; **~ delle Finanze** Ministry of Finance, ≈ Treasury.

**mi'nistro** *sm* (POL, REL) minister; **~ delle Finanze** Minister of Finance, ≈ Chancellor of the Exchequer.

**mino'ranza** [mino'rantsa] *sf* minority.

**mino'rato, a** *ag* handicapped // *sm/f* physically (*o* mentally) handicapped person.

**mi'nore** *ag* (*comparativo*) less; (*più piccolo*) smaller; (*numero*) lower; (*inferiore*) lower, inferior; (*meno importante*) minor; (*più giovane*) younger; (*superlativo*) least; smallest; lowest; youngest // *sm/f* (*minorenne*) minor, person under age.

**mino'renne** *ag* under age // *sm/f* minor, person under age.

**mi'nuscolo, a** *ag* (*scrittura, carattere*) small; (*piccolissimo*) tiny // *sf* small letter.

**mi'nuta** *sf* rough copy, draft.

**mi'nuto, a** *ag* tiny, minute; (*pioggia*) fine; (*corporatura*) delicate, fine; (*lavoro*) detailed // *sm* (*unità di misura*) minute; **al ~** (COMM) retail.

**'mio, 'mia, mi'ei, 'mie** *det*: **il ~, la mia** *etc* my // *pronome*: **il ~, la mia** *etc* mine; **i miei** my family; **un ~ amico** a friend of mine.

**'miope** *ag* short-sighted.

**'mira** *sf* (*anche fig*) aim; **prendere la ~** to take aim; **prendere di ~ qn**

(fig) to pick on sb.

**mi'rabile** ag admirable, wonderful.

**mi'racolo** sm miracle.

**mi'raggio** [mi'radd3o] sm mirage.

**mi'rare** vi: ~ a to aim at.

**mi'rino** sm (TECN) sight; (FOT) viewer, viewfinder.

**mir'tillo** sm bilberry (Brit), blueberry (US), whortleberry.

**mi'scela** [miʃʃela] sf mixture; (di caffè) blend.

**miscel'lanea** [miʃʃel'lanea] sf miscellany.

**'mischia** ['miskja] sf scuffle; (RUGBY) scrum, scrummage.

**mischi'are** [mis'kjare] vt, ~rsi vr to mix, blend.

**mis'cuglio** [mis'kuʎʎo] sm mixture, hotchpotch, jumble.

**mise'rabile** ag (infelice) miserable, wretched; (povero) poverty-stricken; (di scarso valore) miserable.

**mi'seria** sf extreme poverty; (infelicità) misery; ~e sfpl (del mondo etc) misfortunes, troubles; porca ~! (fam) blast!, damn!

**miseri'cordia** sf mercy, pity.

**'misero, a** ag miserable, wretched; (povero) poverty-stricken; (insufficiente) miserable.

**mis'fatto** sm misdeed, crime.

**mi'sogino** [mi'zɔdʒino] sm misogynist.

**'missile** sm missile.

**missio'nario, a** ag, smf missionary.

**missi'one** sf mission.

**misteri'oso, a** ag mysterious.

**mis'tero** sm mystery.

**mistifi'care** vt to fool, bamboozle.

**'misto, a** ag mixed; (scuola) mixed, coeducational // sm mixture.

**mis'tura** sf mixture.

**mi'sura** sf measure; (misurazione, dimensione) measurement; (taglia) size; (provvedimento) measure, step; (moderazione) moderation; (MUS) time; (: divisione) bar; (fig: limite) bounds pl, limit; **nella ~ in cui** inasmuch as, insofar as; **su ~** made to measure.

**misu'rare** vt (ambiente, stoffa) to measure; (terreno) to survey; (abito) to try on; (pesare) to weigh; (fig: parole etc) to weigh up; (: spese, cibo) to limit // vi to measure; ~**rsi** vr: ~**rsi con qn** to have a confrontation with sb; to compete with sb; **misu'rato, a** ag (ponderato) measured; (prudente) cautious; (moderato) moderate.

**'mite** ag mild; (prezzo) moderate, reasonable.

**miti'gare** vt to mitigate, lessen; (lenire) to soothe, relieve; ~**rsi** vr (odio) to subside; (tempo) to become milder.

**'mito** sm myth; **mitolo'gia, 'gie** sf mythology.

**'mitra** sf (REL) mitre // sm inv (arma) sub-machine gun.

**mitraglia'trice** [mitraʎʎa'tritʃe] sf machine gun.

**mit'tente** smf sender.

**'mobile** ag mobile; (parte di macchina) moving; (DIR: bene) movable, personal // sm (arredamento) piece of furniture; ~**i** smpl furniture sg.

**mo'bilia** sf furniture.

**mobili'are** ag (DIR) personal, movable.

**mo'bilio** sm = **mobilia**.

**mobili'tare** vt to mobilize.

**mocas'sino** sm moccasin.

**'moccolo** sm (di candela) candle-end; (fam: bestemmia) oath; (: moccio) snot; **reggere il ~** to play gooseberry (Brit), act as chaperon.

**'moda** sf fashion; **alla ~, di ~** fashionable, in fashion.

**modalità** sf inv formality.

**mo'della** sf model.

**model'lare** vt (creta) to model, shape; ~**rsi** vr: ~**rsi su** to model o.s. on.

**mo'dello** sm model; (stampo) mould // ag inv model cpd.

**'modem** sm inv modem.

**mode'rare** vt to moderate; ~**rsi**

to restrain o.s.; **mode'rato, a** *ag* moderate.

**modera'tore, 'trice** *sm/f* moderator.

**mo'derno, a** *ag* modern.

**mo'destia** *sf* modesty.

**mo'desto, a** *ag* modest.

**'modico, a, ci, che** *ag* reasonable, moderate.

**mo'difica, che** *sf* modification.

**modifi'care** *vt* to modify, alter; ~**rsi** *vr* to alter, change.

**mo'dista** *sf* milliner.

**'modo** *sm* way, manner; (*mezzo*) means, way; (*occasione*) opportunity; (*LING*) mood; (*MUS*) mode; ~**i** *smpl* manners; **a suo ~, a ~ suo** in his own way; **ad** *o* **in ogni ~** anyway; **di** *o* **in ~ che** so that; **in ~ da** so as to; **in tutti i ~i** at all costs; (*comunque sia*) anyway; (*in ogni caso*) in any case; **in qualche ~** somehow or other; ~ **di dire** turn of phrase; **per ~ di dire** so to speak.

**modu'lare** *vt* to modulate; **modulazi'one** *sf* modulation; **modulazione di frequenza** frequency modulation.

**'modulo** *sm* (*modello*) form; (*ARCHIT, lunare, di comando*) module.

**'mogano** *sm* mahogany.

**'mogio, a, gi, gie** ['mɔdʒo] *ag* down in the dumps, dejected.

**'moglie** ['mɔʎʎe] *sf* wife.

**mo'ine** *sfpl* cajolery *sg*; (*leziosità*) affectation *sg*.

**'mola** *sf* millstone; (*utensile abrasivo*) grindstone.

**mo'lare** *sm* (*dente*) molar.

**'mole** *sf* mass; (*dimensioni*) size; (*edificio grandioso*) massive structure.

**moles'tare** *vt* to bother, annoy; **mo'lestia** *sf* annoyance, bother; **recar molestia a qn** to bother sb; **mo'lesto, a** *ag* annoying.

**'molla** *sf* spring; ~**e** *sfpl* tongs.

**mol'lare** *vt* to release, let go; (*NAUT*) to ease; (*fig: ceffone*) to

give // *vi* (*cedere*) to give in.

**'molle** *ag* soft; (*muscoli*) flabby; (*fig: debole*) weak, feeble.

**mol'letta** *sf* (*per capelli*) hairgrip; (*per panni stesi*) clothes peg; ~**e** *sfpl* (*per zucchero*) tongs.

**mollica, che** *sf* crumb, soft part.

**mol'lusco, schi** *sm* mollusc.

**'molo** *sm* mole, breakwater; jetty.

**mol'teplice** [mol'tɛpliʃe] *ag* (*formato di più elementi*) complex; ~**i** *pl* (*svariati: interessi, attività*) numerous, various.

**moltipli'care** *vt* to multiply; ~**rsi** *vr* to multiply; to increase in number; **moltiplicazi'one** *sf* multiplication.

┌─────────────────────────────────┐
│ *PAROLA CHIAVE* │
└─────────────────────────────────┘

**'molto, a,** ◆ *det* (*quantità*) a lot of, much; (*numero*) a lot of, many; ~ **pane/carbone** a lot of bread/coal; ~**a gente** a lot of people, many people; ~**i libri** a lot of books, many books; **non ho ~ tempo** I haven't got much time; **per ~ (tempo)** for a long time

◆ *av* **1** a lot, (very) much; **viaggia ~** he travels a lot; **non viaggia ~** he doesn't travel much *o* a lot

**2** (*intensivo: con aggettivi, avverbi*) very; (: *con participio passato*) (very) much; ~ **buono** very good; ~ **migliore,** ~ **meglio** much *o* a lot better

◆ *pronome* much, a lot; ~**i(e)** *pronome pl* many, a lot; ~**i pensano che ...** many (people) think ....

**momen'taneo, a** *ag* momentary, fleeting.

**mo'mento** *sm* moment; **da un ~ all'altro** at any moment; (*all'improvviso*) suddenly; **al ~ di fare** just as I was (*o* you were *o* he was *etc*) doing; **per il ~** for the time being; **dal ~ che** ever since; (*dato che*) since; **a ~i** (*da un ~ all'altro*) any time *o* moment now; (*quasi*) nearly.

'**monaca, che** *sf* nun.
'**Monaco** *sf* Monaco; ~ (**di** Baviera) Munich.
'**monaco, ci** *sm* monk.
mo'**narca, chi** *sm* monarch; **monar'chia** *sf* monarchy.
monas'**tero** (*di monaci*) monastery; (*di monache*) convent; mo'**nastico, a, ci, che** *ag* monastic.
'**monco, a, chi, che** *ag* maimed; (*fig*) incomplete; ~ **d'un braccio** one-armed.
mon'**dana** *sf* prostitute.
mon'**dano, a** *ag* (*anche fig*) worldly; (*dell'alta società*) society *cpd*; fashionable.
mon'**dare** *vt* (*frutta, patate*) to peel; (*piselli*) to shell; (*pulire*) to clean.
mondi'**ale** *ag* (*campionato, popolazione*) world *cpd*; (*influenza*) world-wide.
'**mondo** *sm* world; (*grande quantità*): **un** ~ **di** lots of, a host of; **il bel** ~ high society.
mo'**nello, a** *sm/f* street urchin; (*ragazzo vivace*) scamp, imp.
mo'**neta** *sf* coin; (*ECON: valuta*) currency; (*denaro spicciolo*) (small) change; ~ **estera** foreign currency; ~ **legale** legal tender; **mone'tario, a** *ag* monetary.
mongo'**loide** *ag, sm/f* (*MED*) mongol.
'**monito** *sm* warning.
'**monitor** *sm inv* (*TECN, TV*) monitor.
monoco'**lore** *ag* (*POL*): **governo** ~ one-party government.
mono'**polio** *sm* monopoly.
mo'**notono, a** *ag* monotonous.
monsi'**gnore** [monsiɲ'ɲore] *sm* (*REL: titolo*) Your (*o* His) Grace.
mon'**sone** *sm* monsoon.
monta'**carichi** [monta'kariki] *sm inv* hoist, goods lift.
mon'**taggio** [mon'taddʒo] *sm* (*TECN*) assembly; (*CINEMA*) editing.

mon'**tagna** [mon'taɲɲa] *sf* mountain; (*zona montuosa*): **la** ~ the mountains *pl*; **andare in** ~ to go to the mountains; ~**e russe** roller coaster *sg*, big dipper *sg* (*Brit*); monta'**gnoso, a** *ag* mountainous.
monta'**naro, a** *ag* mountain *cpd // sm/f* mountain dweller.
mon'**tano, a** *ag* mountain *cpd*; alpine.
mon'**tare** *vt* to go (*o* come) up; (*cavallo*) to ride; (*apparecchiatura*) to set up, assemble; (*CUC*) to whip; (*ZOOL*) to cover; (*incastonare*) to mount, set; (*CINEMA*) to edit; (*FOT*) to mount // *vi* to go (*o* come) up; (*a cavallo*): ~ **bene/male** to ride well/badly; (*aumentare di livello, volume*) to rise; ~**rsi** *vr* to become big-headed; ~ **qc** to exaggerate sth; ~ **qn** *o* **la testa a qn** to turn sb's head; ~ **in bicicletta/macchina/treno** to get on a bicycle/into a car/on a train; ~ **a cavallo** to get on *o* mount a horse.
monta'**tura** *sf* assembling *q*; (*di occhiali*) frames *pl*; (*di gioiello*) mounting, setting; (*fig*): ~ **pubblicitaria** publicity stunt.
'**monte** *sm* mountain; **a** ~ upstream; **mandare a** ~ **qc** to upset sth, cause sth to fail; **il M**~ **Bianco** Mont Blanc; ~ **di pietà** pawnshop.
mon'**tone** *sm* (*ZOOL*) ram; **carne di** ~ mutton.
montu'**oso, a** *ag* mountainous.
monu'**mento** *sm* monument.
'**mora** *sf* (*del rovo*) blackberry; (*del gelso*) mulberry; (*DIR*) delay; (: *somma*) arrears *pl*.
mo'**rale** *ag* moral // *sf* (*scienza*) ethics *sg*, moral philosophy; (*complesso di norme*) moral standards *pl*, morality; (*condotta*) morals *pl*; (*insegnamento morale*) moral // *sm* morale; **essere giù di** ~ to be feeling down; **moralità** *sf* morality; (*condotta*) morals *pl*.
'**morbido, a** *ag* soft; (*pelle*) soft, smooth.

**mor'billo** sm (MED) measles sg.

**'morbo** sm disease.

**mor'boso, a** ag (fig) morbid.

**mor'dace** [mor'datʃe] ag biting, cutting.

**mor'dente** sm (fig: di satira, critica) bite; (: di persona) drive.

**'mordere** vt to bite; (addentare) to bite into; (corrodere) to eat into.

**mori'bondo, a** ag dying, moribund.

**morige'rato, a** [moridʒe'rato] ag of good morals.

**mo'rire** vi to die; (abitudine, civiltà) to die out; ~ **di fame** to die of hunger; (fig) to be starving; ~ **di noia/paura** to be bored/scared to death; **fa un caldo da** ~ it's terribly hot.

**mormo'rare** vi to murmur; (brontolare) to grumble.

**'moro, a** ag dark(-haired); dark(-complexioned); **i M~i** smpl (STORIA) the Moors.

**mo'roso, a** ag in arrears // smf (fam: innamorato) sweetheart.

**'morsa** sf (TECN) vice; (fig: stretta) grip.

**morsi'care** vt to nibble (at), gnaw (at); (sog: insetto) to bite.

**'morso, a** pp di **mordere** // sm bite; (di insetto) sting; (parte della briglia) bit; ~i **della fame** pangs of hunger.

**mor'taio** sm mortar.

**mor'tale** ag, sm mortal; **mortalità** sf mortality, death rate.

**'morte** sf death.

**mortifi'care** vt to mortify.

**'morto, a** pp di **morire** // ag dead // smf dead man/woman; **i ~i** the dead; **fare il** ~ (nell'acqua) to float on one's back; **il Mar M~** the Dead Sea.

**mor'torio** sm (anche fig) funeral.

**mo'saico, ci** sm mosaic.

**'mosca, sche** sf fly; ~ **cieca** blind-man's-buff.

**'Mosca** sf Moscow.

**mos'cato** sm muscatel (wine).

**mosce'rino** [moʃʃe'rino] sm midge,

gnat.

**mos'chea** [mos'kea] sf mosque.

**mos'chetto** [mos'ketto] sm musket.

**'moscio, a, sci, sce** ['moʃʃo] ag (fig) lifeless.

**mos'cone** sm (ZOOL) bluebottle; (barca) pedalo; (: a remi) kind of pedalo with oars.

**'mossa** sf movement; (nel gioco) move.

**'mosso, a** pp di **muovere** // ag (mare) rough; (capelli) wavy; (FOT) blurred; (ritmo, prosa) animated.

**mos'tarda** sf mustard.

**'mostra** sf exhibition, show; (ostentazione) show; **in** ~ on show; **far** ~ **di** (fingere) to pretend; **far** ~ **di sé** to show off.

**mos'trare** vt to show // vi: ~ **di fare** to pretend to do; ~**rsi** vr to appear.

**'mostro** sm monster; **mostru'oso, a** ag monstrous.

**mo'tel** sm inv motel.

**moti'vare** vt (causare) to cause; (giustificare) to justify, account for; **motivazi'one** sf justification; motive; (PSIC) motivation.

**mo'tivo** sm (causa) reason, cause; (movente) motive; (letterario) (central) theme; (disegno) motif, design, pattern; (MUS) motif; **per quale** ~? why?, for what reason?

**'moto** sm (anche FISICA) motion; (movimento, gesto) movement; (esercizio fisico) exercise; (sommossa) rising, revolt; (commozione) feeling, impulse // sf inv (motocicletta) motorbike; **mettere in** ~ to set in motion; (AUT) to start up.

**motoci'cletta** [mototʃi'kletta] sf motorcycle; **motoci'clismo** sm motorcycling, motorcycle racing; **motoci'clista, i, e** smf motorcyclist.

**mo'tore, 'trice** ag motor; (TECN) driving // sm engine, motor; **a** ~ motor cpd, power-driven; ~ **a combustione interna/a reazione**

internal combustion/jet engine; **moto'rino** sm moped; **motorino di avviamento** (AUT) starter;

**motoriz'zato, a** ag (truppe) motorized; (persona) having a car o transport.

**motos'cafo** sm motorboat.

**mot'teggio** [mot'tedd3o] sm banter.

**'motto** sm (battuta scherzosa) witty remark; (frase emblematica) motto, maxim.

**mo'vente** sm motive.

**movimen'tare** vt to liven up.

**movi'mento** sm movement; (fig) activity, hustle and bustle; (MUS) tempo, movement.

**mozi'one** [mot'tsjone] sf (POL) motion.

**moz'zare** [mot'tsare] vt to cut off; (coda) to dock; ~ **il fiato** o **il respiro a qn** (fig) to take sb's breath away.

**mozza'rella** [mottsa'rɛlla] sf mozzarella (a moist Neapolitan curd cheese).

**mozzi'cone** [mottsi'kone] sm stub, butt, end; (anche: ~ **di sigaretta**) cigarette end.

**'mozzo** [mɔddzo] sm (MECCANICA) hub; ['mottso] (NAUT) ship's boy; ~ **di stalla** stable boy.

**'mucca, che** sf cow.

**'mucchio** [mukkjo] sm pile, heap; (fig): **un** ~ **di** lots of, heaps of.

**'muco, chi** sm mucus.

**'muffa** sf mould, mildew.

**mug'gire** [mud'd3ire] vi (vacca) to low, moo; (toro) to bellow; (fig) to roar; **mug'gito** sm low, moo; bellow; roar.

**mu'ghetto** [mu'getto] sm lily of the valley.

**mu'gnaio, a** [muɲ'najo] sm/f miller.

**mugo'lare** vi (cane) to whimper, whine; (fig: persona) to moan.

**muli'nare** vi to whirl, spin (round and round).

**muli'nello** sm (moto vorticoso) eddy, whirl; (di canna da pesca)

reel; (NAUT) windlass.

**mu'lino** sm mill; ~ **a vento** windmill.

**'mulo** sm mule.

**'multa** sf fine; **mul'tare** vt to fine.

**'multiplo, a** ag, sm multiple.

**'mummia** sf mummy.

**'mungere** ['mund3ere] vt (anche fig) to milk.

**munici'pale** [munitʃi'pale] ag municipal; town cpd.

**muni'cipio** [muni'tʃipjo] sm town council, corporation; (edificio) town hall.

**mu'nire** vt: ~ **qc/qn di** to equip sth/sb with.

**munizi'oni** [munit'tsjoni] sfpl (MIL) ammunition sg.

**'munto, a** pp di **mungere**.

**mu'overe** vt to move; (ruota, macchina) to drive; (sollevare: questione, obiezione) to raise, bring up (: accusa) to make, bring forward; **~rsi** vr to move; **muoviti!** hurry up!, get a move on!

**'mura** sfpl vedi **muro**.

**mu'raglia** [mu'raʎʎa] sf (high) wall.

**mu'rale** ag wall cpd; mural.

**mu'rare** vt (persona, porta) to wall up.

**mura'tore** sm mason; bricklayer.

**'muro** sm wall; **~a** sfpl (cinta cittadina) walls; **a** ~ wall cpd; (armadio etc) built-in; ~ **del suono** sound barrier; **mettere al** ~ (fucilare) to shoot o execute (by firing squad).

**'muschio** ['muskjo] sm (ZOOL) musk; (BOT) moss.

**musco'lare** ag muscular, muscle cpd.

**'muscolo** sm (ANAT) muscle.

**mu'seo** sm museum.

**museru'ola** sf muzzle.

**'musica** sf music; ~ **da ballo/ camera** dance/chamber music; **musi'cale** ag musical; **musi'cista, i, e** sm/f musician.

**'muso** sm muzzle; (di auto, aereo) nose; **tenere il** ~ to sulk; **mu'sone,**

**a** *sm/f* sulky person.

'**mussola** *sf* muslin.

'**muta** *sf* (*di animali*) moulting; (*di serpenti*) sloughing; (*per immersioni subacquee*) diving suit; (*gruppo di cani*) pack.

**muta'mento** *sm* change.

**mu'tande** *sfpl* (*da uomo*) (under)pants; **mutan'dine** *sfpl* (*da donna, bambino*) pants (*Brit*), briefs; **mutandine di plastica** plastic pants.

**mu'tare** *vt, vi* to change, alter; **mutazi'one** *sf* change, alteration; (*BIOL*) mutation; **mu'tevole** *ag* changeable.

**muti'lare** *vt* to mutilate, maim; (*fig*) to mutilate, deface; **muti'lato, a** *sm/f* disabled person (*through loss of limbs*).

**mu'tismo** *sm* (*MED*) mutism; (*atteggiamento*) (stubborn) silence.

'**muto, a** *ag* (*MED*) dumb; (*emozione, dolore, CINEMA*) silent; (*LING*) silent, mute; (*carta geografica*) blank; ~ **per lo stupore** *etc* speechless with amazement *etc*.

'**mutua** *sf* (*anche:* **cassa** ~) health insurance scheme.

**mutu'are** *vt* (*fig*) to borrow.

**mutu'ato, a** *sm/f* member of a health insurance scheme.

'**mutuo, a** *ag* (*reciproco*) mutual // *sm* (*ECON*) (long-term) loan.

# N

**N.** *abbr* (= *nord*) N.

'**nacchere** ['nakkere] *sfpl* castanets.

'**nafta** *sf* naphtha; (*per motori diesel*) diesel oil.

**nafta'lina** *sf* (*CHIM*) naphthalene; (*tarmicida*) mothballs *pl.*

'**naia** *sf* (*ZOOL*) cobra; (*MIL*) slang term for national service.

'**nailon** *sm* nylon.

'**nanna** *sf* (*linguaggio infantile*): **andare a** ~ to go to beddy-byes.

'**nano, a** *ag, sm/f* dwarf.

**napole'tano, a** *ag, sm/f* Neapolitan.

'**Napoli** *sf* Naples.

'**nappa** *sf* tassel.

**nar'ciso** [nar'tfizo] *sm* narcissus.

**nar'cosi** *sf* narcosis.

**nar'cotico, ci** *sm* narcotic.

**na'rice** [na'ritfe] *sf* nostril.

**nar'rare** *vt* to tell the story of, recount; **narra'tivo, a** *ag* narrative // *sf* (*branca letteraria*) fiction; **narra'tore, 'trice** *sm/f* narrator; **narrazi'one** *sf* narration; (*racconto*) story, tale.

**na'sale** *ag* nasal.

**'nascere** ['naffere] *vi* (*bambino*) to be born; (*pianta*) to come *o* spring up; (*fiume*) to rise, have its source; (*sole*) to rise; (*dente*) to come through; (*fig: derivare, conseguire*): ~ **da** to arise from, be born out of; **è nata nel 1952** she was born in 1952; '**nascita** *sf* birth.

**nas'condere** *vt* to hide, conceal; ~**rsi** *vr* to hide; **nascon'diglio** *sm* hiding place; **nascon'dino** *sm* (*gioco*) hide-and-seek; **nas'costo, a** *pp di* **nascondere** // *ag* hidden; **di nascosto** secretly.

**na'sello** *sm* (*ZOOL*) hake.

'**naso** *sm* nose.

'**nastro** *sm* ribbon; (*magnetico, isolante, SPORT*) tape; ~ **adesivo** adhesive tape; ~ **trasportatore** conveyor belt.

**nas'turzio** [nas'turtsjo] *sm* nasturtium.

**na'tale** *ag* of one's birth // *sm* (*REL*): N~ Christmas; (*giorno della nascita*) birthday; **natalità** *sf* birth rate; **nata'lizio, a** *ag* (*del Natale*) Christmas *cpd.*

**na'tante** *sm* craft *inv*, boat.

'**natica, che** *sf* (*ANAT*) buttock.

**na'tio, a, 'tii, 'tie** *ag* native.

**Natività** *sf* (*REL*) Nativity.

**na'tivo, a** *ag, sm/f* native.

'**nato, a** *pp di* **nascere** // *ag*: **un attore** ~ a born actor; ~**a Pieri** née Pieri.

**na'tura** *sf* nature; **pagare in** ~ **to**

pay in kind; ~ **morta** still life.

**natu'rale** *ag* natural; **natura'lezza** *sf* naturalness; **natura'lista, i, e** *sm/f* naturalist.

**naturaliz'zare** [naturalid'dzare] *vt* to naturalize.

**natural'mente** *av* naturally; *(certamente, si)* of course.

**naufra'gare** *vi (nave)* to be wrecked; *(persona)* to be shipwrecked; *(fig)* to fall through; **nau'fragio** *sm* shipwreck; *(fig)* ruin, failure; **'naufrago, ghi** *sm* castaway, shipwreck victim.

**'nausea** *sf* nausea; **nausea'bondo, a** *ag* nauseating, sickening; **nause'are** *vt* to nauseate, make (feel) sick.

**'nautico, a, ci, che** *ag* nautical // *sf* (art of) navigation.

**na'vale** *ag* naval.

**na'vata** *sf (anche:* ~ **centrale)** nave; *(anche:* ~ **laterale)** aisle.

**'nave** *sf* ship, vessel; ~ **cisterna** tanker; ~ **da guerra** warship; ~ **passeggeri** passenger ship; ~ **spaziale** spaceship.

**na'vetta** *sf* shuttle; *(servizio di collegamento)* shuttle (service).

**navi'cella** [navi't∫ella] *sf (di aerostato)* gondola.

**navi'gabile** *ag* navigable.

**navi'gare** *vi* to sail; **navigazi'one** *sf* navigation.

**na'viglio** [na'viλλo] *sm* fleet, ships *pl*; *(canale artificiale)* canal; ~ **da pesca** fishing fleet.

**nazio'nale** [nattsjo'nale] *ag* national // *sf (SPORT)* national team; **naziona'lismo** *sm* nationalism; **nazionalità** *sf inv* nationality.

**nazi'one** [nat'tsjone] *sf* nation.

---

│ *PAROLA CHIAVE* │

**ne** ◆ *pronome* **1** *(di lui, lei, loro)* of him/her/them; about him/her/them; ~ **riconosco la voce** I recognize his *(o* her) voice

**2** *(di questa, quella cosa)* of it; about it; ~ **voglio ancora** I want some

more (of it *o* them); **non parliamone più!** let's not talk about it any more!

**3** *(con valore partitivo)*: **hai dei libri?** — sì, ~ **ho** have you any books? — yes, I have (some); **hai del pane?** — no, **non** ~ **ho** have you any bread? — no, I haven't any; **quanti anni hai?** — ~ **ho 17** how old are you? — I'm 17

◆ *av (moto da luogo: da lì)* from there; ~ **vengo ora** I've just come from there.

**né** *cong*: ~ ... ~ neither ... nor; ~ **l'uno** ~ **l'altro lo vuole** neither of them wants it; **non parla** ~ **l'italiano** ~ **il tedesco** he speaks neither Italian nor German, he doesn't speak either Italian or German; **non piove** ~ **nevica** it isn't raining or snowing.

**ne'anche** [ne'anke] *av, cong* not even; **non** ... ~ not even; ~ **se volesse potrebbe venire** he couldn't come even if he wanted to; **non l'ho visto** — ~ **io** I didn't see him — neither did I *o* I didn't either; ~ **per idea** *o* **sogno!** not on your life!

**'nebbia** *sf* fog; *(foschia)* mist; **nebbi'oso, a** *ag* foggy; misty.

**nebu'loso, a** *ag (atmosfera)* hazy; *(fig)* hazy, vague.

**necessaria'mente** [net∫essarja'mente] *av* necessarily.

**neces'sario, a** *ag* necessary.

**necessità** [net∫essi'ta] *sf inv* necessity; *(povertà)* need, poverty; **necessi'tare** *vi* to require // *vi (aver bisogno)*: **necessitare di** to need.

**necro'logio** [nekro'lɔdʒo] *sm* obituary notice; *(registro)* register of deaths.

**ne'fando, a** *ag* infamous, wicked.

**ne'fasto, a** *ag* inauspicious, ill-omened.

**ne'gare** *vt* to deny; *(rifiutare)* to deny, refuse; ~ **di aver fatto/che** to deny having done/that; **nega'tivo, a**

*ag, sf, sm* negative: **negazi'one** *sf* negation.

**ne'gletto, a** [ne'gletto] *ag* (*trascurato*) neglected.

**'negli** ['neʎʎi] *prep* + *det vedi* **in**.

**negli'gente** [negli'dʒɛnte] *ag* negligent, careless; **negli'genza** *sf* negligence, carelessness.

**negozi'ante** [negot'tsjante] *sm/f* trader, dealer; (*bottegaio*) shopkeeper (*Brit*), storekeeper (*Brit*).

**negozi'are** [negot'tsjare] *vt* to negotiate // *vi*: ~ **in** to trade *o* deal in; **negozi'ato** *sm* negotiation.

**ne'gozio** [ne'gɔttsjo] *sm* (*locale*) shop (*Brit*), store (*US*); (*affare*) (piece of) business *q*.

**'negro, a** *ag, sm/f* Negro.

**'nei, nel, nell', 'nella, 'nelle, 'nello** *prep* + *det vedi* **in**.

**'nembo** *sm* (*METEOR*) nimbus.

**ne'mico, a, ci, che** *ag* hostile; (*MIL*) enemy *cpd* // *sm/f* enemy; **essere** ~ **di** to be strongly averse *o* opposed to.

**nem'meno** *av, cong* = **neanche**.

**'nenia** *sf* dirge; (*motivo monotono*) monotonous tune.

**'neo** *sm* mole; (*fig*) (slight) flaw.

**'neo...** *prefisso* neo... .

**'neon** *sm* (*CHIM*) neon.

**neo'nato, a** *ag* newborn // *sm/f* newborn baby.

**neozelan'dese** [neoddzelan'dese] *ag* New Zealand *cpd* // *sm/f* New Zealander.

**nep'pure** *av, cong* = **neanche**.

**'nerbo** *sm* lash; (*fig*) strength, backbone; **nerbo'ruto, a** *ag* muscular; robust.

**ne'retto** *sm* (*TIP*) bold type.

**'nero, a** *ag* black; (*scuro*) dark // *sm* black; **il Mar N~** the Black Sea.

**nerva'tura** *sf* (*ANAT*) nervous system; (*BOT*) veining; (*ARCHIT, TECN*) rib.

**'nervo** *sm* (*ANAT*) nerve; (*BOT*) vein; avere i ~i to be on edge; dare sui ~i a qn to get on sb's nerves; **ner'voso, a** *ag* nervous; (*irritabile*)

irritable // *sm* (*fam*): **far venire il nervoso a qn** to get on sb's nerves.

**'nespola** *sf* (*BOT*) medlar; (*fig*) blow, punch; **'nespolo** *sm* medlar tree.

**'nesso** *sm* connection, link.

**nes'suno, a** *det* (*dav sm* **nessun** + *C, V,* **nessuno** + *s impura, gn, pn, ps, x, z; dav sf* **nessuna** + *C,* **nessun'** + *V*) (*non uno*) no, espressione negativa + any; (*qualche*) any // *pronome* (*non uno*) no one, nobody, espressione negativa + any(one); (: *cosa*) none, espressione negativa + any; (*qualcuno*) anyone, anybody; (*qualcosa*) anything; non c'è nessun libro there isn't any book, there is no book; hai ~a obiezione? do you have any objections?; ~ è venuto, non è venuto ~ nobody came; nessun altro no one else, nobody else; **nessun'altra cosa** nothing else; in nessun luogo nowhere.

**net'tare** *vt* to clean // *sm* ['nɛttare] nectar.

**net'tezza** [net'tettsa] *sf* cleanness, cleanliness; ~ **urbana** cleansing department.

**'netto, a** *ag* (*pulito*) clean; (*chiaro*) clear, clear-cut; (*deciso*) definite; (*ECON*) net.

**nettur'bino** *sm* dustman (*Brit*), garbage collector (*US*).

**neu'rosi** *sf* = **nevrosi**.

**neu'trale** *ag* neutral; **neutralità** *sf* neutrality; **neutraliz'zare** *vt* to neutralize.

**'neutro, a** *ag* neutral; (*LING*) neuter // *sm* (*LING*) neuter.

**ne'vaio** *sm* snowfield.

**'neve** *sf* snow; **nevi'care** *vb impers* to snow; **nevi'cata** *sf* snowfall.

**ne'vischio** [ne'viskjo] *sm* sleet.

**ne'voso, a** *ag* snowy; snow-covered.

**neural'gia** [nevral'dʒia] *sf* neuralgia.

**nevras'tenico, a, ci, che** *ag* (*MED*) neurasthenic; (*fig*) hottempered.

**ne'vrosi** *sf* neurosis.

'**nibbio** *sm* (*ZOOL*) kite.

'**nicchia** ['nikkja] *sf* niche; (*naturale*) cavity, hollow.

**nicchi'are** [nik'kjare] *vi* to shilly-shally, hesitate.

'**nichel** ['nikel] *sm* nickel.

**nico'tina** *sf* nicotine.

'**nido** *sm* nest; **a ~ d'ape** (*tessuto etc*) honeycomb *cpd*.

---
PAROLA CHIAVE
---

**ni'ente** ◆ *pronome* **1** (*nessuna cosa*) nothing; ~ **può fermarlo** nothing can stop him; ~ **di** ~ absolutely nothing; **nient'altro** nothing else; **nient'altro che** nothing but, just, only; ~ **affatto** not at all, not in the least; **come se** ~ **fosse** as if nothing had happened; **cosa da** ~ trivial matters; **per** ~ (*gratis, invano*) for nothing

**2** (*qualcosa*): **hai bisogno di** ~? do you need anything?

**3**: **non ... ** ~ nothing, *espressione negativa* + anything; **non ho visto** ~ I saw nothing, I didn't see anything; **non ho** ~ **da dire** I have nothing o haven't anything to say

◆ *sm* nothing; **un bel** ~ absolutely nothing; **basta un** ~ **per farla piangere** the slightest thing is enough to make her cry

◆ *av* (*in nessuna misura*): **non ... ** ~ not ... at all; **non è (per)** ~ **buono** it isn't good at all.

**nientedi'meno**, **niente'meno** *av* actually, even // *escl* really!, I say!

'**Nilo** *sm*: **il** ~ the Nile.

'**ninfa** *sf* nymph.

**nin'fea** *sf* water lily.

**ninna-'nanna** *sf* lullaby.

'**ninnolo** *sm* (*balocco*) plaything; (*gingillo*) knick-knack.

**ni'pote** *smf* (*di zii*) nephew/niece; (*di nonni*) grandson/daughter, grandchild.

'**nitido**, **a** *ag* clear; (*specchio*) bright.

**ni'trato** *sm* nitrate.

'**nitrico**, **a**, **ci**, **che** *ag* nitric.

**ni'trire** *vi* to neigh.

**ni'trito** *sm* (*di cavallo*) neighing *q*; neigh; (*CHIM*) nitrite.

**nitroglice'rina** [nitroglitʃe'rina] *sf* nitroglycerine.

'**niveo**, **a** *ag* snow-white.

**no** *av* (*risposta*) no; **vieni o** ~? are you coming or not?; **perché** ~? why not?; **lo conosciamo?** — **tu** ~ **ma io sì do we know him?** — you don't but I do; **verrai**, ~? you'll come, won't you?

'**nobile** *ag* noble // *smf* noble, nobleman/woman; **nobili'are** *ag* noble; **nobiltà** *sf* nobility; (*di azione etc*) nobleness.

'**nocca**, **che** *sf* (*ANAT*) knuckle.

**nocci'ola** [not'tʃɔla] *ag* inv (*colore*) hazel, light brown // *sf* hazelnut.

**nocci'olo** [not'tʃɔlo] *sm* (*di frutto*) stone; (*fig*) heart, core; [not'tʃɔlo] (*albero*) hazel.

'**noce** ['notʃe] *sm* (*albero*) walnut tree // *sf* (*frutto*) walnut; ~ **moscata** nutmeg.

**no'civo**, **a** [no'tʃivo] *ag* harmful, noxious.

'**nodo** *sm* (*di cravatta, legname, NAUT*) knot; (*AUT, FERR*) junction; (*MED, ASTR, BOT*) node; (*fig: legame*) bond, tie; (: *punto centrale*) heart, crux; **avere un** ~ **alla gola** to have a lump in one's throat; **no'doso**, **a** *ag* (*tronco*) gnarled.

'**noi** *pronome* (*soggetto*) we; (*oggetto: per dare rilievo, con preposizione*) us; ~ **stessi(e)** we ourselves; (*oggetto*) ourselves.

'**noia** *sf* boredom; (*disturbo, impaccio*) bother *q*, trouble *q*; **avere qn/qc a** ~ not to like sb/sth; **mi è venuto a** ~ I'm tired of it; **dare** ~ **a** to annoy; **avere delle** ~**e con qn** to have trouble with sb.

**noi'altri** *pronome* we.

**noi'oso**, **a** *ag* boring; (*fastidioso*) annoying, troublesome.

**noleggi'are** [noled'dʒare] *vt* (*prendere a noleggio*) to hire (*Brit*), rent;

(*dare a noleggio*) to hire out (*Brit*), rent (out); (*aereo, nave*) to charter; **no'leggio** *sm* hire (*Brit*), rental; charter.

**'nolo** *sm* hire (*Brit*), rental; charter; (*per trasporto merci*) freight; **prendere/dare a ~ qc** to hire/hire out sth.

**'nomade** *ag* nomadic // *sm/f* nomad.

**'nome** *sm* name; (*LING*) noun; **in/a ~ di** in the name of; **di o per ~** (*chiamato*) called, named; **conoscere qn di ~** to know sb by name; **~ d'arte** stage name; **~ di battesimo** Christian name; **~ depositato** trade name; **~ di famiglia** surname.

**no'mea** *sf* notoriety.

**no'mignolo** [no'miɲɲolo] *sm* nickname.

**'nomina** *sf* appointment.

**nomi'nale** *ag* nominal; (*LING*) noun *cpd*.

**nomi'nare** *vt* to name; (*eleggere*) to appoint; (*citare*) to mention.

**nomina'tivo, a** *ag* (*LING*) nominative; (*ECON*) registered // *sm* (*LING*: *anche*: **caso ~**) nominative (case); (*AMM*) name.

**non** *av* not // *prefisso* non-; *vedi* **affatto, appena** *etc*.

**nonché** [non'ke] *cong* (*tanto più, tanto meno*) let alone; (*e inoltre*) as well as.

**noncu'rante** *ag*: **~ (di)** careless (of), indifferent (to); **noncu'ranza** *sf* carelessness, indifference.

**nondi'meno** *cong* (*tuttavia*) however; (*nonostante*) nevertheless.

**'nonno, a** *sm/f* grandfather/mother; (*in senso più familiare*) grandma/grandpa; **~i** *smpl* grandparents.

**non'nulla** *sm inv*: **un ~** nothing, a trifle.

**'nono, a** *ag, sm* ninth.

**nonos'tante** *prep* in spite of, notwithstanding // *cong* although, even though.

**nontiscordardimé** *sm inv* (*BOT*) forget-me-not.

**nord** *sm* North // *ag inv* north; northern; **il Mare del N~** the North Sea; **nor'dest** *sm* north-east; **'nordico, a, ci, che** *ag* nordic, northern European; **nor'dovest** *sm* north-west.

**'norma** *sf* (*principio*) norm; (*regola*) regulation, rule; (*consuetudine*) custom, rule; **a ~ di legge** according to law, as laid down by law.

**nor'male** *ag* normal; standard *cpd*; **normalità** *sf* normality; **normaliz'zare** *vt* to normalize, bring back to normal.

**normal'mente** *av* normally.

**norve'gese** [norve'dʒese] *ag, sm/f, sm* Norwegian.

**Nor'vegia** [nor'vedʒa] *sf*: **la ~** Norway.

**nostal'gia** [nostal'dʒia] *sf* (*di casa, paese*) homesickness; (*del passato*) nostalgia; **nos'talgico, a, ci, che** *ag* homesick; nostalgic.

**nos'trano, a** *ag* local; national; home-produced.

**'nostro, a** *det*: **il(la) ~(a)** *etc* our // *pronome*: **il(la) ~(a)** *etc* ours // *sm*: **il ~** our money; our belongings; **i ~i** our family; our own people; **è dei ~i** he's one of us.

**'nota** *sf* (*segno*) mark; (*comunicazione scritta, MUS*) note; (*fattura*) bill; (*elenco*) list; **degno di ~** noteworthy, worthy of note.

**no'tabile** *ag* notable; (*persona*) important // *sm* prominent citizen.

**no'taio** *sm* notary.

**no'tare** *vt* (*segnare: errori*) to mark; (*registrare*) to note (down), write down; (*rilevare, osservare*) to note, notice; **farsi ~** to get o.s. noticed.

**notazi'one** [notat'tsjone] *sf* (*MUS*) notation.

**no'tevole** *ag* (*talento*) notable, remarkable; (*peso*) considerable.

**no'tifica, che** *sf* notification.

**notifi'care** *vt* (*DIR*): **~ qc a qn** to notify sb of sth, give sb notice of sth.

**no'tizia** [no'tittsja] *sf* (*piece of*) news

*sg;* (*informazione*) piece of information; ~e *sfpl* news *sg;* information *sg;* **notizi'ario** *sm* (*RADIO, TV, STAMPA*) news *sg.*

**'noto, a** *ag* (well-)known.

**notorietà** *sf* fame; notoriety.

**no'torio, a** *ag* well-known; (*peg*) notorious.

**not'tambulo, a** *sm/f* night-bird (*fig*).

**not'tata** *sf* night.

**'notte** *sf* night; **di** ~ at night; (*durante la notte*) in the night, during the night; **peggio che andar di** ~ worse than ever; ~ **bianca** sleepless night; **notte'tempo** *av* at night; during the night.

**not'turno, a** *ag* nocturnal; (*servizio, guardiano*) night *cpd.*

**no'vanta** *num* ninety; **novan'tesimo, a** *ag* ninetieth; **novan'tina** *sf:* una novantina (di) about ninety.

**'nove** *num* nine.

**nove'cento** [nove'tʃɛnto] *num* nine hundred // *sm:* il N~ the twentieth century.

**no'vella** *sf* (*LETTERATURA*) short story.

**novel'lino, a** *ag* (*pivello*) green, inexperienced.

**no'vello, a** *ag* (*piante, patate*) new; (*insalata, verdura*) early; (*sposo*) newly-married.

**no'vembre** *sm* November.

**novi'lunio** *sm* (*ASTR*) new moon.

**novità** *sf inv* novelty; (*innovazione*) innovation; (*cosa originale, insolita*) something new; (*notizia*) (piece) of news *sg;* le ~ **della moda** the latest fashions.

**novizi'ato** [novit'tsjato] *sm* (*REL*) novitiate; (*tirocinio*) apprenticeship.

**no'vizio, a** [no'vittsjo] *sm/f* (*REL*) novice; (*tirocinante*) beginner, apprentice.

**nozi'one** [not'tsjone] *sf* notion, idea; ~i *sfpl* basic knowledge *sg*, rudiments.

**'nozze** ['nɔttse] *sfpl* wedding *sg*,

marriage *sg;* ~ **d'argento/d'oro** silver/golden wedding *sg.*

**ns.** *abbr* (*COMM*) = nostro.

**'nube** *sf* cloud; **nubi'fragio** *sm* cloudburst.

**'nubile** *ag* (*donna*) unmarried, single.

**'nuca** *sf* nape of the neck.

**nucle'are** *ag* nuclear.

**'nucleo** *sm* nucleus; (*gruppo*) team, unit, group; (*MIL, POLIZIA*) squad; **il ~ familiare** the family unit.

**nu'dista** *a, e* *sm/f* nudist.

**'nudo, a** (*persona*) bare, naked, nude; (*membra*) bare, naked; (*montagna*) bare // *sm* (*ARTE*) nude.

**'nugolo** *sm:* **un** ~ **di** a whole host of.

**'nulla** *pronome, av* = niente // *sm:* **il** ~ nothing.

**nulla'osta** *sm inv* authorization.

**nullità** *sf inv* nullity; (*persona*) nonentity.

**'nullo, a** *ag* useless, worthless; (*DIR*) null (and void); (*SPORT*): **incontro** ~ draw.

**nume'rale** *ag, sm* numeral.

**nume'rare** *vt* to number; **numerazi'one** *sf* numbering; (*araba, decimale*) notation.

**nu'merico, a, ci, che** *ag* numerical.

**'numero** *sm* number; (*romano, arabo*) numeral; (*di spettacolo*) act, turn; ~ **civico** house number; **nume'roso, a** *ag* numerous, many; (*con sostantivo sg: adunanza etc*) large.

**'nunzio** ['nuntsjo] *sm* (*REL*) nuncio.

**nu'ocere** ['nwɔtʃere] *vi:* ~ **a** to harm, damage; **nuoci'uto, a** *pp di* nuocere.

**nu'ora** *sf* daughter-in-law.

**nuo'tare** *vi* to swim; (*galleggiare: oggetti*) to float; **nuota'tore, 'trice** *sm/f* swimmer; **nu'oto** *sm* swimming.

**nu'ova** *sf vedi* nuovo.

**nuova'mente** *av* again.

**Nu'ova Ze'landa** [-dze'landa] *sf:* la

~ New Zealand.

**nu'ovo, a** *ag* new // *sf* (*notizia*) (piece of) news *sg*; **di** ~ again; ~ **fiammante** *o* **di zecca** brand-new.

**nutri'ente** *ag* nutritious, nourishing.

**nutri'mento** *sm* food, nourishment.

**nu'trire** *vt* to feed; (*fig: sentimenti*) to harbour, nurse; **nutri'tivo, a** *ag* nutritional; (*alimento*) nutritious; **nutrizi'one** *sf* nutrition.

**'nuvola** *sf* cloud; **'nuvolo, a** *ag*, **nuvo'loso, a** *ag* cloudy.

**nuzi'ale** [nut'tsjale] *ag* nuptial; wedding *cpd*.

# O

**o** *cong* (*dav V spesso* **od**) or; ~ ... ~ either ... or; ~ **l'uno** ~ **l'altro** either (of them).

**O.** *abbr* (= *ovest*) W.

**'oasi** *sf inv* oasis.

**obbedi'ente** *etc vedi* **ubbidiente** *etc.*

**obbli'gare** *vt* (*costringere*): ~ **qn a fare** to force *o* oblige sb to do; (*DIR*) to bind; **~rsi** *vr*: **~rsi a fare** to undertake to do; **obbli'gato, a** *ag* (*costretto, grato*) obliged; (*percorso, tappa*) set, fixed; **obbliga'torio, a** *ag* compulsory, obligatory; **obbligazi'one** *sf* obligation; (*COMM*) bond, debenture; **'obbligo, ghi** *sm* obligation; (*dovere*) duty; **avere l'obbligo di fare, essere nell'obbligo di fare** to be obliged to do; **essere d'obbligo** (*discorso, applauso*) to be called for.

**ob'brobrio** *sm* disgrace; (*fig*) mess, eyesore.

**o'beso, a** *ag* obese.

**obiet'tare** *vt*: ~ **che** to object that; ~ **su qc** to object to sth, raise objections concerning sth.

**obiet'tivo, a** *ag* objective // *sm* (*OTTICA, FOT*) lens *sg*, objective; (*MIL, fig*) objective.

**obiet'tore** *sm* objector; ~ **di coscienza** conscientious objector.

**obiezi'one** [objet'tsjone] *sf* objection.

**obi'torio** *sm* morgue, mortuary.

**o'bliquo, a** *ag* oblique; (*inclinato*) slanting; (*fig*) devious, underhand; **sguardo** ~ sidelong glance.

**oblò** *sm inv* porthole.

**o'blungo, a, ghi, ghe** *ag* oblong.

**'oboe** *sm* (*MUS*) oboe.

**obsole'scenza** [obsolef'fentsa] *sf* (*ECON*) obsolescence.

**'oca, pl 'oche** *sf* goose.

**occasi'one** *sf* (*caso favorevole*) opportunity; (*causa, motivo, circostanza*) occasion; (*COMM*) bargain; **d'**~ (*a buon prezzo*) bargain *cpd*; (*usato*) secondhand.

**occhi'aia** [ok'kjaja] *sf* eye socket; **~e** *sfpl* shadows (under the eyes).

**occhi'ali** [ok'kjali] *smpl* glasses, spectacles; ~ **da sole** sunglasses.

**occhi'ata** [ok'kjata] *sf* look, glance; **dare un'**~ **a** to have a look at.

**occhieggi'are** [okkjed'dʒare] *vi* (*apparire qua e là*) to peep (out).

**occhi'ello** [ok'kjɛllo] *sm* buttonhole; (*asola*) eyelet.

**'occhio** ['ɔkkjo] *sm* eye; ~! careful!, watch out!; **a** ~ **nudo** with the naked eye; **a quattr'~i** privately, tête-à-tête; **dare all'**~ *o* **nell'**~ **a qn** to catch sb's eye; **fare l'**~ **a qc** to get used to sth; **tenere d'**~ **qn** to keep an eye on sb; **vedere di buon/mal** ~ **qc** to look favourably/unfavourably on sth.

**occhio'lino** [okkjo'lino] *sm*: **fare l'**~ **a qn** to wink at sb.

**occiden'tale** [ottfiden'tale] *ag* western *// smf* Westerner.

**occi'dente** [ottfi'dɛnte] *sm* west; (*POL*) **l'O**~ the West; **a** ~ **in** the west.

**oc'cipite** [ot'tfipite] *sm* back of the head, occiput.

**oc'cludere** *vt* to block; **occlusi'one** *sf* blockage, obstruction; **oc'cluso, a** *pp di* **occludere**.

**occor'rente** *ag* necessary // *sm* all that is necessary.

**occor'renza** [okkor'rɛntsa] *sf*

necessity, need; **all'**~ in case of need.

**oc'correre** *vi* to be needed, be required // *vb impers:* **occorre farlo** it must be done; **occorre che tu parta** you must leave, you'll have to leave; **mi occorrono i soldi** I need the money; **oc'corso, a** *pp* di **occorrere**.

**occul'tare** *vt* to hide, conceal.

**oc'culto, a** *ag* hidden, concealed; (*scienze, forze*) occult.

**occu'pare** *vt* to occupy; (*manodopera*) to employ; (*ingombrare*) to occupy, take up; ~**rsi** *vr* to occupy o.s., keep o.s. busy; (*impiegarsi*) to get a job; ~**rsi di** (*interessarsi*) to take an interest in; (*prendersi cura di*) to look after, take care of; **occu'pato, a** *ag* (*MIL, POL*) occupied; (*persona: affaccendato*) busy; (*posto, sedia*) taken; (*toilette, TEL*) engaged; **occupazi'one** *sf* occupation; (*impiego, lavoro*) job; (*ECON*) employment.

**o'ceano** [o'tʃeano] *sm* ocean.

**'ocra** *sf* ochre.

**ocu'lare** *ag* ocular, eye *cpd*; **te-stimone** ~ eye witness.

**ocu'lato, a** *ag* (*attento*) cautious, prudent; (*accorto*) shrewd.

**ocu'lista, i, e** *sm/f* eye specialist, oculist.

**'ode** *sf* ode.

**odi'are** *vt* to hate, detest.

**odi'erno, a** *ag* today's, of today; (*attuale*) present.

**'odio** *sm* hatred; **avere in** ~ **qc/qn** to hate o detest sth/sb; **odi'oso, a** *ag* hateful, odious.

**odo'rare** *vt* (*annusare*) to smell; (*profumare*) to perfume, scent // *vi:* ~ (**di**) to smell (of); **odo'rato** *sm* sense of smell.

**o'dore** *sm* smell; **gli** ~**i** *smpl* (*CUC*) (aromatic) herbs; **odo'roso, a** *ag* sweet-smelling.

**of'fendere** *vt* to offend; (*violare*) to break, violate; (*insultare*) to insult;

(*ferire*) to hurt; ~**rsi** *vr* (*con senso reciproco*) to insult one another; (*risentirsi*): ~**rsi** (**di**) to take offence (at), be offended (by); **offen'sivo, a** *ag, sf* offensive.

**offe'rente** (*sm in aste*): **al maggior** ~ to the highest bidder.

**of'ferto, a** *pp* di **offrire** // *sf* offer; (*donazione, anche REL*) offering; (*in gara d'appalto*) tender; (*in aste*) bid; (*ECON*) supply; **''~e d'impiego''** ''situations vacant''; **fare un'**~**a** to make an offer; to tender; to bid.

**of'feso, a** *pp* di **offendere** // *ag* offended; (*fisicamente*) hurt, injured // *smf* offended party // *sf* insult, affront; (*MIL*) attack; (*DIR*) offence; **essere** ~ **con qn** to be annoyed with sb; **parte** ~**a** (*DIR*) plaintiff.

**offi'cina** [offi'tʃina] *sf* workshop.

**of'frire** *vt* to offer; ~**rsi** *vr* (*proporsi*) to offer (o.s.), volunteer; (*occasione*) to present itself; (*esporsi*): ~**rsi a** to expose o.s. to; **ti offro da bere** I'll buy you a drink.

**offus'care** *vt* to obscure, darken; (*fig: intelletto*) to dim, cloud; (: *fama*) to obscure, overshadow; ~**rsi** *vr* to grow dark; to cloud, grow dim; to be obscured.

**of'talmico, a, ci, che** *ag* ophthalmic.

**oggettività** [oddʒettivi'ta] *sf* objectivity.

**ogget'tivo, a** [oddʒet'tivo] *ag* objective.

**og'getto** [od'dʒɛtto] *sm* object; (*materia, argomento*) subject (matter); ~**i smarriti** lost property *sg*.

**'oggi** ['ɔddʒi] *av, sm* today; ~ **a otto** a week today; **oggigi'orno** *av* nowadays.

**o'giva** [o'dʒiva] *sf* ogive, pointed arch.

**'ogni** ['oɲɲi] *det* every, each; (*tutti*) all; (*con valore distributivo*) every; ~ **uomo è mortale** all men are mortal; **viene** ~ **due giorni** he comes every two days; ~ **cosa**

everything; **ad ~ costo** at all costs, at any price; **in ~ luogo** everywhere; **~ tanto** every so often; **~ volta che** every time that.

**Ognis'santi** [oɲɲis'santi] *sm* All Saints' Day.

**o'gnuno** [oɲ'ɲuno] *pronome* everyone, everybody.

**'ohi** *escl* oh!; *(esprimere dolore)* ow!

**ohimè** *escl* oh dear!

**O'landa** *sf:* **l'~** Holland; **olan'dese** *ag* Dutch // *sm (LING)* Dutch // *sm/f* Dutchman/woman; **gli Olandesi** the Dutch.

**oleo'dotto** *sm* oil pipeline.

**ole'oso, a** *ag* oily; *(che contiene olio)* oil-yielding.

**ol'fatto** *sm* sense of smell.

**oli'are** *vt* to oil.

**oli'era** *sf* oil cruet.

**olim'piadi** *sfpl* Olympic games; **o'limpico, a, ci, che** *ag* Olympic.

**'olio** *sm* oil; **sott'~** *(CUC)* in oil; **~ di fegato di merluzzo** cod liver oil; **~ d'oliva** olive oil; **~ di semi** vegetable oil.

**o'liva** *sf* olive; **oli'vastro, a** *ag* olive(-coloured); *(carnagione)* sallow; **oli'veto** *sm* olive grove; **o'livo** *sm* olive tree.

**'olmo** *sm* elm.

**oltraggi'are** [oltradʤare] *vt* to outrage; to offend gravely.

**ol'traggio** [ol'tradʤo] *sm* outrage; offence, insult; **~ a pubblico ufficiale** *(DIR)* insulting a public official; **~ al pudore** *(DIR)* indecent behaviour; **oltraggi'oso, a** *ag* offensive.

**ol'tralpe** *av* beyond the Alps.

**ol'tranza** [ol'trantsa] *sf:* **a ~** to the last, to the bitter end.

**'oltre** *av (più in là)* further; *(di più: aspettare)* longer, more // *prep (di là da)* beyond, over, on the other side of; *(più di)* more than, over; *(in aggiunta a)* besides; *(eccetto):* **~ a** except, apart from; **oltre'mare** *av* overseas; **oltrepas'sare** *vt* to go

beyond, exceed.

**o'maggio** [o'madʤo] *sm (dono)* gift; *(segno di rispetto)* homage, tribute; **~i** *smpl* compliments; respects; **rendere ~ a** to pay homage *o* tribute to; **in ~** *(copia, biglietto)* complimentary.

**ombeli'cale** *ag* umbilical.

**ombe'lico, chi** *sm* navel.

**'ombra** *sf (zona non assolata, fantasma)* shade; *(sagoma scura)* shadow; **sedere all'~** to sit in the shade; **restare nell'~** *(fig)* to remain in obscurity.

**ombreggi'are** [ombred'ʤare] *vt* to shade.

**om'brello** *sm* umbrella; **ombrel'lone** *sm* beach umbrella.

**om'bretto** *sm* eyeshadow.

**om'broso, a** *ag* shady, shaded; *(cavallo)* nervous, skittish; *(persona)* touchy, easily offended.

**ome'lia** *sf (REL)* homily, sermon.

**omeopa'tia** *sf* homoeopathy.

**omertà** *sf* conspiracy of silence.

**o'messo, a** *pp di* **omettere**.

**o'mettere** *vt* to omit, leave out; **~ di fare** *o* **fare** to omit *o* fail to do.

**omi'cida, i, e** [omi'tʃida] *ag* homicidal, murderous // *smf* murderer/eress.

**omi'cidio** [omi'tʃidjo] *sm* murder; **~ colposo** culpable homicide.

**omissi'one** *sf* omission; **~ di soccorso** *(DIR)* failure to stop and give assistance.

**omogeneiz'zato** [omodʒeneid'dzato] *sm* baby food.

**omo'geneo, a** [omo'dʒɛneo] *ag* homogeneous.

**omolo'gare** *vt* to approve, recognize; to ratify.

**o'monimo, a** *sm/f* namesake // *sm (LING)* homonym.

**omosessu'ale** *ag, sm/f* homosexual.

**'oncia, ce** ['ontʃa] *sf* ounce.

**'onda** *sf* wave; **mettere** *o* **mandare in ~** *(RADIO, TV)* to broadcast; **andare in ~** *(RADIO, TV)* to go on the air; **~e corte/medie/lunghe**

short/medium/long wave; **on'data** sf wave, billow; (fig) wave, surge; a **ondate** in waves; **ondata di caldo** heatwave.

**'onde** cong (affinché: con il congiuntivo) so that, in order that; (: con l'infinito) so as to, in order to.

**ondeggi'are** [onded'dʒare] vi (acqua) to ripple; (muoversi sulle onde: barca) to rock, roll; (fig: muoversi come le onde, barcollare) to sway; (: essere incerto) to waver.

**ondula'torio, a** ag undulating; (FISICA) undulatory, wave cpd.

**ondulazi'one** [ondulat'tsjone] sf undulation; (acconciatura) wave.

**'onere** sm burden; **~i fiscali** taxes; **one'roso, a** ag (fig) heavy, onerous.

**onestà** sf honesty.

**o'nesto, a** ag (probo, retto) honest; (giusto) fair; (casto) chaste, virtuous.

**'onice** ['onitʃe] sf onyx.

**onnipo'tente** ag omnipotent.

**onnisci'ente** [onniʃ'ʃente] ag omniscient.

**onniveg'gente** [onnived'dʒente] ag all-seeing.

**ono'mastico, ci** sm name-day.

**ono'ranze** [ono'rantse] sfpl honours.

**ono'rare** vt to honour; (far onore a) to do credit to; **~rsi** vr: **~rsi di** to feel honoured at, be proud of.

**ono'rario, a** ag honorary // sm fee.

**o'nore** sm honour; **in ~ di** in honour of; **fare gli ~i di casa** to play host (o hostess); **fare ~ a** to honour; (pranzo) to do justice to; (famiglia) to be a credit to; **farsi ~** to distinguish o.s.; **ono'revole** ag honourable // sm/f (POL) ≈ Member of Parliament (Brit), ≈ Congressman/woman (US); **onorifi'cenza** sf honour; decoration; **ono'rifico, a, ci, che** ag honorary.

**'onta** sf shame, disgrace.

**'O.N.U.** ['ɔnu] sigla f = Organizzazione delle Nazioni Unite) UN, UNO.

**o'paco, a, chi; che** ag (vetro) opaque; (metallo) dull, matt.

**o'pale** sm o f opal.

**'opera** sf work; (azione rilevante) action, deed, work; (MUS) work; opus; (: melodramma) opera; (: teatro) opera house; (ente) institution, organization; **~ d'arte** work of art; **~ lirica** (grand) opera; **~e pubbliche** public works.

**ope'raio, a** ag working-class; workers' // sm/f worker; **classe ~a** a working class.

**ope'rare** vt to carry out, make; (MED) to operate on // vi to operate, work; (rimedio) to act, work; (MED) to operate; **~rsi** vr to occur, take place; (MED) to have an operation; **~rsi d'appendicite** to have one's appendix out; **opera'tivo, a** ag operative, operating; **opera'tore, 'trice** sm/f operator; (TV, CINEMA) cameraman; **operatore economico** agent, broker; **operatore turistico** tour operator; **opera'torio, a** ag (MED) operating; **operazi'one** sf operation.

**ope'retta** sf (MUS) operetta, light opera.

**ope'roso, a** ag busy, active, hard-working.

**opi'ficio** [opi'fitʃo] sm factory, works pl.

**opini'one** sf opinion.

**'oppio** sm opium.

**oppo'nente** ag opposing // sm/f opponent.

**op'porre** vt to oppose; **opporsi** vr: **opporsi (a qc)** to oppose (sth); (: object (to sth)); **~ resistenza/un rifiuto** to offer resistance/refuse.

**opportu'nista, i, e** sm/f opportunist.

**opportunità** sf inv opportunity; (convenienza) opportuneness, timeliness.

**oppor'tuno, a** ag timely, opportune.

**opposi'tore, 'trice** sm/f opposer, opponent.

**opposizi'one** [oppozit'tsjone] *sf* opposition; (*DIR*) objection.

**op'posto, a** *pp di* **opporre** // *ag* opposite; (*opinioni*) conflicting // *sm* opposite, contrary; **all'~** on the contrary.

**oppressi'one** *sf* oppression.

**oppres'sivo, a** *ag* oppressive.

**op'presso, a** *pp di* **opprimere**.

**oppres'sore** *sm* oppressor.

**op'primere** *vt* (*premere, gravare*) to weigh down; (*estenuare: sog: caldo*) to suffocate, oppress; (*tiranneggiare: popolo*) to oppress.

**oppu'gnare** [oppu\ɲ'nare] *vt* (*fig*) to refute.

**op'pure** *cong or* else.

**op'tare** *vi*: ~ **per** to opt for.

**o'puscolo** *sm* booklet, pamphlet.

**opzi'one** [opt'sjone] *sf* option.

**'ora** *sf* (*60 minuti*) hour; (*momento*) time; **che** ~ **è?, che** ~**e sono?** what time is it?; **non** è well'~ **di fare** to long to do, look forward to doing; **di buon'**~ early; **alla buon'**~! at last!; ~ **legale** *o* **estiva** summer time (*Brit*), daylight saving time (*US*); ~ **locale** local time; ~ **di punta** (*AUT*) rush hour // *av* (*adesso*) now; (*poco fa*): **è uscito proprio** ~ he's just gone out; (*tra poco*) presently, in a minute; (*correlativo*): ~ ... ~ now ... now; **d'**~ **in avanti** *o* **poi** from now on; *or* ~ just now, a moment ago; **5 anni** *or* **sono** 5 years ago; ~ **come** ~ right now, at present.

**o'racolo** *sm* oracle.

**'orafo** *sm* goldsmith.

**o'rale** *ag, sm* oral.

**ora'mai** *av* = **ormai**.

**o'rario, a** *ag* hourly; (*fuso, segnale*) time *cpd*; (*velocità*) per hour // *sm* timetable, schedule; (*di ufficio, visite etc*) hours *pl*, time(s *pl*).

**ora'tore, 'trice** *smf* speaker; orator.

**ora'torio, a** *ag* oratorical // *sm* (*REL*) oratory; (*MUS*) oratorio // *sf* (*arte*) oratory.

**ora'zione** [orat'tsjone] *sf* (*REL*) prayer; (*discorso*) speech, oration.

**or'bene** *cong* so, well (then).

**'orbita** *sf* (*ASTR, FISICA*) orbit; (*ANAT*) (eye-)socket.

**or'chestra** [or'kɛstra] *sf* orchestra; **orches'trale** *ag* orchestral // *smf* orchestra player; **orches'trare** *vt* to orchestrate; (*fig*) to mount, stage-manage.

**orchi'dea** [orki'dɛa] *sf* orchid.

**'orco, chi** *sm* ogre.

**'orda** *sf* horde.

**or'digno** [or'diɲno] *sm* (*esplosivo*) explosive device.

**ordi'nale** *ag, sm* ordinal.

**ordina'mento** *sm* order, arrangement; (*regolamento*) regulations *pl*, rules *pl*; ~ **scolastico/giuridico** education/legal system.

**ordi'nanza** [ordi'nantsa] *sf* (*DIR, MIL*) order; (*persona: MIL*) orderly, batman; **d'**~ (*MIL*) regulation *cpd*.

**ordi'nare** *vt* (*mettere in ordine*) to arrange, organize; (*COMM*) to order; (*prescrivere: medicina*) to prescribe; (*comandare*): ~ **a qn di fare qc** to order *o* command sb to do sth; (*REL*) to ordain.

**ordi'nario, a** *ag* (*comune*) ordinary; everyday; standard; (*grossolano*) coarse, common // *sm* ordinary; (*INS: di università*) full professor.

**ordi'nato, a** *ag* tidy, orderly.

**ordinazi'one** [ordinat'tsjone] *sf* (*COMM*) order; (*REL*) ordination; **eseguire qc su** ~ to make sth to order.

**'ordine** *sm* order; (*carattere*): **d'**~ **pratico** of a practical nature; **all'**~ (*COMM: assegno*) to order; **di prim'**~ first-class; **fino a nuovo** ~ until further notice; **essere in** ~ (*documenti*) to be in order; (*stanza, persona*) to be tidy; **mettere in** ~ to put in order, tidy (up); ~ **del giorno** (*di seduta*) agenda; (*MIL*) order of the day; ~ **di pagamento** (*COMM*) order for payment; **l'**~ **pubblico** law and order; ~i (sacri) (REL) holy orders.

or'dire vt (fig) to plot, scheme; or'dito sm (di tessuto) warp.

orec'chino [orek'kino] sm earring.

o'recchio [o'rɛkkjo], pl(f) o'recchie sm (ANAT) ear.

orecchi'oni [orek'kjoni] smpl (MED) mumps sg.

o'refice [o'rɛfitʃe] sm goldsmith; jeweller; orefice'ria sf (arte) goldsmith's art; (negozio) jeweller's (shop).

'orfano, a ag orphan(ed) // smlf orphan; ~ di padre/madre fatherless/motherless; orfano'trofio sm orphanage.

orga'netto sm barrel organ; (fam: armonica a bocca) mouth organ; (: fisarmonica) accordion.

or'ganico, a ci, che ag organic // sm personnel, staff.

organi'gramma, i sm organization chart.

orga'nismo sm (BIOL) organism; (corpo umano) body; (AMM) body, organism.

organiz'zare [organid'dzare] vt to organize; ~rsi vr to get organized; organizza'tore, 'trice ag organizing // smlf organizer; organizza-zi'one sf organization.

'organo sm organ; (di congegno) part; (portavoce) spokesman, mouthpiece.

or'gasmo sm (FISIOL) orgasm; (fig) agitation, anxiety.

'orgia, ge ['ordʒa] sf orgy.

or'goglio [or'gɔʎʎo] sm pride; orgogli'oso, a ag proud.

orien'tale ag oriental; eastern; east.

orienta'mento sm positioning; orientation; direction; senso di ~ sense of direction; perdere l'~ to lose one's bearings; ~ professionale careers guidance.

orien'tare vt (situare) to position; (fig) to direct, orientate; ~rsi vr to find one's bearings; (fig: tendere) to tend, lean; (: indirizzarsi): ~rsi

verso to take up, go in for.

ori'ente sm east; l'O~ the East, the Orient; a ~ in the east.

o'rigano sm oregano.

origi'nale [oridʒi'nale] ag original; (bizzarro) eccentric // sm original; originalità sf originality; eccentricity.

origi'nare [oridʒi'nare] vt to bring about, produce // vi: ~ da to arise o spring from.

origi'nario, a [oridʒi'narjo] ag original; essere ~ di to be a native of; (provenire da) to originate from; to be native to.

o'rigine [o'ridʒine] sf origin; all'~ originally; d'~ inglese of English origin; dare ~ a to give rise to.

origli'are [oriʎ'ʎare] vi: ~ (a) to eavesdrop (on).

o'rina sf urine; ori'nale sm chamberpot.

ori'nare vi to urinate // vt to pass; orina'toio sm (public) urinal.

ori'undo, a ag: essere ~ di Milano etc to be of Milanese etc extraction o origin // smlf person of foreign extraction o origin.

orizzon'tale [oriddzon'tale] ag horizontal.

oriz'zonte [orid'dzonte] sm horizon.

or'lare vt to hem.

'orlo sm edge, border; (di recipiente) rim, brim; (di vestito etc) hem.

'orma sf (di persona) footprint; (di animale) track; (impronta, traccia) mark, trace.

or'mai av by now, by this time; (adesso) now; (quasi) almost, nearly.

ormeggi'are [ormed'dʒare] vt (NAUT) to moor; or'meggio sm (atto) mooring q; (luogo) moorings pl.

or'mone sm hormone.

ornamen'tale ag ornamental, decorative.

orna'mento sm ornament, decoration.

or'nare vt to adorn, decorate; ~rsi vr: ~rsi (di) to deck o.s. (out) (with); **or'nato, a** *ag* ornate.

**ornitolo'gia** [ornitolo'dʒia] *sf* ornithology.

**'oro** *sm* gold; **d'~, in ~** gold *cpd*; **d'~** (*colore, occasione*) golden; (*persona*) marvellous.

**orologe'ria** [orolodʒe'ria] *sf* watchmaking *q*; watchmaker's (shop); clockmaker's (shop); **bomba a ~** time bomb.

**orologi'aio** [orolo'dʒajo] *sm* watchmaker; clockmaker.

**oro'logio** [oro'lɔdʒo] *sm* clock; (*da tasca, da polso*) watch; **~ da polso** wristwatch; **~ al quarzo** quartz watch; **~ a sveglia** alarm clock.

**o'roscopo** *sm* horoscope.

**or'rendo, a** *ag* (*spaventoso*) horrible, awful; (*bruttissimo*) hideous.

**or'ribile** *ag* horrible.

**'orrido, a** *ag* fearful, horrid.

**orripi'lante** *ag* hair-raising, horrifying.

**or'rore** *sm* horror; **avere in ~** *qn/ qc* to loathe *o* detest sb/sth; **mi fanno ~** I loathe *o* detest them.

**orsacchi'otto** [orsak'kjɔtto] *sm* teddy bear.

**'orso** *sm* bear; **~ bruno/bianco** brown/polar bear.

**or'taggio** [or'taddʒo] *sm* vegetable.

**or'tica, che** *sf* (*stinging*) nettle.

**orti'caria** *sf* nettle rash.

**orticol'tura** *sf* horticulture.

**'orto** *sm* vegetable garden, kitchen garden; (*AGR*) market garden (*Brit*), truck farm (*US*).

**ortogra'fia** *sf* spelling.

**orto'lano, a** *sm/f* (*venditore*) greengrocer (*Brit*), produce dealer (*US*).

**ortope'dia** *sf* orthopaedics *sg*; **orto'pedico, a, ci, che** *ag* orthopaedic // *sm* orthopaedic specialist.

**orzai'olo** [ordza'jɔlo] *sm* (*MED*) stye.

**or'zata** [or'dzata] *sf* barley water.

**'orzo** ['ordzo] *sm* barley.

**o'sare** *vt, vi* to dare; **~ fare** to dare (to) do.

**osce'nità** [oʃʃeni'ta] *sf inv* obscenity.

**o'sceno, a** [oʃ'ʃeno] *ag* obscene; (*ripugnante*) ghastly.

**oscil'lare** [oʃʃil'lare] *vi* (*pendolo*) to swing; (*dondolare: al vento etc*) to rock; (*variare*) to fluctuate; (*TECN*) to oscillate; (*fig*): **~ fra** to waver *o* hesitate between; **oscillazi'one** *sf* oscillation; (*di prezzi, temperatura*) fluctuation.

**oscura'mento** *sm* darkening; obscuring; (*in tempo di guerra*) blackout.

**oscu'rare** *vt* to darken, obscure; (*fig*) to obscure; **~rsi** *vr* (*cielo*) to darken, cloud over; (*persona*): **si oscurò in volto** his face clouded over.

**os'curo, a** *ag* dark; (*fig*) obscure; humble, lowly // *sm*: **all'~ in** the dark; **tenere qn all'~ di qc** to keep sb in the dark about sth.

**ospe'dale** *sm* hospital; **ospedali'ero, a** *ag* hospital *cpd*.

**ospi'tale** *ag* hospitable; **ospitalità** *sf* hospitality.

**ospi'tare** *vt* to give hospitality to; (*sog: albergo*) to accommodate.

**'ospite** *sm/f* (*persona che ospita*) host/hostess; (*persona ospitata*) guest.

**os'pizio** [os'pittsjo] *sm* (*per vecchi etc*) home.

**'ossa** *sfpl vedi* **osso**.

**ossa'tura** *sf* (*ANAT*) skeletal structure, frame; (*TECN, fig*) framework.

**'osseo, a** *ag* bony; (*tessuto etc*) bone *cpd*.

**os'sequio** *sm* deference, respect; **~i** *smpl* (*saluto*) respects, regards; **ossequi'oso, a** *ag* obsequious.

**osser'vanza** [osser'vantsa] *sf* observance.

**osser'vare** *vt* to observe, watch; (*esaminare*) to examine; (*notare, rilevare*) to notice, observe; (*DIR: la legge*) to observe, respect;

*(mantenere: silenzio)* to keep, observe; **far ~ qc a qn** to point sth out to sb; **osserva'tore, 'trice** *ag* observant, perceptive // *smf* observer; **osserva'torio** *sm (ASTR)* observatory; *(MIL)* observation post; **osservazi'one** *sf* observation; *(di legge etc)* observance; *(considerazione critica)* observation, remark; *(rimprovero)* reproof; **in osservazione** under observation.

**ossessio'nare** *vt* to obsess, haunt; *(tormentare)* to torment, harass.

**ossessi'one** *sf* obsession.

**os'sesso, a** *ag (spiritato)* possessed.

**os'sia** *cong* that is, to be precise.

**ossi'dare** *vt, ~rsi vr* to oxidize.

**'ossido** *sm* oxide; **~ di carbonio** carbon monoxide.

**ossige'nare** [ossidʒe'nare] *vt* to oxygenate; *(decolorare)* to bleach; **acqua ossigenata** hydrogen peroxide.

**os'sigeno** *sm* oxygen.

**'osso** *sm (pl(f) ossa nel senso ANAT)* bone; **d'~** *(bottone etc)* of bone, bone *cpd.*

**osso'buco**, *pl* **ossi'buchi** *sm (CUC)* marrowbone; (: *piatto)* stew made with knuckle of veal in tomato sauce.

**os'suto, a** *ag* bony.

**ostaco'lare** *vt* to block, obstruct.

**os'tacolo** *sm* obstacle; *(EQUITAZIONE)* hurdle, jump.

**os'taggio** [os'taddʒo] *sm* hostage.

**'oste, os'tessa** *smf* innkeeper.

**osteggi'are** [osted'dʒare] *vt* to oppose, be opposed to.

**os'tello** *sm*: **~ della gioventù** youth hostel.

**osten'tare** *vt* to make a show of, flaunt; **ostentazi'one** *sf* ostentation, show.

**oste'ria** *sf* inn.

**os'tessa** *sf vedi* **oste.**

**os'tetrico, a, ci, che** *ag* obstetric // *sm* obstetrician // *sf* midwife.

**'ostia** *sf (REL)* host; *(per medicinali)* wafer.

**'ostico, a, ci, che** *ag (fig)* harsh; hard, difficult; unpleasant.

**os'tile** *ag* hostile; **ostilità** *sf inv* hostility // *sfpl (MIL)* hostilities.

**osti'narsi** *vr* to insist, dig one's heels in; **~ a fare** to persist (obstinately) in doing; **osti'nato, a** *ag (caparbio)* obstinate; *(tenace)* persistent, determined; **ostinazi'one** *sf* obstinacy; persistence.

**ostra'cismo** [ostra'tʃizmo] *sm* ostracism.

**'ostrica, che** *sf* oyster.

**ostru'ire** *vt* to obstruct, block; **ostruzi'one** *sf* obstruction, blockage.

**'otre** *sm (recipiente)* goatskin.

**ottago'nale** *ag* octagonal.

**ot'tagono** *sm* octagon.

**ot'tanta** *num* eighty; **ottan'tesimo, a** *num* eightieth; **ottan'tina** *sf*: **una ottantina (di)** about eighty.

**ot'tavo, a** *num* eighth // *sf* octave.

**ottempe'rare** *vi*: **~ a** to comply with, obey.

**ottene'brare** *vt* to darken; *(fig)* to cloud.

**ot'tenere** *vt* to obtain, get; *(risultato)* to achieve, obtain.

**'ottico, a, ci, che** *ag (della vista: nervo)* optic; *(dell'ottica)* optical // *sm* optician // *sf (scienza)* optics *sg*; *(FOT: lenti, prismi etc)* optics *pl.*

**ottima'mente** *av* excellently, very well.

**otti'mismo** *sm* optimism; **otti'mista, i, e** *smf* optimist.

**'ottimo, a** *ag* excellent, very good.

**'otto** *num* eight.

**ot'tobre** *sm* October.

**otto'cento** [otto'tʃɛnto] *num* eight hundred // *sm*: **l'O~** the nineteenth century.

**ot'tone** *sm* brass; **gli ~i** *(MUS)* the brass.

**ottun'dere** *vt (fig)* to dull.

**ottu'rare** *vt* to close (up); *(dente)* to fill; **ottura'tore** *sm (FOT)* shutter; *(nelle armi)* breechblock; **otturazi'one** *sf* closing (up);

*(dentaria)* filling.

**ot'tuso, a** *pp di* **ottundere** // *ag* (*MAT, fig*) obtuse; *(suono)* dull.

**o'vaia** *sf*, **o'vaio** *sm* (*ANAT*) ovary.

**o'vale** *ag, sm* oval.

**o'vatta** *sf* cotton wool; *(per imbottire)* padding, wadding; **ovat'tare** *vt* (*fig: smorzare*) to muffle.

**ovazi'one** [ovat'tsjone] *sf* ovation.

**'ovest** *sm* west.

**o'vile** *sm* pen, enclosure.

**o'vino, a** *ag* sheep *cpd*, ovine.

**ovulazi'one** [ovulat'tsjone] *sf* ovulation.

**'ovulo** *sm* (*FISIOL*) ovum.

**o'vunque** *av* = **dovunque**.

**ov'vero** *cong (ossia)* that is, to be precise; *(oppure)* or (else).

**ovvi'are** *vi*: ~ a to obviate.

**'ovvio, a** *ag* obvious.

**ozi'are** [ot'tsjare] *vi* to laze, idle.

**'ozio** ['ɔttsjo] *sm* idleness; *(tempo libero)* leisure; **ore d'~** leisure time; **stare in ~** to be idle; **ozi'oso, a** *ag* idle.

**o'zono** [o'dzɔno] *sm* ozone.

# P

**pa'cato, a** *ag* quiet, calm.

**pac'chetto** [pak'ketto] *sm* packet; ~ **azionario** (*COMM*) shareholding.

**'pacco, chi** *sm* parcel; *(involto)* bundle.

**'pace** ['patʃe] *sf* peace; **darsi** ~ to resign o.s.

**pacifi'care** [patʃifi'kare] *vt* (*riconciliare*) to reconcile, make peace between; *(mettere in pace)* to pacify.

**pa'cifico, a, ci, che** [pa'tʃifiko] *ag (persona)* peaceable; *(vita)* peaceful; *(fig: indiscusso)* indisputable; *(: ovvio)* obvious, clear // *sm*: **il P~**, **l'Oceano P~** the Pacific (Ocean).

**paci'fista, i, e** [patʃi'fista] *sm/f* pacifist.

**pa'della** *sf* frying pan; *(per infermi)*

bedpan.

**padigli'one** [padiʎ'ʎone] *sm* pavilion; *(AUT)* roof.

**'Padova** *sf* Padua.

**'padre** *sm* father; ~**i** *smpl (antenati)* forefathers; **pa'drino** *sm* godfather.

**padro'nanza** [padro'nantsa] *sf* command, mastery.

**pa'drone, a** *sm/f* master/mistress; *(proprietario)* owner; *(datore di lavoro)* employer; **essere** ~ **di sé** to be in control of o.s.; ~ **di casa** master/mistress of the house; *(per gli inquilini)* landlord/lady; **pa-droneggi'are** *vt* (*fig: sentimenti*) to master, control; *(: materia)* to master, know thoroughly; **pa-droneggiarsi** *vr* to control o.s.

**pae'saggio** [pae'zaddʒo] *sm* landscape.

**pae'sano, a** *ag* country *cpd* // *sm/f* villager; countryman/woman.

**pa'ese** *sm (nazione)* country, nation; *(terra)* country, land; *(villaggio)* village; ~ **di provenienza** country of origin; **i P~i Bassi** the Netherlands.

**paf'futo, a** *ag* chubby, plump.

**'paga, ghe** *sf* pay, wages *pl*.

**paga'mento** *sm* payment.

**pa'gano, a** *ag, sm/f* pagan.

**pa'gare** *vt* to pay; *(acquisto, fig: colpa)* to pay for; *(contraccambiare)* to repay, pay back // *vi* to pay; **quanto l'hai pagato?** how much did you pay for it?; ~ **con carta di credito** to pay by credit card; ~ **in contanti** to pay cash.

**pa'gella** [pa'dʒella] *sf* (*INS*) report card.

**'paggio** ['paddʒo] *sm* page(boy).

**pagherò** [page'rɔ] *sm inv* acknowledgement of a debt, IOU.

**'pagina** ['padʒina] *sf* page.

**'paglia** ['paʎʎa] *sf* straw.

**pagliac'cetto** [paʎʎat'tʃetto] *sm (per bambini)* rompers *pl*.

**pagli'accio** [paʎ'ʎattʃo] *sm* clown.

**pagli'etta** [paʎ'ʎetta] *sf (cappello*

*per uomo)* (straw) boater; *(per tegami etc)* steel wool.

pa'gnotta [pan'nɔtta] *sf* round loaf.

'paio, *pl(f)* 'paia *sm* pair; un ~ di *(alcuni)* a couple of.

pai'olo, paiu'olo *sm* (copper) pot.

'pala *sf* shovel; *(di remo, ventilatore, elica)* blade; *(di ruota)* paddle.

pa'lato *sm* palate.

pa'lazzo [pa'lattso] *sm (reggia)* palace; *(edificio)* building; ~ di giustizia courthouse; ~ dello sport sports stadium.

pal'chetto [pal'ketto] *sm* shelf.

'palco, chi *sm (TEATRO)* box; *(tavolato)* platform, stand; *(ripiano)* layer.

palco'scenico, ci [palkoʃ'ʃeniko] *sm (TEATRO)* stage.

pale'sare *vt* to reveal, disclose; ~rsi *vr* to reveal o show o.s.

pa'lese *ag* clear, evident.

Pales'tina *sf*: la ~ Palestine.

pa'lestra *sf* gymnasium; *(esercizio atletico)* exercise, training; *(fig)* training ground, school.

pa'letta *sf* spade; *(per il focolare)* shovel; *(del capostazione)* signalling disc.

pa'letto *sm* stake, peg; *(spranga)* bolt.

'palio *sm (gara)*: il P~ horserace run at Siena; mettere qc in ~ to offer sth as a prize.

'palla *sf* ball; *(pallottola)* bullet; ~ canestro *sm* basketball; ~ nuoto *sm* water polo; ~ volo *sm* volleyball.

palleggi'are [palled'dʒare] *vi (CALCIO)* to practise with the ball; *(TENNIS)* to knock up.

pallia'tivo *sm* palliative; *(fig)* stopgap measure.

'pallido, a *ag* pale.

pal'lina *sf (bilia)* marble.

pallon'cino [pallon'tʃino] *sm* balloon; *(lampioncino)* Chinese lantern.

pal'lone *sm (palla)* ball; *(CALCIO)* football; *(aerostato)* balloon; gioco

del ~ football.

pal'lore *sm* pallor, paleness.

pal'lottola *sf* pellet; *(proiettile)* bullet.

'palma *sf (ANAT)* = palmo; *(BOT, simbolo)* palm; ~ da datteri date palm.

'palmo *sm (ANAT)* palm; restare con un ~ di naso to be badly disappointed.

'palo *sm (legno appuntito)* stake; *(sostegno)* pole; fare da o il ~ *(fig)* to act as look-out.

palom'baro *sm* diver.

pa'lombo *sm (pesce)* dogfish.

pal'pare *vt* to feel, finger.

'palpebra *sf* eyelid.

palpi'tare *vi (cuore, polso)* to beat; (: più forte) to pound, throb; *(fremere)* to quiver; 'palpito *sm (del cuore)* beat; *(fig: d'amore etc)* throb.

paltò *sm inv* overcoat.

pa'lude *sf* marsh, swamp; palu'doso, a *ag* marshy, swampy.

pa'lustre *ag* marsh *cpd*, swamp *cpd*.

pam'pino *sm* vine leaf.

'panca, che *sf* bench.

pan'cetta [pan'tʃetta] *sf (CUC)* bacon.

pan'chetto [pan'ketto] *sm* stool; footstool.

pan'china [pan'kina] *sf* garden seat; *(di giardino pubblico)* (park) bench.

'pancia, ce [pantʃa] *sf* belly, stomach; mettere o fare ~ to be getting a paunch; avere mal di ~ to have stomach ache o a sore stomach.

panci'otto [pan'tʃɔtto] *sm* waistcoat.

'pancreas *sm inv* pancreas.

'panda *sm inv* panda.

pande'monio *sm* pandemonium.

'pane *sm* bread; *(pagnotta)* loaf (of bread); *(forma)*: un ~ di burro/cera *etc* a pat of butter/bar of wax *etc*; guadagnarsi il ~ to earn one's living; ~ a cassetta sliced bread; ~ integrale wholemeal bread; ~ tostato toast.

**panette'ria** *sf* (*forno*) bakery; (*negozio*) baker's (shop), bakery.

**panetti'ere,** a *sm/f* baker.

**panet'tone** *sm* *a kind of spiced brioche with sultanas, eaten at Christmas.*

**pangrat'tato** *sm* breadcrumbs *pl.*

**'panico, a, ci, che** *ag, sm* panic.

**pani'ere** *sm* basket.

**pani'ficio** [pani'fitʃo] *sm* (*forno*) bakery; (*negozio*) baker's (shop), bakery.

**pa'nino** *sm* roll; ~ **imbottito** filled roll; sandwich; **panino'teca** *sf* sandwich bar.

**'panna** *sf* (*CUC*) cream; (*TECN*) = **panne**; ~ **da cucina** cooking cream; ~ **montata** whipped cream.

**'panne** *sf inv*: essere in ~ (*AUT*) to have broken down.

**pan'nello** *sm* panel.

**'panno** *sm* cloth; ~i *smpl* (*abiti*) clothes; **mettiti nei miei ~i** (*fig*) put yourself in my shoes.

**pan'nocchia** [pan'nɔkkja] *sf* (*di mais etc*) ear.

**panno'lino** *sm* (*per bambini*) nappy (*Brit*), diaper (*US*).

**pano'rama,** i *sm* panorama; **pano'ramico, a, ci, che** *ag* panoramic; **strada panoramica** scenic route.

**panta'loni** *smpl* trousers (*Brit*), pants (*US*), pair *sg* of trousers o pants.

**pan'tano** *sm* bog.

**pan'tera** *sf* panther.

**pan'tofola** *sf* slipper.

**panto'mima** *sf* pantomime.

**pan'zana** [pan'tsana] *sf* fib, tall story.

**pao'nazzo, a** [pao'nattso] *ag* purple.

**'papa,** i *sm* pope.

**papà** *sm inv* dad(dy).

**pa'pale** *ag* papal.

**pa'pato** *sm* papacy.

**pa'pavero** *sm* poppy.

**'papero, a,** *sm/f* (*ZOOL*) gosling // *sf* (*fig*) slip of the tongue, blunder.

**pa'piro** *sm* papyrus.

**'pappa** *sf* baby cereal.

**pappa'gallo** *sm* parrot; (*fig*: *uomo*) Romeo, wolf.

**pappa'gorgia, ge** [pappa'gɔrdʒa] *sf* double chin.

**pap'pare** *vt* (*fam*: *anche*: ~rsi) to gobble up.

**'para** *sf*: suole di ~ crepe soles.

**pa'rabola** *sf* (*MAT*) parabola; (*REL*) parable.

**para'brezza** [para'breddza] *sm inv* (*AUT*) windscreen (*Brit*), windshield (*US*).

**paraca'dute** *sm inv* parachute.

**para'carro** *sm* kerbstone (*Brit*), curbstone (*US*).

**para'diso** *sm* paradise.

**parados'sale** *ag* paradoxical.

**para'dosso** *sm* paradox.

**para'fango, ghi** *sm* mudguard.

**paraf'fina** *sf* paraffin, paraffin wax.

**para'fulmine** *sm* lightning conductor.

**pa'raggi** [pa'raddʒi] *smpl*: **nei ~ in** the vicinity, in the neighbourhood.

**parago'nare** *vt*: ~ **con/a** to compare with/to.

**para'gone** *sm* comparison; (*esempio analogo*) analogy, parallel; **reggere al ~** to stand comparison.

**pa'ragrafo** *sm* paragraph.

**pa'ralisi** *sf* paralysis; **para'litico, a, ci, che** *ag, sm/f* paralytic.

**paraliz'zare** [paralid'dzare] *vt* to paralyze.

**paral'lelo, a** *ag* parallel // *sm* (*GEO*) parallel; (*comparazione*): **fare un ~ tra** to draw a parallel between // *sf* parallel (line); ~e *sfpl* (*attrezzo ginnico*) parallel bars.

**para'lume** *sm* lampshade.

**pa'rametro** *sm* parameter.

**para'noia** *sf* paranoia; **para'noico, a, ci, che** *ag, sm/f* paranoid.

**para'occhi** [para'ɔkki] *smpl* blinkers.

**para'piglia** [para'piʎʎa] *sm* commotion, uproar.

**pa'rare** *vt* (*addobbare*) to adorn, deck; (*proteggere*) to shield, protect; (*scansare*: *colpo*) to parry;

(CALCIO) to save // vi: **dove vuole andare a ~?** what are you driving at?; **~rsi** vr (presentarsi) to appear, present o.s.

**para'sole** sm inv parasol, sunshade.

**paras'sita, i** sm parasite.

**pa'rata** sf (SPORT) save; (MIL) review, parade.

**para'tia** sf (di nave) bulkhead.

**para'urti** sm inv (AUT) bumper.

**para'vento** sm folding screen; **fare da ~ a qn** (fig) to shield sb.

**par'cella** [par'tʃɛlla] sf account, fee (of lawyer etc).

**parcheggi'are** [parked'dʒare] vt to park; **par'cheggio** sm parking q; (luogo) car park; (singolo posto) parking space.

**par'chimetro** [par'kimetro] sm parking meter.

**'parco, chi** sm park; (spazio per deposito) depot; (complesso di veicoli) fleet.

**'parco, a, chi, che** ag: **~ (in)** (sobrio) moderate (in); (avaro) sparing (with).

**pa'recchio, a** [pa'rekkjo] det quite a lot of; (tempo) quite a lot of, a long; **~i(e)** det pl quite a lot of, several // pronome quite a lot, quite a bit; (tempo) quite a while, a long time; **~i(e)** pronome pl quite a lot, several // av (con ag) quite, rather; (con vb) quite a lot, quite a bit.

**pareggi'are** [pared'dʒare] vt to make equal; (terreno) to level, make level; (bilancio, conti) to balance // vi (SPORT) to draw; **pa'reggio** sm (ECON) balance; (SPORT) draw.

**paren'tado** sm relatives pl, relations pl.

**pa'rente** sm/f relative, relation.

**paren'tela** sf (vincolo di sangue, fig) relationship; (insieme dei parenti) relations pl, relatives pl.

**pa'rentesi** sf (segno grafico) bracket, parenthesis; (frase incisa) parenthesis; (digressione) parenthesis, digression.

**pa'rere** sm (opinione) opinion; (consiglio) advice, opinion; **a mio ~ in my opinion** // vi to seem, appear // vb impers: **pare che** it seems o appears that, they say that; **mi pare che** it seems to me that; **mi pare di sì** I think so; **fai come ti pare** do as you like; **che ti pare del mio libro?** what do you think of my book?

**pa'rete** sf wall.

**'pari** ag inv (uguale) drawn, same; (in giochi) equal; drawn, tied; (MAT) even // sm inv (POL: di Gran Bretagna) peer // sm/f inv peer, equal; **copiato ~ ~** copied word for word; **alla ~** on the same level; **ragazza alla ~** au pair girl; **mettersi alla ~ con** to place o.s. on the same level as; **mettersi in ~ con** to catch up with; **andare di ~ passo con qn** to keep pace with sb.

**Pa'rigi** [pa'ridʒi] sf Paris.

**pa'riglia** [pa'riʎʎa] sf pair; **rendere la ~** to give tit for tat.

**parità** sf parity, equality; (SPORT) draw, tie.

**parlamen'tare** ag parliamentary // sm/f ≈ Member of Parliament (Brit), ≈ Congressman/woman (US) // vi to negotiate, parley.

**parla'mento** sm parliament.

**parlan'tina** sf (fam) talkativeness; **avere una buona ~** to have the gift of the gab.

**par'lare** vi to speak, talk; (confidare cose segrete) to talk // vt to speak; **~ (a qn) di** to speak o talk (to sb) about; **parla'torio** sm (di carcere etc) visiting room; (REL) parlour.

**parmigi'ano** [parmi'dʒano] sm (grana) Parmesan (cheese).

**paro'dia** sf parody.

**pa'rola** sf word; (facoltà) speech; **~e** sfpl (chiacchiere) talk sg; **chiedere la ~** to ask permission to speak; **prendere la ~** to take the floor; **~ d'onore** word of honour; **~ d'ordine** (MIL) password; **~e incrociate** crossword (puzzle) sg; **paro'laccia, ce** sf bad word, swearword.

**par'rocchia** [par'rɔkkja] sf parish; parish church.

**'parroco, ci** sm parish priest.

**par'rucca, che** sf wig.

**parrucchi'ere, a** [parruk'kjɛre] sm/f hairdresser // sm barber.

**parsi'monia** sf frugality, thrift.

**'parso, a** pp di **parere**.

**'parte** sf part; (lato) side; (quota spettante a ciascuno) share; (direzione) direction; (POL) party; faction; (DIR) party; **a ~** ag separate / av separately; **scherzi a ~** joking aside; **a ~ ciò** apart from that; **da ~** (in disparte) to one side, aside; **d'altra ~** on the other hand; **da ~ di** (per conto di) on behalf of; **da ~ mia** as far as I'm concerned, as for me; **da ~ a ~** right through; **da ogni ~** on all sides, everywhere; (moto da luogo) from all sides; **da nessuna ~** nowhere; **da questa ~** (in questa direzione) this way; **prendere ~ a qc** to take part in sth; **mettere da ~** to put aside; **mettere qn a ~ di qc** to inform sb of sth.

**parteci'pare** [partetʃi'pare] vi: **~ a** to take part in, participate in; (utili etc) to share in; (spese etc) to contribute to; (dolore, successo di qn) to share (in); **partecipazi'one** sf participation; sharing; (ECON) interest; **partecipazione agli utili** profit-sharing; **partecipazioni di nozze** wedding announcement card; **par'tecipe** ag participating; essere **partecipe di** to take part in, participate in; to share (in); (consapevole) to be aware of.

**parteggi'are** [parted'dʒare] vi: **~ per** to side with, be on the side of.

**par'tenza** [par'tɛntsa] sf departure; (SPORT) start; **essere in ~** to be about to leave, to be leaving.

**parti'cella** [parti'tʃɛlla] sf particle.

**parti'cipio** [parti'tʃipjo] sm participle.

**partico'lare** ag (specifico) particular; (proprio) personal,

private; (speciale) special, particular; (caratteristico) distinctive, characteristic; (fuori dal comune) peculiar // sm detail, particular; **in ~** in particular, particularly; **particolarità** sf inv particularity; detail; characteristic, feature.

**partigi'ano, a** [parti'dʒano] ag partisan // sm (fautore) supporter, champion; (MIL) partisan.

**par'tire** vi to go, leave; (allontanarsi) to go (o drive etc) away o off; (petardo, colpo) to go off; (fig: avere inizio, SPORT) to start; **sono partita da Roma alle 7** I left Rome at 7; **il volo parte da Ciampino** the flight leaves from Ciampino; **a ~ da** from.

**par'tita** sf (COMM) lot, consignment; (ECON: registrazione) entry, item; (CARTE, SPORT: gioco) game; (: competizione) match, game; **~ di caccia** hunting party; **~ IVA** VAT registration number.

**par'tito** sm (POL) party; (decisione) decision, resolution; (persona da maritare) match.

**parti'tura** sf (MUS) score.

**'parto** sm (MED) delivery, (child)birth; labour; **parto'rire** vt to give birth to; (fig) to produce.

**parzi'ale** [par'tsjale] ag (limitato) partial; (non obiettivo) biased, partial.

**'pascere** ['paʃʃere] vi to graze // vt (brucare) to graze on; (far pascolare) to graze, pasture; **pasci'uto, a** pp di **pascere**.

**pasco'lare** vt, vi to graze.

**'pascolo** sm pasture.

**'Pasqua** sf Easter; **pas'quale** ag Easter cpd.

**pas'sabile** ag fairly good, passable.

**pas'saggio** [pas'saddʒo] sm passing q, passage; (traversata) crossing q, passage; (luogo, prezzo della traversata, brano di libro etc) passage; (su veicolo altrui) lift (Brit), ride; (SPORT) pass; **di ~**

(*persona*) passing through; ~ **pedonale/a livello** pedestrian/level (*Brit*) o grade (*US*) crossing.

**pas'sante** *sm/f* passer-by // *sm* loop.

**passa'porto** *sm* passport.

**pas'sare** *vi* (*andare*) to go; (*veicolo*, *pedone*) to pass (by), go by; (*fare una breve sosta: postino etc*) to come, call; (: *amico: per fare una visita*) to call o drop in; (*sole*, *aria*, *luce*) to get through; (*trascorrere: giorni, tempo*) to pass, go by; (*fig: proposta di legge*) to be passed; (: *dolore*) to pass, go away; (*CARTE*) to pass // *vt* (*attraversare*) to cross; (*trasmettere: messaggio*): ~ qc a qn to pass sth to sb; (*dare*): ~ qc a qn to pass sth to sb, give sb sth; (*trascorrere: tempo*) to spend; (*superare: esame*) to pass; (*tritu-rare: verdura*) to strain; (*approvare*) to pass, approve; (*oltrepassare, sorpassare: anche fig*) to go beyond, pass; (*fig: subire*) to go through; ~ da ... a to pass from ... to; ~ di pa-dre in figlio to be handed down o to pass from father to son; ~ per (*anche fig*) to go through; ~ per stupido/un genio to be taken for a fool/a genius; ~ sopra (*anche fig*) to pass over; ~ attraverso (*anche fig*) to go through; ~ alla storia to pass into history; ~ a un esame to go up (to the next class) after an exam; ~ inosservato to go unnoticed; ~ di moda to go out of fashion; le passo il Signor X (*al telefono*) here is Mr X; I'm putting you through to Mr X; lasciar ~ qn/qc to let sb/sth through; passarsela: come te la passi? how are you getting on o along?

**pas'sata** *sf*: dare una ~ di vernice a qc to give sth a coat of paint; dare una ~ al giornale to have a look at the paper, skim through the paper.

**passa'tempo** *sm* pastime, hobby.

**pas'sato, a** *ag* past; (*sfiorito*) faded // *sm* past; (*LING*) past (tense); ~

**prossimo** (*LING*) present perfect; ~ **remoto** (*LING*) past historic; ~ di **verdura** (*CUC*) vegetable purée.

**passaver'dura** *sm inv* vegetable mill.

**passeg'gero, a** [passed'dʒɛro] *ag* passing // *sm/f* passenger.

**passeggi'are** [passed'dʒare] *vi* to go for a walk; (*in veicolo*) to go for a drive; **passeggi'ata** *sf* walk; drive; (*luogo*) promenade; **fare una passeggiata** to go for a walk (o drive); **passeg'gino** *sm* pushchair (*Brit*), stroller (*US*); **pas'seggio** *sm* walk, stroll; (*luogo*) promenade.

**passe'rella** *sf* footbridge; (*di nave*, *aereo*) gangway; (*pedana*) catwalk.

**'passero** *sm* sparrow.

**pas'sibile** *ag*: ~ di liable to.

**passi'one** *sf* passion.

**pas'sivo, a** *ag* passive // *sm* (*LING*) passive; (*ECON*) debit; (: *complesso dei debiti*) liabilities *pl*.

**'passo** *sm* step; (*andatura*) pace; (*rumore*) (foot)step; (*orma*) footprint; (*passaggio, fig: brano*) passage; (*valico*) pass; a ~ d'uomo at walking pace; ~ (a) ~ step by step; fare due o quattro ~i to go for a walk o stroll; di questo ~ at this rate; "~ carraio" "vehicle en-trance — keep clear".

**'pasta** *sf* (*CUC*) dough; (: *impasto per dolce*) pastry; (: *anche*: ~ **alimentare**) pasta; (*massa molle di materia*) paste; (*fig: indole*) nature; ~e *sfpl* (*pasticcini*) pastries; ~ in **brodo** noodle soup.

**pastasci'utta** [pastaʃˈʃutta] *sf* pasta.

**pas'tella** *sf* batter.

**pas'tello** *sm* pastel.

**pas'tetta** *sf* (*CUC*) = **pastella**.

**pas'ticca, che** *sf* = **pastiglia**.

**pastic'ceria** [pastitʃeˈria] *sf* (*pasticcini*) pastries *pl*, cakes *pl*; (*negozio*) cake shop; (*arte*) con-fectionery.

**pasticci'are** [pastitʃare] *vt* to mess up, make a mess of // *vi* to make a mess.

**pasticci'ere, a** [pastit'tʃere] *sm/f* pastrycook; confectioner.

**pas'ticcio** [pas'tittʃo] *sm* (*CUC*) pie; (*lavoro disordinato, imbroglio*) mess; **trovarsi nei ~i** to get into trouble.

**pasti'ficio** [pasti'fitʃo] *sm* pasta factory.

**pas'tiglia** [pas'tiʎʎa] *sf* pastille, lozenge.

**pas'tina** *sf* small pasta shapes used in soup.

**pasti'naca, che** *sf* parsnip.

**'pasto** *sm* meal.

**pas'tore** *sm* shepherd; (*REL*) pastor, minister; (*anche:* **cane ~**) sheepdog.

**pastoriz'zare** [pastorid'dzare] *vt* to pasteurize.

**pas'toso, a** *ag* doughy; pasty; (*fig: voce, colore*) mellow, soft.

**pas'trano** *sm* greatcoat.

**pas'tura** *sf* pasture.

**pa'tata** *sf* potato; **~e fritte** chips (*Brit*), French fries; **pata'tine** *sfpl* (*potato*) crisps.

**pata'trac** *sm* (*crollo: anche fig*) crash.

**pa'tella** *sf* (*ZOOL*) limpet.

**pa'tema, i** *sm* anxiety, worry.

**pa'tente** *sf* licence; (*anche:* **~ di guida**) driving licence (*Brit*), driver's license (*US*).

**paternità** *sf* paternity, fatherhood.

**pa'terno, a** *ag* (*affetto, consigli*) fatherly; (*casa, autorità*) paternal.

**pa'tetico, a, ci, che** *ag* pathetic; (*commovente*) moving, touching.

**pa'tibolo** *sm* gallows *sg*, scaffold.

**'patina** *sf* (*su rame etc*) patina; (*sulla lingua*) fur, coating.

**pa'tire** *vt, vi* to suffer.

**pa'tito, a** *sm/f* enthusiast, fan, lover.

**patolo'gia** [patolo'dʒia] *sf* pathology; **pato'logico, a, ci, che** *ag* pathological.

**'patria** *sf* homeland.

**patri'arca, chi** *sm* patriarch.

**pa'trigno** [pa'triɲɲo] *sm* stepfather.

**patri'monio** *sm* estate, property; (*fig*) heritage.

**patri'ota, i, e** *sm/f* patriot; **pa-tri'ottico, a, ci, che** *ag* patriotic; **patriot'tismo** *sm* patriotism.

**patroci'nare** [patrotʃi'nare] *vt* (*DIR: difendere*) to defend; (*sostenere*) to sponsor, support; **patro'cinio** *sm* defence; support, sponsorship.

**patro'nato** *sm* patronage; (*istituzione benefica*) charitable institution *o* society.

**pa'trono** *sm* (*REL*) patron saint; (*socio di patronato*) patron; (*DIR*) counsel.

**'patta** *sf* flap; (*dei pantaloni*) fly.

**patteggi'are** [patted'dʒare] *vt, vi* to negotiate.

**patti'naggio** [patti'naddʒo] *sm* skating.

**patti'nare** *vi* to skate; **~ sul ghiaccio** to ice-skate; **pattina'tore, 'trice** *sm/f* skater; **'pattino** *sm* skate; (*di slitta*) runner; (*AER*) skid; (*TECN*) sliding block; **pattini (da ghiaccio)** (ice) skates; **pattini a rotelle** roller skates; [pat'tino] (*barca*) kind of pedalo with oars.

**'patto** *sm* (*accordo*) pact, agreement; (*condizione*) term, condition; **a ~ che** on condition that.

**pat'tuglia** [pat'tuʎʎa] *sf* (*MIL*) patrol.

**pattu'ire** *vt* to reach an agreement on.

**pattumi'era** *sf* (dust)bin (*Brit*), ashcan (*US*).

**pa'ura** *sf* fear; **aver ~ di/di fare/ che** to be frightened *o* afraid of/of doing/that; **far ~ a** to frighten; **per ~ di/che** for fear of/that; **pau'roso, a** *ag* (*che fa paura*) frightening; (*che ha paura*) fearful, timorous.

**'pausa** *sf* (*sosta*) break; (*nel parlare, MUS*) pause.

**pavi'mento** *sm* floor.

**pa'vone** *sm* peacock; **pavoneg-gi'arsi** *vr* to strut about, show off.

**pazien'tare** [pattsjen'tare] *vi* to patient.

**pazi'ente** [pat'tsjɛnte] *ag, sm/f* patient; **pazi'enza** *sf* patience.

**paz'zesco, a, schi, sche** [pat'tsesko] *ag* mad, crazy.

**paz'zia** [pat'tsia] *sf* (*MED*) madness, insanity; (*azione*) folly; (*di azione, decisione*) madness, folly.

**'pazzo, a** ['pattso] *ag* (*MED*) mad, insane; (*strano*) wild, mad // *sm/f* madman/woman; **~ di** (*gioia, amore etc*) mad o crazy with; **~ per qc/qn** mad o crazy about sth/sb.

**PCI** *sigla m* = *Partito Comunista Italiano*.

**'pecca, che** *sf* defect, flaw, fault.

**peccami'noso, a** *ag* sinful.

**pec'care** *vi* to sin; (*fig*) to err.

**pec'cato** *sm* sin; **è un ~ che** it's a pity that; **che ~!** what a shame o pity!

**pecca'tore, 'trice** *sm/f* sinner.

**'pece** ['petʃe] *sf* pitch.

**Pe'chino** [pe'kino] *sf* Peking.

**'pecora** *sf* sheep; **peco'raio** *sm* shepherd; **peco'rino** *sm* sheep's milk cheese.

**peculi'are** *ag*: **~ di** peculiar to.

**pe'daggio** [pe'daddʒo] *sm* toll.

**pedago'gia** [pedago'dʒia] *sf* pedagogy, educational methods *sg*.

**peda'lare** *vi* to pedal; (*andare in bicicletta*) to cycle.

**pe'dale** *sm* pedal.

**pe'dana** *sf* footboard; (*SPORT: nel salto*) springboard; (*: nella scherma*) piste.

**pe'dante** *ag* pedantic // *sm/f* pedant.

**pe'data** *sf* (*impronta*) footprint; (*colpo*) kick; **prendere a ~e qn/qc** to kick sb/sth.

**pede'rasta, i** *sm* pederast; homosexual.

**pedi'atra, i, e** *sm/f* paediatrician; **pedia'tria** *sf* paediatrics *sg*.

**pedi'cure** *sm/f inv* chiropodist.

**pe'dina** *sf* (*della dama*) draughtsman (*Brit*), draftsman (*US*); (*fig*) pawn.

**pedi'nare** *vt* to shadow, tail.

**pedo'nale** *ag* pedestrian.

**pe'done, a** *sm/f* pedestrian // *sm* (*SCACCHI*) pawn.

**'peggio** ['pɛddʒo] *av, ag inv* worse // *sm o f*: **il o la ~** the worst; **alla ~** at worst, if the worst comes to the worst; **peggiora'mento** *sm* worsening; **peggio'rare** *vt* to make worse, worsen // *vi* to grow worse, worsen; **peggiora'tivo, a** *ag* pejorative; **peggi'ore** *ag* (*comparativo*) worse; (*superlativo*) worst // *sm/f*: **il(la) peggiore** the worst (person).

**'pegno** ['peɲɲo] *sm* (*DIR*) security, pledge; (*nei giochi di società*) forfeit; (*fig*) pledge, token; **dare in ~ qc** to pawn sth.

**pe'lame** *sm* (*di animale*) coat, fur.

**pe'lare** *vt* (*spennare*) to pluck; (*spellare*) to skin; (*sbucciare*) to peel; (*fig*) to make pay through the nose; **~rsi** *vr* to go bald.

**pel'lame** *sm* skins *pl*, hides *pl*.

**'pelle** *sf* skin; (*di animale*) skin, hide; (*cuoio*) leather; **avere la ~ d'oca** to have goose pimples o goose flesh.

**pellegri'naggio** [pellegri'naddʒo] *sm* pilgrimage.

**pelle'grino, a** *sm/f* pilgrim.

**pelle'rossa, pelli'rossa,** *pl* **pelli'rosse** *sm/f* Red Indian.

**pellette'ria** *sf* leather goods *pl*; (*negozio*) leather goods shop.

**pelli'cano** *sm* pelican.

**pellicce'ria** [pellittʃe'ria] *sf* (*negozio*) furrier's (shop); (*quantità di pellicce*) furs *pl*.

**pel'liccia, ce** [pel'littʃa] *sf* (*mantello di animale*) coat, fur; (*indumento*) fur coat.

**pel'licola** *sf* (*membrana sottile*) film, layer; (*FOT, CINEMA*) film.

**'pelo** *sm* hair; (*pelame*) coat, hair; (*pelliccia*) fur; (*di tappeto*) pile; (*di liquido*) surface; **per un ~:** **per un ~ non ho perduto il treno** I very nearly missed the train; **c'è mancato un ~ che affogasse** he escaped drowning by the skin of his teeth; **pe'loso, a** *ag* hairy.

**'peltro** *sm* pewter.

**pe'luria** *sf* down.

'**pena** *sf* (*DIR*) sentence; (*punizione*) punishment; (*sofferenza*) sadness *q*, sorrow; (*fatica*) trouble *q*, effort; (*difficoltà*) difficulty; **far** ~ **to** be pitiful; **mi fai** ~ I feel sorry for you; **prendersi** *o* **darsi la** ~ **di fare** to go to the trouble of doing; ~ **di morte** death sentence; ~ **pecuniaria** fine; **pe'nale** *ag* penal; **penalità** *sf inv* penalty; **penaliz'zare** *vt* (*SPORT*) to penalize.

**pe'nare** *vi* (*patire*) to suffer; (*faticare*) to struggle.

**pen'dente** *ag* hanging; leaning // *sm* (*ciondolo*) pendant; (*orecchino*) drop earring; **pen'denza** *sf* slope, slant; (*grado d'inclinazione*) gradient; (*ECON*) outstanding account.

'**pendere** *vi* (*essere appeso*): ~ **da** to hang from; (*essere inclinato*) to lean; (*fig: incombere*): ~ **su** to hang over.

**pen'dio, 'dii** *sm* slope, slant; (*luogo in pendenza*) slope.

'**pendola** *sf* pendulum clock.

**pendo'lare** *smf* commuter.

'**pendolo** *sm* (*peso*) pendulum; (*anche*: **orologio a** ~) pendulum clock.

'**pene** *sm* penis.

**pene'trante** *ag* piercing, penetrating.

**pene'trare** *vi* to come *o* get in // *vt* to penetrate; ~ **in** to enter; (*sog: proiettile*) to penetrate; (:*acqua, aria*) to go *o* come into.

**penicil'lina** [penitʃil'lina] *sf* penicillin.

**pe'nisola** *sf* peninsula.

**peni'tenza** [peni'tɛntsa] *sf* penitence; (*punizione*) penance.

**penitenzi'ario** [peniten'tsjarjo] *sm* prison.

'**penna** *sf* (*di uccello*) feather; (*per scrivere*) pen; ~**e** *sfpl* (*CUC*) quills (*type of pasta*); ~ **a feltro/ stilografica/a sfera** felt-tip/fountain/ ballpoint pen.

**penna'rello** *sm* felt(-tip) pen.

**pennel'lare** *vi* to paint.

**pen'nello** *sm* brush; (*per dipingere*) (paint) brush; **a** ~ (*perfettamente*) to perfection, perfectly; ~ **per la barba** shaving brush.

**pen'nino** *sm* nib.

**pen'none** *sm* (*NAUT*) yard; (*stendardo*) banner, standard.

**pe'nombra** *sf* half-light, dim light.

**pe'noso, a** *ag* painful, distressing; (*faticoso*) tiring, laborious.

**pen'sare** *vi* to think // *vt* to think; (*inventare, escogitare*) to think out; ~ **a** to think of; (*amico, vacanze*) to think of *o* about; (*problema*) to think about; ~ **di fare qc** to think of doing sth; **ci penso io** I'll see to *o* take care of it.

**pensi'ero** *sm* thought; (*modo di pensare, dottrina*) thinking *q*; (*preoccupazione*) worry, care, trouble; **stare in** ~ **per qn** to be worried about sb; **pensie'roso, a** *ag* thoughtful.

'**pensile** *ag* hanging.

**pensio'nante** *smf* (*presso una famiglia*) lodger; (*di albergo*) guest.

**pensio'nato, a** *smf* pensioner.

**pensi'one** *sf* (*al prestatore di lavoro*) pension; (*vitto e alloggio*) board and lodging; (*albergo*) boarding house; **andare in** ~ to retire; **mezza** ~ half board; ~ **completa** full board.

**pen'soso, a** *ag* thoughtful, pensive, lost in thought.

**pentapar'tito** *sm* five-party government.

**Pente'coste** *sf* Pentecost, Whit Sunday (*Brit*).

**penti'mento** *sm* repentance, contrition.

**pen'tirsi** *vr*: ~ **di** to repent of; (*rammaricarsi*) to regret, be sorry for.

'**pentola** *sf* pot; ~ **a pressione** pressure cooker.

**pe'nultimo, a** *ag* last but one (*Brit*), next to last, penultimate.

**pe'nuria** *sf* shortage.

**penzo'lare** [pendzo'lare] *vi* to dangle, hang loosely; **penzo'loni** *av* dangling, hanging down; **stare penzoloni** to dangle, hang down.

'**pepe** *sm* pepper; ~ **macinato/in grani** ground/whole pepper.

**pepe'rone** *sm* pepper, capsicum; (*piccante*) chili.

**pe'pita** *sf* nugget.

---
**PAROLA CHIAVE**

**per** *prep* **1** (*moto attraverso luogo*) through; **i ladri sono passati ~ la finestra** the thieves got in (o out) through the window; **l'ho cercato ~ tutta la casa** I've searched the whole house o all over the house for it

**2** (*moto a luogo*) for, to; **partire ~ la Germania/il mare** to leave for Germany/the sea; **il treno ~ Roma** the Rome train, the train for o to Rome

**3** (*stato in luogo*): **seduto/sdraiato ~ terra** sitting/lying on the ground

**4** (*tempo*) for; ~ **anni/lungo tempo** for years/a long time; ~ **tutta l'estate** throughout the summer, all summer long; **lo rividi ~ Natale** I saw him again at Christmas; **lo faccio ~ lunedì** I'll do it for Monday

**5** (*mezzo, maniera*) by; ~ **lettera/ via aerea/ferrovia** by letter/ airmail/rail; **prendere qn ~ un braccio** to take sb by the arm

**6** (*causa, scopo*) for; **assente ~ malattia** absent because of o through o owing to illness; **ottimo ~ il mal di gola** excellent for sore throats

**7** (*limitazione*) for; **è troppo difficile ~ lui** it's too difficult for him; ~ **quel che mi riguarda** as far as I'm concerned; ~ **poco che sia** however little it may be; ~ **questa volta ti perdono** I'll forgive you this time

**8** (*prezzo, misura*) for; (*distributivo*) a, per; **venduto ~ 3 milioni** sold for 3 million; **1000 lire ~ persona** 1000

lira a o per person; **uno ~ volta** one at a time; **uno ~ uno** one by one; **5 ~ cento** 5 per cent; **3 ~ 4 fa** 12 **3 times** 4 **equals** 12; **dividere/ moltiplicare** 12 ~ **4** to divide/ multiply 12 by 4

**9** (*in qualità di*) as; (*al posto di*) for; **avere qn ~ professore** to have sb as a teacher; **ti ho preso ~ Mario** I mistook you for Mario, I though you were Mario; **dare ~ morto qn** to give sb up for dead

**10** (*seguito da vb: finale*): ~ **fare qc** (*so as*) to do sth, in order to do sth; (: *causale*): ~ **aver fatto qc** for having done sth; (: *consecutivo*): **è abbastanza grande ~ andarci da solo** he's big enough to go on his own.

'**pera** *sf* pear.

**pe'raltro** *av* moreover, what's more.

**per'bene** *ag inv* respectable, decent // *av* (*con cura*) properly, well.

**percentu'ale** [pertʃentu'ale] *sf* percentage.

**perce'pire** [pertʃe'pire] *vt* (*sentire*) to perceive; (*ricevere*) to receive; **percezi'one** *sf* perception.

---
**PAROLA CHIAVE**

**perché** [per'ke] ◆ *av* why; ~ **no?** why not?; ~ **non vuoi andarci?** why don't you want to go?; **spiegami ~ l'hai fatto** tell me why you did it

◆ *cong* **1** (*causale*) because; **non posso uscire ~ ho da fare** I can't go out because o as I've a lot to do

**2** (*finale*) in order that, so that; **te lo do ~ tu lo legga** I'm giving it to you so (that) you can read it

**3** (*consecutivo*): **è troppo forte ~ si possa batterlo** he's too strong to be beaten

◆ *sm inv* reason; **il ~ di** the reason for.

**perciò** [per'tʃɔ] *cong* so, for this (o that) reason.

**per'correre** vt (luogo) to go all over; (: paese) to travel up and down, go all over; (distanza) to cover.

**per'corso, a** pp di **percorrere** // sm (tragitto) journey; (tratto) route.

**per'cosso, a** pp di **percuotere** // sf blow.

**percu'otere** vt to hit, strike.

**percussi'one** sf percussion; **strumenti a ~** (MUS) percussion instruments.

**'perdere** vt to lose; (lasciarsi sfuggire) to miss; (sprecare: tempo, denaro) to waste; (mandare in rovina: persona) to ruin // vi to lose; (serbatoio etc) to leak; **~rsi** vr (smarrirsi) to get lost; (svanire) to disappear, vanish; **saper ~** to be a good loser; **lascia ~!** forget it!, never mind!

**perdigi'orno** [perdi'dʒorno] sm/f inv idler, waster.

**'perdita** sf loss; (spreco) waste; (fuoriuscita) leak; **siamo in ~** (COMM) we are running at a loss; **a ~ d'occhio** as far as the eye can see.

**perdi'tempo** sm/f inv waster, idler.

**perdo'nare** vt to pardon, forgive; (scusare) to excuse, pardon.

**per'dono** sm forgiveness; (DIR) pardon.

**perdu'rare** vi to go on, last; (perseverare) to persist.

**perduta'mente** av desperately, passionately.

**per'duto, a** pp di **perdere**.

**peregri'nare** vi to wander, roam.

**pe'renne** ag eternal, perpetual, perennial; (BOT) perennial.

**peren'torio, a** ag peremptory; (definitivo) final.

**per'fetto, a** ag perfect // sm (LING) perfect (tense).

**perfezio'nare** vt to improve, perfect; **~rsi** vr to improve.

**perfezi'one** [perfet'tsjone] sf perfection.

**'perfido, a** ag perfidious, treacherous.

**per'fino** av even.

**perfo'rare** vt to perforate; to punch a hole (o holes) in; (banda, schede) to punch; (trivellare) to drill; **perfora'tore, 'trice** sm/f punch-card operator // sm (utensile) punch; (INFORM): **perforatore di schede card punch** // sf (TECN) boring o drilling machine; (INFORM) card punch; **perforazi'one** sf perforation; punching; drilling; (INFORM) punch; (MED) perforation.

**perga'mena** sf parchment.

**perico'lante** ag precarious.

**pe'ricolo** sm danger; **mettere in ~** to endanger, put in danger; **perico'loso, a** ag dangerous.

**perife'ria** sf periphery; (di città) outskirts pl.

**peri'frasi** sf circumlocution.

**pe'rimetro** sm perimeter.

**peri'odico, a, ci, che** ag periodic(al); (MAT) recurring // sm periodical.

**pe'riodo** sm period.

**peripe'zie** [peripet'tsie] sfpl ups and downs, vicissitudes.

**pe'rire** vi to perish, die.

**pe'rito, a** ag expert, skilled // sm/f expert; (agronomo, navale) surveyor; **un ~ chimico** a qualified chemist.

**pe'rizia** [pe'rittsja] sf (abilità) ability; (giudizio tecnico) expert opinion; expert's report.

**'perla** sf pearl; **per'lina** sf bead.

**perlu'strare** vt to patrol.

**perma'loso, a** ag touchy.

**perma'nente** ag permanent // sf permanent wave, perm; **perma'nenza** sf permanence; (soggiorno) stay.

**perma'nere** vi to remain.

**perme'are** vt to permeate.

**per'messo, a** pp di **permettere** // sm (autorizzazione) permission, leave; (dato a militare, impiegato) leave; (licenza) licence, permit;

(MIL: foglio) pass; ~?, è ~? (posso entrare?) may I come in?; (posso passare?) excuse me; ~ di lavoro/pesca work/fishing permit.

per'mettere vt to allow, permit; ~ a qn qc/di fare to allow sb sth/to do; ~rsi qc/di fare to allow o.s. sth/to do; (avere la possibilità) to afford sth/to do.

per'nacchia [per'nakkja] sf (fam): fare una ~ to blow a raspberry.

per'nice [per'nitʃe] sf partridge.

'perno sm pivot.

pernot'tare vi to spend the night, stay overnight.

'però sm pear tree.

però cong (ma) but; (tuttavia) however, nevertheless.

pero'rare vt (DIR, fig): ~ la causa di qn to plead sb's case.

perpendico'lare ag, sf perpendicular.

perpe'trare vt to perpetrate.

perpetu'are vt to perpetuate.

per'petuo, a ag perpetual.

per'plesso, a ag perplexed; uncertain, undecided.

perqui'sire vt to search; perquisizi'one sf (police) search.

persecu'tore sm persecutor.

persecuzi'one [persekut'tsjone] sf persecution.

persegu'ire vt to pursue.

persegui'tare vt to persecute.

perseve'rante ag persevering.

perseve'rare vi to persevere.

'Persia sf: la ~ Persia.

persi'ano, a ag, sm/f Persian // sf shutter; ~a avvolgibile Venetian blind.

'persico, a, ci, che ag: il golfo P~ the Persian Gulf.

per'sino av = perfino.

persis'tente ag persistent.

per'sistere vi to persist; ~ a fare to persist in doing; persis'tito, a pp di persistere.

'perso, a pp di perdere.

per'sona sf person; (qualcuno): una ~ someone, somebody, espressione

interrogativa + anyone o anybody; ~e sfpl people; non c'è ~ che ... there's nobody who ..., there isn't anybody who ....

perso'naggio [perso'naddʒo] sm (persona ragguardevole) personality, figure; (tipo) character, individual; (LETTERATURA) character.

perso'nale ag personal // sm staff; personnel; (figura fisica) build.

personalità sf inv personality.

personifi'care vt to personify; to embody.

perspi'cace [perspi'katʃe] ag shrewd, discerning.

persu'adere vt: ~ qn (di qc/a fare) to persuade sb (of sth/to do); persuasi'one sf persuasion; persua'siva, a ag persuasive; persu'aso, a pp di persuadere.

per'tanto cong (quindi) so, therefore.

'pertica, che sf pole.

perti'nente ag: ~ (a) relevant (to), pertinent (to).

per'tosse sf whooping cough.

per'tugio [per'tudʒo] sm hole, opening.

pertur'bare vt to disrupt; (persona) to disturb, perturb; perturbazi'one sf disruption; perturbation; perturbazione atmosferica atmospheric disturbance.

per'vadere vt to pervade; per'vaso, a pp di pervadere.

perve'nire vi: ~ a to reach, arrive at, come to; (venire in possesso): gli pervenne una fortuna he inherited a fortune; far ~ qc a to have sth sent to; perve'nuto, a pp di pervenire.

per'verso, a ag depraved; perverse.

perver'tire vt to pervert.

p. es. abbr (= per esempio) e.g.

'pesa sf weighing q; weighbridge.

pe'sante ag heavy; (fig: noioso) dull, boring.

pe'sare vt to weigh // vi (avere un peso) to weigh; (essere pesante) to be heavy; (fig) to carry weight; ~

su (fig) to lie heavy on; to influence; to hang over; **mi pesa sgridarlo** I find it hard to scold him.

'**pesca** sf (pl **pesche**: frutto) peach; (il pescare) fishing; **andare a ~** to go fishing; **~ di beneficenza** (lotteria) lucky dip; **~ con la lenza** angling.

**pes'care** vt (pesce) to fish for; to catch; (qc nell'acqua) to fish out; (fig: trovare) to get hold of, find.

**pesca'tore** sm fisherman; angler.

'**pesce** ['peʃʃe] sm fish gen inv; **P~i** (dello zodiaco) Pisces; **~ d'aprile!** April Fool!; **~ spada** swordfish; **pesce'cane** sm shark.

**pesche'reccio** [peske'rettʃo] sm fishing boat.

**pesche'ria** [peske'ria] sf fishmonger's (shop) (Brit), fish store (US).

**peschi'era** [pes'kjɛra] sf fishpond.

**pesci'vendolo, a** [peʃʃi'vendolo] sm/f fishmonger (Brit), fish merchant (US).

'**pesco, schi** sm peach tree.

**pes'coso, a** ag abounding in fish.

'**peso** sm weight; (SPORT) shot; **rubare sul ~** to give short weight; **essere di ~ a qn** (fig) to be a burden to sb; **~ lordo/netto** gross/net weight; **~ piuma/mosca/gallo/medio/massimo** (PUGILATO) feather/fly/bantam/middle/heavyweight.

**pessi'mismo** sm pessimism; **pessi'mista, i, e** ag pessimistic // sm/f pessimist.

'**pessimo, a** ag very bad, awful.

**pes'tare** vt to tread on, trample on; (sale, pepe) to grind; (uva, aglio) to crush; (fig: picchiare): **~ qn** to beat sb up.

'**peste** sf plague; (persona) nuisance, pest.

**pes'tello** sm pestle.

**pesti'lenza** [pesti'lɛntsa] sf pestilence; (fetore) stench.

'**pesto, a** ag: **c'è buio ~** it's pitch-dark; **occhio ~** black eye // sm (CUC) sauce made with basil, garlic,

cheese and oil.

'**petalo** sm (BOT) petal.

**pe'tardo** sm firecracker, banger (Brit).

**petizi'one** [petit'tsjone] sf petition.

'**peto** sm (fam!) fart (!).

**petrol'chimica** [petrol'kimika] sf petrochemical industry.

**petroli'era** sf (nave) oil tanker.

**petro'lifero, a** ag oil-bearing; oil cpd.

**pe'trolio** sm oil, petroleum; (per lampada, fornello) paraffin.

**pettego'lare** vi to gossip.

**pettego'lezzo** [pettego'leddzo] sm gossip q; **fare ~i** to gossip.

**pet'tegolo, a** ag gossipy // sm/f gossip.

**petti'nare** vt to comb (the hair of); **~rsi** vr to comb one's hair; **pettina'tura** sf (acconciatura) hairstyle.

'**pettine** sm comb; (ZOOL) scallop.

**petti'rosso** sm robin.

'**petto** sm chest; (seno) breast, bust; (CUC: di carne bovina) brisket; (: di pollo etc) breast; **a doppio ~** (abito) double-breasted; **petto'ruto, a** ag broad-chested; full-breasted.

**petu'lante** ag insolent.

'**pezza** ['pettsa] sf piece of cloth; (toppa) patch; (cencio) rag, cloth.

**pez'zato, a** [pet'tsato] ag piebald.

**pez'zente** [pet'tsɛnte] sm/f beggar.

'**pezzo** ['pettso] sm (gen) piece; (brandello, frammento) piece, bit; (di macchina, arnese etc) part; (STAMPA) article; (di tempo): **aspettare un ~** to wait quite a while o some time; **in o a ~i** in pieces; **andare in ~i** to break into pieces; **un bel ~ d'uomo** a fine figure of a man; **abito a due ~i** two-piece suit; **~ di cronaca** (STAMPA) report; **~ grosso** (fig) bigwig; **~ di ricambio** spare part.

**pia'cente** [pja'tʃɛnte] ag attractive, pleasant.

**pia'cere** [pja'tʃere] vi to please; **una ragazza che piace** a likeable girl;

an attractive girl; ~ a: mi piace I like it; quei ragazzi non mi piacciono I don't like those boys; gli piacerebbe andare al cinema he would like to go to the cinema // sm pleasure; (favore) favour; "~!" (nelle presentazioni) "pleased to meet you!"; con ~ certainly, with pleasure; per ~! please; fare un ~ a qn to do sb a favour; pia'cevole ag pleasant, agreeable; piaci'uto, a pp di piacere.

pi'aga, ghe sf (lesione) sore; (ferita: anche fig) wound; (fig: flagello) scourge, curse; (: persona) pest, nuisance.

piagnis'teo [pjaɲɲis'teo] sm whining, whimpering.

piagnuco'lare [pjaɲɲuko'lare] vi to whimper.

pia'lla sf (arnese) plane; pial'lare vt to plane.

pia'na sf stretch of level ground; (più esteso) plain.

pianeggi'ante [pjaned'dʒante] ag flat, level.

piane'rottolo sm landing.

pia'neta sm (ASTR) planet.

pi'angere ['pjandʒere] vi to cry, weep; (occhi) to water // vt to cry, weep; (lamentare) to bewail, lament; ~ la morte di qn to mourn sb's death.

pianifi'care vt to plan; pianificazi'one sf planning.

pia'nista, i, e smf pianist.

pi'ano, a ag (piatto) flat, level; (MAT) plane; (facile) straightforward, simple; (chiaro) clear, plain // av (adagio) slowly; (a bassa voce) softly; (con cautela) slowly, carefully // sm (MAT) plane; (GEO) plain; (livello) level, plane; (di edificio) floor; (programma) plan; (MUS) piano; pian ~ very slowly; (poco a poco) little by little; in primo/secondo ~ in the foreground/background; di primo ~ (fig) prominent, high-ranking.

piano'forte sm piano, pianoforte.

pi'anta sf (BOT) plant; (ANAT: anche: ~ del piede) sole (of the foot); (grafico) plan; (topografica) map; in ~ stabile on the permanent staff; piantagi'one sf plantation; pian'tare vt to plant; (conficcare) to drive o hammer in; (tenda) to put up, pitch; (fig: lasciare) to leave, desert; ~rsi vr: ~rsi davanti a qn to plant o.s. in front of sb; piantala! (fam) cut it out!

pianter'reno sm ground floor.

pi'anto, a pp di piangere // sm tears pl, crying.

pian'tone sm (vigilante) sentry, guard; (soldato) orderly; (AUT) steering column.

pia'nura sf plain.

pi'astra sf plate; (di pietra) slab; (di fornello) hotplate; ~ di registrazione tape deck; panino alla ~ ≈ toasted sandwich.

pias'trella sf tile.

pias'trina sf (MIL) identity disc.

piatta'forma sf (anche fig) platform.

piat'tino sm saucer.

pi'atto, a ag flat; (fig: scialbo) dull // sm (recipiente, vivanda) dish; (portata) course; (parte piana) flat (part); ~i smpl (MUS) cymbals; ~ fondo soup dish; ~ forte main course; ~ del giorno dish of the day, plat du jour; ~ dei giradischi turntable; ~i già pronti (CULIN) ready-cooked dishes.

pi'azza ['pjatsa] sf square; (COMM) market; far ~ pulita to make a clean sweep; ~ d'armi (MIL) parade ground; piaz'zale sm (large) square.

piaz'zare [pjat'tsare] vt to place; (COMM) to market, sell; ~rsi vr (SPORT) to be placed.

piaz'zista, i [pjat'tsista] sm (COMM) commercial traveller.

piaz'zola [pjat'tsɔla] sf (AUT) lay-by.

'picca, che sf pike; ~che sfpl (CARTE) spades.

pic'cante ag hot, pungent; (fig)

racy; biting.

**pic'carsi** *vr*: ~ **di** fare to pride o.s. on one's ability to do; ~ **per qc** to take offence at sth.

**pic'chetto** [pik'ketto] *sm* (MIL, *di scioperanti*) picket.

**picchi'are** [pik'kjare] *vt* (*persona: colpire*) to hit, strike; (: *prendere a botte*) to beat (up); (*battere*) to beat; (*sbattere*) to bang // *vi* (*bussare*) to knock; (: *con forza*) to bang; (*colpire*) to hit, strike; (*sole*) to beat down; **picchi'ata** *sf* (*percosse*) beating, thrashing; (AER) dive.

**picchiet'tare** [pikkjet'tare] *vt* (*punteggiare*) to spot, dot; (*colpire*) to tap.

**picchio** ['pikkjo] *sm* woodpecker.

**pic'cino, a** [pit'tʃino] *ag* tiny, very small.

**piccio'naia** [pittʃo'naja] *sf* pigeon-loft; (TEATRO): **la** ~ **the gods** *sg*.

**picci'one** [pit'tʃone] *sm* pigeon.

**picco, chi** *sm* peak; **a** ~ vertically.

**'piccolo, a** *ag* small; (*oggetto, mano, di età: bambino*) small, little (*dav sostantivo*); (*di breve durata: viaggio*) short; (*fig*) mean, petty // *smf* child, little one; ~**i** *smpl* (*di animale*) young *pl*; **in** ~ **in miniature.

**pic'cone** *sm* pick(-axe).

**pic'cozza** [pik'kottsa] *sf* ice-axe.

**pic'nic** *sm inv* picnic.

**pi'docchio** [pi'dokkjo] *sm* louse.

**pi'ede** *sm* foot; (*di mobile*) leg; **in** ~**i** standing; **a** ~**i** on foot; **a** ~**i** nudi barefoot; **su due** ~**i** (*fig*) at once; **prendere** ~ (*fig*) to gain ground, catch on; **sul** ~ **di guerra** (MIL) ready for action; ~ **di porco** crowbar.

**piedis'tallo, piedes'tallo** *sm* pedestal.

**pi'ega, ghe** *sf* (*piegatura*, GEO) fold; (*di gonna*) pleat; (*di pantaloni*) crease; (*grinza*) wrinkle, crease; **prendere una brutta** ~ (*avvenimento*) to take a turn for the worse.

**pie'gare** *vt* to fold; (*braccia, gambe, testa*) to bend // *vi* to bend; ~**rsi** *vr* to bend; (*fig*): ~**rsi (a)** to yield (to), submit (to); **pieghet'tare** *vt* to pleat; **pie'ghevole** *ag* pliable, flexible; (*porta*) folding; (*fig*) yielding, docile.

**Pie'monte** *sm*: **il** ~ Piedmont.

**pi'ena** *sf vedi* pieno.

**pi'eno, a** *ag* full; (*muro, mattone*) solid // *sm* (*colmo*) height, peak; (*carico*) full load // *sf* (*di fiume*) flood, spate; (*gran folla*) crowd, throng; ~ **di** full of; **in** ~ **giorno** in broad daylight; **fare il** ~ (**di benzina**) to fill up (with petrol).

**pietà** *sf* pity; (REL) piety; **senza** ~ pitiless, merciless; **avere** ~ **di** (*compassione*) to pity, feel sorry for; (*misericordia*) to have pity o mercy on.

**pie'tanza** [pje'tantsa] *sf* dish; (*main*) course.

**pie'toso, a** *ag* (*compassionevole*) pitying, compassionate; (*che desta pietà*) pitiful.

**pi'etra** *sf* stone; ~ **preziosa** precious stone, gem; **pie'traia** *sf* (*terreno*) stony ground; **pietrifi'care** *vt* to petrify; (*fig*) to transfix, paralyze.

**'piffero** *sm* (MUS) pipe.

**pigi'ama** [pi'dʒama] *sm* pyjamas *pl*.

**'pigia 'pigia** ['pidʒa'pidʒa] *sm* crowd, press.

**pigi'are** [pi'dʒare] *vt* to press.

**pigi'one** [pi'dʒone] *sf* rent.

**pigli'are** [piʎ'ʎare] *vt* to take, grab; (*afferrare*) to catch.

**'piglio** ['piʎʎo] *sm* look, expression.

**pig'meo, a** *smf* pygmy.

**'pigna** ['pinɲa] *sf* pine cone.

**pig'nolo, a** [pin'ɲɔlo] *ag* pernickety.

**pigo'lare** *vi* to cheep, chirp.

**pi'grizia** [pi'grittsja] *sf* laziness.

**'pigro, a** *ag* lazy.

**'pila** *sf* (*catasta, di ponte*) pile; (ELETTR) battery; (*fam*: *torcia*) torch (Brit), flashlight.

**pi'lastro** sm pillar.

**'pillola** sf pill; **prendere la** ~ to be on the pill.

**pi'lone** sm (di ponte) pier; (di linea elettrica) pylon.

**pi'lota, i, e** smf/f pilot; (AUT) driver // ag inv pilot cpd; ~ **automatico** automatic pilot; **pilo'tare** vt to pilot; to drive.

**pi'mento** sm pimento, allspice.

**pinaco'teca, che** sf art gallery.

**pi'neta** sf pinewood.

**ping-'pong** [piŋ'pɔŋ] sm table tennis.

**'pingue** ag fat, corpulent.

**pingu'ino** sm (ZOOL) penguin.

**'pinna** sf fin; (di pinguino, spatola di gomma) flipper.

**'pino** sm pine (tree); **pi'nolo** sm pine kernel.

**'pinza** ['pintsa] sf pliers pl; (MED) forceps pl; (ZOOL) pincer.

**pinzette** [pin'tsette] sfpl tweezers.

**'pio, a, 'pii, 'pie** ag pious; (opere, istituzione) charitable, charity cpd.

**pi'oggia, ge** ['pjɔddʒa] sf rain; ~ **acida** acid rain.

**pi'olo** sm peg; (di scala) rung.

**piom'bare** vi to fall heavily; (gettarsi con impeto): ~ **su** to fall upon, assail // vt (dente) to fill; **piomba'tura** sf (di dente) filling.

**piom'bino** sm (sigillo) (lead) seal; (del filo a piombo) plummet; (PESCA) sinker.

**pi'ombo** sm (CHIM) lead; (sigillo) (lead) seal; (proiettile) (lead) shot; **a** ~ (cadere) straight down.

**pioni'ere, a** smf pioneer.

**pi'oppo** sm poplar.

**pi'overe** vb impers to rain // vi (fig: scendere dall'alto) to rain down; (: affluire in gran numero): ~ **in** to pour into; **pioviggi'nare** vb impers to drizzle; **pio'voso, a** ag rainy.

**pi'ovra** sf octopus.

**'pipa** sf pipe.

**pipì** sf (fam): **fare** ~ to have a wee (wee).

**pipis'trello** sm (ZOOL) bat.

**pi'ramide** sf pyramid.

**pi'rata, i** sm pirate; ~ **della strada** hit-and-run driver.

**Pire'nei** smpl: **i** ~ the Pyrenees.

**'pirico, a, ci, che** ag: **polvere** ~**a** gunpowder.

**pi'rite** sf pyrite.

**pi'rofilo, a** ag heat-resistant.

**pi'roga, ghe** sf dug-out canoe.

**pi'romane** smf/f pyromaniac; arsonist.

**pi'roscafo** sm steamer, steamship.

**pisci'are** [piʃ'ʃare] vi (fam!) to piss (!), pee (!).

**pi'scina** [piʃ'ʃina] sf (swimming) pool; (stabilimento) (swimming) baths pl.

**pi'sello** sm pea.

**piso'lino** sm nap.

**'pista** sf (traccia) track, trail; (di stadio) track; (di pattinaggio) rink; (da sci) run; (AER) runway; (di circo) ring; ~ **da ballo** dance floor.

**pis'tacchio** [pis'takkjo] sm pistachio (tree); pistachio (nut).

**pis'tola** sf pistol, gun.

**pis'tone** sm piston.

**pi'tone** sm python.

**pit'tore, 'trice** smf/f painter; **pitto'resco, a, schi, sche** ag picturesque.

**pit'tura** sf painting; **pittu'rare** vt to paint.

**più** ♦ av **1** (in maggiore quantità) more; ~ **del solito** more than usual; **in** ~ **, di** ~ more; **ne voglio di** ~ I want some more; **ci sono 3 persone in** o **di** ~ there are 3 more o extra people; ~ **o meno** more or less; **per di** ~ (inoltre) what's more, moreover

**2** (comparativo) more, aggettivo corto + ...er; ~ ... **di/che** more ... than; **lavoro** ~ **di te/Paola** I work harder than you/Paola; **è** ~ **intelligente che ricco** he's more intelligent than rich

**3** (*superlativo*) most, *aggettivo corto* + ..est; **il ~ grande/intelligente** the biggest/most intelligent; **è quello che compro ~** spesso that's the one I buy most often; **al ~ presto as soon as possible; al ~ tardi** at the latest

**4** (*negazione*): **non ... ~** no more, no longer; **non ho ~ soldi** I've got no more money, I don't have any more money; **non lavoro ~** I'm no longer working, I don't work any more; **a ~ non posso** (*gridare*) at the top of one's voice; (*correre*) as fast as one can

**5** (*MAT*) plus; **4 ~ 5 fa 9** 4 plus 5 equals 9; **~ 5 gradi** 5 degrees above freezing, plus 5

◆ *prep* plus

◆ *ag inv* **1**: **~ ... (di)** more ... (than); **~ denaro/tempo** more money/time; **~ persone di quante ci aspettassimo** more people than we expected

**2** (*numerosi, diversi*) several; **l'aspettai per ~ giorni** I waited for it for several days

◆ *sm* **1** (*la maggior parte*): **il ~ è fatto** most of it is done

**2** (*MAT*) sign

**3**: **i ~** the majority.

**piuccchepper'fetto** [pjukkepper-'fetto] *sm* (*LING*) pluperfect, past perfect.

**pi'uma** *sf* feather; **~** *sfpl* down *sg*; (*piumaggio*) plumage *sg*, feathers; **piu'maggio** *sm* plumage, feathers *pl*; **piu'mino** *sm* (*eider*)down; (*per letto*) eiderdown; (: *tipo danese*) duvet, continental quilt; (*giacca*) quilted jacket (with *goose-feather padding*); (*per cipria*) powder puff; (*per spolverare*) feather duster.

**piut'tosto** *av* rather; **~ che** (*anziché*) rather than.

**pi'vello, a** *smlf* greenhorn.

**'pizza** ['pittsa] *sf* pizza; **pizze'ria** *sf* place where pizzas are made, sold or eaten.

**pizzi'cagnolo, a** [pittsi'kaɲnolo] *smlf* specialist grocer.

**pizzi'care** [pittsi'kare] *vt* (*stringere*) to nip, pinch; (*pungere*) to sting; to bite; (*MUS*) to pluck // *vi* (*prudere*) to itch, be itchy; (*cibo*) to be hot o spicy.

**pizziche'ria** [pittsike'ria] *sf* delicatessen (shop).

**'pizzico, chi** ['pittsiko] *sm* (*pizzicotto*) pinch, nip; (*piccola quantità*) pinch, dash; (*d'insetto*) sting; bite.

**pizzi'cotto** [pittsi'kɔtto] *sm* pinch, nip.

**'pizzo** ['pittso] *sm* (*merletto*) lace; (*barbetta*) goatee beard.

**pla'care** *vt* to placate, soothe; **~rsi** *vr* to calm down.

**'placca, che** *sf* plate; (*con iscrizione*) plaque; (*anche: ~ dentaria*) (dental) plaque; **plac'care** *vt* to plate; **placcato in oro/argento** gold-/silver-plated.

**'placido, a** ['platʃido] *ag* placid, calm.

**plagi'are** [pla'dʒare] *vt* (*copiare*) to plagiarize; **'plagio** *sm* plagiarism.

**pla'nare** *vi* (*AER*) to glide.

**plane'tario, a** *ag* planetary // *sm* (*locale*) planetarium.

**'plasma** *sm* plasma.

**plas'mare** *vt* to mould, shape.

**'plastico, a, ci, che** *ag* plastic // *sm* (*rappresentazione*) relief model; (*esplosivo*): **bomba al ~** plastic bomb // *sf* (*arte*) plastic arts *pl*; (*MED*) plastic surgery; (*sostanza*) plastic.

**plasti'lina** *sf* ® plasticine ®.

**'platano** *sm* plane tree.

**pla'tea** *sf* (*TEATRO*) stalls *pl*.

**'platino** *sm* platinum.

**pla'tonico, a, ci, che** *ag* platonic *av*.

**plau'sibile** *ag* plausible.

**'plauso** *sm* (*fig*) approval.

**ple'baglia** [ple'baʎʎa] *sf* (*peg*) rabble, mob.

'plebe *sf* common people; ple'beo, a *ag* plebeian; (*volgare*) coarse, common.

ple'nario, a *ag* plenary.

pleni'lunio *sm* full moon.

'plettro *sm* plectrum.

pleu'rite *sf* pleurisy.

'plico, chi *sm* (*pacco*) parcel; in ~ a parte (*COMM*) under separate cover.

plo'tone *sm* (*MIL*) platoon; ~ d'esecuzione firing squad.

'plumbeo, a *ag* leaden.

plu'rale *ag*, *sm* plural; pluralità *sf* plurality; (*maggioranza*) majority.

plusva'lore *sm* (*ECON*) surplus.

pneu'matico, a, ci, che *ag* inflatable; pneumatic // *sm* (*AUT*) tyre (*Brit*), tire (*US*).

po' *av*, *sm vedi* poco.

PAROLA CHIAVE

'poco, a, chi, che ◆ *ag* 1 (*quantità*) little, not much; (*numero*) few, not many; ~ pane/denaro/spazio little *o* not much bread/money/space; ~che persone/idee few *o* not many people/ideas; ci vediamo tra ~ (*sottinteso: tempo*) see you soon

◆ *av* 1 (*in piccola quantità*) little, not much; (*numero limitato*) few, not many; guadagna ~ he doesn't earn much, he earns little

2 (*con ag, av*) (a) little, not very; sta ~ bene he isn't very well; è ~ più vecchia di lui she's a little *o* slightly older than him

3 (*tempo*): ~ dopo/prima shortly afterwards/before; il film dura ~ the film doesn't last very long; ci vediamo molto ~ we don't see each other very often, we hardly ever see each other

4: un po' a little, a bit; è un po' corto it's a little *o* a bit short; arriverà fra un po' he'll arrive shortly *o* in a little while

5: a dir ~ to say the least; a ~ a ~ little by little; per ~ non cadevo I

nearly fell; è una cosa da ~ it's nothing, it's of no importance; una persona da ~ a worthless person

◆ *pronome* (a) little; ~chi/che *pronome pl* (*persone*) few (people); (*cose*) few

◆ *sm* 1 little; vive del ~ che ha he lives on the little he has

2: un po' a little; un po'di zucchero a little sugar; un bel po' di denaro quite a lot of money; un po' per ciascuno a bit each.

po'dere *sm* (*AGR*) farm.

pode'roso, a *ag* powerful.

podestà *sm inv* (*nel fascismo*) podesta, mayor.

'podio *sm* dais, platform; (*MUS*) podium.

po'dismo *sm* (*SPORT*) track events *pl*.

po'ema, i *sm* poem.

poe'sia *sf* (*arte*) poetry; (*componimento*) poem.

po'eta, 'essa *sm/f* poet/poetess; po'etico, a, ci, che *ag* poetic(al).

poggi'are [pod'dʒare] *vt* to lean, rest; (*posare*) to lay, place; poggia'testa *sm inv* (*AUT*) headrest.

'poggio ['pɔddʒo] *sm* hillock, knoll.

'poi *av* then; (*alla fine*) finally, at last; e ~ (*inoltre*) and besides; questa ~ (è bella)! (*ironico*) that's a good one!

poiché (*PdO*) *cong* since, as.

'poker *sm* poker.

po'lacco, a, chi, che *ag* Polish // *sm/f* Pole.

po'lare *ag* polar.

po'lemico, a, ci, che *ag* polemic(al), controversial // *sf* controversy.

po'lenta *sf* (*CUC*) sort of thick porridge made with maize flour.

poli'clinico, ci *sm* general hospital, polyclinic.

poli'estere *sm* polyester.

'polio(mie'lite) *sf* polio(myelitis).

'polipo *sm* polyp.

polisti'rolo *sm* polystyrene.

**poli'tecnico, ci** sm postgraduate technical college.

**politiciz'zare** [politit∫id'dzare] vt to politicize.

**po'litico, a, ci, che** ag political // sm/f politician // sf politics sg; (linea di condotta) policy.

**poli'zia** [polit'tsia] sf police; ~ **giudiziaria** ≈ Criminal Investigation Department (CID) (Brit), ≈ Federal Bureau of Investigation (FBI) (US); ~ **stradale** traffic police; **polizi'esco, a, schi, sche** ag police cpd; (film, romanzo) detective cpd; **polizi'otto** sm policeman; **cane poliziotto** police dog; **donna poliziotto** policewoman.

**'polizza** ['polittsa] sf (COMM) bill; ~ **di assicurazione** insurance policy; ~ **di carico** bill of lading.

**pol'laio** sm henhouse.

**pol'lame** sm poultry.

**pol'lastro** (ZOOL) cockerel.

**'pollice** ['pollit∫e] sm thumb.

**'polline** sm pollen.

**'pollo** sm chicken.

**pol'mone** sm lung; **polmo'nite** sf pneumonia.

**'polo** sm (GEO, FISICA) pole; (gioco) polo; **il ~ sud/nord** the South/North Pole.

**Po'lonia** sf: **la ~** Poland.

**'polpa** sf flesh, pulp; (carne) lean meat.

**pol'paccio** [pol'patt∫o] sm (ANAT) calf.

**pol'petta** sf (CUC) meatball; **polpet'tone** sm (CUC) meatloaf.

**'polpo** sm octopus.

**pol'poso, a** ag fleshy.

**pol'sino** sm cuff.

**'polso** sm (ANAT) wrist; (pulsazione) pulse; (fig: forza) drive, vigour.

**pol'tiglia** [pol'tiʎʎa] sf (composto) mash, mush; (di fango e neve) slush.

**pol'trire** vi to laze about.

**pol'trona** sf armchair; (TEATRO: posto) seat in the front stalls (Brit) o orchestra (US).

**pol'trone** ag lazy, slothful.

**'polvere** sf dust; (anche: ~ **da sparo**) (gun)powder; (sostanza ridotta minutissima) powder, dust; **latte in ~** dried o powdered milk; **caffè in ~** instant coffee; **sapone in ~** soap powder; **polveri'era** sf powder magazine; **polveriz'zare** vt to pulverize; (nebulizzare) to atomize; (fig) to crush, pulverize; to smash; **polve'rone** sm thick cloud of dust; **polve'roso, a** ag dusty.

**po'mata** sf ointment, cream.

**po'mello** sm knob.

**pomeridi'ano, a** ag afternoon cpd; **nelle ore ~e** in the afternoon.

**pome'riggio** [pome'riddʒo] sm afternoon.

**'pomice** ['pomit∫e] sf pumice.

**'pomo** sm (mela) apple; (ornamentale) knob; (di sella) pommel; ~ **d'Adamo** (ANAT) Adam's apple.

**pomo'doro** sm tomato.

**'pompa** sf pump; (sfarzo) pomp (and ceremony); ~**e funebri** funeral parlour sg (Brit), undertaker's sg; **pom'pare** vt to pump; (trarre) to pump out; (gonfiare d'aria) to pump up.

**pom'pelmo** sm grapefruit.

**pompi'ere** sm fireman.

**pom'poso, a** ag pompous.

**ponde'rare** vt to ponder over, consider carefully.

**ponde'roso, a** ag (anche fig) weighty.

**po'nente** sm west.

**'ponte** sm bridge; (di nave) deck; (: anche: ~ **di comando**) bridge; (impalcatura) scaffold; **fare il ~** (fig) to take the extra day off (between 2 public holidays); ~ **aereo** airlift; ~ **interim government**; ~ **aereo** airlift; ~ **sospeso** suspension bridge.

**pon'tefice** [pon't∫efit∫e] sm (REL) pontiff.

**pontifi'care** vi (anche fig) to pontificate.

**ponti'ficio, a, ci, cie** [ponti'fit∫o] ag papal.

**popo'lano, a** *ag* popular, of the people.

**popo'lare** *ag* popular; *(quartiere, clientela)* working-class // *vt (rendere abitato)* to populate; ~**rsi** *vr* to fill with people, get crowded; **popolarità** *sf* popularity; **popolazi'one** *sf* population.

**'popolo** *sm* people; **popo'loso, a** *ag* densely populated.

**po'pone** *sm* melon.

**'poppa** *sf (di nave)* stern; *(mammella)* breast.

**pop'pare** *vt* to suck.

**poppa'toio** *sm* (feeding) bottle.

**porcel'lana** [portʃel'lana] *sf* porcelain, china; piece of china.

**porcel'lino, a** [portʃel'lino] *sm/f* piglet.

**porche'ria** [porke'ria] *sf* filth, muck; *(fig: oscenità)* obscenity; *(: azione disonesta)* dirty trick; *(: cosa mal fatta)* rubbish.

**por'cile** [por'tʃile] *sm* pigsty.

**por'cino, a** [por'tʃino] *ag* of pigs, pork *cpd* // *sm (fungo)* type of edible mushroom.

**'porco, ci** *sm* pig; *(carne)* pork.

**porcos'pino** *sm* porcupine.

**'porgere** ['pɔrdʒere] *vt* to hand, give; *(tendere)* to hold out.

**pornogra'fia** *sf* pornography; **porno'grafico, a, ci, che** *ag* pornographic.

**'poro** *sm* pore; **po'roso, a** *ag* porous.

**'porpora** *sf* purple.

**'porre** *vt (mettere)* to put; *(collocare)* to place; *(posare)* to lay (down), put (down); *(fig: supporre)*: **poniamo (il caso) che ...** let's suppose that ...; **porsi** *vr (mettersi)*: **porsi a sedere/in cammino** to sit down/set off; ~ **una domanda a qn** to ask sb a question, put a question to sb.

**'porro** *sm (BOT)* leek; *(MED)* wart.

**'porta** *sf* door; *(SPORT)* goal; ~**e chiuse** *sfpl (di città)* gates; **a** ~**e chiuse** *(DIR)* in camera.

**'porta...** *prefisso*: **portaba'gagli** *sm inv (facchino)* porter; *(AUT, FERR)* luggage rack; **portabandi'era** *sm inv* standard bearer; **porta'cenere** *sm inv* ashtray; **portachi'avi** *sm inv* keyring; **porta'cipria** *sm inv* powder compact; **porta'erei** *sf inv (nave)* aircraft carrier // *sm inv (aereo)* aircraft transporter; **portafi'nestra, pl portefi'nestre** *sf* French window; **porta'foglio** *sm (busta)* wallet; *(cartella)* briefcase; *(POL, BORSA)* portfolio; **portafor'tuna** *sm inv* lucky charm; mascot; **portagi'oie** *sm inv*, **portagioi'elli** *sm inv* jewellery box.

**porta'lettere** *sm/f inv* postman/woman *(Brit)*, mailman/woman *(US)*.

**porta'mento** *sm* carriage, bearing.

**portamo'nete** *sm inv* purse.

**por'tante** *ag (muro etc)* supporting, load-bearing.

**portan'tina** *sf* sedan chair; *(per ammalati)* stretcher.

**por'tare** *vt (sostenere, sorreggere: peso, bambino, pacco)* to carry; *(indossare: abito, occhiali)* to wear; *(: capelli lunghi)* to have; *(avere: nome, titolo)* to have, bear; *(recare)*: ~ **qc a qn** to take (o bring) sth to sb; *(fig: sentimenti)* to bear; ~**rsi** *vr (recarsi)* to go; ~ **avanti** *(discorso, idea)* to pursue; ~ **via** to take away; *(rubare)* to take; ~ **i bambini a spasso** to take the children for a walk; ~ **fortuna** to bring good luck.

**portasi'garette** *sm inv* cigarette case.

**por'tata** *sf (vivanda)* course; *(AUT) carrying (o loading)* capacity; *(di arma)* range; *(volume d'acqua)* (rate of) flow; *(fig: limite)* scope, capability; *(: importanza)* impact, import; **alla** ~ **di tutti** *(conoscenza)* within everybody's capabilities; *(prezzo)* within everybody's means; **a/fuori** ~ **(di)** within/out of reach (of); **a** ~ **di mano** within (arm's) reach.

**por'tatile** *ag* portable.

**por'tato, a** *ag* (*incline*): ~ **a** inclined *o* apt to.

**porta'tore, 'trice** *sm/f* (*anche* COMM) bearer; (MED) carrier.

**portau'ovo** *sm inv* eggcup.

**porta'voce** [porta'votʃe] *sm/f inv* spokesman/woman.

**por'tento** *sm* wonder, marvel.

**'portico, ci** *sm* portico.

**porti'era** *sf* (AUT) door.

**porti'ere** *sm* (*portinaio*) concierge, caretaker; (*di hotel*) porter; (*nel calcio*) goalkeeper.

**porti'naio, a** *sm/f* concierge, caretaker.

**portine'ria** *sf* caretaker's lodge.

**'porto, a** *pp di* **porgere** ♦ *sm* (NAUT) harbour, port; (*spesa di trasporto*) carriage ♦ *sm inv* port (*wine*); ~ **d'armi** (*documento*) gun licence.

**Porto'gallo** *sm*: **il** ~ Portugal; **porto'ghese** *ag, sm/f, sm* Portuguese *inv*.

**por'tone** *sm* main entrance, main door.

**portu'ale** *ag* harbour *cpd*, port *cpd* ♦ *sm* dock worker.

**porzi'one** [por'tsjone] *sf* portion, share; (*di cibo*) portion, helping.

**'posa** *sf* (FOT) exposure; (*atteggiamento, di modello*) pose.

**po'sare** *vt* to put (down), lay (down) ♦ *vi* (*ponte, edificio, teoria*): ~ **su** to rest on; (FOT, *atteggiarsi*) to pose; ~**rsi** *vr* (*aereo*) to land; (*uccello*) to alight; (*sguardo*) to settle.

**po'sata** *sf* piece of cutlery; ~**e** *sfpl* cutlery *sg*.

**po'sato, a** *ag* serious.

**pos'critto** *sm* postscript.

**posi'tivo, a** *ag* positive.

**posizi'one** [pozit'tsjone] *sf* position; **prendere** ~ (*fig*) to take a stand; **luci di** ~ (AUT) sidelights.

**posolo'gia, 'gie** [pozolo'dʒia] *sf* dosage, directions *pl* for use.

**pos'porre** *vt* to place after; (*differire*) to postpone, defer; **pos'posto,**

**a** *pp di* **posporre**.

**posse'dere** *vt* to own, possess; (*qualità, virtù*) to have, possess; (*conoscere a fondo: lingua etc*) to have a thorough knowledge of; (*sog: ira etc*) to possess; **possedi'mento** *sm* possession.

**posses'sivo, a** *ag* possessive.

**pos'sesso** *sm* ownership *q*; possession.

**posses'sore** *sm* owner.

**pos'sibile** *ag* possible ♦ *sm*: **fare tutto il** ~ to do everything possible; **nei limiti del** ~ as far as possible; **al più tardi** ~ as late as possible; **possibilità** *sf inv* possibility ♦ *sfpl* (*mezzi*) means; **aver la possibilità di fare** to be in a position to do; to have the opportunity to do.

**possi'dente** *sm/f* landowner.

**'posta** *sf* (*servizio*) post, postal service; (*corrispondenza*) post, mail; (*ufficio postale*) post office; (*nei giochi d'azzardo*) stake; ~**e** *sfpl* (*amministrazione*) post office; ~ **aerea** airmail; **ministro delle P~e e Telecomunicazioni** Postmaster General; **posta'giro** *sm* post office cheque, postal giro (Brit); **pos'tale** *ag* postal, post office *cpd*.

**post'bellico, a, ci, che** *ag* postwar.

**posteggi'are** [posted'dʒare] *vt, vi* to park; **pos'teggio** *sm* car park (Brit), parking lot (US); (*di taxi*) rank (Brit), stand (US).

**postelegra'fonico, a, ci, che** *ag* postal and telecommunications *cpd*.

**posteri'ore** *ag* (*dietro*) back; (*dopo*) later ♦ *sm* (*fam: sedere*) behind.

**pos'ticcio, a, ci, ce** [pos'tittʃo] *ag* false ♦ *sm* hairpiece.

**postici'pare** [postitʃi'pare] *vt* to defer, postpone.

**pos'tilla** *sf* marginal note.

**pos'tino** *sm* postman (Brit), mailman (US).

**'posto, a** *pp di* **porre** ♦ *sm* (*sito, posizione*) place; (*impiego*) job; (*spazio libero*) room, space; (*di* _parcheggio_) space; (_sedile: al teatro, in treno etc_) seat; (MIL) post; **a ~** (_in ordine_) in place, tidy; (_fig_) settled; (: _persona_) reliable; **al ~ di** in place of; **sul ~** on the spot; **mettere a ~** to tidy (up), put in order; (_faccende_) to straighten out; **~ di blocco** roadblock; **~ di polizia** police station.

**pos'tribolo** _sm_ brothel.

**'postumo, a** _ag_ posthumous; (_tardivo_) belated; **~i** _smpl_ (_conseguenze_) after-effects, consequences.

**po'tabile** _ag_ drinkable; **acqua ~** drinking water.

**po'tare** _vt_ to prune.

**po'tassio** _sm_ potassium.

**po'tente** _ag_ (_nazione_) strong, powerful; (_veleno, farmaco_) potent, strong; **po'tenza** _sf_ power; (_forza_) strength.

**potenzi'ale** [poten'tsjale] _ag, sm_ potential.

_PAROLA CHIAVE_

**po'tere** ◆ _sm_ power; **al ~** (_partito etc_) in power; **~ d'acquisto** purchasing power

◆ _vb ausiliare_ **1** (_essere in grado di_) can, be able to; **non ha potuto ripararlo** he couldn't _o_ he wasn't able to repair it; **non è potuto venire** he couldn't _o_ he wasn't able to come; **spiacente di non poter aiutare** sorry not to be able to help **2** (_avere il permesso_) can, may, be allowed to; **posso entrare?** can _o_ may I come in?; **si può sapere dove sei stato?** where on earth have you been?

**3** (_eventualità_) may, might, could; **potrebbe essere vero** it might _o_ could be true; **può aver avuto un incidente** he may _o_ might _o_ could have had an accident; **può darsi** perhaps; **può darsi o essere che non venga** he may _o_ might not come **4** (_augurio_): **potessi almeno parlargli!** if only I could speak to him!

**5** (_suggerimento_): **potresti almeno**

**scusarti!** you could at least apologize!

◆ _vt_ can, be able to; **può molto per noi** he can do a lot for us; **non ne posso più** (_per stanchezza_) I'm exhausted; (_per rabbia_) I can't take any more.

**potestà** _sf_ (_potere_) power; (DIR) authority.

**'povero, a** _ag_ poor; (_disadorno_) plain, bare // _sm/f_ poor man/woman; **i ~i** the poor; **~ di** lacking in, having little; **povertà** _sf_ poverty.

**'pozza** ['pottsa] _sf_ pool.

**poz'zanghera** [pot'tsangera] _sf_ puddle.

**'pozzo** ['pottso] _sm_ well; (_cava: di carbone_) pit; (_di miniera_) shaft; **~ petrolifero** oil well.

**pran'zare** [pran'dzare] _vi_ to dine, have dinner; to lunch, have lunch.

**'pranzo** ['prandzo] _sm_ dinner; (a mezzogiorno) lunch.

**'prassi** _sf_ usual procedure.

**'pratica, che** _sf_ practice; (_esperienza_) experience; (_conoscenza_) knowledge, familiarity; (_tirocinio_) training, practice; (AMM: _affare_) matter, case; (: _incartamento_) file, dossier; **in ~** (_praticamente_) in practice; **mettere in ~** to put into practice.

**prati'cabile** _ag_ (_progetto_) practicable, feasible; (_luogo_) passable, practicable.

**prati'cante** _sm/f_ apprentice, trainee; (REL) regular churchgoer.

**prati'care** _vt_ to practise; (SPORT: _tennis etc_) to play; (: _nuoto, scherma etc_) to go in for; (_eseguire: apertura, buco_) to make; **~ uno sconto** to give a discount.

**'pratico, a, ci, che** _ag_ practical; **~ di** (_esperto_) experienced _o_ skilled in; (_familiare_) familiar with.

**'prato** _sm_ meadow; (_di giardino_) lawn.

**preav'viso** _sm_ notice; **telefonata con ~** personal _o_ person to person call.

**pre'cario, a** ag precarious; (INS) temporary.

**precauzi'one** [prekaut'tsjone] sf caution, care; (misura) precaution.

**prece'dente** [pretʃe'dɛnte] ag previous o sm precedent; **il discorso/ film** ~ the previous o preceding speech/film; **senza** ~**i** unprecedented; ~**i penali** criminal record sg; **prece'denza** sf priority, precedence; (AUT) right of way.

**pre'cedere** [pre'tʃɛdere] vt to precede, go (o come) before.

**pre'cetto** [pre'tʃɛtto] sm precept; (MIL) call-up notice.

**precet'tore** [pretʃet'tore] sm (private) tutor.

**precipi'tare** [pretʃipi'tare] vi (cadere) to fall headlong; (fig: situazione) to get out of control o vt (gettare dall'alto in basso) to hurl, fling; (fig: affrettare) to rush; ~**rsi** vr (gettarsi) to hurl o fling o.s.; (affrettarsi) to rush; **precipitazi'one** sf (METEOR) precipitation; (fig) haste; **precipi'toso, a** ag (caduta, fuga) headlong; (fig: avventato) rash, reckless; (: affrettato) hasty, rushed.

**preci'pizio** [pretʃi'pittsjo] sm precipice; **a** ~ (fig: correre) headlong.

**preci'sare** [pretʃi'zare] vt to state, specify; (spiegare) to explain (in detail).

**precisi'one** [pretʃi'zjone] sf precision; accuracy.

**pre'ciso, a** [pre'tʃizo] ag (esatto) precise; (accurato) accurate, precise; (deciso: idee) precise, definite; (uguale): **2 vestiti** ~**i 2 dresses exactly the same; sono le 9** ~**e** it's exactly 9 o'clock.

**pre'cludere** vt to block, obstruct; **pre'cluso, a** pp di **precludere**.

**pre'coce** [pre'kɔtʃe] ag early; (bambino) precocious; (vecchiaia) premature.

**precon'cetto** [prekon'tʃetto] sm preconceived idea, prejudice.

**precur'sore** sm forerunner, precursor.

'**preda** sf (bottino) booty; (animale, fig) prey; **essere** ~ **di** to fall prey to; **essere in** ~ **a** to be prey to; **preda'tore** sm predator.

**predeces'sore, a** [predetʃes'sore] sm/f predecessor.

**predesti'nare** vt to predestine.

**pre'detto, a** pp di **predire**.

'**predica, che** [ʃ] sf sermon; (fig) lecture, talking-to.

**predi'care** vt, vi to preach.

**predi'cato** sm (LING) predicate.

**predi'letto, a** pp di **prediligere** // ag, sm/f favourite.

**predilezi'one** [predilet'tsjone] sf fondness, partiality; **avere una** ~ **per qc/qn** to be partial to sth/fond of sb.

**predi'ligere** [predi'lidʒere] vt to prefer, have a preference for.

**pre'dire** vt to foretell, predict.

**predis'porre** vt to get ready, prepare; ~ **qn a qc** to predispose sb to sth; **predis'posto, a** pp di **predisporre**.

**predizi'one** [predit'tsjone] sf prediction.

**predomi'nare** vi to predominate; **predo'minio** sm predominance; supremacy.

**prefabbri'cato, a** ag (EDIL) prefabricated.

**prefazi'one** [prefat'tsjone] sf preface, foreword.

**prefe'renza** [prefe'rɛntsa] sf preference; **preferenzi'ale** ag preferential; **corsia** ~ bus and taxi lane.

**prefe'rire** vt to prefer, like better; ~ **il caffè al tè** to prefer coffee to tea, like coffee better than tea.

**pre'fetto** sm prefect; **prefet'tura** sf prefecture.

**pre'figgersi** [pre'fiddʒersi] vr: ~**rsi uno scopo** to set o.s. a goal.

**pre'fisso, a** pp di **prefiggere** // sm (LING) prefix; (TEL) dialling (Brit) o dial (US) code.

**pre'gare** vi to pray // vt (REL) to

pray to; (*implorare*) to beg; (*chiedere*): ~ **qn di fare** to ask sb to do; **farsi** ~ to need coaxing *o* persuading.

**pre'gevole** [pre'dʒevole] *ag* valuable.

**preghi'era** [pre'gjɛra] *sf* (REL) prayer; (*domanda*) request.

**pregi'ato, a** [pre'dʒato] *ag* (*di valore*) valuable; **vino** ~ vintage wine.

**'pregio** ['prɛdʒo] *sm* (*stima*) esteem, regard; (*qualità*) (good) quality, merit; (*valore*) value, worth.

**pregiudi'care** [predʒudi'kare] *vt* to prejudice, harm, be detrimental to; **pregiudi'cato, a** *smf* (DIR) previous offender.

**pregiu'dizio** [predʒu'dittsjo] *sm* (*idea errata*) prejudice; (*danno*) harm *q*.

**'pregno, a** ['preɲɲo] *ag* (*gravido*) pregnant; (*saturo*): ~ **di** full of, saturated with.

**'prego** *escl* (*a chi ringrazia*) don't mention it!; (*invitando qn ad accomodarsi*) please sit down!; (*invitando qn ad andare prima*) after you!

**pregus'tare** *vt* to look forward to.

**preis'torico, a, ci, che** *ag* prehistoric.

**pre'lato** *sm* prelate.

**prele'vare** *vt* (*denaro*) to withdraw; (*campione*) to take; (*sog: polizia*) to take, capture.

**preli'evo** *sm* (MED): **fare un** ~ (**di**) to take a sample (of).

**prelimi'nare** *ag* preliminary; ~**i** *smpl* preliminary talks; preliminaries.

**pre'ludio** *sm* prelude.

**pré-ma'man** [prema'mã] *sm inv* maternity dress.

**prema'turo, a** *ag* premature.

**premedi'tazi'one** [premeditat'tsjone] *sf* (DIR) premeditation; **con** ~ *ag* premeditated // *av* with intent.

**'premere** *vt* to press // *vi*: ~ **su** to

press down on; (*fig*) to put pressure on; ~ **a** (*fig: importare*) to matter to.

**pre'messo, a** *pp di* **premettere** // *sf* introductory statement, introduction.

**pre'mettere** *vt* to put before; (*dire prima*) to start by saying, state first.

**premi'are** *vt* to give a prize to; (*fig: merito, onestà*) to reward.

**'premio** *sm* prize; (*ricompensa*) reward; (COMM) premium; (AMM: *indennità*) bonus.

**premu'nirsi** *vr*: ~ **di** to provide o.s. with; ~ **contro** to protect o.s. from, guard o.s. against.

**pre'mura** *sf* (*fretta*) haste, hurry; (*riguardo*) attention, care; **premu'roso, a** *ag* thoughtful, considerate.

**prena'tale** *ag* antenatal.

**'prendere** *vt* to take; (*andare a prendere*) to get, fetch; (*ottenere*) to get; (*guadagnare*) to get, earn; (*catturare: ladro, pesce*) to catch; (*collaboratore, dipendente*) to take on; (*passeggero*) to pick up; (*chiedere: somma, prezzo*) to charge, ask; (*trattare: persona*) to handle // *vi* (*colla, cemento*) to set; (*pianta*) to take; (*fuoco: nel camino*) to catch; (*voltare*): ~ **a destra** to turn (to the) right; ~**rsi** *vr* (*azzuffarsi*): ~**rsi a pugni** to come to blows; **prendi qualcosa?** (*da bere, da mangiare*) would you like something to eat (*o* drink)?; **prendo un caffè** I'll have a coffee; ~ **a fare qc** to start doing sth; ~ **qn/qc per** (*scambiare*) to take sb/sth for; ~ **fuoco** to catch fire; ~ **parte a** to take part in; ~**rsi cura di qn/qc** to look after sb/sth; **prendersela** (*adirarsi*) to get annoyed; (*preoccuparsi*) to get upset, worry.

**prendi'sole** *sm inv* sundress.

**preno'tare** *vt* to book, reserve; **prenotazi'one** *sf* booking, reservation.

**preoccu'pare** *vt* to worry; to preoccupy; ~**rsi** *vr*: ~**rsi di qn/qc** to worry about sb/sth; ~**rsi per qn** to be anxious for sb; **preoccupazi'one** *sf* worry, anxiety.

**prepa'rare** *vt* to prepare; (*esame, concorso*) to prepare for; ~**rsi** *vr* (*vestirsi*) to get ready; ~**rsi a qc/a fare** to get ready *o* prepare (o.s.) for sth/to do; ~ **da mangiare** to prepare a meal; **prepara'tivi** *smpl* preparations; **prepa'rato** *sm* (*prodotto*) preparation; **preparazi'one** *sf* preparation.

**preposizi'one** [prepozit'tsjone] *sf* (*LING*) preposition.

**prepo'tente** *ag* (*persona*) domineering, arrogant; (*bisogno, desiderio*) overwhelming, pressing // *sm/f* bully; **prepo'tenza** *sf* arrogance; arrogant behaviour.

'**presa** *sf* taking *q*; catching *q*; (*di città*) capture; (*indurimento: di cemento*) setting; (*appiglio, SPORT*) hold; (*di acqua, gas*) (supply) point; (*ELETTR*): ~ (**di corrente**) socket; (: *al muro*) point; (*piccola quantità: di sale etc*) pinch; (*CARTE*) trick; **far** ~ (*colla*) to set; **far** ~ **sul pubblico** to catch the public's imagination; ~ **d'aria** air inlet; **essere alle** ~**e con qc** (*fig*) to be struggling with sth.

**pre'sagio** [pre'zadʒo] *sm* omen.

**presa'gire** [preza'dʒire] *vt* to foresee.

'**presbite** *ag* long-sighted.

**presbi'terio** *sm* presbytery.

**pre'scindere** [preʃ'ʃindere] *vi*: ~ **da** to leave out of consideration; **a** ~ **da** apart from.

**pres'critto, a** *pp di* **prescrivere**.

**pres'crivere** *vt* to prescribe; **prescrizi'one** *sf* (*MED, DIR*) prescription; (*norma*) rule, regulation.

**presen'tare** *vt* to present; (*far conoscere*): ~ **qn** (**a**) to introduce sb (to); (*AMM: inoltrare*) to submit; ~**rsi** *vr* (*recarsi, farsi vedere*) to present o.s., appear; (*farsi conoscere*) to introduce o.s.; (*occasione*) to arise; ~**rsi come**

**candidato** (*POL*) to stand as a candidate; ~**rsi bene/male** to have a good/poor appearance; **presentazi'one** *sf* presentation; introduction.

**pre'sente** *ag* present; (*questo*) this // *sm* present; **i** ~**i** those present; **aver** ~ **qc/qn** to remember sth/sb.

**presenti'mento** *sm* premonition.

**pre'senza** [pre'zɛntsa] *sf* presence; (*aspetto esteriore*) appearance; ~ **di spirito** presence of mind.

**pre'sepio, pre'sepe** *sm* crib.

**preser'vare** *vt* to protect; to save; **preserva'tivo** *sm* sheath, condom.

'**preside** *sm/f* (*INS*) head (teacher) (*Brit*), principal (*US*); (*di facoltà universitaria*) dean.

**presi'dente** *sm* (*POL*) president; (*di assemblea, COMM*) chairman; ~ **del consiglio** prime minister; **presiden'tessa** *sf* president; president's wife; chairwoman; **presi'denza** *sf* presidency; office of president; chairmanship.

**presidi'are** *vt* to garrison; **pre'sidio** *sm* garrison.

**presi'edere** *vt* to preside over // *vi*: ~ **a** to direct, be in charge of.

'**preso, a** *pp di* **prendere**.

'**pressa** *sf* (*TECN*) press.

**pressap'poco** *av* about, roughly.

**pres'sare** *vt* to press.

**pressi'one** *sf* pressure; **far** ~ **su qn** to put pressure on sb; ~ **sanguigna** blood pressure.

'**presso** *av* (*vicino*) nearby, close at hand // *prep* (*vicino a*) near; (*accanto a*) beside, next to; (*in casa di*): ~ **qn** at sb's home; (*nelle lettere*) care of (*abbr* c/o); (*alle dipendenze di*): **lavora** ~ **di noi** he works for *o* with us // *smpl*: **nei** ~**i di near**, in the vicinity of.

**pressuriz'zare** [pressurid'dzare] *vt* to pressurize.

**presta'nome** *sm/f inv* (*peg*) figurehead.

**pres'tante** *ag* good-looking.

**pres'tare** *vt*: ~ (**qc a qn**) to lend

(sb sth o sth to sb); ~**rsi** vr (offrirsi): ~**rsi a fare** to offer to do; (essere adatto): ~**rsi a** to lend itself to, to be suitable for; ~ **aiuto** to lend a hand; ~ **attenzione** to pay attention; ~ **fede a qc/qn** to give credence to sth/sb; ~ **orecchio** to listen; **prestazi'one** sf (TECN, SPORT) performance; **prestazioni** sfpl (di persona: servizi) services.

**prestigia'tore, 'trice** [prestidʒa-'tore] sm/f conjurer.

**pres'tigio** [pres'tidʒo] sm (potere) prestige; (illusione): **gioco di** ~ conjuring trick.

**'prestito** sm lending q; loan; **dar in** ~ to lend; **prendere in** ~ to borrow.

**'presto** av (tra poco) soon; (in fretta) quickly; (di buon'ora) early; **a** ~ see you soon; **a fare qc** to hurry up and do sth; (non costare fatica) to have no trouble doing sth; **si fa** ~ **a criticare** it's easy to criticize.

**pre'sumere** vt to presume, assume; **pre'sunto, a** pp di **presumere**

**presuntu'oso, a** ag presumptuous.

**presunzi'one** [prezun'tsjone] sf presumption.

**presup'porre** vt to suppose; to presuppose.

**'prete** sm priest.

**preten'dente** sm/f pretender // sm (corteggiatore) suitor.

**pre'tendere** vt (esigere) to demand, require; (sostenere): ~ **che** to claim that; **pretende di aver sempre ragione** he thinks he's always right.

**pretenzi'oso, a** [preten'tsjoso] ag pretentious.

**pre'teso, a** pp di **pretendere** // sf (esigenza) claim, demand; (presunzione, sfarzo) pretentiousness; **senza** ~**e** unpretentious.

**pre'testo** sm pretext, excuse.

**pre'tore** sm magistrate.

**preva'lente** ag prevailing; **preva'lenza** sf predominance.

**preva'lere** vi to prevail; **pre'valso, a** pp di **prevalere**.

**preve'dere** vt (indovinare) to foresee; (presagire) to foretell; (considerare) to make provision for.

**preve'nire** vt (anticipare) to forestall; to anticipate; (evitare) to avoid, prevent; (avvertire): ~ **qn (di)** to warn sb (of); to inform sb (of).

**preven'tivo, a** ag preventive // sm (COMM) estimate.

**prevenzi'one** [preven'tsjone] sf prevention; (preconcetto) prejudice.

**previ'dente** ag showing foresight; prudent; **previ'denza** sf foresight; **istituto di previdenza** provident institution; **previdenza sociale** social security (Brit), welfare (US).

**previsi'one** sf forecast, prediction; ~**i meteorologiche** o **del tempo** weather forecast sg.

**pre'visto, a** pp di **prevedere** // sm: **più/meno del** ~ more/less than expected.

**prezi'oso, a** [pret'tsjoso] ag precious; invaluable // sm jewel; valuable.

**prez'zemolo** [pret'tsemolo] sm parsley.

**'prezzo** ['prettso] sm price; ~ **d'acquisto/di vendita** buying/selling price.

**prigi'one** [pri'dʒone] sf prison; **prigio'nia** sf imprisonment; **prigioni'ero, a** ag captive // sm/f prisoner.

**'prima** sf vedi **primo** // av before; (in anticipo) in advance, beforehand; (per l'addietro) at one time, formerly; (più presto) sooner, earlier; (in primo luogo) first // cong: ~ **di fare/che parta** before doing/he leaves; ~ **di** prep before; ~ **o poi** sooner or later.

**pri'mario, a** ag (primo); (principale) chief, leading, primary // sm (MED) chief physician.

**pri'mate** sm (REL, ZOOL) primate.

**pri'mato** sm supremacy; (SPORT) record.

**prima'vera** sf spring; **primave'rile**

*ag* spring *cpd*.

**primeggi'are** [primed'dʒare] *vi* to excel, be one of the best.

**primi'tivo, a** *ag* primitive; original.

**pri'mizie** [pri'mittsje] *sfpl* early produce *sg*.

**'primo, a** *ag* first; (*fig*) initial; basic; prime // *smf* first (one) // *sm* (*CUC*) first course; (*in date*) il ~ luglio the first of July // *sf* (*TEATRO*) first night; (*CINEMA*) première; (*AUT*) first (gear); **le ~e ore del mattino** the early hours of the morning; **ai ~i di maggio** at the beginning of May; **viaggiare in ~a** to travel first-class; **in ~ luogo** first of all, in the first place; **di prim'ordine** *o* **~a qualità** first-class, first-rate; **in un ~ tempo** at first; **~a donna** leading lady; (*di opera lirica*) prima donna.

**primo'genito, a** [primo'dʒɛnito] *ag, smf* firstborn.

**primordi'ale** *ag* primordial.

**'primula** *sf* primrose.

**princi'pale** [printʃi'pale] *ag* main, principal // *sm* manager, boss.

**princi'pato** [printʃi'pato] *sm* principality.

**'principe** ['printʃipe] *sm* prince; ~ **ereditario** crown prince; **princi'pessa** *sf* princess.

**principi'ante** [printʃi'pjante] *smf* beginner.

**prin'cipio** [prin'tʃipjo] *sm* (*inizio*) beginning, start; (*origine*) origin, cause; (*concetto, norma*) principle; **al** *o* **in ~ at first**; **per ~ on** principle.

**pri'ore** *sm* (*REL*) prior.

**priorità** *sf* priority.

**'prisma, i** *sm* prism.

**pri'vare** *vt*: ~ **qn di** to deprive sb of; **~rsi di** to go *o* do without.

**priva'tiva** *sf* (*ECON*) monopoly.

**pri'vato, a** *ag* private // *smf* private citizen; **in ~** in private.

**privazi'one** [privat'tsjone] *sf* privation, hardship.

**privilegi'are** [privile'dʒare] *vt* to

grant a privilege to.

**privi'legio** [privi'lɛdʒo] *sm* privilege.

**'privo, a** *ag*: ~ **di** without, lacking.

**pro** *prep* for, on behalf of // *sm inv* (*utilità*) advantage, benefit; **a che ~?** what's the use?; **il ~ e il contro** the pros and cons.

**pro'babile** *ag* probable, likely; **probabilità** *sf inv* probability.

**pro'blema, i** *sm* problem.

**pro'boscide** [pro'bɔʃʃide] *sf* (*di elefante*) trunk.

**procacci'are** [prokat'tʃare] *vt* to get, obtain.

**pro'cedere** [pro'tʃedere] *vi* to proceed; (*comportarsi*) to behave; (*iniziare*): ~ **a** to start; ~ **contro** (*DIR*) to start legal proceedings against; **procedi'mento** *sm* (*modo di condurre*) procedure; (*di avvenimenti*) course; (*TECN*) process; **procedimento penale** (*DIR*) criminal proceedings; **proce'dura** *sf* (*DIR*) procedure.

**proces'sare** [protʃes'sare] *vt* (*DIR*) to try.

**processi'one** [protʃes'sjone] *sf* procession.

**pro'cesso** [pro'tʃɛsso] *sm* (*DIR*) trial; proceedings *pl*; (*metodo*) process.

**pro'cinto** [pro'tʃinto] *sm*: **in ~ di** fare about to do, on the point of doing.

**pro'clama, i** *sm* proclamation.

**procla'mare** *vt* to proclaim.

**procre'are** *vt* to procreate.

**pro'cura** *sf* (*DIR*) proxy; power of attorney; (*ufficio*) attorney's office.

**procu'rare** *vt*: ~ **qc a qn** (*fornire*) to get *o* obtain sth for sb; (*causare*: *noie etc*) to bring *o* give sb sth.

**procura'tore, 'trice** *smf* (*DIR*) ≈ solicitor; (: *chi ha la procura*) attorney, proxy; ~ **generale** (*in corte d'appello*) public prosecutor; (*in corte di cassazione*) Attorney General; ~ **della Repubblica** (*in corte d'assise, tribunale*) public prosecutor.

**prodi'gare** vt to be lavish with; ~rsi per qn to do all one can for sb.

**pro'digio** [pro'did3o] sm marvel, wonder; (persona) prodigy; **prodi-gi'oso, a** ag prodigious; phenomenal.

**'prodigo, a, ghi, ghe** ag lavish, extravagant.

**pro'dotto, a** pp di **produrre** // sm product; ~i **agricoli** farm produce sg.

**pro'durre** vt to produce; **produt-tività** sf productivity; **produt'tivo, a** ag productive; **produt'tore, 'trice** smf producer; **produzi'one** sf production; (rendimento) output.

**pro'emio** sm introduction, preface.

**Prof.** abbr (= professore) Prof.

**profa'nare** vt to desecrate.

**pro'fano, a** ag (mondano) secular; profane; (sacrilego) profane.

**profe'rire** vt to utter.

**profes'sare** vt to profess; (medicina etc) to practise.

**professio'nale** ag professional.

**professi'one** sf profession; **profes-sio'nista, i, e** smf professional.

**profes'sore, 'essa** smf (INS) teacher; (: di università) lecturer; (: titolare di cattedra) professor.

**pro'feta, i** sm prophet; **profe'zia** sf prophecy.

**pro'ficuo, a** ag useful, profitable.

**profi'lare** vt to outline; (ornare: vestito) to edge; ~rsi vr to stand out, be silhouetted; (: to loom up.

**pro'filo** sm profile; (breve de-scrizione) sketch, outline; **di** ~ in profile.

**profit'tare** vi: ~ **di** (trarre profitto) to profit by; (approfittare) to take advantage of.

**pro'fitto** sm advantage, profit, benefit; (fig: progresso) progress; (COMM) profit.

**profondità** sf inv depth.

**pro'fondo, a** ag deep; (rancore, meditazione) profound // sm depth (gen pl), bottom; ~ 8 metri 8 metres deep.

**'profugo, a, ghi, ghe** smf refugee.

**profu'mare** vt to perfume // vi to be fragrant; ~rsi vr to put on perfume o scent.

**profume'ria** sf perfumery; (negozio) perfume shop.

**pro'fumo** sm (prodotto) perfume, scent; (fragranza) scent, fragrance.

**profusi'one** sf profusion; **a** ~ in plenty.

**proget'tare** [prod3et'tare] vt to plan; (TECN: edificio) to plan, design; **pro'getto** sm plan; (idea) plan, project; **progetto di legge** bill.

**pro'gramma, i** sm programme; (TV, RADIO) programmes pl; (INS) syllabus, curriculum; (INFORM) program; **program'mare** vt (TV, RADIO) to put on; (INFORM) to program; (ECON) to plan; **pro-gramma'tore, 'trice** smf (IN-FORM) computer programmer.

**progre'dire** vi to progress, make progress.

**progres'sivo, a** ag progressive.

**pro'gresso** sm progress q; fare ~i to make progress.

**proi'bire** vt to forbid, prohibit; **proibi'tivo, a** ag prohibitive; **proibizi'one** sf prohibition.

**proiet'tare** vt (gen, GEOM, CINEMA) to project; (: presentare) to show, screen; (luce, ombra) to throw, cast, project; **proi'ettile** sm projectile, bullet (o shell etc); **proiet'tore** sm (CINEMA) projec-tor; (AUT) headlamp; (MIL) search-light; **proiezi'one** sf (CINEMA) projection; showing.

**'prole** sf children pl, offspring.

**prole'tario, a** sm, ag proletarian.

**prolife'rare** vi (fig) to proliferate.

**pro'lisso, a** ag verbose.

**'prologo, ghi** sm prologue.

**pro'lunga, ghe** sf (di cavo elettrico etc) extension.

**prolun'gare** vt (discorso, attesa) to prolong; (linea, termine) to extend.

**prome'moria** sm inv memorandum.

**pro'messa** sf promise.

**pro'messo, a** *pp di* **promettere**.

**pro'mettere** *vt* to promise // *vi* to be *o* look promising; ~ **a qn di fare** to promise sb that one will do.

**promi'nente** *ag* prominent.

**promiscuità** *sf* promiscuousness.

**promon'torio** *sm* promontory, headland.

**pro'mosso, a** *pp di* **promuovere**.

**promo'tore, trice** *smf* promoter, organizer.

**promozi'one** [promot'tsjone] *sf* promotion.

**promul'gare** *vt* to promulgate.

**promu'overe** *vt* to promote.

**proni'pote** *smf* (*di nonni*) great-grandchild, great-grandson/grand-daughter; (*di zii*) great-nephew/niece; ~**i** *smpl* (*discendenti*) descendants.

**pro'nome** *sm* (LING) pronoun.

**pron'tezza** [pron'tettsa] *sf* readiness; quickness, promptness.

**'pronto, a** *ag* ready; (*rapido*) fast, quick, prompt; ~**!** (TEL) hello!; ~ **all'ira** quick-tempered; ~ **soccorso** first aid.

**prontu'ario** *sm* manual, handbook.

**pro'nuncia** [pro'nuntʃa] *etc* = **pronunzia** *etc*.

**pro'nunzia** [pro'nuntsja] *sf* pronunciation; **pronunzi'are** *vt* (*parola, sentenza*) to pronounce; (*dire*) to utter; (*discorso*) to deliver; **pronunziarsi** *vr* to declare one's opinion; **pronunzi'ato, a** *ag* (*spiccato*) pronounced, marked; (*sporgente*) prominent.

**propa'ganda** *sf* propaganda.

**propa'gare** *vt* (*notizia, malattia*) to spread; (REL, BIOL) to propagate; ~**rsi** *vr* to spread; (BIOL) to propagate; (FISICA) to be propagated.

**pro'pendere** *vi*: ~ **per** to favour, lean towards; **propensi'one** *sf* inclination, propensity; **pro'penso, a** *pp di* **propendere**.

**propi'nare** *vt* to administer.

**pro'pizio, a** [pro'pittsjo] *ag* favour-able.

**pro'porre** *vt* (*suggerire*): ~ **qc** (a **qn**) to suggest sth (to sb); (*candidato*) to put forward; (*legge, brindisi*) to propose; ~ **di fare** to suggest *o* propose doing; **proporsi di fare** to propose *o* intend to do; **proporsi una meta** to set o.s. a goal.

**proporzio'nale** [proportsjo'nale] *ag* proportional.

**proporzio'nare** [proportsjo'nare] *vt*: ~ **qc a** to proportion *o* adjust sth to.

**proporzi'one** [propor'tsjone] *sf* proportion; **in** ~ **a** in proportion to.

**pro'posito** *sm* (*intenzione*) intention, aim; (*argomento*) subject, matter; **a** ~ **di** regarding, with regard to; **di** ~ (*apposta*) deliberately, on purpose; **a** ~ **by the way; capitare a** ~ (*cosa, persona*) to turn up at the right time.

**proposizi'one** [propozit'tsjone] *sf* (LING) clause; (: *periodo*) sentence.

**pro'posto, a** *pp di* **proporre** // *sf* proposal; (*suggerimento*) suggestion; ~**a di legge** bill.

**proprietà** *sf inv* (*ciò che si possiede*) property *gen q*, estate; (*caratteristica*) property; (*correttezza*) correctness; **proprie'tario, a** *smf* owner; (*di albergo etc*) proprietor, owner; (*per l'inquilino*) landlord/lady.

**'proprio, a** *ag* (*possessivo*) own; (: *impersonale*) one's; (*esatto*) exact, correct, proper; (*senso, significato*) literal; (LING: *nome*) proper; (*particolare*): ~ **di** characteristic of, peculiar to // *av* (*precisamente*) just, exactly; (*davvero*) really; (*affatto*): **non ... ~ not ... at all; l'ha visto con i (suoi) ~i occhi** he saw it with his own eyes.

**prora** *sf* (NAUT) bow(s *pl*), prow.

**'proroga, ghe** *sf* extension; postponement; **proro'gare** *vt* to extend; (*differire*) to postpone, defer.

**pro'rompere** *vi* to burst out; **pro'rotto, a** *pp di* **prorompere**.

'**prosa** sf prose; **pro'saico, a, ci, che** ag (fig) prosaic, mundane.

**pro'sciogliere** [proʃʃɔλλere] vt to release; (DIR) to acquit; **pro-sci'olto, a** pp di **prosciogliere**.

**prosciu'gare** [proʃʃu'gare] vt (terreni) to drain, reclaim; ~rsi vr to dry up.

**prosci'utto** [proʃ'ʃutto] sm ham.

**prosegui'mento** sm continuation; **buon** ~! all the best!; (a chi viaggia) enjoy the rest of your journey!

**prosegu'ire** vt to carry on with, continue // vi to carry on, go on.

**prospe'rare** vi to thrive; **pro-sperità** sf prosperity; '**prospero, a** ag (fiorente) flourishing, thriving, prosperous; **prospe'roso, a** ag (robusto) hale and hearty; (: ragazza) buxom.

**prospet'tare** vt (esporre) to point out, show; ~rsi vr to look, appear.

**prospet'tiva** sf (ARTE) perspective; (veduta) view; (fig: previsione, possibilità) prospect.

**pros'petto** sm (DISEGNO) eleva-tion; (veduta) view, prospect; (facciata) façade, front; (tabella) table; (sommario) summary.

**prospici'ente** [prospi'ʃɛnte] ag: ~ qc facing o overlooking sth.

**prossimità** sf nearness, proximity; in ~ di near (to), close to.

'**prossimo, a** ag (vicino): ~ a near (to), close to; (che viene subito dopo) next; (parente) close // sm ~ neighbour, fellow man.

**prosti'tuta** sf prostitute; **pro-stituzi'one** sf prostitution.

**pros'trare** vt (fig) to exhaust, wear out; ~rsi vr (fig) to humble o.s.

**protago'nista, i, e** smf protago-nist.

**pro'teggere** [pro'teddʒere] vt to protect.

**prote'ina** sf protein.

**pro'tendere** vt to stretch out; **pro'teso, a** pp di **protendere**.

**pro'testa** sf protest.

**protes'tante** ag, smf Protestant.

**protes'tare** vt, vi to protest; ~rsi vr: ~rsi **innocente** etc to protest one's innocence o that one is innocent etc.

**protet'tivo, a** ag protective.

**pro'tetto, a** pp di **proteggere**.

**protet'tore, 'trice** smf protector; (sostenitore) patron.

**protezi'one** [protet'tsjone] sf protec-tion; (patrocinio) patronage.

**protocol'lare** vt to register // ag for-mal; of protocol.

**proto'collo** sm protocol; (registro) register of documents.

**pro'totipo** sm prototype.

**pro'trarre** vt (prolungare) to pro-long; **pro'tratto, a** pp di **protrarre**.

**protube'ranza** [protube'rantsa] sf protuberance, bulge.

'**prova** sf (esperimento, cimento) test, trial; (tentativo) attempt, try; (MAT, testimonianza, documento etc) proof; (DIR) evidence q, proof; (INS) exam, test; (TEATRO) rehearsal; (di abito) fitting; **a** ~ **di** (in testimonianza di) as proof of; **a** ~ **di fuoco** fireproof; **fino a** ~ **contraria** until it is proved otherwise; **mettere alla** ~ to put to the test; **giro di** ~ test o trial run; ~ **generale** (TEA-TRO) dress rehearsal.

**pro'vare** vt (sperimentare) to test; (tentare) to try, attempt; (assaggiare) to try, taste; (spe-rimentare in sé) to experience; (sentire) to feel; (cimentare) to put to the test; (dimostrare) to prove; (abito) to try on; ~rsi vr: ~rsi (a fare) to try o attempt (to do); ~ a fare to try o attempt to do.

**proveni'enza** [prove'njɛntsa] sf origin, source.

**prove'nire** vi: ~ **da** to come from.

**pro'venti** smpl revenue pl.

**prove'nuto, a** pp di **provenire**.

**pro'verbio** sm proverb.

**pro'vetta** sf test tube; **bambino in** ~ test-tube baby.

**pro'vetto, a** ag skilled, experienced.

**pro'vincia, ce** $o$ **cie** [pro'vintʃa] $sf$ province; **provinci'ale** $ag$ provincial; **(strada) provinciale** main road (Brit), highway (US).

**pro'vino** $sm$ (CINEMA) screen test; (campione) specimen.

**provo'cante** $ag$ (attraente) provocative.

**provo'care** $vt$ (causare) to cause, bring about; (eccitare: riso, pietà) to arouse; (irritare, sfidare) to provoke; **provoca'torio, a** $ag$ provocative; **provocazi'one** $sf$ provocation.

**provve'dere** $vi$ (disporre): ~ **(a)** to provide (for); (prendere un provvedimento) to take steps, act // $vt$: ~ **qc a qn** to supply sth to sb; ~**rsi** $vr$: ~**rsi di** to provide o.s. with; **provvedi'mento** $sm$ measure; (di previdenza) precaution.

**provvi'denza** [provvi'dɛntsa] $sf$: **la** ~ providence; **provvidenzi'ale** $ag$ providential.

**provvigi'one** [provvi'dʒone] $sf$ (COMM) commission.

**provvi'sorio, a** $ag$ temporary.

**prov'vista** $sf$ provision, supply.

**'prua** $sf$ (NAUT) = **prora**.

**pru'dente** $ag$ cautious, prudent; (assennato) sensible, wise; **pru'denza** $sf$ prudence; caution; wisdom.

**'prudere** $vi$ to itch, be itchy.

**'prugna** ['pruɲɲa] $sf$ plum; ~ **secca** prune.

**pruri'gi'noso, a** [pruridʒi'noso] $ag$ itchy.

**pru'rito** $sm$ itchiness $q$; itch.

**P.S.** $abbr$ (= postscriptum) P.S.; (POLIZIA) = **Pubblica Sicurezza.**

**pseu'donimo** $sm$ pseudonym.

**PSI** $sigla$ $m$ = Partito Socialista Italiano.

**psicana'lista, i, e** $smf$ psychoanalyst.

**'psiche** ['psike] $sf$ (PSIC) psyche.

**psichi'atra, i, e** [psi'kjatra] $smf$ psychiatrist; **psichi'atrico, a, ci, che** $ag$ psychiatric.

**'psichico, a, ci, che** ['psikiko] $ag$ psychological.

**psico'gia** [psikolo'dʒia] $sf$ psychology; **psico'logico, a, ci** $ag$ psychological; **psi'cologo, a, gi, ghe** $smf$ psychologist.

**psico'patico, a, ci, che** $ag$ psychopathic // $smf$ psychopath.

**P.T.** $abbr$ = Posta e Telegrafi.

**pubbli'care** $vt$ to publish.

**pubblicazi'one** [pubblikat'tsjone] $sf$ publication; ~**i (matrimoniali)** $sfpl$ (marriage) banns.

**pubbli'cista, i, e** [pubbli'tʃista] $smf$ (STAMPA) occasional contributor.

**pubblicità** [pubblitʃi'ta] $sf$ (diffusione) publicity; (attività) advertising; (annunci nei giornali) advertisements $pl$; **pubbli'citario, a** $ag$ advertising $cpd$; (trovata, film) publicity $cpd$.

**'pubblico, a, ci, che** $ag$ public; (statale: scuola etc) state $cpd$ // $sm$ public; (spettatori) audience; **in** ~ **in** public; ~ **funzionario** civil servant; **P~ Ministero** Public Prosecutor's Office; **la P~a Sicurezza** the police.

**'pube** $sm$ (ANAT) pubis.

**pubertà** $sf$ puberty.

**'pudico, a, ci, che** $ag$ modest.

**pu'dore** $sm$ modesty.

**pueri'cul'tura** $sf$ paediatric nursing; infant care.

**pue'rile** $ag$ childish.

**pugi'lato** [pudʒi'lato] $sm$ boxing.

**pugile** ['pudʒile] $sm$ boxer.

**pugna'lare** [puɲɲa'lare] $vt$ to stab.

**pu'gnale** [puɲ'ɲale] $sm$ dagger.

**'pugno** ['puɲɲo] $sm$ fist; (colpo) punch; (quantità) fistful.

**'pulce** ['pultʃe] $sf$ flea.

**pul'cino** [pul'tʃino] $sm$ chick.

**pu'ledro, a** $sm/f$ colt/filly.

**pu'leggia, ge** [pu'leddʒa] $sf$ pulley.

**pu'lire** $vt$ to clean; (lucidare) to polish; **pu'lito, a** $ag$ (anche fig) clean; (ordinato) neat, tidy // $sf$ quick clean; **puli'tura** $sf$ cleaning; **pulitura a secco** dry cleaning; **pu'lizia** $sf$ cleaning; cleanness; **fare le pulizie** to do the cleaning, do the housework.

'**pullman** sm inv coach.

pul'lover sm inv pullover, jumper.

pullu'lare vi to swarm, teem.

pul'mino sm minibus.

'pulpito sm pulpit.

pul'sante sm (push-)button.

pul'sare vi to pulsate, beat; pulsazi'one sf beat.

pul'viscolo sm fine dust.

'puma sm inv puma.

pun'gente ag prickly; stinging; (anche fig) biting.

'pungere ['pundʒere] vt to prick; (sog: insetto, ortica) to sting; (: freddo) to bite.

pungigli'one [pundʒiʎ'ʎone] sm sting.

pu'nire vt to punish; punizi'one sf punishment; (SPORT) penalty.

'punta sf point; (parte terminale) tip, end; (di monte) peak; (di costa) promontory; (minima parte) touch, trace; in ~ di piedi on tip-toe; ore di ~ peak hours; uomo di ~ front-rank o leading man.

pun'tare vt (piedi a terra, gomiti sul tavolo) to plant; (dirigere: pistola) to point; (commettere) to bet // vi (mirare): ~ a to aim at; (avviarsi): ~ su to head o make for; (fig: contare): ~ su to count o rely on.

pun'tata sf (gita) short trip; (scommessa) bet; (parte di opera) instalment; romanzo a ~ serial.

punteggia'tura [punteddʒa'tura] sf (LING) punctuation.

pun'teggio [pun'teddʒo] sm score.

puntel'lare vt to support.

pun'tello sm prop, support.

puntigli'oso, a [puntiʎ'ʎoso] ag punctilious.

pun'tina sf: ~ da disegno drawing pin.

pun'tino sm dot; fare qc a ~ to do sth properly.

'punto, a pp di pungere // sm (segno, macchiolina) dot; (LING) full stop; (MAT, momento, di punteggio, fig: argomento) point; (posto) spot; (a scuola) mark; (nel cucire, nella maglia, MED) stitch // av: non ... ~ not at all; due ~i sm (LING) colon; sul ~ di fare (just) about to do; fare il ~ (NAUT) to take a bearing; (fig): fare il ~ della situazione to take stock of the situation; to sum up the situation; alle 6 in ~ at 6 o'clock sharp o on the dot; essere a buon ~ to have reached a satisfactory stage; mettere a ~ to adjust; (motore) to tune; (cannocchiale) to focus; (fig) to settle; di ~ in bianco point-blank; ~ cardinale point of the compass, cardinal point; ~ debole weak point; ~ esclamativo/interrogativo exclamation/question mark; ~ di riferimento landmark; (fig) point of reference; ~ di vendita retail outlet; ~ e virgola semicolon; ~ di vista (fig) point of view; ~i di sospensione suspension points.

puntu'ale ag punctual; puntualità sf punctuality.

pun'tura sf (di ago) prick; (di insetto) sting, bite; (MED) puncture; (: iniezione) injection; (dolore) sharp pain.

punzecchi'are [puntsek'kjare] vt to prick; (fig) to tease.

pun'zone [pun'tsone] sm (per metalli) stamp, die.

'pupa sf doll.

pu'pazzo [pu'pattso] sm puppet.

pu'pillo, a sm/f (DIR) ward; (prediletto) favourite, pet // sf (ANAT) pupil.

purché [pur'ke] cong provided that, on condition that.

'pure cong (tuttavia) and yet, nevertheless; (anche se) even if // av (anche) too, also; pur di (al fine di) just to; faccia ~! go ahead!, please do!

purè sm, pu'rea sf (CUC) purée; (: di patate) mashed potatoes.

'purga, ghe sf (MED) purging q; purge; (POL) purge.

pur'gante sm (MED) purgative, purge.

**pur'gare** vt (MED, POL) to purge; (pulire) to clean.

**purga'torio** sm purgatory.

**purifi'care** vt to purify; (metallo) to refine.

**puri'tano, a** ag, sm/f puritan.

**'puro, a** ag pure; (acqua) clear, limpid; (vino) undiluted; **puro-'sangue** sm/f inv thoroughbred.

**pur'troppo** av unfortunately.

**'pustola** sf pimple.

**puti'ferio** sm rumpus, row.

**putre'fare** vi to putrefy, rot; **pu-tre'fatto, a** pp di putrefare.

**'putrido, a** ag putrid, rotten.

**put'tana** sf (fam!) whore (!).

**'puzza** ['puttsa] sf = **puzzo.**

**puz'zare** [put'tsare] vi to stink.

**'puzzo** ['puttso] sm stink, foul smell.

**'puzzola** ['puttsola] sf polecat.

**puzzo'lente** [puttso'lɛnte] ag stinking.

# Q

**qua** av here; in ~ (verso questa parte) this way; **da un anno in ~** for a year now; **da quando in ~?** since when?; **da quando in ~** (passare) this way; **al di ~ di** (fiume, strada) on this side of; ~ **dentro/fuori** etc in/out here etc; vedi **questo.**

**qua'derno** sm notebook; (per scuola) exercise book.

**qua'drante** sm quadrant; (di oro-logio) face.

**qua'drare** vi (bilancio) to balance, tally; (descrizione) to correspond; (fig): ~ a to please, be to one's liking // vt (MAT) to square; **non mi quadra** I don't like it; **qua'drato, a** ag square; (fig: equilibrato) level-headed, sensible; (: peg) square // sm (MAT) square; (PUGILATO) ring; **5 al quadrato** 5 squared.

**qua'dretto** sm: a ~i (tessuto) checked; (foglio) squared.

**quadri'foglio** [kwadri'fɔʎʎo] sm four-leaf clover.

**'quadro** sm (pittura) painting, picture; (quadrato) square; (tabella) table, chart; (TECN) board, panel; (TEATRO) scene; (fig: scena, spettacolo) sight; (: descrizione) outline, description; **~i** smpl (POL) party organizers; (MIL) cadres; (COMM) managerial staff; (CARTE) diamonds.

**'quadruplo, a** ag, sm quadruple.

**quaggiù** [kwad'dʒu] av down here.

**'quaglia** ['kwaʎʎa] sf quail.

PAROLA CHIAVE

**'qualche** ['kwalke] det **1** some, a few; (in interrogative) any; **ho comprato ~ libro** I've bought some o a few books; ~ **volta** sometimes; **hai ~ sigaretta?** have you any cigarettes?
**2** (uno): **c'è ~ medico?** is there a doctor?; **in ~ modo** somehow
**3** (un certo, parecchio) some; **un personaggio di ~ rilievo** a figure of some importance
**4**: ~ **cosa** = **qualcosa.**

**qualche'duno** [kwalke'duno] pronome = **qualcuno.**

**qual'cosa** pronome something; (in espressioni interrogative) anything; **qualcos'altro** something else; anything else; ~ **di nuovo** something new; anything new; ~ **da mangiare** something to eat; anything to eat; **c'è ~ che non va?** is there something o anything wrong?

**qual'cuno** pronome (persona) someone, somebody; (: in espressioni interrogative) anyone, anybody; (alcuni) some; ~ **è favorevole a noi** some are on our side; **qualcun altro** someone o somebody else; anyone o anybody else.

PAROLA CHIAVE

**'quale** (spesso troncato in qual) ◆
det **1** (interrogativo) what; (: scegliendo tra due o più cose o persone) which; ~ **uomo/denaro?**

what man/money?; which man/money?; ~i sono i tuoi programmi? what are your plans?; ~ stanza preferisci? which room do you prefer?
2 (relativo: come): il risultato fu ~ ci si aspettava the result was as expected
3 (esclamativo) what; ~ disgrazia! what bad luck!
◆ pronome 1 (interrogativo) which; ~ dei due scegli? which of the two do you want?
2 (relativo: il(la) ~ (persona: soggetto) who; (: oggetto, con preposizione) whom; (cosa) which; (possessivo) whose; suo padre, il ~ è avvocato, ... his father, who is a lawyer, ...; il signore con il ~ parlavo the gentleman to whom I was speaking; l'albergo al ~ ci siamo fermati the hotel where we stayed o which we stayed at; la signora della ~ ammiriamo la bellezza the lady whose beauty we admire
3 (relativo: in elenchi) such as, like; piante ~i l'edera plants like o such as ivy; ~ sindaco di questa città as mayor of this town.

**qua'lifica, che** sf qualification; (titolo) title.
**qualifi'care** vt to qualify; (definire): ~ qn/qc come to describe sb/sth as; ~rsi vr (anche SPORT) to qualify; **qualifica'tivo, a** ag qualifying; **qualificazi'one** sf qualification; gara di qualificazione (SPORT) qualifying event.
**qualità** sf inv quality; in ~ di in one's capacity as.
**qua'lora** cong in case, if.
**qual'siasi, qua'lunque** det inv any; (quale che sia) whatever; (discriminativo) whichever; (posposto: mediocre) poor, indifferent; ordinary; **metti un vestito** ~ put on any old dress; ~ **cosa** anything; ~ **cosa accada** whatever happens; a

~ **costo** at any cost, whatever the cost; **l'uomo** ~ the man in the street; ~ **persona** anyone, anybody.
**'quando** cong, av when; ~ **sarò ricco** when I'm rich; **da** ~ (dacché) since; (interrogativo): **da** ~ **sei qui?** how long have you been here?; **quand'anche** even if.
**quantità** sf inv quantity; (gran numero): **una** ~ **di** a great deal of; a lot of; **in grande** ~ in large quantities; **quantita'tivo** sm (COMM) amount, quantity.

┌─────────────────────────────┐
│ PAROLA CHIAVE │

**'quanto, a** ◆ det 1 (interrogativo: quantità) how much; (: numero) how many; ~ **pane/denaro?** how much bread/money?; ~i **libri/ragazzi?** how many books/boys?; ~ **tempo?** how long?; ~i **anni hai?** how old are you?
2 (esclamativo): ~e **storie!** what a lot of nonsense!; ~ **tempo sprecato!** what a waste of time!
3 (relativo: quantità) as much ... as; (: numero) as many ... as; **ho** ~ **denaro mi occorre** I have as much money as I need; **prendi** ~i **libri vuoi** take as many books as you like
◆ pronome 1 (interrogativo: quantità) how much; (: numero) how many; (: tempo) how long; ~ **mi dai?** how much will you give me?; ~i **me ne hai portati?** how many did you bring me?; **da** ~ **sei qui?** how long have you been here?; ~i **ne abbiamo oggi?** what's the date today?
2 (relativo: quantità) as much as; (: numero) as many as; **farò** ~ **posso** I'll do as much as I can; **possono venire** ~i **sono stati invitati** all those who have been invited can come
◆ av 1 (interrogativo: con ag, av) how; (: con vb) how much; ~ **stanco ti sembrava?** how tired did he seem to you?; ~ **corre la tua moto?** how fast can your motorbike

go?; ~ **costa?** how much does it cost?; **quant'è?** how much is it?

**2** (esclamativo: con ag, av) how; (: con vb) how much; ~ **sono felice!** how happy I am!; **quanti ~ abbiamo camminato!** if you knew how far we've walked!; **studierò ~ posso** I'll study as much as o all I can; ~ **prima** as soon as possible

**3: in** ~ (in qualità di) as; (perché, per il fatto che) as, since; **(in)** ~ **a** (per ciò che riguarda) as for, as regards

**4: per** ~ (nonostante, anche se) however; **per** ~ **si sforzi, non ce la farà** try as he may, he won't manage it; **per** ~ **sia brava, fa degli errori** however good she may be, she makes mistakes; **per** ~ **io sappia** as far as I know.

**quan'tunque** cong although, though.

**qua'ranta** num forty.

**quaran'tena** sf quarantine.

**quaran'tesimo, a** num fortieth.

**quaran'tina** sf: una ~ **(di)** about forty.

**qua'resima** sf: la ~ Lent.

**'quarta** sf vedi **quarto**.

**quar'tetto** sm quartet(te).

**quarti'ere** sm district, area; (MIL) quarters pl; ~ **generale** headquarters pl, HQ.

**'quarto, a** ag fourth // sm fourth; (quarta parte) quarter // sf (AUT) fourth (gear); **le 6 e un** ~ a quarter past six; ~ **d'ora** quarter of an hour; ~**i di finale** quarter final.

**'quarzo** ['kwartso] sm quartz.

**'quasi** av almost, nearly // cong (anche: ~ **che**) as if; **(non)** ... ~ **mai** hardly ever; ~ ~ **me ne andrei** I've half a mind to leave.

**quassù** av up here.

**'quatto, a** ag crouched, squatting; (silenzioso) silent; ~ ~ very quietly; stealthily.

**quat'tordici** [kwat'torditʃi] num

fourteen.

**quat'trini** smpl money sg, cash sg.

**'quattro** num four; **in** ~ **e quattr'otto** in less than no time; **quattro'cento** num four hundred // sm: **il Quattrocento** the fifteenth century; **quattro'mila** num four thousand.

┌─────────────────────────┐
│ **PAROLA CHIAVE**       │
└─────────────────────────┘

**'quello, a ◆** det (dav sm **quel** + C, **quell'** + V, **quello** + s impura, gn, pn, ps, x, z; pl **quei** + C, **quegli** + V o s impura, gn, pn, ps, x, z; dav sf **quella** + C, **quell'** + V; pl **quelle**) that; those pl; ~**a casa** that house; **quegli uomini** those men; **voglio** ~**a camicia** (lì o là) I want that shirt

**◆** pronome **1** (dimostrativo) that (one); those (ones) pl; (ciò) that; **conosci** ~**a?** do you know that woman?; **prendo** ~ **bianco** I'll take the white one; **chi è** ~? who's that?; **prendiamo** ~ (lì o là) let's take that one (there)

**2** (relativo): ~**(a) che** (persona) the one (who); (cosa) the one (which), the one (that); ~**i(e) che** (persone) those who; (cose) those which; **è lui** ~ **che non voleva venire** he's the one who didn't want to come; **ho fatto** ~ **che potevo** I did what I could.

**'quercia, ce** ['kwertʃa] sf oak (tree); (legno) oak.

**que'rela** sf (DIR) (legal) action; **querere** vt to bring an action against.

**que'sito** sm question; query; problem.

**questio'nare** vi: ~ **di/su qc** to argue about/over sth.

**questio'nario** sm questionnaire.

**questi'one** sf problem, question; (controversia) issue; (litigio) quarrel; **in** ~ in question; **fuor di** ~ out of the question; **è** ~ **di tempo** it's a matter o question of time.

*PAROLA CHIAVE*

**'questo, a ◆** *det* **1** (*dimostrativo*) this; these *pl*; ~ **libro** (**qui** *o* **qua**) this book; **io prendo** ~ **cappotto, tu quello** I'll take this coat, you take that one; **quest'oggi** today; ~**a sera** this evening

**2** (*enfatico*): **non fatemi più prendere di** ~**e paure** don't frighten me like that again

**◆** *pronome* (*dimostrativo*) this (one); these (ones) *pl*; (*ciò*) this; **prendo** ~ (**qui** *o* **qua**) I'll take this one; **preferisci** ~**i o quelli?** do you prefer these (ones) or those (ones)?; ~ **intendevo** **io** this is what I meant; **vengono Paolo e Luca:** ~ **da Roma, quello da Palermo** Paolo and Luca are coming: the former from Palermo, the latter from Rome.

**ques'tore** *sm* ≈ chief constable (*Brit*), ≈ police commissioner (*US*).

**'questua** *sf* collection (of alms).

**ques'tura** *sf* police headquarters *pl*.

**qui** *av* here; **da** *o* **di** ~ from here; **di** ~ **in avanti** from now on; **di** ~ **a poco/una settimana** in a little while/a week's time; ~ **dentro/sopra/vicino** in/up/near here; **vieni** **questo.**

**quie'tanza** [kwje'tantsa] *sf* receipt.

**quie'tare** *vt* to calm, soothe.

**qui'ete** *sf* quiet, quietness; calmness; stillness; peace.

**qui'eto, a** *ag* quiet; (*notte*) calm, still; (*mare*) calm.

**'quindi** *av* then // *cong* therefore, so.

**'quindici** ['kwinditʃi] *num* fifteen; ~ **giorni** a fortnight (*Brit*), two weeks.

**quindi'cina** [kwindi'tʃina] *sf* (*serie*): **una** ~ (**di**) about fifteen; **fra una** ~ **di giorni** in a fortnight.

**quin'quennio** *sm* period of five years.

**quin'tale** *sm* quintal (*100 kg*).

**'quinte** *sfpl* (*TEATRO*) wings.

**'quinto, a** *num* fifth.

**'quota** *sf* (*parte*) quota, share; (*AER*) height, altitude; (*IPPICA*) odds *pl*; **prendere/perdere** ~ (*AER*) to gain/lose height *o* altitude; ~ **d'iscrizione** enrolment fee; (*ad un club*) membership fee.

**quo'tare** *vt* (*BORSA*) to quote; **quotazi'one** *sf* quotation.

**quotidi'ano, a** *ag* daily; (*banale*) everyday // *sm* (*giornale*) daily (paper).

**quozi'ente** [kwot'tsjɛnte] *sm* (*MAT*) quotient; ~ **d'intelligenza** intelligence quotient, IQ.

# R

**ra'barbaro** *sm* rhubarb.

**'rabbia** *sf* (*ira*) anger, rage; (*accanimento, furia*) fury; (*MED:* *idrofobia*) rabies *sg*.

**rab'bino** *sm* rabbi.

**rabbi'oso, a** *ag* angry, furious; (*facile* *all'ira*) quick-tempered; (*forze, acqua etc*) furious, raging; (*MED*) rabid, mad.

**rabbo'nire** *vt*, ~**rsi** *vr* to calm down.

**rabbrivi'dire** *vi* to shudder, shiver.

**rabbui'arsi** *vr* to grow dark.

**raccapez'zarsi** [rakkapet'tsarsi] *vr*: **non** ~ to be at a loss.

**raccapricci'ante** [rakkaprit'tʃante] *ag* horrifying.

**raccatta'palle** *sm inv* (*SPORT*) ballboy.

**raccat'tare** *vt* to pick up.

**rac'chetta** [rak'ketta] *sf* (*per tennis*) racket; (*per ping-pong*) bat; ~ **da neve** snowshoe; ~ **da sci** ski stick.

**racchi'udere** [rak'kjudere] *vt* to contain; **racchi'uso, a** *pp di* **racchiudere.**

**rac'cogliere** [rak'kɔʎʎere] *vt* to collect; (*raccattare*) to pick up; (*frutti, fiori*) to pick, pluck; (*AGR*) to harvest; (*approvazione, voti*) to win; (*profughi*) to take in; ~**rsi** *vr* to gather; (*fig*) to gather one's thoughts; to meditate; **raccogli'mento** sm meditation; **raccogli'tore** sm (cartella) folder, binder; raccoglitore a fogli mobili looseleaf binder.

rac'colto, a pp di raccogliere // ag (persona: pensoso) thoughtful; (luogo: appartato) secluded, quiet // sm (AGR) crop, harvest // sf collecting q; collection; (AGR) harvesting q, gathering q; harvest, crop; (adunata) gathering.

raccoman'dare vt to recommend; (affidare) to entrust; (esortare): ~ a qn di non fare to tell o warn sb not to do; ~rsi vr: ~rsi a qn to commend o.s. to sb; mi raccomando! don't forget!; raccoman-'data sf (anche: lettera raccomandata) recorded-delivery letter; raccomandazi'one sf recommendation.

raccon'tare vt: ~ (a qn) (dire) to tell (sb); (narrare) to relate to (sb), tell (sb) about; rac'conto sm telling q, relating q; (fatto raccontato) story, tale.

raccorci'are [rakkor'tʃare] vt to shorten.

rac'cordo sm (TECN: giunzione) connection, joint; (AUT: di autostrada) slip road (Brit), entrance (o exit) ramp (US); ~ anulare (AUT) ring road (Brit), beltway (US).

ra'chitico, a, ci, che [ra'kitiko] ag suffering from rickets; (fig) scraggy, scrawny.

racimo'lare [ratʃimo'lare] vt (fig) to scrape together, glean.

'rada sf (natural) harbour.

'radar sm radar.

raddol'cire [raddol'tʃire] vt (persona, carattere) to soften; ~rsi vr (tempo) to grow milder; (persona) to soften, mellow.

raddoppi'are vt, vi to double.

raddriz'zare [raddrit'tsare] vt to straighten; (fig: correggere) to put straight, correct.

'radere vt (barba) to shave off;

(mento) to shave; (fig: rasentare) to graze; to skim; ~rsi vr to shave (o.s.); ~ al suolo to raze to the ground.

radi'ale ag radial.

radi'are vt to strike off.

radia'tore sm radiator.

radiazi'one [radjat'tsjone] sf (FISICA) radiation; (cancellazione) striking off.

radi'cale ag radical // sm (LING) root.

ra'dicchio [ra'dikkjo] sm chicory.

ra'dice [ra'ditʃe] sf root.

'radio sf inv radio // sm (CHIM) radium; radioat'tivo, a ag radioactive; radiodiffusi'one sf (radio) broadcasting; radiogra'fare vt to X-ray; radiogra'fia sf radiography; (foto) X-ray photograph.

radi'oso, a ag radiant.

radiostazi'one [radjostat'tsjone] sf radio station.

radiotera'pia sf radiotherapy.

'rado, a ag (capelli) sparse, thin; (visite) infrequent; di ~ rarely.

radu'nare vt, ~rsi vr to gather, assemble.

ra'dura sf clearing.

'rafano sm horseradish.

raffazzo'nare [raffattso'nare] vt to patch up.

raf'fermo, a ag stale.

'raffica, che sf (METEOR) gust of wind); (di colpi: scarica) burst of gunfire.

raffigu'rare vt to represent.

raffi'nare vt to refine; raffina'tezza sf refinement; raffi'nato, a ag refined; raffine'ria sf refinery.

raffor'zare [raffor'tsare] vt to reinforce.

raffredda'mento sm cooling.

raffred'dare vt to cool; (fig) to dampen, have a cooling effect on; ~rsi vr to grow cool o cold; (prendere un raffreddore) to catch a cold; (fig) to cool (off).

raffred'dato, a ag (MED): essere ~ to have a cold.

**raffred'dore** sm (MED) cold.

**raf'fronto** sm comparison.

**'rafia** sf (fibra) raffia.

**ra'gazzo, a** [ra'gattso] sm/f boy/girl; (fam: fidanzato) boyfriend/girlfriend.

**raggi'ante** [rad'dʒante] ag radiant, shining.

**'raggio** ['raddʒo] sm (di sole etc) ray; (MAT, distanza) radius; (di ruota etc) spoke; ~ **d'azione** range; ~**i X** X-rays.

**raggi'rare** [raddʒi'rare] vt to take in, trick; **rag'giro** sm trick.

**raggi'ungere** [rad'dʒundʒere] vt to reach; (persona: riprendere) to catch up (with); (bersaglio) to hit; (fig: meta) to achieve; **raggi'unto, a** pp di **raggiungere**.

**raggomi'tolarsi** vr to curl up.

**raggranel'lare** vt to scrape together.

**raggrin'zare** [raggrin'tsare] vt, vi (anche: ~**rsi**) to wrinkle.

**raggrup'pare** vt to group (together).

**raggu'aglio** [rag'gwaʎʎo] sm comparison; (informazione, relazione) piece of information.

**ragguar'devole** ag (degno di riguardo) distinguished, notable; (notevole: somma) considerable.

**ragiona'mento** [radʒona'mento] sm reasoning q; arguing q; argument.

**ragio'nare** [radʒo'nare] vi (usare la ragione) to reason; (discorrere): ~ (di) to argue (about).

**ragi'one** [ra'dʒone] sf reason; (dimostrazione, prova) argument, reason; (diritto) right; aver ~ to be right; aver ~ di qn to get the better of sb; dare ~ a qn to agree with sb; to prove sb right; perdere la ~ to become insane; (fig) to take leave of one's senses; in ~ di at the rate of; to the amount of; according to; a o con ~ rightly, justly; ~ sociale (COMM) corporate name; a ragion veduta after due consideration.

**ragione'ria** [radʒone'ria] sf accountancy; accounts department.

**ragio'nevole** [radʒo'nevole] ag reasonable.

**ragioni'ere, a** [radʒo'njɛre] sm/f accountant.

**ragli'are** [raʎ'ʎare] vi to bray.

**ragna'tela** [raɲɲa'tela] sf cobweb, spider's web.

**'ragno** ['raɲɲo] sm spider.

**ragù** sm inv (CUC) meat sauce; stew.

**RAI-TV** [raiti'vu] sigla f = Radio televisione italiana.

**rallegra'menti** smpl congratulations.

**ralle'grare** vt to cheer up; ~**rsi** vr to cheer up; (provare allegrezza) to rejoice; ~**rsi con qn** to congratulate sb.

**rallen'tare** vt to slow down; (fig) to slow down // vi to slow down.

**rallen'tare** vt to slow down; (fig) to lessen, slacken // vi to slow down.

**raman'zina** [raman'dzina] sf lecture, telling-off.

**'rame** sm (CHIM) copper.

**rammari'carsi** vr: ~ (di) (rincrescersi) to be sorry (about); (lamentarsi) to complain (about); **ram'marico, chi** sm regret.

**rammen'dare** vt to mend; (calza) to darn; **ram'mendo** sm mending q; darning q; mend; darn.

**rammen'tare** vt to remember, recall; (richiamare alla memoria): ~ **qc a qn** to remind sb of sth; ~**rsi** vr: ~**rsi (di) qc** to remember (sth).

**rammol'lire** vt to soften // vi (anche: ~**rsi**) to go soft.

**'ramo** sm branch.

**ramo'scello** [ramoʃ'ʃɛllo] sm twig.

**'rampa** sf flight (of stairs); ~ **di lancio** launching pad.

**rampi'cante** ag (BOT) climbing.

**ram'pone** sm harpoon; (ALPINISMO) crampon.

**'rana** sf frog.

**'rancido, a** ['rantʃido] ag rancid.

**ran'core** sm rancour, resentment.

**ran'dagio, a, gi, gie o ge** [ran'dadʒo] ag (gatto, cane) stray.

**ran'dello** sm club, cudgel.

'**rango**, **ghi** sm (condizione sociale, MIL: riga) rank.

**rannicchi'arsi** [rannik'kjarsi] vr to crouch, huddle.

**rannuvo'larsi** vr to cloud over, become overcast.

**ra'nocchio** [ra'nɔkkjo] sm (edible) frog.

'**rantolo** sm wheeze; (di agonizzanti) death rattle.

'**rapa** sf (BOT) turnip.

**ra'pace** [ra'patʃe] ag (animale) predatory; (fig) rapacious, grasping // sm bird of prey.

**ra'pare** vt (capelli) to crop, cut very short.

'**rapida** sf vedi **rapido**.

**rapida'mente** av quickly, rapidly.

**rapidità** sf speed.

'**rapido**, **a** ag fast; (esame, occhiata) quick, rapid // sm (FERR) express (train) // sf (di fiume) rapid.

**rapi'mento** sm kidnapping; (fig) rapture.

**ra'pina** sf robbery; ~ a mano armata armed robbery; **rapi'nare** vt to rob; **rapina'tore**, '**trice** sm/f robber.

**ra'pire** vt (cose) to steal; (persone) to kidnap; (fig) to enrapture, delight; **rapi'tore**, '**trice** sm/f kidnapper.

**rappor'tare** vt (confrontare) to compare; (riprodurre) to reproduce.

**rap'porto** sm (resoconto) report; (legame) relationship; (MAT, TECN) ratio; ~i smpl (fra persone, paesi) relations; ~i sessuali sexual intercourse sg.

**rap'prendersi** vr to coagulate, clot; (latte) to curdle.

**rappre'saglia** [rappre'saʎʎa] sf reprisal, retaliation.

**rappresen'tante** sm/f representative; **rappresen'tanza** sf delegation, deputation; (COMM: ufficio, sede) agency.

**rappresen'tare** vt to represent; (TEATRO) to perform; **rappresenta'tivo**, **a** ag representative; **rappresentazi'one** sf representa-

tion; performing q; (spettacolo) performance.

**rap'preso**, **a** pp di **rapprendere**.

**rapso'dia** sf rhapsody.

**rara'mente** av seldom, rarely.

**rare'fatto**, **a** ag rarefied.

'**raro**, **a** ag rare.

**ra'sare** vt (barba etc) to shave off; (siepi, erba) to trim, cut; ~rsi vr to shave (o.s.).

**raschi'are** [ras'kjare] vt to scrape; (macchia, fango) to scrape off // vi to clear one's throat.

**rasen'tare** vt (andar rasente) to keep close to; (sfiorare) to skim along (o over); (fig) to border on.

**ra'sente** prep: ~ (a) close to, very near.

'**raso**, **a** pp di **radere** // ag (barba) shaved; (capelli) cropped; (con misure di capacità) level; (pieno: bicchiere) full to the brim // sm (tessuto) satin; ~ terra close to the ground; **un cucchiaio** ~ a level spoonful.

**ra'soio** sm razor; ~ elettrico electric shaver o razor.

**ras'segna** [ras'seɲɲa] sf (MIL) inspection, review; (esame) inspection; (resoconto) review, survey; (pubblicazione letteraria etc) review; (mostra) exhibition, show; passare in ~ (MIL, fig) to review.

**rasse'gnare** [rasseɲ'ɲare] vt: ~ le dimissioni to resign, hand in one's resignation; ~rsi vr (accettare): ~rsi (a qc/a fare) to resign o.s. (to sth/to doing); **rassegnazi'one** sf resignation.

**rasse'renarsi** vr (tempo) to clear up.

**rasset'tare** vt to tidy, put in order; (aggiustare) to repair, mend.

**rassicu'rare** vt to reassure.

**rasso'dare** vt to harden, stiffen.

**rassomigli'anza** [rassomiʎ'ʎantsa] sf resemblance.

**rassomigli'are** [rassomiʎ'ʎare] vi: ~ a to resemble, look like.

**rastrel'lare** vt to rake; (fig:

*perlustrare*) to comb.

**rastrelli'era** *sf* rack; (*per piatti*) dish rack.

**ras'trello** *sm* rake.

**'rata** *sf* (*quota*) instalment; **pagare a ~e** to pay by instalments *o* on hire purchase (*Brit*).

**ratifi'care** *vt* (*DIR*) to ratify.

**'ratto** *sm* (*DIR*) abduction; (*ZOOL*) rat.

**rattop'pare** *vt* to patch; **rat'toppo** *sm* patching *q*; patch.

**rattrap'pire** *vt* to make stiff; **~rsi** *vr* to be stiff.

**rattris'tare** *vt* to sadden; **~rsi** *vr* to become sad.

**'rauco, a, chi, che** *ag* hoarse.

**rava'nello** *sm* radish.

**ravi'oli** *smpl* ravioli *sg*.

**ravve'dersi** *vr* to mend one's ways.

**ravvici'nare** [ravvitʃi'nare] *vt* (*avvicinare*): **~ qc** to bring sth nearer to; (: *due tubi*) to bring closer together; (*riconciliare*) to reconcile, bring together.

**ravvi'sare** *vt* to recognize.

**ravvi'vare** *vt* to revive; (*fig*) to brighten up, enliven; **~rsi** *vr* to revive; to brighten up.

**razio'cinio** [ratsjo'tʃinjo] *sm* reasoning *q*; reason; (*buon senso*) common sense.

**razio'nale** [rattsjo'nale] *ag* rational.

**razio'nare** [rattsjo'nare] *vt* to ration.

**razi'one** [rat'tsjone] *sf* ration; (*porzione*) portion, share.

**'razza** ['rattsa] *sf* race; (*ZOOL*) breed; (*discendenza, stirpe*) stock, race; (*sorta*) sort, kind.

**raz'zia** [rat'tsia] *sf* raid, foray.

**razzi'ale** [rat'tsjale] *ag* racial.

**raz'zismo** [rat'tsizmo] *sm* racism, racialism.

**raz'zista, i, e** [rat'tsista] *ag, smf* racist, racialist.

**'razzo** ['raddzo] *sm* rocket.

**razzo'lare** [rattso'lare] *vi* (*galline*) to scratch about.

**re** *sm inv* king; (*MUS*) D; (: *solfeggiando la scala*) re.

**rea'gire** [rea'dʒire] *vi* to react.

**re'ale** *ag* real; (*di, da re*) royal // *sm*: **il ~** reality; **rea'lismo** *sm* realism; **rea'lista, i, e** *smf* realist; (*POL*) royalist.

**realiz'zare** [realid'dzare] *vt* (*progetto etc*) to realize, carry out; (*sogno, desiderio*) to realize, fulfil; (*scopo*) to achieve; (*COMM: titoli etc*) to realize; (*CALCIO etc*) to score; **~rsi** *vr* to be realized; **realizzazi'one** *sf* realization; fulfilment; achievement.

**real'mente** *av* really, actually.

**realtà** *sf inv* reality.

**re'ato** *sm* offence.

**reat'tore** *sm* (*FISICA*) reactor; (*AER: aereo*) jet; (: *motore*) jet engine.

**reazio'nario, a** [reattsjo'narjo] *ag* (*POL*) reactionary.

**reazi'one** [reat'tsjone] *sf* reaction.

**'rebbio** *sm* prong.

**recapi'tare** *vt* to deliver.

**re'capito** *sm* (*indirizzo*) address; (*consegna*) delivery.

**re'care** *vt* (*portare*) to bring; (*avere su di sé*) to carry, bear; (*cagionare*) to cause, bring; **~rsi** *vr* to go.

**re'cedere** [re'tʃedere] *vi* to withdraw.

**recensi'one** [retʃen'sjone] *sf* review; **recen'sire** *vt* to review.

**re'cente** [re'tʃente] *ag* recent; **di ~** recently; **recente'mente** *av* recently.

**recessi'one** [retʃes'sjone] *sf* (*ECON*) recession.

**re'cidere** [re'tʃidere] *vt* to cut off, chop off.

**reci'divo, a** [retʃi'divo] *smf* (*DIR*) second (*o* habitual) offender, recidivist.

**re'cinto** [re'tʃinto] *sm* enclosure; (*ciò che recinge*) fence; surrounding wall.

**recipi'ente** [retʃi'pjente] *sm* container.

**re'ciproco, a, ci, che** [re'tʃiproko] *ag* reciprocal.

**re'ciso, a** [re'tʃizo] *pp di* **recidere**.

'**recita** ['rɛtʃita] *sf* performance.

**reci'tare** [retʃi'tare] *vt* (*poesia, lezione*) to recite; (*dramma*) to perform; (*ruolo*) to play o act (the part of); **recitazi'one** *sf* recitation; (*di attore*) acting.

**recla'mare** *vi* to complain // *vt* (*richiedere*) to demand.

**ré'clame** [re'klam] *sf inv* advertising *q*; advertisement, advert (*Brit*), ad (*fam*).

**re'clamo** *sm* complaint.

**reclusi'one** *sf* (*DIR*) imprisonment.

'**recluta** *sf* recruit; **reclu'tare** *vt* to recruit.

**re'condito, a** *ag* secluded; (*fig*) secret, hidden.

**recriminazi'one** [rekriminat'tsjone] *sf* recrimination.

**recrude'scenza** [rekrudeʃ'ʃɛntsa] *sf* fresh outbreak.

**recupe'rare** *vt* = ricuperare.

**redargu'ire** *vt* to rebuke.

**re'datto, a** *pp di* **redigere**; **redat'tore, 'trice** *smf* (*STAMPA*) editor; (: *di articolo*) writer; (*di dizionario etc*) compiler; **redattore capo** chief editor; **redazi'one** *sf* editing; writing; (*sede*) editorial office(s); (*personale*) editorial staff; (*versione*) version.

**reddi'tizio, a** [reddi'tittsjo] *ag* profitable.

'**reddito** *sm* income; (*dello Stato*) revenue; (*di un capitale*) yield.

**re'dento, a** *pp di* **redimere**.

**redenzi'one** [reden'tsjone] *sf* redemption.

**re'digere** [re'didʒere] *vt* to write; (*contratto*) to draw up.

**re'dimere** *vt* to deliver; (*REL*) to redeem.

'**redini** *sfpl* reins.

'**reduce** ['rɛdutʃe] *ag*: ~ **da** returning from, back from // *smf* survivor.

**refe'rendum** *sm inv* referendum.

**refe'renza** [refe'rɛntsa] *sf* reference.

**re'ferto** *sm* medical report.

**refet'torio** *sm* refectory.

**refrat'tario, a** *ag* refractory.

**refrige'rare** [refridʒe'rare] *vt* to refrigerate; (*rinfrescare*) to cool, refresh.

**rega'lare** *vt* to give (as a present), make a present of.

**re'gale** *ag* regal.

**re'galo** *sm* gift, present.

**re'gata** *sf* regatta.

**reg'gente** [red'dʒɛnte] *smf* regent.

'**reggere** ['reddʒere] *vt* (*tenere*) to hold; (*sostenere*) to support, bear, hold up; (*portare*) to carry, bear; (*resistere*) to withstand; (*dirigere: impresa*) to manage, run; (*governare*) to rule, govern; (*LING*) to take, be followed by // *vi* (*resistere*): ~ **a** to stand up to, hold out against; (*sopportare*): ~ **a** to stand; (*durare*) to last; (*fig: teoria etc*) to hold water; ~rsi *vr* (*stare ritto*) to stand; (*fig: dominarsi*) to control o.s.; ~rsi **sulle gambe** *o* **in piedi** to stand up.

'**reggia, ge** ['reddʒa] *sf* royal palace.

**reggi'calze** [reddʒi'kaltse] *sm inv* suspender belt.

**reggi'mento** [reddʒi'mento] *sm* (*MIL*) regiment.

**reggi'petto** [reddʒi'petto] *sm*, **reggi'seno** [reddʒi'seno] *sm* bra.

**re'gia, gie** [re'dʒia] *sf* (*TV, CINEMA etc*) direction.

**re'gime** [re'dʒime] *sm* (*POL*) regime; (*DIR: aureo, patrimoniale etc*) system; (*MED*) diet; (*TECN*) (engine) speed.

**re'gina** [re'dʒina] *sf* queen.

'**regio, a, gi, gie** ['rɛdʒo] *ag* royal.

**regio'nale** [redʒo'nale] *ag* regional.

**regi'one** [re'dʒone] *sf* region; (*territorio*) region, district, area.

**re'gista, i, e** [re'dʒista] *smf* (*TV, CINEMA etc*) director.

**regis'trare** [redʒis'trare] *vt* (*AMM*) to register; (*COMM*) to enter; (*notare*) to note, take note of; (*canzone, conversazione, sog: strumento di misura*) to record; (*mettere a punto*) to adjust, regulate; (*bagagli*) to check in; **registra'tore** *sm* (*strumento*) recorder, register;

(*magnetofono*) tape recorder; **registratore di cassa** cash register; **registrazi'one** *sf* recording; (*AMM*) registration; (*COMM*) entry; (*di bagagli*) check-in.

re'gistro [re'dʒistro] *sm* (*libro*) register; ledger; logbook; (*DIR*) registry; (*MUS, TECN*) register.

re'gnare [reɲ'nare] *vi* to reign, rule; (*fig*) to reign.

'regno ['reɲɲo] *sm* kingdom; (*periodo*) reign; (*fig*) realm; **il ~ animale/vegetale** the animal/vegetable kingdom; **il R~ Unito** the United Kingdom.

'regola *sf* rule; **a ~ d'arte** duly; perfectly; **in ~** in order.

regola'mento *sm* (*complesso di norme*) regulations *pl*; (*di debito*) settlement; **~ di conti** (*fig*) settling of scores.

rego'lare *ag* regular; (*in regola: domanda*) in order, lawful // *vt* to regulate, control; (*apparecchio*) to adjust, regulate; (*questione, conto, debito*) to settle; **~rsi** *vr* (*moderarsi*): **~rsi nel bere/nello spendere** to control one's drinking/spending; (*comportarsi*) to behave, act; **regolarità** *sf inv* regularity.

'regolo *sm* ruler; **~ calcolatore** slide rule.

reinte'grare *vt* (*energie*) to recover; (*in una carica*) to reinstate.

rela'tivo, a *ag* relative.

relazi'one [relat'tsjone] *sf* (*fra cose, persone*) relation(ship); (*resoconto*) report, account; **~i** *sfpl* (*conoscenze*) connections.

rele'gare *vt* to banish; (*fig*) to relegate.

religi'one [reli'dʒone] *sf* religion; **religi'oso, a** *ag* religious // *sm/f* monk/nun.

re'liquia *sf* relic.

re'litto *sm* wreck; (*fig*) down-and-out.

re'mare *vi* to row.

remini'scenze [reminiʃ'ʃentse] *sfpl* reminiscences.

remissi'one *sf* remission.

remis'sivo, a *ag* submissive, compliant.

'remo *sm* oar.

re'moto, a *ag* remote.

'rendere *vt* (*ridare*) to return, give back; (: *saluto etc*) to return; (*produrre*) to yield, bring in; (*esprimere, tradurre*) to render; (*far diventare*): **~ qc possibile** to make sth possible; **~ grazie a qn** to thank sb; **~rsi utile** to make o.s. useful; **~rsi conto di qc** to realize sth.

rendi'conto *sm* (*rapporto*) report, account; (*AMM, COMM*) statement of account.

rendi'mento *sm* (*reddito*) yield; (*di manodopera, TECN*) efficiency; (*capacità di produrre*) output; (*di studenti*) performance.

'rendita *sf* (*di individuo*) private o unearned income; (*COMM*) revenue; **~ annua** annuity.

'rene *sm* kidney.

'reni *sfpl* back *sg*.

reni'tente *ag* reluctant, unwilling; **~ ai consigli di qn** unwilling to follow sb's advice; **essere ~ alla leva** (*MIL*) to fail to report for military service.

'renna *sf* reindeer *inv*.

'Reno *sm*: **il ~** the Rhine.

'reo, a *sm/f* (*DIR*) offender.

re'parto *sm* department, section; (*MIL*) detachment.

repel'lente *ag* repulsive.

repen'taglio [repen'taʎʎo] *sm*: **mettere a ~** to jeopardize, risk.

repen'tino, a *ag* sudden, unexpected.

repe'rire *vt* to find, trace.

re'perto *sm* (*ARCHEOLOGIA*) find; (*MED*) report; (*DIR: anche*: **~ giudiziario**) exhibit.

reper'torio *sm* (*TEATRO*) repertory; (*elenco*) index, (alphabetical) list.

'replica, *sf* (*ripetizione*) reply, answer; (*obiezione*) objection; (*TEATRO, CINEMA*) repeat performance;

(*copia*) replica.

**repli'care** *vt* (*ripetere*) to repeat; (*rispondere*) to answer, reply.

**repressi'one** *sf* repression.

**re'presso, a** *pp di* **reprimere**.

**re'primere** *vt* to suppress, repress.

**re'pubblica, che** *sf* republic; **repubbli'cano, a** *ag, smf* republican.

**repu'tare** *vt* to consider, judge.

**reputazi'one** [reputat'tsjone] *sf* reputation.

**'requie** *sf*: senza ~ unceasingly.

**requi'sire** *vt* to requisition.

**requi'sito** *sm* requirement.

**requisizi'one** [rekwizit'tsjone] *sf* requisition.

**'resa** *sf* (*l'arrendersi*) surrender; (*restituzione, rendimento*) return; ~ **dei conti** rendering of accounts; (*fig*) day of reckoning.

**resi'dente** *ag* resident; **resi'denza** *sf* residence; **residenzi'ale** *ag* residential.

**re'siduo, a** *ag* residual, remaining // *sm* remainder; (*CHIM*) residue.

**'resina** *sf* resin.

**resis'tente** *ag* (*che resiste*): ~ **a** resistant to; (*forte*) strong; (*duraturo*) long-lasting, durable; ~ **al caldo** heat-resistant; **resis'tenza** *sf* resistance; (*di persona: fisica*) stamina, endurance; (*: mentale*) endurance, resistance.

**re'sistere** *vi* to resist; ~ **a** (*assalto, tentazioni*) to resist; (*dolore, sog: pianta*) to withstand; (*non patir danno*) to be resistant to; **resis'tito, a** *pp di* **resistere**.

**'reso, a** *pp di* **rendere**.

**reso'conto** *sm* report, account.

**res'pingere** [res'pindʒere] *vt* to drive back, repel; (*rifiutare*) to reject; (*INS: bocciare*) to fail; **res'pinto, a** *pp di* **respingere**.

**respi'rare** *vi* to breathe; (*fig*) to get one's breath; to breathe again // *vt* to breathe (in), inhale; **respira'tore** *sm* respirator; **respirazi'one** *sf* breathing; **respirazione artificiale**

artificial respiration; **res'piro** *sm* breathing *q*; (*singolo atto*) breath; (*fig*) respite, rest; **mandare un respiro di sollievo** to give a sigh of relief.

**respon'sabile** *ag* responsible // *smf* person responsible; (*capo*) person in charge; ~ **di** responsible for; (*DIR*) liable for; **responsabilità** *sf inv* responsibility; (*legale*) liability.

**res'ponso** *sm* answer.

**'ressa** *sf* crowd, throng.

**res'tare** *vi* (*rimanere*) to remain, stay; (*diventare*): ~ **orfano/cieco** to become o be left an orphan/become blind; (*trovarsi*): ~ **sorpreso** to be surprised; (*avanzare*) to be left, remain; ~ **d'accordo** to agree; **non resta più niente** there's nothing left; **restano pochi giorni** there are only a few days left.

**restau'rare** *vt* to restore; **restaurazi'one** *sf* (*POL*) restoration; **res'tauro** *sm* (*di edifici etc*) restoration.

**res'tio, a, 'tii, 'tie** *ag* restive; (*persona*): ~ **a** reluctant to.

**restitu'ire** *vt* to return, give back; (*energie, forze*) to restore.

**'resto** *sm* remainder, rest; (*denaro*) change; (*MAT*) remainder; ~**i** *smpl* leftovers; (*di città*) remains; **del** ~ moreover, besides; ~**i mortali** (*mortal*) remains.

**res'tringere** [res'trindʒere] *vt* to reduce; (*vestito*) to take in; (*stoffa*) to shrink; (*fig*) to restrict, limit; ~**rsi** *vr* (*strada*) to narrow; (*stoffa*) to shrink; **restrizi'one** *sf* restriction.

**'rete** *sf* net; (*fig*) trap, snare; (*di recinzione*) wire netting; (*AUT, FERR, di spionaggio etc*) network; **segnare una** ~ (*CALCIO*) to score a goal; ~ **del letto** (*sprung*) bed base.

**reti'cente** [reti'tʃɛnte] *ag* reticent.

**retico'lato** *sm* grid; (*rete metallica*) wire netting; (*di filo spinato*) barbed wire (fence).

**'retina** *sf* (*ANAT*) retina.

**re'torico, a, ci, che** *ag* rhetorical

// sf rhetoric.

**retribu'ire** vt to pay; (premiare) to reward; **retribuzi'one** sf payment; reward.

'**retro** sm inv back // av (dietro): **vedi** ~ see over(leaf).

**retro'cedere** vi to withdraw // vt (CALCIO) to relegate; (MIL) to degrade.

**re'trogrado, a** ag (fig) reactionary, backward-looking.

**retro'marcia** [retro'martʃa] sf (AUT) reverse; (: dispositivo) reverse gear.

**retrospet'tivo, a** ag retrospective.

**retrovi'sore** sm (AUT) (rear-view) mirror.

'**retta** sf (MAT) straight line; (di convitto) charge for bed and board; (fig: ascolto): **dar** ~ **a** to listen to, pay attention to.

**rettango'lare** ag rectangular.

**ret'tangolo, a** ag right-angled // sm rectangle.

**ret'tifica, che** sf rectification, correction.

**rettifi'care** vt (curva) to straighten; (fig) to rectify, correct.

'**rettile** sm reptile.

**retti'lineo, a** ag rectilinear.

**retti'tudine** sf rectitude, uprightness.

'**retto, a** pp di **reggere** // ag straight; (MAT): **angolo** ~ right angle; (onesto) honest, upright; (giusto, esatto) correct, proper, right.

**ret'tore** sm (REL) rector; (di università) ≈ chancellor.

**reuma'tismo** sm rheumatism.

**reve'rendo, a** ag: **il** ~ **padre Belli** the Reverend Father Belli.

**rever'sibile** ag reversible.

**revisio'nare** vt (conti) to audit; (TECN) to overhaul, service; (DIR: processo) to review; (componimento) to revise.

**revisi'one** sf auditing q; audit; servicing q; overhaul; review; revision.

**revi'sore** sm: ~ **di conti/bozze** auditor/proofreader.

'**revoca** sf revocation.

**revo'care** vt to revoke.

**re'volver** sm inv revolver.

**riabili'tare** vt to rehabilitate; (fig) to restore to favour.

**rial'zare** [rial'tsare] vt to raise, lift; (alzare di più) to heighten, raise; (aumentare: prezzi) to increase, raise // vi (prezzi) to rise, increase; **ri'alzo** sm (di prezzi) increase, rise; (sporgenza) rise.

**rianimazi'one** [rianimat'tsjone] sf (MED) resuscitation; **centro di** ~ intensive care unit.

**riap'pendere** vt to rehang; (TEL) to hang up.

**ria'prire** vt, ~rsi vr to reopen, open again.

**ri'armo** sm (MIL) rearmament.

**rias'setto** sm (di stanza etc) rearrangement; (ordinamento) reorganization.

**rias'sumere** vt (riprendere) to resume; (impiegare di nuovo) to reemploy; (sintetizzare) to summarize; **rias'sunto, a** pp di **riassumere** // sm summary.

**ria'vere** vt to have again; (avere indietro) to get back; (riacquistare) to recover; ~rsi vr to recover.

**riba'dire** vt (fig) to confirm.

**ri'balta** sf flap; (TEATRO: proscenio) front of the stage; (: apparecchio d'illuminazione) footlights pl; (fig) limelight.

**ribal'tabile** ag (sedile) tip-up.

**ribal'tare** vt, vi (anche: ~rsi) to turn over, tip over.

**ribas'sare** vt to lower, bring down // vi to come down, fall; **ri'basso** sm reduction, fall.

**ri'battere** vt to return, hit back; (confutare) to refute; ~ **che** to retort that.

**ribel'larsi** vr: ~ **(a)** to rebel (against); **ri'belle** ag (soldati) rebel; (ragazzo) rebellious // smf rebel; **ribelli'one** sf rebellion.

'**ribes** sm inv currant; ~ **nero** blackcurrant; ~ **rosso** redcurrant.

**ribol'lire** vi (fermentare) to ferment; (fare bolle) to bubble, boil; (fig) to seethe.

**ri'brezzo** [ri'breddzo] sm disgust, loathing; **far** ~ **a** to disgust.

**ribut'tante** ag disgusting, revolting.

**rica'dere** vi to fall again; (scendere a terra, fig: nel peccato etc) to fall back; (vestiti, capelli etc) to hang (down); (riversarsi: fatiche, colpe): ~ **su** to fall on; **rica'duta** sf (MED) relapse.

**rical'care** vt (disegni) to trace; (fig) to follow faithfully.

**rica'mare** vt to embroider.

**ricambi'are** vt to change again; (contraccambiare) to repay, return; **ri'cambio** sm exchange, return; (FISIOL) metabolism; **ricambi** smpl, **pezzi di ricambio** spare parts.

**ri'camo** sm embroidery.

**ricapito'lare** vt to recapitulate, sum up.

**ricari'care** vt (arma, macchina fotografica) to reload; (pipa) to refill; (orologio) to rewind; (batteria) to recharge.

**ricat'tare** vt to blackmail; **ricatta'tore**, **'trice** smf blackmailer; **ri'catto** sm blackmail.

**rica'vare** vt (estrarre) to draw out, extract; (ottenere) to obtain, gain; **ri'cavo** sm proceeds pl.

**ric'chezza** [rik'kettsa] sf wealth; (fig) richness; ~**e** sfpl (beni) wealth sg, riches.

**'riccio, a** ['rittfo] ag curly // sm (ZOOL) hedgehog; (: anche: ~ **di mare**) sea urchin; **'ricciolo** sm curl; **ricci'uto, a** ag curly.

**'ricco, a, chi, che** ag rich; (persona, paese) rich, wealthy // smf rich man/woman; **i** ~**chi** the rich; ~ **di** full of; rich in.

**ri'cerca, che** [ri'tferka] sf search; (indagine) investigation, inquiry; (studio): **la** ~ research; **una** ~ piece of research.

**ricer'care** [ritfer'kare] vt (motivi, cause) to look for, try to determine;

(successo, piacere) to pursue; (onore, gloria) to seek; **ricer'cato, a** ag (apprezzato) much sought-after; (affettato) studied, affected // smf (POLIZIA) wanted man/woman.

**ri'cetta** [ri'tfetta] sf (MED) prescription; (CUC) recipe.

**ricettazi'one** [ritfettat'tsjone] sf (DIR) receiving (stolen goods).

**ri'cevere** [ri'tfevere] vt to receive; (stipendio, lettera) to get, receive; (accogliere: ospite) to welcome; (vedere: cliente, rappresentante etc) to see; **ricevi'mento** sm receiving q; (trattenimento) reception; **rice-vi'tore** sm (TECN) receiver; **ricevitore delle imposte** tax collector; **rice'vuta** sf receipt; **ricevuta fiscale** receipt for tax purposes; **ricezi'one** sf (RADIO, TV) reception.

**richia'mare** [rikja'mare] vt (chiamare indietro, ritelefonare) to call back; (ambasciatore, truppe) to recall; (rimproverare) to reprimand; (attirare) to attract, draw; ~**rsi a** (riferirsi a) to refer to; **richi'amo** sm call; recall; reprimand; attraction.

**richi'edere** [ri'kjedere] vt to ask again for; (chiedere indietro): ~ **qc** to ask for sth back; (chiedere: per sapere) to ask; (: per avere) to ask for; (AMM: documenti) to apply for; (esigere) to need, require; **ri-chi'esto, a** pp di **richiedere** // sf (domanda) request; (AMM) application, request; (esigenza) demand, request; **a richiesta** on request.

**'ricino** ['ritfino] sm: **olio di** ~ castor oil.

**ricognizi'one** [rikoɲɲit'tsjone] sf (MIL) reconnaissance; (DIR) recognition, acknowledgement.

**ricominci'are** [rikomin'tfare] vt, vi to start again, begin again.

**ricom'pensa** sf reward.

**ricompen'sare** vt to reward.

**riconcili'are** [rikontʃi'ljare] vt to reconcile; ~**rsi** vr to be reconciled;

**riconciliazi'one** sf reconciliation.

**ricono'scente** [rikonoʃ'fɛnte] ag grateful; **ricono'scenza** sf gratitude.

**rico'noscere** [riko'noʃʃere] vt to recognize; (DIR: figlio, debito) to acknowledge; (ammettere: errore) to admit, acknowledge; **riconosci'mento** sm recognition; acknowledgement; (identificazione) identification; **riconosci'uto, a** pp di **riconoscere**.

**rico'prire** vt (coprire) to cover; (occupare: carica) to hold.

**ricor'dare** vt to remember, recall; (richiamare alla memoria): ~ qc a qn to remind sb of sth; ~rsi vr: ~rsi (di) to remember; ~rsi di qc/ di aver fatto to remember sth/ having done.

**ri'cordo** sm memory; (regalo) keepsake, souvenir; (di viaggio) souvenir; ~i smpl (memorie) memoirs.

**ricor'rente** ag recurrent, recurring; **ricor'renza** sf recurrence; (festività) anniversary.

**ri'correre** vi (ripetersi) to recur; ~ a (rivolgersi) to turn to; (: DIR) to appeal to; (servirsi di) to have recourse to; **ri'corso, a** pp di **ricorrere** (DIR) sm recurrence; (DIR) appeal; **far ricorso a** = **ricorrere a**.

**ricostru'ire** vt (casa) to rebuild; (fatti) to reconstruct; **ricostruzi'one** sf rebuilding; reconstruction.

**ri'cotta** sf soft white unsalted cheese made from sheep's milk.

**ricove'rare** vt to give shelter to; ~ qn in ospedale to admit sb to hospital.

**ri'covero** sm shelter, refuge; (MIL) shelter; (MED) admission (to hospital).

**ricre'are** vt to recreate; (rinvigorire) to restore; (fig: distrarre) to amuse.

**ricreazi'one** sf [rikreat'tsjone] sf recreation, entertainment; (INS) break.

**ri'credersi** vr to change one's mind.

**ricupe'rare** vt (rientrare in possesso di) to recover, get back; (tempo perduto) to make up for; (NAUT) to salvage; (: naufraghi) to rescue; (delinquente) to rehabilitate; ~ lo svantaggio (SPORT) to close the gap.

**ridacchi'are** [ridak'kjare] vi to snigger.

**ri'dare** vt to return, give back.

**'ridere** vi to laugh; (deridere, beffare): ~ di to laugh at, make fun of.

**ri'detto, a** pp di ridire.

**ri'dicolo, a** ag ridiculous, absurd.

**ridimensio'nare** vt to reorganize; (fig) to see in the right perspective.

**ri'dire** vt to repeat; (criticare) to find fault with; to object to; **trova sempre qualcosa da ~** he always manages to find fault.

**ridon'dante** ag redundant.

**ri'dotto, a** pp di ridurre.

**ri'durre** vt (anche CHIM, MAT) to reduce; (prezzo, spese) to cut, reduce; (accorciare: opera letteraria) to abridge; (: RADIO, TV) to adapt; **ridursi** vr (diminuirsi) to be reduced, shrink; **ridursi a** to be reduced to; **ridursi pelle e ossa** to be reduced to skin and bone; **riduzi'one** sf reduction; abridgement; adaptation.

**riem'pire** vt to fill (up); (modulo) to fill in o out; ~rsi vr to fill (up); (mangiare troppo) to stuff o.s.; ~ qc di to fill sth (up) with.

**rien'tranza** [rien'trantsa] sf recess; indentation.

**rien'trare** vi (entrare di nuovo) to go (o come) back in; (tornare) to return; (fare una rientranza) to go in, curve inwards; (to be indented; (riguardare): ~ in to be included among, form part of; **ri'entro** sm (ritorno) return; (di astronave) re-entry.

**riepilo'gare** vt to summarize // vi to recapitulate.

**ri'fare** vt to do again; (ricostruire) to make again; (nodo) to tie again, do up again; (imitare) to imitate, copy; ~rsi vr (riarcirsi): ~rsi di to make up for; (vendicarsi): ~rsi di qc su qn to get one's own back on sb for sth; (riferirsi): ~rsi a to go back to; to follow; ~ il letto to make the bed; ~rsi una vita to make a new life for o.s.; **ri'fatto, a** pp di **rifare**.

**riferi'mento** sm reference; **in** o **con ~ a** with reference to.

**rife'rire** vt (riportare) to report; (ascrivere): ~ **qc a** to attribute sth to // vi to do a report; ~rsi vr: ~rsi **a** to refer to.

**rifi'nire** vt to finish off, put the finishing touches to; **rifini'tura** sf finishing touch; **rifiniture** sfpl (di mobile, auto) finish sg.

**rifiu'tare** vt to refuse; ~ **di fare** to refuse to do; **rifi'uto** sm refusal; **rifiuti** smpl (spazzatura) rubbish sg, refuse sg.

**riflessi'one** sf (FISICA, meditazione) reflection; (il pensare) thought, reflection; (osservazione) remark.

**rifles'sivo, a** ag (persona) thoughtful, reflective; (LING) reflexive.

**ri'flesso, a** pp di **riflettere** // sm (di luce, rispecchiamento) reflection; (FISIOL) reflex; **di** o **per ~** indirectly.

**ri'flettere** vt to reflect // vi to think; ~rsi vr to be reflected; ~ **su** to think over.

**riflet'tore** sm reflector; (proiettore) floodlight; searchlight.

**ri'flusso** sm flowing back; (della marea) ebb; **un'epoca di ~** an era of nostalgia.

**ri'fondere** vt (rimborsare) to refund, repay.

**ri'forma** sf reform; **la R~** (REL) the Reformation.

**rifor'mare** vt to re-form; (cambiare, innovare) to reform; (MIL: recluta) to declare unfit for service; (: soldato) to invalid out, discharge; **riforma'torio** sm (DIR) community

home (Brit), reformatory (US).

**riforni'mento** sm supplying, providing; restocking; ~**i** smpl supplies, provisions.

**rifor'nire** vt (provvedere): ~ **di** to supply o provide with; (fornire di nuovo: casa etc) to restock.

**ri'frangere** [ri'frandʒere] vt to refract; **ri'fratto, a** pp di **rifrangere**; **rifrazi'one** sf refraction.

**rifug'gire** [rifud'dʒire] vi to escape again; (fig): ~ **da** to shun.

**rifugi'arsi** [rifu'dʒarsi] vr to take refuge; **rifugi'ato, a** sm/f refugee.

**ri'fugio** [ri'fudʒo] sm refuge, shelter; (in montagna) shelter; ~ **antiaereo** air-raid shelter.

**'riga, ghe** sf line; (striscia) stripe; (di persone, cose) line, row; (regolo) ruler; (scriminatura) parting; mettersi in ~ to line up; **a ~ghe** (foglio) lined; (vestito) striped.

**ri'gagnolo** [ri'gaɲɲolo] sm rivulet.

**ri'gare** vt (foglio) to rule // vi: ~ **diritto** (fig) to toe the line.

**rigat'tiere** sm junk dealer.

**riget'tare** [ridʒet'tare] vt (gettare indietro) to throw back; (fig: respingere) to reject; (vomitare) to bring o throw up; **ri'getto** sm (anche MED) rejection.

**rigidità** [ridʒidi'ta] sf rigidity; stiffness; severity, rigours pl; strictness.

**'rigido, a** ['ridʒido] ag rigid, stiff; (membra etc: indurite) stiff; (METEOR) harsh, severe; (fig) strict.

**rigi'rare** [ridʒi'rare] vt to turn; ~rsi vr to turn round; (nel letto) to turn over; ~ **qc tra le mani** to turn sth over in one's hands; ~ **il discorso** to change the subject.

**'rigo, ghi** sm line; (MUS) staff, stave.

**rigogli'oso, a** [rigoʎ'ʎoso] ag (pianta) luxuriant; (fig: commercio, sviluppo) thriving.

**ri'gonfio, a** ag swollen.

**ri'gore** sm (METEOR) harshness, rigours pl; (fig) severity, strictness; (anche: **calcio di ~**) penalty; **di ~**

compulsory; **a rigor di termini** strictly speaking; **rigo'roso, a** ag (severo: persona, ordine) strict; (preciso) rigorous.

**rigover'nare** vt to wash (up).

**riguar'dare** vt to look at again; (considerare) to regard, consider; (concernere) to regard, concern; ~rsi vr (aver cura di sé) to look after o.s.

**rigu'ardo** sm (attenzione) care; (considerazione) regard, respect; ~ **a** concerning, with regard to; **non aver ~i nell'agire/nel parlare** to act/speak freely.

**rilasci'are** [rilaʃˈʃare] vt (rimettere in libertà) to release; (AMM: documenti) to issue; **ri'lascio** sm release; issue.

**rilas'sare** vt to relax; ~rsi vr to relax; (fig: disciplina) to become slack.

**rile'gare** vt (libro) to bind; **rilega'tura** sf binding.

**ri'leggere** [riˈlɛddʒere] vt to reread, read again; (rivedere) to read over.

**ri'lento: a ~** av slowly.

**rileva'mento** sm (topografico, statistico) survey; (NAUT) bearing.

**rile'vante** ag considerable; important.

**rile'vare** vt (ricavare) to find; (notare) to notice; (mettere in evidenza) to point out; (venire a conoscere: notizia) to learn; (raccogliere: dati) to gather, collect; (TOPOGRAFIA) to survey; (MIL) to relieve; (COMM) to take over.

**rili'evo** sm (ARTE, GEO) relief; (fig: rilevanza) importance; (osservazione) point, remark; (TOPOGRAFIA) survey; **dar ~ a o mettere in ~ qc** (fig) to bring sth out, highlight sth.

**rilut'tante** ag reluctant; **rilut'tanza** sf reluctance.

**'rima** sf rhyme; (verso) verse.

**riman'dare** vt to send again; (restituire, rinviare) to send back, return; (differire): ~ **qc (a)** to postpone sth o put sth off (till); (fare rife-

rimento): ~ **qn a** to refer sb to; **essere rimandato** (INS) to have to repeat one's exams; **ri'mando** sm (rinvio) return; (dilazione) postponement; (riferimento) cross-reference.

**rima'nente** ag remaining // sm rest, remainder; **i ~i** (persone) the rest of them, the others; **rima'nenza** sf rest, remainder; **rimanenze** sfpl (COMM) unsold stock sg.

**rima'nere** vi (restare) to remain, stay; (avanzare) to be left, remain; (restare stupito) to be amazed; (restare, mancare): **rimangono poche settimane a Pasqua** there are only a few weeks left till Easter; **rimane da vedere se** it remains to be seen whether; (diventare): ~ **vedovo** to be left a widower; (trovarsi): ~ **confuso/sorpreso** to be confused/surprised.

**ri'mare** vt, vi to rhyme.

**rimargi'nare** [rimardʒiˈnare] vt, vi (anche: ~rsi) to heal.

**ri'masto, a** pp di **rimanere**.

**rima'sugli** [rimaˈsuʎʎi] smpl leftovers.

**rimbal'zare** [rimbalˈtsare] vi to bounce back, rebound; (proiettile) to ricochet; **rim'balzo** sm rebound; ricochet.

**rimbam'bito, a** ag senile, in one's dotage.

**rimboc'care** vt (orlo) to turn up; (coperta) to tuck in; (maniche, pantaloni) to turn o roll up.

**rimbom'bare** vi to resound.

**rimbor'sare** vt to pay back, repay; **rim'borso** sm repayment.

**rimedi'are** vi: ~ **a** to remedy // vt (fam: procurarsi) to get o scrape together.

**ri'medio** sm (medicina) medicine; (cura, fig) remedy, cure.

**rimesco'lare** vt to mix well, stir well; (carte) to shuffle; **sentirsi ~ il sangue** (per paura) to feel one's blood run cold; (per rabbia) to feel one's blood boil.

**ri'messa** sf (locale: per veicoli) garage; (: *per aerei*) hangar; (*COMM*: *di merce*) consignment; (: *di denaro*) remittance; (*TENNIS*) return; (*CALCIO*: *anche*: ~ **in gioco**) throw-in.

**ri'messo, a** *pp* di **rimettere**.

**ri'mettere** *vt* (*mettere di nuovo*) to put back; (*indossare di nuovo*): ~ **qc** to put sth back on, put sth on again; (*restituire*) to return, give back; (*affidare*) to entrust; (: *decisione*) to refer; (*condonare*) to remit; (*COMM*: *merci*) to deliver; (: *denaro*) to remit; (*vomitare*) to bring up; (*perdere*: *anche*: **rimetterci**) to lose; ~**rsi al bello** (*tempo*) to clear up; ~**rsi in salute** to get better, recover one's health.

**'rimmel** *sm inv* ® mascara.

**rimoder'nare** *vt* to modernize.

**rimon'tare** *vt* (*meccanismo*) to reassemble; (: *tenda*) to put up again // *vi* (*salire di nuovo*): ~ **in** (*macchina, treno*) to get back into; (*SPORT*) to close the gap.

**rimorchi'are** [rimor'kjare] *vt* to tow; (*fig*: *ragazza*) to pick up; **rimorchia'tore** *sm* (*NAUT*) tug(boat).

**ri'morchio** [ri'morkjo] *sm* tow; (*veicolo*) trailer.

**ri'morso** *sm* remorse.

**rimozi'one** [rimot'tsjone] *sf* removal; (*da un impiego*) dismissal; (*PSIC*) repression.

**rim'pasto** *sm* (*POL*) reshuffle.

**rimpatri'are** *vi* to return home // *vt* to repatriate; **rim'patrio** *sm* repatriation.

**rimpi'angere** [rim'pjandʒere] *vt* to regret; (*persona*) to miss; **rimpi'anto, a** *pp* di **rimpiangere** // *sm* regret.

**rimpiat'tino** *sm* hide-and-seek.

**rimpiaz'zare** [rimpjat'tsare] *vt* to replace.

**rimpiccio'lire** [rimpittʃo'lire] *vt* to make smaller // *vi* (*anche*: ~**rsi**) to become smaller.

**rimpin'zare** [rimpin'tsare] *vt*: ~ **di** to cram o stuff with.

**rimprove'rare** *vt* to rebuke, rep-

rimand; **rim'provero** *sm* rebuke, reprimand.

**rimugi'nare** [rimudʒi'nare] *vt* (*fig*) to turn over in one's mind.

**rimunerazi'one** [rimunerat'tsjone] *sf* remuneration; (*premio*) reward.

**rimu'overe** *vt* to remove; (*destituire*) to dismiss.

**Rinasci'mento** [rinaʃʃi'mento] *sm*: **il** ~ the Renaissance.

**ri'nascita** [ri'naʃʃita] *sf* rebirth, revival.

**rincal'zare** [rinkal'tsare] *vt* (*palo, albero*) to support, prop up; (*lenzuola*) to tuck in.

**rinca'rare** *vt* to increase the price of // *vi* to go up, become more expensive.

**rinca'sare** *vi* to go home.

**rinchi'udere** [rin'kjudere] *vt* to shut (o lock) up; ~**rsi** *vr*: ~**rsi in** to shut o.s. up in; ~**rsi in se stesso** to withdraw into o.s.; **rinchi'uso, a** *pp* di **rinchiudere**.

**rin'correre** *vt* to chase, run after; **rin'corso, a** *pp* di **rincorrere** // *sf* short run.

**rin'crescere** [rin'kreʃʃere] *vb impers*: **mi rincresce che/di non poter fare** I'm sorry that/I can't do, I regret that/being unable to do; **rincresci'mento** *sm* regret; **rincresci'uto, a** *pp* di **rincrescere**.

**rincu'lare** *vi* to draw back; (*arma*) to recoil.

**rinfacci'are** [rinfat'tʃare] *vt* (*fig*): ~ **qc a qn** to throw sth in sb's face.

**rinfor'zare** [rinfor'tsare] *vt* to reinforce, strengthen // *vi* (*anche*: ~**rsi**) to grow stronger; **rin'forzo** *sm*: **mettere un rinforzo a** to strengthen; **di rinforzo** (*asse, sbarra*) strengthening; (*esercito*) supporting; (*personale*) extra, additional; **rinforzi** *smpl* (*MIL*) reinforcements.

**rinfran'care** *vt* to encourage, reassure.

**rinfres'care** *vt* (*atmosfera, temperatura*) to cool (down); (*abito, pa-*

*reti*) to freshen up // *vi* (*tempo*) to grow cooler; **~rsi** *vr* (*ristorarsi*) to refresh o.s.; (*lavarsi*) to freshen up; **rin'fresco, schi** *sm* (*festa*) party; **rinfreschi** *smpl* refreshments.

**rin'fusa** *sf*: **alla ~** in confusion, higgledy-piggledy.

**ringhi'are** [riŋ'gjare] *vi* to growl, snarl.

**ringhi'era** [riŋ'gjɛra] *sf* railing; (*delle scale*) banister(s *pl*).

**ringiova'nire** [rindʒova'nire] *vt* (*sog: vestito, acconciatura etc*): **~ qn** to make sb look younger; (: *vacanze etc*) to rejuvenate // *vi* (*anche:* **~rsi**) to become (*o* look) younger.

**ringrazia'mento** [ringrattsja'mento] *sm* thanks *pl*.

**ringrazi'are** [ringrat'tsjare] *vt* to thank; **~ qn di qc** to thank sb for sth.

**rinne'gare** *vt* (*fede*) to renounce; (*figlio*) to disown, repudiate; **rinne'gato, a** *sm/f* renegade.

**rinnova'mento** *sm* renewal; (*economico*) revival.

**rinno'vare** *vt* to renew; (*ripetere*) to repeat, renew; **~rsi** *vr* (*fenomeno*) to be repeated, recur; **rin'novo** *sm* (*di contratto*) renewal; "chiuso per rinnovo dei locali" "closed for alterations".

**rinoce'ronte** [rinotʃe'ronte] *sm* rhinoceros.

**rino'mato, a** *ag* renowned, celebrated.

**rinsal'dare** *vt* to strengthen.

**rintoc'care** *vi* (*campana*) to toll; (*orologio*) to strike.

**rintracci'are** [rintrat'tʃare] *vt* to track down.

**rintro'nare** *vi* to boom, roar // *vt* (*assordare*) to deafen; (*stordire*) to stun.

**ri'nuncia** [ri'nuntʃa] *etc* = **rinunzia** *etc*.

**ri'nunzia** [ri'nuntsja] *sf* renunciation.

**rinunzi'are** [rinun'tsjare] *vi*: **~ a** to give up, renounce.

**rinve'nire** *vt* to find, recover; (*scoprire*) to discover, find out // *vi* (*riprendere i sensi*) to come round; (*riprendere l'aspetto naturale*) to revive.

**rinvi'are** *vt* (*rimandare indietro*) to send back, return; (*differire*): **~ qc (a)** to postpone sth **o** put sth off (till); to adjourn sth (till); (*fare un rimando*): **~ qn a** to refer sb to.

**rinvigo'rire** *vt* to strengthen.

**rin'vio, 'vii** *sm* (*rimando*) return; (*differimento*) postponement; (: *di seduta*) adjournment; (*in un testo*) cross-reference.

**ri'one** *sm* district, quarter.

**riordi'nare** *vt* (*rimettere in ordine*) to tidy; (*riorganizzare*) to reorganize.

**riorganiz'zare** [riorganid'dzare] *vt* to reorganize.

**ripa'gare** *vt* to repay.

**ripa'rare** *vt* (*proteggere*) to protect, defend; (*correggere: male, torto*) to make up for; (: *errore*) to put right; (*aggiustare*) to repair // *vi* (*mettere rimedio*): **~ a** to make up for; **~rsi** *vr* (*rifugiarsi*) to take refuge *o* shelter; **riparazi'one** *sf* (*di un torto*) reparation; (*di guasto, scarpe*) repairing *q*; repair; (*risarcimento*) compensation.

**ri'paro** *sm* (*protezione*) shelter, protection; (*rimedio*) remedy.

**ripar'tire** *vt* (*dividere*) to divide up; (*distribuire*) to share out // *vi* to set off again; to leave again.

**ripas'sare** *vi* to come (*o* go) back // *vt* (*scritto, lezione*) to go over (again).

**ripen'sare** *vi* to think; (*cambiare pensiero*) to change one's mind; (*tornare col pensiero*) to recall.

**ripercu'otersi** *vr*: **~ su** (*fig*) to have repercussions on.

**ripercussi'one** *sf* (*fig*): avere una **~ o** delle **~i su** to have repercussions on.

**ripes'care** *vt* (*pesce*) to catch again; (*persona, cosa*) to fish out; (*fig: ritrovare*) to dig out.

**ri'petere** *vt* to repeat; (*ripassare*) to go over; **ripetizi'one** *sf* repetition; (*di lezione*) revision; **ripetizi'oni** *sfpl* (*INS*) private tutoring *o* coaching *sg*.

**ripi'ano** *sm* (*GEO*) terrace; (*di mobile*) shelf.

**ri'picca** *sf*: per ~ out of spite.

**'ripido, a** *ag* steep.

**ripie'gare** *vt* to refold; (*piegare più volte*) to fold (up) // *vi* (*MIL*) to retreat, fall back; (*fig: accontentarsi*): ~ su to make do with; **~rsi** *vr* to bend; **ripi'ego, gli** *sm* expedient.

**ripi'eno, a** *ag* full; (*CUC*) stuffed; (: *panino*) filled // *sm* (*CUC*) stuffing.

**ri'porre** *vt* (*porre al suo posto*) to put back, replace; (*mettere via*) to put away; (*fiducia, speranza*): ~ qc in qn to place *o* put sth in sb.

**ripor'tare** *vt* (*portare indietro*) to bring (*o* take) back; (*riferire*) to report; (*citare*) to quote; (*ricevere*) to receive, get; (*vittoria*) to gain; (*successo*) to have; (*MAT*) to carry; **~rsi** a (*anche fig*) to go back to; (*riferirsi a*) to refer to; ~ danni *o* suffer damage.

**ripo'sare** *vt* (*bicchiere, valigia*) to put down; (*dare sollievo*) to rest // *vi* to rest; **~rsi** *vr* to rest; **ri'poso** *sm* rest; (*MIL*): **riposo!** at ease!; a riposo (*in pensione*) retired; giorno di riposo day off.

**ripos'tiglio** [ripos'tiʎʎo] *sm* lumberroom.

**ri'posto, a** *pp di* riporre.

**ri'prendere** *vt* (*prigioniero, fortezza*) to recapture; (*prendere indietro*) to take back; (*ricominciare: lavoro*) to resume; (*andare a prendere*) to fetch, come back for; (*assumere di nuovo: impiegati*) to take on again, re-employ; (*rimproverare*) to tell off; (*restringere: abito*) to take in; (*CINEMA*) to shoot; **~rsi** *vr* to recover; (*correggersi*) to correct o.s.; **ri'preso, a** *pp di* riprendere // *sf* recapture; resumption; (*economica, da malattia, emozione*) recovery;

(*AUT*) acceleration *q*; (*TEATRO, CINEMA*) rerun; (*CINEMA: presa*) shooting *q*; shot; (*SPORT*) second half; (: *PUGILATO*) round; a più riprese on several occasions, several times.

**ripristi'nare** *vt* to restore.

**ripro'durre** *vt* to reproduce; **riprodursi** *vr* (*BIOL*) to reproduce; (*riformarsi*) to form again; **riprodut'tivo, a** *ag* reproductive; **riproduzi'one** *sf* reproduction; **riproduzione vietata** all rights reserved.

**ripudi'are** *vt* to repudiate, disown.

**ripu'gnante** [ripuɲ'ɲante] *ag* disgusting, repulsive.

**ripu'gnare** [ripuɲ'ɲare] *vi*: ~ a qn to repel *o* disgust sb.

**ripu'lire** *vt* to clean up; (*sog: ladri*) to clean out; (*perfezionare*) to polish, refine.

**ri'quadro** *sm* square; (*ARCHIT*) panel.

**ri'saia** *sf* paddy field.

**risa'lire** *vi* (*ritornare in su*) to go back up; ~ a (*ritornare con la mente*) to go back to; (*datare da*) to date back to, go back to.

**risal'tare** *vi* (*fig: distinguersi*) to stand out; (*ARCHIT*) to project, jut out; **ri'salto** *sm* prominence; (*sporgenza*) projection; mettere *o* porre in risalto qc to make sth stand out.

**risa'nare** *vt* (*guarire*) to heal, cure; (*palude*) to reclaim; (*economia*) to improve; (*bilancio*) to reorganize.

**risa'puto, a** *ag*: è ~ che ... everyone knows that ..., it is common knowledge that ....

**risarci'mento** [risartʃi'mento] *sm*: ~ (di) compensation (for).

**risar'cire** [risar'tʃire] *vt* (*cose*) to pay compensation for; (*persona*): ~ qn di qc to compensate sb for sth.

**ri'sata** *sf* laugh.

**riscalda'mento** *sm* heating; ~ **centrale** central heating.

**riscal'dare** *vt* (*scaldare*) to heat; (:

*mani, persona*) to warm; (*minestra*) to reheat; ~**rsi** *vr* to warm up.

**riscat'tare** *vt* (*prigioniero*) to ransom, pay a ransom for; (*DIR*) to redeem; ~**rsi** *vr* (*da disonore*) to redeem o.s.; **ris'catto** *sm* ransom; redemption.

**rischia'rare** [riskja'rare] *vt* (*illuminare*) to light up; (*colore*) to make lighter; ~**rsi** *vr* (*tempo*) to clear up; (*cielo*) to clear; (*fig: volto*) to brighten up; ~**rsi la voce** to clear one's throat.

**rischi'are** [ris'kjare] *vt* to risk // *vi*: ~ **di fare qc** to risk o run the risk of doing sth.

**'rischio** [ˈriskjo] *sm* risk; **rischi'oso, a** *ag* risky, dangerous.

**riscia'cquare** [riʃʃaˈkware] *vt* to rinse.

**riscon'trare** *vt* (*confrontare: due cose*) to compare; (*esaminare*) to check, verify; (*rilevare*) to find; **ris'contro** *sm* comparison; check, verification; (*AMM: lettera di risposta*) reply.

**riscossi'one** *sf* collection.

**ris'cosso, a** *pp di* **riscuotere** // *sf* (*riconquista*) recovery, reconquest.

**riscu'otere** *vt* (*ritirare una somma dovuta*) to collect; (: *stipendio*) to draw, collect; (*assegno*) to cash; (*fig: successo etc*) to win, earn; ~**rsi** *vr*: ~**rsi (da)** to shake o.s. (out of), rouse o.s. (from).

**risenti'mento** *sm* resentment.

**risen'tire** *vt* to hear again; (*provare*) to feel // *vi*: ~ **di** to feel (o show) the effects of; ~**rsi** *vr*: ~**rsi di o per** to take offence at, resent; **risen'tito, a** *ag* resentful.

**ri'serbo** *sm* reserve.

**ri'serva** *sf* reserve; (*di caccia, pesca*) preserve; (*restrizione, di indigeni*) reservation; **di** ~ (*provviste etc*) in reserve.

**riser'vare** *vt* (*tenere in serbo*) to keep, put aside; (*prenotare*) to book, reserve; ~**rsi** *vr*: ~**rsi di fare qc** to intend to do sth; **riser'vato, a** *ag*

(*prenotato, fig: persona*) reserved; (*confidenziale*) confidential; **riserva'tezza** *sf* reserve.

**risi'edere** *vi*: ~ **a o in** to reside in.

**'risma** *sf* (*di carta*) ream; (*fig*) kind, sort.

**'riso, a** *pp di* **ridere** // *sm* (*pl(f)* ~**a**: *il ridere*): **un** ~ **a laugh; il** ~ laughter; (*pianta*) rice.

**riso'lino** *sm* snigger.

**ri'solto, a** *pp di* **risolvere**.

**risolu'tezza** [risolu'tettsa] *sf* determination.

**riso'luto, a** *ag* determined, resolute.

**risoluzi'one** [risolut'tsjone] *sf* solving *q*; (*MAT*) solution; (*decisione, di immagine*) resolution.

**ri'solvere** *vt* (*difficoltà, controversia*) to resolve; (*problema*) to solve; (*decidere*): ~ **di fare** to resolve to do; ~**rsi** *vr* (*decidersi*): ~**rsi a fare** to make up one's mind to do; (*andare a finire*): ~**rsi in** to end up, turn out; ~**rsi in nulla** to come to nothing.

**riso'nanza** [riso'nantsa] *sf* resonance; **aver vasta** ~ (*fig: fatto etc*) to be known far and wide.

**riso'nare** *vt, vi* = **risuonare**.

**ri'sorgere** [ri'sordʒere] *vi* to rise again; **risorgi'mento** *sm* revival; **il Risorgimento** (*STORIA*) the Risorgimento.

**ri'sorsa** *sf* expedient, resort; ~**e** *sfpl* (*naturali, finanziarie etc*) resources; **persona piena di** ~**e** a resourceful person.

**ri'sorto, a** *pp di* **risorgere**.

**ri'sotto** *sm* (*CUC*) risotto.

**risparmi'are** *vt* to save; (*non uccidere*) to spare // *vi* to save; ~ **qc a qn** to spare sb sth.

**ris'parmio** *sm* saving *q*; (*denaro*) savings *pl*.

**rispec'chiare** [rispek'kjare] *vt* to reflect.

**rispet'tabile** *ag* respectable.

**rispet'tare** *vt* to respect; **farsi** ~ to command respect.

**rispet'tivo, a** *ag* respective.

**ris'petto** *sm* respect; ~**i** *smpl* (*saluti*) respects, regards; ~ **a** (*in paragone a*) compared to; (*in relazione a*) as regards, as for; **rispet'toso, a** *ag* respectful.

**ris'plendere** *vi* to shine.

**ris'pondere** *vi* to answer, reply; (*freni*) to respond; ~ **a** (*domanda*) to answer, reply to; (*persona*) to answer; (*invito*) to reply to; (*provocazione*, *sog*: *veicolo, apparecchio*) to respond to; (*corrispondere a*) to correspond to; (: *speranze, bisogno*) to answer; ~ **di** to answer for; **ris'posta, a** *pp di* **rispondere** // *sf* answer, reply; **in risposta a** in reply to.

**'rissa** *sf* brawl.

**ristabi'lire** *vt* to re-establish, restore; (*persona*: *sog*: *riposo etc*) to restore to health; ~**rsi** *vr* to recover.

**rista'gnare** *vi* (*acqua*) to become stagnant; (*sangue*) to cease flowing; (*fig*: *industria*) to stagnate; **ris'tagno** *sm* stagnation.

**ris'tampa** *sf* reprinting *q*; reprint.

**risto'rante** *sm* restaurant.

**risto'rarsi** *vr* to have something to eat and drink; (*riposarsi*) to rest, have a rest; **ris'toro** *sm* (*bevanda, cibo*) refreshment; **servizio di ristoro** (*FERR*) refreshments *pl*.

**ristret'tezza** [ristret'tettsa] *sf* (*strettezza*) narrowness; (*: scarsezza*) scarcity, lack; (*: meschinità*) meanness; ~**e** *sfpl* (*povertà*) financial straits.

**ris'tretto, a** *pp di* **restringere** // *ag* (*racchiuso*) enclosed, hemmed in; (*angusto*) narrow; (*limitato*): ~ (**a**) restricted *o* limited (to); (*CUC*: *brodo*) thick; (: *caffè*) extra strong.

**risucchi'are** [risuk'kjare] *vt* to suck in.

**risul'tare** *vi* (*dimostrarsi*) to prove (to be), turn out (to be); (*riuscire*): ~ **vincitore** to emerge as the winner; ~ **da** (*provenire*) to result from, be the result of; **mi risulta che** ... I understand that ...; **non mi**

risulta not as far as I know; **risul'tato** *sm* result.

**risuo'nare** *vi* (*rimbombare*) to resound.

**risurrezi'one** [risurret'tsjone] *sf* (*REL*) resurrection.

**risusci'tare** [risuʃʃi'tare] *vt* to resuscitate, restore to life; (*fig*) to revive, bring back // *vi* to rise (from the dead).

**ris'veglio** [riz'veλλo] *sm* waking up; (*fig*) revival.

**ris'volto** *sm* (*di giacca*) lapel; (*di pantaloni*) turn-up; (*di manica*) cuff; (*di tasca*) flap; (*di libro*) inside flap; (*fig*) implication.

**ritagli'are** [ritaʎ'ʎare] *vt* (*tagliar via*) to cut out; **ri'taglio** *sm* (*di giornale*) cutting, clipping; (*di stoffa etc*) scrap; **nei ritagli di tempo** in one's spare time.

**ritar'dare** *vi* (*persona, treno*) to be late; (*orologio*) to be slow // *vt* (*rallentare*) to slow down; (*impedire*) to delay, hold up; (*differire*) to postpone, delay; **ritarda'tario, a** *sm/f* latecomer.

**ri'tardo** *sm* delay; (*di persona aspettata*) lateness *q*; (*fig*: *mentale*) backwardness; **in** ~ late.

**rite'nere** *vt* (*trattenere*) to hold back; (: *somma*) to deduct; (*giudicare*) to consider, believe; **rite'nuta** *sf* (*sul salario*) deduction.

**riti'rare** *vt* to withdraw; (*POL*: *richiamare*) to recall; (*andare a prendere*: *pacco etc*) to collect, pick up; ~**rsi** *vr* to withdraw; (*da un'attività*) to retire; (*stoffa*) to shrink; (*marea*) to recede; **riti'rata** *sf* (*MIL*) retreat; (*latrina*) lavatory; **ri'tiro** *sm* withdrawal; recall; collection; (*luogo appartato*) retreat.

**'ritmo** *sm* rhythm; (*fig*) rate; (: *della vita*) pace, tempo.

**'rito** *sm* rite; **di** ~ usual, customary.

**ritoc'care** *vt* (*disegno, fotografia*) to touch up; (*testo*) to alter; **ri'tocco, chi** *sm* touching up *q*; alteration.

**ritor'nare** *vi* to return, go (*o come*) back; (*ripresentarsi*) to recur; (*ridiventare*): ~ **ricco** to become rich again // *vt* (*restituire*) to return, give back.

**ritor'nello** *sm* refrain.

**ri'torno** *sm* return; **essere di** ~ to be back; **avere un** ~ **di fiamma** (*AUT*) to backfire; (*fig: persona*) to be back in love again.

**ri'trarre** *vt* (*trarre indietro, via*) to withdraw; (*distogliere: sguardo*) to turn away; (*rappresentare*) to portray, depict; (*ricavare*) to get, obtain.

**ritrat'tare** *vt* (*disdire*) to retract, take back; (*trattare nuovamente*) to deal with again.

**ri'tratto, a** *pp di* **ritrarre** // *sm* portrait.

**ri'troso, a** *ag* (*restìo*): ~ **(a)** reluctant (to); (*schivo*) shy; **andare a** ~ to go backwards.

**ritro'vare** *vt/o* to find; (*salute*) to regain; (*persona*) to find; to meet again; ~**rsi** *vr* (*essere, capitare*) to find o.s.; (*raccapezzarsi*) to find one's way; (*con senso reciproco*) to meet (again); **ri'trovo** *sm* meeting place; **ritrovo notturno** night club.

**'ritto, a** *ag* (*in piedi*) standing, on one's feet; (*levato in alto*) erect, raised; (: *capelli*) standing on end; (*posto verticalmente*) upright.

**ritu'ale** *ag, sm* ritual.

**riuni'one** *sf* (*adunanza*) meeting; (*riconciliazione*) reunion.

**riu'nire** *vt* (*ricongiungere*) to join (together); (*riconciliare*) to reunite, bring together (again); ~**rsi** *vr* (*adunarsi*) to meet; (*tornare a stare insieme*) to be reunited.

**riu'scire** [rjuʃ'ʃire] *vi* (*uscire di nuovo*) to go out again, go back out; (*aver esito: fatti, azioni*) to go, turn out; (*aver successo*) to succeed, be successful; (*essere, apparire*) to be, prove; (*raggiungere il fine*) to manage, succeed; ~ **a fare qc** to manage to do *o* succeed in doing *o* be

able to do sth; **questo mi riesce nuovo** this is new to me; **riu'scita** *sf* (*esito*) result, outcome; (*buon esito*) success.

**'riva** *sf* (*di fiume*) bank; (*di lago, mare*) shore.

**ri'vale** *sm/f* rival; **rivalità** *sf* rivalry.

**ri'valsa** *sf* (*rivincita*) revenge; (*risarcimento*) compensation.

**rivalu'tare** *vt* (*ECON*) to revalue.

**rivan'gare** *vt* (*ricordi etc*) to dig up (again).

**rive'dere** *vt* *o* to see again; (*ripassare*) to revise; (*verificare*) to check.

**rive'lare** *vt* to reveal; (*divulgare*) to reveal, disclose; (*dare indizio*) to reveal, show; ~**rsi** *vr* (*manifestarsi*) to be revealed; ~**rsi onesto** *etc* to prove to be honest *etc*; **rivela'tore, 'trice** *sm* (*TECN*) detector; (*FOT*) developer; **rivelazi'one** *sf* revelation.

**rivendi'care** *vt* to claim, demand.

**ri'vendita** *sf* (*bottega*) retailer's (shop).

**rivendi'tore, 'trice** *sm/f* retailer; ~ **autorizzato** (*COMM*) authorized dealer.

**ri'verbero** *sm* (*di luce, calore*) reflection; (*di suono*) reverberation.

**rive'renza** [rive'rɛntsa] *sf* reverence; (*inchino*) bow; curtsey.

**rive'rire** *vt* (*rispettare*) to revere; (*salutare*) to pay one's respects to.

**river'sare** *vt* (*anche fig*) to pour; ~**rsi** *vr* (*fig: persone*) to pour out.

**rivesti'mento** *sm* covering; coating.

**rives'tire** *vt* to dress again; (*ricoprire*) to cover; to coat; (*fig: carica*) to hold; ~**rsi** *vr* to get dressed again; to change (one's clothes).

**rivi'era** *sf* coast; **la** ~ **italiana** the Italian Riviera.

**ri'vincita** [ri'vintʃita] *sf* (*SPORT*) return match; (*fig*) revenge.

**rivis'suto, a** *pp di* **rivivere**.

**ri'vista** *sf* review; (*periodico*) magazine, review; (*TEATRO*) revue;

variety show.

**ri'vivere** vi (riacquistare forza) to come alive again; (tornare in uso) to be revived // vt to relive.

**ri'volgere** [ri'vɔldʒere] vt (attenzione, sguardo) to turn, direct; (parole) to address; ~**rsi** vr to turn round; (fig: dirigersi per informazioni): ~**rsi a** to go and see, go and speak to; (: ufficio) to enquire at.

**ri'volta** sf revolt, rebellion.

**rivol'tare** vt to turn over; (con l'interno all'esterno) to turn inside out; (disgustare: stomaco) to upset, turn; ~**rsi** vr (ribellarsi): ~**rsi (a)** to rebel (against).

**rivol'tella** sf revolver.

**ri'volto, a** pp di **rivolgere**.

**rivoluzio'nare** [rivoluttsjo'nare] vt to revolutionize.

**rivoluzio'nario, a** [rivoluttsjo'narjo] ag, sm/f revolutionary.

**rivoluzi'one** [rivolut'tsjone] sf revolution.

**riz'zare** [rit'tsare] vt to raise, erect; ~**rsi** vr to stand up; (capelli) to stand on end.

**'roba** sf stuff, things pl; (possessi, beni) belongings pl, things pl, possessions pl; ~ **da mangiare** things pl to eat, food; ~ **da matti** sheer madness o lunacy.

**'robot** sm inv robot.

**ro'busto, a** ag robust, sturdy; (solido: catena) strong.

**'rocca, che** sf fortress.

**rocca'forte** sf stronghold.

**roc'chetto** [rok'ketto] sm reel, spool.

**'roccia, ce** ['rɔttʃa] sf rock; **fare** ~ (SPORT) to go rock climbing; **roc'cioso, a** ag rocky.

**ro'daggio** [ro'daddʒo] sm running (Brit) o breaking (US) in; **in** ~ running (Brit) o breaking (US) in.

**'Rodano** sm: **il** ~ the Rhone.

**'rodere** vt to gnaw (at); (distruggere a poco) to eat into.

**rodi'tore** sm (ZOOL) rodent.

**rodo'dendro** sm rhododendron.

**'rogna** ['rɔɲɲa] sf (MED) scabies sg; (fig) bother, nuisance.

**ro'gnone** [roɲ'ɲone] sm (CUC) kidney.

**'rogo, ghi** sm (per cadaveri) (funeral) pyre; (supplizio): **il** ~ the stake.

**rol'lio** sm roll(ing).

**'Roma** sf Rome.

**Roma'nia** sf: **la** ~ Romania.

**ro'manico, a, ci, che** ag Romanesque.

**ro'mano, a** ag, sm/f Roman.

**romanti'cismo** [romanti'tʃizmo] sm romanticism.

**ro'mantico, a, ci, che** ag romantic.

**ro'manza** [ro'mandza] sf (MUS, LETTERATURA) romance.

**roman'zesco, a, schi, sche** [roman'dzesko] ag (stile, personaggi) fictional; (fig) storybook cpd.

**romanzi'ere** [roman'dzjere] sm novelist.

**ro'manzo, a** [ro'mandzo] ag (LING) romance cpd // sm (medievale) romance; (moderno) novel; ~ **d'appendice** serial (story).

**rom'bare** vi to rumble, thunder, roar.

**'rombo** sm rumble, thunder, roar; (MAT) rhombus; (ZOOL) turbot, brill.

**ro'meno, a** ag, sm/f, sm = **rumeno, a**.

**'rompere** vt to break; (conversazione, fidanzamento) to break off // vi to break; ~**rsi** vr to break; **mi rompe le scatole** (fam) he (o she) is a pain in the neck; ~**rsi un braccio** to break an arm; **rompi'capo** sm worry, headache; (indovinello) puzzle; (in enigmistica) brainteaser; **rompighi'accio** sm (NAUT) icebreaker; **rompis'catole** sm/f inv (fam) pest, pain in the neck.

**'ronda** sf (MIL) rounds pl, patrol.

**ron'della** sf (TECN) washer.

**'rondine** sf (ZOOL) swallow.

**ron'done** *sm* (*ZOOL*) swift.

**ron'zare** [ron'dzare] *vi* to buzz, hum.

**ron'zino** [ron'dzino] *sm* (*peg: cavallo*) nag.

**'rosa** *sf* rose // *ag inv, sm* pink;

**ro'saio** *sm* (*pianta*) rosebush, rose tree; (*giardino*) rose garden; **ro'sario** *sm* (*REL*) rosary; **ro'sato, a** *ag* pink, rosy // *sm* (*vino*) rosé (wine); **ro'seo, a** *ag* (*anche fig*) rosy.

**rosicchi'are** [rosik'kjare] *vt* to gnaw (at); (*mangiucchiare*) to nibble (at).

**rosma'rino** *sm* rosemary.

**'roso, a** *pp di* **rodere**.

**roso'lare** *vt* (*CUC*) to brown.

**roso'lia** *sf* (*MED*) German measles *sg*, rubella.

**ro'sone** *sm* rosette; (*vetrata*) rose window.

**'rospo** *sm* (*ZOOL*) toad.

**ros'setto** *sm* (*per labbra*) lipstick; (*per guance*) rouge.

**'rosso, a** *ag, sm, sm/f* red; **il mar R~** the Red Sea; **~ d'uovo** egg yolk; **ros'sore** *sm* flush, blush.

**rostic'ceria** [rostitʃe'ria] *sf* shop selling roast meat and other cooked food.

**'rostro** *sm* rostrum; (*becco*) beak.

**ro'tabile** *ag* (*percorribile*): **strada ~** roadway; (*FERR*): **materiale** *m* **~** rolling stock.

**ro'taia** *sf* rut, track; (*FERR*) rail.

**ro'tare** *vt, vi* to rotate; **rotazi'one** *sf* rotation.

**rote'are** *vt, vi* to whirl; **~ gli occhi** to roll one's eyes.

**ro'tella** *sf* small wheel; (*di mobile*) castor.

**roto'lare** *vt, vi* to roll; **~rsi** *vr* to roll (about).

**'rotolo** *sm* roll; **andare a ~i** (*fig*) to go to rack and ruin.

**ro'tondo, a** *ag* round // *sf* rotunda.

**ro'tore** *sm* rotor.

**'rotta** *sf* (*AER, NAUT*) course, route; (*MIL*) rout; **a ~ di collo** at breakneck speed; **essere in ~ con qn** to be on bad terms with sb.

**rot'tame** *sm* fragment, scrap, broken bit; **~i** *smpl* (*di nave, aereo etc*) wreckage *sg*; **~i di ferro** scrap iron *sg*.

**'rotto, a** *pp di* **rompere** // *ag* broken; (*calzoni*) torn, split; (*persona: pratico, resistente*): **~ a** accustomed *o* inured to; **per il ~ della cuffia** by the skin of one's teeth.

**rot'tura** *sf* breaking *q*; break; breaking off; (*MED*) fracture, break.

**rou'lotte** [ru'lɔt] *sf* caravan.

**ro'vente** *ag* red-hot.

**'rovere** *sm* oak.

**rovesci'are** [rovef'ʃare] *vt* (*versare in giù*) to pour; (: *accidentalmente*) to spill; (*capovolgere*) to turn upside down; (*gettare a terra*) to knock down; (: *fig: governo*) to overthrow; (*piegare all'indietro: testa*) to throw back; **~rsi** *vr* (*sedia, macchina*) to overturn; (*barca*) to capsize; (*liquido*) to spill; (*fig: situazione*) to be reversed.

**ro'vescio, sci** [ro'veʃʃo] *sm* other side, wrong side; (*della mano*) back; (*di moneta*) reverse; (*pioggia*) sudden downpour; (*fig*) setback; (*MAGLIA: anche*: **punto ~**) purl (stitch); (*TENNIS*) backhand (stroke); **a ~** upside-down; inside-out; **capire qc a ~** to misunderstand sth.

**ro'vina** *sf* ruin; **~e** *sfpl* ruins; **andare in ~** (*andare a pezzi*) to collapse; (*fig*) to go to rack and ruin.

**rovi'nare** *vi* to collapse, fall down // *vt* (*far cadere giù: casa*) to demolish; (*danneggiare, fig*) to ruin; **rovi'noso, a** *ag* disastrous; damaging; violent.

**rovis'tare** *vt* (*casa*) to ransack; (*tasche*) to rummage in (*o* through).

**'rovo** *sm* (*BOT*) blackberry bush, bramble bush.

**'rozzo, a** ['rɔddzo] *ag* rough, coarse.

**'ruba** *sf*: **andare a ~** to sell like hot cakes.

**ru'bare** *vt* to steal; **~ qc a qn** to steal sth from sb.

**rubi'netto** sm tap, faucet (US).

**ru'bino** sm ruby.

**ru'brica, che** sf (STAMPA) column; (quadernetto) index book; address book.

**'rude** ag tough, rough.

**'rudere** sm (rovina) ruins pl.

**rudimen'tale** ag rudimentary, basic.

**rudi'menti** smpl rudiments; basic principles; basic knowledge sg.

**ruffi'ano** sm pimp.

**'ruga, ghe** sf wrinkle.

**'ruggine** ['ruddʒine] sf rust.

**rug'gire** [rud'dʒire] vi to roar.

**rugi'ada** [ru'dʒada] sf dew.

**ru'goso, a** ag wrinkled.

**rul'lare** vi (tamburo, nave) to roll; (aereo) to taxi.

**'rullo** sm (di tamburi) roll; (arnese cilindrico, TIP) roller; ~ compressore steam roller; ~ di pellicola roll of film.

**rum** sm rum.

**ru'meno, a** ag, sm/f, sm Romanian.

**rumi'nare** vt (ZOOL) to ruminate.

**ru'more** sm: un ~ a noise, a sound; (fig) a rumour; il ~ noise; **rumo'roso, a** ag noisy.

**ru'olo** sm (TEATRO, fig) role, part; (elenco) roll, register, list; di ~ permanent, on the permanent staff.

**ru'ota** sf wheel; a ~ (forma) circular; ~ anteriore/posteriore front/back wheel; ~ di scorta spare wheel.

**ruo'tare** vt, vi = rotare.

**'rupe** sf cliff.

**ru'rale** ag rural, country cpd.

**ru'scello** [ruʃ'ʃɛllo] sm stream.

**'ruspa** sf excavator.

**rus'sare** vi to snore.

**'Russia** sf: la ~ Russia; **'russo, a** ag, sm/f, sm Russian.

**'rustico, a, ci, che** ag rustic; (fig) rough, unrefined.

**rut'tare** vi to belch; **'rutto** sm belch.

**'ruvido, a** ag rough, coarse.

**ruzzo'lare** [ruttso'lare] vi to tumble

down; **ruzzo'loni** av: **cadere ruzzoloni** to tumble down; **fare le scale ruzzoloni** to tumble down the stairs.

# S

**S.** abbr (= sud) S.

**sa** vb vedi sapere.

**'sabato** sm Saturday; di o il ~ on Saturdays.

**'sabbia** sf sand; ~e mobili quicksand(s); **sabbi'oso, a** ag sandy.

**sabo'taggio** [sabo'taddʒo] sm sabotage.

**sabo'tare** vt to sabotage.

**'sacca, che** sf bag; (bisaccia) haversack; (insenatura) inlet; ~ da viaggio travelling bag.

**sacca'rina** sf saccharin(e).

**sac'cente** [sat'tʃɛnte] sm/f know-all (Brit), know-it-all (US).

**saccheggi'are** [sakked'dʒare] vt to sack, plunder; **sac'cheggio** sm sack(ing).

**sac'chetto** [sak'ketto] sm (small) bag; (small) sack.

**'sacco, chi** sm bag; (per carbone etc) sack; (ANAT, BIOL) sac; (tela) sacking; (saccheggio) sack(ing); (fig: grande quantità): un ~ di lots of, heaps of; ~ a pelo sleeping bag; ~ per i rifiuti bin bag.

**sacer'dote** [satʃer'dote] sm priest; **sacer'dozio** sm priesthood.

**sacra'mento** sm sacrament.

**sacrifi'care** vt to sacrifice; ~rsi vr to sacrifice o.s.; (privarsi di qc) to make sacrifices.

**sacri'ficio** [sakri'fitʃo] sm sacrifice.

**sacri'legio** [sacri'lɛdʒo] sm sacrilege.

**'sacro, a** ag sacred.

**'sadico, a, ci, che** ag sadistic // sm/f sadist.

**sa'etta** sf arrow; (fulmine // anche fig) thunderbolt; flash of lightning.

**sa'fari** sm inv safari.

**sa'gace** [sa'gatʃe] *ag* shrewd, sagacious.

**sag'gezza** [sad'dʒettsa] *sf* wisdom.

**saggi'are** [sad'dʒare] *vt* (*metalli*) to assay; (*fig*) to test.

**'saggio, a, gi, ge** [] *ag* wise // *sm* (*persona*) sage; (*operazione sperimentale*) test; (: *dell'oro*) assay; (*fig: prova*) proof; (*campione indicativo*) sample; (*ricerca, esame critico*) essay.

**Sagit'tario** [sadʒit'tarjo] *sm* Sagittarius.

**'sagoma** *sf* (*profilo*) outline, profile; (*forma*) form, shape; (*TECN*) template; (*bersaglio*) target; (*fig: persona*) character.

**'sagra** *sf* festival.

**sagres'tano** *sm* sacristan; sexton.

**sagres'tia** *sf* sacristy; (*culto protestante*) vestry.

**Sa'hara** [sa'ara] *sm:* il (*deserto del*) ~ the Sahara (Desert).

**'sai** *vb vedi* **sapere**.

**'sala** *sf* hall; (*stanza*) room; ~ d'aspetto waiting room; ~ da ballo ballroom; ~ **per concerti** concert hall; ~ **da gioco** gaming room; ~ operatoria operating theatre; ~ **da pranzo** dining room.

**sa'lame** *sm* salami *q*, salami sausage.

**sala'moia** *sf* (*CUC*) brine.

**sa'lare** *vt* to salt.

**salari'ato, a** *sm/f* wage-earner.

**sa'lario** *sm* pay, wages *pl*.

**sa'lato, a** *ag* (*sapore*) salty; (*CUC*) salted, salt *cpd*; (*fig: discorso etc*) biting, sharp; (: *prezzi*) steep, stiff.

**sal'dare** *vt* (*congiungere*) to join, bind; (*parti metalliche*) to solder; (: *con saldatura autogena*) to weld; (*conto*) to settle, pay; **salda'tura** *sf* soldering; welding; (*punto saldato*) soldered joint; weld.

**sal'dezza** [sal'dettsa] *sf* firmness; strength.

**'saldo, a** *ag* (*resistente, forte*) strong, firm; (*fermo*) firm, steady, stable; (*fig*) firm, steadfast // *sm*

(*svendita*) sale; (*di conto*) settlement; (*ECON*) balance.

**'sale** *sm* salt; (*fig*): **ha poco ~ in zucca** he doesn't have much sense; ~ fino/grosso table/cooking salt.

**'salice** ['salitʃe] *sm* willow; ~ piangente weeping willow.

**sali'ente** *ag* (*fig*) salient, main.

**sali'era** *sf* salt cellar.

**sa'lino, a** *ag* saline // *sf* saltworks *sg*.

**sa'lire** *vi* to go (*o come*) up; (*aereo etc*) to climb, go up; (*passeggero*) to get on; (*sentiero, prezzi, livello*) to go up, rise // *vt* (*scale, gradini*) to go (*o come*) up; ~ **su** to climb (up); ~ **sul treno/sull'autobus** to board the train/the bus; ~ **in macchina** to get into the car; **sa'lita** *sf* climb, ascent; (*erta*) hill, slope; **in salita** *ag*, *av* uphill.

**sa'liva** *sf* saliva.

**'salma** *sf* corpse.

**'salmo** *sm* psalm.

**sal'mone** *sm* salmon.

**sa'lone** *sm* (*stanza*) sitting room, lounge; (*in albergo*) lounge; (*su nave*) lounge, saloon; (*mostra*) show, exhibition; ~ **di bellezza** beauty salon.

**sa'lotto** *sm* lounge, sitting room; (*mobilio*) lounge suite.

**sal'pare** *vi* (*NAUT*) to set sail; (*anche*: ~ **l'ancora**) to weigh anchor.

**'salsa** *sf* (*CUC*) sauce; ~ **di pomodoro** tomato sauce.

**sal'siccia, ce** [sal'sittʃa] *sf* pork sausage.

**sal'tare** *vi* to jump, leap; (*esplodere*) to blow up, explode; (: *valvola*) to blow; (*venir via*) to pop off; (*non aver luogo: corso etc*) to be cancelled // *vt* to jump (over), leap (over); (*fig: pranzo, capitolo*) to skip, miss (out); (*CUC*) to sauté; **far** ~ to blow up; to burst open; ~ **fuori** (*fig: apparire all'improvviso*) to turn up.

**saltel'lare** *vi* to skip; to hop.

**saltim'banco** *sm* acrobat.

**'salto** sm jump; (SPORT) jumping; fare un ~ to jump, leap; fare un ~ da qn to pop over to sb's (place); ~ in alto/lungo high/long jump; ~ con l'asta pole vaulting; ~ mortale somersault.

**saltu'ario, a** ag occasional, irregular.

**sa'lubre** ag healthy, salubrious.

**salume'ria** sf delicatessen.

**sa'lumi** smpl salted pork meats.

**salu'tare** ag healthy; (fig) salutary, beneficial // vt (per dire buon giorno, fig) to greet; (per dire addio) to say goodbye to; (MIL) to salute.

**sa'lute** sf health; ~! (a chi starnutisce) bless you!; (nei brindisi) cheers!; bere alla ~ di qn to drink (to) sb's health.

**sa'luto** sm (gesto) wave; (parola) greeting; (MIL) salute; ~i smpl greetings; cari ~i best regards; vogliate gradire i nostri più distinti ~i Yours faithfully.

**salvacon'dotto** sm (MIL) safe-conduct.

**salva'gente** [salva'dʒɛnte] sm (NAUT) lifebuoy; (stradale) traffic island; ~ a ciambella life belt; ~ a giubbotto lifejacket.

**salvaguar'dare** vt to safeguard.

**sal'vare** vt to save; (trarre da un pericolo) to rescue; (proteggere) to protect; ~rsi vr to save o.s.; to escape; **salva'taggio** sm rescue; **salva'tore, 'trice** sm/f saviour.

**'salve** escl (fam) hi!

**sal'vezza** [sal'vettsa] sf salvation; (sicurezza) safety.

**'salvia** sf (BOT) sage.

**'salvo, a** ag safe, unhurt, unharmed; (fuori pericolo) safe, out of danger // sm: in ~ safe // prep (eccetto) except; **mettere qc in** ~ to put sth in a safe place; ~ **che** cong (a meno che) unless; (eccetto) except (that); ~ **imprevisti** barring accidents.

**sam'buco** sm elder (tree).

**sa'nare** vt to heal, cure; (economia

to put right.

**san'cire** [san'tʃire] vt to sanction.

**'sandalo** sm (BOT) sandalwood; (calzatura) sandal.

**'sangue** sm blood; **farsi cattivo** ~ to fret, get in a state; ~ **freddo** (fig) sang-froid, calm; a ~ **freddo** in cold blood; **sangu'igno, a** ag blood cpd; (colore) blood-red; **sangui'nare** vi to bleed; **sangui'noso, a** ag bloody; **sangui'suga** sf leech.

**sanità** sf health; (salubrità) healthiness; **Ministero della S~** Department of Health; ~ **mentale** sanity.

**sani'tario, a** ag health cpd; (condizioni) sanitary // sm (AMM) doctor; (impianti) ~i smpl bathroom o sanitary fittings.

**'sanno** vb vedi **sapere**.

**'sano, a** ag healthy; (denti, costituzione) healthy, sound; (integro) whole, unbroken; (fig: politica, consigli) sound; ~ **di mente** sane; ~ **di ~ a pianta** completely, entirely; ~ **e salvo** safe and sound.

**santifi'care** vt to sanctify; (feste) to observe.

**santità** sf sanctity; holiness; **Sua/Vostra** ~ (titolo di Papa) His/Your Holiness.

**'santo, a** ag holy; (fig) saintly; (seguito da nome proprio): dav sm **san** + C, **sant'** + V, **santo** + s impura, gn, pn, ps, x, z; dav sf **santa** + C, **sant'** + V) saint // sm/f saint; la S~a Sede the Holy See.

**santu'ario** sm sanctuary.

**sanzio'nare** [santsjo'nare] vt to sanction.

**sanzi'one** [san'tsjone] sf sanction; (penale, civile) sanction, penalty.

**sa'pere** vt to know; (essere capace di): so nuotare I know how to swim, I can swim // vi: ~ **di** (aver sapore) to taste of; (aver odore) to smell of // sm knowledge; far ~ qc a qn to inform sb about sth, let sb know sth; mi sa che non sia vero I don't think that's true.

**sapi'enza** [sa'pjɛntsa] sf wisdom.

**sa'pone** *sm* soap; ~ **da bucato** washing soap; **sapo'netta** *sf* cake *o* bar *o* tablet of soap.

**sa'pore** *sm* taste, flavour; **sapo'rito, a** *ag* tasty.

**sappi'amo** *vb vedi* **sapere**.

**saraci'nesca** [sarat∫i'neska] *sf* (*serranda*) rolling shutter.

**sar'casmo** *sm* sarcasm *q*; sarcastic remark.

**Sar'degna** [sar'deɲɲa] *sf*: **la** ~ Sardinia.

**sar'dina** *sf* sardine.

**'sardo, a** *ag*, *sm/f* Sardinian.

**'sarto, a** *sm/f* tailor/dressmaker; **sarto'ria** *sf* tailor's (shop); dressmaker's (shop); (*casa di moda*) fashion house; (*arte*) couture.

**'sasso** *sm* stone; (*ciottolo*) pebble; (*masso*) rock.

**sas'sofono** *sm* saxophone.

**sas'soso, a** *ag* stony; pebbly.

**'Satana** *sm* Satan; **sa'tanico, a, ci, che** *ag* satanic, fiendish.

**sa'tellite** *sm*, *ag* satellite.

**'satira** *sf* satire.

**'saturo, a** *ag* saturated; (*fig*): ~ **di** full of.

**S.A.U.B.** ['saub] *sigla f* (= *Struttura Amministrativa Unificata di Base*) *state welfare system*.

**'sauna** *sf* sauna.

**Sa'voia** *sf*: **la** ~ Savoy.

**savoi'ardo, a** *ag* of Savoy, Savoyard // *sm* (*biscotto*) sponge finger.

**sazi'are** [sat'tsjare] *vt* to satisfy, satiate; ~**rsi** *vr* (*riempirsi di cibo*): ~**rsi (di)** to eat one's fill (of); (*fig*): ~**rsi di** to grow tired *o* weary of.

**'sazio, a** ['sattsjo] *ag* (*di*) sated (with), full (of); (*fig*: *stufo*) fed up (with), sick (of).

**sba'dato, a** *ag* careless, inattentive.

**sbadigli'are** [zbadiʎ'ʎare] *vi* to yawn; **sba'diglio** *sm* yawn.

**sbagli'are** [zbaʎ'ʎare] *vt* to make a mistake in, get wrong // *vi* to make a mistake, be mistaken, be wrong; (*operare in modo non giusto*) to err; ~**rsi** *vr* to make a mistake, be mis-

taken, be wrong; ~ **la mira/strada** to miss one's aim/take the wrong road; **'sbaglio** *sm* mistake, error; (*morale*) error; **fare uno sbaglio** to make a mistake.

**sbal'lare** *vt* (*merce*) to unpack // *vi* (*nel fare un conto*) to overestimate; (*fam*: *gergo della droga*) to get high.

**sballot'tare** *vt* to toss (about).

**sbalor'dire** *vt* to stun, amaze // *vi* to be stunned, be amazed; **sbalordi'tivo, a** *ag* amazing; (*prezzo*) incredible, absurd.

**sbal'zare** [zbal'tsare] *vt* to throw, hurl // *vi* (*balzare*) to bounce; (*saltare*) to leap, bound; **'sbalzo** *sm* (*spostamento improvviso*) jolt, jerk; **a sbalzi** jerkily; (*fig*) in fits and starts; **uno sbalzo di temperatura** a sudden change in temperature.

**sban'dare** *vi* (*NAUT*) to list; (*AER*) to bank; (*AUT*) to skid; ~**rsi** *vr* (*folla*) to disperse; (*fig*: *famiglia*) to break up.

**sbandie'rare** *vt* (*bandiera*) to wave; (*fig*) to parade, show off.

**sbaragli'are** [zbaraʎ'ʎare] *vt* (*MIL*) to rout; (*in gare sportive etc*) to beat, defeat.

**sba'raglio** [zba'raʎʎo] *sm* rout; defeat; **gettarsi allo** ~ to risk everything.

**sbaraz'zarsi** [zbarat'tsarsi] *vr*: ~ **di** to get rid of, rid o.s. of.

**sbar'care** *vt* (*passeggeri*) to disembark; (*merci*) to unload // *vi* to disembark; **'sbarco** *sm* disembarkation; unloading; (*MIL*) landing.

**'sbarra** *sf* bar; (*di passaggio a livello*) barrier; (*DIR*): **presentarsi alla** ~ to appear before the court.

**sbarra'mento** *sm* (*stradale*) barrier; (*diga*) dam, barrage; (*MIL*) barrage.

**sbar'rare** *vt* (*strada etc*) to block, bar; (*assegno*) to cross; ~ **il passo** to bar the way; ~ **gli occhi** to open one's eyes wide.

**'sbattere** *vt* (*porta*) to slam, bang; (*tappeti, ali, CUC*) to beat; (*urtare*) to knock, hit // vi (porta, finestra) to bang; (agitarsi: ali, vele etc) to flap; **me ne sbatto!** (fam) I don't give a damn!; **sbat'tuto**, a ag (viso, aria) dejected, worn out; (uovo) beaten.

**sba'vare** vi to dribble; (colore) to smear, smudge.

**sbia'dire** vi (anche: ~rsi), vt to fade; **sbia'dito**, a ag faded; (fig) colourless, dull.

**sbian'care** vt to whiten; (tessuto) to bleach // vi (impallidire) to grow pale o white.

**sbi'eco, a, chi, che** ag (storto) squint, askew; **di ~: guardare qn di ~** (fig) to look askance at sb; **tagliare una stoffa di ~** to cut a material on the bias.

**sbigot'tire** vt to dismay, stun // vi (anche: ~rsi) to be dismayed.

**sbilanci'are** [zbilan'tʃare] vt to throw off balance; **~rsi** vr (perdere l'equilibrio) to overbalance, lose one's balance; (fig: compromettersi) to compromise o.s.

**sbirci'are** [zbir'tʃare] vt to cast sidelong glances at, eye.

**'sbirro** sm (peg) cop.

**sbizzar'rirsi** [zbiddzar'rirsi] vr to indulge one's whims.

**sbloc'care** vt to unblock, free; (freno) to release; (prezzi, affitti) to decontrol.

**sboc'care** vi: **~ in** (fiume) to flow into; (strada) to lead into; (persona) to come (out) into; (fig: concludersi) to end (up) in.

**sboc'cato, a** ag (persona) foulmouthed; (linguaggio) foul.

**sbocci'are** [zbot'tʃare] vi (fiore) to bloom, open (out).

**'sbocco, chi** sm (di fiume) mouth; (di strada) end; (di tubazione, COMM) outlet; (uscita: anche fig) way out; **siamo in una situazione senza ~chi** there's no way out of this for us.

**sbol'lire** vi (fig) to cool down, calm down.

**'sbornia** sf (fam): **prendersi una ~**

to get plastered.

**sbor'sare** vt (denaro) to pay out.

**sbot'tare** vi: **~ in una risata/per la collera** to burst out laughing/ explode with anger.

**sbotto'nare** vt to unbutton, undo.

**sbracci'ato, a** [zbrat'tʃato] ag (camicia) sleeveless; (persona) bare-armed.

**sbrai'tare** vi to yell, bawl.

**sbra'nare** vt to tear to pieces.

**sbricio'lare** [zbritʃo'lare] vt, **~rsi** vr to crumble.

**sbri'gare** vt to deal with, get through; (cliente) to attend to, deal with; **~rsi** vr to hurry (up); **sbriga'tivo, a** ag (persona, modo) quick, expeditious; (giudizio) hasty.

**sbrindel'lato, a** ag tattered, in tatters.

**sbrodo'lare** vt to stain, dirty.

**'sbronzo, a** ['zbrontso] ag (fam: ubriaco) tight // sf: **prendersi una ~a** to get tight o plastered.

**sbu'care** vi to come out, emerge; (apparire improvvisamente) to pop out (o up).

**sbucci'are** [zbut'tʃare] vt (arancia, patata) to peel; (piselli) to shell; **~rsi un ginocchio** to graze one's knee.

**sbudel'larsi** vr: **~ dalle risa** to split one's sides laughing.

**sbuf'fare** vi (persona, cavallo) to snort; (: ansimare) to puff, pant; (treno) to puff; **'sbuffo** sm (di aria, fumo, vapore) puff; **maniche a sbuffo** puff(ed) sleeves.

**'scabbia** sf (MED) scabies sg.

**sca'broso, a** ag (fig: difficile) difficult, thorny; (: imbarazzante) embarrassing; (: sconcio) indecent.

**scacchi'era** [skak'kjera] sf chessboard.

**scacci'are** [skat'tʃare] vt to chase away o out, drive away o out.

**'scacco, chi** sm (pezzo del gioco) chessman; (quadretto di scacchiera) square; (fig) setback, reverse; **~chi** smpl (gioco) chess sg; **a ~chi**

*(tessuto)* check(ed); **scacco'matto** *sm* checkmate.

**sca'dente** *ag* shoddy, of poor quality.

**sca'denza** [ska'dɛntsa] *sf* *(di cambiale, contratto)* maturity; *(di passaporto)* expiry date; **a breve/ lunga ~** short-/long-term; **data di ~** expiry date.

**sca'dere** *vi (contratto etc)* to expire; *(debito)* to fall due; *(valore, forze, peso)* to decline, go down.

**sca'fandro** *sm (di palombaro)* diving suit; *(di astronauta)* space-suit.

**scaf'fale** *sm* shelf; *(mobile)* set of shelves.

**'scafo** *sm (NAUT, AER)* hull.

**scagio'nare** [skadʒo'nare] *vt* to exonerate, free from blame.

**'scaglia** ['skaʎʎa] *sf (ZOOL)* scale; *(scheggia)* chip, flake.

**scagli'are** [skaʎ'ʎare] *vt (lanciare: anche fig)* to hurl, fling; **~rsi** *vr*: **~rsi su** *o* **contro** to hurl *o* fling o.s. at; *(fig)* to rail at.

**scaglio'nare** [skaʎʎo'nare] *vt (pagamenti)* to space out, spread out; *(MIL)* to echelon; **scagli'one** *sm* echelon; *(GEO)* terrace; **a sca- glioni** in groups.

**'scala** *sf (a gradini etc)* staircase, stairs *pl*; *(a pioli, di corda)* ladder; *(MUS, GEO, di colori, valori, fig)* scale; **~e** *sfpl (scalinata)* stairs; **su vasta ~/~ ridotta** on a large/small scale; **~ a libretto** stepladder; **~ mobile** escalator; *(ECON)* sliding scale; **~ mobile (dei salari)** index- linked pay scale.

**sca'lare** *vt (ALPINISMO, muro)* to climb, scale; *(debito)* to scale down, reduce; **sca'lata** *sf* scaling *q*, climbing *q*; *(arrampicata, fig)* climb; **scala'tore, 'trice** *smf* climber.

**scalda'bagno** [skalda'baɲɲo] *sm* water-heater.

**scal'dare** *vt* to heat; **~rsi** *vr* to warm up, heat up; *(al fuoco, al sole)* to warm o.s.; *(fig)* to get excited.

**scal'fire** *vt* to scratch.

**scali'nata** *sf* staircase.

**sca'lino** *sm (anche fig)* step; *(di scala a pioli)* rung.

**'scalo** *sm (NAUT)* slipway; *(: porto d'approdo)* port of call; *(AER)* stop- over; **fare ~ (a)** *(NAUT)* to call (at), put in (at); *(AER)* to land (at), make a stop (at); **~ merci** *(FERR)* goods *(Brit) o* freight yard.

**scalop'pina** *sf (CUC)* escalope.

**scal'pello** *sm* chisel.

**scal'pore** *sm* noise, row; **far ~** *(notizia)* to cause a sensation *o* a stir.

**'scaltro, a** *ag* cunning, shrewd.

**scal'zare** [skal'tsare] *vt (albero)* to bare the roots of; *(muro, fig: auto- rità)* to undermine.

**'scalzo, a** ['skaltso] *ag* barefoot.

**scambi'are** *vt* to exchange; *(con- fondere)*: **~ qn/qc per** to take *o* mis- take sb/sth for; **mi hanno scambiato il cappello** they've given me the wrong hat.

**scambi'evole** *ag* mutual, re- ciprocal.

**'scambio** *sm* exchange; *(FERR)* points *pl*; **fare (uno) ~** to make a swap.

**scampa'gnata** [skampaɲ'nata] *sf* trip to the country.

**scampa'nare** *vi* to peal.

**scam'pare** *vt (salvare)* to rescue, save; *(evitare: morte, prigione)* to escape *// vi*: **~ (a qc)** to survive (sth), escape (sth); **scamparla bella** to have a narrow escape.

**'scampo** *sm (salvezza)* escape; *(ZOOL)* prawn; **cercare ~ nella fuga** to seek safety in flight.

**scampolo** *sm* remnant.

**scanala'tura** *sf (incavo)* channel, groove.

**scandagli'are** [skanda'ʎʎare] *vt (NAUT)* to sound; *(fig)* to sound out; **~** to probe.

**scandaliz'zare** [skandali'dzare] *vt* to shock, scandalize; **~rsi** *vr* to be shocked.

**'scandalo** *sm* scandal.

**Scandi'navia** *sf*: **la ~** Scandinavia;

**scandi'navo, a** *ag, sm/f* Scandinavian.

**scan'dire** *vt* (*versi*) to scan; (*parole*) to articulate, pronounce distinctly; ~ **il tempo** (*MUS*) to beat time.

**scan'nare** *vt* (*animale*) to butcher, slaughter; (*persona*) to cut o slit the throat of.

**'scanno** *sm* seat, bench.

**scansafa'tiche** [skansafa'tike] *sm/f inv* idler, loafer.

**scan'sare** *vt* (*rimuovere*) to move (aside), shift; (*schivare: schiaffo*) to dodge; (*sfuggire*) to avoid; ~**rsi** *vr* to move aside.

**scan'sia** *sf* shelves *pl*; (*per libri*) bookcase.

**'scanso** *sm*: **a ~ di** in order to avoid, as a precaution against.

**scanti'nato** *sm* basement.

**scanto'nare** *vi* to turn the corner; (*svignarsela*) to sneak off.

**scapes'trato, a** *ag* dissolute.

**'scapito** *sm* (*perdita*) loss; (*danno*) damage, detriment; **a ~ di** to the detriment of.

**'scapola** *sf* shoulder blade.

**'scapolo** *sm* bachelor.

**scappa'mento** *sm* (*AUT*) exhaust.

**scap'pare** *vi* (*fuggire*) to escape; (*andare via in fretta*) to rush off; **lasciarsi ~ un'occasione** to let an opportunity go by; ~ **di prigione** to escape from prison; ~ **di mano** (*oggetto*) to slip out of one's hands; ~ **di mente** a qn to slip sb's mind; **mi scappò detto** I let it slip; **scap'pata** *sf* quick visit o call; **scappa'tella** *sf* escapade; **scappa'toia** *sf* way out.

**scara'beo** *sm* beetle.

**scarabocchi'are** [skarabok'kjare] *vt* to scribble, scrawl; **scara'bocchio** *sm* scribble, scrawl.

**scara'faggio** [skara'faddʒo] *sm* cockroach.

**scaraven'tare** *vt* to fling, hurl.

**scarce'rare** [skartʃe'rare] *vt* to release (from prison).

**'scarica, che** *sf* (*di più armi*) volley of shots; (*di sassi, pugni*) hail, shower; (*ELETTR*) discharge; ~ **di mitra** burst of machine-gun fire.

**scari'care** *vt* (*merci, camion etc*) to unload; (*passeggeri*) to set down, put off; (*arma*) to unload; (: *sparare, ELETTR*) to discharge; (*sog: corso d'acqua*) to empty, pour; (*fig: liberare da un peso*) to unburden, relieve; ~**rsi** *vr* (*orologio*) to run o wind down; (*batteria, accumulatore*) to go flat o dead; (*fig: rilassarsi*) to unwind; (: *sfogarsi*) to let off steam; **il fulmine si scaricò su un albero** the lightning struck a tree; **scarica'tore** *sm* loader; (*di porto*) docker.

**'scarico, a, chi, che** *ag* (*unloaded*); (*orologio*) run down; (*accumulatore*) dead, flat // *sm* (*di merci, materiali*) unloading; (*di immondizie*) dumping, tipping (*Brit*); (: *luogo*) rubbish dump; (*TECN: deflusso*) draining; (: *dispositivo*) drain; (*AUT*) exhaust.

**scar'latto, a** *ag* scarlet.

**'scarno, a** *ag* thin, bony.

**'scarpa** *sf* shoe; ~**e da ginnastica/tennis** gym/tennis shoes.

**scar'pata** *sf* escarpment.

**scarseggi'are** [skarsed'dʒare] *vi* to be scarce; ~ **di** to be short of, lack.

**scar'sezza** [skar'settsa] *sf* scarcity, lack.

**'scarso, a** *ag* (*insufficiente*) insufficient, meagre; (*povero: annata*) poor, lean; (*INS: voto*) poor; ~ **di** lacking in; **3 chili ~i** just under 3 kilos, barely 3 kilos.

**scarta'mento** *sm* (*FERR*) gauge; ~ **normale/ridotto** standard/narrow gauge.

**scar'tare** *vt* (*pacco*) to unwrap; (*idea*) to reject; (*MIL*) to declare unfit for military service; (*carte da gioco*) to discard; (*CALCIO*) to dodge (*past*) // *vi* to swerve.

**'scarto** *sm* (*cosa scartata, anche COMM*) reject; (*di veicolo*) swerve; (*differenza*) gap, difference.

**scassi'nare** vt to break, force.

**'scasso** sm vedi **furto**.

**scate'nare** vt (fig) to incite, stir up; ~**rsi** vr (temporale) to break; (rivolta) to break out; (persona: infuriarsi) to rage.

**'scatola** sf box; (di latta) tin (Brit), can; **cibi in ~** tinned (Brit) o canned foods; ~ **cranica** cranium.

**scat'tare** vt (fotografia) to take // vi (congegno, molla etc) to be released; (balzare) to spring up; (SPORT) to put on a spurt; (fig: per l'ira) to fly into a rage; ~ **in piedi** to spring to one's feet.

**'scatto** sm (dispositivo) release; (: di arma da fuoco) trigger mechanism; (rumore) click; (balzo) jump, start; (SPORT) spurt; (fig: di ira etc) fit; (: di stipendio) increment; **di ~** suddenly.

**scatu'rire** vi to gush, spring.

**scaval'care** vt (ostacolo) to pass (o climb) over; (fig) to get ahead of, overtake.

**sca'vare** vt (terreno) to dig; (legno) to hollow out; (pozzo, galleria) to bore; (città sepolta etc) to excavate.

**'scavo** sm excavating q; excavation.

**'scegliere** ['ʃeʎʎere] vt to choose, select.

**sce'icco, chi** [ʃe'ikko] sm sheik.

**scelle'rato, a** [ʃelle'rato] ag wicked, evil.

**scel'lino** [ʃel'lino] sm shilling.

**'scelto, a** ['ʃelto] pp di **scegliere** // ag (gruppo) carefully selected; (frutta, verdura) choice, top quality; (MIL: specializzato) crack cpd, highly skilled // sf choice; selection: **di prima** ~**a** top grade o quality; **frutta o formaggi a** ~**a** a choice of fruit or cheese.

**sce'mare** [ʃe'mare] vt, vi to diminish.

**'scemo, a** ['ʃemo] ag stupid, silly.

**'scempio** ['ʃempjo] sm slaughter, massacre; (fig) ruin; **far** ~ **di** (fig) to play havoc with, ruin.

**'scena** ['ʃena] sf (gen) scene;

(palcoscenico) stage; **le** ~**e** (fig: teatro) the stage; **fare una** ~ to make a scene; **andare in** ~ to be staged o put on o performed; **mettere in** ~ to stage.

**sce'nario** [ʃe'narjo] sm scenery; (di film) scenario.

**sce'nata** [ʃe'nata] sf row, scene.

**'scendere** ['ʃendere] vi to go (o come) down; (strada, sole) to go down; (notte) to fall; (passeggero: fermarsi) to get out, alight; (fig: temperatura, prezzi) to go o come down, fall, drop // vt (scale, pendio) to go (o come) down; ~ **dalle scale** to go (o come) down the stairs; ~ **dal treno** to get off o out of the train; ~ **dalla macchina** to get out of the car; ~ **da cavallo** to dismount, get off one's horse.

**'scenico, a, ci, che** ['ʃeniko] ag stage cpd, scenic.

**scervel'lato, a** [ʃervel'lato] ag feather-brained, scatterbrained.

**'sceso, a** ['ʃeso] pp di **scendere**.

**'scettico, a, ci, che** ['ʃettiko] ag sceptical.

**'scettro** ['ʃettro] sm sceptre.

**'scheda** ['skeda] sf (index) card; ~ **elettorale** ballot paper; ~ **perforata** punch card; **sche'dare** vt (dati) to file; (libri) to catalogue; (registrare: anche POLIZIA) to put on one's files; **sche'dario** sm file; (mobile) filing cabinet.

**scheggia, ge** ['skeddʒa] sf splinter, sliver.

**'scheletro** ['skeletro] sm skeleton.

**'schema, i** ['skema] sm (diagramma) diagram, sketch; (progetto, abbozzo) outline, plan.

**'scherma** ['skerma] sf fencing.

**scher'maglia** [sker'maʎʎa] sf (fig) skirmish.

**'schermo** ['skermo] sm shield, screen; (CINEMA, TV) screen.

**scher'nire** [sker'nire] vt to mock, sneer at; **'scherno** sm mockery, derision.

**scher'zare** [sker'tsare] vi to joke.

'**scherzo** ['skertso] *sm* joke; (*tiro*) trick; (*MUS*) scherzo; **è uno ~!** (*una cosa facile*) it's child's play!; it's easy!; **per ~** in jest; for a joke *o* a laugh; **fare un brutto ~ a qn** to play a nasty trick on sb; **scher'zoso, a** *ag* (*tono, gesto*) playful; (*osservazione*) facetious; **è un tipo scherzoso** he likes a joke.

**schiaccia'noci** [skjattʃa'notʃi] *sm inv* nutcracker.

**schiacci'are** [skjat'tʃare] *vt* (*dito*) to crush; (*noci*) to crack; **~ un pisolino** to have a nap.

**schiaffeggi'are** [skjaffed'dʒare] *vt* to slap.

**schi'affo** ['skjaffo] *sm* slap.

**schiamaz'zare** [skjamat'tsare] *vi* to squawk, cackle.

**schian'tare** [skjan'tare] *vt* to break, tear apart; **~rsi** *vr* to break (up), shatter; **schi'anto** *sm* (*rumore*) crash; tearing sound; **è uno schianto!** (*fam*) it's *o* he's *o* she's terrific!; **di schianto** all of a sudden.

**schia'rire** [skja'rire] *vt* to lighten, make lighter // *vi* (*anche*: **~rsi**) to grow lighter; (*tornar sereno*) to clear, brighten up; **~rsi la voce** to clear one's throat.

**schiavitù** [skjavi'tu] *sf* slavery.

**schi'avo, a** ['skjavo] *sm/f* slave.

**schi'ena** [skj'ɛna] *sf* (*ANAT*) back; **schie'nale** *sm* (*di sedia*) back.

**schi'era** [skj'ɛra] *sf* (*MIL*) rank; (*gruppo*) group, band.

**schiera'mento** [skjɛra'mento] *sm* (*MIL*, *SPORT*) formation; (*fig*) alliance.

**schie'rare** [skje'rare] *vt* (*esercito*) to line up, draw up, marshal; **~rsi** *vr* to line up; (*fig*): **~rsi con o dalla parte di/contro qn** to side with/ oppose sb.

**schi'etto, a** ['skjɛtto] *ag* (*puro*) pure; (*fig*) frank, straightforward; sincere.

'**schifo** ['skifo] *sm* disgust; **fare ~** (*essere fatto male, dare pessimi risultati*) to be awful; **mi fa ~** it

makes me sick, it's disgusting; **quel libro è uno ~** that book's rotten; **schi'foso, a** *ag* disgusting, revolting; (*molto scadente*) rotten, lousy.

**schioc'care** [skjok'kare] *vt* (*frusta*) to crack; (*dita*) to snap; (*lingua*) to click; **~ le labbra** to smack one's lips.

**schi'udere** [skj'udere] *vt*, **~rsi** *vr* to open.

**schi'uma** ['skjuma] *sf* foam; (*di sapone*) lather; (*di latte*) froth; (*fig*: *feccia*) scum; **schiu'mare** *vt* to skim // *vi* to foam.

**schi'uso, a** ['skjuso] *pp di* **schiudere**.

**schi'vare** [ski'vare] *vt* to dodge, avoid.

'**schivo, a** ['skivo] *ag* (*ritroso*) stand-offish, reserved; (*timido*) shy.

**schiz'zare** [skit'tsare] *vt* (*spruzzare*) to spurt, squirt; (*sporcare*) to splash, spatter; (*fig*: *abbozzare*) to sketch // *vi* to spurt, squirt; (*saltar fuori*) to dart up (*o* off *etc*).

**schizzi'noso, a** [skittsi'noso] *ag* fussy, finicky.

'**schizzo** ['skittso] *sm* (*di liquido*) spurt; splash, spatter; (*abbozzo*) sketch.

**sci** [ʃi] *sm* (*attrezzo*) ski; (*attività*) skiing; **~ nautico** water-skiing.

'**scia**, *pl* '**scie** ['ʃia] *sf* (*imbarcazione*) wake; (*di profumo*) trail.

**scià** [ʃa] *sm inv* shah.

**sci'abola** ['ʃabola] *sf* sabre.

**sci'acallo** [ʃa'kallo] *sm* jackal.

**sciac'quare** [ʃak'kware] *vt* to rinse.

**scia'gura** [ʃa'gura] *sf* disaster, calamity; misfortune; **sciagu'rato, a** *ag* unfortunate; (*malvagio*) wicked.

**scialac'quare** [ʃalak'kware] *vt* to squander.

**scia'lare** [ʃa'lare] *vi* to lead a life of luxury.

**sci'albo, a** ['ʃalbo] *ag* pale, dull; (*fig*) dull, colourless.

**sci'alle** ['ʃalle] *sm* shawl.

**scia'luppa** [ʃa'luppa] *sf* (*NAUT*) sloop; (*anche*: ~ **di salvataggio**) lifeboat.

**sci'ame** [ʃ'ame] *sm* swarm.

**scian'cato, a** [ʃan'kato] *ag* lame; (*mobile*) rickety.

**sci'are** [ʃi'are] *vi* to ski.

**sci'arpa** [ʃ'arpa] *sf* scarf; (*fascia*) sash.

**scia'tore, 'trice** [ʃia'tore] *smf* skier.

**sci'atto, a** [ʃ'atto] *ag* (*persona: nell'aspetto*) slovenly, unkempt; (: *nel lavoro*) sloppy, careless.

**scien'tifico, a, ci, che** [ʃen'tifiko] *ag* scientific.

**sci'enza** [ʃ'entsa] *sf* science; (*sapere*) knowledge; ~e *sfpl* (*INS*) science *sg*; ~e **naturali** natural sciences; **scienzi'ato, a** *smf* scientist.

**'scimmia** [ʃ'immja] *sf* monkey; **scimmiot'tare** *vt* to ape, mimic.

**scimpanzé** [ʃimpan'tse] *sm inv* chimpanzee.

**scimu'nito, a** [ʃimu'nito] *ag* silly, idiotic.

**'scindere** [ʃ'indere] *vt*, ~**rsi** *vr* to split (up).

**scin'tilla** [ʃin'tilla] *sf* spark; **scintil'lare** *vi* to spark; (*acqua, occhi*) to sparkle.

**scioc'chezza** [ʃok'kettsa] *sf* stupidity *q*; (*stupid o foolish thing*) **dire** ~e to talk nonsense.

**sci'occo, a, chi, che** [ʃ'ɔkko] *ag* stupid, foolish.

**sci'ogliere** [ʃ'ɔʎʎere] *vt* (*nodo*) to untie; (*capelli*) to loosen; (*persona, animale*) to untie, release; (*fig: persona*): ~ **da** to release from; (*neve*) to melt; (*nell'acqua: zucchero etc*) to dissolve; (*fig: mistero*) to solve; (*porre fine a: contratto*) to cancel; (: *società, matrimonio*) to dissolve; (: *riunione*) to bring to an end; ~**rsi** *vr* to loosen, come untied; to melt; to dissolve; (*assemblea etc*) to break up; ~ **i muscoli** to limber up.

**sciol'tezza** [ʃol'tettsa] *sf* agility; suppleness; ease.

**sci'olto, a** [ʃ'ɔlto] *pp di* **sciogliere** // *ag* loose; (*agile*) agile, nimble; supple; (*disinvolto*) free and easy; **versi** ~**i** (*POESIA*) blank verse.

**sciope'rante** [ʃope'rante] *smf* striker.

**sciope'rare** [ʃope'rare] *vi* to strike, go on strike.

**sci'opero** [ʃ'ɔpero] *sm* strike; **fare** ~ to strike; ~ **bianco** work-to-rule (*Brit*), slowdown (*US*); ~ **selvaggio** wildcat strike; ~ **a singhiozzo** on-off strike.

**sci'rocco** [ʃi'rɔkko] *sm* sirocco.

**sci'roppo** [ʃi'rɔppo] *sm* syrup.

**'scisma, i** [ʃ'izma] *sm* (*REL*) schism.

**scissi'one** [ʃis'sjone] *sf* (*anche fig*) split, division; (*FISICA*) fission.

**'scisso, a** [ʃ'isso] *pp di* **scindere**.

**sciu'pare** [ʃu'pare] *vt* (*abito, libro, appetito*) to spoil, ruin; (*tempo, denaro*) to waste; ~**rsi** *vr* to get spoilt o ruined; (*rovinarsi la salute*) to ruin one's health.

**scivo'lare** [ʃivo'lare] *vi* to slide o glide along; (*involontariamente*) to slip, slide; **'scivolo** *sm* slide; (*TECN*) chute.

**scle'rosi** *sf* sclerosis.

**scoc'care** *vt* (*freccia*) to shoot // *vi* (*guizzare*) to shoot up; (*battere: ora*) to strike.

**scocci'are** [skot'tʃare] (*fam*) *vt* to bother, annoy; ~**rsi** *vr* to be bothered o annoyed.

**sco'della** *sf* bowl.

**scodinzo'lare** [skodintso'lare] *vi* to wag its tail.

**scogli'era** [skoʎ'ʎera] *sf* reef; cliff.

**'scoglio** [sk'ɔʎʎo] *sm* (*al mare*) rock.

**scoi'attolo** *sm* squirrel.

**sco'lare** *ag*: **età** ~ school age // *vt* to drain // *vi* to drip.

**scola'resca** *sf* schoolchildren *pl*, pupils *pl*.

**sco'laro, a** *smf* pupil, schoolboy/girl.

**sco'lastico, a, ci, che** *ag* school *cpd*; scholastic.

**scol'lare** *vt* (*staccare*) to unstick; ~rsi *vr* to come unstuck.

**scolla'tura** *sf* neckline.

**'scolo** *sm* drainage.

**scolo'rire** *vt* to fade; to discolour // *vi* (*anche*: ~rsi) to fade; to become discoloured; (*impallidire*) to turn pale.

**scol'pire** *vt* to carve, sculpt.

**scombi'nare** *vt* to mess up, upset.

**scombusso'lare** *vt* to upset.

**scom'messo, a** *pp di* **scommettere** // *sf* bet, wager.

**scom'mettere** *vt, vi* to bet.

**scomo'dare** *vt* to trouble, bother; to disturb; ~rsi *vr* to put o.s. out; ~rsi a fare to go to the bother *o* trouble of doing.

**'scomodo, a** *ag* uncomfortable; (*sistemazione, posto*) awkward, inconvenient.

**scompa'rire** *vi* (*sparire*) to disappear, vanish; (*fig*) to be insignificant; **scom'parso, a** *pp di* **scomparire** // *sf* disappearance.

**scomparti'mento** *sm* (*FERR*) compartment.

**scom'parto** *sm* compartment, division.

**scompigli'are** [skompiʎ'ʎare] *vt* (*cassetto, capelli*) to mess up, disarrange; (*fig: piani*) to upset; **scom'piglio** *sm* mess, confusion.

**scom'porre** *vt* (*parola, numero*) to break up; (*CHIM*) to decompose; **scomporsi** *vr* (*fig*) to get upset, lose one's composure; **scom'posto, a** *pp di* **scomporre** // *ag* (*gesto*) unseemly; (*capelli*) ruffled, dishevelled.

**sco'munica** *sf* excommunication.

**scomuni'care** *vt* to excommunicate.

**sconcer'tare** [skontʃer'tare] *vt* to disconcert, bewilder.

**'sconcio, a, ci, ce** [skontʃo] *ag* (*osceno*) indecent, obscene // *sm* (*cosa riprovevole, mal fatta*) disgrace.

**sconfes'sare** *vt* to renounce, disavow; to repudiate.

**scon'figgere** [skon'fiddʒere] *vt* to defeat, overcome.

**sconfi'nare** *vi* to cross the border; (*in proprietà privata*) to trespass; (*fig*): ~ da to stray *o* digress from; **sconfi'nato, a** *ag* boundless, unlimited.

**scon'fitta, a** *pp di* **sconfiggere** // *sf* defeat.

**scon'forto** *sm* despondency.

**scongiu'rare** [skondʒu'rare] *vt* (*implorare*) to entreat, beseech, implore; (*eludere: pericolo*) to ward off, avert; **scongi'uro** *sm* entreaty; (*esorcismo*) exorcism; **fare gli scongiuri** to touch wood (*Brit*), knock on wood (*US*).

**scon'nesso, a** *ag* (*fig: discorso*) incoherent, rambling.

**sconosci'uto, a** [skonoʃ'ʃuto] *ag* unknown; new, strange // *sm/f* stranger; unknown person.

**sconquas'sare** *vt* to shatter, smash.

**sconside'rato, a** *ag* thoughtless, rash.

**sconsigli'are** [skonsiʎ'ʎare] *vt*: ~ qc a qn to advise sb against sth; ~ qn dal fare qc to advise sb not to do *o* against doing sth.

**sconso'lato, a** *ag* inconsolable; desolate.

**scon'tare** *vt* (*COMM: detrarre*) to deduct; (*: debito*) to pay off; (*: cambiale*) to discount; (*pena*) to serve; (*colpa, errori*) to pay for, suffer for.

**scon'tato, a** *ag* (*previsto*) foreseen, taken for granted; **dare per ~ che** to take it for granted that.

**scon'tento, a** *ag*: ~ (**di**) discontented *o* dissatisfied (with) // *sm* discontent, dissatisfaction.

**'sconto** *sm* discount; **fare uno ~** to give a discount.

**scon'trarsi** *vr* (*treni etc*) to crash, collide; (*venire ad uno scontro, fig*) to clash; ~ **con** to crash into, collide with.

**scon'trino** sm ticket.

**'scontro** sm clash, encounter; crash, collision.

**scon'troso, a** ag sullen, surly; (permaloso) touchy.

**sconveni'ente** ag unseemly, improper.

**scon'volgere** [skon'vɔldʒere] vt to throw into confusion, upset; (turbare) to shake, disturb, upset; **scon'volto, a** pp di **sconvolgere**.

**'scopa** sf broom; (CARTE) Italian card game; **sco'pare** vt to sweep.

**sco'perto, a** pp di **scoprire** // ag uncovered; (capo) uncovered, bare; (macchina) open; (MIL) exposed, without cover; (conto) overdrawn // sf discovery.

**'scopo** sm aim, purpose; **a che ~?** what for?

**scoppi'are** vi (spaccarsi) to burst; (esplodere) to explode; (fig) to break out; **~ in pianto** o **a piangere** to burst out crying; **~ dalle risa** o **dal ridere** to split one's sides laughing.

**scoppiet'tare** vi to crackle.

**'scoppio** sm explosion; (di tuono, arma etc) crash, bang; (fig: di risa, ira) fit, outburst; (: di guerra) outbreak; **a ~ ritardato** delayed-action.

**sco'prire** vt to discover; (liberare da ciò che copre) to uncover; (: monumento) to unveil; **~rsi** vr to put on lighter clothes; (fig) to give o.s. away.

**scoraggi'are** [skorad'dʒare] vt to discourage; **~rsi** vr to become discouraged, lose heart.

**scorcia'toia** [skortʃa'toja] sf short cut.

**'scorcio** ['skortʃo] sm (ARTE) foreshortening; (di secolo, periodo) end, close.

**scor'dare** vt to forget; **~rsi** vr: **~rsi di qc/di fare** to forget sth/to do.

**'scorgere** ['skɔrdʒere] vt to make out, distinguish, see.

**sco'ria** sf (di metalli) slag; (vulcanica) scoria; **~e radioattive**

(FISICA) radioactive waste sg.

**'scorno** sm ignominy, disgrace.

**scorpacci'ata** [skorpat'tʃata] sf: **fare una ~ (di)** to stuff o.s. (with), eat one's fill (of).

**scorpi'one** sm scorpion; (dello zodiaco) **S~** Scorpio.

**scorraz'zare** [skorrat'tsare] vi to run about.

**'scorrere** vt (giornale, lettera) to run o skim through // vi (liquido, fiume) to run, flow; (fune) to run; (cassetto, porta) to slide easily; (tempo) to pass (by).

**scor'retto, a** ag incorrect; (sgarbato) impolite; (sconveniente) improper.

**scor'revole** ag (porta) sliding; (fig: stile) fluent, flowing.

**scorri'banda** sf (MIL) raid; (escursione) trip, excursion.

**'scorso, a** pp di **scorrere** // ag last // sf quick look, glance.

**scor'soio, a** ag: **nodo ~** noose.

**'scorta** sf (di personalità, convoglio) escort; (provvista) supply, stock; **scor'tare** vt to escort.

**scor'tese** ag discourteous, rude; **scorte'sia** sf discourtesy, rudeness; (azione) discourtesy.

**scorti'care** vt to skin.

**'scorto, a** pp di **scorgere**.

**'scorza** ['skɔrdza] sf (di albero) bark; (di agrumi) peel, skin.

**sco'sceso, a** [skoʃ'ʃeso] ag steep.

**'scosso, a** pp di **scuotere** // ag (turbato) shaken, upset // sf jerk, jolt, shake; (ELETTR, fig) shock.

**scos'tante** ag (fig) off-putting (Brit), unpleasant.

**scos'tare** vt to move (away), shift; **~rsi** vr to move away.

**scostu'mato, a** ag immoral, dissolute.

**scot'tare** vt (ustionare) to burn; (: con liquido bollente) to scald // vi to burn; (caffè) to be too hot; **scotta'tura** sf burn; scald.

**'scotto, a** ag overcooked // sm (fig): **pagare lo ~ (di)** to pay the penalty (for).

**sco'vare** vt to drive out, flush out; (fig) to discover.

'**Scozia** ['skɔttsja] sf: la ~ Scotland; **scoz'zese** ag Scottish // sm/f Scot.

**scredi'tare** vt to discredit.

**screpo'lare** vt, ~**rsi** vr to crack; **screpola'tura** sf cracking q; crack.

**screzi'ato, a** [skret'tsjato] ag streaked.

'**screzio** ['skrɛttsjo] sm disagreement.

**scricchio'lare** [skrikkjo'lare] vi to creak, squeak.

'**scricciolo** ['skrittʃolo] sm wren.

'**scrigno** ['skriɲɲo] sm casket.

**scrimina'tura** sf parting.

'**scritto, a** pp di **scrivere** // ag written // sm writing; (lettera) letter, note // gl inscription; ~**i** smpl (letterari etc) writing sg; **per** o **in** ~ in writing.

**scrit'toio** sm writing desk.

**scrit'tore, 'trice** sm/f writer.

**scrit'tura** sf writing; (COMM) entry; (contratto) contract; (REL): la **Sacra S**~ the Scriptures pl; ~**e** sfpl (COMM) accounts, books.

**scrittu'rare** vt (TEATRO, CINEMA) to sign up, engage; (COMM) to enter.

**scriva'nia** sf desk.

**scri'vente** sm/f writer.

'**scrivere** vt to write; **come si scrive?** how is it spelt?, how do you write it?

**scroc'cone, a** sm/f scrounger.

'**scrofa** sf (ZOOL) sow.

**scrol'lare** vt to shake; ~**rsi** vr (anche fig) to give o.s. a shake; ~ **le spalle/il capo** to shrug one's shoulders/shake one's head.

**scrosci'are** [skroʃ'ʃare] vi (pioggia) to pour down, pelt down; (torrente, fig: applausi) to thunder, roar; '**scroscio** sm pelting; thunder, roar; (di applausi) burst.

**scros'tare** vt (intonaco) to scrape off, strip; ~**rsi** vr to peel off, flake off.

'**scrupolo** sm scruple; (meticolosità) care, conscientiousness.

**scru'tare** vt to scrutinize; (intenzioni, causa) to examine, scrutinize.

**scruti'nare** vt (voti) to count; **scru'tinio** sm (votazione) ballot; (insieme delle operazioni) poll; (INS) (meeting for) assignment of marks at end of a term or year.

**scu'cire** [sku'tʃire] vt (orlo etc) to unpick, undo.

**scude'ria** sf stable.

**scu'detto** sm (SPORT) (championship) shield; (distintivo) badge.

'**scudo** sm shield.

**scul'tore, 'trice** sm/f sculptor.

**scul'tura** sf sculpture.

**scu'ola** sf school; ~ **elementare/ materna/media** primary (Brit) o grade (US)/nursery/secondary (Brit) o high (US) school; ~ **guida** driving school; ~ **dell'obbligo** compulsory education; ~**e serali** evening classes, night school sg; ~ **tecnica** technical college.

**scu'otere** vt to shake; ~**rsi** vr to jump, be startled; (fig: muoversi) to rouse o.s., stir o.s.; (: turbarsi) to be shaken.

'**scure** sf axe.

'**scuro, a** ag dark; (fig: espressione) grim // sm darkness; dark colour; (imposta) (window) shutter; **verde/ rosso** etc ~ dark green/red etc.

**scur'rile** ag scurrilous.

'**scusa** sf excuse; ~**e** sfpl apology sg, apologies; **chiedere** ~ **a qn (per)** to apologize to sb (for); **chiedo** ~ I'm sorry; (disturbando etc) excuse me.

**scu'sare** vt to excuse; ~**rsi** vr: ~**rsi (di)** to apologize (for); (**mi**) **scusi** I'm sorry; (per richiamare l'attenzione) excuse me.

**sde'gnato, a** [zdeɲ'ɲato] ag indignant, angry.

'**sdegno** ['zdeɲɲo] sm scorn, disdain; **sde'gnoso, a** ag scornful, disdainful.

**sdoga'nare** vt (merci) to clear through customs.

**sdolci'nato, a** [zdoltʃi'nato] *ag* mawkish, oversentimental.

**sdoppi'are** *vt* (*dividere*) to divide o split in two.

**sdrai'arsi** *vr* to stretch out, lie down.

**'sdraio** *sm*: **sedia a ~** deck chair.

**sdruccio'levole** [zdruttʃo'levole] *ag* slippery.

PAROLA CHIAVE

**se** ♦ *pronome vedi* **si**
♦ *cong* **1** (*condizionale, ipotetica*) if; **~ nevica non vengo** I won't come if it snows; **sarei rimasto ~ me l'avessero chiesto** I would have stayed if they'd asked me; **non puoi fare altro ~ non telefonare** all you can do is phone; **~ mai** if, if ever; **siamo noi ~ mai che le siamo grati** it is we who should be grateful to you; **~ no** (*altrimenti*) or (else), otherwise
**2** (*in frasi dubitative, interrogative indirette*) if, whether; **non so ~ scrivere o telefonare** I don't know whether o if I should write or phone.

**sé** *pronome* (*gen*) oneself; (*esso, essa, lui, lei, loro*) itself; himself; herself; themselves; **~ stesso(a)** *pronome* oneself; itself; himself; herself; **~ stessi(e)** *pronome pl* themselves.

**seb'bene** *cong* although, though.

**sec.** *abbr* (= *secolo*) c.

**'secca** *sf vedi* **secco.**

**sec'care** *vt* to dry; (*prosciugare*) to dry up; (*fig: importunare*) to annoy, bother // *vi* to dry; to dry up; **~rsi** *vr* to dry; to dry up; (*fig*) to grow annoyed; **secca'tura** *sf* (*fig*) bother *q*, trouble *q*.

**'secchia** ['sekkja] *sf* bucket, pail.

**'secco, a, chi, che** *ag* dry; (*fichi, pesce*) dried; (*foglie, ramo*) withered; (*magro: persona*) thin, skinny; (*fig: risposta, modo di fare*) curt, abrupt; (: *colpo*) clean, sharp // *sm* (*siccità*) drought // *sf* (*del mare*) shallows *pl*; **restarci ~** (*fig: morire*

sul colpo) to drop dead; **mettere in ~** (*barca*) to beach; **rimanere in o a ~** (*NAUT*) to run aground; (*fig*) to be left in the lurch.

**seco'lare** *ag* age-old, centuries-old; (*laico, mondano*) secular.

**'secolo** *sm* century; (*epoca*) age.

**se'conda** *sf vedi* **secondo.**

**secon'dario, a** *ag* secondary.

**se'condo, a** *ag* second // *sm* second; (*di pranzo*) main course // *sf* (*AUT*) second (gear) // *prep* according to; (*nel modo prescritto*) in accordance with; **~ me** in my opinion, to my mind; **di ~a classe** second-class; **di ~a mano** second-hand; **viaggiare in ~a** to travel second-class; **a ~a di** *prep* according to; in accordance with.

**'sedano** *sm* celery.

**seda'tivo, a** *ag, sm* sedative.

**'sede** *sf* seat; (*di ditta*) head office; (*di organizzazione*) headquarters *pl*; **in ~ di** (*in occasione di*) during; **~ sociale** registered office.

**seden'tario, a** *ag* sedentary.

**se'dere** *vi* to sit, be seated; **~rsi** *vr* to sit down // *sm* (*deretano*) behind, bottom.

**'sedia** *sf* chair.

**sedi'cente** [sedi'tʃente] *ag* self-styled.

**'sedici** ['seditʃi] *num* sixteen.

**se'dile** *sm* seat; (*panchina*) bench.

**sedizi'one** [sedit'tsjone] *sf* revolt, rebellion.

**se'dotto, a** *pp di* **sedurre.**

**sedu'cente** [sedu'tʃente] *ag* seductive; (*proposta*) very attractive.

**se'durre** *vt* to seduce.

**se'duta** *sf* session, sitting; (*riunione*) meeting; **~ spiritica** séance; **~ stante** (*fig*) immediately.

**seduzi'one** [sedut'tsjone] *sf* seduction; (*fascino*) charm, appeal.

**'sega, ghe** *sf* saw.

**'segale** *sf* rye.

**se'gare** *vt* to saw; (*recidere*) to saw off; **sega'tura** *sf* (*residuo*) sawdust.

**'seggio** ['seddʒo] *sm* seat; **~**

elettorale polling station.

**'seggiola** ['sɛddʒola] sf chair; **seggio'lino** sm seat; (per bambini) child's chair; **seggio'lone** sm (per bambini) highchair.

**seggio'via** [sɛddʒo'via] sf chairlift.

**seghe'ria** [sege'ria] sf sawmill.

**segna'lare** [seɲɲa'lare] vt (manovra etc) to signal; to indicate; (annunciare) to announce; to report; (fig: far conoscere) to point out; (: persona) to single out; **~rsi** vr (distinguersi) to distinguish o.s.

**se'gnale** [seɲ'ɲale] sm signal; (cartello): ~ **stradale** road sign; ~ **d'allarme** alarm; (FERR) communication cord; ~ **orario** (RADIO) time signal; **segna'letica** sf signalling, signposting; **segnaletica stradale** road signs pl.

**se'gnare** [seɲ'ɲare] vt to mark; (prendere nota) to note; (indicare) to indicate, mark; (SPORT: goal) to score; **~rsi** vr (REL) to make the sign of the cross, cross o.s.

**'segno** ['seɲɲo] sm sign; (impronta, contrassegno) mark; (limite) limit, bounds pl; (bersaglio) target; **fare ~ di si/no** to nod (one's head)/shake one's head; **fare ~ a qn di fermarsi** to motion (to) sb to stop; **cogliere o colpire nel ~** (fig) to hit the mark.

**segre'gare** vt to segregate, isolate; **segregazi'one** sf segregation.

**segre'tario, a** smf secretary; ~ **comunale** town clerk; ~ **di Stato** Secretary of State.

**segrete'ria** sf (di ditta, scuola) (secretary's) office; (d'organizzazione internazionale) secretariat; (POL etc: carica) office of Secretary; ~ **telefonica** answering service.

**segre'tezza** [segre'tettsa] sf secrecy.

**se'greto, a** ag secret // sm secret; secrecy q; **in ~** in secret, secretly.

**segu'ace** [se'gwatʃe] smf follower, disciple.

**segu'ente** ag following, next.

**segu'ire** vt to follow; (frequentare:

corso) to attend // vi to follow; (continuare: testo) to continue.

**segui'tare** vt to continue, carry on with // vi to continue, carry on.

**'seguito** sm (scorta) suite, retinue; (discepoli) followers pl; (favore) following; (serie) sequence, series sg; (continuazione) continuation; (conseguenza) result; **di ~** at a stretch, on end; **in ~** later on; **in ~ a, a ~ di** following; (a causa di) as a result of, owing to.

**'sei** vb vedi **essere** // num six.

**sei'cento** [sei'tʃɛnto] num six hundred // sm: **il S~** the seventeenth century.

**selci'ato** [sel'tʃato] sm cobbled surface.

**selezio'nare** [selettsjo'nare] vt to select.

**selezi'one** [selet'tsjone] sf selection.

**'sella** sf saddle; **sel'lare** vt to saddle.

**selvag'gina** [selvad'dʒina] sf (animali) game.

**sel'vaggio, a, gi, ge** [sel'vaddʒo] ag wild; (tribù) savage, uncivilized; (fig) savage, brutal // sm/f savage.

**sel'vatico, a, ci, che** ag wild.

**se'maforo** sm (AUT) traffic lights pl.

**sem'brare** vi to seem // vb impers: **sembra che** it seems that; **mi sembra che** it seems to me that; **I think** (that); ~ **di essere** to seem to be.

**'seme** sm seed; (sperma) semen; (CARTE) suit.

**se'mestre** sm half-year, six-month period.

**'semi...** prefisso semi...; **semi'cerchio** sm semicircle; **semifi'nale** sf semifinal; **semi'freddo, a** ag (CUC) chilled // sm ice-cream cake.

**'semina** sf (AGR) sowing.

**semi'nare** vt to sow.

**semi'nario** sm seminar; (REL) seminary.

**seminter'rato** sm basement; (appartamento) basement flat.

**se'mitico, a, ci, che** ag semitic.

**sem'mai = se mai;** *vedi* **se.**

**'semola** *sf* bran; ~ **di grano duro** durum wheat.

**semo'lino** *sm* semolina.

**'semplice** ['semplitʃe] *ag* simple; (*di un solo elemento*) single; **sem- plice'mente** *av* simply; **semplicità** *sf* simplicity.

**'sempre** *av* always; (*ancora*) still; **posso ~ tentare** I can always *o* still try; **da ~** always; **per ~** forever; **una volta per ~** once and for all; ~ **che** *cong* provided (that); ~ **più** more and more; ~ **meno** less and less.

**sempre'verde** *ag, sm o f* (*BOT*) evergreen.

**'senape** *sf* (*CUC*) mustard.

**se'nato** *sm* senate; **sena'tore, 'trice** *sm/f* senator.

**'senno** *sm* judgment, (*common*) sense; **col ~ di poi** with hindsight.

**sennò** *av* = **se no;** *vedi* **se.**

**'seno** *sm* (*ANAT: petto, mammella*) breast; (: *grembo, fig*) womb; (: *cavità*) sinus; (*GEO*) inlet, creek; (*MAT*) sine.

**sen'sato, a** *ag* sensible.

**sensazio'nale** [sensattsjo'nale] *ag* sensational.

**sensazi'one** [sensat'tsjone] *sf* feeling, sensation; **avere la ~ che** to have a feeling that; **fare ~** to cause a sensation, create a stir.

**sen'sibile** *ag* sensitive; (*ai sensi*) perceptible; (*rilevante, notevole*) appreciable, noticeable; ~ **a** sensitive to; **sensibilità** *sf* sensitivity.

**'senso** *sm* (*FISIOL, istinto*) sense; (*impressione, sensazione*) feeling, sensation; (*significato*) meaning, sense; (*direzione*) direction; ~**i** *smpl* (*coscienza*) consciousness *sg;* (*sensualità*) senses; **ciò non ha ~** that doesn't make sense; **fare ~ a** (*ripugnare*) to disgust, repel; ~ **comune** common sense; **in ~ orario/antiorario** clockwise/anti-clockwise; **a ~ unico** (*strada*) one-way; "~ **vietato**" (*AUT*) "no en-

try".

**sensu'ale** *ag* sensual; sensuous; **sensualità** *sf* sensuality; sensuous-ness.

**sen'tenza** [sen'tentsa] *sf* (*DIR*) sentence; (*massima*) maxim; **sentenzi'are** *vi* (*DIR*) to pass judg-ment.

**senti'ero** *sm* path.

**sentimen'tale** *ag* sentimental; (*vita, avventura*) love *cpd.*

**senti'mento** *sm* feeling.

**senti'nella** *sf* sentry.

**sen'tire** *vt* (*percepire al tatto, fig*) to feel; (*udire*) to hear; (*ascoltare*) to listen to; (*odore*) to smell; (*avvertire con il gusto, assaggiare*) to taste // *vi:* ~ **di** (*avere sapore*) to taste of; (*avere odore*) to smell of; ~**rsi** *vr* (*uso reciproco*) to be in touch; ~**rsi bene/male** to feel well/unwell *o* ill; ~**rsi di fare qc** (*essere disposto*) to feel like doing sth.

**sen'tito, a** *ag* (*sincero*) sincere, warm; **per ~ dire** by hearsay.

**'senza** ['sentsa] *prep, cong* without; ~ **dir nulla** without saying a word; **fare ~ qc** to do without sth; ~ **di me** without me; ~ **che io lo sappesi** without me *o* my knowing; **senz'al- tro** of course, certainly; ~ **dubbio** no doubt; ~ **scrupoli** unscrupulous; ~ **amici** friendless.

**sepa'rare** *vt* to separate; (*dividere*) to divide; (*tenere distinto*) to distinguish; ~**rsi** *vr* (*coniugi*) to separate, part; (*amici*) to part, leave each other; ~**rsi da** (*coniuge*) to separate *o* part from; (*amico, socio*) to part company with; (*oggetto*) to part with; **sepa'rato, a** *ag* (*letti, conto etc*) separate; (*coniugi*) separated; **separazi'one** *sf* separa-tion.

**se'polcro** *sm* sepulchre.

**se'polto, a** *pp di* **seppellire.**

**seppel'lire** *vt* to bury.

**'seppia** *sf* cuttlefish // *ag inv* sepia.

**se'quenza** [se'kwentsa] *sf* sequence.

**seques'trare** *vt* (*DIR*) to impound;

*(rapire)* to kidnap; *(costringere in un luogo)* to keep, confine; **se'questro** *sm (DIR)* impoundment; **sequestro di persona** kidnapping.

**'sera** *sf* evening; **di** ~ in the evening; **domani** ~ tomorrow evening, tomorrow night; **se'rale** *ag* evening *cpd*; **se'rata** *sf* evening; *(ricevimento)* party.

**ser'bare** *vt* to keep; *(mettere da parte)* to put aside; ~ **rancore/odio verso qn** to bear sb a grudge/hate sb.

**serba'toio** *sm* tank; *(cisterna)* cistern.

**'serbo** *sm*: mettere/tenere *o* avere in ~ qc to put/keep sth aside.

**se'reno, a** *ag (tempo, cielo)* clear; *(fig)* serene, calm.

**ser'gente** [ser'dʒɛnte] *sm (MIL)* sergeant.

**'serie** *sf inv (successione)* series *inv*; *(gruppo, collezione: di chiavi etc)* set; *(SPORT)* division; league; *(COMM)*: **modello di** ~/**fuori** ~ standard/custom-built model; **in** ~ in quick succession; *(COMM)* mass *cpd*.

**serietà** *sf* seriousness; reliability.

**'serio, a** *ag* serious; *(impiegato)* responsible, reliable; *(ditta, cliente)* reliable, dependable; **sul** ~ *(davvero)* really, truly; *(seriamente)* seriously, in earnest.

**ser'mone** *sm* sermon.

**serpeggi'are** [serped'dʒare] *vi* to wind; *(fig)* to spread.

**ser'pente** *sm* snake; ~ **a sonagli** rattlesnake.

**'serra** *sf* greenhouse; hothouse.

**ser'randa** *sf* roller shutter.

**ser'rare** *vt* to close, shut; *(a chiave)* to lock; *(stringere)* to tighten; *(premere: nemico)* to close in on; ~ **i pugni/i denti** to clench one's fists/teeth; ~ **le file** to close ranks.

**serra'tura** *sf* lock.

**'serva** *sf vedi* **servo**.

**ser'vire** *vt* to serve; *(clienti: al ristorante)* to wait on; *(: al negozio)* to serve, attend to; *(fig: giovare)* to

aid, help; *(CARTE)* to deal // *vi (TENNIS)* to serve; *(essere utile)*: ~ **a qn** to be of use to sb; ~ **a qc/a fare** *(utensile etc)* to be used for sth/for doing; ~ **(a qn) da** to serve as (for sb); ~**rsi** *vr (usare)*: ~**rsi di** to use; *(prendere: cibo)*: ~**rsi (di)** to help o.s. (to); *(essere cliente abituale)*: ~**rsi da** to be a regular customer at, go to.

**servitù** *sf* servitude; slavery; *(personale di servizio)* servants *pl*, domestic staff.

**servi'zievole** [servit'tsjevole] *ag* obliging, willing to help.

**ser'vizio** [ser'vittsjo] *sm* service; *(al ristorante: sul conto)* service (charge); *(STAMPA, TV, RADIO)* report; *(da tè, caffè etc)* set, service; ~**i** *smpl (di casa)* kitchen and bathroom; *(ECON)* services; **essere di** ~ to be on duty; **fuori** ~ *(telefono etc)* out of order; ~ **compreso** service included; ~ **militare** military service; ~**i segreti** secret service *sg*.

**'servo, a** *sm/f* servant.

**ses'santa** *num* sixty; **sessan'tesimo, a** *num* sixtieth.

**sessan'tina** *sf*: **una** ~ **(di)** about sixty.

**sessi'one** *sf* session.

**'sesso** *sm* sex; **sessu'ale** *ag* sexual, sex *cpd*.

**ses'tante** *sm* sextant.

**'sesto, a** *ag, sm* sixth.

**'seta** *sf* silk.

**'sete** *sf* thirst; **avere** ~ to be thirsty.

**'setola** *sf* bristle.

**'setta** *sf* sect.

**set'tanta** *num* seventy; **settan'tesimo, a** *num* seventieth.

**settan'tina** *sf*: **una** ~ **(di)** about seventy.

**'sette** *num* seven.

**sette'cento** [sette'tʃɛnto] *num* seven hundred // *sm*: **il S**~ the eighteenth century.

**set'tembre** *sm* September.

**settentrio'nale** *ag* northern.

**settentri'one** *sm* north.

**'settico, a, ci, che** *ag* (*MED*) septic.

**setti'mana** *sf* week; **settima'nale** *ag*, *sm* weekly.

**'settimo, a** *ag*, *sm* seventh.

**set'tore** *sm* sector.

**severità** *sf* severity.

**se'vero, a** *ag* severe.

**se'vizie** [se'vittsje] *sfpl* torture *sg*; **sevizi'are** *vt* to torture.

**sezio'nare** [settsjo'nare] *vt* to divide into sections; (*MED*) to dissect.

**sezi'one** [set'tsjone] *sf* section; (*MED*) dissection.

**sfaccen'dato, a** [sfattʃen'dato] *ag* idle.

**sfacci'ato, a** [sfat'tʃato] *ag* (*maleducato*) cheeky, impudent; (*vistoso*) gaudy.

**sfa'celo** [sfa'tʃelo] *sm* (*fig*) ruin, collapse.

**sfal'darsi** *vr* to flake (off).

**'sfarzo** ['sfartso] *sm* pomp, splendour.

**sfasci'are** [sfaʃ'ʃare] *vt* (*ferita*) to unbandage; (*distruggere: porta*) to smash, shatter; **~rsi** *vr* (*rompersi*) to smash, shatter.

**sfa'tare** *vt* (*leggenda*) to explode.

**sfavil'lare** *vi* to spark, send out sparks; (*risplendere*) to sparkle.

**sfavo'revole** *ag* unfavourable.

**'sfera** *sf* sphere; **'sferico, a, ci, che** *ag* spherical.

**sfer'rare** *vt* (*fig: colpo*) to land, deal; (: *attacco*) to launch.

**sfer'zare** [sfer'tsare] *vt* to whip; (*fig*) to lash out at.

**sfi'brare** *vt* (*indebolire*) to exhaust, enervate.

**'sfida** *sf* challenge; **sfi'dare** *vt* to challenge; (*fig*) to defy, brave.

**sfi'ducia** [sfi'dutʃa] *sf* distrust, mistrust.

**sfigu'rare** *vt* (*persona*) to disfigure; (*quadro, statua*) to deface // *vi* (*far cattiva figura*) to make a bad impression.

**sfi'lare** *vt* (*ago*) to unthread; (*abito, scarpe*) to slip off // *vi* (*truppe*) to march past; (*atleti*) to parade; **~rsi**

*vr* (*perle etc*) to come unstrung; (*orlo, tessuto*) to fray; (*calza*) to run, ladder; **sfi'lata** *sf* march past; parade; **sfilata di moda** fashion show.

**'sfinge** ['sfindʒe] *sf* sphinx.

**sfi'nito, a** *ag* exhausted.

**sfio'rare** *vt* to brush (against); (*argomento*) to touch upon.

**sfio'rire** *vi* to wither, fade.

**sfo'cato, a** *ag* (*FOT*) out of focus.

**sfoci'are** [sfo'tʃare] *vi*: **~ in** to flow into; (*fig: malcontento*) to develop into.

**sfo'gare** *vt* to vent, pour out; **~rsi** *vr* (*sfogare la propria rabbia*) to give vent to one's anger; (*confidarsi*): **~rsi (con)** to pour out one's feelings (to); **non sfogarti su di me!** don't take your bad temper out on me!

**sfoggi'are** [sfod'dʒare] *vt*, *vi* to show off.

**'sfoglia** ['sfoʎʎa] *sf* sheet of pasta dough; **pasta ~** (*CUC*) puff pastry.

**sfogli'are** [sfoʎ'ʎare] *vt* (*libro*) to leaf through.

**'sfogo, ghi** *sm* outlet; (*eruzione cutanea*) rash; (*fig*) outburst; **dare ~ a** (*fig*) to give vent to.

**sfol'gorante** *ag* (*luce*) blazing; (*fig: vittoria*) brilliant.

**sfol'lare** *vt* to empty, clear // *vi* to disperse; **~ da** (*città*) to evacuate.

**sfon'dare** *vt* (*porta*) to break down; (*scarpe*) to wear a hole in; (*cesto, scatola*) to burst, knock the bottom out of; (*MIL*) to break through // *vi* (*riuscire*) to make a name for o.s.

**'sfondo** *sm* background.

**sfor'mato** *sm* (*CUC*) type of soufflé.

**sfor'nito, a** *ag*: **~ di** lacking in, without; (*negozio*) out of.

**sfor'tuna** *sf* misfortune, ill luck *q*; **avere ~** to be unlucky; **sfortu'nato, a** *ag* unlucky; (*impresa, film*) unsuccessful.

**sfor'zare** [sfor'tsare] *vt* to force; (*voce, occhi*) to strain; **~rsi** *vr*: **~rsi di** *o* **a** *o* **per fare** to try hard to do.

**'sforzo** ['sfɔrtso] *sm* effort; *(tensione eccessiva, TECN)* strain; **fare uno ~** to make an effort.

**sfrat'tare** *vt* to evict; **'sfratto** *sm* eviction.

**sfrecci'are** [sfret'tʃare] *vi* to shoot *o* flash past.

**sfregi'are** [sfre'dʒare] *vt* to slash, gash; *(persona)* to disfigure; *(quadro)* to deface; **'sfregio** *sm* gash; scar; *(fig)* insult.

**sfre'nato, a** *ag (fig)* unrestrained, unbridled.

**sfron'tato, a** *ag* shameless.

**sfrutta'mento** *sm* exploitation.

**sfrut'tare** *vt (terreno)* to overwork, exhaust; *(miniera)* to exploit, work; *(fig: operai, occasione, potere)* to exploit.

**sfug'gire** [sfud'dʒire] *vi* to escape; **~ a** *(custode)* to escape *(from)*; *(morte)* to escape; **~ a qn** *(dettaglio, nome)* to escape sb; **~ di mano a qn** to slip out of sb's hand *(o* hands); **sfug'gita** *di sfuggita* *ad (rapidamente, in fretta)* in passing.

**sfu'mare** *vt (colori, contorni)* to soften, shade off // *vi* to shade (off), fade; *(fig: svanire)* to vanish, disappear; *(: speranze)* to come to nothing; **sfuma'tura** *sf* shading off *q*; *(tonalità)* shade, tone; *(fig)* touch, hint.

**sfuri'ata** *sf (scatto di collera)* fit of anger; *(rimprovero)* sharp rebuke.

**sga'bello** *sm* stool.

**sgabuz'zino** [sgabud'dzino] *sm* lumber room.

**sgambet'tare** *vi* to kick one's legs about.

**sgam'betto** *sm*: **far lo ~ a qn** to trip sb up; *(fig)* to oust sb.

**sganasci'arsi** [zganaʃ'ʃarsi] *vr*: **~ dalle risa** to roar with laughter.

**sganci'are** [zgan'tʃare] *vt* to unhook; *(FERR)* to uncouple; *(bombe: da aereo)* to release, drop; *(fig: fam: soldi)* to fork out; **~rsi** *vr (fig)*: **~rsi (da)** to get away (from).

**sganghe'rato, a** [zgange'rato] *ag (porta)* off its hinges; *(auto)* ramshackle; *(risata)* wild, boisterous.

**sgar'bato, a** *ag* rude, impolite.

**'sgarbo** *sm*: **fare uno ~ a qn** to be rude to sb.

**sgattaio'lare** *vi* to sneak away *o* off.

**sge'lare** [zdʒe'lare] *vi, vt* to thaw.

**'sghembo, a** ['zgembo] *ag (obliquo)* slanting; *(storto)* crooked.

**sghignaz'zare** [zgiɲɲat'tsare] *vi* to laugh scornfully.

**sgob'bare** *vi (fam: scolaro)* to swot; *(: operaio)* to slog.

**sgoccio'lare** [zgottʃo'lare] *vt (vuotare)* to drain (to the last drop) // *vi (acqua)* to drip; *(recipiente)* to drain.

**sgo'larsi** *vr* to talk *(o* shout *o* sing) o.s. hoarse.

**sgomb(e)'rare** *vt* to clear; *(andarsene da: stanza)* to vacate; *(evacuare)* to evacuate.

**'sgombro, a** *ag*: **~ (di)** clear (of), free (from) // *sm (ZOOL)* mackerel; *(anche:* **sgombero**) clearing; vacating; evacuation; *(: trasloco)* removal.

**sgomen'tare** *vt* to dismay; **~rsi** *vr* to be dismayed; **sgo'mento, a** *ag* dismayed // *sm* dismay, consternation.

**sgonfi'are** *vt* to let down, deflate; **~rsi** *vr* to go down.

**'sgorbio** *sm* blot; scribble.

**sgor'gare** *vi* to gush (out).

**sgoz'zare** [zgot'tsare] *vt* to cut the throat of.

**sgra'devole** *ag* unpleasant, disagreeable.

**sgra'dito, a** *ag* unpleasant, unwelcome.

**sgra'nare** *vt (piselli)* to shell; **~ gli occhi** to open one's eyes wide.

**sgran'chirsi** [zgran'kirsi] *vr* to stretch; **~ le gambe** to stretch one's legs.

**sgranocchi'are** [zgranok'kjare] *vt* to munch.

**'sgravio** sm: ~ fiscale tax relief.

**sgrazi'ato, a** [zgrat'tsjato] ag clumsy, ungainly.

**sgreto'lare** vt to cause to crumble; ~rsi vr to crumble.

**sgri'dare** vt to scold; **sgri'data** sf scolding.

**sguai'ato, a** ag coarse, vulgar.

**sgual'cire** [zgwal'tʃire] vt to crumple (up), crease.

**sgual'drina** sf (peg) slut.

**sgu'ardo** sm (occhiata) look, glance; (espressione) look (in one's eye).

**sguaz'zare** [zgwat'tsare] vi (nell'acqua) to splash about; (nella melma) to wallow; ~ nell'oro to be rolling in money.

**sguinzagli'are** [zgwintsaʎ'ʎare] vt to let off the leash; (fig: persona): ~ qn dietro a qn to set sb on sb.

**sgusci'are** [zguʃ'ʃare] vt to shell // vi (sfuggire di mano) to slip; ~ via to slip o slink away.

**'shampoo** ['ʃampo] sm inv shampoo.

**shock** [ʃɔk] sm inv shock.

---

PAROLA CHIAVE

---

**si** ♦ sm (MUS) B; (solfeggiando la scala) ti

♦ pronome (dav lo, la, li, le, ne diventa **se**) 1 (riflessivo: maschile) himself; (: femminile) herself; (: neutro) itself; (: impersonale) one-self; (: pl) themselves; **lavarsi** to wash (oneself); ~ **è tagliato** he has cut himself; ~ **credono importanti** they think a lot of themselves

2 (riflessivo: con complemento oggetto): **lavarsi le mani** to wash one's hands; ~ **sta lavando i capelli he** (o she) is washing his (o her) hair

3 (reciproco) one another, each other; **si amano** they love one another o each other

4 (passivo): ~ **ripara facilmente** it is easily repaired

5 (impersonale): ~ **dice che ...**

they o people say that ...; ~ **vede che è vecchio** one o you can see that it's old

6 (noi) we; **tra poco ~ parte** we're leaving soon.

**si** av yes; **un giorno ~ e uno no** every other day.

**'sia** cong: ~ ... ~ (o ... o): ~ **che lavori, ~ che non lavori** whether he works or not; (tanto ... quanto): **verranno ~ Luigi ~ suo fratello** both Luigi and his brother will be coming.

**si'amo** vb vedi **essere**.

**sibi'lare** vi to hiss; (fischiare) to whistle; **'sibilo** sm hiss; whistle.

**si'cario** sm hired killer.

**sicché** [sik'ke] cong (perciò) so (that), therefore; (e quindi) (and) so.

**siccità** [sittʃi'ta] sf drought.

**sic'come** cong since, as.

**Si'cilia** [si'tʃilja] sf: **la ~** Sicily; **sicili'ano, a** ag, sm/f Sicilian.

**sicu'rezza** [siku'rettsa] sf safety; security; (fiducia) confidence; (certezza) certainty; **di ~** safety cpd; **la ~ stradale** road safety.

**si'curo, a** ag safe; (ben difeso) secure; (fiducioso) confident; (certo) sure, certain; (notizia, amico) reli-able; (esperto) skilled // av (anche: **di ~**) certainly; **essere/mettere al ~** to be safe/put in a safe place; ~ **di sé** self-confident, sure of o.s.; **sentirsi ~** to feel safe o secure.

**siderur'gia** [siderur'dʒia] sf iron and steel industry.

**'sidro** sm cider.

**si'epe** sf hedge.

**si'ero** sm (MED) serum.

**si'esta** sf siesta, (afternoon) nap.

**si'ete** vb vedi **essere**.

**si'filide** sf syphilis.

**si'fone** sm siphon.

**Sig.** abbr (= signore) Mr.

**siga'retta** sf cigarette.

**'sigaro** sm cigar.

**Sigg.** abbr (= signori) Messrs.

**sigil'lare** [sidʒil'lare] vt to seal.

**si'gillo** [si'dʒillo] *sm* seal.

**'sigla** *sf* initials *pl*; acronym, abbreviation; ~ **automobilistica** *abbreviation of province on vehicle number plate*; ~ **musicale** signature tune.

**si'glare** *vt* to initial.

**Sig.na** *abbr* (= *signorina*) Miss.

**signifi'care** [siɲɲifi'kare] *vt* to mean; **significa'tivo, a** *ag* significant; **signifi'cato** *sm* meaning.

**si'gnora** [siɲ'ɲora] *sf* lady; **la ~ X** Mrs ['mɪsɪz] X; **buon giorno S~/ Signore/Signorina** good morning; *(deferente)* good morning Madam/ Sir/Madam; *(quando si conosce il nome)* good morning Mrs/Mr/Miss X; **Gentile S~/Signore/Signorina** *(in una lettera)* Dear Madam/Sir/ Madam; **il signor Rossi e ~ Mr** Rossi and his wife; **~e e signori** ladies and gentlemen.

**si'gnore** [siɲ'ɲore] *sm* gentleman; *(padrone)* lord, master; *(REL)*: **il S~ the Lord; il signor X Mr** ['mɪstə*] X; **i ~i Bianchi** *(coniugi)* Mr and Mrs Bianchi; *vedi anche* **signora**.

**signo'rile** [siɲɲo'rile] *ag* refined.

**signo'rina** [siɲɲo'rina] *sf* young lady; **la ~ X** Miss X; *vedi anche* **signora**.

**Sig.ra** *abbr* (= *signora*) Mrs.

**silenzia'tore** [silentsja'tore] *sm* silencer.

**si'lenzio** [si'lentsjo] *sm* silence; **fare ~** to be quiet, stop talking; **silenzi'oso, a** *ag* silent, quiet.

**si'licio** [si'litʃo] *sm* silicon; **piastrina di ~** silicon chip.

**'sillaba** *sf* syllable.

**silu'rare** *vt* to torpedo; *(fig: privare del comando)* to oust.

**si'luro** *sm* torpedo.

**simboleggi'are** [simboled'dʒare] *vt* to symbolize.

**'simbolo** *sm* symbol.

**'simile** *ag* (*analogo*) similar; *(di questo tipo)*: **un uomo ~** such a man, a man like this; **libri ~i** such books; **~ a** similar to; **i suoi ~i** one's fellow men; one's peers.

**simme'tria** *sf* symmetry.

**simpa'tia** *sf* (*qualità*) pleasantness; *(inclinazione)* liking; **avere ~ per qn** to like sb, have a liking for sb; **sim'patico, a, ci, che** *ag* (*persona*) nice, pleasant, likeable; *(casa, albergo etc)* nice, pleasant.

**simpatiz'zare** [simpatid'dzare] *vi*: **~ con** to take a liking to.

**sim'posio** *sm* symposium.

**simu'lare** *vt* to sham, simulate; *(TECN)* to simulate; **simulazi'one** *sf* shamming; simulation.

**simul'taneo, a** *ag* simultaneous.

**sina'goga, ghe** *sf* synagogue.

**since'rità** [sintʃeri'ta] *sf* sincerity.

**sin'cero, a** [sin'tʃero] *ag* sincere; genuine; heartfelt.

**'sincope** *sf* syncopation; *(MED)* blackout.

**sinda'cale** *ag* (trade-)union *cpd*; **sinda'calista, i, e** *sm/f* trade unionist.

**sinda'cato** *sm* (*di lavoratori*) (trade) union; *(AMM, ECON, DIR)* syndicate, trust, pool; **~ dei datori di lavoro** employers' association, employers' federation.

**'sindaco, ci** *sm* mayor.

**sinfo'nia** *sf* (*MUS*) symphony.

**singhioz'zare** [singjot'tsare] *vi* to sob; to hiccup.

**singhi'ozzo** [sin'gjottso] *sm* sob; *(MED)* hiccup; **avere il ~** to have the hiccups; **a ~** *(fig)* by fits and starts.

**singo'lare** *ag* (*insolito*) remarkable, singular; *(LING)* singular // *sm* (*LING*) singular; *(TENNIS)*: **~ maschile/femminile** men's/women's singles.

**'singolo, a** *ag* single, individual // *sm* (*persona*) individual; *(TENNIS)* = **singolare**.

**si'nistro, a** *ag* left, left-hand; *(fig)* sinister // *sm* (*incidente*) accident // *sf* (*POL*) left (wing); **a ~a** on the left;

*(direzione)* to the left.

'**sino** *prep* = **fino.**

si'**nonimo, a** *ag* synonymous // *sm* synonym; ~ **di** synonymous with.

sin'**tassi** *sf* syntax.

'**sintesi** *sf* synthesis; *(riassunto)* summary, résumé.

sin'**tetico, a, ci, che** *ag* synthetic.

sintetiz'**zare** [sintetid'dzare] *vt* to synthesize; *(riassumere)* to summarize.

sinto'**matico, a, ci, che** *ag* symptomatic.

'**sintomo** *sm* symptom.

sinu'**oso, a** *ag* (strada) winding.

**S.I.P.** *sigla f (= Società italiana per l'esercizio telefonico)* Italian telephone company.

si'**pario** *sm (TEATRO)* curtain.

si'**rena** *sf (apparecchio)* siren; *(nella mitologia, fig)* siren, mermaid.

'**Siria** *sf*: **la** ~ Syria.

si'**ringa, ghe** *sf* syringe.

'**sismico, a, ci, che** *ag* seismic.

sis'**mografo** *sm* seismograph.

sis'**tema, i** *sm* system; method, way; ~ **di vita** way of life.

siste'**mare** *vt (mettere a posto)* to tidy, put in order; *(risolvere: questione)* to sort out, settle; *(procurare un lavoro a)* to find a job for; *(dare un alloggio a)* to settle, find accommodation for; ~**rsi** *vr (problema)* to be settled; *(persona: trovare alloggio)* to find accommodation (Brit) o accommodations (US); *(: trovarsi un lavoro)* to get fixed up with a job; **ti sistemo io!** I'll soon sort you out!

siste'**matico, a, ci, che** *ag* systematic.

sistemazi'**one** [sistemat'tsjone] *sf* arrangement, order; settlement; employment; accommodation (Brit), accommodations (US).

'**sito** *sm (letterario)* place.

situ'**are** *vt* to site, situate; **situ'ato, a** *ag*: **situato** a/su situated at/on.

situazi'**one** [situat'tsjone] *sf* situation.

slacci'**are** [zlat'tʃare] *vt* to undo, unfasten.

slanci'**arsi** [zlan'tʃarsi] *vr* to dash, fling o.s.; **slanci'ato, a** *ag* slender; '**slancio** *sm* dash, leap; *(fig)* surge; **di slancio** impetuously.

sla'**vato, a** *ag* faded, washed out; *(fig: viso, occhi)* pale, colourless.

'**slavo, a** *ag* Slav(onic), Slavic.

sle'**ale** *ag* disloyal; *(concorrenza etc)* unfair.

sle'**gare** *vt* to untie.

'**slitta** *sf* sledge; *(trainata)* sleigh.

slit'**tare** *vi* to slip, slide; *(AUT)* to skid.

slo'**gare** *vt (MED)* to dislocate.

sloggi'**are** [zlod'dʒare] *vt (inquilino)* to turn out; *(nemico)* to drive out, dislodge // *vi* to move out.

smacchi'**are** [zmak'kjare] *vt* to remove stains from.

'**smacco, chi** *sm* humiliating defeat.

smagli'**ante** [zmaʎʎante] *ag* brilliant, dazzling.

smaglia'**tura** [zmaʎʎa'tura] *sf (su maglia, calza)* ladder; *(della pelle)* stretch mark.

smali'**ziato, a** [zmalit'tsjato] *ag* shrewd, cunning.

smal'**tare** *vt* to enamel; *(ceramica)* to glaze; *(unghie)* to varnish.

smal'**tire** *vt (merce)* to sell off; *(rifiuti)* to dispose of; *(cibo)* to digest; *(peso)* to lose; *(rabbia)* to get over; ~ **la sbornia** to sober up.

'**smalto** *sm (anche: di denti)* enamel; *(per ceramica)* glaze; ~ **per unghie** nail varnish.

'**smania** *sf* agitation, restlessness; *(fig)*: ~ **di** thirst for, craving for; **avere la** ~ **addosso** to have the fidgets; **avere la** ~ **di fare** o to be desperate to do.

smantel'**lare** *vt* to dismantle.

smarri'**mento** *sm* loss; *(fig)* bewilderment; dismay.

smar'**rire** *vt* to lose; *(non riuscire a trovare)* to mislay; ~**rsi** *vr (perdersi)* to lose one's way, get lost; *(: oggetto)* to go astray; **smar'rito,**

**a** *ag (sbigottito)* bewildered.

**smasche'rare** [zmaske'rare] *vt* to unmask.

**smemo'rato, a** *ag* forgetful.

**smen'tire** *vt (negare)* to deny; *(testimonianza)* to refute; *(reputazione)* to give the lie to; ~**rsi** *vr* to be inconsistent; **smen'tita** *sf* denial; retraction.

**sme'raldo** *sm* emerald.

**smerci'are** [zmer'tfare] *vt (COMM)* to sell; *(: svendere)* to sell off.

**sme'riglio** [zmer'riλλo] *sm* emery.

**'smesso, a** *pp di* smettere.

**'smettere** *vt* to stop; *(vestiti)* to stop wearing // *vi* to stop, cease; ~ **di** fare to stop doing.

**'smilzo, a** ['zmiltso] *ag* thin, lean.

**sminu'ire** *vt* to diminish, lessen; *(fig)* to belittle.

**sminuz'zare** [zminut'tsare] *vt* to break into small pieces; to crumble.

**smis'tare** *vt (pacchi etc)* to sort; *(FERR)* to shunt.

**smisu'rato, a** *ag* boundless, immeasurable; *(grandissimo)* immense, enormous.

**smobili'tare** *vt* to demobilize.

**smo'dato, a** *ag* immoderate.

**smoking** ['smɔukiŋ] *sm inv* dinner jacket.

**smon'tare** *vt (mobile, macchina etc)* to take to pieces, dismantle; *(fig: scoraggiare)* to dishearten // *vi (scendere: da cavallo)* to dismount; *(: da treno)* to get off; *(terminare il lavoro)* to stop (work); ~**rsi** *vr* to lose heart; to lose one's enthusiasm.

**'smorfia** *sf* grimace; *(atteggiamento lezioso)* simpering; **fare** ~**e** to make faces; to simper; **smorfi'oso, a** *ag* simpering.

**'smorto, a** *ag (viso)* pale, wan; *(colore)* dull.

**smor'zare** [zmor'tsare] *vt (suoni)* to deaden; *(colori)* to tone down; *(luce)* to dim; *(sete)* to quench; *(entusiasmo)* to dampen; ~**rsi** *vr (suono, luce)* to fade; *(entusiasmo)* to dampen.

**'smosso, a** *pp di* smuovere.

**smotta'mento** *sm* landslide.

**'smunto, a** *ag* haggard, pinched.

**smu'overe** *vt* to move, shift; *(fig: commuovere)* to move; *(: dall'inerzia)* to rouse, stir; ~**rsi** *vr* to move, shift.

**smus'sare** *vt (angolo)* to round off, smooth; *(lama etc)* to blunt; ~**rsi** *vr* to become blunt.

**snatu'rato, a** *ag* inhuman, heartless.

**'snello, a** *ag (agile)* agile; *(svelto)* slender, slim.

**sner'vare** *vt* to enervate, wear out; ~**rsi** *vr* to become enervated.

**sni'dare** *vt* to drive out, flush out.

**snob'bare** *vt* to snub.

**sno'bismo** *sm* snobbery.

**snoccio'lare** [znottʃo'lare] *vt (frutta)* to stone; *(fig: orazioni)* to rattle off; *(: verità)* to blab.

**sno'dare** *vt (rendere agile, mobile)* to loosen; ~**rsi** *vr* to come loose; *(articolarsi)* to bend; *(strada, fiume)* to wind.

**so** *vb vedi* sapere.

**so'ave** *ag* sweet, gentle, soft.

**sobbal'zare** [sobbal'tsare] *vi* to jolt, jerk; *(trasalire)* to jump, start; **sob'balzo** *sm* jerk, jolt; jump, start.

**sobbar'carsi** *vr*: ~ **a** to take on, undertake.

**sob'borgo, ghi** *sm* suburb.

**sobil'lare** *vt* to stir up, incite.

**'sobrio, a** *ag* sober.

**socchi'udere** [sok'kjudere] *vt (porta)* to leave ajar; *(occhi)* to half-close; **socchi'uso, a** *pp di* socchiudere.

**soc'correre** *vt* to help, assist; **soc'corso, a** *pp di* soccorrere // *sm* help, aid, assistance; **soccorsi** *smpl* relief *sg*, aid *sg*; **soccorso stradale** breakdown service.

**socialdemo'cratico, a, ci, che** [sotʃaldemo'kratiko] *sm/f* Social Democrat.

**soci'ale** [so'tʃale] *ag* social; *(di associazione)* club *cpd*, association *cpd.*

**socia'lismo** [sotʃa'lizmo] *sm* socialism; **socia'lista, i, e** *ag, smf* socialist.

**società** [sotʃe'ta] *sf inv* society; (*sportiva*) club; (*COMM*) company; ~ **per azioni (S.p.A.)** limited (*Brit*) *o* incorporated (*US*) company; ~ **a responsabilità limitata (S.r.l.)** *type of limited liability company.*

**soci'evole** [so'tʃevole] *ag* sociable.

**'socio** [sɔtʃo] *sm* (*DIR, COMM*) partner; (*membro di associazione*) member.

**'soda** *sf* (*CHIM*) soda; (*acqua gassata*) soda (water).

**soda'lizio** [soda'littsjo] *sm* association, society.

**soddisfa'cente** [soddisfa'tʃɛnte] *ag* satisfactory.

**soddis'fare** *vt, vi:* ~ a to satisfy; (*impegno*) to fulfil; (*debito*) to pay off; (*richiesta*) to meet, comply with; (*offesa*) to make amends for; **soddis'fatto, a** *pp di* **soddisfare** // *ag* satisfied; soddisfatto di happy *o* satisfied with; pleased with; **soddisfazi'one** *sf* satisfaction.

**'sodo, a** *ag* firm, hard // *av* (*picchiare, lavorare*) hard; **dormire** ~ to sleep soundly.

**sofa** *sm inv* sofa.

**soffe'renza** [soffe'rɛntsa] *sf* suffering.

**sof'ferto, a** *pp di* **soffrire.**

**soffi'are** *vt* to blow; (*notizia, segreto*) to whisper // *vi* to blow; (*sbuffare*) to puff (and blow); ~**rsi** il naso to blow one's nose; ~ qc/qn a qn (*fig*) to pinch *o* steal sth/sb from sb; ~ **via** qc to blow sth away.

**'soffice** ['sɔffitʃe] *ag* soft.

**'soffio** *sm* (*di vento*) breath; (*di fumo*) puff; (*MED*) murmur.

**sof'fitta** *sf* attic.

**sof'fitto** *sm* ceiling.

**soffo'care** *vi* (*anche:* ~**rsi**) to suffocate, choke // *vt* to suffocate, choke; (*fig*) to stifle, suppress.

**sof'friggere** [sof'friddʒere] *vt* to fry

lightly.

**sof'frire** *vt* to suffer, endure; (*sopportare*) to bear, stand // *vi* to suffer; to be in pain; ~ (**di**) qc (*MED*) to suffer from etc.

**sof'fritto, a** *pp di* **soffriggere** // *sm* (*CUC*) fried mixture of herbs, bacon and onions.

**sofisti'cato, a** *ag* sophisticated; (*vino*) adulterated.

**sogget'tivo, a** [soddʒet'tivo] *ag* subjective.

**sog'getto, a** [sod'dʒetto] *ag:* ~ a (*sottomesso*) subject to; (*esposto: a variazioni, danni etc*) subject *o* liable to // *sm* subject.

**soggezi'one** [soddʒet'tsjone] *sf* subjection; (*timidezza*) awe; **avere** ~ **di** qn to stand in awe of sb; to be ill at ease in sb's presence.

**sogghi'gnare** [soggiɲ'ɲare] *vi* to sneer.

**soggior'nare** [soddʒor'nare] *vi* to stay; **soggi'orno** *sm* (*invernale, marino*) stay; (*stanza*) living room.

**sog'giungere** [sod'dʒundʒere] *vt* to add.

**'soglia** ['sɔʎʎa] *sf* doorstep; (*anche fig*) threshold.

**'sogliola** ['sɔʎʎola] *sf* (*ZOOL*) sole.

**so'gnare** [soɲ'ɲare] *vt, vi* to dream; ~ a occhi aperti to daydream; **sogna'tore, 'trice** *smf* dreamer.

**'sogno** ['soɲɲo] *sm* dream.

**'soia** *sf* (*BOT*) soya.

**sol** *sm* (*MUS*) G; (: *solfeggiando la scala*) so(h).

**so'laio** *sm* (*soffitta*) attic.

**sola'mente** *av* only, just.

**so'lare** *ag* solar, sun *cpd.*

**'solco, chi** *sm* (*scavo, fig: ruga*) furrow; (*incavo*) rut, track; (*di disco*) groove; (*scia*) wake.

**sol'dato** *sm* soldier; ~ **semplice** private.

**'soldo** *sm* (*fig*): non avere un ~ to be penniless; **non vale un** ~ it's not worth a penny; ~**i** *smpl* (*denaro*) money *sg.*

**'sole** *sm* sun; (*luce*) sun(light);

(*tempo assolato*) sun(shine); **prendere il** ~ to sunbathe.

**soleggi'ato, a** [soled'dʒato] *ag* sunny.

**so'lenne** *ag* solemn; **solennità** *sf* solemnity; (*festività*) holiday, feast day.

**sol'fato** *sm* (*CHIM*) sulphate.

**soli'dale** *ag*: **essere ~ (con)** to be in agreement (with).

**solidarietà** *sf* solidarity.

**'solido, a** *ag* solid; (*forte, robusto*) sturdy, solid; (*fig: ditta*) sound, solid // *sm* (*MAT*) solid.

**soli'loquio** *sm* soliloquy.

**so'lista, i, e** *ag* solo // *sm/f* soloist.

**'solita'mente** *av* usually, as a rule.

**soli'tario, a** *ag* (*senza compagnia*) solitary, lonely; (*solo, isolato*) solitary, lone; (*deserto*) lonely // *sm* (*gioiello, gioco*) solitaire.

**'solito, a** *ag* usual; **essere ~ fare** to be in the habit of doing; **di ~** usually; **più tardi del ~** later than usual; **come al ~** as usual.

**soli'tudine** *sf* solitude.

**solleci'tare** [sollet∫i'tare] *vt* (*lavoro*) to speed up; (*persona*) to urge on; (*chiedere con insistenza*) to press for, request urgently; (*stimolare*): ~ **qn a fare** to urge sb to do; (*TECN*) to stress; **sollecitazi'one** *sf* entreaty, request; (*fig*) incentive; (*TECN*) stress.

**sol'lecito, a** [sol'let∫ito] *ag* prompt, quick // *sm* (*lettera*) reminder; **solleci'tudine** *sf* promptness, speed.

**solleti'care** *vt* to tickle.

**sol'letico** *sm* tickling; **soffrire il ~** to be ticklish.

**solleva'mento** *sm* raising; lifting; revolt; ~ **pesi** (*SPORT*) weightlifting.

**solle'vare** *vt* to lift, raise; (*fig: persona: alleggerire*): ~ (**da**) to relieve (of); (: *dar conforto*) to comfort, relieve; (: *questione*) to raise; (: *far insorgere*) to stir (to revolt); ~**rsi** *vr* to rise; (*fig: riprendersi*) to recover; (: *ribellarsi*)

to rise up.

**solli'evo** *sm* relief; (*conforto*) comfort.

**'solo, a** *ag* alone; (*in senso spirituale: isolato*) lonely; (*unico*): **un ~ libro** only one book, a single book; (*con ag numerale*): **veniamo noi tre ~i** just o only the three of us are coming // *av* (*soltanto*) only, just; **non ~ ... ma anche** not only ... but also; **fare qc da ~** to do sth (all) by oneself; **da me ~** single-handed, on my own.

**sol'tanto** *av* only.

**so'lubile** *ag* (*sostanza*) soluble.

**soluzi'one** [solut'tsjone] *sf* solution.

**sol'vente** *ag, sm* solvent.

**'soma** *sf*: **bestia da ~** beast of burden.

**so'maro** *sm* ass, donkey.

**somigli'anza** [somi∆'∆antsa] *sf* resemblance.

**somigli'are** [somi∆'∆are] *vi*: ~ **a** to be like, resemble; (*nell'aspetto fisico*) to look like; ~**rsi** *vr* to be (o look) alike.

**'somma** *sf* (*MAT*) sum; (*di denaro*) sum (of money); (*complesso di varie cose*) whole amount, sum total.

**som'mare** *vt* to add up; (*aggiungere*) to add; **tutto sommato** all things considered.

**som'mario, a** *ag* (*racconto, indagine*) brief; (*giustizia*) summary // *sm* summary.

**som'mergere** [som'merdʒere] *vt* to submerge.

**sommer'gibile** [sommer'dʒibile] *sm* submarine.

**som'merso, a** *pp di* **sommergere**

**som'messo, a** *ag* (*voce*) soft, subdued.

**somminis'trare** *vt* to give, administer.

**sommità** *sf inv* summit, top; (*fig*) height.

**'sommo, a** *ag* highest; (*rispetto etc*) highest, greatest; (*poeta, artista*) great, outstanding // *sm* (*fig*) height; **per ~i capi** briefly, covering the main points.

**som'mossa** *sf* uprising.

**so'nare** *etc* = **suonare** *etc*.

**son'daggio** [son'daddʒo] *sm* sounding; probe; boring, drilling; (*indagine*) survey; ~ **d'opinioni** opinion poll.

**son'dare** *vt* (*NAUT*) to sound; (*atmosfera, piaga*) to probe; (*MINERALOGIA*) to bore, drill; (*fig: opinione etc*) to survey, poll.

**so'netto** *sm* sonnet.

**son'nambulo, a** *sm/f* sleepwalker.

**sonnecchi'are** [sonnek'kjare] *vi* to doze, nod.

**son'nifero** *sm* sleeping drug (*o* pill).

**'sonno** *sm* sleep; **prendere** ~ to fall asleep; **aver** ~ to be sleepy.

**'sono** *vb vedi* **essere**.

**so'noro, a** *ag* (*ambiente*) resonant; (*voce*) sonorous, ringing; (*onde, film*) sound *cpd*.

**sontu'oso, a** *ag* sumptuous; lavish.

**sopo'rifero, a** *ag* soporific.

**soppe'sare** *vt* to weigh in one's hand(s), feel the weight of; (*fig*) to weigh up.

**soppi'atto: di** ~ *av* secretly; furtively.

**soppor'tare** *vt* (*reggere*) to support; (*subire: perdita, spese*) to bear, sustain; (*soffrire: dolore*) to bear, endure; (*sog: cosa: freddo*) to withstand; (*sog: persona: freddo, vino*) to take; (*tollerare*) to put up with, tolerate.

**sop'presso, a** *pp di* **sopprimere**.

**sop'primere** *vt* (*carica, privilegi, testimone*) to do away with; (*pubblicazione*) to suppress; (*parola, frase*) to delete.

**'sopra** *prep* (*gen*) on; (*al di sopra di, più in alto di*) above; over; (*riguardo a*) on, about *// av* on top; (*attaccato, scritto*) on it; (*al di sopra*) above; (*al piano superiore*) upstairs; **dormir** ~ **i 30 anni** women over 30 (years of age); **abito di** ~ **I** I live upstairs; **dormirci** ~ (*fig*) to sleep on it.

**so'prabito** *sm* overcoat.

**soprac'ciglio** [soprat'tʃiʎʎo], *pl(f)* **soprac'ciglia** *sm* eyebrow.

**sopracco'perta** *sf* (*di letto*) bedspread; (*di libro*) jacket.

**soprad'detto, a** *ag* aforesaid.

**sopraf'fare** *vt* to overcome, overwhelm; **sopraf'fatto, a** *pp di* **sopraffare**.

**sopraf'fino, a** *ag* (*pranzo, vino*) excellent.

**sopraggi'ungere** [soprad'dʒundʒere] *vi* (*giungere all'improvviso*) to arrive (unexpectedly); (*accadere*) to occur (unexpectedly).

**sopral'luogo, ghi** *sm* (*di esperti*) inspection; (*di polizia*) on-the-spot investigation.

**sopram'mobile** *sm* ornament.

**soprannatu'rale** *ag* supernatural.

**sopran'nome** *sm* nickname.

**so'prano, a** *sm/f* (*persona*) soprano *// sm* (*voce*) soprano.

**soprappensi'ero** *av* lost in thought.

**sopras'salto** *sm*: **di** ~ with a start; suddenly.

**soprasse'dere** *vi*: ~ **a** to delay, put off.

**soprat'tutto** *av* (*anzitutto*) above all; (*specialmente*) especially.

**soprav'vento** *sm*: **avere/prendere il** ~ **su** to have/get the upper hand over.

**sopravvis'suto, a** *pp di* **sopravvivere**.

**soprav'vivere** *vi* to survive; (*continuare a vivere*): ~ (**in**) to live on (in); ~ **a** (*incidente etc*) to survive; (*persona*) to outlive.

**soprinten'dente** *sm/f* supervisor; (*statale: di belle arti etc*) keeper; **soprinten'denza** *sf* supervision; (*ente*): **soprintendenza alle Belle Arti** government department responsible for monuments and artistic treasures.

**so'pruso** *sm* abuse of power; **subire un** ~ to be abused.

**soq'quadro** *sm*: **mettere a** ~ to turn upside-down.

**sor'betto** *sm* sorbet, water ice.

**sor'bire** vt to sip; (fig) to put up with.

**'sorcio, ci** ['sortʃo] sm mouse.

**'sordido, a** ag sordid; (fig: gretto) stingy.

**sor'dina** sf: **in ~** softly; (fig) on the sly.

**sordità** sf deafness.

**'sordo, a** ag deaf; (rumore) muffled; (dolore) dull; (odio, rancore) veiled // (dolore) dull; (odio, rancore) veiled // dif deaf person; **sordo'muto, a** ag deaf-and-dumb // sm/f deaf-mute.

**so'rella** sf sister; **sorel'lastra** sf stepsister.

**sor'gente** [sor'dʒɛnte] sf (acqua che sgorga) spring; (di fiume, FISICA, fig) source.

**'sorgere** ['sordʒere] vi to rise; (scaturire) to spring, rise; (fig: difficoltà) to arise.

**sormon'tare** vt (fig) to overcome, surmount.

**sorni'one, a** ag sly.

**sorpas'sare** vt (AUT) to overtake; (fig) to surpass; (: eccedere) to exceed, go beyond; **~ in altezza** to be higher than; (persona) to be taller than.

**sorpren'dente** ag surprising.

**sor'prendere** vt (cogliere: in flagrante etc) to catch; (stupire) to surprise; **~rsi** vr: **~rsi (di)** to be surprised (at); **sor'presa, a** pp di **sorprendere** // sf surprise; **fare una sorpresa a qn** to give sb a surprise.

**sor'reggere** [sor'rɛddʒere] vt to support, hold up; (fig) to sustain; **sor'retto, a** pp di **sorreggere**.

**sor'ridere** vi to smile; **sor'riso, a** pp di **sorridere** // sm smile.

**'sorso** sm sip.

**'sorta** sf sort, kind; **di ~** whatever, of any kind, at all.

**'sorte** sf (fato) fate, destiny; (evento fortuito) chance; **tirare a ~** to draw lots.

**sor'teggio** [sor'teddʒo] sm draw.

**sorti'legio** [sorti'ledʒo] sm witch-

craft q; (incantesimo) spell; **fare un ~ a qn** to cast a spell on sb.

**sor'tita** sf (MIL) sortie.

**'sorto, a** pp di **sorgere**.

**sorvegli'anza** [sorveʎ'ʎantsa] sf watch; supervision; (POLIZIA, MIL) surveillance.

**sorvegli'are** [sorveʎ'ʎare] vt (bambino, bagagli, prigioniero) to watch, keep an eye on; (malato) to watch over; (territorio, casa) to watch o keep watch over; (lavori) to supervise.

**sorvo'lare** vt (territorio) to fly over // vi: **~ su** (fig) to skim over.

**'sosia** sm inv double.

**sos'pendere** vt (appendere) to hang (up); (interrompere, privare di una carica) to suspend; (rimandare) to defer; **~ un quadro al muro/un lampadario al soffitto** to hang a picture on the wall/a chandelier from the ceiling; **sospensi'one** sf (anche CHIM, AUT) suspension; deferment; **sos'peso, a** pp di **sospendere** // ag (appeso): **sospeso a** hanging on (o from); (treno, autobus) cancelled; **in sospeso** in abeyance; (conto) outstanding; **tenere in sospeso** (fig) to keep in suspense.

**sospet'tare** vt to suspect // vi: **~ di** to suspect; (diffidare) to be suspicious of.

**sos'petto, a** ag suspicious // sm suspicion; **sospet'toso, a** ag suspicious.

**sos'pingere** [sos'pindʒere] vt to drive, push; **sos'pinto, a** pp di **sospingere**.

**sospi'rare** vi to sigh // vt to long for, yearn for; **sos'piro** sm sigh.

**'sosta** sf (fermata) stop, halt; (pausa) pause, break; **senza ~** nonstop, without a break.

**sostan'tivo** sm noun, substantive.

**sos'tanza** [sos'tantsa] sf substance; **~e** sfpl (ricchezze) wealth sg, possessions; **in ~** in short, to sum up; **sostanzi'oso, a** ag (cibo) nourishing, substantial.

**sos'tare** vi (fermarsi) to stop (for a while), stay; (fare una pausa) to take a break.

**sos'tegno** [sos'tɛɲɲo] sm support.

**soste'nere** vt to support; (prendere su di sé) to take on, bear; (resistere) to withstand, stand up to; (affermare): ~ che to maintain that; ~rsi vr to hold o.s. up, support o.s.; (fig) to keep up one's strength; ~ gli esami to sit exams; **soste'ni'tore, 'trice** smf supporter.

**sostenta'mento** sm maintenance, support.

**soste'nuto, a** ag (stile) elevated; (velocità, ritmo) sustained; (prezzo) high // smf: fare il(la) ~(a) to be standoffish, keep one's distance.

**sostitu'ire** vt (mettere al posto di): ~ qn/qc a to substitute sb/sth for; (prendere il posto di: persona) to substitute for; (: cosa) to take the place of.

**sosti'tuto, a** smf substitute.

**sostituzi'one** [sostitut'tsjone] sf substitution; **in ~ di** as a substitute for, in place of.

**sotta'ceti** [sotta'tʃeti] smpl pickles.

**sot'tana** sf (sottoveste) underskirt; (gonna) skirt; (REL) soutane, cassock.

**sotter'fugio** [sotter'fudʒo] sm subterfuge.

**sotter'raneo, a** ag underground // sm cellar.

**sotter'rare** vt to bury.

**sottigli'ezza** [sottiʎ'ʎettsa] sf thinness; slimness; (fig: acutezza) subtlety; shrewdness; **~e** sfpl (pedanteria) quibbles.

**sot'tile** ag thin; (figura, caviglia) thin, slim, slender; (fine: polvere, capelli) fine; (fig: leggero) light; (: vista) sharp, keen; (: olfatto) fine, discriminating; (: mente) subtle; shrewd // sm: **non andare per il ~** not to mince matters.

**sottin'tendere** vt (intendere qc non espresso) to understand; (implicare) to imply; **sottin'teso, a** pp di

**sottintendere** // sm allusion; **parlare senza sottintesi** to speak plainly.

**'sotto** prep (gen) under; (più in basso di) below // av underneath, beneath; below; (al piano inferiore): **(al piano) di ~** downstairs; ~ **forma di** in the form of; ~ **il monte** at the foot of the mountain; **siamo ~ Natale** it's nearly Christmas; ~ **la pioggia/il sole** in the rain/sun(shine); ~ **terra** underground; ~ **voce** in a low voice; **chiuso ~ vuoto** vacuum-packed.

**sottoline'are** vt to underline; (fig) to emphasize, stress.

**sotto'rino, a** ag (flora) submarine; (cavo, navigazione) underwater // sm (NAUT) submarine.

**sotto'messo, a** pp di **sottomettere.**

**sotto'mettere** vt to subdue, subjugate; ~**rsi** vr to submit.

**sottopas'saggio** [sottopas'saddʒo] sm (AUT) underpass; (pedonale) subway, underpass.

**sotto'porre** vt (costringere) to subject; (fig: presentare) to submit; **sottoporsi** vr to submit; **sottoporsi a** (subire) to undergo; **sotto'posto, a** pp di **sottoporre.**

**sottos'critto, a** pp di **sottoscrivere.**

**sottos'crivere** vt to sign // vi: ~ **a** to subscribe to; **sottoscrizi'one** sf signing; subscription.

**sottosegre'tario** sm: ~ **di Stato** Under-Secretary of State (Brit), Assistant Secretary of State (US).

**sotto'sopra** av upside-down.

**sotto'terra** av underground.

**sotto'titolo** sm subtitle.

**sotto'veste** sf underskirt.

**sotto'voce** [sotto'votʃe] av in a low voice.

**sot'trarre** vt (MAT) to subtract, take away; ~ **qn/qc a** (togliere) to remove sb/sth from; (salvare) to save o rescue sb/sth from; ~ **qc a qn** (rubare) to steal sth from sb; **sot-**

trarsi *vr*: **sottrarsi a** (*sfuggire*) to escape; (*evitare*) to avoid; **sot'tratto, a** *pp* di **sottrarre**; **sottrazi'one** *sf* subtraction; removal.

**sovi'etico, a, ci, che** *ag* Soviet // *sm/f* Soviet citizen.

**sovraccari'care** *vt* to overload.

**sovrannatu'rale** *ag* = **sopranna'turale**.

**so'vrano, a** *ag* sovereign; (*fig: sommo*) supreme // *sm/f* sovereign, monarch.

**sovrap'porre** *vt* to place on top of, put on top of.

**sovras'tare** *vi*: ~ **a**, *vt* (*vallata, fiume*) to overhang; (*fig*) to hang over, threaten.

**sovrinten'dente** *sm/f* = **soprintendente**; **sovrinten'denza** *sf* = **soprintendenza**.

**sovru'mano, a** *ag* superhuman.

**sovvenzi'one** [sovven'tsjone] *sf* subsidy, grant.

**sovver'sivo, a** *ag* subversive.

**'sozzo, a** ['sottso] *ag* filthy, dirty.

**S.p.A.** *abbr* = **società per azioni**.

**spac'care** *vt* to split, break; (*legna*) to chop; **~rsi** *vr* to split, break; **spacca'tura** *sf* split.

**spacci'are** [spat'tʃare] *vt* (*vendere*) to sell (off); (*mettere in circolazione*) to circulate; (*droga*) to peddle, push; **~rsi** *vr*: **~rsi per** (*farsi credere*) to pass o.s. off as, pretend to be; **spaccia'tore, 'trice** *sm/f* (*di droga*) pusher; (*di denaro falso*) dealer; **'spaccio** *sm* (*di merce rubata, droga*): **spaccio (di)** trafficking (in); (*in denaro falso*): **spaccio (di)** passing (of); (*vendita*) sale; (*bottega*) shop.

**'spacco, chi** *sm* (*fenditura*) split, crack; (*strappo*) tear; (*di gonna*) slit.

**spac'cone** *sm/f* boaster, braggart.

**'spada** *sf* sword.

**spae'sato, a** *ag* disorientated, lost.

**spa'ghetti** [spa'getti] *smpl* (*CUC*) spaghetti *sg*.

**'Spagna** ['spaɲɲa] *sf*: **la ~** Spain;

**spa'gnolo, a** *ag* Spanish // *sm/f* Spaniard // *sm* (*LING*) Spanish; **gli Spagnoli** the Spanish.

**'spago, ghi** *sm* string, twine.

**spai'ato, a** *ag* (*calza, guanto*) odd.

**spalan'care** *vt*, **~rsi** *vr* to open wide.

**spa'lare** *vt* to shovel.

**'spalla** *sf* shoulder; (*fig: TEATRO*) stooge; **~e** *sfpl* (*dorso*) back; **spalleggi'are** *vt* to back up, support.

**spal'letta** *sf* (*parapetto*) parapet.

**spalli'era** *sf* (*di sedia etc*) back; (*di letto: da capo*) head(board); (: *da piedi*) foot(board); (*GINNASTICA*) wall bars *pl*.

**spal'mare** *vt* to spread.

**'spalti** *smpl* (*di stadio*) terracing.

**'spandere** *vt* to spread; (*versare*) to pour (out); **~rsi** *vr* to spread; **'spanto, a** *pp* di **spandere**.

**spa'rare** *vt* to fire // *vi* (*far fuoco*) to fire; (*tirare*) to shoot; **spara'tore** *sm* gunman; **spara'toria** *sf* exchange of shots.

**sparecchi'are** [sparek'kjare] *vt*: ~ **(la tavola)** to clear the table.

**spa'reggio** [spa'reddʒo] *sm* (*SPORT*) play-off.

**'spargere** ['spardʒere] *vt* (*spargagliare*) to scatter; (*versare: vino*) to spill; (: *lacrime, sangue*) to shed; (*diffondere*) to spread; (*emanare*) to give off (*o* out); **~rsi** *vr* to spread; **spargi'mento** *sm* scattering, strewing; spilling; shedding; **spargimento di sangue** bloodshed.

**spa'rire** *vi* to disappear, vanish.

**spar'lare** *vi*: ~ **di** to run down, speak ill of.

**'sparo** *sm* shot.

**sparpagli'are** [sparpaʎ'ʎare] *vt*, **~rsi** *vr* to scatter.

**'sparso, a** *pp* di **spargere** // *ag* scattered; (*sciolto*) loose.

**spar'tire** *vt* (*eredità, bottino*) to share out; (*avversari*) to separate.

**sparti'traffico** *sm inv* (*AUT*) central reservation (*Brit*), median (strip) (US).

**spa'ruto, a** ag (viso etc) haggard.

**sparvi'ero** sm (ZOOL) sparrow-hawk.

**spasi'mare** vi to be in agony; ~ di fare (fig) to yearn to do; ~ **per qn** to be madly in love with sb.

**'spasimo** sm pang; **'spasmo** sm (MED) spasm; **spas'modico, a, ci, che** ag (angoscioso) agonizing; (MED) spasmodic.

**spassio'nato, a** ag dispassionate, impartial.

**'spasso** sm (divertimento) amusement, enjoyment; **andare a** ~ to go out for a walk; **essere a** ~ (fig) to be out of work; **mandare qn a** ~ (fig) to give sb the sack.

**spau'racchio** [spau'rakkjo] sm scarecrow.

**spau'rire** vt to frighten, terrify.

**spa'valdo, a** ag arrogant, bold.

**spaventa'passeri** sm inv scarecrow.

**spaven'tare** vt to frighten, scare; ~**rsi** vr to be frightened, be scared; to get a fright; **spa'vento** sm fear, fright; **far spavento a qn** to give sb a fright; **spaven'toso, a** ag frightening, terrible; (fig: fam) tremendous, fantastic.

**spazien'tire** [spattsjen'tire] vi (anche: ~**rsi**) to lose one's patience.

**'spazio** ['spattsjo] sm space; ~ **aereo** airspace; **spazi'oso, a** ag spacious.

**spazzaca'mino** [spattsaka'mino] sm chimney sweep.

**spaz'zare** [spat'tsare] vt to sweep; (foglie etc) to sweep up; (cacciare) to sweep away; **spazza'tura** sf sweepings pl; (immondizia) rubbish; **spaz'zino** sm street sweeper.

**'spazzola** ['spattsola] sf brush; ~ **per abiti** clothesbrush; ~ **da capelli** hairbrush; **spazzo'lare** vt to brush; **spazzo'lino** sm (small) brush; spazzolino da denti toothbrush.

**specchi'arsi** [spek'kjarsi] vr to look at o.s. in a mirror; (riflettersi) to be

mirrored, be reflected.

**'specchio** ['spekkjo] sm mirror.

**speci'ale** [spe'tʃale] ag special; **specia'lista, i, e** sm/f specialist; **specialità** sf inv speciality; (branca di studio) special field, speciality; **specializ'zarsi** vr: **specializzarsi** (in) to specialize (in); **special'mente** av especially, particularly.

**'specie** ['spetʃe] sf inv (BIOL, BOT, ZOOL) species inv; (tipo) kind, sort // av especially, particularly; **una** ~ **di** a kind of; **fare** ~ **a qn** to surprise sb; **la** ~ **umana** mankind.

**specifi'care** [spetʃifi'kare] vt to specify, state.

**spe'cifico, a, ci, che** [spe'tʃifiko] ag specific.

**specu'lare** vi: ~ **su** (COMM) to speculate in; (sfruttare) to exploit; (meditare) to speculate on; **speculazi'one** sf speculation.

**spe'dire** vt to send; **spedizi'one** sf sending; (collo) consignment; (scientifica etc) expedition.

**'spegnere** ['spɛɲɲere] vt (fuoco, sigaretta) to put out, extinguish; (apparecchio elettrico) to turn o switch off; (gas) to turn off; (fig: suoni, passioni) to stifle; (debito) to extinguish; ~**rsi** vr to go out; to go off; (morire) to pass away.

**spel'lare** vt (scuoiare) to skin; (scorticare) to graze; ~**rsi** vr to peel.

**'spendere** vt to spend.

**spen'nare** vt to pluck.

**spensie'rato, a** ag carefree.

**'spento, a** pp di **spegnere** // ag (suono) muffled; (colore) dull; (sigaretta) out; (civiltà, vulcano) extinct.

**spe'ranza** [spe'rantsa] sf hope.

**spe'rare** vt to hope for // vi: ~ **in** to trust in; ~ **che/di fare** to hope that/ to do; **lo spero, spero di sì** I hope so.

**sper'duto, a** ag (isolato) out-of-the-way; (persona: smarrita, a disagio) lost.

**spergi'uro, a** [sper'dʒuro] *sm/f* perjurer // *sm* perjury.

**sperimen'tale** *ag* experimental.

**sperimen'tare** *vt* to experiment with, test; *(fig)* to test, put to the test.

**'sperma, i** *sm* (BIOL) sperm.

**spe'rone** *sm* spur.

**sperpe'rare** *vt* to squander.

**'spesa** *sf* (*somma di denaro*) expense; (*costo*) cost; (*acquisto*) purchase; (*fam: acquisto del cibo quotidiano*) shopping; ~**e** *sfpl* expenses; (COMM) costs; charges; fare la ~ to do the shopping; a ~**e di** (*a carico di*) at the expense of; ~**e generali** overheads; ~**e postali** postage *sg*; ~**e di viaggio** travelling expenses.

**'speso, a** *pp di* **spendere**.

**'spesso, a** *ag* (*fitto*) thick; (*frequente*) frequent // *av* often; ~**e volte** frequently, often.

**spes'sore** *sm* thickness.

**spet'tabile** *ag* (*abbr:* Spett.: *in lettere*): ~ **ditta X** Messrs X and Co.

**spet'tacolo** *sm* (*rappresentazione*) performance, show; (*vista, scena*) sight; dare ~ di sé to make an exhibition o a spectacle of o.s.; **spettaco'loso, a** *ag* spectacular.

**spet'tare** *vi*: ~ a (*decisione*) to be up to; (*stipendio*) to be due to; **spetta a te decidere** it's up to you to decide.

**spetta'tore, 'trice** *sm/f* (CINEMA, TEATRO) member of the audience; (*di avvenimento*) onlooker, witness.

**spetti'nare** *vt*: ~ **qn** to ruffle sb's hair; ~**rsi** *vr* to get one's hair in a mess.

**'spettro** *sm* (*fantasma*) spectre; (FISICA) spectrum.

**'spezie** [spettsje] *sfpl* (CUC) spices.

**spez'zare** [spet'tsare] *vt* (*rompere*) to break; (*fig: interrompere*) to break up; ~**rsi** *vr* to break.

**spezza'tino** [spettsa'tino] *sm* (CUC) stew.

**spezzet'tare** [spettset'tare] *vt* to break up (o chop) into small pieces.

**'spia** *sf* spy; (*confidente della polizia*) informer; (ELETTR) indicating light; warning light; (*fessura*) peep-hole; (*fig: sintomo*) sign, indication.

**spia'cente** [spja'tʃɛnte] *ag* sorry; **essere** ~ **di qc/di fare qc** to be sorry about sth/for doing sth.

**spia'cevole** [spja'tʃevole] *ag* unpleasant, disagreeable.

**spi'aggia, ge** [spˈjaddʒa] *sf* beach.

**spia'nare** *vt* (*terreno*) to level, make level; (*edificio*) to raze to the ground; (*pasta*) to roll out; (*rendere liscio*) to smooth (out).

**spi'ano** *sm*: a tutto ~ (*lavorare*) non-stop, without a break; (*spendere*) lavishly.

**spian'tato, a** *ag* penniless, ruined.

**spi'are** *vt* to spy on; (*occasione etc*) to watch o wait for.

**spi'azzo** [spjattso] *sm* open space; (*radura*) clearing.

**spic'care** *vt* (*assegno, mandato di cattura*) to issue // *vi* (*risaltare*) to stand out; ~ **il volo** to fly off; (*fig*) to spread one's wings; ~ **un balzo** to leap; **spic'cato, a** *ag* (*marcato*) marked, strong; (*notevole*) remarkable.

**'spicchio** [spikkjo] *sm* (*di agrumi*) segment; (*di aglio*) clove; (*parte*) piece, slice.

**spicci'arsi** [spit'tʃarsi] *vr* to hurry up.

**'spicciolo, a** [spittʃolo] *ag*: **moneta** ~**a**, ~**i** *smpl* (small) change.

**'spicco, chi** *sm* (*di*) ~ outstanding; (*tema*) main, principal; fare ~ to stand out.

**spi'edo** *sm* (CUC) spit.

**spie'gare** *vt* (*far capire*) to explain; (*tovaglia*) to unfold; (*vele*) to unfurl; ~**rsi** *vr* to explain; ~ **qc a qn** to explain sth to sb; **il problema si spiega** one can understand the problem; **spiegazi'one** *sf* explanation.

**spiegaz'zare** [spjegat'tsare] *vt* to

crease, crumple.

**spie'tato, a** *ag* ruthless, pitiless.

**spiffe'rare** *vt* (*fam*) to blurt out, blab.

**'spiga, ghe** *sf* (*BOT*) ear.

**spigli'ato, a** [spiʎ'ʎato] *ag* self-possessed, self-confident.

**'spigolo** *sm* corner; (*MAT*) edge.

**'spilla** *sf* brooch; (*da cravatta, cappello*) pin.

**spil'lare** *vt* (*vino, fig*) to tap; ~ **denaro/notizie a qn** to tap sb for money/information.

**'spillo** *sm* pin; (*spilla*) brooch; ~ **di sicurezza** *o* **da balia** safety pin; ~ **di sicurezza** (*MIL*) (safety) pin.

**spi'lorcio, a, ci, ce** [spi'lortʃo] *ag* mean, stingy.

**'spina** *sf* (*BOT*) thorn; (*ZOOL*) spine, prickle; (*di pesce*) bone; (*ELETTR*) plug; (*di botte*) bunghole; **birra alla** ~ draught beer; ~ **dorsale** (*ANAT*) backbone.

**spi'nacio** [spi'natʃo] *sm* spinach; (*CUC*): ~**i** spinach *sg*.

**spi'nale** *ag* (*ANAT*) spinal.

**'spingere** ['spindʒere] *vt* to push; (*condurre: anche fig*) to drive; (*stimolare*): ~ **qn a fare** to urge *o* press sb to do; ~**rsi** *vr* (*inoltrarsi*) to push on, carry on; ~**rsi troppo lontano** (*anche fig*) to go too far.

**spi'noso, a** *ag* thorny, prickly.

**'spinto, a** *pp di* **spingere** // *sf* (*urto*) push; (*FISICA*) thrust; (*fig: stimolo*) incentive, spur; (: *appoggio*) string-pulling *q*; **dare una** ~**a a qn** (*fig*) to pull strings for sb.

**spio'naggio** [spio'naddʒo] *sm* espionage, spying.

**spi'overe** *vi* (*scorrere*) to flow down; (*ricadere*) to hang down, fall.

**'spira** *sf* coil.

**spi'raglio** [spi'raʎʎo] *sm* (*fessura*) chink, narrow opening; (*raggio di luce, fig*) glimmer, gleam.

**spi'rale** *sf* spiral; (*contraccettivo*) coil; **a** ~ spiral(-shaped).

**spi'rare** *vi* (*vento*) to blow; (*morire*) to expire, pass away.

**spiri'tato, a** *ag* possessed; (*fig: persona, espressione*) wild.

**spiri'tismo** *sm* spiritualism.

**'spirito** *sm* (*REL, CHIM, disposizione d'animo, di legge etc, fantasma*) spirit; (*pensieri, intelletto*) mind; (*arguzia*) wit; (*umorismo*) humour, wit; **lo S**~ **Santo** the Holy Spirit *o* Ghost.

**spirito'saggine** [spirito'saddʒine] *sf* witticism; (*peg*) wisecrack.

**spiri'toso, a** *ag* witty.

**spiritu'ale** *ag* spiritual.

**'splendere** *vi* to shine.

**'splendido, a** *ag* splendid; (*splendente*) shining; (*sfarzoso*) magnificent, splendid.

**splen'dore** *sm* splendour; (*luce intensa*) brilliance, brightness.

**spodes'tare** *vt* to deprive of power; (*sovrano*) to depose.

**'spoglia** ['spɔʎʎa] *sf vedi* **spoglio**.

**spogli'are** [spoʎ'ʎare] *vt* (*svestire*) to undress; (*privare, fig: depredare*): ~ **qn di qc** to deprive sb of sth; (*togliere ornamenti: anche fig*): ~ **qn/qc di** to strip sb/sth of; ~**rsi** *vr* to undress, strip; ~**rsi di** (*ricchezze etc*) to deprive o.s. of, give up; (*pregiudizi*) to rid o.s. of; **spoglia'toio** *sm* dressing room; (*di scuola etc*) cloakroom; (*SPORT*) changing room; **'spoglio, a** *ag* (*pianta, terreno*) bare; (*privo*): **spoglio di** stripped of; lacking in, without // *sm* (*di voti*) counting // *sf* (*ZOOL*) skin, hide; (: *di rettile*) slough; **'spoglie** *sfpl* (*salma*) remains; (*preda*) spoils, booty *sg*.

**'spola** *sf* shuttle; (*bobina di filo*) cop; **fare la** ~ (**fra**) to go to and fro *o* shuttle (between).

**spol'pare** *vt* to strip the flesh off.

**spolve'rare** *vt* (*anche CUC*) to dust; (*con spazzola*) to brush; (*con battipanni*) to beat; (*fig*) to polish off // *vi* to dust.

**'sponda** *sf* (*di fiume*) bank; (*di mare, lago*) shore; (*bordo*) edge.

**spon'taneo, a** *ag* spontaneous;

(persona) unaffected, natural.

**spopo'lare** vt to depopulate // vi (attirare folla) to draw the crowds; ~rsi vr to become depopulated.

**spor'care** vt to dirty, make dirty; (fig) to sully, soil; ~rsi vr to get dirty.

**spor'cizia** [spor'tʃittsja] sf (stato) dirtiness; (sudiciume) dirt, filth; (cosa sporca) dirt q, something dirty; (fig: cosa oscena) obscenity.

**'sporco, a, chi, che** ag dirty, filthy.

**spor'genza** [spor'dʒɛntsa] sf projection.

**'sporgere** ['spɔrdʒere] vt to put out, stretch out // vi (venire in fuori) to stick out; ~rsi vr to lean out; ~ querela contro qn (DIR) to take legal action against sb.

**sport** sm inv sport.

**'sporta** sf shopping bag.

**spor'tello** sm (di treno, auto etc) door; (di banca, ufficio) window, counter; ~ automatico (BANCA) cash dispenser, automated telling machine.

**spor'tivo, a** ag (gara, giornale) sports cpd; (persona) sporty; (abito) casual; (spirito, atteggiamento) sporting.

**'sporto, a** pp di sporgere.

**'sposa** sf bride; (moglie) wife.

**sposa'lizio** [spoza'littsjo] sm wedding.

**spo'sare** vt to marry; (fig: idea, fede) to espouse; ~rsi vr to get married, marry; ~rsi con qn to marry sb, get married to sb; **spo'sato, a** ag married.

**'sposo** sm (bride)groom; (marito) husband; gli ~i smpl the newlyweds.

**spos'sato, a** ag exhausted, weary.

**spos'tare** vt to move, shift; (cambiare: orario) to change; ~rsi vr to move.

**'spranga, ghe** sf (sbarra) bar.

**'sprazzo** ['sprattso] sm (di sole etc) flash; (fig: di gioia etc) burst.

**spre'care** vt to waste; ~rsi vr

(persona) to waste one's energy; **'spreco** sm waste.

**spre'gevole** [spre'dʒevole] ag contemptible, despicable.

**spregiudi'cato, a** [spredʒudi'kato] ag unprejudiced, unbiased; (peg) unscrupulous.

**'spremere** vt to squeeze.

**spre'muta** sf fresh juice; ~ d'arancia fresh orange juice.

**sprez'zante** [spret'tsante] ag scornful, contemptuous.

**sprigio'nare** [spridʒo'nare] vt to give off, emit; ~rsi vr to emanate; (uscire con impeto) to burst out.

**spriz'zare** [sprit'tsare] vt, vi to spurt; ~ gioia/salute to be bursting with joy/health.

**sprofon'dare** vi to sink; (casa) to collapse; (suolo) to give way, subside; ~rsi vr: ~rsi in (poltrona) to sink into; (fig) to become immersed o absorbed in.

**spro'nare** vt to spur (on).

**'sprone** sm (sperone, fig) spur.

**sproporzio'nato, a** [sproportsjo'nato] ag disproportionate, out of all proportion.

**sproporzi'one** [spropor'tsjone] sf disproportion.

**sproposi'tato, a** ag (lettera, discorso) full of mistakes; (fig: costo) excessive, enormous.

**spro'posito** sm blunder; a ~ at the wrong time; (rispondere, parlare) irrelevantly.

**sprovve'duto, a** ag inexperienced, naive.

**sprov'visto, a** ag (mancante): ~ di lacking in, without; **alla** ~a unawares.

**spruz'zare** [sprut'tsare] vt (a nebulizzazione) to spray; (aspergere) to sprinkle; (inzaccherare) to splash; **'spruzzo** sm spray; splash.

**'spugna** ['spuɲɲa] sf (ZOOL) sponge; (tessuto) towelling; **spu'gnoso, a** ag spongy.

**'spuma** sf (schiuma) foam; (bibita) mineral water.

**spu'mante** sm sparkling wine.

**spumeggi'ante** [spumed'dʒante] ag (birra) foaming; (vino, fig) sparkling.

**spu'mone** sm (CUC) mousse.

**spun'tare** vt (coltello) to break the point of; (capelli) to trim // vi (uscire: germogli) to sprout; (: capelli) to begin to grow; (: denti) to come through; (apparire) to appear (suddenly); ~rsi vr to become blunt, lose its point; **spuntarla** (fig) to make it, win through.

**spun'tino** sm snack.

**'spunto** sm (TEATRO, MUS) cue; (fig) starting point; **dare lo ~ a** (fig) to give rise to.

**spur'gare** vt (fogna) to clean, clear; ~rsi vr (MED) to expectorate.

**spu'tare** vt to spit out; (fig) to belch (out) // vi to spit; **'sputo** sm spittle q, spit q.

**'squadra** sf (strumento) (set) square; (gruppo) team, squad; (di operai) gang, squad; (MIL) squad; (: AER, NAUT) squadron; (SPORT) team; **lavoro a ~e** teamwork.

**squa'drare** vt to square, make square; (osservare) to look at closely.

**squa'driglia** [skwa'driʎʎa] sf (AER) flight; (NAUT) squadron.

**squa'drone** sm squadron.

**squagli'arsi** [skwaʎ'ʎarsi] vr to melt; (fig) to sneak off.

**squa'lifica** sf disqualification.

**squalifi'care** vt to disqualify.

**'squallido, a** ag wretched, bleak.

**squal'lore** sm wretchedness, bleakness.

**'squalo** sm shark.

**'squama** sf scale; **squa'mare** vt to scale; **squamarsi** vr to flake o peel (off).

**squarcia'gola** [skwartʃa'gola]: **a ~** av at the top of one's voice.

**squar'tare** vt to quarter, cut up.

**squattri'nato, a** ag penniless.

**squili'brare** vt to unbalance; **squili'brato, a** ag (PSIC) un-

balanced; **squi'librio** sm (differenza, sbilancio) imbalance; (PSIC) unbalance.

**squil'lante** ag shrill, sharp.

**squil'lare** vi (campanello, telefono) to ring (out); (tromba) to blare; **'squillo** sm ring, ringing q; blare; **ragazza f squillo** inv call girl.

**squi'sito, a** ag exquisite; (cibo) delicious; (persona) delightful.

**squit'tire** vi (uccello) to squawk; (topo) to squeak.

**sradi'care** vt to uproot; (fig) to eradicate.

**sragio'nare** [zradʒo'nare] vi to talk nonsense, rave.

**srego'lato, a** ag (senza ordine: vita) disorderly; (smodato) immoderate; (dissoluto) dissolute.

**S.r.l.** abbr = **società a responsabilità limitata**.

**'stabile** ag stable, steady; (tempo: non variabile) settled; (TEATRO: compagnia) resident // sm (edificio) building.

**stabili'mento** sm (edificio) establishment; (fabbrica) plant, factory.

**stabi'lire** vt to establish; (fissare: prezzi, data) to fix; (decidere) to decide; ~rsi vr (prendere dimora) to settle.

**stac'care** vt (levare) to detach, remove; (separare: anche fig) to separate, divide; (strappare) to tear off (o out); (scandire: parole) to pronounce clearly; (SPORT) to leave behind; ~rsi vr (bottone etc) to come off; (scostarsi): ~rsi (da) to move away (from); (fig: separarsi): ~rsi da to leave; **non ~ gli occhi da qn** not to take one's eyes off sb.

**'stadio** sm (SPORT) stadium; (periodo, fase) phase, stage.

**'staffa** sf (di sella, TECN) stirrup; **perdere le ~e** (fig) to fly off the handle.

**staf'fetta** sf (messo) dispatch rider; (SPORT) relay race.

**stagio'nale** [stadʒo'nale] ag seasonal.

**stagio'nare** [stadʒo'nare] *vt* (*legno*) to season; (*formaggi, vino*) to mature.

**stagi'one** [sta'dʒone] *sf* season; **alta/bassa** ~ high/low season.

**stagli'arsi** [staʎ'ʎarsi] *vr* to stand out, be silhouetted.

**sta'gnare** [staɲ'ɲare] *vt* (*vaso, tegame*) to tin-plate; (*barca, botte*) to make watertight; (*sangue*) to stop // *vi* to stagnate.

**'stagno, a** ['staɲɲo] *ag* watertight; (*a tenuta d'aria*) airtight // *sm* (*acquitrino*) pond; (*CHIM*) tin.

**sta'gnola** [staɲ'ɲɔla] *sf* tinfoil.

**'stalla** *sf* (*per bovini*) cowshed; (*per cavalli*) stable.

**stal'lone** *sm* stallion.

**sta'mani, stamat'tina** *av* this morning.

**'stampa** *sf* (*TIP, FOT: tecnica*) printing; (*impressione, copia fotografica*) print; (*insieme di quotidiani, giornalisti etc*) press; ~**e** *sfpl* printed matter.

**stam'pante** *sf* (*INFORM*) printer.

**stam'pare** *vt* to print; (*pubblicare*) to publish; (*coniare*) to strike, coin; (*imprimere: anche fig*) to impress.

**stampa'tello** *sm* block letters *pl*.

**stam'pella** *sf* crutch.

**'stampo** *sm* mould; (*fig: indole*) type, kind, sort.

**sta'nare** *vt* to drive out.

**stan'care** *vt* to tire, make tired; (*annoiare*) to bore; (*infastidire*) to annoy; ~**rsi** *vr* to get tired, tire o.s. out; ~**rsi** (**di**) to grow weary (of), grow tired (of).

**stan'chezza** [stan'kettsa] *sf* tiredness, fatigue.

**'stanco, a, chi, che** *ag* tired; ~ **di** tired of, fed up with.

**'stanga, ghe** *sm* bar; (*di carro*) shaft.

**stan'gata** *sf* (*colpo: anche fig*) blow; (*cattivo risultato*) poor result; (*CALCIO*) shot.

**sta'notte** *av* tonight; (*notte passata*) last night.

**'stante** *prep*: **a sé** ~ (*appartamento, casa*) independent, separate.

**stan'tio, a, 'tii, 'tie** *ag* stale; (*burro*) rancid; (*fig*) old.

**stan'tuffo** *sm* piston.

**'stanza** ['stantsa] *sf* room; (*POESIA*) stanza; ~ **da letto** bedroom.

**stanzi'are** [stan'tsjare] *vt* to allocate.

**stap'pare** *vt* to uncork; to uncap.

**'stare** *vi* (*restare in un luogo*) to stay, remain; (*abitare*) to stay, live; (*essere situato*) to be, be situated; (*anche:* ~ **in piedi**) to be, stand; (*essere, trovarsi*) to be; (*dipendere*): **se stesse in me** if it were up to me, if it depended on me; (*seguito da gerundio*): **sta studiando** he's studying; **starci** (*esserci spazio*): **nel baule non ci sta più niente** there's no more room in the boot; (*accettare*) to accept; **ci stai?** is that okay with you?; ~ **a** (*attenersi a*) to follow, stick to; (*seguito dall'infinito*): **stiamo a discutere** we're talking; (*toccare a*): **sta a te giocare** it's your turn to play; ~ **per fare qc** to be about to do sth; **come sta?** how are you?; **io sto bene/male** I'm very well/not very well; ~ **a qn** (*abiti etc*) to fit sb; **queste scarpe mi stanno strette** these shoes are tight for me; **il rosso ti sta bene** red suits you.

**starnu'tire** *vi* to sneeze; **star'nuto** *sm* sneeze.

**sta'sera** *av* this evening, tonight.

**sta'tale** *ag* state *cpd*; government *cpd* // *sm/f* state employee, local authority employee; (*nell'amministrazione*) ≈ civil servant.

**sta'tista, i** *sm* statesman.

**sta'tistica** *sf* statistics *sg*.

**'stato, a** *pp di* **essere, stare** // *sm* (*condizione*) state, condition; (*POL*) state; (*DIR*) status; **essere in** ~ **d'accusa** (*DIR*) to be committed for trial; ~ **d'assedio/d'emergenza** state of siege/emergency; ~ **civile** (*AMM*) marital status; ~ **maggiore**

(*MIL*) staff; **gli S~i Uniti (d'America)** the United States (of America).

**'statua** *sf* statue.

**statuni'tense** *ag* United States *cpd*, of the United States.

**sta'tura** *sf* (*ANAT*) height, stature; (*fig*) stature.

**sta'tuto** *sm* (*DIR*) statute; constitution.

**sta'volta** *av* this time.

**stazio'nario, a** [stattsjo'narjo] *ag* stationary; (*fig*) unchanged.

**stazi'one** [stat'tsjone] *sf* station; (*balneare, termale*) resort; **~ degli autobus** bus station; **~ balneare** seaside resort; **~ ferroviaria** railway (*Brit*) *o* railroad (*US*) station; **~ invernale** winter sports resort; **~ di polizia** police station (*in small town*); **~ di servizio** service *o* petrol (*Brit*) *o* filling station.

**'stecca, che** *sf* stick; (*di ombrello*) rib; (*di sigarette*) carton; (*MED*) splint; (*stonatura*): **fare una ~** to sing (*o* play) a wrong note.

**stec'cato** *sm* fence.

**stec'chito, a** [stek'kito] *ag* dried up; (*persona*) skinny; **lasciar ~ qn** (*fig*) to leave sb flabbergasted; **morto ~** stone dead.

**'stella** *sf* star; **~ alpina** (*BOT*) edelweiss; **~ di mare** (*ZOOL*) starfish.

**'stelo** *sm* stem; (*asta*) rod; **lampada a ~** standard lamp.

**'stemma, i** *sm* coat of arms.

**stempe'rare** *vt* to dilute; to dissolve; (*colori*) to mix.

**sten'dardo** *sm* standard.

**'stendere** *vt* (*braccia, gambe*) to stretch (out); (*tovaglia*) to spread (out); (*bucato*) to hang out; (*mettere a giacere*) to lay (down); (*spalmare: colore*) to spread; (*mettere per iscritto*) to draw up; **~rsi** *vr* (*coricarsi*) to stretch out, lie down; (*estendersi*) to extend, stretch.

**stenodatti'lografo, a** *smf* shorthand typist (*Brit*), stenographer

(*US*).

**stenogra'fare** *vt* to take down in shorthand; **stenogra'fia** *sf* shorthand.

**sten'tare** *vi*: **~ a fare** to find it hard to do, have difficulty doing.

**'stento** *sm* (*fatica*) difficulty; **~i** *smpl* (*privazioni*) hardship *sg*, privation *sg*; **a ~** *av* with difficulty, barely.

**'sterco** *sm* dung.

**stereo('fonico, a, ci, che)** *ag* stereo(phonic).

**'sterile** *ag* sterile; (*terra*) barren; (*fig*) futile, fruitless; **sterilità** *sf* sterility.

**steriliz'zare** [sterilid'dzare] *vt* to sterilize; **sterilizzazi'one** *sf* sterilization.

**ster'lina** *sf* pound (sterling).

**stermi'nare** *vt* to exterminate, wipe out.

**stermi'nato, a** *ag* immense; endless.

**ster'minio** *sm* extermination, destruction.

**'sterno** *sm* (*ANAT*) breastbone.

**ster'zare** [ster'tsare] *vt, vi* (*AUT*) to steer; **'sterzo** *sm* steering; (*volante*) steering wheel.

**'steso, a** *pp di* **stendere**.

**'stesso, a** *ag* same; (*rafforzativo: in persona, proprio*): **il re ~** the king himself *o* in person // *pronome*: **lo(la) ~(a)** the same (one); **i suoi ~i avversari lo ammirano** even his enemies admire him; **fa lo ~ it** doesn't matter; **per me è lo ~** it's all the same to me, it doesn't matter to me; *vedi* **io, tu** etc.

**ste'sura** *sf* drafting *q*, drawing up *q*; draft.

**'stigma, i** *sm* stigma.

**'stigmate** *sfpl* (*REL*) stigmata.

**sti'lare** *vt* to draw up, draft.

**'stile** *sm* style; **sti'lista, i** *sm* designer.

**stil'lare** *vi* (*trasudare*) to ooze; (*gocciolare*) to drip; **stilli'cidio** *sm* (*fig*) continual pestering (*o* moaning etc).

**stilo'grafica, che** sf (anche: **penna ~**) fountain pen.

'**stima** sf esteem; valuation; assessment, estimate.

**sti'mare** vt (persona) to esteem, hold in high regard; (terreno, casa etc) to value; (stabilire in misura approssimativa) to estimate, assess; (ritenere): ~ **che** to consider that; **~rsi fortunato** to consider o.s. (to be) lucky.

**stimo'lare** vt to stimulate; (incitare): ~ **qn (a fare)** to spur sb on (to do).

'**stimolo** sm (anche fig) stimulus.

'**stinco, chi** sm shin; shinbone.

'**stingere** ['stindʒere] vt, vi (anche: **~rsi**) to fade; '**stinto, a** pp di **stingere**.

**sti'pare** vt to cram, pack; **~rsi** vr (accalcarsi) to crowd, throng.

**sti'pendio** sm salary.

'**stipite** sm (di porta, finestra) jamb.

**stipu'lare** vt (redigere) to draw up.

**sti'rare** vt (abito) to iron; (distendere) to stretch; (strappare: muscolo) to strain; **~rsi** vr to stretch (o.s.); **stira'tura** sf ironing.

'**stirpe** sf birth, stock; descendants pl.

**stiti'chezza** [stiti'kettsa] sf constipation.

'**stitico, a, ci, che** ag constipated.

'**stiva** sf (di nave) hold.

**sti'vale** sm boot.

'**stizza** ['stittsa] sf anger, vexation; **stiz'zirsi** vr to lose one's temper; **stiz'zoso, a** ag (persona) quick-tempered, irascible; (risposta) angry.

**stocca'fisso** sm stockfish, dried cod.

**stoc'cata** sf (colpo) stab, thrust; (fig) gibe, cutting remark.

'**stoffa** sf material, fabric; (fig): aver la ~ di to have the makings of.

'**stola** sf stole.

'**stolto, a** ag stupid, foolish.

'**stomaco, chi** sm stomach; dare di ~ to vomit, be sick.

**sto'nare** vt to sing (o play) out of tune // vi to be out of tune, sing (o play) out of tune; (fig) to be out of place, jar; (: colori) to clash; **stona'tura** sf (suono) false note.

'**stoppa** sf tow.

'**stoppia** sf (AGR) stubble.

**stop'pino** sm wick; (miccia) fuse.

'**storcere** ['stortʃere] vt to twist; **~rsi** vr to writhe, twist; ~ **il naso** (fig) to turn up one's nose; **~rsi la caviglia** to twist one's ankle.

**stor'dire** vt (intontire) to stun, daze; **~rsi** vr: **~rsi col bere** to dull one's senses with drink; **stor'dito, a** ag stunned; (sventato) scatterbrained, heedless.

'**storia** sf (scienza, avvenimenti) history; (racconto, bugia) story; (faccenda, questione) business g; (pretesto) excuse, pretext; **~e** sfpl (smancerie) fuss sg; '**storico, a, ci, che** ag historic(al) // sm historian.

**stori'one** sm (ZOOL) sturgeon.

**stor'mire** vi to rustle.

'**stormo** sm (di uccelli) flock.

**stor'nare** vt (COMM) to transfer.

'**storno** sm starling.

**storpi'are** vt to cripple, maim; (fig: parole) to mangle; (: significato) to twist.

'**storpio, a** ag crippled, maimed.

'**storto, a** pp di **storcere** // ag (chiodo) twisted, bent; (gamba, quadro) crooked; (fig: ragionamento) false, wrong // sf (distorsione) sprain, twist; (recipiente) retort.

**sto'viglie** [sto'viʎʎe] sfpl dishes pl, crockery.

**strabico, a, ci, che** ag squint-eyed; (occhi) squint.

**stra'bismo** sm squinting.

**stra'carico, a, chi, che** ag overloaded.

**stracci'are** [strat'tʃare] vt to tear.

'**straccio, a, ci, ce** ['strattʃo] ag: **carta ~a** waste paper // sm rag;

(*per pulire*) cloth, duster; **stracci-'vendolo** *sm* ragman.

**stra'cotto, a** *ag* overcooked // *sm* (*CUC*) beef stew.

'**strada** *sf* road; (*di città*) street; (*cammino, via, fig*) way; **farsi ~** (*fig*) to do well for o.s.; **essere fuori ~** (*fig*) to be on the wrong track; **~ facendo** on the way; **~ senza uscita** dead end; **stra'dale** *ag* road *cpd*.

**strafalci'one** [strafal'tʃone] *sm* blunder, howler.

**stra'fare** *vi* to overdo it; **stra'fatto, a** *pp di* **strafare**.

**strafot'tente** *ag*: **è ~** he doesn't give a damn, he couldn't care less.

'**strage** ['stradʒe] *sf* massacre, slaughter.

**stralu'nato, a** *ag* (*occhi*) rolling; (*persona*) beside o.s., very upset.

**stramaz'zare** [stramat'tsare] *vi* to fall heavily.

'**strambo, a** *ag* strange, queer.

**strampa'lato, a** *ag* odd, eccentric.

**stra'nezza** [stra'nettsa] *sf* strangeness.

**strango'lare** *vt* to strangle; **~rsi** *vr* to choke.

**strani'ero, a** *ag* foreign // *sm/f* foreigner.

'**strano, a** *ag* strange, odd.

**straordi'nario, a** *ag* extraordinary; (*treno etc*) special // *sm* (*lavoro*) overtime.

**strapaz'zare** [strapat'tsare] *vt* to ill-treat; **~rsi** *vr* to tire o.s. out, overdo things; **stra'pazzo** *sm* strain, fatigue; **da strapazzo** (*fig*) third-rate.

**strapi'ombo** *sm* overhanging rock; **a ~** overhanging.

**strapo'tere** *sm* excessive power.

**strap'pare** *vt* (*gen*) to tear, rip; (*pagina etc*) to tear off, tear out; (*sradicare*) to pull up; (*togliere*): **~ qc a qn** to snatch sth from sb; (*fig*) to wrest sth from sb; **~rsi** *vr* (*lacerarsi*) to rip, tear; (*rompersi*) to break; **~rsi un muscolo** to tear a

muscle; '**strappo** *sm* pull, tug; tear, rip; **fare uno strappo alla regola** to make an exception to the rule; **strappo muscolare** torn muscle.

**strapun'tino** *sm* jump *o* foldaway seat.

**strari'pare** *vi* to overflow.

**strasci'care** [straʃʃi'kare] *vt* to trail; (*piedi*) to drag; **~ le parole** to drawl.

'**strascico, chi** ['straʃʃiko] *sm* (*di abito*) train; (*conseguenza*) after-effect.

**strata'gemma, i** [strata'dʒemma] *sm* stratagem.

**strate'gia, 'gie** [strate'dʒia] *sf* strategy; **stra'tegico, a, ci, che** *ag* strategic.

'**strato** *sm* layer; (*rivestimento*) coat, coating; (*GEO, fig*) stratum; (*METEOR*) stratus.

**stratos'fera** *sf* stratosphere.

**strava'gante** *ag* odd, eccentric; **strava'ganza** *sf* eccentricity.

**stra'vecchio, a** [stra'vekkjo] *ag* very old.

**stra'vizio** [stra'vittsjo] *sm* excess.

**stra'volgere** [stra'voldʒere] *vt* (*volto*) to contort; (*fig: animo*) to trouble deeply; (: *verità*) to twist, distort; **stra'volto, a** *pp di* **stravolgere**.

**strazi'are** [strat'tsjare] *vt* to torture, torment; '**strazio** *sm* torture; (*fig: cosa fatta male*): **essere uno ~** to be appalling.

'**strega, ghe** *sf* witch.

**stre'gare** *vt* to bewitch.

**stre'gone** *sm* (*mago*) wizard; (*di tribù*) witch doctor.

'**stregua** *sf*: **alla ~ di** by the same standard as.

**stre'mare** *vt* to exhaust.

'**stremo** *sm* very end; **essere allo ~** to be at the end of one's tether.

'**strenna** *sf* Christmas present.

'**strenuo, a** *ag* brave, courageous.

**strepi'toso, a** *ag* clamorous, deafening; (*fig: successo*) resounding.

**stres'sante** *ag* stressful.

'**stretta** *sf vedi* **stretto**.

**stretta'mente** *av* tightly; (*rigorosamente*) strictly.

**stret'tezza** [stret'tettsa] *sf* narrowness; ~e *sfpl* poverty *sg*, straitened circumstances.

'**stretto, a** *pp di* **stringere** // *ag* (*corridoio, limiti*) narrow; (*gonna, scarpe, nodo, curva*) tight; (*intimo: parente, amico*) close; (*rigoroso: osservanza*) strict; (*preciso: significato*) precise, exact // *sm* (*braccio di mare*) strait // *sf* (*di mano*) grasp; (*finanziaria*) squeeze; (*fig: dolore, turbamento*) pang; **a denti** ~**i** with clenched teeth; **lo** ~ **necessario** the bare minimum; **una** ~**a di mano** a handshake; **essere alle** ~**e** to have one's back to the wall; **stret'toia** *sf* bottleneck; (*fig*) tricky situation.

**stri'ato, a** *ag* streaked.

'**stridere** *vi* (*porta*) to squeak; (*animale*) to screech, shriek; (*colori*) to clash; '**strido,** *pl(f)* **strida** *sm* screech, shriek; **stri'dore** *sm* screeching, shrieking; '**stridulo, a** *ag* shrill.

**stril'lare** *vt, vi* to scream, shriek; '**strillo** *sm* scream, shriek.

**stril'lone** *sm* newspaper seller.

**strimin'zito, a** [strimin'tsito] *ag* (*misero*) shabby; (*molto magro*) skinny.

**strimpel'lare** *vt* (*MUS*) to strum.

'**stringa, ghe** *sf* lace.

**strin'gato, a** *ag* (*fig*) concise.

'**stringere** ['strindʒere] *vt* (*avvicinare due cose*) to press (together), squeeze (together); (*tenere stretto*) to hold tight, clasp, clutch; (*pugno, mascella, denti*) to clench; (*labbra*) to compress; (*avvitare*) to tighten; (*abito*) to take in; (*sog: scarpe*) to pinch, be tight for; (*fig: concludere: patto*) to make; (: *accelerare: passo, tempo*) to quicken // *vi* (*essere stretto*) to be tight; (*tempo: incalzare*) to be pressing; ~**rsi** *vr* (*accostarsi*): ~**rsi a** to

press o.s. up against; ~ **la mano a qn** to shake sb's hand; ~ **gli occhi** to screw up one's eyes.

'**striscia, sce** ['striʃʃa] *sf* (*di carta, tessuto etc*) strip; (*riga*) stripe; ~**sce (pedonali)** zebra crossing *sg*.

**strisci'are** [striʃ'ʃare] *vt* (*piedi*) to drag; (*muro, macchina*) to graze // *vi* to crawl, creep.

'**striscio** ['striʃʃo] *sm* graze; (*MED*) smear; **colpire di** ~ to graze.

**strito'lare** *vt* to grind.

**striz'zare** [strit'tsare] *vt* (*arancia*) to squeeze; (*panni*) to wring (out); ~ **l'occhio** to wink.

'**strofa** *sf*, '**strofe** *sf inv* strophe.

**strofi'naccio** [strofi'nattʃo] *sm* duster, cloth; (*per piatti*) dishcloth; (*per pavimenti*) floorcloth.

**strofi'nare** *vt* to rub.

**stron'care** *vt* to break off; (*fig: ribellione*) to suppress, put down; (: *film, libro*) to tear to pieces.

**stropicci'are** [stropit'tʃare] *vt* to rub.

**stroz'zare** [strot'tsare] *vt* (*soffocare*) to choke, strangle; ~**rsi** *vr* to choke; **strozza'tura** *sf* (*restringimento*) narrowing; (*di strada etc*) bottleneck.

'**struggere** ['struddʒere] *vt* (*fig*) to consume; ~**rsi** *vr* (*fig*): ~**rsi di** to be consumed with.

**strumen'tale** *ag* (*MUS*) instrumental.

**strumentaliz'zare** [strumentalid'dzare] *vt* to exploit, use to one's own ends.

**stru'mento** *sm* (*arnese, fig*) instrument, tool; (*MUS*) instrument; ~ **a corda** o **ad arco/a fiato** stringed/wind instrument.

'**strutto** *sm* lard.

**strut'tura** *sf* structure; **struttu'rare** *vt* to structure.

'**struzzo** ['struttso] *sm* ostrich.

**stuc'care** *vt* (*muro*) to plaster; (*vetro*) to putty; (*decorare con stucchi*) to stucco.

**stuc'chevole** [stuk'kevole] *ag*

nauseating; (*fig*) tedious, boring.

**'stucco, chi** *sm* plaster; (*da vetri*) putty; (*ornamentale*) stucco; **rimanere di ~** (*fig*) to be dumbfounded.

**stu'dente, 'essa** *sm/f* student; (*scolaro*) pupil, schoolboy/girl; **studen'tesco, a, schi, sche** *ag* student *cpd*; school *cpd*.

**studi'are** *vt* to study.

**'studio** *sm* studying; (*ricerca, saggio, stanza*) study; (*di professionista*) office; (*di artista, CINEMA, TV, RADIO*) studio; **~i** *smpl* (*INS*) studies; **~ medico** doctor's surgery (*Brit*) *o* office (*US*).

**studi'oso, a** *ag* studious, hard-working // *sm/f* scholar.

**'stufa** *sf* stove; **~ elettrica** electric fire *o* heater.

**stu'fare** *vt* (*CUC*) to stew; (*fig: fam*) to bore; **stu'fato** *sm* (*CUC*) stew; **'stufo, a** *ag* (*fam*): **essere stufo di** to be fed up with, be sick and tired of.

**stu'oia** *sf* mat.

**stupefa'cente** [stupefa'tʃɛnte] *ag* stunning, astounding // *sm* drug, narcotic.

**stu'pendo, a** *ag* marvellous, wonderful.

**stupi'daggine** [stupi'daddʒine] *sf* stupid thing (to do *o* say).

**stupidità** *sf* stupidity.

**'stupido, a** *ag* stupid.

**stu'pire** *vt* to amaze, stun // *vi* (*anche: ~rsi*): **~ (di)** to be amazed (at), be stunned (by).

**stu'pore** *sm* amazement, astonishment.

**'stupro** *sm* rape.

**stu'rare** *vt* (*lavandino*) to clear.

**stuzzica'denti** [stuttsika'denti] *sm* toothpick.

**stuzzi'care** [stuttsi'kare] *vt* (*ferita etc*) to poke (at), prod (at); (*fig*) to tease; (: *appetito*) to whet; (: *curiosità*) to stimulate; **~ i denti** to pick one's teeth.

---

PAROLA CHIAVE

**su** *prep* (*su + il =* **sul**, *su + lo =* **sullo**, *su + l' =* **sull'**, *su + la =* **sulla**, *su + i =* **sui**, *su + gli =* **sugli**, *su + le =* **sulle**) **1** (*gen*) on; (*moto*) on(to); (*in cima a*) on (top of); **mettilo sul tavolo** put it on the table; **un paesino sul mare** a village by the sea

**2** (*argomento*) about, on; **un libro ~** Cesare a book on *o* about Caesar

**3** (*circa*) about; **costerà sui 3 milioni** it will cost about 3 million; **una ragazza sui 17 anni** a girl of about 17 (years of age)

**4: ~ misura** made to measure; **~ richiesta** on request; **3 casi ~ dieci** 3 cases out of 10

♦ *av* **1** (*in alto, verso l'alto*) up; **vieni ~** come on up; **guarda ~** look up; **~ le mani!** hands up!; **in ~** (*verso l'alto*) up(wards); (*in poi*) onwards; **dai 20 anni in ~** from the age of 20 onwards

**2** (*addosso*) on; **cos'hai ~?** what have you got on?

♦ *escl* come on!; **~ coraggio!** come on, cheer up!

---

**'sua** *vedi* **suo**.

**su'bacqueo, a** *ag* underwater // *sm* skindiver.

**sub'buglio** [sub'buʎʎo] *sm* confusion, turmoil.

**subcosci'ente** [subkoʃ'ʃɛnte] *ag, sm* subconscious.

**'subdolo, a** *ag* underhand, sneaky.

**suben'trare** *vi*: **~ a qn in qc** to take over sth from sb.

**su'bire** *vt* to suffer, endure.

**subis'sare** *vt* (*fig*): **~ di** to overwhelm with, load with.

**subi'taneo, a** *ag* sudden.

**'subito** *av* immediately, at once, straight away.

**subodo'rare** *vt* (*insidia etc*) to smell, suspect.

**subordi'nato, a** *ag* subordinate; (*dipendente*): **~ a** dependent on, subject to.

**subur'bano, a** *ag* suburban.

**succe'daneo** [suttʃe'daneo] *sm* substitute.

**suc'cedere** [sut'tʃɛdere] *vi* (*prendere il posto di qn*): ~ **a** to succeed; (*venire dopo*): ~ **a** to follow; (*accadere*) to happen; **~rsi** *vr* to follow each other; ~ **al trono** to succeed to the throne; **successi'one** *sf* succession; **succes'sivo, a** *ag* successive; **suc'cesso, a** *pp di* **succedere** // *sm* (*esito*) outcome; (*buona riuscita*) success; **di successo** (*libro, personaggio*) successful.

**succhi'are** [suk'kjare] *vt* to suck (up).

**suc'cinto, a** [sut'tʃinto] *ag* (*discorso*) succinct; (*abito*) brief.

**'succo, chi** *sm* juice; (*fig*) essence, gist; ~ **di frutta** fruit juice; **suc'coso, a** *ag* juicy; (*fig*) pithy.

**succur'sale** *sf* branch (office).

**sud** *sm* south // *ag inv* south; (*lato*) south, southern.

**Su'dafrica** *sm*: **il** ~ South Africa; **sudafri'cano, a** *ag, sm/f* South African.

**Suda'merica** *sm*: **il** ~ South America; **sudameri'cano, a** *ag, sm/f* South American.

**su'dare** *vi* to perspire, sweat; ~ **freddo** to come out in a cold sweat; **su'data** *sf* sweat; **ho fatto una bella sudata per finirlo in tempo** it was a real sweat to get it finished in time.

**sud'detto, a** *ag* above-mentioned.

**sud'dito, a** *sm/f* subject.

**suddi'videre** *vt* to subdivide.

**su'dest** *sm* south-east.

**'sudicio, a, ci, ce** ['suditʃo] *ag* dirty, filthy; **sudici'ume** *sm* dirt, filth.

**su'dore** *sm* perspiration, sweat.

**su'dovest** *sm* south-west.

**'sue** *vedi* **suo.**

**suffici'ente** [suffi'tʃɛnte] *ag* enough, sufficient; (*borioso*) self-important;

(*INS*) satisfactory; **suffici'enza** *sf* self-importance; pass mark; **a sufficienza** *av* enough; **ne ho avuto a sufficienza!** I've had enough of this!

**suf'fisso** *sm* (*LING*) suffix.

**suf'fragio** [suf'fradʒo] *sm* (*voto*) vote; ~ **universale** universal suffrage.

**suggel'lare** [suddʒel'lare] *vt* (*fig*) to seal.

**suggeri'mento** [suddʒeri'mento] *sm* suggestion; (*consiglio*) piece of advice, advice *q*.

**sugge'rire** [suddʒe'rire] *vt* (*risposta*) to tell; (*consigliare*) to advise; (*proporre*) to suggest; (*TEATRO*) to prompt; **suggeri'tore, 'trice** *sm/f* (*TEATRO*) prompter.

**suggestio'nare** [suddʒestjo'nare] *vt* to influence.

**suggesti'one** [suddʒes'tjone] *sf* (*PSIC*) suggestion; (*istigazione*) instigation.

**sugges'tivo, a** [suddʒes'tivo] *ag* (*paesaggio*) evocative; (*teoria*) interesting, attractive.

**'sughero** ['sugero] *sm* cork.

**'sugli** ['suʎʎi] *prep* + *det vedi* **su.**

**'sugo, ghi** *sm* (*succo*) juice; (*di carne*) gravy; (*condimento*) sauce; (*fig*) gist, essence.

**'sui** *prep* + *det vedi* **su.**

**sui'cida, i, e** [sui'tʃida] *ag* suicidal // *sm/f* suicide.

**suici'darsi** [suitʃi'darsi] *vr* to commit suicide.

**sui'cidio** [sui'tʃidjo] *sm* suicide.

**su'ino, a** *ag*: **carne ~a** pork // *sm* pig; **~i** *smpl* swine *pl*.

**sul, sull', 'sulla, 'sulle, 'sullo** *prep* + *det vedi* **su.**

**sulta'nina** *ag f*: (**uva**) ~ sultana.

**sul'tano, a** *sm/f* sultan/sultana.

**'sunto** *sm* summary.

**'suo, 'sua, 'sue, su'oi** *det*: **il** ~, **la sua** *etc* (*di lui*) his; (*di lei*) her; (*di esso*) its; (*con valore indefinito*) one's, his/her; (*forma di cortesia: anche*: **S~**) your // *pronome*: **il** ~, **la**

sua *etc* his; hers; yours; **i suoi** (*parenti*) his (*o* her *o* one's *o* your) family.

**su'ocero, a** ['swɔtʃero] *sm/f* father/mother-in-law; **i ~i** *smpl* father-and mother-in-law.

**su'oi** *vedi* **suo**.

**su'ola** *sf* (*di scarpa*) sole.

**su'olo** *sm* (*terreno*) ground; (*terra*) soil.

**suo'nare** *vt* (*MUS*) to play; (*campana*) to ring; (*ore*) to strike; (*clacson, allarme*) to sound // *vi* to play; (*telefono, campana*) to ring; (*ore*) to strike; (*clacson, fig: parole*) to sound.

**su'ono** *sm* sound.

**su'ora** *sf* (*REL*) sister.

**'super** *sf* (*anche:* **benzina ~**) four-star (petrol) (*Brit*), premium (*US*).

**supe'rare** *vt* (*oltrepassare: limite*) to exceed, surpass; (*percorrere*) to cover; (*attraversare: fiume*) to cross; (*sorpassare: veicolo*) to overtake; (*fig: essere più bravo di*) to surpass, outdo; (: *difficoltà*) to overcome; (: *esame*) to get through; ~ **qn in altezza/peso** to be taller/heavier than sb; **ha superato la cinquantina** he's over fifty (years of age).

**su'perbia** *sf* pride.

**su'perbo, a** *ag* proud; (*fig*) magnificent, superb.

**superfici'ale** [superfi'tʃale] *ag* superficial.

**super'ficie, ci** [super'fitʃe] *sf* surface.

**su'perfluo, a** *ag* superfluous.

**superi'ore** *ag* (*piano, arto, classi*) upper; (*più elevato: temperatura, livello*): ~ **(a)** higher (than); (*migliore*): ~ **(a)** superior (to); ~, **a** *sm/f* (*anche REL*) superior; **superiorità** *sf* superiority.

**superla'tivo, a** *ag, sm* superlative.

**super'mercato** *sm* supermarket.

**su'perstite** *ag* surviving // *sm/f* survivor.

**superstizi'one** [superstit'tsjone] *sf* superstition; **superstizi'oso, a** *ag* superstitious.

**su'pino, a** *ag* supine.

**suppel'lettile** *sf* furnishings *pl*.

**suppergiù** [supper'dʒu] *av* more or less, roughly.

**supplemen'tare** *ag* extra; (*treno*) relief *cpd*; (*entrate*) additional.

**supple'mento** *sm* supplement.

**sup'plente** *ag* temporary; (*insegnante*) supply *cpd* (*Brit*), substitute *cpd* (*US*) // *sm/f* temporary member of staff; supply (*o* substitute) teacher.

**'supplica, che** *sf* (*preghiera*) plea; (*domanda scritta*) petition, request.

**suppli'care** *vt* to implore, beseech.

**sup'plire** *vi*: ~ **a** to make up for, compensate for.

**sup'plizio** [sup'plittsjo] *sm* torture.

**sup'porre** *vt* to suppose.

**sup'porto** *sm* (*sostegno*) support.

**sup'posta** *sf* (*MED*) suppository.

**sup'posto, a** *pp di* **supporre**.

**su'premo, a** *ag* supreme.

**surge'lare** [surdʒe'lare] *vt* to (deep-)freeze; **surge'lati** *smpl* frozen food *sg*.

**sur'plus** *sm inv* (*ECON*) surplus.

**surriscal'dare** *vt* to overheat.

**surro'gato** *sm* substitute.

**suscet'tibile** [suʃʃet'tibile] *ag* (*sensibile*) touchy, sensitive; (*soggetto*): ~ **di miglioramento** that can be improved, open to improvement.

**susci'tare** [suʃʃi'tare] *vt* to provoke, arouse.

**su'sina** *sf* plum; **su'sino** *sm* plum (tree).

**sussegu'ire** *vt* to follow; **~rsi** *vr* to follow one another.

**sussidi'ario, a** *ag* subsidiary; auxiliary.

**sus'sidio** *sm* subsidy.

**sussis'tenza** [sussis'tɛntsa] *sf* subsistence.

**sussi'stere** *vi* to exist; (*essere fondato*) to be valid *o* sound.

**sussul'tare** *vi* to shudder.

**sussur'rare** *vt, vi* to whisper, murmur; **sus'surro** *sm* whisper, murmur.

**sutu'rare** *vt* (*MED*) to stitch up, suture.

**sva'gare** *vt* (*distrarre*) to distract; (*divertire*) to amuse; **~rsi** *vr* to amuse o.s.; to enjoy o.s.

**'svago, ghi** *sm* (*riposo*) relaxation; (*ricreazione*) amusement; (*passatempo*) pastime.

**svaligi'are** *vt* to rob, burgle (*Brit*), burglarize (*US*).

**svalu'tare** *vt* (*ECON*) to devalue; (*fig*) to belittle; **~rsi** *vr* (*ECON*) to be devalued; **svalutazi'one** *sf* devaluation.

**sva'nire** *vi* to disappear, vanish.

**svan'taggio** [zvan'taddʒo] *sm* disadvantage; (*inconveniente*) drawback, disadvantage.

**svapo'rare** *vi* to evaporate.

**svari'ato, a** *ag* varied; various.

**'svastica** *sf* swastika.

**sve'dese** *ag* Swedish // *sm/f* Swede // *sm* (*LING*) Swedish.

**'sveglia** ['zveʎʎa] *sf* waking up; (*orologio*) alarm (clock); **suonare la ~** (*MIL*) to sound the reveille.

**svegli'are** [zveʎ'ʎare] *vt* to wake up; (*fig*) to awaken, arouse; **~rsi** *vr* to wake up; (*fig*) to be revived, re-awaken.

**'sveglio, a** ['zveʎʎo] *ag* awake; (*fig*) quick-witted.

**sve'lare** *vt* to reveal.

**'svelto, a** *ag* (*passo*) quick; (*mente*) quick, alert; (*linea*) slim, slender; **alla ~a** *av* quickly.

**'svendita** *sf* (*COMM*) (clearance) sale.

**sveni'mento** *sm* fainting fit, faint.

**sve'nire** *vi* to faint.

**sven'tare** *vt* to foil, thwart.

**sven'tato, a** *ag* (*distratto*) scatter-brained; (*imprudente*) rash.

**svento'lare** *vt, vi* to wave, flutter.

**sven'trare** *vt* to disembowel.

**sven'tura** *sf* misfortune; **sventu'ra-**

**to, a** *ag* unlucky, unfortunate.

**sve'nuto, a** *pp di* **svenire**.

**svergo'gnato, a** [zvergoɲ'ɲato] *ag* shameless.

**sver'nare** *vi* to spend the winter.

**sves'tire** *vt* to undress; **~rsi** *vr* to get undressed.

**'Svezia** ['zvɛttsja] *sf*: **la ~** Sweden.

**svez'zare** [zvet'tsare] *vt* to wean.

**svi'are** *vt* to divert; (*fig*) to lead astray; **~rsi** *vr* to go astray.

**svi'gnarsela** [zviɲ'ɲarsela] *vr* to slip away, sneak off.

**svilup'pare** *vt, ~rsi vr* to develop.

**svi'luppo** *sm* development.

**svincolo** *sm* (*COMM*) clearance; (*stradale*) motorway (*Brit*) o expressway (*US*) intersection.

**svisce'rare** [zviʃʃe'rare] *vt* (*fig*: *argomento*) to examine in depth; **svisce'rato, a** *ag* (*amore*) passionate; (*lodi*) obsequious.

**'svista** *sf* oversight.

**svi'tare** *vt* to unscrew.

**'Svizzera** ['zvittsera] *sf*: **la ~** Switzerland.

**'svizzero, a** ['zvittsero] *ag, sm/f* Swiss.

**svogli'ato, a** [zvoʎ'ʎato] *ag* listless; (*pigro*) lazy.

**svolaz'zare** [zvolat'tsare] *vi* to flutter.

**'svolgere** ['zvɔldʒere] *vt* to unwind; (*srotolare*) to unroll; (*fig*: *argomento*) to develop; (: *piano, programma*) to carry out; **~rsi** *vr* to unwind; to unroll; (*fig*: *aver luogo*) to take place; (: *procedere*) to go on; **svolgi'mento** *sm* development; carrying out; (*andamento*) course.

**'svolta** *sf* (*atto*) turning *q*; (*curva*) turn, bend; (*fig*) turning-point.

**svol'tare** *vi* to turn.

**'svolto, a** *pp di* **svolgere**.

**svuo'tare** *vt* to empty (out).

# T

**tabac'caio, a** sm/f tobacconist.

**tabacche'ria** [tabakke'ria] sf tobacconist's (shop).

**ta'bacco, chi** sm tobacco.

**ta'bella** sf (tavola) table; (elenco) list.

**taber'nacolo** sm tabernacle.

**tabu'lato** sm (INFORM) printout.

**'tacca, che** sf notch, nick; **di mezza ~** (fig) mediocre.

**tac'cagno, a** [tak'kaɲɲo] ag mean, stingy.

**tac'cheggio** [tak'keddʒo] sm shoplifting.

**tac'chino** [tak'kino] sm turkey.

**tacci'are** [tat'tʃare] vt: **~ qn di** to accuse sb of.

**'tacco, chi** sm heel.

**taccu'ino** sm notebook.

**ta'cere** [ta'tʃere] vi to be silent o quiet; (smettere di parlare) to fall silent // vt to keep to oneself, say nothing about; **far ~ qn** to make sb be quiet; (fig) to silence sb.

**ta'chimetro** [ta'kimetro] sm speedometer.

**'tacito, a** [ta'tʃito] ag silent; (sottinteso) tacit, unspoken.

**ta'fano** sm horsefly.

**taffe'ruglio** [taffe'ruʎʎo] sm brawl, scuffle.

**taffettà** sm taffeta.

**taglia** ['taʎʎa] sf (statura) height; (misura) size; (riscatto) ransom; (ricompensa) reward.

**taglia'carte** [taʎʎa'karte] sm inv paperknife.

**tagli'ando** [taʎ'ʎando] sm coupon.

**tagli'are** [taʎ'ʎare] vt to cut; (recidere, interrompere) to cut off; (intersecare) to cut across, intersect; (carne) to carve; (vini) to blend // vi to cut; (prendere una scorciatoia) to take a short-cut; **~ corto** (fig) to cut short.

**taglia'telle** [taʎʎa'tɛlle] sfpl

tagliatelle pl.

**tagli'ente** [taʎ'ʎɛnte] ag sharp.

**'taglio** ['taʎʎo] sm cutting q; cut; (parte tagliente) cutting edge; (di abito) cut, style; (di stoffa: lunghezza) length; (di vini) blending; **di ~** on edge, edgeways; **banconote di piccolo/grosso ~** notes of small/ large denomination.

**tagli'ola** [taʎ'ʎola] sf trap, snare.

**tagliuz'zare** [taʎʎut'tsare] vt to cut into small pieces.

**'talco** sm talcum powder.

---

*PAROLA CHIAVE*

**'tale ♦** det **1** (simile, così grande) such; **un(a) ~** ... such (a) ...; **non accetto ~i discorsi** I won't allow such talk; **è di una ~ arroganza** he is so arrogant; **fa una ~ confusione!** he makes such a mess! **2** (persona o cosa indeterminata) such-and-such; **il giorno ~ all'ora ~** on such-and-such a day at such-and-such a time; **la tal persona** that person; **ha telefonato una ~ Giovanna** somebody called Giovanna phoned **3** (nelle similitudini): **~** ... **~** like ... like; **~ padre ~ figlio** like father, like son; **hai il vestito ~ quale il mio** your dress is just o exactly like mine

**♦** pronome (indefinito: persona): **un(a) ~** someone; **quel** (o **quella**) **~** that person, that man (o woman); **il tal dei ~i** what's-his-name.

**ta'lento** sm talent.

**talis'mano** sm talisman.

**tallon'cino** [tallon'tʃino] sm counterfoil.

**tal'lone** sm heel.

**tal'mente** av so.

**ta'lora** av = talvolta.

**'talpa** sf (ZOOL) mole.

**tal'volta** av sometimes, at times.

**tambu'rello** sm tambourine.

**tam'buro** sm drum.

**Ta'migi** [ta'midʒi] sm: **il ~ the**

Thames.

**tampo'nare** vt (otturare) to plug; (urtare: macchina) to crash o ram into.

**tam'pone** sm (MED) wad, pad; (per timbri) ink-pad; (respingente) buffer; ~ **assorbente** tampon.

**'tana** sf lair, den.

**'tanfo** sm stench; musty smell.

**tan'gente** [tan'dʒɛntɛ] ag (MAT): ~ a tangential to // sf tangent; (quota) share.

**tan'tino**: **un** ~ av a little, a bit.

---
**PAROLA CHIAVE**

**'tanto, a** ♦ det **1** (molto: quantità) a lot of, much; (: numero) a lot of, many; (così ~: quantità) so much, such a lot of; (: numero) so many, such a lot of; **~e volte** so many times, so often; **~i auguri!** all the best!; **~e grazie** many thanks; **~ tempo** so long, such a long time; **ogni ~i chilometri** every so many kilometres

**2**: ~ ... **quanto** (quantità) as much ... as; (numero) as many ... as; **ho ~a pazienza quanta ne hai tu** I have as much patience as you have o as you; **ha ~i amici quanti nemici** he has as many friends as he has enemies

**3** (rafforzativo) such; **ho aspettato per ~ tempo** I waited so long o for such a long time

♦ pronome **1** (molto) much, a lot; (così ~) so much, such a lot; **~i(e)** many, a lot; such a lot; **credevo ce ne fosse ~** I thought there was (such) a lot, I thought there was plenty

**2**: ~ **quanto** (denaro) as much as; (cioccolatini) as many as; **ne ho ~ quanto basta** I have as much as I need; **due volte ~** twice as much

**3** (indeterminato) so much; ~ **per l'affitto, ~ per il gas** so much for the rent, so much for the gas; **costa un ~ al metro** it costs so much per metre; **di ~ in ~, ogni ~** every so

often; ~ **vale che ... I** (o we etc) may as well ...; ~ **meglio!** so much the better!; ~ **peggio per lui!** so much the worse for him!

♦ av **1** (molto) very; **vengo ~ volentieri** I'd be very glad to come; **non ci vuole ~ a capirlo** it doesn't take much to understand it

**2** (così ~: con ag, av) so; (: con vb) so much, such a lot; **è ~ bella!** she's so beautiful!; **non urlare ~** don't shout so much; **sto ~ meglio adesso** I'm so much better now; ~ ... **che** so ... (that); ~ ... **da** so ... as

**3**: ~ ... **quanto** as ... as; **conosco ~ Carlo quanto suo padre** I know both Carlo and his father; **non è poi ~ complicato quanto sembri** it's not as difficult as it seems; **~ più insisti, ~ più non mollerà** the more you insist, the more stubborn he'll be; **quanto più ... ~ meno** the more ... the less

**4** (solamente) just; ~ **per cambiare/scherzare** just for a change/a joke; **una volta** ~ for once

**5** (a lungo) (for) long

♦ cong after all.

**'tappa** sf (luogo di sosta, fermata) stop, halt; (parte di un percorso) stage, leg; (SPORT) lap; **a ~e in** stages.

**tap'pare** vt to plug, stop up; (bottiglia) to cork.

**tap'peto** sm carpet; (anche: tappetino) rug; (di tavolo) cloth; (SPORT): **andare al ~** to go down for the count; **mettere sul ~** (fig) to bring up for discussion.

**tappez'zare** [tappet'tsare] vt (con carta) to paper; (rivestire): ~ **qc (di)** to cover sth (with);

**tappezze'ria** sf (tessuto) tapestry; (carta da parato) wallpaper; (arte) upholstery; **far da tappezzeria** (fig) to be a wallflower; **tappezzi'ere** sm upholsterer.

**'tappo** sm stopper; (in sughero)

cork.

**tarchi'ato, a** [tar'kjato] *ag* stocky, thickset.

**tar'dare** *vi* to be late // *vt* to delay; ~ **a fare** to delay doing.

**'tardi** *av* late; **più** ~ later (on); **al più** ~ at the latest; **sul** ~ (*verso sera*) late in the day; **far** ~ to be late; (*restare alzato*) to stay up late.

**tar'divo, a** *ag* (*primavera*) late; (*rimedio*) belated, tardy; (*fig: bambino*) retarded.

**'tardo, a** *ag* (*lento, fig: ottuso*) slow; (*tempo: avanzato*) late.

**'targa, ghe** *sf* plate; (*AUT*) number (*Brit*) o license (*US*) plate.

**ta'riffa** *sf* (*gen*) rate, tariff; (*di trasporti*) fare; (*elenco*) price list; tariff.

**'tarlo** *sm* woodworm.

**'tarma** *sf* moth.

**ta'rocco, chi** *sm* tarot card; ~**chi** *smpl* (*gioco*) tarot *sg*.

**tartagli'are** [tarta'ʎʎare] *vi* to stutter, stammer.

**'tartaro, a** *ag, sm* (*in tutti i sensi*) tartar.

**tarta'ruga, ghe** *sf* tortoise; (*di mare*) turtle; (*materiale*) tortoise-shell.

**tar'tina** *sf* canapé.

**tar'tufo** *sm* (*BOT*) truffle.

**'tasca, sche** *sf* pocket; **tas'cabile** *ag* (*libro*) pocket *cpd*; **tasca'pane** *sm* haversack; **tas'chino** *sm* breast pocket.

**'tassa** *sf* (*imposta*) tax; (*doganale*) duty; (*per iscrizione: a scuola etc*) fee; ~ **di circolazione/di soggiorno** road/tourist tax.

**tas'sametro** *sm* taximeter.

**tas'sare** *vt* to tax; to levy a duty on.

**tassa'tivo, a** *ag* peremptory.

**tassazi'one** [tassat'tsjone] *sf* taxation.

**tas'sello** *sm* plug; wedge.

**tassi** *sm inv* = taxi; **tas'sista, i, e** *sm/f* taxi driver.

**'tasso** *sm* (*di natalità, d'interesse etc*) rate; (*BOT*) yew; (*ZOOL*) badger; ~ **di cambio/d'interesse** rate of exchange/interest.

**tas'tare** *vt* to feel; ~ **il terreno** (*fig*) to see how the land lies.

**tasti'era** *sf* keyboard.

**'tasto** *sm* key; (*tatto*) touch, feel.

**tas'toni** *av*: **procedere (a)** ~ to grope one's way forward.

**'tattico, a, ci, che** *ag* tactical // *sf* tactics *pl*.

**'tatto** *sm* (*senso*) touch; (*fig*) tact; **duro al** ~ hard to the touch; **aver** ~ to be tactful, have tact.

**tatu'aggio** [tatu'addʒo] *sm* tattooing; (*disegno*) tattoo.

**tatu'are** *vt* to tattoo.

**'tavola** *sf* table; (*asse*) plank, board; (*lastra*) tablet; (*quadro*) panel (painting); (*illustrazione*) table; ~ **calda** snack bar; ~ **pieghevole** folding table.

**tavo'lato** *sm* boarding; (*pavimento*) wooden floor.

**tavo'letta** *sf* tablet, bar; **a** ~ (*AUT*) flat out.

**tavo'lino** *sm* small table; (*scrivania*) desk.

**'tavolo** *sm* table.

**tavo'lozza** [tavo'lɔttsa] *sf* (*ARTE*) palette.

**'taxi** *sm inv* taxi.

**'tazza** [ˈtattsa] *sf* cup; ~ **da caffè/tè** coffee/tea cup; **una** ~ **di caffè/tè** a cup of coffee/tea.

**te** *pronome* (*soggetto: in forme comparative, oggetto*) you.

**tè** *sm inv* tea; (*trattenimento*) tea party.

**tea'trale** *ag* theatrical.

**te'atro** *sm* theatre.

**'tecnico, a, ci, che** *ag* technical // *sm/f* technician // *sf* technique; (*tecnologia*) technology.

**tecnolo'gia** [teknolo'dʒia] *sf* technology.

**te'desco, a, schi, sche** *ag, sm/f, sm* German.

**'tedio** *sm* tedium, boredom.

**te'game** *sm* (*CUC*) pan.

**'tegola** *sf* tile.

**tei'era** sf teapot.

**'tela** sf (tessuto) cloth; (per vele, quadri) canvas; (dipinto) canvas, painting; **di** ~ (calzoni) (heavy) cotton cpd; (scarpe, borsa) canvas cpd; ~ **cerata** oilcloth; (copertone) tarpaulin.

**te'laio** sm (apparecchio) loom; (struttura) frame.

**tele'camera** sf television camera.

**tele'cronaca** sf television report.

**tele'ferica, che** sf cableway.

**telefo'nare** vi to telephone, ring; to make a phone call // vt to telephone; ~ **a** to phone up, ring up, call up.

**telefo'nata** sf (telephone) call; ~ **a carico del destinatario** reverse charge (Brit) o collect (US) call.

**tele'fonico, a, ci, che** ag (tele)phone cpd.

**telefo'nista, a** e sm/f telephonist; (d'impresa) switchboard operator.

**te'lefono** sm telephone; ~ **a gettoni** ≈ pay phone.

**telegior'nale** [teledʒor'nale] sm television news (programme).

**te'legrafo** sm telegraph; (ufficio) telegraph office.

**tele'gramma, i** sm telegram.

**tele'matica** sf data transmission; telematics sg.

**telepa'tia** sf telepathy.

**teles'copio** sm telescope.

**teleselezi'one** [teleselet'tsjone] sf direct dialling.

**telespetta'tore, 'trice** sm/f (television) viewer.

**televisi'one** sf television.

**televi'sore** sm television set.

**'telex** sm inv telex.

**'tema, i** sm theme; (INS) essay, composition.

**teme'rario, a** ag rash, reckless.

**te'mere** vt to fear, be afraid of; (essere sensibile a: freddo, calore) to be sensitive to // vi to be afraid; (essere preoccupato): ~ **per** to worry about, fear for; ~ **di/che** to be afraid of/that.

**temperama'tite** sm inv pencil

sharpener.

**tempera'mento** sm temperament.

**tempe'rare** vt (aguzzare) to sharpen; (fig) to moderate, control, temper.

**tempe'rato, a** ag moderate, temperate; (clima) temperate.

**tempera'tura** sf temperature.

**tempe'rino** sm penknife.

**tem'pesta** sf storm; ~ **di sabbia/ neve** sand/snowstorm.

**tempes'tare** vt: ~ **qn di domande** to bombard sb with questions; ~ **qn di colpi** to rain blows on sb.

**tempes'tivo, a** ag timely.

**tempes'toso, a** ag stormy.

**'tempia** sf (ANAT) temple.

**'tempio** sm (edificio) temple.

**'tempo** sm (METEOR) weather; (cronologico) time; (epoca) time, times pl; (di film, gioco: parte) part; (MUS) time; (: battuta) beat; (LING) tense; **un** ~ once; ~ **fa** some time ago; **al** ~ **stesso** o **a un** ~ at the same time; **per** ~ early; **aver fatto il suo** ~ to have had its (o his etc) day; **primo/secondo** ~ (TEATRO) first/second part; (SPORT) first/second half; **in** ~ **utile** in due time o course.

**tempo'rale** ag temporal // sm (METEOR) (thunder)storm.

**tempo'raneo, a** ag temporary.

**temporeggi'are** [tempored'dʒare] vi to play for time, temporize.

**tem'prare** vt to temper.

**te'nace** [te'natʃe] ag strong, tough; (fig) tenacious.

**te'nacia** sf tenacity.

**te'naglie** [te'naʎʎe] sfpl pincers pl.

**'tenda** sf (riparo) awning; (di finestra) curtain; (per campeggio etc) tent.

**ten'denza** sf tendency; (orientamento) trend; **avere** ~ **a** o **per qc** to have a bent for sth.

**'tendere** vt (allungare al massimo) to stretch, draw tight; (porgere: mano) to hold out; (fig: trappola) to lay, set // vi: ~ **a qc/a fare** to tend towards sth/to do; ~ **l'orecchio** to prick up one's ears; **il tempo tende al caldo** the weather is getting hot; **un blu che tende al verde** a greenish blue.

**ten'dina** sf curtain.

**'tendine** sm tendon, sinew.

**ten'done** sm (da circo) tent.

**'tenebre** sfpl darkness sg; **tene'broso, a** ag dark, gloomy.

**te'nente** sm lieutenant.

**te'nere** vt to hold; (conservare, mantenere) to keep; (ritenere, considerare) to consider; (spazio: occupare) to take up, occupy; (seguire: strada) to keep to // vi to hold; (colori) to be fast; (dare importanza): ~ **a** to care about; ~ **a fare** to want to do, be keen to do; ~**rsi** vr (stare in una determinata posizione) to stand; (stimarsi) to consider o.s.; (aggrapparsi): ~**rsi a** to hold on to; (attenersi): ~**rsi a** to stick to; ~ **una conferenza** to give a lecture; ~ **conto di qc** to take sth into consideration; ~ **presente qc** to bear sth in mind.

**'tenero, a** ag tender; (pietra, cera, colore) soft; (fig) tender, loving.

**'tenia** sf tapeworm.

**'tennis** sm tennis.

**te'nore** sm (tono) tone; (MUS) tenor; ~ **di vita** way of life; (livello) standard of living.

**tensi'one** sf tension.

**ten'tare** vt (indurre) to tempt; (provare): ~ **qc/di fare** to attempt o try sth/to do; **tenta'tivo** sm attempt; **tentazi'one** sf temptation.

**tenten'nare** vi to shake, be unsteady; (fig) to hesitate, waver // vt: ~ **il capo** to shake one's head.

**ten'toni** av: **andare a** ~ (anche fig) to grope one's way.

**te'nue** ag (sottile) fine; (colore) soft; (fig) slender, slight.

**te'nuta** sf (capacità) capacity; (divisa) uniform; (abito) dress; (AGR) estate; ~ **d'aria** airtight; ~ **di strada** roadholding power.

**teolo'gia** [teolo'dʒia] sf theology;

**te'ologo, gi** sm theologian.

**teo'rema, i** sm theorem.

**teo'ria** sf theory; **te'orico, a, ci, che** ag theoretic(al).

**'tepido, a** ag = tiepido.

**te'pore** sm warmth.

**'teppa** sf mob, hooligans pl; **tep'pismo** sm hooliganism; **tep'pista, i** sm hooligan.

**tera'pia** sf therapy.

**tergicris'tallo** [terdʒikris'tallo] sm windscreen (Brit) o windshield (US) wiper.

**tergiver'sare** [terdʒiver'sare] vi to shilly-shally.

**'tergo** sm: **a** ~ behind; **vedi a** ~ please turn over.

**ter'male** ag thermal; **stazione** f ~ spa.

**'terme** sfpl thermal baths.

**'termico, a, ci, che** ag thermic; (unità) thermal.

**termi'nale** ag, sm terminal.

**termi'nare** vt to end; (lavoro) to finish // vi to end.

**'termine** sm term; (fine, estremità) end; (di territorio) boundary, limit; **contratto a** ~ (COMM) forward contract; **a breve/lungo** ~ short-/long-term; **parlare senza mezzi** ~**i** to talk frankly, not to mince one's words.

**ter'mometro** sm thermometer.

**termonucle'are** ag thermonuclear.

**'termos** sm inv = **thermos**.

**termosi'fone** sm radiator; (riscaldamento a) ~ central heating.

**ter'mostato** sm thermostat.

**'terra** sf (gen, ELETTR) earth; (sostanza) soil, earth; (opposto al mare) land g; (regione, paese) land; (argilla) clay; ~ **e** sfpl (possedimento) lands, land sg; **a o per** ~ (stato) on the ground (o floor); (moto) to the ground, down; **mettere a** ~ (ELETTR) to earth.

**terra'cotta** sf terracotta; **vasellame m di** ~ earthenware.

**terra'ferma** sf dry land, terra firma; (continente) mainland.

**terrapi'eno** sm embankment, bank.

**ter'razza** [ter'rattsa] sf, **ter'razzo** [ter'rattso] sm terrace.

**terre'moto** sm earthquake.

**ter'reno, a** ag (vita, beni) earthly // sm (suolo, fig) ground; (COMM) land q, plot (of land); site; (SPORT, MIL) field.

**ter'restre** ag (superficie) of the earth, earth's; (di terra: battaglia, animale) land cpd; (REL) earthly, worldly.

**ter'ribile** ag terrible, dreadful.

**terrifi'cante** ag terrifying.

**territori'ale** ag territorial.

**terri'torio** sm territory.

**ter'rore** sm terror; **terro'rismo** sm terrorism; **terro'rista, i, e** smf terrorist.

**'terso, a** ag clear.

**'terzo, a** ['tɛrtso] ag third // sm (frazione) third; (DIR) third party; ~i smpl (altri) others, other people; **la ~a pagina** (STAMPA) the Arts page.

**'tesa** sf brim.

**'teschio** ['tɛskjo] sm skull.

**'tesi** sf thesis.

**'teso, a** pp di **tendere** // ag (tirato) taut, tight; (fig) tense.

**tesore'ria** sf treasury.

**tesori'ere** sm treasurer.

**te'soro** sm treasure; **il Ministero del T~** the Treasury.

**'tessera** sf (documento) card.

**'tessere** vt to weave; **'tessile** ag, sm textile; **tessi'tore, 'trice** smf weaver; **tessi'tura** sf weaving.

**tes'suto** sm fabric, material; (BIOL) tissue; (fig) web.

**'testa** sf head; (di cose: estremità, parte anteriore) head, front; (di vettura etc) front; **tenere ~ a qn** (nemico etc) to stand up to sb; **fare di ~ propria** to go one's own way; **in ~** (SPORT) in the lead; **~ o croce?** heads or tails?; **avere la ~ dura** to be stubborn; **~ di serie** (TENNIS) seed, seeded player.

**testa'mento** sm (atto) will;

l'Antico/il Nuovo T~ (REL) the Old/New Testament.

**tes'tardo, a** ag stubborn, pigheaded.

**tes'tata** sf (parte anteriore) head; (intestazione) heading.

**'teste** smf witness.

**tes'ticolo** sm testicle.

**testi'mone** smf (DIR) witness.

**testimoni'anza** [testimo'njantsa] sf testimony.

**testimoni'are** vt to testify; (fig) to bear witness to, testify to // vi to give evidence, testify.

**'testo** sm text; **fare ~** (opera, autore) to be authoritative; **questo libro non fa ~** this book is not essential reading; **testu'ale** ag textual; literal, word for word.

**tes'tuggine** [tes'tuddʒine] sf tortoise; (di mare) turtle.

**'tetano** sm (MED) tetanus.

**'tetro, a** ag gloomy.

**'tetto** sm roof; **tet'toia** sf roofing; canopy.

**'Tevere** sm: **il ~** the Tiber.

**Tg.** abbr = **telegiornale**.

**'thermos** ® ['tɛrmos] sm inv vacuum o Thermos ® flask.

**ti** pronome (dav lo, la, li, le, ne diventa **te**) (oggetto) you; (complemento di termine) (to) you; (riflessivo) yourself.

**ti'ara** sf (REL) tiara.

**'tibia** sf tibia, shinbone.

**tic** sm inv tic, (nervous) twitch; (fig) mannerism.

**ticchet'tio** [tikket'tio] sm (di macchina da scrivere) clatter; (di orologio) ticking; (della pioggia) patter.

**'ticchio** ['tikkjo] sm (ghiribizzo) whim; (tic) tic, (nervous) twitch.

**ti'epido, a** ag lukewarm, tepid.

**ti'fare** vi: **~ per** to be a fan of; (parteggiare) to side with.

**'tifo** sm (MED) typhus; (fig): **fare il ~ per** to be a fan of.

**tifoi'dea** sf typhoid.

**ti'fone** sm typhoon.

**ti'foso, a** smf (SPORT etc) fan.

'**tiglio** ['tiλλo] *sm* lime (tree), linden (tree).

'**tigre** *sf* tiger.

**tim'ballo** *sm* (*strumento*) kettle-drum; (*CUC*) timbale.

'**timbro** *sm* stamp; (*MUS*) timbre, tone.

'**timido, a** *ag* shy; timid.

'**timo** *sm* thyme.

**ti'mone** *sm* (*NAUT*) rudder; **timoni'ere** *sm* helmsman.

**ti'more** *sm* (*paura*) fear; (*rispetto*) awe; **timo'roso, a** *ag* timid, timorous.

'**timpano** *sm* (*ANAT*) eardrum; (*MUS*): ~**i** *smpl* kettledrums, timpani.

'**tingere** ['tindʒere] *vt* to dye.

'**tino** *sm* vat.

**ti'nozza** [ti'nɔttsa] *sf* tub.

'**tinta** *sf* (*materia colorante*) dye; (*colore*) colour, shade; **tinta'rella** *sf* (*fam*) (sun)tan.

**tintin'nare** *vi* to tinkle.

'**tinto, a** *pp di* **tingere**.

**tinto'ria** *sf* (*officina*) dyeworks *sg*; (*lavasecco*) dry cleaner's (shop).

**tin'tura** *sf* (*operazione*) dyeing; (*colorante*) dye; ~ **di iodio** tincture of iodine.

'**tipico, a, ci, che** *ag* typical.

'**tipo** *sm* type; (*genere*) kind, type; (*fam*) chap, fellow.

**tipogra'fia** *sf* typography; (*procedimento*) letterpress (printing); (*officina*) printing house; **tipo'grafico, a, ci, che** *ag* typographic(al); letterpress *cpd*; **ti'pografo** *sm* typographer.

**ti'ranno, a** *ag* tyrannical // *sm* tyrant.

**ti'rante** *sm* (*per tenda*) guy.

**ti'rare** *vt* (*gen*) to pull; (*estrarre*): ~ **qc da** to take *o* pull sth out of; to get sth out of; to extract sth from; (*chiudere: tenda etc*) to draw, pull; (*tracciare, disegnare*) to draw, trace; (*lanciare: sasso, palla*) to throw; (*stampare*) to print; (*pistola, freccia*) to fire // *vi* (*pipa, camino*) to draw; (*vento*) to blow; (*abito*) to be tight; (*fare fuoco*) to fire; (*fare del tiro, CALCIO*) to shoot; ~ **avanti** *vi* to struggle on // *vt* to keep going; ~ **fuori** *vt* (*estrarre*) to take out, pull out; ~ **giù** *vt* (*abbassare*) to bring down; ~ **su** *vt* to pull up; (*capelli*) to put up; (*fig: bambino*) to bring up; ~**rsi indietro** to move back.

**tira'tore** *sm* gunman; **un buon** ~ a good shot; ~ **scelto** marksman.

**tira'tura** *sf* (*azione*) printing; (*di libro*) (print) run; (*di giornale*) circulation.

'**tirchio, a** ['tirkjo] *ag* mean, stingy.

'**tiro** *sm* shooting *q*, firing *q*; (*colpo, sparo*) shot; (*di palla: lancio*) throwing *q*; throw; (*fig*) trick; **cavallo da** ~ **draught** (*Brit*) *o* draft (*US*) horse; ~ **a segno** target shooting; (*luogo*) shooting range.

**tiro'cinio** [tiro'tʃinjo] *sm* apprenticeship; (*professionale*) training.

**ti'roide** *sf* thyroid (gland).

**Tir'reno** *sm*: **il** (**mar**) ~ the Tyrrhenian Sea.

**ti'sana** *sf* herb tea.

**tito'lare** *ag* appointed; (*sovrano*) titular // *sm/f* incumbent; (*proprietario*) owner; (*CALCIO*) regular player.

'**titolo** *sm* title; (*di giornale*) headline; (*diploma*) qualification; (*COMM*) security; (: *azione*) share; **a che** ~? for what reason? **a** ~ **di amicizia** out of friendship; **a** ~ **di premio** as a prize; ~ **di credito** share; ~ **di proprietà** title deed.

**titu'bante** *ag* hesitant, irresolute.

'**tizio, a** ['tittsjo] *sm/f* fellow, chap.

**tiz'zone** [tit'tsone] *sm* brand.

**toc'cante** *ag* touching.

**toc'care** *vt* to touch; (*tastare*) to feel; (*fig: riguardare*) to concern; (: *commuovere*) to touch, move; (: *pungere*) to hurt, wound; (: *far cenno a: argomento*) to touch on, mention // *vi*: ~ **a** (*accadere*) to happen to; (*spettare*) to be up to; (**il fondo**) (*in acqua*) to touch the bottom; **tocca a te difenderci** it's up to you to defend us; **a chi tocca?** whose turn is it?; **mi toccò pagare** I had to pay.

**'tocco, chi** sm touch; (ARTE) stroke, touch.

**'toga, ghe** sf toga; (di magistrato, professore) gown.

**togliere** ['tɔʎʎere] vt (rimuovere) to take away (o off), remove; (riprendere, non concedere più) to take away, remove; (MAT) to take away, subtract; (liberare) to free; **qc a qn** to take sth (away) from sb; **ciò non toglie che** nevertheless, be that as it may; **~rsi il cappello** to take off one's hat.

**toi'lette** [twa'lɛt] sf inv, **to'letta** sf toilet; (mobile) dressing table.

**tolle'ranza** [tolle'rantsa] sf tolerance.

**tolle'rare** vt to tolerate.

**'tolto, a** pp di **togliere**.

**to'maia** sf (di scarpa) upper.

**'tomba** sf tomb.

**tom'bino** sm manhole cover.

**'tombola** sf (gioco) tombola; (ruzzolone) tumble.

**'tomo** sm volume.

**'tonaca, che** sf (REL) habit.

**to'nare** vi = **tuonare**.

**'tondo, a** ag round.

**'tonfo** sm splash; (rumore sordo) thud; (caduta): **fare un ~** to take a tumble.

**'tonico, a, ci, che** ag, sm tonic.

**tonifi'care** vt (muscoli, pelle) to tone up; (irrobustire) to invigorate, brace.

**tonnel'laggio** [tonnel'laddʒo] sm (NAUT) tonnage.

**tonnel'lata** sf ton.

**'tonno** sm tuna (fish).

**'tono** sm (gen) tone; (MUS: di pezzo) key; (di colore) shade, tone.

**ton'silla** sf tonsil; **tonsil'lite** sf tonsillitis.

**'tonto, a** ag dull, stupid.

**to'pazio** [to'pattsjo] sm topaz.

**'topo** sm mouse.

**topogra'fia** sf topography.

**'toppa** sf (serratura) keyhole; (pezza) patch.

**to'race** [to'ratʃe] sm chest.

**'torba** sf peat.

**'torbido, a** ag (liquido) cloudy; (: fiume) muddy; (fig) dark; troubled // sm: **pescare nel ~** (fig) to fish in troubled water.

**'torcere** ['tɔrtʃere] vt to twist; (biancheria) to wring (out); **~rsi** vr to twist, writhe.

**torchi'are** [tor'kjare] vt to press; **'torchio** sm press; **torchio tipografico** printing press.

**'torcia, ce** ['tɔrtʃa] sf torch; **~ elettrica** torch (Brit), flashlight (US).

**torci'collo** [tortʃi'kɔllo] sm stiff neck.

**'tordo** sm thrush.

**To'rino** sf Turin.

**tor'menta** sf snowstorm.

**tormen'tare** vt to torment; **~rsi** vr to fret, worry o.s.; **tor'mento** sm torment.

**torna'conto** sm advantage, benefit.

**tor'nado** sm tornado.

**tor'nante** sm hairpin bend.

**tor'nare** vi to return, go (o come) back; (ridiventare: anche fig) to become (again); (riuscire giusto, esatto: conto) to work out; (risultare) to turn out (to be), prove (to be); **~ utile** to prove o turn out (to be) useful; **~ a casa** to go (o come) home.

**torna'sole** sm inv litmus.

**tor'neo** sm tournament.

**'tornio** sm lathe.

**'toro** sm bull; (dello zodiaco): **T~** Taurus.

**tor'pedine** sf torpedo; **torpedi'ni'era** sf torpedo boat.

**'torre** sf tower; (SCACCHI) rook, castle; **~ di controllo** (AER) control tower.

**torrefazi'one** [torrefat'tsjone] sf roasting.

**tor'rente** sm torrent.

**tor'retta** sf turret.

**torri'one** sm keep.

**tor'rone** sm nougat.

**torsi'one** sf twisting; torsion.

**'torso** sm torso, trunk; (ARTE) torso.

**'torsolo** sm (di cavolo etc) stump; (di frutta) core.

**'torta** sf cake.

**'torto, a** pp di **torcere** // ag (ritorto) twisted; (storto) twisted, crooked // sm (ingiustizia) wrong; (colpa) fault; **a ~** wrongly; **aver ~** to be wrong.

**'tortora** sf turtle dove.

**tortu'oso, a** ag (strada) twisting; (fig) tortuous.

**tor'tura** sf torture; **tortu'rare** vt to torture.

**'torvo, a** ag menacing, grim.

**tosa'erba** sm o f inv (lawn)mower.

**to'sare** vt (pecora) to shear; (siepe) to clip, trim.

**Tos'cana** sf: **la ~** Tuscany; **tos'cano, a** ag, sm/f Tuscan // sm (sigaro) strong Italian cigar.

**'tosse** sf cough.

**'tossico, a, ci, che** ag toxic.

**tossicodipen'dente, tossi'comane** sm/f drug addict.

**tos'sire** vi to cough.

**tosta'pane** sm inv toaster.

**tos'tare** vt to toast; (caffè) to roast.

**'tosto, a** ag: **faccia ~** a cheek.

**to'tale** ag, sm total; **totalità** sf: la totalità di all of, the total amount (o number) of; **the whole + sg**; **totaliz'zare** vt to total; (SPORT: punti) to score.

**toto'calcio** [toto'kaltʃo] sm gambling pool betting on football results, ≈ (football) pools pl (Brit).

**to'vaglia** [to'vaʎʎa] sf tablecloth; **tovagli'olo** sm napkin.

**'tozzo, a** ['tɔttso] ag squat // sm: **~ di pane** crust of bread.

**tra** prep (di due persone, cose) between; (di più persone, cose) among(st); (tempo: entro) within, in; **~ 5 giorni** in 5 days' time; **sia detto ~ noi ...** between you and me ...; **litigano ~ (di) loro** they're

fighting amongst themselves; **~ breve** soon; **~ sé e sé** (parlare etc) to oneself.

**trabal'lare** vi to stagger, totter.

**traboc'care** vi to overflow.

**traboc'chetto** [trabok'ketto] sm (fig) trap.

**tracan'nare** vt to gulp down.

**'traccia, ce** ['trattʃa] sf (segno, striscia) trail, track; (orma) tracks pl; (residuo, testimonianza) trace, sign; (abbozzo) outline.

**tracci'are** [trat'tʃare] vt to trace, mark (out); (disegnare) to draw; (fig: abbozzare) to outline; **tracci'ato** sm (grafico) layout, plan.

**tra'chea** [tra'kɛa] sf windpipe, trachea.

**tra'colla** sf shoulder strap; **borsa a ~** shoulder bag.

**tra'collo** sm (fig) collapse, crash.

**traco'tante** ag overbearing, arrogant.

**tradi'mento** sm betrayal; (DIR, MIL) treason.

**tra'dire** vt to betray; (coniuge) to be unfaithful to; (doveri: mancare) to fail in; (rivelare) to give away, reveal; **tradi'tore, 'trice** sm/f traitor.

**tradizio'nale** [tradittsjo'nale] ag traditional.

**tradizi'one** [tradit'tsjone] sf tradition.

**tra'dotto, a** pp di **tradurre**.

**tra'durre** vt to translate; (spiegare) to render, convey; **tradut'tore, 'trice** sm/f translator; **traduzi'one** sf translation.

**tra'ente** sm/f (ECON) drawer.

**trafe'lato, a** ag out of breath.

**traffi'cante** sm/f dealer; (peg) trafficker.

**traffi'care** vi (commerciare): **~ (in)** to trade (in), deal (in); (affaccendarsi) to busy o.s. // vt (peg) to traffic in.

**'traffico, ci** sm traffic; (commercio) trade, traffic.

**tra'figgere** [tra'fiddʒere] vt to run through, stab; (fig) to pierce;

**tra'fitto, a** *pp di* **trafiggere**.

**trafo'rare** *vt* to bore, drill; **'traforo** *sm (azione)* boring, drilling; *(galleria)* tunnel.

**tra'gedia** [tra'dʒɛdja] *sf* tragedy.

**tra'ghetto** [tra'getto] *sm* crossing; *(barca)* ferry(boat).

**'tragico, a, ci, che** ['tradʒiko] *ag* tragic.

**tra'gitto** [tra'dʒitto] *sm (passaggio)* crossing; *(viaggio)* journey.

**tragu'ardo** *sm (SPORT)* finishing line; *(fig)* goal, aim.

**traiet'toria** *sf* trajectory.

**trai'nare** *vt* to drag, haul; *(rimorchiare)* to tow; **'traino** *sm (carro)* wagon; *(slitta)* sledge; *(carico)* load.

**tralasci'are** [tralaʃ'ʃare] *vt (studi)* to neglect; *(dettagli)* to leave out, omit.

**'tralcio** ['traltʃo] *sm (BOT)* shoot.

**tra'liccio** [tra'littʃo] *sm (tela)* ticking; *(struttura)* trellis; *(ELETTR)* pylon.

**tram** *sm inv* tram.

**'trama** *sf (filo)* weft, woof; *(fig: argomento, maneggio)* plot.

**traman'dare** *vt* to pass on, hand down.

**tra'mare** *vt (fig)* to scheme, plot.

**tram'busto** *sm* turmoil.

**trames'tio** *sm* bustle.

**tramez'zino** [tramed'dzino] *sm* sandwich.

**tra'mezzo** [tra'meddzo] *sm (EDIL)* partition.

**'tramite** *prep* through.

**tramon'tare** *vi* to set, go down; **tra'monto** *sm* setting; *(del sole)* sunset.

**tramor'tire** *vi* to faint // *vt* to stun.

**trampo'lino** *sm (per tuffi)* springboard, diving board; *(per lo sci)* ski-jump.

**'trampolo** *sm* stilt.

**tramu'tare** *vt*: ~ **in** to change into, turn into.

**tra'nello** *sm* trap.

**trangugi'are** [trangu'dʒare] *vt* to gulp down.

**'tranne** *prep* except (for), but (for); ~ **che** *cong* unless.

**tranquil'lante** *sm (MED)* tranquillizer.

**tranquillità** *sf* calm, stillness; quietness; peace of mind.

**tranquilliz'zare** [trankwillid'dzare] *vt* to reassure.

**tran'quillo, a** *ag* calm, quiet; *(bambino, scolaro)* quiet; *(sereno)* with one's mind at rest; **sta'** ~ don't worry.

**transat'lantico, a, ci, che** *ag* transatlantic // *sm* transatlantic liner.

**tran'satto, a** *pp di* **transigere**.

**transazi'one** [transat'tsjone] *sf* compromise; *(DIR)* settlement; *(COMM)* transaction, deal.

**tran'senna** *sf* barrier.

**tran'sigere** [tran'sidʒere] *vi (DIR)* to reach a settlement; *(venire a patti)* to compromise, come to an agreement.

**tran'sistor** *sm*, **transis'tore** *sm* transistor.

**transi'tabile** *ag* passable.

**transi'tare** *vi* to pass.

**transi'tivo, a** *ag* transitive.

**'transito** *sm* transit; **di** ~ *(merci)* in transit; *(stazione)* transit *cpd*; **"divieto di** ~**"** "no entry".

**transi'torio, a** *ag* transitory, transient; *(provvisorio)* provisional.

**tran'via** *sf* tramway *(Brit)*, streetcar line *(US)*.

**'trapano** *sm (utensile)* drill; *(: MED)* trepan.

**trapas'sare** *vt* to pierce.

**tra'passo** *sm* passage.

**trape'lare** *vi* to leak, drip; *(fig)* to leak out.

**tra'pezio** [tra'pɛttsjo] *sm (MAT)* trapezium; *(attrezzo ginnico)* trapeze.

**trapian'tare** *vt* to transplant; **trapi'anto** *sm* transplanting; *(MED)* transplant.

**'trappola** *sf* trap.

**tra'punta** *sf* quilt.

**'trarre** *vt* to draw, pull; *(portare)* to

take; (*prendere, tirare fuori*) to take (out), draw; (*derivare*) to obtain; ~ **origine da qc** to have its origins *o* originate in sth.

**trasa'lire** *vi* to start, jump.

**trasan'dato, a** *ag* shabby.

**trasbor'dare** *vt* to transfer; (*NAUT*) to tran(s)ship // *vi* (*NAUT*) to change ship; (*AER*) to change plane; (*FERR*) to change (trains).

**trasci'nare** [traʃʃi'nare] *vt* to drag; ~**rsi** *vr* to drag o.s. along; (*fig*) to drag on.

**tras'correre** *vt* (*tempo*) to spend, pass // *vi* to pass; **tras'corso, a** *pp di* trascorrere.

**tras'critto, a** *pp di* trascrivere.

**tras'crivere** *vt* to transcribe.

**trascu'rare** *vt* to neglect; (*non considerare*) to disregard; **trascura'tezza** *sf* carelessness, negligence; **trascu'rato, a** *ag* (*casa*) neglected; (*persona*) careless, negligent.

**traseco'lato, a** *ag* astounded, amazed.

**trasferi'mento** *sm* transfer; (*trasloco*) removal, move.

**trasfe'rire** *vt* to transfer; ~**rsi** *vr* to move; **tras'ferta** *sf* transfer; (*indennità*) travelling expenses *pl*; (*SPORT*) away game.

**trasfigu'rare** *vt* to transfigure.

**trasfor'mare** *vt* to transform, change.

**trasfusi'one** *sf* (*MED*) transfusion.

**trasgre'dire** *vt* to disobey, contravene.

**tras'lato, a** *ag* metaphorical, figurative.

**traslo'care** *vt* to move, transfer; ~**rsi** *vr* to move; **tras'loco, chi** *sm* removal.

**tras'messo, a** *pp di* trasmettere.

**tras'mettere** *vt* (*passare*): ~ **qc a qn** to pass sth on to sb; (*mandare*) to send; (*TECN, TEL, MED*) to transmit; (*TV, RADIO*) to broadcast; **trasmetti'tore** *sm* transmitter; **trasmissi'one** *sf* (*gen, FISICA, TECN*) transmission; (*passaggio*) transmis-

sion, passing on; (*TV, RADIO*) broadcast; **trasmit'tente** *sf* transmitting *o* broadcasting station.

**traso'gnato, a** [trasoɲ'ɲato] *ag* dreamy.

**traspa'rente** *ag* transparent.

**traspa'rire** *vi* to show (through).

**traspi'rare** *vi* to perspire; (*fig*) to come to light, leak out; **traspirazi'one** *sf* perspiration.

**traspor'tare** *vt* to carry, move; (*merce*) to transport, convey; **lasciarsi** ~ (**da qc**) (*fig*) to let o.s. be carried away (by sth); **tras'porto** *sm* transport.

**trastul'lare** *vt* to amuse; ~**rsi** *vr* to amuse o.s.

**trasu'dare** *vi* (*filtrare*) to ooze; (*sudare*) to sweat // *vt* to ooze with.

**trasver'sale** *ag* transverse, cross(-); running at right angles.

**trasvo'lare** *vt* to fly over.

**'tratta** *sf* (*ECON*) draft; (*di persone*): **la** ~ **delle bianche** the white slave trade.

**tratta'mento** *sm* treatment; (*servizio*) service.

**trat'tare** *vt* (*gen*) to treat; (*commerciare*) to deal in; (*svolgere: argomento*) to discuss, deal with; (*negoziare*) to negotiate // *vi*: ~ **di** to deal with; ~ **con** (*persona*) to deal with; **si tratta di** ... it's about ...; **tratta'tive** *sfpl* negotiations; **trat'tato** *sm* (*testo*) treatise; (*accordo*) treaty; **trattazi'one** *sf* treatment.

**tratteggi'are** [tratted'dʒare] *vt* (*disegnare: a tratti*) to sketch, outline; (*: col tratteggio*) to hatch.

**tratte'nere** *vt* (*far rimanere: persona*) to detain; (*intrattenere: ospiti*) to entertain; (*tenere, frenare, reprimere*) to hold back, keep back; (*astenersi dal consegnare*) to hold, keep; (*detrarre: somma*) to deduct; ~**rsi** *vr* (*astenersi*) to restrain o.s., stop o.s.; (*soffermarsi*) to stay, remain.

**tratteni'mento** *sm* entertainment;

(festa) party.

**tratte'nuta** sf deduction.

**trat'tino** sm dash; (in parole composte) hyphen.

'**tratto, a** pp di **trarre** // sm (di penna, matita) stroke; (parte) part, piece; (di strada) stretch; (di mare, cielo) expanse; (di tempo) period (of time); ~i smpl (caratteristiche) features; (modo di fare) ways, manners; **a un ~, d'un ~** suddenly.

**trat'tore** sm tractor.

**tratto'ria** sf restaurant.

'**trauma, i** sm trauma; **trau'matico, a, ci, che** ag traumatic.

**tra'vaglio** [tra'vaλλo] sm (angoscia) pain, suffering; (MED) pains pl; ~ **di parto** labour pains.

**trava'sare** vt to decant.

'**trave** sf beam.

**tra'versa** sf (trave) crosspiece; (via) sidestreet; (FERR) sleeper (Brit), (railroad) tie (US); (CALCIO) crossbar.

**traver'sare** vt to cross; **traver'sata** sf crossing; (AER) flight, trip.

**traver'sie** sfpl mishaps, misfortunes.

**traver'sina** sf (FERR) sleeper (Brit), (railroad) tie (US).

**tra'verso, a** ag oblique; **di ~ ag** askew // av sideways; **andare di ~** (cibo) to go down the wrong way; **guardare di ~** to look askance at.

**travesti'mento** sm disguise.

**traves'tire** vt to disguise; ~**rsi** vr to disguise o.s.

**travi'are** vt (fig) to lead astray.

**travi'sare** vt (fig) to distort, misrepresent.

**tra'volgere** [tra'vɔldʒere] vt to sweep away, carry away; (fig) to overwhelm; **tra'volto, a** pp di **travolgere**.

**tre** num three.

**trebbi'are** vt to thresh.

'**treccia, ce** ['trettʃa] sf plait, braid.

**tre'cento** [tre'tʃɛnto] num three hundred // sm: **il T~** the fourteenth century.

'**tredici** ['treditʃi] num thirteen.

'**tregua** sf truce; (fig) respite.

**tre'mare** vi: ~ **di** (freddo etc) to shiver o tremble with; (paura, rabbia) to shake o tremble with.

**tre'mendo, a** ag terrible, awful.

**tre'mila** num three thousand.

**'tremito** sm trembling q; shaking q; shivering q.

**tremo'lare** vi to tremble; (luce) to flicker; (foglie) to quiver.

**tre'more** sm tremor.

'**treno** sm train; ~ **di gomme** set of tyres (Brit) o tires (US); ~ **merci** goods (Brit) o freight train; ~ **viaggiatori** passenger train.

'**trenta** num thirty; **tren'tesimo, a** num thirtieth; **tren'tina** sf: **una trentina (di)** thirty or so, about thirty.

'**trepido, a** ag anxious.

**treppi'ede** sm tripod; (CUC) trivet.

'**tresca, sche** sf (fig) intrigue; (: relazione amorosa) affair.

'**trespolo** sm trestle.

**tri'angolo** sm triangle.

**tribù** sf inv tribe.

**tri'buna** sf (podio) platform; (in aule etc) gallery; (di stadio) stand.

**tribu'nale** sm court.

**tribu'tare** vt to bestow.

**tri'buto** sm tax; (fig) tribute.

**tri'checo, chi** [tri'kɛko] sm (ZOOL) walrus.

**tri'ciclo** [tri'tʃiklo] sm tricycle.

**trico'lore** ag three-coloured // sm tricolour; (bandiera italiana) Italian flag.

**tri'dente** sm trident.

**tri'foglio** [tri'fɔλλo] sm clover.

'**triglia** [triλλa] sf red mullet.

**tril'lare** vi (MUS) to trill.

**tri'mestre** sm period of three months; (INS) term, quarter (US); (COMM) quarter.

'**trina** sf lace.

**trin'cea** [trin'tʃɛa] sf trench; **trince'rare** vt to entrench.

**trinci'are** [trin'tʃare] vt to cut up.

**trion'fare** vi to triumph, win; ~ **su** to triumph over, overcome; **tri'onfo**

*sm* triumph.

**tripli'care** *vt* to triple.

**'triplice** ['triplitʃe] *ag* triple; **in ~ copia** in triplicate.

**'triplo, a** *ag* triple; treble // *sm*: **il ~ (di)** three times as much (as); **la spesa è ~a** it costs three times as much.

**'tripode** *sm* tripod.

**'trippa** *sf* (CUC) tripe.

**'triste** *ag* sad; (*luogo*) dreary, gloomy; **tris'tezza** *sf* sadness; gloominess.

**trita'carne** *sm inv* mincer, grinder (US).

**tri'tare** *vt* to mince, grind (US).

**'trito, a** *ag* (*tritato*) minced, ground (US); **~ e ritrito** (*fig*) trite, hackneyed.

**'trittico, ci** *sm* (ARTE) triptych.

**trivel'lare** *vt* to drill.

**trivi'ale** *ag* vulgar, low.

**tro'feo** *sm* trophy.

**'trogolo** *sm* (*per maiali*) trough.

**'tromba** *sf* (MUS) trumpet; (AUT) horn; **~ d'aria** whirlwind; **~ delle scale** stairwell.

**trom'bone** *sm* trombone.

**trom'bosi** *sf* thrombosis.

**tron'care** *vt* to cut off; (*spezzare*) to break off.

**'tronco, a, chi, che** *ag* cut off; broken off; (LING) truncated; (*fig*) cut short // *sm* (BOT, ANAT) trunk; (*fig: tratto*) section; (: *pezzo: di lancia*) stump; **licenziare qn in ~** to fire sb on the spot.

**troneggi'are** [troned'dʒare] *vi:* **~ (su)** to tower (over).

**'tronfio, a** *ag* conceited.

**'trono** *sm* throne.

**tropi'cale** *ag* tropical.

**'tropico, ci** *sm* tropic; **~ci** *smpl* tropics.

PAROLA CHIAVE

**'troppo, a ♦** *det* (*in eccesso: quantità*) too much; (: *numero*) too many; **c'era ~a gente** there were too many people; **fa ~ caldo** it's too

hot

**♦** *pronome* (*in eccesso: quantità*) too much; (: *numero*) too many; **ne hai messo ~** you've put in too much; **meglio ~i che pochi** better too many than too few

**♦** *av* (*eccessivamente: con ag, av*) too; (: *con vb*) too much; **~ amaro/tardi** too bitter/late; **lavora ~** he works too much; **di ~** too much; too many; **qualche tazza di ~** a few cups too many; **3000 lire di ~** 3000 lire too much; **essere di ~** to be in the way.

**'trota** *sf* trout.

**trot'tare** *vi* to trot; **trotterel'lare** *vi* to trot along; (*bambino*) to toddle; **'trotto** *sm* trot.

**'trottola** *sf* spinning top.

**tro'vare** *vt* to find; (*giudicare*): **trovo che** I find *o* think that; **~rsi** *vr* (*reciproco: incontrarsi*) to meet; (*essere, stare*) to be; (*arrivare, capitare*) to find o.s.; **andare a ~ qn** to go and see sb; **~ qn colpevole** to find sb guilty; **~rsi bene** (*in un luogo, con qn*) to get on well; **tro'vata** *sf* good idea.

**truc'care** *vt* (*falsare*) to fake; (*attore etc*) to make up; (*travestire*) to disguise; (SPORT) to fix; (AUT) to soup up; **~rsi** *vr* to make up (one's face); **trucca'tore, 'trice** *smf* (CINEMA, TEATRO) make-up artist.

**'trucco, chi** *sm* trick; (*cosmesi*) make-up.

**'truce** ['trutʃe] *ag* fierce.

**truci'dare** [trutʃi'dare] *vt* to slaughter.

**'truciolo** ['trutʃolo] *sm* shaving.

**'truffa** *sf* fraud, swindle; **truf'fare** *vt* to swindle, cheat.

**'truppa** *sf* troop.

**tu** *pronome* you; **~ stesso(a)** you yourself; **dare del ~ a qn** to address sb as "tu".

**'tua** *vedi* **tuo.**

**'tuba** *sf* (MUS) tuba; (*cappello*) top hat.

**tu'bare** *vi* to coo.

**tuba'tura** *sf*, **tubazi'one** [tubat-'tsjone] *sf* piping *q*, pipes *pl*.

**tu'betto** *sm* tube.

**'tubo** *sm* tube; pipe; ~ **digerente** (*ANAT*) alimentary canal, digestive tract; ~ **di scappamento** (*AUT*) exhaust pipe.

**'tue** *vedi* **tuo**.

**tuf'fare** *vt* to plunge, dip; ~**rsi** *vr* to plunge, dive; **'tuffo** *sm* dive; (*breve bagno*) dip.

**tu'gurio** *sm* hovel.

**tuli'pano** *sm* tulip.

**tume'farsi** *vr* (*MED*) to swell.

**'tumido, a** *ag* swollen.

**tu'more** *sm* (*MED*) tumour.

**tu'multo** *sm* uproar, commotion; (*sommossa*) riot; (*agitazione*) turmoil; **tumultu'oso, a** *ag* rowdy, unruly; (*fig*) turbulent, stormy.

**'tunica, che** *sf* tunic.

**Tuni'sia** *sf*: **la** ~ Tunisia.

**'tuo, 'tua, tu'oi, 'tue** *det*: **il** ~, **la tua** *etc* your // *pronome*: **il** ~, **la tua** *etc* yours.

**tuo'nare** *vi* to thunder; **tuona** it is thundering, there's some thunder.

**tu'ono** *sm* thunder.

**tu'orlo** *sm* yolk.

**tu'racciolo** [tu'rattʃolo] *sm* cap, top; (*di sughero*) cork.

**tu'rare** *vt* to stop, plug; (*con sughero*) to cork; ~**rsi il naso** to hold one's nose.

**turba'mento** *sm* disturbance; (*di animo*) anxiety, agitation.

**tur'bante** *sm* turban.

**tur'bare** *vt* to disturb, trouble.

**turbi'nare** *vi* to whirl.

**'turbine** *sm* whirlwind; ~ **di neve** swirl of snow; ~ **di polvere/sabbia** dust/sandstorm.

**turbo'lento, a** *ag* turbulent; (*ragazzo*) boisterous, unruly; **turbo'lenza** [turbo'lɛntsa] *sf* turbulence.

**tur'chese** [tur'kese] *sf* turquoise.

**Tur'chia** [tur'kia] *sf*: **la** ~ Turkey.

**tur'chino, a** [tur'kino] *ag* deep blue.

**'turco, a, chi, che** *ag* Turkish // *smf* Turk/Turkish woman // *sm* (*LING*) Turkish; **parlare** ~ (*fig*) to talk double-dutch.

**tu'rismo** *sm* tourism; tourist industry; **tu'rista, i, e** *smf* tourist; **tu'ristico, a, ci, che** *ag* tourist *cpd*.

**'turno** *sm* turn; (*di lavoro*) shift; **di** ~ (*soldato, medico, custode*) on duty; **a** ~ (*rispondere*) in turn; (*lavorare*) in shifts; **fare a** ~ **a fare qc** to take turns to do sth; **è il suo** ~ it's your (*o* his *etc*) turn.

**'turpe** *ag* filthy, vile; **turpi'loquio** *sm* obscene language.

**'tuta** *sf* overalls *pl*; (*SPORT*) track-suit.

**tu'tela** *sf* (*DIR*: *di minore*) guardianship; (: *protezione*) protection; (*difesa*) defence; **tute'lare** *vt* to protect, defend.

**tu'tore, 'trice** *smf* (*DIR*) guardian.

**tutta'via** *cong* nevertheless, yet.

---

**PAROLA CHIAVE**

**'tutto, a** ♦ *det* **1** (*intero*) all; ~ **il latte** all the milk; ~**a la notte** all night, the whole night; ~ **il libro** the whole book; ~**a una bottiglia** a whole bottle

**2** (*pl, collettivo*) all; every; ~**i i libri** all the books; ~**e le notti** every night; ~**i i venerdì** every Friday; ~**i gli uomini** all the men; (*collettivo*) all men; ~**i e due** both *o* each of us (*o* them *o* you); ~**i e cinque** all five of us (*o* them *o* you)

**3** (*completamente*): **era** ~**a sporca** she was all dirty; **tremava** ~ he was trembling all over; **è** ~**a sua madre** she's just *o* exactly like her mother

**4: a tutt'oggi** so far, up till now; **a** ~**a velocità** at full *o* top speed

♦ *pronome* **1** (*ogni cosa*) everything, all; (*qualsiasi cosa*) anything; **ha mangiato** ~ he's eaten everything; ~ **considerato** all things considered; **in** ~: **10.000 lire in** ~ 10.000 lire in all; **in** ~ **eravamo 50** there were 50

of us in all
**2: ~i(e)** (ognuno) all, everybody;
**vengono ~i** they are all coming,
everybody's coming; **~i quanti** all
and sundry

◆ av (completamente) entirely,
quite; **è ~ il contrario** it's quite o
exactly the opposite; **tutt'al più:**
**saranno stati tutt'al più una**
**cinquantina** there were about fifty of
them at (the very) most; **tutt'al più**
**possiamo prendere un treno** if the
worst comes to the worst we can take
a train; **tutt'altro** on the contrary; **è**
**tutt'altro che felice** he's anything
but happy; **tutt'a un tratto** suddenly

◆ sm: **il ~** the whole lot, all of it.

**tutto'fare** ag inv: **domestica ~**
general maid; **ragazzo ~** office boy
// sm/f inv handyman/woman.

**tutt'tora** av still.

# U

**ubbidi'ente** ag obedient; **ubbi-**
**di'enza** sf obedience.

**ubbi'dire** vi to obey; **~ a** to obey;
(sog: veicolo, macchina) to respond
to.

**ubiquità** sf: **non ho il dono dell'~**
I can't be everywhere at once.

**ubria'care** vt: **~ qn** to get sb
drunk; (sog: alcool) to make sb
drunk; (fig) to make sb's head spin o
reel; **~rsi** vr to get drunk; **~rsi di**
(fig) to become intoxicated with.

**ubri'aco, a, chi, che** ag, sm/f
drunk.

**uccelli'era** [uttʃel'ljera] sf aviary.

**uccel'lino** [uttʃel'lino] sm baby bird,
chick.

**uc'cello** [ut'tʃɛllo] sm bird.

**uc'cidere** [ut'tʃidere] vt to kill; **~rsi**
vr (suicidarsi) to kill o.s.; (perdere
la vita) to be killed; **uccisi'one** sf
killing; **ucci'so, a** pp di **uccidere**;
**ucci'sore, uccidi'trice** sm/f killer.

**udi'enza** [u'djɛntsa] sf audience;

(DIR) hearing; **dare ~ (a)** to grant
an audience (to).

**u'dire** vt to hear; **udi'tivo, a** ag
auditory; **u'dito** sm (sense of) hearing; **udi'tore, 'trice** sm/f listener;
(INS) unregistered student (attending
lectures); **udi'torio** sm (persone)
audience.

**uffa** escl tut!

**uffici'ale** [uffi'tʃale] ag official // sm
(AMM) official, officer; (MIL) officer;
**~ di stato civile** registrar.

**uf'ficio** [uf'fitʃo] sm (gen) office;
(dovere) duty; (mansione) task,
function, job; (agenzia) agency, bureau; (REL) service; **d'~** ag office
cpd; official // av officially; **~ di**
**collocamento** employment office; **~**
**oggetti smarriti** lost property office
(Brit), lost and found (US); **~ po-**
**stale** post office.

**uffici'oso, a** [uffi'tʃoso] ag unofficial.

**'ufo** av: **a ~** av free, for nothing.

**uggi'oso, a** [ud'dʒoso] ag tiresome;
(tempo) dull.

**uguagli'anza** [ugwaʎ'ʎantsa] sf
equality.

**uguagli'are** [ugwaʎ'ʎare] vt to make
equal; (essere uguale) to equal, be
equal to; (livellare) to level; **~rsi**
**o con qn** (paragonarsi) to compare
o.s. to sb.

**ugu'ale** ag equal; (identico)
identical, the same; (uniforme) level,
even // av: **costano ~** they cost the
same; **sono bravi ~** they're equally
good; **ugual'mente** av equally; (lo
stesso) all the same.

**'ulcera** ['ultʃera] sf ulcer.

**u'liva** etc = **oliva** etc.

**ulteri'ore** ag further.

**ulti'mare** vt to finish, complete.

**'ultimo, a** ag (finale) last;
(estremo) farthest, utmost; (recente:
notizia, moda) latest; (fig: sommo,
fondamentale) ultimate // sm/f last
(one); **fino all'~** to the last, until the
end; **da ~, in ~** in the end; **abitare**

all'~ piano to live on the top floor; per ~ (entrare, arrivare) last.

ulu'lare vi to howl; ulu'lato sm howling q; howl.

umanità sf humanity; umani'tario, a ag humanitarian.

u'mano, a ag human; (comprensivo) humane.

umbi'lico sm = ombelico.

umet'tare vt to dampen, moisten.

umidità sf dampness; humidity.

'umido, a ag damp; (mano, occhi) moist; (clima) humid // sm dampness, damp; carne in ~ stew.

'umile ag humble.

umili'are vt to humiliate; ~rsi vr to humble o.s.; umiliazi'one sf humiliation.

umiltà sf humility, humbleness.

u'more sm (disposizione d'animo) mood; (carattere) temper; di buon/cattivo ~ in a good/bad mood.

umo'rismo sm humour; avere il senso dell'~ to have a sense of humour; umo'rista, i, e smf humorist; umo'ristico, a, ci, che ag humorous, funny.

un, un', una vedi uno.

u'nanime ag unanimous; unanimità sf unanimity; all'unanimità unanimously.

unci'netto [untʃi'netto] sm crochet hook.

un'cino [un'tʃino] sm hook.

'undici ['unditʃi] num eleven.

'ungere ['undʒere] vt to grease, oil; (REL) to anoint; (fig) to flatter, butter up; ~rsi vr (sporcarsi) to get covered in grease; ~rsi con la crema to put on cream.

unghe'rese [unge'rese] ag, smf, sm Hungarian.

Unghe'ria [unge'ria] sf: l'~ Hungary.

'unghia ['ungja] sf (ANAT) nail; (di animale) claw; (di rapace) talon; (di cavallo) hoof; unghi'ata sf (graffio) scratch.

ungu'ento sm ointment.

'unico, a, ci, che ag (solo) only;

(ineguagliabile) unique; (singolo: binario) single; figlio(a) ~(a) only son/daughter, only child.

unifi'care vt to unite, unify; (sistemi) to standardize; unificazi'one sf uniting; unification; standardization.

uni'forme ag uniform; (superficie) even // sf (divisa) uniform.

unilate'rale ag one-sided; (DIR) unilateral.

uni'one sf union; (fig: concordia) unity, harmony; l'U~ Sovietica the Soviet Union.

u'nire vt to unite; (congiungere) to join, connect; (: ingredienti, colori) to combine; (in matrimonio) to unite, join together; ~rsi vr to unite; (in matrimonio) to be joined together; ~ qc a to unite sth with; to join o connect sth with; to combine sth with; ~rsi a (gruppo, società) to join.

unità sf inv (unione, concordia) unity; (MAT, MIL, COMM, di misura) unit; uni'tario, a ag unitary; prezzo unitario price per unit.

u'nito, a ag (paese) united; (amici, famiglia) close; in tinta ~a plain, self-coloured.

univer'sale ag universal; general.

università sf inv university; universi'tario, a ag university cpd // smf (studente) university student; (insegnante) academic, university lecturer.

uni'verso sm universe.

┌─────────────────────┐
│ PAROLA CHIAVE       │
└─────────────────────┘

'uno, a (dav sm un + C, V, uno + s impura, gn, pn, ps, x, z; dav sf un' + V, una + C) ◆ articolo indefinito 1 a; (dav vocale) an; un bambino a child; ~a strada a street; ~ zingaro a gypsy

2 (intensivo): ho avuto ~a paura! you had such a fright!

◆ pronome 1 one; prendine ~ take one (of them); l'~ o l'altro either (of them); l'~ e l'altro both (either (of them); aiutarsi l'un l'altro to help one another o each other; **sono entrati l'~ dopo l'altro** they came in one after the other

**2** (*un tale*) someone, somebody

**3** (*con valore impersonale*) one, you; **se ~ vuole** if one wants, if you want

♦ *num* one; **~a mela e due pere** one apple and two pears; **~ più ~ fa due** one plus one equals two, one and one are two

♦ *sf*: **è l'~a** it's one (o'clock).

**'unto, a** *pp* di **ungere** // *ag* greasy, oily // *sm* grease; **untu'oso, a** *ag* greasy, oily.

**u'omo,** *pl* **u'omini** *sm* man; **da ~** (*abito, scarpe*) men's, for men; **~ d'affari** businessman; **~ di paglia** stooge; **~ rana** frogman.

**u'opo** *sm*: **all'~** if necessary.

**u'ovo,** *pl*(*f*) **u'ova** *sm* egg; **~ affogato** poached egg; **~ bazzotto/sodo** soft-/hard-boiled egg; **~ alla coque** boiled egg; **~ di Pasqua** Easter egg; **uova strapazzate** scrambled eggs.

**ura'gano** *sm* hurricane.

**urba'nistica** *sf* town planning.

**ur'bano, a** *ag* urban, city (*cpd*, town *cpd*; (*TEL*: *chiamata*) local; (*fig*) urbane.

**ur'gente** [ur'dʒɛnte] *ag* urgent; **ur'genza** *sf* urgency; **in caso d'urgenza** in (case of) an emergency; **d'urgenza** *ag* emergency // *av* urgently, as a matter of urgency.

**'urgere** ['urdʒere] *vi* to be urgent; to be needed urgently.

**u'rina** *sf* = **orina**.

**ur'lare** *vi* (*persona*) to scream, yell; (*animale, vento*) to howl // *vt* to scream, yell.

**'urlo,** *pl*(*m*) **'urli,** *pl*(*f*) **'urla** *sm* scream, yell; howl.

**'urna** *sf* urn; (*elettorale*) ballot-box; **andare alle ~e** to go to the polls.

**urrà** *escl* hurrah!

**U.R.S.S.** *abbr f*: **l'~** the USSR.

**ur'tare** *vt* to bump into, knock

against; (*fig*: *irritare*) to annoy // *vi*: **~ contro o in** to bump into, knock against, crash into; (*fig*: *imbattersi*) to come up against; **~rsi** *vr* (*reciproco*: *scontrarsi*) to collide; (: *fig*) to clash; (*irritarsi*) to get annoyed; **'urto** *sm* (*colpo*) knock, bump; (*scontro*) crash, collision; (*fig*) clash.

**U.S.A.** ['uza] *smpl*: **gli ~** the USA.

**u'sanza** [u'zantsa] *sf* custom; (*moda*) fashion.

**u'sare** *vt* to use, employ // *vi* (*servirsi*): **~ di** to use; (: *diritto*) to exercise; (*essere di moda*) to be fashionable; (*essere solito*): **~ fare** to be in the habit of doing, be accustomed to doing // *vb impersonale*: **qui usa così** it's the custom round here; **u'sato, a** *ag* used; (*consumato*) worn; (*di seconda mano*) used, second-hand // *sm* second-hand goods *pl*.

**usci'ere** [uʃ'ɛre] *sm* usher.

**'uscio** ['uʃʃo] *sm* door.

**u'scire** [uʃ'ʃire] *vi* (*gen*) to come out; (*partire, andare a passeggio, a uno spettacolo etc*) to go out; (*essere sorteggiato*: *numero*) to come up; **~ da** (*gen*) to leave; (*posto*) to go (o come) out of, leave; (*solco, vasca etc*) to come out of; (*muro*) to stick out of; (*competenza etc*) to be outside; (*infanzia, adolescenza*) to come out of; (*muro*) to stick out of; (*competenza etc*) to be outside; (*infanzia, adolescenza*) to come from; **~ da** o **di casa** to go out; (*fig*) to leave home; **~ in automobile** to go out in the car, go for a drive; **~ di strada** (*AUT*) to go off o leave the road.

**u'scita** [uʃ'ʃita] *sf* (*passaggio, varco*) exit, way out; (*per divertimento*) outing; (*ECON*: *somma*) expenditure; (*TEATRO*) entrance; (*fig*: *battuta*) witty remark; **~ di sicurezza** emergency exit.

**usi'gnolo** [uziɲ'ɲɔlo] *sm* nightingale.

**U.S.L.** [uzl] *sigla f* (= *unità sanitaria locale*) local health centre.

**'uso** *sm* (*utilizzazione*) use; (*esercizio*) practice; (*abitudine*) custom; **a ~ di** for (the use of); **d'~** (corrente) in use; **fuori ~** out of use.

**usti'one** sf burn.

**usu'ale** ag common, everyday.

**u'sura** sf usury; (logoramento) wear (and tear).

**uten'sile** sm tool, implement; **~i da cucina** kitchen utensils.

**u'tente** smf user.

**'utero** sm uterus.

**'utile** ag useful // sm (vantaggio) advantage, benefit; (ECON: profitto) profit; **utilità** sf usefulness q; use; (vantaggio) benefit; **utili'tario, a** ag utilitarian // sf (AUT) economy car.

**utiliz'zare** [utilid'dzare] vt to use, make use of, utilize.

**'uva** sf grapes pl; **~ passa** raisins pl; **~ spina** gooseberry.

# V

**v.** abbr (= vedi) v.

**va** vb vedi **andare**.

**va'cante** ag vacant.

**va'canza** [va'kantsa] sf (l'essere vacante) vacancy; (riposo, ferie) holiday(s pl) (Brit), vacation (US); (giorno di permesso) day off, holiday; **~e** sfpl (periodo di ferie) holidays (Brit), vacation sg (US); **essere/andare in ~** to be/go on holiday o vacation; **~e estive** summer holiday(s) o vacation.

**'vacca, che** sf cow.

**vacci'nare** [vattʃi'nare] vt to vaccinate.

**vacil'lare** [vatʃil'lare] vi to sway, wobble; (luce) to flicker; (fig: memoria, coraggio) to be failing, falter.

**'vacuo, a** ag (fig) empty, vacuous // sm vacuum.

**'vado** vb vedi **andare**.

**vaga'bondo, a** sm/f tramp, vagrant; (fannullone) idler, loafer.

**va'gare** vi to wander.

**vagheggi'are** [vaged'dʒare] vt to long for, dream of.

**va'gina** [va'dʒina] sf vagina.

**va'gire** [va'dʒire] vi to whimper.

**'vaglia** ['vaʎʎa] sm inv money order; **~ postale** postal order.

**vagli'are** [vaʎ'ʎare] vt to sift; (fig) to weigh up; **'vaglio** sm sieve.

**'vago, a, ghi, ghe** ag vague.

**va'gone** sm (FERR: per passeggeri) coach; (: per merci) truck, wagon; **~ letto** sleeper, sleeping car; **~ ristorante** dining o restaurant car.

**'vai** vb vedi **andare**.

**va'iolo** sm smallpox.

**va'langa, ghe** sf avalanche.

**va'lente** ag able, talented.

**va'lere** vi (avere forza, potenza) to have influence; (essere valido) to be valid; (avere vigore, autorità) to hold, apply; (essere capace: poeta, studente) to be good, be able // vt (prezzo, sforzo) to be worth; (corrispondere) to correspond to; (procurare): **~ qc a qn** to earn sb sth; **~rsi di** to make use of, take advantage of; **far ~** (autorità etc) to assert; **vale a dire** that is to say; **~ la pena** to be worth the effort o worth it.

**va'levole** ag valid.

**vali'care** vt to cross.

**'valico, chi** sm (passo) pass.

**'valido, a** ag valid; (rimedio) effective; (aiuto) real; (persona) worthwhile.

**valige'ria** [validʒe'ria] sf leather goods pl; leather goods factory; leather goods shop.

**va'ligia, gie** o **ge** [va'lidʒa] sf (suit)case; **fare le ~gie** to pack (up); **~ diplomatica** diplomatic bag.

**val'lata** sf valley.

**'valle** sf valley; **a ~** (di fiume) downstream; **scendere a ~** to go downhill.

**val'letto** sm valet.

**va'lore** sm (gen) value; (merito) merit, worth; (coraggio) valour, courage; (COMM: titolo) security; **~i** smpl (oggetti preziosi) valuables.

**valoriz'zare** [valorid'dzare] *vt* (*terreno*) to develop; (*fig*) to make the most of.

**'valso, a** *pp di* **valere.**

**va'luta** *sf* currency, money; (*BANCA*): ~ 15 gennaio interest to run from January 15th.

**valu'tare** *vt* (*casa, gioiello, fig*) to value; (*stabilire: peso, entrate, fig*) to estimate; **valutazi'one** *sf* valuation; estimate.

**'valvola** *sf* (*TECN, ANAT*) valve; (*ELETTR*) fuse.

**'valzer** ['valtser] *sm inv* waltz.

**vam'pata** *sf* (*di fiamma*) blaze; (*di calore*) blast; (: *al viso*) flush.

**vam'piro** *sm* vampire.

**vanda'lismo** *sm* vandalism.

**'vandalo** *sm* vandal.

**vaneggi'are** [vaned'dʒare] *vi* to rave.

**'vanga, ghe** *sf* spade; **van'gare** *vt* to dig.

**van'gelo** [van'dʒɛlo] *sm* gospel.

**va'niglia** [va'niʎʎa] *sf* vanilla.

**vanità** *sf* vanity; (*di promessa*) emptiness; (*di sforzo*) futility; **vani'toso, a** *ag* vain, conceited.

**'vanno** *vb vedi* **andare.**

**'vano, a** *ag* vain // *sm* (*spazio*) space; (*apertura*) opening; (*stanza*) room.

**van'taggio** [van'taddʒo] *sm* advantage; **essere/portarsi in ~** (*SPORT*) to be in/take the lead; **vantaggi'oso, a** *ag* advantageous; favourable.

**van'tare** *vt* to praise, speak highly of; ~**rsi** *vr*: ~**rsi** (**di/di aver fatto**) to boast o brag (about/about having done); **vante'ria** *sf* boasting; **'vanto** *sm* boasting; (*merito*) virtue, merit; (*gloria*) pride.

**'vanvera** *sf*: **a** ~ haphazardly; **parlare a** ~ to talk nonsense.

**va'pore** *sm* vapour; (*anche:* ~ **acqueo**) steam; (*nave*) steamer; **a** ~ (*turbina etc*) steam *cpd*; **al** ~ (*CUC*) steamed; **vapo'retto** *sm* steamer; **vapori'era** *sf* (*FERR*)

steam engine; **vaporiz'zare** *vt* to vaporize; **vapo'roso, a** *ag* (*tessuto*) filmy; (*capelli*) soft and full.

**va'rare** *vt* (*NAUT, fig*) to launch; (*DIR*) to pass.

**var'care** *vt* to cross.

**'varco, chi** *sm* passage; **aprirsi un** ~ **tra la folla** to push one's way through the crowd.

**vari'abile** *ag* variable; (*tempo, umore*) changeable, variable // *sf* (*MAT*) variable.

**vari'are** *vt, vi* to vary; ~ **di opinione** to change one's mind; **variazi'one** *sf* variation; change.

**va'rice** [va'ritʃe] *sf* varicose vein.

**vari'cella** [vari'tʃɛlla] *sf* chickenpox.

**vari'coso, a** *ag* varicose.

**varie'gato, a** *ag* variegated.

**varietà** *sf inv* variety // *sm inv* variety show.

**'vario, a** *ag* varied; (*parecchi: col sostantivo al pl*) various; (*mutevole: umore*) changeable; **vario'pinto, a** *ag* multicoloured.

**'varo** *sm* (*NAUT, fig*) launch; (*di leggi*) passing.

**va'saio** *sm* potter.

**'vasca, sche** *sf* basin; (*anche:* ~ **da bagno**) bathtub, bath.

**va'scello** [vaʃ'ʃello] *sm* (*NAUT*) vessel, ship.

**vase'lina** *sf* vaseline.

**vasel'lame** *sm* (*stoviglie*) crockery; (: *di porcellana*) china; ~ **d'oro/d'argento** gold/silver plate.

**'vaso** *sm* (*recipiente*) pot; (: *barattolo*) jar; (: *decorativo*) vase; (*ANAT*) vessel; ~ **da fiori** vase; (*per piante*) flowerpot.

**vas'soio** *sm* tray.

**'vasto, a** *ag* vast, immense.

**Vati'cano** *sm*: **il** ~ **the** Vatican.

**ve** *pronome, av vedi* **vi.**

**vecchi'aia** [vek'kjaja] *sf* old age.

**'vecchio, a** ['vekkjo] *ag* old // *sm/f* old man/woman; **i** ~**i** the old.

**'vece** ['vetʃe] *sf*: **in** ~ **di** in the place of, for; **fare le** ~**i di qn** to take sb's place.

**ve'dere** *vt*, *vi* to see; ~**rsi** *vr* to meet, see one another; **avere a che ~ con** to have something to do with; **far ~ qc a qn** to show sb sth; **farsi ~** to show o.s.; (*farsi vivo*) to show one's face; **vedi di non farlo** make sure *o* see you don't do it; **non (ci) si vede** (*è buio etc*) you can't see a thing; **non lo posso ~** (*fig*) I can't stand him.

**ve'detta** *sf* (*sentinella, posto*) look-out; (*NAUT*) patrol boat.

**'vedovo, a** *sm/f* widower/widow.

**ve'duta** *sf* view.

**vee'mente** *ag* vehement; violent.

**vege'tale** [vedʒe'tale] *ag, sm* vegetable.

**vegetari'ano, a** [vedʒeta'rjano] *ag, sm/f* vegetarian.

**'vegeto, a** ['vedʒeto] *ag* (*pianta*) thriving; (*persona*) strong, vigorous.

**'veglia** ['veʎʎa] *sf* wakefulness; (*sorveglianza*) watch; (*trattenimento*) evening gathering; **fare la ~ a un malato** to watch over a sick person.

**vegli'are** [veʎ'ʎare] *vi* to be awake; to stay *o* sit up; (*stare vigile*) to watch; to keep watch // *vt* (*malato, morto*) to watch over, sit up with.

**ve'icolo** *sm* vehicle; ~ **spaziale** spacecraft *inv.*

**'vela** *sf* (*NAUT: tela*) sail; (*sport*) sailing.

**ve'lare** *vt* to veil; ~**rsi** *vr* (*occhi, luna*) to mist over; (*voce*) to become husky; ~**rsi il viso** to cover one's face (with a veil); **ve'lato, a** *ag* veiled.

**veleggi'are** [veled'dʒare] *vi* to sail; (*AER*) to glide.

**ve'leno** *sm* poison; **vele'noso, a** *ag* poisonous.

**veli'ero** *sm* sailing ship.

**ve'lina** *sf* (*anche:* **carta ~:** *per imballare*) tissue paper; (: *per copie*) flimsy paper; (*copia*) carbon copy.

**ve'livolo** *sm* aircraft.

**velleità** *sf inv* vain ambition, vain desire.

**'vello** *sm* fleece.

**vel'luto** *sm* velvet; ~ **a coste** cord.

**'velo** *sm* veil; (*tessuto*) voile.

**ve'loce** [ve'lotʃe] *ag* fast, quick // *av* fast, quickly; **velo'cista, i, e** *sm/f* (*sport*) sprinter; **velocità** *sf* speed; **a forte velocità** at high speed; **velocità di crociera** cruising speed.

**ve'lodromo** *sm* velodrome.

**'vena** *sf* (*gen*) vein; (*filone*) vein, seam; (*fig: ispirazione*) inspiration; (: *umore*) mood; **essere in ~ di qc** to be in the mood for sth.

**ve'nale** *ag* (*prezzo, valore*) market *cpd*; (*fig*) venal; mercenary.

**ven'demmia** *sf* (*raccolta*) grape harvest; (*quantità d'uva*) grape crop, grapes *pl*; (*vino ottenuto*) vintage; **vendemmi'are** *vt* to harvest // *vi* to harvest the grapes.

**'vendere** *vt* to sell; **"vendesi"** "for sale".

**ven'detta** *sf* revenge.

**vendi'care** *vt* to avenge; ~**rsi** *vr*: ~**rsi (di)** to avenge o.s. (for); (*per rancore*) to take one's revenge (for); ~**rsi su qn** to revenge o.s. on sb; **vendica'tivo, a** *ag* vindictive.

**'vendita** *sf* sale; **la ~** (*attività*) selling; (*smercio*) sales *pl*; **in ~** on sale; ~ **all'asta** sale by auction; **vendi'tore** *sm* seller, vendor; (*gestore di negozio*) trader, dealer.

**ve'nefico, a, ci, che** *ag* poisonous.

**vene'rabile** *ag*, **vene'rando, a** *ag* venerable.

**vene'rare** *vt* to venerate.

**venerdì** *sm inv* Friday; **di** *o* **il ~ on** Fridays; **V~ Santo** Good Friday.

**ve'nereo, a** *ag* venereal.

**'veneto, a** *ag, sm/f* Venetian.

**Ve'nezia** [ve'nettsja] *sf* Venice; **venezi'ano, a** *ag, sm/f* Venetian.

**veni'ale** *ag* venial.

**ve'nire** *vi* to come; (*riuscire: dolce, fotografia*) to turn out; (*come ausiliare: essere*): **viene ammirato da tutti** he is admired by everyone;

~ da to come from; **quanto viene?** how much does it cost?; **far** ~ (*mandare a chiamare*) to send for; ~ **giù** to come down; ~ **meno** (*svenire*) to faint; **venir meno a qc** not to fulfil sth; ~ **su** to come up; ~ **a trovare qn** to come and see sb; ~ **via** to come away.

**ven'taglio** [ven'taʎʎo] sm fan.

**ven'tata** sf gust (of wind).

**ven'tenne** ag: **una ragazza** ~ a twenty-year-old girl, a girl of twenty.

**ven'tesimo, a** num twentieth.

**'venti** num twenty.

**venti'lare** vt (*stanza*) to air, ventilate; (*fig: idea, proposta*) to air; **ventila'tore** sm ventilator, fan.

**ven'tina** sf: **una** ~ (**di**) around twenty, twenty or so.

**venti'sette** num twenty-seven; **il** ~ (*giorno di paga*) (monthly) pay day.

**'vento** sm wind.

**'ventola** sf (AUT, TECN) fan.

**ven'tosa** sf (ZOOL) sucker; (*di gomma*) suction pad.

**ven'toso, a** ag windy.

**'ventre** sm stomach.

**ven'tura** sf: **andare alla** ~ to trust to luck; **soldato di** ~ mercenary.

**ven'turo, a** ag next, coming.

**ve'nuto, a** pp di **venire** // sf coming, arrival.

**vera'mente** av really.

**ver'bale** ag verbal // sm (*di riunione*) minutes pl.

**'verbo** sm (LING) verb; (*parola*) word; (REL): **il V**~ the Word.

**'verde** ag, sm green; **essere al** ~ to be broke; ~ **bottiglia/oliva** ag inv bottle/olive green.

**verde'rame** sm verdigris.

**ver'detto** sm verdict.

**ver'dura** sf vegetables pl.

**vere'condo, a** ag modest.

**'verga, ghe** sf rod.

**ver'gato a** ag (*foglio*) ruled.

**'vergine** ['verdʒine] sf virgin; (*dello zodiaco*) **V**~ Virgo // ag virgin; (*ragazza*): **essere** ~ to be a virgin.

**ver'gogna** [ver'ɡoɲɲa] sf shame;

(*timidezza*) shyness, embarrassment; **vergo'gnarsi** vr: **vergognarsi (di)** to be o feel ashamed (of); to be shy (about), be embarrassed (about); **vergo'gnoso, a** ag ashamed; (*timido*) shy, embarrassed; (*causa di vergogna: azione*) shameful.

**ve'rifica, che** sf checking q, check.

**verifi'care** vt (*controllare*) to check; (*confermare*) to confirm, bear out.

**verità** sf inv truth.

**veriti'ero, a** ag (*che dice la verità*) truthful; (*conforme a verità*) true.

**'verme** sm worm.

**vermi'celli** [vermi't ʃelli] smpl vermicelli sg.

**ver'miglio** [ver'miʎʎo] sm vermilion, scarlet.

**'vermut** sm inv vermouth.

**ver'nice** [ver'nit ʃe] sf (*colorazione*) paint; (*trasparente*) varnish; (*pelle*) patent leather; "~ **fresca**" "wet paint"; **vernici'are** vt to paint; to varnish.

**'vero, a** ag (*veridico: fatti, testimonianza*) true; (*autentico*) real // sm (*verità*) truth; (*realtà*) real life; **un** ~ **e proprio delinquente** a real criminal, an out and out criminal.

**vero'simile** ag likely, probable.

**ver'ruca, che** sf wart.

**versa'mento** sm (*pagamento*) payment; (*deposito di denaro*) deposit.

**ver'sante** sm slopes pl, side.

**ver'sare** vt (*fare uscire: vino, farina*) to pour (out); (*spargere: lacrime, sangue*) to shed; (*rovesciare*) to spill; (ECON) to pay; (: *depositare*) to deposit, pay in; ~**rsi** vr (*rovesciarsi*) to spill; (*fiume, folla*): ~**rsi (in)** to pour (into).

**versa'tile** ag versatile.

**ver'setto** sm (REL) verse.

**versi'one** sf version; (*traduzione*) translation.

**'verso** sm (*di poesia*) verse, line; (*di animale, uccello, venditore ambulante*) cry; (*direzione*) direction; (*modo*) way; (*di foglio di carta*) verso;

(di moneta) reverse; ~i smpl (poesia) verse sg; **non c'è ~ di persuaderlo** there's no way of persuading him, he can't be persuaded // prep (in direzione di) toward(s); (nei pressi di) near, around (about); (in senso temporale) around, around (about); (nei confronti di) for; ~ **di me** towards me; ~ **sera** towards evening.

**verti'cale** ag, sf vertical.

**'vertice** ['vertitʃe] sm summit, top; (MAT) vertex; **conferenza al ~** (POL) summit conference.

**ver'tigine** [ver'tidʒine] sf dizziness q; dizzy spell; (MED) vertigo; **avere le ~i** to feel dizzy; **vertigi'noso, a** ag (altezza) dizzy; (fig) breathtakingly high (o deep etc).

**ve'scica** (**ve**[veʃ'ʃika] sf (ANAT) bladder; (MED) blister.

**'vescovo** sm bishop.

**'vespa** sf wasp.

**'vespro** sm (REL) vespers pl.

**ves'sillo** sm standard; (bandiera) flag.

**ves'taglia** [ves'taʎʎa] sf dressing gown.

**'veste** sf garment; (rivestimento) covering; (qualità, facoltà) capacity; ~**i** sfpl clothes, clothing sg; **in ~ ufficiale** (fig) in an official capacity; **in ~ di** in the guise of, as; **ve-sti'ario** sm wardrobe, clothes pl.

**ves'tibolo** sm (entrance) hall.

**ves'tire** vt (bambino, malato) to dress; (avere indosso) to have on, wear; ~**rsi** vr to dress, get dressed; **ves'tito, a** ag dressed // sm garment; (da donna) dress; (da uomo) suit; **vestiti** smpl clothes; **vestito di bianco** dressed in white.

**Ve'suvio** sm: **il ~** Vesuvius.

**vete'rano** a ag, smf veteran.

**veteri'nario, a** ag veterinary // sm veterinary surgeon (Brit), veterinarian (US), vet // sf veterinary medicine.

**'veto** sm inv veto.

**ve'traio** sm glassmaker; glazier.

**ve'trato, a** ag (porta, finestra)

glazed; (che contiene vetro) glass cpd // sf glass door (o window); (di chiesa) stained glass window.

**vetre'ria** sf (stabilimento) glass-works sg; (oggetti di vetro) glass-ware.

**ve'trina** sf (di negozio) (shop) window; (armadio) display cabinet; **vetri'nista, i, e** smf window dresser.

**vetri'olo** sm vitriol.

**'vetro** sm glass; (per finestra, porta) pane (of glass).

**'vetta** sf peak, summit, top.

**vet'tore** sm (MAT, FISICA) vector; (chi trasporta) carrier.

**vetto'vaglie** [vetto'vaʎʎe] sfpl supplies.

**vet'tura** sf (carrozza) carriage; (FERR) carriage (Brit), car (US); (auto) car (Brit), automobile (US).

**vezzeggi'are** [vettsed'dʒare] vt to fondle, caress; **vezzeggia'tivo** sm (LING) term of endearment.

**'vezzo** ['vettso] sm habit; ~**i** smpl (smancerie) affected ways; (leggiadria) charms; **vez'zoso, a** ag (grazioso) charming, pretty; (lezioso) affected.

**vi**, dav lo, la, li, le, ne diventa **ve** pronome (oggetto) you; (complemento di termine) (to) you; (riflessivo) yourselves; (reciproco) each other // av (li) there; (qui) here; (per questo/quel luogo) through here/there; ~ **è/sono** there is/are.

**'via** sf (gen) way; (strada) street; (sentiero, pista) path, track; (AMM: procedimento) channels pl // prep (passando per) via, by way of // sf away // escl go away!; (suvvia) come on!; (SPORT) go! // sm (SPORT) starting signal; **in ~ di guarigione** on the road to recovery; **per ~ di** (a causa di) because of, on account of; **in o per ~** on the way; **per ~ aerea** by air; (lettere) by airmail; **andare/essere ~** to go/be away; ~ **che** (a mano a mano) as; **dare il ~** (SPORT) to give the starting signal; **dare il ~ a** (*fig*) to start; **V~ lattea** (*ASTR*) Milky Way; **~ di mezzo** middle course; **in ~ provvisoria** provisionally.

**viabilità** *sf* (*di strada*) practicability; (*rete stradale*) roads *pl*, road network.

**via'dotto** *sm* viaduct.

**viaggi'are** [viad'dʒare] *vi* to travel; **viaggia'tore, 'trice** *ag* travelling // *sm* traveller; (*passeggero*) passenger.

**vi'aggio** ['vjaddʒo] *sm* travel(ling); (*tragitto*) journey, trip; **buon ~!** have a good trip!; **~ di nozze** honeymoon.

**vi'ale** *sm* avenue.

**via'vai** *sm* coming and going, bustle.

**vi'brare** *vi* to vibrate; (*agitarsi*): **~ (di)** to quiver (with).

**vi'cario** *sm* (*apostolico etc*) vicar.

**'vice** [vitʃe] *smf* deputy // *prefisso*: **~'console** *sm* vice-consul; **~diret'tore** *sm* assistant manager.

**vi'cenda** [vi'tʃenda] *sf* event; **a ~** in turn; **vicen'devole** *ag* mutual, reciprocal.

**vice'versa** [vitʃe'versa] *av* vice versa; **da Roma a Pisa e ~** from Rome to Pisa and back.

**vici'nanza** [vitʃi'nantsa] *sf* nearness, closeness; **~e** *sfpl* neighbourhood, vicinity.

**vici'nato** [vitʃi'nato] *sm* neighbourhood; (*vicini*) neighbours *pl*.

**vi'cino, a** [vi'tʃino] *ag* (*gen*) near; (*nello spazio*) near, nearby; (*accanto*) next; (*nel tempo*) near, close at hand // *smf* neighbour // *av* near, close; **da ~** (*guardare*) close up; (*esaminare, seguire*) closely; (*conoscere*) well, intimately; **~ a** *prep* near (to), close to; (*accanto a*) beside; **~ di casa** neighbour.

**'vicolo** *sm* alley; **~ cieco** blind alley.

**'video** *sm inv* (*TV: schermo*) screen; **~cas'setta** *sf* videocassette; **~regi-stra'tore** *sm* video (recorder).

**vie'tare** *vt* to forbid; (*AMM*) to prohibit; **~ a qn di fare** to forbid sb to do; to prohibit sb from doing; "**vietato fumare/l'ingresso**" "no smoking/admittance".

**Viet'nam** *sm*: **il ~** Vietnam; **vietna'mita, i, e** *ag*, *smf*, *sm* Vietnamese *inv*.

**vi'gente** [vi'dʒente] *ag* in force.

**vigi'lante** [vidʒi'lante] *ag* vigilant, watchful.

**vigi'lare** [vidʒi'lare] *vt* to watch over, keep an eye on; **~ che** to make sure that, see to it that.

**'vigile** ['vidʒile] *ag* watchful // *sm* (*anche: ~ urbano*) policeman (*in towns*); **~ del fuoco** fireman.

**vi'gilia** [vi'dʒilja] *sf* (*giorno antecedente*) eve; **la ~ di Natale** Christmas Eve.

**vi'gliacco, a, chi, che** [viʎ'ʎakko] *ag* cowardly // *smf* coward.

**'vigna** ['viɲɲa] *sf*, **vi'gneto** [viɲ'ɲeto] *sm* vineyard.

**vi'gnetta** [viɲ'ɲetta] *sf* cartoon.

**vi'gore** *sm* vigour; (*DIR*): **essere/entrare in ~** to be in/come into force; **vigo'roso, a** *ag* vigorous.

**'vile** *ag* (*spregevole*) low, mean, base; (*codardo*) cowardly.

**vili'pendio** *sm* contempt, scorn; public insult.

**'villa** *sf* villa.

**vil'laggio** [vil'laddʒo] *sm* village.

**villa'nia** *sf* rudeness, lack of manners; **fare** (*o* **dire**) **una ~ a qn** to be rude to sb.

**vil'lano, a** *ag* rude, ill-mannered // *sm* boor.

**villeggia'tura** [villeddʒa'tura] *sf* holiday(s *pl*) (*Brit*), vacation (*US*).

**vil'lino** *sm* small house (with a garden), cottage.

**vil'loso, a** *ag* hairy.

**viltà** *sf* cowardice *q*; cowardly act.

**'vimine** *sm* wicker; **mobili di ~i** wicker furniture *sg*.

**'vincere** ['vintʃere] *vt* (*in guerra, al gioco, a una gara*) to defeat, beat; (*premio, guerra, partita*) to win; (*fig*) to overcome, conquer // *vi* to win; ~ **qn in bellezza** to be better-looking than sb; **'vincita** sf win; (denaro vinto) winnings pl; **vinci'tore** sm winner; (MIL) victor.

**vinco'lare** vt to bind; (COMM: denaro) to tie up; **'vincolo** sm (fig) bond, tie; (DIR: servitù) obligation.

**vi'nicolo, a** ag wine cpd.

**'vino** sm wine; ~ **bianco/rosso** white/red wine.

**'vinto, a** pp di **vincere**.

**vi'ola** sf (BOT) violet; (MUS) viola // ag, sm inv (colore) purple.

**vio'lare** vt (chiesa) to desecrate, violate; (giuramento, legge) to violate.

**violen'tare** vt to use violence on; (donna) to rape.

**vio'lento, a** ag violent; **vio'lenza** sf violence; **violenza carnale** rape.

**vio'letto, a** ag, sm (colore) violet // sf (BOT) violet.

**violi'nista, i, e** sm/f violinist.

**vio'lino** sm violin.

**violon'cello** sm/f violin cello.

**vi'ottolo** sm path, track.

**'vipera** sf viper, adder.

**vi'raggio** [vi'raddʒo] sm (NAUT, AER) turn; (FOT) toning.

**vi'rare** vt (NAUT) to haul (in), heave (in) // vi (NAUT, AER) to turn; (FOT) to tone; ~ **di bordo** (NAUT) to tack.

**'virgola** sf (LING) comma; (MAT) point; (fig) **virgo'lette** sfpl inverted commas, quotation marks.

**vi'rile** ag (proprio dell'uomo) masculine; (non puerile, da uomo) manly, virile.

**virtù** sf inv virtue; **in** o **per** ~ **di** by virtue of, by.

**virtu'ale** ag virtual.

**virtu'oso, a** ag virtuous // sm/f (MUS etc) virtuoso.

**'virus** sm inv virus.

**'viscere** ['viʃʃere] sm (ANAT) internal organ // sfpl (di animale) entrails pl; (fig) bowels pl.

**'vischio** ['viskjo] sm (BOT) mistletoe; (pania) birdlime; **vischi'oso, a**

**'viscido, a** ['viʃʃido] ag slimy.

**vi'sibile** ag visible.

**visi'bilio** sm: **andare in** ~ to go into raptures.

**visibilità** sf visibility.

**visi'era** sf (di elmo) visor; (di berretto) peak.

**visi'one** sf vision; **prendere** ~ **di qc** to examine sth, look sth over; **prima/seconda** ~ (CINEMA) first/second showing.

**'visita** sf visit; (MED) visit, call; (: esame) examination; **visi'tare** vt to visit; (MED) to visit, call on; (: esaminare) to examine; **visita'tore, 'trice** sm/f visitor.

**vi'sivo, a** ag visual.

**'viso** sm face.

**vi'sone** sm mink.

**'vispo, a** ag quick, lively.

**vis'suto, a** pp di **vivere** // ag (aria, modo di fare) experienced.

**'vista** sf (facoltà) (eye)sight; (fatto di vedere): **la** ~ **di** the sight of; (veduta) view; **sparare a** ~ to shoot on sight; **in** ~ in sight; **perdere qc di** ~ to lose sight of sb; (fig) to lose touch with sb; **a** ~ **d'occhio** as far as the eye can see; (fig) before one's very eyes; **far** ~ **di fare** to pretend to do.

**'visto, a** pp di **vedere** // sm visa; ~ **che** cong seeing (that).

**vis'toso, a** ag gaudy, garish; (ingente) considerable.

**visu'ale** ag visual; **visualizza'tore** sm (INFORM) visual display unit, VDU.

**'vita** sf life; (ANAT) waist; **a** ~ for life.

**vi'tale** ag vital; **vita'lizio, a** ag life cpd // sm life annuity.

**vita'mina** sf vitamin.

**'vite** sf (BOT) vine; (TECN) screw.

**vi'tello** sm (ZOOL) calf; (carne) veal; (pelle) calfskin.

**vi'ticcio** [vi'tittʃo] sm (BOT) tendril.

**viticol'tore** sm wine grower; **viticol'tura** sf wine growing.

**'vitreo, a** ag vitreous; (occhio, sguardo) glassy.

**'vittima** sf victim.

**'vitto** sm food; (in un albergo etc) board; ~ e alloggio board and lodging.

**vit'toria** sf victory.

**'viva** escl: ~ il re! long live the king!

**vi'vace** [vi'vatfe] ag (vivo, animato) lively; (: mente) lively, sharp; (colore) bright; **vivacità** sf vivacity; liveliness; brightness.

**vi'vaio** sm (di pesci) hatchery; (AGR) nursery.

**vi'vanda** sf food; (piatto) dish.

**vi'vente** ag living, alive; **i ~i** the living.

**'vivere** vi to 'live // vt to live; (passare: brutto momento) to live through, go through; (sentire: gioie, pene di qn) to share // sm life; (anche: modo di ~) way of life; ~ smpl food sg, provisions; ~ di to live on.

**'vivido, a** ag (colore) vivid, bright.

**'vivo, a** ag (vivente) alive, living; (: animale) live; (fig) lively; (: colore) bright, brilliant; **i ~i** the living; ~ e vegeto hale and hearty; **farsi ~** to show one's face; to be heard from; **ritrarre dal ~** to paint from life; **pungere qn nel ~** (fig) to cut sb to the quick.

**vizi'are** [vit'tsjare] vt (bambino) to spoil; (corrompere moralmente) to corrupt; **vizi'ato, a** ag spoilt; (aria, acqua) polluted.

**'vizio** [vittsjo] sm (morale) vice; (cattiva abitudine) bad habit; (imperfezione) flaw, defect; (errore) fault, mistake; **vizi'oso, a** ag depraved; defective; (inesatto) incorrect, wrong.

**vocabo'lario** sm (dizionario) dictionary; (lessico) vocabulary.

**vo'cabolo** sm word.

**vo'cale** ag vocal // sf vowel.

**vocazi'one** [vokat'tsjone] sf vocation; (fig) natural bent.

**'voce** ['votfe] sf voice; (diceria) rumour; (di un elenco, in bilancio) item; aver ~ in capitolo (fig) to have a say in the matter.

**voci'are** [vo'tfare] vi to shout, yell.

**'voga** sf (NAUT) rowing; (usanza): essere in ~ to be in fashion o in vogue.

**vo'gare** vi to row.

**'voglia** ['voʎʎa] sf desire, wish; (macchia) birthmark; aver ~ di qc/di fare to feel like sth/like doing; (più forte) to want sth/to do.

**'voi** pronome you; **voi'altri** pronome you.

**vo'lano** sm (SPORT) shuttlecock; (TECN) flywheel.

**vo'lante** ag flying // sm (steering) wheel.

**volan'tino** sm leaflet.

**vo'lare** vi (uccello, aereo, fig) to fly; (cappello) to blow away o off, fly away o off; ~ via to fly away o off.

**vo'latile** ag (CHIM) volatile // sm (ZOOL) bird.

**volente'roso, a** ag willing.

**volenti'eri** av willingly; "~" "with pleasure", "I'd be glad to".

PAROLA CHIAVE

**vo'lere** ♦ sm will, wish(es); contro il ~ di against the wishes of; per ~ di qn in obedience to sb's will o wishes

♦ vt 1 (esigere, desiderare) to want; voler fare/che qn faccia to want to do/sb to do; volete del caffè? would you like o do you want some coffee?; vorrei questo/fare I would o I'd like this/to do; come vuoi as you like; senza ~ (inavvertitamente) without meaning to, unintentionally

2 (consentire): vogliate attendere, per piacere please wait; vogliamo andare? shall we go?; vuole essere così gentile da ...? would you be so kind as to ...?; non ha voluto ricevermi he wouldn't see me

3: volerci (essere necessario:

*materiale, attenzione*) to need; (: *tempo*) to take; **quanta farina ci vuole per questa torta?** how much flour do you need for this cake?; **ci vuole un'ora per arrivare a Venezia** it takes an hour to get to Venice

**4: voler bene a qn** (*amore*) to love sb; (*affetto*) to be fond of sb, like sb very much; **voler male a qn** to dislike sb; **volerne a qn** to bear sb a grudge; **voler dire** to mean.

**vol'gare** *ag* vulgar; **volgariz'zare** *vt* to popularize.

**'volgere** ['vɔldʒere] *vt* to turn // *vi* to turn; (*tendere*): ~ **a: il tempo volge al brutto** the weather is breaking; **un rosso che volge al viola** a red verging on purple; ~**rsi** *vr* to turn; ~ **al peggio** to take a turn for the worse; ~ **al termine** to draw to an end.

**'volgo** *sm* common people.

**voli'era** *sf* aviary.

**voli'tivo, a** *ag* strong-willed.

**'volo** *sm* flight; **al** ~: **colpire qc al** ~ to hit sth as it flies past; **capire al** ~ to understand straight away.

**volontà** *sf* will; **a** ~ (*mangiare, bere*) as much as one likes; **buona/cattiva** ~ goodwill/lack of goodwill.

**volon'tario, a** *ag* voluntary // *sm* (*MIL*) volunteer.

**'volpe** *sf* fox.

**'volta** *sf* (*momento, circostanza*) time; (*turno, giro*) turn; (*curva*) turn, bend; (*ARCHIT*) vault; (*direzione*): **partire alla** ~ **di** to set off for; **a mia** (*o* **tua** *etc*) ~ in turn; **una** ~ once; **una** ~ **sola** only once; **due** ~ **e** twice; **una cosa per** ~ one thing at a time; **una** ~ **per tutte** once and for all; **a** ~**e** at times, sometimes; **una** ~ **che** (*temporale*) once; (*causale*) since; **3** ~**e 4 3** times 4.

**volta'faccia** [vɔlta'fattʃa] *sm inv* (*fig*) volte-face.

**vol'taggio** [vol'taddʒo] *sm*

(*ELETTR*) voltage.

**vol'tare** *vt* to turn; (*girare: moneta*) to turn over; (*rigirare*) to turn round // *vi* to turn; ~**rsi** *vr* to turn; to turn over; to turn round.

**volteggi'are** [volted'dʒare] *vi* (*volare*) to circle; (*in equitazione*) to do trick riding; (*in ginnastica*) to vault; to perform acrobatics.

**'volto, a** *pp di* **volgere** // *sm* face.

**vo'lubile** *ag* changeable, fickle.

**vo'lume** *sm* volume; **volumi'noso, a** *ag* voluminous, bulky.

**voluttà** *sf* sensual pleasure *o* delight; **voluttu'oso, a** *ag* voluptuous.

**vomi'tare** *vt, vi* to vomit; **'vomito** *sm* vomiting *q*; vomit.

**'vongola** *sf* clam.

**vo'race** [vo'ratʃe] *ag* voracious, greedy.

**vo'ragine** [vo'radʒine] *sf* abyss, chasm.

**'vortice** ['vɔrtitʃe] *sm* whirlwind; whirlpool; (*fig*) whirl.

**'vostro, a** *det*: **il(la)** ~**(a)** *etc* your *// pronome*: **il(la)** ~**(a)** *etc* yours.

**vo'tante** *sm/f* voter.

**vo'tare** *vi* to vote // *vt* (*sottoporre a votazione*) to take a vote on; (*approvare*) to vote for; (*REL*): ~ **qc a** to dedicate sth to; **votazi'one** *sf* vote, voting; **votazioni** *sfpl* (*POL*) votes; (*INS*) marks.

**'voto** *sm* (*POL*) vote; (*INS*) mark; (*REL*) vow; (: *offerta*) votive offering; **aver** ~ **i belli/brutti** (*INS*) to get good/bad marks.

**vs.** *abbr* (*COMM*) = **vostro.**

**vul'cano** *sm* volcano.

**vulne'rabile** *ag* vulnerable.

**vuo'tare** *vt,* ~**rsi** *vr* to empty.

**vu'oto, a** *ag* empty; (*fig: privo*): ~ **di** (*senso etc*) devoid of // *sm* empty space, gap; (*spazio in bianco*) blank; (*FISICA*) vacuum; (*fig: mancanza*) gap, void; **a mani** ~ **e** empty-handed; ~ **d'aria** air pocket; ~ **a rendere** returnable bottle.

# W X Y

**watt** [vat] *sm inv* watt.

**'weekend** ['wi:kend] *sm inv* weekend.

**'whisky** ['wiski] *sm inv* whisky.

**'xeres** [ˈksɛres] *sm inv* sherry.

**xero'copia** [kseroˈkɔpja] *sf* xerox ®, photocopy.

**xi'lofono** [ksiˈlɔfono] *sm* xylophone.

**yacht** [jɔt] *sm inv* yacht.

**'yoghurt** ['jɔgurt] *sm inv* yoghurt.

# Z

**zabai'one** [dzabaˈjone] *sm* dessert made of egg yolks, sugar and marsala.

**zaf'fata** [tsafˈfata] *sf* (*tanfo*) stench.

**zaffe'rano** [dzaffeˈrano] *sm* saffron.

**zaf'firo** [dzafˈfiro] *sm* sapphire.

**'zaino** [ˈdzaino] *sm* rucksack.

**'zampa** [ˈtsampa] *sf* (*di animale: gamba*) leg; (*: piede*) paw; a quattro ~e on all fours.

**zampil'lare** [tsampilˈlare] *vi* to gush, spurt; **zam'pillo** *sm* gush, spurt.

**zam'pogna** [tsamˈpoɲɲa] *sf* instrument similar to bagpipes.

**'zanna** [ˈtsanna] *sf* (*di elefante*) tusk; (*di carnivori*) fang.

**zan'zara** [dzanˈdzara] *sf* mosquito; **zanzari'era** *sf* mosquito net.

**'zappa** [ˈtsappa] *sf* hoe; **zap'pare** *vt* to hoe.

**zar, za'rina** [tsar, tsaˈrina] *sm/f* tsar/tsarina.

**'zattera** [ˈdzattera] *sf* raft.

**za'vorra** [dzaˈvorra] *sf* ballast.

**'zazzera** [ˈtsattsera] *sf* shock of hair.

**'zebra** [ˈdzebra] *sf* zebra; ~e *sfpl* (*AUT*) zebra crossing *sg* (*Brit*), crosswalk *sg* (*US*).

**'zecca, che** [ˈtsekka] *sf* (*ZOOL*) tick; (*officina di monete*) mint.

**'zelo** [ˈdzelo] *sm* zeal.

**'zenit** [ˈdzenit] *sm* zenith.

**'zenzero** [ˈdzendzero] *sm* ginger.

**'zeppa** [ˈtseppa] *sf* wedge.

**'zeppo, a** [ˈtseppo] *ag*: ~ di crammed o packed with.

**zer'bino** [dzerˈbino] *sm* doormat.

**'zero** [ˈdzɛro] *sm* zero, nought; vincere per tre a ~ (*SPORT*) to win three-nil.

**'zeta** [ˈdzɛta] *sm o f* zed, (the letter) z.

**'zia** [ˈtsia] *sf* aunt.

**zibel'lino** [dzibelˈlino] *sm* sable.

**'zigomo** [ˈdzigomo] *sm* cheekbone.

**zig'zag** [dzigˈdzag] *sm inv* zigzag; andare a ~ to zigzag.

**zim'bello** [dzimˈbello] *sm* (*oggetto di burle*) laughing-stock.

**'zinco** [ˈdzinko] *sm* zinc.

**'zingaro, a** [ˈdzingaro] *sm/f* gipsy.

**'zio** [ˈtsio] *pl* **'zii** *sm* uncle; zii *smpl* (*zio e zia*) uncle and aunt.

**zi'tella** [dziˈtella] *sf* spinster; (*peg*) old maid.

**'zitto, a** [ˈtsitto] *ag* quiet, silent; sta' ~! be quiet!

**ziz'zania** [dzidˈdzanja] *sf* (*fig*): gettare o seminare ~ to sow discord.

**'zoccolo** [ˈtsɔkkolo] *sm* (*calzatura*) clog; (*di cavallo etc*) hoof; (*basamento*) base; plinth.

**zo'diaco** [dzoˈdiako] *sm* zodiac.

**'zolfo** [ˈtsolfo] *sm* sulphur.

**'zolla** [ˈdzɔlla] *sf* clod (of earth).

**zol'letta** [dzolˈletta] *sf* sugar lump.

**'zona** [ˈdzɔna] *sf* zone, area; ~ di depressione (*METEOR*) trough of low pressure; ~ pedonale pedestrian precinct; ~ verde (*di abitato*) green area.

**'zonzo** [ˈdzondzo]: a ~ *av*: andare a ~ to wander about, stroll about.

**zoo** [ˈdzɔo] *sm inv* zoo.

**zoolo'gia** [dzooloˈdʒia] *sf* zoology.

**zoppi'care** [tsoppiˈkare] *vi* to limp; to be shaky, rickety.

**'zoppo, a** [ˈtsɔppo] *ag* lame; (*fig: mobile*) shaky, rickety.

**zoti'cone** [dzotiˈkone] *sm* lout.

**'zucca, che** [ˈtsukka] *sf* (*BOT*)

marrow; pumpkin.

**zucche'rare** [tsukke'rare] vt to put sugar in; **zucche'rato, a** ag sweet, sweetened.

**zuccheri'era** [tsukke'rjɛra] sf sugar bowl.

**zuccheri'ficio** [tsukkeri'fitʃo] sm sugar refinery.

**zucche'rino, a** [tsukke'rino] ag sugary, sweet.

**'zucchero** ['tsukkero] sm sugar.

**zuc'china** [tsuk'kina] sf, **zuc'chino** [tsuk'kino] sm courgette (Brit), zucchini (US).

**'zuffa** ['tsuffa] sf brawl.

**'zuppa** ['tsuppa] sf soup; (fig) mixture, muddle; ~ **inglese** (CUC) dessert made with sponge cake, custard and chocolate, ≈ trifle (Brit);

**zuppi'era** sf soup tureen.

**'zuppo, a** ['tsuppo] ag: ~ **(di)** drenched (with), soaked (with).

# ENGLISH - ITALIAN
# INGLESE - ITALIANO
## A

**A** [eɪ] n (MUS) la m; (AUT): ~ **road** ≈ strada statale.

---
### KEYWORD
---

**a** indefinite article (before vowel or silent h: **an**) [eɪ, ə æn, ən, n] **1** un (uno + s impure, gn, pn, ps, x, z), f una (un' + vowel); ~ **book** un libro; ~ **mirror** uno specchio; **an apple** una mela; **she's** ~ **doctor** è medico

**2** (instead of the number 'one') un(o), f una; ~ **year** ago un anno fa; ~ **hundred/thousand** etc pounds cento/mille etc sterline

**3** (in expressing ratios, prices etc) a, per; **3** ~ **day/week** 3 al giorno/alla settimana; **10 km an hour** 10 km all'ora; **£5** ~ **person** 5 sterline a persona or per persona.

**A.A.** n abbr (= Alcoholics Anonymous) AA; (Brit: = Automobile Association) ≈ A.C.I. m.
**A.A.A.** n abbr (US: = American Automobile Association) ≈ A.C.I. m.
**aback** [əˈbæk] ad: **to be taken** ~ essere sbalordito(a).
**abandon** [əˈbændən] vt abbandonare // n abbandono; **with** ~ sfrenatamente, spensieratamente.
**abashed** [əˈbæʃt] a imbarazzato(a).
**abate** [əˈbeɪt] vi calmarsi.
**abattoir** [ˈæbətwɑ:ˈ] n (Brit) mattatoio.
**abbey** [ˈæbɪ] n abbazia, badia.
**abbot** [ˈæbət] n abate m.
**abbreviation** [əbriːvɪˈeɪʃən] n abbreviazione f.
**abdicate** [ˈæbdɪkeɪt] vt abdicare a // vi abdicare.
**abdomen** [ˈæbdəmən] n addome m.
**abduct** [æbˈdʌkt] vt rapire.
**aberration** [æbəˈreɪʃən] n aberrazione f.

**abet** [əˈbɛt] vt see **aid**.
**abeyance** [əˈbeɪəns] n: **in** ~ (law) in disuso; (matter) in sospeso.
**abide** [əˈbaɪd] vt: **I can't** ~ **it/him** non lo posso soffrire or sopportare; **to** ~ **by** vt fus conformarsi a.
**ability** [əˈbɪlɪtɪ] n abilità f inv.
**abject** [ˈæbdʒɛkt] a (poverty) abietto(a); (apology) umiliante.
**ablaze** [əˈbleɪz] a in fiamme.
**able** [ˈeɪbl] a capace; **to be** ~ **to do** sth essere capace di fare qc, poter fare qc; **ably** ad abilmente.
**abnormal** [æbˈnɔːməl] a anormale.
**aboard** [əˈbɔːd] ad a bordo // prep a bordo di.
**abode** [əˈbəud] n: **of no fixed** ~ senza fissa dimora.
**abolish** [əˈbɒlɪʃ] vt abolire.
**abominable** [əˈbɒmɪnəbl] a abominevole.
**aborigine** [æbəˈrɪdʒɪnɪ] n aborigeno/a.
**abort** [əˈbɔːt] vt abortire; **~ion** [əˈbɔːʃən] n aborto; **to have an** ~ion abortire; **~ive** a abortivo(a).
**abound** [əˈbaund] vi abbondare; **to** ~ **in** abbondare di.

---
### KEYWORD
---

**about** [əˈbaut] ◆ ad **1** (approximately) circa, quasi; ~ **a hundred/thousand** etc un centinaio/migliaio etc, circa cento/mille etc; **it takes** ~ **10 hours** ci vogliono circa 10 ore; **at** ~ **2 o'clock** verso le 2; **I've just** ~ **finished** ho quasi finito

**2** (referring to place) qua e là, in giro; **to leave things lying** ~ lasciare delle cose in giro; **to run** ~ correre qua e là; **to walk** ~ camminare

**3**: **to be** ~ **to do** sth stare per fare qc

◆ *prep* **1** (*relating to*) su, di; a book ~ London un libro su Londra; what is it ~? di che si tratta?; (*book, film etc*) di cosa tratta?; we talked ~ it ne abbiamo parlato; what *or* how ~ doing this? che ne dici di fare questo?
**2** (*referring to place*): to walk ~ the town camminare per la città ; her clothes were scattered ~ the room i suoi vestiti erano sparsi *or* in giro per tutta la stanza.

**about-face** [ə'baut'feɪs] *n*, **about-turn** [ə'baut'tə:n] *n* dietro front *m inv*.

**above** [ə'bʌv] *ad*, *prep* sopra; mentioned ~ suddetto; ~ all soprattutto; ~board *a* aperto(a); onesto(a).

**abrasive** [ə'breɪzɪv] *a* abrasivo(a); (*fig*) caustico(a).

**abreast** [ə'brɛst] *ad* di fianco; to keep ~ of tenersi aggiornato su.

**abridge** [ə'brɪdʒ] *vt* ridurre.

**abroad** [ə'brɔ:d] *ad* all'estero.

**abrupt** [ə'brʌpt] *a* (*steep*) erto(a); (*sudden*) improvviso(a); (*gruff, blunt*) brusco(a).

**abscess** ['æbsɪs] *n* ascesso.

**abscond** [əb'skɔnd] *vi* scappare.

**absence** ['æbsəns] *n* assenza.

**absent** ['æbsənt] *a* assente; ~ee [-'ti:] *n* assente *m/f*; ~-minded *a* distratto(a).

**absolute** ['æbsəlu:t] *a* assoluto(a); ~ly [-'lu:tlɪ] *ad* assolutamente.

**absolve** [əb'zɔlv] *vt*: to ~ sb (from) (*sin*) assolvere qn (da) ; (*oath*) sciogliere qn (da).

**absorb** [əb'zɔ:b] *vt* assorbire; to be ~ed in a book essere immerso in un libro; ~ent cotton *n* (*US*) cotone *m* idrofilo.

**absorption** [əb'sɔ:pʃən] *n* assorbimento.

**abstain** [əb'steɪn] *vi*: to ~ (from) astenersi (da).

**abstemious** [əb'sti:mɪəs] *a* astemio(a).

**abstract** ['æbstrækt] *a* astratto(a).

**absurd** [əb'sə:d] *a* assurdo(a).

**abuse** *n* [ə'bju:s] abuso; (*insults*) ingiurie *fpl* // *vt* [ə'bju:z] abusare di; **abusive** *a* ingiurioso(a).

**abysmal** [ə'bɪzməl] *a* spaventoso(a).

**abyss** [ə'bɪs] *n* abisso.

**AC** *abbr* (= *alternating current*) c.a.

**academic** [ækə'dɛmɪk] *a* accademico(a); (*pej: issue*) puramente formale // *n* universitario/a.

**academy** [ə'kædəmɪ] *n* (*learned body*) accademia; (*school*) scuola privata; ~ of music conservatorio.

**accelerate** [æk'sɛləreɪt] *vt*, *vi* accelerare; **accelerator** *n* acceleratore *m*.

**accent** ['æksɛnt] *n* accento.

**accept** [ək'sɛpt] *vt* accettare; ~**ance** *n* accettazione *f*.

**access** ['æksɛs] *n* accesso; ~**ible** [æk'sɛsəbl] *a* accessibile(a).

**accessory** [æk'sɛsərɪ] *n* accessorio; toilet accessories *npl* articoli *mpl* da toilette.

**accident** ['æksɪdənt] *n* incidente *m*; (*chance*) caso; by ~ per caso; ~**al** [-'dɛntl] *a* accidentale; ~**ally** [-'dɛntəlɪ] *ad* per caso; ~**-prone** *a*: he's very ~-prone è un vero passaguai.

**acclaim** [ə'kleɪm] *vt* acclamare // *n* acclamazione *f*.

**accommodate** [ə'kɔmədeɪt] *vt* alloggiare; (*oblige, help*) favorire.

**accommodating** [ə'kɔmədeɪtɪŋ] *a* compiacente.

**accommodation** [əkɔmə'deɪʃən] *n* (*US*: ~s) alloggio.

**accompany** [ə'kʌmpənɪ] *vt* accompagnare.

**accomplice** [ə'kʌmplɪs] *n* complice *m/f*.

**accomplish** [ə'kʌmplɪʃ] *vt* compiere; ~**ed** *a* (*person*) esperto(a); ~**ment** *n* compimento; realizzazione *f*; ~**ments** *npl* doti *fpl*.

**accord** [ə'kɔ:d] *n* accordo // *vt* accordare; of his own ~ di propria

iniziativa; ~**ance** n: in ~ance with in conformità con; ~**ing to** prep secondo; ~**ingly** ad in conformità.
**accordion** [ə'kɔːdɪən] n fisarmonica.
**accost** [ə'kɒst] vt avvicinare.
**account** [ə'kaunt] n (COMM) conto; (report) descrizione f; ~**s** npl (COMM) conti mpl; of little ~ di poca importanza; **on** ~ in acconto; **on no** ~ per nessun motivo; **on** ~ **of** a causa di; **to take into** ~, **take** ~ **of** tener conto di; **to** ~ **for** spiegare; giustificare; ~**able** a responsabile.
**accountancy** [ə'kauntənsɪ] n ragioneria.
**accountant** [ə'kauntənt] n ragioniere/a.
**account number** n numero di conto.
**accumulate** [ə'kjuːmjuleɪt] vt accumulare // vi accumularsi.
**accuracy** ['ækjurəsɪ] n precisione f.
**accurate** ['ækjurɪt] a preciso(a); ~**ly** ad precisamente.
**accusation** [ækjuːˈzeɪʃən] n accusa.
**accuse** [ə'kjuːz] vt accusare; ~**d** n accusato/a.
**accustom** [ə'kʌstəm] vt abituare; ~**ed** a (usual) abituale; ~**ed to** abituato(a) a.
**ace** [eɪs] n asso.
**ache** [eɪk] n male m, dolore m // vi (be sore) far male, dolere; **my head** ~**s** mi fa male la testa.
**achieve** [ə'tʃiːv] vt (aim) raggiungere; (victory, success) ottenere; (task) compiere; ~**ment** n compimento; successo.
**acid** ['æsɪd] a acido(a) // n acido; ~ **rain** n pioggia acida.
**acknowledge** [ək'nɒlɪdʒ] vt (letter: also: ~ **receipt of**) confermare la ricevuta di; (fact) riconoscere; ~**ment** n conferma; riconoscimento.
**acne** ['æknɪ] n acne f.
**acorn** ['eɪkɔːn] n ghianda.
**acoustic** [ə'kuːstɪk] a acustico(a); ~**s** n, npl acustica.
**acquaint** [ə'kweɪnt] vt: **to** ~ **sb with sth** far sapere qc a qn; **to be**

~**ed with** (person) conoscere; ~**ance** n conoscenza; (person) conoscente m/f.
**acquiesce** [ækwɪ'es] vi: **to** ~ (**in**) acconsentire (a).
**acquire** [ə'kwaɪə*] vt acquistare.
**acquisition** [ækwɪ'zɪʃən] n acquisto.
**acquit** [ə'kwɪt] vt assolvere; **to** ~ **o.s. well** comportarsi bene; ~**tal** n assoluzione f.
**acre** ['eɪkə*] n acro (= 4047 m2).
**acrid** ['ækrɪd] a acre; pungente.
**acrimonious** [ækrɪ'məunɪəs] a astioso/a.
**acrobat** ['ækrəbæt] n acrobata m/f.
**across** [ə'krɒs] prep (on the other side) dall'altra parte di; (crosswise) attraverso // ad dall'altra parte; in larghezza; **to walk** ~ (**the road**) attraversare (la strada); ~ **from** di fronte a.
**acrylic** [ə'krɪlɪk] a acrilico(a) // n acrilico.
**act** [ækt] n atto; (in music-hall etc) numero; (LAW) decreto // vi agire; (THEATRE) recitare; (pretend) fingere // vt (part) recitare; **to** ~ **as** agire da; ~**ing** a che fa le funzioni di // n (of actor) recitazione f; (activity): **to do some** ~**ing** fare del teatro (or del cinema).
**action** ['ækʃən] n azione f; (MIL) combattimento; (LAW) processo; **out of** ~ fuori combattimento; fuori servizio; **to take** ~ agire; ~ **replay** n (TV) replay m inv.
**activate** ['æktɪveɪt] vt (mechanism) fare funzionare; (CHEM, PHYSICS) rendere attivo/a.
**active** ['æktɪv] a attivo(a); ~**ly** ad (participate) attivamente; (discourage, dislike) vivamente.
**activity** [æk'tɪvɪtɪ] n attività f inv.
**actor** ['æktə*] n attore m.
**actress** ['æktrɪs] n attrice f.
**actual** ['æktjuəl] a reale, vero(a); ~**ly** ad veramente; (even) addirittura.
**acumen** ['ækjumən] n acume m.
**acute** [ə'kjuːt] a acuto(a); (mind,

*person)* perspicace.

**ad** [æd] *n abbr* = **advertisement**.

**A.D.** *ad abbr* (= *Anno Domini*) d.C.

**adamant** ['ædəmənt] *a* irremovibile.

**adapt** [ə'dæpt] *vt* adattare // *vi*: **to ~** (**to**) adattarsi (a); **~able** *a* (*device*) adattabile; (*person*) che sa adattarsi; **~er** or **~or** *n* (*ELEC*) adattatore *m*.

**add** [æd] *vt* aggiungere; (*figures*: *also*: **to ~ up**) addizionare // *vi*: **to ~** (*increase*) aumentare; **it doesn't ~ up** (*fig*) non quadra, non ha senso.

**adder** ['ædə*] *n* vipera.

**addict** ['ædɪkt] *n* tossicomane *m/f*; (*fig*) fanatico/a; **~ed** [ə'dɪktɪd] *a*: **to be ~ed to** (*drink etc*) essere dedito a; (*fig*: football etc) essere tifoso di; **~ion** [ə'dɪkʃən] *n* (*MED*) tossicomania; **~ive** [ə'dɪktɪv] *a* che dà assuefazione.

**addition** [ə'dɪʃən] *n* addizione *f*; **in ~** inoltre; **in ~ to** oltre; **~al** *a* supplementare.

**additive** ['ædɪtɪv] *n* additivo.

**address** [ə'drɛs] *n* indirizzo; (*talk*) discorso // *vt* indirizzare; (*speak to*) fare un discorso a.

**adept** ['ædɛpt] *a*: **~ at** esperto(a) in.

**adequate** ['ædɪkwɪt] *a* adeguato(a); sufficiente.

**adhere** [əd'hɪə*] *vi*: **to ~ to** aderire a; (*fig*: rule, decision) seguire.

**adhesion** [əd'hiːʒən] *n* adesione *f*.

**adhesive** [əd'hiːzɪv] *a* adesivo // *n* adesivo; **~ tape** *n* (*Brit*: for parcels etc) nastro adesivo; (*US*: *MED*) cerotto adesivo.

**adjective** ['ædʒɛktɪv] *n* aggettivo.

**adjoining** [ə'dʒɔɪnɪŋ] *a* accanto *inv*, adiacente.

**adjourn** [ə'dʒəːn] *vt* rimandare // *vi* essere aggiornato(a); (*go*) spostarsi.

**adjudicate** [ə'dʒuːdɪkeɪt] *vt* (*contest*) giudicare; (*claim*) decidere su.

**adjust** [ə'dʒʌst] *vt* aggiustare; (*COMM*) rettificare // *vi*: **to ~** (**to**) adattarsi a; **~able** *a* regolabile.

**ad-lib** [æd'lɪb] *vt*, *vi* improvvisare //

*ad*: **ad lib** a piacere, a volontà.

**administer** [əd'mɪnɪstə*] *vt* amministrare; (*justice*) somministrare.

**administration** [ədmɪnɪs'treɪʃən] *n* amministrazione *f*.

**administrative** [əd'mɪnɪstrətɪv] *a* amministrativo(a).

**admiral** ['ædmərəl] *n* ammiraglio; **A~ty** *n* (*Brit*: *also*: **A~ty Board**) Ministero della Marina.

**admiration** [ædmə'reɪʃən] *n* ammirazione *f*.

**admire** [əd'maɪə*] *vt* ammirare.

**admission** [əd'mɪʃən] *n* ammissione *f*; (*to exhibition, night club etc*) ingresso; (*confession*) confessione *f*.

**admit** [əd'mɪt] *vt* ammettere; far entrare; (*agree*) riconoscere; **to ~ to** riconoscere; **~tance** *n* ingresso; **~tedly** *ad* bisogna pur riconoscere (che).

**admonish** [əd'mɔnɪʃ] *vt* ammonire.

**ad nauseam** [æd'nɔːsɪæm] *ad* fino alla nausea, a non finire.

**ado** [ə'duː] *n*: **without (any) more ~** senza più indugi.

**adolescence** [ædəu'lɛsns] *n* adolescenza.

**adolescent** [ædəu'lɛsnt] *a*, *n* adolescente (*m/f*).

**adopt** [ə'dɔpt] *vt* adottare; **~ed** *a* adottivo(a); **~ion** [ə'dɔpʃən] *n* adozione *f*.

**adore** [ə'dɔː*] *vt* adorare.

**Adriatic (Sea)** [eɪdrɪ'ætɪk('siː)] *n* Adriatico.

**adrift** [ə'drɪft] *ad* alla deriva.

**adroit** [ə'drɔɪt] *a* abile, destro(a).

**adult** ['ædʌlt] *n* adulto/a.

**adultery** [ə'dʌltərɪ] *n* adulterio.

**advance** [əd'vɑːns] *n* avanzamento; (*money*) anticipo // *vt* avanzare; (*date, money*) anticipare // *vi* avanzare; **in ~** in anticipo; **~d** *a* avanzato(a); (*SCOL*: *studies*) superiore.

**advantage** [əd'vɑːntɪdʒ] *n* (*also* TENNIS) vantaggio; **to take ~ of** approfittarsi di.

**advent** ['ædvənt] *n* avvento; **A~**

Avvento.

**adventure** [əd'vɛntʃə*] n avventura.

**adverb** ['ædvə:b] n avverbio.

**adverse** ['ædvə:s] a avverso(a); ~ to contrario(a) a.

**advert** ['ædvə:t] n abbr (Brit) = **advertisement**.

**advertise** ['ædvətaɪz] vi (vt) fare pubblicità or réclame (a); fare un'inserzione (per vendere); to ~ for (staff) mettere un annuncio sul giornale per trovare.

**advertisement** [əd'və:tɪsmənt] n (COMM) réclame f inv, pubblicità f inv; (in classified ads) inserzione f.

**advertiser** ['ædvətaɪzə*] n (in newspaper etc) inserzionista m/f.

**advertising** ['ædvətaɪzɪŋ] n pubblicità.

**advice** [əd'vaɪs] n consigli mpl; (notification) avviso; **piece of** ~ consiglio; **to take legal** ~ consultare un avvocato.

**advisable** [əd'vaɪzəbl] a consigliabile.

**advise** [əd'vaɪz] vt consigliare; **to** ~ **sb of sth** informare qn di qc; **to** ~ **sb against sth/doing sth** sconsigliare qc a qn/a qn di fare qc; ~**dly** [-ədlɪ] ad (deliberately) di proposito; ~**r** n consigliere/a; **advisory** [-ərɪ] a consultivo(a).

**advocate** n ['ædvəkɪt] (upholder) sostenitore/trice; (LAW) avvocato (difensore) // vt ['ædvəkeɪt] propugnare; **to be an** ~ **of** essere a favore di.

**aerial** ['ɛərɪəl] n antenna // a aereo(a).

**aerobics** [ɛə'rəubɪks] n aerobica.

**aeroplane** ['ɛərəpleɪn] n (Brit) aeroplano.

**aerosol** ['ɛərəsɔl] n (Brit) aerosol m inv.

**aesthetic** [ɪs'θɛtɪk] a estetico(a).

**afar** [ə'fɑ:*] ad: **from** ~ da lontano.

**affair** [ə'fɛə*] n affare m; (also: love ~) relazione f amorosa.

**affect** [ə'fɛkt] vt toccare; (feign) fingere; ~**ed** a affettato(a).

**affection** [ə'fɛkʃən] n affezione f; ~**ate** a affettuoso(a).

**affirmation** [æfə'meɪʃən] n affermazione f.

**affix** [ə'fɪks] vt apporre; attaccare.

**afflict** [ə'flɪkt] vt affliggere.

**affluence** ['æfluəns] n abbondanza; opulenza.

**affluent** ['æfluənt] a abbondante; opulente; (person) ricco(a).

**afford** [ə'fɔ:d] vt permettersi; (provide) fornire.

**afield** [ə'fi:ld] ad: **far** ~ lontano.

**afloat** [ə'fləut] a, ad a galla.

**afoot** [ə'fut] ad: **there is something** ~ si sta preparando qualcosa.

**afraid** [ə'freɪd] a impaurito(a); **to be** ~ **of or to** aver paura di; **I am** ~ **that I'll be late** mi dispiace, ma farò tardi.

**afresh** [ə'frɛʃ] ad di nuovo.

**Africa** ['æfrɪkə] n Africa; ~**n** a, n africano(a).

**aft** [ɑ:ft] ad a poppa, verso poppa.

**after** ['ɑ:ftə*] prep, ad dopo // cj dopo che; **what/who are you** ~? che/chi cerca?; ~ **he left/having done** dopo che se ne fu andato/dopo aver fatto; ~ **all** dopo tutto; ~ **you!** dopo di lei!; ~**effects** npl conseguenze fpl; (of illness) postumi mpl; ~**life** n vita dell'al di là ; ~**math** n conseguenze fpl; **in the** ~**math of** nel periodo dopo; ~**noon** n pomeriggio; ~**s** n (col: dessert) dessert m inv; ~**sales service** n (Brit) servizio assistenza clienti; ~**shave (lotion)** n dopobarba m inv; ~**thought** n: **as an** ~**thought** come aggiunta; ~**wards** ad dopo.

**again** [ə'gɛn] ad di nuovo; **to begin/see** ~ ricominciare/rivedere; **not** ... ~ non ... più; ~ **and** ~ ripetutamente.

**against** [ə'gɛnst] prep contro; ~ **a blue background** su uno sfondo azzurro.

**age** [eɪdʒ] n età f inv // vt, vi invecchiare; **it's been** ~**s since** sono secoli che; **he is 20 years of** ~ ha

20 anni; **to come of** ~ diventare maggiorenne; **~d** 10 di 10 anni; **the ~d** ('eɪdʒɪd) gli anziani; ~ **group** n generazione f; ~ **limit** n limite m d'età.

**agency** ['eɪdʒənsɪ] n agenzia; **through** or **by the** ~ **of** grazie a.

**agenda** [ə'dʒɛndə] n ordine m del giorno.

**agent** ['eɪdʒənt] n agente m.

**aggregate** ['ægrɪgeɪt] n aggregato.

**aggressive** [ə'grɛsɪv] a aggressivo(a).

**aggrieved** [ə'griːvd] a addolorato(a).

**aghast** [ə'gɑːst] a sbigottito(a).

**agitate** ['ædʒɪteɪt] vt turbare; agitare; **to** ~ **for** agitarsi per.

**ago** [ə'gəʊ] ad: **2 days** ~ 2 giorni fa; **not long** ~ poco tempo fa; **how long** ~? quanto tempo fa?

**agog** [ə'gɒg] a ansioso(a), emozionato(a).

**agonizing** ['ægənaɪzɪŋ] a straziante.

**agony** ['ægənɪ] n agonia.

**agree** [ə'griː] vt (price) pattuire // vi: **to** ~ (**with**) essere d'accordo (con); (LING) concordare (con); **to** ~ **to sth/to do sth** accettare qc/di fare qc; **to** ~ **that** (admit) ammettere che; **to** ~ **on sth** accordarsi su qc; **garlic doesn't** ~ **with me** l'aglio non mi va; **~able** a gradevole; (willing) disposto(a); **are you ~able to this?** è d'accordo con questo?; **~d** a (time, place) stabilito(a); **~ment** n accordo; **in ~ment** d'accordo.

**agricultural** [ægrɪ'kʌltʃərəl] a agricolo(a).

**agriculture** ['ægrɪkʌltʃə*] n agricoltura.

**aground** [ə'graʊnd] ad: **to run** ~ arenarsi.

**ahead** [ə'hɛd] ad avanti; davanti; ~ **of** davanti a; (fig: schedule etc) in anticipo su; ~ **of time** in anticipo; **go right** or **straight** ~ tiri diritto; **they were** (right) ~ **of us** erano (proprio) davanti a noi.

**aid** [eɪd] n aiuto // vt aiutare; **in** ~ **of** a favore di; **to** ~ **and abet** (LAW)

essere complice di.

**aide** [eɪd] n (person) aiutante m.

**AIDS** [eɪdz] n abbr (= acquired immune deficiency syndrome) AIDS m.

**ailing** ['eɪlɪŋ] a sofferente.

**ailment** ['eɪlmənt] n indisposizione f.

**aim** [eɪm] vt: **to** ~ **sth at** (such as gun) mirare qc a, puntare qc a; (camera, remark) rivolgere qc a; (missile) tirare qc a // vi (also: **to take** ~) prendere la mira // n mira; **to** ~ **at** mirare; **to** ~ **to do** aver l'intenzione di fare; **~less** a senza scopo.

**ain't** [eɪnt] (col) = **am not**; **aren't**; **isn't**.

**air** [ɛə*] n aria // vt aerare; (grievances, ideas) esprimere pubblicamente // cpd (currents) d'aria; (attack) aereo(a); **to throw sth into the** ~ lanciare qc in aria; **by** ~ (travel) in aereo; **on the** ~ (RADIO, TV) in onda; **~bed** n (Brit) materassino; **~borne** a in volo; aerotrasportato(a); ~ **conditioning** n condizionamento d'aria; **~craft** n (pl inv) apparecchio; **~craft carrier** n portaerei f inv; **~field** n campo d'aviazione; **A~ Force** n aviazione f militare; **~ freshener** n deodorante m per ambienti; **~gun** n fucile m ad aria compressa; ~ **hostess** n (Brit) hostess f inv; **~ letter** n (Brit) aerogramma m; **~lift** n ponte m aereo; **~line** n linea aerea; **~liner** n aereo di linea; **~lock** n cassa d'aria; **~mail** n: **by ~mail** per via aerea; **~ mattress** n materassino; **~plane** n (US) aeroplano; **~port** n aeroporto; ~ **raid** n incursione f aerea; **~sick** a che ha il mal d'aereo; **~space** n spazio aereo; **~strip** n pista d'atterraggio; ~ **terminal** n air-terminal m inv; **~tight** a ermetico(a); ~ **traffic controller** n controllore m del traffico aereo; **~y** a arioso(a); (manners) noncurante.

**aisle** [aɪl] n (of church) navata laterale; navata centrale; (of plane) corridoio.

**ajar** [ə'dʒɑ:*] a socchiuso(a).

**akin** [ə'kɪn] a: ~ to simile a.

**alacrity** [ə'lækrɪtɪ] n: with ~ con prontezza.

**alarm** [ə'lɑ:m] n allarme m // vt allarmare; ~ **clock** n sveglia.

**alas** [ə'læs] excl ohimè!, ahimè!

**albeit** [ɔ:l'bi:ɪt] cj sebbene+ sub, benché + sub.

**album** ['ælbəm] n album m inv; (L.P.) 33 giri m inv, L.P. m inv.

**alcohol** ['ælkəhɔl] n alcool m; ~**ic** [-'hɔlɪk] a alcolico(a) // n alcolizzato/a.

**alderman** ['ɔ:ldəmən] n consigliere m comunale.

**ale** [eɪl] n birra.

**alert** [ə'lə:t] a vivo(a), (watchful) vigile // n allarme m // vt avvertire; mettere in guardia; **on the** ~ all'erta.

**algebra** ['ældʒɪbrə] n algebra.

**alias** ['eɪlɪəs] ad alias // n pseudonimo, falso nome m.

**alibi** ['ælɪbaɪ] n alibi m inv.

**alien** ['eɪlɪən] n straniero/a // a: ~ (**to**) estraneo(a) (a); ~**ate** vt alienare.

**alight** [ə'laɪt] a acceso(a) // vi scendere; (bird) posarsi.

**align** [ə'laɪn] vt allineare.

**alike** [ə'laɪk] a simile // ad sia ... sia; **to look** ~ assomigliarsi.

**alimony** ['ælɪmənɪ] n (payment) alimenti mpl.

**alive** [ə'laɪv] a vivo(a); (active) attivo(a).

KEYWORD

**all** [ɔ:l] ♦ a tutto(a); ~ **day** tutto il giorno; ~ **night** tutta la notte; ~ **men** tutti gli uomini; ~ **five came** sono venuti tutti e cinque; ~ **the books** tutti i libri; ~ **the food** tutto il cibo; ~ **the time** sempre; tutto il tempo; ~ **his life** tutta la vita

♦ pronoun **1** tutto(a); I **ate it** ~, I

**ate** ~ **of it** l'ho mangiato tutto; ~ **of us went** tutti noi siamo andati; ~ **of the boys went** tutti i ragazzi sono andati

**2** (in phrases): **above** ~ soprattutto; **after** ~ dopotutto; **at** ~: **not at** ~ (in answer to question) niente affatto; (in answer to thanks) prego!, di niente!, s'immagini!; **I'm not at** ~ **tired** non sono affatto stanco(a); **anything at** ~ **will do** andrà bene qualsiasi cosa; ~ **in** ~ tutto sommato

♦ ad: ~ **alone** tutto(a) solo(a); **it's not as hard as** ~ **that** non è poi così difficile; ~ **the more/the better** tanto più/meglio; ~ **but** quasi; **the score is two** ~ il punteggio è di due a due.

**allay** [ə'leɪ] vt (fears) dissipare.

**all clear** n (also fig) segnale m di cessato allarme.

**allegation** [ælɪ'geɪʃən] n asserzione f.

**allege** [ə'lɛdʒ] vt asserire; ~**dly** [ə'lɛdʒɪdlɪ] ad secondo quanto si asserisce.

**allegiance** [ə'li:dʒəns] n fedeltà.

**allergic** [ə'lə:dʒɪk] a: ~ **to** allergico(a) a.

**allergy** ['ælədʒɪ] n allergia.

**alleviate** [ə'li:vɪeɪt] vt sollevare.

**alley** ['ælɪ] n vicolo; (in garden) vialetto.

**alliance** [ə'laɪəns] n alleanza.

**allied** ['ælaɪd] a alleato(a).

**all-in** ['ɔ:lɪn] a (Brit: also ad: charge) tutto compreso; ~ **wrestling** n lotta americana.

**all-night** ['ɔ:l'naɪt] a aperto(a) (or che dura) tutta la notte.

**allocate** ['æləkeɪt] vt (share out) distribuire; (duties, sum, time): **to** ~ **sth to** assegnare qc a qc; **to** ~ **sth for** stanziare qc per.

**allot** [ə'lɔt] vt (share out) spartire; **to** ~ **sth to** (time) dare qc a; (duties) assegnare qc a; ~**ment** n (share) spartizione f; (garden) lotto di terra.

**all-out** ['ɔ:laut] a (effort etc) totale // ad: **to go all out for** mettercela tutta per.

**allow** [ə'lau] vt (practice, behaviour) permettere; (sum to spend etc) accordare; (sum, time estimated) dare; (concede): **to ~ that** ammettere che; **to ~ sb to do** permettere a qn di fare; **he is ~ed** to lo può fare; **to ~ for** vt fus tener conto di; **~ance** n (money received) assegno; indennità f inv; (TAX) detrazione f di imposta; **to make ~ances for** tener conto di.

**alloy** ['æloɪ] n lega.

**all right** ad (feel, work) bene; (as answer) va bene.

**all-round** ['ɔ:l'raund] a completo(a).

**all-time** ['ɔ:l'taɪm] a (record) assoluto(a).

**allude** [ə'lu:d] vi: **to ~ to** alludere a.

**alluring** [ə'ljuərɪŋ] a seducente.

**ally** ['ælaɪ] n alleato.

**almighty** [ɔ:l'maɪtɪ] a onnipotente.

**almond** ['ɑ:mənd] n mandorla.

**almost** ['ɔ:lməust] ad quasi.

**alms** [ɑ:mz] npl elemosina sg.

**aloft** [ə'lɔft] ad in alto; (NAUT) sull'alberatura.

**alone** [ə'ləun] a, ad solo(a); **to leave sb ~** lasciare qn in pace; **to leave sth ~** lasciare stare qc; **let ~ ...** figuriamoci poi ..., tanto meno ... .

**along** [ə'lɔŋ] prep lungo // ad: **is he coming ~?** viene con noi?; **he was hopping/limping ~** veniva saltellando/zoppicando; **~ with** insieme con; **all ~** (all the time) sempre, fin dall'inizio; **~side** prep accanto a; lungo // ad accanto.

**aloof** [ə'lu:f] a distaccato(a) // ad: **to stand ~** tenersi a distanza or in disparte.

**aloud** [ə'laud] ad ad alta voce.

**alphabet** ['ælfəbet] n alfabeto.

**alpine** ['ælpaɪn] a alpino(a).

**Alps** [ælps] npl: **the ~** le Alpi.

**already** [ɔ:l'redɪ] ad già.

**alright** ['ɔ:l'raɪt] ad (Brit) = **all**

right.

**Alsatian** [æl'seɪʃən] n (Brit: dog) pastore m tedesco, (cane m) lupo.

**also** ['ɔ:lsəu] ad anche.

**altar** ['ɔltə*] n altare m.

**alter** ['ɔltə*] vt, vi alterare.

**alternate** a [ɔl'tə:nɪt] alterno(a) // vb ['ɔltə:neɪt] vi: **to ~ (with)** alternarsi (a) // vt alternare; **on ~ days** ogni due giorni; **alternating** a (current) alterno(a).

**alternative** [ɔl'tə:nətɪv] a (solutions) alternativo(a); (solution) altro(a) // n (choice) alternativa; (other possibility) altra possibilità; **~ly** ad alternativamente.

**alternator** ['ɔltə:neɪtə*] n (AUT) alternatore m.

**although** [ɔ:l'ðəu] cj benché + sub, sebbene + sub.

**altitude** ['æltɪtju:d] n altitudine f.

**alto** ['æltəu] n contralto; (male) contraltino.

**altogether** [ɔ:ltə'geðə*] ad del tutto, completamente; (on the whole) tutto considerato; (in all) in tutto.

**aluminium** [ælju'mɪnɪəm], (US) **aluminum** [ə'lu:mɪnəm] n alluminio.

**always** ['ɔ:lweɪz] ad sempre.

**am** [æm] vb see **be**.

**a.m.** ad abbr (= ante meridiem) della mattina.

**amalgamate** [ə'mælgəmeɪt] vt amalgamare // vi amalgamarsi.

**amateur** ['æmətə*] n dilettante m/f // a (SPORT) dilettante; **~ish** a (pej) da dilettante.

**amaze** [ə'meɪz] vt stupire; **to be ~d (at)** essere sbalordito (da); **~ment** n stupore m; **amazing** a sorprendente, sbalorditivo(a); (bargain) sensazionale.

**ambassador** [æm'bæsədə*] n ambasciatore/trice.

**amber** ['æmbə*] n ambra; **at ~** (Brit AUT) giallo.

**ambiguous** [æm'bɪgjuəs] a ambiguo(a).

**ambition** [æm'bɪʃən] n ambizione f.

**ambitious** [æm'bɪʃəs] a

ambizioso(a).

**amble** ['æmbl] *vi* (*gen*: to ~ along) camminare tranquillamente.

**ambulance** ['æmbjuləns] *n* ambulanza.

**ambush** ['æmbuʃ] *n* imboscata // *vt* fare un'imboscata a.

**amenable** [ə'mi:nəbl] *a*: ~ to (*advice etc*) ben disposto(a) a.

**amend** [ə'mɛnd] *vt* (*law*) emendare; (*text*) correggere // *vi* emendarsi; to **make** ~s fare ammenda.

**amenities** [ə'mi:nɪtɪz] *npl* attrezzature *fpl* ricreative e culturali.

**America** [ə'mɛrɪkə] *n* America; ~n *a*, *n* americano(a).

**amiable** ['eɪmɪəbl] *a* amabile, gentile.

**amicable** ['æmɪkəbl] *a* amichevole.

**amid(st)** [ə'mɪd(st)] *prep* fra, tra, in mezzo a.

**amiss** [ə'mɪs] *a*, *ad*: there's something ~ c'è qualcosa che non va bene; **don't take it** ~ non prendertela (a male).

**ammonia** [ə'məunɪə] *n* ammoniaca.

**ammunition** [æmju'nɪʃən] *n* munizioni *fpl*.

**amok** [ə'mɔk] *ad*: to **run** ~ diventare pazzo(a) furioso(a).

**among(st)** [ə'mʌŋ(st)] *prep* fra, tra, in mezzo a.

**amorous** ['æmərəs] *a* amoroso(a).

**amount** [ə'maunt] *n* somma; ammontare *m*; quantità *f inv* // *vi*: to ~ to (*total*) ammontare a; (*be same as*) essere come.

**amp(ère)** ['æmp(ɛə*)] *n* ampère *m inv*.

**ample** ['æmpl] *a* ampio(a); spazioso(a); (*enough*): this is ~ questo è più che sufficiente; to have ~ time/room avere assai tempo/posto.

**amplifier** ['æmplɪfaɪə*] *n* amplificatore *m*.

**amuck** [ə'mʌk] *ad* = **amok**.

**amuse** [ə'mju:z] *vt* divertire; ~ment *n* divertimento; ~ment arcade *n* sala giochi.

**an** [æn, ən, n] *indefinite article see* **a**.

**anaemic** [ə'ni:mɪk] *a* anemico(a).

**anaesthetic** [ænɪs'θɛtɪk] *a* anestetico(a) // *n* anestetico.

**analog(ue)** ['ænəlɔg] *a* (*watch*, *computer*) analogico(a).

**analyse** ['ænəlaɪz] *vt* (*Brit*) analizzare.

**analysis**, *pl* **analyses** [ə'næləsɪs, -sɪːz] *n* analisi *f inv*.

**analyst** ['ænəlɪst] *n* (*POL etc*) analista *m/f*; (*US*) (psic)analista *m/f*.

**analyze** ['ænəlaɪz] *vt* (*US*) = **analyse**.

**anarchist** ['ænəkɪst] *a*, *n* anarchico(a).

**anarchy** ['ænəkɪ] *n* anarchia.

**anathema** [ə'næθɪmə] *n*: that is ~ to him non vuole nemmeno sentirne parlare.

**anatomy** [ə'nætəmɪ] *n* anatomia.

**ancestor** ['ænsɪstə*] *n* antenato/a.

**ancestral** [æn'sɛstrəl] *a* avito(a).

**anchor** ['æŋkə*] *n* ancora // *vi* (*also*: to **drop** ~) gettare l'ancora // *vt* ancorare; to **weigh** ~ salpare or levare l'ancora.

**anchovy** ['æntʃəvɪ] *n* acciuga.

**ancient** ['eɪnʃənt] *a* antico(a); (*fig*) anziano(a).

**ancillary** [æn'sɪlərɪ] *a* ausiliario(a).

**and** [ænd] *cj* e (*often ed before vowel*); ~ so on e così via; try ~ come cerca di venire; he talked ~ talked non la finiva di parlare; better ~ better sempre meglio.

**anew** [ə'nju:] *ad* di nuovo.

**angel** ['eɪndʒəl] *n* angelo.

**anger** ['æŋgə*] *n* rabbia // *vt* arrabbiare.

**angina** [æn'dʒaɪnə] *n* angina pectoris.

**angle** ['æŋgl] *n* angolo; from their ~ dal loro punto di vista; ~r *n* pescatore *m* con la lenza.

**Anglican** ['æŋglɪkən] *a*, *n* anglicano(a).

**angling** ['æŋglɪŋ] *n* pesca con la lenza.

**Anglo-** ['æŋgləu] *prefix* anglo... .

**angry** ['æŋgrɪ] *a* arrabbiato(a,

furioso(a); **to be ~ with** sb/at sth essere in collera con qn/per qc; **to get ~** arrabbiarsi; **to make** sb **~** fare arrabbiare a.

**anguish** ['æŋgwɪʃ] n angoscia.

**animal** ['ænɪməl] a, n animale (m).

**animate** vt ['ænɪmeɪt] animare // a ['ænɪmɪt] animato(a); **~d** a animato(a).

**aniseed** ['ænɪsiːd] n semi mpl di anice.

**ankle** ['æŋkl] n caviglia; **~ sock** n calzino.

**annex** n ['æneks] (also: Brit: **annexe**) edificio annesso // vt [ə'neks] annettere.

**annihilate** [ə'naɪəleɪt] vt annientare.

**anniversary** [ænɪ'vɜːsərɪ] n anniversario.

**announce** [ə'nauns] vt annunciare; **~ment** n annuncio; (letter, card) partecipazione f; **~r** n (RADIO, TV: between programmes) annunciatore/trice; (: in a programme) presentatore/trice.

**annoy** [ə'nɔɪ] vt dare fastidio a; **don't get ~ed!** non irritarti!; **~ance** n fastidio; (cause of ~ance) noia; **~ing** a noioso(a).

**annual** ['ænjuəl] a annuale // n (BOT) pianta annua; (book) annuario.

**annul** [ə'nʌl] vt annullare; (law) rescindere.

**annum** ['ænəm] n see per.

**anonymous** [ə'nɒnɪməs] a anonimo(a).

**anorak** ['ænəræk] n giacca a vento.

**another** [ə'nʌðə*] a: **~ book** (one more) un altro libro, ancora un libro; (a different one) un altro libro // pronoun un altro(un'altra), ancora uno(a); see also **one**.

**answer** ['ɑːnsə*] n risposta; soluzione f // vi rispondere // vt (reply to) rispondere a; (problem) risolvere; (prayer) esaudire; **to ~ the phone** rispondere (al telefono); **in ~ to your letter** in risposta alla sua lettera; **to ~ the bell** rispondere al campanello; **to ~ the door** aprire

la porta; **to ~ back** vi ribattere; **to ~ for** vt fus essere responsabile di; **to ~ to** vt fus (description) corrispondere a; **~able** a: **~able (to** sb/ **for** sth) responsabile (verso qn/di qc); **~ing machine** n segreteria (telefonica) automatica.

**ant** [ænt] n formica.

**antagonism** [æn'tægənɪzəm] n antagonismo.

**antagonize** [æn'tægənaɪz] vt provocare l'ostilità di.

**Antarctic** [ænt'ɑːktɪk] n: **the ~** l'Antartide f // a antartico(a).

**antenatal** ['æntɪ'neɪtl] a prenatale: **~ clinic** n assistenza medica preparto.

**anthem** ['ænθəm] n antifona; **national ~** inno nazionale.

**anthology** [æn'θɒlədʒɪ] n antologia.

**antibiotic** ['æntɪbaɪ'ɒtɪk] n antibiotico(a) // n antibiotico.

**antibody** ['æntɪbɒdɪ] n anticorpo.

**anticipate** [æn'tɪsɪpeɪt] vt prevedere; pregustare; (wishes, request) prevenire.

**anticipation** [æntɪsɪ'peɪʃən] n anticipazione f; (expectation) aspettativa fpl.

**anticlimax** ['æntɪ'klaɪmæks] n: **it was an ~** fu una completa delusione.

**anticlockwise** ['æntɪ'klɒkwaɪz] a, ad in senso antiorario.

**antics** ['æntɪks] npl buffonerie fpl.

**antifreeze** ['æntɪ'friːz] n anticongelante m.

**antihistamine** [æntɪ'hɪstəmɪn] n antistaminico.

**antiquated** ['æntɪkweɪtɪd] a antiquato(a).

**antique** [æn'tiːk] n antichità f inv // a antico(a); **~ shop** n negozio d'antichità.

**antiquity** [æn'tɪkwɪtɪ] n antichità f inv.

**anti-Semitism** ['æntɪ'semɪtɪzəm] n antisemitismo.

**antiseptic** [æntɪ'septɪk] n antisettico(a) // n antisettico.

**antisocial** ['ænti'səuʃəl] a asociale; (against society) antisociale.

**antlers** ['æntləz] npl palchi mpl.

**anvil** ['ænvil] n incudine f.

**anxiety** [æŋ'zaiəti] n ansia; (keenness): ~ to do smania di fare.

**anxious** ['æŋkʃəs] a ansioso(a), inquieto(a), (keen): ~ to do/that impaziente di fare/che + sub.

KEYWORD

**any** ['ɛni] ♦ a 1 (in questions etc): have you ~ butter? hai del burro?, hai un po' di burro?; have you ~ children? hai bambini?; if there are ~ tickets left se ci sono ancora (dei) biglietti, se c'è ancora qualche biglietto
2 (with negative): I haven't ~ money/books non ho soldi/libri
3 (no matter which) qualsiasi, qualunque; choose ~ book you like scegli un libro qualsiasi
4 (in phrases): in ~ case in ogni caso; ~ day now da un giorno all'altro; at ~ moment in qualsiasi momento, da un momento all'altro; at ~ rate ad ogni modo
♦ pronoun 1 (in questions, with negative): have you got ~? ne hai?; can ~ of you sing? qualcuno di voi sa cantare?; I haven't ~ (of them) non ne ho
2 (no matter which one(s)): take ~ of those books (you like) prendi uno qualsiasi di quei libri
♦ ad 1 (in questions etc): do you want ~ more soup/sandwiches? vuoi ancora un po' di minestra/degli altri panini?; are you feeling ~ better? ti senti meglio?
2 (with negative): I can't hear him ~ more non lo sento più; don't wait ~ longer non aspettare più.

**anybody** ['ɛnibɔdi] pronoun (in questions etc) qualcuno, nessuno; (with negative) nessuno; (no matter who) chiunque; can you see ~? vedi qualcuno or nessuno?; if ~ should

**phone** ... se telefona qualcuno ...; I can't see ~ non vedo nessuno; ~ could do it chiunque potrebbe farlo.

**anyhow** ['ɛnihau] ad (at any rate) ad ogni modo, comunque; (haphazard): do it ~ you like fallo come ti pare; I shall go ~ ci andrò lo stesso or comunque; she leaves things just ~ lascia tutto come capita.

**anyone** ['ɛniwʌn] pronoun = anybody.

**anything** ['ɛniθiŋ] pronoun (in question etc) qualcosa, niente; (with negative) niente; (no matter what): you can say ~ you like puoi dire quello che ti pare; can you see ~? vedi niente or qualcosa?; if ~ happens to me ... se mi dovesse succedere qualcosa ...; I can't see ~ non vedo niente; ~ will do va bene qualsiasi cosa or tutto.

**anyway** ['ɛniwei] ad (at any rate) ad ogni modo, comunque; (besides) ad ogni modo.

**anywhere** ['ɛniwɛə] ad (in questions etc) da qualche parte; (with negative) da nessuna parte; (no matter where) da qualsiasi or qualunque parte, dovunque; can you see him ~? lo vedi da qualche parte?; I can't see him ~ non lo vedo da nessuna parte; ~ in the world dovunque nel mondo.

**apart** [ə'pɑ:t] ad (to one side) a parte; (separately) separatamente; with one's legs ~ con le gambe divaricate; 10 miles ~ a 10 miglia di distanza (l'uno dall'altro); to take ~ smontare; ~ from prep a parte, eccetto.

**apartheid** [ə'pɑ:teit] n apartheid f.

**apartment** [ə'pɑ:tmənt] n (US) appartamento; ~ building n (US) stabile m, caseggiato.

**apathetic** [æpə'θɛtik] a apatico(a).

**ape** [eip] n scimmia // vt scimmiottare.

**aperture** ['æpətʃuə*] n apertura.

**apex** ['eipɛks] n apice m.

**apiece** [ə'pi:s] *ad* ciascuno(a).

**apologetic** [əpɔlə'dʒɛtɪk] *a* (*tone, letter*) di scusa.

**apologize** [ə'pɔlədʒaɪz] *vi*: to ~ (for sth to sb) scusarsi (di qc a qn), chiedere scusa (a qn per qc).

**apology** [ə'pɔlədʒɪ] *n* scuse *fpl*.

**apostle** [ə'pɔsl] *n* apostolo.

**apostrophe** [ə'pɔstrəfɪ] *n* (*sign*) apostrofo.

**appalling** [ə'pɔ:lɪŋ] *a* spaventoso(a).

**apparatus** [æpə'reɪtəs] *n* apparato; (*in gymnasium*) attrezzatura.

**apparel** [ə'pærl] *n* (*US*) abbigliamento, confezioni *fpl*.

**apparent** [ə'pærənt] *a* evidente; ~ly *ad* evidentemente.

**apparition** [æpə'rɪʃən] *n* apparizione *f*.

**appeal** [ə'pi:l] *vi* (*LAW*) appellarsi alla legge // *n* (*LAW*) appello; (*request*) richiesta; (*charm*) attrattiva; to ~ for chiedere (con insistenza); to ~ to (*subj: person*) appellarsi a; (*subj: thing*) piacere a; to ~ to sb for mercy chiedere pietà a qn; it doesn't ~ to me dice poco; ~ing *a* (*nice*) attraente; (*touching*) commovente.

**appear** [ə'pɪə*] *vi* apparire; (*LAW*) comparire; (*publication*) essere pubblicato(a); (*seem*) sembrare; it would ~ that sembra che; to ~ in Hamlet recitare nell'Amleto; to ~ on TV presentarsi in televisione; ~ance *n* apparizione *f*; apparenza; (*look, aspect*) aspetto.

**appease** [ə'pi:z] *vt* calmare, appagare.

**appendage** [ə'pendɪdʒ] *n* aggiunta.

**appendicitis** [əpendɪ'saɪtɪs] *n* appendicite *f*.

**appendix,** *pl* **appendices** [ə'pendɪks, -si:z] *n* appendice *f*.

**appetite** ['æpɪtaɪt] *n* appetito.

**appetizer** ['æpɪtaɪzə*] *n* stuzzichino.

**applaud** [ə'plɔ:d] *vt, vi* applaudire.

**applause** [ə'plɔ:z] *n* applauso.

**apple** ['æpl] *n* mela; ~ **tree** *n* melo.

**appliance** [ə'plaɪəns] *n* apparecchio.

**applicant** ['æplɪkənt] *n* candidato/a.

**application** [æplɪ'keɪʃən] *n* applicazione *f*; (*for a job, a grant etc*) domanda; ~ **form** *n* modulo per la domanda.

**applied** [ə'plaɪd] *a* applicato(a).

**apply** [ə'plaɪ] *vi*: to ~ (to) (*paint, ointment*) dare (a); (*theory, technique*) applicare (a) // *vi*: to ~ to (*ask*) rivolgersi a; (*be suitable for, relevant to*) riguardare, riferirsi a; to ~ (for) (*permit, grant, job*) fare domanda (per); to ~ the brakes frenare; to ~ o.s. to dedicarsi a.

**appoint** [ə'pɔɪnt] *vt* nominare; ~ment *n* nomina; (*arrangement to meet*) appuntamento; **to make an** ~ment (with) prendere un appuntamento (con).

**appraisal** [ə'preɪzl] *n* valutazione *f*.

**appreciate** [ə'pri:ʃɪeɪt] *vt* (*like*) apprezzare; (*be grateful for*) essere riconoscente di; (*be aware of*) rendersi conto di // *vi* (*FINANCE*) aumentare.

**appreciation** [əpri:ʃɪ'eɪʃən] *n* apprezzamento; (*FINANCE*) aumento del valore.

**appreciative** [ə'pri:ʃɪətɪv] *a* (*person*) sensibile; (*comment*) elogiativo(a).

**apprehend** [æprɪ'hend] *vt* (*arrest*) arrestare.

**apprehension** [æprɪ'henʃən] *n* (*fear*) inquietudine *f*.

**apprehensive** [æprɪ'hensɪv] *a* apprensivo(a).

**apprentice** [ə'prentɪs] *n* apprendista *m/f*; ~**ship** *n* apprendistato.

**approach** [ə'prəutʃ] *vi* avvicinarsi // *vt* (*come near*) avvicinarsi a; (*ask, apply to*) rivolgersi a; (*subject, passer-by*) avvicinare // *n* approccio; accesso; (*to problem*) modo di affrontare; ~**able** *a* accessibile.

**appropriate** [ə'prəuprɪɪt] *a* appropriato(a); adatto(a) // [ə'prəuprɪeɪt] (*take*) appropriarsi.

**approval** [ə'pru:vəl] *n* approvazione

$f$; on ~ (COMM) in prova, in esame.

**approve** [əˈpruːv] vt, vi approvare; **to ~ of** vt fus approvare; **~d school** n (Brit) riformatorio.

**approximate** [əˈprɒksɪmɪt] a approssimativo(a); **~ly** ad circa.

**apricot** [ˈeɪprɪkɒt] n albicocca.

**April** [ˈeɪprəl] n aprile m; ~ **fool!** pesce d'aprile!

**apron** [ˈeɪprən] n grembiule m.

**apt** [æpt] a (suitable) adatto(a); (able) capace; (likely): **to be ~ to** do avere tendenza a fare.

**aptitude** [ˈæptɪtjuːd] n abilità f inv.

**aqualung** [ˈækwəlʌŋ] n autorespiratore m.

**aquarium** [əˈkweərɪəm] n acquario.

**Aquarius** [əˈkweərɪəs] n Acquario.

**Arab** [ˈærəb] n arabo/a.

**Arabian** [əˈreɪbɪən] a arabo(a).

**Arabic** [ˈærəbɪk] a arabico(a) // n arabo; ~ **numerals** numeri npl arabi, numerazione f araba.

**arbitrary** [ˈɑːbɪtrərɪ] a arbitrario(a).

**arbitration** [ɑːbɪˈtreɪʃən] n (LAW) arbitrato; (INDUSTRY) arbitraggio.

**arcade** [ɑːˈkeɪd] n portico; (passage with shops) galleria.

**arch** [ɑːtʃ] n arco; (of foot) arco plantare // vt inarcare // a malizioso(a).

**archaeologist** [ɑːkɪˈɒlədʒɪst] n archeologo/a.

**archaeology** [ɑːkɪˈɒlədʒɪ] n archeologia.

**archbishop** [ɑːtʃˈbɪʃəp] n arcivescovo.

**arch-enemy** [ˈɑːtʃˈɛnəmɪ] n arcinemico/a.

**archeology** [ɑːkɪˈɒlədʒɪ] etc = **archaeology** etc.

**archer** [ˈɑːtʃə*] n arciere m; **~y** n tiro all'arco.

**architect** [ˈɑːkɪtɛkt] n architetto; **~ure** [ˈɑːkɪtɛktʃə*] n architettura.

**archives** [ˈɑːkaɪvz] npl archivi mpl.

**archway** [ˈɑːtʃweɪ] n arco.

**Arctic** [ˈɑːktɪk] a artico(a) // n: **the ~** l'Artico.

**ardent** [ˈɑːdənt] a ardente.

**are** [ɑː*] vb see **be**.

**area** [ˈɛərɪə] n (GEOM) area; (zone) zona; (: smaller) settore m.

**aren't** [ɑːnt] = **are not**.

**Argentina** [ɑːdʒənˈtiːnə] n Argentina; **Argentinian** [-ˈtɪnɪən] a, n argentino(a).

**arguably** [ˈɑːɡjʊəblɪ] ad: it is ~ ... si può sostenere che sia ... .

**argue** [ˈɑːɡjuː] vi (quarrel) litigare; (reason) ragionare; **to ~ that** sostenere che.

**argument** [ˈɑːɡjʊmənt] n (reasons) argomento; (quarrel) lite f; (debate) discussione f; **~ative** [ɑːɡjuːˈmɛntətɪv] a litigioso(a).

**Aries** [ˈɛəriːz] n Ariete m.

**arise**, pt **arose**, pp **arisen** [əˈraɪz, -ˈrəʊz, -ˈrɪzn] vi alzarsi; (opportunity, problem) presentarsi; **to ~ from** risultare da.

**aristocrat** [ˈærɪstəkræt] n aristocratico/a.

**arithmetic** [əˈrɪθmətɪk] n aritmetica.

**ark** [ɑːk] n: **Noah's A~** l'arca di Noè.

**arm** [ɑːm] n braccio // vt armare; **~s** npl (weapons) armi fpl; **~ in ~** a braccetto.

**armaments** [ˈɑːməmənts] npl armamenti mpl.

**arm: ~chair** n poltrona; **~ed** a armato(a); **~ed robbery** n rapina a mano armata.

**armour**, (US) **armor** [ˈɑːmə*] n armatura; (also: **~-plating**) corazza, blindatura; (MIL: tanks) mezzi mpl blindati; **~ed car** n autoblinda f inv; **~y** n arsenale m.

**armpit** [ˈɑːmpɪt] n ascella.

**armrest** [ˈɑːmrɛst] n bracciolo.

**army** [ˈɑːmɪ] n esercito.

**aroma** [əˈrəʊmə] n aroma.

**arose** [əˈrəʊz] pt of **arise**.

**around** [əˈraʊnd] ad attorno, intorno // prep intorno a; (fig: about): ~ **3 o'clock** circa le 3; **is he ~?** è in giro?

**arouse** [əˈraʊz] vt (sleeper) svegliare; (curiosity, passions) suscitare.

**arrange** [əˈreɪndʒ] vt sistemare; (programme) preparare; **to ~ to do** sth mettersi d'accordo per fare qc; **~ment** n sistemazione f; (plans etc): **~ments** progetti mpl, piani mpl.

**array** [əˈreɪ] n: **~ of** fila di.

**arrears** [əˈrɪəz] npl arretrati mpl; **to be in ~ with** one's rent essere in arretrato con l'affitto.

**arrest** [əˈrest] vt arrestare; (sb's attention) attirare // n arresto; **under ~** in arresto.

**arrival** [əˈraɪvəl] n arrivo; (person) arrivato/a; **a new ~** un nuovo venuto; (baby) un neonato.

**arrive** [əˈraɪv] vi arrivare; **to ~ at** vt fus (fig) raggiungere.

**arrogant** [ˈærəgənt] a arrogante.

**arrow** [ˈærəʊ] n freccia.

**arse** [ɑːs] n (col!) culo (!).

**arson** [ˈɑːsn] n incendio doloso.

**art** [ɑːt] n arte f; (craft) mestiere m; **A~s** npl (SCOL) Lettere fpl.

**artefact** [ˈɑːtɪfækt] n manufatto.

**artery** [ˈɑːtərɪ] n arteria.

**art gallery** n galleria d'arte.

**arthritis** [ɑːˈθraɪtɪs] n artrite f.

**artichoke** [ˈɑːtɪtʃəʊk] n carciofo; **Jerusalem ~** topinambur m inv.

**article** [ˈɑːtɪkl] n articolo; (Brit LAW: training): **~s** npl contratto di tirocinio; **~ of clothing** capo di vestiario.

**articulate** a [ɑːˈtɪkjʊlɪt] (person) che si esprime forbitamente; (speech) articolato(a) // vi [ɑːˈtɪkjʊleɪt] articolare; **~d lorry** n (Brit) autotreno.

**artificial** [ɑːtɪˈfɪʃəl] a artificiale; **~ respiration** n respirazione f artificiale.

**artillery** [ɑːˈtɪlərɪ] n artiglieria.

**artisan** [ˈɑːtɪzæn] n artigiano/a.

**artist** [ˈɑːtɪst] n artista m/f; **~ic** [ɑːˈtɪstɪk] a artistico(a); **~ry** n arte f.

**artless** [ˈɑːtlɪs] a semplice, naturale.

**art school** n scuola d'arte.

KEYWORD

**as** [æz] ♦ cj 1 (referring to time) mentre; **~ the years went by** col passare degli anni; **he came in ~ I was leaving** arrivò mentre stavo uscendo; **~ from tomorrow** da domani

2 (in comparisons): **~ big ~** grande come; **twice ~ big ~** due volte più grande di; **~ much/many ~** tanto quanto/tanti quanti; **~ soon ~ possible** prima possibile

3 (since, because) dal momento che, siccome

4 (referring to manner, way) come; **do ~ you wish** fa' come vuoi; **~ she said** come ha detto lei

5 (concerning): **~ for** or **to that** per quanto riguarda or quanto a quello

6: **~ if** or **though** come se; **he looked ~ if he was ill** sembrava stare male; see also **long, such, well**

♦ prep: **he works ~ a driver** fa l'autista; **~ chairman of the company, he ...** come presidente della compagnia, lui ...; **he gave me it ~ a present** me lo ha regalato.

**a.s.a.p.** abbr (= as soon as possible) prima possibile.

**ascend** [əˈsend] vt salire.

**ascent** [əˈsent] n salita.

**ascertain** [æsəˈteɪn] vt accertare.

**ash** [æʃ] n (dust) cenere f; (also: ~ tree) frassino.

**ashamed** [əˈʃeɪmd] a vergognoso(a); **to be ~ of** vergognarsi di.

**ashen** [ˈæʃn] a (pale) livido(a).

**ashore** [əˈʃɔː] ad a terra.

**ashtray** [ˈæʃtreɪ] n portacenere m.

**Ash Wednesday** n mercoledì m inv delle Ceneri.

**Asia** [ˈeɪʃə] n Asia; **~n a,** n asiatico(a).

**aside** [əˈsaɪd] ad da parte // n a parte m.

**ask** [ɑːsk] vt (request) chiedere; (question) domandare; (invite) invitare; **to ~ sb sth/sb to do sth** chiedere qc a qn/a qn di fare qc; **to ~ sb about sth** chiedere a qn di qc; **to ~ (sb) a question** fare una domanda (a qn); **to ~ sb out to dinner** invitare qn a mangiare fuori; **to ~ after** *vt fus* chiedere di; **to ~ for** *vt fus* chiedere.

**askance** [ə'skɑːns] *ad*: **to look ~ at sb** guardare qn di traverso.

**askew** [ə'skjuː] *ad* di traverso, storto.

**asleep** [ə'sliːp] *a* addormentato(a); **to be ~** dormire; **to fall ~** addormentarsi.

**asparagus** [əs'pærəgəs] *n* asparagi *mpl*.

**aspect** ['æspɛkt] *n* aspetto.

**aspersions** [əs'pəːʃənz] *npl*: **to cast ~ on** diffamare.

**asphyxiation** [æsfɪksɪ'eɪʃən] *n* asfissia.

**aspire** [əs'paɪə*] *vi*: **to ~ to** aspirare a.

**aspirin** ['æsprɪn] *n* aspirina.

**ass** [æs] *n* asino; (*col*) scemo/a; (*US col!*) culo (!).

**assailant** [ə'seɪlənt] *n* assalitore *m*.

**assassinate** [ə'sæsɪneɪt] *vt* assassinare; **assassination** [əsæsɪ'neɪʃən] *n* assassinio.

**assault** [ə'sɔːlt] *n* (*MIL*) assalto; (*gen*: *attack*) aggressione *f* // *vt* assaltare; aggredire; (*sexually*) violentare.

**assemble** [ə'sɛmbl] *vt* riunire; (*TECH*) montare // *vi* riunirsi.

**assembly** [ə'sɛmblɪ] *n* (*meeting*) assemblea; (*construction*) montaggio; **~ line** *n* catena di montaggio.

**assent** [ə'sɛnt] *n* assenso, consenso.

**assert** [ə'səːt] *vt* asserire; (*insist on*) far valere.

**assess** [ə'sɛs] *vt* valutare; **~ment** *n* valutazione *f*.

**asset** ['æsɛt] *n* vantaggio; **~s** *npl* beni *mpl*; disponibilità *fpl*; attivo.

**assign** [ə'saɪn] *vt*: **to ~ (to)** (*task*) assegnare (a); (*resources*) riservare (a); (*cause*, *meaning*) attribuire (a); **to ~ a date to sth** fissare la data di qc; **~ment** *n* compito.

**assist** [ə'sɪst] *vt* assistere, aiutare; **~ance** *n* assistenza, aiuto; **~ant** *n* assistente *m/f*; (*Brit*: *also*: **shop ~ant**) commesso/a.

**associate** [ə'səʊʃɪɪt] *a* associato(a); (*member*) aggiunto(a) // *n* collega *m/f*; (*in business*) socio/a // *vb* [ə'səʊʃɪeɪt] *vt* associare // *vi*: **to ~ with sb** frequentare qn.

**association** [əsəʊsɪ'eɪʃən] *n* associazione *f*.

**assorted** [ə'sɔːtɪd] *a* assortito(a).

**assortment** [ə'sɔːtmənt] *n* assortimento.

**assume** [ə'sjuːm] *vt* supporre; (*responsibilities etc*) assumere; (*attitude*, *name*) prendere; **~d name** *n* nome *m* falso.

**assumption** [ə'sʌmpʃən] *n* supposizione *f*, ipotesi *f inv*.

**assurance** [ə'ʃʊərəns] *n* assicurazione *f*; (*self-confidence*) fiducia in se stesso.

**assure** [ə'ʃʊə*] *vt* assicurare.

**astern** [ə'stəːn] *ad* a poppa.

**asthma** ['æsmə] *n* asma.

**astonish** [əs'tɔnɪʃ] *vt* stupire; **~ment** *n* stupore *m*.

**astound** [əs'taʊnd] *vt* sbalordire.

**astray** [ə'streɪ] *ad*: **to go ~** smarrirsi; (*fig*) traviarsi.

**astride** [ə'straɪd] *prep* a cavalcioni di.

**astrology** [əs'trɔlədʒɪ] *n* astrologia.

**astronaut** ['æstrənɔːt] *n* astronauta *m/f*.

**astronomy** [əs'trɔnəmɪ] *n* astronomia.

**astute** [əs'tjuːt] *a* astuto(a).

**asylum** [ə'saɪləm] *n* asilo; (*building*) manicomio.

KEYWORD

**at** [æt] *prep* **1** (*referring to position, direction*) a; **~ the top** in cima; **~ the desk** al banco, alla scrivania; **~ home/school** a casa/scuola; **~ the**

baker's dal panettiere; **to look ~ sth** guardare qc; **to throw sth ~ sb** lanciare qc a qn
**2** (referring to time) a; **~ 4 o'clock** alle 4; **~ night** di notte; **~ Christmas** a Natale; **~ times** a volte
**3** (referring to rates, speed etc) a; **~ £1 a kilo** a 1 sterlina al chilo; **two ~ a time** due alla volta, due per volta; **~ 50 km/h** a 50 km/h
**4** (referring to manner): **~ a stroke** d'un solo colpo; **~ peace** in pace
**5** (referring to activity): **to be ~ work** essere al lavoro; **to play ~ cowboys** giocare ai cowboy; **to be good ~ sth/doing sth** essere bravo in qc/a fare qc
**6** (referring to cause): **shocked/ surprised/annoyed ~ sth** colpito da/sorpreso da/arrabbiato per qc; **I went ~ his suggestion** ci sono andato dietro suo consiglio.

**ate** [eɪt] pt of **eat**.
**atheist** ['eɪθɪɪst] n ateo/a.
**Athens** ['æθɪnz] n Atene f.
**athlete** ['æθliːt] n atleta m/f.
**athletic** [æθ'letɪk] a atletico(a); **~s** n atletica.
**Atlantic** [ət'læntɪk] a atlantico(a) // n: **the ~ (Ocean)** l'Atlantico, l'Oceano Atlantico.
**atlas** ['ætləs] n atlante m.
**atmosphere** ['ætməsfɪə*] n atmosfera.
**atom** ['ætəm] n atomo; **~ic** [ə'tɒmɪk] a atomico(a); **~(ic) bomb** n bomba atomica; **~izer** ['ætəmaɪzə*] n atomizzatore m.
**atone** [ə'təun] vi: **to ~ for** espiare.
**atrocious** [ə'trəuʃəs] a pessimo(a), atroce.
**attach** [ə'tætʃ] vt attaccare; (document, letter) allegare; (MIL: troops) assegnare; **to be ~ed to sb/ sth** (to like) essere affezionato(a) a qn/qc.
**attaché case** [ə'tæʃeɪ-] n valigetta per documenti.
**attachment** [ə'tætʃmənt] n (tool)

accessorio; (love): **~ (to)** affetto (per).
**attack** [ə'tæk] vt attaccare; (task etc) iniziare; (problem) affrontare // n attacco; (also: **heart ~**) infarto.
**attain** [ə'teɪn] vt (also: **~ to**) arrivare a, raggiungere; **~ments** npl cognizioni fpl.
**attempt** [ə'tempt] n tentativo // vt tentare; **to make an ~ on sb's life** attentare alla vita di qn.
**attend** [ə'tend] vt frequentare; (meeting, talk) andare a; (patient) assistere; **to ~ to** vt fus (needs, affairs etc) prendersi cura di; (customer) occuparsi di; **~ance** n (being present) presenza; (people present) gente f presente; **~ant** n custode m/ f; persona di servizio // a concomitante.
**attention** [ə'tenʃən] n attenzione f; **~!** (MIL) attenti!; **for the ~ of** (ADMIN) per l'attenzione di.
**attentive** [ə'tentɪv] a attento(a); (kind) premuroso(a).
**attic** ['ætɪk] n soffitta.
**attitude** ['ætɪtjuːd] n atteggiamento, posa.
**attorney** [ə'tɜːnɪ] n (lawyer) avvocato; (having proxy) mandatario; **A~ General** n (Brit) Procuratore m Generale; (US) Ministro della Giustizia.
**attract** [ə'trækt] vt attirare; **~ion** [ə'trækʃən] n (gen pl: pleasant things) attrattiva; (PHYSICS, fig: towards sth) attrazione f; **~ive** a attraente.
**attribute** n ['ætrɪbjuːt] attributo // vt [ə'trɪbjuːt]: **to ~ sth to** attribuire qc a.
**attrition** [ə'trɪʃən] n: **war of ~** guerra di logoramento.
**aubergine** ['əubəʒiːn] n melanzana.
**auburn** ['ɔːbən] a tizianesco(a).
**auction** ['ɔːkʃən] n (also: **sale by ~**) asta // vt (also: **to sell by ~**) vendere all'asta; (also: **to put up for ~**) mettere all'asta; **~eer** [-'nɪə*] n banditore m.

**audible** ['ɔ:dɪbl] *a* udibile.

**audience** ['ɔ:dɪəns] *n* (*people*) pubblico; spettatori *mpl*; ascoltatori *mpl*; (*interview*) udienza.

**audio-typist** ['ɔ:dɪəu'taɪpɪst] *n* dattilografo/a che trascrive da nastro.

**audio-visual** ['ɔ:dɪəu'vɪʒuəl] *a* audiovisivo(a); ~ **aid** *n* sussidio audiovisivo.

**audit** ['ɔ:dɪt] *vt* rivedere, verificare.

**audition** [ɔ:'dɪʃən] *n* audizione *f*.

**auditor** ['ɔ:dɪtə*] *n* revisore *m*.

**augment** [ɔ:g'ment] *vt*, *vi* aumentare.

**augur** ['ɔ:gə*] *vi*: it ~s well promette bene.

**August** ['ɔ:gəst] *n* agosto.

**aunt** [ɑ:nt] *n* zia; ~**ie**, ~**y** *n* zietta.

**au pair** ['əu'peə*] *n* (*also*: ~ **girl**) (ragazza *f*) alla pari *inv*.

**aura** ['ɔ:rə] *n* aura.

**auspicious** [ɔ:s'pɪʃəs] *a* propizio(a).

**austerity** [ɔs'terɪtɪ] *n* austerità.

**Australia** [ɔs'treɪlɪə] *n* Australia; ~**n** *a*, *n* australiano(a).

**Austria** ['ɔstrɪə] *n* Austria; ~**n** *a*, *n* austriaco(a).

**authentic** [ɔ:'θentɪk] *a* autentico(a).

**author** ['ɔ:θə*] *n* autore/trice.

**authoritarian** [ɔ:θɔrɪ'teərɪən] *a* autoritario(a).

**authoritative** [ɔ:'θɔrɪtətɪv] *a* (*account etc*) autorevole; (*manner*) autoritario(a).

**authority** [ɔ:'θɔrɪtɪ] *n* autorità *f inv*; (*permission*) autorizzazione *f*; **the authorities** *npl* le autorità .

**authorize** ['ɔ:θəraɪz] *vt* autorizzare.

**auto** ['ɔ:təu] *n* (*US*) auto *f inv*.

**autobiography** ['ɔ:təbaɪ'ɔgrəfɪ] *n* autobiografia.

**autograph** ['ɔ:təgrɑ:f] *n* autografo // *vt* firmare.

**automatic** [ɔ:tə'mætɪk] *a* automatico(a) // *n* (*gun*) arma automatica; (*Brit AUT*) automobile *f* con cambio automatico; ~**ally** *ad* automaticamente.

**automaton,** *pl* **automata** [ɔ:'tɔmətən, -tə] *n* automa *m*.

**automobile** ['ɔ:təməbi:l] *n* (*US*) automobile *f*.

**autonomy** [ɔ:'tɔnəmɪ] *n* autonomia.

**autumn** ['ɔ:təm] *n* autunno.

**auxiliary** [ɔ:g'zɪlɪərɪ] *a* ausiliario(a) // *n* ausiliare *m/f*.

**Av.** *abbr* = **avenue**.

**avail** [ə'veɪl] *vt*: to ~ o.s. of servirsi di; approfittarsi di // *n*: to no ~ inutilmente.

**available** [ə'veɪləbl] *a* disponibile.

**avalanche** ['ævəlɑ:nʃ] *n* valanga.

**avant-garde** ['ævãŋ'gɑ:d] *a* d'avanguardia.

**Ave.** *abbr* = **avenue**.

**avenge** [ə'vendʒ] *vt* vendicare.

**avenue** ['ævənju:] *n* viale *m*.

**average** ['ævərɪdʒ] *n* media // *a* medio(a) // *vt* (*a certain figure*) fare di or in media; on ~ in media; to ~ **out** *vi*: to ~ **out** at aggirarsi in media su, essere in media di.

**averse** [ə'və:s] *a*: to be ~ to sth/ doing essere contrario a qc/a fare.

**avert** [ə'və:t] *vt* evitare, prevenire; (*one's eyes*) distogliere.

**aviary** ['eɪvɪərɪ] *n* voliera, uccelliera.

**avocado** [ævə'kɑ:dəu] *n* (*also*: *Brit*: ~ **pear**) avocado *m inv*.

**avoid** [ə'vɔɪd] *vt* evitare.

**await** [ə'weɪt] *vt* aspettare.

**awake** [ə'weɪk] *a* sveglio(a) // *vb* (*pt* **awoke,** *pp* **awoken, awaked**) *vt* svegliare // *vi* svegliarsi; ~**ning** [ə'weɪknɪŋ] *n* risveglio.

**award** [ə'wɔ:d] *n* premio; (*LAW*) decreto // *vt* assegnare; (*LAW*: *damages*) decretare.

**aware** [ə'weə*] *a*: ~ **of** (*conscious*) conscio(a) di; (*informed*) informato(a) di; to become ~ of accorgersi di; ~**ness** *n* consapevolezza.

**awash** [ə'wɔʃ] *a*: ~ (**with**) inondato(a) da.

**away** [ə'weɪ] *a*, *ad* via; lontano(a); **two kilometres** ~ a due chilometri di distanza; **two hours** ~ **by car** a due ore di distanza in macchina; **the holiday was two weeks ~** mancavano due settimane alle vacanze; **~ from** lontano da; **he's ~ for a week** è andato via per una settimana; **he was working/pedalling** etc ~ *la particella indica la continuità e l'energia dell'azione*: lavorava/pedalava etc più che poteva; **to fade/wither** etc ~ *la particella rinforza l'idea della diminuzione*; **~ game** n (SPORT) partita fuori casa.

**awe** [ɔ:] n timore m; **~-inspiring, ~some** a imponente.

**awful** [ˈɔ:fəl] a terribile; **~-ly** ad (very) terribilmente.

**awhile** [əˈwail] ad (per) un po'.

**awkward** [ˈɔ:kwəd] a (clumsy) goffo(a); (inconvenient) scomodo(a); (embarrassing) imbarazzante.

**awning** [ˈɔ:niŋ] n (of shop, hotel etc) tenda.

**awoke, awoken** [əˈwəuk, -kən] pt, pp of **awake**.

**awry** [əˈrai] ad di traverso // a storto(a); **to go ~** andare a monte.

**axe**, (US) **ax** [æks] n scure f // vt (project etc) abolire; (jobs) sopprimere.

**axis**, pl **axes** [ˈæksis, -si:z] n asse m.

**axle** [ˈæksl] n (also: **~-tree**) asse m.

**ay(e)** [ai] excl (yes) sì.

## B

**B** [bi:] n (MUS) si m.

**B.A.** n abbr = **Bachelor of Arts**.

**baby** [ˈbeibi] n bambino/a; **~ carriage** n (US) carrozzina; **~-sit** vi fare il (or la) babysitter; **~-sitter** n baby-sitter m/f inv.

**bachelor** [ˈbætʃələ*] n scapolo; **B~ of Arts/Science (B.A./B.Sc.)** = laureato/a in lettere/scienze.

**back** [bæk] n (of person, horse) dorso, schiena; (of hand) dorso; (of house, car) dietro(a); (of train) coda; (of chair) schienale m; (of page)

rovescio; (FOOTBALL) difensore m // vt (candidate: also: **~ up**) appoggiare; (horse: at races) puntare su; (car) guidare a marcia indietro // vi indietreggiare; (car etc) fare marcia indietro // a (in compounds) posteriore, di dietro; **~ seats/wheels** (AUT) sedili mpl/ruote fpl posteriori; **~ payments** arretrati mpl // ad (not forward) indietro; (returned): **he's ~** è tornato; **he ran ~** tornò indietro di corsa; (restitution): **throw the ball ~** ritira la palla; **can I have it ~?** posso riaverlo?; (again): **he called ~** ha richiamato; **to ~ down** vi fare marcia indietro; **to ~ out** vi (of promise) tirarsi indietro; **to ~ up** vt (support) appoggiare, sostenere; (COMPUT) fare una copia di riserva di; **~bencher** n (Brit) membro del Parlamento senza potere amministrativo; **~bone** n spina dorsale; **~cloth** n scena di sfondo; **~date** vt (letter) retrodatare; **~dated pay rise** aumento retroattivo; **~drop** n = **~cloth**; **~fire** vi (AUT) dar ritorni di fiamma; (plans) fallire; **~ground** n sfondo; (of events) background m inv; (basic knowledge) base f; (experience) esperienza; **family ~ground** ambiente m familiare; **~hand** n (TENNIS: also: **~hand stroke**) rovescio; **~handed** a (fig) ambiguo(a); **~hander** n (Brit: bribe) bustarella; **~ing** n (fig) appoggio; **~lash** n contraccolpo, ripercussione f; **~log** n: **~log of work** lavoro arretrato; **~ number** n (of magazine etc) numero arretrato; **~pack** n zaino; **~ pay** n arretrato di paga; **~side** n (col) sedere m; **~stage** ad nel retroscena; **~stroke** n nuoto sul dorso; **~up** a (train, plane) supplementare; (COMPUT) di riserva // n (support) appoggio, sostegno; (also: **~up file**) file m inv di riserva; **~ward** a (movement) indietro inv; (person) tardivo(a); (country) arretrato(a)

~**wards** *ad* indietro; *(fall, walk)* all'indietro; ~**water** *n (fig)* posto morto; ~**yard** *n* cortile *m* dietro la casa.

**bacon** ['beɪkən] *n* pancetta.

**bad** [bæd] *a* cattivo(a); *(child)* cattivello(a); *(meat, food)* andato(a) a male; **his** ~ **leg** la sua gamba malata; **to go** ~ andare a male.

**bade** [bæd] *pt of* **bid**.

**badge** [bædʒ] *n* insegna; *(of policeman)* stemma *m*.

**badger** ['bædʒə*] *n* tasso.

**badly** ['bædlɪ] *ad (work, dress etc)* male; ~ **wounded** gravemente ferito; **he needs it** ~ ne ha gran bisogno; ~ **off** *a* povero(a).

**badminton** ['bædmɪntən] *n* badminton *m*.

**bad-tempered** ['bæd'tɛmpəd] *a* irritabile; di malumore.

**baffle** ['bæfl] *vt (puzzle)* confondere.

**bag** [bæg] *n* sacco; *(handbag etc)* borsa; *(of hunter)* carniere *m*; bottino // *vt (col: take)* mettersi in tasca; prendersi; ~**s of** *(col: lots of)* un sacco di; ~**gage** *n* bagagli *mpl*; ~**gy** *a* largo(a), sformato(a); ~**pipes** *npl* cornamusa.

**bail** [beɪl] *n* cauzione *f* // *vt (prisoner: also:* ~ **grant** ~ *to)* concedere la libertà provvisoria su cauzione a; *(boat: also:* ~ **out)** aggottare; **on** ~ *(accused person)* in libertà provvisoria su cauzione; **to** ~ **out** *vt (prisoner)* ottenere la libertà provvisoria su cauzione di; *see also* **bale**.

**bailiff** ['beɪlɪf] *n* usciere *m*; fattore *m*.

**bait** [beɪt] *n* esca // *vt (fig)* tormentare.

**bake** [beɪk] *vt* cuocere al forno // *vi* cuocersi al forno; ~**d beans** *npl* fagioli *mpl* all'uccelletto; ~**r** *n* fornaio/a, panettiere/a; ~**ry** *n* panetteria; **baking** *n* cottura (al forno).

**balance** ['bæləns] *n* equilibrio; *(COMM: sum)* bilancio; *(scales)*

bilancia // *vt* tenere in equilibrio; *(pros and cons)* soppesare; *(budget)* far quadrare; *(account)* pareggiare; *(compensate)* contrappesare; ~ **of trade/payments** bilancia commerciale/dei pagamenti; ~**d** *(personality, diet)* equilibrato(a); ~ **sheet** *n* bilancio.

**balcony** ['bælkənɪ] *n* balcone *m*.

**bald** [bɔːld] *a* calvo(a).

**bale** [beɪl] *n* balla; **to** ~ **out** *vi (of a plane)* gettarsi col paracadute.

**baleful** ['beɪlful] *a* funesto(a).

**ball** [bɔːl] *n* palla; *(football)* pallone *m*; *(for golf)* pallina; *(dance)* ballo.

**ballast** ['bæləst] *n* zavorra.

**ball bearings** *npl* cuscinetti a sfere.

**ballerina** [bælə'riːnə] *n* ballerina.

**ballet** ['bæleɪ] *n* balletto; *(art)* danza classica.

**balloon** [bə'luːn] *n* pallone *m*; *(in comic strip)* fumetto.

**ballot** ['bælət] *n* scrutinio.

**ball-point pen** [bɔːl'pɔɪnt-] *n* penna a sfera.

**ballroom** ['bɔːlrum] *n* sala da ballo.

**balm** [bɑːm] *n* balsamo.

**ban** [bæn] *n* interdizione *f* // *vt* interdire.

**banana** [bə'nɑːnə] *n* banana.

**band** [bænd] *n* banda; *(at a dance)* orchestra; *(MIL)* fanfara; **to** ~ **together** *vi* collegarsi.

**bandage** ['bændɪdʒ] *n* benda.

**bandaid** ['bændeɪd] *n (US)* cerotto.

**bandwagon** ['bændwægən] *n:* **to jump on the** ~ *(fig)* seguire la corrente.

**bandy** ['bændɪ] *vt (jokes, insults)* scambiare.

**bandy-legged** ['bændɪ'legɪd] *a* dalle gambe storte.

**bang** [bæŋ] *n* botta; *(of door)* lo sbattere; *(blow)* colpo // *vt* battere *(violentemente)*; *(door)* sbattere // *vi* scoppiare; sbattere.

**bangle** ['bæŋgl] *n* braccialetto.

**bangs** [bæŋz] *npl (US: fringe)* frangia, frangetta.

**banish** ['bænɪʃ] *vt* bandire.

**banister(s)** ['bænistə(z)] $n(pl)$ ringhiera.

**bank** [bæŋk] $n$ banca, banco; (of river, lake) riva, sponda; (of earth) banco // $vi$ (AVIAT) inclinarsi in virata; **to ~ on** $vt$ $fus$ contare su; **~ account** $n$ conto in banca; **~ card** $n$ carta assegni; **~er** $n$ banchiere $m$; **~er's card** $n$ (Brit) = **~ card; B~ holiday** $n$ (Brit) giorno di festa (in cui le banche sono chiuse); **~ing** $n$ attività bancaria; professione $f$ di banchiere; **~note** $n$ banconota; **~ rate** $n$ tasso bancario.

**bankrupt** ['bæŋkrʌpt] $a$ fallito(a); **to go ~** fallire; **~cy** $n$ fallimento.

**bank statement** $n$ estratto conto.

**banner** ['bænə*] $n$ bandiera.

**banns** [bænz] $npl$ pubblicazioni $fpl$ di matrimonio.

**baptism** ['bæptizəm] $n$ battesimo.

**bar** [ba:*] $n$ barra; (of window etc) sbarra; (of chocolate) tavoletta; (fig) ostacolo; restrizione $f$; (pub) bar $m$ $inv$; (counter: in pub) banco; (MUS) battuta // $vt$ (road, window) sbarrare; (person) escludere; (activity) interdire; **~ of soap** saponetta; **the B~** (LAW) l'Ordine $m$ degli avvocati; **behind ~s** (prisoner) dietro le sbarre; **~ none** senza eccezione.

**barbaric** [ba:'bærik] $a$ barbarico(a).

**barbecue** ['ba:bikju:] $n$ barbecue $m$ $inv$.

**barbed wire** [ba:bd-] $n$ filo spinato.

**barber** ['ba:bə*] $n$ barbiere $m$.

**bar code** $n$ (on goods) codice $m$ a barre.

**bare** [beə*] $a$ nudo(a) // $vt$ scoprire, denudare; (teeth) mostrare; **~back** $ad$ senza sella; **~faced** $a$ sfacciato(a); **~foot** $a$, $ad$ scalzo(a); **~ly** $ad$ appena.

**bargain** ['ba:gin] $n$ (transaction) contratto; (good buy) affare $m$ // $vi$ trattare; **into the ~** per giunta; **to ~ for** $vt$ $fus$: **he got more than he ~ed for** gli è andata peggio di quel che si aspettasse or che avesse

calcolato.

**barge** [ba:dʒ] $n$ chiatta; **to ~ in** $vi$ (walk in) piombare dentro; (interrupt talk) intromettersi a sproposito; **to ~ into** $vt$ $fus$ urtare contro.

**bark** [ba:k] $n$ (of tree) corteccia; (of dog) abbaio // $vi$ abbaiare.

**barley** ['ba:li] $n$ orzo.

**barmaid** ['ba:meid] $n$ cameriera al banco.

**barman** ['ba:mən] $n$ barista $m$.

**barn** [ba:n] $n$ granaio.

**barometer** [bə'rɔmitə*] $n$ barometro.

**baron** ['bærən] $n$ barone $m$; **~ess** $n$ baronessa.

**barracks** ['bærəks] $npl$ caserma.

**barrage** ['bæra:ʒ] $n$ (MIL, dam) sbarramento; (fig) fiume $m$.

**barrel** ['bærəl] $n$ barile $m$; (of gun) canna.

**barren** ['bærən] $a$ sterile; (soil) arido(a).

**barricade** [bæri'keid] $n$ barricata.

**barrier** ['bæriə*] $n$ barriera.

**barring** ['ba:riŋ] $prep$ salvo.

**barrister** ['bæristə*] $n$ (Brit) avvocato/essa (con diritto di parlare davanti a tutte le corti).

**barrow** ['bærəu] $n$ (cart) carriola.

**bartender** ['ba:tendə*] $n$ (US) barista $m$.

**barter** ['ba:tə*] $n$ baratto // $vt$: **to ~ sth for** barattare qc con.

**base** [beis] $n$ base $f$ // $vt$: **to ~ sth on** basare qc su // $a$ vile.

**baseball** ['beisbo:l] $n$ baseball $m$.

**basement** ['beismənt] $n$ seminterrato; (of shop) interrato.

**bases** ['beisi:z] $npl$ of **basis**; ['beisiz] $npl$ of **base**.

**bash** [bæʃ] $vt$ (col) picchiare.

**bashful** ['bæʃful] $a$ timido(a).

**basic** ['beisik] $a$ rudimentale; essenziale; **~ally** [-li] $ad$ fondamentalmente; sostanzialmente.

**basil** ['bæzl] $n$ basilico.

**basin** ['beisn] $n$ (vessel, also GEO) bacino; (also: **wash~**) lavabo.

**basis**, pl **bases** ['beɪsɪs, -siːz] n base f.

**bask** [bɑːsk] vi: to ~ in the sun crogiolarsi al sole.

**basket** ['bɑːskɪt] n cesta; (smaller) cestino; (with handle) paniere m; ~**ball** n pallacanestro f.

**bass** [beɪs] n (MUS) basso.

**bassoon** [bə'suːn] n fagotto.

**bastard** ['bɑːstəd] n bastardo/a; (col!) stronzo (!).

**bat** [bæt] n pipistrello; (for baseball etc) mazza; (Brit: for table tennis) racchetta // vt: he didn't ~ an eyelid non battè ciglio.

**batch** [bætʃ] n (of bread) infornata; (of papers) cumulo.

**bated** ['beɪtɪd] a: with ~ breath col fiato sospeso.

**bath** [bɑːθ, pl bɑːðz] n (see also **baths**) bagno; (bathtub) vasca da bagno // vt far fare il bagno a; to have a ~ fare un bagno.

**bathe** [beɪð] vi fare il bagno // vt bagnare.

**bathing** ['beɪðɪŋ] n bagni mpl; ~**cap** n cuffia da bagno; ~ **costume**, (US) ~ **suit** n costume m da bagno.

**bath**: ~**robe** n accappatoio; ~**room** n stanza da bagno.

**baths** [bɑːðz] npl bagni mpl pubblici.

**bath towel** n asciugamano da bagno.

**baton** ['bætən] n (MUS) bacchetta; (club) manganello.

**batter** ['bætə*] vt battere // n pastetta; ~**ed** a (hat) sformato/a; (pan) ammaccato/a.

**battery** ['bætərɪ] n batteria; (of torch) pila.

**battle** ['bætl] n battaglia // vi battagliare, lottare; ~**field** n campo di battaglia; ~**ship** n nave f da guerra.

**bawdy** ['bɔːdɪ] a piccante.

**bawl** [bɔːl] vi urlare.

**bay** [beɪ] n (of sea) baia; to hold sb at ~ tenere qn a bada.

**bay window** n bovindo.

**bazaar** [bə'zɑː*] n bazar m inv; vendita di beneficenza.

**b. & b., B. & B.** abbr = **bed and breakfast**.

**BBC** n abbr (= British Broadcasting Corporation) rete nazionale di radiotelevisione in Gran Bretagna.

**B.C.** ad abbr (= before Christ) a.C.

KEYWORD

**be** [biː], pt **was, were**, pp **been** ♦ auxiliary vb **1** (with present participle: forming continuous tenses): what are you doing? che fa?, che sta facendo?; they're coming tomorrow vengono domani; I've been waiting for her for hours sono ore che l'aspetto

**2** (with pp: forming passives) essere; to ~ killed essere or venire ucciso(a); the box had been opened la scatola era stata aperta; the thief was nowhere to ~ seen il ladro non si trovava da nessuna parte

**3** (in tag questions): it was fun, wasn't it? è stato divertente, no?; he's good-looking, isn't he? è un bell'uomo, vero?; she's back, isn't she? così è tornata, eh?

**4** (+ to + infinitive): the house is to ~ sold abbiamo (or hanno etc) intenzione di vendere casa; you're to ~ congratulated for all your work dovremo farvi i complimenti per tutto il vostro lavoro; he's not to open it non deve aprirlo

♦ vb + complement **1** (gen) essere; I'm English sono inglese; I'm tired sono stanco(a); I'm hot/cold ho caldo/freddo; he's a doctor è medico; **2 and 2 are 4** 2 più 2 fa 4; ~ **careful!** sta attento(a)!; ~ **good** sii buono(a)

**2** (of health) stare; how are you? come sta?; he's very ill sta molto male

**3** (of age): how old are you? quanti anni hai?; I'm sixteen (years old) ho sedici anni

**4** (cost) costare; how much was the meal? quant'era or quanto costava il pranzo?; that'll ~ £5,

**please** (fa) 5 sterline, per favore

◆ vi 1 (exist, occur etc) essere, esistere; **the best singer that ever was** il migliore cantante mai esistito or di tutti tempi; ~ **that as it may** comunque sia, sia come sia; **so ~ it** sia pure, e sia

2 (referring to place) essere, trovarsi; **I won't ~ here tomorrow** non ci sarò domani; **Edinburgh is in Scotland** Edimburgo si trova in Scozia

3 (referring to movement): **where have you been?** dov'è stato?; **I've been to China** sono stato in Cina

◆ impersonal vb 1 (referring to time, distance) essere; **it's 5 o'clock** sono le 5; **it's the 28th of April** è il 28 aprile; **it's 10 km to the village** di qui al paese sono 10 km

2 (referring to the weather) fare; **it's too hot/cold** fa troppo caldo/freddo; **it's windy** c'è vento

3 (emphatic): **it's me** sono io; **it was Maria who paid the bill** è stata Maria che ha pagato il conto.

**beach** [biːtʃ] n spiaggia // vt tirare in secco.

**beacon** ['biːkən] n (lighthouse) faro; (marker) segnale m.

**bead** [biːd] n perlina.

**beak** [biːk] n becco.

**beaker** ['biːkə*] n coppa.

**beam** [biːm] n trave f; (of light) raggio // vi brillare.

**bean** [biːn] n fagiolo; (of coffee) chicco; **runner ~** fagiolino; **broad ~** fava; **~sprouts** npl germogli mpl di soia.

**bear** [bɛə*] n orso // vb (pt **bore**, pp **borne**) vt portare; (endure) sopportare // vi: **to ~ right/left** piegare a destra/sinistra; **to ~ out** vt (suspicions) confermare, convalidare; (person) dare il proprio appoggio a; **to ~ up** vi (person) fare buon viso a cattiva sorte.

**beard** [bɪəd] n barba.

**bearer** ['bɛərə*] n portatore m.

**bearing** ['bɛərɪŋ] n portamento; (connection) rapporto; **~s** npl (also: **ball ~s**) cuscinetti mpl a sfere; **to take a ~** fare un rilevamento; **to find one's ~s** orientarsi.

**beast** [biːst] n bestia; **~ly** a meschino(a); (weather) da cani.

**beat** [biːt] n colpo; (of heart) battito; (MUS) tempo; battuta; (of policeman) giro // vt (pt **beat**, pp **beaten**) battere; **off the ~en track** fuori mano; **to ~ time** battere il tempo; **~ it!** (col) fila!, fuori dai piedi!; **to ~ off** vt respingere; **to ~ up** vt (col: person) picchiare; (eggs) sbattere; **~ing** n bastonata.

**beautiful** ['bjuːtɪful] a bello(a); **~ly** ad splendidamente.

**beauty** ['bjuːtɪ] n bellezza; **~ salon** n istituto di bellezza; **~ spot** n neo; (Brit: TOURISM) luogo pittoresco.

**beaver** ['biːvə*] n castoro.

**became** [bɪ'keɪm] pt of **become**.

**because** [bɪ'kɒz] cj perché; **~ of** prep a causa di.

**beck** [bɛk] n: **to be at sb's ~ and call** essere a completa disposizione di qn.

**beckon** ['bɛkən] vt (also: **~ to**) chiamare con un cenno.

**become** [bɪ'kʌm] vt (irg: like **come**) diventare // vi: **to ~ fat/thin** ingrassarsi/dimagrire; **what has ~ of him?** che gli è successo?

**becoming** [bɪ'kʌmɪŋ] a (behaviour) che si conviene; (clothes) grazioso(a).

**bed** [bɛd] n letto; (of flowers) aiuola; (of coal, clay) strato; **single/double ~** letto a una piazza/a due piazze or matrimoniale; **~ and breakfast (b. & b.)** n (place) ≈ pensione f familiare; (terms) camera con colazione; **~clothes** npl biancheria e coperte fpl da letto; **~ding** n coperte e lenzuola fpl.

**bedlam** ['bɛdləm] n baraonda.

**bedraggled** [bɪ'dræɡld] a fradicio(a).

**bed: ~ridden** a costretto(a) a letto;

~**room** n camera da letto; ~**side** n: at sb's ~**side** al capezzale di qn; ~**sit(ter)** n (Brit) monolocale m; ~**spread** n copriletto; ~**time** n: it's ~**time** è ora di andare a letto.

**bee** [biː] n ape f.

**beech** [biːtʃ] n faggio.

**beef** [biːf] n manzo; roast ~ arrosto di manzo; ~**burger** n hamburger m inv; ~**eater** n guardia della Torre di Londra.

**beehive** ['biːhaɪv] n alveare m.

**beeline** ['biːlaɪn] n: to make a ~ for buttarsi a capo fitto verso.

**been** [biːn] pp of **be**.

**beer** [bɪəʳ] n birra.

**beetle** ['biːtl] n scarafaggio; coleottero.

**beetroot** ['biːtruːt] n (Brit) barbabietola.

**before** [bɪˈfɔːʳ] prep (in time) prima di; (in space) davanti a // cj prima che + sub; prima di // ad prima; ~ going prima di andare; ~ she goes prima che vada; the week ~ la settimana prima; I've seen it ~ l'ho già visto; I've never seen it ~ è la prima volta che lo vedo; ~**hand** ad in anticipo.

**beg** [beg] vi chiedere l'elemosina // vt chiedere in elemosina; (favour) chiedere; (entreat) pregare.

**began** [bɪˈgæn] pt of **begin**.

**beggar** ['begəʳ] n mendicante m/f.

**begin** [bɪˈgɪn], pt **began**, pp **begun** vt, vi cominciare; to ~ **doing** or to do sth incominciare or iniziare a fare qc; ~**ner** n principiante m/f; ~**ning** n inizio, principio.

**begun** [bɪˈgʌn] pp of **begin**.

**behalf** [bɪˈhɑːf] n: on ~ of per conto di; a nome di.

**behave** [bɪˈheɪv] vi comportarsi; (well: also: ~ o.s.) comportarsi bene.

**behaviour**, (US) **behavior** [bɪˈheɪvjəʳ] n comportamento, condotta.

**behead** [bɪˈhed] vt decapitare.

**beheld** [bɪˈheld] pt, pp of **behold**.

**behind** [bɪˈhaɪnd] prep dietro; (followed by pronoun) dietro di; (time) in ritardo con // ad dietro; in ritardo // n didietro; to be ~ (schedule) essere in ritardo rispetto al programma; ~ the scenes (fig) dietro le quinte.

**behold** [bɪˈhəʊld] vt (irg: like **hold**) vedere, scorgere.

**beige** [beɪʒ] a beige inv.

**being** ['biːɪŋ] n essere m; to come into ~ cominciare ad esistere.

**belated** [bɪˈleɪtɪd] a tardo(a).

**belch** [beltʃ] vi ruttare // vt (gen: ~ out: smoke etc) eruttare.

**belfry** ['belfrɪ] n campanile m.

**Belgian** ['beldʒən] a, n belga (m/f).

**Belgium** ['beldʒəm] n Belgio.

**belie** [bɪˈlaɪ] vt smentire.

**belief** [bɪˈliːf] n (opinion) opinione f, convinzione f; (trust, faith) fede f; (acceptance as true) credenza.

**believe** [bɪˈliːv] vt, vi credere; to ~ in (God) credere in; (ghosts) credere a; (method) avere fiducia in; ~**r** n (REL) credente m/f; (in idea, activity): to be a ~**r** in credere in.

**belittle** [bɪˈlɪtl] vt sminuire.

**bell** [bel] n campana; (small, on door, electric) campanello.

**bellow** ['beləʊ] vi muggire.

**bellows** ['beləʊz] npl soffietto.

**belly** ['belɪ] n pancia.

**belong** [bɪˈlɒŋ] vi: to ~ to appartenere a; (club etc) essere socio di; this book ~s here questo libro va qui; ~**ings** npl cose fpl, roba.

**beloved** [bɪˈlʌvɪd] a adorato(a).

**below** [bɪˈləʊ] prep sotto, al di sotto di // ad sotto, di sotto; giù; see ~ vedi sotto or oltre.

**belt** [belt] n cintura; (TECH) cinghia // vt (thrash) picchiare // vi (col) filarsela; ~**way** n (US AUT: ring road) circonvallazione f; (: motorway) autostrada.

**bemused** [bɪˈmjuːzd] a perplesso(a), stupito(a).

**bench** [bentʃ] n panca; (in

*workshop*) banco; **the B~** (*LAW*) la Corte.

**bend** [bɛnd] *vb* (*pt*, *pp* **bent**) *vt* curvare; (*leg*, *arm*) piegare // *vi* curvarsi; piegarsi // *n* (*Brit*: *in road*) curva; (*in pipe*, *river*) gomito; **to ~ down** *vi* chinarsi; **to ~ over** *vi* piegarsi.

**beneath** [bɪˈniːθ] *prep* sotto, al di sotto di; (*unworthy of*) indegno(a) di // *ad* sotto, di sotto.

**benefactor** [ˈbɛnɪfæktə*] *n* benefattore *m*.

**beneficial** [bɛnɪˈfɪʃəl] *a* che fa bene; vantaggioso(a).

**benefit** [ˈbɛnɪfɪt] *n* beneficio, vantaggio; (*allowance of money*) indennità *f inv* // *vt* far bene a // *vi*: **he'll ~ from it** ne trarrà beneficio *or* profitto.

**benevolent** [bɪˈnɛvələnt] *a* benevolo(a).

**benign** [bɪˈnaɪn] *a* (*person*, *smile*) benevolo(a); (*MED*) benigno(a).

**bent** [bɛnt] *pt*, *pp of* **bend** // *n* inclinazione *f* // *a* (*col*: *dishonest*) losco(a); **to be ~ on** essere deciso(a) a.

**bequest** [bɪˈkwɛst] *n* lascito.

**bereaved** [bɪˈriːvd] *n*: **the ~ i** familiari in lutto.

**beret** [ˈbɛreɪ] *n* berretto.

**berm** [bɑːm] *n* (*US AUT*) corsia d'emergenza.

**berry** [ˈbɛrɪ] *n* bacca.

**berserk** [bəˈsɜːk] *a*: **to go ~** montare su tutte le furie.

**berth** [bɜːθ] *n* (*bed*) cuccetta; (*for ship*) ormeggio // *vi* (*in harbour*) entrare in porto; (*at anchor*) gettare l'ancora.

**beseech** [bɪˈsiːtʃ], *pt*, *pp* **besought** *vt* implorare.

**beset**, *pt*, *pp* **beset** [bɪˈsɛt] *vt* assalire.

**beside** [bɪˈsaɪd] *prep* accanto a; **to be ~ o.s.** (*with anger*) essere fuori di sé; **that's ~ the point** non c'entra.

**besides** [bɪˈsaɪdz] *ad* inoltre, per di più // *prep* oltre a; a parte.

**besiege** [bɪˈsiːdʒ] *vt* (*town*) assediare; (*fig*) tempestare.

**besought** [bɪˈsɔːt] *pt*, *pp of* **beseech**.

**best** [bɛst] *a* migliore // *ad* meglio; **the ~ part of** (*quantity*) la maggior parte di; **at ~** tutt'al più; **to make the ~ of sth** cavare il meglio possibile da qc; **to do one's ~** fare del proprio meglio; **to the ~ of my knowledge** per quel che ne so; **to the ~ of my ability** al massimo delle mie capacità; **~ man** *n* testimone *m* dello sposo.

**bestow** [bɪˈstəu] *vt* accordare; (*title*) conferire.

**bet** [bɛt] *n* scommessa // *vt*, *vi* (*pt*, *pp* **bet** *or* **betted**) scommettere.

**betray** [bɪˈtreɪ] *vt* tradire; **~al** *n* tradimento.

**better** [ˈbɛtə*] *a* migliore // *ad* meglio // *vt* migliorare // *n*: **to get the ~ of** avere la meglio su; **you had ~ do it** è meglio che lo faccia; **he thought ~ of it** cambiò idea; **to get ~** migliorare; **~ off** a più ricco(a); (*fig*): **you'd be ~ off this way** starebbe meglio così.

**betting** [ˈbɛtɪŋ] *n* scommesse *fpl*; **~ shop** *n* (*Brit*) ufficio dell'allibratore.

**between** [bɪˈtwiːn] *prep* tra // *ad* in mezzo, nel mezzo.

**beverage** [ˈbɛvərɪdʒ] *n* bevanda.

**bevy** [ˈbɛvɪ] *n* banda.

**beware** [bɪˈwɛə*] *vt*, *vi*: **to ~ (of)** stare attento(a) (a).

**bewildered** [bɪˈwɪldəd] *a* sconcertato(a), confuso(a).

**bewitching** [bɪˈwɪtʃɪŋ] *a* affascinante.

**beyond** [bɪˈjɔnd] *prep* (*in space*) oltre; (*exceeding*) al di sopra di // *ad* di là; **~ doubt** senza dubbio.

**bias** [ˈbaɪəs] *n* (*prejudice*) pregiudizio; (*preference*) preferenza; **~(s)ed** *a* parziale.

**bib** [bɪb] *n* bavaglino.

**Bible** [ˈbaɪbl] *n* Bibbia.

**bicarbonate of soda**

[baɪˈkɑːbənɪt-] n bicarbonato (di sodio).

**bicker** [ˈbɪkə*] vi bisticciare.

**bicycle** [ˈbaɪsɪkl] n bicicletta.

**bid** [bɪd] n offerta; (attempt) tentativo // vb (pt **bade** [bæd] or **bid**, pp **bidden** [ˈbɪdn] or **bid**) vi fare un'offerta // vt dare un'offerta di; to ~ sb good day dire buon giorno a qn; ~**der** n: the highest ~**der** il maggior offerente; ~**ding** n offerte fpl.

**bide** [baɪd] vt: to ~ one's time aspettare il momento giusto.

**bier** [bɪə*] n bara.

**bifocals** [baɪˈfəuklz] npl occhiali mpl bifocali.

**big** [bɪg] a grande; grosso(a).

**big dipper** [-ˈdɪpə*] n montagne fpl russe, otto m inv volante.

**bigheaded** [ˈbɪgˈhɛdɪd] a presuntuoso(a).

**bigot** [ˈbɪgət] n persona gretta; ~**ed** a gretto(a); ~**ry** n grettezza.

**big top** n tendone m del circo.

**bike** [baɪk] n bici f inv.

**bikini** [bɪˈkiːnɪ] n bikini m inv.

**bilingual** [baɪˈlɪŋgwəl] a bilingue.

**bill** [bɪl] n conto; (POL) atto; (US: banknote) banconota; (of bird) becco; "post no ~s" "divieto di affissione"; to fit or fill the ~ (fig) fare al caso; ~**board** n tabellone m.

**billet** [ˈbɪlɪt] n alloggio.

**billfold** [ˈbɪlfəuld] n (US) portafoglio.

**billiards** [ˈbɪljədz] n biliardo.

**billion** [ˈbɪljən] n (Brit) bilione m; (US) miliardo.

**bin** [bɪn] n (for coal, rubbish) bidone m; (for bread) cassetta; (dust~) pattumiera; (litter ~) cestino.

**bind** [baɪnd], pt, pp **bound** vt legare; (oblige) obbligare; ~**ing** n (of book) legatura // a (contract) vincolante.

**binge** [bɪndʒ] n (col): to go on a ~ fare baldoria.

**bingo** [ˈbɪŋgəu] n gioco simile alla tombola.

**binoculars** [bɪˈnɔkjuləz] npl binocolo.

**bio...** [baɪə'...] prefix: ~**chemistry** n biochimica; ~**graphy** [baɪˈɔgrəfɪ] n biografia; ~**logical** a biologico(a); ~**logy** [baɪˈɔlədʒɪ] n biologia.

**birch** [bəːtʃ] n betulla.

**bird** [bəːd] n uccello; (Brit: col: girl) bambola; ~**'s eye view** n vista panoramica; ~ **watcher** n ornitologo/a dilettante.

**Biro** [ˈbaɪrəu] n ® biro f inv ®.

**birth** [bəːθ] n nascita; ~ **certificate** n certificato di nascita; ~ **control** n controllo delle nascite; contraccezione f; ~**day** n compleanno; ~ **rate** n indice m di natalità.

**biscuit** [ˈbɪskɪt] n (Brit) biscotto.

**bisect** [baɪˈsɛkt] vt tagliare in due (parti).

**bishop** [ˈbɪʃəp] n vescovo.

**bit** [bɪt] pt of **bite** n pezzo; (of tool) punta; (COMPUT) bit m inv; (of horse) morso; a ~ of un po' di; a ~ mad un po' matto; ~ by ~ a poco a poco.

**bitch** [bɪtʃ] n (dog) cagna; (col!) vacca.

**bite** [baɪt] vt, vi (pt **bit** [bɪt], pp **bitten** [ˈbɪtn]) mordere // n morso; (insect ~) puntura; (mouthful) boccone m; let's have a ~ (to eat) mangiamo un boccone; to ~ one's nails mangiarsi le unghie.

**bitter** [ˈbɪtə*] a amaro(a); (wind, criticism) pungente // n (Brit: beer) birra amara; ~**ness** n amarezza; gusto amaro.

**blab** [blæb] vi parlare troppo.

**black** [blæk] a nero(a); (person): B~ negro/a // vt (Brit INDUSTRY) boicottare; to give sb a ~ eye fare un occhio nero a qn; in the ~ (bank account) in attivo; ~ **and blue** a tutto(a) pesto(a); ~**berry** n mora; ~**bird** n merlo; ~**board** n lavagna; ~**currant** n ribes m inv; ~**en** vt annerire; ~**ice** n strato trasparente di ghiaccio; ~**leg** n (Brit) crumiro; ~**list** n lista nera; ~**mail** n ricatto // vt ricattare; ~ **market** n mercato nero; ~**out** n oscuramente; (*fainting*) svenimento; **the B~ Sea** *n* il Mar Nero; **~ sheep** *n* pecora nera; **~smith** *n* fabbro ferraio; **~ spot** *n* (*AUT*) luogo famigerato per gli incidenti; (*for unemployment etc*) zona critica.

**bladder** ['blædə*] *n* vescica.

**blade** [bleɪd] *n* lama; (*of oar*) pala; **~ of grass** filo d'erba.

**blame** [bleɪm] *n* colpa // *vt*: **to ~ sb/ sth for sth** dare la colpa di qc a qn/ qc; **who's to ~?** chi è colpevole?

**bland** [blænd] *a* mite; (*taste*) blando(a).

**blank** [blæŋk] *a* bianco(a); (*look*) distratto(a) // *n* spazio vuoto; (*cartridge*) cartuccia a salve; **~ cheque** *n* assegno in bianco.

**blanket** ['blæŋkɪt] *n* coperta.

**blare** [bleə*] *vi* strombettare.

**blasphemy** ['blæsfɪmɪ] *n* bestemmia.

**blast** [blɑːst] *n* raffica di vento; esplosione *f* // *vt* far saltare; **~-off** *n* (*SPACE*) lancio.

**blatant** ['bleɪtənt] *a* flagrante.

**blaze** [bleɪz] *n* (*fire*) incendio; (*fig*) vampata // *vi* (*fire*) · ardere, fiammeggiare; (*fig*) infiammarsi // *vt*: **to ~ a trail** (*fig*) tracciare una via nuova.

**blazer** ['bleɪzə*] *n* blazer *m inv*.

**bleach** [bliːtʃ] *n* (*also*: **household ~**) varechina // *vt* (*material*) candeggiare; **~ed** *a* (*hair*) decolorato(a); **~ers** *npl* (*US SPORT*) posti *mpl* di gradinata.

**bleak** [bliːk] *a* tetro(a).

**bleary-eyed** ['blɪərɪˌaɪd] *a* dagli occhi offuscati.

**bleat** [bliːt] *vi* belare.

**bleed**, *pt*, *pp* **bled** [bliːd, blɛd] *vt* dissanguare // *vi* sanguinare; **my nose is ~ing** mi viene fuori sangue dal naso.

**bleeper** ['bliːpə*] *n* (*device*) cicalino.

**blemish** ['blɛmɪʃ] *n* macchia.

**blend** [blɛnd] *n* miscela // *vt* mescolare // *vi* (*colours etc*) armonizzare.

**bless**, *pt*, *pp* **blessed** *or* **blest** [blɛs,

blɛst] *vt* benedire; **~ing** *n* benedizione *f*; fortuna.

**blew** [bluː] *pt of* **blow**.

**blight** [blaɪt] *n* (*of plants*) golpe *f* // *vt* (*hopes etc*) deludere; (*life*) rovinare.

**blimey** ['blaɪmɪ] *excl* (*Brit col*) accidenti!

**blind** [blaɪnd] *a* cieco(a) // *n* (*for window*) avvolgibile *m*; (*Venetian ~*) veneziana // *vt* accecare; **~ alley** *n* vicolo cieco; **~ corner** *n* (*Brit*) svolta cieca; **~fold** *n* benda // *a*, *ad* bendato(a) // *vt* bendare gli occhi a; **~ly** *ad* ciecamente; **~ness** *n* cecità; **~ spot** *n* (*AUT etc*) punto cieco; (*fig*) punto debole.

**blink** [blɪŋk] *vi* battere gli occhi; (*light*) lampeggiare; **~ers** *npl* paraocchi *mpl*.

**bliss** [blɪs] *n* estasi *f*.

**blister** ['blɪstə*] *n* (*on skin*) vescica; (*on paintwork*) bolla // *vi* (*paint*) coprirsi di bolle.

**blithely** ['blaɪðlɪ] *ad* allegramente.

**blizzard** ['blɪzəd] *n* bufera di neve.

**bloated** ['bləutɪd] *a* gonfio(a).

**blob** [blɔb] *n* (*drop*) goccia; (*stain, spot*) macchia.

**bloc** [blɔk] *n* (*POL*) blocco.

**block** [blɔk] *n* blocco; (*in pipes*) ingombro; (*toy*) cubo; (*of buildings*) isolato // *vt* bloccare; **~ade** [-'keɪd] *n* blocco // *vt* assediare; **~age** *n* ostacolo; **~buster** *n* (*film, book*) grande successo; **~ of flats** *n* (*Brit*) caseggiato; **~ letters** *npl* stampatello.

**bloke** [bləuk] *n* (*Brit col*) tizio.

**blonde** [blɔnd] *a*, *n* biondo(a).

**blood** [blʌd] *n* sangue *m*; **~ donor** *n* donatore/trice di sangue; **~ group** *n* gruppo sanguigno; **~hound** *n* segugio; **~ poisoning** *n* setticemia; **~ pressure** *n* pressione *f* sanguigna; **~shed** *n* spargimento di sangue; **~shot** *a*: **~shot eyes** occhi iniettati di sangue; **~stream** *n* flusso del sangue; **~ test** *n* analisi *f inv* del sangue; **~thirsty** *a* assetato(a) di sangue; **~y** a sanguinoso(a); (Brit col!): **this ~y** ... questo maledetto ...; **~y awful/ good** (col!) veramente terribile/ forte; **~y-minded** a (Brit col) indisponente.

**bloom** [blu:m] n fiore m // vi essere in fiore.

**blossom** ['blɔsəm] n fiore m; (with pl sense) fiori mpl // vi essere in fiore.

**blot** [blɔt] n macchia // vt macchiare; **to ~ out** (memories) cancellare; (view) nascondere; (nation, city) annientare.

**blotchy** ['blɔtʃi] a (complexion) coperto(a) di macchie.

**blotting paper** ['blɔtiŋ-] n carta assorbente.

**blouse** [blauz] n (feminine garment) camicetta.

**blow** [bləu] n colpo // vb (pt blew, pp blown [blu:, bləun]) vi soffiare // vt (fuse) far saltare; **to ~ one's nose** soffiarsi il naso; **to ~ a whistle** fischiare; **to ~ away** vt portare via; **to ~ down** vt abbattere; **to ~ off** vt far volare via; **to ~ out** vi scoppiare; **to ~ over** vi calmarsi; **to ~ up** vi saltare in aria // vt far saltare in aria; (tyre) gonfiare; (PHOT) ingrandire; **~-dry** n messa in piega a föhn; **~lamp** n (Brit) lampada a benzina per saldare; **~-out** n (of tyre) scoppio; **~torch** n = **~lamp**.

**blue** [blu:] a azzurro(a); **~ film/joke** film/barzelletta pornografico(a); **out of the ~** (fig) all'improvviso; **to have the ~s** essere depresso(a); **~bottle** n moscone m; **~ jeans** mpl blue-jeans mpl; **~print** n (fig): **~print (for)** formula (di).

**bluff** [blʌf] vi bluffare // n bluff m inv // a (person) brusco(a); **to call sb's ~** mettere alla prova il bluff di qn.

**blunder** ['blʌndə*] n abbaglio // vi prendere un abbaglio.

**blunt** [blʌnt] a smussato(a); spuntato(a); (person) brusco(a) // vt

smussare; spuntare.

**blur** [blə:*] n cosa offuscata // vt offuscare.

**blurb** [blə:b] n trafiletto pubblicitario.

**blurt** [blə:t]: **to ~ out** vt lasciarsi sfuggire.

**blush** [blʌʃ] vi arrossire // n rossore m.

**blustery** ['blʌstəri] a (weather) burrascoso(a).

**boar** [bɔ:*] n cinghiale m.

**board** [bɔ:d] n tavola; (on wall) tabellone m; (committee) consiglio, comitato; (in firm) consiglio d'amministrazione // vt (ship) salire a bordo di; (train) salire su; (NAUT, AVIAT): **on ~** a bordo; **full ~** (Brit) pensione completa; **half ~** (Brit) mezza pensione; **~ and lodging** vitto e alloggio; **which goes by the ~** (fig) che viene abbandonato; **to ~ up** vt (door) chiudere con assi; **~er** n pensionante m/f; (SCOL) convittore/trice; **~ing card** n (AVIAT, NAUT) carta d'imbarco; **~ing house** n pensione f; **~ing school** n collegio; **~ room** n sala del consiglio.

**boast** [bəust] vi: **to ~** (about or of) vantarsi (di) // vt vantare // n vanteria; vanto.

**boat** [bəut] n nave f; (small) barca; **~er** n (hat) paglietta; **~swain** ['bəusn] n nostromo.

**bob** [bɔb] vi (boat, cork on water: also: **~ up and down**) andare su e giù // n (Brit col) = **shilling**; **to ~ up** vi saltare fuori.

**bobby** ['bɔbi] n (Brit col) poliziotto.

**bobsleigh** ['bɔbsleɪ] n bob m inv.

**bode** [bəud] vi: **to ~ well/ill (for)** essere di buon/cattivo auspicio (per).

**bodily** ['bɔdili] a fisico(a), corporale // ad corporalmente; interamente; in persona.

**body** ['bɔdi] n corpo; (of car) carrozzeria; (of plane) fusoliera; (fig: quantity) quantità f inv; **a wine with ~** un vino corposo; **~building** n culturismo; **~guard** n guardia del corpo; **~work** n carrozzeria.

**bog** [bɔg] n palude f // vt: **to get ~ged down** (fig) impantanarsi.

**boggle** ['bɔgəl] vi: **the mind ~s** è incredibile.

**bogus** ['bəugəs] a falso(a); finto(a).

**boil** [bɔɪl] vt, vi bollire // n (MED) foruncolo; **to come to the** (Brit) or a (US) **~** raggiungere l'ebollizione; **to ~ down** vi (fig): **to ~ down to** ridursi a; **to ~ over** vi traboccare (bollendo); **~ed egg** n uovo alla coque; **~ed potatoes** npl patate fpl bollite or lesse; **~er** n caldaia; **~er suit** n (Brit) tuta; **~ing point** n punto di ebollizione.

**boisterous** ['bɔɪstərəs] a chiassoso(a).

**bold** [bəuld] a audace; (child) impudente; (outline) chiaro(a); (colour) deciso(a).

**bollard** ['bɔləd] n (Brit AUT) colonnina luminosa.

**bolster** ['bəulstə*] n capezzale m; **to ~ up** vt sostenere.

**bolt** [bəult] n chiavistello; (with nut) bullone m // ad: **~ upright** diritto(a) come un fuso // vt serrare; (food) mangiare in fretta // vi scappare via.

**bomb** [bɔm] n bomba // vt bombardare; **~ disposal unit** n corpo degli artificieri; **~er** n (AVIAT) bombardiere m; **~shell** n (fig) notizia bomba.

**bona fide** ['bəunə'faɪdɪ] a sincero(a); (offer) onesto(a).

**bond** [bɔnd] n legame m; (binding promise, FINANCE) obbligazione f; (COMM): **in ~** in attesa di sdoganamento.

**bondage** ['bɔndɪdʒ] n schiavitù f.

**bone** [bəun] n osso; (of fish) spina, lisca // vt disossare; togliere le spine a; **~ idle**, **~ lazy** a pigrissimo(a).

**bonfire** ['bɔnfaɪə*] n falò m inv.

**bonnet** ['bɔnɪt] n cuffia; (Brit: of car) cofano.

**bonus** ['bəunəs] n premio.

**bony** ['bəunɪ] a (arm, face, MED:

tissue) osseo(a); (meat) pieno(a) di ossi; (fish) pieno(a) di spine.

**boo** [bu:] excl ba! // vt fischiare // n fischio.

**booby trap** ['bu:bɪ-] n trappola.

**book** [buk] n libro; (of stamps etc) blocchetto // vt (ticket, seat, room) prenotare; (driver) multare; (football player) ammonire; **~s** npl (COMM) conti mpl; **~case** n scaffale m; **~ing office** n (Brit RAIL) biglietteria; (: THEATRE) botteghino; **~keeping** n contabilità; **~let** n libricino; **~maker** n allibratore m; **~seller** n libraio; **~shop**, **~ store** n libreria.

**boom** [bu:m] n (noise) rimbombo; (busy period) boom m inv // vi rimbombare; andare a gonfie vele.

**boon** [bu:n] n vantaggio.

**boost** [bu:st] n spinta // vt spingere; **~er** n (MED) richiamo.

**boot** [bu:t] n stivale m; (for hiking) scarpone m da montagna; (for football etc) scarpa; (Brit: of car) portabagagli m inv // vt (COMPUT) inizializzare; **to ~** (in addition) per giunta, in più.

**booth** [bu:ð] n (at fair) baraccone m; (of cinema, telephone, voting ~) cabina.

**booty** ['bu:tɪ] n bottino.

**booze** [bu:z] n (col) alcool m.

**border** ['bɔ:də*] n orlo; margine m; (of a country) frontiera; the **B~s** la zona di confine tra l'Inghilterra e la Scozia; **to ~ on** vt fus confinare con; **~line** n (fig) linea di demarcazione; **~line case** n caso limite.

**bore** [bɔ:*] pt of **bear** // vt (hole) perforare; (person) annoiare // n (person) seccatore/trice; (of gun) calibro; **to be ~d** annoiarsi; **~dom** n noia; **boring** a noioso(a).

**born** [bɔ:n] a: **to be ~** nascere; **I was ~ in 1960** sono nato nel 1960.

**borne** [bɔ:n] pp of **bear**.

**borough** ['bʌrə] n comune m.

**borrow** ['bɔrəu] vt: **to ~ sth** (from

sb) prendere in prestito qc (da qn).

**bosom** ['buzəm] $n$ petto; ($fig$) seno.

**boss** [bɔs] $n$ capo // $vt$ comandare; **~y** $a$ prepotente.

**bosun** ['bəusn] $n$ nostromo.

**botany** ['bɔtəni] $n$ botanica.

**botch** [bɔtʃ] $vt$ ($also:$ ~ **up**) fare un pasticcio di.

**both** [bəuθ] $a$ entrambi(e), tutt'e due // $pronoun:$ ~ (**of them**) entrambi(e); ~ **of us went, we** ~ **went** ci siamo andati tutt'e due // $ad:$ **they sell** ~ **meat and poultry** vendono insieme la carne ed il pollame.

**bother** ['bɔðə*] $vt$ ($worry$) preoccupare; ($annoy$) infastidire // $vi$ ($gen:$ ~ **o.s.**) preoccuparsi // $n:$ **it is a** ~ **to have to do** è una seccatura dover fare; **it was no** ~ non c'era problema; **to** ~ **doing sth** darsi la pena di fare qc.

**bottle** ['bɔtl] $n$ bottiglia; ($baby's$) biberon $m$ $inv$ // $vt$ imbottigliare; **to** ~ **up** $vt$ contenere; **~neck** $n$ ingorgo; **~-opener** $n$ apribottiglie $m$ $inv$.

**bottom** ['bɔtəm] $n$ fondo; ($buttocks$) sedere $m$ // $a$ più basso(a); ultimo(a); **at the** ~ **of** in fondo a.

**bough** [bau] $n$ ramo.

**bought** [bɔːt] $pt$, $pp$ of **buy**.

**boulder** ['bəuldə*] $n$ masso (tondeggiante).

**bounce** [bauns] $vi$ ($ball$) rimbalzare; ($cheque$) essere restituito(a) // $vt$ far rimbalzare // $n$ ($rebound$) rimbalzo; **~r** $n$ ($col$) buttafuori $m$ $inv$.

**bound** [baund] $pt$, $pp$ of **bind** // $n$ ($gen$ $pl$) limite $m$; ($leap$) salto // $vi$ ($leap$) saltare; ($limit$) delimitare // $a:$ **to be** ~ **to do sth** ($obliged$) essere costretto(a) a fare qc; **he's** ~ **to fail** ($likely$) è certo di fallire; ~ **for** diretto(a) a; **out of** ~**s** il cui accesso è vietato.

**boundary** ['baundrı] $n$ confine $m$.

**bourgeois** ['buəʒwa:] $a$, $n$ borghese ($m/f$).

**bout** [baut] $n$ periodo; ($of$ $malaria$

$etc$) attacco; ($BOXING$ $etc$) incontro.

**bow** $n$ [bəu] nodo; ($weapon$) arco; ($MUS$) archetto; [bau] ($with$ $body$) inchino; ($NAUT:$ $also:$ ~**s**) prua // $vi$ [bau] inchinarsi; ($yield$): **to** ~ **to** $or$ **before** sottomettersi a.

**bowels** ['bauəlz] $npl$ intestini $mpl$; ($fig$) viscere $fpl$.

**bowl** [bəul] $n$ ($for$ $eating$) scodella; ($for$ $washing$) bacino; ($ball$) boccia; ($of$ $pipe$) fornello // $vi$ ($CRICKET$) servire (la palla); ~**s** $n$ gioco delle bocce.

**bow-legged** ['bəu'lεgid] $a$ dalle gambe storte.

**bowler** ['bəulə*] $n$ giocatore $m$ di bocce; ($CRICKET$) giocatore che serve la palla; ($Brit:$ $also:$ ~ **hat**) bombetta.

**bowling** ['bəulıŋ] $n$ ($game$) gioco delle bocce; ~ **alley** $n$ pista da bowling; ~ **green** $n$ campo di bocce.

**bow tie** $n$ cravatta a farfalla.

**box** [bɔks] $n$ scatola; ($also:$ **cardboard** ~) cartone $m$; ($THEATRE$) palco // $vi$ fare del pugilato; ~**er** $n$ ($person$) pugile $m$; ~**ing** $n$ ($SPORT$) pugilato; **B~ing Day** $n$ ($Brit$) Santo Stefano; ~**ing gloves** $npl$ guantoni $mpl$ da pugile; ~**ing ring** $n$ ring $m$ $inv$; ~ **office** $n$ biglietteria; ~ **room** $n$ ripostiglio.

**boy** [bɔı] $n$ ragazzo.

**boycott** ['bɔıkɔt] $n$ boicottaggio // $vt$ boicottare.

**boyfriend** ['bɔıfrεnd] $n$ ragazzo.

**B.R.** $abbr$ = **British Rail**.

**bra** [bra:] $n$ reggipetto, reggiseno.

**brace** [breıs] $n$ sostegno; ($on$ $teeth$) apparecchio correttore; ($tool$) trapano // $vt$ rinforzare, sostenere; ~**s** $npl$ ($Brit$) bretelle $fpl$; **to** ~ **o.s.** ($fig$) farsi coraggio.

**bracelet** ['breıslıt] $n$ braccialetto.

**bracing** ['breısıŋ] $a$ invigorante.

**bracken** ['brækən] $n$ felce $f$.

**bracket** ['brækıt] $n$ ($TECH$) mensola; ($group$) gruppo; ($TYP$) parentesi $f$ $inv$ // $vt$ mettere fra parentesi.

**brag** [bræg] $vi$ vantarsi.

**braid** [breɪd] n (trimming) passamano; (of hair) treccia.

**brain** [breɪn] n cervello; ~s npl cervella fpl; he's got ~s è intelligente; ~child n creatura, creazione f; ~wash vt fare un lavaggio di cervello a; ~wave n lampo di genio; ~y a intelligente.

**braise** [breɪz] vt brasare.

**brake** [breɪk] n (on vehicle) freno // vt, vi frenare; ~ fluid n liquido dei freni; ~ light n (fanalino dello) stop m inv.

**bramble** ['bræmbl] n rovo.

**bran** [bræn] n crusca.

**branch** [brɑːntʃ] n ramo; (COMM) succursale f // vi diramarsi.

**brand** [brænd] n marca // vt (cattle) marcare (a ferro rovente).

**brand-new** ['brænd'njuː] a nuovo(a) di zecca.

**brandy** ['brændɪ] n brandy m inv.

**brash** [bræʃ] a sfacciato(a).

**brass** [brɑːs] n ottone m; the ~ (MUS) gli ottoni; ~ band n fanfara.

**brassière** ['bræsɪə*] n reggipetto, reggiseno.

**brat** [bræt] n (pej) marmocchio, monello(a).

**bravado** [brəˈvɑːdəu] n spavalderia.

**brave** [breɪv] a coraggioso(a) // n guerriero m pelle rossa inv // vt affrontare; ~ry n coraggio.

**brawl** [brɔːl] n rissa.

**brawn** [brɔːn] n muscolo; (meat) carne f di testa di maiale.

**bray** [breɪ] vi ragliare.

**brazen** ['breɪzn] a svergognato(a) // vt: to ~ it out fare lo sfacciato.

**brazier** ['breɪzɪə*] n braciere m.

**Brazil** [brəˈzɪl] n Brasile m.

**breach** [briːtʃ] vt aprire una breccia in // n (gap) breccia, varco; (breaking): ~ of contract rottura di contratto; ~ of the peace violazione f dell'ordine pubblico.

**bread** [bred] n pane m; ~ and butter n pane e burro; (fig) mezzi mpl di sussistenza; ~bin, (US) ~box n cassetta f portapane inv;

~crumbs npl briciole fpl; (CULIN) pangrattato; ~line n: to be on the ~line avere appena denaro per vivere.

**breadth** [brɛtθ] n larghezza.

**breadwinner** ['brɛdwɪnə*] n chi guadagna il pane per tutta la famiglia.

**break** [breɪk] vb (pt broke [brəuk], pp broken ['brəukən]) vt rompere; (law) violare // vi rompersi; (weather) cambiare // n (gap) breccia; (fracture) rottura; (rest, also SCOL) intervallo; (: short) pausa; (chance) possibilità f inv; to ~ one's leg etc rompersi la gamba etc; to ~ a record battere un primato; to ~ the news to sb comunicare per primo la notizia a qn; to ~ down vt (figures, data) analizzare // vi crollare; (MED) avere un esaurimento (nervoso); (AUT) guastarsi; to ~ even vi coprire le spese; to ~ free or loose vi spezzare i legami; to ~ in vt (horse etc) domare // vi (burglar) fare irruzione; to ~ into vt fus (house) fare irruzione in; to ~ off vi (speaker) interrompersi; (branch) troncarsi; to ~ open vt (door etc) sfondare; to ~ out vi evadere; to ~ out in spots coprirsi di macchie; to ~ up vi (partnership) sciogliersi; (friends) separarsi // vt fare in pezzi, spaccare; (fight etc) interrompere, far cessare; ~age n rottura; ~down n (AUT) guasto; (in communications) interruzione f; (MED: also: nervous ~down) esaurimento nervoso; ~down van n (Brit) carro m attrezzi inv; ~er n frangente m.

**breakfast** ['brɛkfəst] n colazione f.

**break: ~in n irruzione f; ~ing and entering n (LAW) violazione f di domicilio con scasso; ~through n (MIL) breccia; (fig) passo avanti; ~water n frangiflutti m inv.

**breast** [brɛst] n (of woman) seno m; (chest) petto; ~feed vt, vi (irg:

*like* **feed**) allattare (al seno); ~ **stroke** *n* nuoto a rana.

**breath** [brɛθ] *n* fiato; **out of** ~ senza fiato.

**Breathalyser** ['brɛθəlaɪzə*] *n* ® (*Brit*) alcoltest *m inv*.

**breathe** [bri:ð] *vt, vi* respirare; **to** ~ **in** *vt* respirare // *vi* inspirare; **to** ~ **out** *vt, vi* espirare; ~**r** *n* attimo di respiro; **breathing** *n* respiro, respirazione *f*.

**breathless** ['brɛθlɪs] *a* senza fiato.

**breath-taking** ['brɛθteɪkɪŋ] *a* sbalorditivo(a).

**breed** [bri:d] *vb* (*pt, pp* **bred** [brɛd]) *vt* allevare // *vi* riprodursi // *n* razza, varietà *f inv*; ~**ing** *n* riproduzione *f*; allevamento; (*upbringing*) educazione *f*.

**breeze** [bri:z] *n* brezza.

**breezy** ['bri:zɪ] *a* arioso(a); allegro(a).

**brew** [bru:] *vt* (*tea*) fare un infuso di; (*beer*) fare; (*plot*) tramare // *vi* (*tea*) essere in infusione; (*beer*) essere in fermentazione; (*fig*) bollire in pentola; ~**er** *n* birraio; ~**ery** *n* fabbrica di birra.

**bribe** [braɪb] *n* bustarella // *vt* comprare; ~**ry** *n* corruzione *f*.

**brick** [brɪk] *n* mattone *m*; ~**layer** *n* muratore *m*.

**bridal** ['braɪdl] *a* nuziale.

**bride** [braɪd] *n* sposa; ~**groom** *n* sposo; ~**smaid** *n* damigella d'onore.

**bridge** [brɪdʒ] *n* ponte *m*; (*NAUT*) ponte di comando; (*of nose*) dorso; (*CARDS, DENTISTRY*) ponte *m inv* // *vt* (*river*) fare un ponte sopra; (*gap*) colmare.

**bridle** ['braɪdl] *n* briglia // *vt* tenere a freno; (*horse*) mettere la briglia a; ~ **path** *n* sentiero (per cavalli).

**brief** [bri:f] *a* breve // *n* (*LAW*) comparsa // *vt* dare istruzioni a; ~**s** *npl* mutande *fpl*; ~**case** *n* cartella; ~**ing** *n* istruzioni *fpl*; ~**ly** *ad* (*glance*) di sfuggita; (*explain, say*) brevemente.

**bright** [braɪt] *a* luminoso(a);

(*person*) sveglio(a); (*colour*) vivace; ~**en** (*also:* ~**en up**) *vt* (*room*) rendere luminoso(a); ornare // *vi* schiarirsi; (*person*) rallegrarsi.

**brilliance** ['brɪljəns] *n* splendore *m*.

**brilliant** ['brɪljənt] *a* splendente.

**brim** [brɪm] *n* orlo.

**brine** [braɪn] *n* acqua salmastra; (*CULIN*) salamoia.

**bring** [brɪŋ], *pt, pp* **brought** *vt* portare; **to** ~ **about** *vt* causare; **to** ~ **back** *vt* riportare; **to** ~ **down** *vt* portare giù; abbattere; **to** ~ **forward** *vt* portare avanti; (*in time*) anticipare; **to** ~ **off** *vt* (*task, plan*) portare a compimento; **to** ~ **out** *vt* (*meaning*) mettere in evidenza; **to** ~ **round** *or* **to** *vt* (*unconscious person*) far rinvenire; **to** ~ **up** *vt* allevare; (*question*) introdurre; (*food: vomit*) rimettere, rigurgitare.

**brink** [brɪŋk] *n* orlo.

**brisk** [brɪsk] *a* vivace.

**bristle** ['brɪsl] *n* setola // *vi* rizzarsi; **bristling with** irto(a) di.

**Britain** ['brɪtən] *n* (*also:* **Great** ~) Gran Bretagna.

**British** ['brɪtɪʃ] *a* britannico(a); **the** ~ *npl* i Britannici; **the** ~ **Isles** *npl* le Isole Britanniche; ~ **Rail (B.R.)** *n* compagnia ferroviaria britannica, ≈ Ferrovie *fpl* dello Stato (F.S.).

**Briton** ['brɪtən] *n* britannico/a.

**brittle** ['brɪtl] *a* fragile.

**broach** [brəʊtʃ] *vt* (*subject*) affrontare.

**broad** [brɔ:d] *a* largo(a); (*distinction*) generale; (*accent*) spiccato(a); **in** ~ **daylight** in pieno giorno; ~**cast** *n* trasmissione // *vb* (*pt, pp* ~**cast**) *vt* trasmettere per radio (*or per television*) // *vi* fare una trasmissione; ~**en** *vt* allargare // *vi* allargarsi; ~**ly** *ad* (*fig*) in generale; ~**-minded** *a* di mente aperta.

**broccoli** ['brɔkəlɪ] *n* broccoli *mpl*.

**brochure** ['brəʊʃjʊə*] *n* dépliant *m inv*.

**broil** [brɔɪl] *vt* cuocere a fuoco vivo.

**broke** [brəuk] *pt of* **break** // *a* (*col*) squattrinato(a).

**broken** ['brəukn] *pp of* **break** // *a*: ~ **leg** *etc* gamba *etc* rotta; **in** ~ **English** in un inglese stentato; ~-**hearted** *a*: **to be** ~**hearted** avere il cuore spezzato.

**broker** ['brəukə*] *n* agente *m*.

**brolly** ['brɔlɪ] *n* (*Brit col*) ombrello.

**bronchitis** [brɔŋ'kaɪtɪs] *n* bronchite *f*.

**bronze** [brɔnz] *n* bronzo.

**brooch** [brəutʃ] *n* spilla.

**brood** [bru:d] *n* covata // *vi* (*hen*) covare; (*person*) rimuginare.

**brook** [bruk] *n* ruscello.

**broom** [brum] *n* scopa; ~**stick** *n* manico di scopa.

**Bros.** *abbr* (= *Brothers*) F.lli.

**broth** [brɔθ] *n* brodo.

**brothel** ['brɔθl] *n* bordello.

**brother** ['brʌðə*] *n* fratello; ~-**in-law** *n* cognato.

**brought** [brɔ:t] *pt, pp of* **bring**.

**brow** [brau] *n* fronte *f*; (*rare, gen*: *eye*~) sopracciglio; (*of hill*) cima.

**brown** [braun] *a* bruno(a), marrone // *n* (*colour*) color *m* bruno *or* marrone // *vt* (*CULIN*) rosolare; ~ **bread** *n* pane *m* integrale, pane nero.

**brownie** ['braunɪ] *n* giovane esploratrice *f*.

**brown paper** *n* carta da pacchi *or* da imballaggio.

**brown sugar** *n* zucchero greggio.

**browse** [brauz] *vi* (*among books*) curiosare fra i libri.

**bruise** [bru:z] *n* ammaccatura // *vt* ammaccare.

**brunette** [bru:'net] *n* bruna.

**brunt** [brʌnt] *n*: **the** ~ **of** (*attack, criticism etc*) il peso maggiore di.

**brush** [brʌʃ] *n* spazzola; (*quarrel*) schermaglia // *vt* spazzolare; ~ **past**, ~ **against** sfiorare; **to** ~ **aside** *vt* scostare; **to** ~ **up** *vt* (*knowledge*) rinfrescare; ~**wood** *n* macchia.

**Brussels** ['brʌslz] *n* Bruxelles *f*; ~

**sprout** *n* cavolo di Bruxelles.

**brutal** ['bru:tl] *a* brutale.

**brute** [bru:t] *n* bestia // *a*: **by** ~ **force** con la forza, a viva forza.

**B.Sc.** *n abbr* = **Bachelor of Science**.

**bubble** ['bʌbl] *n* bolla // *vi* ribollire; (*sparkle, fig*) essere effervescente; ~ **bath** *n* bagnoschiuma *m inv*.

**buck** [bʌk] *n* maschio (*di camoscio, caprone, coniglio etc*); (*US col*) dollaro // *vi* sgroppare; **to pass the** ~ (**to sb**) scaricare (su di qn) la propria responsabilità; **to** ~ **up** *vi* (*cheer up*) rianimarsi.

**bucket** ['bʌkɪt] *n* secchio.

**buckle** ['bʌkl] *n* fibbia // *vt* affibbiare; (*warp*) deformare.

**bud** [bʌd] *n* gemma; (*of flower*) boccio // *vi* germogliare; (*flower*) sbocciare.

**Buddhism** ['budɪzəm] *n* buddismo.

**budding** ['bʌdɪŋ] *a* (*poet etc*) in erba.

**buddy** ['bʌdɪ] *n* (*US*) compagno.

**budge** [bʌdʒ] *vt* scostare // *vi* spostarsi.

**budgerigar** ['bʌdʒərɪga:*] *n* pappagallino.

**budget** ['bʌdʒɪt] *n* bilancio preventivo // *vi*: **to** ~ **for sth** fare il bilancio per qc.

**budgie** ['bʌdʒɪ] *n* = **budgerigar**.

**buff** [bʌf] *a* color camoscio // *n* (*enthusiast*) appassionato/a.

**buffalo**, *pl* ~ *or* ~**es** ['bʌfələu] *n* bufalo; (*US*) bisonte *m*.

**buffer** ['bʌfə*] *n* respingente *m*; (*COMPUT*) memoria tampone, buffer *m inv*.

**buffet** *n* ['bufeɪ] (*food, Brit: bar*) buffet *m inv* // *vt* ['bʌfɪt] schiaffeggiare; scuotere; urtare; ~ **car** *n* (*Brit RAIL*) = servizio ristoro.

**bug** [bʌg] *n* (*insect*) cimice *f*; (: *gen*) insetto; (*fig: germ*) virus *m inv*; (*spy device*) microfono spia // *vt* mettere sotto controllo; ~**bear** *n* spauracchio.

**bugle** ['bju:gl] *n* tromba.

**build** [bɪld] n (of person) corporatura // vt (pt, pp **built**) costruire; **to ~ up** vt accumulare; aumentare; **~er** n costruttore m; **~ing** n costruzione f; edificio; (also: **~ing trade**) edilizia; **~ing society** n (Brit) società f inv immobiliare.

**built** [bɪlt] pt, pp of build; **~-in** a (cupboard) a muro; (device) incorporato(a); **~-up area** n abitato.

**bulb** [bʌlb] n (BOT) bulbo; (ELEC) lampadina.

**bulge** [bʌldʒ] n rigonfiamento // vi essere protuberante or rigonfio(a); **to be bulging with** essere pieno(a) or zeppo(a) di.

**bulk** [bʌlk] n massa, volume m; **in ~** a pacchi (or cassette etc); (COMM) all'ingrosso; **the ~** of il grosso di; **~y** a grosso(a); voluminoso(a).

**bull** [bʊl] n toro; **~dog** n bulldog m inv.

**bulldozer** ['bʊldəʊzə*] n bulldozer m inv.

**bullet** ['bʊlɪt] n pallottola.

**bulletin** ['bʊlɪtɪn] n bollettino.

**bulletproof** ['bʊlɪtpruːf] a (car) blindato(a); (vest etc) antiproiettile inv.

**bullfight** ['bʊlfaɪt] n corrida; **~er** n torero; **~ing** n tauromachia.

**bullion** ['bʊljən] n oro or argento in lingotti.

**bullock** ['bʊlək] n giovenco.

**bullring** ['bʊlrɪŋ] n arena (per corride).

**bull's-eye** ['bʊlzaɪ] n centro del bersaglio.

**bully** ['bʊlɪ] n prepotente m // vt angariare; (frighten) intimidire.

**bum** [bʌm] n (col: backside) culo; (tramp) vagabondo/a.

**bumblebee** ['bʌmblbiː] n bombo.

**bump** [bʌmp] n (blow) colpo; (jolt) scossa; (on road etc) protuberanza; (on head) bernoccolo // vt battere; **to ~ into** vt fus scontrarsi con; **~er** n paraurti m inv // a: **~er harvest** raccolto eccezionale.

**bumptious** ['bʌmpʃəs] a presuntuoso(a).

**bumpy** ['bʌmpɪ] a (road) dissestato(a).

**bun** [bʌn] n focaccia; (of hair) crocchia.

**bunch** [bʌntʃ] n (of flowers, keys) mazzo; (of bananas) ciuffo; (of people) gruppo; **~ of grapes** grappolo d'uva.

**bundle** [bʌndl] n fascio // vt (also: **~ up**) legare in un fascio; (put): **to ~ sth/sb into** spingere qc/qn in.

**bungalow** ['bʌŋgələʊ] n bungalow m inv.

**bungle** ['bʌŋgl] vt abborracciare.

**bunion** ['bʌnjən] n callo (al piede).

**bunk** [bʌŋk] n cuccetta; **~ beds** npl letti mpl a castello.

**bunker** ['bʌŋkə*] n (coal store) ripostiglio per il carbone; (MIL, GOLF) bunker m inv.

**bunny** ['bʌnɪ] n (also: **~ rabbit**) coniglietto.

**bunting** ['bʌntɪŋ] n pavesi mpl, bandierine fpl.

**buoy** [bɔɪ] n boa; **to ~ up** vt tenere a galla; (fig) sostenere; **~ant** a galleggiante; (fig) vivace.

**burden** ['bəːdn] n carico, fardello // vt caricare; (oppress) opprimere.

**bureau** ['bjʊə~x [bjuə'rəu, -z] n (Brit: writing desk) scrivania; (US: chest of drawers) cassettone m; (office) ufficio, agenzia.

**bureaucracy** [bjuə'rɔkrəsɪ] n burocrazia.

**burglar** ['bəːglə*] n scassinatore m; **~ alarm** n campanello antifurto; **~y** n furto con scasso.

**burial** ['bɛrɪəl] n sepoltura.

**burly** ['bəːlɪ] a robusto(a).

**Burma** ['bəːmə] n Birmania.

**burn** [bəːn] vt, vi (pt, pp **burned** or **burnt**) bruciare // n bruciatura, scottatura; **to ~ down** vt distruggere col fuoco; **~er** n (on cooker) fornello; (TECH) bruciatore m, becco (a gas).

**burnt** [bəːnt] pt, pp of burn.

**burrow** ['bʌrəu] n tana // vt scavare.

**bursar** ['bɜːsə*] n economo/a; (Brit: student) borsista m/f; **~y** n (Brit) borsa di studio.

**burst** [bɜːst] vb (pt, pp **burst**) vt far scoppiare (or esplodere) // vi esplodere; (tyre) scoppiare // n scoppio; (also: ~ **pipe**) rottura nel tubo, perdita; **to ~ into flames/ tears** scoppiare in fiamme/lacrime; **to ~ out laughing** scoppiare a ridere; **to be ~ing with** essere pronto a scoppiare di; **to ~ into** vt fus (room etc) irrompere in; **to ~ open** vi aprirsi improvvisamente; (door) spalancarsi.

**bury** ['bɛrɪ] vt seppellire.

**bus, ~es** [bʌs, 'bʌsɪz] n autobus m inv.

**bush** [buʃ] n cespuglio; (scrub land) macchia; **to beat about the ~** menare il cane per l'aia.

**bushy** ['buʃɪ] a cespuglioso(a).

**busily** ['bɪzɪlɪ] ad con impegno, alacremente.

**business** ['bɪznɪs] n (matter) affare m; (trading) affari mpl; (firm) azienda; (job, duty) lavoro; **to be away on ~** essere andato via per affari; **it's none of my ~** questo non mi riguarda; **he means ~** non scherza; **~like** a serio(a); efficiente; **~man/woman** n uomo/ donna d'affari; **~ trip** n viaggio d'affari.

**busker** ['bʌskə*] n (Brit) suonatore/ trice ambulante.

**bus-stop** ['bʌsstɔp] n fermata d'autobus.

**bust** [bʌst] n busto; (ANAT) seno // a (col: broken) rotto(a); **to go ~** fallire.

**bustle** ['bʌsl] n movimento, attività // vi darsi da fare; **bustling** a (person) indaffarato(a); (town) animato(a).

**busy** ['bɪzɪ] a occupato(a); (shop, street) molto frequentato(a) // vt: **~ o.s.** darsi da fare; **~body** n ficcanaso; **~ signal** n (US TEL) se-

gnale m di occupato.

---

KEYWORD

---

**but** [bʌt] ◆ cj ma; **I'd love to come, ~ I'm busy** vorrei tanto venire, ma ho da fare
◆ prep (apart from, except) eccetto, tranne, meno; **he was nothing ~ trouble** non dava altro che guai; **no-one ~ him can do it** nessuno può farlo tranne lui; **~ for you/your help** se non fosse per te/per il tuo aiuto; **anything ~ that** tutto ma non questo
◆ ad (just, only) solo, soltanto; **she's ~ a child** è solo una bambina; **had I ~ known** se solo avessi saputo; **I can ~ try** tentar non nuoce; **all ~ finished** quasi finito.

**butcher** ['butʃə*] n macellaio // vt macellare.

**butler** ['bʌtlə*] n maggiordomo.

**butt** [bʌt] n (cask) grossa botte f; (thick end) estremità f più grossa; (of gun) calcio; (of cigarette) mozzicone m; (Brit fig: target) oggetto // vt cozzare; **to ~ in** vi (interrupt) interrompere.

**butter** ['bʌtə*] n burro // vt imburrare; **~cup** n ranuncolo.

**butterfly** ['bʌtəflaɪ] n farfalla; (SWIMMING: also: ~ **stroke**) (nuoto a) farfalla.

**buttocks** ['bʌtəks] npl natiche fpl.

**button** ['bʌtn] n bottone m // vt (also: ~ **up**) abbottonare // vi abbottonarsi.

**buttress** ['bʌtrɪs] n contrafforte f.

**buxom** ['bʌksəm] a formoso(a).

**buy** [baɪ], pt, pp **bought** vt comprare; **to ~ sb sth/sth from sb** comprare qc per qn/qc da qn; **to ~ sb a drink** offrire da bere a qn; **~er** n compratore/trice.

**buzz** [bʌz] n ronzio; (col: phone call) colpo di telefono // vi ronzare.

**buzzer** ['bʌzə*] n cicalino.

**buzz word** n (col) termine m di gran moda.

KEYWORD

**by** [baɪ] ♦ prep **1** (referring to cause, agent) da; killed ~ lightning ucciso da un fulmine; surrounded ~ a fence circondato da uno steccato; a painting ~ Picasso un quadro di Picasso

**2** (referring to method, manner, means): ~ bus/car/train in autobus/macchina/treno, con l'autobus/la macchina/il treno; to pay ~ cheque pagare con (un) assegno; ~ moonlight al chiaro di luna; ~ saving hard, he ... risparmiando molto, lui ...

**3** (via, through) per; we came ~ Dover siamo venuti via Dover

**4** (close to, past) accanto a; the house ~ the river la casa sul fiume; a holiday ~ the sea una vacanza al mare; she sat ~ his bed si sedette accanto al suo letto; she rushed ~ me mi è passata accanto correndo; I go ~ the post office every day passo davanti all'ufficio postale ogni giorno

**5** (not later than) per, entro; ~ 4 o'clock per o entro le 4; ~ this time tomorrow domani a quest'ora; ~ the time I got here it was too late quando sono arrivato era ormai troppo tardi

**6** (during): ~ day/night di giorno/notte

**7** (amount) a; ~ the kilo/metre a chili/metri; paid ~ the hour pagato all'ora; one ~ one uno per uno; little ~ little a poco a poco

**8** (MATH, measure): to divide/multiply ~ 3 dividere/moltiplicare per 3; it's broader ~ a metre è un metro più largo; è più largo di un metro

**9** (according to) per; to play ~ the rules attenersi alle regole; it's all right ~ me per me va bene

**10:** (all) ~ oneself etc (tutto(a)) solo(a); he did it (all) ~ himself lo ha fatto (tutto) da solo

**11:** ~ the way a proposito; this wasn't my idea ~ the way tra l'altro l'idea non è stata mia
♦ ad **1** see go, pass etc

**2:** ~ and ~ (in past) poco dopo; (in future) fra breve; ~ and large nel complesso.

**bye(-bye)** ['baɪ'baɪ] excl ciao!, arrivederci!

**by(e)-law** ['baɪlɔ:] n legge f locale.

**by-election** ['baɪɪlekʃən] n (Brit) elezione f straordinaria.

**bygone** ['baɪɡɒn] a passato(a) // n: let ~s be ~s mettiamoci una pietra sopra.

**bypass** ['baɪpɑ:s] n circonvallazione f; (MED) by-pass m inv // vt fare una deviazione intorno a.

**by-product** ['baɪprɒdʌkt] n sottoprodotto; (fig) conseguenza secondaria.

**bystander** ['baɪstændə*] n spettatore/trice.

**byte** [baɪt] n (COMPUT) byte m inv, bicarattere m.

**byword** ['baɪwɜ:d] n: to be a ~ for essere sinonimo di.

**by-your-leave** ['baɪjɔ:'li:v] n: without so much as a ~ senza nemmeno chiedere il permesso.

# C

**C** [si:] n (MUS) do.
**C.A.** n abbr = chartered accountant.

**cab** [kæb] n taxi m inv; (of train, truck) cabina; (horse-drawn) carrozza.

**cabaret** ['kæbəreɪ] n cabaret m inv.

**cabbage** ['kæbɪdʒ] n cavolo.

**cabin** ['kæbɪn] n capanna; (on ship) cabina.

**cabinet** ['kæbɪnɪt] n (POL) consiglio dei ministri; (furniture) armadietto; (also: display ~) vetrinetta; ~-maker n stipettaio.

**cable** ['keɪbl] n cavo; fune f; (TEL)

cablogramma *m* // *vt* telegrafare; **~-car** *n* funivia; **~ television** *n* televisione *f* via cavo.

**cache** [kæʃ] *n*: **a ~ of** food *etc* un deposito segreto di viveri *etc*.

**cackle** ['kækl] *vi* schiamazzare.

**cactus,** *pl* **cacti** ['kæktəs, -taɪ] *n* cactus *m inv*.

**cadet** [kə'dɛt] *n* (*MIL*) cadetto.

**cadge** [kædʒ] *vt* (*col*) scroccare.

**café** ['kæfeɪ] *n* caffè *m inv*.

**cafeteria** [kæfɪ'tɪərɪə] *n* self-service *m inv*.

**cage** [keɪdʒ] *n* gabbia.

**cagey** ['keɪdʒɪ] *a* (*col*) chiuso(a); guardingo(a).

**cagoule** [kə'guːl] *n* K-way *m inv* ®.

**cajole** [kə'dʒəul] *vt* allettare.

**cake** [keɪk] *n* torta; **~ of** soap saponetta; **~d** *a*: **~d with** incrostato(a) di.

**calculate** ['kælkjuleɪt] *vt* calcolare; **calculation** [-'leɪʃən] *n* calcolo; **calculator** *n* calcolatrice *f*.

**calendar** ['kæləndə*] *n* calendario; **~ year** *n* anno civile.

**calf** [kɑːf], *pl* **calves** *n* (*of* cow) vitello; (*of other animals*) piccolo; (*also:* **~skin**) (pelle *f* di) vitello; (*ANAT*) polpaccio.

**calibre,** (*US*) **caliber** ['kælɪbə*] *n* calibro.

**call** [kɔːl] *vt* (*gen, also TEL*) chiamare // *vi* chiamare; (*visit: also:* **~ in, ~ round**): **to ~ (for)** passare (a prendere) // *n* (*shout*) grido, urlo; (*visit*) visita; (*also:* **telephone ~**) telefonata; **to be ~ed** (*person, object*) chiamarsi; **to be on ~** essere a disposizione; **to ~ back** *vi* (*return*) ritornare; (*TEL*) ritelefonare, richiamare; **to ~ for** *vt fus* richiedere; **to ~ off** *vt* disdire; **to ~ on** *vt fus* (*visit*) passare da; (*request*): **to ~ on sb to do** chiedere a qn di fare; **to ~ out** *vi* (*in pain*) urlare; (*shout*) chiamare; **to ~ up** *vt* (*MIL*) richiamare; **~box** *n* (*Brit*) cabina telefonica; **~er** *n* persona che

chiama; visitatore/trice; **~ girl** *n* ragazza *f* squillo *inv*; **~-in** *n* (*US: phone-in*) trasmissione *f* a filo diretto con gli ascoltatori; **~ing** *n* vocazione *f*; **~ing card** *n* (*US*) biglietto da visita.

**callous** ['kæləs] *a* indurito(a), insensibile.

**calm** [kɑːm] *a* calmo(a) // *n* calma // *vt* calmare; **to ~ down** *vi* calmarsi // *vt* calmare.

**Calor gas** ['kælə*-] *n* ® butano.

**calorie** ['kælərɪ] *n* caloria.

**calves** [kɑːvz] *npl of* **calf**.

**camber** ['kæmbə*] *n* (*of* road) bombatura.

**Cambodia** [kæm'bəudjə] *n* Cambogia.

**came** [keɪm] *pt of* **come**.

**camel** ['kæməl] *n* cammello.

**camera** ['kæmərə] *n* macchina fotografica; (*also:* **cine~, movie ~**) cinepresa; **in ~** a porte chiuse; **~man** *n* cameraman *m inv*.

**camouflage** ['kæməflɑːʒ] *n* camuffamento; (*MIL*) mimetizzazione *f* // *vt* camuffare; mimetizzare.

**camp** [kæmp] *n* campeggio; (*MIL*) campo // *vi* campeggiare; accamparsi.

**campaign** [kæm'peɪn] *n* (*MIL, POL etc*) campagna // *vi* (*also fig*) fare una campagna.

**campbed** ['kæmp'bɛd] *n* (*Brit*) brandina.

**camper** ['kæmpə*] *n* campeggiatore/ trice.

**camping** ['kæmpɪŋ] *n* campeggio; **to go ~** andare in campeggio.

**campsite** ['kæmpsaɪt] *n* campeggio.

**campus** ['kæmpəs] *n* campus *m inv*.

**can** [kæn] *n* (*of* milk) scatola; (*of* oil) bidone *m*; (*of* water) tanica; (*tin*) scatola // *vt* mettere in scatola.

*KEYWORD*

**can** [kæn] ♦ *n, vt see previous headword*

♦ *auxiliary vb* (*negative* **cannot,**

**can't**; *conditional and pt* **could) 1**
(*be able to*) potere; **I ~'t go any
further** non posso andare oltre; **you
~ do it if you try** sei in grado di
farlo — basta provarci; **I'll help you
all I ~** ti aiuterò come potrò; **I ~'t
see** you non ti vedo
**2** (*know how to*) sapere, essere
capace di; **I ~ swim** so nuotare; **~
you speak French?** parla francese?
**3** (*may*) potere; **could I have a
word with you?** posso parlarle un
momento?
**4** (*expressing disbelief, puzzlement
etc*): **it ~'t be true!** non può essere
vero!; **what CAN he want?** cosa
può mai volere?
**5** (*expressing possibility, suggestion
etc*): **he could be in the library**
può darsi che sia in biblioteca; **she
could have been delayed** può aver
avuto un contrattempo.

**Canada** ['kænədə] *n* Canada *m*.
**Canadian** [kə'neɪdɪən] *a*, *n* canadese
(*m/f*).
**canal** [kə'næl] *n* canale *m*.
**canary** [kə'neərɪ] *n* canarino.
**cancel** ['kænsəl] *vt* annullare; (*train*)
sopprimere; (*cross out*) cancellare;
**~lation** [-'leɪʃən] *n* annullamento;
soppressione *f*; cancellazione *f*;
(*TOURISM*) prenotazione *f* annullata.
**cancer** ['kænsə*] *n* cancro; **C~**
(*sign*) Cancro.
**candid** ['kændɪd] *a* onesto(a).
**candidate** ['kændɪdeɪt] *n* candidato/
a.
**candle** ['kændl] *n* candela; (*in
church*) cero; **by ~light** a lume di
candela; **~stick** *n* (*also: ~ holder*)
bugia; (*bigger, ornate*) candeliere *m*.
**candour**, (*US*) **candor** ['kændə*] *n*
sincerità.
**candy** ['kændɪ] *n* zucchero candito;
(*US*) caramella, caramelle *fpl*; **~
floss** *n* (*Brit*) zucchero filato.
**cane** [keɪn] *n* canna; (*SCOL*) verga //
*vt* (*Brit SCOL*) punire a colpi di
verga.

**canister** ['kænɪstə*] *n* scatola
metallica.
**cannabis** ['kænəbɪs] *n* canapa
indiana.
**canned** ['kænd] *a* (*food*) in scatola.
**cannon**, *pl* ~ *or* **~s** ['kænən] *n*
(*gun*) cannone *m*.
**cannot** ['kænɔt] = **can not**.
**canny** ['kænɪ] *a* furbo(a).
**canoe** [kə'nu:] *n* canoa; (*SPORT*)
canotto.
**canon** ['kænən] *n* (*clergyman*)
canonico; (*standard*) canone *m*.
**can opener** [-'əupnə*] *n* apriscatole
*m inv*.
**canopy** ['kænəpɪ] *n* baldacchino.
**can't** [kænt] = **can not**.
**cantankerous** [kæn'tæŋkərəs] *a*
stizzoso(a).
**canteen** [kæn'ti:n] *n* mensa; (*Brit:
of cutlery*) portaposate *m inv*.
**canter** ['kæntə*] *n* piccolo galoppo.
**canvas** ['kænvəs] *n* tela.
**canvassing** ['kænvəsɪŋ] *n* (*POL*)
sollecitazione *f*; (*COMM*) indagine *f*
di mercato.
**canyon** ['kænjən] *n* canyon *m inv*.
**cap** [kæp] *n* (*also Brit FOOTBALL*)
berretto; (*of pen*) coperchio; (*of bottle*) tappo // *vt* tappare; (*outdo*)
superare.
**capability** [keɪpə'bɪlɪtɪ] *n* capacità *f
inv*, abilità *f inv*.
**capable** ['keɪpəbl] *a* capace.
**capacity** [kə'pæsɪtɪ] *n* capacità *f inv*;
(*of lift etc*) capienza.
**cape** [keɪp] *n* (*garment*) cappa; (*GEO*) capo.
**capital** ['kæpɪtl] *n* (*also: ~ city*)
capitale *f*; (*money*) capitale *m*;
(*also: ~ letter*) (lettera) maiuscola;
**~ gains tax** *n* imposta sulla plus-
valenza; **~ism** *n* capitalismo; **~ist**
*a*, *n* capitalista (*m/f*); **~ize: to ~ize
on** *vt fus* trarre vantaggio da; **~
punishment** *n* pena di morte.
**Capricorn** ['kæprɪkɔ:n] *n* Capricorno.
**capsize** [kæp'saɪz] *vt* capovolgere //
*vi* capovolgersi.
**capsule** ['kæpsju:l] *n* capsula.

**captain** ['kæptɪn] n capitano.

**caption** ['kæpʃən] n leggenda.

**captivate** ['kæptɪveɪt] vt avvincere.

**captive** ['kæptɪv] a, n prigioniero(a).

**captivity** [kæp'tɪvɪtɪ] n prigionia; in ~ (animal) in cattività.

**capture** ['kæptʃə*] vt catturare, prendere; (attention) attirare // n cattura; (data ~) registrazione f or rilevazione f di dati.

**car** [kɑ:*] n macchina, automobile f.

**carafe** [kə'ræf] n caraffa.

**caramel** ['kærəməl] n caramello.

**caravan** ['kærəvæn] n (Brit) roulotte f inv; (of camels) carovana; ~ **site** n (Brit) campeggio per roulotte.

**carbohydrates** ['kɑ:bəʊ'haɪdreɪts] npl (foods) carboidrati mpl.

**carbon** ['kɑ:bən] n carbonio; ~ **paper** n carta carbone.

**carburettor**, (US) **carburetor** [kɑ:bjʊ'retə*] n carburatore m.

**card** [kɑ:d] n carta; (visiting ~ etc) biglietto; (Christmas ~ etc) cartolina; ~**board** n cartone m; ~ **game** n gioco di carte.

**cardiac** ['kɑ:dɪæk] a cardiaco(a).

**cardigan** ['kɑ:dɪgən] n cardigan m inv.

**cardinal** ['kɑ:dɪnl] a, n cardinale (m).

**card index** n schedario.

**care** [kɛə*] n cura, attenzione f; (worry) preoccupazione f // vi: to ~ **about** interessarsi di; ~ **of** (c/o) presso (c/o); in sb's ~ alle cure di qn; **to take** ~ (**to do**) fare attenzione (a fare); **to take** ~ **of** curarsi di; **I don't** ~ non me ne importa; **to** ~ **for** vt fus aver cura di; (like) volere bene a.

**career** [kə'rɪə*] n carriera // vi (also: ~ **along**) andare di (gran) carriera.

**carefree** ['kɛəfri:] a sgombro(a) di preoccupazioni.

**careful** ['kɛəful] a attento(a); (cautious) cauto(a); **(be)** ~! attenzione!; ~**ly** ad con cura; cautamente.

**careless** ['kɛəlɪs] a negligente;

(heedless) spensierato(a).

**caress** [kə'rɛs] n carezza // vt accarezzare.

**caretaker** ['kɛəteɪkə*] n custode m.

**car-ferry** ['kɑ:fɛrɪ] n traghetto.

**cargo**, pl ~**es** ['kɑ:gəʊ] n carico.

**car hire** n autonoleggio.

**Caribbean** [kærɪ'bi:ən] a: **the** ~ **(Sea)** il Mar dei Caraibi.

**caring** ['kɛərɪŋ] a (person) premuroso(a); (society, organization) umanitario(a).

**carnage** ['kɑ:nɪdʒ] n carneficina.

**carnation** [kɑ:'neɪʃən] n garofano.

**carnival** ['kɑ:nɪvəl] n (public celebration) carnevale m; (US: funfair) luna park m inv.

**carol** ['kærəl] n: **(Christmas)** ~ canto di Natale.

**carp** [kɑ:p] n (fish) carpa; **to** ~ **at** vt fus trovare a ridire su.

**car park** n (Brit) parcheggio.

**carpenter** ['kɑ:pɪntə*] n carpentiere m.

**carpentry** ['kɑ:pɪntrɪ] n carpenteria.

**carpet** ['kɑ:pɪt] n tappeto // vt coprire con tappeto; ~ **slippers** npl pantofole fpl; ~ **sweeper** n scopatappeti m inv.

**carriage** ['kærɪdʒ] n vettura; (of goods) trasporto; (of typewriter) carrello; (bearing) portamento; ~ **return** n (on typewriter etc) leva (or tasto) del ritorno a capo; ~**way** n (Brit: part of road) carreggiata.

**carrier** ['kærɪə*] n (of disease) portatore/trice; (COMM) impresa di trasporti; (NAUT) portaerei f inv; (on car, bicycle) portabagagli m inv; ~ **bag** n (Brit) sacchetto.

**carrot** ['kærət] n carota.

**carry** ['kærɪ] vt (subj: person) portare; (: vehicle) trasportare; (a motion, bill) far passare; (involve: responsibilities) etc) comportare // vi (sound) farsi sentire; **to be** or **get carried away** (fig) entusiasmarsi; **to** ~ **on** vi: **to** ~ **on with sth/doing** continuare qc/a fare // vt mandare avanti; **to** ~ **out** vt (*orders*) eseguire; (*investigation*) svolgere; ~**cot** n culla portabile; ~**-on** n (col: *fuss*) casino, confusione f.

**cart** [kɑːt] n carro // vt (col) trascinare.

**carton** ['kɑːtən] n (box) scatola di cartone; (of *yogurt*) cartone m; (of *cigarettes*) stecca.

**cartoon** [kɑː'tuːn] n (PRESS) disegno umoristico; (*satirical*) caricatura; (*comic strip*) fumetto; (CINEMA) disegno animato.

**cartridge** ['kɑːtrɪdʒ] n (for gun, pen) cartuccia; (for *camera*) caricatore m; (*music tape*) cassetta.

**carve** [kɑːv] vt (meat) trinciare; (*wood, stone*) intagliare; **to ~ up** vt (meat) tagliare; (fig: *country*) suddividere; **carving** n (in *wood etc*) scultura; **carving knife** n trinciante m.

**car wash** n lavaggio auto.

**case** [keɪs] n caso; (LAW) causa, processo; (box) scatola; (Brit: also: suit~) valigia; **he hasn't put forward his ~ very well** non ha dimostrato bene il suo caso; **in ~ of** in caso di; **in ~ he** caso mai lui; **just in ~** in caso di bisogno.

**cash** [kæʃ] n denaro; (coins, notes) denaro liquido // vt incassare; **to pay (in) ~** pagare in contanti; **~ on delivery (C.O.D.)** (COMM) pagamento alla consegna; ~**book** n giornale m di cassa; ~ **card** n tesserino di prelievo; ~ **desk** n (Brit) cassa; ~ **dispenser** n sportello automatico.

**cashew** [kæ'ʃuː] n (also: ~ **nut**) anacardio.

**cashier** [kæ'ʃɪə*] n cassiere/a.

**cashmere** ['kæʃmɪə*] n cachemire m.

**cash register** n registratore m di cassa.

**casing** ['keɪsɪŋ] n rivestimento.

**casino** [kə'siːnəu] n casinò m inv.

**cask** [kɑːsk] n botte f.

**casket** ['kɑːskɪt] n cofanetto; (US:

coffin) bara.

**casserole** ['kæsərəul] n casseruola; (food): **chicken ~** pollo in casseruola.

**cassette** [kæ'sɛt] n cassetta; ~ **player** n riproduttore m a cassette; **~ recorder** n registratore m a cassette.

**cast** [kɑːst] vt (pt, pp cast) (throw) gettare; (shed) perdere; spogliarsi di; (metal) gettare, fondere; (THEATRE): **to ~ sb as Hamlet** scegliere qn per la parte di Amleto // n (THEATRE) complesso di attori; (mould) forma; (also: **plaster ~**) ingessatura; **to ~ one's vote** votare, dare il voto; **to ~ off** vi (NAUT) salpare.

**castaway** ['kɑːstəwei] n naufrago/a.

**caster sugar** ['kɑːstə*-] n (Brit) zucchero semolato.

**casting** ['kɑːstɪŋ] a: ~ **vote** (Brit) voto decisivo.

**cast iron** n ghisa.

**castle** ['kɑːsl] n castello; (fortified) rocca.

**castor** ['kɑːstə*] n (wheel) rotella; ~ **oil** n olio di ricino.

**castrate** [kæs'treɪt] vt castrare.

**casual** ['kæʒjul] a (by chance) casuale, fortuito(a); (irregular: work etc) avventizio(a); (unconcerned) noncurante, indifferente; ~ **wear** casual m; ~**ly** ad con disinvoltura; casualmente.

**casualty** ['kæʒjultɪ] n ferito/a; (dead) morto/a, vittima.

**cat** [kæt] n gatto.

**catalogue**, (US) **catalog** ['kætələg] n catalogo // vt catalogare.

**catalyst** ['kætəlɪst] n catalizzatore m.

**catapult** ['kætəpʌlt] n catapulta; fionda.

**cataract** ['kætərækt] n (also MED) cateratta.

**catarrh** [kə'tɑː*] n catarro.

**catastrophe** [kə'tæstrəfi] n catastrofe f.

**catch** [kætʃ] vb (pt, pp caught) vt (train, thief, cold) acchiappare;

(*ball*) afferrare; (*person: by surprise*) sorprendere; (*understand*) comprendere; (*get entangled*) impigliare // *vi* (*fire*) prendere // *n* (*fish etc caught*) retata, presa; (*trick*) inganno; (*TECH*) gancio; **to ~ sb's attention** *or* **eye** attirare l'attenzione di qn; **to ~ fire** prendere fuoco; **to ~ sight of** scorgere; **to ~ on** *vi* capire; (*become popular*) affermarsi, far presa; **to ~ up** *vi* mettersi in pari // *vt* (*also*: **~ up with**) raggiungere.

**catching** ['kætʃɪŋ] *a* (*MED*) contagioso(a).

**catchment area** ['kætʃmənt-] *n* (*Brit SCOL*) circoscrizione *f* scolare; (*GEO*) bacino pluviale.

**catch phrase** *n* slogan *m inv*; frase *f* fatta.

**catchy** ['kætʃɪ] *a* orecchiabile.

**category** ['kætɪgərɪ] *n* categoria.

**cater** ['keɪtə*] *vi* (*gen*: **~ for**) provvedere da mangiare (per); **to ~ for** *vt fus* (*Brit: needs*) provvedere a; (: *readers, consumers*) incontrare i gusti di; **~er** *n* fornitore *m*; **~ing** *n* approvvigionamento.

**caterpillar** ['kætəpɪlə*] *n* bruco; **~ track** *n* catena a cingoli.

**cathedral** [kə'θiːdrəl] *n* cattedrale *f*, duomo.

**catholic** ['kæθəlɪk] *a* universale; aperto(a); eclettico(a); **C~** *a*, *n* (*REL*) cattolico(a).

**cat's-eye** [kæts'aɪ] *n* (*Brit AUT*) catarifrangente *m*.

**cattle** ['kætl] *npl* bestiame *m*, bestie *fpl*.

**catty** ['kætɪ] *a* maligno(a), dispettoso(a).

**caucus** ['kɔːkəs] *n* (*POL*: *group*) comitato di dirigenti; (: *US*) (riunione *f* del) comitato elettorale.

**caught** [kɔːt] *pt*, *pp* *of* **catch**.

**cauliflower** ['kɒlɪflaʊə*] *n* cavolfiore *m*.

**cause** [kɔːz] *n* causa // *vt* causare.

**caution** ['kɔːʃən] *n* prudenza; (*warning*) avvertimento // *vt*

avvertire; ammonire.

**cautious** ['kɔːʃəs] *a* cauto(a), prudente.

**cavalry** ['kævəlrɪ] *n* cavalleria.

**cave** [keɪv] *n* caverna, grotta; **to ~ in** *vi* (*roof etc*) crollare; **~man** *n* uomo delle caverne.

**caviar(e)** ['kævɪɑː*] *n* caviale *m*.

**cavort** [kə'vɔːt] *vi* far capriole.

**CB** *n abbr* (= *Citizens' Band* (*Radio*)): **~ radio** (*set*) baracchino.

**CBI** *n abbr* (= *Confederation of British Industries*) ≈ Confindustria.

**cc** *abbr* = *cubic centimetres*; *carbon copy*.

**cease** [siːs] *vt*, *vi* cessare; **~fire** *n* cessate il fuoco *m inv*; **~less** *a* incessante, continuo(a).

**cedar** ['siːdə*] *n* cedro.

**ceiling** ['siːlɪŋ] *n* soffitto.

**celebrate** ['sɛlɪbreɪt] *vt*, *vi* celebrare; **~d** *a* celebre; **celebration** [-'breɪʃən] *n* celebrazione *f*.

**celery** ['sɛlərɪ] *n* sedano.

**cell** [sɛl] *n* cella; (*BIOL*) cellula; (*ELEC*) elemento (di batteria).

**cellar** ['sɛlə*] *n* sottosuolo, cantina.

**'cello** ['tʃɛləʊ] *n* violoncello.

**Celt** [kɛlt, sɛlt] *n* celta *m/f*.

**Celtic** ['kɛltɪk, 'sɛltɪk] *a* celtico(a).

**cement** [sə'mɛnt] *n* cemento // *vt* cementare; **~ mixer** *n* betoniera.

**cemetery** ['sɛmɪtrɪ] *n* cimitero.

**censor** ['sɛnsə*] *n* censore *m* // *vt* censurare; **~ship** *n* censura.

**censure** ['sɛnʃə*] *vt* riprovare, censurare.

**census** ['sɛnsəs] *n* censimento.

**cent** [sɛnt] *n* (*US: coin*) centesimo (= *1:100 di un dollaro*); *see also* **per**.

**centenary** [sɛn'tiːnərɪ] *n* centenario.

**center** ['sɛntə*] *n*, *vt* (*US*) = **centre**.

**centi...** ['sɛntɪ] *prefix*: **~grade** *a* centigrado(a); **~metre**, (*US*) **~meter** *n* centimetro.

**centipede** ['sɛntɪpiːd] *n* centopiedi *m inv*.

**central** ['sɛntrəl] *a* centrale; **C~ America** *n* America centrale; **~ heating** *n* riscaldamento centrale;

~**ize** vt accentrare.

**centre**, (US) **center** ['sɛntə*] n centro // vt centrare; ~**-forward** n (SPORT) centroavanti m inv; ~**-half** n (SPORT) centromediano.

**century** ['sɛntjʊrɪ] n secolo; 20th ~ ventesimo secolo.

**ceramic** [sɪ'ræmɪk] a ceramico(a); ~**s** npl ceramica.

**cereal** ['sɪːrɪəl] n cereale m.

**ceremony** ['sɛrɪmənɪ] n cerimonia; to stand on ~ fare complimenti.

**certain** ['səːtən] a certo(a); to make ~ of assicurarsi di; for ~ per certo, di sicuro; ~**ly** ad certamente, certo; ~**ty** n certezza.

**certificate** [sə'tɪfɪkɪt] n certificato; diploma m.

**certified** ['səːtɪfaɪd]: ~ **mail** n (US) posta raccomandata con ricevuta di ritorno; ~ **public accountant (CPA)** n (US) ≈ commercialista m/f.

**cervical** ['səːvɪkl] a: ~ **cancer** cancro della cervice; ~ **smear** Pap-test m inv.

**cervix** ['səːvɪks] n cervice f.

**cesspit** ['sɛspɪt], **cesspool** ['sɛspuːl] n pozzo nero.

**cf.** abbr (= compare) cfr.

**ch.** abbr (= chapter) cap.

**chafe** [tʃeɪf] vt fregare, irritare.

**chaffinch** ['tʃæfɪntʃ] n fringuello.

**chain** [tʃeɪn] n catena // vt (also: ~ up) incatenare; ~ **reaction** n reazione f a catena; ~ **smoke** vi fumare una sigaretta dopo l'altra; ~ **store** n negozio a catena.

**chair** [tʃɛə*] n sedia; (armchair) poltrona; (of university) cattedra // (meeting) presiedere; ~**lift** n seggiovia; ~**man** n presidente m.

**chalice** ['tʃælɪs] n calice m.

**chalk** [tʃɔːk] n gesso.

**challenge** ['tʃælɪndʒ] n sfida // vt sfidare; (statement, right) mettere in dubbio; to ~ sb to do sfidare qn a fare; **challenging** a sfidante; provocatorio(a).

**chamber** ['tʃeɪmbə*] n camera; ~ **of commerce** n camera di

commercio; ~**maid** n cameriera; ~ **music** n musica da camera.

**chamois** ['ʃæmwɑ:] n camoscio; ~ **leather** ['ʃæmɪ-] n pelle f di camoscio.

**champagne** [ʃæm'peɪn] n champagne m inv.

**champion** ['tʃæmpɪən] n campione/essa; ~**ship** n campionato.

**chance** [tʃɑːns] n caso; (opportunity) occasione f; (likelihood) possibilità f inv // vt: to ~ it rischiare, provarci // a fortuito(a); to take a ~ rischiarlo; by ~ per caso.

**chancellor** ['tʃɑːnsələ*] n cancelliere // **C~ of the Exchequer** n (Brit) Cancelliere dello Scacchiere.

**chandelier** [ʃændə'lɪə*] n lampadario.

**change** [tʃeɪndʒ] vt cambiare; (transform): to ~ sb into trasformare qn in // vi cambiarsi; (be transformed): to ~ into trasformarsi in // n cambiamento; (money) resto; to ~ one's mind cambiare idea; a ~ of clothes un cambio (di vestiti); for a ~ tanto per cambiare; small ~ spiccioli mpl, moneta; ~**able** a (weather) variabile; ~ **machine** n distributore automatico di monete; ~**over** n cambiamento, passaggio.

**changing** ['tʃeɪndʒɪŋ] a che cambia; (colours) cangiante; ~ **room** n (Brit: in shop) camerino; (: SPORT) spogliatoio.

**channel** ['tʃænl] n canale m; (of river, sea) alveo // vt canalizzare; through the usual ~s per le solite vie; the (English) C~ la Manica; the C~ **Islands** npl le isole Normanne.

**chant** [tʃɑːnt] n canto; salmodia // vt cantare; salmodiare.

**chaos** ['keɪɔs] n caos m.

**chaotic** [keɪ'ɔtɪk] a caotico(a).

**chap** [tʃæp] n (Brit col: man) tipo.

**chapel** ['tʃæpəl] n cappella.

**chaperon** ['ʃæpərəun] n accompagnatrice f // vt accompagnare.

**chaplain** ['tʃæplɪn] n cappellano.

**chapped** [tʃæpt] a (skin, lips) screpolato(a).

**chapter** ['tʃæptə*] n capitolo.

**char** [tʃɑ:*] vt (burn) carbonizzare // n (Brit:) = **charlady**.

**character** ['kærɪktə*] n carattere m; (in novel, film) personaggio; (eccentric) originale m; ~**istic** [-'rɪstɪk] a caratteristico(a) // n caratteristica.

**charade** [ʃə'rɑ:d] n sciarada.

**charcoal** ['tʃɑ:kəul] n carbone m di legna.

**charge** [tʃɑ:dʒ] n accusa; (cost) prezzo; (of gun, battery, MIL: attack) carica // vt (gun, battery, MIL: enemy) caricare; (customer) fare pagare a; (sum) fare pagare; (LAW): **to ~ sb with** accusare qn (di) // vi (gen with: up, along etc) lanciarsi; ~**s** npl: **bank ~s** commissioni fpl bancarie; **is there a ~?** c'è da pagare?; **to reverse the ~s** (TEL) fare una telefonata a carico del destinatario; **to take ~ of** incaricarsi di; **to be in ~ of** essere responsabile per; **to ~ an expense (up) to sb** addebitare una spesa a qn; ~ **card** n carta f clienti inv.

**chariot** ['tʃærɪət] n carro.

**charitable** ['tʃærɪtəbl] a caritatevole.

**charity** ['tʃærɪtɪ] n carità; (organization) opera pia.

**charlady** ['tʃɑ:leɪdɪ] n (Brit) domestica a ore.

**charlatan** ['ʃɑ:lətən] n ciarlatano.

**charm** [tʃɑ:m] n fascino; (on bracelet) ciondolo // vt affascinare, incantare; ~**ing** a affascinante.

**chart** [tʃɑ:t] n tabella; grafico; (map) carta nautica // vt fare una carta nautica di.

**charter** ['tʃɑ:tə*] vt (plane) noleggiare // n (document) carta; ~**ed accountant (C.A.)** n (Brit) ragioniere/a professionista; ~ **flight** n volo m charter inv.

**chase** [tʃeɪs] vt inseguire; (away) cacciare // n caccia.

**chasm** ['kæzəm] n abisso.

**chassis** ['ʃæsɪ] n telaio.

**chastity** ['tʃæstɪtɪ] n castità.

**chat** [tʃæt] vi (also: **have a ~**) chiacchierare // n chiacchierata; ~ **show** n (Brit) talk show m inv.

**chatter** ['tʃætə*] vi (person) ciarlare // n ciarle fpl; **her teeth were ~ing** batteva i denti; ~**box** n chiacchierone/a.

**chatty** ['tʃætɪ] a (style) familiare; (person) chiacchierino(a).

**chauffeur** ['ʃəufə*] n autista m.

**chauvinist** ['ʃəuvɪnɪst] n (male ~) maschilista m; (nationalist) sciovinista m/f.

**cheap** [tʃi:p] a a buon mercato; (joke) grossolano(a); (poor quality) di cattiva qualità // ad (a buon mercato; ~**en** vt ribassare; (fig) avvilire; ~**er** a meno caro(a) // ~**ly** ad a buon prezzo, a buon mercato.

**cheat** [tʃi:t] vi imbrogliare; (at school) copiare // vt ingannare; (rob) defraudare // n imbroglione m; copione m; (trick) inganno.

**check** [tʃek] vt verificare; (passport, ticket) controllare; (halt) fermare; (restrain) contenere // n verifica; controllo; (curb) freno; (bill) conto; (pattern: gen pl) quadretti mpl; (US) = **cheque** // a (also: ~**ed**: pattern, cloth) a quadretti; **to ~ in** vi (in hotel) registrare; (at airport) presentarsi all'accettazione // vt (luggage) depositare; **to ~ out** vi (in hotel) saldare il conto // vt (luggage) ritirare; **to ~ up** vi: **to ~ up on** (sth) investigare (qc); **to ~ up on sb** informarsi sul conto di qn; ~**ered** a (US) = **chequered**; ~**ers** n (US) dama; ~**in (desk)** n check-in m inv, accettazione f (bagagli inv); ~**ing account** n (US) conto corrente; ~**mate** n scaccomatto; ~**out** n (in supermarket) cassa; ~**point** n posto di blocco; ~**room** n (US) deposito m bagagli inv; ~**up** n (MED) controllo medico.

**cheek** [tʃi:k] n guancia; (impudence)

faccia tosta; ~**bone** $n$ zigomo; ~**y** $a$ sfacciato(a).

**cheep** [tʃiːp] $vi$ pigolare.

**cheer** [tʃɪə*] $vt$ applaudire; (gladden) rallegrare // $vi$ applaudire // $n$ (gen pl) applausi mpl; evviva mpl; ~**s**! salute!; **to ~ up** $vi$ rallegrarsi, farsi animo // $vt$ rallegrare; ~**ful** $a$ allegro(a).

**cheerio** ['tʃɪərɪ'əu] excl (Brit) ciao!

**cheese** [tʃiːz] $n$ formaggio; ~**board** $n$ piatto del (or per il) formaggio.

**cheetah** ['tʃiːtə] $n$ ghepardo.

**chef** [ʃef] $n$ capocuoco.

**chemical** ['kemɪkəl] $a$ chimico(a) // $n$ prodotto chimico.

**chemist** ['kemɪst] $n$ (Brit: pharmacist) farmacista m/f; (scientist) chimico/a; ~**ry** $n$ chimica; ~**'s (shop)** $n$ (Brit) farmacia.

**cheque** [tʃek] $n$ (Brit) assegno; ~**book** $n$ libretto degli assegni; ~ **card** $n$ carta $f$ assegni inv.

**chequered** ['tʃekəd] $a$ (fig) movimentato(a).

**cherish** ['tʃerɪʃ] $vt$ aver caro; (hope etc) nutrire.

**cherry** ['tʃerɪ] $n$ ciliegia.

**chess** [tʃes] $n$ scacchi mpl; ~**board** $n$ scacchiera; ~**man** $n$ pezzo degli scacchi.

**chest** [tʃest] $n$ petto; (box) cassa; ~ **of drawers** $n$ cassettone m.

**chestnut** ['tʃesnʌt] $n$ castagna; (also: ~ **tree**) castagno m.

**chew** [tʃuː] $vt$ masticare; ~**ing gum** $n$ chewing gum m.

**chic** [ʃiːk] $a$ elegante.

**chick** [tʃɪk] $n$ pulcino; (US col) pollastrella.

**chicken** ['tʃɪkɪn] $n$ pollo; **to ~ out** $vi$ (col) avere fifa; ~**pox** $n$ varicella.

**chicory** ['tʃɪkərɪ] $n$ cicoria.

**chief** [tʃiːf] $n$ capo $m$ // $a$ principale; ~ **constable** $n$ (Brit) ≈ questore m; ~ **executive** $n$ direttore $m$ generale; ~**ly** ad per lo più, soprattutto.

**chilblain** ['tʃɪlbleɪn] $n$ gelone m.

**child**, pl ~**ren** [tʃaɪld, 'tʃɪldrən] $n$

bambino/a; ~**birth** $n$ parto; ~**hood** $n$ infanzia; ~**ish** $a$ puerile; ~**like** $a$ fanciullesco(a); ~ **minder** $n$ (Brit) bambinaia.

**Chile** ['tʃɪlɪ] $n$ Cile m.

**chill** [tʃɪl] $n$ freddo; (MED) infreddatura $f$ a freddo(a), gelido(a) // $vt$ raffreddare.

**chil(l)i** ['tʃɪlɪ] $n$ peperoncino.

**chilly** ['tʃɪlɪ] $a$ freddo(a), fresco(a); **to feel** ~ sentirsi infreddolito(a).

**chime** [tʃaɪm] $n$ carillon m inv // $vi$ suonare, scampanare.

**chimney** ['tʃɪmnɪ] $n$ camino; ~ **sweep** $n$ spazzacamino.

**chimpanzee** [tʃɪmpæn'ziː] $n$ scimpanzé m inv.

**chin** [tʃɪn] $n$ mento.

**China** ['tʃaɪnə] $n$ Cina.

**china** ['tʃaɪnə] $n$ porcellana.

**Chinese** [tʃaɪ'niːz] $a$ cinese // $n$ (pl inv) cinese m/f; (LING) cinese m.

**chink** [tʃɪŋk] $n$ (opening) fessura; (noise) tintinnio.

**chip** [tʃɪp] $n$ (gen pl: CULIN) patatina fritta; (: US: also: **potato** ~) patatina; (of wood, glass, stone) scheggia; (also: **micro**~) chip m inv // $vt$ (cup, plate) scheggiare; **to ~ in** $vi$ (col: contribute) contribuire; (: interrupt) intromettersi.

**chiropodist** [kɪ'rɔpədɪst] $n$ (Brit) pedicure m/f inv.

**chirp** [tʃəːp] $vi$ cinguettare.

**chisel** ['tʃɪzl] $n$ cesello.

**chit** [tʃɪt] $n$ biglietto.

**chivalry** ['ʃɪvəlrɪ] $n$ cavalleria; cortesia.

**chives** [tʃaɪvz] npl erba cipollina.

**chock** [tʃɔk] $n$ zeppa; ~**a-block**, ~**full** $a$ pieno(a) zeppo(a).

**chocolate** ['tʃɔklɪt] $n$ (substance) cioccolato, cioccolata; (drink) cioccolata; (a sweet) cioccolatino.

**choice** [tʃɔɪs] $n$ scelta // $a$ scelto(a).

**choir** ['kwaɪə*] $n$ coro; ~**boy** $n$ corista m fanciullo.

**choke** [tʃəuk] $vi$ soffocare // $vt$ soffocare; (block) ingombrare // $n$ (AUT) valvola dell'aria.

**cholera** ['kɔlərə] n colera m.

**cholesterol** [kə'lɛstərɔl] n colesterolo.

**choose** [tʃuːz], pt **chose**, pp **chosen** vt scegliere; **to ~ to do** decidere di fare; preferire fare.

**choosy** ['tʃuːzɪ] a schizzinoso(a).

**chop** [tʃɔp] vt (wood) spaccare; (CULIN: also: ~ **up**) tritare // n colpo netto; (CULIN) costoletta; ~s npl (jaws) mascelle fpl.

**chopper** ['tʃɔpə*] n (helicopter) elicottero.

**choppy** ['tʃɔpɪ] a (sea) mosso(a).

**chopsticks** ['tʃɔpstɪks] npl bastoncini mpl cinesi.

**choral** ['kɔːrəl] a corale.

**chord** [kɔːd] n (MUS) accordo.

**chore** [tʃɔː*] n faccenda; **household** ~s faccende fpl domestiche.

**choreographer** [kɔrɪ'ɔgrəfə*] n coreografo/a.

**chorister** ['kɔrɪstə*] n corista m/f.

**chortle** ['tʃɔːtl] vi ridacchiare.

**chorus** ['kɔːrəs] n coro; (repeated part of song, also fig) ritornello.

**chose** [tʃəuz] pt of **choose**.

**chosen** ['tʃəuzn] pp of **choose**.

**Christ** [kraɪst] n Cristo.

**christen** ['krɪsn] vt battezzare.

**Christian** ['krɪstɪən] a, n cristiano(a); ~**ity** [-'ænɪtɪ] n cristianesimo; ~ **name** n nome m (di battesimo).

**Christmas** ['krɪsməs] n Natale m; **Merry ~!** Buon Natale!; ~ **card** n cartolina di Natale; ~ **Day** n il giorno di Natale; ~ **Eve** n la vigilia di Natale; ~ **tree** n albero di Natale.

**chrome** [krəum], **chromium** ['krəumɪəm] n cromo.

**chronic** ['krɔnɪk] a cronico(a).

**chronicle** ['krɔnɪkl] n cronaca.

**chronological** [krɔnə'lɔdʒɪkəl] a cronologico(a).

**chrysanthemum** [krɪ'sænθəməm] n crisantemo.

**chubby** ['tʃʌbɪ] a paffuto(a).

**chuck** [tʃʌk] vt buttare, gettare; **to ~ out** vt buttar fuori; **to ~ (up)** vt ritornello.

(Brit) piantare.

**chuckle** ['tʃʌkl] vi ridere sommessamente.

**chug** [tʃʌg] vi fare ciuf ciuf.

**chum** [tʃʌm] n compagno/a.

**chunk** [tʃʌŋk] n pezzo; (of bread) tocco.

**church** [tʃəːtʃ] n chiesa; ~**yard** n sagrato.

**churlish** ['tʃəːlɪʃ] a rozzo(a), sgarbato(a).

**churn** [tʃəːn] n (for butter) zangola; (for transport: also: **milk ~**) bidone m; **to ~ out** vt sfornare.

**chute** [ʃuːt] n cascata; (also: **rubbish ~**) canale m di scarico; (Brit: children's slide) scivolo.

**chutney** ['tʃʌtnɪ] n salsa piccante (di frutta, zucchero e spezie).

**CIA** n abbr (US: = Central Intelligence Agency) CIA f.

**CID** n abbr (Brit: = Criminal Investigation Department) ≈ polizia giudiziaria.

**cider** ['saɪdə*] n sidro.

**cigar** [sɪ'gɑː*] n sigaro.

**cigarette** [sɪgə'rɛt] n sigaretta; ~ **case** n portasigarette m inv; ~ **end** n mozzicone m.

**cinder** ['sɪndə*] n cenere f.

**Cinderella** [sɪndə'rɛlə] n Cenerentola.

**cine** ['sɪnɪ]: ~**-camera** n (Brit) cinepresa; ~**-film** n (Brit) pellicola.

**cinema** ['sɪnəmə] n cinema m inv.

**cinnamon** ['sɪnəmən] n cannella.

**cipher** ['saɪfə*] n cifra; (fig: faceless employee etc) persona di nessun conto.

**circle** ['səːkl] n cerchio; (of friends etc) circolo; (in cinema) galleria // vi girare in circolo // vt (surround) circondare; (move round) girare intorno a.

**circuit** ['səːkɪt] n circuito; ~**ous** [səː'kjuɪtəs] a indiretto(a).

**circular** ['səːkjulə*] a, n circolare (f).

**circulate** ['səːkjuleɪt] vi circolare // vt far circolare; **circulation** [-'leɪʃən] n circolazione f; (of news-

*paper*) tiratura.

**circumstances** ['sə:kəmstənsiz] *npl* circostanze *fpl*; (*financial condition*) condizioni *fpl* finanziarie.

**circumvent** [sə:kəm'vent] *vt* aggirare.

**circus** ['sə:kəs] *n* circo.

**cistern** ['sistən] *n* cisterna; (*in toilet*) serbatoio d'acqua.

**citizen** ['sitizn] *n* (POL) cittadino/a; (*resident*): **the ~s of this town** gli abitanti di questa città; **~ship** *n* cittadinanza.

**citrus fruit** ['sitrəs-] *n* agrume *m*.

**city** ['siti] *n* città *f inv*; **the C~** la Città di Londra (*centro commerciale*).

**civic** ['sivik] *a* civico(a); **~ centre** *n* (Brit) centro civico.

**civil** ['sivil] *a* civile; **~ engineer** *n* ingegnere *m* civile; **~ian** [si'viliən] *a, n* borghese (m/f).

**civilization** [sivilai'zeifən] *n* civiltà *f inv*.

**civilized** ['sivilaizd] *a* civilizzato(a); (*fig*) cortese.

**civil: ~ law** *n* codice *m* civile; (*study*) diritto civile; **~ servant** *n* impiegato/a statale; **C~ Service** *n* amministrazione *f* statale; **~ war** *n* guerra civile.

**clad** [klæd] *a*: **~ (in)** vestito/a (di).

**claim** [kleim] *vt* rivendicare; sostenere, pretendere; (*damages*) richiedere // *vi* (*for insurance*) fare una domanda d'indennizzo // *n* rivendicazione *f*; pretesa; (*right*) diritto; (*insurance*) ~ domanda d'indennizzo; **~ant** *n* (ADMIN, LAW) richiedente *m/f*.

**clairvoyant** [kleə'vɔiənt] *n* chiaroveggente *m*.

**clam** [klæm] *n* vongola.

**clamber** ['klæmbə*] *vi* arrampicarsi.

**clammy** ['klæmi] *a* (*weather*) caldo(a) umido(a); (*hands*) viscido(a).

**clamour** (US) **clamor** ['klæmə*] *vi*: **to ~ for** chiedere a gran voce.

**clamp** [klæmp] *n* pinza; morsa // *vt*

ammorsare; **to ~ down on** *vt fus* dare un giro di vite a.

**clan** [klæn] *n* clan *m inv*.

**clang** [klæŋ] *n* fragore *m*, suono metallico.

**clap** [klæp] *vi* applaudire; **~ping** *n* applausi *mpl*.

**claret** ['klærət] *n* vino di Bordeaux.

**clarify** ['klærifai] *vt* chiarificare, chiarire.

**clarinet** [klæri'net] *n* clarinetto.

**clarity** ['klæriti] *n* chiarità.

**clash** [klæʃ] *n* frastuono; (*fig*) scontro // *vi* scontrarsi; cozzare.

**clasp** [klɑːsp] *n* fermaglio, fibbia // *vt* stringere.

**class** [klɑːs] *n* classe *f* // *vt* classificare.

**classic** ['klæsik] *a* classico(a) // *n* classico; **~al** *a* classico(a).

**classified** ['klæsifaid] *a* (*information*) segreto(a), riservato(a); **~ advertisement, ~ ad** *n* annuncio economico.

**classmate** ['klɑːsmeit] *n* compagno/a di classe.

**classroom** ['klɑːsrum] *n* aula.

**clatter** ['klætə*] *n* acciottolio; scalpitio // *vi* acciottolare; scalpitare.

**clause** [klɔːz] *n* clausola; (LING) proposizione *f*.

**claw** [klɔː] *n* tenaglia; (*of bird of prey*) artiglio; (*of lobster*) pinza // *vt* (*also: ~ at*) graffiare; afferrare.

**clay** [klei] *n* argilla.

**clean** [kliːn] *a* pulito(a); (*clear, smooth*) liscio(a) // *vt* pulire; **to ~ out** *vt* ripulire; **to ~ up** *vi* far pulizia // *vt* (*also fig*) ripulire; **~er** *n* (*person*) donna delle pulizie; (*also: dry ~er*) tintore/a; (*product*) smacchiatore *m*; **~ing** *n* pulizia; **~liness** ['klenlinis] *n* pulizia.

**cleanse** [klenz] *vt* pulire; purificare; **~r** *n* detergente *m*.

**clean-shaven** ['kliːn'ʃeivn] *a* sbarbato(a).

**cleansing department** ['klenziŋ-] *n* (Brit) nettezza urbana.

**clear** [kliə*] *a* chiaro(a); (*road, way*

libero(a) // vt sgombrare; liberare; (table) sparecchiare; (COMM: goods) liquidare; (: debt) liquidare, saldare; (: cheque) fare la compensazione di; (LAW: suspect) discolpare; (obstacle) superare // vi (weather) rasserenarsi; (fog) andarsene // ad: ~ of distante da; to ~ up vi schiarirsi // vt mettere in ordine; (mystery) risolvere; ~ance n (removal) sgombro; (free space) spazio; (permission) autorizzazione f, permesso; ~-cut a ben delineato(a), distinto(a); ~ing n radura; ~ing bank n (Brit) banca (che fa uso della camera di compensazione); ~ly ad chiaramente; ~way n (Brit) strada con divieto di sosta.

cleaver ['kliːvə*] n mannaia.

clef [klef] n (MUS) chiave f.

cleft [kleft] n (in rock) crepa, fenditura.

clench [klɛntʃ] vt stringere.

clergy ['klɜːdʒi] n clero; ~man n ecclesiastico.

clerical ['klɛrikəl] a d'impiegato; (REL) clericale.

clerk [klɑːk, (US) klɜːrk] n impiegato/a; (US: sales person) commesso/a.

clever ['klɛvə*] a (mentally) intelligente; (deft, skilful) abile; (device, arrangement) ingegnoso(a).

click [klik] vi scattare // vt (heels etc) battere; (tongue) far schioccare.

client ['klaɪənt] n cliente m/f.

cliff [klif] n scogliera scoscesa, rupe f.

climate ['klaimit] n clima m.

climax ['klaimæks] n culmine m.

climb [klaim] vi salire; (clamber) arrampicarsi // vt salire; (CLIMBING) scalare // n salita; arrampicata; scalata; ~-down n marcia indietro; ~er n (also: rock ~er) rocciatore/trice; alpinista m/f; ~ing n (also: rock ~ing) alpinismo.

clinch [klintʃ] vt (deal) concludere.

cling [klin], pt, pp clung vi: to ~ (to) tenersi stretto(a) (a); (of

clothes) aderire strettamente (a).

clinic ['klinik] n clinica.

clink [klink] vi tintinnare.

clip [klip] n (for hair) forcina; (also: paper ~) graffetta; (holding hose etc) anello d'attacco // vt (also: ~ together: papers) attaccare insieme; (hair, nails) tagliare; (hedge) tosare; ~pers npl macchinetta per capelli; (also: nail ~pers) forbicine fpl per le unghie; ~ping n (from newspaper) ritaglio.

clique [kliːk] n cricca.

cloak [kləuk] n mantello // vt avvolgere; ~room n (for coats etc) guardaroba m inv; (Brit: W.C.) gabinetti mpl.

clock [klɔk] n orologio; to ~ in or on vi timbrare il cartellino (all'entrata); to ~ off or out vi timbrare il cartellino (all'uscita); ~wise ad in senso orario; ~work n movimento or meccanismo a orologeria // a a molla.

clog [klɔg] n zoccolo // vt intasare // vi intasarsi, bloccarsi.

cloister ['klɔistə*] n chiostro.

clone n clone m.

close a, ad and derivatives [kləus] a: ~ (to) vicino(a) (a); (writing, texture) fitto(a); (watch) stretto(a); (examination) attento(a); (weather) afoso(a) // ad vicino, dappresso; ~ to prep vicino a; by, ~ at hand a, ad a portata di mano; a ~ friend un amico intimo; to have a ~ shave (fig) scamparla bella // vb and derivatives [kləuz] vt chiudere // vi (shop etc) chiudere; (lid, door etc) chiudersi; (end) finire // n (end) fine f; to ~ down vt chiudere (definitivamente) // vi cessare (definitivamente); ~d a chiuso(a); ~d shop n azienda o fabbrica che impiega solo aderenti ai sindacati; ~knit a (family, community) molto unito(a); ~ly ad (examine, watch) da vicino.

closet ['klɔzit] n (cupboard) armadio.

**close-up** ['kləusʌp] n primo piano.

**closure** ['kləuʒə*] n chiusura.

**clot** [klɔt] n (also: **blood** ~) coagulo; (col: idiot) scemo/a // vi coagularsi.

**cloth** [klɔθ] n (material) tessuto, stoffa; (also: **tea**~) strofinaccio.

**clothe** [kləuð] vt vestire; ~**s** npl abiti mpl, vestiti mpl; ~**s brush** n spazzola per abiti; ~**s line** n corda (per stendere il bucato); ~**s peg**, (US) ~**s pin** n molletta.

**clothing** ['kləuðiŋ] n = **clothes**.

**cloud** [klaud] n nuvola; ~**y** a nuvoloso(a); (liquid) torbido(a).

**clout** [klaut] vt dare un colpo a.

**clove** [kləuv] n chiodo di garofano; ~ **of garlic** spicchio d'aglio.

**clover** ['kləuvə*] n trifoglio.

**clown** [klaun] n pagliaccio // vi (also: ~ **about**, ~ **around**) fare il pagliaccio.

**cloying** ['klɔiiŋ] a (taste, smell) nauseabondo(a).

**club** [klʌb] n (society) club m inv, circolo; (weapon, GOLF) mazza // vt bastonare // vi: **to** ~ **together** associarsi; ~**s** npl (CARDS) fiori mpl; ~ **car** n (US RAIL) vagone m ristorante; ~**house** n sede f del circolo.

**cluck** [klʌk] vi chiocciare.

**clue** [klu:] n indizio; (in crosswords) definizione f; **I haven't a** ~ non ho la minima idea.

**clump** [klʌmp] n: ~ **of trees** folto d'alberi.

**clumsy** ['klʌmzi] a (person) goffo(a), maldestro(a); (object) malfatto/a, mal costruito(a).

**clung** [klʌŋ] pt, pp of **cling**.

**cluster** ['klʌstə*] n gruppo // vi raggrupparsi.

**clutch** [klʌtʃ] n (grip, grasp) presa, stretta; (AUT) frizione f // vt afferrare, stringere forte; **to** ~ **at** aggrapparsi a.

**clutter** ['klʌtə*] vt ingombrare.

**CND** n abbr = Campaign for Nuclear Disarmament.

**Co.** abbr = **county**; **company**.

**c/o** abbr (= care of) presso.

**coach** [kəutʃ] n (bus) pullman m inv; (horse-drawn, of train) carrozza; (SPORT) allenatore/trice // vt allenare; ~ **trip** n viaggio in pullman.

**coagulate** [kəu'ægjuleit] vi coagularsi.

**coal** [kəul] n carbone m; ~ **face** n fronte f; ~**field** n bacino carbonifero.

**coalition** [kəuə'liʃən] n coalizione f.

**coalman, coal merchant** ['kəulmən, 'kəulmə:tʃənt] n negoziante m di carbone.

**coalmine** ['kəulmain] n miniera di carbone.

**coarse** [kɔ:s] a (salt, sand etc) grosso(a); (cloth, person) rozzo(a).

**coast** [kəust] n costa // vi (with cycle etc) scendere a ruota libera; ~**al** a costiero(a); ~**guard** n guardia costiera; ~**line** n linea costiera.

**coat** [kəut] n cappotto; (of animal) pelo; (of paint) mano f // vt coprire; ~ **of arms** n stemma m; ~**hanger** n attaccapanni m inv; ~**ing** n rivestimento.

**coax** [kəuks] vt indurre (con moine).

**cob** [kɔb] n see **corn**.

**cobbler** ['kɔblə*] n calzolaio.

**cobbles, cobblestones** ['kɔblz, 'kɔblstəunz] npl ciottoli mpl.

**cobweb** ['kɔbweb] n ragnatela.

**cocaine** [kə'kein] n cocaina.

**cock** [kɔk] n (rooster) gallo; (male bird) maschio // vt (gun) armare; ~**erel** n galletto; ~**eyed** a (fig) storto(a); strampalato(a).

**cockle** ['kɔkl] n cardio.

**cockney** ['kɔkni] n cockney m/f inv (abitante dei quartieri popolari dell'East End di Londra).

**cockpit** ['kɔkpit] n (in aircraft) abitacolo.

**cockroach** ['kɔkrəutʃ] n blatta.

**cocktail** ['kɔkteil] n cocktail m inv; ~ **cabinet** n mobile m bar inv; ~ **party** n cocktail m inv.

**cocoa** ['kəukəu] n cacao.

**coconut** ['kəukənʌt] $n$ noce $f$ di cocco.

**cocoon** [kə'ku:n] $n$ bozzolo.

**cod** [kɔd] $n$ merluzzo.

**C.O.D.** *abbr* = **cash on delivery**.

**code** [kəud] $n$ codice $m$.

**cod-liver oil** ['kɔdlivə*-] $n$ olio di fegato di merluzzo.

**coercion** [kəu'ə:ʃən] $n$ coercizione $f$.

**coffee** ['kɔfi] $n$ caffè $m$ *inv*; ~ **bar** $n$ (*Brit*) caffè $m$ *inv*; ~ **break** $n$ pausa per il caffè; ~**pot** $n$ caffettiera; ~ **table** $n$ tavolino.

**coffin** ['kɔfin] $n$ bara.

**cog** [kɔg] $n$ dente $m$.

**cogent** ['kəudʒənt] $a$ convincente.

**coherent** [kəu'hiərənt] $a$ coerente.

**coil** [kɔil] $n$ rotolo; (*one loop*) anello; (*contraceptive*) spirale $f$ // $vt$ avvolgere.

**coin** [kɔin] $n$ moneta // $vt$ (*word*) coniare; ~**age** $n$ sistema $m$ monetario; ~-**box** $n$ (*Brit*) telefono a gettoni.

**coincide** [kəuin'said] $vi$ coincidere; ~**nce** [kəu'insidəns] $n$ combinazione $f$.

**coke** [kəuk] $n$ coke $m$.

**colander** ['kɔləndə*] $n$ colino.

**cold** [kəuld] $a$ freddo // $n$ freddo; (*MED*) raffreddore $m$; **it's** ~ fa freddo; **to be** ~ aver freddo; **to catch** ~ prendere freddo; **to catch a** ~ prendere un raffreddore; **in** ~ **blood** a sangue freddo; ~ **sore** $n$ erpete $m$.

**coleslaw** ['kəulslɔ:] $n$ insalata di cavolo bianco.

**colic** ['kɔlik] $n$ colica.

**collapse** [kə'læps] $vi$ crollare // $n$ crollo; (*MED*) collasso.

**collapsible** [kə'læpsəbl] $a$ pieghevole.

**collar** ['kɔlə*] $n$ (*of coat, shirt*) colletto; ~**bone** $n$ clavicola.

**collateral** [kɔ'lætərl] $n$ garanzia.

**colleague** ['kɔli:g] $n$ collega $m/f$.

**collect** [kə'lekt] $vt$ (*gen*) raccogliere; (*as a hobby*) fare collezione di; (*Brit: call and pick up*) prendere;

(*money owed, pension*) riscuotere; (*donations, subscriptions*) fare una colletta di // $vi$ adunarsi, riunirsi; ammucchiarsi; **to call** ~ (*US TEL*) fare una chiamata a carico del destinatario; ~**ion** [kə'lekʃən] $n$ collezione $f$; raccolta; (*for money*) colletta.

**collector** [kə'lektə*] $n$ collezionista $m/f$; (*of taxes*) esattore $m$.

**college** ['kɔlidʒ] $n$ (*US SCOL*) college $m$ *inv*; (*of technology etc*) istituto superiore; (*body*) collegio.

**collide** [kə'laid] $vi$: **to** ~ (**with**) scontrarsi (con).

**collie** ['kɔli] $n$ (*dog*) collie $m$ *inv*.

**colliery** ['kɔliəri] $n$ (*Brit*) miniera di carbone.

**collision** [kə'liʒən] $n$ collisione $f$, scontro.

**colloquial** [kə'ləukwiəl] $a$ familiare.

**colon** ['kəulən] $n$ (*sign*) due punti $mpl$; (*MED*) colon $m$ *inv*.

**colonel** ['kə:nl] $n$ colonnello.

**colonial** [kə'ləuniəl] $a$ coloniale.

**colony** ['kɔləni] $n$ colonia.

**colour**, (*US*) **color** ['kʌlə*] $n$ colore $m$ // $vt$ colorare; (*tint, dye*) tingere; (*fig: affect*) influenzare // $vi$ (*blush: also:* ~ **up**) arrossire; ~**s** $npl$ (*of party, club*) emblemi $mpl$; ~ **bar** $n$ discriminazione $f$ razziale (*in locali etc*); ~-**blind** $a$ daltonico(a); ~**ed** $a$ colorato(a); (*photo*) a colori // $n$: ~**eds** gente $f$ di colore; ~ **film** $n$ (*for camera*) pellicola a colori; ~**ful** $a$ pieno(a) di colore, a vivaci colori; (*personality*) colorato(a); ~**ing** $n$ colorazione $f$; (*substance*) colorante $m$; (*complexion*) colorito; ~ **scheme** $n$ combinazione $f$ di colori; ~ **television** $n$ televisione $f$ a colori.

**colt** [kəult] $n$ puledro.

**column** ['kɔləm] $n$ colonna; ~**ist** ['kɔləmnist] $n$ articolista $m/f$.

**coma** ['kəumə] $n$ coma $m$ *inv*.

**comb** [kəum] $n$ pettine $m$ // $vt$ (*hair*) pettinare; (*area*) battere a tappeto.

**combat** ['kɔmbæt] $n$ combattimento // $vt$ combattere, lottare contro.

**combination** [kombɪ'neɪʃən] n combinazione f.

**combine** vb [kəm'baɪn] vt: to ~ (with) combinare (con); (one quality with another) unire (a) // vi unirsi; (CHEM) combinarsi // n ['kɔmbaɪn] lega; (ECON) associazione f; ~ (harvester) n mietitrebbia.

**come** [kʌm], pt came, pp come vi venire; arrivare; to ~ to (decision etc) raggiungere; to ~ undone slacciarsi; to ~ loose allentarsi; to ~ about vi succedere; to ~ across vt fus trovare per caso; to ~ along vi = to come on; to ~ away vi venire via; staccarsi; to ~ back vi ritornare; to ~ by vt fus (acquire) ottenere; procurarsi; to ~ down vi scendere; (prices) calare; (buildings) essere demolito(a); to ~ forward vi farsi avanti; presentarsi; to ~ from vt fus venire da; provenire da; to ~ in vi entrare; to ~ in for vt fus (criticism etc) ricevere; to ~ into vt fus (money) ereditare; to ~ off vi (button) staccarsi; (stain) andar via; (attempt) riuscire; to ~ on vi (pupil, work, project) fare progressi; (lights) accendersi; (electricity) entrare in funzione; ~ on! avanti!, andiamo!, forza!; to ~ out vi uscire; (strike) entrare in sciopero; to ~ round vi (after faint, operation) riprendere conoscenza, rinvenire; to ~ to vi rinvenire; to ~ up vi venire su; to ~ up against vt fus (resistance, difficulties) urtare contro; to ~ up with vt fus: he came up with an idea venne fuori con un'idea; to ~ upon vt fus trovare per caso; ~back n (THEATRE etc) ritorno.

**comedian** [kə'miːdɪən] n comico.

**comedown** ['kʌmdaun] n rovescio.

**comedy** ['kɔmɪdɪ] n commedia.

**comeuppance** [kʌm'ʌpəns] n: to get one's ~ ricevere ciò che si merita.

**comfort** ['kʌmfət] n comodità f inv, benessere m; (solace) consolazione f, conforto // vt consolare, confortare; ~s npl comodità fpl; ~able a comodo(a); ~ably ad (sit etc) comodamente; (live) bene; ~ station n (US) gabinetti mpl.

**comic** ['kɔmɪk] a (also: ~al) comico(a) // n comico; (magazine) giornaletto; ~ strip n fumetto.

**coming** ['kʌmɪŋ] n arrivo // a (next) prossimo(a); (future) futuro(a); ~(s) and going(s) n(pl) andirivieni m inv.

**comma** ['kɔmə] n virgola.

**command** [kə'maːnd] n ordine m, comando; (MIL: authority) comando; (mastery) padronanza // vt comandare; to ~ sb to do ordinare a qn di fare; ~eer [kɔmən'dɪəˈ] vt requisire; ~er n capo; (MIL) comandante m.

**commando** [kə'maːndəu] n commando m inv; membro di un commando.

**commemorate** [kə'meməreɪt] vt commemorare.

**commence** [kə'mens] vt, vi cominciare.

**commend** [kə'mend] vt lodare; raccomandare.

**commensurate** [kə'menʃərɪt] a: ~ with proporzionato(a) a.

**comment** ['kɔment] n commento // vi: to ~ (on) fare commenti (su); ~ary ['kɔməntəri] n commentario; (SPORT) radiocronaca; telecronaca; ~ator ['kɔmənteɪtəˈ] n commentatore/trice; radiocronista m/f; telecronista m/f.

**commerce** ['kɔməːs] n commercio.

**commercial** [kə'məːʃəl] a commerciale // n (TV: also: ~ break) pubblicità f inv.

**commiserate** [kə'mɪzəreɪt] vi: to ~ with condolersi con.

**commission** [kə'mɪʃən] n commissione f // vt (MIL) nominare (al comando); (work of art) commissionare; out of ~ (NAUT) in disarmo; ~**aire** [kəmiʃə'neə*] n (Brit: at shop, cinema etc) portiere m in livrea; ~**er** n commissionaire; (POLICE) questore m.

**commit** [kə'mɪt] vt (act) commettere; (to sb's care) affidare; **to ~ o.s.** (to do) impegnarsi (a fare); **to ~ suicide** suicidarsi; ~**ment** n impegno; promessa.

**committee** [kə'mɪtɪ] n comitato.

**commodity** [kə'mɒdɪtɪ] n prodotto, articolo; (food) derrata.

**common** ['kɒmən] a comune; (pej) volgare; (usual) normale // n terreno comune; **the C~s** npl (Brit) la Camera dei Comuni; **in ~** in comune; ~**er** n cittadino/a (non nobile); ~ **ground** n (fig) terreno comune; ~ **law** n diritto consuetudinario; ~**ly** ad comunemente, usualmente; **C~ Market** n Mercato Comune; ~**place** a banale, ordinario(a); ~**room** n sala di riunione; (SCOL) sala dei professori; ~ **sense** n buon senso; **the C~wealth** n il Commonwealth.

**commotion** [kə'məuʃən] n confusione f, tumulto.

**communal** ['kɒmju:nl] a (life) comunale; (for common use) pubblico(a).

**commune** n ['kɒmju:n] (group) comune f // vi [kə'mju:n]: **to ~ with** mettersi in comunione con.

**communicate** [kə'mju:nɪkeɪt] vt comunicare, trasmettere // vi: **to ~ (with)** comunicare (con).

**communication** [kəmju:nɪ'keɪʃən] n comunicazione f; ~ **cord** n (Brit) segnale m d'allarme.

**communion** [kə'mju:nɪən] n (also: Holy C~) comunione f.

**communiqué** [kə'mju:nɪkeɪ] n comunicato.

**communism** ['kɒmjunɪzəm] n comunismo; **communist** a, n comunista (m/f).

**community** [kə'mju:nɪtɪ] n comunità f inv; ~ **centre** n circolo ricreativo; ~ **chest** n (US) fondo di beneficenza.

**commutation ticket** [kɒmju-'teɪʃən-] n (US) biglietto di abbonamento.

**commute** [kə'mju:t] vi fare il pendolare // vt (LAW) commutare; ~**r** n pendolare m/f.

**compact** a [kəm'pækt] compatto(a) // n ['kɒmpækt] (also: **powder ~**) portacipria m inv; ~ **disk** n compact disc m inv.

**companion** [kəm'pænɪən] n compagno/a; ~**ship** n compagnia.

**company** ['kʌmpənɪ] n (also COMM, MIL, THEATRE) compagnia; **to keep sb ~** tenere compagnia a qn; ~ **secretary** n (Brit) segretario/a generale.

**comparative** [kəm'pærətɪv] a relativo(a); (adjective etc) comparativo(a); ~**ly** ad relativamente.

**compare** [kəm'pɛə*] vt: **to ~ sth/sb with/to** confrontare qc/qn con/a // vi: **to ~ (with)** reggere il confronto (con); **comparison** [-'pærɪsn] n confronto.

**compartment** [kəm'pɑ:tmənt] n compartimento; (RAIL) scompartimento.

**compass** ['kʌmpəs] n bussola; ~**es** npl compasso.

**compassion** [kəm'pæʃən] n compassione f.

**compatible** [kəm'pætɪbl] a compatibile.

**compel** [kəm'pel] vt costringere, obbligare; ~**ling** a (fig: argument) irresistibile.

**compendium** [kəm'pendɪəm] n compendio.

**compensate** ['kɒmpənseɪt] vt risarcire // vi: **to ~ for** compensare; **compensation** [-'seɪʃən] n compensazione f; (money) risarcimento.

**compère** ['kɒmpɛə*] n presentatore/trice.

**compete** [kəm'pi:t] vi (take part) concorrere; (vie): **to ~ (with)** fare concorrenza (a).

**competence** ['kɒmpɪtəns] n

competenza.

**competent** ['kɔmpitənt] *a* competente.

**competition** [kɔmpı'tıʃən] *n* gara; concorso; (*ECON*) concorrenza.

**competitive** [kəm'petitiv] *a* (*ECON*) concorrenziale; (*sport*) agonistico(a); (*person*) che ha spirito di competizione; che ha spirito agonistico; ~ **exam** concorso.

**competitor** [kəm'petitə*] *n* concorrente *m/f*.

**complacency** [kəm'pleisnsi] *n* compiacenza di sé.

**complain** [kəm'plein] *vi*: to ~ (about) lagnarsi (di); (*in shop etc*) reclamare (per); ~**t** *n* lamento; reclamo; (*MED*) malattia.

**complement** *n* ['kɔmplimənt] complemento; (*especially of ship's crew etc*) effettivo // *vt* ['kɔmpliment] (*enhance*) accompagnarsi bene a; ~**ary** [kɔmpli'mentəri] *a* complementare.

**complete** [kəm'pli:t] *a* completo(a) // *vt* completare; (*a form*) riempire; ~**ly** *ad* completamente; **completion** *n* completamento.

**complex** ['kɔmpleks] *a* complesso(a) // *n* (*PSYCH, buildings etc*) complesso.

**complexion** [kəm'plekʃən] *n* (*of face*) carnagione *f*; (*of event etc*) aspetto.

**compliance** [kəm'plaiəns] *n* acquiescenza; in ~ with (*orders, wishes etc*) in conformità con.

**complicate** ['kɔmplikeit] *vt* complicare; ~**d** *a* complicato(a); **complication** [-'keiʃən] *n* complicazione *f*.

**compliment** *n* ['kɔmplimənt] complimento // *vt* ['kɔmpliment] fare un complimento a; ~**s** *npl* complimenti *mpl*; rispetti *mpl*; to pay sb a ~ fare un complimento a qn; ~**ary** ['mentəri] *a* complimentoso(a), elogiativo(a); (*free*) in omaggio; ~**ary ticket** *n* biglietto d'omaggio;

**comply** [kəm'plai] *vi*: to ~ with

assentire a; conformarsi a.

**component** [kəm'pəunənt] *n* componente *m*.

**compose** [kəm'pəuz] *vt* comporre; to ~ o.s. ricomporsi; ~**d** *a* calmo(a); ~**r** *n* (*MUS*) compositore/trice.

**composition** [kɔmpə'ziʃən] *n* composizione *f*.

**composure** [kəm'pəuʒə*] *n* calma.

**compound** ['kɔmpaund] *n* (*CHEM, LING*) composto; (*enclosure*) recinto // *a* composto(a); ~ **fracture** *n* frattura esposta.

**comprehend** [kɔmprı'hend] *vt* comprendere, capire; **comprehension** [-'henʃən] *n* comprensione *f*.

**comprehensive** [kɔmprı'hensıv] *a* comprensivo(a); ~ **policy** *n* (*INSURANCE*) polizza che copre tutti i rischi; ~ (**school**) *n* (*Brit*) scuola secondaria aperta a tutti.

**compress** *vt* [kəm'pres] comprimere // *n* ['kɔmpres] (*MED*) compressa.

**comprise** [kəm'praiz] *vt* (*also*: be ~**d of**) comprendere.

**compromise** ['kɔmprəmaiz] *n* compromesso // *vt* compromettere // *vi* venire a un compromesso.

**compulsion** [kəm'pʌlʃən] *n* costrizione *f*.

**compulsive** [kəm'pʌlsıv] *a* (*PSYCH*) incontrollabile.

**compulsory** [kəm'pʌlsəri] *a* obbligatorio(a).

**computer** [kəm'pju:tə*] *n* computer *m inv*, elaboratore *m* elettronico; ~**ize** *vt* computerizzare; ~ **programmer** *n* programmatore/trice; ~ **programming** *n* programmazione *f* di computer; ~ **science, computing** *n* informatica.

**comrade** ['kɔmrid] *n* compagno/a.

**con** [kɔn] *vt* (*col*) truffare // *n* truffa.

**conceal** [kən'si:l] *vt* nascondere.

**conceit** [kən'si:t] *n* presunzione *f*, vanità; ~**ed** *a* presuntuoso(a), vanitoso(a).

**conceive** [kən'si:v] *vt* concepire // *vi* concepire un bambino.

**concentrate** ['kɒnsəntreɪt] *vi* concentrarsi // *vt* concentrare.

**concentration** [kɒnsən'treɪʃən] *n* concentrazione *f*; ~ **camp** *n* campo di concentramento.

**concept** ['kɒnsɛpt] *n* concetto.

**conception** [kən'sɛpʃən] *n* concezione *f*.

**concern** [kən'sə:n] *n* affare *m*; (*COMM*) azienda, ditta; (*anxiety*) preoccupazione *f* // *vt* riguardare; to be ~ed (about) preoccuparsi (di); ~ing *prep* riguardo a, circa.

**concert** ['kɒnsət] *n* concerto; ~ed [kən'sə:tɪd] *a* concertato(a); ~ hall *n* sala da concerti.

**concertina** [kɒnsə'ti:nə] *n* piccola fisarmonica // *vi* ridursi come una fisarmonica.

**concerto** [kən'tʃə:təu] *n* concerto.

**conclude** [kən'klu:d] *vt* concludere; **conclusion** [-'klu:ʒən] *n* conclusione *f*; **conclusive** [-'klu:sɪv] *a* conclusivo(a).

**concoct** [kən'kɒkt] *vt* inventare; ~**ion** [-'kɒkʃən] *n* miscuglio.

**concourse** ['kɒŋkɔ:s] *n* (*hall*) atrio.

**concrete** ['kɒŋkri:t] *n* calcestruzzo // *a* concreto(a); di calcestruzzo.

**concur** [kən'kə:] *vi* concordare.

**concurrently** [kən'kʌrntlɪ] *ad* simultaneamente.

**concussion** [kən'kʌʃən] *n* commozione *f* cerebrale.

**condemn** [kən'dɛm] *vt* condannare; ~**ation** [kɒndɛm'neɪʃən] *n* condanna.

**condensation** [kɒndɛn'seɪʃən] *n* condensazione *f*.

**condense** [kən'dɛns] *vi* condensarsi // *vt* condensare; ~**d milk** *n* latte *m* condensato.

**condition** [kən'dɪʃən] *n* condizione *f* // *vt* condizionare, regolare; on ~ that a condizione che + *sub*, a condizione di; ~**al** *a* condizionale; ~**er** *n* (*for hair*) balsamo.

**condolences** [kən'dəulənsɪz] *npl* condoglianze *fpl*.

**condom** ['kɒndəm] *n* preservativo.

**condominium** [kɒndə'mɪnɪəm] *n* (*US*) condominio.

**condone** [kən'dəun] *vt* condonare.

**conducive** [kən'dju:sɪv] *a*: ~ to favorevole a.

**conduct** *n* ['kɒndʌkt] condotta // *vt* [kən'dʌkt] condurre; (*manage*) dirigere; amministrare; (*MUS*) dirigere; **to** ~ **o.s.** comportarsi; ~**ed tour** *n* gita accompagnata; ~**or** *n* (*of orchestra*) direttore *m* d'orchestra; (*on bus*) bigliettaio; (*US: on train*) controllore *m*; (*ELEC*) conduttore *m*; ~**ress** *n* (*on bus*) bigliettaia.

**conduit** ['kɒndɪt] *n* condotto; tubo.

**cone** [kəun] *n* cono; (*BOT*) pigna.

**confectioner** [kən'fɛkʃənə*] *n* pasticciere *m*; ~**'s (shop)** *n* = pasticceria; ~**y** *n* dolciumi *mpl*.

**confer** [kən'fə:*] *vt*: to ~ sth on conferire qc a // *vi* conferire.

**conference** ['kɒnfərns] *n* congresso.

**confess** [kən'fɛs] *vt* confessare, ammettere // *vi* confessarsi; ~**ion** [-'fɛʃən] *n* confessione *f*.

**confetti** [kən'fɛtɪ] *n* coriandoli *mpl*.

**confide** [kən'faɪd] *vi*: to ~ in confidarsi con.

**confidence** ['kɒnfɪdns] *n* confidenza; (*trust*) fiducia; (*also*: self~) sicurezza di sé; in ~ (*speak, write*) in confidenza, confidenzialmente; ~ **trick** *n* truffa; **confident** *a* sicuro(a); sicuro(a) di sé; **confidential** [kɒnfɪ'dɛnʃəl] *a* riservato(a).

**confine** [kən'faɪn] *vt* limitare; (*shut up*) rinchiudere; ~**s** ['kɒnfaɪnz] *npl* confini *mpl*; ~**d** *a* (*space*) ristretto(a); ~**ment** *n* prigionia; (*MIL*) consegna; (*MED*) parto.

**confirm** [kən'fə:m] *vt* confermare; (*REL*) cresimare; ~**ation** [kɒnfə'meɪʃən] *n* conferma; cresima; ~**ed** *a* inveterato(a).

**confiscate** ['kɒnfɪskeɪt] *vt* confiscare.

**conflict** *n* ['kɒnflɪkt] conflitto // *vi* [kən'flɪkt] essere in conflitto; ~**ing** *a* contrastante.

**conform** [kən'fɔːm] vi: to ~ (to) conformarsi (a).

**confound** [kən'faund] vt confondere.

**confront** [kən'frʌnt] vt confrontare; (enemy, danger) affrontare; ~ation [kɔnfrən'teɪʃən] n confronto.

**confuse** [kən'fjuːz] vt imbrogliare; (one thing with another) confondere; ~d a confuso(a); **confusing** a che fa confondere; **confusion** [-'fjuːʒən] n confusione f.

**congeal** [kən'dʒiːl] vi (blood) congelarsi.

**congenial** [kən'dʒiːnɪəl] a (person) simpatico(a); (thing) congeniale.

**congested** [kən'dʒɛstɪd] a congestionato(a).

**congestion** [kən'dʒɛstʃən] n congestione f.

**congratulate** [kən'grætjuleɪt] vt: to ~ sb (on) congratularsi con qn (per or di); **congratulations** [-'leɪʃənz] npl auguri mpl; (on success) complimenti mpl.

**congregate** ['kɔŋgrɪgeɪt] vi congregarsi, riunirsi.

**congress** ['kɔŋgres] n congresso; ~**man** n (US) membro del Congresso.

**conjecture** [kən'dʒɛktʃə*] n congettura.

**conjunction** [kən'dʒʌŋkʃən] n congiunzione f.

**conjunctivitis** [kəndʒʌŋktɪ'vaɪtɪs] n congiuntivite f.

**conjure** ['kʌndʒə*] vi fare giochi di prestigio; **to ~ up** vt (ghost, spirit) evocare; (memories) rievocare; ~**r** n prestidigitatore/trice, prestigiatore/trice.

**conk out** [kɔŋk-] vi (col) andare in panne.

**conman** ['kɔnmæn] n truffatore m.

**connect** [kə'nɛkt] vt connettere, collegare; (ELEC) collegare; (fig) associare // vi (train): to ~ with essere in coincidenza con; to be ~ed with (associated) aver rapporti con; (by birth, marriage) essere imparentato con; ~**ion** [-ʃən] n

relazione f, rapporto; (ELEC) connessione f; (TEL) collegamento; **in ~ion with** con riferimento a.

**connive** [kə'naɪv] vi: to ~ at essere connivente in.

**connoisseur** [kɔnɪ'sə*] n conoscitore/trice.

**conquer** ['kɔŋkə*] vt conquistare; (feelings) vincere.

**conquest** ['kɔŋkwest] n conquista.

**cons** [kɔnz] npl see **convenience**, **pro**.

**conscience** ['kɔnʃəns] n coscienza.

**conscientious** [kɔnʃɪ'ɛnʃəs] a coscienzioso(a).

**conscious** ['kɔnʃəs] a consapevole; (MED) conscio(a); ~**ness** n consapevolezza; coscienza.

**conscript** [kən'skrɪpt] n coscritto.

**consent** [kən'sɛnt] n consenso // vi: to ~ (to) acconsentire (a).

**consequence** ['kɔnsɪkwəns] n conseguenza, risultato; importanza.

**consequently** ['kɔnsɪkwəntlɪ] ad di conseguenza, dunque.

**conservation** [kɔnsə'veɪʃən] n conservazione f.

**conservative** [kən'sə:vətɪv] a conservatore(trice); (cautious) cauto(a); (ELEC) **C~** a, n (Brit POL) conservatore(trice).

**conservatory** [kən'sə:vətrɪ] n (greenhouse) serra.

**conserve** [kən'sə:v] vt conservare // n conserva.

**consider** [kən'sɪdə*] vt considerare; (take into account) tener conto di; **to ~ doing sth** considerare la possibilità di fare qc.

**considerable** [kən'sɪdərəbl] a considerevole, notevole; **considerably** ad notevolmente, decisamente.

**considerate** [kən'sɪdərɪt] a premuroso(a).

**consideration** [kənsɪdə'reɪʃən] n considerazione f; (reward) rimunerazione f.

**considering** [kən'sɪdərɪŋ] prep in considerazione di.

**consign** [kən'saɪn] vt consegnare;

(send: goods) spedire; ~ment n consegna; spedizione f.

**consist** [kən'sıst] vi: to ~ of constare di, essere composto(a) di.

**consistency** [kən'sıstənsı] n consistenza; (fig) coerenza.

**consistent** [kən'sıstənt] a coerente; (constant) costante; ~ with compatibile con.

**consolation** [kɔnsə'leıʃən] n consolazione f.

**console** vt [kən'səul] consolare // n ['kɔnsəul] quadro di comando.

**consonant** ['kɔnsənənt] n consonante f.

**consortium** [kən'sɔ:tıəm] n consorzio.

**conspicuous** [kən'spıkjuəs] a cospicuo(a).

**conspiracy** [kən'spırəsı] n congiura, cospirazione f.

**constable** ['kʌnstəbl] n (Brit) = poliziotto, agente m di polizia.

**constabulary** [kən'stæbjulərı] n forze fpl dell'ordine.

**constant** ['kɔnstənt] a costante; continuo(a); ~ly ad costantemente; continuamente.

**constipated** ['kɔnstıpeıtıd] a stitico(a).

**constipation** [kɔnstı'peıʃən] n stitichezza.

**constituency** [kən'stıtjuənsı] n collegio elettorale.

**constituent** [kən'stıtjuənt] n elettore/trice; (part) elemento componente.

**constitution** [kɔnstı'tju:ʃən] n costituzione f; ~al a costituzionale.

**constraint** [kən'streınt] n costrizione f.

**construct** [kən'strʌkt] vt costruire; ~ion [-ʃən] n costruzione f; ~ive a costruttivo(a).

**construe** [kən'stru:] vt interpretare.

**consul** ['kɔnsl] n console m; ~ate ['kɔnsjulıt] n consolato.

**consult** [kən'sʌlt] vt consultare // vi consultarsi; ~ant n (MED) consulente m medico; (other

specialist) consulente; ~ing room n (Brit) ambulatorio.

**consume** [kən'sju:m] vt consumare; ~r n consumatore/trice; ~r goods npl beni mpl di consumo; ~r society n società dei consumi.

**consummate** ['kɔnsʌmeıt] vt consumare.

**consumption** [kən'sʌmpʃən] n consumo; (MED) consunzione f.

**cont.** abbr = continued.

**contact** ['kɔntækt] n contatto; (person) conoscenza // vt mettersi in contatto con; ~ lenses npl lenti fpl a contatto.

**contagious** [kən'teıdʒəs] a contagioso(a).

**contain** [kən'teın] vt contenere; to ~ o.s. contenersi; ~er n recipiente m; (for shipping etc) container m.

**contaminate** [kən'tæmıneıt] vt contaminare.

**cont'd** abbr = continued.

**contemplate** ['kɔntəmpleıt] vt contemplare; (consider) pensare a (or di).

**contemporary** [kən'tempərərı] a contemporaneo(a); (design) moderno(a) // n contemporaneo(a).

**contempt** [kən'tempt] n disprezzo; ~ of court (LAW) oltraggio alla Corte; ~uous a sdegnoso(a).

**contend** [kən'tend] vt: to ~ that sostenere che // vi: to ~ with lottare contro; ~er n contendente m/f; concorrente m/f.

**content** [kən'tent] a contento(a), soddisfatto(a) // vt contentare, soddisfare // n ['kɔntent] contenuto; ~s npl contenuto; (of barrel etc: capacity) capacità f inv; (table of) ~s indice m; ~ed a contento(a), soddisfatto(a).

**contention** [kən'tenʃən] n contesa; (assertion) tesi f inv.

**contentment** [kən'tentmənt] n contentezza.

**contest** n ['kɔntest] lotta; (competition) gara, concorso // vt [kən'test] contestare; impugnare;

(*compete for*) contendere; ~**ant** [kən'testənt] *n* concorrente *m/f*; (*in fight*) avversario/a.

**context** ['kɔntekst] *n* contesto.

**continent** ['kɔntinənt] *n* continente *m*; **the C~** (*Brit*) l'Europa continentale; ~**al** [-'nentl] *a* continentale *n* abitante *m/f* dell'Europa continentale; ~**al quilt** *n* (*Brit*) piumino.

**contingency** [kən'tindʒənsi] *n* eventualità *f inv*; ~ **plan** *n* misura d'emergenza.

**continual** [kən'tinjuəl] *a* continuo(a).

**continuation** [kəntinju'eiʃən] *n* continuazione *f*; (*after interruption*) ripresa; (*of story*) seguito.

**continue** [kən'tinju:] *vi* continuare // *vt* continuare; (*start again*) riprendere.

**continuous** [kən'tinjuəs] *a* continuo(a), ininterrotto(a); ~ **stationery** *n* carta a moduli continui.

**contort** [kən'tɔ:t] *vt* contorcere.

**contour** ['kɔntuə*] *n* contorno, profilo; (*also:* ~ **line**) curva di livello.

**contraband** ['kɔntrəbænd] *n* contrabbando.

**contraceptive** [kɔntrə'septiv] *a* traccettivo(a) // *n* contraccettivo.

**contract** *n* ['kɔntrækt] contratto // *vi* [kən'trækt] (*become smaller*) contrarre; (*COMM*): **to ~ to do sth** fare un contratto per fare qc; ~**ion** [-ʃən] *n* contrazione *f*; ~**or** *n* imprenditore *m*.

**contradict** [kɔntrə'dikt] *vt* contraddire.

**contraption** [kən'træpʃən] *n* (*pej*) aggeggio.

**contrary** ['kɔntrəri] *a* contrario(a); (*unfavourable*) avverso(a), contrario(a); [kən'trɛəri] (*perverse*) bisbetico(a) // *n* contrario; **on the ~** al contrario; **unless you hear to the** ~ a meno che non si disdica.

**contrast** *n* ['kɔntra:st] contrasto // *vt* [kən'tra:st] mettere in contrasto.

**contribute** [kən'tribju:t] *vi* con-

tribuire // *vt*: **to ~ £10/an article to** dare 10 sterline/un articolo a; **to ~ to** contribuire a; (*newspaper*) scrivere per; ~ **contribution** [kɔntri'bju:ʃən] *n* ~**contribuzione** *f*; **contributor** *n* (*to newspaper*) collaboratore/trice.

**contrivance** [kən'traivəns] *n* congegno; espediente *m*.

**contrive** [kən'traiv] *vt* inventare; escogitare // *vi*: **to ~ to do** fare in modo di fare.

**control** [kən'trəul] *vt* dominare; (*firm, operation etc*) dirigere; (*check*) controllare // *n* controllo; ~**s** *npl* comandi *mpl*; **under** ~ sotto controllo; **to be in** ~ **of** aver autorità su; essere responsabile di; controllare; **to go out of** ~ (*car*) non rispondere ai comandi; (*situation*) sfuggire di mano; ~ **panel** *n* quadro dei comandi; ~ **room** *n* (*NAUT, MIL*) sala di comando; (*RADIO, TV*) sala di regia; ~ **tower** *n* (*AVIAT*) torre *f* di controllo.

**controversial** [kɔntrə'və:ʃl] *a* controverso(a), polemico(a).

**controversy** ['kɔntrəvə:si] *n* controversia, polemica.

**convalesce** [kɔnvə'les] *vi* rimettersi in salute.

**convene** [kən'vi:n] *vt* convocare // *vi* convenire, adunarsi.

**convenience** [kən'vi:niəns] *n* comodità *f inv*; **at your** ~ a suo comodo; **all modern** ~**s**, (*Brit*) **all mod cons** tutte le comodità moderne.

**convenient** [kən'vi:niənt] *a* conveniente, comodo(a).

**convent** ['kɔnvənt] *n* convento.

**convention** [kən'venʃən] *n* convenzione *f*; (*meeting*) convegno; ~**al** *a* convenzionale.

**conversant** [kən'və:snt] *a*: **to be** ~ **with** essere al corrente di; essere pratico(a) di.

**conversation** [kɔnvə'seiʃən] *n* conversazione *f*; ~**al** *a* non formale.

**converse** *n* ['kɔnvə:s] contrario,

opposto // *vi* [kən'vɜːs] conversare; ~**ly** [-'vɜːslɪ] *ad* al contrario, per contro.

**convert** *vt* [kən'vɜːt] (*REL, COMM*) convertire; (*alter*) trasformare // *n* ['kɒnvɜːt] convertito/a; ~**ible** *a* (*currency*) convertibile // *n* macchina decappottabile.

**convex** ['kɒnveks] *a* convesso(a).

**convey** [kən'veɪ] *vt* trasportare; (*thanks*) comunicare; (*idea*) dare; ~**or belt** *n* nastro trasportatore.

**convict** *vt* [kən'vɪkt] dichiarare colpevole // *n* ['kɒnvɪkt] carcerato/a; ~**ion** [-ʃən] *n* condanna; (*belief*) convinzione *f*.

**convince** [kən'vɪns] *vt* convincere, persuadere; **convincing** *a* convincente.

**convivial** [kən'vɪvɪəl] *a* allegro(a).

**convoluted** [kɒnvə'luːtɪd] *a* (*argument etc*) involuto(a).

**convoy** ['kɒnvɔɪ] *n* convoglio.

**convulse** [kən'vʌls] *vt* sconvolgere; **to be** ~**d with laughter** contorcersi dalle risa.

**coo** [kuː] *vi* tubare.

**cook** [kuk] *vt* cucinare, cuocere // *vi* cuocere; (*person*) cucinare // *n* cuoco/a; ~**book** *n* libro di cucina; ~**er** *n* fornello, cucina; ~**ery** *n* cucina; ~**ery book** *n* (*Brit*) = ~**book**; ~**ie** *n* (*US*) biscotto; ~**ing** *n* cucina.

**cool** [kuːl] *a* fresco(a); (*not afraid*) calmo(a); (*unfriendly*) freddo(a); (*impertinent*) sfacciato(a) // *vt* raffreddare, rinfrescare // *vi* raffreddarsi, rinfrescarsi.

**coop** [kuːp] *n* stia // *vt*: **to** ~ **up** (*fig*) rinchiudere.

**cooperate** [kəʊ'ɒpəreɪt] *vi* cooperare, collaborare; **cooperation** [-'reɪʃən] *n* cooperazione *f*, collaborazione *f*.

**cooperative** [kəʊ'ɒpərətɪv] *a* cooperativo(a) // *n* cooperativa.

**coordinate** *vt* [kəʊ'ɔːdɪneɪt] coordinare // *n* [kəʊ'ɔːdɪnət] (*MATH*) coordinata; ~**s** *npl* (*clothes*)

coordinati *mpl.*

**cop** [kɒp] *n* (*col*) sbirro.

**cope** [kəʊp] *vi* farcela; **to** ~ **with** (*problems*) far fronte a.

**copper** ['kɒpə*] *n* rame *m*; (*col: policeman*) sbirro; ~**s** *npl* spiccioli *mpl.*

**coppice** ['kɒpɪs] *n*, **copse** [kɒps] *n* bosco ceduo.

**copulate** ['kɒpjuleɪt] *vi* accoppiarsi.

**copy** ['kɒpɪ] *n* copia; (*book etc*) esemplare *m* // *vt* copiare; ~**right** *n* diritto d'autore.

**coral** ['kɒrəl] *n* corallo.

**cord** [kɔːd] *n* corda; (*fabric*) velluto a coste.

**cordial** ['kɔːdɪəl] *a*, *n* cordiale (*m*).

**cordon** ['kɔːdn] *n* cordone *m*; **to** ~ **off** *vt* fare cordone a.

**corduroy** ['kɔːdərɔɪ] *n* fustagno.

**core** [kɔː*] *n* (*of fruit*) torsolo; (*TECH*) centro // *vt* estrarre il torsolo da.

**cork** [kɔːk] *n* sughero; (*of bottle*) tappo; ~**screw** *n* cavatappi *m inv.*

**corn** [kɔːn] *n* (*Brit: wheat*) grano; (*US: maize*) granturco; (*on foot*) callo; ~ **on the cob** (*CULIN*) pannocchia cotta.

**corned beef** ['kɔːnd-] *n* carne *f* di manzo in scatola.

**corner** ['kɔːnə*] *n* angolo; (*AUT*) curva // *vt* intrappolare; mettere con le spalle al muro; (*COMM: market*) accaparrare // *vi* prendere una curva; ~**stone** *n* pietra angolare.

**cornet** ['kɔːnɪt] *n* (*MUS*) cornetta; (*Brit: of ice-cream*) cono.

**cornflakes** ['kɔːnfleɪks] *npl* fiocchi *mpl* di granturco.

**cornflour** ['kɔːnflaʊə*] *n* (*Brit*) farina finissima di granturco.

**cornstarch** ['kɔːnstɑːtʃ] *n* (*US*) = **cornflour.**

**Cornwall** ['kɔːnwəl] *n* Cornovaglia.

**corny** ['kɔːnɪ] *a* (*col*) trito(a).

**coronary** ['kɒrənərɪ] *n*: ~ (**thrombosis**) trombosi *f* coronaria.

**coronation** [kɒrə'neɪʃən] *n* incoronazione *f*.

**coroner** ['kɒrənə\*] n magistrato incaricato di indagare la causa di morte in circostanze sospette.

**coronet** ['kɒrənt] n diadema m.

**corporal** ['kɔːpərl] n caporalmaggiore m // a: ~ **punishment** pena corporale.

**corporate** ['kɔːpərit] a costituito(a) (in corporazione); comune.

**corporation** [kɔːpə'reiʃən] n (of town) consiglio comunale; (COMM) ente m.

**corps** [kɔː\*], pl **corps** [kɔːz] n corpo.

**corpse** [kɔːps] n cadavere m.

**corral** [kə'rɑːl] n recinto.

**correct** [kə'rɛkt] a (accurate) corretto(a), esatto(a); (proper) corretto(a) // vt correggere; **~ion** [-ʃən] n correzione f.

**correspond** [kɒris'pɒnd] vi corrispondere; **~ence** n corrispondenza; **~ence course** n corso per corrispondenza; **~ent** n corrispondente m/f.

**corridor** ['kɒridɔː\*] n corridoio.

**corrode** [kə'rəud] vt corrodere // vi corrodersi.

**corrugated** ['kɒrəgeitid] a increspato(a); ondulato(a); ~ **iron** n lamiera di ferro ondulata.

**corrupt** [kə'rʌpt] a corrotto(a) // vt corrompere; **~ion** [-ʃən] n corruzione f.

**corset** ['kɔːsit] n busto.

**cortège** [kɔː'teiʒ] n corteo.

**cosh** [kɒʃ] n (Brit) randello (corto).

**cosmetic** [kɒz'mɛtik] n cosmetico.

**cosset** ['kɒsit] vt vezzeggiare.

**cost** [kɒst] n costo // vb (pt, pp **cost**) vi costare // vt stabilire il prezzo di; ~s npl (LAW) spese fpl; it ~s £5/too much costa 5 sterline/troppo; at all ~s a ogni costo.

**co-star** ['kəustɑː\*] n attore/trice della stessa importanza del protagonista.

**cost-effective** [kɒsti'fɛktiv] a conveniente.

**costly** ['kɒstli] a costoso(a), caro(a).

**cost-of-living** [kɒstəv'liviŋ] a: ~ **allowance** indennità f inv di

contingenza; ~ **index** indice m della scala mobile.

**cost price** n (Brit) prezzo all'ingrosso.

**costume** ['kɒstjuːm] n costume m; (lady's suit) tailleur m inv; (Brit: also: swimming ~) costume da bagno; ~ **jewellery** n bigiotteria.

**cosy,** (US) **cozy** ['kəuzi] a intimo(a).

**cot** [kɒt] n (Brit: child's) lettino; (US: campbed) brandina.

**cottage** ['kɒtidʒ] n cottage m inv; ~ **cheese** n fiocchi mpl di latte magro; ~ **industry** n industria artigianale basata sul lavoro a cottimo; ~ **pie** n piatto a base di carne macinata in sugo e purè di patate.

**cotton** ['kɒtn] n cotone m; **to ~ on to** vt fus (col) afferrare; ~ **candy** n (US) zucchero filato; ~ **wool** n (Brit) cotone idrofilo.

**couch** [kautʃ] n sofà m inv // vt esprimere.

**couchette** [kuː'ʃɛt] n (on train, boat) cuccetta.

**cough** [kɒf] vi tossire // n tosse f; ~ **drop** n pasticca per la tosse.

**could** [kud] pt of **can**; **~n't** = could not.

**council** ['kaunsl] n consiglio; **city** or **town** ~ consiglio comunale; ~ **estate** n (Brit) quartiere m di case popolari; ~ **house** n (Brit) casa popolare; **~lor** n consigliere/a.

**counsel** ['kaunsl] n avvocato; consultazione f; **~lor** n consigliere/a.

**count** [kaunt] vt, vi contare // n conto; (nobleman) conte m; **to ~ on** vt fus contare su; **~down** n conto alla rovescia.

**countenance** ['kauntinəns] n volto, aspetto // vt approvare.

**counter** ['kauntə\*] n banco // vt opporsi a; (blow) parare // ad: ~ **to** contro; in opposizione a; **~act** vt agire in opposizione a; (poison etc) annullare gli effetti di; **~espionage** n controspionaggio.

**counterfeit** ['kauntəfit] n contraffazione f, falso // vt contraffare, falsificare // a falso(a).

**counterfoil** ['kauntəfɔil] n matrice f.

**countermand** [kauntə'mɑ:nd] vt annullare.

**counterpart** ['kauntəpɑ:t] n (of document etc) copia; (of person) corrispondente m/f.

**counter-productive** [kauntəprə-'dʌktiv] a controproducente.

**countersign** ['kauntəsain] vt controfirmare.

**countess** ['kauntis] n contessa.

**countless** ['kauntlis] a innumerevole.

**country** ['kʌntri] n paese m; (native land) patria; (as opposed to town) campagna; (region) regione f; ~ **dancing** n (Brit) danza popolare; ~ **house** n villa in campagna; ~**man** n (national) compatriota m; (rural) contadino; ~**side** n campagna.

**county** ['kaunti] n contea.

**coup** [ku:], ~**s** [ku:, -z] n colpo; (also: ~ d'état) colpo di Stato.

**couple** ['kʌpl] n coppia // vt (carriages) agganciare; (TECH) accoppiare; (ideas, names) associare; **a** ~ **of** un paio di.

**coupon** ['ku:pɔn] n buono; (COMM) coupon m inv.

**courage** ['kʌridʒ] n coraggio.

**courgette** [kuə'ʒɛt] n (Brit) zucchina.

**courier** ['kuriə*] n corriere m; (for tourists) guida.

**course** [kɔ:s] n corso; (of ship) rotta; (for golf) campo; (part of meal) piatto; **first** ~ primo piatto; **of** ~ ad senz'altro, naturalmente; ~ **of action** modo d'agire; ~ **of lectures** corso di lezioni; **a** ~ **of treatment** (MED) una cura.

**court** [kɔ:t] n corte f; (TENNIS) campo // vt (woman) fare la corte a; **to take to** ~ citare in tribunale.

**courteous** ['kə:tiəs] a cortese.

**courtesan** [kɔ:ti'zæn] n cortigiana.

**courtesy** ['kə:təsi] n cortesia; **by** ~ **of** per gentile concessione di.

**court-house** ['kɔ:thaus] n (US)

palazzo di giustizia.

**courtier** ['kɔ:tiə*] n cortigiano/a.

**court-martial**, pl **courts-martial** ['kɔ:t'mɑ:ʃəl] n corte f marziale.

**courtroom** ['kɔ:trum] n tribunale m.

**courtyard** ['kɔ:tjɑ:d] n cortile m.

**cousin** ['kʌzn] n cugino/a; **first** ~ cugino di primo grado.

**cove** [kəuv] n piccola baia.

**covenant** ['kʌvənənt] n accordo.

**cover** ['kʌvə*] vt coprire // n (of pan) coperchio; (over furniture) fodera; (of book) copertina; (shelter) riparo; (COMM, INSURANCE) copertura; **to take** ~ (shelter) ripararsi; **under** ~ al riparo; **under** ~ **of darkness** protetto dall'oscurità; **under separate** ~ (COMM) a parte, in plico separato; **to** ~ **up for sb** coprire qn; ~**age** n (PRESS, TV, RADIO): **to give full** ~**age to sth** fare un ampio servizio su qc; ~ **charge** n coperto; ~**ing** n copertura; ~**ing letter**, (US) ~ **letter** n lettera d'accompagnamento; ~ **note** n (INSURANCE) polizza di assicurazione provvisoria.

**covert** ['kʌvət] a (hidden) nascosto(a); (glance) furtivo(a).

**cover-up** ['kʌvərʌp] n occultamento (di informazioni).

**covet** ['kʌvit] vt bramare.

**cow** [kau] n vacca // vt (person) intimidire.

**coward** ['kauəd] n vigliacco/a; ~**ice** [-is] n vigliaccheria; ~**ly** a vigliacco(a).

**cowboy** ['kaubɔi] n cow-boy m inv.

**cower** ['kauə*] vi acquattarsi.

**coxswain** ['kɔksn] n (abbr: **cox**) timoniere m.

**coy** [kɔi] a falsamente timido(a).

**cozy** ['kəuzi] a (US) = **cosy**.

**CPA** n abbr (US) = **certified public accountant**.

**crab** [kræb] n granchio; ~ **apple** n mela selvatica.

**crack** [kræk] n fessura, crepa; incrinatura; (noise) schiocco; (: of gun) scoppio; (joke) battuta; (col:

*attempt*): **to have a ~ at** sth tentare qc // *vt* spaccare; incrinare; (*whip*) schioccare; (*nut*) schiacciare // *a* (*troops*) fuori classe; **to ~ down on** sth *vi fus* porre freno a; **to ~ up** *vi* crollare; **~er** *n* cracker *m inv*; petardo.

**crackle** ['krækl] *vi* crepitare.

**cradle** ['kreɪdl] *n* culla.

**craft** [krɑːft] *n* mestiere *m*; (*cunning*) astuzia; (*boat*) naviglio; **~sman** *n* artigiano; **~smanship** *n* abilità; **~y** *a* furbo(a), astuto(a).

**crag** [kræg] *n* roccia.

**cram** [kræm] *vt* (*fill*): **to ~** sth with riempire qc di; (*put*): **to ~** sth into stipare qc in // *vi* (*for exams*) prepararsi (in gran fretta).

**cramp** [kræmp] *n* crampo; **~ed** *a* ristretto(a).

**crampon** ['kræmpən] *n* (*CLIMBING*) rampone *m*.

**cranberry** ['krænbəri] *n* mirtillo.

**crane** [kreɪn] *n* gru *f inv*.

**crank** [kræŋk] *n* manovella; (*person*) persona strana; **~shaft** *n* albero a gomiti.

**cranny** ['kræni] *n see* **nook**.

**crash** [kræʃ] *n* fragore *m*; (*of car*) incidente *m*; (*of plane*) caduta // *vt* fracassare // *vi* (*plane*) fracassarsi; (*car*) avere un incidente; (*two cars*) scontrarsi; (*fig*) fallire, andare in rovina; **to ~ into** scontrarsi con; **~ course** *n* corso intensivo; **~ helmet** *n* casco; **~ landing** *n* atterraggio di fortuna.

**crate** [kreɪt] *n* gabbia.

**cravat(e)** [krə'væt] *n* fazzoletto da collo.

**crave** [kreɪv] *vt*, *vi*: **to ~** (**for**) desiderare ardentemente.

**crawl** [krɔːl] *vi* strisciare carponi; (*vehicle*) avanzare lentamente // *n* (*SWIMMING*) crawl *m*.

**crayfish** ['kreɪfɪʃ] *n* (*pl inv*) (*freshwater*) gambero (d'acqua dolce); (*saltwater*) gambero.

**crayon** ['kreɪən] *n* matita colorata.

**craze** [kreɪz] *n* mania.

**crazy** ['kreɪzi] *a* matto(a); **~ paving** *n* lastricato a mosaico irregolare.

**creak** [kriːk] *vi* cigolare, scricchiolare.

**cream** [kriːm] *n* crema; (*fresh*) panna // *a* (*colour*) color crema *inv*; **~ cake** *n* torta alla panna; **~ cheese** *n* formaggio fresco; **~y** *a* cremoso(a).

**crease** [kriːs] *n* grinza; (*deliberate*) piega // *vt* sgualcire.

**create** [kriː'eɪt] *vt* creare; **creation** [-ʃən] *n* creazione *f*; **creative** *a* creativo(a).

**creature** ['kriːtʃə*] *n* creatura.

**crèche, creche** [kreʃ] *n* asilo infantile.

**credence** ['kriːdns] *n*: **to lend** *or* **give ~ to** prestare fede a.

**credentials** [krɪ'dɛnʃlz] *npl* (*papers*) credenziali *fpl*.

**credit** ['krɛdɪt] *n* credito; onore *m* // *vt* (*COMM*) accreditare; (*believe: also*: **give ~ to**) credere, prestar fede a; **~s** *npl* (*CINEMA*) titoli *mpl*; **to ~** sb **with** (*fig*) attribuire a qn; **to be in ~** (*person*) essere creditore (trice); (*bank account*) essere coperto(a); **~ card** *n* carta di credito; **~or** *n* creditore/trice.

**creed** [kriːd] *n* credo; dottrina.

**creek** [kriːk] *n* insenatura; (*US*) piccolo fiume *m*.

**creep** [kriːp], *pt*, *pp* **crept** *vi* avanzare furtivamente (*or* pian piano); (*plant*) arrampicarsi; **~er** *n* pianta rampicante; **~y** *a* (*frightening*) che fa accapponare la pelle.

**cremate** [krɪ'meɪt] *vt* cremare.

**crematorium**, *pl* **crematoria** [krɛmə'tɔːrɪəm, -'tɔːrɪə] *n* forno crematorio.

**crêpe** [kreɪp] *n* crespo; **~ bandage** *n* (*Brit*) fascia elastica.

**crept** [krɛpt] *pt*, *pp of* **creep**.

**crescent** ['krɛsnt] *n* (*shape*) mezzaluna; (*street*) strada semicircolare.

**cress** [krɛs] *n* crescione *m*.

**crest** [krɛst] n cresta; (of helmet) pennacchiera; (of coat of arms) cimiero; ~**fallen** a mortificato(a).

**crevasse** [krɪ'væs] n crepaccio.

**crevice** ['krɛvɪs] n fessura, crepa.

**crew** [kru:] n equipaggio; **to have a** ~**cut** avere i capelli a spazzola; ~**neck** n girocollo.

**crib** [krɪb] n culla; (REL) presepio // vt (col) copiare.

**crick** [krɪk] n crampo.

**cricket** ['krɪkɪt] n (insect) grillo; (game) cricket m.

**crime** [kraɪm] n crimine m; **criminal** ['krɪmɪnl] a, n criminale (m/f).

**crimson** ['krɪmzn] a color cremisi inv.

**cringe** [krɪndʒ] vi acquattarsi; (fig) essere servile.

**crinkle** ['krɪŋkl] vt arricciare, increspare.

**cripple** ['krɪpl] n zoppo/a // vt azzoppare.

**crisis**, pl **crises** ['kraɪsɪs, -sɪːz] n crisi f inv.

**crisp** [krɪsp] a croccante; (fig) frizzante; vivace; deciso(a); ~**s** npl (Brit) patatine fpl.

**criss-cross** ['krɪskrɔs] a incrociato(a).

**criterion**, pl **criteria** [kraɪ'tɪərɪən, -'tɪərɪə] n criterio.

**critic** ['krɪtɪk] n critico; ~**al** a critico(a); ~**ally** ad (speak etc) criticamente; ~**ally ill** gravemente malato; ~**ism** ['krɪtɪsɪzm] n critica; ~**ize** ['krɪtɪsaɪz] vt criticare.

**croak** [krəuk] vi gracchiare; (frog) gracidare.

**crochet** ['krəuʃeɪ] n lavoro all'uncinetto.

**crockery** ['krɔkərɪ] n vasellame m.

**crocodile** ['krɔkədaɪl] n coccodrillo.

**crocus** ['krəukəs] n croco.

**croft** [krɔft] n (Brit) piccolo podere m.

**crony** ['krəunɪ] n (col) amicone/a.

**crook** [kruk] n truffatore m; (of shepherd) bastone m; ~**ed** ['krukɪd] a curvo(a), storto(a); (action)

disonesto(a).

**crop** [krɔp] n (produce) coltivazione f; (amount produced) raccolto; (riding ~) frustino; **to** ~ **up** vi presentarsi.

**croquette** [krə'kɛt] n crocchetta.

**cross** [krɔs] n croce f; (BIOL) incrocio // vt (street etc) attraversare; (arms, legs, BIOL) incrociare; (cheque) sbarrare // a di cattivo umore; **to** ~ **o.s.** fare il segno della croce, segnarsi; **to** ~ **out** vt cancellare; **to** ~ **over** vi attraversare; ~**bar** n traversa; ~**country (race)** n cross-country m inv; ~**examine** vt (LAW) interrogare in contraddittorio; ~**eyed** a strabico(a); ~**fire** n fuoco incrociato; ~**ing** n incrocio; (sea passage) traversata; (also: **pedestrian** ~**ing**) passaggio pedonale; ~**ing guard** n (US) dipendente comunale che aiuta i bambini ad attraversare la strada; ~**purposes** npl: **to be at** ~**purposes** non parlare della stessa cosa; ~**reference** n rinvio, rimando; ~**roads** n incrocio; ~**section** n (BIOL) sezione f trasversale; (in population) settore m rappresentativo; ~**walk** n (US) strisce fpl pedonali, passaggio pedonale; ~**wind** n vento di traverso; ~**wise** ad di traverso; ~**word** n cruciverba m inv.

**crotch** [krɔtʃ] n (of garment) pattina.

**crotchety** ['krɔtʃɪtɪ] a (person) burbero(a).

**crouch** [krautʃ] vi acquattarsi; rannicchiarsi.

**crouton** ['kru:tɔn] n crostino.

**crow** [krəu] n (bird) cornacchia; (of cock) canto del gallo // vi (cock) cantare; (fig) vantarsi; cantar vittoria.

**crowbar** ['krəubɑ:*] n piede m di porco.

**crowd** [kraud] n folla // vt affollare, stipare // vi affollarsi; ~**ed** a affollato(a); ~**ed with** stipato(a) di.

**crown** [kraun] $n$ corona; (of head) calotta cranica; (of hat) cocuzzolo; (of hill) cima // $vt$ incoronare; ~ **jewels** $npl$ gioielli $mpl$ della Corona; ~ **prince** $n$ principe $m$ ereditario.

**crow's feet** $npl$ zampe $fpl$ di gallina.

**crucial** ['kru:ʃl] $a$ cruciale, decisivo(a).

**crucifix** ['kru:sɪfɪks] $n$ crocifisso; ~**ion** [-'fɪkʃən] $n$ crocifissione $f$.

**crude** [kru:d] $a$ (materials) greggio(a); non raffinato(a); (fig: basic) crudo(a), primitivo(a); (: vulgar) rozzo(a), grossolano(a); ~ **(oil)** $n$ (petrolio) greggio.

**cruel** ['kruəl] $a$ crudele; ~**ty** $n$ crudeltà $f$ $inv$.

**cruet** ['kru:ɪt] $n$ ampolla.

**cruise** [kru:z] $n$ crociera // $vi$ andare a velocità di crociera; (taxi) circolare; ~**r** $n$ incrociatore $m$.

**crumb** [krʌm] $n$ briciola.

**crumble** ['krʌmbl] $vt$ sbriciolare // $vi$ sbriciolarsi; (plaster etc) sgretolarsi; (land, earth) franare; (building, fig) crollare; **crumbly** $a$ friabile.

**crumpet** ['krʌmpɪt] $n$ specie di frittella.

**crumple** ['krʌmpl] $vt$ raggrinzare, spiegazzare.

**crunch** [krʌntʃ] $vt$ sgranocchiare; (underfoot) scricchiolare // $n$ (fig) punto $or$ momento cruciale; ~**y** $a$ croccante.

**crusade** [kru:'seɪd] $n$ crociata.

**crush** [krʌʃ] $n$ folla // $vt$ schiacciare; (crumple) sgualcire.

**crust** [krʌst] $n$ crosta.

**crutch** [krʌtʃ] $n$ gruccia.

**crux** [krʌks] $n$ nodo.

**cry** [kraɪ] $vi$ piangere; (shout: also: ~ **out**) urlare // $n$ urlo, grido; **to** ~ **off** $vi$ ritirarsi.

**cryptic** ['krɪptɪk] $a$ ermetico(a).

**crystal** ['krɪstl] $n$ cristallo; ~**-clear** $a$ cristallino(a).

**cub** [kʌb] $n$ cucciolo; (also: ~ **scout**) lupetto.

**Cuba** ['kju:bə] $n$ Cuba.

**cubbyhole** ['kʌbɪhəul] $n$ angolino.

**cube** [kju:b] $n$ cubo // $vt$ (MATH) elevare al cubo; **cubic** $a$ cubico(a); (metre, foot) cubo(a); **cubic capacity** $n$ cilindrata.

**cubicle** ['kju:bɪkl] $n$ scompartimento separato; cabina.

**cuckoo** ['kuku:] $n$ cucù $m$ $inv$; ~ **clock** $n$ orologio a cucù.

**cucumber** ['kju:kʌmbə*] $n$ cetriolo.

**cuddle** ['kʌdl] $vt$ abbracciare, coccolare // $vi$ abbracciarsi.

**cue** [kju:] $n$ (snooker ~) stecca; (THEATRE etc) segnale $m$.

**cuff** [kʌf] $n$ (Brit: of shirt, coat etc) polsino; (US: of trousers) risvolto; **off the** ~ $ad$ improvvisando; ~**link** $n$ gemello.

**cuisine** [kwɪ'zi:n] $n$ cucina.

**cul-de-sac** ['kʌldəsæk] $n$ vicolo cieco.

**culminate** ['kʌlmɪneɪt] $vi$: **to** ~ **in** culminare con; **culmination** [-'neɪʃən] $n$ culmine $m$.

**culottes** [kju:'lɒts] $npl$ gonna $f$ pantalone $inv$.

**culpable** ['kʌlpəbl] $a$ colpevole.

**culprit** ['kʌlprɪt] $n$ colpevole $m/f$.

**cult** [kʌlt] $n$ culto.

**cultivate** ['kʌltɪveɪt] $vt$ (also fig) coltivare; **cultivation** [-'veɪʃən] $n$ coltivazione $f$.

**cultural** ['kʌltʃərəl] $a$ culturale.

**culture** ['kʌltʃə*] $n$ (also fig) cultura; ~**d** $a$ colto(a).

**cumbersome** ['kʌmbəsəm] $a$ ingombrante.

**cunning** ['kʌnɪŋ] $n$ astuzia, furberia // $a$ astuto(a), furbo(a).

**cup** [kʌp] $n$ tazza; (prize) coppa.

**cupboard** ['kʌbəd] $n$ armadio.

**cup-tie** ['kʌptaɪ] $n$ (Brit) partita di coppa.

**curate** ['kjuərɪt] $n$ cappellano.

**curator** [kjuə'reɪtə*] $n$ direttore $m$ (di museo etc).

**curb** [kə:b] $vt$ tenere a freno // $n$ freno; (US) = **kerb**.

**curdle** ['kə:dl] $vi$ cagliare.

**cure** [kjuə*] vt guarire; (CULIN) trattare; affumicare; essiccare // n rimedio.

**curfew** ['kə:fju:] n coprifuoco.

**curio** ['kjuəriəu] n curiosità f inv.

**curiosity** [kjuəri'ɔsiti] n curiosità.

**curious** ['kjuəriəs] a curioso(a).

**curl** [kə:l] n riccio // vt ondulare; (tightly) arricciare // vi arricciarsi; **to ~ up** vi avvolgersi a spirale; rannicchiarsi; **~er** n bigodino.

**curly** ['kə:lɪ] a ricciuto(a).

**currant** ['kʌrnt] n uva passa.

**currency** ['kʌrnsɪ] n moneta; **to gain ~** (fig) acquistare larga diffusione.

**current** ['kʌrnt] a, n corrente (f); **~ account** a (Brit) conto corrente; **~ affairs** npl attualità fpl; **~ly** ad attualmente.

**curriculum, pl ~s or curricula** [kə'rɪkjuləm, -lə] n curriculum m inv; **~ vitae (CV)** n curriculum vitae m inv.

**curry** ['kʌrɪ] n curry m inv // vt: **to ~ favour with** cercare di attirarsi i favori di.

**curse** [kə:s] vt maledire // vi bestemmiare // n maledizione f; bestemmia f.

**cursor** ['kə:sə*] n (COMPUT) cursore m.

**cursory** ['kə:sərɪ] a superficiale.

**curt** [kə:t] a secco(a).

**curtail** [kə:'teɪl] vt (visit etc) accorciare; (expenses etc) ridurre, decurtare.

**curtain** ['kə:tn] n tenda.

**curts(e)y** ['kə:tsɪ] n inchino, riverenza // vi fare un inchino or una riverenza.

**curve** [kə:v] n curva // vi curvarsi.

**cushion** ['kuʃən] n cuscino // vt (shock) fare da cuscinetto a.

**custard** ['kʌstəd] n (for pouring) crema.

**custodian** [kʌs'təudɪən] n custode m/f.

**custody** ['kʌstədɪ] n (of child) tutela; (for offenders) arresto.

**custom** ['kʌstəm] n costume m, usanza; (LAW) consuetudine f; (COMM) clientela; **~ary** a consueto(a).

**customer** ['kʌstəmə*] n cliente m/f.

**customized** ['kʌstəmaɪzd] a (car etc) fuoriserie inv.

**custom-made** ['kʌstəm'meɪd] a (clothes) fatto(a) su misura; (other goods) fatto(a) su ordinazione.

**customs** ['kʌstəmz] npl dogana; **~ officer** n doganiere m.

**cut** [kʌt] vb (pt, pp cut) vt tagliare; (shape, make) intagliare; (reduce) ridurre // vi tagliare; (intersect) tagliarsi // n taglio; (in salary etc) riduzione f; **to ~ a tooth** mettere un dente; **to ~ down** vt (tree etc) abbattere // vt fus (also: **~ down on**) ridurre; **to ~ off** vt tagliare; (fig) isolare; **to ~ out** vt tagliare fuori; eliminare; ritagliare; **to ~ up** vt (paper, meat) tagliare a pezzi; **~back** n riduzione f.

**cute** [kju:t] a grazioso(a); (clever) astuto(a).

**cuticle** ['kju:tɪkl] n (on nail) pellicina, cuticola.

**cutlery** ['kʌtlərɪ] n posate fpl.

**cutlet** ['kʌtlɪt] n costoletta.

**cut: ~out** n interruttore m; (cardboard ~) ritaglio; **~price**, (US) **~rate** a a prezzo ridotto; **~throat** n assassino // a (razor) da barbiere; (competition) spietato(a).

**cutting** ['kʌtɪŋ] a tagliente; (fig) pungente // n (Brit: from newspaper) ritaglio (di giornale).

**CV** n abbr = **curriculum vitae.**

**cwt** abbr = **hundredweight(s).**

**cyanide** ['saɪənaɪd] n cianuro.

**cycle** ['saɪkl] n ciclo; (bicycle) bicicletta // vi andare in bicicletta.

**cycling** ['saɪklɪŋ] n ciclismo.

**cyclist** ['saɪklɪst] n ciclista m/f.

**cygnet** ['sɪgnɪt] n cigno giovane.

**cylinder** ['sɪlɪndə*] n cilindro; **~head gasket** n guarnizione f della testata del cilindro.

**cymbals** ['sɪmblz] npl cembali mpl.

**cynic** ['sɪnɪk] *n* cinico/a; ~**al** *a* cinico(a); ~**ism** ['sɪnɪsɪzəm] *n* cinismo.

**Cypriot** ['sɪprɪət] *a, n* cipriota (*m/f*).

**Cyprus** ['saɪprəs] *n* Cipro.

**cyst** [sɪst] *n* cisti *f inv*.

**cystitis** [sɪs'taɪtɪs] *n* cistite *f*.

**czar** [zɑ:*] *n* zar *m inv*.

**Czech** [tʃɛk] *a* ceco(a) // *n* ceco/a; (*LING*) ceco.

**Czechoslovakia** [tʃɛkəslə'vækɪə] *n* Cecoslovacchia; ~**n** *a*, *n* cecoslovacco(a).

# D

**D** [di:] *n* (*MUS*) re *m*.

**dab** [dæb] *vt* (*eyes, wound*) tamponare; (*paint, cream*) applicare (con leggeri colpetti).

**dabble** ['dæbl] *vi*: to ~ in occuparsi (da dilettante) di.

**dad, daddy** [dæd, 'dædɪ] *n* babbo, papà *m inv*.

**daffodil** ['dæfədɪl] *n* trombone *m*, giunchiglia.

**daft** [dɑːft] *a* sciocco(a).

**dagger** ['dægə*] *n* pugnale *m*.

**daily** ['deɪlɪ] *a* quotidiano(a), giornaliero(a) // *n* quotidiano *m* // *ad* tutti i giorni.

**dainty** ['deɪntɪ] *a* delicato(a), grazioso(a).

**dairy** ['dɛərɪ] *n* (*shop*) latteria; (*on farm*) caseificio // *a* caseario(a); ~ **produce** *n* latticini *mpl*.

**dais** ['deɪɪs] *n* pedana, palco.

**daisy** ['deɪzɪ] *n* margherita; ~ **wheel** *n* (*on printer*) margherita.

**dale** [deɪl] *n* valle *f*.

**dam** [dæm] *n* diga // *vt* sbarrare; costruire dighe su.

**damage** ['dæmɪdʒ] *n* danno, danni *mpl*; (*fig*) danno // *vt* danneggiare; (*fig*) recar danno a; ~**s** *npl* (*LAW*) danni.

**damn** [dæm] *vt* condannare; (*curse*) maledire // *n* (*col*): **I don't give a** ~ non me ne importa un fico // *a* (*col*:

*also*: ~**ed**): **this** ~ ... questo maledetto ...; ~ (**it**)! accidenti!

**damp** [dæmp] *a* umido(a) // *n* umidità, umido // *vt* (*also*: ~**en**: *cloth, rag*) inumidire, bagnare; (*enthusiasm etc*) spegnere.

**damson** ['dæmzən] *n* susina damaschina.

**dance** [dɑːns] *n* danza, ballo; (*ball*) ballo // *vi* ballare; ~ **hall** *n* dancing *m inv*, sala da ballo; ~**r** *n* danzatore/trice; (*professional*) ballerino/a.

**dancing** ['dɑːnsɪŋ] *n* danza, ballo.

**dandelion** ['dændɪlaɪən] *n* dente *m* di leone.

**dandruff** ['dændrəf] *n* forfora.

**Dane** [deɪn] *n* danese *m/f*.

**danger** ['deɪndʒə*] *n* pericolo; **there is a** ~ **of fire** c'è pericolo di incendio; **in** ~ in pericolo; **he was in** ~ **of falling** rischiava di cadere; ~**ous** *a* pericoloso(a).

**dangle** ['dæŋgl] *vt* dondolare; (*fig*) far balenare // *vi* pendolare.

**Danish** ['deɪnɪʃ] *a* danese // *n* (*LING*) danese *m*.

**dapper** ['dæpə*] *a* lindo(a).

**dare** [dɛə*] *vt*: to ~ **sb to do** sfidare qn a fare // *vi*: to ~ (**to**) **do sth** osare fare qc; **I** ~ **say** (*I suppose*) immagino (che); ~**devil** *n* scavezzacollo *m/f*; **daring** *a* audace, ardito(a) // *n* audacia.

**dark** [dɑːk] *a* (*night, room*) buio(a), scuro(a); (*colour, complexion*) scuro(a); (*fig*) cupo(a), tetro(a), nero(a) // *n*: **in the** ~ al buio; **in the** ~ **about** (*fig*) all'oscuro di; **after** ~ a notte fatta; ~**en** *vt* (*room*) oscurare; (*photo, painting*) far scuro(a) // *vi* oscurarsi; imbrunirsi; ~ **glasses** *npl* occhiali *mpl* scuri; ~**ness** *n* oscurità, buio; ~ **room** *n* camera oscura.

**darling** ['dɑːlɪŋ] *a* caro(a) // *n* tesoro.

**darn** [dɑːn] *vt* rammendare.

**dart** [dɑːt] *n* freccetta // *vi*: to ~ **towards** precipitarsi verso; **to** ~ **away** guizzare via; ~**s** *n* tiro al bersaglio (con freccette); ~**board** n bersaglio (per freccette).

**dash** [dæʃ] n (sign) lineetta; (small quantity) punta // vt (missile) gettare; (hopes) infrangere // vi: to ~ **towards** precipitarsi verso; **to ~ away** or **off** vi scappare via.

**dashboard** ['dæʃbɔːd] n (AUT) cruscotto.

**dashing** ['dæʃɪŋ] a ardito(a).

**data** ['deɪtə] npl dati mpl; ~**base** n base f di dati, data base m inv; ~ **processing** n elaborazione f (elettronica) dei dati.

**date** [deɪt] n data; appuntamento; (fruit) dattero // vt datare; ~ **of birth** data di nascita; **to ~ ad** fino a oggi; **out of ~** scaduto(a); (old-fashioned) passato(a) di moda; ~**d a** passato(a) di moda.

**daub** [dɔːb] vt imbrattare.

**daughter** ['dɔːtə*] n figlia; ~**-in-law** n nuora.

**daunt** [dɔːnt] vt intimidire; ~**ing** a non invidiabile.

**dawdle** ['dɔːdl] vi bighellonare.

**dawn** [dɔːn] n alba // vi (day) spuntare; (fig) venire in mente; it ~**ed on him** that ... gli è venuto in mente che ...

**day** [deɪ] n giorno; (as duration) giornata; (period of time, age) tempo, epoca; **the ~ before** il giorno avanti or prima; **the ~ after, the following ~** il giorno dopo or seguente; **the ~ after tomorrow** dopodomani; **the ~ before yesterday** l'altroieri; **by ~** di giorno; ~**break** n spuntar m del giorno; ~**dream** vi sognare a occhi aperti; ~**light** n luce f del giorno; ~ **return** n (Brit) biglietto giornaliero di andata e ritorno; ~**time** n giorno; ~**-to-** a (life, organization) quotidiano(a).

**daze** [deɪz] vt (subject: drug) inebetire; (: blow) stordire // n: **in a ~** inebetito(a); stordito(a).

**dazzle** ['dæzl] vt abbagliare.

**DC** abbr (= direct current) c.c.

**deacon** ['diːkən] n diacono.

**dead** [dɛd] a morto(a); (numb) intirizzito(a) // ad assolutamente, perfettamente; **he was shot ~** fu colpito a morte; **~ on time** in perfetto orario; ~ **tired** stanco(a) morto(a); **to stop ~** fermarsi in tronco; **the ~** i morti; **~en** vt (blow, sound) ammortire; (make numb) intirizzire; **~ end** n vicolo cieco; **~ heat** n (SPORT): **to finish in a ~ heat** finire alla pari; **~line** n scadenza; **~lock** n punto morto; **~ loss** n: **to be a ~ loss** (col: person, thing) non valere niente; **~ly a** mortale; (weapon, poison) micidiale; **~pan** a a faccia impassibile.

**deaf** [dɛf] a sordo(a); **~en** vt assordare; **~mute** n sordomuto(a); **~ness** n sordità.

**deal** [diːl] n accordo; (business ~) affare m // vt (pt, pp **dealt** [dɛlt]) (blow, cards) dare; **a great ~ (of)** molto(a); **to ~ in** vt fus occuparsi di; **to ~ with** vt fus (COMM) fare affari con, trattare con; (handle) occuparsi di; (be about: book etc) trattare di; **~er** n commerciante m/f; **~ings** npl (COMM) relazioni fpl; (relations) rapporti mpl.

**dean** [diːn] n (REL) decano; (SCOL) preside m di facoltà (or di collegio).

**dear** [dɪə*] a caro(a) // n: my ~ caro mio/cara mia; ~ **me!** Dio mio!; D~ **Sir/Madam** (in letter) Egregio Signore/Egregia Signora, D~ **Mr/Mrs X** Gentile Signor/Signora X; **~ly** ad (love) moltissimo; (pay) a caro prezzo.

**death** [dɛθ] n morte f; (ADMIN) decesso; ~ **certificate** n atto di decesso; ~ **duties** npl (Brit) imposta or tassa di successione; **~ly a** di morte; ~ **penalty** n pena di morte; ~ **rate** n indice m di mortalità.

**debacle** [dɪ'bækl] n fiasco.

**debar** [dɪ'bɑː*] vt: **to ~ sb from doing** impedire a qn di fare.

**debase** [dɪ'beɪs] vt (currency) adulterare; (person) degradare.

**debatable** [dɪˈbeɪtəbl] a discutibile.

**debate** [dɪˈbeɪt] n dibattito // vt dibattere; discutere.

**debauchery** [dɪˈbɔːtʃərɪ] n dissolutezza.

**debit** [ˈdɛbɪt] n debito // vt: to ~ a sum to sb or to sb's account addebitare una somma a qn.

**debris** [ˈdɛbriː] n detriti mpl.

**debt** [dɛt] n debito; to be in ~ essere indebitato(a); ~or n debitore/trice.

**debunk** [diːˈbʌŋk] vt (theory, claim) smentire.

**début** [ˈdeɪbjuː] n debutto.

**decade** [ˈdɛkeɪd] n decennio.

**decadence** [ˈdɛkədəns] n decadenza.

**decaffeinated** [dɪˈkæfɪneɪtɪd] a decaffeinato(a).

**decanter** [dɪˈkæntə*] n caraffa.

**decay** [dɪˈkeɪ] n decadimento; (mi-tridimento; (fig) rovina; (also: tooth ~) carie f // vi (rot) imputridire; (fig) andare in rovina.

**deceased** [dɪˈsiːst] n defunto/a.

**deceit** [dɪˈsiːt] n inganno; ~ful a ingannevole, perfido(a).

**deceive** [dɪˈsiːv] vt ingannare.

**December** [dɪˈsɛmbə*] n dicembre m.

**decent** [ˈdiːsənt] a decente; they were very ~ about it si sono comportati da signori riguardo a ciò.

**deception** [dɪˈsɛpʃən] n inganno.

**deceptive** [dɪˈsɛptɪv] a ingannevole.

**decide** [dɪˈsaɪd] vt (person) far prendere una decisione a; (question, argument) risolvere, decidere // vi decidere, decidersi; to ~ to do/that decidere di fare/che; to ~ on decidere per; ~d a (resolute) deciso(a); (clear, definite) netto(a), chiaro(a); ~dly [-dɪdlɪ] ad indubbiamente; decisamente.

**decimal** [ˈdɛsɪməl] a, n decimale (m); ~ point n ~ virgola.

**decipher** [dɪˈsaɪfə*] vt decifrare.

**decision** [dɪˈsɪʒən] n decisione f.

**decisive** [dɪˈsaɪsɪv] a decisivo(a).

**deck** [dɛk] n (NAUT) ponte m; (of

bus): top ~ imperiale m; (of cards) mazzo; ~chair n sedia a sdraio.

**declaration** [dɛkləˈreɪʃən] n dichiarazione f.

**declare** [dɪˈklɛə*] vt dichiarare.

**decline** [dɪˈklaɪn] n (decay) declino; (lessening) ribasso // vt declinare; rifiutare // vi declinare; diminuire.

**decode** [diːˈkəʊd] vt decifrare.

**decompose** [diːkəmˈpəʊz] vi decomporre.

**décor** [ˈdeɪkɔː*] n decorazione f.

**decorate** [ˈdɛkəreɪt] vt (adorn, give a medal to) decorare; (paint and paper) tinteggiare e tappezzare; **decoration** [-ˈreɪʃən] n (medal etc, adornment) decorazione f; **decorator** n decoratore m.

**decorum** [dɪˈkɔːrəm] n decoro.

**decoy** [ˈdiːkɔɪ] n zimbello.

**decrease** n [ˈdiːkriːs] diminuzione f // vt, vi [diːˈkriːs] diminuire.

**decree** [dɪˈkriː] n decreto; ~ nisi [-ˈnaɪsaɪ] n sentenza provvisoria di divorzio.

**dedicate** [ˈdɛdɪkeɪt] vt consacrare; (book etc) dedicare.

**dedication** [dɛdɪˈkeɪʃən] n (devotion) dedizione f.

**deduce** [dɪˈdjuːs] vt dedurre.

**deduct** [dɪˈdʌkt] vt: to ~ sth (from) dedurre qc (da); (from wage etc) trattenere qc (da); ~ion [dɪˈdʌkʃən] n (deducting) deduzione f; (from wage etc) trattenuta; (deducing) deduzione f, conclusione f.

**deed** [diːd] n azione f, atto; (LAW) atto.

**deep** [diːp] a profondo(a); 4 metres ~ profondo(a) 4 metri // ad: spectators stood 20 ~ c'erano 20 file di spettatori; ~en vt (hole) approfondire // vi approfondirsi; (darkness) farsi più buio; ~freeze n congelatore m // vt congelare; ~fry vt friggere in olio abbondante; ~ly ad profondamente; ~sea diving n immersione f in alto mare.

**deer** [dɪə*] n (pl inv): the ~ i cervidi; (red) ~ cervo; (fallow) ~

daino; **(roe)** ~ capriolo.

**deface** |dɪ'feɪs| vt imbrattare.

**default** |dɪ'fɔːlt| vi (LAW) essere contumace; (gen) essere inadempiente // n (COMPUT: also: ~ **value**) default m inv; **by** ~ (LAW) in contumacia; (SPORT) per abbandono.

**defeat** |dɪ'fiːt| n sconfitta // vt (team, opponents) sconfiggere; (fig: plans, efforts) frustrare; ~**ist** a, n disfattista (m/f).

**defect** n |'diːfɛkt| difetto // vi |dɪ'fɛkt|: **to** ~ **to the enemy** passare al nemico; ~**ive** |dɪ'fɛktɪv| a difettoso(a).

**defence**, (US) **defense** |dɪ'fɛns| n difesa; **in** ~ **of** in difesa di; ~**less** a senza difesa.

**defend** |dɪ'fɛnd| vt difendere; ~**ant** n imputato/a; ~**er** n difensore/a.

**defense** |dɪ'fɛns| n (US) = **defence**.

**defer** |dɪ'fɜː| vt (postpone) differire, rinviare // vi: **to** ~ **to** rimettersi a.

**defiance** |dɪ'faɪəns| n sfida; **in** ~ **of** a dispetto di.

**defiant** |dɪ'faɪənt| a (attitude) di sfida; (person) ribelle.

**deficiency** |dɪ'fɪʃənsɪ| n deficienza; carenza.

**deficit** |'dɛfɪsɪt| n disavanzo.

**defile** vb |dɪ'faɪl| vt contaminare // vi sfilare // n |dɪ'faɪl| gola, stretta.

**define** |dɪ'faɪn| vt definire.

**definite** |'dɛfɪnɪt| a (fixed) definito(a), preciso(a); (clear, obvious) ben definito(a), netto(a); (LING) determinativo(a); **he was** ~ **about it** ne era sicuro; ~**ly** ad indubbiamente.

**definition** |dɛfɪ'nɪʃən| n definizione f.

**deflate** |diː'fleɪt| vt sgonfiare.

**deflect** |dɪ'flɛkt| vt deflettere, deviare.

**deformed** |dɪ'fɔːmd| a deforme.

**defraud** |dɪ'frɔːd| vt defraudare.

**defray** |dɪ'freɪ| vt: **to** ~ **sb's expenses** sostenere le spese di qn.

**defrost** |diː'frɔst| vt (fridge) disgelare; ~**er** n (US: demister) sbrinatore m.

**deft** |dɛft| a svelto(a), destro(a).

**defunct** |dɪ'fʌŋkt| a defunto(a).

**defuse** |diː'fjuːz| vt disinnescare.

**defy** |dɪ'faɪ| vt sfidare; (efforts etc) resistere a.

**degenerate** vi |dɪ'dʒɛnəreɪt| degenerare // a |dɪ'dʒɛnərɪt| degenere.

**degree** |dɪ'griː| n grado; (SCOL) laurea (universitaria); **a (first)** ~ **in maths** una laurea in matematica; **by** ~**s** (gradually) gradualmente, a poco a poco; **to some** ~ fino a un certo punto, in certa misura.

**dehydrated** |diːhaɪ'dreɪtɪd| a disidratato(a); (milk, eggs) in polvere.

**de-ice** |diː'aɪs| vt (windscreen) disgelare.

**deign** |deɪn| vi: **to** ~ **to do** degnarsi di fare.

**deity** |'diːɪtɪ| n divinità f inv.

**dejected** |dɪ'dʒɛktɪd| a abbattuto(a), avvilito(a).

**delay** |dɪ'leɪ| vt (journey, operation) ritardare, rinviare; (travellers, trains) ritardare // vi: **to** ~ (**in doing sth**) ritardare (a fare qc) // n ritardo.

**delectable** |dɪ'lɛktəbl| a (person, food) delizioso/a.

**delegate** n |'dɛlɪgɪt| delegato/a // vt |'dɛlɪgeɪt| delegare.

**delete** |dɪ'liːt| vt cancellare.

**deliberate** a |dɪ'lɪbərɪt| (intentional) intenzionale; (slow) misurato(a) // vi |dɪ'lɪbəreɪt| deliberare, riflettere; ~**ly** ad (on purpose) deliberatamente.

**delicacy** |'dɛlɪkəsɪ| n delicatezza.

**delicate** |'dɛlɪkɪt| a delicato(a).

**delicatessen** |dɛlɪkə'tɛsn| n = salumeria.

**delicious** |dɪ'lɪʃəs| a delizioso(a), squisito(a).

**delight** |dɪ'laɪt| n delizia, gran piacere m // vt dilettare; ~**ed** a: ~**ed (at or with)** contentissimo(a) (di), felice (di); ~**ed to do** felice di fare; ~**ful** a delizioso(a); incantevole.

**delinquent** |dɪ'lɪŋkwənt| a, n

delinquente (m/f).

**delirious** [dɪˈlɪrɪəs] a: to be ~ delirare.

**deliver** [dɪˈlɪvə*] vt (mail) distribuire; (goods) consegnare; (speech) pronunciare; (free) liberare; (MED) far partorire; ~y n distribuzione f; consegna; (of speaker) dizione f; (MED) parto.

**delude** [dɪˈluːd] vt deludere, illudere.

**deluge** [ˈdeljuːdʒ] n diluvio.

**delusion** [dɪˈluːʒən] n illusione f.

**delve** [delv] vi: to ~ into frugare in; (subject) far ricerche in.

**demand** [dɪˈmɑːnd] vt richiedere // n domanda; (ECON, claim) richiesta; in ~ ricercato(a), richiesto(a); on ~ a richiesta; ~ing a (boss) esigente; (work) impegnativo(a).

**demean** [dɪˈmiːn] vt: to ~ o.s. umiliarsi.

**demeanour**, (US) **demeanor** [dɪˈmiːnə*] n comportamento; contegno.

**demented** [dɪˈmɛntɪd] a demente, impazzito(a).

**demise** [dɪˈmaɪz] n decesso.

**demister** [diːˈmɪstə*] n (AUT) sbrinatore m.

**demo** [ˈdɛməʊ] n abbr (col: = demonstration) manifestazione f.

**demobilize** [diːˈməʊbɪlaɪz] vt smobilitare.

**democracy** [dɪˈmɔkrəsɪ] n democrazia.

**democrat** [ˈdɛməkræt] n democratico(a); ~ic [dɛmə'krætɪk] a democratico(a).

**demolish** [dɪˈmɔlɪʃ] vt demolire.

**demonstrate** [ˈdɛmənstreɪt] vt dimostrare, provare // vi: to ~ (for/against) dimostrare (per/contro), manifestare (per/contro); **demonstration** [-ˈstreɪʃən] n dimostrazione f; (POL) manifestazione f, dimostrazione; **demonstrator** n (POL) dimostrante m/f.

**demote** [dɪˈməʊt] vt far retrocedere.

**demure** [dɪˈmjʊə*] a contegnoso(a).

**den** [dɛn] n tana, covo.

**denatured alcohol** [diːˈneɪtʃəd-] n (US) alcool m inv denaturato.

**denial** [dɪˈnaɪəl] n diniego; rifiuto.

**denim** [ˈdɛnɪm] n tessuto di cotone ritorto; ~s npl blue jeans mpl.

**Denmark** [ˈdɛnmɑːk] n Danimarca.

**denomination** [dɪnɔmɪˈneɪʃən] n (money) valore m; (REL) confessione f.

**denounce** [dɪˈnaʊns] vt denunciare.

**dense** [dɛns] a fitto(a); (stupid) ottuso(a), duro(a).

**density** [ˈdɛnsɪtɪ] n densità f inv.

**dent** [dɛnt] n ammaccatura // vt (also: **make a ~ in**) ammaccare.

**dental** [ˈdɛntl] a dentale; ~ **surgeon** n medico/a dentista.

**dentist** [ˈdɛntɪst] n dentista m/f; ~ry n odontoiatria.

**denture(s)** [ˈdɛntʃə(z)] n(pl) dentiera.

**deny** [dɪˈnaɪ] vt negare; (refuse) rifiutare.

**deodorant** [diːˈəʊdərənt] n deodorante m.

**depart** [dɪˈpɑːt] vi partire; to ~ from (fig) deviare da.

**department** [dɪˈpɑːtmənt] n (COMM) reparto; (SCOL) sezione f, dipartimento; (POL) ministero; ~ **store** n grande magazzino.

**departure** [dɪˈpɑːtʃə*] n partenza; (fig): ~ **from** deviazione f da; a new ~ una svolta (decisiva); ~ **lounge** n (at airport) sala d'attesa.

**depend** [dɪˈpɛnd] vi: to ~ **on** dipendere da; (rely on) contare su; it ~s dipende; ~ing on the result ... a seconda del risultato ...; ~able a fidato(a); (car etc) affidabile; ~ant n persona a carico; ~ent a: to be ~ent on dipendere da; (child, relative) essere a carico di // n = ~ant.

**depict** [dɪˈpɪkt] vt (in picture) dipingere; (in words) descrivere.

**depleted** [dɪˈpliːtɪd] a diminuito(a).

**deploy** [dɪˈplɔɪ] vt dispiegare.

**depopulation** [ˈdiːpɔpjuˈleɪʃən] n spopolamento.

**deport** [dɪˈpɔːt] vt deportare; espellere.

**deportment** [dɪˈpɔːtmənt] n portamento.

**depose** [dɪˈpəʊz] vt deporre.

**deposit** [dɪˈpɔzɪt] n (COMM, GEO) deposito; (of ore, oil) giacimento; (CHEM) sedimento; (part payment) acconto; (for hired goods etc) cauzione f // vt depositare; dare in acconto; mettere or lasciare in deposito; ~ **account** n conto vincolato.

**depot** [ˈdɛpəʊ] n deposito.

**depreciate** [dɪˈpriːʃɪeɪt] vt svalutare // vi svalutarsi.

**depress** [dɪˈpres] vt deprimere; (press down) premere; ~**ed** a (person) depresso(a), abbattuto(a); (area) depresso(a); ~**ing** a deprimente; ~**ion** [dɪˈpreʃən] n depressione f.

**deprivation** [dɛprɪˈveɪʃən] n privazione f; (loss) perdita.

**deprive** [dɪˈpraɪv] vt: to ~ sb of privare qn di; ~**d** a disgraziato(a).

**depth** [dɛpθ] n profondità f inv; in the ~s nel profondo di; nel cuore di; in the ~s of winter in pieno inverno.

**deputize** [ˈdɛpjutaɪz] vi: to ~ for svolgere le funzioni di.

**deputy** [ˈdɛpjutɪ] a: ~ **head** (SCOL) vicepreside m/f // n (replacement) supplente m/f; (second in command) vice m/f.

**derail** [dɪˈreɪl] vt far deragliare; to be ~**ed** deragliare.

**deranged** [dɪˈreɪndʒd] a: to be (mentally) ~ essere pazzo(a).

**derby** [ˈdɑːbɪ] n (US: bowler hat) bombetta.

**derelict** [ˈdɛrɪlɪkt] a abbandonato(a).

**deride** [dɪˈraɪd] vt deridere.

**derisory** [dɪˈraɪsərɪ] a (sum) irrisorio(a); (laughter, person) beffardo(a).

**derive** [dɪˈraɪv] vt: to ~ sth from derivare qc da; trarre qc da // vi: to ~ from derivare da.

**derogatory** [dɪˈrɔgətərɪ] a denigratorio(a).

**derrick** [ˈderɪk] n gru f inv; (for oil) derrick m inv.

**derv** [dəːv] n (Brit) gasolio.

**descend** [dɪˈsend] vt, vi discendere, scendere; to ~ **from** discendere da; ~**ant** n discendente m/f.

**descent** [dɪˈsent] n discesa; (origin) discendenza, famiglia.

**describe** [dɪsˈkraɪb] vt descrivere; **description** [-ˈkrɪpʃən] n descrizione f; (sort) genere m, specie f.

**desecrate** [ˈdesɪkreɪt] vt profanare.

**desert** n [ˈdezət] deserto // vb [dɪˈzəːt] vt lasciare, abbandonare // vi (MIL) disertare; ~**er** n disertore m; ~ **island** n isola deserta; ~**s** [dɪˈzəːts] npl: to get one's just ~s avere ciò che si merita.

**deserve** [dɪˈzəːv] vt meritare; **deserving** a (person) meritevole, degno(a); (cause) meritorio(a).

**design** [dɪˈzaɪn] n (sketch) disegno; (layout, shape) linea; (pattern) fantasia; (COMM) disegno tecnico; (intention) intenzione f // vt disegnare; progettare; to **have** ~ **s on** aver mire su.

**designer** [dɪˈzaɪnə*] n (ART, TECH) disegnatore/trice; (of fashion) modellista m/f.

**desire** [dɪˈzaɪə*] n desiderio, voglia // vt desiderare, volere.

**desk** [desk] n (in office) scrivania; (for pupil) banco; (Brit: in shop, restaurant) cassa; (in hotel) ricevimento; (at airport) accettazione f.

**desolate** [ˈdesəlɪt] a desolato(a).

**despair** [dɪsˈpeə*] n disperazione f // vi: to ~ **of** disperare di.

**despatch** [dɪsˈpætʃ] n, vt = **dispatch.**

**desperate** [ˈdespərɪt] a disperato(a); (fugitive) capace di tutto; ~**ly** ad disperatamente; (very) terribilmente, estremamente.

**desperation** [despəˈreɪʃən] n disperazione f.

**despicable** [dɪsˈpɪkəbl] a disprezzabile.

**despise** [dɪs'paɪz] vt disprezzare, sdegnare.

**despite** [dɪs'paɪt] prep malgrado, a dispetto di, nonostante.

**despondent** [dɪs'pɔndənt] a abbattuto(a), scoraggiato(a).

**dessert** [dɪ'zə:t] n dolce m; frutta; ~**spoon** n cucchiaio da dolci.

**destination** [dɛstɪ'neɪʃən] n destinazione f.

**destiny** ['dɛstɪnɪ] n destino.

**destitute** ['dɛstɪtjuːt] a indigente, bisognoso(a).

**destroy** [dɪs'trɔɪ] vt distruggere; ~**er** n (NAUT) cacciatorpediniere m.

**destruction** [dɪs'trʌkʃən] n distruzione f.

**detach** [dɪ'tætʃ] vt staccare, distaccare; ~**ed** a (attitude) distante; ~**ed house** n villa; ~**ment** n (MIL) distaccamento; (fig) distacco.

**detail** ['diːteɪl] n particolare m, dettaglio // vt dettagliare, particolareggiare; **in** ~ nei particolari; ~**ed** a particolareggiato(a).

**detain** [dɪ'teɪn] vt trattenere; (in captivity) detenere.

**detect** [dɪ'tɛkt] vt scoprire, scorgere; (MED, POLICE, RADAR etc) individuare; ~**ion** [dɪ'tɛkʃən] n scoperta; individuazione f; ~**ive** n investigatore/trice; **private** ~**ive** investigatore m privato; ~**ive story** n giallo.

**detention** [dɪ'tɛnʃən] n detenzione f; (SCOL) permanenza forzata per punizione.

**deter** [dɪ'təː] vt dissuadere.

**detergent** [dɪ'təːdʒənt] n detersivo.

**deteriorate** [dɪ'tɪərɪəreɪt] vi deteriorarsi.

**determine** [dɪ'təːmɪn] vt determinare; **to** ~ **to do** decidere di fare; ~**d** a (person) risoluto(a), deciso(a).

**detour** ['diːtuə*] n deviazione f // vt (US: traffic) deviare.

**detract** [dɪ'trækt] vt: **to** ~ **from** detrarre da.

**detriment** ['dɛtrɪmənt] n: **to the** ~ **of** a detrimento di; ~**al** [dɛtrɪ'mɛntl] a: ~**al to** dannoso(a) a, nocivo(a) a.

**devaluation** [dɪvæljuˈeɪʃən] n svalutazione f.

**devastating** ['dɛvəsteɪtɪŋ] a devastatore(trice).

**develop** [dɪ'vɛləp] vt sviluppare; (habit) prendere (gradualmente) // vi svilupparsi; (facts, symptoms: appear) manifestarsi, rivelarsi; ~**ing country** paese m in via di sviluppo; ~**ment** n sviluppo.

**device** [dɪ'vaɪs] n (apparatus) congegno.

**devil** ['dɛvl] n diavolo; demonio.

**devious** ['dɪːvɪəs] a (means) indiretto(a), tortuoso(a); (person) subdolo(a).

**devise** [dɪ'vaɪz] vt escogitare, concepire.

**devoid** [dɪ'vɔɪd] a: ~ **of** privo(a) di.

**devolution** [diːvə'luːʃən] n (POL) decentramento.

**devote** [dɪ'vəut] vt: **to** ~ **sth to** dedicare qc a; ~**d** a devoto(a); **to be** ~**d to** essere molto affezionato(a) a; ~**e** [dɛvəu'tiː] n (MUS, SPORT) appassionato/a.

**devotion** [dɪ'vəuʃən] n devozione f, attaccamento; (REL) atto di devozione, preghiera.

**devour** [dɪ'vauə*] vt divorare.

**devout** [dɪ'vaut] a pio(a), devoto(a).

**dew** [djuː] n rugiada.

**dexterity** [dɛks'tɛrɪtɪ] n destrezza.

**DHSS** n abbr (= Department of Health and Social Security) = ministero della Sanità e della Previdenza sociale.

**diabetes** [daɪə'biːtiːz] n diabete m; **diabetic** [-'bɛtɪk] a, n diabetico(a).

**diabolical** [daɪə'bɔlɪkl] a (col: weather, behaviour) orribile.

**diagnosis** [daɪəg'nəusɪs, -siːz] n diagnosi f inv.

**diagonal** [daɪ'ægənl] n, a diagonale (f).

**diagram** ['daɪəgræm] n diagramma m.

**dial** ['daɪəl] n quadrante m; (on telephone) disco combinatore // vt (number) fare.

**dialect** ['daɪəlɛkt] n dialetto.

**dialling** ['daɪəlɪŋ]: ~ **code**, (US) **dial code** n prefisso; ~ **tone**, (US) **dial tone** n segnale m di linea libera.

**dialogue** ['daɪələg] n dialogo.

**diameter** [daɪ'æmɪtə*] n diametro.

**diamond** ['daɪəmənd] n diamante m; (shape) rombo; ~s npl (CARDS) quadri mpl.

**diaper** ['daɪəpə*] n (US) pannolino.

**diaphragm** ['daɪəfræm] n diaframma m.

**diarrhoea**, (US) **diarrhea** [daɪə'riːə] n diarrea.

**diary** ['daɪərɪ] n (daily account) diario; (book) agenda.

**dice** [daɪs] n (pl inv) dado // vt (CULIN) tagliare a dadini.

**Dictaphone** ['dɪktəfəun] n ® dittafono ®.

**dictate** vt [dɪk'teɪt] dettare // n ['dɪkteɪt] dettame m.

**dictation** [dɪk'teɪʃən] n dettato.

**dictator** [dɪk'teɪtə*] n dittatore m; ~**ship** n dittatura.

**dictionary** ['dɪkʃənrɪ] n dizionario.

**did** [dɪd] pt of **do**.

**didn't** = did not.

**die** [daɪ] n (pl **dies**) conio; matrice f; stampo // vi morire; **to be dying for** sth/**to do** sth morire dalla voglia di qc/di fare qc; **to ~ away** vi spegnersi a poco a poco; **to ~ down** vi abbassarsi; **to ~ out** vi estinguersi.

**diehard** ['daɪhɑːd] n reazionario/a.

**Diesel** ['diːzəl]: ~ **engine** n motore m diesel inv; ~ **(oil)** n gasolio (per motori diesel).

**diet** ['daɪət] n alimentazione f; (restricted food) dieta // vi (also: **be on a ~**) stare a dieta.

**differ** ['dɪfə*] vi: **to ~ from** sth differire da qc; essere diverso(a) da qc; **to ~ from** sb **over** sth essere in disaccordo con qn su qc; ~**ence** n differenza; (quarrel) screzio; ~**ent**

a diverso(a); ~**entiate** [-'ɛnʃɪeɪt] vi differenziarsi; **to ~entiate between** discriminare or fare differenza fra.

**difficult** ['dɪfɪkəlt] a difficile; ~**y** n difficoltà f inv.

**diffident** ['dɪfɪdənt] a sfiduciato(a).

**dig** [dɪg] vt (pt, pp **dug**) (hole) scavare; (garden) vangare // n (prod) gomitata; (fig) frecciata; **to ~ in** vi (MIL: also: ~ **o.s. in**) trincerarsi; (col: eat) attaccare a mangiare; **to ~ into** vt fus (snow, soil) scavare; **to ~ one's nails into** conficcare le unghie in; **to ~ up** vt scavare; (tree etc) sradicare.

**digest** [daɪ'dʒɛst] vt digerire; ~**ion** [dɪ'dʒɛstʃən] n digestione f; ~**ive** a (juices, system) digerente.

**digit** ['dɪdʒɪt] n cifra; (finger) dito; ~**al** a digitale.

**dignified** ['dɪgnɪfaɪd] a dignitoso(a).

**dignity** ['dɪgnɪtɪ] n dignità.

**digress** [daɪ'grɛs] vi: **to ~ from** divagare da.

**digs** [dɪgz] npl (Brit col) camera ammobiliata.

**dilapidated** [dɪ'læpɪdeɪtɪd] a cadente.

**dilemma** [daɪ'lɛmə] n dilemma m.

**diligent** ['dɪlɪdʒənt] a diligente.

**dilute** [daɪ'luːt] vt diluire; (with water) annacquare.

**dim** [dɪm] a (light, eyesight) debole; (memory, outline) vago(a); (stupid) lento(a) d'ingegno // vt (light) abbassare.

**dime** [daɪm] n (US) = 10 cents.

**dimension** [daɪ'mɛnʃən] n dimensione f.

**diminish** [dɪ'mɪnɪʃ] vt, vi diminuire.

**diminutive** [dɪ'mɪnjutɪv] a minuscolo(a) // n (LING) diminutivo.

**dimmers** ['dɪməz] npl (US AUT) anabbaglianti mpl; luci fpl di posizione.

**dimple** ['dɪmpl] n fossetta.

**din** [dɪn] n chiasso, fracasso.

**dine** [daɪn] vi pranzare.

**dinghy** ['dɪŋgɪ] n battello pneumatico; (also: **rubber ~**)

gommone $m$; (also: **sailing** ~) dinghy $m$ inv.

**dingy** ['dɪndʒɪ] $a$ grigio(a).

**dining** ['daɪnɪŋ] $cpd$: ~ **car** $n$ (Brit) vagone $m$ ristorante; ~ **room** $n$ sala da pranzo.

**dinner** ['dɪnə*] $n$ (lunch) pranzo; (evening meal) cena; (public) banchetto; ~'**s ready!** a tavola!; ~ **jacket** $n$ smoking $m$ inv; ~ **party** $n$ cena; ~ **time** $n$ ora di pranzo (or cena).

**dint** [dɪnt] $n$: **by ~ of** a forza di.

**dip** [dɪp] $n$ discesa; (in sea) bagno // $vt$ immergere; bagnare; (Brit AUT: lights) abbassare // $vi$ abbassarsi.

**diphthong** ['dɪfθɒŋ] $n$ dittongo.

**diploma** [dɪ'pləʊmə] $n$ diploma $m$.

**diplomacy** [dɪ'pləʊməsɪ] $n$ diplomazia.

**diplomat** ['dɪpləmæt] $n$ diplomatico; ~**ic** [dɪplə'mætɪk] $a$ diplomatico(a).

**dipstick** ['dɪpstɪk] $n$ (AUT) indicatore $m$ di livello dell'olio.

**dire** [daɪə*] $a$ terribile; estremo(a).

**direct** [daɪ'rɛkt] $a$ diretto(a) // $vt$ dirigere; **can you ~ me to ...?** mi può indicare la strada per ...?

**direction** [dɪ'rɛkʃən] $n$ direzione $f$; **sense of ~** senso dell'orientamento; ~**s** npl (advice) chiarimenti mpl; ~**s for use** istruzioni fpl.

**directly** [dɪ'rɛktlɪ] $ad$ (in straight line) direttamente; (at once) subito.

**director** [dɪ'rɛktə*] $n$ direttore/trice; amministratore/trice; (THEATRE, CINEMA) regista $m/f$.

**directory** [dɪ'rɛktərɪ] $n$ elenco.

**dirt** [də:t] $n$ sporcizia; immondizia; ~**-cheap** $a$ da due soldi; ~**y** $a$ sporco(a) // $vt$ sporcare; ~**y trick** $n$ brutto scherzo.

**disability** [dɪsə'bɪlɪtɪ] $n$ invalidità $f$ inv; (LAW) incapacità $f$ inv.

**disabled** [dɪs'eɪbld] $a$ invalido(a); (maimed) mutilato(a); (through illness, old age) inabile.

**disadvantage** [dɪsəd'vɑ:ntɪdʒ] $n$ svantaggio.

**disagree** [dɪsə'gri:] $vi$ (differ) di-

scordare; (be against, think otherwise): **to ~ (with)** essere in disaccordo (con), dissentire (da); ~**able** $a$ sgradevole; (person) antipatico(a); ~**ment** $n$ disaccordo.

**disappear** [dɪsə'pɪə*] $vi$ scomparire; ~**ance** $n$ scomparsa.

**disappoint** [dɪsə'pɔɪnt] $vt$ deludere; ~**ed** $a$ deluso(a); ~**ing** $a$ deludente; ~**ment** $n$ delusione $f$.

**disapproval** [dɪsə'pru:vəl] $n$ disapprovazione $f$.

**disapprove** [dɪsə'pru:v] $vi$: **to ~ of** disapprovare.

**disarm** [dɪs'ɑ:m] $vt$ disarmare; ~**ament** $n$ disarmo.

**disarray** [dɪsə'reɪ] $n$: **in ~** (army) in rotta; (organization) in uno stato di confusione; (clothes, hair) in disordine.

**disaster** [dɪ'zɑ:stə*] $n$ disastro.

**disband** [dɪs'bænd] $vt$ sbandare; (MIL) congedare // $vi$ sciogliersi.

**disbelief** [dɪsbə'li:f] $n$ incredulità.

**disc** [dɪsk] $n$ disco; (COMPUT) = **disk**.

**discard** [dɪs'kɑ:d] $vt$ (old things) scartare; (fig) abbandonare.

**discern** [dɪ'sə:n] $vt$ discernere, distinguere; ~**ing** $a$ perspicace.

**discharge** [dɪs'tʃɑ:dʒ] (duties) compiere; (ELEC, waste etc) scaricare; (MED) emettere; (patient) dimettere; (employee) licenziare; (soldier) congedare; (defendant) liberare // $n$ ['dɪstʃɑ:dʒ] (ELEC) scarica; (MED) emissione $f$; (dismissal) licenziamento; congedo; liberazione $f$.

**disciple** [dɪ'saɪpl] $n$ discepolo.

**discipline** ['dɪsɪplɪn] $n$ disciplina // $vt$ disciplinare; (punish) punire.

**disc jockey** $n$ disc jockey $m$ inv.

**disclaim** [dɪs'kleɪm] $vt$ negare, smentire.

**disclose** [dɪs'kləʊz] $vt$ rivelare, svelare; **disclosure** [-'kləʊʒə*] $n$ rivelazione $f$.

**disco** ['dɪskəʊ] $n$ abbr = **discothèque**.

**discoloured,** (US) **discolored** [dɪsˈkʌləd] a scolorito(a); ingiallito(a).

**discomfort** [dɪsˈkʌmfət] n disagio; (lack of comfort) scomodità f inv.

**disconcert** [dɪskənˈsəːt] vt sconcertare.

**disconnect** [dɪskəˈnɛkt] vt sconnettere, staccare; (ELEC. RADIO) staccare; (gas, water) chiudere.

**disconsolate** [dɪsˈkɔnsəlɪt] a sconsolato(a).

**discontent** [dɪskənˈtɛnt] n scontentezza; **~ed** a scontento(a).

**discontinue** [dɪskənˈtɪnjuː] vt smettere, cessare.

**discord** [ˈdɪskɔːd] n disaccordo; (MUS) dissonanza.

**discothèque** [ˈdɪskəʊtɛk] n discoteca.

**discount** n [ˈdɪskaʊnt] sconto // vt [dɪsˈkaʊnt] scontare.

**discourage** [dɪsˈkʌrɪdʒ] vt scoraggiare.

**discourteous** [dɪsˈkəːtɪəs] a scortese.

**discover** [dɪsˈkʌvə*] vt scoprire; **~y** n scoperta.

**discredit** [dɪsˈkrɛdɪt] vt screditare; mettere in dubbio.

**discreet** [dɪsˈkriːt] a discreto(a).

**discrepancy** [dɪˈskrɛpənsɪ] n discrepanza.

**discriminate** [dɪˈskrɪmɪneɪt] vi: to ~ between distinguere tra; to ~ against discriminare contro; **discriminating** a fine, giudizioso(a); **discrimination** [-ˈneɪʃən] n discriminazione f; (judgment) discernimento.

**discuss** [dɪˈskʌs] vt discutere; (debate) dibattere; **~ion** [dɪˈskʌʃən] n discussione f.

**disdain** [dɪsˈdeɪn] n disdegno.

**disease** [dɪˈziːz] n malattia.

**disembark** [dɪsɪmˈbɑːk] vt, vi sbarcare.

**disengage** [dɪsɪnˈgeɪdʒ] vt disimpegnare; (TECH) distaccare; (AUT: clutch) disinnestare.

**disfigure** [dɪsˈfɪgə*] vt sfigurare.

**disgrace** [dɪsˈgreɪs] n vergogna; (disfavour) disgrazia // vt disonorare, far cadere in disgrazia; **~ful** a scandaloso(a), vergognoso(a).

**disgruntled** [dɪsˈgrʌntld] a scontento(a), di cattivo umore.

**disguise** [dɪsˈgaɪz] n travestimento // vt travestire; in ~ travestito(a).

**disgust** [dɪsˈgʌst] n disgusto, nausea // vt disgustare, far schifo a; **~ing** a disgustoso(a); ripugnante.

**dish** [dɪʃ] n piatto; to do or wash the ~es fare i piatti; to ~ up vt servire; (facts, statistics) presentare; **~cloth** n strofinaccio.

**dishearten** [dɪsˈhɑːtn] vt scoraggiare.

**dishevelled** [dɪˈʃɛvəld] a arruffato(a); scapigliato(a).

**dishonest** [dɪsˈɔnɪst] a disonesto(a).

**dishonour,** (US) **dishonor** [dɪsˈɔnə*] n disonore m; **~able** a disonorevole.

**dish towel** [US] n strofinaccio dei piatti.

**dishwasher** [ˈdɪʃwɔʃə*] n lavastoviglie f inv; (person) sguattero/a.

**disillusion** [dɪsɪˈluːʒən] n disilludere, disingannare // n disillusione f.

**disincentive** [dɪsɪnˈsɛntɪv] n: to be a ~ essere demotivante; to be a ~ to sb demotivare qn.

**disinfect** [dɪsɪnˈfɛkt] vt disinfettare; **~ant** n disinfettante m.

**disintegrate** [dɪsˈɪntɪgreɪt] vi disintegrarsi.

**disinterested** [dɪsˈɪntrəstɪd] a disinteressato(a).

**disjointed** [dɪsˈdʒɔɪntɪd] a sconnesso(a).

**disk** [dɪsk] n (COMPUT) disco; single-/double-sided ~ disco a facciata singola/doppia; ~ **drive** n lettore m; **~ette** n (US) = **disk**.

**dislike** [dɪsˈlaɪk] n antipatia, avversione f // vt: he ~s it non gli piace.

**dislocate** ['dɪsləkeɪt] vt slogare; disorganizzare.

**dislodge** [dɪs'lɔdʒ] vt rimuovere, staccare; (enemy) sloggiare.

**disloyal** [dɪs'lɔɪəl] a sleale.

**dismal** ['dɪzml] a triste, cupo(a).

**dismantle** [dɪs'mæntl] vt smantellare, smontare; (fort, warship) disarmare.

**dismay** [dɪs'meɪ] n costernazione f // vt sgomentare.

**dismiss** [dɪs'mɪs] vt congedare; (employee) licenziare; (idea) scacciare; (LAW) respingere; **~al** n congedo; licenziamento.

**dismount** [dɪs'maunt] vi scendere.

**disobedience** [dɪsə'bi:dɪəns] n disubbidienza.

**disobedient** [dɪsə'bi:dɪənt] a disubbidiente.

**disobey** [dɪsə'beɪ] vt disubbidire.

**disorder** [dɪs'ɔ:də*] n disordine m; (rioting) tumulto; (MED) disturbo; **~ly** a disordinato(a); tumultuoso(a).

**disorientated** [dɪs'ɔ:rɪenteɪtɪd] a disorientato(a).

**disown** [dɪs'əun] vt ripudiare.

**disparaging** [dɪs'pærɪdʒɪŋ] a spregiativo(a), sprezzante.

**dispassionate** [dɪs'pæʃənət] a calmo(a), freddo(a); imparziale.

**dispatch** [dɪs'pætʃ] vt spedire, inviare // n spedizione f, invio; (MIL, PRESS) dispaccio.

**dispel** [dɪs'pel] vt dissipare, scacciare.

**dispensary** [dɪs'pensərɪ] n farmacia; (in chemist's) dispensario.

**dispense** [dɪs'pens] vt distribuire, amministrare; **to ~ with** vt fus fare a meno di; **~r** n (container) distributore m; **dispensing chemist** n (Brit) farmacista m/f.

**disperse** [dɪs'pə:s] vt disperdere; (knowledge) disseminare // vi disperdersi.

**dispirited** [dɪs'pɪrɪtɪd] a scoraggiato(a), abbattuto(a).

**displace** [dɪs'pleɪs] vt spostare; **~d person** n (POL) profugo/a.

**display** [dɪs'pleɪ] n mostra; esposizione f; (of feeling etc) manifestazione f; (screen) schermo; (pej) ostentazione f // vt mostrare; (goods) esporre; (results) affiggere; (departure times) indicare.

**displease** [dɪs'pli:z] vt dispiacere a, scontentare; **~d with** scontento di; **displeasure** [-'pleʒə*] n dispiacere m.

**disposable** [dɪs'pəuzəbl] a (pack etc) a perdere; (income) disponibile; **~ nappy** n pannolino di carta.

**disposal** [dɪs'pəuzl] n (of rubbish) evacuazione f; distruzione f; **at one's ~** alla sua disposizione.

**dispose** [dɪs'pəuz] vt disporre; **to ~ of** vt (time, money) disporre di; (unwanted goods) sbarazzarsi di; (problem) eliminare; **~d** a: **~d to do** disposto(a) a fare; **disposition** [-'zɪʃən] n disposizione f; (temperament) carattere m.

**disproportionate** [dɪsprə'pɔ:ʃənət] a sproporzionato(a).

**disprove** [dɪs'pru:v] vt confutare.

**dispute** [dɪs'pju:t] n disputa; (also: **industrial ~**) controversia (sindacale) // vt contestare; (matter) discutere; (victory) disputare.

**disqualify** [dɪs'kwɔlɪfaɪ] vt (SPORT) squalificare; **to ~ sb from sth/from doing** rendere qn incapace a qc/a fare; squalificare qn da qc/da fare; **to ~ sb from driving** ritirare la patente a qn.

**disquiet** [dɪs'kwaɪət] n inquietudine f.

**disregard** [dɪsrɪ'gɑ:d] vt non far caso a, non badare a.

**disrepair** [dɪsrɪ'peə*] n cattivo stato; **to fall into ~** (building) andare in rovina; (street) deteriorarsi.

**disreputable** [dɪs'repjutəbl] a (person) di cattiva fama.

**disrupt** [dɪs'rʌpt] vt mettere in disordine.

**dissatisfaction** [dɪssætɪs'fækʃən] n scontentezza, insoddisfazione f.

**dissect** [dɪ'sekt] vt sezionare.

**dissent** [dɪˈsɛnt] n dissenso.
**dissertation** [dɪsəˈteɪʃən] n tesi f inv, dissertazione f.
**disservice** [dɪsˈsəːvɪs] n: **to do sb a** ~ fare un cattivo servizio a qn.
**dissimilar** [dɪˈsɪmɪlə] a: ~ (**to**) dissimile or diverso(a) (da).
**dissipate** [ˈdɪsɪpeɪt] vt dissipare; **~d** a dissipato(a).
**dissolute** [ˈdɪsəluːt] a dissoluto(a), licenzioso(a).
**dissolution** [dɪsəˈluːʃən] n (of organization, marriage, POL) scioglimento.
**dissolve** [dɪˈzɔlv] vt dissolvere, sciogliere; (POL, marriage etc) sciogliere // vi dissolversi, sciogliersi; (fig) svanire.
**distance** [ˈdɪstns] n distanza; **in the** ~ in lontananza.
**distant** [ˈdɪstnt] a lontano(a), distante; (manner) riservato(a), freddo(a).
**distaste** [dɪsˈteɪst] n ripugnanza; **~ful** a ripugnante, sgradevole.
**distended** [dɪsˈtɛndɪd] a (stomach) dilatato(a).
**distil** [dɪsˈtɪl] vt distillare; **~lery** n distilleria.
**distinct** [dɪsˈtɪŋkt] a distinto(a); (preference, progress) definito(a); **as** ~ **from** a differenza di; **~ion** [dɪsˈtɪŋkʃən] n distinzione f; (in exam) lode f; **~ive** a distintivo(a).
**distinguish** [dɪsˈtɪŋgwɪʃ] vt distinguere; discernere; **~ed** a (eminent) eminente; **~ing** a (feature) distinto(a), caratteristico(a).
**distort** [dɪsˈtɔːt] vt distorcere; (TECH) deformare.
**distract** [dɪsˈtrækt] vt distrarre; **~ed** a distratto(a); **~ion** [dɪsˈtrækʃən] n distrazione f.
**distraught** [dɪsˈtrɔːt] a stravolto(a).
**distress** [dɪsˈtrɛs] n angoscia; (pain) dolore m // vt affliggere; **~ing** a doloroso(a).
**distribute** [dɪsˈtrɪbjuːt] vt distribuire; **distribution** [-ˈbjuːʃən] n

distribuzione f; **distributor** n stributore m.
**district** [ˈdɪstrɪkt] n (of country) regione f; (of town) quartiere m; (ADMIN) distretto; ~ **attorney** n (US) ≈ sostituto procuratore m della Repubblica; ~ **nurse** n (Brit) infermiera di quartiere.
**distrust** [dɪsˈtrʌst] n diffidenza, sfiducia // vt non aver fiducia in.
**disturb** [dɪsˈtəːb] vt disturbare; (inconvenience) scomodare; **~ance** n disturbo; (political etc) tumulto; (by drunks etc) disordini mpl; **~ed** a (worried, upset) turbato(a); **emotionally ~ed** con turbe emotive; **~ing** a sconvolgente.
**disuse** [dɪsˈjuːs] n: **to fall into** ~ cadere in disuso.
**disused** [dɪsˈjuːzd] a abbandonato(a).
**ditch** [dɪtʃ] n fossa // vt (col) piantare in asso.
**dither** [ˈdɪðə] vi vacillare.
**ditto** [ˈdɪtəu] ad idem.
**dive** [daɪv] n tuffo; (of submarine) immersione f; (AVIAT) picchiata; (pej) buco // vi tuffarsi; **~r** n tuffatore/trice; palombaro.
**diverse** [daɪˈvəːs] a vario(a).
**diversion** [daɪˈvəːʃən] n (Brit AUT) deviazione f; (distraction) divertimento.
**divert** [daɪˈvəːt] vt deviare; (amuse) divertire.
**divide** [dɪˈvaɪd] vt dividere; (separate) separare // vi dividersi; **~d highway** n (US) strada a doppia carreggiata.
**dividend** [ˈdɪvɪdɛnd] n dividendo.
**divine** [dɪˈvaɪn] a divino(a).
**diving** [ˈdaɪvɪŋ] n tuffo; ~ **board** n trampolino.
**divinity** [dɪˈvɪnɪtɪ] n divinità f inv; teologia.
**division** [dɪˈvɪʒən] n divisione f; separazione f.
**divorce** [dɪˈvɔːs] n divorzio // vt divorziare da; **~d** a divorziato(a); **~e** [-ˈsiː] n divorziato/a.
**D.I.Y.** n abbr (Brit) = **do-it-**

yourself.

**dizzy** ['dɪzɪ] *a (height)*
vertiginoso(a); **to feel** ~ avere il
capogiro; **to make sb** ~ far venire
il capogiro a qn.

**DJ** *n abbr* = **disc jockey**.

_KEYWORD_

**do** [du:] ◆ *n (col: party etc)* festa; **it
was rather a grand** ~ è stato un
ricevimento piuttosto importante
◆ *vb (pt* **did**, *pp* **done) 1** *(in
negative constructions)* non tradotto;
**I don't understand** non capisco
**2** *(to form questions)* non tradotto;
**didn't you know?** non lo sapevi?;
**why didn't you come?** perché non
sei venuto?
**3** *(for emphasis, in polite expressions)*: **she does seem rather
late** sembra essere piuttosto in
ritardo; ~ **sit down** si accomodi la
prego, prego si sieda; ~ **take care!**
mi raccomando, sta attento!
**4** *(used to avoid repeating vb)*: **she
swims better than I** ~ lei nuota
meglio di me; ~ **you agree?** —
**yes, I** ~**/no, I don't** sei d'accordo?
— sì/no; **she lives in Glasgow** — **so
~ I** lei vive a Glasgow — anch'io; **he
asked me to help him and I did**
mi ha chiesto di aiutarlo ed io l'ho
fatto
**5** *(in question tags)*: **you like him,
don't you?** ti piace, vero?; **I don't
know him,** ~ **I?** non lo conosco,
vero?
◆ *vt (gen, carry out, perform etc)*
fare; **what are you** ~**ing tonight?**
che fa stasera?; **to** ~ **the cooking**
cucinare; **to** ~ **the washing-up fare
i piatti; **to** ~ **one's teeth lavarsi i
denti; **to** ~ **one's hair/nails** farsi i
capelli/le unghie; **the car was** ~**ing
100** la macchina faceva i 100 all'ora
◆ *vi* **1** *(act, behave)* fare; ~ **as I** ~
faccia come me, faccia come faccio
io
**2** *(get on, fare)* andare; **he's** ~**ing
well/badly at school** va bene/male a

scuola; **how** ~ **you** ~? piacere!
**3** *(suit)* andare bene; **this room will**
~ questa stanza va bene
**4** *(be sufficient)* bastare; **will £10**
~? basteranno 10 sterline?; **that'll**
~ basta così; **that'll** ~! *(in
annoyance)* ora basta!; **to make** ~
**(with)** arrangiarsi (con)

**to do away with** *vt fus (kill)* far
fuori; *(abolish)* abolire

**to do up** *vt (laces)* allacciare;
*(dress, buttons)* abbottonare;
*(renovate: room, house)* rimettere a
nuovo, rifare

**to do with** *vt fus (need)* aver bisogno di; *(be connected)*: **what has it
got to** ~ **with you?** e tu che c'en-
tri?; **I won't have anything to** ~
**with it** non voglio avere niente a che
farci; **it has to** ~ **with money** si
tratta di soldi

**to do without** *vi* fare senza ◆ *vt
fus* fare a meno di.

**dock** [dɔk] *n* bacino; *(LAW)* banco
degli imputati // *vi* entrare in bacino;
~**er** *n* scaricatore *m*; ~**yard** *n*
cantiere *m* (navale).

**doctor** ['dɔktə*] *n* medico/a; *(Ph.D.
etc)* dottore/essa // *vt (fig)* alterare,
manipolare; *(drink etc)* adulterare;
**D~ of Philosophy (Ph.D.)** *n*
dottorato di ricerca; *(person)* titolare
*m/f* di un dottorato di ricerca.

**doctrine** ['dɔktrɪn] *n* dottrina.

**document** ['dɔkjumənt] *n*
documento; ~**ary** [-'mɛntərɪ] *a*
documentario(a); *(evidence)* docu-
mentato(a) // *n* documentario.

**dodge** [dɔdʒ] *n* trucco; schivata // *vt*
schivare, eludere.

**doe** [dəu] *n (deer)* femmina di daino;
*(rabbit)* coniglia.

**does** [dʌz] *vb see* do; **doesn't** =
does not.

**dog** [dɔg] *n* cane *m* // *vt (follow
closely)* pedinare; *(fig: memory etc)*
perseguitare; ~ **collar** *n* collare *m*
di cane; *(fig)* collarino; ~**-eared** *a
(book)* con orecchie.

**dogged** ['dɔgid] *a* ostinato(a), tenace.

**dogsbody** ['dɔgzbɔdɪ] *n* factotum *m inv*.

**doings** ['duɪŋz] *npl* attività *fpl*.

**do-it-yourself** [du:ɪtjɔ:'self] *n* il far da sé.

**doldrums** ['dɔldrəmz] *npl* (*fig*): to be in the ~ essere giù.

**dole** [dəul] *n* (*Brit*) sussidio di disoccupazione; **to be on the ~** vivere del sussidio; **to ~ out** *vt* distribuire.

**doleful** ['dəulful] *a* triste, doloroso(a).

**doll** [dɔl] *n* bambola; **to ~ o.s. up** farsi bello(a).

**dollar** ['dɔlə*] *n* dollaro.

**dolphin** ['dɔlfin] *n* delfino.

**domain** [də'meɪn] *n* dominio.

**dome** [dəum] *n* cupola.

**domestic** [də'mɛstɪk] *a* (*duty, happiness, animal*) domestico(a); (*policy, affairs, flights*) nazionale; **~ated** *a* addomesticato(a).

**dominate** ['dɔmineɪt] *vt* dominare.

**domineering** [dɔmɪ'nɪərɪŋ] *a* dispotico(a), autoritario(a).

**dominion** [də'mɪnɪən] *n* dominio; sovranità; dominion *m inv*.

**domino** ['dɔmɪnəu] *n* domino; **~es** *n* (*game*) gioco del domino.

**don** [dɔn] *n* (*Brit*) docente *m/f* universitario/a.

**donate** [də'neɪt] *vt* donare.

**done** [dʌn] *pp* of **do**.

**donkey** ['dɔŋkɪ] *n* asino.

**donor** ['dəunə*] *n* donatore/trice.

**don't** [dəunt] *vb* = **do not**.

**doodle** ['du:dl] *vi* scarabocchiare.

**doom** [du:m] *n* destino; rovina // *vt*: to be **~ed** (to failure) essere predestinato(a) (a fallire); **~sday** *n* il giorno del Giudizio.

**door** [dɔ:*] *n* porta; **~bell** *n* campanello; **~man** *n* (*in hotel*) portiere *m* in livrea; (*in block of flats*) portinaio; **~mat** *n* stuoia della porta; **~step** *n* gradino della porta; **~way** *n* porta.

**dope** [dəup] *n* (*col: drugs*) roba // *vt* (*horse etc*) drogare.

**dopey** ['dəupɪ] *a* (*col*) inebetito(a).

**dormant** ['dɔ:mənt] *a* inattivo(a); (*fig*) latente.

**dormitory** ['dɔ:mɪtrɪ] *n* dormitorio.

**dose** [dəus] *n* dose *f*; (*bout*) attacco.

**doss house** ['dɔs-] *n* (*Brit*) asilo notturno.

**dot** [dɔt] *n* punto; macchiolina; **~ted with** punteggiato(a) di; **on the ~** in punto.

**dote** [dəut]: **to ~ on** *vt fus* essere infatuato/a di.

**dot-matrix printer** [dɔt'meɪtrɪks-] *n* stampante *f* a matrice a punti.

**dotted line** ['dɔtɪd-] *n* linea punteggiata.

**double** ['dʌbl] *a* doppio(a) // *ad* (*fold*) in due, doppio; (*twice*): to cost ~ (sth) costare il doppio (di qc) // *n* sosia *m inv*; (*CINEMA*) controfigura // *vt* raddoppiare; (*fold*) piegare doppio *or* in due // *vi* raddoppiarsi; **on the ~**, (*Brit*) at the ~ a passo di corsa; **~s** *n* (*TENNIS*) doppio; **~ bass** *n* contrabbasso; **~ bed** *n* letto matrimoniale; **~-breasted** *a* a doppio petto; **~cross** *vt* fare il doppio gioco con; **~-decker** *n* autobus *m inv* a due piani; **~ glazing** *n* (*Brit*) doppi vetri *mpl*; **~ room** *n* camera per due; **doubly** *ad* doppiamente.

**doubt** [daut] *n* dubbio // *vt* dubitare di; **to ~ that** dubitare che + *sub*; **~ful** *a* dubbioso(a), incerto(a); (*person*) equivoco(a); **~less** *ad* indubbiamente.

**dough** [dəu] *n* pasta, impasto; **~nut** *n* bombolone *m*.

**douse** [dauz] *vt* (*drench*) inzuppare; (*extinguish*) spegnere.

**dove** [dʌv] *n* colombo/a.

**dovetail** ['dʌvteɪl] *vi* (*fig*) combaciare.

**dowdy** ['daudɪ] *a* trasandato(a); malvestito(a).

**down** [daun] *n* (*fluff*) piumino // *ad* giù, di sotto // *prep* giù per // *vt* (*col*:

*drink*) scolarsi; ~ **with** X! abbasso X!; ~**-and-out** *n* barbone *m*; ~**at-heel** *a* scalcagnato(a); (*fig*) trasandato(a); ~**cast** *a* abbattuto(a); ~**fall** *n* caduta; rovina; ~**hearted** *a* scoraggiato(a); ~**hill** *ad*: **to go** ~**hill** andare in discesa // *n* (*SKI*: *also*: ~**hill race**) discesa libera; ~ **payment** *n* acconto; ~**pour** *n* scroscio di pioggia; ~**right** *a* franco(a); (*refusal*) assoluto(a); ~**stairs** *ad* di sotto; al piano inferiore; ~**stream** *ad* a valle; ~**-to-earth** *a* pratico(a); ~**town** *ad* in città; ~ **under** *ad* (*Australia etc*) agli antipodi; ~**ward** ['daunwəd] *a*, *ad*, ~**wards** ['daunwədz] *ad* in giù, in discesa.

**dowry** ['dauri] *n* dote *f*.

**doz.** *abbr* = **dozen.**

**doze** [dəuz] *vi* sonnecchiare; ~ **off** *vi* appisolarsi.

**dozen** ['dʌzn] *n* dozzina; **a** ~ **books** una dozzina di libri; ~**s of** decine *fpl* di.

**Dr.** *abbr* = **doctor; drive** (*n*).

**drab** [dræb] *a* tetro(a), grigio(a).

**draft** [drɑːft] *n* abbozzo; (*COMM*) tratta; (*US MIL*) contingente *m*; (: *call-up*) leva // *vt* abbozzare; *see also* **draught.**

**draftsman** ['drɑːftsmən] *n* (*US*) = **draughtsman.**

**drag** [dræg] *vt* trascinare; (*river*) dragare // *vi* trascinarsi // *n* (*col*) noioso(a): noia, fatica; (*women's clothing*): **in** ~ travestito (da donna); **to** ~ **on** *vi* tirar avanti lentamente.

**dragon** ['drægən] *n* drago.

**dragonfly** ['drægənflai] *n* libellula.

**drain** [drein] *n* canale *m* di scolo; (*for sewage*) fogna; (*on resources*) salasso // *vt* (*land, marshes*) prosciugare; (*vegetables*) scolare; (*reservoir etc*) vuotare // *vi* (*water*) defluire (via); ~**age** *n* prosciugamento: fognatura; ~**ing board**, (*US*) ~**board** *n* piano del lavello; ~**pipe** *n* tubo di scarico.

**dram** [dræm] *n* bicchierino.

**drama** ['drɑːmə] *n* (*art*) dramma *m*, teatro; (*play*) commedia; (*event*) dramma; ~**tic** [drə'mætik] *a* drammatico(a); ~**tist** ['dræmətist] *n* drammaturgo/a; ~**tize** *vt* (*events*) drammatizzare; (*adapt*: *for TV/ cinema*) ridurre or adattare per la televisione/lo schermo.

**drank** [dræŋk] *pt* of **drink.**

**drape** [dreip] *vt* drappeggiare; ~**s** *npl* (*US*) tende *fpl*; ~**r** *n* (*Brit*) negoziante *m/f* di stoffe.

**drastic** ['dræstik] *a* drastico(a).

**draught**, (*US*) **draft** [drɑːft] *n* corrente *f* d'aria; (*NAUT*) pescaggio; ~**s** *n* (*Brit*) (gioco della) dama; **on** ~ (*beer*) alla spina; ~**board** *n* (*Brit*) scacchiera.

**draughtsman**, (*US*) **draftsman** ['drɑːftsmən] *n* disegnatore *m*.

**draw** [drɔː] *vb* (*pt* **drew**, *pp* **drawn**) *vt* tirare; (*attract*) attirare; (*picture*) disegnare; (*line, circle*) tracciare; (*money*) ritirare // *vi* (*SPORT*) pareggiare // *n* pareggio; (*in lottery*) estrazione *f*; (*attraction*) attrazione *f*; **to** ~ **near** *vi* avvicinarsi; **to** ~ **out** *vi* (*lengthen*) allungarsi // *vt* (*money*) ritirare; **to** ~ **up** *vi* (*stop*) arrestarsi, fermarsi // *vt* (*document*) compilare; ~**back** *n* svantaggio, inconveniente *m*; ~**bridge** *n* ponte *m* levatoio.

**drawer** [drɔː*] *n* cassetto; ['drɔːə*] (*of cheque*) traente *m/f*.

**drawing** ['drɔːiŋ] *n* disegno; ~ **board** *n* tavola da disegno; ~ **pin** *n* (*Brit*) puntina da disegno; ~ **room** *n* salotto.

**drawl** [drɔːl] *n* pronuncia strascicata.

**drawn** [drɔːn] *pp* of **draw.**

**dread** [dred] *n* terrore *m* // *vt* tremare all'idea di; ~**ful** *a* terribile.

**dream** [driːm] *n* sogno // *vt*, *vi* (*pt*, *pp* **dreamed** or **dreamt** [dremt]) sognare; ~**y** *a* sognante.

**dreary** ['driəri] *a* tetro(a); monotono(a).

**dredge** [dredʒ] *vt* dragare.

**dregs** [drεgz] *npl* feccia.

**drench** [drεntʃ] *vt* inzuppare.

**dress** [drεs] *n* vestito; (*clothing*) abbigliamento // *vt* vestire; (*wound*) fasciare; (*food*) condire; preparare // *vi* vestirsi; to ~ **up** *vi* vestirsi a festa; (*in fancy dress*) vestirsi in costume; ~ **circle** *n* (*Brit*) prima galleria; ~**er** *n* (*THEATRE*) assistente *m/f* del camerino; (*furniture*) credenza; ~**ing** *n* (*MED*) benda; (*CULIN*) condimento; ~**ing gown** *n* (*Brit*) vestaglia; ~**ing room** *n* (*THEATRE*) camerino; (*SPORT*) spogliatoio; ~**ing table** *n* toilette *f inv*; ~**maker** *n* sarta; ~ **rehearsal** *n* prova generale; ~**y** *a* (*col*) elegante.

**drew** [dru:] *pt of* **draw**.

**dribble** ['drɪbl] *vi* gocciolare; (*baby*) sbavare; (*FOOTBALL*) dribblare.

**dried** [draɪd] *a* (*fruit, beans*) secco(a); (*eggs, milk*) in polvere.

**drier** ['draɪə*] *n* = **dryer**.

**drift** [drɪft] *n* (*of current etc*) direzione *f*; forza; (*of sand etc*) turbine *m*; (*of snow*) cumulo; turbine; (*general meaning*) senso // *vi* (*boat*) essere trasportato(a) dalla corrente; (*sand, snow*) ammucchiarsi; ~**wood** *n* resti *mpl* della mareggiata.

**drill** [drɪl] *n* trapano; (*MIL*) esercitazione *f* // *vt* trapanare // *vi* (*for oil*) fare trivellazioni.

**drink** [drɪŋk] *n* bevanda, bibita // *vt*, *vi* (*pt* **drank**, *pp* **drunk**) bere; to have a ~ bere qualcosa; a ~ of water un po' d'acqua; ~**er** *n* bevitore/trice; ~**ing water** *n* acqua potabile.

**drip** [drɪp] *n* goccia; gocciolamento; (*MED*) fleboclisi *f inv* // *vi* gocciolare; (*washing*) sgocciolare; (*wall*) trasudare; ~**-dry** *a* (*shirt*) che non si stira; ~**ping** *n* grasso d'arrosto.

**drive** [draɪv] *n* passeggiata *or* giro in macchina; (*also*: ~**way**) viale *m* d'accesso; (*energy*) energia; (*PSYCH*) impulso; bisogno; (*push*)

sforzo eccezionale; campagna; (*SPORT*) drive *m inv*; (*TECH*) trasmissione *f*; propulsione *f*; presa; (*also*: **disk** ~) lettore *m* // *vb* (*pt* **drove**, *pp* **driven**) *vt* guidare; (*nail*) piantare; (*push*) cacciare, spingere; (*TECH*: *motor*) azionare; far funzionare // *vi* (*AUT*: *at controls*) guidare; (: *travel*) andare in macchina; **left-/right-hand** ~ guida a sinistra/destra; to ~ **sb mad** far impazzire qn.

**drivel** ['drɪvl] *n* idiozie *fpl*.

**driven** ['drɪvn] *pp of* **drive**.

**driver** ['draɪvə*] *n* conducente *m/f*; (*of taxi*) tassista *m*; (*of bus*) autista *m*; ~**'s license** *n* (*US*) patente *f* di guida.

**driveway** ['draɪvweɪ] *n* viale *m* d'accesso.

**driving** ['draɪvɪŋ] *a*: ~ **rain** pioggia sferzante // *n* guida; ~ **instructor** *n* istruttore/trice di scuola guida; ~ **lesson** *n* lezione *f* di guida; ~ **licence** *n* (*Brit*) patente *f* di guida; ~ **mirror** *n* specchietto retrovisore; ~ **school** *n* scuola *f* guida *inv*; ~ **test** *n* esame *m* di guida.

**drizzle** ['drɪzl] *n* pioggerella.

**droll** [drəʊl] *a* buffo(a).

**drone** [drəʊn] *n* ronzio; (*male bee*) fuco.

**drool** [dru:l] *vi* sbavare.

**droop** [dru:p] *vi* abbassarsi; languire.

**drop** [drɒp] *n* goccia; (*fall*) caduta; (*also*: **parachute** ~) lancio; (*steep incline*) salto // *vt* lasciare cadere; (*voice, eyes, price*) abbassare; (*set down from car*) far scendere // *vi* cascare; ~**s** *npl* (*MED*) gocce *fpl*; to ~ **off** *vi* (*sleep*) addormentarsi; to ~ **out** *vi* (*withdraw*) ritirarsi; (*student etc*) smettere di studiare; ~**-out** *n* (*from society/from university*) chi ha abbandonato (la società/gli studi); ~**pings** *npl* sterco.

**drought** [draʊt] *n* siccità *f inv*.

**drove** [drəʊv] *pt of* **drive**.

**drown** [draʊn] *vt* affogare // *vi*

affogarsi.

**drowsy** ['drauzı] *a* sonnolento(a), assonnato(a).

**drudgery** ['drʌdʒərı] *n* lavoro faticoso.

**drug** [drʌg] *n* farmaco; (*narcotic*) droga // *vt* drogare; ~ **addict** *n* tossicomane *m/f*; ~**gist** *n* (*US*) persona che gestisce un drugstore; ~**store** *n* (*US*) drugstore *m inv*.

**drum** [drʌm] *n* tamburo; (*for oil, petrol*) fusto // *vi* tamburellare; ~**s** *npl* batteria; ~**mer** *n* batterista *m/f*.

**drunk** [drʌŋk] *pp of* **drink** // *a* ubriaco(a); ebbro(a) // *n* (*also*: ~**ard**) ubriacone/a; ~**en** *a* ubriaco(a); da ubriaco.

**dry** [draı] *a* secco(a); (*day, clothes*) asciutto(a) // *vt* seccare; (*clothes, hair, hands*) asciugare // *vi* asciugarsi; **to** ~ **up** *vi* seccarsi; ~**-cleaner's** *n* lavasecco *m inv*; ~**er** *n* (*for hair*) föhn *m inv*, asciugacapelli *m inv*; (*for clothes*) asciugabiancheria; (*US*: *spin-dryer*) centrifuga; ~ **goods store** *n* (*US*) negozio di stoffe; ~ **rot** *n* fungo del legno.

**dual** ['djuəl] *a* doppio(a); ~ **carriageway** *n* (*Brit*) strada a doppia carreggiata.

**dubbed** [dʌbd] *a* (*CINEMA*) doppiato(a); (*nicknamed*) soprannominato(a).

**dubious** ['dju:bıəs] *a* dubbio(a).

**Dublin** ['dʌblın] *n* Dublino *f*.

**duchess** ['dʌtʃıs] *n* duchessa.

**duck** [dʌk] *n* anatra // *vi* abbassare la testa; ~**ling** *n* anatroccolo.

**duct** [dʌkt] *n* condotto; (*ANAT*) canale *m*.

**dud** [dʌd] *n* (*shell*) proiettile *m* che fa cilecca; (*object, tool*): **it's a** ~ è inutile, non funziona // *a* (*Brit*: *cheque*) a vuoto; (: *note, coin*) falso(a).

**due** [dju:] *a* dovuto(a); (*expected*) atteso(a); (*fitting*) giusto(a) // *n* dovuto // *ad*: ~ **north** diritto verso nord; ~**s** *npl* (*for club, union*) quota;

(*in harbour*) diritti *mpl* di porto; **in** ~ **course** a tempo debito; finalmente; ~ **to** dovuto a; a causa di; **to be** ~ **to do** dover fare.

**duet** [dju:'ɛt] *n* duetto.

**duffel** [dʌfl] *a*: ~ **bag** sacca da viaggio di tela; ~ **coat** montgomery *m inv*.

**dug** [dʌg] *pt, pp of* **dig**.

**duke** [dju:k] *n* duca *m*.

**dull** [dʌl] *a* (*boring*) noioso(a); (*slow-witted*) ottuso(a); (*sound, pain*) sordo(a); (*weather, day*) fosco(a), scuro(a); (*blade*) smussato(a) // *vt* (*pain, grief*) attutire; (*mind, senses*) intorpidire.

**duly** ['dju:lı] *ad* (*on time*) a tempo debito; (*as expected*) debitamente.

**dumb** [dʌm] *a* muto(a); (*stupid*) stupido(a); **dumbfounded** [dʌm-'faundıd] *a* stupito(a), stordito(a).

**dummy** ['dʌmı] *n* (*tailor's model*) manichino; (*SPORT*) finto; (*Brit*: *for baby*) tettarella // *a* falso(a), finto(a).

**dump** [dʌmp] *n* mucchio di rifiuti; (*place*) luogo di scarico; (*MIL*) deposito // *vt* (*put down*) scaricare; mettere giù; (*get rid of*) buttar via; ~**ing** *n* (*ECON*) dumping *m*; (*of rubbish*): **"no** ~**ing"** "vietato lo scarico".

**dumpling** ['dʌmplıŋ] *n* specie di gnocco.

**dumpy** ['dʌmpı] *a* tracagnotto(a).

**dung** [dʌŋ] *n* concime *m*.

**dungarees** [dʌŋgə'ri:z] *npl* tuta.

**dungeon** ['dʌndʒən] *n* prigione *f* sotterranea.

**dupe** [dju:p] *vt* gabbare, ingannare.

**duplex** ['dju:plɛks] *n* (*US*: *house*) casa con muro divisorio in comune con un'altra; (: *apartment*) appartamento su due piani.

**duplicate** *n* ['dju:plıkət] doppio // *vt* ['dju:plıkeıt] raddoppiare; (*on machine*) ciclostilare.

**durable** ['djuərəbl] *a* durevole; (*clothes, metal*) resistente.

**duration** [djuə'reıʃən] *n* durata.

**duress** [djuə'rɛs] *n*: **under** ~ sotto

costrizione.

**during** ['djʊərɪŋ] *prep* durante, nel corso di.

**dusk** [dʌsk] *n* crepuscolo.

**dust** [dʌst] *n* polvere *f* // *vt* (*furniture*) spolverare; (*cake etc*): **to ~ with** cospargere con; **~bin** *n* (*Brit*) pattumiera; **~er** *n* straccio per la polvere; **~ jacket** *n* sopraccoperta; **~man** *n* (*Brit*) netturbino; **~y** *a* polveroso(a).

**Dutch** [dʌtʃ] *a* olandese // *n* (*LING*) olandese *m*; **the ~** *npl* gli Olandesi; **to go ~** fare alla romana; **~man/woman** *n* olandese *m/f*.

**dutiful** ['dju:tɪful] *a* (*child*) rispettoso(a).

**duty** ['dju:tɪ] *n* dovere *m*; (*tax*) dazio, tassa; **duties** *npl* mansioni *fpl*; **on ~** di servizio; **off ~** libero(a), fuori servizio; **~-free** *a* esente da dazio.

**duvet** ['du:veɪ] *n* (*Brit*) piumino, piumone *m*.

**dwarf** [dwɔ:f] *n* nano/a // *vt* far apparire piccolo.

**dwell**, *pt*, *pp* **dwelt** [dwɛl, dwɛlt] *vi* dimorare; **to ~ on** *vt fus* indugiare su; **~ing** *n* dimora.

**dwindle** ['dwɪndl] *vi* diminuire, decrescere.

**dye** [daɪ] *n* tinta // *vt* tingere.

**dying** ['daɪɪŋ] *a* morente, moribondo(a).

**dyke** [daɪk] *n* (*Brit*) diga.

**dynamic** [daɪ'næmɪk] *a* dinamico(a).

**dynamite** ['daɪnəmaɪt] *n* dinamite *f*.

**dynamo** ['daɪnəməʊ] *n* dinamo *f inv*.

**dysentery** ['dɪsɪntrɪ] *n* dissenteria.

**dyslexia** [dɪs'lɛksɪə] *n* dislessia.

# E

**E** [i:] *n* (*MUS*) mi *m*.

**each** [i:tʃ] *a* ogni, ciascuno(a) // *pronoun* ciascuno(a), ognuno(a); **~ one** ognuno(a); **~ other** si (*or* ci *etc*); **they hate ~ other** si odiano (l'un l'altro); **you are jealous of ~**

other siete gelosi l'uno dell'altro; **they have 2 books ~** hanno 2 libri ciascuno.

**eager** ['i:gə*] *a* impaziente; desideroso(a); ardente; **to be ~ for** essere desideroso di, aver gran voglia di.

**eagle** ['i:gl] *n* aquila.

**ear** [ɪə*] *n* orecchio; (*of corn*) pannocchia; **~ache** *n* mal *m* d'orecchi; **~drum** *n* timpano.

**earl** [ə:l] *n* conte *m*.

**earlier** ['ə:lɪə*] *a* precedente // *ad* prima.

**early** ['ə:lɪ] *ad* presto, di buon'ora; (*ahead of time*) in anticipo // *a* precoce; anticipato(a); che si fa vedere di buon'ora; **to have an ~ night** andare a letto presto; **in the ~ or ~ in the spring/19th century** all'inizio della primavera/dell'Ottocento; **~ retirement** *n* ritiro anticipato.

**earmark** ['ɪəmɑ:k] *vt*: **to ~ sth for** destinare qc a.

**earn** [ə:n] *vt* guadagnare; (*rest, reward*) meritare.

**earnest** ['ə:nɪst] *a* serio(a); **in ~** *ad* sul serio.

**earnings** ['ə:nɪŋz] *npl* guadagni *mpl*; (*salary*) stipendio.

**earphones** ['ɪəfəʊnz] *npl* cuffia.

**earring** ['ɪərɪŋ] *n* orecchino.

**earshot** ['ɪəʃɔt] *n*: **out of/within ~** fuori portata/a portata d'orecchio.

**earth** [ə:θ] *n* (*gen, also Brit ELEC*) terra; (*of fox etc*) tana // *vt* (*Brit ELEC*) mettere a terra; **~enware** *n* terracotta; stoviglie *fpl* di terracotta // *a* di terracotta; **~quake** *n* terremoto; **~y** *a* (*fig*) grossolano(a).

**ease** [i:z] *n* agio, comodo // *vt* (*soothe*) calmare; (*loosen*) allentare; **to ~ sth out/in** tirare fuori/infilare qc con delicatezza; facilitare l'uscita/l'entrata di qc; **at ~** a proprio agio; (*MIL*) a riposo; **to ~ off** *or* **up** *vi* diminuire; (*slow down*) rallentarsi; (*fig*) rilassarsi.

**easel** ['i:zl] *n* cavalletto.

**east** [i:st] $n$ est $m$ // a dell'est // ad a oriente; **the E~** l'Oriente $m$.

**Easter** ['i:stə*] $n$ Pasqua; **~ egg** $n$ uovo di Pasqua.

**easterly** ['i:stəli] $a$ dall'est, d'oriente.

**eastern** ['i:stən] $a$ orientale, d'oriente.

**East Germany** $n$ Germania dell'Est.

**eastward(s)** ['i:stwəd(z)] $ad$ verso est, verso levante.

**easy** ['i:zi] $a$ facile; (manner) disinvolto(a) // ad: **to take it** or **things ~** prendersela con calma; **~ chair** $n$ poltrona; **~-going** $a$ accomodante.

**eat** $pt$ **ate**, $pp$ **eaten** [i:t, eit, 'i:tn] $vt$, $vi$ mangiare; **to ~ into, to ~ away at** $vt$ fus rodere.

**eaves** [i:vz] $npl$ gronda.

**eavesdrop** ['i:vzdrɔp] $vi$: **to ~ (on a conversation)** origliare (una conversazione).

**ebb** [eb] $n$ riflusso // $vi$ rifluire; (fig: also: **~ away**) declinare.

**ebony** ['ebəni] $n$ ebano.

**eccentric** [ik'sentrik] $a$, $n$ eccentrico(a).

**echo**, **~es** ['ekəu] $n$ eco $m$ or $f$ // $vt$ ripetere; fare eco a // $vi$ echeggiare; dare un eco.

**eclipse** [i'klips] $n$ eclissi $f$ inv // $vt$ eclissare.

**ecology** [i'kɔlədʒi] $n$ ecologia.

**economic** [i:kə'nɔmik] $a$ economico(a); **~al** $a$ economico(a); (person) economo(a); **~s** $n$ economia.

**economize** [i'kɔnəmaiz] $vi$ risparmiare, fare economia.

**economy** [i'kɔnəmi] $n$ economia.

**ecstasy** ['ekstəsi] $n$ estasi $f$ inv.

**eczema** ['eksimə] $n$ eczema $m$.

**edge** [edʒ] $n$ margine $m$; (of table, plate, cup) orlo; (of knife etc) taglio // $vt$ bordare; **on ~** (fig) = **edgy**; **to ~ away from** scattaiolare da; **~ways** ad di fianco; **he couldn't get a word in** ~ways non riuscì a dire una parola.

**edgy** ['edʒi] $a$ nervoso(a).

**edible** ['edibl] $a$ commestibile; (meal) mangiabile.

**edict** ['i:dikt] $n$ editto.

**Edinburgh** ['edinbərə] $n$ Edimburgo $f$.

**edit** ['edit] $vt$ curare; **~ion** [i'diʃən] $n$ edizione $f$; **~or** $n$ (in newspaper) redattore/trice; redattore/trice capo; (of sb's work) curatore/trice; **~orial** [-'tɔ:riəl] $a$ redazionale, editoriale // $n$ editoriale $m$.

**educate** ['edjukeit] $vt$ istruire; educare.

**education** [edju'keiʃən] $n$ educazione $f$; (schooling) istruzione $f$; **~al** $a$ pedagogico(a); scolastico(a); istruttivo(a).

**EEC** $n$ abbr (= European Economic Community) C.E.E. $f$ (= Comunità Economica Europea).

**eel** [i:l] $n$ anguilla.

**eerie** ['iəri] $a$ che fa accapponare la pelle.

**effect** [i'fekt] $n$ effetto // $vt$ effettuare; **~s** $npl$ (THEATRE) effetti $mpl$ scenici; **to take** (law) entrare in vigore; (drug) fare effetto; **in ~** effettivamente; **~ive** $a$ efficace; **~ively** ad efficacemente; (in reality) effettivamente; **~iveness** $n$ efficacia.

**effeminate** [i'feminit] $a$ effeminato(a).

**efficiency** [i'fiʃənsi] $n$ efficienza; rendimento effettivo.

**efficient** [i'fiʃənt] $a$ efficiente.

**effort** ['efət] $n$ sforzo.

**effrontery** [i'frʌntəri] $n$ sfrontatezza.

**effusive** [i'fju:siv] $a$ (person) espansivo(a); (welcome, letter) caloroso(a); (thanks, apologies) interminabile.

**e.g.** ad abbr (= exempli gratia) per esempio, p.es.

**egg** [eg] $n$ uovo; **to ~ on** $vt$ incitare; **~cup** $n$ portauovo $m$ inv; **~plant** $n$ (especially US) melanzana; **~shell** $n$ guscio d'uovo.

**ego** ['i:gəu] $n$ ego $m$ inv.

**egotism** ['egəʊtızəm] n egotismo.

**egotist** ['egəʊtıst] n egotista m/f.

**Egypt** ['i:dʒıpt] n Egitto; **~ian** [ı'dʒıpʃən] a, n egiziano(a).

**eiderdown** ['aıdədaʊn] n piumino.

**eight** [eıt] num otto; **~een** num diciotto; **eighth** [eıtθ] num ottavo(a); **~y** num ottanta.

**Eire** ['eərə] n Repubblica d'Irlanda.

**either** ['aıðə*] a l'uno(a) o l'altro(a), (both, each) ciascuno(a); **on ~ side** su ciascun lato // pronoun: **~ (of them)** (o) l'uno(a) o l'altro(a); **I don't like ~** non mi piace né l'uno né l'altro // ad neanche; **no, I don't ~** no, neanch'io // cj: **~ good or bad** o buono o cattivo.

**eject** [ı'dʒekt] vt espellere; lanciare.

**eke** [i:k]: **to ~ out** vt far durare; aumentare.

**elaborate** a [ı'læbərıt] elaborato(a), minuzioso(a) // vb [ı'læbəreıt] vt elaborare // vi fornire i particolari.

**elapse** [ı'læps] vi trascorrere, passare.

**elastic** [ı'læstık] a elastico(a) // n elastico; **~ band** n (Brit) elastico.

**elated** [ı'leıtıd] a pieno(a) di gioia.

**elbow** ['elbəʊ] n gomito.

**elder** ['eldə*] a maggiore, più vecchio(a) // n (tree) sambuco; **one's ~s** i più anziani; **~ly** a anziano(a) // npl: **the ~ly** gli anziani.

**eldest** ['eldıst] a, n: **the ~ (child)** il(la) maggiore (dei bambini).

**elect** [ı'lekt] vt eleggere; **to ~ to do** decidere di fare // a: **the president ~** il presidente designato; **~ion** [ı'lekʃən] n elezione f; **~ioneering** [ılekʃə'nıərıŋ] n propaganda elettorale; **~or** n elettore/trice; **~orate** n elettorato.

**electric** [ı'lektrık] a elettrico(a); **~ blanket** n coperta elettrica; **~ fire** n stufa elettrica.

**electrician** [ılek'trıʃən] n elettricista m.

**electricity** [ılek'trısıtı] n elettricità.

**electrify** [ı'lektrıfaı] vt (RAIL) elettrificare; (audience) elettrizzare.

**electrocute** [ı'lektrəʊkju:t] vt fulminare.

**electronic** [ılek'trɒnık] a elettronico(a); **~ mail** n posta elettronica; **~s** n elettronica.

**elegant** ['elıgənt] a elegante.

**element** ['elımənt] n elemento; (of heater, kettle etc) resistenza; **~ary** [-'mentərı] a elementare.

**elephant** ['elıfənt] n elefante/essa.

**elevate** ['elıveıt] vt elevare.

**elevator** ['elıveıtə*] n elevatore m; (US: lift) ascensore m.

**eleven** [ı'levn] num undici; **~ses** npl (Brit) caffè m a metà mattina; **~th** a undicesimo(a).

**elicit** [ı'lısıt] vt: **to ~ (from)** trarre (da), cavare fuori (da).

**eligible** ['elıdʒəbl] a eleggibile; (for membership) che ha i requisiti.

**ellipse** [ı'lıps] n ellisse f.

**elm** [elm] n olmo.

**elongated** ['i:lɒŋgeıtıd] a allungato(a).

**elope** [ı'ləʊp] vi (lovers) scappare.

**eloquent** ['eləkwənt] a eloquente.

**else** [els] ad altro; **something ~** qualcos'altro; **somewhere ~** altrove; **everywhere ~** in qualsiasi altro luogo; **nobody ~** nessun altro; **where ~?** in quale altro luogo?; **little ~** poco altro; **~where** ad altrove.

**elucidate** [ı'lu:sıdeıt] vt delucidare.

**elude** [ı'lu:d] vt eludere.

**elusive** [ı'lu:sıv] a elusivo(a).

**emaciated** [ı'meısıeıtıd] a emaciato(a).

**emancipate** [ı'mænsıpeıt] vt emancipare.

**embankment** [ım'bæŋkmənt] n (of road, railway) terrapieno; (riverside) argine m; (dyke) diga.

**embark** [ım'ba:k] vi: **to ~ (on)** imbarcarsi (su) // vt imbarcare; **to ~ on** (fig) imbarcarsi in; **~ation** [embɑ:'keıʃən] n imbarco.

**embarrass** [ım'bærəs] vt imbarazzare; **~ed** a imbarazzato(a); **~ing** a imbarazzante; **~ment** a imbarazzante;

imbarazzo.

**embassy** ['embəsi] n ambasciata.

**embed** [im'bɛd] vt conficcare, incastrare.

**embellish** [im'bɛlɪʃ] vt abbellire.

**embers** ['embəz] npl braci fpl.

**embezzle** [im'bɛzl] vt appropriarsi indebitamente di.

**embitter** [im'bitə*] vt amareggiare; inasprire.

**embody** [im'bɒdi] vt (features) racchiudere, comprendere; (ideas) dar forma concreta a, esprimere.

**embossed** [im'bɒst] a in rilievo; goffrato(a).

**embrace** [im'breis] vt abbracciare // vi abbracciarsi // n abbraccio.

**embroider** [im'brɔidə*] vt ricamare; (fig: story) abbellire; **~y** n ricamo.

**embryo** ['embriəu] n (also fig) embrione m.

**emerald** ['emərəld] n smeraldo.

**emerge** [i'mə:dʒ] vi apparire, sorgere.

**emergence** [i'mə:dʒəns] n apparizione f.

**emergency** [i'mə:dʒənsi] n emergenza; **in an ~** in caso di emergenza; **~ cord** n (US) segnale m d'allarme; **~ exit** n uscita di sicurezza; **~ landing** n atterraggio forzato; **the ~ services** npl (fire, police, ambulance) servizi mpl di pronto intervento.

**emery board** ['eməri-] n limetta di carta smerigliata.

**emigrate** ['emigreit] vi emigrare.

**eminent** ['eminənt] a eminente.

**emit** [i'mit] vt emettere.

**emotion** [i'məuʃən] n emozione f; **~al** a (person) emotivo(a); (scene) commovente; (tone, speech) carico(a) d'emozione.

**emperor** ['empərə*] n imperatore m.

**emphasis**, pl **-ases** ['emfəsis, -si:z] n enfasi f inv; importanza.

**emphasize** ['emfəsaiz] vt (word, point) sottolineare; (feature) mettere in evidenza.

**emphatic** [em'fætik] a (strong) vigoroso(a); (unambiguous, clear) netto(a); **~ally** ad vigorosamente; nettamente.

**empire** ['empaiə*] n impero.

**employ** [im'plɔi] vt impiegare; **~ee** [-'i:] n impiegato/a; **~er** n principale m/f, datore m di lavoro; **~ment** n impiego; **~ment agency** n agenzia di collocamento.

**empower** [im'pauə*] vt: **to ~ sb to do** concedere autorità a qn di fare.

**empress** ['empris] n imperatrice f.

**emptiness** ['emptinis] n vuoto.

**empty** ['empti] a vuoto(a); (threat, promise) vano(a) // vt vuotare; (liquid) scaricarsi // vi vuotarsi; (liquid) scaricarsi // n (bottle) vuoto; **~-handed** a a mani vuote.

**emulate** ['emjuleit] vt emulare.

**emulsion** [i'mʌlʃən] n emulsione f; **~ (paint)** n colore m a tempera.

**enable** [i'neibl] vt: **to ~ sb to do** permettere a qn di fare.

**enact** [in'ækt] vt (law) emanare; (play, scene) rappresentare.

**enamel** [i'næməl] n smalto.

**encased** [in'keist] a: **~ in** racchiuso(a) in; rivestito(a) di.

**enchant** [in'tʃɑ:nt] vt incantare; (subj: magic spell) catturare; **~ing** a incantevole, affascinante.

**encircle** [in'sə:kl] vt accerchiare.

**encl.** abbr (= enclosed) all.

**enclave** ['enkleiv] n enclave f.

**enclose** [in'kləuz] vt (land) circondare, recingere; (letter etc): **to ~ (with)** allegare (con); **please find ~d** trovi qui accluso.

**enclosure** [in'kləuʒə*] n recinto; (COMM) allegato.

**encompass** [in'kʌmpəs] vt comprendere.

**encore** [ɔŋ'kɔ:*] excl, n bis (m inv).

**encounter** [in'kauntə*] n incontro // vt incontrare.

**encourage** [in'kʌridʒ] vt incoraggiare; **~ment** n incoraggiamento.

**encroach** [in'krəutʃ] vi: **to ~**

**(up)on** (*rights*) usurpare; (*time*) abusare di; (*land*) oltrepassare i limiti di.

**encyclop(a)edia** [ɛnsaɪklou'pi:dɪə] *n* enciclopedia.

**end** [ɛnd] *n* fine *f*; (*aim*) fine *m*; (*of table*) bordo estremo // *vt* finire; (*also*: **bring to an ~, put an ~ to**) mettere fine a // *vi* finire; **in the ~** alla fine; **on ~** (*object*) ritto(a); **to stand on ~** (*hair*) rizzarsi; **for 5 hours on ~** per 5 ore di fila; **to ~ up** *vi*: **to ~ up in** finire in.

**endanger** [ɪn'deɪndʒə*] *vt* mettere in pericolo.

**endearing** [ɪn'dɪərɪŋ] *a* accattivante.

**endeavour,** (*US*) **endeavor** [ɪn'devə*] *n* sforzo, tentativo // *vi*: **to ~ to do** cercare *or* sforzarsi di fare.

**ending** ['ɛndɪŋ] *n* fine *f*, conclusione *f*; (*LING*) desinenza.

**endive** ['ɛndaɪv] *n* (*curly*) indivia (riccia); (*smooth, flat*) indivia belga.

**endless** ['ɛndlɪs] *a* senza fine; (*patience, resources*) infinito(a).

**endorse** [ɪn'dɔ:s] *vt* (*cheque*) girare; (*approve*) approvare, appoggiare; **~ment** *n* (*on driving licence*) contravvenzione registrata sulla patente.

**endow** [ɪn'dau] *vt* (*provide with money*) devolvere denaro a; (*equip*): **to ~** with fornire di, dotare di.

**endurance** [ɪn'djuərəns] *n* resistenza; pazienza.

**endure** [ɪn'djuə*] *vt* sopportare, resistere a // *vi* durare.

**enemy** ['ɛnəmɪ] *a, n* nemico(a).

**energetic** [ɛnə'dʒɛtɪk] *a* energico(a); attivo(a).

**energy** ['ɛnədʒɪ] *n* energia.

**enforce** [ɪn'fɔ:s] *vt* (*LAW*) applicare, far osservare; **~d** *a* forzato(a).

**engage** [ɪn'geɪdʒ] *vt* (*hire*) assumere; (*lawyer*) incaricare; (*attention, interest*) assorbire; (*MIL*) attaccare; (*TECH*): **to ~ gear/the clutch** innestare la marcia/la frizione // *vi* (*TECH*) ingranare; **to ~ in** impegnarsi in; **~d** *a* (*Brit*: *busy, in use*) occupato(a); (*betrothed*)

fidanzato(a); **to get ~d** fidanzarsi; **~d tone** *n* (*Brit TEL*) segnale *m* di occupato; **~ment** *n* impegno, obbligo; appuntamento; (*to marry*) fidanzamento; (*MIL*) combattimento; **~ment ring** *n* anello di fidanzamento.

**engaging** [ɪn'geɪdʒɪŋ] *a* attraente.

**engender** [ɪn'dʒɛndə*] *vt* produrre, causare.

**engine** ['ɛndʒɪn] *n* (*AUT*) motore *m*; (*RAIL*) locomotiva; **~ driver** *n* (*of train*) macchinista *m*.

**engineer** [ɛndʒɪ'nɪə*] *n* ingegnere *m*; (*US RAIL*) macchinista *m*; **~ing** *n* ingegneria.

**England** ['ɪŋglənd] *n* Inghilterra.

**English** ['ɪŋglɪʃ] *a* inglese // *n* (*LING*) inglese *m*; **the ~** *npl* gli Inglesi; **the ~ Channel** *n* la Manica; **~man/woman** *n* inglese *m/f*.

**engraving** [ɪn'greɪvɪŋ] *n* incisione *f*.

**engrossed** [ɪn'grəust] *a*: **~ in** assorbito(a) da, preso(a) da.

**engulf** [ɪn'gʌlf] *vt* inghiottire.

**enhance** [ɪn'hɑ:ns] *vt* accrescere.

**enjoy** [ɪn'dʒɔɪ] *vt* godere; (*have: success, fortune*) avere; **to ~ o.s.** godersela, divertirsi; **~able** *a* piacevole; **~ment** *n* piacere *m*, godimento.

**enlarge** [ɪn'lɑ:dʒ] *vt* ingrandire // *vi*: **to ~ on** (*subject*) dilungarsi su.

**enlighten** [ɪn'laɪtn] *vt* illuminare; dare schiarimenti a; **~ed** *a* illuminato(a); **~ment** *n*: **the E~ment** (*HISTORY*) l'Illuminismo.

**enlist** [ɪn'lɪst] *vt* arruolare; (*support*) procurare // *vi* arruolarsi.

**enmity** ['ɛnmɪtɪ] *n* inimicizia.

**enormous** [ɪ'nɔ:məs] *a* enorme.

**enough** [ɪ'nʌf] *a, n*: **~ time/books** assai tempo/libri; **have you got ~?** ne ha abbastanza *or* a sufficienza? // *ad*: **big ~** abbastanza grande; **he has not worked ~** non ha lavorato abbastanza; **~!** basta!; **that's ~, thanks** basta così, grazie; **I've had ~ of him** ne ho abbastanza di lui; ... **which, funnily ~** ... che, strano a dirsi.

**enquire** [ɪn'kwaɪə*] vt, vi = **inquire**.

**enrage** [ɪn'reɪdʒ] vt fare arrabbiare.

**enrich** [ɪn'rɪtʃ] vt arricchire.

**enrol** [ɪn'rəul] vt iscrivere // vi iscriversi; ~**ment** n iscrizione f.

**ensign** n (NAUT) ['ensən] bandiera; (MIL) ['ensaɪn] portabandiera m inv.

**ensue** [ɪn'sju:] vi seguire, risultare.

**ensure** [ɪn'ʃuə*] vt assicurare; garantire; **to ~ that** assicurarsi che.

**entail** [ɪn'teɪl] vt comportare.

**entangle** [ɪn'tæŋgl] vt impigliare.

**enter** ['entə*] vt (room) entrare in; (club) associarsi a; (army) arruolarsi in; (competition) partecipare a; (sb for a competition) iscrivere; (write down) registrare; (COMPUT) inserire // vi entrare; **to ~ for** vt fus iscriversi a; **to ~ into** vt fus (explanation) cominciare a dare; (debate) partecipare a; (agreement) concludere; **to ~ (up)on** vt fus cominciare.

**enterprise** ['entəpraɪz] n (undertaking, company) impresa; (spirit) iniziativa; **free ~** liberalismo economico; **private ~** iniziativa privata.

**enterprising** ['entəpraɪzɪŋ] a intraprendente.

**entertain** [entə'teɪn] vt divertire; (invite) ricevere; (idea, plan) nutrire; ~**er** n comico/a; ~**ing** a divertente; ~**ment** n (amusement) divertimento; (show) spettacolo.

**enthralled** [ɪn'θrɔ:ld] a affascinato(a).

**enthusiasm** [ɪn'θu:zɪæzəm] n entusiasmo.

**enthusiast** [ɪn'θu:zɪæst] n entusiasta m/f; ~**ic** [-'æstɪk] a entusiasta, entusiastico(a); **to be ~ic about** sth/sb essere appassionato di qc/ entusiasta di qn.

**entice** [ɪn'taɪs] vt allettare, sedurre.

**entire** [ɪn'taɪə*] a intero(a); ~**ly** ad completamente, interamente; ~**ty** [ɪn'taɪərətɪ] n: **in its ~ty** nel suo complesso.

**entitle** [ɪn'taɪtl] vt (give right): **to ~ sb to sth/to do** dare diritto a qn a qc/a fare; ~**d** a (book) che si intitola; **to be ~d to do** avere il diritto di fare.

**entrails** ['entreɪlz] npl interiora fpl.

**entrance** n ['entrəns] entrata, ingresso; (of person) entrata // vi [ɪn'trɑ:ns] incantare, rapire; **to gain ~ to** (university etc) essere ammesso a; ~ **examination** n esame m di ammissione; ~ **fee** n tassa d'iscrizione; (to museum etc) prezzo d'ingresso; ~ **ramp** n (US AUT) rampa di accesso.

**entrant** ['entrnt] n partecipante m/f; concorrente m/f.

**entreat** [en'tri:t] vt supplicare.

**entrenched** [en'trentʃt] a radicato(a).

**entrepreneur** [ɔntrəprə'nə:*] n imprenditore m.

**entrust** [ɪn'trʌst] vt: **to ~ sth to** affidare qc a.

**entry** ['entrɪ] n entrata; (way in) entrata, ingresso; (item: on list) iscrizione f; (in dictionary) voce f; **no ~** vietato l'ingresso; (AUT) divieto di accesso; ~ **form** n modulo d'iscrizione; ~ **phone** n citofono.

**envelop** [ɪn'vɛləp] vt avvolgere, avviluppare.

**envelope** ['ɛnvələup] n busta.

**envious** ['ɛnvɪəs] a invidioso(a).

**environment** [ɪn'vaɪərnmənt] n ambiente m; ~**al** [-'mentl] a ecologico(a); ambientale.

**envisage** [ɪn'vɪzɪdʒ] vt immaginare; prevedere.

**envoy** ['ɛnvɔɪ] n inviato/a.

**envy** ['ɛnvɪ] n invidia // vt invidiare; **to ~ sb sth** invidiare qn per qc.

**epic** ['ɛpɪk] n poema m epico // a epico(a).

**epidemic** [ɛpɪ'demɪk] n epidemia.

**epilepsy** ['ɛpɪlepsɪ] n epilessia.

**episode** ['ɛpɪsəud] n episodio.

**epistle** [ɪ'pɪsl] n epistola.

**epitome** [ɪ'pɪtəmɪ] n epitome f; quintessenza; **epitomize** vt (fig) incarnare.

**equable** ['ɛkwəbl] *a* uniforme; equilibrato(a).

**equal** ['iːkwl] *a*, *n* uguale (*m/f*) // *vt* uguagliare; ~ **to** (task) all'altezza di; ~**ity** [iːˈkwɔlɪtɪ] *n* uguaglianza; ~**ize** *vt*, *vi* pareggiare; ~**izer** *n* pareggio; ~**ly** *ad* ugualmente.

**equanimity** [ɛkwəˈnɪmɪtɪ] *n* serenità.

**equate** [ɪˈkweɪt] *vt*: **to** ~ **sth with** considerare qc uguale a; (compare) paragonare qc con; **equation** [ɪˈkweɪʃən] *n* (MATH) equazione *f*.

**equator** [ɪˈkweɪtə*] *n* equatore *m*.

**equilibrium** [iːkwɪˈlɪbrɪəm] *n* equilibrio.

**equip** [ɪˈkwɪp] *vt* equipaggiare, attrezzare; **to** ~ **sb/sth with** fornire qn/qc di; **to be well** ~**ped** (office etc) essere ben attrezzato(a); **he is well** ~**ped for the job** ha i requisiti necessari per quel lavoro; ~**ment** *n* attrezzatura; (electrical etc) apparecchiatura.

**equitable** ['ɛkwɪtəbl] *a* equo(a), giusto(a).

**equities** ['ɛkwɪtɪz] *npl* (Brit COMM) azioni *fpl* ordinarie.

**equivalent** [ɪˈkwɪvələnt] *a*, *n* equivalente (*m*); **to be** ~ **to** equivalere a.

**equivocal** [ɪˈkwɪvəkl] *a* equivoco(a); (open to suspicion) dubbio(a).

**era** ['ɪərə] *n* era, età *f inv*.

**eradicate** [ɪˈrædɪkeɪt] *vt* sradicare.

**erase** [ɪˈreɪz] *vt* cancellare; ~**r** *n* gomma.

**erect** [ɪˈrɛkt] *a* eretto(a) // *vt* costruire; (monument, tent) alzare; ~**ion** [ɪˈrɛkʃən] *n* erezione *f*.

**ermine** ['əːmɪn] *n* ermellino.

**erode** [ɪˈrəud] *vt* erodere; (metal) corrodere.

**erotic** [ɪˈrɔtɪk] *a* erotico(a).

**err** [əː*] *vi* errare; (REL) peccare.

**errand** ['ɛrnd] *n* commissione *f*.

**erratic** [ɪˈrætɪk] *a* imprevedibile; (person, mood) incostante.

**error** ['ɛrə*] *n* errore *m*.

**erupt** [ɪˈrʌpt] *vi* erompere; (volcano) mettersi (or essere) in eruzione; ~**ion** [ɪˈrʌpʃən] *n* eruzione *f*.

**escalate** ['ɛskəleɪt] *vi* intensificarsi.

**escalator** ['ɛskəleɪtə*] *n* scala mobile.

**escapade** [ɛskəˈpeɪd] *n* scappatella; avventura.

**escape** [ɪˈskeɪp] *n* evasione *f*; fuga; (of gas etc) fuga, fuoriuscita // *vi* fuggire; (from jail) evadere, scappare; (fig) sfuggire; (leak) uscire // *vt* sfuggire a; **to** ~ **from sb** sfuggire a qn; **escapism** *n* evasione *f* (dalla realtà).

**escort** *n* ['ɛskɔːt] scorta; (male companion) cavaliere *m* // *vt* [ɪˈskɔːt] scortare; accompagnare.

**Eskimo** ['ɛskɪməu] *n* eschimese *m/f*.

**especially** [ɪˈspɛʃlɪ] *ad* specialmente; soprattutto; espressamente.

**espionage** ['ɛspɪənɑːʒ] *n* spionaggio.

**Esquire** [ɪˈskwaɪə*] *n* (abbr Esq.): **J. Brown,** ~ Signor J. Brown.

**essay** ['ɛseɪ] *n* (SCOL) composizione *f*; (LITERATURE) saggio.

**essence** ['ɛsns] *n* essenza.

**essential** [ɪˈsɛnʃl] *a* essenziale; (basic) fondamentale // *n* essenziale; ~**ly** *ad* essenzialmente.

**establish** [ɪˈstæblɪʃ] *vt* stabilire; (business) mettere su; (one's power etc) confermare; ~**ment** *n* stabilimento; **the E~ment** la classe dirigente, l'establishment *m*.

**estate** [ɪˈsteɪt] *n* proprietà *f inv*; beni *mpl*, patrimonio; ~ **agent** *n* (Brit) agente *m* immobiliare; ~ **car** *n* (Brit) giardiniera.

**esteem** [ɪˈstiːm] *n* stima // *vt* (think highly of) stimare; (consider) considerare.

**esthetic** [ɪsˈθɛtɪk] *a* (US) = **aesthetic**.

**estimate** *n* ['ɛstɪmət] stima; (COMM) preventivo // *vt* ['ɛstɪmeɪt] stimare, valutare; **estimation** [-ˈmeɪʃən] *n* stima; opinione *f*.

**estranged** [ɪˈstreɪndʒd] *a*

separato(a).

**etc** abbr (= et cetera) etc., ecc.

**etching** ['etʃɪŋ] n acquaforte f.

**eternal** [ɪ'tɜːnl] a eterno(a).

**eternity** [ɪ'tɜːnɪtɪ] n eternità.

**ether** ['iːθəˀ] n etere m.

**ethical** ['eθɪkl] a etico(a), morale.

**ethics** ['eθɪks] n etica // npl morale f.

**Ethiopia** [iːθɪ'əupɪə] n Etiopia.

**ethnic** ['eθnɪk] a etnico(a).

**ethos** ['iːθɒs] n norma di vita.

**etiquette** ['etɪket] n etichetta.

**Eurocheque** ['juərəutʃek] n euro-chèque m inv.

**Europe** ['juərəp] n Europa; **~an** [-'piːən] a, n europeo(a).

**evacuate** [ɪ'vækjueɪt] vt evacuare.

**evade** [ɪ'veɪd] vt eludere; (duties etc) sottrarsi a.

**evaluate** [ɪ'væljueɪt] vt valutare.

**evaporate** [ɪ'væpəreɪt] vi evaporare // vi far evaporare; **~d milk** n latte m concentrato.

**evasion** [ɪ'veɪʒən] n evasione f.

**evasive** [ɪ'veɪsɪv] a evasivo(a).

**eve** [iːv] n: **on the ~ of** alla vigilia di.

**even** ['iːvn] a regolare; (number) pari inv // ad anche, perfino; ~ **if,** ~ **though** anche se; ~ **more** ancora di più; ~ **so** ciò nonostante; **not** ~ nemmeno; **to get** ~ **with sb** dare la pari a qn; **to** ~ **out** vi pareggiare.

**evening** ['iːvnɪŋ] n sera; (as duration, event) serata; **in the** ~ la sera; ~ **class** n corso serale; ~ **dress** n (woman's) abito da sera; **in** ~ **dress** (man) in abito scuro; (woman) in abito lungo.

**event** [ɪ'vent] n avvenimento; (SPORT) gara; **in the** ~ **of** in caso di; **~ful** a denso(a) di eventi.

**eventual** [ɪ'ventʃuəl] a finale; **~ity** [-'ælɪtɪ] n possibilità f inv, eventualità f inv; **~ly** ad finalmente.

**ever** ['evəˀ] ad mai; (at all times) sempre; **the best** ~ il migliore che ci sia mai stato; **have you** ~ **seen it?** l'ha mai visto?; ~ **since** ad da allora // cj sin da quando; ~ **so**

**pretty** così bello(a); **~green** n sempreverde m; **~lasting** a eterno(a).

**every** ['evrɪ] a ogni; ~ **day** tutti i giorni, ogni giorno; ~ **other/third day** ogni due/tre giorni; ~ **other car** una macchina su due; ~ **now and then** ogni tanto, di quando in quando; **~body** pronoun ognuno, tutti pl; **~day** a quotidiano(a); di ogni giorno; **~one** = **~body**; **~thing** pronoun tutto, ogni cosa; **~where** ad (gen) dappertutto; (wherever) ovunque.

**evict** [ɪ'vɪkt] vt sfrattare.

**evidence** ['evɪdns] n (proof) prova; (of witness) testimonianza; (sign): **to show** ~ **of** dare segni di; **to give** ~ deporre.

**evident** ['evɪdnt] a evidente; **~ly** ad evidentemente.

**evil** ['iːvl] a cattivo(a), maligno(a) // n male m.

**evoke** [ɪ'vəuk] vt evocare.

**evolution** [iːvə'luːʃən] n evoluzione f.

**evolve** [ɪ'vɒlv] vt elaborare // vi svilupparsi, evolversi.

**ewe** [juː] n pecora.

**ex-** [eks] prefix ex.

**exacerbate** [eks'æsəbeɪt] vt aggravare.

**exact** [ɪg'zækt] a esatto(a) // vt: **to** ~ **sth (from)** estorcere qc (da); esigere qc (da); **~ing** a esigente; (work) faticoso(a); **~itude** n esattezza, precisione f; **~ly** ad esattamente.

**exaggerate** [ɪg'zædʒəreɪt] vt, vi esagerare; **exaggeration** [-'reɪʃən] n esagerazione f.

**exalted** [ɪg'zɔːltɪd] a esaltato(a); elevato(a).

**exam** [ɪg'zæm] n abbr (SCOL) = **examination.**

**examination** [ɪgzæmɪ'neɪʃən] n (SCOL) esame m; (MED) controllo.

**examine** [ɪg'zæmɪn] vt esaminare; (LAW: person) interrogare; **~r** n esaminatore/trice.

**example** [ɪg'zɑːmpl] n esempio; **for**

~ ad or per esempio.

**exasperate** [ɪgˈzɑːspəreɪt] vt esasperare; **exasperating** a esasperante; **exasperation** [-ˈreɪʃən] n esasperazione f.

**excavate** [ˈekskəveɪt] vt scavare.

**exceed** [ɪkˈsiːd] vt superare; (one's powers, time limit) oltrepassare; ~**ingly** ad eccessivamente.

**excellent** [ˈeksələnt] a eccellente.

**except** [ɪkˈsept] prep (also: ~ for, ~ing) salvo, all'infuori di, eccetto // vt escludere; ~ **if/when** salvo se/ quando; ~ **that** salvo che; ~**ion** [ɪkˈsepʃən] n eccezione f; to take ~**ion** to trovare a ridire su; ~**ional** [ɪkˈsepʃənl] a eccezionale.

**excerpt** [ˈeksəːpt] n estratto.

**excess** [ɪkˈses] n eccesso; ~ **baggage** n bagaglio in eccedenza; ~ **fare** n supplemento; ~**ive** a eccessivo(a).

**exchange** [ɪksˈtʃeɪndʒ] n scambio; (also: **telephone** ~) centralino // vt: to ~ (**for**) scambiare (con); ~ **rate** n tasso di cambio.

**Exchequer** [ɪksˈtʃekə*] n: the ~ (Brit) lo Scacchiere, ≈ il ministero delle Finanze.

**excise** [ˈeksaɪz] n imposta, dazio.

**excite** [ɪkˈsaɪt] vt eccitare; to get ~**d** eccitarsi; ~**ment** n eccitazione f; agitazione f; **exciting** a avventuroso(a); (film, book) appassionante.

**exclaim** [ɪksˈkleɪm] vi esclamare; **exclamation** [ekskləˈmeɪʃən] n esclamazione f; **exclamation mark** n punto esclamativo.

**exclude** [ɪksˈkluːd] vt escludere.

**exclusive** [ɪksˈkluːsɪv] a esclusivo(a); (club) selettivo(a); (district) snob inv; ~ **of VAT** I.V.A. esclusa.

**excommunicate** [ekskəˈmjuːnɪkeɪt] vt scomunicare.

**excruciating** [ɪkˈskruːʃɪeɪtɪŋ] a straziante, atroce.

**excursion** [ɪkˈskəːʃən] n escursione f, gita.

**excuse** n [ɪkˈskjuːs] scusa // vt

**ex-directory** [ˈeksdɪˈrektərɪ] a (Brit TEL): to be ~ non essere sull'elenco.

**execute** [ˈeksɪkjuːt] vt (prisoner) giustiziare; (plan etc) eseguire.

**execution** [eksɪˈkjuːʃən] n esecuzione f; ~**er** n boia m inv.

**executive** [ɪgˈzekjutɪv] n (COMM) dirigente m; (POL) esecutivo // a esecutivo(a).

**exemplify** [ɪgˈzemplɪfaɪ] vt esemplificare.

**exempt** [ɪgˈzempt] a esentato(a) // vt: to ~ **sb from** esentare qn da; ~**ion** [ɪgˈzempʃən] n esenzione f.

**exercise** [ˈeksəsaɪz] n esercizio // vt esercitare; (dog) portar fuori // vi fare del movimento or moto; ~ **book** n quaderno.

**exert** [ɪgˈzəːt] vt esercitare; to ~ o.s. sforzarsi; ~**ion** [-ʃən] n sforzo.

**exhaust** [ɪgˈzɔːst] n (also: ~ **fumes**) scappamento; (also: ~ **pipe**) tubo di scappamento // vt esaurire; ~**ed** a esaurito(a); ~**ion** [ɪgˈzɔːstʃən] n esaurimento; **nervous** ~**ion** sovraffaticamento mentale; ~**ive** a esauriente.

**exhibit** [ɪgˈzɪbɪt] n (ART) oggetto esposto; (LAW) documento or oggetto esibito // vt esporre; (courage, skill) dimostrare; ~**ion** [eksɪˈbɪʃən] n mostra, esposizione f.

**exhilarating** [ɪgˈzɪləreɪtɪŋ] a esilarante; stimolante.

**exhort** [ɪgˈzɔːt] vt esortare.

**exile** [ˈeksaɪl] n esilio; (person) esiliato/a // vt esiliare.

**exist** [ɪgˈzɪst] vi esistere; ~**ence** n esistenza; to be in ~**ence** esistere; ~**ent** a esistente.

**exit** [ˈeksɪt] n uscita // vi (THEATRE, COMPUT) uscire; ~ **ramp** n (US AUT) rampa di uscita.

**exodus** [ˈeksədəs] n esodo.

**exonerate** [ɪgˈzɔnəret] vt: to ~

from discolpare da.

**exotic** [ɪg'zɔtɪk] a esotico(a).

**expand** [ɪk'spænd] vt espandere; estendere; allargare // vi (trade etc) svilupparsi, ampliarsi; espandersi; (gas) espandersi; (metal) dilatarsi.

**expanse** [ɪk'spæns] n distesa, estensione f.

**expansion** [ɪk'spænʃən] n (gen) espansione f; (of town, economy) sviluppo; (of metal) dilatazione f.

**expect** [ɪk'spɛkt] vt (anticipate) prevedere, aspettarsi, prevedere or aspettarsi che + sub; (count on) contare su; (hope for) sperare; (require) richiedere, esigere; (suppose) supporre; (await, also baby) aspettare // vi: to be ~ing essere in stato interessante; to ~ sb to do aspettarsi che qn faccia; ~ancy n (anticipation) attesa; life ~ancy probabilità fpl di vita; ~ant mother n gestante f; ~ation [ɛkspɛk'teɪʃən] n aspettativa; speranza.

**expedience, expediency** [ɪk'spi:dɪəns, ɪk'spi:dɪənsɪ] n convenienza.

**expedient** [ɪk'spi:dɪənt] a conveniente; vantaggioso(a) // n espediente m.

**expedite** ['ɛkspədaɪt] vt sbrigare; facilitare.

**expedition** [ɛkspə'dɪʃən] n spedizione f.

**expel** [ɪk'spɛl] vt espellere.

**expend** [ɪk'spɛnd] vt spendere; (use up) consumare; ~able a sacrificabile; ~iture [ɪk'spɛndɪtʃə*] n spesa.

**expense** [ɪk'spɛns] n spesa; (high cost) costo; ~s npl (COMM) spese fpl, indennità fpl; at the ~ of a spese di; ~ account n conto m spese inv.

**expensive** [ɪk'spɛnsɪv] a caro(a), costoso(a).

**experience** [ɪk'spɪərɪəns] n (knowledge, activity) vt (pleasure) provare; (hardship) soffrire; ~d a esperto(a).

**experiment** n [ɪk'spɛrɪmənt] esperimento, esperienza // vi [ɪk'spɛrɪment] fare esperimenti; to ~ with sperimentare.

**expert** ['ɛkspə:t] a, n esperto(a); ~ise [-'ti:z] n competenza.

**expire** [ɪk'spaɪə*] vi (period of time, licence) scadere; **expiry** n scadenza.

**explain** [ɪk'spleɪn] vt spiegare; **explanation** [ɛksplə'neɪʃən] n spiegazione f; **explanatory** [ɪk'splænətrɪ] a esplicativo(a).

**explicit** [ɪk'splɪsɪt] a esplicito(a); (definite) netto(a).

**explode** [ɪk'spləud] vi esplodere.

**exploit** n ['ɛksplɔɪt] impresa // vt [ɪk'splɔɪt] sfruttare; ~ation [-'teɪʃən] n sfruttamento.

**exploratory** [ɪk'splɔrətrɪ] a (fig: talks) esplorativo(a).

**explore** [ɪk'splɔ:*] vt esplorare; (possibilities) esaminare; ~r n esploratore/trice.

**explosion** [ɪk'spləuʒən] n esplosione f.

**explosive** [ɪk'spləusɪv] a esplosivo(a) // n esplosivo.

**exponent** [ɛk'spəunənt] n esponente m/f.

**export** vt [ɛk'spɔ:t] esportare // n ['ɛkspɔ:t] esportazione f; articolo di esportazione // cpd d'esportazione; ~er n esportatore m.

**expose** [ɪk'spəuz] vt esporre; (unmask) smascherare; ~d a (position) esposto(a).

**exposure** [ɪk'spəuʒə*] n esposizione f; (PHOT) posa; (MED) assideramento; ~ meter n esposimetro.

**expound** [ɪk'spaund] vt esporre.

**express** [ɪk'sprɛs] a (definite) chiaro(a), espresso(a); (Brit: letter etc) espresso inv // n (train) espresso // ad (send) espresso // vt esprimere; ~ion [ɪk'sprɛʃən] n espressione f; ~ive a espressivo(a); ~ly ad espressamente; ~way n (US: urban motorway) autostrada che attraversa la città.

**exquisite** [ɛk'skwɪzɪt] a squisito(a).

**extend** [ɪk'stɛnd] vt (visit) protrarre; (road, deadline) prolungare; (building) ampliare; (offer) offrire, porgere // vi (land) estendersi.

**extension** [ɪk'stɛnʃən] n (of road, term) prolungamento; (of contract, deadline) proroga; (building) annesso; (to wire, table) prolunga; (telephone) interno; (: in private house) apparecchio supplementare.

**extensive** [ɪk'stɛnsɪv] a vaste(a), ampio(a); (damage) su larga scala; (alterations) notevole; (inquiries) esauriente; (use) grande; ~ly ad: he's travelled ~ly ha viaggiato molto.

**extent** [ɪk'stɛnt] n estensione f; to some ~ fino a un certo punto; to what ~? fino a che punto?; to the ~ of ... fino al punto di ...

**extenuating** [ɪks'tɛnjueɪtɪŋ] a: ~ circumstances attenuanti fpl.

**exterior** [ɛk'stɪərɪə*] a esteriore, esterno(a) // n esteriore m, esterno; aspetto (esteriore).

**exterminate** [ɪk'stɜːmɪneɪt] vt sterminare.

**external** [ɪk'stɜːnl] a esterno(a), esteriore.

**extinct** [ɪk'stɪŋkt] a estinto(a).

**extinguish** [ɪk'stɪŋwɪʃ] vt estinguere; ~er n estintore m.

**extort** [ɪk'stɔːt] vt: to ~ sth (from) estorcere qc (da); ~ionate [ɪk'stɔːʃnət] a esorbitante.

**extra** ['ɛkstrə] a extra inv, supplementare // ad (in addition) di più // n supplemento; (THEATRE) comparso.

**extra...** ['ɛkstrə] prefix extra... .

**extract** vt [ɪk'strækt] estrarre; (money, promise) strappare // n ['ɛkstrækt] estratto; (passage) brano.

**extracurricular** ['ɛkstrəkə'rɪkjulə*] a parascolastico(a).

**extradite** ['ɛkstrədaɪt] vt estradare.

**extramarital** [ɛkstrə'mærɪtl] a extraconiugale.

**extramural** [ɛkstrə'mjuərl] a fuori dell'università.

**extraordinary** [ɪk'strɔːdnrɪ] a straordinario(a).

**extravagance** [ɪk'strævəgəns] n sperpero; stravaganza.

**extravagant** [ɪk'strævəgənt] a stravagante; (in spending) dispendioso(a).

**extreme** [ɪk'striːm] a estremo(a) // n estremo; ~ly ad estremamente.

**extricate** ['ɛkstrɪkeɪt] vt: to ~ sth (from) districare qc (da).

**extrovert** ['ɛkstrəvəːt] n estroverso/a.

**exude** [ɪg'zjuːd] vt trasudare; (fig) emanare.

**eye** [aɪ] n occhio; (of needle) cruna // vt osservare; to keep an ~ on tenere d'occhio; ~ball n globo dell'occhio; ~bath n occhino; ~brow n sopracciglio; ~brow pencil n matita per le sopracciglia; ~drops npl gocce fpl oculari, collirio; ~lash n ciglio; ~lid n palpebra; ~ liner n eye-liner m inv; ~opener n rivelazione f; ~shadow n ombretto; ~sight n vista; ~sore n pugno nell'occhio; ~ witness n testimone m/f oculare.

# F

**F** [ɛf] n (MUS) fa m.

**fable** ['feɪbl] n favola.

**fabric** ['fæbrɪk] n stoffa, tessuto.

**fabrication** [fæbrɪ'keɪʃən] n fabricazione f; falsificazione f.

**fabulous** ['fæbjuləs] a favoloso(a); (col: super) favoloso(a), fantastico(a).

**façade** [fə'sɑːd] n facciata.

**face** [feɪs] n faccia, viso, volto; (expression) faccia; (grimace) smorfia; (of clock) quadrante m; (of building) facciata; (side, surface) faccia // vt essere di fronte a; (fig) affrontare; ~ down a (person) faccia a terra; to make or pull a ~ fare una smorfia; in the ~ of (difficulties etc) di fronte a; on the ~ of it a prima vista; ~ to ~ to faccia a faccia; **to ~ up to** vt fus affrontare, far fronte a; **~ cloth** n (Brit) guanto di spugna; **~ cream** n crema per il viso; **~ lift** n lifting m inv; (of façade etc) ripulita.

**facet** ['fæsɪt] n faccetta, sfaccettatura; (fig) sfaccettatura.

**facetious** [fə'si:ʃəs] a faceto(a).

**face value** n (of coin) valore m facciale or nominale; **to take sth at** ~ (fig) giudicare qc dalle apparenze.

**facilities** [fə'sɪlɪtz] npl attrezzature fpl; **credit ~** facilitazioni fpl di credito.

**facing** ['feɪsɪŋ] prep di fronte a // n (of wall etc) rivestimento; (SEWING) paramontura.

**facsimile** [fæk'sɪmɪlɪ] n facsimile m inv; ~ **machine** n telecopiatrice f.

**fact** [fækt] n fatto; **in** ~ infatti.

**factor** ['fæktə*] n fattore m.

**factory** ['fæktərɪ] n fabbrica, stabilimento.

**factual** ['fæktjuəl] a che si attiene ai fatti.

**faculty** ['fækəltɪ] n facoltà f inv.

**fad** [fæd] n mania; capriccio.

**fade** [feɪd] vi sbiadire, sbiadirsi; (light, sound, hope) attenuarsi, affievolirsi; (flower) appassire.

**fag** [fæg] n (col: cigarette) cicca.

**fail** [feɪl] vt (exam) non superare; (candidate) bocciare; (subj: courage, memory) mancare a // vi fallire; (student) essere respinto(a); (supplies) mancare; (eyesight, health, light) venire a mancare; **to ~ to do sth** (neglect) mancare di fare qc; (be unable) non riuscire a fare qc; **without ~** senza fallo; certamente; ~**ing** n difetto // prep in mancanza di; ~**ure** ['feɪljə*] n fallimento; (person) fallito(a); (mechanical etc) guasto.

**faint** [feɪnt] a debole; (recollection) vago(a); (mark) indistinto(a) // vi svenire; **to feel** ~ sentirsi svenire.

**fair** [fɛə*] a (person, decision) giusto(a), equo(a); (hair etc) biondo(a); (skin, complexion) bianco(a);

(weather) bello(a), clemente; (good enough) assai buono(a); (sizeable) bello(a) // ad (play) lealmente // n fiera; (Brit: funfair) luna park m inv; ~**ly** ad equamente; (quite) abbastanza; ~**ness** n equità, giustizia; ~ **play** n correttezza.

**fairy** ['fɛərɪ] n fata; ~ **tale** n fiaba.

**faith** [feɪθ] n fede f; (trust) fiducia; (sect) religione f, fede f; ~**ful** a fedele; ~**fully** ad fedelmente; **yours** ~**fully** (Brit: in letters) distinti saluti.

**fake** [feɪk] n imitazione f; (picture) falso; (person) impostore/a // a falso(a) // vt (accounts) falsificare; (illness) fingere; (painting) contraffare.

**falcon** ['fɔ:lkən] n falco, falcone m.

**fall** [fɔ:l] n caduta; (in temperature) abbassamento; (in price) ribasso; (US: autumn) autunno // vi (pt fell, pp fallen) cadere; (temperature, price) abbassare; ~**s** npl (waterfall) cascate fpl; **to ~ flat** vi (on one's face) cadere bocconi; (joke) fare cilecca; (plan) fallire; **to ~ back** vi (retreat) indietreggiare; (MIL) ritirarsi; **to ~ back on** vt fus (remedy etc) ripiegare su; **to ~ behind** vi rimanere indietro; **to ~ down** vi (person) cadere; (building) crollare; **to ~ for** vt fus (person) prendere una cotta per; **to ~ for a trick** (or a story etc) cascarci; **to ~ in** vi crollare; (MIL) mettersi in riga; **to ~ off** vi cadere; (diminish) diminuire, abbassarsi; **to ~ out** vi (friends etc) litigare; **to ~ through** vi (plan, project) fallire.

**fallacy** ['fæləsɪ] n errore m.

**fallen** ['fɔ:lən] pp of **fall**.

**fallout** ['fɔ:laut] n fall-out m; ~ **shelter** n rifugio antiatomico.

**fallow** ['fæləu] a incolto(a), a maggese.

**false** [fɔ:ls] a falso(a); **under ~ pretences** con l'inganno; ~ **teeth** npl (Brit) denti mpl finti.

**falter** ['fɔ:ltə*] vi esitare, vacillare.

**fame** [feɪm] n fama, celebrità.

**familiar** [fə'mɪlɪə*] a familiare; (common) comune; (close) intimo(a); **to be ~ with** (subject) conoscere; **~ity** [fəmɪlɪ'ærɪtɪ] n familiarità; intimità; **~ize** [fə'mɪlɪəraɪz] vt: **to ~ize sb with sth** far conoscere qc a qn.

**family** ['fæmɪlɪ] n famiglia.

**famine** ['fæmɪn] n carestia.

**famished** ['fæmɪʃt] a affamato(a).

**famous** ['feɪməs] a famoso(a); **~ly** ad (get on) a meraviglia.

**fan** [fæn] n (folding) ventaglio; (ELEC) ventilatore m; (person) ammiratore/trice; tifoso/a // vt far vento a; (fire, quarrel) alimentare; **to ~ out** vi spargersi a ventaglio).

**fanatic** [fə'nætɪk] n fanatico/a.

**fan belt** n cinghia del ventilatore.

**fanciful** ['fænsɪful] a fantasioso(a); (object) di fantasia.

**fancy** ['fænsɪ] n immaginazione f, fantasia; (whim) capriccio // a (di) fantasia inv // vt (feel like, want) aver voglia di; (imagine) immaginare, pensare; **to ~ that ~** credere, pensare; **to take a ~ to** incapricciarsi di; **~ dress** n costume m (per maschera); **~-dress ball** n ballo in maschera.

**fang** [fæŋ] n zanna; (of snake) dente m.

**fantastic** [fæn'tæstɪk] a fantastico(a).

**fantasy** ['fæntəsɪ] n fantasia, immaginazione f; fantasticheria; chimera.

**far** [fɑ:*] a: the **~ side/end** l'altra parte/l'altro capo // ad lontano; **~ away**, **~ off** lontano, distante; **~ better** assai migliore; **~ from** lontano da; **by ~** di gran lunga; **go as ~ as the farm** vada fino alla fattoria; **as ~ as I know** per quel che so; **~away** a lontano(a).

**farce** [fɑ:s] n farsa.

**farcical** ['fɑ:sɪkəl] a farsesco(a).

**fare** [fɛə*] n (on trains, buses) tariffa; (in taxi) prezzo della corsa; (food) vitto, cibo // vi passarsela; **half ~** metà tariffa; **full ~** tariffa intera.

**Far East** n: the **~** l'Estremo Oriente m.

**farewell** [fɛə'wɛl] excl, n addio.

**farm** [fɑ:m] n fattoria, podere m // vt coltivare; **~er** n coltivatore/trice; agricoltore/trice; **~hand** n bracciante m agricolo; **~house** n fattoria; **~ing** n agricoltura; **~ worker** n = **~hand**; **~yard** n aia.

**far-reaching** ['fɑ:'ri:tʃɪŋ] a di vasta portata.

**fart** [fɑ:t] (col!) n scoreggia(!) // vi scoreggiare (!).

**farther** ['fɑ:ðə*] ad più lontano // a più lontano(a).

**farthest** ['fɑ:ðɪst] superlative of **far**.

**fascinate** ['fæsɪneɪt] vt affascinare; **fascinating** a affascinante; **fascination** [-'neɪʃən] n fascino.

**fascism** ['fæʃɪzəm] n fascismo.

**fascist** ['fæʃɪst] a, n fascista (m/f).

**fashion** ['fæʃən] n moda; (manner) maniera, modo // vt foggiare, formare; **in ~** alla moda; **out of ~** passato(a) di moda; **~able** a alla moda, di moda; **~ show** n sfilata di moda.

**fast** [fɑ:st] a rapido(a), svelto(a), veloce; (clock): **to be ~** andare avanti; (dye, colour) solido(a) // ad rapidamente; (stuck, held) saldamente // n digiuno // vi digiunare; **~ asleep** profondamente addormentato.

**fasten** ['fɑ:sn] vt chiudere, fissare; (coat) abbottonare, allacciare // vi chiudersi, fissarsi; **~er**, **~ing** n fermaglio, chiusura.

**fast food** n fast food m.

**fastidious** [fæs'tɪdɪəs] a esigente, difficile.

**fat** [fæt] a grasso(a) // n grasso.

**fatal** ['feɪtl] a fatale; mortale; disastroso(a); **~ity** [fə'tælɪtɪ] n (road death etc) morto/a, vittima; **~ly** ad a morte.

**fate** [feɪt] n destino; (of person) sorte f; **~ful** a fatidico(a).

**father** ['fɑ:ðə*] n padre m; **~-in-law** n suocero; **~ly** a paterno(a).

**fathom** ['fæðəm] n braccio (= 1828 mm) // vt (mystery) penetrare, sondare.

**fatigue** [fə'ti:g] n stanchezza; (MIL) corvé f.

**fatten** ['fætn] vt, vi ingrassare.

**fatty** ['fæti] a (food) grasso(a) // n (col) ciccione/a.

**fatuous** ['fætjuəs] a fatuo(a).

**faucet** ['fɔ:sɪt] n (US) rubinetto.

**fault** [fɔ:lt] n colpa; (TENNIS) fallo; (defect) difetto; (GEO) faglia // vt criticare; it's my ~ è colpa mia; to find ~ with trovare da ridire su; at ~ in fallo; to a ~ eccessivamente; ~less a perfetto(a); senza difetto, impeccabile; ~y a difettoso(a).

**fauna** ['fɔ:nə] n fauna.

**faux pas** ['fou'pɑ:] n gaffe f inv.

**favour, favor** ['feɪvə*] n favore m, cortesia, piacere m // vt (proposition) favorire, essere favorevole a; (pupil etc) favorire; (team, horse) dare per vincente; to do sb a ~ fare un favore or una cortesia a qn; to find ~ with (subj: person) entrare nelle buone grazie di; (: suggestion) avere l'approvazione di; in ~ of in favore di; ~able a favorevole; ~ite [-rɪt] a, n favorito(a).

**fawn** [fɔ:n] n daino // a (also: ~-coloured) marrone chiaro inv // vi: to ~ (up)on adulare servilmente.

**fax** [fæks] n (document) facsimile m inv, telecopia; (machine) telecopiatrice f.

**FBI** n abbr (US: = Federal Bureau of Investigation) F.B.I. f.

**fear** [fɪə*] n paura, timore m // vt aver paura di, temere; for ~ of per paura di; ~ful a pauroso(a); (sight, noise) terribile, spaventoso(a).

**feasibility** [fi:zə'bɪlɪtɪ] n praticabilità.

**feasible** ['fi:zəbl] a possibile, realizzabile.

**feast** [fi:st] n festa, banchetto; (REL: also: ~ day) festa // vi banchettare.

**feat** [fi:t] n impresa, fatto insigne.

**feather** ['feðə*] n penna.

**feature** ['fi:tʃə*] n caratteristica; (article) articolo // vt (subj: film) avere come protagonista // vi figurare; ~s npl (of face) fisionomia; ~ film n film m inv principale.

**February** ['februərɪ] n febbraio.

**fed** [fed] pt, pp of **feed**.

**federal** ['fedərəl] a federale.

**fed-up** [fed'ʌp] a: to be ~ essere stufo(a).

**fee** [fi:] n pagamento; (of doctor, lawyer) onorario; (for examination) tassa d'esame; **school** ~s tasse fpl scolastiche.

**feeble** ['fi:bl] a debole.

**feed** [fi:d] n (of baby) pappa; (of animal) mangime m; (on printer) meccanismo di alimentazione // vt (pt, pp **fed**) nutrire; (Brit: baby) allattare; (horse etc) dare da mangiare a; (fire, machine) alimentare; to ~ material into introdurre materiale in; to ~ data/information into inserire dati/informazioni in; to ~ on vt fus nutrirsi di; ~back n feed-back m; ~ing bottle n (Brit) biberon m inv.

**feel** [fi:l] n (sense of touch) tatto; (of substance) consistenza // vt (pt, pp **felt**) toccare; palpare; tastare; (cold, pain, anger) sentire; (grief) provare; (think, believe); to ~ (that) pensare che; to ~ hungry/cold aver fame/freddo; to ~ lonely/better sentirsi solo/meglio; I don't ~ well non mi sento bene; to ~ like (want) aver voglia di; to ~ about or around for cercare a tastoni; ~er n (of insect) antenna; to put out ~ers (fig) fare un sondaggio; ~ing n sensazione f; sentimento.

**feet** [fi:t] npl of **foot**.

**feign** [feɪn] vt fingere, simulare.

**fell** [fel] pt of **fall** // vt (tree) abbattere.

**fellow** ['felou] n individuo, tipo; compagno; (of learned society) membro // cpd: ~ **countryman** n compatriota m; ~ **men** npl simili *mpl;* ~**ship** *n* associazione *f;* compagnia; *specie di borsa di studio universitaria.*

**felony** ['fɛlənɪ] *n* reato, crimine *m.*

**felt** [fɛlt] *pt, pp of* feel *// n* feltro; ~**tip pen** *n* pennarello.

**female** ['fi:meɪl] *n* (ZOOL) femmina; (pej: woman) donna, femmina *// a* femminile; (BIOL, ELEC) femmina *inv;* (sex, character) femminile; (vote etc) di donne.

**feminine** ['fɛmɪnɪn] *a, n* femminile (*m*).

**feminist** ['fɛmɪnɪst] *n* femminista *m/f.*

**fence** [fɛns] *n* recinto; (col: person) ricettatore/trice *// vt* (also: ~ **in**) recingere *// vi* schermire; **fencing** *n* (SPORT) scherma.

**fend** [fɛnd] *vi:* to ~ **for o.s.** arrangiarsi; **to ~ off** *vt* (attack, attacker) respingere, difendersi da; (questions) eludere.

**fender** ['fɛndə*] *n* parafuoco; (US) parafango; paraurti *m inv.*

**ferment** *vi* [fə'mɛnt] fermentare *// n* ['fɜ:mɛnt] agitazione *f,* eccitazione *f.*

**fern** [fɜ:n] *n* felce *f.*

**ferocious** [fə'rəʊʃəs] *a* feroce.

**ferret** ['fɛrɪt] *n* furetto.

**ferry** ['fɛrɪ] *n* (small) traghetto; (large: also: ~**boat**) nave *f* traghetto *inv // vt* traghettare.

**fertile** ['fɜ:taɪl] *a* fertile; (BIOL) fecondo(a); **fertilizer** ['fɜ:tɪlaɪzə*] *n* fertilizzante *m.*

**fester** ['fɛstə*] *vi* suppurare.

**festival** ['fɛstɪvəl] *n* (REL) festa; (ART, MUS) festival *m inv.*

**festive** ['fɛstɪv] *a* di festa; **the ~ season** (Brit: Christmas) il periodo delle feste.

**festivities** [fɛs'tɪvɪtɪz] *npl* festeggiamenti *mpl.*

**festoon** [fɛs'tu:n] *vt:* **to ~ with** ornare di.

**fetch** [fɛtʃ] *vt* andare a prendere; (sell for) essere venduto(a) per.

**fetching** ['fɛtʃɪŋ] *a* attraente.

**fête** [feɪt] *n* festa.

**fetish** ['fɛtɪʃ] *n* feticcio.

**fetus** ['fi:təs] *n* (US) = foetus.

**feud** [fju:d] *n* contesa, lotta *// vi* essere in lotta.

**feudal** ['fju:dl] *a* feudale.

**fever** ['fi:və*] *n* febbre *f;* ~**ish** *a* febbrile.

**few** [fju:] *a* pochi(e); **they were ~** erano pochi; **a ~** *a* qualche *inv* // *pronoun* alcuni(e); ~**er** *a* meno *inv;* meno numerosi(e); ~**est** *a* il minor numero di.

**fiancé** [fɪ'ɑ:ŋseɪ] *n* fidanzato; ~**e** *n* fidanzata.

**fib** [fɪb] *n* piccola bugia.

**fibre**, (US) **fiber** ['faɪbə*] *n* fibra; ~**glass** *n* fibra di vetro.

**fickle** ['fɪkl] *a* incostante, capriccioso(a).

**fiction** ['fɪkʃən] *n* narrativa, romanzi *mpl;* (sth made up) finzione *f;* ~**al** *a* immaginario(a).

**fictitious** [fɪk'tɪʃəs] *a* fittizio(a).

**fiddle** ['fɪdl] *n* (MUS) violino; (cheating) imbroglio; truffa *// vt* (Brit: accounts) falsificare, falsare; **to ~ with** *vt fus* gingillarsi con.

**fidelity** [fɪ'dɛlɪtɪ] *n* fedeltà; (accuracy) esattezza.

**fidget** ['fɪdʒɪt] *vi* agitarsi.

**field** [fi:ld] *n* campo; ~ **marshal** *n* feldmaresciallo; ~**work** *n* ricerche *fpl* esterne.

**fiend** [fi:nd] *n* demonio.

**fierce** [fɪəs] *a* (look, fighting) fiero(a); (wind) furioso(a); (attack) feroce; (enemy) acerrimo(a).

**fiery** ['faɪərɪ] *a* ardente, infocato(a).

**fifteen** [fɪf'ti:n] *num* quindici.

**fifth** [fɪfθ] *num* quinto(a).

**fifty** ['fɪftɪ] *num* cinquanta; ~-~ *a:* **a ~-~ chance** una possibilità su due *// ad* fifty-fifty, metà per ciascuno.

**fig** [fɪg] *n* fico.

**fight** [faɪt] *n* zuffa, rissa; (MIL) battaglia, combattimento; (against cancer etc) lotta *// vb* (pt, pp fought) *vt* picchiare; combattere; (cancer, alcoholism) lottare contro, combattere // *vi* battersi, combattere; ~**er** n combattente m; (plane) aeroplano da caccia; ~**ing** n combattimento.

**figment** ['figmənt] n: a ~ **of the imagination** un parto della fantasia.

**figurative** ['figjurətiv] a figurato(a).

**figure** ['figə*] n (DRAWING, GEOM) figura; (number, cipher) cifra; (body, outline) forma // vi (appear) figurare; (US: make sense) spiegarsi; **to** ~ **out** vt riuscire a capire; calcolare; ~**head** n (NAUT) polena; (pej) prestanome m/f inv; ~ **of speech** n figura retorica.

**file** [fail] n (tool) lima; (dossier) incartamento; (folder) cartellina; (for loose leaf) raccoglitore m; (COMPUT) archivio; (row) fila // vt (nails, wood) limare; (papers) archiviare; (LAW: claim) presentare; passare agli atti; **to** ~ **in/out** vi entrare/uscire in fila; **to** ~ **past** vt fus marciare in fila davanti a.

**filing** ['failiŋ] n archiviare m; ~ **cabinet** n casellario.

**fill** [fil] vt riempire; (tooth) otturare; (job) coprire // n: **to eat one's** ~ mangiare a sazietà; **to** ~ **in** vt (hole) riempire; (form) compilare; **to** ~ **up** vt riempire // vi (AUT) fare il pieno; ~ **it up, please** (AUT) mi faccia il pieno, per piacere.

**fillet** ['filit] n filetto; ~ **steak** n bistecca di filetto.

**filling** ['filiŋ] n (CULIN) impasto, ripieno; (for tooth) otturazione f; ~ **station** n stazione f di rifornimento.

**film** [film] n (CINEMA) film m; (PHOT) pellicola; (thin layer) velo // vt (scene) filmare; ~ **star** n divo/a dello schermo; ~ **strip** n filmina.

**filter** ['filtə*] n filtro // vt filtrare; ~ **lane** n (Brit AUT) corsia di svincolo; ~**tipped** a con filtro.

**filth** [filθ] n sporcizia; (fig) oscenità; ~**y** a lordo(a), sozzo(a); (language) osceno(a).

**fin** [fin] n (of fish) pinna.

**final** ['fainl] a finale, ultimo(a); definitivo(a) // n (SPORT) finale f; ~**s**

npl (SCOL) esami mpl finali; ~**e** [fi'nɑ:li] n finale m; ~**ize** vt mettere a punto; ~**ly** ad (lastly) alla fine; (eventually) finalmente.

**finance** [fai'næns] n finanza // vt finanziare; ~**s** npl finanze fpl.

**financial** [fai'nænʃəl] a finanziario(a).

**financier** [fai'nænsiə*] n finanziatore m.

**find** [faind] vt (pt, pp **found**) trovare; (lost object) ritrovare // n trovata, scoperta; **to** ~ **sb guilty** (LAW) giudicare qn colpevole; **to** ~ **out** vt informarsi di; (truth, secret) scoprire; (person) cogliere in fallo; **to** ~ **out about** informarsi di; (by chance) scoprire; ~**ings** npl (LAW) sentenza, conclusioni fpl; (of report) conclusioni.

**fine** [fain] a bello(a); ottimo(a); (thin, subtle) fine // ad (well) molto bene; (small) finemente // n (LAW) multa // vt (LAW) multare; **to be** ~ (weather) far bello; ~ **arts** npl belle arti fpl.

**finery** ['fainəri] n abiti mpl eleganti.

**finger** ['fiŋgə*] n dito // vt toccare, tastare; **little/index** ~ mignolo/(dito) indice m; ~**nail** n unghia; ~**print** n impronta digitale; ~**tip** n punta del dito.

**finicky** ['finiki] a esigente, pignolo(a); minuzioso(a).

**finish** ['finiʃ] n fine f; (polish etc) finitura // vt finire; (use up) esaurire // vi finire; (session) terminare; **to** ~ **doing sth** finire di fare qc; **to** ~ **third** arrivare terzo(a); **to** ~ **off** vt compiere; (kill) uccidere; **to** ~ **up** vi, vt finire; ~**ing line** n linea d'arrivo; ~**ing school** n scuola privata di perfezionamento (per signorine).

**finite** ['fainait] a limitato(a); (verb) finito(a).

**Finland** ['finlənd] n Finlandia.

**Finn** [fin] n finlandese m/f; ~**ish** a finlandese // n (LING) finlandese m.

**fir** [fə:*] n abete m.

**fire** [faɪə\*] n fuoco; incendio // vt (discharge): **to ~ a gun** scaricare un fucile; (fig) infiammare; (dismiss) licenziare // vi sparare, far fuoco; **on ~** in fiamme; **~ alarm** n allarme m d'incendio; **~arm** n arma da fuoco; **~ brigade,** (US) **~ department** n (corpo dei) pompieri mpl; **~ engine** n autopompa; **~ escape** n scala di sicurezza; **~ extinguisher** n estintore m; **~man** n pompiere m; **~place** n focolare m; **~side** n angolo del focolare; **~ station** n caserma dei pompieri; **~wood** n legna; **~work** n fuoco d'artificio; **~works display** n spettacolo pirotecnico.

**firing** ['faɪərɪŋ] n (MIL) spari mpl, tiro; **~ squad** n plotone m d'esecuzione.

**firm** [fə:m] a fermo(a) // n ditta, azienda; **~ly** ad fermamente.

**first** [fə:st] a primo(a) // ad (before others) il primo, la prima; (before other things) per primo; (when listing reasons etc) per prima cosa // n (person: in race) primo/a; (SCOL) laurea con lode; (AUT) prima // ad: dapprima, all'inizio; **~ of all** prima di tutto; **~ aid** n pronto soccorso; **~-aid kit** n cassetta pronto soccorso; **~-class** a di prima classe; **~-hand** a di prima mano; **~ lady** n (US) moglie f del presidente; **~ly** ad in primo luogo; **~ name** n prenome m; **~-rate** a di prima qualità, ottimo(a).

**fish** [fɪʃ] n (pl inv) pesce m // vi pescare; **to go ~ing** andare a pesca; **~erman** n pescatore m; **~ farm** n vivaio; **~ fingers** npl (Brit) bastoncini mpl di pesce (surgelati); **~ing boat** n barca da pesca; **~ing line** n lenza; **~ing rod** n canna da pesca; **~monger** n pescivendolo; **~monger's (shop)** n pescheria; **~ sticks** npl (US) = **~ fingers**; **~y** a (fig) sospetto(a).

**fist** [fɪst] n pugno.

**fit** [fɪt] a (MED, SPORT) in forma;

(proper) adatto(a), appropriato(a); conveniente // vt (subj: clothes) stare bene a; (adjust) aggiustare; (put in, attach) mettere; installare; (equip) fornire, equipaggiare // vi (clothes) stare bene; (parts) andare bene, adattarsi; (in space, gap) entrare // n (MED) accesso, attacco; **~ to** in grado di; **~ for** adatto(a) a; degno(a) di; **a ~ of anger** un accesso d'ira; **this dress is a tight/good ~** questo vestito è stretto/sta bene; **by ~s and starts** a sbalzi; **to ~ in** vi accordarsi; adattarsi; **to ~ out** vt (Brit: also: **~ up**) equipaggiare; **~ful** a saltuario(a); **~ment** n componibile m; **~ness** n (MED) forma fisica; (of remark) appropriatezza; **~ted carpet** n moquette f; **~ted kitchen** n cucina componibile; **~ter** n aggiustatore m or montatore m meccanico; (DRESS-MAKING) sarto/a; **~ting** a appropriato(a) // n (of dress) prova; (of piece of equipment) montaggio, aggiustaggio; **~ting room** n camerino; **~tings** npl impianti mpl.

**five** [faɪv] num cinque; **~r** n (col: Brit) biglietto da cinque sterline; (US) biglietto da cinque dollari.

**fix** [fɪks] vt fissare; mettere in ordine; (mend) riparare // n: **to be in a ~** essere nei guai; **to ~ up** vt (meeting) fissare; **to ~ sb up with sth** procurare qc a qn; **~ation** n fissazione f; **~ed** [fɪkst] a (prices etc) fisso(a); **~ture** ['fɪkstʃə\*] n impianto (fisso); (SPORT) incontro (del calendario sportivo).

**fizz** [fɪz] vi frizzare.

**fizzle** ['fɪzl] vi frizzare; **to ~ out** vi finire in nulla.

**fizzy** ['fɪzɪ] a frizzante; gassato(a).

**flabbergasted** ['flæbəgɑːstɪd] a sbalordito(a).

**flabby** ['flæbɪ] a flaccido(a).

**flag** [flæg] n bandiera; (also: **~stone**) pietra da lastricare // vi stancarsi; affievolirsi; **to ~ down** vt fare segno (di fermarsi) a.

**flagpole** ['flægpəul] n albero.

**flair** [fleə*] n (for business etc) fiuto; (for languages etc) facilità.

**flak** [flæk] n (MIL) fuoco d'artiglieria; (col: criticism) critiche fpl.

**flake** [fleɪk] n (of rust, paint) scaglia; (of snow, soap powder) fiocco // vi (also: ~ off) sfaldarsi.

**flamboyant** [flæm'bɔɪənt] a sgargiante.

**flame** [fleɪm] n fiamma.

**flamingo** [flə'mɪŋgəu] n fenicottero, fiammingo.

**flammable** ['flæməbl] a infiammabile.

**flan** [flæn] n (Brit) flan m inv.

**flank** [flæŋk] n fianco.

**flannel** ['flænl] n (Brit: also: face ~) guanto di spugna; (fabric) flanella; ~s npl pantaloni mpl di flanella.

**flap** [flæp] n (of pocket) patta; (of envelope) lembo // vt (wings) battere // vi (sail, flag) sbattere; (col: also: be in a ~) essere in agitazione.

**flare** [fleə*] n razzo; (in skirt etc) svasatura; to ~ up vi andare in fiamme; (fig: person) infiammarsi di rabbia; (: revolt) scoppiare.

**flash** [flæʃ] n vampata; (also: news ~) notizia f lampo inv; (PHOT) flash m inv // vt accendere e spegnere; (send: message) trasmettere // vi brillare; (light on ambulance, eyes etc) lampeggiare; in a ~ in un lampo; to ~ one's headlights lampeggiare; he ~ed by or past ci passò davanti come un lampo; ~bulb n cubo m flash inv; ~cube n flash m inv; ~light n lampadina tascabile.

**flashy** ['flæʃɪ] a (pej) vistoso(a).

**flask** [flɑːsk] n fiasco; (CHEM) beuta; (also: vacuum ~) thermos m inv ®.

**flat** [flæt] a piatto(a); (tyre) sgonfio(a), a terra; (denial) netto(a); (MUS) bemolle inv; (: voice) stonato(a) // n (Brit: rooms) appartamento; (AUT) pneumatico sgonfio; (MUS) bemolle m inv; to work ~ out lavorare a più non posso; ~ly

ad categoricamente; ~ten vt (also: ~ten out) appiattire.

**flatter** ['flætə*] vt lusingare; ~ing a lusinghiero(a); ~y n adulazione f.

**flaunt** [flɔːnt] vt fare mostra di.

**flavour**, (US) **flavor** ['fleɪvə*] n gusto, sapore m // vt insaporire, aggiungere sapore a; **vanilla**-~ed al gusto di vaniglia; ~ing n essenza (artificiale).

**flaw** [flɔː] n difetto.

**flax** [flæks] n lino; ~en a biondo(a).

**flea** [fliː] n pulce f.

**fleck** [flek] n (mark) macchiolina; (pattern) screziatura.

**flee**, pt, pp **fled** [fliː, fled] vt fuggire da // vi fuggire, scappare.

**fleece** [fliːs] n vello // vt (col) pelare.

**fleet** [fliːt] n flotta; (of lorries etc) convoglio; parco.

**fleeting** ['fliːtɪŋ] a fugace, fuggitivo(a); (visit) volante.

**Flemish** ['flemɪʃ] a fiammingo(a) // n (LING) fiammingo.

**flesh** [fleʃ] n carne f; (of fruit) polpa; ~ **wound** n ferita superficiale.

**flew** [fluː] pt of fly.

**flex** [fleks] n filo (flessibile) // vt flettere; (muscles) contrarre; ~ible a flessibile.

**flick** [flik] n colpetto; scarto; to ~ through vt fus sfogliare.

**flicker** ['flikə*] vi tremolare // n tremolio.

**flier** ['flaɪə*] n aviatore m.

**flight** [flaɪt] n volo; (escape) fuga; (also: ~ of steps) scalinata; ~ **attendant** n (US) steward m inv, hostess f inv; ~ **deck** n (AVIAT) cabina di controllo; (NAUT) ponte m di comando.

**flimsy** ['flimzɪ] a (fabric) inconsistente; (excuse) meschino(a).

**flinch** [flintʃ] vi ritirarsi; to ~ from tirarsi indietro di fronte a.

**fling** [fliŋ], pt, pp **flung** vt lanciare, gettare.

**flint** [flint] n selce f; (in lighter) pietrina.

**flip** [flip] n colpetto.

**flippant** ['flɪpənt] a senza rispetto, irriverente.

**flipper** ['flɪpə*] n pinna.

**flirt** [flə:t] vi flirtare // n civetta.

**flit** [flɪt] vi svolazzare.

**float** [fləut] n galleggiante m; (in procession) carro; (money) somma // vi galleggiare // vt far galleggiare; (loan, business) lanciare.

**flock** [flɔk] n gregge m; (of people) folla.

**flog** [flɔg] vt flagellare.

**flood** [flʌd] n alluvione m; (of words, tears etc) diluvio // vt allagare; ~ing n inondazione f; ~light n riflettore m // vt illuminare a giorno.

**floor** [flɔ:*] n pavimento; (storey) piano; (fig: at meeting): the ~ il pubblico // vt pavimentare; (knock down) atterrare; **on the** ~ per terra; **ground** ~, (US) **first** ~ pianterreno; **first** ~, (US) **second** ~ primo piano; ~**board** n tavellone m di legno; ~ **show** n spettacolo di varietà.

**flop** [flɔp] n fiasco.

**floppy** ['flɔpɪ] a floscio(a), molle; ~ **(disk)** n (COMPUT) floppy disk m inv.

**flora** ['flɔ:rə] n flora.

**Florence** ['flɔrəns] n Firenze f; **Florentine** ['flɔrəntaɪn] a fiorentino(a).

**florid** ['flɔrɪd] a (complexion) florido(a); (style) fiorito(a).

**florist** ['flɔrɪst] n fioraio/a.

**flounce** [flauns] n balzo.

**flounder** ['flaundə*] vi annaspare // n (ZOOL) passera di mare.

**flour** ['flauə*] n farina.

**flourish** ['flʌrɪʃ] vi fiorire // vt brandire // n abbellimento; svolazzo; (of trumpets) fanfara.

**flout** [flaut] vt (order) contravvenire a; (convention) sfidare.

**flow** [fləu] n flusso; circolazione f // vi fluire; (traffic, blood in veins) circolare; (hair) scendere; ~ **chart** n schema m di flusso.

**flower** ['flauə*] n fiore m // vi fiorire; ~ **bed** n aiuola; ~**pot** n vaso da

fiori; ~**y** a fiorito(a).

**flown** [fləun] pp of **fly**.

**flu** [flu:] n influenza.

**fluctuate** ['flʌktjueɪt] vi fluttuare, oscillare.

**fluency** ['flu:ənsɪ] n facilità, scioltezza; **his** ~ **in English** la sua scioltezza nel parlare l'inglese.

**fluent** ['flu:ənt] a (speech) facile, sciolto(a); corrente; **he speaks** ~ **Italian** parla l'italiano correntemente.

**fluff** [flʌf] n lanugine f; ~**y** a lanuginoso(a); (toy) di peluche.

**fluid** ['flu:ɪd] a fluido(a) // n fluido.

**fluke** [flu:k] n (col) colpo di fortuna.

**flung** [flʌŋ] pt, pp of **fling**.

**fluoride** ['fluəraɪd] n fluoruro.

**flurry** ['flʌrɪ] n (of snow) tempesta; a ~ **of activity/excitement** una febbre di attività/improvvisa agitazione.

**flush** [flʌʃ] n rossore m; (fig) ebbrezza; (: of youth, beauty etc) rigoglio, pieno vigore // vt ripulire con un getto d'acqua // vi arrossire // a: ~ **with** a livello di, pari a; **to** ~ **the toilet** tirare l'acqua; **to** ~ **out** (birds) far alzare in volo; (animals, fig) stanare; ~**ed** a tutto(a) rosso(a).

**flustered** ['flʌstəd] a sconvolto(a).

**flute** [flu:t] n flauto.

**flutter** ['flʌtə*] n agitazione f; (of wings) frullio // vi (bird) battere le ali.

**flux** [flʌks] n: **in a state of** ~ in continuo mutamento.

**fly** [flaɪ] n (insect) mosca; (on trousers: also: **flies**) bracchetta // vb (pt **flew**, pp **flown**) vt pilotare; (passengers, cargo) trasportare (in aereo); (distances) percorrere // vi volare; (passengers) andare in aereo; (escape) fuggire; (flag) sventolare; **to** ~ **away or off** vi volare via; ~**ing** n (activity) aviazione f; (action) volo // a: ~**ing visit** visita volante; **with** ~**ing colours** con risultati brillanti; ~**ing saucer** n disco volante; ~**ing start**

*n*: to get off to a ~ing start partire come un razzo; ~**over** *n* (*Brit*: *bridge*) cavalcavia *m inv*; ~**sheet** *n* (*for tent*) sopratetto.

**foal** [fəul] *n* puledro.

**foam** [fəum] *n* schiuma // *vi* schiumare; ~ **rubber** *n* gommapiuma ®.

**fob** [fɔb] *vt*: to ~ sb off with appioppare qn con; sbarazzarsi di qn con.

**focus** ['fəukəs] *n* (*pl* ~**es**) fuoco; (*of interest*) centro // *vt* (*field glasses etc*) mettere a fuoco // *vi*: to ~ **on** (*with camera*) mettere a fuoco; (*person*) fissare lo sguardo su; **in** ~ a fuoco; **out of** ~ sfocato(a).

**fodder** ['fɔdə*] *n* foraggio.

**foe** [fəu] *n* nemico.

**foetus**, (*US*) **fetus** ['fi:təs] *n* feto.

**fog** [fɔg] *n* nebbia; ~**gy** *a* nebbioso(a); **it's** ~**gy** c'è nebbia; ~ **lamp** *n* (*AUT*) faro *m* antinebbia *inv*.

**foil** [fɔil] *vt* confondere, frustrare // *n* lamina di metallo; (*kitchen* ~) foglio di alluminio; (*FENCING*) fioretto.

**fold** [fəuld] *n* (*bend*, *crease*) piega; (*AGR*) ovile *m*; (*fig*) gregge *m* // *vt* piegare; **to** ~ **up** *vi* (*business*) crollare // *vt* (*map etc*) piegare, ripiegare; ~**er** *n* (*for papers*) cartella; cartellina; (*brochure*) dépliant *m inv*; ~**ing** *a* (*chair*, *bed*) pieghevole.

**foliage** ['fəuliidʒ] *n* fogliame *m*.

**folk** [fəuk] *npl* gente *f* // *a* popolare; ~**s** *npl* famiglia; ~**lore** ['fəuklɔ:*] *n* folclore *m*; ~ **song** *n* canto popolare.

**follow** ['fɔləu] *vt* seguire // *vi* seguire; (*result*) conseguire, risultare; **he** ~**ed suit** lui ha fatto lo stesso; **to** ~ **up** *vi* (*victory*) sfruttare; (*letter*, *offer*) fare seguito a; (*case*) seguire; ~**er** *n* seguace *m/f*, discepolo/a; ~**ing** *a* seguente, successivo(a) // *n* seguito, discepoli *mpl*.

**folly** ['fɔli] *n* pazzia, follia.

**fond** [fɔnd] *a* (*memory*, *look*) tenero(a), affettuoso(a); **to be** ~ **of** volere bene a.

**fondle** ['fɔndl] *vt* accarezzare.

**food** [fu:d] *n* cibo; ~ **mixer** *n* frullatore *m*; ~ **poisoning** *n* intossicazione *f*; ~ **processor** *n* tritatutto *m inv* elettrico; ~**stuffs** *npl* generi *fpl* alimentari.

**fool** [fu:l] *n* sciocco/a; (*HISTORY*: *of king*) buffone *m*; (*CULIN*) frullato // *vt* ingannare // *vi* (*gen*: ~ *around*) fare lo sciocco; ~**hardy** *a* avventato(a); ~**ish** *a* scemo(a), stupido(a); imprudente; ~**proof** *a* (*plan etc*) sicurissimo(a).

**foot** [fut] *n* (*pl* **feet**) piede *m*; (*measure*) piede (= 304 *mm*; 12 *inches*); (*of animal*) zampa // *vt* (*bill*) pagare; **on** ~ a piedi; ~**age** *n* (*CINEMA*: *length*) ~ metraggio; (: *material*) sequenza; ~**ball** *n* pallone *m*; (*sport*: *Brit*) calcio; (: *US*) football *m* americano; ~**baller** *n* (*Brit*) = ~**ball player**; ~**ball ground** *n* campo di calcio; ~**ball player** *n* (*Brit*) calciatore *m*; (*US*) giocatore *m* di football americano; ~**brake** *n* freno a pedale; ~**bridge** *n* passerella; ~**hills** *npl* contrafforti *fpl*; ~**hold** *n* punto d'appoggio; ~**ing** *n* (*fig*) posizione *f*; **to lose one's** ~**ing** mettere un piede in fallo; ~**lights** *npl* luci *fpl* della ribalta; ~**man** *n* lacchè *m inv*; ~**note** *n* nota (a piè di pagina); ~**path** *n* sentiero; (*in street*) marciapiede *m*; ~**print** *n* orma, impronta; ~**step** *n* passo; ~**wear** *n* calzatura.

┌─────────────┐
│ KEYWORD │
└─────────────┘

**for** [fɔ:*] ◆ *prep* **1** (*indicating destination*, *intention*, *purpose*) per; **the train** ~ London il treno per Londra; **he went** ~ **the paper** è andato a prendere il giornale; **it's time** ~ **lunch** è ora di pranzo; **what's it** ~? a che serve?; **what** ~? (*why*) perché?

**2** (*on behalf of, representing*) per; **to work ~ sb/sth** lavorare per qn/qc; **I'll ask him ~ you** glielo chiederò a nome tuo; **G ~ George** G come George

**3** (*because of*) per, a causa di; **~ this reason** per questo motivo

**4** (*with regard to*) per; **it's cold ~ July** è freddo per luglio; **~ everyone who voted yes, 50 voted no** per ogni voto a favore ce n'erano 50 contro

**5** (*in exchange for*) per; **I sold it ~ £5** l'ho venduto per 5 sterline

**6** (*in favour of*) per, a favore di; **are you ~ or against us?** è con noi o contro di noi?; **I'm all ~ it** sono completamente a favore

**7** (*referring to distance, time*) per; **there are roadworks ~ 5 km** ci sono lavori in corso per 5 km; **he was away ~ 2 years** è stato via per 2 anni; **she will be away ~ a month** starà via un mese; **it hasn't rained ~ 3 weeks** non piove da 3 settimane; **can you do it ~ tomorrow?** può farlo per domani?

**8** (*with infinitive clauses*): **it is not ~ me to decide** non sta a me decidere; **it would be best ~ you to leave** sarebbe meglio che lei se ne andasse; **there is still time ~ you to do it** ha ancora tempo per farlo; **~ this to be possible ...** perché ciò sia possibile ...

**9** (*in spite of*) nonostante; **~ all his complaints, he's very fond of her** nonostante tutte le sue lamentele, le vuole molto bene

◆ *cj* (*since, as: rather formal*) dal momento che, poiché.

**forage** ['fɔrɪdʒ] *vi* foraggiare.

**foray** ['fɔreɪ] *n* incursione *f*.

**forbid** *pt* **forbad(e)**, *pp* **forbidden** [fə'bɪd, -'bæd, -'bɪdn] *vt* vietare, interdire; **to ~ sb to do sth** proibire a qn di fare qc; **~den** *a* vietato(a); **~ding** *a* arcigno(a), d'aspetto minaccioso.

**force** [fɔːs] *n* forza // *vt* forzare; **the F~s** *npl* (*Brit*) le forze armate; **to ~ o.s. to do** costringersi a fare; **in ~** (*in large numbers*) in gran numero; (*law*) in vigore; **to come into ~** entrare in vigore; **~-feed** *vt* (*animal, prisoner*) sottoporre ad alimentazione forzata; **~ful** *a* forte, vigoroso(a).

**forceps** ['fɔːsɛps] *npl* forcipe *m*.

**forcibly** ['fɔːsəblɪ] *ad* con la forza; (*vigorously*) vigorosamente.

**ford** [fɔːd] *n* guado // *vt* guadare.

**fore** [fɔː*] *n*: **to the ~** in prima linea; **to come to the ~** mettersi in evidenza.

**forearm** ['fɔːrɑːm] *n* avambraccio.

**foreboding** [fɔː'bəudɪŋ] *n* presagio di male.

**forecast** ['fɔːkɑːst] *n* previsione *f* // *vt* (*irg: like* **cast**) prevedere.

**forecourt** ['fɔːkɔːt] *n* (*of garage*) corte *f* esterna.

**forefathers** ['fɔːfɑːðəz] *npl* antenati *mpl*, avi *mpl*.

**forefinger** ['fɔːfɪŋgə*] *n* (dito) indice *m*.

**forefront** ['fɔːfrʌnt] *n*: **in the ~ of** all'avanguardia in.

**forego** [fɔː'gəu] *vt* = **forgo**.

**foregone** [fɔː'gɒn] *a*: **it's a ~ conclusion** è una conclusione scontata.

**foreground** ['fɔːgraund] *n* primo piano.

**forehead** ['fɔrɪd] *n* fronte *f*.

**foreign** ['fɒrɪn] *a* straniero(a); (*trade*) estero(a); **~ body** *n* corpo estraneo; **~er** *n* straniero/a; **F~ Office** *n* (*Brit*) Ministero degli Esteri; **~ secretary** *n* (*Brit*) ministro degli Affari esteri.

**foreleg** ['fɔːlɛg] *n* zampa anteriore.

**foreman** ['fɔːmən] *n* caposquadra *m*.

**foremost** ['fɔːməust] *a* principale; **più in vista** // *ad*: **first and ~** innanzitutto.

**forensic** [fə'rɛnsɪk] *a*: **~ medicine** medicina legale.

**forerunner** ['fɔːrʌnə*] *n* precursore *m*.

**foresee**, *pt* **foresaw**, *pp* **foreseen**

[fɔːˈsiː, -ˈsɔː, -ˈsiːn] vt prevedere; ~**able** a prevedibile.

**foreshadow** [fɔːˈʃædəʊ] vt presagire, far prevedere.

**foresight** [ˈfɔːsaɪt] n previdenza.

**forest** [ˈfɒrɪst] n foresta.

**forestall** [fɔːˈstɔːl] vt prevenire.

**forestry** [ˈfɒrɪstrɪ] n silvicoltura.

**foretaste** [ˈfɔːteɪst] n pregustazione f.

**foretell**, pt, pp **foretold** [fɔːˈtel, -ˈtəʊld] vt predire.

**forever** [fəˈrevə*] ad per sempre; (fig) sempre, di continuo.

**foreword** [ˈfɔːwəːd] n prefazione f.

**forfeit** [ˈfɔːfɪt] n ammenda, pena // vt perdere; (one's happiness, health) giocarsi.

**forgave** [fəˈɡeɪv] pt of **forgive**.

**forge** [fɔːdʒ] n fucina // vt (signature, Brit: money) contraffare, falsificare; (wrought iron) fucinare, foggiare; to ~ **ahead** vi tirare avanti; ~**r** n contraffattore m; ~**ry** n falso; (activity) contraffazione f.

**forget** [fəˈɡet], pt **forgot**, pp **forgotten** vt, vi dimenticare; ~**ful** a di corta memoria; ~**ful of** dimentico di; ~-**me-not** n nontiscordardimé m inv.

**forgive** [fəˈɡɪv], pt **forgave**, pp **forgiven** vt perdonare; to ~ sb for sth perdonare qc a qn; ~**ness** n perdono.

**forgo** [fɔːˈɡəʊ], pt **forwent**, pp **forgone** vt rinunciare a.

**forgot** [fəˈɡɒt] pt of **forget**.

**forgotten** [fəˈɡɒtn] pp of **forget**.

**fork** [fɔːk] n (for eating) forchetta; (for gardening) forca; (of roads) bivio; (of railways) inforcazione f // vi (road) biforcarsi; to ~ **out** (col: pay) vt sborsare // vi pagare; ~-**lift truck** n carrello elevatore.

**forlorn** [fəˈlɔːn] a (person) sconsolato(a); (place) abbandonato(a); (attempt) disperato(a); (hope) vano(a).

**form** [fɔːm] n forma; (SCOL) classe f; (questionnaire) scheda // vt

formare; **in top** ~ in gran forma.

**formal** [ˈfɔːməl] a (offer, receipt) vero(a) e proprio(a); (person) cerimonioso(a); (occasion, dinner) formale, ufficiale; (ART, PHILOSOPHY) formale; ~**ly** ad ufficialmente; formalmente; cerimoniosamente.

**format** [ˈfɔːmæt] n formato // vt (COMPUT) formattare.

**formation** [fɔːˈmeɪʃən] n formazione f.

**formative** [ˈfɔːmətɪv] a: ~ **years** anni mpl formativi.

**former** [ˈfɔːmə*] a (before n), ex inv (before n); the ~ ... the latter quello ... questo; ~**ly** ad in passato.

**formula** [ˈfɔːmjulə] n formula.

**forsake**, pt **forsook**, pp **forsaken** [fəˈseɪk, -ˈsuk, -ˈseɪkən] vt abbandonare.

**fort** [fɔːt] n forte m.

**forth** [fɔːθ] ad in avanti; **to go back and** ~ andare avanti e indietro; **and so** ~ e così via; ~**coming** a prossimo(a); (character) aperto(a), comunicativo(a); ~**right** a franco(a), schietto(a); ~**with** ad immediatamente, subito.

**fortify** [ˈfɔːtɪfaɪ] vt fortificare; **fortified wine** n vino ad alta gradazione alcolica.

**fortnight** [ˈfɔːtnaɪt] n quindici giorni mpl, due settimane fpl; ~**ly** a bimensile // ad ogni quindici giorni.

**fortress** [ˈfɔːtrɪs] n fortezza, rocca.

**fortunate** [ˈfɔːtʃənɪt] a fortunato(a); **it is** ~ **that** è una fortuna che; ~**ly** ad fortunatamente.

**fortune** [ˈfɔːtʃən] n fortuna; ~**teller** n indovino/a.

**forty** [ˈfɔːtɪ] num quaranta.

**forum** [ˈfɔːrəm] n foro.

**forward** [ˈfɔːwəd] a (ahead of schedule) in anticipo; (movement, position) in avanti; (not shy) aperto(a); diretto(a); sfacciato(a) // n (SPORT) avanti m inv // vt (letter) inoltrare; (parcel, goods) spedire;

(*fig*) promuovere, appoggiare; **to move** ~ avanzare; ~**(s)** *ad* avanti.

**forwent** [fɔː'went] *pt of* **forgo**.

**fossil** ['fɔsl] *a, n* fossile (*m*).

**foster** ['fɔstə*] *vt* incoraggiare, nutrire; (*child*) avere in affidamento; ~ **child** *n* bambino/a preso(a) in affidamento; ~ **mother** *n* madre *f* affidataria.

**fought** [fɔːt] *pt, pp of* **fight**.

**foul** [faul] *a* (*smell, food*) cattivo(a); (*weather*) brutto(a); (*language*) osceno(a); (*deed*) infame // *n* (*FOOTBALL*) fallo // *vt* sporcare; (*football player*) commettere un fallo su.

**found** [faund] *pt, pp of* **find** // *vt* (*establish*) fondare; ~**ation** [-'deɪʃən] *n* (*act*) fondazione *f*; (*base*) base *f*; (*also*: ~**ation cream**) fondo tinta; ~**ations** *npl* (*of building*) fondamenta *fpl*.

**founder** ['faundə*] *n* fondatore/trice // *vi* affondare.

**foundry** ['faundrɪ] *n* fonderia.

**fount** [faunt] *n* fonte *f*.

**fountain** ['fauntɪn] *n* fontana; ~ **pen** *n* penna stilografica.

**four** [fɔː*] *num* quattro; **on all** ~**s** a carponi; ~**poster** *n* (*also*: ~**poster bed**) letto a quattro colonne; ~**some** ['fɔːsəm] *n* partita a quattro; uscita in quattro; ~**teen** *num* quattordici; ~**th** *num* quarto(a).

**fowl** [faul] *n* pollame *m*; volatile *m*.

**fox** [fɔks] *n* volpe *f* // *vt* confondere.

**foyer** ['fɔɪeɪ] *n* atrio; (*THEATRE*) ridotto.

**fraction** ['frækʃən] *n* frazione *f*.

**fracture** ['fræktʃə*] *n* frattura.

**fragile** ['frædʒaɪl] *a* fragile.

**fragment** ['frægmənt] *n* frammento.

**fragrant** ['freɪgrənt] *a* fragrante, profumato(a).

**frail** [freɪl] *a* debole, delicato(a).

**frame** [freɪm] *n* (*of building*) armatura; (*of human, animal*) ossatura, corpo; (*of picture*) cornice *f*; (*of door, window*) telaio; (*of spectacles: also*: ~**s**) montatura; ~

**of mind** *n* stato d'animo; ~**work** *n* struttura.

**France** [frɑːns] *n* Francia.

**franchise** ['fræntʃaɪz] *n* (*POL*) diritto di voto; (*COMM*) concessione *f*.

**frank** [fræŋk] *a* franco(a), aperto(a) // *vt* (*letter*) affrancare; ~**ly** *ad* francamente, sinceramente.

**frantic** ['fræntɪk] *a* frenetico(a).

**fraternity** [frə'tɜːnɪtɪ] *n* (*club*) associazione *f*; (*spirit*) fratellanza.

**fraud** [frɔːd] *n* truffa; (*LAW*) frode *f*; (*person*) impostore/a.

**fraught** [frɔːt] *a*: ~ **with** pieno(a) di, intriso(a) da.

**fray** [freɪ] *n* baruffa // *vt* logorare // *vi* logorarsi; **her nerves were** ~**ed** aveva i nervi a pezzi.

**freak** [friːk] *n* fenomeno, mostro // *cpd* fenomenale.

**freckle** ['frekl] *n* lentiggine *f*.

**free** [friː] *a* libero(a); (*gratis*) gratuito(a); (*liberal*) generoso(a) // *vt* (*prisoner, jammed person*) liberare; (*jammed object*) districare; ~ **of charge**, **for** ~ *ad* gratuitamente; ~**dom** ['friːdəm] *n* libertà; ~**for-all** *n* parapiglia *m* generale; ~ **gift** *n* regalo, omaggio; ~**hold** *n* proprietà assoluta; ~ **kick** *n* calcio libero; ~**lance** *a* indipendente; (*liberally*) liberamente; ~**ly** *ad* liberamente; ~**mason** *n* massone *m*; ~**post** *n* affrancatura a carico del destinatario; ~**range** *a* (*hen*) ruspante; (*eggs*) di gallina ruspante; ~ **trade** *n* libero scambio; ~**way** *n* (*US*) superstrada; ~**wheel** *vi* andare a ruota libera; ~ **will** *n* libero arbitrio; **of one's own** ~ **will** di spontanea volontà.

**freeze** [friːz] *vb* (*pt* **froze**, *pp* **frozen**) *vi* gelare // *vt* gelare; (*food*) congelare; (*prices, salaries*) bloccare // *n* gelo; blocco; ~**dried** *a* liofilizzato(a); ~**r** *n* congelatore *m*.

**freezing** ['friːzɪŋ] *a*: **I'm** ~ mi sto congelando // *n* (*also*: ~ **point**) punto di congelamento; **3 degrees below** ~ 3 gradi sotto zero.

**freight** [freɪt] n (goods) merce f, merci fpl; (money charged) spese fpl di trasporto; ~ **train** n (US) treno m merci inv.

**French** [frɛntʃ] a francese // n (LING) francese m; **the** ~ npl i Francesi; ~ **bean** n fagiolino; ~ **fried potatoes**, (US) ~ **fries** npl patate fpl fritte; ~**man** n francese m; ~ **window** n portafinestra; ~**woman** n francese f.

**frenzy** ['frɛnzɪ] n frenesia.

**frequent** a ['fri:kwənt] frequente // a [frɪ'kwɛnt] frequentare; ~**ly** ad frequentemente, spesso.

**fresco** ['frɛskəu] n affresco.

**fresh** [frɛʃ] a fresco(a); (new) nuovo(a); (cheeky) sfacciato(a); ~**en** vi (wind, air) rinfrescare; **to** ~**en up** vi rinfrescarsi; ~**er** n (BRIT SCOL: col) matricola; ~**ly** ad di recente, di fresco; ~**man** n (US) = ~**er**; ~**ness** n freschezza; ~**water** a (fish) d'acqua dolce.

**fret** [frɛt] vi agitarsi, affliggersi.

**friar** ['fraɪə*] n frate m.

**friction** ['frɪkʃən] n frizione f, attrito.

**Friday** ['fraɪdɪ] n venerdì m inv.

**fridge** [frɪdʒ] n (Brit) frigo, frigorifero.

**fried** [fraɪd] pt, pp of **fry** // a fritto(a).

**friend** [frɛnd] n amico/a; ~**ly** a amichevole; ~**ship** n amicizia.

**frieze** [fri:z] n fregio.

**fright** [fraɪt] n paura, spavento; **to** **take** ~ spaventarsi; ~**en** vt spaventare, far paura a; ~**ened** a spaventato(a); ~**ening** a spaventoso(a), pauroso(a); ~**ful** a orribile.

**frigid** ['frɪdʒɪd] a (woman) frigido(a).

**frill** [frɪl] n balza.

**fringe** [frɪndʒ] n (Brit: of hair) frangia; (edge: of forest etc) margine m; (fig: of surface) al margine; ~ **benefits** npl vantaggi mpl.

**frisk** [frɪsk] vt perquisire.

**frisky** ['frɪskɪ] a vivace, vispo(a).

**fritter** ['frɪtə*] n frittella; **to** ~

**away** vt sprecare.

**frivolity** [frɪ'vɔlɪtɪ] n frivolezza.

**frivolous** ['frɪvələs] a frivolo(a).

**frizzy** ['frɪzɪ] a crespo(a).

**fro** [frəu] ad: **to and** ~ avanti e indietro.

**frock** [frɔk] n vestito.

**frog** [frɔg] n rana; ~**man** n uomo m rana inv.

**frolic** ['frɔlɪk] vi sgambettare.

┌─────────────────┐
│ **KEYWORD** │
└─────────────────┘

**from** [frɔm] prep **1** (indicating starting place, origin etc) da; **where do you come** ~?, **where are you** ~? da dove viene?, di dov'è?; ~ **London to Glasgow** da Londra a Glasgow; **a letter** ~ **my sister** una lettera da mia sorella; **tell him** ~ **me that** ... gli dica da parte mia che ...

**2** (indicating time) da; ~ **one o'clock to** or **until** or **till two** dall'una alle due; ~ **January** (on) da gennaio, a partire da gennaio

**3** (indicating distance) da; **the hotel is 1 km** ~ **the beach** l'albergo è a 1 km dalla spiaggia

**4** (indicating price, number etc) da; **prices range** ~ **£10 to £50** i prezzi vanno dalle 10 alle 50 sterline

**5** (indicating difference) da; **he can't tell red** ~ **green** non sa distinguere il rosso dal verde

**6** (because of, on the basis of): ~ **what he says** da quanto dice lui; **weak** ~ **hunger** debole per la fame.

**front** [frʌnt] n (of house, dress) davanti m inv; (of train) testa; (of book) copertina; (promenade: also: sea ~) lungomare m; (MIL, POL, METEOR) fronte m; (fig: appearances) fronte f // a primo(a); anteriore, davanti inv; **in** ~ **of** davanti a; ~ **door** n porta d'entrata; (of car) sportello anteriore; ~**ier** ['frʌntɪə*] n frontiera; ~ **page** n prima pagina; ~ **room** n (Brit) salotto; ~**wheel drive** n trasmissione *f* anteriore.

**frost** [frɔst] *n* gelo; (*also:* hoar~) brina; ~**bite** *n* congelamento; ~**ed** *a* (*glass*) smerigliato(a); ~**y** *a* (*window*) coperto(a) di ghiaccio; (*welcome*) gelido(a).

**froth** [frɔθ] *n* spuma; schiuma.

**frown** [fraun] *n* cipiglio // *vi* accigliarsi.

**froze** [frəuz] *pt of* freeze; ~**n** *pp of* freeze // *a* (*food*) congelato(a).

**fruit** [fru:t] *n* (*pl inv*) frutto; (*collectively*) frutta; ~**erer** *n* fruttivendolo; ~**erer's (shop)** *n*: at the ~**erer's (shop)** dal fruttivendolo; ~**ful** *a* fruttuoso(a); (*plant*) fruttifero(a); (*soil*) fertile; ~**ion** [fru:'ɪʃən] *n*: to come to ~**ion** realizzarsi; ~ **juice** *n* succo di frutta; ~ **machine** *n* (*Brit*) macchina *f* mangiasoldi *inv*; ~ **salad** *n* macedonia.

**frustrate** [frʌs'treit] *vt* frustrare; ~**d** *a* frustrato(a).

**fry** [frai], *pt, pp* **fried** *vt* friggere; **the small** ~ i pesci piccoli; ~**ing pan** *n* padella.

**ft.** *abbr* = **foot, feet.**

**fuddy-duddy** ['fʌdɪdʌdɪ] *n* matusa.

**fudge** [fʌdʒ] *n* (*CULIN*) specie di caramella a base di latte, burro e zucchero.

**fuel** [fjuəl] *n* (*for heating*) combustibile *m*; (*for propelling*) carburante *m*; ~ **tank** *n* deposito *m* nafta *inv*; (*on vehicle*) serbatoio (della benzina).

**fugitive** ['fju:dʒɪtɪv] *n* fuggitivo/a, profugo/a.

**fulfil** [ful'fil] *vt* (*function*) compiere; (*order*) eseguire; (*wish, desire*) soddisfare, appagare; ~**ment** *n* (*of wishes*) soddisfazione *f*, appagamento.

**full** [ful] *a* pieno(a); (*details, skirt*) ampio(a) // *ad*: **to know ~ well that** sapere benissimo che; **I'm ~ (up)** sono pieno; ~ **employment** piena occupazione; **a ~ two hours** due ore intere; **at ~ speed** a tutta velocità;

**in ~** per intero; **to pay in ~** pagare tutto; ~ **moon** *n* luna piena; ~**scale** *a* (*attack, war*) su larga scala; (*model*) in grandezza naturale; ~ **stop** *n* punto; ~**time** *a, ad* (*work*) a tempo pieno // *n* (*SPORT*) fine *f* partita; ~**y** *ad* interamente, pienamente, completamente; ~**y-fledged** *a* (*teacher, member etc*) a tutti gli effetti.

**fulsome** ['fulsəm] *a* (*pej: praise, gratitude*) esagerato(a).

**fumble** ['fʌmbl] *vi* brancolare, andare a tentoni; **to ~ with** *vt fus* trafficare.

**fume** [fju:m] *vi* essere furioso(a); ~**s** *npl* esalazioni *fpl*, vapori *mpl*.

**fumigate** ['fju:mɪgeɪt] *vt* suffumicare.

**fun** [fʌn] *n* divertimento, spasso; **to have ~** divertirsi; **for ~** per scherzo; **to make ~ of** *vt fus* prendersi gioco di.

**function** ['fʌŋkʃən] *n* funzione *f*; cerimonia, ricevimento // *vi* funzionare; ~**al** *a* funzionale.

**fund** [fʌnd] *n* fondo, cassa; (*source*) fondo; (*store*) riserva; ~**s** *npl* (*money*) fondi *mpl*.

**fundamental** [fʌndə'mɛntl] *a* fondamentale.

**funeral** ['fju:nərəl] *n* funerale *m*; ~ **parlour** *n* impresa di pompe funebri; ~ **service** *n* ufficio funebre.

**fun fair** *n* (*Brit*) luna park *m inv*.

**fungus** ['fʌŋgəs], *pl* **fungi** [-gaɪ] *n* fungo; (*mould*) muffa.

**funnel** ['fʌnl] *n* imbuto; (*of ship*) ciminiera.

**funny** ['fʌnɪ] *a* divertente, buffo(a); (*strange*) strano(a), bizzarro(a).

**fur** [fə:*] *n* pelo; pelliccia; (*Brit: in kettle etc*) deposito calcare; ~ **coat** *n* pelliccia.

**furious** ['fjuərɪəs] *a* furioso(a); (*effort*) accanito(a).

**furlong** ['fə:lɔŋ] *n* = 201.17 *m* (*termine ippico*).

**furlough** ['fə:ləu] *n* congedo, permesso.

**furnace** ['fə:nɪs] n fornace f.

**furnish** ['fə:nɪʃ] vt ammobiliare; (supply) fornire; ~**ings** npl mobili mpl, mobilia.

**furniture** ['fə:nɪtʃə*] n mobili mpl; piece of ~ mobile m.

**furrow** ['fʌrəu] n solco.

**furry** ['fə:rɪ] a (animal) peloso(a).

**further** ['fə:ðə*] a supplementare, altro(a); nuovo(a); più lontano(a) // ad più lontano; (more) di più; (moreover) inoltre // vt favorire, promuovere; **college of** ~ **education** n istituto statale con corsi specializzati (di formazione professionale, aggiornamento professionale etc); ~**more** [fə:ðə'mɔ:*] ad inoltre, per di più.

**furthest** ['fə:ðɪst] superlative of **far**.

**fury** ['fjuərɪ] n furore m.

**fuse** [fju:z] n fusibile m; (for bomb etc) miccia, spoletta // vt fondere; (Brit ELEC): **to** ~ **the lights** far saltare i fusibili // vi fondersi; ~ **box** n cassetta dei fusibili.

**fuselage** ['fju:zəlɑ:ʒ] n fusoliera.

**fuss** [fʌs] n chiasso, trambusto, confusione f; (complaining) storie fpl; **to make a** ~ fare delle storie; ~**y** a (person) puntiglioso(a), esigente; che fa le storie; (dress) carico(a) di fronzoli; (style) elaborato(a).

**future** ['fju:tʃə*] a futuro(a) // n futuro, avvenire m; (LING) futuro; **in** ~ in futuro.

**fuze** [fju:z] (US) = **fuse**.

**fuzzy** ['fʌzɪ] a (PHOT) indistinto(a), sfocato(a); (hair) crespo(a).

# G

**G** [dʒi:] n (MUS) sol m.

**gabble** ['gæbl] vi borbottare; farfugliare.

**gable** ['geɪbl] n frontone m.

**gadget** ['gædʒɪt] n aggeggio.

**Gaelic** ['geɪlɪk] a gaelico(a) // n (LING) gaelico.

**gag** [gæg] n bavaglio; (joke) facezia, scherzo // vt imbavagliare.

**gaiety** ['geɪtɪ] n gaiezza.

**gaily** ['geɪlɪ] ad allegramente.

**gain** [geɪn] n guadagno, profitto // vt guadagnare // vi (watch) andare avanti; **to** ~ **in/by** aumentare di/con; **to** ~ **3lbs (in weight)** aumentare di 3 libbre.

**gait** [geɪt] n andatura.

**gal.** abbr = **gallon**.

**galaxy** ['gæləksɪ] n galassia.

**gale** [geɪl] n vento forte; burrasca.

**gallant** ['gælənt] a valoroso(a); (towards ladies) galante, cortese.

**gall bladder** ['gɔ:l-] n cistifellea.

**gallery** ['gælərɪ] n galleria.

**galley** ['gælɪ] n (ship's kitchen) cambusa; (ship) galea.

**gallon** ['gælən] n gallone m (= 8 pints; Brit = 4.543l; US = 3.785l).

**gallop** ['gæləp] n galoppo // vi galoppare.

**gallows** ['gæləuz] n forca.

**gallstone** ['gɔ:lstəun] n calcolo biliare.

**galore** [gə'lɔ:*] ad a iosa, a profusione.

**galvanize** ['gælvənaɪz] vt galvanizzare.

**gambit** ['gæmbɪt] n (fig): (opening) ~ prima mossa.

**gamble** ['gæmbl] n azzardo, rischio calcolato // vt, vi giocare; **to** ~ **on** (fig) giocare su; ~**r** n giocatore/trice d'azzardo; **gambling** n gioco d'azzardo.

**game** [geɪm] n gioco; (event) partita; (HUNTING) selvaggina // a coraggioso(a); (ready): **to be** ~ (**for** sth/to do) essere pronto(a) (a qc/a fare); **big** ~ n selvaggina grossa; ~**keeper** n guardacaccia m inv.

**gammon** ['gæmən] n (bacon) quarto di maiale; (ham) prosciutto affumicato.

**gamut** ['gæmət] n gamma.

**gang** [gæŋ] n banda, squadra // vi: **to** ~ **up on sb** far combutta contro qn.

**gangrene** ['gæŋgriːn] n cancrena.

**gangster** ['gæŋstə*] n gangster m inv.

**gangway** ['gæŋweɪ] n passerella; (Brit: of bus) corridoio.

**gaol** [dʒeɪl] n, vt (Brit) = jail.

**gap** [gæp] n buco; (in time) intervallo; (fig) lacuna; vuoto.

**gape** [geɪp] vi restare a bocca aperta; **gaping** a (hole) squarciato(a).

**garage** ['gærɑːʒ] n garage m inv.

**garbage** ['gɑːbɪdʒ] n immondizie fpl, rifiuti mpl; ~ **can** n (US) bidone m della spazzatura.

**garbled** ['gɑːbld] a deformato(a); ingarbugliato(a).

**garden** ['gɑːdn] n giardino // vi lavorare nel giardino; ~**er** n giardiniere/a; ~**ing** n giardinaggio.

**gargle** ['gɑːgl] vi fare gargarismi // n gargarismo.

**gargoyle** ['gɑːgɔɪl] n gargouille f inv.

**garish** ['gɛərɪʃ] a vistoso(a).

**garland** ['gɑːlənd] n ghirlanda; corona.

**garlic** ['gɑːlɪk] n aglio.

**garment** ['gɑːmənt] n indumento.

**garrison** ['gærɪsn] n guarnigione f.

**garrulous** ['gærjuləs] a ciarliero(a), loquace.

**garter** ['gɑːtə*] n giarrettiera.

**gas** [gæs] n gas m inv; (US: gasoline) benzina // vt asfissiare con il gas; (MIL) gasare; ~ **cooker** n (Brit) cucina a gas; ~ **cylinder** n bombola del gas; ~ **fire** n radiatore m a gas.

**gash** [gæʃ] n sfregio // vt sfregiare.

**gasket** ['gæskɪt] n (AUT) guarnizione f.

**gas mask** n maschera f antigas inv.

**gas meter** n contatore m del gas.

**gasoline** ['gæsəliːn] n (US) benzina.

**gasp** [gɑːsp] vi ansare, boccheggiare; (in surprise) restare senza fiato; **to** ~ **out** vt dire affannosamente.

**gas ring** n fornello a gas.

**gassy** ['gæsɪ] a gassoso(a).

**gas tap** n rubinetto del gas.

**gate** [geɪt] n cancello; ~**crash** vt

(Brit) partecipare senza invito a; ~**way** n porta.

**gather** ['gæðə*] vt (flowers, fruit) cogliere; (pick up) raccogliere; (assemble) radunare; raccogliere; (understand) capire // vi (assemble) radunarsi; **to** ~ **speed** acquistare velocità; ~**ing** n adunanza.

**gauche** [gəuʃ] a goffo(a), maldestro(a).

**gaudy** ['gɔːdɪ] a vistoso(a).

**gauge** [geɪdʒ] n (standard measure) calibro; (RAIL) scartamento; (instrument) indicatore m // vt misurare.

**gaunt** [gɔːnt] a scarno(a); (grim, desolate) desolato(a).

**gauntlet** ['gɔːntlɪt] n (fig): **to run the** ~ **through an angry crowd** passare sotto il fuoco di una folla ostile; **to throw down the** ~ gettare il guanto.

**gauze** [gɔːz] n garza.

**gave** [geɪv] pt of **give**.

**gay** [geɪ] a (person) gaio(a), allegro(a); (colour) vivace, vivo(a); (col) omosessuale.

**gaze** [geɪz] n sguardo fisso // vi: **to** ~ **at** guardare fisso.

**GB** abbr = **Great Britain**.

**GCE** n abbr (Brit): = General Certificate of Education) = maturità.

**GCSE** n abbr (Brit) = General Certificate of Secondary Education.

**gear** [gɪə*] n attrezzi mpl, equipaggiamento; (belongings) roba; (TECH) ingranaggio; (AUT) marcia // vt (fig: adapt): **to** ~ **sth to** adattare qc a; **in top or** (US) **high/ low/bottom** ~ in quarta (or quinta)/ seconda/prima; **in** ~ in marcia; ~ **box** n scatola del cambio; ~ **lever**, (US) ~ **shift** n leva del cambio.

**geese** [giːs] npl of **goose**.

**gel** [dʒel] n gel m inv.

**gelignite** ['dʒelɪgnaɪt] n nitroglicerina.

**gem** [dʒem] n gemma.

**Gemini** ['dʒemɪnaɪ] n Gemelli mpl.

**gender** ['dʒendə*] n genere m.

**general** ['dʒɛnərl] n generale m // a generale; **in** ~ in genere; ~ **delivery** n (US) fermo posta m; ~ **election** n elezioni fpl generali; **~ize** vi generalizzare; **~ly** ad generalmente; ~ **practitioner** (G.P.) n medico generico.

**generate** ['dʒɛnəreɪt] vt generare.

**generation** [dʒɛnə'reɪʃən] n generazione f.

**generator** ['dʒɛnəreɪtə*] n generatore m.

**generosity** [dʒɛnə'rɒsɪtɪ] n generosità.

**generous** ['dʒɛnərəs] a generoso(a); (copious) abbondante.

**genetic** [dʒɪ'nɛtɪk] a genetico(a).

**Geneva** [dʒɪ'niːvə] n Ginevra.

**genial** ['dʒiːnɪəl] a geniale, cordiale.

**genitals** ['dʒɛnɪtlz] npl genitali mpl.

**genius** ['dʒiːnɪəs] n genio.

**Genoa** ['dʒɛnəuə] n Genova.

**gent** [dʒɛnt] n abbr = **gentleman**.

**genteel** [dʒɛn'tiːl] a raffinato(a), distinto(a).

**gentle** ['dʒɛntl] a delicato(a); (persona) dolce.

**gentleman** ['dʒɛntlmən] n signore m; (well-bred man) gentiluomo.

**gently** ['dʒɛntlɪ] ad delicatamente.

**gentry** ['dʒɛntrɪ] n nobiltà minore.

**gents** [dʒɛnts] n W.C. m (per signori).

**genuine** ['dʒɛnjuɪn] a autentico(a); sincero(a).

**geography** [dʒɪ'ɒgrəfɪ] n geografia.

**geology** [dʒɪ'ɒlədʒɪ] n geologia.

**geometric(al)** [dʒɪə'mɛtrɪk(l)] a geometrico(a).

**geometry** [dʒɪ'ɒmətrɪ] n geometria.

**geranium** [dʒɪ'reɪnjəm] n geranio.

**geriatric** [dʒɛrɪ'ætrɪk] a geriatrico(a).

**germ** [dʒəːm] n (MED) microbo; (BIOL, fig) germe m.

**German** ['dʒəːmən] a tedesco(a) // n tedesco/a; (LING) tedesco; ~ **measles** n rosolia.

**Germany** ['dʒəːmənɪ] n Germania.

**gesture** ['dʒɛstʃə*] n gesto.

KEYWORD

**get** [gɛt], pt, pp **got**, pp **gotten** (US)
♦ vi 1 (become, be) diventare, farsi; to ~ **old** invecchiare; to ~ **tired** stancarsi; to ~ **drunk** ubriacarsi; to ~ **killed** venire or rimanere ucciso(a); **when do I ~ paid?** quando mi pagate?; **it's ~ting late** si sta facendo tardi

**2** (go): to ~ **to/from** andare a/da; to ~ **home** arrivare or tornare a casa; **how did you ~ here?** come sei venuto?

**3** (begin) mettersi a, cominciare a; to ~ **to know sb** incominciare a conoscere qn; **let's ~ going** or **started** muoviamoci

**4** (modal auxiliary vb): **you've got to do it** devi farlo

♦ vt 1: to ~ **sth done** (do) fare qc; (have done) far fare qc; to ~ **one's hair cut** farsi tagliare i capelli; to ~ **sb to do sth** far fare qc a qn

**2** (obtain: money, permission, results) ottenere; (find: job, flat) trovare; (fetch: person, doctor) chiamare; (: object) prendere; to ~ **sth for sb** prendere or procurare qc a qn; ~ **me Mr Jones, please** (TEL) mi passi il signor Jones, per favore; **can I ~ you a drink?** le posso offrire da bere?

**3** (receive: present, letter, prize) ricevere; (acquire: reputation) farsi; **how much did you ~ for the painting?** quanto te lo hanno dato per il quadro?

**4** (catch) prendere; (hit: target etc) colpire; to ~ **sb by the arm/throat** afferrare qn per un braccio/alla gola; ~ **him!** prendetelo!

**5** (take, move) portare; to ~ **sth to sb** far avere qc a qn; **do you think we'll ~ it through the door?** pensi che riusciremo a farlo passare per la porta?

**6** (catch, take: plane, bus etc) prendere

**7** (understand) afferrare; (hear)

sentire; **I've got it!** ci sono arrivato!, ci sono!; **I'm sorry, I didn't ~ your name** scusi, non ho capito (or sentito) il suo nome
**8** (have, possess): **to have got** avere; **how many have you got?** quanti ne ha?
**to get about** vi muoversi; (news) diffondersi
**to get along** vi (agree) andare d'accordo; (depart) andarsene; (manage) = **to get by**
**to get at** vt fus (attack) prendersela con; (reach) raggiungere, arrivare a
**to get away** vi partire, andarsene; (escape) scappare
**to get away with** vt fus cavarsela; farla franca
**to get back** vi (return) ritornare, tornare ◆ vt riottenere, riavere
**to get by** vi (pass) passare; (manage) farcela
**to get down** vi, vt fus scendere ◆ vt far scendere; (depress) buttare giù
**to get down to** vt fus (work) mettersi a (fare)
**to get in** vi entrare; (train) arrivare; (arrive home) ritornare, tornare
**to get into** vt fus entrare in; **to ~ into a rage** incavolarsi
**to get off** vi (from train etc) scendere; (depart: person, car) andare via; (escape) cavarsela ◆ vt (remove: clothes, stain) levare ◆ vt fus (train, bus) scendere da
**to get on** vi (at exam etc) andare; (agree): **to ~ on (with)** andare d'accordo (con) ◆ vt fus montare in; (horse) montare su
**to get out** vi uscire; (of vehicle) scendere ◆ vt tirar fuori, far uscire
**to get out of** vt fus uscire da; (duty etc) evitare
**to get over** vt fus (illness) riaversi da
**to get round** vt fus aggirare; (fig: person) rigirare

**to get through** vi (TEL) avere la linea
**to get through to** vt fus (TEL) parlare a
**to get together** vi riunirsi ◆ vt raccogliere; (people) adunare
**to get up** vi (rise) alzarsi ◆ vt fus salire su per
**to get up to** vt fus (reach) raggiungere; (prank etc) fare.

**getaway** ['getəweɪ] n fuga.
**geyser** ['gi:zə*] n scaldabagno; (GEO) geyser m inv.
**Ghana** ['gɑ:nə] n Ghana m.
**ghastly** ['gɑ:stlɪ] a orribile, orrendo(a).
**gherkin** ['gə:kɪn] n cetriolino.
**ghost** [gəust] n fantasma m, spettro.
**giant** ['dʒaɪənt] n gigante/essa // a gigante, enorme.
**gibberish** ['dʒɪbərɪʃ] n parole fpl senza senso.
**gibe** [dʒaɪb] n frecciata.
**giblets** ['dʒɪblɪts] npl frattaglie fpl.
**Gibraltar** [dʒɪ'brɔ:ltə*] n Gibilterra.
**giddy** ['gɪdɪ] a (dizzy): **to be ~** aver le vertigini; (height) vertiginoso(a).
**gift** [gɪft] n regalo; (donation, ability) dono; **~ed** a dotato(a); **~ token** or **voucher** n buono m omaggio inv.
**gigantic** [dʒaɪ'gæntɪk] a gigantesco(a).
**giggle** ['gɪgl] vi ridere scioccamente.
**gill** [dʒɪl] n (measure) = 0.25 pints (Brit = 0.148l, US = 0.118l).
**gills** [gɪlz] npl (of fish) branchie fpl.
**gilt** [gɪlt] n doratura // a dorato(a); **~-edged** a (COMM) della massima sicurezza.
**gimmick** ['gɪmɪk] n trucco.
**gin** [dʒɪn] n (liquor) gin m inv.
**ginger** ['dʒɪndʒə*] n zenzero; **~ ale, ~ beer** n bibita gassosa allo zenzero; **~bread** n pan m di zenzero.
**gingerly** ['dʒɪndʒəlɪ] ad cautamente.
**gipsy** ['dʒɪpsɪ] n zingaro/a.
**giraffe** [dʒɪ'rɑ:f] n giraffa.
**girder** ['gə:də*] n trave f.

**girdle** ['gə:dl] $n$ (corset) guaina.

**girl** [gə:l] $n$ ragazza; (young unmarried woman) signorina; (daughter) figlia, figliola; ~**friend** $n$ (of girl) amica; (of boy) ragazza; ~**ish** $a$ da ragazza.

**giro** ['dʒaɪrəu] $n$ (bank ~) versamento bancario; (post office ~) postagiro.

**girth** [gə:θ] $n$ circonferenza; (of horse) cinghia.

**gist** [dʒɪst] $n$ succo.

**give** [gɪv] $vb$ (pt gave, pp given) $vt$ dare // vi cedere; to ~ sb sth, ~ sth to sb dare qc a qn; to ~ a cry/ sigh emettere un grido/sospiro; to ~ away $vt$ dare via; (give free) fare dono di; (betray) tradire; (disclose) rivelare; (bride) condurre all'altare; to ~ back $vt$ rendere; to ~ in $vi$ cedere // $vt$ consegnare; to ~ off $vt$ emettere; to ~ out $vt$ distribuire; annunciare; to ~ up $vi$ rinunciare // $vt$ rinunciare a; to ~ up smoking smettere di fumare; to ~ o.s. up arrendersi; to ~ way $vi$ cedere; (Brit AUT) dare la precedenza.

**glacier** ['glæsɪə*] $n$ ghiacciaio.

**glad** [glæd] $a$ lieto(a), contento(a).

**gladly** ['glædlɪ] $ad$ volentieri.

**glamorous** ['glæmərəs] $a$ affascinante, seducente.

**glamour** ['glæmə*] $n$ fascino.

**glance** [glɑːns] $n$ occhiata, sguardo // $vi$: to ~ at dare un'occhiata a; to ~ off (bullet) rimbalzare su; **glancing** $a$ (blow) che colpisce di striscio.

**gland** [glænd] $n$ ghiandola.

**glare** [glɛə*] $n$ riverbero, luce $f$ abbagliante; (look) sguardo furioso // $vi$ abbagliare; to ~ at guardare male; **glaring** $a$ (mistake) madornale.

**glass** [glɑːs] $n$ (substance) vetro; (tumbler) bicchiere $m$; (also: looking ~) specchio; ~**es** $npl$ (spectacles) occhiali $mpl$; ~**ware** $n$ vetrame $m$; ~**y** $a$ (eyes) vitreo(a).

**glaze** [gleɪz] $vt$ (door) fornire di vetro; (pottery) smaltare // $n$ smalto.

**glazier** ['gleɪzɪə*] $n$ vetraio.

**gleam** [gliːm] $n$ barlume $m$; raggio // $vi$ luccicare; ~**ing** $a$ lucente.

**glean** [gliːn] $vt$ (information) racimolare.

**glee** [gliː] $n$ allegrezza, gioia.

**glen** [glɛn] $n$ valletta.

**glib** [glɪb] $a$ dalla parola facile; facile.

**glide** [glaɪd] $vi$ scivolare; (AVIAT, birds) planare; ~**r** $n$ (AVIAT) aliante $m$; **gliding** $n$ (AVIAT) volo a vela.

**glimmer** ['glɪmə*] $vi$ luccicare // $n$ barlume $m$.

**glimpse** [glɪmps] $n$ impressione $f$ fugace // $vt$ vedere al volo.

**glint** [glɪnt] $n$ luccichio // $vi$ luccicare.

**glisten** ['glɪsn] $vi$ luccicare.

**glitter** ['glɪtə*] $vi$ scintillare // $n$ scintillio.

**gloat** [gləut] $vi$: to ~ (over) gongolare di piacere (per).

**global** ['gləubl] $a$ globale.

**globe** [gləub] $n$ globo, sfera.

**gloom** [gluːm] $n$ oscurità, buio; (sadness) tristezza, malinconia; ~**y** $a$ fosco(a), triste.

**glorious** ['glɔːrɪəs] $a$ glorioso(a); magnifico(a).

**glory** ['glɔːrɪ] $n$ gloria; splendore $m$ // $vi$: to ~ in gloriarsi di or in.

**gloss** [glɔs] $n$ (shine) lucentezza; to ~ **over** $vt$ fus scivolare su.

**glossary** ['glɔsərɪ] $n$ glossario.

**glossy** ['glɔsɪ] $a$ lucente.

**glove** [glʌv] $n$ guanto; ~ **compartment** $n$ (AUT) vano portaoggetti.

**glow** [gləu] $vi$ ardere; (face) essere luminoso(a) // $n$ bagliore $m$; (of face) colorito acceso.

**glower** ['glauə*] $vi$: to ~ (at sb) guardare (qn) in cagnesco.

**glue** [gluː] $n$ colla // $vt$ incollare.

**glum** [glʌm] $a$ abbattuto(a).

**glut** [glʌt] $n$ eccesso // $vt$ saziare; (market) saturare.

**glutton** ['glʌtn] $n$ ghiottone/a; $a$ ~ **for work** uno(a) patito(a) del lavoro.

**gnarled** [nɑːld] $a$ nodoso(a).

**gnat** [næt] $n$ moscerino.

**gnaw** [nɔː] $vt$ rodere.

**go** [gəʊ] *vb* (*pt* **went**, *pp* **gone**) *vi* andare; (*depart*) partire, andarsene; (*work*) funzionare; (*break etc*) cedere; (*be sold*): **to ~ for £10** essere venduto per 10 sterline; (*fit, suit*): **to ~ with** andare bene con; (*become*): **to ~ pale** diventare pallido(a); **to ~ mouldy** ammuffire // *n* (*pl* **~es**): **to have a ~** (*at*) provare; **to be on the ~** essere in moto; **whose ~ is it?** a chi tocca?; **he's going to do** sta per fare; **to ~ for a walk** andare a fare una passeggiata; **to ~ dancing/shopping** andare a ballare/fare la spesa; **how did it ~?** com'è andato?; **to ~ round the back/by the shop** passare da dietro/davanti al negozio; **to ~ about** *vi* (*rumour*) correre, circolare // *vt fus*: **how do I ~ about this?** qual'è la prassi per questo?; **to ~ ahead** *vi* andare avanti; **~ ahead!** faccia pure!; **to ~ along** *vi* andare, avanzare // *vt fus* percorrere; **to ~ away** *vi* partire, andarsene; **to ~ back** *vi* tornare, ritornare; (*go again*) andare di nuovo; **to ~ back on** *vt fus* (*promise*) non mantenere; **to ~ by** *vi* (*years, time*) scorrere // *vt fus* attenersi a, seguire (alla lettera); prestar fede a; **to ~ down** *vi* scendere; (*ship*) affondare; (*sun*) tramontare // *vt fus* scendere; **to ~ for** *vt fus* (*fetch*) andare a prendere; (*col: like*) andar matto(a) per; (*attack*) attaccare; saltare addosso a; **to ~ in** *vi* entrare; **to ~ in for** *vt fus* (*competition*) iscriversi a; (*be interested in*) interessarsi di; **to ~ into** *vt fus* entrare in; (*investigate*) indagare, esaminare; (*embark on*) lanciarsi in; **to ~ off** *vi* partire, andar via; (*food*) guastarsi; (*explode*) esplodere, scoppiare; (*event*) passare // *vt fus*: **I've gone off chocolate** la cioccolata non mi piace più; **the gun went off** il fucile si è scaricò; **to ~ on** *vi* continuare; (*happen*) succedere; **to ~ on doing**

continuare a fare; **to ~ out** *vi* uscire; (*fire, light*) spegnersi; **to ~ over** *vi* (*ship*) ribaltarsi // *vt fus* (*check*) esaminare; **to ~ through** *vt fus* (*town etc*) attraversare; **to ~ up** *vi* salire // *vt fus* salire su per; **to ~ without** *vt fus* fare a meno di.

**goad** [gəʊd] *vt* spronare.

**go-ahead** ['gəʊəhɛd] *a* intraprendente // *n* via *m*.

**goal** [gəʊl] *n* (SPORT) gol *m*, rete *f*; (*: place*) porta; (*fig: aim*) fine *m*, scopo; **~keeper** *n* portiere *m*; **~post** *n* palo (della porta).

**goat** [gəʊt] *n* capra.

**gobble** ['gɔbl] *vt* (*also: ~ down, ~ up*) ingoiare.

**goblet** ['gɔblɪt] *n* calice *m*, coppa.

**god** [gɔd] *n* dio; **G~** *n* Dio; **~child** *n* figlioccio/a; **~daughter** *n* figlioccia; **~dess** *n* dea; **~father** *n* padrino; **~forsaken** *a* desolato(a), sperduto(a); **~mother** *n* madrina; **~send** *n* dono del cielo; **~son** *n* figlioccio.

**goggles** ['gɔglz] *npl* occhiali *mpl* (di protezione).

**going** ['gəʊɪŋ] *n* (*conditions*) andare *m*, stato del terreno // *a*: **the ~ rate** la tariffa in vigore.

**gold** [gəʊld] *n* oro // *a* d'oro; **~en** *a* (*made of gold*) d'oro; (*gold in colour*) dorato(a); **~fish** *n* pesce *m* dorato *or* rosso; **~plated** *a* placcato(a) oro *inv*; **~smith** *n* orefice *m*, orafo.

**golf** [gɔlf] *n* golf *m*; **~ ball** *n* (*for game*) pallina da golf; (*on typewriter*) pallina; **~ club** *n* circolo di golf; (*stick*) bastone *m* or mazza da golf; **~ course** *n* campo di golf; **~er** *n* giocatore/trice di golf.

**gondola** ['gɔndələ] *n* gondola.

**gone** [gɔn] *pp of* **go** // *a* partito(a).

**gong** [gɔŋ] *n* gong *m inv*.

**good** [gʊd] *a* buono(a); (*kind*) buono(a), gentile; (*child*) bravo(a) // *n* bene *m*; **~s** *npl* (COMM *etc*) beni *mpl*; merci *fpl*; **~ bene!**, ottimo!; **to be ~ at** essere bravo(a) in;

~ **for** andare bene per; **it's** ~ **for you** fa bene; **would you be** ~ **enough to** ...? avrebbe la gentilezza di ...?; **a** ~ **deal (of)** molto(a), una buona quantità (di); **a** ~ **many** molti(e); **to make** ~ *vi* (*succeed*) aver successo // *vt* (*deficit*) colmare; (*losses*) compensare; **it's no** ~ **complaining** brontolare non serve a niente; **for** ~ per sempre, definitivamente; ~ **morning!** buon giorno!; ~ **afternoon/evening!** buona sera!; ~ **night!** buona notte!; ~**bye** *excl* arrivederci!; **G**~ **Friday** *n* Venerdì Santo; ~**looking** *a* bello(a); ~**-natured** *a* affabile; (*discussion*) amichevole, cordiale; ~**ness** *n* (*of person*) bontà; **for** ~**ness sake!** per amor di Dio!; ~**ness gracious!** santo cielo!, mamma mia!; ~**s train** *n* (*Brit*) treno *m* merci *inv*; ~**will** *n* amicizia, benevolenza; (*COMM*) avviamento.

**goose** [gu:s], *pl* **geese** *n* oca.
**gooseberry** ['guzbərı] *n* uva spina; **to play** ~ tenere la candela.
**gooseflesh** ['gu:sfleʃ] *n*, **goose pimples** *npl* pelle *f* d'oca.
**gore** [gɔ:*] *vt* incornare // *n* sangue *m* (coagulato).
**gorge** [gɔ:dʒ] *n* gola // *vt*: **to** ~ **o.s. (on)** ingozzarsi (di).
**gorgeous** ['gɔ:dʒəs] *a* magnifico(a).
**gorilla** [gə'rılə] *n* gorilla *m inv*.
**gorse** [gɔ:s] *n* ginestrone *m*.
**gory** ['gɔ:rı] *a* sanguinoso(a).
**go-slow** ['gəu'sləu] *n* (*Brit*) rallentamento dei lavori (*per agitazione sindacale*).
**gospel** ['gɔspl] *n* vangelo.
**gossip** ['gɔsıp] *n* chiacchiere *fpl*; pettegolezzi *mpl*; (*person*) pettegolo/a // *vi* chiacchierare; (*maliciously*) pettegolare.
**got** [gɔt] *pt, pp of* **get**; ~**ten** (*US*) *pp of* **get**.
**gout** [gaut] *n* gotta.
**govern** ['gʌvən] *vt* governare; (*LING*) reggere.

**governess** ['gʌvənıs] *n* governante *f*.
**government** ['gʌvnmənt] *n* governo.
**governor** ['gʌvənə*] *n* (*of state, bank*) governatore *m*; (*of school, hospital*) amministratore *m*.
**gown** [gaun] *n* vestito lungo; (*of teacher, Brit: of judge*) toga.
**G.P.** *n abbr* = **general practitioner**.
**grab** [græb] *vt* afferrare, arraffare; (*property, power*) impadronirsi di.
**grace** [greıs] *n* grazia // *vt* onorare; **5 days'** ~ dilazione *f* di 5 giorni; **to say** ~ dire il benedicite; ~**ful** *a* elegante, aggraziato(a); ~**ious** ['greıʃəs] *a* grazioso(a); misericordioso(a).
**grade** [greıd] *n* (*COMM*) qualità *f inv*; classe *f*; categoria; (*in hierarchy*) grado; (*US: SCOL*) voto; classe // *vt* classificare; ordinare; graduare; ~ **crossing** *n* (*US*) passaggio a livello; ~ **school** *n* (*US*) scuola elementare.
**gradient** ['greıdıənt] *n* pendenza, inclinazione *f*.
**gradual** ['grædjuəl] *a* graduale; ~**ly** *ad* man mano, a poco a poco.
**graduate** *n* ['grædjuıt] laureato/a // *vi* ['grædjueıt] laurearsi; **graduation** [-'eıʃən] *n* cerimonia del conferimento della laurea.
**graffiti** [grə'fi:tı] *npl* graffiti *mpl*.
**graft** [grɑ:ft] *n* (*AGR, MED*) innesto // *vt* innestare; **hard** ~ *n* (*col*): **by sheer hard** ~ lavorando da matti.
**grain** [greın] *n* grano; (*of sand*) granello; (*of wood*) venatura.
**gram** [græm] *n* grammo.
**grammar** ['græmə*] *n* grammatica; ~ **school** *n* (*Brit*) = liceo.
**grammatical** [grə'mætıkl] *a* grammaticale.
**gramme** [græm] *n* = **gram**.
**grand** [grænd] *a* grande, magnifico(a); grandioso(a); ~**children** *npl* nipoti *mpl*; ~**dad** *n* (*col*) nonno; ~**daughter** *n* nipote *f*; ~**father** *n* nonno; ~**ma** *n* (*col*) nonna; ~**mother** *n* nonna; ~**pa** *n* (*col*) = ~**dad**; ~**parents** *npl* nonni *mpl*; ~

~ **piano** $n$ pianoforte $m$ a coda; ~**son** $n$ nipote $m$; ~**stand** $n$ (SPORT) tribuna.

**granite** ['grænɪt] $n$ granito.

**granny** ['grænɪ] $n$ (col) nonna.

**grant** [grɑ:nt] $vt$ accordare; (a request) accogliere; (admit) ammettere, concedere // $n$ (SCOL) borsa; (ADMIN) sussidio, sovvenzione $f$; **to take sth for** ~**ed** dare qc per scontato.

**granulated** ['grænjuleɪtɪd] $a$: ~ **sugar** zucchero cristallizzato.

**grape** [greɪp] $n$ chicco d'uva, acino.

**grapefruit** ['greɪpfru:t] $n$ pompelmo.

**graph** [grɑ:f] $n$ grafico; ~**ic** $a$ grafico(a); (vivid) vivido(a); ~**ics** $n$ grafica // $npl$ illustrazioni $fpl$.

**grapple** ['græpl] $vi$: **to** ~ **with** essere alle prese con.

**grasp** [grɑ:sp] $vt$ afferrare // $n$ (grip) presa; (fig) potere $m$; comprensione $f$; ~**ing** $a$ avido(a).

**grass** [grɑ:s] $n$ erba; ~**hopper** $n$ cavalletta; ~-**roots** $a$ di base; ~ **snake** $n$ natrice $f$.

**grate** [greɪt] $n$ graticola (del focolare) // $vi$ cigolare, stridere // $vt$ (CULIN) grattugiare.

**grateful** ['greɪtful] $a$ grato(a), riconoscente; ~**ly** $ad$ con gratitudine.

**grater** ['greɪtə*] $n$ grattugia.

**gratify** ['grætɪfaɪ] $vt$ appagare; (whim) soddisfare.

**grating** ['greɪtɪŋ] $n$ (iron bars) grata // $a$ (noise) stridente, stridulo(a).

**gratitude** ['grætɪtju:d] $n$ gratitudine $f$.

**gratuity** [grə'tju:ɪtɪ] $n$ mancia.

**grave** [greɪv] $n$ tomba // $a$ grave, serio(a).

**gravel** ['grævl] $n$ ghiaia.

**gravestone** ['greɪvstəun] $n$ pietra tombale.

**graveyard** ['greɪvjɑ:d] $n$ cimitero.

**gravity** ['grævɪtɪ] $n$ (PHYSICS) gravità; pesantezza; (seriousness) gravità, serietà.

**gravy** ['greɪvɪ] $n$ intingolo della carne; salsa.

**gray** [greɪ] $a$ = **grey**.

**graze** [greɪz] $vi$ pascolare, pascere // $vt$ (touch lightly) sfiorare; (scrape) escoriare // $n$ (MED) escoriazione $f$.

**grease** [gri:s] $n$ (fat) grasso; (lubricant) lubrificante $m$ // $vt$ ingrassare; lubrificare; ~-**proof paper** $n$ (Brit) carta oleata; **greasy** $a$ grasso(a), untuoso(a).

**great** [greɪt] $a$ grande; (col) magnifico(a), meraviglioso(a); **G**~ **Britain** $n$ Gran Bretagna; ~**grandfather** $n$ bisnonno; ~**grandmother** $n$ bisnonna; ~**ly** $ad$ molto; ~**ness** $n$ grandezza.

**Greece** [gri:s] $n$ Grecia.

**greed** [gri:d] $n$ (also: ~**iness**) avarizia; (for food) golosità, ghiottoneria; ~**y** $a$ avido(a); goloso(a), ghiotto(a).

**Greek** [gri:k] $a$ greco(a) // $n$ greco(a); (LING) greco.

**green** [gri:n] $a$ verde; (inexperienced) inesperto(a), ingenuo(a) // $n$ verde $m$; (stretch of grass) prato; (also: village ~) ≈ piazza del paese; ~**s** $npl$ (vegetables) verdura; ~ **belt** $n$ (round town) cintura di verde; ~ **card** $n$ (AUT) carta verde; ~**ery** $n$ verde $m$; ~**gage** $n$ susina Regina Claudia; ~**grocer** $n$ (Brit) fruttivendolo/a, erbivendolo/a; ~**house** $n$ serra.

**Greenland** ['gri:nlənd] $n$ Groenlandia.

**greet** [gri:t] $vt$ salutare; ~**ing** $n$ saluto; ~**ing(s) card** $n$ cartolina d'auguri.

**grenade** [grə'neɪd] $n$ granata.

**grew** [gru:] $pt$ of **grow**.

**grey** [greɪ] $a$ grigio(a); ~**hound** $n$ levriere $m$.

**grid** [grɪd] $n$ grata; (ELEC) rete $f$.

**grief** [gri:f] $n$ dolore $m$.

**grievance** ['gri:vəns] $n$ doglianza, lagnanza.

**grieve** [gri:v] $vi$ addolorarsi; rattristarsi // $vt$ addolorare; **to** ~ **for sb** (dead person) piangere qn.

**grievous** ['gri:vəs] $a$: ~ **bodily**

harm (*LAW*) aggressione *f*.

grill [grɪl] *n* (*on cooker*) griglia // *vt* (*Brit*) cuocere ai ferri; (*question*) interrogare senza sosta.

grille [grɪl] *n* grata; (*AUT*) griglia.

grim [grɪm] *a* sinistro(a), brutto(a).

grimace [grɪ'meɪs] *n* smorfia // *vi* fare smorfie; fare boccacce.

grime [graɪm] *n* sudiciume *m*.

grimy ['graɪmɪ] *a* sudicio(a).

grin [grɪn] *n* sorriso smagliante // *vi* fare un gran sorriso.

grind [graɪnd] *vt* (*pt, pp* ground) macinare; (*make sharp*) arrotare // *n* (*work*) sgobbata; to ~ one's teeth digrignare i denti.

grip [grɪp] *n* impugnatura; presa; (*holdall*) borsa da viaggio // *vt* impugnare; afferrare; to come to ~s with affrontare; cercare di risolvere.

gripping ['grɪpɪŋ] *a* avvincente.

grisly ['grɪzlɪ] *a* macabro(a), orrido(a).

gristle ['grɪsl] *n* cartilagine *f*.

grit [grɪt] *n* ghiaia; (*courage*) fegato // *vt* (*road*) coprire di sabbia; to ~ one's teeth stringere i denti.

groan [grəʊn] *n* gemito // *vi* gemere.

grocer ['grəʊsə] *n* negoziante *m* di generi alimentari; ~ies *npl* provviste *fpl*.

groggy ['grɔgɪ] *a* barcollante.

groin [grɔɪn] *n* inguine *m*.

groom [gruːm] *n* palafreniere *m*; (*also*: bride~) sposo // *vt* (*horse*) strigliare; (*fig*): to ~ sb for avviare qn a.

groove [gruːv] *n* scanalatura, solco.

grope [grəʊp] *vi* andare a tentoni; to ~ for *vt fus* cercare a tastoni.

gross [grəʊs] *a* grossolano(a); (*COMM*) lordo(a) // *n* (*pl inv*) (*twelve dozen*) grossa; ~ly *ad* (*greatly*) molto.

grotesque [grəʊ'tɛsk] *a* grottesco(a).

grotto ['grɔtəʊ] *n* grotta.

ground [graʊnd] *pt, pp of* grind // *n* suolo, terra; (*land*) terreno; (*SPORT*) campo; (*reason*: *gen pl*) ragione *f*;

(*US*: *also*: ~ wire) terra // *vt* (*plane*) tenere a terra // *vi* (*ship*) arenarsi; ~s *npl* (*of coffee etc*) fondi *mpl*; (*gardens etc*) terreno, giardini *mpl*; on/to the ~ per/a terra; to gain/lose ~ guadagnare/perdere terreno; ~ cloth *n* (*US*) = ~sheet; ~ing *n* (*in education*) basi *fpl*; ~less *a* infondato(a); ~sheet *n* (*Brit*) telone *m* impermeabile; ~ staff *n* personale *m* di terra; ~ swell *n* maremoto; (*fig*) movimento d'opinione; ~work *n* preparazione *f*.

group [gruːp] *n* gruppo // *vt* (*also*: ~ together) raggruppare // *vi* (*also*: ~ together) raggrupparsi.

grouse [graʊs] *n* (*pl inv*) (*bird*) tetraone *m* // *vi* (*complain*) brontolare.

grove [grəʊv] *n* boschetto.

grovel ['grɔvl] *vi* (*fig*): to ~ (before) strisciare (di fronte a).

grow [grəʊ], *pt* grew, *pp* grown *vi* crescere; (*increase*) aumentare; (*become*): to ~ rich/weak arricchirsi/indebolirsi // *vt* coltivare, far crescere; to ~ up *vi* farsi grande, crescere; ~er *n* coltivatore/trice; ~ing *a* (*fear, amount*) crescente.

growl [graʊl] *vi* ringhiare.

grown [grəʊn] *pp of* grow // *a* adulto(a), maturo(a); ~-up *n* adulto/a, grande *m/f*.

growth [grəʊθ] *n* crescita, sviluppo; (*what has grown*) crescita; (*MED*) escrescenza, tumore *m*.

grub [grʌb] *n* larva; (*col*: *food*) roba (da mangiare).

grubby ['grʌbɪ] *a* sporco(a).

grudge [grʌdʒ] *n* rancore *m* // *vt*: to ~ sb sth dare qc a qn di malavoglia; invidiare qc a qn; to bear sb a ~ (for) serbar rancore a qn (per).

gruelling ['grʊəlɪŋ] *a* estenuante.

gruesome ['gruːsəm] *a* orribile.

gruff [grʌf] *a* rozzo(a).

grumble ['grʌmbl] *vi* brontolare, lagnarsi.

grumpy ['grʌmpɪ] *a* stizzito(a).

**grunt** [grʌnt] vi grugnire // n grugnito.

**G-string** ['dʒi:strɪŋ] n tanga m inv.

**guarantee** [gærən'ti:] n garanzia // vt garantire.

**guard** [gɑ:d] n guardia; (BOXING) difesa; (one man) sentinella; (Brit RAIL) capotreno // vt fare la guardia a; **~ed** a (fig) cauto(a), guardingo(a); **~ian** n custode m; (of minor) tutore/trice; **~'s van** n (Brit RAIL) vagone m di servizio.

**guerrilla** [gə'rɪlə] n guerrigliero; **~ warfare** n guerriglia.

**guess** [gɛs] vi indovinare // vt indovinare; (US) credere, pensare // n congettura; **~work** n: I got the answer by ~work ho azzeccato la risposta.

**guest** [gɛst] n ospite m/f; (in hotel) cliente m/f; **~-house** n pensione f; **~ room** n camera degli ospiti.

**guffaw** [gʌ'fɔ:] vi scoppiare in una risata sonora.

**guidance** ['gaɪdəns] n guida, direzione f.

**guide** [gaɪd] n (person, book etc) guida; (also: **girl ~**) giovane esploratrice f // vt guidare; **~book** n guida; **~ dog** n cane m guida inv; **~lines** npl (fig) indicazioni fpl, linee fpl direttive.

**guild** [gɪld] n arte f, corporazione f; associazione f.

**guile** [gaɪl] n astuzia.

**guillotine** ['gɪləti:n] n ghigliottina.

**guilt** [gɪlt] n colpevolezza; **~y** a colpevole.

**guinea pig** ['gɪnɪ-] n cavia.

**guise** [gaɪz] n maschera.

**guitar** [gɪ'tɑ:*] n chitarra.

**gulf** [gʌlf] n golfo; (abyss) abisso.

**gull** [gʌl] n gabbiano.

**gullet** ['gʌlɪt] n gola.

**gullible** ['gʌlɪbl] a credulo(a).

**gully** ['gʌlɪ] n burrone m; gola; canale m.

**gulp** [gʌlp] vi deglutire; (from emotion) avere il nodo in gola // vt

(also: **~ down**) tracannare, inghiottire.

**gum** [gʌm] n (ANAT) gengiva; (glue) colla; (sweet) gelatina di frutta; (also: **chewing-~**) chewing-gum m // vt incollare; **~boots** npl (Brit) stivali mpl di gomma.

**gun** [gʌn] n fucile m; (small) pistola, rivoltella; (rifle) carabina; (shotgun) fucile da caccia; (cannon) cannone m; **~boat** n cannoniera; **~fire** n spari mpl; **~man** n bandito armato; **~ner** n artigliere m; **~point** n: at **~point** sotto minaccia di fucile; **~powder** n polvere f da sparo; **~shot** n sparo; **~smith** n armaiolo.

**gurgle** ['gə:gl] vi gorgogliare.

**guru** ['guru:] n guru m inv.

**gush** [gʌʃ] vi sgorgare; (fig) abbandonarsi ad effusioni.

**gusset** ['gʌsɪt] n gherone m.

**gust** [gʌst] n (of wind) raffica; (of smoke) buffata.

**gusto** ['gʌstəu] n entusiasmo.

**gut** [gʌt] n intestino, budello; (MUS etc) minugia; **~s** npl (courage) fegato.

**gutter** ['gʌtə*] n (of roof) grondaia; (in street) cunetta.

**guy** [gaɪ] n (also: **~rope**) cavo o corda di fissaggio; (col: man) tipo, elemento; (figure) effigie di Guy Fawkes.

**guzzle** ['gʌzl] vi gozzovigliare // vt trangugiare.

**gym** [dʒɪm] n (also: **gymnasium**) palestra; (also: **gymnastics**) ginnastica.

**gymnast** ['dʒɪmnæst] n ginnasta m/f; **~ics** [-'næstɪks] n, npl ginnastica.

**gym shoes** npl scarpe fpl da ginnastica.

**gym slip** n (Brit) grembiule m da scuola (per ragazze).

**gynaecologist**, (US) **gynecologist** [gaɪnɪ'kɔlədʒɪst] n ginecologo/a.

**gypsy** ['dʒɪpsɪ] n = **gipsy**.

**gyrate** [dʒaɪ'reɪt] vi girare.

# H

**haberdashery** [ˈhæbəˈdæʃərɪ] n (Brit) merceria.

**habit** [ˈhæbɪt] n abitudine f; (costume) abito; (REL) tonaca.

**habitation** [hæbɪˈteɪʃən] n abitazione f.

**habitual** [həˈbɪtjuəl] a abituale; (drinker, liar) inveterato(a); ~ly ad abitualmente, di solito.

**hack** [hæk] vt tagliare, fare a pezzi // n (cut) taglio; (blow) colpo; (pej: writer) negro.

**hackneyed** [ˈhæknɪd] a comune, trito(a).

**had** [hæd] pt, pp of **have**.

**haddock** pl ~ or ~s [ˈhædək] n eglefino.

**hadn't** [ˈhædnt] = **had not**.

**haemorrhage**, (US) **hemorrhage** [ˈhemərɪdʒ] n emorragia.

**haemorrhoids**, (US) **hemorrhoids** [ˈhemərɔɪdz] npl emorroidi fpl.

**haggard** [ˈhægəd] a smunto(a).

**haggle** [ˈhægl] vi mercanteggiare.

**Hague** [heɪg] n: The ~ L'Aia.

**hail** [heɪl] n grandine f // vt (call) chiamare; (greet) salutare // vi grandinare; ~**stone** n chicco di grandine.

**hair** [heə*] n capelli mpl; (single hair: on head) capello; (: on body) pelo; **to do one's** ~ pettinarsi; ~**brush** n spazzola per capelli; ~**cut** n taglio di capelli; ~**do** [ˈheədu:] n acconciatura, pettinatura; ~**dresser** n parrucchiere/a; ~**dryer** n asciugacapelli m inv; ~**grip** n forcina; ~**pin** n forcina; ~**pin bend**, (US) ~**pin curve** n tornante m; ~**raising** a orripilante; ~ **remover** n crema depilatoria; ~ **spray** n lacca per capelli; ~**style** n pettinatura, acconciatura; ~**y** a irsuto(a); peloso(a); (col: frightening) spaventoso(a).

**hake**, pl ~ or ~s [heɪk] n nasello.

**half** [hɑ:f] n (pl **halves**) mezzo, metà f inv // a mezzo(a) // ad a mezzo, a metà; ~ **an hour** mezz'ora; ~ **a dozen** mezza dozzina; ~ **a pound** mezza libbra; **two and a** ~ due e mezzo; **a week and a** ~ una settimana e mezza; ~ (**of it**) la metà; ~ (**of**) la metà di; **to cut sth in** ~ tagliare qc in due; ~ **asleep** mezzo(a) addormentato(a); ~**back** n (SPORT) mediano; ~**-breed**, ~**caste** n meticcio/a; ~**-hearted** a tiepido(a); ~**-hour** n mezz'ora; ~ **mast** n: **at** ~**-mast** (flag) a mezz'asta; ~**penny** [ˈheɪpnɪ] n prezzo a, ad a metà prezzo; ~ **term** n (Brit SCOL) vacanza a or di metà trimestre; ~**-time** n (SPORT) intervallo; ~**way** ad a metà strada.

**halibut** [ˈhælɪbət] n (pl inv) ippoglosso.

**hall** [hɔ:l] n sala, salone m; (entrance way) entrata; (corridor) corridoio; (mansion) grande villa, maniero; ~ **of residence** n (Brit) casa dello studente.

**hallmark** [ˈhɔ:lmɑ:k] n marchio di garanzia; (fig) caratteristica.

**hallo** [həˈləʊ] excl = **hello**.

**Hallowe'en** [hæləʊˈi:n] n vigilia d'Ognissanti.

**hallucination** [həlu:sɪˈneɪʃən] n allucinazione f.

**hallway** [ˈhɔ:lweɪ] n corridoio; (entrance) ingresso.

**halo** [ˈheɪləʊ] n (of saint etc) aureola; (of sun) alone m.

**halt** [hɔ:lt] n fermata // vt fermare // vi fermarsi.

**halve** [hɑ:v] vt (apple etc) dividere a metà; (expense) ridurre di metà.

**halves** [hɑ:vz] npl of **half**.

**ham** [hæm] n prosciutto.

**hamburger** [ˈhæmbə:gə*] n hamburger m inv.

**hamlet** [ˈhæmlɪt] n paesetto.

**hammer** [ˈhæmə*] n martello // vt martellare; (fig) sconfiggere duramente // vi: to ~ on or at the door picchiare alla porta.

**hammock** ['hæmək] n amaca.

**hamper** ['hæmpə*] vt impedire // n cesta.

**hamster** ['hæmstə*] n criceto.

**hand** [hænd] n mano f; (of clock) lancetta; (handwriting) scrittura; (at cards) mano; (: game) partita; (worker) operaio/a // vt dare, passare; to give sb a ~ dare una mano a qn; at ~ a portata di mano; in ~ a disposizione; (work) in corso; on ~ (person) disponibile; (services) pronto(a) a intervenire; to ~ (information etc) a portata di mano; on the one ~ ..., on the other ~ da un lato ..., dall'altro; to ~ in vt consegnare; to ~ out vt distribuire; to ~ over vt passare; cedere; ~bag n borsetta; ~book n manuale m; ~brake n freno a mano; ~cuffs npl manciette fpl; ~ful n manciata, pugno.

**handicap** ['hændɪkæp] n handicap m inv // vt handicappare; to be physically ~ped essere handicappato(a); to be mentally ~ped essere un(a) handicappato(a) mentale.

**handicraft** ['hændɪkrɑ:ft] n lavoro d'artigiano.

**handiwork** ['hændɪwɔ:k] n opera.

**handkerchief** ['hæŋkətʃɪf] n fazzoletto.

**handle** ['hændl] n (of door etc) maniglia; (of cup etc) ansa; (of knife etc) impugnatura; (of saucepan) manico; (for winding) manovella // vt toccare, maneggiare; (deal with) occuparsi di; (treat: people) trattare; "~ with care" "fragile"; to fly off the ~ (fig) perdere le staffe, uscire dai gangheri; ~bar(s) n|pl manubrio.

**hand:** ~ **luggage** n bagagli mpl a mano; ~**made** a fatto(a) a mano; ~**out** n (leaflet) volantino; (at lecture) prospetto; ~**rail** n corrimano; ~**shake** n stretta di mano.

**handsome** ['hænsəm] a bello(a).

(reward) generoso(a); (profit, fortune) considerevole.

**handwriting** ['hændraɪtɪŋ] n scrittura.

**handy** ['hændɪ] a (person) bravo(a); (close at hand) a portata di mano; (convenient) comodo(a); ~**man** n tuttofare m inv.

**hang** [hæŋ], pt, pp **hung** vt appendere; (criminal: pt, pp **hanged**) impiccare // vi pendere; (hair) scendere; (drapery) cadere; to get the ~ of sth (col) capire come qc funziona; to ~ about vi bighellonare, ciondolare; to ~ on vi (wait) aspettare; to ~ up vi (TEL) riattaccare // vt appendere.

**hangar** ['hæŋə*] n hangar m inv.

**hanger** ['hæŋə*] n gruccia.

**hanger-on** [hæŋər'ɔn] n parassita m.

**hang-gliding** ['hæŋglaɪdɪŋ] n volo col deltaplano.

**hangover** ['hæŋəuvə*] n (after drinking) postumi mpl di sbornia.

**hang-up** ['hæŋʌp] n complesso.

**hanker** ['hæŋkə*] vi: to ~ **after** bramare.

**hankie, hanky** ['hæŋkɪ] n abbr = **handkerchief.**

**haphazard** [hæp'hæzəd] a a casaccio, alla carlona.

**happen** ['hæpən] vi accadere, succedere; as it ~s guarda caso; ~**ing** n avvenimento.

**happily** ['hæpɪlɪ] ad felicemente; fortunatamente.

**happiness** ['hæpɪnɪs] n felicità, contentezza.

**happy** ['hæpɪ] a felice, contento(a); ~ **with** (arrangements etc) soddisfatto(a) di; ~ **birthday!** buon compleanno!; ~**go-lucky** a spensierato(a).

**harangue** [hə'ræŋ] vt arringare.

**harass** ['hærəs] vt molestare; ~**ment** n molestia.

**harbour,** (US) **harbor** ['hɑ:bə*] n porto // vt dare rifugio a.

**hard** [hɑ:d] a duro(a) // ad (work) sodo; (think, try) bene; to look ~ at guardare fissamente; esaminare attentamente; **no ~ feelings!** senza rancore!; **to be ~ of hearing** essere duro(a) d'orecchio; **to be ~ done by** essere trattato(a) ingiustamente; **~back** n libro rilegato; **~ cash** n denaro in contanti; **~ disk** n (COMPUT) disco rigido; **~en** vt, vi indurire; **~-headed** a pratico(a); **~ labour** n lavori forzati mpl.

**hardly** ['hɑːdlɪ] ad (scarcely) appena; **it's ~ the case** non è proprio il caso; **that can ~ be true** non può essere vero; **~ anyone/ anywhere** quasi nessuno/da nessuna parte; **~ ever** quasi mai.

**hardship** ['hɑːdʃɪp] n avversità f inv; privazioni fpl.

**hard-up** [hɑːd'ʌp] a (col) al verde.

**hardware** ['hɑːdwɛə*] n ferramenta fpl; (COMPUT) hardware m; **~ shop** n (negozio di) ferramenta fpl.

**hard-wearing** [hɑːd'wɛərɪŋ] a resistente; (shoes) robusto(a).

**hard-working** [hɑːd'wəːkɪŋ] a lavoratore(trice).

**hardy** ['hɑːdɪ] a robusto(a); (plant) resistente al gelo.

**hare** [hɛə*] n lepre f; **~-brained** a folle; scervellato(a).

**harm** [hɑːm] n male m; (wrong) danno n; vt (person) fare male a; (thing) danneggiare; **out of ~'s way** al sicuro; **~ful** a dannoso(a); **~less** a innocuo(a); inoffensivo(a).

**harmonica** [hɑː'mɔnɪkə] n armonica.

**harmonious** [hɑː'məʊnɪəs] a armonioso(a).

**harmony** ['hɑːmənɪ] n armonia.

**harness** ['hɑːnɪs] n bardatura, finimenti mpl // vt (horse) bardare; (resources) sfruttare.

**harp** [hɑːp] n arpa // vi: **to ~ on about** insistere tediosamente su.

**harpoon** [hɑː'puːn] n arpione m.

**harrowing** ['hærəʊɪŋ] a straziante.

**harsh** [hɑːʃ] a (hard) duro(a); (severe) severo(a); (unpleasant: sound) rauco(a); (: colour)

chiassoso(a); violento(a); **~ly** ad duramente; severamente.

**harvest** ['hɑːvɪst] n raccolto; (of grapes) vendemmia // vt fare il raccolto di, raccogliere; vendemmiare.

**has** [hæz] vb see **have**.

**hash** [hæʃ] n (CULIN) specie di spezzatino fatto con carne già cotta; (fig: mess) pasticcio.

**hashish** ['hæʃɪʃ] n hascisc m.

**hasn't** ['hæznt] = **has not**.

**hassle** ['hæsl] n (col) sacco di problemi.

**haste** [heɪst] n fretta; precipitazione f; **~n** ['heɪsn] vt affrettare // vi affrettarsi; **hastily** in fretta; precipitosamente; **hasty** a affrettato(a); precipitoso(a).

**hat** [hæt] n cappello.

**hatch** [hætʃ] n (NAUT: also: **~way**) boccaporto; (also: **service ~**) portello di servizio // vi schiudersi // vt covare.

**hatchback** ['hætʃbæk] n (AUT) tre (or cinque) porte f inv.

**hatchet** ['hætʃɪt] n accetta.

**hate** [heɪt] vt odiare, detestare // n odio; **~ful** a odioso(a), detestabile.

**hatred** ['heɪtrɪd] n odio.

**hat trick** n: **to get a ~** segnare tre punti consecutivi (or vincere tre volte consecutive).

**haughty** ['hɔːtɪ] a altero(a), arrogante.

**haul** [hɔːl] vt trascinare, tirare // n (of fish) pescata; (of stolen goods etc) bottino; **~age** n trasporto; autotrasporto; **~ier**, (US) **~er** n trasportatore m.

**haunch** [hɔːntʃ] n anca.

**haunt** [hɔːnt] vt (subj: fear) pervadere; (: person) frequentare // n rifugio; **a ghost ~s this house** questa casa è abitata da un fantasma.

┌─────────────┐
│ **KEYWORD** │
└─────────────┘

**have** [hæv], pt, pp **had** ♦ auxiliary vb **1** (gen) avere; essere; **to ~**

arrived/gone essere arrivato(a)/ andato(a); to ~ eaten/slept avere mangiato/dormito; he has been kind/promoted è stato gentile/ promosso; having finished or when he had finished, he left dopo aver finito, se n'è andato

2 (*in tag questions*): you've done it, ~n't you? l'ha fatto, (non è) vero?; he hasn't done it, has he? non l'ha fatto, vero?

3 (*in short answers and questions*): you've made a mistake — no I ~n't/so I ~ ha fatto un errore — ma no, niente affatto/sì, è vero; we ~n't paid — yes we ~! non abbiamo pagato — ma sì che abbiamo pagato; I've been there before, ~ you? ci sono già stato, e lei?

♦ *modal auxiliary vb* (*be obliged*): to ~ (got) to do sth dover fare qc; I ~n't got *or* I don't ~ to wear glasses non ho bisogno di portare gli occhiali

♦ *vt* 1 (*possess, obtain*) avere; he has (got) blue eyes/dark hair ha gli occhi azzurri/i capelli scuri; do you ~ *or* ~ you got a car/phone? ha la macchina/il telefono?; may I ~ your address? potrebbe darmi il suo indirizzo?; you can ~ it for £5 te lo lascio per 5 sterline

2 (+ *noun: take, hold etc*): to ~ breakfast/a swim/a bath fare colazione/una nuotata/un bagno; to ~ lunch pranzare; to ~ dinner cenare; to ~ a drink bere qualcosa; to ~ a cigarette fumare una sigaretta

3: to ~ sth done far fare qc; to ~ one's hair cut farsi tagliare i capelli; to ~ sb do sth far fare qc a qn

4 (*experience, suffer*) avere; to ~ a cold/flu avere il raffreddore/ l'influenza; she had her bag stolen le hanno rubato la borsa

5 (*col: dupe*): you've been had! ci sei cascato!

to have out *vt*: to ~ it out with sb (*settle a problem etc*) mettere le cose in chiaro con qn

haven ['heɪvn] *n* porto; (*fig*) rifugio.

haven't ['hævnt] = have not.

haversack ['hævəsæk] *n* zaino.

havoc ['hævək] *n* caos *m*.

hawk [hɔːk] *n* falco.

hay [heɪ] *n* fieno; ~ fever *n* febbre *f* da fieno; ~stack *n* pagliaio.

haywire ['heɪwaɪə] *a* (*col*): to go ~ perdere la testa; impazzire.

hazard ['hæzəd] *n* azzardo, ventura; pericolo, rischio; ~ (warning) lights *npl* (*AUT*) luci *fpl* di emergenza.

haze [heɪz] *n* foschia.

hazelnut ['heɪzlnʌt] *n* nocciola.

hazy ['heɪzɪ] *a* fosco(a); (*idea*) vago(a); (*photograph*) indistinto(a).

he [hiː] *pronoun* lui, egli; it is ~ who ... è lui che ....

head [hed] *n* testa, capo; (*leader*) capo // *vt* (*list*) essere in testa a; (*group*) essere a capo di; ~s (or tails) testa (o croce), pari (o dispari); ~ first *a* capofitto, di testa; ~ over heels in love pazzamente innamorato(a); to ~ the ball dare di testa alla palla; to ~ for *vt fus* dirigersi verso; ~ache *n* mal *m* di testa; ~dress *n* (*of Indian etc*) copricapo; (*of bride*) acconciatura; ~ing *n* titolo; intestazione *f*; ~lamp *n* (*Brit*) = ~light; ~land *n* promontorio; ~light *n* fanale *m*; ~line *n* titolo; ~long *ad* (*fall*) a capofitto; (*rush*) precipitosamente; ~master *n* preside *m*; ~mistress *n* preside *f*; ~ office *n* sede *f* (centrale); ~-on *a* (*collision*) frontale; ~phones *npl* cuffia; ~quarters (HQ) *npl* ufficio centrale; (*MIL*) quartiere *m* generale; ~-rest *n* poggiacapo; ~room *n* (*in car*) altezza dell'abitacolo; (*under bridge*) altezza limite; ~scarf *n* foulard *m inv*; ~strong *a* testardo(a); ~waiter *n* capocameriere *m*; ~way *n*: to make ~way fare progressi

~**wind** n controvento; ~**y** a (experience, period) inebriante.

**heal** [hi:l] vt, vi guarire.

**health** [hɛlθ] n salute f; ~ **food**s n(pl) alimenti mpl integrali; **the H~ Service** n (Brit) = il Servizio Sanitario Statale; ~**y** a (person) in buona salute; (climate) salubre; (food) salutare; (attitude etc) sano(a).

**heap** [hi:p] n mucchio // vt ammucchiare.

**hear**, pt, pp **heard** [hɪə*, hə:d] vt sentire; (news) ascoltare; (lecture) assistere a // vi sentire; **to** ~ **about** avere notizie di; sentire parlare di; **to** ~ **from sb** ricevere notizie da qn; ~**ing** n (sense) udito; (of witnesses) audizione f; (of a case) udienza; ~**ing aid** n apparecchio acustico; ~**say** n dicerie fpl, chiacchiere fpl.

**hearse** [hə:s] n carro funebre.

**heart** [hɑ:t] n cuore m; ~**s** npl (CARDS) cuori mpl; **at** ~ in fondo; **by** ~ (learn, know) a memoria; ~ **attack** n attacco di cuore; ~**beat** n battito del cuore; ~**broken**: **to be** ~**broken** avere il cuore spezzato; ~**burn** n bruciore m di stomaco; ~ **failure** n arresto cardiaco; ~**felt** a sincero(a).

**hearth** [hɑ:θ] n focolare m.

**heartily** ['hɑ:tɪlɪ] ad (laugh) di cuore; (eat) di buon appetito; (agree) in pieno, completamente.

**hearty** ['hɑ:tɪ] a caloroso(a); robusto(a), sano(a); vigoroso(a).

**heat** [hi:t] n calore m; (fig) ardore m; fuoco; (SPORT: also: **qualifying** ~) prova eliminatoria // vt scaldare; **to** ~ **up** vi (liquids) scaldarsi; (room) riscaldarsi // vt riscaldare; ~**ed** a riscaldato(a); (fig) appassionato(a); acceso(a), eccitato(a); ~**er** n stufa; radiatore m.

**heath** [hi:θ] n (Brit) landa.

**heathen** ['hi:ðn] a, n pagano(a).

**heather** ['hɛðə*] n erica.

**heating** ['hi:tɪŋ] n riscaldamento.

**heatstroke** ['hi:tstrəuk] n colpo di sole.

**heatwave** ['hi:tweɪv] n ondata di caldo.

**heave** [hi:v] vt sollevare (con forza) // vi sollevarsi; (retch) aver conati di vomito // n (push) grande spinta.

**heaven** ['hɛvn] n paradiso, cielo; ~**ly** a divino(a), celeste.

**heavily** ['hɛvɪlɪ] ad pesantemente; (drink, smoke) molto.

**heavy** ['hɛvɪ] a pesante; (sea) grosso(a); (rain) forte; (drinker, smoker) gran (before noun); ~ **goods vehicle (HGV)** n veicolo per trasporti pesanti; ~**weight** n (SPORT) peso massimo.

**Hebrew** ['hi:bru:] a ebreo(a) // n (LING) ebraico.

**Hebrides** ['hɛbrɪdi:z] npl: **the** ~ le Ebridi.

**heckle** ['hɛkl] vt interpellare e dare noia a (un oratore).

**hectic** ['hɛktɪk] a movimentato(a).

**he'd** [hi:d] = **he would**, **he had**.

**hedge** [hɛdʒ] n siepe f // vi essere elusivo(a); **to** ~ **one's bets** (fig) coprirsi dai rischi.

**hedgehog** ['hɛdʒhɒg] n riccio.

**heed** [hi:d] vt (also: **take** ~ **of**) badare a, far conto di; ~**less** a sbadato(a).

**heel** [hi:l] n (ANAT) calcagno; (of shoe) tacco // vt (shoe) rifare i tacchi a.

**hefty** ['hɛftɪ] a (person) solido(a); (parcel) pesante; (piece, price) grosso(a).

**heifer** ['hɛfə*] n giovenca.

**height** [haɪt] n altezza; (high ground) altura; (fig: of glory) apice m; (: of stupidity) colmo; ~**en** vt innalzare; (fig) accrescere.

**heir** [ɛə*] n erede m; ~**ess** n erede f; ~**loom** n mobile m (or gioiello or quadro) di famiglia.

**held** [hɛld] pt, pp of **hold**.

**helicopter** ['hɛlɪkɒptə*] n elicottero.

**heliport** ['hɛlɪpɔ:t] n eliporto.

**helium** ['hi:lɪəm] n elio.

**hell** [hɛl] n inferno; ~! (col) porca

miseria!, accidenti!

**he'll** [hi:l] = **he will, he shall**.

**hellish** ['helɪʃ] a infernale.

**hello** [hə'ləu] excl buon giorno!; ciao! (to sb one addresses as "tu"); (surprise) ma guarda!

**helm** [helm] n (NAUT) timone m.

**helmet** ['helmɪt] n casco.

**help** [help] n aiuto; (charwoman) donna di servizio; (assistant etc) impiegato/a // vt aiutare; ~! aiuto!; ~ yourself (to bread) si serva (del pane); he can't ~ it non ci può far niente; ~er n aiutante m/f, assistente m/f; ~ful a di grande aiuto; (useful) utile; ~ing n porzione f; ~less a impotente; debole.

**hem** [hem] n orlo // vt fare l'orlo a; to ~ in vt circondare.

**he-man** ['hi:mæn] n fusto.

**hemisphere** ['hemɪsfɪə*] n emisfero.

**hemorrhage** ['hemərɪdʒ] n (US) = **haemorrhage**.

**hemorrhoids** ['hemərɔɪdz] npl (US) = **haemorrhoids**.

**hen** [hen] n gallina.

**hence** [hens] ad (therefore) dunque; 2 years ~ di qui a 2 anni; ~forth ad d'ora in poi.

**henchman** ['hentʃmən] n (pej) caudatario.

**henpecked** ['henpekt] a dominato dalla moglie.

**hepatitis** [hepə'taɪtɪs] n epatite f.

**her** [hə:*] pronoun (direct) la, l' + vowel; (indirect) le; (stressed, after prep) lei; see note at **she** // a il(la) suo(a), i(le) suoi(sue); see also **me, my**.

**herald** ['herəld] n araldo // vt annunciare.

**heraldry** ['herəldrɪ] n araldica.

**herb** [hə:b] n erba.

**herd** [hə:d] n mandria.

**here** [hɪə*] ad qui, qua // excl ehi!; ~! (at roll call) presente!; ~ is/are ecco; ~'s my sister ecco mia sorella; ~ he/she is eccolo/eccola; ~ she comes eccola che viene; ~after ad in futuro; dopo questo // n: the

~after l'al di là m; ~by ad (in letter) con la presente.

**hereditary** [hɪ'redɪtrɪ] a ereditario(a).

**heresy** ['herəsɪ] n eresia.

**heretic** ['herətɪk] n eretico/a.

**heritage** ['herɪtɪdʒ] n eredità; (fig) retaggio.

**hermetically** [hə:'metɪklɪ] ad: ~ sealed ermeticamente chiuso(a).

**hermit** ['hə:mɪt] n eremita m.

**hernia** ['hə:nɪə] n ernia.

**hero**, ~es ['hɪərəu] n eroe m.

**heroin** ['herəuɪn] n eroina.

**heroine** ['herəuɪn] n eroina.

**heron** ['herən] n airone m.

**herring** ['herɪŋ] n aringa.

**hers** [hə:z] pronoun il(la) suo(a), i(le) suoi(sue); see also **mine**.

**herself** [hə:'self] pronoun (reflexive) si; (emphatic) lei stessa; (after prep) se stessa, sé; see also **oneself**.

**he's** [hi:z] = **he is, he has**.

**hesitant** ['hezɪtənt] a esitante, indeciso(a).

**hesitate** ['hezɪteɪt] vi: to ~ (about/to do) esitare (su/a fare); **hesitation** [-'teɪʃən] n esitazione f.

**heterosexual** ['hetərəu'seksjuəl] a, n eterosessuale (m/f).

**hexagon** ['heksəgən] n esagono.

**heyday** ['heɪdeɪ] n: the ~ of i bei giorni di, l'età d'oro di.

**HGV** n abbr = **heavy goods vehicle**.

**hi** [haɪ] excl ciao!

**hiatus** [haɪ'eɪtəs] n vuoto; (LING) iato.

**hibernate** ['haɪbəneɪt] vi ibernare.

**hiccough, hiccup** ['hɪkʌp] vi singhiozzare // n singhiozzo.

**hide** [haɪd] n (skin) pelle f // vb (pt hid, pp hidden [haɪd, 'hɪdn]) vt: to ~ sth (from sb) nascondere qc (a qn) // vi: to ~ (from sb) nascondersi (da qn); ~-and-seek n rimpiattino; ~away n nascondiglio.

**hideous** ['hɪdɪəs] a laido(a); orribile.

**hiding** ['haɪdɪŋ] n (beating) bastonata; to be in ~ (concealed) tenersi nascosto(a).

**hierarchy** ['haɪərɑːkɪ] n gerarchia.

**hi-fi** ['haɪfaɪ] n stereo // a ad alta fedeltà, hi-fi inv.

**high** [haɪ] a alto(a); (speed, respect, number) grande; (wind) forte // ad alto, in alto; 20m ~ alto(a) 20m; ~**boy** n (US: tallboy) cassettone m; ~**brow** a, n intellettuale (m/f); ~**chair** n seggiolone m; ~**er education** n studi mpl superiori; ~-**handed** a prepotente; ~**jack** vt = **hijack**; ~ **jump** n (SPORT) salto in alto; **the H~lands** npl le Highlands scozzesi; ~**light** n (fig: of event) momento culminante // vt mettere in evidenza; ~**ly** ad molto; ~**ly strung** a teso(a) di nervi, eccitabile; ~**ness** n altezza; Her H~ness Sua Altezza; ~-**pitched** a acuto(a); ~-**rise block** n palazzone m; ~ **school** n scuola secondaria; (US) istituto superiore d'istruzione; ~ **season** n (Brit) alta stagione; ~ **street** n (Brit) strada principale.

**highway** ['haɪweɪ] n strada maestra; H~ **Code** n (Brit) codice m della strada.

**hijack** ['haɪdʒæk] vt dirottare; ~**er** n dirottatore/trice.

**hike** [haɪk] vi fare un'escursione a piedi // n escursione f a piedi; (in prices) aumento; ~**r** n escursionista m/f.

**hilarious** [hɪ'lɛərɪəs] a (behaviour, event) che fa schiantare dal ridere.

**hilarity** [hɪ'lærɪtɪ] n ilarità.

**hill** [hɪl] n collina, colle m; (fairly high) montagna; (on road) salita; ~**side** n fianco della collina; ~**y** a collinoso(a); montagnoso(a).

**hilt** [hɪlt] n (of sword) elsa; **to the** ~ (fig: support) fino in fondo.

**him** [hɪm] pronoun (direct) lo, l' + vowel; (indirect) gli; (stressed, after prep) lui; see also **me**; ~**self** pronoun (reflexive) si; (emphatic) lui stesso; (after prep) se stesso, sé; see also **oneself**.

**hind** [haɪnd] a posteriore // n cerva.

**hinder** ['hɪndə*] vt ostacolare; (delay) tardare; (prevent): **to** ~ **sb from doing** impedire a qn di fare; **hindrance** ['hɪndrəns] n ostacolo, impedimento.

**hindsight** ['haɪndsaɪt] n: **with** ~ con il senno di poi.

**Hindu** ['hɪnduː] n indù m/f inv.

**hinge** [hɪndʒ] n cardine m // vi (fig): **to** ~ **on** dipendere da.

**hint** [hɪnt] n accenno, allusione f; (advice) consiglio // vt: **to** ~ **that** lasciar capire che // vi: **to** ~ **at** accennare a.

**hip** [hɪp] n anca, fianco.

**hippopotamus**, pl ~**es** or **hippopotami** [hɪpə'pɒtəməs, -'pɒtəmaɪ] n ippopotamo.

**hire** ['haɪə*] vt (Brit: car, equipment) noleggiare; (worker) assumere, dare lavoro a // n nolo, noleggio; **for** ~ da nolo; (taxi) libero(a); ~ **purchase (H.P.)** n (Brit) acquisto (or vendita) rateale.

**his** [hɪz] a, pronoun il(la) suo(sua), i(le) suoi(sue); see also **my**, **mine**.

**hiss** [hɪs] vi fischiare; (cat, snake) sibilare // n fischio; sibilo.

**historic(al)** [hɪ'stɒrɪk(l)] a storico(a).

**history** ['hɪstərɪ] n storia.

**hit** [hɪt] vt (pt, pp **hit**) colpire, picchiare; (knock against) battere; (reach: target) raggiungere; (collide with: car) urtare contro; (fig: affect) colpire; (find: problem etc) incontrare // n colpo; (success, song) successo; **to** ~ **it off with sb** andare molto d'accordo con qn; ~-**and-run driver** n pirata m della strada.

**hitch** [hɪtʃ] vt (fasten) attaccare; (also: ~ **up**) tirare su // n (difficulty) intoppo, difficoltà f inv; **to** ~ **a lift** fare l'autostop.

**hitch-hike** ['hɪtʃhaɪk] vi fare l'autostop; ~**r** n autostoppista m/f.

**hi-tech** ['haɪ'tɛk] a di alta tecnologia // n alta tecnologia.

**hitherto** [hɪðə'tuː] ad in precedenza.

**hive** [haɪv] n alveare m; **to** ~ **off** vt separare.

**H.M.S.** abbr = His (Her) Majesty's Ship.

**hoard** [hɔːd] n (of food) provviste fpl; (of money) gruzzolo // vt ammassare.

**hoarding** ['hɔːdɪŋ] n (Brit: for posters) tabellone m per affissioni.

**hoarfrost** ['hɔːfrɔst] n brina.

**hoarse** [hɔːs] a rauco(a).

**hoax** [həʊks] n scherzo; falso allarme.

**hob** [hɔb] n piastra (con fornelli).

**hobble** ['hɔbl] vi zoppicare.

**hobby** ['hɔbɪ] n hobby m inv, passatempo; ~**horse** n (fig) chiodo fisso.

**hobo** ['həʊbəʊ] n (US) vagabondo.

**hockey** ['hɔkɪ] n hockey m.

**hoe** [həʊ] n zappa.

**hog** [hɔg] n maiale m // vt (fig) arraffare; **to go the whole ~** farlo fino in fondo.

**hoist** [hɔɪst] n paranco // vt issare.

**hold** [həʊld] vb (pt, pp held) vt tenere; (contain) contenere; (keep back) trattenere; (believe) mantenere; considerare; (possess) avere, possedere; detenere // vi (withstand pressure) tenere; (be valid) essere valido(a) // n presa; (fig) potere m; (NAUT) stiva; ~ **the line!** (TEL) resti in linea!; **to ~ one's own** (fig) difendersi bene; **to catch or get (a) ~ of** afferrare; **to get ~ of** (fig) trovare; **to ~ back** vt trattenere; (secret) tenere celato(a); **to ~ down** vt (person) tenere a terra; (job) tenere; **to ~ off** vt tener lontano; **to ~ on** vi tener fermo; (wait) aspettare; **to ~ on!** (TEL) resti in linea!; **to ~ on to** vt fus tenersi stretto/a a; (keep) conservare; **to ~ out** vi offrire // vi (resist) resistere; **to ~ up** vt (raise) alzare; (support) sostenere; (delay) ritardare; ~**all** n (Brit) borsone m; ~**er** n (of ticket, title) possessore/posseditrice; (of office etc) incaricato/a; (of record) detentore/trice; ~**ing** n (share)

azioni fpl, titoli mpl; (farm) podere m, tenuta; ~**up** n (robbery) rapina a mano armata; (delay) ritardo; (Brit: in traffic) blocco.

**hole** [həʊl] n buco, buca // vt bucare.

**holiday** ['hɔlədɪ] n vacanza; (day off) giorno di vacanza; (public) giorno festivo; **on ~** in vacanza; ~ **camp** n (for children) colonia (di villeggiatura); (also: ~ **centre**) = villaggio (di vacanze); ~**maker** n (Brit) villeggiante m/f; ~ **resort** n luogo di villeggiatura.

**holiness** ['həʊlɪnɪs] n santità.

**Holland** ['hɔlənd] n Olanda.

**hollow** ['hɔləʊ] a cavo(a), vuoto(a); (fig) falso(a); vano(a) // n cavità f inv; (in land) valletta, depressione f // vt: **to ~ out** scavare.

**holly** ['hɔlɪ] n agrifoglio.

**holocaust** ['hɔləkɔːst] n olocausto.

**holster** ['həʊlstə*] n fondina (di pistola).

**holy** ['həʊlɪ] a santo(a); (bread) benedetto(a), consacrato(a); (ground) consacrato(a); **H~ Ghost** or **Spirit** n Spirito Santo; ~ **orders** npl ordini mpl (sacri).

**homage** ['hɔmɪdʒ] n omaggio; **to pay ~ to** rendere omaggio a.

**home** [həʊm] n casa; (country) patria; (institution) casa, ricovero // a familiare; (cooking etc) casalingo(a); (ECON, POL) nazionale, interno(a) // ad a casa; in patria; (right in: nail etc) fino in fondo; **at ~** a casa; to go (or come) ~ tornare a casa (or in patria); **make yourself at ~** si metta a suo agio; ~ **address** n indirizzo di casa; ~ **computer** n home computer m inv; ~**land** n patria; ~**less** a senza tetto; casalingo(a); ~**ly** a semplice, alla buona; accogliente; ~**made** a casalingo(a); **H~ Office** n (Brit) ministero degli Interni; ~ **rule** n autogoverno; **H~ Secretary** n (Brit) ministro degli Interni; ~**sick** a: **to be ~sick** avere la nostalgia; ~ **town** n città f inv natale; ~**ward**

['haʊmwəd] a (journey) di ritorno; ~**work** n compiti mpl (per casa).
**homicide** ['hɒmɪsaɪd] n (US) omicidio.
**homoeopathy** [hɒmɪ'ɒpəθɪ] n omeopatia.
**homogeneous** [hɒməʊ'dʒiːnɪəs] a omogeneo(a).
**homosexual** [hɒməʊ'sɛksjʊəl] a, n omossessuale (m/f).
**honest** ['ɒnɪst] a onesto(a); sincero(a); ~**ly** ad onestamente; sinceramente; ~**y** n onestà.
**honey** ['hʌnɪ] n miele m; ~**comb** n favo; ~**moon** n luna di miele, viaggio di nozze; ~**suckle** n (BOT) caprifoglio.
**honk** [hɒŋk] vi suonare il clacson.
**honorary** ['ɒnərərɪ] a onorario(a); (duty, title) onorifico(a).
**honour,** (US **honor**) ['ɒnə*] vt onorare // n onore m; ~**able** a onorevole; ~**s degree** n (SCOL) laurea specializzata.
**hood** [hʊd] n cappuccio; (Brit AUT) capote f; (US AUT) cofano.
**hoodlum** ['huːdləm] n teppista m/f.
**hoodwink** ['hʊdwɪŋk] vt infinocchiare.
**hoof** [huːf], pl ~**s** or **hooves** n zoccolo.
**hook** [hʊk] n gancio; (for fishing) amo // vt uncinare; (dress) agganciare.
**hooligan** ['huːlɪgən] n giovinastro, teppista m.
**hoop** [huːp] n cerchio.
**hoot** [huːt] vi (AUT) suonare il clacson; ~**er** n (Brit AUT) clacson m inv; (NAUT) sirena.
**hoover** ['huːvə*] ® (Brit) n aspirapolvere m inv // vt pulire con l'aspirapolvere.
**hooves** [huːvz] npl of **hoof.**
**hop** [hɒp] vi saltellare, saltare; (on one foot) saltare su una gamba // n salto.
**hope** [həʊp] vt, vi sperare // n speranza; **I** ~ **so/not** spero di sì/no; ~**ful** a (person) pieno(a) di

speranza; (situation) promettente; ~**fully** ad con speranza; ~**fully he will recover** speriamo che si prenda; ~**less** a senza speranza, disperato(a); (useless) inutile.
**hops** [hɒps] npl luppoli mpl.
**horde** [hɔːd] n orda.
**horizon** [hə'raɪzn] n orizzonte m; ~**tal** [hɔrɪ'zɒntl] a orizzontale.
**hormone** ['hɔːməʊn] n ormone m.
**horn** [hɔːn] n (ZOOL, MUS) corno; (AUT) clacson m inv.
**hornet** ['hɔːnɪt] n calabrone m.
**horny** ['hɔːnɪ] a corneo(a); (hands) calloso(a); (col) arrapato(a).
**horoscope** ['hɒrəskəʊp] n oroscopo.
**horrendous** [hə'rɛndəs] a orrendo(a).
**horrible** ['hɒrɪbl] a orribile, tremendo(a).
**horrid** ['hɒrɪd] a orrido(a); (person) antipatico(a).
**horrify** ['hɒrɪfaɪ] vt scandalizzare.
**horror** ['hɒrə*] n orrore m; ~ **film** n film m inv dell'orrore.
**hors d'œuvre** [ɔː'dɜːvrə] n antipasto.
**horse** [hɔːs] n cavallo; ~ **back: on** ~**back** a cavallo; ~ **chestnut** n ippocastano; ~**man** n cavaliere m; ~**power (h.p.)** n cavallo (vapore); ~**racing** n ippica; ~**radish** n rafano; ~**shoe** n ferro di cavallo; ~**woman** n amazzone f.
**horticulture** ['hɔːtɪkʌltʃə*] n orticoltura.
**hose** [həʊz] n (also: ~**pipe**) tubo; (also: **garden** ~) tubo per annaffiare.
**hospice** ['hɒspɪs] n ricovero, ospizio.
**hospitable** [hɒs'pɪtəbl] a ospitale.
**hospital** ['hɒspɪtl] n ospedale m.
**hospitality** [hɒspɪ'tælɪtɪ] n ospitalità.
**host** [həʊst] n ospite m; (REL) ostia; (large number): **a** ~ **of** una schiera di.
**hostage** ['hɒstɪdʒ] n ostaggio/a.
**hostel** ['hɒstl] n ostello; (also: **youth** ~) ostello della gioventù.
**hostess** ['həʊstɪs] n ospite f; (Brit

*air* ~) hostess *f inv*; (*in nightclub*) entraîneuse *f inv*.

**hostile** ['hɔstail] *a* ostile.

**hostility** [hɔ'stiliti] *n* ostilità *f inv*.

**hot** [hɔt] *a* caldo(a); (*as opposed to only warm*) molto caldo(a); (*spicy*) piccante; (*fig*) accanito(a); ardente; violento(a), focoso(a); **to be** ~ (*person*) aver caldo; (*object*) essere caldo(a); (*weather*) far caldo; ~**bed** *n* (*fig*) focolaio; ~ **dog** *n* hot dog *m inv*.

**hotel** [həu'tel] *n* albergo; ~**ier** *n* albergatore/trice.

**hot:** ~**headed** *a* focoso(a), eccitabile; ~**house** *n* serra; ~ **line** *n* (*POL*) telefono rosso; ~**ly** *ad* violentemente; ~**plate** *n* (*on cooker*) piastra riscaldante; ~**-water bottle** *n* borsa dell'acqua calda.

**hound** [haund] *vt* perseguitare // *n* segugio.

**hour** ['auə*] *n* ora; ~**ly** *a* all'ora // *ad* ogni ora; ~**ly paid** *a* pagato(a) a ore.

**house** *n* [haus] (*pl* ~**s** [ˈhauzɪz]) (*also*: *firm*) casa; (*POL*) camera; (*THEATRE*) sala; pubblico; spettacolo // *vt* [hauz] (*person*) ospitare, alloggiare; **on the** ~ (*fig*) offerto(a) dalla casa; ~**boat** *n* house boat *f inv*; ~**breaking** *n* furto con scasso; ~**coat** *n* vestaglia; ~**hold** *n* famiglia; casa; ~**keeper** *n* governante *f*; ~**keeping** *n* (*work*) governo della casa; ~**keeping** (*money*) soldi *mpl* per le spese di casa; ~**-warming party** *n* festa per inaugurare la casa nuova; ~**wife** *n* massaia, casalinga; ~**work** *n* faccende *fpl* domestiche.

**housing** ['hauziŋ] *n* alloggio; ~ **development**, (*Brit*) ~ **estate** *n* zona residenziale con case popolari e/o private.

**hovel** ['hɔvl] *n* casupola.

**hover** ['hɔvə*] *vi* librarsi; (*helicopter*) volare a punto fisso; ~**craft** *n* hovercraft *m inv*.

**how** [hau] *ad* come; ~ **are you?** come sta?; ~ **do you do?** piacere!; ~ **far is it to the river?** quanto è lontano il fiume?; ~ **long have you been here?** da quando è qui?; ~ **lovely!/awful!** che bello!/orrore!; ~ **many?** quanti(e)?; ~ **much?** quanto(a)?; ~ **much milk?** quanto latte?; ~ **many people?** quante persone?; ~ **old are you?** quanti anni ha?; ~**ever** *ad* in qualsiasi modo *or* maniera che; (+ *adjective*) per quanto + *sub*; (*in questions*) come // *cj* comunque, però.

**howl** [haul] *n* ululato // *vi* ululare.

**h.p., H.P.** *abbr* = **hire purchase, horsepower.**

**hub** [hʌb] *n* (*of wheel*) mozzo; (*fig*) fulcro.

**hubbub** ['hʌbʌb] *n* baccano.

**hub cap** *n* coprimozzo.

**huddle** ['hʌdl] *vi*: **to** ~ **together** rannicchiarsi l'uno contro l'altro.

**hue** [hju:] *n* tinta; ~ **and cry** *n* clamore *m*.

**huff** [hʌf] *n*: **in a** ~ stizzito(a).

**hug** [hʌg] *vt* abbracciare; (*shore, kerb*) stringere // *n* abbraccio, stretta.

**huge** [hju:dʒ] *a* enorme, immenso(a).

**hulk** [hʌlk] *n* (*ship*) nave *f* in disarmo; (*building, car*) carcassa; (*person*) mastodonte *m*.

**hull** [hʌl] *n* (*of ship*) scafo.

**hullo** ['hʌ'ləu] *excl* = **hello.**

**hum** [hʌm] *vt* (*tune*) canticchiare // *vi* canticchiare; (*insect, plane, tool*) ronzare.

**human** ['hju:mən] *a* umano(a) // *n* essere *m* umano.

**humane** [hju:'mein] *a* umanitario(a).

**humanitarian** [hju:mænɪˈtɛəriən] *a* umanitario(a).

**humanity** [hju:'mæniti] *n* umanità.

**humble** ['hʌmbl] *a* umile, modesto(a) // *vt* umiliare.

**humbug** ['hʌmbʌg] *n* inganno; sciocchezze *fpl*.

**humdrum** ['hʌmdrʌm] *a* monotono(a), tedioso(a).

**humid** ['hju:mɪd] a umido(a).

**humiliate** [hju:'mɪlɪeɪt] vt umiliare; **humiliation** [-'eɪʃən] n umiliazione f.

**humility** [hju:'mɪlɪtɪ] n umiltà.

**humorous** ['hju:mərəs] a umoristico(a); (person) buffo(a).

**humour**, (US) **humor** ['hju:mə*] n umore m // vt (person) compiacere; (sb's whims) assecondare.

**hump** [hʌmp] n gobba.

**hunch** [hʌntʃ] n gobba; (premonition) intuizione f; ~**back** n gobbo/a; ~**ed** a incurvato(a).

**hundred** ['hʌndrəd] num cento; ~**s of** centinaia fpl di; ~**weight** n (Brit) = 50.8 kg; 112 lb; (US) = 45.3 kg; 100 lb.

**hung** [hʌŋ] pt, pp of hang.

**Hungary** ['hʌŋgərɪ] n Ungheria.

**hunger** ['hʌŋgə*] n fame f // vi: to ~ **for** desiderare ardentemente.

**hungry** ['hʌŋgrɪ] a affamato(a); to be ~ aver fame.

**hunk** [hʌŋk] n (of bread etc) bel pezzo.

**hunt** [hʌnt] vt (seek) cercare; (SPORT) cacciare // vi andare a caccia // n caccia; ~**er** n cacciatore m; ~**ing** n caccia.

**hurdle** ['hə:dl] n (SPORT, fig) ostacolo.

**hurl** [hə:l] vt lanciare con violenza.

**hurrah, hurray** [hu'rɑ:, hu'reɪ] excl urra!, evviva!

**hurricane** ['hʌrɪkən] n uragano.

**hurried** ['hʌrɪd] a affrettato(a); (work) fatto(a) in fretta; ~**ly** ad in fretta.

**hurry** ['hʌrɪ] n fretta // vb (also: ~ **up**) vi affrettarsi // vt (person) affrettare; (work) far in fretta; to be in a ~ aver fretta; to do sth in a ~ fare qc in fretta; to ~ in/out entrare/uscire in fretta.

**hurt** [hə:t] vb (pt, pp hurt) vt (cause pain to) far male a; (injure, fig) ferire // vi far male // a ferito(a); ~**ful** a (remark) che ferisce.

**hurtle** ['hə:tl] vt scagliare // vi: to ~

past/down passare/scendere a razzo.

**husband** ['hʌzbənd] n marito.

**hush** [hʌʃ] n silenzio, calma // vt zittire; ~! zitto(a)!

**husk** [hʌsk] n (of wheat) cartoccio; (of rice, maize) buccia.

**husky** ['hʌskɪ] a roco(a) // n cane m eschimese.

**hustle** ['hʌsl] vt spingere, incalzare // n pigia pigia m inv; ~ **and bustle** n trambusto.

**hut** [hʌt] n rifugio; (shed) ripostiglio.

**hutch** [hʌtʃ] n gabbia.

**hyacinth** ['haɪəsɪnθ] n giacinto.

**hybrid** ['haɪbrɪd] a ibrido(a) // n ibrido.

**hydrant** ['haɪdrənt] n (also: fire ~) idrante m.

**hydraulic** [haɪ'drɔ:lɪk] a idraulico(a).

**hydroelectric** [haɪdrəu'lektrɪk] a idroelettrico(a).

**hydrofoil** ['haɪdrəufɔɪl] n aliscafo.

**hydrogen** ['haɪdrədʒən] n idrogeno.

**hyena** [haɪ'i:nə] n iena.

**hygiene** ['haɪdʒi:n] n igiene f.

**hymn** [hɪm] n inno; cantica.

**hype** [haɪp] n (col) campagna pubblicitaria.

**hypermarket** ['haɪpəmɑ:kɪt] n ipermercato.

**hyphen** ['haɪfn] n trattino.

**hypnotism** ['hɪpnətɪzm] n ipnotismo.

**hypnotize** ['hɪpnətaɪz] vt ipnotizzare.

**hypocrisy** [hɪ'pɔkrɪsɪ] n ipocrisia.

**hypocrite** ['hɪpəkrɪt] n ipocrita m/f; **hypocritical** [-'krɪtɪkl] a ipocrita.

**hypothermia** [haɪpəu'θə:mɪə] n ipotermia.

**hypothesis**, pl **hypotheses** [haɪ'pɔθɪsɪs, -si:z] n ipotesi f inv.

**hypothetical** [haɪpəu'θetɪkl] a ipotetico(a).

**hysterical** [hɪ'sterɪkl] a isterico(a).

**hysterics** [hɪ'sterɪks] npl accesso di isteria; (laughter) attacco di riso.

**I**

**I** [aɪ] *pronoun* io.

**ice** [aɪs] *n* ghiaccio; (*on road*) gelo // *vt* (*cake*) glassare; (*drink*) mettere in fresco // *vi* (*also:* ~ **over**) ghiacciare; (*also:* ~ **up**) gelare; ~ **axe** *n* piccozza da ghiaccio; ~**berg** *n* iceberg *m inv*; ~**box** *n* (*US*) frigorifero; (*Brit*) reparto ghiaccio; (*insulated box*) frigo portatile; ~ **cream** *n* gelato; ~ **hockey** *n* hockey *m* su ghiaccio.

**Iceland** [ˈaɪslənd] *n* Islanda.

**ice:** ~ **lolly** *n* (*Brit*) ghiacciolo; ~ **rink** *n* pista di pattinaggio; ~ **skating** *n* pattinaggio sul ghiaccio.

**icicle** [ˈaɪsɪkl] *n* ghiacciolo.

**icing** [ˈaɪsɪŋ] *n* (*AVIAT etc*) patina di ghiaccio; (*CULIN*) glassa; ~ **sugar** *n* (*Brit*) zucchero a velo.

**icy** [ˈaɪsɪ] *a* ghiacciato(a); (*weather, temperature*) gelido(a).

**I'd** [aɪd] = **I would, I had**.

**idea** [aɪˈdɪə] *n* idea.

**ideal** [aɪˈdɪəl] *a, n* ideale (m).

**identical** [aɪˈdɛntɪkl] *a* identico(a).

**identification** [aɪdɛntɪfɪˈkeɪʃən] *n* identificazione *f*; **means of** ~ carta d'identità.

**identify** [aɪˈdɛntɪfaɪ] *vt* identificare.

**identikit picture** [aɪˈdɛntɪkɪt-] *n* identikit *m inv*.

**identity** [aɪˈdɛntɪtɪ] *n* identità *f inv*; ~ **card** *n* carta d'identità.

**idiom** [ˈɪdɪəm] *n* idioma *m*; (*phrase*) espressione *f* idiomatica.

**idiot** [ˈɪdɪət] *n* idiota *m/f*; ~**ic** [-ˈɔtɪk] *a* idiota.

**idle** [ˈaɪdl] *a* inattivo(a); (*lazy*) pigro(a), ozioso(a); (*unemployed*) disoccupato(a); (*question, pleasures*) ozioso(a); **to lie** ~ stare fermo, non funzionare; **to** ~ **away** *vt* (*time*) sprecare, buttar via.

**idol** [ˈaɪdl] *n* idolo; ~**ize** *vt* idoleggiare.

**i.e.** *ad abbr* (= *that is*) cioè.

**if** [ɪf] *cj* se; ~ **I were you** ... se fossi in te ..., io al tuo posto ...; ~ **so** se è così; ~ **not** se no; ~ **only** se solo *or* soltanto.

**ignite** [ɪgˈnaɪt] *vt* accendere // *vi* accendersi.

**ignition** [ɪgˈnɪʃən] *n* (*AUT*) accensione *f*; **to switch on/off the** ~ accendere/spegnere il motore; ~ **key** *n* (*AUT*) chiave *f* dell'accensione.

**ignorant** [ˈɪgnərənt] *a* ignorante; **to be** ~ **of** (*subject*) essere ignorante in; (*events*) essere ignaro(a) di.

**ignore** [ɪgˈnɔː] *vt* non tener conto di; (*person, fact*) ignorare.

**I'll** [aɪl] = **I will, I shall.**

**ill** [ɪl] *a* (*sick*) malato(a); (*bad*) cattivo(a) // *n* male *m* // *ad*: **to speak** *etc* ~ **of sb** parlare *etc* male di qn; **to take** *or* **be taken** ~ ammalarsi; ~**-advised** *a* (*decision*) poco giudizioso(a); (*person*) mal consigliato(a); ~**-at-ease** *a* a disagio.

**illegal** [ɪˈliːgl] *a* illegale.

**illegible** [ɪˈlɛdʒɪbl] *a* illeggibile.

**illegitimate** [ɪlɪˈdʒɪtɪmət] *a* illegittimo(a).

**ill-fated** [ɪlˈfeɪtɪd] *a* nefasto(a).

**ill feeling** *n* rancore *m*.

**illiterate** [ɪˈlɪtərət] *a* analfabeta, illetterato(a); (*letter*) scorretto(a).

**illness** [ˈɪlnɪs] *n* malattia.

**ill-treat** [ɪlˈtriːt] *vt* maltrattare.

**illuminate** [ɪˈluːmɪneɪt] *vt* illuminare; **illumination** [-ˈneɪʃən] *n* illuminazione *f*.

**illusion** [ɪˈluːʒən] *n* illusione *f*; **to be under the** ~ **that** avere l'impressione che.

**illustrate** [ˈɪləstreɪt] *vt* illustrare; **illustration** [-ˈstreɪʃən] *n* illustrazione *f*.

**ill will** *n* cattiva volontà.

**I'm** [aɪm] = **I am.**

**image** [ˈɪmɪdʒ] *n* immagine *f*; (*public face*) immagine (pubblica); ~**ry** *n* immagini *fpl*.

**imaginary** [ɪˈmædʒɪnərɪ] *a* immaginario(a).

**imagination** [imædʒi'neiʃən] n immaginazione f, fantasia.

**imaginative** [i'mædʒinətiv] a immaginoso(a).

**imagine** [i'mædʒin] vt immaginare.

**imbalance** [im'bæləns] n squilibrio.

**imitate** ['imiteit] vt imitare; **imitation** [-'teiʃən] n imitazione f.

**immaculate** [i'mækjulət] a immacolato(a); (dress, appearance) impeccabile.

**immaterial** [imə'tiəriəl] a immateriale, indifferente.

**immature** [imə'tjuə*] a immaturo(a).

**immediate** [i'mi:diət] a immediato(a); ~ly ad (at once) subito, immediatamente; ~ly next to proprio accanto a.

**immense** [i'mens] a immenso(a); enorme.

**immerse** [i'mə:s] vt immergere.

**immersion heater** [i'mə:ʃən-] n (Brit) scaldacqua m inv a immersione.

**immigrant** ['imigrənt] n immigrante m/f; immigrato/a.

**immigration** [imi'greiʃən] n immigrazione f.

**imminent** ['iminənt] a imminente.

**immoral** [i'mɔrl] a immorale.

**immortal** [i'mɔ:tl] a, n immortale (m/f).

**immune** [i'mju:n] a: ~ (to) immune (da).

**immunity** [i'mju:niti] n immunità.

**imp** [imp] n folletto, diavoletto; (child) diavoletto.

**impact** ['impækt] n impatto.

**impair** [im'peə*] vt danneggiare.

**impart** [im'pa:t] vt (make known) comunicare; (bestow) impartire.

**impartial** [im'pa:ʃl] a imparziale.

**impassable** [im'pɑ:səbl] a insuperabile; (road) impraticabile.

**impassive** [im'pæsiv] a impassibile.

**impatience** [im'peiʃəns] n impazienza.

**impatient** [im'peiʃənt] a impaziente; **to get** or **grow** ~ perdere la pazienza.

**impeccable** [im'pekəbl] a impeccabile.

**impede** [im'pi:d] vt impedire.

**impediment** [im'pedimənt] n impedimento; (also: **speech** ~) difetto di pronuncia.

**impending** [im'pendiŋ] a imminente.

**imperative** [im'perətiv] a imperativo(a); necessario(a), urgente; (voice) imperioso(a) // n (LING) imperativo.

**imperfect** [im'pə:fikt] a imperfetto(a); (goods etc) difettoso(a).

**imperial** [im'piəriəl] a imperiale; (measure) legale.

**impersonal** [im'pə:sənl] a impersonale.

**impersonate** [im'pə:səneit] vt impersonare; (THEATRE) fare la mimica di.

**impertinent** [im'pə:tinənt] a insolente, impertinente.

**impervious** [im'pə:viəs] a impermeabile; (fig): ~ **to** insensibile a; impassibile di fronte a.

**impetuous** [im'petjuəs] a impetuoso(a), precipitoso(a).

**impetus** ['impətəs] n impeto.

**impinge** [im'pindʒ]: **to ~ on** vt fus (person) colpire; (rights) ledere.

**implement** n ['implimənt] attrezzo; (for cooking) utensile m // vt ['impliment] effettuare.

**implicit** [im'plisit] a implicito(a); (complete) completo(a).

**imply** [im'plai] vt insinuare; suggerire.

**impolite** [impə'lait] a scortese.

**import** vt [im'pɔ:t] importare // n ['impɔ:t] (COMM) importazione f; (meaning) significato, senso.

**importance** [im'pɔ:tns] n importanza.

**important** [im'pɔ:tnt] a importante; it's not ~ non ha importanza.

**importer** [im'pɔ:tə*] n importatore/trice.

**impose** [ɪmˈpəʊz] vt imporre // vi: to ~ on sb sfruttare la bontà di qn.

**imposing** [ɪmˈpəʊzɪŋ] a imponente.

**imposition** [ɪmpəˈzɪʃən] n (of tax etc) imposizione f; to be an ~ on (person) abusare della gentilezza di.

**impossibility** [ɪmpɒsəˈbɪlɪtɪ] n impossibilità.

**impossible** [ɪmˈpɒsɪbl] a impossibile.

**impotent** [ˈɪmpətnt] a impotente.

**impound** [ɪmˈpaʊnd] vt confiscare.

**impoverished** [ɪmˈpɒvərɪʃt] a impoverito(a).

**impractical** [ɪmˈpræktɪkl] a non pratico(a).

**impregnable** [ɪmˈpregnəbl] a (fortress) inespugnabile; (fig) inoppugnabile; irrefutabile.

**impress** [ɪmˈpres] vt impressionare; (mark) imprimere, stampare; to ~ sth on sb far capire qc a qn.

**impression** [ɪmˈpreʃən] n impressione f; to be under the ~ that avere l'impressione che.

**impressive** [ɪmˈpresɪv] a impressionante.

**imprint** [ˈɪmprɪnt] n (PUBLISHING) sigla editoriale.

**imprison** [ɪmˈprɪzn] vt imprigionare; ~ment n imprigionamento.

**improbable** [ɪmˈprɒbəbl] a improbabile; (excuse) inverosimile.

**impromptu** [ɪmˈprɒmptjuː] a improvvisato(a).

**improper** [ɪmˈprɒpə*] a scorretto(a); (unsuitable) inadatto(a), improprio(a); sconveniente, indecente.

**improve** [ɪmˈpruːv] vt migliorare // vi migliorare; (pupil etc) fare progressi; ~ment n miglioramento; progresso.

**improvise** [ˈɪmprəvaɪz] vt, vi improvvisare.

**impudent** [ˈɪmpjʊdnt] a impudente, sfacciato(a).

**impulse** [ˈɪmpʌls] n impulso; on ~ d'impulso, impulsivamente.

**impulsive** [ɪmˈpʌlsɪv] a impulsivo(a).

---

KEYWORD

**in** [ɪn] ♦ prep 1 (indicating place, position) in; ~ the house/garden in casa/giardino; ~ the box nella scatola; ~ the fridge nel frigorifero; I have it ~ my hand ce l'ho in mano; ~ town/the country in città/campagna; ~ school a scuola; ~ here/there qui/li dentro

2 (with place names: of town, region, country): ~ London a Londra; ~ England in Inghilterra; ~ the United States negli Stati Uniti; ~ Yorkshire nello Yorkshire

3 (indicating time: during, in the space of) in; ~ spring/summer in primavera/estate; ~ 1988 nel 1988; ~ May in or a maggio; I'll see you ~ July ci vediamo a luglio; ~ the afternoon nel pomeriggio; at 4 o'clock ~ the afternoon alle 4 del pomeriggio; I did it ~ 3 hours/days l'ho fatto in 3 ore/giorni; I'll see you ~ 2 weeks or ~ 2 weeks' time ci vediamo tra 2 settimane

4 (indicating manner etc) a; ~ a loud/soft voice a voce alta/bassa; ~ pencil a matita; ~ English/French in inglese/francese; the boy ~ the blue shirt il ragazzo con la camicia blu

5 (indicating circumstances): ~ the sun al sole; ~ the shade all'ombra; ~ the rain sotto la pioggia; a rise ~ prices un aumento dei prezzi

6 (indicating mood, state): ~ tears in lacrime; ~ anger per la rabbia; ~ despair disperato(a); ~ good condition in buono stato, in buone condizioni; to live ~ luxury vivere nel lusso

7 (with ratios, numbers): 1 ~ 10 1 su 10; 20 pence ~ the pound 20 pence per sterlina; they lined up ~ twos si misero in fila a due a due

8 (referring to people, works) in; the disease is common ~ children la malattia è comune nei bambini; ~ (the works of) Dickens in Dickens

**9** (indicating profession etc) in; **to be ~ teaching** fare l'insegnante, insegnare; **to be ~ publishing** essere nell'editoria **10** (after superlative) di; **the best ~ the class** il migliore della classe **11** (with present participle): **~ saying this** dicendo questo, nel dire questo

♦ ad: **to be ~** (person: at home, work) esserci; (train, ship, plane) essere arrivato(a); (in fashion) essere di moda; **to ask sb ~** invitare qn ad entrare; **to run/limp** etc **~** entrare di corsa/zoppicando etc ♦ n: **the ~s and outs of** the problem tutti i particolari del problema.

**in., ins** abbr = **inch(es)**.

**inability** [ɪnə'bɪlɪtɪ] n inabilità, incapacità.

**inaccurate** [ɪn'ækjurət] a inesatto(a), impreciso(a).

**inadequate** [ɪn'ædɪkwət] a insufficiente.

**inadvertently** [ɪnəd'vɜːtntlɪ] ad senza volerlo.

**inane** [ɪ'neɪn] a vacuo(a), stupido(a).

**inanimate** [ɪn'ænɪmət] a inanimato(a).

**inappropriate** [ɪnə'prəuprɪət] a disadatto(a); (word, expression) improprio(a).

**inarticulate** [ɪnɑː'tɪkjulət] a (person) che si esprime male; (speech) inarticolato(a).

**inasmuch as** [ɪnəz'mʌtʃæz] ad in quanto che; (seeing that) poiché.

**inaudible** [ɪn'ɔːdɪbl] a non si riesce a sentire.

**inauguration** [ɪnɔː'gjuːreɪʃən] n inaugurazione f; insediamento in carica.

**in-between** [ɪnbɪ'twiːn] a fra i (or le) due.

**inborn** [ɪn'bɔːn] a (feeling) innato(a); (defect) congenito(a).

**inbred** [ɪn'bred] a innato(a); (family) connaturato(a).

**Inc.** abbr = **incorporated**.

**incapable** [ɪn'keɪpəbl] a incapace.

**incapacitate** [ɪnkə'pæsɪtet] vt: **to ~ sb from doing** rendere qn incapace di fare.

**incense** n ['ɪnsens] incenso // vt [ɪn'sens] (anger) infuriare.

**incentive** [ɪn'sentɪv] n incentivo.

**incessant** [ɪn'sesnt] a incessante; **~ly** ad di continuo, senza sosta.

**inch** [ɪntʃ] n pollice m (= 25 mm; 12 in a foot); **within an ~ of** a un pelo da; **he didn't give an ~** non ha ceduto di un millimetro; **to ~ forward** vi avanzare pian piano.

**incidence** ['ɪnsɪdns] n (of crime, disease) incidenza.

**incident** ['ɪnsɪdnt] n incidente m; (in book) episodio.

**incidental** [ɪnsɪ'dentl] a accessorio(a), d'accompagnamento; (unplanned) incidentale; **~ to** marginale a; **~ly** [-'dentəlɪ] ad (by the way) a proposito.

**inclination** [ɪnklɪ'neɪʃən] n inclinazione f.

**incline** n ['ɪnklaɪn] pendenza, pendio // vb [ɪn'klaɪn] vt inclinare // vi: **to ~ to tendere** a; **to be ~d to do** tendere a fare; essere propenso(a) a fare.

**include** [ɪn'kluːd] vt includere, comprendere; **including** prep compreso(a), incluso(a).

**inclusive** [ɪn'kluːsɪv] a incluso(a), compreso(a) // ad: **~ of tax** etc tasse etc comprese.

**incoherent** [ɪnkəu'hɪərənt] a incoerente.

**income** ['ɪnkʌm] n reddito; **~ tax** n imposta sul reddito.

**incompetent** [ɪn'kɒmpɪtnt] a incompetente, incapace.

**incomplete** [ɪnkəm'pliːt] a incompleto(a).

**incongruous** [ɪn'kɒngruəs] a poco appropriato(a); (remark, act) incongruo(a).

**inconsiderate** [ɪnkən'sɪdərət] a sconsiderato(a).

**inconsistency** [ɪnkən'sɪstənsɪ] n (of actions, statement) incoerenza; (of work) irregolarità.

**inconspicuous** [ɪnkən'spɪkjuəs] a incospicuo(a); (colour) poco appariscente; (dress) dimesso(a).

**inconvenience** [ɪnkən'viːnjəns] n inconveniente m; (trouble) disturbo // vt disturbare.

**inconvenient** [ɪnkən'viːnjənt] a scomodo(a).

**incorporate** [ɪn'kɔːpəreɪt] vt incorporare; (contain) contenere; ~d a: ~d company (US: abbr Inc.) società f inv anonima (S.A.).

**incorrect** [ɪnkə'rɛkt] a scorretto(a); (statement) impreciso(a).

**increase** n ['ɪnkriːs] aumento // vi, vt [ɪn'kriːs] aumentare.

**increasing** [ɪn'kriːsɪŋ] a (number) crescente; ~ly ad sempre più.

**incredible** [ɪn'krɛdɪbl] a incredibile.

**incredulous** [ɪn'krɛdjuləs] a incredulo(a).

**increment** ['ɪnkrɪmənt] n aumento, incremento.

**incriminate** [ɪn'krɪmɪneɪt] vt compromettere.

**incubator** ['ɪnkjubeɪtə*] n incubatrice f.

**incumbent** [ɪn'kʌmbənt] n titolare m/f // a: to be ~ on sb spettare a qn.

**incur** [ɪn'kəː*] vt (expenses) incorrere; (anger, risk) esporsi a; (debt) contrarre; (loss) subire.

**indebted** [ɪn'dɛtɪd] a: to be ~ to sb (for) essere obbligato(a) verso qn (per).

**indecent** [ɪn'diːsnt] a indecente; ~ assault n (Brit) aggressione f a scopo di violenza sessuale; ~ exposure n atti mpl osceni in luogo pubblico.

**indecisive** [ɪndɪ'saɪsɪv] a indeciso(a); (discussion) non decisivo(a).

**indeed** [ɪn'diːd] ad infatti; veramente; yes ~! certamente!

**indefinite** [ɪn'dɛfɪnɪt] a indefinito(a); (answer) vago(a); (period, number)

indeterminato(a); ~ly ad (wait) indefinitamente.

**indemnity** [ɪn'dɛmnɪtɪ] n (insurance) assicurazione f; (compensation) indennità, indennizzo.

**independence** [ɪndɪ'pɛndns] n indipendenza.

**independent** [ɪndɪ'pɛndnt] a indipendente.

**index** ['ɪndɛks] n (pl ~es: in book) indice m; (: in library etc) catalogo; (pl indices: ratio, sign) indice m; ~ card n scheda; ~ finger n (dito) indice m; ~-linked, (US) ~ed a legato(a) al costo della vita.

**India** ['ɪndɪə] n India; ~n a, n indiano(a); Red ~n pellerossa m/f.

**indicate** ['ɪndɪkeɪt] vt indicare; **indication** [-'keɪʃən] n indicazione f, segno.

**indicative** [ɪn'dɪkətɪv] a: ~ of indicativo(a) di // n (LING) indicativo.

**indicator** ['ɪndɪkeɪtə*] n indicatore m.

**indices** ['ɪndɪsiːz] npl of **index**.

**indictment** [ɪn'daɪtmənt] n accusa.

**indifference** [ɪn'dɪfrəns] n indifferenza.

**indifferent** [ɪn'dɪfrənt] a indifferente; (poor) mediocre.

**indigenous** [ɪn'dɪdʒɪnəs] a indigeno(a).

**indigestible** [ɪndɪ'dʒɛstɪbl] a indigeribile.

**indigestion** [ɪndɪ'dʒɛstʃən] n indigestione f.

**indignant** [ɪn'dɪgnənt] a: ~ (at sth/with sb) indignato(a) (per qc/contro qn).

**indignity** [ɪn'dɪgnɪtɪ] n umiliazione f.

**indirect** [ɪndɪ'rɛkt] a indiretto(a).

**indiscreet** [ɪndɪ'skriːt] a indiscreto(a); (rash) imprudente.

**indiscriminate** [ɪndɪ'skrɪmɪnət] a (person) che non sa discernere; (admiration) cieco(a); (killings) indiscriminato(a).

**indisputable** [ɪndɪ'spjuːtəbl] a incontestabile, indiscutibile.

**individual** [ɪndɪ'vɪdjʊəl] n individuo // a individuale; (characteristic) particolare, originale; ~ist n individualista m/f; ~ity [-'ælɪtɪ] n individualità.

**indoctrination** [ɪndɒktrɪ'neɪʃən] n indottrinamento.

**Indonesia** [ɪndə'niːzɪə] n Indonesia.

**indoor** ['ɪndɔː*] a interno; (plant) d'appartamento; (swimming pool) coperto(a); (sport, games) fatto(a) al coperto; ~s [ɪn'dɔːz] ad all'interno; (at home) in casa.

**induce** [ɪn'djuːs] vt persuadere; (bring about) provocare; ~ment n incitamento; (incentive) stimolo, incentivo.

**induction** [ɪn'dʌkʃən] n (MED: of birth) parto indotto; ~ course n (Brit) corso di avviamento.

**indulge** [ɪn'dʌldʒ] vt (whim) compiacere, soddisfare; (child) viziare // vi: to ~ in sth concedersi qc; abbandonarsi a qc; (leniency) indulgenza; ~nt a indulgente.

**industrial** [ɪn'dʌstrɪəl] a industriale; (injury) sul lavoro; (dispute) di lavoro; ~ action n azione f rivendicativa; ~ estate n (Brit) zona industriale; ~ist n industriale m; ~ park n (US) = ~ estate.

**industrious** [ɪn'dʌstrɪəs] a industrioso(a), assiduo(a).

**industry** ['ɪndəstrɪ] n industria; (diligence) operosità.

**inebriated** [ɪ'niːbrɪeɪtɪd] a ubriaco(a).

**inedible** [ɪn'edɪbl] a immangiabile.

**ineffective** [ɪnɪ'fektɪv], **ineffectual** [ɪnɪ'fektʃʊəl] a inefficace; incompetente.

**inefficiency** [ɪnɪ'fɪʃənsɪ] n inefficienza.

**inefficient** [ɪnɪ'fɪʃənt] a inefficiente.

**inept** [ɪ'nept] a inetto(a).

**inequality** [ɪnɪ'kwɒlɪtɪ] n ineguaglianza.

**inescapable** [ɪnɪ'skeɪpəbl] a inevitabile.

**inevitable** [ɪn'evɪtəbl] a inevitabile; **inevitably** ad inevitabilmente.

**inexact** [ɪnɪg'zækt] a inesatto(a).

**inexpensive** [ɪnɪk'spensɪv] a poco costoso(a).

**inexperienced** [ɪnɪks'pɪərɪənst] a inesperto(a), senza esperienza.

**infallible** [ɪn'fælɪbl] a infallibile.

**infamous** ['ɪnfəməs] a infame.

**infancy** ['ɪnfənsɪ] n infanzia.

**infant** ['ɪnfənt] n bambino/a; ~ school n (Brit) scuola elementare (per bambini dall'età di 5 a 7 anni).

**infantry** ['ɪnfəntrɪ] n fanteria.

**infatuated** [ɪn'fætjʊeɪtɪd] a: ~ with infatuato(a) di.

**infatuation** [ɪnfætjʊ'eɪʃən] n infatuazione f.

**infect** [ɪn'fekt] vt infettare; ~ion [ɪn'fekʃən] n infezione f; ~ious [ɪn'fekʃəs] a (disease) infettivo(a), contagioso(a); (person, laughter) contagioso(a).

**infer** [ɪn'fɜː*] vt inferire, dedurre.

**inferior** [ɪn'fɪərɪə*] a inferiore; (goods) di qualità scadente // n inferiore m/f; (in rank) subalterno/a; ~ity [ɪnfɪərɪ'ɒrɪtɪ] n inferiorità; ~ity complex n complesso di inferiorità.

**infertile** [ɪn'fɜːtaɪl] a sterile.

**in-fighting** ['ɪnfaɪtɪŋ] n lotte fpl intestine.

**infinite** ['ɪnfɪnɪt] a infinito(a).

**infinitive** [ɪn'fɪnɪtɪv] n infinito.

**infinity** [ɪn'fɪnɪtɪ] n infinità; (also MATH) infinito.

**infirmary** [ɪn'fɜːmərɪ] n ospedale m; (in school, factory) infermeria.

**infirmity** [ɪn'fɜːmɪtɪ] n infermità f inv.

**inflamed** [ɪn'fleɪmd] a infiammato(a).

**inflammable** [ɪn'flæməbl] a (Brit) infiammabile.

**inflammation** [ɪnflə'meɪʃən] n infiammazione f.

**inflatable** [ɪn'fleɪtəbl] a gonfiabile.

**inflate** [ɪn'fleɪt] vt (tyre, balloon) gonfiare; (fig) esagerare; gonfiare; **inflation** [ɪn'fleɪʃən] n (ECON) inflazione *f*; **inflationary** [ɪnˈfleɪʃnərɪ] *a* inflazionistico(a).

**inflict** [ɪnˈflɪkt] *vt*: to ~ on infliggere a.

**influence** [ˈɪnfluəns] *n* influenza // *vt* influenzare; **under the** ~ **of** sotto l'influenza di.

**influential** [ɪnfluˈɛnʃl] *a* influente.

**influenza** [ɪnfluˈɛnzə] *n* (MED) influenza.

**influx** [ˈɪnflʌks] *n* afflusso.

**inform** [ɪnˈfɔːm] *vt*: to ~ sb (of) informare qn (di) // *vi* to ~ on sb denunciare qn; to ~ sb about mettere qn al corrente di.

**informal** [ɪnˈfɔːml] *a* (person, manner) alla buona, semplice; (visit, discussion) informale; (announcement, invitation) non ufficiale; ~**ity** [-ˈmælɪtɪ] *n* semplicità, informalità; carattere *m* non ufficiale.

**informant** [ɪnˈfɔːmənt] *n* informatore/trice.

**information** [ɪnfəˈmeɪʃən] *n* informazioni *fpl*; particolari *mpl*; **a piece of** ~ un'informazione; ~ **office** *n* ufficio *m* informazioni *inv*.

**informative** [ɪnˈfɔːmətɪv] *a* istruttivo(a).

**informer** [ɪnˈfɔːmə*] *n* informatore/trice; **to turn** ~ (POLICE) denunciare i complici.

**infringe** [ɪnˈfrɪndʒ] *vt* infrangere // *vi*: to ~ on calpestare; ~**ment** *n*: ~**ment (of)** infrazione *f* (di).

**infuriating** [ɪnˈfjuərieɪtɪŋ] *a* molto irritante.

**ingenious** [ɪnˈdʒiːnjəs] *a* ingegnoso(a).

**ingenuity** [ɪndʒɪˈnjuːɪtɪ] *n* ingegnosità.

**ingenuous** [ɪnˈdʒɛnjuəs] *a* ingenuo(a).

**ingot** [ˈɪŋgət] *n* lingotto.

**ingrained** [ɪnˈgreɪnd] *a* radicato(a).

**ingratiate** [ɪnˈgreɪʃɪeɪt] *vt*: to ~ o.s. with sb ingraziarsi qn.

**ingredient** [ɪnˈgriːdɪənt] *n* ingrediente *m*; elemento.

**inhabit** [ɪnˈhæbɪt] *vt* abitare.

**inhabitant** [ɪnˈhæbɪtnt] *n* abitante *m/f*.

**inhale** [ɪnˈheɪl] *vt* inalare // *vi* (in smoking) aspirare.

**inherent** [ɪnˈhɪərənt] *a*: ~ (in or to) inerente a.

**inherit** [ɪnˈhɛrɪt] *vt* ereditare; ~**ance** *n* eredità.

**inhibit** [ɪnˈhɪbɪt] *vt* (PSYCH) inibire; to ~ sb from doing impedire a qn di fare; ~**ion** [-ˈbɪʃən] *n* inibizione *f*.

**inhospitable** [ɪnhɔsˈpɪtəbl] *a* inospitale.

**inhuman** [ɪnˈhjuːmən] *a* inumano(a).

**initial** [ɪˈnɪʃl] *a* iniziale // *n* iniziale *f* // *vt* siglare; ~**s** *npl* iniziali *fpl*; (as signature) sigla; ~**ly** *ad* inizialmente, all'inizio.

**initiate** [ɪˈnɪʃɪeɪt] *vt* (start) avviare; intraprendere; iniziare; (person) iniziare.

**initiative** [ɪˈnɪʃətɪv] *n* iniziativa.

**inject** [ɪnˈdʒɛkt] *vt* (liquid) iniettare; (person) fare una puntura a; ~**ion** [ɪnˈdʒɛkʃən] *n* iniezione *f*, puntura.

**injure** [ˈɪndʒə*] *vt* ferire; (wrong) fare male *or* torto a; (damage: reputation etc) nuocere a; ~**d** *a* (person, arm) ferito(a).

**injury** [ˈɪndʒərɪ] *n* ferita; (wrong) torto; ~ **time** *n* (SPORT) tempo di recupero.

**injustice** [ɪnˈdʒʌstɪs] *n* ingiustizia.

**ink** [ɪŋk] *n* inchiostro.

**inkling** [ˈɪŋklɪŋ] *n* sentore *m*, vaga idea.

**inlaid** [ˈɪnleɪd] *a* incrostato(a); (table etc) intarsiato(a).

**inland** *a* [ˈɪnlənd] interno(a) // *ad* [ɪnˈlænd] all'interno; **I~ Revenue** *n* (Brit) Fisco.

**in-laws** [ˈɪnlɔːz] *npl* suoceri *mpl*; famiglia del marito (*or* della moglie).

**inlet** [ˈɪnlɛt] *n* (GEO) insenatura, baia.

**inmate** [ˈɪnmeɪt] *n* (in prison) carcerato/a; (in asylum) ricoverato/a.

**inn** [ɪn] *n* locanda.

**innate** [ɪˈneɪt] *a* innato(a).

**inner** ['ɪnə*] a interno(a), interiore; ~ **city** n centro di una zona urbana; ~ **tube** n camera d'aria.

**innings** ['ɪnɪŋz] n (CRICKET) turno di battuta.

**innocence** ['ɪnəsns] n innocenza.

**innocent** ['ɪnəsnt] a innocente.

**innocuous** [ɪ'nɔkjuəs] a innocuo(a).

**innuendo,** ~es [ɪnju'ɛndəu] n insinuazione f.

**innumerable** [ɪ'njuːmrəbl] a innumerevole.

**inordinately** [ɪ'nɔːdɪnətlɪ] ad smoderatamente.

**in-patient** ['ɪnpeɪʃənt] n ricoverato/a.

**input** ['ɪnput] n (ELEC) energia, potenza; (of machine) alimentazione f; (of computer) input m.

**inquest** ['ɪnkwɛst] n inchiesta.

**inquire** [ɪn'kwaɪə*] vi informarsi // vt domandare, informarsi su; **to ~ about** vt fus informarsi di or su; **to ~ into** vt fus fare indagini su; **inquiry** n domanda; (LAW) indagine f, investigazione f; **inquiry office** n (Brit) ufficio m informazioni inv.

**inquisitive** [ɪn'kwɪzɪtɪv] a curioso(a).

**inroad** ['ɪnrəud] n incursione f.

**insane** [ɪn'seɪn] a matto(a), pazzo(a); (MED) alienato(a).

**insanity** [ɪn'sænɪtɪ] n follia; (MED) alienazione f mentale.

**inscription** [ɪn'skrɪpʃən] n iscrizione f; dedica.

**inscrutable** [ɪn'skruːtəbl] a imperscrutabile.

**insect** ['ɪnsɛkt] n insetto; ~**icide** [ɪn'sɛktɪsaɪd] n insetticida m.

**insecure** [ɪnsɪ'kjuə*] a malsicuro(a); (person) insicuro(a).

**insemination** [ɪnsɛmɪ'neɪʃən] n: **artificial ~** fecondazione f artificiale.

**insensible** [ɪn'sɛnsɪbl] a insensibile; (unconscious) privo(a) di sensi.

**insensitive** [ɪn'sɛnsɪtɪv] a insensibile.

**insert** vt [ɪn'sɜːt] inserire, introdurre // n ['ɪnsɜːt] inserto; ~**ion** [ɪn'sɜːʃən] n inserzione f.

**in-service** [ɪn'sɜːvɪs] a (training, course) durante l'orario di lavoro.

**inshore** [ɪn'ʃɔː*] a costiero(a) // ad presso la riva; verso la riva.

**inside** [ɪn'saɪd] n interno, parte f interiore // a interno(a), interiore // ad dentro, all'interno // prep dentro, all'interno di; (of time): ~ **10 minutes** entro 10 minuti; ~**s** npl (col) ventre m; ~ **forward** n (SPORT) mezzala, interno; ~ **lane** n (AUT) corsia di marcia; ~ **out** ad (turn) a rovescio; (know) a fondo; **to turn sth ~ out** rivoltare qc.

**insight** ['ɪnsaɪt] n acume m, perspicacia; (glimpse, idea) percezione f.

**insignia** [ɪn'sɪgnɪə] npl insegne fpl.

**insignificant** [ɪnsɪg'nɪfɪknt] a insignificante.

**insincere** [ɪnsɪn'sɪə*] a insincero(a).

**insinuate** [ɪn'sɪnjuːeɪt] vt insinuare.

**insist** [ɪn'sɪst] vi insistere; **to ~ on doing** insistere per fare; **to ~ that** insistere perché + sub; (claim) sostenere che; ~**ent** a insistente.

**insole** ['ɪnsəul] n soletta.

**insolent** ['ɪnsələnt] a insolente.

**insomnia** [ɪn'sɔmnɪə] n insonnia.

**inspect** [ɪn'spɛkt] vt ispezionare; (ticket) controllare; ~**ion** [ɪn'spɛkʃən] n ispezione f; controllo; ~**or** n ispettore/trice; (Brit: on buses, trains) controllore m.

**inspire** [ɪn'spaɪə*] vt ispirare.

**install** [ɪn'stɔːl] vt installare; ~**ation** [ɪnstə'leɪʃən] n installazione f.

**instalment,** (US) **installment** [ɪn'stɔːlmənt] n rata; (of TV serial etc) puntata; **in ~s** (pay) a rate; (receive) una parte per volta; (: publication) a fascicoli.

**instance** ['ɪnstəns] n esempio, caso; **for ~** per or ad esempio; **in many ~s** in molti casi; **in the first ~** in primo luogo.

**instant** ['ɪnstənt] n istante m, attimo // a immediato(a); urgente; (coffee, food) in polvere; ~**ly** ad immediatamente, subito.

**instead** [ɪnˈsted] ad invece; ~ **of** invece di; ~ **of sb** al posto di qn.

**instep** [ˈɪnstep] n collo del piede; (of shoe) collo della scarpa.

**instil** [ɪnˈstɪl] vt: **to** ~ (**into**) inculcare (in).

**instinct** [ˈɪnstɪŋkt] n istinto.

**institute** [ˈɪnstɪtjuːt] n istituto // vt istituire, stabilire; (inquiry) avviare; (proceedings) iniziare.

**institution** [ɪnstɪˈtjuːʃən] n istituzione f; istituto (d'istruzione); istituto (psichiatrico).

**instruct** [ɪnˈstrʌkt] vt istruire; **to** ~ **sb in sth** insegnare qc a qn; **to** ~ **sb to do** dare ordini a qn di fare; ~**ion** [ɪnˈstrʌkʃən] n istruzione f; ~**ions** (for use) istruzioni per l'uso; ~**or n** istruttore/trice; (for skiing) maestro/a.

**instrument** [ˈɪnstrəmənt] n strumento; ~**al** [-ˈmentl] a (MUS) strumentale; **to be** ~**al in** essere d'aiuto in; ~ **panel** n quadro m portastrumenti inv.

**insufficient** [ɪnsəˈfɪʃənt] a insufficiente.

**insular** [ˈɪnsjulə*] a insulare; (person) di mente ristretta.

**insulate** [ˈɪnsjuleɪt] vt isolare; **insulating tape** n nastro isolante; **insulation** [-ˈleɪʃən] n isolamento.

**insulin** [ˈɪnsjuˈə*] n insulina.

**insult** n [ˈɪnsʌlt] insulto, affronto // vt [ɪnˈsʌlt] insultare; ~**ing** a offensivo(a), ingiurioso(a).

**insuperable** [ɪnˈsjuːprəbl] a insormontabile, insuperabile.

**insurance** [ɪnˈʃuərəns] n assicurazione f; **fire/life** ~ assicurazione contro gli incendi/sulla vita; ~ **policy** n polizza d'assicurazione.

**insure** [ɪnˈʃuə*] vt assicurare.

**intact** [ɪnˈtækt] a intatto(a).

**intake** [ˈɪnteɪk] n (TECH) immissione f; (of food) consumo; (Brit: of pupils etc) afflusso.

**integral** [ˈɪntɪɡrəl] a integrale; (part) integrante.

**integrate** [ˈɪntɪɡreɪt] vt integrare.

**integrity** [ɪnˈtɛɡrɪtɪ] n integrità.

**intellect** [ˈɪntəlɛkt] n intelletto; ~**ual** [-ˈlɛktjuəl] a, n intellettuale (m/f).

**intelligence** [ɪnˈtɛlɪdʒəns] n intelligenza; (MIL etc) informazioni fpl.

**intelligent** [ɪnˈtɛlɪdʒənt] a intelligente.

**intend** [ɪnˈtend] vt (gift etc): **to** ~ **sth for** destinare qc a; **to** ~ **to do** aver l'intenzione di fare; ~**ed** a (effect) voluto(a).

**intense** [ɪnˈtens] a intenso(a); (person) di forti sentimenti; ~**ly** ad intensamente; profondamente.

**intensive** [ɪnˈtensɪv] a intensivo(a); ~ **care unit** n reparto terapia intensiva.

**intent** [ɪnˈtent] n intenzione f // a: ~ (**on**) intento(a) (a), immerso(a) (in); **to all** ~**s and purposes** a tutti gli effetti; **to be** ~ **on doing sth** essere deciso a fare qc.

**intention** [ɪnˈtenʃən] n intenzione f; ~**al** a intenzionale, deliberato(a); ~**ally** ad apposta.

**intently** [ɪnˈtentlɪ] ad attentamente.

**inter** [ɪnˈtəː*] vt sotterrare.

**interact** [ɪntərˈækt] vi agire reciprocamente, interagire.

**interchange** n [ˈɪntətʃeɪndʒ] (exchange) scambio; (on motorway) incrocio pluridirezionale // vt [ɪntəˈtʃeɪndʒ] scambiare; sostituire l'uno(a) per l'altro(a); ~**able** a intercambiabile.

**intercom** [ˈɪntəkɔm] n interfono.

**intercourse** [ˈɪntəkɔːs] n rapporti mpl.

**interest** [ˈɪntrɪst] n interesse m; (COMM: stake, share) interessi mpl // vt interessare; ~**ed** a interessato(a); **to be** ~**ed in** interessarsi di; ~**ing** a interessante; ~ **rate** n tasso di interesse.

**interface** [ˈɪntəfeɪs] n (COMPUT) interfaccia.

**interfere** [ɪntəˈfɪə*] vi: **to** ~ **in** (quarrel, other people's business) immischiarsi in; **to ~ with** (*object*) toccare; (*plans*) ostacolare; (*duty*) interferire con.

**interference** [intəˈfiərəns] *n* interferenza.

**interim** [ˈintərim] *a* provvisorio(a) // *n*: in the ~ nel frattempo.

**interior** [inˈtiəriə*] *n* interno; (*of country*) entroterra // *a* interiore, interno(a); **~ designer** *n* arredatore/trice.

**interlock** [intəˈlɔk] *vi* ingranarsi // *vt* ingranare.

**interloper** [ˈintələupə*] *n* intruso/a.

**interlude** [ˈintəluːd] *n* intervallo; (*THEATRE*) intermezzo.

**intermediate** [intəˈmiːdiət] *a* intermedio(a); (*SCOL: course, level*) medio(a).

**intermission** [intəˈmiʃən] *n* pausa; (*THEATRE, CINEMA*) intermissione *f*, intervallo.

**intern** *vt* [inˈtəːn] internare // *n* [ˈintəːn] (*US*) medico interno.

**internal** [inˈtəːnl] *a* interno(a); **~ly** *ad* all'interno; **"not to be taken ~ly"** "per uso esterno"; **I~ Revenue Service (IRS)** *n* (*US*) Fisco.

**international** [intəˈnæʃənl] *a* internazionale.

**interplay** [ˈintəpleɪ] *n* azione e reazione *f*.

**interpret** [inˈtəːprit] *vt* interpretare // *vi* fare da interprete; **~er** *n* interprete *m/f*.

**interrelated** [intərriˈleitid] *a* correlato(a).

**interrogate** [inˈterəugeit] *vt* interrogare; **interrogation** [-ˈgeiʃən] *n* interrogazione *f*; (*of suspect etc*) interrogatorio; **interrogative** [intəˈrɔgətiv] *a* interrogativo(a).

**interrupt** [intəˈrʌpt] *vt* interrompere; **~ion** [-ˈrʌpʃən] *n* interruzione *f*.

**intersect** [intəˈsekt] *vt* intersecare // *vi* (*roads*) intersecarsi; **~ion** [-ˈsekʃən] *n* intersezione *f*; (*of roads*) incrocio.

**intersperse** [intəˈspəːs] *vt*: **to ~**

with costellare di.

**intertwine** [intəˈtwain] *vt* intrecciare // *vi* intrecciarsi.

**interval** [ˈintəvl] *n* intervallo; **at ~s** a intervalli.

**intervene** [intəˈviːn] *vi* (*time*) intercorrere; (*event, person*) intervenire; **intervention** [-ˈvenʃən] *n* intervento.

**interview** [ˈintəvjuː] *n* (*RADIO, TV etc*) intervista; (*for job*) colloquio // *vt* intervistare; avere un colloquio con; **~er** *n* intervistatore/trice.

**intestine** [inˈtestin] *n* intestino.

**intimacy** [ˈintiməsi] *n* intimità.

**intimate** *a* [ˈintimət] intimo(a); (*knowledge*) profondo(a) // *vt* [ˈintimeit] lasciar capire.

**into** [ˈintu] *prep* dentro, in; **come ~ the house** vieni dentro la casa; **~ Italian** in italiano.

**intolerable** [inˈtɔlərəbl] *a* intollerabile.

**intolerance** [inˈtɔlərns] *n* intolleranza.

**intolerant** [inˈtɔlərnt] *a*: **~ of** intollerante di.

**intoxicate** [inˈtɔksikeit] *vt* inebriare; **~d** *a* inebriato(a); **intoxication** [-ˈkeiʃən] *n* ebbrezza.

**intractable** [inˈtræktəbl] *a* intrattabile.

**intransitive** [inˈtrænsitiv] *a* intransitivo(a).

**intravenous** [intrəˈviːnəs] *a* endovenoso(a).

**in-tray** [ˈintrei] *n* contenitore *m* per la corrispondenza in arrivo.

**intricate** [ˈintrikət] *a* intricato(a), complicato(a).

**intrigue** [inˈtriːg] *n* intrigo // *vt* affascinare // *vi* complottare, tramare; **intriguing** *a* affascinante.

**intrinsic** [inˈtrinsik] *a* intrinseco(a).

**introduce** [intrəˈdjuːs] *vt* introdurre; **to ~ sb (to sb)** presentare qn (a qn); **to ~ sb to** (*pastime, technique*) iniziare qn a; **introduction** [-ˈdʌkʃən] *n* introduzione *f*; (*of person*) presentazione *f*; **intro-**

ductory $a$ introduttivo(a).

**intrude** [ɪn'truːd] $vi$ (person): to ~ (on) intromettersi (in); **am I intruding?** disturbo?; ~**r** $n$ intruso/a.

**intuition** [ɪntjuː'ɪʃən] $n$ intuizione $f$.

**inundate** ['ɪnʌndeɪt] $vt$: to ~ **with** inondare di.

**invade** [ɪn'veɪd] $vt$ invadere.

**invalid** $n$ ['ɪnvəlɪd] malato/a; (with disability) invalido // $a$ [ɪn'vælɪd] (not valid) invalido(a), non valido(a).

**invaluable** [ɪn'væljuəbl] $a$ prezioso(a); inestimabile.

**invariably** [ɪn'vɛərɪəblɪ] $ad$ invariabilmente; sempre.

**invasion** [ɪn'veɪʒən] $n$ invasione $f$.

**invent** [ɪn'vɛnt] $vt$ inventare; ~**ion** [ɪn'vɛnʃən] $n$ invenzione $f$; ~**ive** $a$ inventivo(a); ~**or** $n$ inventore $m$.

**inventory** ['ɪnvəntrɪ] $n$ inventario.

**invert** [ɪn'vɜːt] $vt$ invertire; (cup, object) rovesciare; ~**ed commas** $npl$ (Brit) virgolette $fpl$.

**invest** [ɪn'vɛst] $vt$ investire // $vi$ fare investimenti.

**investigate** [ɪn'vɛstɪgeɪt] $vt$ investigare, indagare; (crime) fare indagini su; **investigation** [-'geɪʃən] $n$ investigazione $f$; (of crime) indagine $f$.

**investment** [ɪn'vɛstmənt] $n$ investimento.

**investor** [ɪn'vɛstə*] $n$ investitore/trice; azionista $m/f$.

**invidious** [ɪn'vɪdɪəs] $a$ odioso(a); (task) spiacevole.

**invigilate** [ɪn'vɪdʒɪleɪt] $vt$, $vi$ (in exam) sorvegliare.

**invigorating** [ɪn'vɪgəreɪtɪŋ] $a$ stimolante; vivificante.

**invisible** [ɪn'vɪzɪbl] $a$ invisibile; ~ **ink** $n$ inchiostro simpatico.

**invitation** [ɪnvɪ'teɪʃən] $n$ invito.

**invite** [ɪn'vaɪt] $vt$ invitare; (opinions etc) sollecitare; (trouble) provocare; **inviting** $a$ invitante, attraente.

**invoice** ['ɪnvɔɪs] $n$ fattura.

**involuntary** [ɪn'vɔləntrɪ] $a$ involontario(a).

**involve** [ɪn'vɔlv] $vt$ (entail) ri-

chiedere, comportare; (associate): to ~ **sb** (**in**) implicare qn (in); coinvolgere qn (in); ~**d** $a$ involuto(a), complesso(a); to feel ~**d** sentirsi coinvolto(a); ~**ment** $n$ implicazione $f$; coinvolgimento; ~**ment** (in) impegno (in); partecipazione $f$ (in).

**inward** ['ɪnwəd] $a$ (movement) verso l'interno; (thought, feeling) interiore, intimo(a); ~(**s**) $ad$ verso l'interno.

**I/O** $abbr$ (COMPUT: = input/output) I/O.

**iodine** ['aɪəʊdiːn] $n$ iodio.

**iota** [aɪ'əʊtə] $n$ (fig) briciolo.

**IOU** $n$ $abbr$ (= I owe you) pagherò $n$ inv.

**IQ** $n$ $abbr$ (= intelligence quotient) quoziente $m$ d'intelligenza.

**IRA** $n$ $abbr$ (= Irish Republican Army) IRA $f$.

**Iran** [ɪ'rɑːn] $n$ Iran $m$.

**Iraq** [ɪ'rɑːk] $n$ Iraq $m$.

**Ireland** ['aɪələnd] $n$ Irlanda.

**iris** ['aɪrɪs, -ɪz] $n$ iride $f$; (BOT) giaggiolo, iride.

**Irish** ['aɪrɪʃ] $a$ irlandese // $npl$: the ~ gli Irlandesi; ~**man** $n$ irlandese $m$; ~ **Sea** $n$ Mar $m$ d'Irlanda; ~**woman** $n$ irlandese $f$.

**irksome** ['ɜːksəm] $a$ seccante.

**iron** ['aɪən] $n$ ferro; (for clothes) ferro da stiro // $a$ di or in ferro // $vt$ (clothes) stirare; **to** ~ **out** $vt$ (crease) appianare; (fig) spianare; far sparire; **the I~ Curtain** $n$ la cortina di ferro.

**ironic(al)** [aɪ'rɔnɪk(l)] $a$ ironico(a).

**ironing** ['aɪənɪŋ] $n$ (act) stirare $m$; (clothes) roba da stirare; ~ **board** $n$ asse $f$ da stiro.

**ironmonger** ['aɪənmʌŋgə*] $n$ (Brit) negoziante $m$ in ferramenta; ~'**s** (**shop**) $n$ negozio di ferramenta.

**ironworks** ['aɪənwɜːks] $n$ ferriera.

**irony** ['aɪrənɪ] $n$ ironia.

**irrational** [ɪ'ræʃənl] $a$ irrazionale; irragionevole; illogico(a).

**irregular** [ɪ'regjulə*] $a$ irregolare.

**irrelevant** [ɪ'rɛləvənt] $a$ non

pertinente.

**irreplaceable** [ɪrɪ'pleɪsəbl] *a* insostituibile.

**irrepressible** [ɪrɪ'presəbl] *a* irrefrenabile.

**irresistible** [ɪrɪ'zɪstɪbl] *a* irresistibile.

**irrespective** [ɪrɪ'spektɪv]: ~ **of** *prep* senza riguardo a.

**irresponsible** [ɪrɪ'spɔnsɪbl] *a* irresponsabile.

**irrigate** ['ɪrɪgeɪt] *vt* irrigare; **irrigation** [-'geɪʃən] *n* irrigazione *f*.

**irritable** ['ɪrɪtəbl] *a* irritabile.

**irritate** ['ɪrɪteɪt] *vt* irritare; **irritating** *a* (*person, sound etc*) irritante; **irritation** [-'teɪʃən] *n* irritazione *f*.

**IRS** *n abbr* = **Internal Revenue Service.**

**is** [ɪz] *vb see* **be.**

**Islam** ['ɪzlɑːm] *n* Islam *m*.

**island** ['aɪlənd] *n* isola; (*also:* **traffic** ~) salvagente *m*; **~er** *n* isolano/a.

**isle** [aɪl] *n* isola.

**isn't** ['ɪznt] = **is not.**

**isolate** ['aɪsəleɪt] *vt* isolare; **~d** *a* isolato(a); **isolation** [-'leɪʃən] *n* isolamento.

**Israel** ['ɪzreɪl] *n* Israele *m*; **~i** [ɪz'reɪlɪ] *a*, *n* israeliano(a).

**issue** ['ɪʃjuː] *n* questione *f*, problema *m*; (*outcome*) esito, risultato; (*of banknotes etc*) emissione *f*; (*of newspaper etc*) numero; (*offspring*) discendenza // *vt* (*rations, equipment*) distribuire; (*orders*) dare; (*book*) pubblicare; (*banknotes, cheques, stamps*) emettere; **at** ~ in gioco, in discussione; **to take** ~ **with sb (over sth)** prendere posizione contro qn (riguardo a qc).

**isthmus** ['ɪsməs] *n* istmo.

*KEYWORD*

**it** [ɪt] *pronoun* **1** (*specific: subject*) esso(a); (: *direct object*) lo(la), l'; (: *indirect object*) gli(le); **where's my book?** - ~**'s on the table** dov'è il mio libro? - è sulla tavola; **I can't find** ~ non lo (*or* la) trovo; **give** ~ **to me** dammelo (*or*

dammela); **about/from/of** ~ ne; **I spoke to him about** ~ gliene ho parlato; **what did you learn from** ~? quale insegnamento ne hai tratto?; **I'm proud of** ~ ne sono fiero; **did you go to** ~? ci sei andato?; **put the book in** ~ mettici il libro

**2** (*impersonal*): ~**'s raining** piove; ~**'s Friday tomorrow** domani è venerdì; ~**'s 6 o'clock** sono le 6; **who is** ~? - ~**'s me** chi è? - sono io.

**Italian** [ɪ'tæljən] *a* italiano(a) // *n* italiano/a; (*LING*) italiano; **the** ~**s** gli Italiani.

**italic** [ɪ'tælɪk] *a* corsivo(a); ~**s** *npl* corsivo.

**Italy** ['ɪtəlɪ] *n* Italia.

**itch** [ɪtʃ] *n* prurito // *vi* (*person*) avere il prurito; (*part of body*) prudere; **to be** ~**ing to do sth** aver una gran voglia di fare qc; ~**y** *a* che prude; **to be** ~**y** = **to** ~.

**it'd** ['ɪtd] = **it would; it had.**

**item** ['aɪtəm] *n* articolo; (*on agenda*) punto; (*in programme*) numero; (*also:* **news** ~) notizia; ~**ize** *vt* specificare, dettagliare.

**itinerant** [ɪ'tɪnərənt] *a* ambulante.

**itinerary** [aɪ'tɪnərərɪ] *n* itinerario.

**it'll** ['ɪtl] = **it will, it shall.**

**its** [ɪts] *a* il(la) suo(a), i(le) suoi(sue).

**it's** [ɪts] = **it is; it has.**

**itself** [ɪt'self] *pronoun* (*emphatic*) esso(a) stesso(a); (*reflexive*) si.

**ITV** *n abbr* (*Brit:* = *Independent Television*) rete televisiva in concorrenza con la BBC.

**I.U.D.** *n abbr* (= *intra-uterine device*) spirale *f*.

**I've** [aɪv] = **I have.**

**ivory** ['aɪvərɪ] *n* avorio.

**ivy** ['aɪvɪ] *n* edera.

# J

**jab** [dʒæb] *vt*: to ~ sth into affondare *or* piantare qc dentro // *n* colpo; (*MED*: *col*) puntura.

**jack** [dʒæk] *n* (*AUT*) cricco; (*CARDS*) fante *m*; to ~ up *vt* sollevare sul cricco.

**jackal** ['dʒækl] *n* sciacallo.

**jackdaw** ['dʒækdɔ:] *n* taccola.

**jacket** ['dʒækɪt] *n* giacca; (*of book*) copertura.

**jack-knife** ['dʒæknaɪf] *vi*: the lorry ~d l'autotreno si è piegato su se stesso.

**jack plug** *n* (*ELEC*) jack *m inv*.

**jackpot** ['dʒækpɔt] *n* primo premio (in denaro).

**jade** [dʒeɪd] *n* (*stone*) giada.

**jaded** ['dʒeɪdɪd] *a* sfinito(a), spossato(a).

**jagged** ['dʒægɪd] *a* sbocconcellato(a); (*cliffs etc*) frastagliato(a).

**jail** [dʒeɪl] *n* prigione *f* // *vt* mandare in prigione; ~er *n* custode *m* del carcere.

**jam** [dʒæm] *n* marmellata; (*of shoppers etc*) ressa; (*also*: traffic ~) ingorgo *m* // (*passage etc*) ingombrare, ostacolare; (*mechanism, drawer etc*) bloccare; (*RADIO*) disturbare con interferenze // *vi* (*mechanism, sliding part*) incepparsi, bloccarsi; (*gun*) incepparsi; to ~ sth into forzare qc dentro; infilare qc a forza dentro.

**Jamaica** [dʒə'meɪkə] *n* Giamaica.

**jangle** ['dʒæŋgl] *vi* risuonare; (*bracelet*) tintinnare.

**janitor** ['dʒænɪtə*] *n* (*caretaker*) portiere *m*; (: *SCOL*) bidello.

**January** ['dʒænjuərɪ] *n* gennaio.

**Japan** [dʒə'pæn] *n* Giappone *m*; ~ese [dʒæpə'ni:z] *a* giapponese // *a* (*pl inv*) giapponese *m/f*; (*LING*) giapponese *m*.

**jar** [dʒɑ:*] *n* (*glass*) barattolo, vasetto

// *vi* (*sound*) stridere; (*colours etc*) stonare.

**jargon** ['dʒɑ:gən] *n* gergo.

**jasmin(e)** ['dʒæzmɪn] *n* gelsomino.

**jaundice** ['dʒɔ:ndɪs] *n* itterizia; ~d *a* (*fig*) invidioso(a) e critico(a).

**jaunt** [dʒɔ:nt] *n* gita; ~y *a* vivace; disinvolto(a).

**javelin** ['dʒævlɪn] *n* giavellotto.

**jaw** [dʒɔ:] *n* mascella.

**jay** [dʒeɪ] *n* ghiandaia.

**jaywalker** ['dʒeɪwɔ:kə*] *n* pedone(a) indisciplinato(a).

**jazz** [dʒæz] *n* jazz *m*; to ~ up *vt* rendere vivace.

**jealous** ['dʒeləs] *a* geloso(a); ~y *n* gelosia.

**jeans** [dʒi:nz] *npl* (blue-)jeans *mpl*.

**jeer** [dʒɪə*] *vi*: to ~ (at) fischiare; beffeggiare.

**jelly** ['dʒelɪ] *n* gelatina; ~fish *n* medusa.

**jeopardy** ['dʒepədɪ] *n*: in ~ in pericolo.

**jerk** [dʒə:k] *n* sobbalzo, scossa; sussulto // *vt* dare una scossa a // *vi* (*vehicles*) sobbalzare.

**jerkin** ['dʒə:kɪn] *n* giubbotto.

**jersey** ['dʒə:zɪ] *n* maglia.

**jest** [dʒest] *n* scherzo.

**Jesus** ['dʒi:zəs] *n* Gesù m.

**jet** [dʒet] *n* (*of gas, liquid*) getto; (*AVIAT*) aviogetto; ~-black *a* nero(a) come l'ebano, corvino(a); ~ engine *n* motore m a reazione; ~ lag *n* (problemi *mpl* dovuti allo) sbalzo dei fusi orari.

**jettison** ['dʒetɪsn] *vt* gettare in mare.

**jetty** ['dʒetɪ] *n* molo.

**Jew** [dʒu:] *n* ebreo.

**jewel** ['dʒu:əl] *n* gioiello; ~ler *n* orefice *m*, gioielliere/a; ~ler's (shop) *n* oreficeria, gioielleria; ~lery *n* gioielli *mpl*.

**Jewess** ['dʒu:ɪs] *n* ebrea.

**Jewish** ['dʒu:ɪʃ] *a* ebreo(a), ebraico(a).

**jib** [dʒɪb] *n* (*NAUT*) fiocco; (*of crane*) braccio.

**jibe** [dʒaɪb] *n* beffa.

**jiffy** ['dʒɪfɪ] n (col): **in a ~** in un batter d'occhio.

**jig** [dʒɪg] n giga.

**jigsaw** ['dʒɪgsɔː] n (also: ~ **puzzle**) puzzle m inv.

**jilt** [dʒɪlt] vt piantare in asso.

**jingle** ['dʒɪŋgl] n (advert) sigla pubblicitaria // vi tintinnare, scampanellare.

**jinx** [dʒɪŋks] n (col) iettatura; (person) iettatore/trice.

**jitters** ['dʒɪtəz] npl (col): **to get the ~** aver fifa.

**job** [dʒɔb] n lavoro; (employment) impiego, posto; **it's a good ~ that ... meno male che ...**; **just the ~!** proprio quello che ci vuole; ~ **centre** n (Brit) ufficio di collocamento; ~**less** a senza lavoro, disoccupato(a).

**jockey** ['dʒɔkɪ] n fantino, jockey m inv // vi: **to ~ for position** manovrare per una posizione di vantaggio.

**jocular** ['dʒɔkjulə*] a gioviale; scherzoso(a).

**jog** [dʒɔg] vt urtare // vi (SPORT) fare footing, fare jogging; **to ~ along** trottare; (fig) andare avanti piano piano; ~**ging** n footing m, jogging m.

**join** [dʒɔɪn] vt unire, congiungere; (become member of) iscriversi a; (meet) raggiungere; riunirsi a // vi (roads, rivers) confluire // n giuntura; **to ~ in** vi partecipare // vt fus unirsi a; **to ~ up** vi arruolarsi.

**joiner** ['dʒɔɪnə*] n falegname m; ~ n falegnameria.

**joint** [dʒɔɪnt] n (TECH) giuntura; giunto; (ANAT) articolazione f, giuntura; (Brit CULIN) arrosto; (col: place) locale m // a comune; ~ **account** n (at bank etc) conto in partecipazione, conto comune; ~**ly** ad in comune, insieme.

**joist** [dʒɔɪst] n trave f.

**joke** [dʒəuk] n scherzo; (funny story) barzelletta; (also: **practical ~**) beffa // vi scherzare; **to play a ~ on**

sb fare uno scherzo a qn; ~**r** n buffone/a, burlone/a; (CARDS) matta, jolly m inv.

**jolly** ['dʒɔlɪ] a allegro(a), gioioso(a) // ad (col) veramente, proprio.

**jolt** [dʒəult] n scossa, sobbalzo // vt urtare.

**Jordan** ['dʒɔːdən] n (country) Giordania; (river) Giordano.

**jostle** ['dʒɔsl] vt spingere coi gomiti // vi farsi spazio coi gomiti.

**jot** [dʒɔt] n: **not one** ~ nemmeno un po'; **to ~ down** vt annotare in fretta, buttare giù; ~**ter** n (Brit) blocco.

**journal** ['dʒəːnl] n giornale m; rivista; diario; ~**ism** n giornalismo; ~**ist** n giornalista m/f.

**journey** ['dʒəːnɪ] n viaggio; (distance covered) tragitto // vi viaggiare.

**joy** [dʒɔɪ] n gioia; ~**ful**, ~**ous** a gioioso(a), allegro(a); ~ **ride** n gita in automobile (specialmente rubata); ~**stick** n (AVIAT) barra di comando; (COMPUT) joystick m inv.

**J.P.** n abbr = **Justice of the Peace.**

**Jr, Jun., Junr** abbr = **junior.**

**jubilant** ['dʒuːbɪlnt] a giubilante; trionfante.

**jubilee** ['dʒuːbɪliː] n giubileo; **silver ~** venticinquesimo anniversario.

**judge** [dʒʌdʒ] n giudice m/f // vt giudicare; **judg(e)ment** n giudizio; (punishment) punizione f.

**judicial** [dʒuː'dɪʃl] a giudiziale, giudiziario(a).

**judiciary** [dʒuː'dɪʃɪərɪ] n magistratura.

**judo** ['dʒuːdəu] n judo.

**jug** [dʒʌg] n brocca, bricco.

**juggernaut** ['dʒʌgənɔːt] n (Brit: huge truck) bestione m.

**juggle** ['dʒʌgl] vi fare giochi di destrezza; ~**r** n giocoliere/a.

**Jugoslav** ['juːgəuslɑːv] etc = **Yugoslav** etc.

**juice** [dʒuːs] n succo.

**juicy** ['dʒuːsɪ] a succoso(a).

**jukebox** ['dʒu:kbɔks] n juke-box m inv.

**July** [dʒu:'laɪ] n luglio.

**jumble** ['dʒʌmbl] n miscuglio // vt (also: ~ **up**) mischiare; ~ **sale** n (Brit) vendita di oggetti per beneficenza.

**jumbo (jet)** ['dʒʌmbəu-] n jumbo-jet m inv.

**jump** [dʒʌmp] vi saltare, balzare; (start) sobbalzare; (increase) rincarare // vt saltare // n salto, balzo; sobbalzo.

**jumper** ['dʒʌmpə*] n (Brit: pullover) maglione m, pullover m inv; (US: dress) scamiciato; ~ **cables** npl (US) = **jump leads**.

**jump leads** npl (Brit) cavi mpl per batteria.

**jumpy** ['dʒʌmpɪ] a nervoso(a), agitato(a).

**junction** ['dʒʌŋkʃən] n (Brit: of roads) incrocio; (of rails) nodo ferroviario.

**juncture** ['dʒʌŋktʃə*] n: at this ~ in questa congiuntura.

**June** [dʒu:n] n giugno.

**jungle** ['dʒʌŋgl] n giungla.

**junior** ['dʒu:nɪə*] a, n: he's ~ to me (by 2 years), he's my ~ (by 2 years) è più giovane di me (di 2 anni); he's ~ to me (seniority) è al di sotto di me, ho più anzianità di lui; ~ **school** n (Brit) scuola elementare (da 8 a 11 anni).

**junk** [dʒʌŋk] n (rubbish) chincaglia; (ship) giunca; ~ **food** n porcherie fpl; ~ **shop** n chincaglieria.

**juror** ['dʒuərə*] n giurato/a.

**jury** ['dʒuərɪ] n giuria.

**just** [dʒʌst] a giusto(a) // ad: he's ~ done it/left lo ha appena fatto/è appena partito; ~ **as I expected** proprio come me lo aspettavo; ~ **right** proprio giusto; ~ **2 o'clock** le 2 precise; she's ~ as clever as you è in gamba proprio quanto te; it's ~ as well that ... meno male che ...; ~ **as I arrived** proprio mentre arrivavo; it was ~ before/enough/

here era poco prima/appena assai/ proprio qui; it's ~ me sono solo io; it's ~ a mistake non è che uno sbaglio; ~ **missed/caught** appena perso/preso; ~ **listen to this!** senta un po' questo!

**justice** ['dʒʌstɪs] n giustizia; **J~ of the Peace (J.P.)** n giudice m conciliatore.

**justify** ['dʒʌstɪfaɪ] vt giustificare.

**jut** [dʒʌt] vi (also: ~ **out**) sporgersi.

**juvenile** ['dʒu:vənaɪl] a giovane, giovanile; (court) dei minorenni; (books) per ragazzi // n giovane m/f, minorenne m/f.

**juxtapose** ['dʒʌkstəpəuz] vt giustapporre.

## K

**K** abbr (= one thousand) mille; (= kilobyte) K.

**kangaroo** [kæŋgə'ru:] n canguro.

**karate** [kə'rɑ:tɪ] n karatè m.

**kebab** [kə'bæb] n spiedino.

**keel** [ki:l] n chiglia; on an even ~ (fig) in uno stato normale.

**keen** [ki:n] a (interest, desire) vivo(a); (eye, intelligence) acuto(a); (competition) serrato(a); (edge) affilato(a); (eager) entusiasta; to be ~ to do or on doing sth avere una gran voglia di fare qc; to be ~ on sth essere appassionato/a di qc; to be ~ on sb avere un debole per qn.

**keep** [ki:p] vb (pt, pp **kept**) vt tenere; (hold back) trattenere; (feed: one's family etc) mantenere, sostentare; (a promise) mantenere; (chickens, bees, pigs etc) allevare // vi (food) mantenersi; (remain: in a certain state or place) restare // n (of castle) maschio; (food etc): enough for his ~ abbastanza per vitto e alloggio; (col): for ~s per sempre; to ~ doing sth continuare a fare qc; fare qc di continuo; to ~ sb from doing/sth from happening impedire a qn di fare/che qc succeda; to ~ sb busy/a **place** tidy tenere qn occupato(a)/un luogo in ordine; **to ~ sth to o.s.** tenere qc per sé; **to ~ sth (back) from sb** celare qc a qn; **to ~ time** (clock) andar bene; **to ~ on** vi continuare; **to ~ on doing** continuare a fare; **to ~ out** vt tener fuori; **"~ out"** "vietato l'accesso"; **to ~ up** vi mantenersi // vt continuare, mantenere; **to ~ up with** tener dietro a, andare di pari passo con; (work etc) farcela a seguire; **~er** n custode m/f, guardiano/a; **~fit** n ginnastica; **~ing** n (care) custodia; **in ~ing with** in armonia con; in accordo con; **~sake** n ricordo.

**keg** [kɛg] n barilotto.

**kennel** ['kɛnl] n canile m.

**kept** [kɛpt] pt, pp of **keep.**

**kerb** [kə:b] n (Brit) orlo del marciapiede.

**kernel** ['kə:nl] n nocciolo.

**kettle** ['kɛtl] n bollitore m.

**kettle drums** npl timpano.

**key** [ki:] n (gen, MUS) chiave f; (of piano, typewriter) tasto // vt (also: ~ **in**) digitare; **~board** n tastiera; **~ed up** a (person) agitato(a); **~hole** n buco della serratura; **~note** n (MUS) tonica; (fig) nota dominante; **~ ring** n portachiavi m inv.

**khaki** ['kɑ:kɪ] a, n cachi (m).

**kick** [kɪk] vt calciare, dare calci a // vi (horse) tirar calci // n calcio; (of rifle) contraccolpo; (thrill): **he does it for ~s** lo fa giusto per il piacere di farlo; **to ~ off** vi (SPORT) dare il primo calcio.

**kid** [kɪd] n (col: child) ragazzino/a; (animal, leather) capretto // vi (col) scherzare // vt (col) prendere in giro.

**kidnap** ['kɪdnæp] vt rapire, seque-strare; **~per** n rapitore/trice; **~ping** n sequestro (di persona).

**kidney** ['kɪdnɪ] n (ANAT) rene m; (CULIN) rognone m.

**kill** [kɪl] vt uccidere, ammazzare; (fig) sopprimere, sopraffare;

ammazzare // n uccisione f; **~er** n uccisore m, killer m inv; assassino/a; **~ing** n assassinio; (massacre) strage f; **~joy** n guastafeste m/f inv.

**kiln** [kɪln] n forno.

**kilo** ['ki:ləu] n chilo; **~byte** n (COMPUT) kilobyte m inv; **~gram(me)** ['kɪləugræm] n chilo-grammo; **~metre**, (US) **~meter** ['kɪləmi:tə*] n chilometro; **~watt** ['kɪləuwɒt] n chilowatt m inv.

**kilt** [kɪlt] n gonnellino scozzese.

**kin** [kɪn] n see **next, kith.**

**kind** [kaɪnd] a gentile, buono(a) // n sorta, specie f; (species) genere m; **to be two of a ~** essere molto simili; **in ~** (COMM) in natura.

**kindergarten** ['kɪndəgɑ:tn] n giardino d'infanzia.

**kind-hearted** [kaɪnd'hɑ:tɪd] a di buon cuore.

**kindle** ['kɪndl] vt accendere, infiammare.

**kindly** ['kaɪndlɪ] a pieno(a) di bontà, benevolo(a) // ad con bontà, gentilmente; **will you ~...** vuole ... per favore.

**kindness** ['kaɪndnɪs] n bontà, gentilezza.

**kindred** ['kɪndrɪd] a imparentato(a); **~ spirit** n spirito affine.

**king** [kɪŋ] n re m inv; **~dom** n re-gno, reame m; **~fisher** n martin m inv pescatore; **~-size** a super inv; gigante.

**kinky** ['kɪŋkɪ] a (fig) eccentrico(a); dai gusti particolari.

**kiosk** ['ki:ɔsk] n edicola, chiosco; (Brit TEL) cabina (telefonica).

**kipper** ['kɪpə*] n aringa affumicata.

**kiss** [kɪs] n bacio // vt baciare; **to ~ (each other)** baciarsi.

**kit** [kɪt] n equipaggiamento, corredo; (set of tools etc) attrezzi mpl; (for assembly) scatola di montaggio.

**kitchen** ['kɪtʃɪn] n cucina; **~ sink** n acquaio.

**kite** [kaɪt] n (toy) aquilone m; (ZOOL) nibbio.

**kith** [kɪθ] n: **~ and kin** amici e

parenti *mpl.*

**kitten** ['kɪtn] *n* gattino/a, micino/a.

**kitty** ['kɪtɪ] *n* (*money*) fondo comune.

**knack** [næk] *n*: **to have the ~ of** avere l'abilità di; **there's a ~ to doing this** c'è un trucco per fare questo.

**knapsack** ['næpsæk] *n* zaino, sacco da montagna.

**knead** [niːd] *vt* impastare.

**knee** [niː] *n* ginocchio; **~cap** *n* rotula.

**kneel**, *pt, pp* **knelt** [niːl, nɛlt] *vi* (*also:* **~ down**) inginocchiarsi.

**knell** [nɛl] *n* rintocco.

**knew** [njuː] *pt of* **know**.

**knickers** ['nɪkəz] *npl* (*Brit*) mutandine *fpl.*

**knife** [naɪf] *n* (*pl* **knives**) coltello // *vt* accoltellare, dare una coltellata a.

**knight** [naɪt] *n* cavaliere *m*; (*CHESS*) cavallo; **~hood** *n* (*title*): **to get a ~hood** essere fatto cavaliere.

**knit** [nɪt] *vt* fare a maglia; (*fig*): **to ~ together** unire // *vi* lavorare a maglia; (*broken bones*) saldarsi; **~ting** *n* lavoro a maglia; **~ting needle** *n* ferro (da calza); **~wear** *n* maglieria.

**knives** [naɪvz] *npl of* **knife**.

**knob** [nɔb] *n* bottone *m*; manopola.

**knock** [nɔk] *vt* colpire; urtare; (*fig: col*) criticare // *vi* (*engine*) battere; (*at door etc*): **to ~ at/on** bussare a // *n* bussata; colpo, botta; **to ~ down** *vt* abbattere; **to ~ off** *vi* (*col: finish*) smettere (di lavorare); **to ~ out** *vt* stendere; (*BOXING*) mettere K.O.; **to ~ over** *vt* (*person*) investire; (*object*) far cadere; **~er** *n* (*on door*) battente *m*; **~-kneed** *a* che ha le gambe ad x; **~out** *n* (*BOXING*) knock out *m inv.*

**knot** [nɔt] *n* nodo // *vt* annodare; **~ty** *a* (*fig*) spinoso(a).

**know** [nəu] *vt* (*pt* **knew**, *pp* **known**) sapere; (*person, author, place*) conoscere; **to ~ how to do** sapere fare; **to ~ about** *or* **of** sth/sb conoscere qc/qn; **~-all** *n* sapientone/

a; **~-how** *n* tecnica; pratica; **~ing** *a* (*look etc*) d'intesa; **~ingly** *ad* (*purposely*) consapevolmente; (*smile, look*) con aria d'intesa.

**knowledge** ['nɔlɪdʒ] *n* consapevolezza; (*learning*) conoscenza, sapere *m*; **~able** *a* ben informato(a).

**known** [nəun] *pp of* **know**.

**knuckle** ['nʌkl] *n* nocca.

**Koran** [kɔ'rɑːn] *n* Corano.

**Korea** [kə'rɪə] *n* Corea.

**kosher** ['kəuʃə*] *a* kasher *inv.*

# L

**lab** [læb] *n abbr* (= *laboratory*) laboratorio.

**label** ['leɪbl] *n* etichetta, cartellino; (*brand: of record*) casa // *vt* etichettare.

**laboratory** [lə'bɔrətərɪ] *n* laboratorio.

**labour**, (*US*) **labor** ['leɪbə*] *n* (*task*) lavoro; (*workmen*) manodopera; (*MED*) travaglio del parto, doglie *fpl* // *vi*: **to ~** (**at**) lavorare duro (a); **in ~** (*MED*) in travaglio; **L~**, **the L~ party** (*Brit*) il partito laburista, i laburisti; **~ed** *a* (*breathing*) affannoso(a); (*style*) pesante; **~er** *n* manovale *m*; (*on farm*) lavoratore *m* agricolo.

**lace** [leɪs] *n* merletto, pizzo; (*of shoe etc*) laccio // *vt* (*shoe*) allacciare.

**lack** [læk] *n* mancanza // *vt* mancare di; **through** *or* **for ~ of** per mancanza di; **to be ~ing** mancare; **to be ~ing in** mancare di.

**lackadaisical** [lækə'deɪzɪkl] *a* disinteressato(a), noncurante.

**lacquer** ['lækə*] *n* lacca.

**lad** [læd] *n* ragazzo, giovanotto.

**ladder** ['lædə*] *n* scala; (*Brit: in tights*) smagliatura // *vt* smagliare // *vi* smagliarsi.

**laden** ['leɪdn] *a*: **~ (with)** carico(a) *or* caricato(a) (di).

**ladle** ['leɪdl] *n* mestolo.

**lady** ['leɪdɪ] *n* signora; dama; L~ Smith lady Smith; **the ladies' (room)** i gabinetti per signore; ~**bird**, (*US*) ~**bug** *n* coccinella; ~**-in-waiting** *n* dama di compagnia; ~**like** *a* da signora, distinto(a); ~**ship** *n*: **your** ~**ship** signora contessa (*or* baronessa *etc*).

**lag** [læg] *vi* (*also*: ~ **behind**) trascinarsi // *vt* (*pipes*) rivestire di materiale isolante.

**lager** ['lɑːgə*] *n* lager *m inv*.

**lagoon** [lə'guːn] *n* laguna.

**laid** [leɪd] *pt, pp* of **lay**; ~ **back** *a* (*col*) rilassato(a), tranquillo(a).

**lain** [leɪn] *pp* of **lie**.

**lair** [lɛə*] *n* covo, tana.

**laity** ['leɪɪtɪ] *n* laici *mpl*.

**lake** [leɪk] *n* lago.

**lamb** [læm] *n* agnello.

**lame** [leɪm] *a* zoppo(a).

**lament** [lə'mɛnt] *n* lamento // *vt* lamentare, piangere.

**laminated** ['læmɪneɪtɪd] *a* laminato(a).

**lamp** [læmp] *n* lampada.

**lampoon** [læm'puːn] *n* satira.

**lamp**: ~**post** *n* (*Brit*) lampione *m*; ~**shade** *n* paralume *m*.

**lance** [lɑːns] *n* lancia // *vt* (*MED*) incidere; ~ **corporal** *n* (*Brit*) caporale *m*.

**land** [lænd] *n* (*as opposed to sea*) terra (ferma); (*country*) paese *m*; (*soil*) terreno; suolo; (*estate*) terreni *mpl*, terre *fpl* // *vi* (*from ship*) sbarcare; (*AVIAT*) atterrare; (*fig: fall*) cadere // *vt* (*obtain*) acchiappare; (*passengers*) sbarcare; (*goods*) scaricare; **to** ~ **up** *vi* andare a finire; ~**ing** *n* sbarco; atterraggio; (*of staircase*) pianerottolo; ~**ing stage** *n* (*Brit*) pontile *m* da sbarco; ~**lady** *n* padrona *or* proprietaria di casa; ~**lord** *n* padrone *m or* proprietario di casa; (*of pub etc*) oste *m*; ~**mark** *n* punto di riferimento; (*fig*) pietra miliare; ~**owner** *n* proprietario(a) terriero(a).

**landscape** ['lænskeɪp] *n* paesaggio.

**landslide** ['lændslaɪd] *n* (*GEO*) frana; (*fig: POL*) valanga.

**lane** [leɪn] *n* (*in country*) viottolo; (*in town*) stradetta; (*AUT, in race*) corsia.

**language** ['læŋgwɪdʒ] *n* lingua; (*way one speaks*) linguaggio; **bad** ~ linguaggio volgare; ~ **laboratory** *n* laboratorio linguistico.

**languid** ['læŋgwɪd] *a* languente; languido(a).

**lank** [læŋk] *a* (*hair*) liscio(a) e opaco(a).

**lanky** ['læŋkɪ] *a* allampanato(a).

**lantern** ['læntn] *n* lanterna.

**lap** [læp] *n* (*of track*) giro; (*of body*): **in** *or* **on one's** ~ in grembo // *vt* (*also*: ~ **up**) papparsi, leccare // *vi* (*waves*) sciabordare.

**lapel** [lə'pɛl] *n* risvolto.

**Lapland** ['læplænd] *n* Lapponia.

**lapse** [læps] *n* lapsus *m inv*; (*longer*) caduta // *vi* (*law, act*) cadere; (*ticket, passport*) scadere; **to** ~ **into bad habits** pigliare cattive abitudini; ~ **of time** spazio di tempo.

**larceny** ['lɑːsənɪ] *n* furto.

**lard** [lɑːd] *n* lardo.

**larder** ['lɑːdə*] *n* dispensa.

**large** [lɑːdʒ] *a* grande; (*person, animal*) grosso(a); **at** ~ (*free*) in libertà; (*generally*) in generale; nell'insieme; ~**ly** *ad* in gran parte.

**largesse** [lɑː'ʒɛs] *n* generosità.

**lark** [lɑːk] *n* (*bird*) allodola; (*joke*) scherzo, gioco; **to** ~ **about** *vi* fare lo stupido.

**laryngitis** [lærɪn'dʒaɪtɪs] *n* laringite *f*.

**laser** ['leɪzə*] *n* laser *m*; ~ **printer** *n* stampante *f* laser *inv*.

**lash** [læʃ] *n* frustata; (*also*: **eye**~) ciglio // *vt* frustare; (*tie*) assicurare con una corda; **to** ~ **out** *vi*: **to** ~ **out** (**at** *or* **against sb/sth**) attaccare violentemente (qn/qc); **to** ~ **out** (**on sth**) (*col: spend*) spendere un sacco di soldi (per qc).

**lass** [læs] *n* ragazza.

**lasso** [læ'su:] *n* laccio.

**last** [lɑːst] *a* ultimo(a); (*week, month, year*) scorso(a), passato(a) // *ad* per ultimo // *vi* durare; ~ **week** la settimana scorsa; ~ **night** ieri sera, la notte scorsa; **at** ~ finalmente, alla fine; ~ **but one** penultimo(a); ~-**ditch** *a* (*attempt*) estremo(a); ~-**ing** *a* durevole; ~**ly** *ad* infine, per finire; ~-**minute** *a* fatto(a) (*or* preso(a) *etc*) all'ultimo momento.

**latch** [lætʃ] *n* serratura a scatto.

**late** [leɪt] *a* (*not on time*) in ritardo; (*far on in day etc*) tardi // *ad* tardo(a); (*recent*) recente, ultimo(a); (*former*) ex; (*dead*) defunto(a) // *ad* tardi; (*behind time, schedule*) in ritardo; **of** ~ di recente; **in the** ~ **afternoon** nel tardo pomeriggio; **in** ~ **May** verso la fine di maggio; ~-**comer** *n* ritardatario/a; ~**ly** *ad* recentemente.

**later** ['leɪtə*] *a* (*date etc*) posteriore; (*version etc*) successivo(a) // *ad* più tardi; ~ **on** più avanti.

**lateral** ['lætərl] *a* laterale.

**latest** ['leɪtɪst] *a* ultimo(a), più recente; **at the** ~ al più tardi.

**lathe** [leɪð] *n* tornio.

**lather** ['lɑːðə*] *n* schiuma di sapone // *vt* insaponare.

**Latin** ['lætɪn] *n* latino // *a* latino(a); ~ **America** *n* America Latina; ~-**American** *a* sudamericano(a).

**latitude** ['lætɪtjuːd] *n* latitudine *f*.

**latter** ['lætə*] *a* secondo(a); più recente // *n*: **the** ~ quest'ultimo, il secondo; ~**ly** *ad* recentemente, negli ultimi tempi.

**lattice** ['lætɪs] *n* traliccio; graticolato.

**laudable** ['lɔːdəbl] *a* lodevole.

**laugh** [lɑːf] *n* risata // *vi* ridere; **to** ~ **at** *vt fus* (*misfortune etc*) ridere di; **to** ~ **off** *vt* prendere alla leggera; ~**able** *a* ridicolo(a); ~**ing stock** *n*: **the** ~**ing stock of** lo zimbello di; ~**ter** *n* riso; risate *fpl*.

**launch** [lɔːntʃ] *n* (*of rocket etc*) lancio; (*of new ship*) varo; (*boat*)

scialuppa; (*also*: **motor** ~) lancia // *vt* (*rocket*) lanciare; (*ship, plan*) varare; ~(**ing**) **pad** *n* rampa di lancio.

**launder** ['lɔːndə*] *vt* lavare e stirare.

**launderette** ['lɔːn'drɛt], (*US*) **laundromat** ['lɔːndrəmæt] *n* lavanderia (automatica).

**laundry** ['lɔːndrɪ] *n* lavanderia; (*clothes*) biancheria.

**laureate** ['lɔːrɪət] *a see* **poet**.

**laurel** ['lɔrl] *n* lauro.

**lava** ['lɑːvə] *n* lava.

**lavatory** ['lævətərɪ] *n* gabinetto.

**lavender** ['lævəndə*] *n* lavanda.

**lavish** ['lævɪʃ] *a* copioso(a); abbondante; (*giving freely*): ~ **with** prodigo(a) di, largo(a) in // *vt*: **to** ~ **on sb/sth** (*care*) profondere a qn/qc.

**law** [lɔː] *n* legge *f*; **civil/criminal** ~ diritto civile/penale; ~-**abiding** *a* ubbidiente alla legge; ~ **and order** *n* l'ordine *m* pubblico; ~ **court** *n* tribunale *m*, corte *f* di giustizia; ~**ful** *a* legale; lecito(a).

**lawn** [lɔːn] *n* tappeto erboso; ~**mower** *n* tosaerba *m or f inv*; ~ **tennis** *n* tennis *m* su prato.

**law school** *n* facoltà *f inv* di legge.

**lawsuit** ['lɔːsuːt] *n* processo, causa.

**lawyer** ['lɔːjə*] *n* (*consultant, with company*) giurista *m/f*; (*for sales, wills etc*) ~ notaio; (*partner, in court*) ~ avvocato/essa.

**lax** [læks] *a* rilassato(a); negligente.

**laxative** ['læksətɪv] *n* lassativo.

**laxity** ['læksɪtɪ] *n* rilassatezza; negligenza.

**lay** [leɪ] *pt* of **lie** // *a* laico(a); secolare // *vt* (*pt, pp* **laid**) posare, mettere; (*eggs*) fare; (*trap*) tendere; (*plans*) fare, elaborare; **to** ~ **the table** apparecchiare la tavola; **to** ~ **aside** *or* **by** *vt* mettere da parte; **to** ~ **down** *vt* mettere giù; **to** ~ **down the law** dettar legge; **to** ~ **off** *vt* (*workers*) licenziare; **to** ~ **on** *vt* (*water, gas*) installare, mettere; (*provide*) fornire; (*paint*) applicare; **to** ~ **out** *vt* (*design*) progettare;

*(display)* presentare; *(spend)* sborsare; **to ~ up** *vt (to store)* accumulare; *(ship)* mettere in disarmo; *(subj: illness)* costringere a letto; **~about** *n* sfaccendato/a, fannullone/a; **~-by** *n (Brit)* piazzola *(di sosta)*.

**layer** ['leɪə*] *n* strato.

**layman** ['leɪmən] *n* laico; profano.

**layout** ['leɪaut] *n* lay-out *m inv*, disposizione *f*; *(PRESS)* impaginazione *f*.

**laze** [leɪz] *vi* oziare.

**lazy** ['leɪzɪ] *a* pigro(a).

**lb.** *abbr* = **pound** *(weight)*.

**lead** [li:d] *n (front position)* posizione *f* di testa; *(distance, time ahead)* vantaggio; *(clue)* indizio; *(ELEC)* filo (elettrico); *(for dog)* guinzaglio; *(THEATRE)* parte *f* principale; [lɛd] *(metal)* piombo; *(in pencil)* mina // *vb (pt, pp* **led***)* menare, guidare, condurre; *(induce)* indurre; *(be leader of)* essere a capo di; *(SPORT)* essere in testa a // *vi* condurre, essere in testa; **to ~ astray** *vt* sviare; **to ~ away** *vt* condurre via; **to ~ back** *vt:* **to ~ back to** ricondurre a; **to ~ on** *vt (tease)* tenere sulla corda; **to ~ on to** *(induce)* portare a; **to ~ to** *vt fus* condurre a; portare a; **to ~ up to** *vt fus* portare a.

**leaden** ['lɛdn] *a (sky, sea)* plumbeo(a); *(heavy: footsteps)* pesante.

**leader** ['li:də*] *n* capo; leader *m inv* *(in newspaper)* articolo di fondo; **~ship** *n* direzione *f*; capacità di comando.

**leading** ['li:dɪŋ] *a* primo(a); principale; **~ man/lady** *n (THEATRE)* primo attore/prima attrice; **~ light** *n (person)* personaggio di primo piano.

**leaf** [li:f] *n (pl* **leaves***)* foglia; *(of table)* ribalta // *vi:* **to ~ through** sfogliare qc; **to turn over a new ~** cambiar vita.

**leaflet** ['li:flɪt] *n* dépliant *m inv*;

*(POL, REL)* volantino.

**league** [li:g] *n* lega; *(FOOTBALL)* campionato; **to be in ~ with** essere in lega con.

**leak** [li:k] *n (out, also fig)* fuga; *(in)* infiltrazione *f* // *vi (roof, bucket)* perdere; *(liquid)* uscire; *(shoes)* lasciar passare l'acqua // *vt (liquid)* spandere; *(information)* divulgare; **to ~ out** *vi* uscire; *(information)* trapelare.

**lean** [li:n] *a* magro(a) // *vb (pt, pp* **leaned** *or* **lent***)* *vt:* **to ~ sth on sth** appoggiare qc su qc // *vi (slope)* pendere; *(rest):* **to ~ against** appoggiarsi contro; essere appoggiato(a) a; **to ~ on** appoggiarsi a; **to ~ back/forward** *vi* sporgersi in avanti/indietro; **to ~ out** *vi* sporgersi; **to ~ over** *vi* inclinarsi; **~ing** *n:* **~ing (towards)** propensione *f* (per); **~to** *n (roof)* tettoia; *(shed)* capanno *con tetto a una falda*.

**leap** [li:p] *n* salto, balzo // *vi (pt, pp* **leaped** *or* **leapt** [lɛpt]*)* saltare, balzare; **~frog** *n* gioco della cavallina; **~ year** *n* anno bisestile.

**learn**, *pt, pp* **learned** *or* **learnt** [lə:n, -t] *vt, vi* imparare; **to ~ how to do sth** imparare a fare qc; **~ed** ['lə:nɪd] *a* erudito(a), dotto(a); **~er** *n* principiante *m/f*; apprendista *m/f*; *(Brit: also:* **~er driver***)* guidatore/trice principiante; **~ing** *n* erudizione *f*, sapienza.

**lease** [li:s] *n* contratto d'affitto // *vt* affittare.

**leash** [li:ʃ] *n* guinzaglio.

**least** [li:st] *a:* **the ~ +** *noun* il(la) più piccolo(a), il(la) minimo(a); *(smallest amount of)* il(la) meno; **the ~ +** *adjective:* **the ~ beautiful girl** la ragazza meno bella; **the ~ expensive** il(la) meno caro(a); **I have the ~ money** ho meno denaro di tutti; **at ~** almeno; **not in the ~** affatto, per nulla.

**leather** ['lɛðə*] *n* cuoio // *cpd* di cuoio.

**leave** [li:v] vb (pt, pp **left**) vt lasciare; (go away from) partire da // vi partire, andarsene // n (time off) congedo; (MIL, also: consent) licenza; **to be left** rimanere; **there's some milk left over** c'è rimasto del latte; **on** ~ in congedo; **to** ~ **behind** vt (person, object) lasciare indietro; (: forget) dimenticare; **to** ~ **out** vt omettere, tralasciare; ~ **of absence** n congedo.

**leaves** [li:vz] npl of **leaf**.

**Lebanon** ['lɛbənən] n Libano.

**lecherous** ['lɛtʃərəs] a lascivo(a), brico(a).

**lecture** ['lɛktʃə*] n conferenza; (SCOL) lezione f // vi fare conferenze; fare lezioni // vt (scold) rimproverare, fare una ramanzina a; **to** ~ **on** fare una conferenza su; **to give a** ~ **on** tenere una conferenza su.

**lecturer** ['lɛktʃərə*] n (speaker) conferenziere/a; (Brit: at university) professore/essa, docente m/f.

**led** [lɛd] pt, pp of **lead**.

**ledge** [lɛdʒ] n (of window) davanzale m; (on wall etc) sporgenza; (of mountain) cornice f, cengia.

**ledger** ['lɛdʒə*] n libro maestro, registro.

**lee** [li:] n lato sottovento.

**leech** [li:tʃ] n sanguisuga.

**leek** [li:k] n porro.

**leer** [lɪə*] vi: **to** ~ **at sb** gettare uno sguardo voglioso (or maligno) su qn.

**leeway** ['li:wei] n (fig): **to have some** ~ avere una certa libertà di agire.

**left** [lɛft] pt, pp of **leave** // a sinistro(a) // ad a sinistra // n sinistra; **on the** ~, **to the** ~ a sinistra; **the L~** (POL) la sinistra; ~-**handed** a mancino(a); ~-**hand side** n lato or fianco sinistro; ~ **luggage** (office) n (Brit) deposito m bagagli inv; ~-**overs** npl avanzi mpl, resti mpl; ~-**wing** a (POL) di sinistra.

**leg** [lɛg] n gamba; (of animal) zampa; (of furniture) piede m;

(CULIN: of chicken) coscia; (of journey) tappa; **lst/2nd** ~ (SPORT) partita di andata/ritorno.

**legacy** ['lɛgəsɪ] n eredità f inv.

**legal** ['li:gl] a legale; ~ **holiday** n (US) giorno festivo, festa nazionale; ~ **tender** n moneta legale.

**legend** ['lɛdʒənd] n leggenda.

**legible** ['lɛdʒəbl] a leggibile.

**legislation** [lɛdʒɪs'leɪʃən] n legislazione f; **legislature** ['lɛdʒɪslətʃə*] n corpo legislativo.

**legitimate** [lɪ'dʒɪtɪmət] a legittimo(a).

**leg-room** ['lɛgru:m] n spazio per le gambe.

**leisure** ['lɛʒə*] n agio, tempo libero; ricreazioni fpl; **at** ~ all'agio; a proprio comodo; ~ **centre** n centro di ricreazione; ~**ly** a tranquillo(a); fatto(a) con comodo or senza fretta.

**lemon** ['lɛmən] n limone m; ~**ade** [-'neɪd] n limonata; ~ **tea** n tè m inv al limone.

**lend** [lɛnd] pt, pp **lent** vt: **to** ~ **sth (to sb)** prestare qc a (qn).

**length** [lɛŋθ] n lunghezza; (section: of road, pipe etc) pezzo, tratto; **at** ~ (at last) finalmente, alla fine; (lengthily) a lungo; ~**en** vt allungare, prolungare // vi allungarsi; ~**ways** ad per il lungo; ~**y** a molto lungo(a).

**lenient** ['li:nɪənt] a indulgente, clemente.

**lens** [lɛnz] n lente f; (of camera) obiettivo.

**Lent** [lɛnt] n Quaresima.

**lent** [lɛnt] pt, pp of **lend**.

**lentil** ['lɛntl] n lenticchia.

**Leo** ['li:əu] n Leone m.

**leotard** ['li:əta:d] n calzamaglia.

**leper** ['lɛpə*] n lebbroso/a.

**leprosy** ['lɛprəsɪ] n lebbra.

**lesbian** ['lɛzbɪən] n lesbica.

**less** [lɛs] a, pronoun, ad meno; ~ **than you/ever** meno di lei/che mai; ~ **than half** meno della metà; ~ **and** ~ sempre meno; **the** ~ **he works** ... meno lavora ... .

**lessen** ['lɛsn] *vi* diminuire, attenuarsi // *vt* diminuire, ridurre.

**lesser** ['lɛsə*] *a* minore, più piccolo(a); **to a ~ extent** in grado or misura minore.

**lesson** ['lɛsn] *n* lezione *f*.

**lest** [lɛst] *cj* per paura di + *infinitive*, per paura che + *sub*.

**let**, *pt, pp* **let** [lɛt] *vt* lasciare; (*Brit: lease*) dare in affitto; **to ~ sb do sth** lasciar fare qc a qn, lasciare che qn faccia qc; **to ~ sb know sth** far sapere qc a qn; **he ~ me go** mi ha lasciato andare; **~'s go** andiamo; **~ him come** lo lasci venire; **"to ~" "affittasi"**; **to ~ down** *vt* (*lower*) abbassare; (*dress*) allungare; (*hair*) sciogliere; (*disappoint*) deludere; **to ~ go** *vt, vi* mollare; **to ~ in** *vt* lasciare entrare; (*visitor etc*) far entrare; **to ~ off** *vt* (*allow to go*) lasciare andare; (*firework etc*) far partire; (*smell etc*) emettere; **to ~ on** *vi* (*col*) dire; **to ~ out** *vt* lasciare uscire; (*dress*) allargare; (*scream*) emettere; **to ~ up** *vi* diminuire.

**lethal** ['li:θl] *a* letale, mortale.

**lethargy** ['lɛθədʒɪ] *n* letargia.

**letter** ['lɛtə*] *n* lettera; **~ bomb** *n* lettera esplosiva; **~box** *n* (*Brit*) buca delle lettere; **~ing** *n* iscrizione *f*; caratteri *mpl*.

**lettuce** ['lɛtɪs] *n* lattuga, insalata.

**leukaemia**, (*US*) **leukemia** [lu:'ki:mɪə] *n* leucemia.

**level** ['lɛvl] *a* piatto(a), piano(a); orizzontale // *n* livello; (*also: spirit ~*) livella (a bolla d'aria) // *vt* livellare, spianare; **to be ~ with** essere alla pari di; **A ~s** *npl* (*Brit*) = esami fini di maturità; **O ~s** *npl* (*Brit*) esami fatti in Inghilterra all'età di 16 anni; **on the ~** piatto(a); (*fig*) onesto(a); **to ~ off** or **out** *vi* (*prices etc*) stabilizzarsi; **~ crossing** *n* (*Brit*) passaggio a livello; **~-headed** *a* equilibrato(a).

**lever** ['li:və*] *n* leva // *vt*: **to ~ up/out** sollevare/estrarre con una leva;

**~age** *n*: **~age** (**on** or **with**) ascendente *m* (su).

**levy** ['lɛvɪ] *n* tassa, imposta // *vt* imporre.

**lewd** [lu:d] *a* osceno(a), lascivo(a).

**liability** [laɪə'bɪlɪtɪ] *n* responsabilità *f inv*; (*handicap*) peso; **liabilities** *npl* debiti *mpl*; (*on balance sheet*) passivo.

**liable** ['laɪəbl] *a* (*subject*): **~ to** soggetto(a) a; passibile di; (*responsible*): **~ (for)** responsabile (di); (*likely*): **~ to do** propenso(a) a fare.

**liaison** [li:'eɪzɔn] *n* relazione *f*; (*MIL*) collegamento.

**liar** ['laɪə*] *n* bugiardo/a.

**libel** ['laɪbl] *n* libello, diffamazione *f* // *vt* diffamare.

**liberal** ['lɪbərl] *a* liberale; (*generous*): **to be ~ with** distribuire liberalmente.

**liberty** ['lɪbətɪ] *n* libertà *f inv*; **at ~ to do** libero(a) di fare.

**Libra** ['li:brə] *n* Bilancia.

**librarian** [laɪ'brɛərɪən] *n* bibliotecario/a.

**library** ['laɪbrərɪ] *n* biblioteca.

**Libya** ['lɪbɪə] *n* Libia.

**lice** [laɪs] *npl* of **louse**.

**licence**, (*US*) **license** ['laɪsns] *n* autorizzazione *f*, permesso; (*COMM*) licenza; (*RADIO, TV*) canone *m*, abbonamento; (*also: driving ~*, (*US*) **driver's ~**) patente *f* di guida; (*excessive freedom*) licenza; **~ number** *n* numero di targa; **~ plate** *n* targa.

**license** ['laɪsns] *n* (*US*) = **licence** // *vt* dare una licenza a; **~d** *a* (*for alcohol*) che ha la licenza di vendere bibite alcoliche.

**lick** [lɪk] *vt* leccare.

**licorice** ['lɪkərɪs] *n* = **liquorice**.

**lid** [lɪd] *n* coperchio.

**lie** [laɪ] *n* bugia, menzogna // *vi* mentire, dire bugie; (*pt* **lay**, *pp* **lain**) (*rest*) giacere, star disteso(a); (*in grave*) giacere, riposare; (*of object: be situated*) trovarsi, essere; (*fig*) latitare; **to ~ about** *vi* *(things)* essere in giro; *(person)* bighellonare; **~down** *n (Brit)*: **to have a ~down** sdraiarsi, riposarsi; **~in** *n (Brit)*: **to have a ~in** rimanere a letto.

**lieutenant** [lefˈtenənt, *(US)* luːˈtɛnənt] *n* tenente *m*.

**life** [laɪf] *n (pl* **lives)** vita // *cpd* di vita; della vita; a vita; **~ assurance** *n (Brit)* assicurazione *f* sulla vita; **~belt** *n (Brit)* salvagente *m*; **~boat** *n* scialuppa di salvataggio; **~guard** *n* bagnino; **~ insurance** *n* = **~ assurance**; **~ jacket** *n* giubbotto di salvataggio; **~less** *a* senza vita; **~like** *a* verosimile; rassomigliante; **~long** *a* per tutta la vita; **~ preserver** *n (US)* salvagente *m*; giubbotto di salvataggio; **~saver** *n* bagnino; **~ sentence** *n* ergastolo; **~sized** *a* a grandezza naturale; **~ span** *n* (durata della) vita; **~style** *n* stile *m* di vita; **~ support system** *n* respiratore *m* automatico; **~time** *n*: **in his ~time** durante la sua vita; **once in a ~time** una volta nella vita.

**lift** [lɪft] *vt* sollevare, levare; *(steal)* prendere, rubare // *vi (fog)* alzarsi // *n (Brit: elevator)* ascensore *m*; **to give sb a ~** *(Brit)* dare un passaggio a qn; **~off** *n* decollo.

**light** [laɪt] *n* luce *f*, lume *m*; *(daylight)* luce *f*, giorno; *(lamp)* lampada; *(AUT: rear ~)* luce *f* di posizione; (: *headlamp)* fanale *m*; *(for cigarette etc)*: **have you got a ~?** ha da accendere? // *vt (pt, pp* **lighted** *or* **lit)** *(candle, cigarette, fire)* accendere; *(room)* illuminare // *a (room, colour)* chiaro(a); *(not heavy, also fig)* leggero(a); **~s** *npl (AUT: traffic ~s)* semaforo; **to come to ~** venire alla luce, emergere; **to ~ up** *vi* illuminarsi // *vt* illuminare; **~ bulb** *n* lampadina; **~en** *vi* schiarirsi // *vt (give light to)* illuminare; *(make lighter)* schiarire; *(make less heavy)* alleggerire; **~er**

*n (also:* **cigarette ~er)** accendino; *(boat)* chiatta; **~headed** *a* stordito(a); **~hearted** *a* gioioso(a), gaio(a); **~house** *n* faro; **~ing** *n* illuminazione *f*; **~ly** *ad* leggermente; **to get off ~ly** cavarsela a buon mercato; **~ness** *n* chiarezza; *(in weight)* leggerezza.

**lightning** [ˈlaɪtnɪŋ] *n* lampo, fulmine *m*; **~ conductor,** *(US)* **~ rod** *n* parafulmine *m*.

**light pen** *n* penna ottica.

**lightweight** [ˈlaɪtweɪt] *a (suit)* leggero(a); *(boxer)* peso leggero *inv* // *n (BOXING)* peso leggero.

**like** [laɪk] *vt (person)* volere bene a; *(activity, object, food)*: **I ~ swimming/that book/chocolate** mi piace nuotare/quel libro/il cioccolato // *prep* come // *a* simile, uguale // *n*: **the ~** uno(a) uguale; **his ~s and dislikes** i suoi gusti; **I would ~, I'd ~** mi piacerebbe, vorrei; **would you ~ a coffee?** gradirebbe un caffè?; **to be/look ~ sb/sth** somigliare a qn/qc; **that's just ~ him** è proprio da lui; **do it ~ this** fallo così; **it is nothing ~ ...** non è affatto come ...; **~able** *a* simpatico(a).

**likelihood** [ˈlaɪklɪhud] *n* probabilità.

**likely** [ˈlaɪklɪ] *a* probabile; plausibile; **he's ~ to leave** probabilmente partirà, è probabile che parta; **not ~!** neanche per sogno!

**likeness** [ˈlaɪknɪs] *n* somiglianza.

**likewise** [ˈlaɪkwaɪz] *ad* similmente, nello stesso modo.

**liking** [ˈlaɪkɪŋ] *n*: **~ (for)** debole *m* (per).

**lilac** [ˈlaɪlək] *n* lilla *m inv* // *a* lilla *inv*.

**lily** [ˈlɪlɪ] *n* giglio; **~ of the valley** *n* mughetto.

**limb** [lɪm] *n* membro.

**limber** [ˈlɪmbə*] : **to ~ up** *vi* riscaldarsi i muscoli.

**limbo** [ˈlɪmbəu] *n*: **to be in ~** *(fig)* essere lasciato(a) nel dimenticatoio.

**lime** [laɪm] *n (tree)* tiglio; *(fruit)* limetta; *(GEO)* calce *f*.

**limelight** [ˈlaɪmlaɪt] *n*: **in the ~**

*(fig)* alla ribalta, in vista.

**limerick** ['lɪmərɪk] *n* poesiola umoristica di 5 versi.

**limestone** ['laɪmstəun] *n* pietra calcarea; *(GEO)* calcare *m*.

**limit** ['lɪmɪt] *n* limite *m // vt* limitare; ~ed *a* limitato(a), ristretto(a); to be ~ed to limitarsi a; ~ed (liability) company (Ltd) *n (Brit)* = società *f inv* a responsabilità limitata (S.r.l.).

**limp** [lɪmp] *n:* to have a ~ zoppicare // *vi* zoppicare // *a* floscio(a), flaccido(a).

**limpet** ['lɪmpɪt] *n* patella.

**line** [laɪn] *n* linea; *(rope)* corda; *(wire)* filo; *(of poem)* verso; *(row, series)* fila, riga; coda // *vt (clothes)* to ~ (with) foderare (di); *(box):* to ~ (with) rivestire *o* foderare (di); *(subj: trees, crowd)* fiancheggiare; ~ of business settore *m or* ramo d'attività; in ~ with in linea con; to ~ up *vi* allinearsi, mettersi in fila // *vt* mettere in fila.

**lined** [laɪnd] *a (face)* rugoso(a); *(paper)* a righe, rigato(a).

**linen** ['lɪnɪn] *n* biancheria, panni *mpl; (cloth)* tela di lino.

**liner** ['laɪnə*] *n* nave *f* di linea.

**linesman** ['laɪnzmən] *n* guardalinee *m inv.*

**line-up** ['laɪnʌp] *n* allineamento, fila; *(SPORT)* formazione *f* di gioco.

**linger** ['lɪŋɡə*] *vi* attardarsi; indugiare; *(smell, tradition)* persistere.

**lingo**, ~es ['lɪŋɡəu] *n (pej)* gergo.

**linguistics** [lɪŋˈɡwɪstɪks] *n* linguistica.

**lining** ['laɪnɪŋ] *n* fodera.

**link** [lɪŋk] *n (of a chain)* anello; *(connection)* legame *m*, collegamento // *vt* collegare, unire, congiungere; ~s *npl (GOLF)* pista *o* terreno da golf; to ~ up *vt* collegare, unire // *vi* riunirsi; associarsi.

**lino** ['laɪnəu], **linoleum** [lɪˈnəuliəm] *n* linoleum *m inv.*

**lion** ['laɪən] *n* leone *m;* ~ess *n*

leonessa.

**lip** [lɪp] *n* labbro; *(of cup etc)* orlo; *(insolence)* sfacciataggine *f;* ~read *vi* leggere sulle labbra; ~ salve *n* burro di cacao; ~ service *n:* to pay ~ service to sth essere favorevole a qc solo a parole; ~stick *n* rossetto.

**liqueur** [lɪˈkjuə*] *n* liquore *m.*

**liquid** ['lɪkwɪd] *n* liquido // *a* liquido(a).

**liquidize** ['lɪkwɪdaɪz] *vt (CULIN)* passare al frullatore; ~r *n* frullatore *m* (a brocca).

**liquor** ['lɪkə*] *n* alcool *m.*

**liquorice** ['lɪkərɪs] *n* liquirizia.

**liquor store** *n (US)* negozio di liquori.

**lisp** [lɪsp] *n* difetto nel pronunciare le sibilanti.

**list** [lɪst] *n* lista, elenco; *(of ship)* sbandamento // *vt (write down)* mettere in lista; fare una lista di; *(enumerate)* elencare // *vi (ship)* sbandare.

**listen** ['lɪsn] *vi* ascoltare; to ~ to ascoltare; ~er *n* ascoltatore/trice.

**listless** ['lɪstlɪs] *a* apatico(a).

**lit** [lɪt] *pt, pp of* **light.**

**liter** ['li:tə*] *n (US)* = **litre.**

**literacy** ['lɪtərəsɪ] *n* il sapere leggere e scrivere.

**literal** ['lɪtərl] *a* letterale.

**literary** ['lɪtərərɪ] *a* letterario(a).

**literate** ['lɪtərət] *a* che sa leggere e scrivere.

**literature** ['lɪtərɪtʃə*] *n* letteratura; *(brochures etc)* materiale *m.*

**lithe** [laɪð] *a* agile, snello(a).

**litigation** [lɪtɪˈɡeɪʃən] *n* causa.

**litre** ['li:tə*] *n (US* **liter** ['li:tə*] *n* litro.

**litter** ['lɪtə*] *n (rubbish)* rifiuti *mpl; (young animals)* figliata // *vt* spargagliare; lasciare rifiuti in; ~ bin *n (Brit)* cestino per rifiuti; ~ed *a:* ~ed with coperto(a) di.

**little** ['lɪtl] *a (small)* piccolo(a); *(not much)* poco(a) *// ad* poco; a ~ un po' (di); a ~ milk un po' di latte; ~ by ~ a poco a poco.

**live** *vi* [lɪv] vivere; *(reside)* vivere,

abitare // *a* [laɪv] (*animal*) vivo(a); (*wire*) sotto tensione; (*broadcast*) diretto(a); **to ~ down** *vt* far dimenticare (alla gente); **to ~ on** *vt fus* (*food*) vivere di // *vi* sopravvivere, continuare a vivere; **to ~ together** *vi* vivere insieme, convivere; **to ~ up to** *vt fus* tener fede a, non venir meno a.

**livelihood** ['laɪvlɪhud] *n* mezzi *mpl* di sostentamento.

**lively** ['laɪvlɪ] *a* vivace, vivo(a).

**liven up** ['laɪvn'ʌp] *vt* (*discussion*, *evening*) animare.

**liver** ['lɪvə*] *n* fegato.

**livery** ['lɪvərɪ] *n* livrea.

**lives** [laɪvz] *npl of* **life.**

**livestock** ['laɪvstɔk] *n* bestiame *m*.

**livid** ['lɪvɪd] *a* livido(a); (*furious*) livido(a) di rabbia, furibondo(a).

**living** ['lɪvɪŋ] *a* vivo(a), vivente // *n*: **to earn** *or* **make a ~** guadagnarsi la vita; **~ conditions** *npl* condizioni *fpl* di vita; **~ room** *n* soggiorno; **~ wage** *n* salario sufficiente per vivere.

**lizard** ['lɪzəd] *n* lucertola.

**load** [ləud] *n* (*weight*) peso; (*ELEC*, *TECH*, *thing carried*) carico // *vt* (*also*: **~ up**): **to ~ (with)** (*lorry*, *ship*) caricare (di); (*gun*, *camera*, *COMPUT*) caricare (con); **a ~ of**, **~s of** (*fig*) un sacco di; **~ed** *a* (*dice*) falsato(a); (*question*) capzioso(a); (*col*: *rich*) carico(a); di soldi; (: *drunk*) ubriaco(a); **~ing bay** *n* piazzola di carico.

**loaf** [ləuf] *n* (*pl* **loaves**) *n* pane *m*, pagnotta // *vi* (*also*: **~ about, ~ around**) bighellonare.

**loan** [ləun] *n* prestito // *vt* dare in prestito; **on ~** in prestito.

**loath** [ləuθ] *a*: **to be ~ to do** essere restio(a) a fare.

**loathe** [ləuð] *vt* detestare, aborrire.

**loaves** [ləuvz] *npl of* **loaf.**

**lobby** ['lɔbɪ] *n* atrio, vestibolo; (*POL*: *pressure group*) gruppo di pressione // *vi* fare pressione su.

**lobster** ['lɔbstə*] *n* aragosta.

**local** ['ləukl] *a* locale // *n* (*Brit*: *pub*) ≈ bar *m inv* all'angolo; **the ~s** *npl* la gente della zona; **~ call** *n* (*TEL*) telefonata urbana; **~ government** *n* amministrazione *f* locale.

**locality** [ləu'kælɪtɪ] *n* località *f inv*; (*position*) posto, luogo.

**locally** ['ləukəlɪ] *ad* da queste parti; nel vicinato.

**locate** [ləu'keɪt] *vt* (*find*) trovare; (*situate*) collocare.

**location** [ləu'keɪʃən] *n* posizione *f*; **on ~** (*CINEMA*) all'esterno.

**loch** [lɔx] *n* lago.

**lock** [lɔk] *n* (*of door*, *box*) serratura; (*of canal*) chiusa; (*of hair*) ciocca, riccio // *vt* (*with key*) chiudere a chiave; (*immobilize*) bloccare // *vi* (*door etc*) chiudersi; (*wheels*) bloccarsi, incepparsi.

**locker** ['lɔkə*] *n* armadietto.

**locket** ['lɔkɪt] *n* medaglione *m*.

**locksmith** ['lɔksmɪθ] *n* magnano.

**lock-up** ['lɔkʌp] *n* (*garage*) box *m inv*.

**locomotive** [ləukə'məutɪv] *n* locomotiva.

**locum** ['ləukəm] *n* (*MED*) medico sostituto.

**locust** ['ləukəst] *n* locusta.

**lodge** [lɔdʒ] *n* casetta, portineria // *vi* (*person*): **to ~ (with)** essere a pensione (presso *or* da) // *vt* (*appeal etc*) presentare, fare; **to ~ a complaint** presentare un reclamo; **~r** *n* affittuario/a; (*with room and meals*) pensionante *m/f*.

**lodgings** ['lɔdʒɪŋz] *npl* camera d'affitto; camera ammobiliata.

**loft** [lɔft] *n* solaio, soffitta; (*AGR*) granaio.

**lofty** ['lɔftɪ] *a* alto(a); (*haughty*) altezzoso(a).

**log** [lɔg] *n* (*of wood*) ceppo; (*book*) = **logbook.**

**logbook** ['lɔgbuk] *n* (*NAUT*, *AVIAT*) diario di bordo; (*AUT*) libretto di circolazione; (*of lorry driver*) registro di viaggio; (*of events, movement of goods etc*) registro.

**loggerheads** [ˈlɔgəhɛdz] npl: at ~ (with) ai ferri corti (con).

**logic** [ˈlɔdʒɪk] n logica; ~al a logico(a).

**loin** [lɔɪn] n (CULIN) lombata.

**loiter** [ˈlɔɪtə*] vi attardarsi; to ~ (about) indugiare, bighellonare.

**loll** [lɔl] vi (also: ~ about) essere stravaccato(a).

**lollipop** [ˈlɔlɪpɔp] n lecca lecca m inv; ~ **man/lady** n (Brit) impiegato/a che aiuta i bambini ad attraversare la strada in vicinanza di scuole.

**London** [ˈlʌndən] n Londra; ~**er** n londinese m/f.

**lone** [ləʊn] a solitario(a).

**loneliness** [ˈləʊnlɪnɪs] n solitudine f, isolamento.

**lonely** [ˈləʊnlɪ] a solo(a); solitario(a), isolato(a).

**long** [lɔŋ] a lungo(a) // ad a lungo, per molto tempo // vi: to ~ for sth/ to do desiderare qc/di fare; di non veder l'ora di aver qc/di fare; so or as ~ as (while) finché; (provided that) sempre che + sub; don't be ~! fai presto!; how ~ is this river/course? quanto è lungo questo fiume/corso?; 6 metres ~ lungo 6 metri; 6 months ~ che dura 6 mesi, di 6 mesi; all night ~ tutta la notte; he no ~er comes non viene più; ~ before molto tempo prima; before ~ (+ future) presto, fra poco; (+ past) poco tempo dopo; at ~ last finalmente; ~distance a (race) di fondo; (call) interurbano(a); ~hand n scrittura normale; ~ing n desiderio, voglia, brama // a di desiderio; pieno(a) di nostalgia.

**longitude** [ˈlɔŋgɪtjuːd] n longitudine f.

**long:** ~ **jump** n salto in lungo; ~**playing record (L.P.)** n (disco) 33 giri m inv; ~**range** a a lunga portata; ~**sighted** a presbite; (fig) lungimirante; ~**standing** a di vecchia data; ~**suffering** a estremamente paziente; infinitamente

tollerante; ~**term** a a lungo termine; ~ **wave** n onde fpl lunghe; ~**winded** a prolisso(a), interminabile.

**loo** [luː] n (Brit col) W.C. m inv, cesso.

**look** [luk] vi guardare; (seem) sembrare, parere; (building etc): to ~ south/on to the sea dare a sud/sul mare // n sguardo; (appearance) aspetto, aria; ~s npl aspetto; bellezza; to ~ after vt fus occuparsi di, prendere cura di; (keep an eye on) guardare, badare a; to ~ at vt fus guardare; to ~ back vi: to ~ back at voltarsi a guardare; to ~ back on (event etc) ripensare a; to ~ down on vt fus (fig) guardare dall'alto, disprezzare; to ~ for vt fus cercare; to ~ forward to vt fus non veder l'ora di; (in letters): we ~ forward to hearing from you in attesa di una vostra gentile risposta; to ~ into vt fus esaminare; to ~ on vi fare da spettatore; to ~ out vi (beware): to ~ out (for) stare in guardia (per); to ~ out for vt fus cercare; (watch for): to ~ out for sb/sth guardare se arriva qn/qc; to ~ round vi (turn) girarsi, voltarsi; (in shop) dare un'occhiata; to ~ up vi fus stare attento a a; (rely on) contare su; to ~ up vi alzare gli occhi; (improve) migliorare // vt (word) cercare; (friend) andare a trovare; to ~ up to vt fus avere rispetto per; ~**out** n posto d'osservazione; guardia; to be on the ~**out** (for) stare in guardia (per).

**loom** [luːm] n telaio // vi sorgere; (fig) minacciare.

**loony** [ˈluːnɪ] n (col) pazzo/a.

**loop** [luːp] n cappio; ~**hole** n via d'uscita; scappatoia.

**loose** [luːs] a (knot) sciolto(a); (screw) allentato(a); (stone) cadente; (clothes) ampio(a), largo(a); (animal) in libertà, scappato(a);

*(life, morals)* dissoluto(a); *(discipline)* allentato(a); *(thinking)* poco rigoroso(a), vago(a); **~ change** n spiccioli mpl, moneta; **~ chippings** npl *(on road)* ghiaino; **~ end** n: to be at a **~** end *or (US)* at **~** ends non saper che fare; **~ly** ad lentamente; approssimativamente; **~n** vt sciogliere.

**loot** [luːt] n bottino // vt saccheggiare.

**lop** [lɔp] vt *(also: ~ off)* tagliare via, recidere.

**lop-sided** ['lɔp'saidid] a non equilibrato(a), asimmetrico(a).

**lord** [lɔːd] n signore m; L~ Smith lord Smith; the L~ il Signore; the (House of) L~s *(Brit)* la Camera dei Lord; **~ship** n: **your** L~**ship** Sua Eccellenza.

**lore** [lɔː*] n tradizioni fpl.

**lorry** ['lɔri] n *(Brit)* camion m inv; **~ driver** n *(Brit)* camionista m.

**lose** [luːz], pt, pp **lost** vt perdere; *(pursuers)* distanziare // vi perdere; **to ~** *(time) (clock)* ritardare; **to get lost** vi perdersi, smarrirsi; **~r** n perdente m/f.

**loss** [lɔs] n perdita; **to be at a ~** essere perplesso(a).

**lost** [lɔst] pt, pp of **lose** // a perduto(a); **~ property**, *(US) ~* **and found** n oggetti mpl smarriti.

**lot** [lɔt] n *(at auctions)* lotto; *(destiny)* destino, sorte f; the **~** tutto(a) quanto(a); tutti(e) quanti(e); a **~** molto; a **~** of una gran quantità di, un sacco di; **~s of** molto(a); **to draw ~s** (for **sth**) tirare a sorte (per qc).

**lotion** ['ləuʃən] n lozione f.

**lottery** ['lɔtəri] n lotteria.

**loud** [laud] a forte, alto(a); *(gaudy)* vistoso(a), sgargiante // ad *(speak etc)* forte; **~hailer** n *(Brit)* portavoce m inv; **~ly** ad fortemente, ad alta voce; **~speaker** n altoparlante m.

**lounge** [laundʒ] n salotto, soggiorno // vi oziare; starsene colle mani in mano; **~ suit** n *(Brit)* completo da uomo.

**louse** [laus], pl **lice** n pidocchio.

**lousy** ['lauzi] a *(fig)* orrendo(a), schifoso(a).

**lout** [laut] n zoticone m.

**louvre**, *(US)* **louver** ['luːvə*] a *(door, window)* con apertura a gelosia.

**lovable** ['lʌvəbl] a simpatico(a), carino(a); amabile.

**love** [lʌv] n amore m // vt amare; voler bene a; **to ~ to do:** I **~** to do mi piace fare; **to be in ~ with** essere innamorato(a) di; **to make ~** fare l'amore; **"15 ~"** *(TENNIS)* "15 a zero"; **~ affair** n relazione f; **~ life** n vita sentimentale.

**lovely** ['lʌvli] a bello(a); *(delicious: smell, meal)* buono(a).

**lover** ['lʌvə*] n amante m/f; *(amateur)*: **a ~ of** un(un')amante di; un(un')appassionato(a) di.

**loving** ['lʌviŋ] a affettuoso(a), amoroso(a), tenero(a).

**low** [ləu] a basso(a) // ad in basso // n *(METEOR)* depressione f // vi *(cow)* muggire; **to feel ~** sentirsi giù; **to turn (down)** ~ vt abbassare; **~-cut** a *(dress)* scollato(a); **~er** vt calare; *(reduce)* abbassare; **~-fat** a magro(a); **~lands** npl *(GEO)* pianura; **~ly** a umile, modesto(a); **~-lying** a a basso livello.

**loyal** ['lɔiəl] a fedele, leale; **~ty** n fedeltà, lealtà.

**lozenge** ['lɔzindʒ] n *(MED)* pastiglia; *(GEOM)* losanga.

**L.P.** n abbr = **long-playing record.**

**L-plates** ['ɛlpleits] npl *(Brit)* cartelli sui veicoli dei guidatori principianti.

**Ltd** abbr = **limited.**

**lubricant** ['luːbrikənt] n lubrificante m.

**lubricate** ['luːbrikeit] vt lubrificare.

**luck** [lʌk] n fortuna, sorte f; **bad ~** sfortuna, mala sorte; **good ~!** buona fortuna!; **~ily** ad fortunatamente, per fortuna; **~y** a fortunato(a); *(number etc)* che porta fortuna.

**ludicrous** ['luːdikrəs] a ridicolo(a),

assurdo(a).

**lug** [lʌg] vt trascinare.

**luggage** ['lʌgɪdʒ] n bagagli mpl; ~ **rack** n portabagagli m inv.

**lukewarm** ['lu:kwɔ:m] a tiepido(a).

**lull** [lʌl] n intervallo di calma // vt (child) cullare; (person, fear) acquietare, calmare.

**lullaby** ['lʌləbaɪ] n ninnananna.

**lumbago** [lʌm'beɪgəu] n lombaggine f.

**lumber** ['lʌmbə*] n roba vecchia; ~**jack** n boscaiolo.

**luminous** ['lu:mɪnəs] a luminoso(a).

**lump** [lʌmp] n pezzo; (in sauce) grumo; (swelling) gonfiore m // vt (also: ~ **together**) riunire, mettere insieme; a ~ **sum** una somma globale.

**lunacy** ['lu:nəsɪ] n demenza, follia, pazzia.

**lunar** ['lu:nə*] a lunare.

**lunatic** ['lu:nətɪk] a, n pazzo(a), matto(a).

**lunch** [lʌntʃ] n pranzo, colazione f.

**luncheon** ['lʌntʃən] n pranzo; ~ **meat** n = mortadella; ~ **voucher** n buono m pasto inv.

**lung** [lʌŋ] n polmone m.

**lunge** [lʌndʒ] vi (also: ~ **forward**) fare un balzo in avanti; to ~ **at** balzare su.

**lurch** [lə:tʃ] vi vacillare, barcollare // n scatto improvviso; to **leave sb in the** ~ piantare in asso qn.

**lure** [luə*] n richiamo; lusinga // vt attirare (con l'inganno).

**lurid** ['luərɪd] a sgargiante; (details etc) impressionante.

**lurk** [lə:k] vi stare in agguato.

**luscious** ['lʌʃəs] a succulento(a); delizioso(a).

**lush** [lʌʃ] a lussureggiante.

**lust** [lʌst] n lussuria; cupidigia; desiderio; (fig): ~ **for** sete f di; to ~ **after** vt fus bramare, desiderare.

**lusty** ['lʌstɪ] a vigoroso(a), robusto(a).

**Luxembourg** ['lʌksəmbə:g] n (state) Lussemburgo m; (city)

Lussemburgo f.

**luxuriant** [lʌg'zjuərɪənt] a lussureggiante.

**luxurious** [lʌg'zjuərɪəs] a sontuoso(a), di lusso.

**luxury** ['lʌkʃərɪ] n lusso // cpd di lusso.

**lying** ['laɪɪŋ] n bugie fpl, menzogne fpl.

**lynch** [lɪntʃ] vt linciare.

**lynx** [lɪŋks] n lince f.

**lyric** ['lɪrɪk] a lirico(a); ~**s** npl (of song) parole fpl; ~**al** a lirico(a).

# M

**m.** abbr = **metre, mile, million.**

**M.A.** abbr = **Master of Arts.**

**mac** [mæk] n (Brit) impermeabile m.

**macaroni** [mækə'rəunɪ] n maccheroni mpl.

**mace** [meɪs] n mazza; (spice) macis m or f.

**machine** [mə'ʃi:n] n macchina // vt (dress etc) cucire a macchina; ~**gun** n mitragliatrice f; ~**ry** n macchinario, macchine fpl; (fig) macchina.

**mackerel** ['mækrl] n (pl inv) sgombro.

**mackintosh** ['mækɪntɔʃ] n (Brit) impermeabile m.

**mad** [mæd] a matto(a), pazzo(a); (foolish) sciocco(a); (angry) furioso(a).

**madam** ['mædəm] n signora.

**madden** ['mædn] vt far infuriare.

**made** [meɪd] pt, pp of **make.**

**Madeira** [mə'dɪərə] n (GEO) Madera; (wine) madera.

**made-to-measure** ['meɪdtə'meʒə*] a (Brit) fatto(a) su misura.

**madly** ['mædlɪ] ad follemente; (love) alla follia.

**madman** ['mædmən] n pazzo, alienato.

**madness** ['mædnɪs] n pazzia.

**magazine** [mægə'zi:n] n (PRESS) rivista; (MIL: store) magazzino, deposito; (of firearm) caricatore m.

**maggot** ['mægət] n baco, verme m.

**magic** ['mædʒɪk] n magia // a magico(a); ~al a magico(a); ~ian [mə'dʒɪʃən] n mago/a.

**magistrate** ['mædʒɪstreɪt] n magistrato; giudice m/f.

**magnet** ['mægnɪt] n magnete m, calamita; ~ic [-'nɛtɪk] a magnetico(a).

**magnificent** [mæg'nɪfɪsnt] a magnifico(a).

**magnify** ['mægnɪfaɪ] vt ingrandire; ~ing glass n lente f d'ingrandimento.

**magnitude** ['mægnɪtjuːd] n grandezza; importanza.

**magpie** ['mægpaɪ] n gazza.

**mahogany** [mə'hɔgənɪ] n mogano // cpd di or in mogano.

**maid** [meɪd] n domestica; (in hotel) cameriera; old ~ (pej) vecchia zitella.

**maiden** ['meɪdn] n fanciulla // a (aunt etc) nubile; (speech, voyage) inaugurale; ~ name n nome m nubile or da ragazza.

**mail** [meɪl] n posta // vt spedire (per posta); ~box n (US) cassetta delle lettere; ~ing list n elenco d'indirizzi; ~-order n vendita (or acquisto) per corrispondenza.

**maim** [meɪm] vt mutilare.

**main** [meɪn] a principale // n (pipe) conduttura principale; the ~s (ELEC) la linea principale; in the ~ nel complesso, nell'insieme; ~frame n (COMPUT) mainframe m inv; ~land n continente m; ~ly ad principalmente, soprattutto; ~ road n strada principale; ~stay n (fig) sostegno principale; ~stream n (fig) corrente f principale.

**maintain** [meɪn'teɪn] vt mantenere; (affirm) sostenere; **maintenance** ['meɪntənəns] n manutenzione f; (alimony) alimenti mpl.

**maize** [meɪz] n granturco, mais m.

**majestic** [mə'dʒɛstɪk] a maestoso(a).

**majesty** ['mædʒɪstɪ] n maestà f inv.

**major** ['meɪdʒə*] n (MIL) maggiore m // a (greater, MUS) maggiore; (in importance) principale, importante.

**Majorca** [mə'jɔːkə] n Maiorca.

**majority** [mə'dʒɔrɪtɪ] n maggioranza.

**make** [meɪk] vt (pt, pp made) fare; (manufacture) fare, fabbricare; (cause to be): to ~ sb sad etc rendere qn triste etc; (force): to ~ sb do sth costringere qn a fare qc, far fare qc a qn; (equal): 2 and 2 ~ 4 2 più 2 fa 4 // n fabbricazione f; (brand) marca; to ~ a fool of sb far fare a qn la figura dello scemo; to ~ a profit realizzare un profitto; to ~ a loss subire una perdita; to ~ it (arrive) arrivare; (achieve sth) farcela; what time do you ~ it? che ora fai?; to ~ do with arrangiarsi con; to ~ for vt fus (place) avviarsi verso; to ~ out vt (write out) scrivere; (: cheque) emettere; (understand) capire; (see) distinguere; (: numbers) decifrare; to ~ up vt (invent) inventare; (parcel) fare // vi conciliarsi; (with cosmetics) truccarsi; to ~ up for vt fus compensare; recuperare; ~believe n: a world of ~-believe un mondo di favole; it's just ~-believe è tutta un'invenzione; ~r n fabbricante m; creatore/trice, autore/trice; ~shift a improvvisato(a); ~up n trucco; ~up remover n struccatore m.

**making** ['meɪkɪŋ] n (fig): in the ~ in formazione; to have the ~s of (actor, athlete etc) avere la stoffa di.

**maladjusted** [mælə'dʒʌstɪd] a disadattato(a).

**malaria** [mə'lɛərɪə] n malaria.

**Malaya** [mə'leɪə] n Malesia.

**male** [meɪl] n (BIOL, ELEC) maschio // a maschile; maschio(a).

**malevolent** [mə'lɛvələnt] a malevolo(a).

**malfunction** [mæl'fʌŋkʃən] n funzione f difettosa.

**malice** ['mælɪs] n malevolenza; **malicious** [mə'lɪʃəs] a malevolo(a);

(LAW) doloso(a).

**malign** [mə'laɪn] vt malignare su; calunniare.

**malignant** [mə'lɪgnənt] a (MED) maligno(a).

**mall** [mɔ:l] n (also: shopping ~) centro commerciale.

**mallet** ['mælɪt] n maglio.

**malnutrition** [mælnju:'trɪʃən] n denutrizione f.

**malpractice** [mæl'præktɪs] n prevaricazione f; negligenza.

**malt** [mɔ:lt] n malto.

**Malta** ['mɔ:ltə] n Malta.

**mammal** ['mæml] n mammifero.

**mammoth** ['mæməθ] n mammut m inv // a enorme, gigantesco(a).

**man** [mæn] n (pl men) uomo; (CHESS) pezzo; (DRAUGHTS) pedina // vt fornire d'uomini; stare a; essere di servizio a; an old ~ un vecchio; ~ and wife marito e moglie.

**manage** ['mænɪdʒ] vi farcela // vt (be in charge of) occuparsi di; gestire; to ~ to do sth riuscire a far qc; ~able a maneggevole; fattibile; ~ment n amministrazione f, direzione f; ~r n direttore m; (of shop, restaurant) gerente m; (of artist) manager m inv; ~ress [-ə'rɛs] n direttrice f; gerente f; ~rial [-ə'dʒɪərɪəl] a dirigenziale; managing a: managing director amministratore m delegato.

**mandarin** ['mændərɪn] n (person, fruit) mandarino.

**mandatory** ['mændətərɪ] a obbligatorio(a); ingiuntivo(a).

**mane** [meɪn] n criniera.

**maneuver** [mə'nu:və*] etc (US) = **manoeuvre** etc.

**manfully** ['mænfəlɪ] ad valorosamente.

**mangle** ['mæŋgl] vt straziare; mutilare // n strizzatoio.

**mango**, ~es ['mæŋgəu] n mango.

**mangy** ['meɪndʒɪ] a rognoso(a).

**manhandle** ['mænhændl] vt malmenare.

**manhole** ['mænhəul] n botola

stradale.

**manhood** ['mænhud] n età virile; virilità.

**man-hour** ['mæn'auə*] n ora di lavoro.

**manhunt** ['mænhʌnt] n caccia all'uomo.

**mania** ['meɪnɪə] n mania; ~c ['meɪnɪæk] n maniaco(a).

**manic** ['mænɪk] a (behaviour, activity) maniacale.

**manicure** ['mænɪkjuə*] n manicure f inv; ~ set n trousse f inv della manicure.

**manifest** ['mænɪfɛst] vt manifestare // a manifesto(a), palese.

**manifesto** [mænɪ'fɛstəu] n manifesto.

**manipulate** [mə'nɪpjuleɪt] vt manipolare.

**mankind** [mæn'kaɪnd] n umanità, genere m umano.

**manly** ['mænlɪ] a virile; coraggioso(a).

**man-made** ['mæn'meɪd] a sintetico(a); artificiale.

**manner** ['mænə*] n maniera, modo; ~s npl maniere fpl; ~ism n vezzo, tic m inv.

**manoeuvre**, (US) **maneuver** [mə'nu:və*] vt manovrare // vi far manovre // n manovra.

**manor** ['mænə*] n (also: ~ house) maniero.

**manpower** ['mænpauə*] n manodopera.

**mansion** ['mænʃən] n casa signorile.

**manslaughter** ['mænslɔ:tə*] n omicidio preterintenzionale.

**mantelpiece** ['mæntlpi:s] n mensola del caminetto.

**Mantua** ['mæntjuə] n Mantova.

**manual** ['mænjuəl] a manuale // n manuale m.

**manufacture** [mænju'fæktʃə*] vt fabbricare // n fabbricazione f, manifattura; ~r n fabbricante m.

**manure** [mə'njuə*] n concime m.

**manuscript** ['mænjuskrɪpt] n manoscritto.

**many** ['mɛnɪ] *a* molti(e) // *pronoun* molti(e), un gran numero; **a great** ~ moltissimi(e), un gran numero (di); ~ **a** ... molti(e) ..., più di un(a) ... .

**map** [mæp] *n* carta (geografica) // *vt* fare una carta di; **to** ~ **out** *vt* tracciare un piano di.

**maple** ['meɪpl] *n* acero.

**mar** [ma:*] *vt* sciupare.

**marathon** ['mærəθən] *n* maratona.

**marauder** [məˈrɔ:də*] *n* saccheggiatore *m*; predatore *m*.

**marble** ['ma:bl] *n* marmo; (*toy*) pallina, bilia; ~**s** *n* (*game*) palline, bilie.

**March** [ma:tʃ] *n* marzo.

**march** [ma:tʃ] *vi* marciare; sfilare // *n* marcia; (*demonstration*) dimostrazione *f*.

**mare** [mɛə*] *n* giumenta.

**margarine** [ma:dʒəˈri:n] *n* margarina.

**margin** ['ma:dʒɪn] *n* margine *m*; ~**al (seat)** *n* (POL) seggio elettorale ottenuto con una stretta maggioranza.

**marigold** ['mærɪɡəuld] *n* calendola.

**marijuana** [mærɪˈwɑ:nə] *n* marijuana.

**marine** [məˈri:n] *a* (*animal, plant*) marino(a); (*forces, engineering*) marittimo(a) // *n* fante *m* di marina; (*US*) marine *m inv*.

**marital** ['mærɪtl] *a* maritale, coniugale; ~ **status** stato coniugale.

**mark** [ma:k] *n* segno; (*stain*) macchia; (*of skid etc*) traccia; (Brit SCOL) voto; (SPORT) bersaglio; (*currency*) marco // *vt* segnare; (*stain*) macchiare; (Brit SCOL) dare un voto a; correggere; **to** ~ **time** segnare il passo; **to** ~ **out** *vt* delimitare; ~**ed** *a* spiccato(a), chiaro(a); ~**er** *n* (*sign*) segno; (*bookmark*) segnalibro.

**market** ['ma:kɪt] *n* mercato // *vt* (COMM) mettere in vendita; ~ **garden** *n* (Brit) orto industriale; ~**ing** *n* marketing *m*; ~ **place** *n*

piazza del mercato; (COMM) piazza, mercato; ~ **research** *n* indagine *f* or ricerca di mercato; ~ **value** *n* valore *m* di mercato.

**marksman** ['ma:ksmən] *n* tiratore *m* scelto.

**marmalade** ['ma:məleɪd] *n* marmellata d'arance.

**maroon** [məˈru:n] *vt* (*fig*): **to be** ~**ed** (**in** *or* **at**) essere abbandonato(a) (in) // *a* bordeaux *inv*.

**marquee** [ma:ˈki:] *n* padiglione *m*.

**marquess, marquis** [ma:kwɪs] *n* marchese *m*.

**marriage** ['mærɪdʒ] *n* matrimonio; ~ **bureau** *n* agenzia matrimoniale; ~ **certificate** *n* certificato di matrimonio.

**married** ['mærɪd] *a* sposato(a); (*life, love*) coniugale, matrimoniale.

**marrow** ['mærəu] *n* midollo; (*vegetable*) zucca.

**marry** ['mærɪ] *vt* sposare, sposarsi con; (*subj: father, priest etc*) dare in matrimonio // *vi* (*also*: **get married**) sposarsi.

**Mars** [ma:z] *n* (*planet*) Marte *m*.

**marsh** [ma:ʃ] *n* palude *f*.

**marshal** ['ma:ʃl] *n* maresciallo; (US: *fire*) capo; (: *police*) capitano // *vt* adunare.

**martyr** ['ma:tə*] *n* martire *m/f* // *vt* martirizzare; ~**dom** *n* martirio.

**marvel** ['ma:vl] *n* meraviglia // *vi*: **to** ~ (**at**) meravigliarsi (di); ~**lous**, (US) ~**ous** *a* meraviglioso(a).

**Marxist** ['ma:ksɪst] *a, n* marxista (*m/f*).

**marzipan** ['ma:zɪpæn] *n* marzapane *m*.

**mascara** [mæsˈka:rə] *n* mascara *m*.

**masculine** ['mæskjulɪn] *a* maschile // *n* genere *m* maschile.

**mashed** [mæʃt] *a*: ~ **potatoes** purè *m* di patate.

**mask** [ma:sk] *n* maschera // *vt* mascherare.

**mason** ['meɪsn] *n* (*also*: **stone**~) scalpellino; (*also*: **free**~) massone

$m$; ~**ry** $n$ muratura.

**masquerade** [mæskə'reid] $n$ ballo in maschera; (fig) mascherata // $vi$: to ~ as farsi passare per.

**mass** [mæs] $n$ moltitudine $f$, massa; (PHYSICS) massa; (REL) messa // $vi$ ammassarsi; **the** ~**es** le masse.

**massacre** ['mæsəkə*] $n$ massacro.

**massage** ['mæsɑːʒ] $n$ massaggio.

**masseur** [mæ'səː*] $n$ massaggiatore $m$; **masseuse** [-'səːz] $n$ massaggiatrice $f$.

**massive** ['mæsiv] $a$ enorme, massiccio(a).

**mass media** $npl$ mass media $mpl$.

**mass-produce** ['mæsprə'djuːs] $vt$ produrre in serie.

**mast** [mɑːst] $n$ albero.

**master** ['mɑːstə*] $n$ padrone $m$; (ART etc, teacher: in primary school) maestro; (: in secondary school) professore $m$; (title for boys): **M~ X** Signorino X // $vt$ domare; (learn) imparare a fondo; (understand) conoscere a fondo; ~**key** $n$ chiave $f$ maestra; ~**ly** $a$ magistrale; ~**mind** $n$ mente $f$ superiore // $vt$ essere il cervello di; **M~ of Arts/Science (M.A./M.Sc.)** $n$ Master $m$ $inv$ in lettere/scienze; ~**piece** $n$ capolavoro; ~**y** $n$ dominio; padronanza.

**mat** [mæt] $n$ stuoia; (also: **door**~) stoino, zerbino // $a$ = **matt**.

**match** [mætʃ] $n$ fiammifero; (game) partita, incontro; (fig) uguale $m/f$; matrimonio; partito // $vt$ intonare; (go well with) andare benissimo con; (equal) uguagliare // $vi$ combaciare; **to be a good** ~ andare bene; ~**box** $n$ scatola per fiammiferi; ~**ing** $a$ ben assortito(a).

**mate** [meit] $n$ compagno/a di lavoro; (col: friend) amico/a; (animal) compagno/a; (in merchant navy) secondo; // $vi$ accoppiarsi // $vt$ accoppiare.

**material** [mə'tiəriəl] $n$ (substance) materiale $m$, materia; (cloth) stoffa // $a$ materiale; (important)

essenziale; ~**s** $npl$ materiali $mpl$.

**maternal** [mə'təːnl] $a$ materno(a).

**maternity** [mə'təːniti] $n$ maternità; ~ **dress** $n$ vestito $m$ pre-maman $inv$; ~ **hospital** $n$ = clinica ostetrica.

**math** [mæθ] $n$ (US) = **maths**.

**mathematical** [mæθə'mætikl] $a$ matematico(a).

**mathematics** [mæθə'mætiks] $n$ matematica.

**maths** [mæθs], (US) **math** [mæθ] $n$ matematica.

**matinée** ['mætinei] $n$ matinée $f$ $inv$.

**mating** ['meitiŋ] $n$ accoppiamento.

**matriculation** [mətrikju'leiʃən] $n$ immatricolazione $f$.

**matrimonial** [mætri'məuniəl] $a$ matrimoniale, coniugale.

**matrimony** ['mætriməni] $n$ matrimonio.

**matron** ['meitrən] $n$ (in hospital) capoinfermiera; (in school) infermiera; ~**ly** $a$ da matrona.

**matt(t)** [mæt] $a$ opaco(a).

**matted** ['mætid] $a$ ingarbugliato(a).

**matter** ['mætə*] $n$ questione $f$; (PHYSICS) materia, sostanza; (content) contenuto; (MED: pus) pus $m$ // $vi$ importare; **it doesn't** ~ non importa; (I don't mind) non fa niente; **what's the** ~? che cosa c'è?; **no** ~ **what** qualsiasi cosa accada; **as a** ~ **of course** come cosa naturale; **as a** ~ **of fact** in verità; ~**-of-fact** $a$ prosaico(a).

**mattress** ['mætris] $n$ materasso.

**mature** [mə'tjuə*] $a$ maturo(a); (cheese) stagionato(a) // $vi$ maturare; stagionare; (COMM) scadere.

**maul** [mɔːl] $vt$ lacerare.

**mauve** [məuv] $a$ malva $inv$.

**maxim** ['mæksim] $n$ massima.

**maximum** ['mæksiməm] $a$ massimo(a) // $n$ (pl **maxima** ['mæksimə]) massimo.

**May** [mei] $n$ maggio.

**may** [mei] $vi$ (conditional: **might**) (indicating possibility): **he** ~ **come**

può darsi che venga; (be allowed to): ~ **I smoke?** posso fumare?; (wishes): ~ **God bless you!** Dio la benedica!

**maybe** ['meɪbɪ] ad forse, può darsi; ~ **he'll** ... può darsi che lui ... + sub, forse lui ....

**May Day** n il primo maggio.

**mayhem** ['meɪhem] n cagnara.

**mayonnaise** [meɪə'neɪz] n maionese f.

**mayor** [mɛə*] n sindaco; ~**ess** n sindaco (donna); moglie f del sindaco.

**maze** [meɪz] n labirinto, dedalo.

**M.D.** abbr = Doctor of Medicine.

**me** [miː] pronoun mi, m' + vowel or silent 'h'; (stressed, after prep) me; **he heard** ~ mi ha or m'ha sentito; **give** ~ **a book** dammi (or mi dia) un libro; **it's** ~ sono io; **with** ~ con me; **without** ~ senza di me.

**meadow** ['mɛdəu] n prato.

**meagre,** (US) **meager** ['miːgə*] a magro(a).

**meal** [miːl] n pasto; (flour) farina; ~**time** n l'ora di mangiare.

**mean** [miːn] a (with money) avaro(a), gretto(a); (unkind) meschino(a), maligno(a); (average) medio(a) // vt (pt, pp **meant**) (signify) significare, voler dire; (intend): **to** ~ **to do** aver l'intenzione di fare // n mezzo; (MATH) media; ~**s** npl mezzi mpl; **by** ~**s of** per mezzo di; (person) a mezzo di; **by all** ~**s ma** certo, prego; **to be meant for** essere destinato(a); **a do you** ~ **it?** dice sul serio?; **what do you** ~? che cosa vuol dire?

**meander** [mɪ'ændə*] vi far meandri; (fig) divagare.

**meaning** ['miːnɪŋ] n significato, senso; ~**ful** a significativo(a); ~**less** a senza senso.

**meant** [ment] pt, pp of **mean**.

**meantime** ['miːntaɪm] ad, **meanwhile** ['miːnwaɪl] ad (also: **in the** ~) nel frattempo.

**measles** ['miːzlz] n morbillo.

**measly** ['miːzlɪ] a (col) miserabile.

**measure** ['mɛʒə*] vt, vi misurare // n misura; (ruler) metro; ~**ments** npl misure fpl; **chest/hip** ~**ment** giro petto/fianchi.

**meat** [miːt] n carne f; ~**ball** n polpetta di carne; ~**y** a che sa di carne; (fig) sostanzioso(a).

**Mecca** ['mɛkə] n Mecca.

**mechanic** [mɪ'kænɪk] n meccanico; ~**al** a meccanico(a); ~**s** n meccanica // npl meccanismo.

**mechanism** ['mɛkənɪzəm] n meccanismo.

**medal** ['mɛdl] n medaglia; ~**lion** [mɪ'dælɪən] n medaglione m.

**meddle** ['mɛdl] vi: **to** ~ **in** immischiarsi in, mettere le mani in; **to** ~ **with** toccare.

**media** ['miːdɪə] npl media mpl.

**mediaeval** [mɛdɪ'iːvl] a = **medieval**.

**median** ['miːdɪən] n mediana; (US: also: ~ **strip**) banchina f spartitraffico.

**mediate** ['miːdɪeɪt] vi interporsi; fare da mediatore/trice.

**Medicaid** ['mɛdɪkeɪd] n (US) assistenza medica ai poveri.

**medical** ['mɛdɪkl] a medico(a).

**Medicare** ['mɛdɪkɛə*] n (US) assistenza medica agli anziani.

**medication** [mɛdɪ'keɪʃən] n medicinali mpl, farmaci mpl.

**medicine** ['mɛdsɪn] n medicina.

**medieval** [mɛdɪ'iːvl] a medievale.

**mediocre** [miːdɪ'əukə*] a mediocre.

**meditate** ['mɛdɪteɪt] vi: **to** ~ **(on)** meditare (su).

**Mediterranean** [mɛdɪtə'reɪnɪən] a mediterraneo(a); **the** ~ (**Sea**) il (mare) Mediterraneo.

**medium** ['miːdɪəm] a medio(a) // n (pl **media**: means) mezzo; (pl **mediums**: person) medium m inv; **the happy** ~ una giusta via di mezzo; ~ **wave** n onde fpl medie.

**medley** ['mɛdlɪ] n selezione f.

**meek** [miːk] a dolce, umile.

**meet** [miːt] pt, pp **met** vt incontrare; (for the first time) fare la conoscenza di; (fig) affrontare; soddisfare; raggiungere // vi incontrarsi; (in session) riunirsi; (join: objects) unirsi; **I'll ~ you at the station** verrò a prenderla alla stazione; **to ~ with** vt fus incontrare; **~ing** n incontro; (session: of club etc) riunione f; (interview) intervista; **she's at a ~ing** (COMM) è in riunione.

**megabyte** ['mɛgəbaɪt] n (COMPUT) megabyte m inv.

**megaphone** ['mɛgəfəun] n megafono.

**melancholy** ['mɛlənkəlɪ] n malinconia // a malinconico(a).

**mellow** ['mɛləu] a (wine, sound) ricco(a); (person, light) dolce; (colour) caldo(a); (fruit) maturo(a) // vi (person) addolcirsi.

**melody** ['mɛlədɪ] n melodia.

**melon** ['mɛlən] n melone m.

**melt** [mɛlt] vi (gen) sciogliersi, struggersi; (metals) fondersi; (fig) intenerirsi // vt sciogliere, struggere; fondere; (person) commuovere; **to ~ away** vi sciogliersi completamente; **to ~ down** vt fondere; **~down** n (in nuclear reactor) fusione f (dovuta a surriscaldamento); **~ing pot** n (fig) crogiolo.

**member** ['mɛmbə*] n membro; **M~ of the European Parliament (MEP)** n (Brit) eurodeputato; **M~ of Parliament (MP)** n (Brit) deputato; **~ship** n iscrizione f; (number of) iscritti mpl, membri mpl; **~ship card** n tessera (di iscrizione).

**memento** [mə'mɛntəu] n ricordo, souvenir m inv.

**memo** ['mɛməu] n appunto; (COMM etc) comunicazione f di servizio.

**memoirs** ['mɛmwɑːz] npl memorie fpl, ricordi mpl.

**memorandum,** pl **memoranda** [mɛmə'rændəm, -də] n appunto; (COMM etc) comunicazione f di servizio; (DIPLOMACY) memoran-

dum m inv.

**memorial** [mɪ'mɔːrɪəl] n monumento commemorativo // a commemorativo(a).

**memorize** ['mɛməraɪz] vt imparare a memoria.

**memory** ['mɛmərɪ] n (also COMPUT) memoria; (recollection) ricordo.

**men** [mɛn] npl of **man**.

**menace** ['mɛnəs] n minaccia // vt minacciare.

**menagerie** [mɪ'nædʒərɪ] n serraglio.

**mend** [mɛnd] vt aggiustare, riparare; (darn) rammendare // n rammendo; **on the ~** in via di guarigione.

**menial** ['miːnɪəl] a da servo, domestico(a); umile.

**meningitis** [mɛnɪn'dʒaɪtɪs] n meningite f.

**menopause** ['mɛnəupɔːz] n menopausa.

**menstruation** [mɛnstruˈeɪʃən] n menstruazione f.

**mental** ['mɛntl] a mentale.

**mentality** [mɛn'tælɪt] n mentalità f inv.

**menthol** ['mɛnθəl] n mentolo.

**mention** ['mɛnʃən] n menzione f // vt menzionare, far menzione di; **don't ~ it!** non c'è di che!, prego!

**menu** ['mɛnjuː] n (set ~, COMPUT) menù m inv; (printed) carta.

**MEP** n abbr = **Member of the European Parliament.**

**mercenary** ['mɜːsɪnərɪ] a venale // n mercenario.

**merchandise** ['mɜːtʃəndaɪz] n merci fpl.

**merchant** ['mɜːtʃənt] n mercante m, commerciante m; **~ bank** n (Brit) banca d'affari; **~ navy,** (US) **~ marine** n marina mercantile.

**merciful** ['mɜːsɪful] a pietoso(a), clemente.

**merciless** ['mɜːsɪlɪs] a spietato(a).

**mercury** ['mɜːkjurɪ] n mercurio.

**mercy** ['mɜːsɪ] n pietà; (REL) misericordia; **at the ~ of** alla mercè di.

**mere** [mɪə*] *a* semplice; by a ~ chance per mero caso; ~**ly** *ad* semplicemente, non ... che.

**merge** [mə:dʒ] *vt* unire // *vi* fondersi, unirsi; (*COMM*) fondersi; ~**r** *n* (*COMM*) fusione *f*.

**meringue** [mə'ræŋ] *n* meringa.

**merit** ['mɛrɪt] *n* merito, valore *m* // *vt* meritare.

**mermaid** ['mə:meɪd] *n* sirena.

**merry** ['mɛrɪ] *a* gaio(a), allegro(a); **M~ Christmas!** Buon Natale!; ~-**go-round** *n* carosello.

**mesh** [mɛʃ] *n* maglia; rete *f*.

**mesmerize** ['mɛzmərɑɪz] *vt* ipnotizzare; affascinare.

**mess** [mɛs] *n* confusione *f*, disordine *m*; (*fig*) pasticcio; (*MIL*) mensa; **to ~ about** or **around** *vi* (*col*) trastullarsi; **to ~ about** or **around with** *vt fus* (*col*) gingillarsi con; (: *plans*) fare un pasticcio di; **to ~ up** *vt* sporcare; fare un pasticcio di; rovinare.

**message** ['mɛsɪdʒ] *n* messaggio.

**messenger** ['mɛsɪndʒə*] *n* messaggero/a.

**Messrs** ['mɛsəz] *abbr* (*on letters*) Spett.

**messy** ['mɛsɪ] *a* sporco(a); disordinato(a).

**met** [mɛt] *pt, pp of* **meet**.

**metal** ['mɛtl] *n* metallo; ~**lic** [-'tælɪk] *a* metallico(a).

**metaphor** ['mɛtəfə*] *n* metafora.

**mete** [mi:t]: **to ~ out** *vt fus* infliggere.

**meteorology** [mi:tɪə'rɔlədʒɪ] *n* meteorologia.

**meter** ['mi:tə*] *n* (*instrument*) contatore *m*; (*US*: *unit*) = **metre**.

**method** ['mɛθəd] *n* metodo; ~**ical** [mɪ'θɔdɪkl] *a* metodico(a).

**Methodist** ['mɛθədɪst] *a, n* metodista (*m/f*).

**methylated spirit** ['mɛθɪleɪtɪd-] *n* (*Brit*: *also*: **meths**) alcool *m* denaturato.

**metre**, (*US*) **meter** ['mi:tə*] *n* metro.

**metric** ['mɛtrɪk] *a* metrico(a).

**metropolitan** [mɛtrə'pɔlɪtən] *a* metropolitano(a); **the M~ Police** *n* (*Brit*) la polizia di Londra.

**mettle** ['mɛtl] *n* coraggio.

**mew** [mju:] *vi* (*cat*) miagolare.

**mews** [mju:z] *n*: ~ **cottage** (*Brit*) villetta ricavata da un'antica scuderia.

**Mexico** ['mɛksɪkəu] *n* Messico.

**miaow** [mi:'au] *vi* miagolare.

**mice** [mɑɪs] *npl of* **mouse**.

**micro** ['mɑɪkrəu] *n* (*also*: ~ **computer**) microcomputer *m inv*.

**microchip** ['mɑɪkrəutʃɪp] *n* microcircuito integrato.

**microfilm** ['mɑɪkrəufɪlm] *n* microfilm *m inv* // *vt* microfilmare.

**microphone** ['mɑɪkrəfəun] *n* microfono.

**microscope** ['mɑɪkrəskəup] *n* microscopio.

**microwave** ['mɑɪkrəuweɪv] *n* (*also*: ~ **oven**) forno a microonde.

**mid** [mɪd] *a*: ~ **May** metà maggio; ~ **afternoon** metà pomeriggio; **in ~ air** a mezz'aria; ~**day** *n* mezzogiorno.

**middle** ['mɪdl] *n* mezzo; centro; (*waist*) vita // *a* di mezzo; **in the ~ of the night** nel bel mezzo della notte; ~-**aged** *a* di mezza età; **the M~ Ages** *npl* il Medioevo; ~-**class** *a* borghese; **the ~ class(es)** *n*(*pl*) ≈ la borghesia; **M~ East** *n* Medio Oriente *m*; ~**man** *n* intermediario; agente *m* rivenditore; ~ **name** *n* secondo nome *m*; ~**weight** *n* (*BOXING*) peso medio.

**middling** ['mɪdlɪŋ] *a* medio(a).

**midge** [mɪdʒ] *n* moscerino.

**midget** ['mɪdʒɪt] *n* nano/a.

**Midlands** ['mɪdləndz] *npl* contee del centro dell'Inghilterra.

**midnight** ['mɪdnɑɪt] *n* mezzanotte *f*.

**midriff** ['mɪdrɪf] *n* diaframma *m*.

**midst** [mɪdst] *n*: **in the ~ of** in mezzo a.

**midsummer** [mɪd'sʌmə*] *n* mezza

or piena estate f.

**midway** [mɪd'weɪ] a, ad: ~ (between) a mezza strada (fra).

**midweek** [mɪd'wiːk] a, ad a metà settimana.

**midwife**, pl **midwives** ['mɪdwaɪf, -vz] n levatrice f; ~**ry** [-wɪfərɪ] n ostetrica.

**might** [maɪt] vb see **may** // n potere m, forza; ~**y** a forte, potente.

**migraine** ['miːɡreɪn] n emicrania.

**migrant** ['maɪɡrənt] a (bird) migratore(trice); (person) nomade; (worker) emigrato(a).

**migrate** [maɪ'ɡreɪt] vi migrare.

**mike** [maɪk] n abbr (= microphone) microfono.

**Milan** [mɪ'læn] n Milano f.

**mild** [maɪld] a mite; (person, voice) dolce; (flavour) delicato(a); (illness) leggero(a) // n birra leggera.

**mildew** ['mɪldjuː] n muffa.

**mildly** ['maɪldlɪ] ad mitemente; dolcemente; delicatamente; leggermente; **to put it** ~ a dire poco.

**mile** [maɪl] n miglio; ~**age** n (of distance in miglia, ≈ chilometraggio; ~**stone** n pietra miliare.

**milieu** ['miːljə:] n ambiente m.

**militant** ['mɪlɪtnt] a, n militante (m/f).

**military** ['mɪlɪtərɪ] a militare.

**militate** ['mɪlɪteɪt] vi: **to** ~ **against** essere d'ostacolo a.

**milk** [mɪlk] n latte m // vt (cow) mungere; (fig) sfruttare; ~ **chocolate** n cioccolato al latte; ~**man** n lattaio; ~ **shake** n frappé m inv; ~**y** a lattiginoso(a); (colour) latteo(a); **M~y Way** n Via Lattea.

**mill** [mɪl] n mulino; (small: for coffee, pepper etc) macinino; (factory) fabbrica; (spinning ~) filatura // vt macinare // vi (also: ~ about) formicolare.

**millennium** [mɪ'lenɪəm], pl ~**s** or **millennia** [mɪ'lenɪəm, -'lenɪə] n millennio.

**miller** ['mɪlə*] n mugnaio.

**millet** ['mɪlɪt] n miglio.

**milli...** ['mɪlɪ] prefix: ~**gram(me)** n

milligrammo; ~**metre**, (US) ~**meter** n millimetro.

**millinery** ['mɪlɪnərɪ] n modisteria.

**million** ['mɪljən] n milione m; ~**aire** n milionario, ≈ miliardario.

**millstone** ['mɪlstəʊn] n macina.

**milometer** [maɪ'lɒmɪtə*] n ≈ contachilometri m inv.

**mime** [maɪm] n mimo // vt, vi mimare.

**mimic** ['mɪmɪk] n imitatore/trice // vt fare la mimica di; ~**ry** n mimica; (ZOOL) mimetismo.

**min.** abbr = **minute(s)**, **minimum**.

**mince** [mɪns] vt tritare, macinare // vi (in walking) camminare a passettini // n (Brit CULIN) carne f tritata or macinata; ~**meat** n frutta secca tritata per uso in pasticceria; ~ **pie** n specie di torta con frutta secca; ~**r** n tritacarne m inv.

**mind** [maɪnd] n mente f // vt (attend to, look after) badare a, occuparsi di; (be careful) fare attenzione a, stare attento(a) a; (object to): **I don't** ~ **the noise** il rumore non mi dà alcun fastidio; **I don't** ~ **non m'importa**; **it is on my** ~ mi preoccupa; **to my** ~ secondo me, a mio parere; **to make up one's** ~ essere uscito(a) di mente; **to keep or bear sth in** ~ non dimenticare qc; **to make up one's** ~ decidersi; ~ **you**, ... sì, però va detto che ...; **never** ~ non importa, non fa niente; "~ **the step**" "attenzione allo scalino"; ~**er** n (child ~er) bambinaia; (bodyguard) guardia del corpo; ~**ful** a: ~**ful of** attento(a) a; memore di; ~**less** a idiota.

**mine** [maɪn] pronoun il(la) mio(a), pl i(le) miei(mie); **that book is** ~ quel libro è mio; **yours is red,** ~ **is green** il tuo è rosso, il mio è verde; **a friend of** ~ un mio amico // n miniera; (explosive) mina // vt (coal) estrarre; (ship, beach) minare.

**miner** ['maɪnə*] n minatore m.

**mineral** ['mɪnərəl] a minerale // n minerale m; ~**s** npl (Brit: soft *drinks*) bevande *fpl* gasate; ~ **water** *n* acqua minerale.

**minesweeper** ['maɪnswiːpə*] *n* dragamine *m inv*.

**mingle** ['mɪŋgl] *vi*: to ~ with mescolarsi a, mischiarsi con.

**miniature** ['mɪnətʃə*] *a* in miniatura // *n* miniatura.

**minibus** ['mɪnɪbʌs] *n* minibus *m inv*.

**minim** ['mɪnɪm] *n* (*MUS*) minima.

**minimum** ['mɪnɪməm] *n* (*pl* **minima** ['mɪnɪmə]) minimo // *a* minimo(a).

**mining** ['maɪnɪŋ] *n* industria mineraria // *a* minerario(a); di minatori.

**miniskirt** ['mɪnɪskəːt] *n* minigonna.

**minister** ['mɪnɪstə*] *n* (*Brit POL*) ministro; (*REL*) pastore *m* // *vi*: to ~ to sb assistere qn; to ~ to sb's needs provvedere ai bisogni di qn; ~ial [-'tɪərɪəl] *a* (*Brit POL*) ministeriale.

**ministry** ['mɪnɪstrɪ] *n* (*Brit POL*) ministero; (*REL*): to go into the ~ diventare pastore.

**mink** [mɪŋk] *n* visone *m*.

**minnow** ['mɪnəʊ] *n* pesciolino d'acqua dolce.

**minor** ['maɪnə*] *a* minore, di poca importanza; (*MUS*) minore // *n* (*LAW*) minorenne *m/f*.

**minority** [maɪ'nɔrɪtɪ] *n* minoranza.

**mint** [mɪnt] *n* (*plant*) menta; (*sweet*) pasticca di menta // *vt* (*coins*) battere; the (**Royal**) **M~**, (*US*) the (**US**) **M~** la Zecca; in ~ **condition** come nuovo/a di zecca.

**minus** ['maɪnəs] *n* (*also*: ~ **sign**) segno meno // *prep* meno.

**minute** *a* [maɪ'njuːt] minuscolo(a); (*detail*) minuzioso(a) // *n* ['mɪnɪt] minuto; (*official record*) processo verbale, resoconto sommario; ~s *npl* verbale *m*, verbali *mpl*.

**miracle** ['mɪrəkl] *n* miracolo.

**mirage** ['mɪrɑːʒ] *n* miraggio.

**mire** ['maɪə*] *n* pantano, melma.

**mirror** ['mɪrə*] *n* specchio // *vt* rispecchiare, riflettere.

**mirth** [məːθ] *n* gaiezza.

**misadventure** [mɪsəd'vɛntʃə*] *n* disavventura; **death by** ~ morte *f* accidentale.

**misapprehension** ['mɪsæprɪ'henʃən] *n* malinteso.

**misbehave** [mɪsbɪ'heɪv] *vi* comportarsi male.

**miscarriage** ['mɪskærɪdʒ] *n* (*MED*) aborto spontaneo; ~ **of justice** errore *m* giudiziario.

**miscellaneous** [mɪsɪ'leɪnɪəs] *a* (*items*) vario(a); (*selection*) misto(a).

**mischief** ['mɪstʃɪf] *n* (*naughtiness*) birichineria; (*harm*) male *m*, danno; (*maliciousness*) malizia; **mischievous** *a* (*naughty*) birichino(a); (*harmful*) dannoso(a).

**misconception** ['mɪskən'sepʃən] *n* idea sbagliata.

**misconduct** [mɪs'kɒndʌkt] *n* cattiva condotta; **professional** ~ reato professionale.

**misconstrue** [mɪskən'struː] *vt* interpretare male.

**misdeed** [mɪs'diːd] *n* misfatto.

**misdemeanour**, (*US*) **misdemeanor** [mɪsdɪ'miːnə*] *n* misfatto; infrazione *f*.

**miser** ['maɪzə*] *n* avaro.

**miserable** ['mɪzərəbl] *a* infelice; (*wretched*) miserabile.

**miserly** ['maɪzəlɪ] *a* avaro(a).

**misery** ['mɪzərɪ] *n* (*unhappiness*) tristezza; (*pain*) sofferenza; (*wretchedness*) miseria.

**misfire** [mɪs'faɪə*] *vi* far cilecca; (*car engine*) perdere colpi.

**misfit** ['mɪsfɪt] *n* (*person*) spostato/a.

**misfortune** [mɪs'fɔːtʃən] *n* sfortuna.

**misgivings** [mɪs'gɪvɪŋ(z)] *n(pl)* dubbi *mpl*, sospetti *mpl*.

**misguided** [mɪs'gaɪdɪd] *a* sbagliato(a); poco giudizioso(a).

**mishandle** [mɪs'hændl] *vt* (*treat roughly*) maltrattare; (*mismanage*) trattare male.

**mishap** ['mɪshæp] *n* disgrazia.

**misinterpret** [mɪsɪn'təːprɪt] *vt* interpretare male.

**misjudge** [mɪs'dʒʌdʒ] vt giudicare male.

**mislay** [mɪs'leɪ] vt irg smarrire.

**mislead** [mɪs'li:d] vt irg sviare; **~ing** a ingannevole.

**misnomer** [mɪs'nəumə*] n termine m sbagliato or improprio.

**misplace** [mɪs'pleɪs] vt smarrire; collocare fuori posto.

**misprint** ['mɪsprɪnt] n errore m di stampa.

**Miss** [mɪs] n Signorina.

**miss** [mɪs] vt (fail to get) perdere; (regret the absence of): **I ~ him/it** sento la sua mancanza, lui/esso mi manca // vi mancare // n (shot) colpo mancato; **to ~ out** vt (Brit) omettere.

**misshapen** [mɪs'ʃeɪpən] a deforme.

**missile** ['mɪsaɪl] n (AVIAT) missile m; (object thrown) proiettile m.

**missing** ['mɪsɪŋ] a perso(a), smarrito(a); (person) scomparso(a); (: after disaster, MIL) disperso(a); **to be ~** mancare.

**mission** ['mɪʃən] n missione f; **~ary** n missionario/a.

**misspent** ['mɪs'spent] a: **his ~ youth** la sua gioventù sciupata.

**mist** [mɪst] n nebbia, foschia // vi (also: **~ over, ~ up**) annebbiarsi; (: Brit: windows) appannarsi.

**mistake** [mɪs'teɪk] n sbaglio, errore m // vt (irg: like take) sbagliarsi di; fraintendere; **to make a ~** fare uno sbaglio, sbagliare; **by ~** per sbaglio; **to ~ for** prendere per; **~n** a (idea etc) sbagliato(a); **to be ~n** sbagliarsi.

**mister** ['mɪstə*] n (col) signore m; see **Mr.**

**mistletoe** ['mɪsltəu] n vischio.

**mistook** [mɪs'tuk] pt of **mistake**.

**mistress** ['mɪstrɪs] n padrona; (lover) amante f; (Brit SCOL) insegnante f; see **Mrs.**

**mistrust** [mɪs'trʌst] vt diffidare di.

**misty** ['mɪstɪ] a nebbioso(a), brumoso(a).

**misunderstand** [mɪsʌndə'stænd] vt, vi irg capire male, fraintendere; **~ing** n malinteso, equivoco.

**misuse** n [mɪs'ju:s] cattivo uso; (of power) abuso // vt [mɪs'ju:z] far cattivo uso di; abusare di.

**mitigate** ['mɪtɪgeɪt] vt mitigare.

**mitt(en)** ['mɪt(n)] n mezzo guanto; manopola.

**mix** [mɪks] vt mescolare // vi mescolarsi // n mescolanza; preparato; **to ~ up** vt mescolare; (confuse) confondere; **~ed** a misto(a); **~ed grill** n misto alla griglia; **~ed-up** a (confused) confuso(a); **~er** n (for food: electric) frullatore m; (: hand) frullino; (person): **he is a good ~er** è molto socievole; **~ture** n mescolanza; (blend: of tobacco etc) miscela; (MED) sciroppo; **~-up** n confusione f.

**moan** [məun] n gemito // vi gemere; (col: complain): **to ~ (about)** lamentarsi (di); **~ing** n gemiti mpl.

**moat** [məut] n fossato.

**mob** [mɔb] n folla; (disorderly) calca; (pej): **the ~** la plebaglia // vt accalcarsi intorno a.

**mobile** ['məubaɪl] a mobile; **~ home** n grande roulotte f inv (utilizzata come domicilio).

**mock** [mɔk] vt deridere, burlarsi di // a falso(a); **~ery** n derisione f.

**mod** [mɔd] a see **convenience**.

**mode** [məud] n modo.

**model** ['mɔdl] n modello; (person: for fashion) indossatore/trice; (: for artist) modello/a // vt fare l'indossatore (or l'indossatrice) // a (small-scale: railway etc) in miniatura; (child, factory) modello inv; **to ~ clothes** presentare degli abiti.

**modem** ['məudem] n modem m inv.

**moderate** a, n ['mɔdərət] moderato(a) // vb ['mɔdəreɪt] vi moderarsi, placarsi // vt moderare.

**modern** ['mɔdən] a moderno(a); **~ize** vt modernizzare.

**modest** ['mɔdɪst] a modesto(a); **~y**

*n* modestia.

**modicum** ['mɔdɪkəm] *n*: **a ~ of** un minimo di.

**modify** ['mɔdɪfaɪ] *vt* modificare.

**mogul** ['məugl] *n* (*fig*) magnate *m*, pezzo grosso.

**mohair** ['məuheə*] *n* mohair *m*.

**moist** [mɔɪst] *a* umido(a); **~en** ['mɔɪsn] *vt* inumidire; **~ure** ['mɔɪstʃə*] *n* umidità; (*on glass*) goccioline *fpl* di vapore; **~urizer** ['mɔɪstʃəraɪzə*] *n* idratante *f*.

**molar** ['məulə*] *n* molare *m*.

**molasses** [məu'læsɪz] *n* molassa.

**mold** [məuld] *n*, *vt* (*US*) = **mould**.

**mole** [məul] *n* (*animal*) talpa; (*spot*) neo.

**molest** [məu'lɛst] *vt* molestare.

**mollycoddle** ['mɔlɪkɔdl] *vt* coccolare, vezzeggiare.

**molt** [məult] *vi* (*US*) = **moult**.

**molten** ['məultən] *a* fuso(a).

**mom** [mɔm] *n* (*US*) = **mum**.

**moment** ['məumənt] *n* momento, istante *m*; importanza; **at the ~** al momento, in questo momento; **~ary** *a* momentaneo(a), passeggero(a); **~ous** [-'mɛntəs] *a* di grande importanza.

**momentum** [məu'mɛntəm] *n* velocità acquisita, slancio; (*PHYSICS*) momento; **to gather ~** aumentare di velocità.

**mommy** ['mɔmɪ] *n* (*US*) = **mummy**.

**Monaco** ['mɔnəkəu] *n* Principato di Monaco.

**monarch** ['mɔnək] *n* monarca *m*; **~y** *n* monarchia.

**monastery** ['mɔnəstərɪ] *n* monastero.

**monastic** [mə'næstɪk] *a* monastico(a).

**Monday** ['mʌndɪ] *n* lunedì *m inv*.

**monetary** ['mʌnɪtərɪ] *a* monetario(a).

**money** ['mʌnɪ] *n* denaro, soldi *mpl*; **~lender** *n* prestatore *m* di denaro; **~ order** *n* vaglia *m inv*; **~-spinner** *n* (*col*) miniera d'oro (*fig*).

**mongol** ['mɔŋgəl] *a*, *n* (*MED*) mongoloide (*m/f*).

**mongrel** ['mʌŋgrəl] *n* (*dog*) cane *m* bastardo.

**monitor** ['mɔnɪtə*] *n* (*SCOL*) capoclasse *m/f*; (*TV*, *COMPUT*) monitor *m inv* // *vt* controllare.

**monk** [mʌŋk] *n* monaco.

**monkey** ['mʌŋkɪ] *n* scimmia; **~ nut** *n* (*Brit*) nocciolina americana; **~ wrench** *n* chiave *f* a rullino.

**mono...** ['mɔnəu] *prefix*: **~chrome** *a* monocromo(a).

**monopoly** [mə'nɔpəlɪ] *n* monopolio.

**monotone** ['mɔnətəun] *n* pronunzia (*or voce f*) monotona.

**monotonous** [mə'nɔtənəs] *a* monotono(a).

**monsoon** [mɔn'su:n] *n* monsone *m*.

**monster** ['mɔnstə*] *n* mostro.

**monstrous** ['mɔnstrəs] *a* mostruoso(a).

**montage** [mɔn'tɑ:ʒ] *n* montaggio.

**month** [mʌnθ] *n* mese *m*; **~ly** *a* mensile // *ad* al mese; ogni mese // *n* (*magazine*) rivista mensile.

**monument** ['mɔnjumənt] *n* monumento.

**moo** [mu:] *vi* muggire, mugghiare.

**mood** [mu:d] *n* umore *m*; **to be in a good/bad ~** essere di buon/cattivo umore; **~y** *a* (*variable*) capriccioso(a), lunatico(a); (*sullen*) imbronciato(a).

**moon** [mu:n] *n* luna; **~light** *n* chiaro di luna; **~lighting** *n* lavoro nero; **~lit** *a*: **a ~lit night** una notte rischiarata dalla luna.

**moor** [muə*] *n* brughiera // *vt* (*ship*) ormeggiare // *vi* ormeggiarsi.

**moorland** ['muələnd] *n* brughiera.

**moose** [mu:s] *n* (*pl inv*) alce *m*.

**mop** [mɔp] *n* lavapavimenti *m inv*; (*also*: **~ of hair**) zazzera // *vt* lavare con lo straccio; **to ~ up** *vt* asciugare con uno straccio.

**mope** [məup] *vi* fare il broncio.

**moped** ['məupɛd] *n* ciclomotore *m*.

**moral** ['mɔrl] *a* morale // *n* morale *f*; **~s** *npl* moralità.

**morale** [mɔ'rɑːl] n morale m.

**morality** [mə'ræltɪ] n moralità.

**morass** [mə'ræs] n palude f, pantano.

**morbid** ['mɔːbɪd] a morboso(a).

KEYWORD

**more** [mɔː'] ♦ a 1 (greater in number etc) più; ~ people/letters than we expected più persone/ lettere di quante ne aspettavamo; I have ~ wine/money than you ho più vino/soldi di te; I have ~ wine than beer ho più vino che birra 2 (additional) altro(a), ancora; do you want (some) ~ tea? vuole dell'altro tè?, vuole ancora del tè?; I have no ~ / don't have any ~ money non ho più soldi
♦ pronoun 1 (greater amount) (di) più; ~ than 10 più di 10; it cost ~ than we expected ha costato più di quanto ci aspettavamo 2 (further or additional amount) ancora; is there any ~? ce n'è ancora?; there's no ~ non ce n'è più; a little ~ ancora un po'; many/much ~ molti(e)/molto(a) di più
♦ ad: ~ dangerous/easily (than) più pericoloso/facilmente (di); ~ and ~ sempre di più; ~ and ~ difficult sempre più difficile; ~ or less più o meno; ~ than ever più che mai.

**moreover** [mɔː'rəuvə'] ad inoltre, di più.

**morgue** [mɔːg] n obitorio.

**morning** ['mɔːnɪŋ] n mattina, mattino; (duration) mattinata; in the ~ la mattina; 7 o'clock in the ~ le 7 di or della mattina.

**Morocco** [mə'rɔkəu] n Marocco.

**moron** ['mɔːrɔn] n deficiente m/f.

**morose** [mə'rəus] a cupo(a), tetro(a).

**Morse** [mɔːs] n (also: ~ code) alfabeto Morse.

**morsel** ['mɔːsl] n boccone m.

**mortal** ['mɔːtl] a, n mortale (m);

~ity [-'tælɪtɪ] n mortalità.

**mortar** ['mɔːtə'] n (CONSTR) malta; (dish) mortaio.

**mortgage** ['mɔːgɪdʒ] n ipoteca; (loan) prestito ipotecario // vt ipotecare; ~ company n (US) società f inv di credito immobiliare.

**mortified** ['mɔːtɪfaɪd] a umiliato(a).

**mortuary** ['mɔːtjuərɪ] n camera mortuaria; obitorio.

**mosaic** [məu'zeɪɪk] n mosaico.

**Moscow** ['mɔskəu] n Mosca.

**Moslem** ['mɔzləm] a, n = **Muslim**.

**mosque** [mɔsk] n moschea.

**mosquito**, ~es [mɔs'kiːtəu] n zanzara.

**moss** [mɔs] n muschio.

**most** [məust] a la maggior parte di; il più di // pronoun la maggior parte // ad più; (work, sleep etc) di più; (very) molto, estremamente; the ~ (also: + adjective) il(la) più; ~ of la maggior parte di; ~ of them quasi tutti; I saw (the) ~ ho visto più io; at the (very) ~ al massimo; to make the ~ of trarre il massimo vantaggio da; a ~ interesting book un libro estremamente interessante; ~ly ad per lo più.

**MOT** n abbr (Brit: = Ministry of Transport): the ~ (test) revisione annuale obbligatoria degli autoveicoli.

**motel** [məu'tel] n motel m inv.

**moth** [mɔθ] n farfalla notturna; tarma; ~ball n pallina di naftalina.

**mother** ['mʌðə'] n madre f // vt (care for) fare da madre a; ~hood n maternità; ~-in-law n suocera; ~ly a materno(a); ~-of-pearl n madreperla; ~-to-be n futura mamma; ~ tongue n madrelingua.

**motion** ['məuʃən] n movimento, moto; (gesture) gesto; (at meeting) mozione f // vt, vi: to ~ (to) sb to do fare cenno a qn di fare; ~less a immobile; ~ picture n film m inv.

**motivated** ['məutɪveɪtɪd] a motivato(a).

**motive** ['məutɪv] n motivo.

**motley** ['mɔtlɪ] *a* eterogeneo(a), molto vario(a).

**motor** ['məutə*] *n* motore *m*; (*Brit col*: *vehicle*) macchina // *a* motore(trice); ~**bike** *n* moto *f inv*; ~**boat** *n* motoscafo; ~**car** *n* (*Brit*) automobile *f*; ~**cycle** *n* motocicletta; ~**cyclist** *n* motociclista *m/f*; ~**ing** *n* (*Brit*) turismo automobilistico; ~**ist** *n* automobilista *m/f*; ~**racing** *n* (*Brit*) corse *fpl* automobilistiche; ~**way** *n* (*Brit*) autostrada.

**mottled** ['mɔtld] *a* chiazzato(a), marezzato(a).

**motto, ~es** ['mɔtəu] *n* motto.

**mould, (US) mold** [məuld] *n* forma, stampo; (*mildew*) muffa // *vt* formare; (*fig*) foggiare; ~**er** *vi* (*decay*) ammuffire; ~**y** *a* ammuffito(a).

**moult, (US) molt** [məult] *vi* far la muta.

**mound** [maund] *n* rialzo, collinetta.

**mount** [maunt] *n* monte *m*, montagna; (*horse*) cavalcatura; (*for jewel etc*) montatura // *vt* montare; (*horse*) montare a // *vi* salire, montare; (*also*: ~ **up**) aumentare.

**mountain** ['mauntɪn] *n* montagna // *cpd* di montagna; ~**eer** [-'nɪə*] *n* alpinista *m/f*; ~**eering** [-'nɪərɪŋ] *n* alpinismo; ~**ous** *a* montagnoso(a); ~**side** *n* fianco della montagna.

**mourn** [mɔ:n] *vt* piangere, lamentare // *vi*: **to ~ (for sb)** piangere (la morte di qn); ~**er** *n* parente *m/f* or amico/a del defunto; persona venuta a rendere omaggio al defunto; ~**ful** *a* triste, lugubre; ~**ing** *n* lutto // *cpd* (*dress*) da lutto; **in ~ing** in lutto.

**mouse** [maus], *pl* **mice** *n* topo; (*COMPUT*) mouse *m inv*; ~**trap** *n* trappola per i topi.

**mousse** [mu:s] *n* mousse *f inv*.

**moustache** [məs'ta:ʃ] *n* baffi *mpl*.

**mousy** ['mausɪ] *a* (*person*) timido(a); (*hair*) né chiaro(a) né scuro(a).

**mouth, ~s** [mauθ, -ðz] *n* bocca; (*of river*) bocca, foce *f*; (*opening*)

orifizio; ~**ful** *n* boccata; ~ **organ** *n* armonica; ~**piece** *n* (*of musical instrument*) imboccatura, bocchino; (*spokesman*) portavoce *m/f inv*; ~**wash** *n* collutorio; ~**watering** *a* che fa venire l'acquolina in bocca.

**movable** ['mu:vəbl] *a* mobile.

**move** [mu:v] *n* (*movement*) movimento; (*in game*) mossa; (: *turn to play*) turno; (*change of house*) trasloco // *vt* muovere, spostare; (*emotionally*) commuovere; (*POL*: *resolution etc*) proporre // *vi* (*gen*) muoversi, spostarsi; (*traffic*) circolare; (*also*: ~ **house**) cambiar casa, traslocare; **to ~ towards** andare verso; **to ~ sb to do sth** indurre or spingere qn a fare qc; **to get a ~ on** affrettarsi, sbrigarsi; **to ~ about** or **around** *vi* (*fidget*) agitarsi; (*travel*) viaggiare; **to ~ along** *vi* muoversi avanti; **to ~ away** *vi* allontanarsi, andarsene; **to ~ back** *vi* indietreggiare; (*return*) ritornare; **to ~ forward** *vi* avanzare // *vt* avanzare, spostare in avanti; (*people*) far avanzare; **to ~ in** *vi* (*to a house*) entrare (in una nuova casa); **to ~ on** *vi* riprendere la strada // *vt* (*onlookers*) far circolare; **to ~ out** *vi* (*of house*) sgombrare; **to ~ over** *vi* spostarsi; **to ~ up** *vi* avanzare.

**movement** ['mu:vmənt] *n* (*gen*) movimento; (*gesture*) gesto; (*of stars, water, physical*) moto.

**movie** ['mu:vɪ] *n* film *m inv*; **the ~s** il cinema; ~ **camera** *n* cinepresa.

**moving** ['mu:vɪŋ] *a* mobile; (*causing emotion*) commovente.

**mow**, *pt* **mowed**, *pp* **mowed** *or* **mown** [məu, -n] *vt* falciare; (*lawn*) mietere; **to ~ down** *vt* falciare; ~**er** *n* (*also*: **lawnmower**) tagliaerba *m inv*.

**MP** *n abbr* = **Member of Parliament.**

**m.p.h.** *abbr* = **miles per hour** (*m.p.h. = 96 km/h*).

**Mr, Mr.** ['mɪstə*] *n*: ~ **X** Signor X,

Sig. X.

**Mrs, Mrs.** ['mɪsɪz] n: ~ X Signora X, Sig.ra X.

**Ms, Ms.** [mɪz] n (= Miss or Mrs): ~ X ≈ Signora X, Sig.ra X.

**M.Sc.** abbr = **Master of Science**.

**much** [mʌtʃ] a molto(a) // ad, n or pronoun molto; **how ~ is it?** quanto costa?; **too ~** troppo.

**muck** [mʌk] n (mud) fango; (dirt) sporcizia; **to ~ about or around** vi (col) fare lo stupido; (: waste time) gingillarsi; **to ~ up** vt (col: ruin) rovinare.

**mud** [mʌd] n fango.

**muddle** ['mʌdl] n confusione f, disordine m; pasticcio // vt (also: ~ **up**) impasticciare; **to be in a ~** (person) non riuscire a raccapezzarsi; **to ~ through** vi cavarsela alla meno peggio.

**muddy** ['mʌdɪ] a fangoso(a).

**mudguard** ['mʌdgɑ:d] n parafango.

**mudslinging** ['mʌdslɪŋɪŋ] n (fig) denigrazione f.

**muff** [mʌf] n manicotto // vt (shot, catch etc) mancare, sbagliare.

**muffin** ['mʌfɪn] n specie di pasticcino soffice da tè.

**muffle** ['mʌfl] vt (sound) smorzare, attutire; (against cold) imbacuccare.

**muffler** ['mʌflə*] n (US AUT) marmitta; (: on motorbike) silenziatore m.

**mug** [mʌg] n (cup) tazzone m; (for beer) boccale m; (col: face) muso; (: fool) scemo/a // vt (assault) assalire; **~ging** n assalto.

**muggy** ['mʌgɪ] a afoso(a).

**mule** [mju:l] n mulo.

**mull** [mʌl] **: to ~ over** vt rimuginare.

**mulled** [mʌld] a: ~ **wine** vino caldo.

**multi-level** ['mʌltɪlevl] a (US) = **multistorey**.

**multiple** ['mʌltɪpl] a multiplo(a); molteplice // n multiplo; ~ **sclerosis** n sclerosi f a placche.

**multiplication** [mʌltɪplɪ'keɪʃən] n moltiplicazione f.

**multiply** ['mʌltɪplaɪ] vt moltiplicare

// vi moltiplicarsi.

**multistorey** ['mʌltɪ'stɔ:rɪ] a (Brit: building, car park) a più piani.

**mum** [mʌm] n (Brit) mamma // a: **to keep ~** non aprire bocca.

**mumble** ['mʌmbl] vt, vi borbottare.

**mummy** ['mʌmɪ] n (Brit: mother) mamma; (embalmed) mummia.

**mumps** [mʌmps] n orecchioni mpl.

**munch** [mʌntʃ] vt, vi sgranocchiare.

**mundane** [mʌn'deɪn] a terra a terra inv.

**municipal** [mju:'nɪsɪpl] a municipale; **~ity** [-'pælɪtɪ] n municipio.

**mural** ['mjuərl] n dipinto murale.

**murder** ['mə:də*] n assassinio, omicidio // vt assassinare; **~er** n omicida m, assassino; **~ous** a micidiale.

**murky** ['mə:kɪ] a tenebroso(a), buio(a).

**murmur** ['mə:mə*] n mormorio // vt, vi mormorare.

**muscle** ['mʌsl] n muscolo; **to ~ in** vi immischiarsi.

**muscular** ['mʌskjulə*] a muscolare; (person, arm) muscoloso(a).

**muse** [mju:z] vi meditare, sognare // n musa.

**museum** [mju:'zɪəm] n museo.

**mushroom** ['mʌʃrum] n fungo.

**music** ['mju:zɪk] n musica; **~al** a musicale // n (show) commedia musicale; **~al box** n carillon m inv; **~al instrument** n strumento musicale; **~ hall** n teatro di varietà; **~ian** [-'zɪʃən] n musicista m/f.

**musk** [mʌsk] n muschio.

**Muslim** ['mʌzlɪm] a, n musulmano(a).

**muslin** ['mʌzlɪn] n mussola.

**mussel** ['mʌsl] n cozza.

**must** [mʌst] auxiliary vb (obligation): **I ~ do it** devo farlo; (probability): **he ~ be there by now** dovrebbe essere arrivato ormai; **I ~ have made a mistake** devo essermi sbagliato // n cosa da non mancare; cosa d'obbligo.

**mustard** ['mʌstəd] n senape f, mostarda.

**muster** ['mʌstə*] vt radunare.

**mustn't** ['mʌsnt] = **must not**.

**musty** ['mʌstɪ] a che sa di muffa or di rinchiuso.

**mutation** [mju:'teɪʃən] n mutazione f.

**mute** [mju:t] a, n muto(a).

**muted** ['mju:tɪd] a (noise) attutito(a), smorzato(a); (criticism) attenuato(a).

**mutiny** ['mju:tɪnɪ] n ammutinamento.

**mutter** ['mʌtə*] vt, vi borbottare, brontolare.

**mutton** ['mʌtn] n carne f di montone.

**mutual** ['mju:tʃuəl] a mutuo(a), reciproco(a).

**muzzle** ['mʌzl] n muso; (protective device) museruola; (of gun) bocca // vt mettere la museruola a.

**my** [maɪ] a il(la) mio(a), pl i(le) miei(mie); ~ **house** la mia casa; ~ **books** i miei libri; ~ **brother** mio fratello; **I've washed** ~ **hair/cut** ~ **finger** mi sono lavato i capelli/ tagliato il dito.

**myself** [maɪ'sɛlf] pronoun (reflexive) mi; (emphatic) io stesso(a); (after prep) me; see also **oneself**.

**mysterious** [mɪs'tɪərɪəs] a misterioso(a).

**mystery** ['mɪstərɪ] n mistero.

**mystify** ['mɪstɪfaɪ] vt mistificare; (puzzle) confondere.

**mystique** [mɪs'ti:k] n fascino.

**myth** [mɪθ] n mito; ~**ology** [mɪ'θɔlədʒɪ] n mitologia.

# N

**n/a** abbr = not applicable.

**nab** [næb] vt (col) beccare, acchiappare.

**nag** [næg] n (pej: horse) ronzino; (: person) brontolone/a // vt tormentare // vi brontolare in continuazione;

~**ging** a (doubt, pain) persistente.

**nail** [neɪl] n (human) unghia; (metal) chiodo // vt inchiodare; **to** ~ **sb down to a date/price** costringere qn a un appuntamento/ad accettare un prezzo; ~**brush** n spazzolino da or per unghie; ~**file** n lima da or per unghie; ~ **polish** n smalto da or per unghie; ~ **polish remover** n acetone m, solvente m; ~ **scissors** npl forbici fpl da or per unghie; ~ **varnish** n (Brit) = ~ **polish**.

**naïve** [naɪ'i:v] a ingenuo(a).

**naked** ['neɪkɪd] a nudo(a).

**name** [neɪm] n nome m; (reputation) nome, reputazione f // vt (baby etc) chiamare; (plant, illness) nominare; (person, object) identificare; (price, date) fissare; **by** ~ di nome; **she knows them all by** ~ li conosce tutti per nome; ~**less** a senza nome; ~**ly** ad cioè; ~**sake** n omonimo.

**nanny** ['nænɪ] n bambinaia.

**nap** [næp] n (sleep) pisolino; (of cloth) peluria; **to be caught** ~**ping** essere preso alla sprovvista.

**nape** [neɪp] n: ~ **of the neck** nuca.

**napkin** ['næpkɪn] n (also: table ~) tovagliolo.

**nappy** ['næpɪ] n (Brit) pannolino; ~ **rash** n arrossamento (causato dal pannolino).

**narcissus**, pl **narcissi** [nɑː'sɪsəs, -saɪ] n narciso.

**narcotic** [nɑː'kɔtɪk] n narcotico // a narcotico(a).

**narrative** ['nærətɪv] n narrativa // a narrativo(a).

**narrow** ['nærəu] a stretto(a); (fig) limitato(a), ristretto(a) // vi restringersi; **to have a** ~ **escape** farcela per un pelo; **to** ~ **sth down to** ridurre qc a q; ~**ly** ad per un pelo; (time) per poco; ~**-minded** a meschino(a).

**nasty** ['nɑ:stɪ] a (person, remark) cattivo(a); (smell, wound, situation) brutto(a).

**nation** ['neɪʃən] n nazione f.

**national** ['næʃənl] a nazionale // n

cittadino/a; ~ **dress** n costume m nazionale; **N~ Health Service (NHS)** n (Brit) servizio nazionale di assistenza sanitaria, = S.A.U.B. f; **N~ Insurance** n (Brit) Previdenza Sociale; **~ism** n nazionalismo; **~ist** [-'næliti] n nazionalità f inv; **~ize** vt nazionalizzare; **~ly** ad a livello nazionale.

**nation-wide** ['neɪʃənwaɪd] a diffuso/a in tutto il paese // ad in tutto il paese.

**native** ['neɪtɪv] n abitante m/f del paese; (in colonies) indigeno/a // a indigeno(a); (country) natio(a); (ability) innato(a); **a ~ of Russia** un nativo della Russia; **a ~ speaker of French** una persona di madrelingua francese; **~ language** n madrelingua.

**NATO** ['neɪtəu] n abbr (= North Atlantic Treaty Organization) N.A.T.O. f.

**natural** ['nætʃrəl] a naturale; (ability) innato(a); (manner) semplice; **~ gas** n gas m metano; **~ize** vt naturalizzare; **to become ~ized** (person) naturalizzarsi; **~ly** ad naturalmente; (by nature: gifted) di natura.

**nature** ['neɪtʃə*] n natura; (character) natura, indole f; **by ~** di natura.

**naught** [nɔ:t] n = **nought.**

**naughty** ['nɔ:tɪ] a (child) birichino(a), cattivello(a); (story, film) spinto(a).

**nausea** ['nɔ:sɪə] n (MED) nausea; (fig: disgust) schifo; **~te** ['nɔ:sɪeɪt] vt nauseare; far schifo a.

**nautical** ['nɔ:tɪkl] a nautico(a).

**naval** ['neɪvl] a navale; **~ officer** n ufficiale m di marina.

**nave** [neɪv] n navata centrale.

**navel** ['neɪvl] n ombelico.

**navigate** ['nævɪgeɪt] vt percorrere navigando // vi navigare; (AUT) fare da navigatore; **navigation** [-'geɪʃən] n navigazione f; **navigator** n

(NAUT, AVIAT) ufficiale m di rotta; (explorer) navigatore m; (AUT) copilota m/f.

**navvy** ['nævɪ] n (Brit) manovale m.

**navy** ['neɪvɪ] n marina; **~(-blue)** a blu scuro inv.

**Nazi** ['nɑ:tsɪ] n nazista m/f.

**NB** abbr (= nota bene) N.B.

**near** [nɪə*] a vicino(a); (relation) prossimo(a) // ad vicino // prep (also: **~ to**) vicino a, presso; (: time) verso // vt avvicinarsi a; **~by** [nɪə'baɪ] a vicino(a) // ad vicino; **~ly** ad quasi; **I ~ly fell** per poco non sono caduto; **~ miss** n: **that was a ~ miss** c'è mancato poco; **~side** n (AUT: in Britain) lato sinistro; (: in Italy etc) lato destro; **~-sighted** a miope.

**neat** [ni:t] a (person, room) ordinato(a); (work) pulito(a); (solution, plan) ben indovinato(a); azzeccato(a); (spirits) liscio(a); **~ly** ad con ordine; (skilfully) abilmente.

**necessarily** ['nɛsɪsrɪlɪ] ad necessariamente.

**necessary** ['nɛsɪsrɪ] a necessario(a).

**necessity** [nɪ'sɛsɪtɪ] n necessità f inv.

**neck** [nɛk] n collo; (of garment) colletto // vi (col) pomiciare, sbaciucchiarsi; **~ and ~** testa a testa.

**necklace** ['nɛklɪs] n collana.

**neckline** ['nɛklaɪn] n scollatura.

**necktie** ['nɛktaɪ] n cravatta.

**née** [neɪ] a: ~ Scott nata Scott.

**need** [ni:d] n bisogno // vt aver bisogno di; **to ~ to do** dover fare; aver bisogno di fare; **you don't ~ to go** non devi andare, non c'è bisogno che tu vada.

**needle** ['ni:dl] n ago // vt punzecchiare.

**needless** ['ni:dlɪs] a inutile.

**needlework** ['ni:dlwə:k] n cucito.

**needn't** ['ni:dnt] = **need not.**

**needy** ['ni:dɪ] a bisognoso(a).

**negative** ['nɛgətɪv] n (answer) risposta negativa; (LING) negazione f; (PHOT) negativo // a negativo(a).

**neglect** [nɪˈglɛkt] vt trascurare // n (of person, duty) negligenza; state of ~ stato di abbandono.

**negligee** [ˈnɛglɪʒeɪ] n négligé m inv.

**negligence** [ˈnɛglɪdʒəns] n negligenza.

**negligible** [ˈnɛglɪdʒɪbl] a insignificante, trascurabile.

**negotiate** [nɪˈgəʊʃɪeɪt] vi: to ~ (with) negoziare (con) // vt (COMM) negoziare; (obstacle) superare; **negotiation** [-ˈeɪʃən] n negoziato, trattativa.

**Negro** [ˈniːgrəʊ] a, n (pl ~es) negro(a).

**neigh** [neɪ] vi nitrire.

**neighbour**, (US) **neighbor** [ˈneɪbə*] n vicino/a; **~hood** n vicinato; **~ing** a vicino(a); **~ly** a: he is a **~ly** person è un buon vicino.

**neither** [ˈnaɪðə*] a, pronoun né l'uno(a) né l'altro(a), nessuno(a) dei(delle) due // cj neanche, nemmeno, neppure // ad: ~ **good nor bad** né buono né cattivo; **I didn't move** and ~ **did Claude** io non mi mossi e nemmeno Claude; ..., ~ **did I refuse** ..., ma non ho nemmeno rifiutato.

**neon** [ˈniːɔn] n neon m; ~ **light** n luce f al neon.

**nephew** [ˈnɛvjuː] n nipote m.

**nerve** [nɜːv] n nervo; (fig) coraggio; (impudence) faccia tosca; a **fit of** ~s una crisi di nervi; **~-racking** a che spezza i nervi.

**nervous** [ˈnɜːvəs] a nervoso(a); (anxious) agitato(a), in apprensione; ~ **breakdown** n esaurimento nervoso.

**nest** [nɛst] n nido // vi fare il nido, nidificare; ~ **egg** n (fig) gruzzolo.

**nestle** [ˈnɛsl] vi accoccolarsi.

**net** [nɛt] n rete f // a netto(a) // vt (fish etc) prendere con la rete; (profit) ricavare un utile netto di; **~ball** n specie di pallacanestro; **~curtains** npl tende fpl di tulle.

**Netherlands** [ˈnɛðələndz] npl: the ~ i Paesi Bassi.

**nett** [nɛt] a = **net**.

**netting** [ˈnɛtɪŋ] n (for fence etc) reticolato.

**nettle** [ˈnɛtl] n ortica.

**network** [ˈnɛtwɜːk] n rete f.

**neurotic** [njʊəˈrɔtɪk] a, n nevrotico(a).

**neuter** [ˈnjuːtə*] a neutro(a) // n neutro // vt (cat etc) castrare.

**neutral** [ˈnjuːtrəl] a neutro(a); (person, nation) neutrale // n (AUT): **in** ~ in folle; **~ize** vt neutralizzare.

**never** [ˈnɛvə*] ad (non...) mai; ~ **again** mai più; **I'll** ~ **go there again** non ci vado più; ~ **in my life** mai in vita mia; see also **mind**; **~-ending** a interminabile; **~theless** [nɛvəðəˈlɛs] ad tuttavia, ciò nonostante, ciò nondimeno.

**new** [njuː] a nuovo(a); (brand new) nuovo(a) di zecca; **~-born** a neonato(a); **~-comer** [ˈnjuːkʌmə*] n nuovo(a) venuto(a); **~-fangled** [ˈnjuːfæŋgld] a (pej) stramoderno(a); **~-found** a (fig) nuovo(a); **~ly** ad di recente; **~ly-weds** npl sposini mpl, sposi novelli.

**news** [njuːz] n notizie fpl; (RADIO) giornale m radio; (TV) telegiornale m; a **piece of** ~ una notizia; ~ **agency** n agenzia di stampa; **~agent** n (Brit) giornalaio; **~caster** n (RADIO, TV) annunciatore/trice; **~dealer** n (US) = **~agent**; ~ **flash** n notizia f lampo inv; **~letter** n bollettino; **~paper** n giornale m; **~print** n carta da giornale; **~reader** n **~caster**; **~reel** n cinegiornale m; ~ **stand** n edicola.

**newt** [njuːt] n tritone m.

**New Year** n Anno Nuovo; **~'s Day** n il Capodanno; **~'s Eve** n la vigilia di Capodanno.

**New Zealand** [-ˈziːlənd] n Nuova Zelanda; **~er** n neozelandese m/f.

**next** [nɛkst] a prossimo(a) // ad accanto; (in time) dopo; **the** ~ **day** il giorno dopo, l'indomani; ~ **year**

l'anno prossimo; **when do we meet ~?** quando ci rincontriamo?; **~ door** ad accanto; **~-of-kin** n parente m/f prossimo(a); **~ to** prep accanto a; **~ to nothing** quasi niente.

**NHS** n abbr = **National Health Service**.

**nib** [nɪb] n (of pen) pennino.

**nibble** ['nɪbl] vt mordicchiare.

**Nicaragua** [nɪkə'rægjuə] n Nicaragua m.

**nice** [naɪs] a (holiday, trip) piacevole; (flat, picture) bello(a); (person) simpatico(a), gentile; (distinction, point) sottile; **~-looking** a bello(a); **~ly** ad bene.

**niceties** ['naɪsɪtɪz] npl finezze fpl.

**niche** [niːʃ] n nicchia; (fig): **to find a ~ for o.s.** trovare la propria strada.

**nick** [nɪk] n tacca // vt (col) rubare; **in the ~ of time** appena in tempo.

**nickel** ['nɪkl] n nichel m; (US) moneta da cinque centesimi di dollaro.

**nickname** ['nɪkneɪm] n soprannome m // vt soprannominare.

**niece** [niːs] n nipote f.

**Nigeria** [naɪ'dʒɪərɪə] n Nigeria m.

**nigger** ['nɪɡə*] n (col!: highly offensive) negro/a.

**niggling** ['nɪɡlɪŋ] a pignolo(a).

**night** [naɪt] n notte f; (evening) sera; **at ~** la sera; **by ~** di notte; **the ~ before last** l'altro ieri notte (or sera); **~cap** n bicchierino prima di andare a letto; **~ club** n locale m notturno; **~dress** n camicia da notte; **~fall** n crepuscolo; **~gown** n, **~ie** ['naɪtɪ] n camicia da notte.

**nightingale** ['naɪtɪŋɡeɪl] n usignolo.

**night life** n vita notturna.

**nightly** ['naɪtlɪ] a di ogni notte or sera; (by night) notturno(a) // ad ogni notte or sera.

**nightmare** ['naɪtmɛə*] n incubo.

**night: ~ porter** n portiere m di notte; **~ school** n scuola serale; **~ shift** n turno di notte; **~-time** n

notte f.

**nil** [nɪl] n nulla m; (Brit SPORT) zero.

**Nile** [naɪl] n: **the ~** il Nilo.

**nimble** ['nɪmbl] a agile.

**nine** [naɪn] num nove; **~teen** num diciannove; **~ty** num novanta.

**ninth** [naɪnθ] a nono(a).

**nip** [nɪp] vt pizzicare.

**nipple** ['nɪpl] n (ANAT) capezzolo.

**nitrogen** ['naɪtrədʒən] n azoto.

---

**KEYWORD**

**no** [nəʊ] ♦ ad (opposite of "yes") no; **are you coming? — ~ (I'm not)** viene? — no (non vengo); **would you like some more? — ~ thank you** ne vuole ancora un po'? — no, grazie

♦ a (not any) nessuno(a); **I have ~ money/time/books** non ho soldi/tempo/libri; **~ student would have done it** nessuno studente lo avrebbe fatto; **"~ parking"** "divieto di sosta"; **"~ smoking"** "vietato fumare"

♦ n (pl **~es**) no m inv.

**nobility** [nəʊ'bɪlɪtɪ] n nobiltà.

**noble** ['nəʊbl] a, n nobile (m).

**nobody** ['nəʊbədɪ] pronoun nessuno.

**nod** [nɒd] vi accennare col capo, fare un cenno; (sleep) sonnecchiare // vt: **to ~ one's head** fare di sì col capo // n cenno; **to ~ off** vi assopirsi.

**noise** [nɔɪz] n rumore m; (din, racket) chiasso; **noisy** a (street, car) rumoroso(a); (person) chiassoso(a).

**no man's land** ['nəʊmænzlænd] n terra di nessuno.

**nominal** ['nɒmɪnl] a nominale.

**nominate** ['nɒmɪneɪt] vt (propose) proporre come candidato; (elect) nominare.

**nominee** [nɒmɪ'niː] n persona nominata; candidato/a.

**non...** [nɒn] prefix non...; **~ alcoholic** a analcolico(a); **~ committal** ['nɒnkə'mɪtl] a evasivo(a).

**nondescript** ['nɔndɪskrɪpt] *a* qualunque *inv*.

**none** [nʌn] *pronoun* (*not one thing*) niente; (*not one person*) nessuno(a); ~ of you nessuno(a) di voi; I've ~ left non ne ho più; he's ~ the worse for it non ne ha risentito.

**nonentity** [nɔ'nentɪtɪ] *n* persona insignificante.

**nonetheless** [nʌnðə'les] *ad* nondimeno.

**non**: ~-**existent** *a* inesistente; ~-**fiction** *n* saggistica.

**nonplussed** [nɔn'plʌst] *a* sconcertato(a).

**nonsense** ['nɔnsəns] *n* sciocchezze *fpl*.

**non**: ~-**smoker** *n* non fumatore/trice; ~-**stick** *a* antiaderente, antiadesivo(a); ~-**stop** *a* continuo(a); (*train, bus*) direttissimo(a) // *ad* senza sosta.

**noodles** ['nu:dlz] *npl* taglierini *mpl*.

**nook** [nuk] *n*: ~**s and crannies** angoli *mpl*.

**noon** [nu:n] *n* mezzogiorno.

**no one** ['nəuwʌn] *pronoun* = **nobody**.

**noose** [nu:s] *n* nodo scorsoio; (*hangman's*) cappio.

**nor** [nɔ:*] *cj* = **neither** // *ad see* **neither**.

**norm** [nɔ:m] *n* norma.

**normal** ['nɔ:ml] *a* normale; ~-**ly** *ad* normalmente.

**north** [nɔ:θ] *n* nord *m*, settentrione *m* // *a* nord *inv*, del nord, settentrionale // *ad* verso nord; **N~ America** *n* America del Nord; ~-**east** *n* nord-est *m*; ~-**erly** ['nɔ:ðəlɪ] *a* (*point, direction*) verso nord; ~-**ern** ['nɔ:ðən] *a* del nord, settentrionale; **N~ Ireland** *n* Irlanda del Nord; **N~ Pole** *n* Polo Nord; **N~ Sea** *n* Mare *m* del Nord; ~-**ward(s)** ['nɔ:θwəd(z)] *ad* verso nord; ~-**west** *n* nord-ovest *m*.

**Norway** ['nɔ:weɪ] *n* Norvegia.

**Norwegian** [nɔ:'wi:dʒən] *a* norvegese // *n* norvegese *m/f*; (*LING*)

norvegese *m*.

**nose** [nəuz] *n* naso; (*of animal*) muso // *vi*: to ~ **about** aggirarsi; ~-**bleed** *n* emorragia nasale; ~-**dive** *n* picchiata; ~-**y** *a* = **nosy**.

**nostalgia** [nɔs'tældʒɪə] *n* nostalgia.

**nostril** ['nɔstrɪl] *n* narice *f*; (*of horse*) frogia.

**nosy** ['nəuzɪ] *a* curioso(a).

**not** [nɔt] *ad* non; he is ~ *or* isn't here non è qui, non c'è; you must ~ *or* you mustn't do that non devi fare quello; it's too late, isn't it *or* is it ~? è troppo tardi, vero?; ~ that I don't like him non che (lui) non mi piaccia; ~ **yet/now** non ancora/ora; *see also* **all, only**.

**notably** ['nəutəblɪ] *ad* (*markedly*) notevolmente; (*particularly*) in particolare.

**notary** ['nəutərɪ] *n* (*also*: ~ **public**) notaio.

**notch** [nɔtʃ] *n* tacca.

**note** [nəut] *n* nota; (*letter, banknote*) biglietto // *vt* (*also*: ~ **down**) prendere nota di; to take ~**s** prendere appunti; ~-**book** *n* taccuino; ~-**d** ['nəutɪd] *a* celebre; ~-**pad** *n* bloc-notes *m inv*; ~-**paper** *n* carta da lettere.

**nothing** ['nʌθɪŋ] *n* nulla *m*, niente *m*; (*zero*) zero; he does ~ non fa niente; ~ **new** niente di nuovo; for ~ per niente.

**notice** ['nəutɪs] *n* avviso; (*of leaving*) preavviso // *vt* notare, accorgersi di; to take ~ of fare attenzione a; to bring sth to sb's ~ far notare qc a qn; at short ~ con un breve preavviso; until further ~ fino a nuovo avviso; to hand in one's ~ licenziarsi; ~-**able** *a* evidente; ~-**board** *n* (*Brit*) tabellone *m* per affissi.

**notify** ['nəutɪfaɪ] *vt*: to ~ sth to sb far sapere qc a qn; to ~ sb of sth avvisare qn di qc.

**notion** ['nəuʃən] *n* idea; (*concept*) nozione *f*.

**notorious** [nəu'tɔ:rɪəs] *a*

famigerato(a).

**notwithstanding** [nɒtwɪθ'stændɪŋ] ad nondimeno // prep nonostante, malgrado.

**nougat** ['nuːgɑː] n torrone m.

**nought** [nɔːt] n zero.

**noun** [naun] n nome m, sostantivo.

**nourish** ['nʌrɪʃ] vt nutrire; ~ing a nutriente; ~ment n nutrimento.

**novel** ['nɒvl] n romanzo // a nuovo(a); ~ist n romanziere/a; ~ty n novità f inv.

**November** [nəʊ'vɛmbə*] n novembre m.

**novice** ['nɒvɪs] n principiante m/f; (REL) novizio/a.

**now** [nau] ad ora, adesso // cj: ~ (that) adesso che, ora che; by ~ ormai; just ~ proprio ora; right ~ subito, immediatamente; ~ and then, ~ and again ogni tanto; from ~ on da ora in poi; ~adays ['nauədeɪz] ad oggidì.

**nowhere** ['nəʊwɛə*] ad in nessun luogo, da nessuna parte.

**nozzle** ['nɒzl] n (of hose etc) boccaglio; (of fire extinguisher) lancia.

**nuance** ['njuːɑːns] n sfumatura.

**nuclear** ['njuːklɪə*] a nucleare.

**nucleus**, pl **nuclei** ['njuːklɪəs, 'njuːklɪaɪ] n nucleo.

**nude** [njuːd] a nudo(a) // n (ART) nudo; in the ~ tutto(a) nudo(a).

**nudge** [nʌdʒ] vt dare una gomitata a.

**nudist** ['njuːdɪst] n nudista m/f.

**nuisance** ['njuːsns] n: it's a ~ è una seccatura; he's a ~ è uno scocciatore; what a ~! che seccatura!

**null** [nʌl] a: ~ and void nullo(a).

**numb** [nʌm] a intorpidito(a); ~ with cold intirizzito(a) (dal freddo).

**number** ['nʌmbə*] n numero // vt numerare; (include) contare; a ~ of un certo numero di; to be ~ed among venire annoverato(a) tra; they were 10 in ~ erano in tutto 10; ~ plate n (Brit AUT) targa.

**numeral** ['njuːmərəl] n numero, ci-

fra.

**numerate** ['njuːmərɪt] a: to be ~ avere nozioni di aritmetica.

**numerical** [njuː'mɛrɪkl] a numerico(a).

**numerous** ['njuːmərəs] a numeroso(a).

**nun** [nʌn] n suora, monaca.

**nurse** [nɜːs] n infermiere/a // vt (patient, cold) curare; (baby: Brit) cullare; (: US) allattare, dare il latte a; (hope) nutrire.

**nursery** ['nɜːsərɪ] n (room) camera dei bambini; (institution) asilo; (for plants) vivaio; ~ rhyme n filastrocca; ~ school n scuola materna; ~ slope n (Brit SKI) pista per principianti.

**nursing** ['nɜːsɪŋ] n (profession) professione f di infermiere (or di infermiera); ~ home n casa di cura.

**nurture** ['nɜːtʃə*] vt allevare; nutrire.

**nut** [nʌt] n (of metal) dado; (fruit) noce f; he's ~s (col) è matto; ~crackers npl schiaccianoci m inv.

**nutmeg** ['nʌtmɛg] n noce f moscata.

**nutritious** [njuː'trɪʃəs] a nutriente.

**nutshell** ['nʌtʃɛl] n guscio di noce; in a ~ in poche parole.

**nylon** ['naɪlɒn] n nailon m // a di nailon.

**nymph** [nɪmf] n ninfa.

# O

**oak** [əʊk] n quercia // a di quercia.

**O.A.P.** abbr = old age pensioner.

**oar** [ɔː*] n remo.

**oasis**, pl **oases** [əʊ'eɪsɪs] n oasi f inv.

**oath** [əʊθ] n giuramento; (swear word) bestemmia.

**oatmeal** ['əʊtmiːl] n farina d'avena.

**oats** [əʊts] npl avena.

**obedience** [ə'biːdɪəns] n ubbidienza.

**obedient** [ə'biːdɪənt] a ubbidiente.

**obey** [ə'beɪ] vt ubbidire a; (instructions, regulations) osservare // vi ubbidire.

**obituary** [ə'bɪtjuərɪ] n necrologia.

**object** n ['ɔbdʒɪkt] oggetto; (purpose) scopo, intento; (LING) complemento oggetto // vi [əb'dʒɛkt]: to ~ to (attitude) disapprovare; (proposal) protestare contro, sollevare delle obiezioni contro; expense is no ~ non si bada a spese; I ~! mi oppongo!; he ~ed that ... obiettò che ...; ~ion [əb'dʒɛkʃən] n obiezione f; (drawback) inconveniente m; ~ionable [əb'dʒɛkʃənəbl] a antipatico(a); (smell) sgradevole; (language) scostumato(a); ~ive n obiettivo // a obiettivo(a).

**obligation** [ɔblɪ'geɪʃən] n obbligo, dovere m; (debt) obbligo (di riconoscenza); without ~ senza impegno.

**oblige** [ə'blaɪdʒ] vt (force): to ~ sb to do costringere qn a fare; (do a favour) fare una cortesia a; to be ~d to sb for sth essere grato a qn per qc; **obliging** a servizievole, compiacente.

**oblique** [ə'bliːk] a obliquo(a); (allusion) indiretto(a).

**obliterate** [ə'blɪtəreɪt] vt cancellare.

**oblivion** [ə'blɪvɪən] n oblio.

**oblivious** [ə'blɪvɪəs] a: ~ of incurante di; inconscio(a) di.

**oblong** ['ɔblɔŋ] a oblungo(a) // n rettangolo.

**obnoxious** [əb'nɔkʃəs] a odioso(a); (smell) disgustoso(a), ripugnante.

**oboe** ['əubəu] n oboe m.

**obscene** [əb'siːn] a osceno(a).

**obscure** [əb'skjuə*] a oscuro(a) // vt oscurare; (hide: sun) nascondere.

**observant** [əb'zə:vnt] a attento(a).

**observation** [ɔbzə'veɪʃən] n osservazione f; (by police etc) sorveglianza.

**observatory** [əb'zə:vətrɪ] n osservatorio.

**observe** [əb'zə:v] vt osservare; (remark) fare osservare; ~r n osservatore/trice.

**obsess** [əb'sɛs] vt ossessionare;

~ive a ossessivo(a).

**obsolescence** [ɔbsə'lɛsns] n obsolescenza.

**obsolete** ['ɔbsəliːt] a obsoleto(a); (word) desueto(a).

**obstacle** ['ɔbstəkl] n ostacolo.

**obstinate** ['ɔbstɪnɪt] a ostinato(a).

**obstruct** [əb'strʌkt] vt (block) ostruire, ostacolare; (halt) fermare; (hinder) impedire.

**obtain** [əb'teɪn] vt ottenere // vi essere in uso; ~able a ottenibile.

**obtrusive** [əb'truːsɪv] a (person) importuno(a), (smell) invadente; (building etc) imponente e invadente.

**obtuse** [əb'tjuːs] a ottuso(a).

**obvious** ['ɔbvɪəs] a ovvio(a), evidente; ~ly ad ovviamente; certo.

**occasion** [ə'keɪʒən] n occasione f; (event) avvenimento // vt cagionare; ~al a occasionale; ~ally ad ogni tanto.

**occupation** [ɔkju'peɪʃən] n occupazione f; (job) mestiere m, professione f; ~al hazard n rischio del mestiere.

**occupier** ['ɔkjupaɪə*] n occupante m/f.

**occupy** ['ɔkjupaɪ] vt occupare; to ~ o.s. with or by doing occuparsi a fare.

**occur** [ə'kə:*] vi accadere; (difficulty, opportunity) capitare; (phenomenon, error) trovarsi; to ~ to sb venire in mente a qn; ~rence n caso, fatto; presenza.

**ocean** ['əuʃən] n oceano; ~-going a d'alto mare.

**o'clock** [ə'klɔk] ad: it is 5 ~ sono le 5.

**OCR** n abbr = optical character recognition/reader.

**octave** ['ɔktɪv] n ottavo.

**October** [ɔk'təubə*] n ottobre m.

**octopus** ['ɔktəpəs] n polpo, piovra.

**odd** [ɔd] a (strange) strano(a), bizzarro(a); (number) dispari inv; (left over) in più; (not of a set) spaiato(a); 60~ 60 e oltre; at ~ times di tanto in tanto; the ~ one

out l'eccezione f; ~s and ends npl
avanzi mpl; ~ity n bizzarria;
(person) originale m; ~ jobs npl
lavori mpl occasionali; ~ly ad
stranamente; ~ments npl (COMM)
rimanenze fpl; ~s npl (in betting)
quota; it makes no ~s non importa;
at ~s in contesa.

**odometer** [ɔ'dɔmitə*] n odometro.

**odour**, (US) **odor** ['əudə*] n odore
m.

---
KEYWORD
---

**of** [ɔv, əv] prep 1 (gen) di; a boy ~
10 un ragazzo di 10 anni; a friend ~
ours un nostro amico; that was
kind ~ you è stato molto gentile da
parte sua
2 (expressing quantity, amount,
dates etc) di; a kilo ~ flour un chilo
di farina; how much ~ this do you
need? quanto gliene serve?; there
were 3 ~ them (people) erano in 3;
(objects) ce n'erano 3; 3 ~ us went
3 di noi sono andati; the 5th ~ July
il 5 luglio
3 (from, out of) di, in; made ~
wood (fatto) di or in legno.

**off** [ɔf] a, ad (engine) spento(a);
(tap) chiuso(a); (Brit: food: bad)
andato(a) a male; (absent) assente;
(cancelled) sospeso(a) // prep da; a
poca distanza di; to be ~ (to leave)
partire, andarsene; to be ~ sick
essere assente per malattia; a day
~ un giorno di vacanza; to have an
~ day non essere in forma; he had
his coat ~ si era tolto il cappotto;
10% ~ (COMM) con uno sconto di
10%; ~ the coast al largo della costa; I'm ~ meat la carne non mi va
più; (no longer eat it) non mangio
più la carne; on the ~ chance a
caso.

**offal** ['ɔfl] n (CULIN) frattaglie fpl.

**offbeat** ['ɔfbiːt] a eccentrico(a).

**off-colour** ['ɔf'kʌlə*] a (Brit: ill)
malato(a), indisposto(a).

**offence**, (US) **offense** [ə'fɛns] n

(LAW) contravvenzione f; (: more
serious) reato; to take ~ at
offendersi per.

**offend** [ə'fɛnd] vt (person)
offendere; ~er n delinquente m/f;
(against regulations) contravventore/
trice.

**offensive** [ə'fɛnsiv] a offensivo(a);
(smell etc) sgradevole, ripugnante //
n (MIL) offensiva.

**offer** ['ɔfə*] n offerta, proposta // vt
offrire; "on ~" (COMM) "in offerta
speciale"; ~ing n offerta.

**offhand** [ɔf'hænd] a disinvolto(a),
noncurante // ad all'improvviso.

**office** ['ɔfis] n (place) ufficio;
(position) carica; doctor's ~ (US)
studio; to take ~ entrare in carica;
~ automation n automazione f
d'ufficio; burotica; ~ block, (US) ~
building n complesso di uffici; ~
hours npl orario d'ufficio; (US
MED) orario di visite.

**officer** ['ɔfisə*] n (MIL etc) ufficiale
m; (of organization) funzionario
m; (also: police ~) agente m di polizia.

**office worker** n impiegato/a
d'ufficio.

**official** [ə'fiʃl] a (authorized) ufficiale
// n ufficiale m; (civil servant)
impiegato/a statale; funzionario;
~dom n burocrazia.

**officiate** [ə'fiʃieit] vi presenziare; to
~ at a marriage celebrare un matrimonio.

**officious** [ə'fiʃəs] a invadente.

**offing** ['ɔfiŋ] n: in the ~ (fig) in vista.

**off**: ~-licence n (Brit: shop) spaccio
di bevande alcoliche; ~-line a, ad
(COMPUT) off-line inv, fuori linea; (:
switched off) spento(a); ~-peak a
(ticket etc) a tariffa ridotta; (time)
non di punta; ~-putting a (Brit)
sgradevole, antipatico(a); ~-season
a, ad fuori stagione.

**offset** ['ɔfsɛt] vt irg (counteract) con-
trobilanciare, compensare.

**offshoot** ['ɔfʃuːt] n (fig) diramazione
f.

**offshore** [ɔf'ʃɔː*] a (breeze) di terra; (island) vicino alla costa; (fishing) costiero(a).

**offside** ['ɔf'saɪd] a (SPORT) fuori gioco; (AUT: in Britain) destro(a); (: in Italy etc) sinistro(a) // n (AUT) lato destro; lato sinistro.

**offspring** ['ɔfsprɪŋ] n prole f, discendenza.

**off**: ~**stage** ad dietro le quinte; ~-**the-peg**, (US) ~-**the-rack** ad prêt-à-porter; ~-**white** a bianco sporco inv.

**often** ['ɔfn] ad spesso; how ~ do you go? quanto spesso ci vai?

**ogle** ['əugl] vt occhieggiare.

**oh** [əu] excl oh!

**oil** [ɔɪl] n olio; (petroleum) petrolio; (for central heating) nafta // vt (machine) lubrificare; ~**can** n oliatore m a mano; (for storing) latta da olio; ~**field** n giacimento petrolifero; ~ **filter** n (AUT) filtro dell'olio; ~ **fired** a a nafta; ~ **level** n livello dell'olio; ~ **painting** n quadro a olio; ~ **refinery** n raffineria di petrolio; ~ **rig** n derrick m inv; (at sea) piattaforma per trivellazioni subacquee; ~**skins** npl indumenti mpl di tela cerata; ~ **tanker** n petroliera; ~ **well** n pozzo petrolifero; ~**y** a unto(a), oleoso(a); (food) untuoso(a).

**ointment** ['ɔɪntmənt] n unguento.

**O.K., okay** ['əu'keɪ] excl d'accordo! // vt approvare; is it ~?, are you ~? tutto bene?

**old** [əuld] a vecchio(a); (ancient) antico(a), vecchio(a); (person) vecchio(a), anziano(a); how ~ are you? quanti anni ha?; he's 10 years ~ ha 10 anni; ~**er brother/sister** fratello/sorella maggiore; ~ **age** n vecchiaia; ~ **age pensioner (O.A.P.)** n (Brit) pensionato/a; ~-**fashioned** a antiquato(a), fuori moda; (person) all'antica.

**olive** ['ɔlɪv] n (fruit) oliva; (tree) olivo // a (also: ~-**green**) verde oliva inv; ~ **oil** n olio d'oliva.

**Olympic** [əu'lɪmpɪk] a olimpico(a); **the** ~ **Games**, **the** ~**s** i giochi olimpici, le Olimpiadi.

**omelet(te)** ['ɔmlɪt] n omelette f inv.

**omen** ['əumən] n presagio, augurio.

**ominous** ['ɔmɪnəs] a minaccioso(a); (event) di malaugurio.

**omit** [əu'mɪt] vt omettere.

KEYWORD

**on** [ɔn] ♦ prep 1 (indicating position) su; ~ **the wall** sulla parete; ~ **the left** a or sulla sinistra
2 (indicating means, method, condition etc): ~ **foot** a piedi; ~ **the train/plane** in treno/aereo; ~ **the telephone** al telefono; ~ **the radio/television** alla radio/televisione; **to be** ~ **drugs** drogarsi; ~ **holiday** in vacanza
3 (referring to time): ~ **Friday** venerdì; ~ **Fridays** il or di venerdì; ~ **June 20th** il 20 giugno; ~ **Friday, June 20th** venerdì, 20 giugno; **a week** ~ **Friday** venerdì a otto; ~ **his arrival** al suo arrivo; ~ **seeing this** vedendo ciò
4 (about, concerning) su, di; **information** ~ **train services** informazioni sui collegamenti ferroviari; **a book** ~ **Goldoni/ physics** un libro su Goldoni/di or sulla fisica
♦ ad 1 (referring to dress, covering): **to have one's coat** ~ avere indosso il cappotto; **to put one's coat** ~ mettersi il cappotto; **what's she got** ~? cosa indossa?; **she put her boots/gloves/hat** ~ si mise gli stivali/i guanti/il cappello; **screw the lid** ~ **tightly** avvita bene il coperchio
2 (further, continuously): **to walk** ~, **go** ~ etc continuare, proseguire etc; **to read** ~ continuare a leggere; ~ **and off** ogni tanto
♦ a 1 (in operation: machine, TV, light) acceso(a); (: tap) aperto(a); (: brake) inserito(a); **is the meeting still** ~? (in progress) la riunione

è ancora in corso?; (*not cancelled*) è confermato l'incontro?; **there's a good film ~ at the cinema** danno un buon film al cinema

**2** (*col*): **that's not ~!** (*not acceptable*) non si fa così!; (*not possible*) non se ne parla neanche!

**once** [wʌns] *ad* una volta // *cj* non appena, quando; **~ he had left/it was done** dopo che se n'era andato/fu fatto; **at ~** subito; (*simultaneously*) a un tempo; **~ more** ancora una volta; **~ and for all** una volta per sempre; **~ upon a time** c'era una volta.

**oncoming** ['ɔnkʌmɪŋ] *a* (*traffic*) che viene in senso opposto.

KEYWORD

**one** [wʌn] ◆ *num* uno(a); **~ hundred and fifty** centocinquanta; **~ day** un giorno

◆ *a* **1** (*sole*) unico(a); **the ~ book which** l'unico libro che; **the ~ man who** l'unico che

**2** (*same*) stesso(a); **they came in the ~ car** sono venuti nella stessa macchina

◆ *pronoun* **1**: **this ~** questo/a; **that ~** quello/a; **I've already got ~/a red ~** ne ho già uno/uno rosso; **~ by ~** uno per uno

**2**: **~ another** l'un l'altro; **to look at ~ another** guardarsi

**3** (*impersonal*) si; **~ never knows** non si sa mai; **to cut ~'s finger** tagliarsi un dito; **~ needs to eat** bisogna mangiare

**one: ~-armed bandit** *n* slot-machine *f inv*; **~-day excursion** *n* (*US*) biglietto giornaliero di andata e ritorno; **~-man** *a* (*business*) diretto(a) *etc* da un solo uomo; **~-man band** *n* suonatore ambulante con vari strumenti; **~-off** *n* (*Brit col*) fatto eccezionale.

**oneself** [wʌn'sɛlf] *pronoun* (*reflexive*) si; (*after prep*) se

stesso(a), sé; **to do sth (by) ~** fare qc da sé; **to hurt ~** farsi male; **to keep sth for ~** tenere qc per sé; **to talk to ~** parlare da solo.

**one: ~-sided** *a* (*argument*) unilaterale; **~-to-~** *a* (*relationship*) univoco(a); **~-upmanship** [-'ʌpmənʃɪp] *n* l'arte di fare sempre meglio degli altri; **~-way** *a* (*street, traffic*) a senso unico.

**ongoing** ['ɔngəʊɪŋ] *a* in corso; in attuazione.

**onion** ['ʌnjən] *n* cipolla.

**on-line** ['ɔnlaɪn] *a, ad* (*COMPUT*) on-line *inv*.

**onlooker** ['ɔnlʊkə*] *n* spettatore/trice.

**only** ['əʊnlɪ] *ad* solo, soltanto // *a* solo(a), unico(a) // *cj* solo che, ma; **an ~ child** un figlio unico; **not ~ ... but also** non solo ... ma anche; **I ~ took one** ne ho preso soltanto uno, non ne ho preso che uno.

**onset** ['ɔnsɛt] *n* inizio; (*of winter, old age*) approssimarsi *m*.

**onshore** ['ɔnʃɔ:*] *a* (*wind*) di mare.

**onslaught** ['ɔnslɔ:t] *n* attacco, assalto.

**onto** ['ɔntu] *prep* su, sopra.

**onus** ['əʊnəs] *n* onere *m*, peso.

**onward(s)** ['ɔnwəd(z)] *ad* (*move*) in avanti.

**onyx** ['ɔnɪks] *n* onice *f*.

**ooze** [u:z] *vi* stillare.

**opaque** [əʊ'peɪk] *a* opaco(a).

**OPEC** ['əʊpɛk] *n abbr* (= *Organization of Petroleum-Exporting Countries*) O.P.E.C. *f*.

**open** ['əʊpn] *a* aperto(a); (*road*) libero(a); (*meeting*) pubblico(a); (*admiration*) evidente, franco(a); (*question*) insoluto(a); (*enemy*) dichiarato(a) // *vt* aprire // *vi* (*eyes, door, debate*) aprirsi; (*flower*) sbocciare; (*shop, bank, museum*) aprire; (*book etc: commence*) cominciare; **in the ~ (air)** all'aperto; **to ~ on to** *vt fus* (*subj: room, door*) dare su; **to ~ up** *vt* aprire; (*blocked road*) sgombrare //

*vi* aprirsi; ~**ing** *n* apertura; (*opportunity*) occasione *f*, opportunità *f inv*; sbocco; (*job*) posto vacante; ~**ly** *ad* apertamente; ~**-minded** *a* che ha la mente aperta; ~**-plan** *a* senza pareti divisorie.

**opera** ['ɔpərə] *n* opera; ~ **house** *n* opera.

**operate** ['ɔpəreɪt] *vt* (*machine*) azionare, far funzionare; (*system*) usare // *vi* funzionare; (*drug*) essere efficace; **to ~ on sb (for)** (*MED*) operare qn (di).

**operatic** [ɔpə'rætɪk] *a* dell'opera, lirico(a).

**operating** ['ɔpəreɪtɪŋ] *a*: ~ **table** tavolo operatorio; ~ **theatre** sala operatoria.

**operation** [ɔpə'reɪʃən] *n* operazione *f*; **to be in** ~ (*machine*) essere in azione *or* funzionamento; (*system*) essere in vigore; **to have an** ~ (*MED*) subire un'operazione; ~**al** *a* in funzione; d'esercizio.

**operative** ['ɔpərətɪv] *a* (*measure*) operativo(a).

**operator** ['ɔpəreɪtə*] *n* (*of machine*) operatore/trice; (*TEL*) centralinista *m/f*.

**opinion** [ə'pɪnɪən] *n* opinione *f*, parere *m*; **in my** ~ secondo me, a mio avviso; ~**ated** *a* dogmatico(a); ~ **poll** *n* sondaggio di opinioni.

**opium** ['ɔupɪəm] *n* oppio.

**opponent** [ə'pəunənt] *n* avversario/a.

**opportunist** [ɔpə'tjuːnɪst] *n* opportunista *m/f*.

**opportunity** [ɔpə'tjuːnɪtɪ] *n* opportunità *f inv*, occasione *f*; **to take the** ~ **of doing** cogliere l'occasione per fare.

**oppose** [ə'pəuz] *vt* opporsi a; ~**d to** *a* contrario(a) a; **as** ~**d to** in contrasto con; **opposing** *a* opposto(a); (*team*) avversario(a).

**opposite** ['ɔpəzɪt] *a* opposto(a); (*house etc*) di fronte // *ad* di fronte, dirimpetto // *prep* di fronte a // *n* opposto, contrario; (*of word*) con-

trario.

**opposition** [ɔpə'zɪʃən] *n* opposizione *f*.

**oppress** [ə'prɛs] *vt* opprimere.

**opt** [ɔpt] *vi*: **to ~ for** optare per; **to ~ to do** scegliere di fare; **to ~ out of** ritirarsi da.

**optical** ['ɔptɪkl] *a* ottico(a); ~ **character recognition (OCR)** *n* lettura ottica; ~ **character reader (OCR)** *n* lettore ottico.

**optician** [ɔp'tɪʃən] *n* ottico.

**optimist** ['ɔptɪmɪst] *n* ottimista *m/f*; ~**ic** [-'mɪstɪk] *a* ottimistico(a).

**optimum** ['ɔptɪməm] *a* ottimale.

**option** ['ɔpʃən] *n* scelta; (*SCOL*) materia facoltativa; (*COMM*) opzione *f*; ~**al** *a* facoltativo(a); (*COMM*) a scelta.

**or** [ɔː*] *cj* o, oppure; (*with negative*): **he hasn't seen ~ heard anything** non ha visto né sentito niente; ~ **else** se no, altrimenti; oppure.

**oral** ['ɔːrəl] *a* orale // *n* esame *m* orale.

**orange** ['ɔrɪndʒ] *n* (*fruit*) arancia // *a* arancione.

**orator** ['ɔrətə*] *n* oratore/trice.

**orbit** ['ɔːbɪt] *n* orbita.

**orchard** ['ɔːtʃəd] *n* frutteto.

**orchestra** ['ɔːkɪstrə] *n* orchestra; (*US: seating*) platea; ~**l** [-'kɛstrəl] *a* orchestrale; (*concert*) sinfonico(a).

**orchid** ['ɔːkɪd] *n* orchidea.

**ordain** [ɔː'deɪn] *vt* (*REL*) ordinare; (*decide*) decretare.

**ordeal** [ɔː'diːl] *n* prova, travaglio.

**order** ['ɔːdə*] *n* ordine *m*; (*COMM*) ordinazione *f* // *vt* ordinare; **in ~** in ordine; (*of document*) in regola; **in (working)** ~ funzionante; **in ~ of size** in ordine di grandezza; **in ~ to do** per fare; **in ~ that** affinché + *sub*; **on ~** (*COMM*) in ordinazione; **to ~ sb to do** ordinare a qn di fare; **the lower ~s** (*pej*) i ceti inferiori; ~ **form** *n* modulo di ordinazione; ~**ly** *n* (*MIL*) attendente *m* // *a* (*room*) in ordine; (*mind*) metodico(a); (*person*) ordinato(a), metodico(a).

**ordinary** ['ɔ:dnrɪ] a normale, comune; (pej) mediocre; **out of the** ~ diverso dal solito, fuori dell'ordinario.

**ore** [ɔ:*] n minerale m grezzo.

**organ** ['ɔ:gən] n organo; ~**ic** [ɔ:'gænɪk] a organico(a).

**organization** [ɔ:gənaɪ'zeɪʃən] n organizzazione f.

**organize** ['ɔ:gənaɪz] vt organizzare; ~**r** n organizzatore/trice.

**orgasm** ['ɔ:gæzəm] n orgasmo.

**orgy** ['ɔ:dʒɪ] n orgia.

**Orient** ['ɔ:rɪənt] n: **the** ~ l'Oriente m; **oriental** [-'entl] a, n orientale (m/f).

**origin** ['ɔrɪdʒɪn] n origine f.

**original** [ə'rɪdʒɪnl] a originale; (earliest) originario(a) // n originale m; ~**ly** ad (at first) all'inizio.

**originate** [ə'rɪdʒɪneɪt] vi: **to** ~ **from** essere originario(a) di; (suggestion) provenire da; **to** ~ **in** avere origine in.

**Orkneys** ['ɔ:knɪz] npl: **the** ~ (also: **the Orkney Islands**) le Orcadi.

**ornament** ['ɔ:nəmənt] n ornamento; (trinket) ninnolo; ~**al** [-'mentl] a ornamentale.

**ornate** [ɔ:'neɪt] a molto ornato(a).

**orphan** ['ɔ:fn] n orfano/a // vt: **to be** ~**ed** diventare orfano; ~**age** n orfanotrofio.

**orthodox** ['ɔ:θədɔks] a ortodosso(a).

**orthopaedic,** (US) **orthopedic** [ɔ:θə'pi:dɪk] a ortopedico(a).

**ostensibly** [ɔs'tensɪblɪ] ad all'apparenza.

**ostentatious** [ɔstən'teɪʃəs] a pretenzioso(a); ostentato(a).

**ostrich** ['ɔstrɪtʃ] n struzzo.

**other** ['ʌðə*] a altro(a) // pronoun: **the** ~ (one) l'altro(a); ~**s** (~ people) altri mpl; ~ **than** altro che; a parte; ~**wise** ad, cj altrimenti.

**otter** ['ɔtə*] n lontra.

**ouch** [autʃ] excl ohi!, ahi!

**ought,** pl **ought** [ɔ:t] auxiliary vb: **I** ~ **to do it** dovrei farlo; **this** ~ **to**

have been corrected questo avrebbe dovuto essere corretto; **he** ~ **to win** dovrebbe vincere.

**ounce** [auns] n oncia (= 28.35 g; 16 in a pound).

**our** ['auə*] a il(la) nostro(a), pl i(le) nostri(e); see also **my**; ~**s** pronoun il(la) nostro(a), pl i(le) nostri(e); see also **mine**; ~**selves** pronoun pl (reflexive) ci; (after preposition) noi; (emphatic) noi stessi(e); see also oneself.

**oust** [aust] vt cacciare, espellere.

**out** [aut] ad fuori; (published, not at home etc) uscito(a); (light, fire) spento(a); ~ **here** qui fuori; ~ **there** là fuori; **he's** ~ è uscito; (unconscious) ha perso conoscenza; **to be** ~ **in one's calculations** essersi sbagliato nei calcoli; **to run/back** etc ~ uscire di corsa/a marcia indietro etc; ~ **loud** ad ad alta voce; ~ **of** (outside) fuori di; (because of: anger etc) per; (from among): ~ **of** 10 su 10; (without): ~ **of petrol** senza benzina, a corto di benzina; ~ **of order** (machine etc) guasto(a); ~**and**~ a (liar, thief etc) vero(a) e proprio(a).

**outback** ['autbæk] n (in Australia) interno, entroterra.

**outboard** ['autbɔ:d] n: ~ (**motor**) (motore m) fuoribordo.

**outbreak** ['autbreɪk] n scoppio, epidemia.

**outburst** ['autbə:st] n scoppio.

**outcast** ['autkɑ:st] n esule m/f; (socially) paria m inv.

**outcome** ['autkʌm] n esito, risultato.

**outcrop** ['autkrɔp] n (of rock) affioramento.

**outcry** ['autkraɪ] n protesta, clamore m.

**outdated** [aut'deɪtɪd] a (custom, clothes) fuori moda; (idea) sorpassato(a).

**outdo** [aut'du:] vt irg sorpassare.

**outdoor** [aut'dɔ:*] a all'aperto; ~**s** ad fuori; all'aria aperta.

**outer** ['autə*] a esteriore; ~ **space**

*n* spazio cosmico.

**outfit** ['autgouɳ] *n* equipaggiamento; (*clothes*) abito; "~**ter's**" (*Brit*) "confezioni da uomo".

**outgoing** ['autgouiɳ] *a* (*character*) socievole; ~**s** *npl* (*Brit: expenses*) spese *fpl*, uscite *fpl*.

**outgrow** [aut'grou] *vt irg* (*clothes*) diventare troppo grande per.

**outhouse** ['authaus] *n* costruzione *f* annessa.

**outing** ['autiɳ] *n* gita; escursione *f*.

**outlandish** [aut'lændiʃ] *a* strano(a).

**outlaw** ['autlɔ:] *n* fuorilegge *m/f*.

**outlay** ['autlei] *n* spese *fpl*; (*investment*) sborsa, spesa.

**outlet** ['autlet] *n* (*for liquid etc*) sbocco, scarico; (*US ELEC*) presa di corrente; (*for emotion*) sfogo; (*for goods*) sbocco; (*also*: retail ~) punto di vendita.

**outline** ['autlain] *n* contorno, profilo; (*summary*) abbozzo, grandi linee *fpl*.

**outlive** [aut'liv] *vt* sopravvivere a.

**outlook** ['autluk] *n* prospettiva, vista.

**outlying** ['autlaiiɳ] *a* periferico(a).

**outmoded** [aut'moudid] *a* passato(a) di moda; antiquato(a).

**outnumber** [aut'nʌmbə*] *vt* superare in numero.

**out-of-date** [autəv'deit] *a* (*passport*) scaduto(a); (*clothes*) fuori moda *inv*.

**out-of-the-way** ['autəvðə'wei] *a* (*place*) fuori mano *inv*.

**outpatient** ['autpeiʃənt] *n* paziente *m/f* esterno(a).

**outpost** ['autpəust] *n* avamposto.

**output** ['autput] *n* produzione *f*; (*COMPUT*) output *m inv*.

**outrage** ['autreidʒ] *n* oltraggio; scandalo // *vt* oltraggiare; ~**ous** [-'reidʒəs] *a* oltraggioso(a); scandaloso(a).

**outright** *ad* [aut'rait] completamente; schiettamente; apertamente; sul colpo // *a* ['autrait] completo(a); schietto(a) e netto(a).

**outset** ['autset] *n* inizio.

**outside** [aut'said] *n* esterno,

esteriore *m* // *a* esterno(a), esteriore // *ad* fuori, all'esterno // *prep* fuori di, all'esterno di; **at the** ~ (*fig*) al massimo; ~ **lane** *n* (*AUT*) corsia di sorpasso; ~**left/right** *n* (*FOOT-BALL*) ala sinistra/destra; ~ **line** *n* (*TEL*) linea esterna; ~**r** *n* (*in race etc*) outsider *m inv*; (*stranger*) straniero/a.

**outsize** ['autsaiz] *a* enorme; (*clothes*) per taglie forti.

**outskirts** ['autskə:ts] *npl* sobborghi *mpl*.

**outspoken** [aut'spəukən] *a* molto franco/a.

**outstanding** [aut'stændiɳ] *a* eccezionale, di rilievo; (*unfinished*) non completo(a); non evaso(a); non regolato(a).

**outstay** [aut'stei] *vt*: **to** ~ **one's welcome** diventare un ospite sgradito.

**outstretched** [aut'stretʃt] *a* (*hand*) teso(a); (*body*) disteso(a).

**outstrip** [aut'strip] *vt* (*competitors, demand*) superare.

**out-tray** ['auttrei] *n* contenitore *m* per la corrispondenza in partenza.

**outward** ['autwəd] *a* (*sign, appearances*) esteriore; (*journey*) d'andata; ~**ly** *ad* esteriormente; in apparenza.

**outweigh** [aut'wei] *vt* avere maggior peso di.

**outwit** [aut'wit] *vt* superare in astuzia.

**oval** ['əuvl] *a, n* ovale (*m*).

**ovary** ['əuvəri] *n* ovaia.

**oven** ['ʌvn] *n* forno; ~**proof** *a* da forno.

**over** ['əuvə*] *ad* al di sopra // *a* (*or ad*) (*finished*) finito(a), terminato(a); (*too*) troppo; (*remaining*) che avanza // *prep* su; sopra; (*above*) al di sopra di; (*on the other side of*) di là di; (*more than*) più di; (*during*) durante; ~ **here** qui; ~ **there** là; **all** ~ (*everywhere*) dappertutto; (*finished*) tutto(a) finito(a); ~ **and** ~ (*again*) più e più volte; ~ **and**

**above** oltre (a); **to ask sb ~** invitare qn (a passare).

**overall** $a$, $n$ ['əuvərɔːl] $a$ totale // $n$ (Brit) grembiule $m$ // $ad$ [əuvər'ɔːl] nell'insieme, complessivamente; **~s** $npl$ tuta (da lavoro).

**overawe** [əuvər'ɔː] $vt$ intimidire.

**overbalance** [əuvə'bæləns] $vi$ perdere l'equilibrio.

**overbearing** [əuvə'bɛərɪŋ] $a$ imperioso(a), prepotente.

**overboard** [əuvə'bɔːd] $ad$ (NAUT) fuori bordo, in mare.

**overbook** [əuvə'buk] $vt$: **the hotel was ~ed** le prenotazioni all'albergo superavano i posti disponibili.

**overcast** ['əuvəkɑːst] $a$ coperto(a).

**overcharge** [əuvə'tʃɑːdʒ] $vt$: **to ~ sb for sth** far pagare troppo caro a qn per qc.

**overcoat** ['əuvəkəut] $n$ soprabito, cappotto.

**overcome** [əuvə'kʌm] $vt$ $irg$ superare; sopraffare.

**overcrowded** [əuvə'kraudɪd] $a$ sovraffollato(a).

**overdo** [əuvə'duː] $vt$ $irg$ esagerare; (overcook) cuocere troppo.

**overdose** ['əuvədəus] $n$ dose $f$ eccessiva.

**overdraft** ['əuvədrɑːft] $n$ scoperto (di conto).

**overdrawn** [əuvə'drɔːn] $a$ (account) scoperto(a).

**overdue** [əuvə'djuː] $a$ in ritardo; (recognition) tardivo(a).

**overestimate** [əuvər'estɪmeɪt] $vt$ sopravvalutare.

**overflow** $vi$ [əuvə'fləu] traboccare // $n$ ['əuvəfləu] troppopieno.

**overgrown** [əuvə'grəun] $a$ (garden) ricoperto(a) di vegetazione.

**overhaul** $vt$ [əuvə'hɔːl] revisionare // $n$ ['əuvəhɔːl] revisione $f$.

**overhead** $ad$ [əuvə'hed] di sopra // $a$ ['əuvəhed] aereo(a); (lighting) verticale; **~s** $npl$, (US) **~** $n$ spese $fpl$ generali.

**overhear** [əuvə'hɪə] $vt$ $irg$ sentire (per caso).

**overheat** [əuvə'hiːt] $vi$ (engine) surriscaldare.

**overjoyed** [əuvə'dʒɔɪd] $a$ pazzo(a) di gioia.

**overkill** ['əuvəkɪl] $n$ (fig) eccessi $mpl$.

**overlap** [əuvə'læp] $vi$ sovrapporsi.

**overleaf** [əuvə'liːf] $ad$ a tergo.

**overload** [əuvə'ləud] $vt$ sovraccaricare.

**overlook** $vt$ [əuvə'luk] (have view of) dare su; (miss) trascurare; (forgive) passare sopra a.

**overnight** [əuvə'naɪt] $ad$ (happen) durante la notte; (fig) tutto ad un tratto // $a$ di notte; fulmineo(a); **he stayed there ~** ci ha passato la notte.

**overpower** [əuvə'pauə] $vt$ sopraffare; **~ing** $a$ irresistibile; (heat, stench) soffocante.

**overrate** [əuvə'reɪt] $vt$ sopravvalutare.

**override** [əuvə'raɪd] $vt$ (irg: like ride) (order, objection) passar sopra a; (decision) annullare; **overriding** $a$ preponderante.

**overrule** [əuvə'ruːl] $vt$ (decision) annullare; (claim) respingere.

**overrun** [əuvə'rʌn] $vt$ (irg: like run) (country) invadere; (time limit) superare.

**overseas** [əuvə'siːz] $ad$ oltremare; (abroad) all'estero // $a$ (trade) estero(a); (visitor) straniero(a).

**overseer** ['əuvəsɪə] $n$ (in factory) caposquadra $m$.

**overshadow** [əuvə'ʃædəu] $vt$ (fig) eclissare.

**overshoot** [əuvə'ʃuːt] $vt$ $irg$ superare.

**oversight** ['əuvəsaɪt] $n$ omissione $f$, svista.

**oversleep** [əuvə'sliːp] $vi$ $irg$ dormire troppo a lungo.

**overstep** [əuvə'step] $vt$: **to ~ the mark** superare ogni limite.

**overt** [əu'vəːt] $a$ palese.

**overtake** [əuvə'teɪk] $vt$ $irg$ sorpassare.

**overthrow** [əuvə'θrəu] *vt irg* (*government*) rovesciare.

**overtime** ['əuvətaım] *n* (*lavoro*) straordinario.

**overtone** ['əuvətəun] *n* (*also*: ~s) sfumatura.

**overture** ['əuvətʃuə*] *n* (*MUS*) ouverture *f inv*; (*fig*) approccio.

**overturn** [əuvə'tə:n] *vt* rovesciare // *vi* rovesciarsi.

**overweight** [əuvə'weɪt] *a* (*person*) troppo grasso(a); (*luggage*) troppo pesante.

**overwhelm** [əuvə'welm] *vt* sopraffare; sommergere; schiacciare; ~**ing** *a* (*victory*, *defeat*) schiacciante; (*desire*) irresistibile.

**overwork** [əuvə'wə:k] *vt* far lavorare troppo // *vi* lavorare troppo, strapazzarsi.

**overwrought** [əuvə'rɔ:t] *a* molto agitato(a).

**owe** [əu] *vt* dovere; to ~ sb sth, to ~ sth to sb dovere qc a qn.

**owing to** ['əuɪŋtu:] *prep* a causa di.

**owl** [aul] *n* gufo.

**own** [əun] *vt* possedere // *a* proprio(a); **a room of my** ~ la mia propria camera; **to get one's** ~ **back** vendicarsi; **on one's** ~ tutto(a) solo(a); **to** ~ **up** *vi* confessare; ~**er** *n* proprietario/a; ~**ership** *n* possesso.

**ox**, *pl* **oxen** [ɔks, 'ɔksn] *n* bue *m*.

**oxtail** ['ɔksteɪl] *n*: ~ **soup** minestra di coda di bue.

**oxygen** ['ɔksɪdʒən] *n* ossigeno; ~ **mask** *n* maschera ad ossigeno.

**oyster** ['ɔɪstə*] *n* ostrica.

**oz.** *abbr* = **ounce(s)**.

**ozone** ['əuzəun] *n* ozono.

# P

**p** [pi:] *abbr* = **penny, pence**.

**pa** [pa:] *n* (*col*) papà *m inv*, babbo.

**P.A.** *n abbr* = **personal assistant, public address system**.

**p.a.** *abbr* = **per annum**.

**pace** [peɪs] *n* passo; (*speed*) passo; velocità // *vi*: **to** ~ **up and down** camminare su e giù; **to keep** ~ **with** camminare di pari passo a; (*events*) tenersi al corrente di; ~**maker** *n* (*MED*) segnapasso.

**pacific** [pə'sɪfɪk] *n*: **the P**~ (**Ocean**) il Pacifico, l'Oceano Pacifico.

**pack** [pæk] *n* pacco; balla; (*of hounds*) muta; (*of thieves etc*) banda; (*of cards*) mazzo // *vt* (*goods*) impaccare, imballare; (*in suitcase etc*) mettere; (*box*) riempire; (*cram*) stipare, pigiare; (*press down*) tamponare; turare; **to** ~ (**one's bags**) fare la valigia; **to** ~ **off** *vt* (*person*) spedire.

**package** ['pækɪdʒ] *n* pacco; balla; (*also*: ~ **deal**) pacchetto; forfait *m inv*; ~ **tour** *n* viaggio organizzato.

**packed lunch** *n* pranzo al sacco.

**packet** ['pækɪt] *n* pacchetto.

**packing** ['pækɪŋ] *n* imballaggio; ~ **case** *n* cassa da imballaggio.

**pact** [pækt] *n* patto, accordo; trattato.

**pad** [pæd] *n* blocco; (*for inking*) tampone *m*; (*col*: *flat*) appartamentino // *vt* imbottire; ~**ding** *n* imbottitura; (*fig*) riempitivo.

**paddle** ['pædl] *n* (*oar*) pagaia; (*US*: *for table tennis*) racchetta da ping-pong // *vi* sguazzare // *vt*: **to** ~ **a canoe** *etc* vogare con la pagaia; ~ **steamer** *n* battello a ruote; **paddling pool** *n* (*Brit*) piscina per bambini.

**paddy field** ['pædɪ-] *n* risaia.

**padlock** ['pædlɔk] *n* lucchetto.

**paediatrics**, (*US*) **pediatrics** [pi:dɪ'ætrɪks] *n* pediatria.

**pagan** ['peɪgən] *a*, *n* pagano(a).

**page** [peɪdʒ] *n* pagina; (*also*: ~ **boy**) fattorino; (*at wedding*) paggio // *vt* (*in hotel etc*) (far) chiamare.

**pageant** ['pædʒənt] *n* spettacolo storico; grande cerimonia; ~**ry** *n* pompa.

**paid** [peɪd] *pt*, *pp of* **pay** // *a* (*work*, *official*) rimunerato(a); **to put** ~ **to**

(*Brit*) mettere fine a.

**pail** [peɪl] *n* secchio.

**pain** [peɪn] *n* dolore *m*; to be in ~ soffrire, aver male; to take ~s to do mettercela tutta per fare; ~ed *a* addolorato(a), afflitto(a); ~ful *a* doloroso(a), che fa male; difficile, penoso(a); ~fully *ad* (*fig*: *very*) fin troppo; ~killer *n* antalgico, antidolorifico; ~less *a* indolore.

**painstaking** ['peɪnzteɪkɪŋ] *a* (*person*) sollecito(a); (*work*) accurato(a).

**paint** [peɪnt] *n* vernice *f*, colore *m* // *vt* dipingere; (*walls, door etc*) verniciare; to ~ the door blue verniciare la porta di azzurro; ~brush *n* pennello; ~er *n* (*artist*) pittore *m*; (*decorator*) imbianchino; ~ing *n* pittura; verniciatura; (*picture*) dipinto, quadro; ~work *n* tinta; (*of car*) vernice *f*.

**pair** [pɛə*] *n* (*of shoes, gloves etc*) paio; (*of people*) coppia; duo *m inv*; a ~ of scissors/trousers un paio di forbici/pantaloni.

**pajamas** [pɪ'dʒɑːməz] *npl* (*US*) pigiama *m*.

**Pakistan** [pɑːkɪˈstɑːn] *n* Pakistan *m*; ~i *a, n* pakistano(a).

**pal** [pæl] *n* (*col*) amico/a, compagno/a.

**palace** ['pæləs] *n* palazzo.

**palatable** ['pælɪtəbl] *a* gustoso(a).

**palate** ['pælɪt] *n* palato.

**palatial** [pə'leɪʃəl] *a* sontuoso(a), sfarzoso(a).

**palaver** [pə'lɑːvə*] *n* chiacchiere *fpl*; storie *fpl*.

**pale** [peɪl] *a* pallido(a) // *n*: to be beyond the ~ aver oltrepassato ogni limite; to grow ~ diventare pallido, impallidire.

**Palestine** ['pælɪstaɪn] *n* Palestina; **Palestinian** [-'tɪnɪən] *a, n* palestinese (*m/f*).

**palette** ['pælɪt] *n* tavolozza.

**paling** ['peɪlɪŋ] *n* (*stake*) palo; (*fence*) palizzata.

**pall** [pɔːl] *n* (*of smoke*) cappa // *vi*: to

~ (on) diventare noioso(a) (a).

**pallet** ['pælɪt] *n* (*for goods*) paletta.

**pallid** ['pælɪd] *a* pallido(a), smorto(a).

**pallor** ['pælə*] *n* pallore *m*.

**palm** [pɑːm] *n* (*ANAT*) palma, palmo; (*also*: ~ tree) palma // *vt*: to ~ sth off on sb (*col*) rifilare qc a qn; **P~ Sunday** *n* Domenica delle Palme.

**palpable** ['pælpəbl] *a* palpabile.

**paltry** ['pɔːltrɪ] *a* derisorio(a); insignificante.

**pamper** ['pæmpə*] *vt* viziare, accarezzare.

**pamphlet** ['pæmflət] *n* dépliant *m inv*.

**pan** [pæn] *n* (*also*: **sauce~**) casseruola; (*also*: **frying ~**) padella // *vi* (*CINEMA*) fare una panoramica.

**panache** [pə'næʃ] *n* stile *m*.

**pancake** ['pænkeɪk] *n* frittella.

**pancreas** ['pæŋkrɪəs] *n* pancreas *m inv*.

**panda** ['pændə] *n* panda *m inv*; ~ **car** *n* (*Brit*) auto *f* della polizia.

**pandemonium** [pændɪ'məʊnɪəm] *n* pandemonio.

**pander** ['pændə*] *vi*: to ~ to lusingare; concedere tutto a.

**pane** [peɪn] *n* vetro.

**panel** ['pænl] *n* (*of wood, cloth etc*) pannello; (*RADIO, TV*) giuria; ~ling, (*US*) ~ing *n* rivestimento a pannelli.

**pang** [pæŋ] *n*: ~s of hunger spasimi *mpl* della fame; ~s of conscience morsi *mpl* di coscienza.

**panic** ['pænɪk] *n* panico // *vi* perdere il sangue freddo; ~ky *a* (*person*) pauroso(a); ~-stricken *a* (*person*) preso(a) dal panico, in preda al panico; (*look*) terrorizzato(a).

**pansy** ['pænzɪ] *n* (*BOT*) viola del pensiero, pensée *f inv*; (*col*) femminuccia.

**pant** [pænt] *vi* ansare.

**panther** ['pænθə*] *n* pantera.

**panties** ['pæntɪz] *npl* slip *m*, mutandine *fpl*.

**pantihose** ['pæntɪhəʊz] *n* (US) collant *m inv.*

**pantomime** ['pæntəmaɪm] *n* (Brit) pantomima.

**pantry** ['pæntrɪ] *n* dispensa.

**pants** [pænts] *npl* mutande *fpl*, slip *m*; (US: trousers) pantaloni *mpl*.

**papal** ['peɪpəl] *a* papale, pontificio(a).

**paper** ['peɪpə*] *n* carta; (also: **wall~**) carta da parati, tappezzeria; (also: **news~**) giornale *m*; (study, article) saggio; (exam) prova scritta // a di carta // *vt* tappezzare; ~s *npl* (also: **identity** ~s) carte *fpl*, documenti *mpl*; ~**back** *n* tascabile *m*; edizione *f* economica; ~ **clip** *n* graffetta, clip *f inv*; ~ **hankie** *n* fazzolettino di carta; ~ **mill** *n* cartiera; ~**weight** *n* fermacarte *m inv*; ~**work** *n* lavoro amministrativo.

**papier-mâché** ['pæpɪeɪ'mæʃeɪ] *n* cartapesta.

**par** [pɑ:*] *n* parità, pari *f*; (GOLF) norma; **on a ~ with** alla pari con.

**parable** ['pærəbl] *n* parabola.

**parachute** ['pærəʃu:t] *n* paracadute *m inv.*

**parade** [pə'reɪd] *n* parata; (inspection) rivista, rassegna // *vt* (fig) fare sfoggio di // *vi* sfilare in parata.

**paradise** ['pærədaɪs] *n* paradiso.

**paradox** ['pærədɔks] *n* paradosso; ~**ically** [-'dɔksɪklɪ] *ad* paradossalmente.

**paraffin** ['pærəfɪn] *n* (Brit): ~ (**oil**) paraffina.

**paragon** ['pærəgən] *n* modello di perfezione *or* di virtù.

**paragraph** ['pærəgrɑ:f] *n* paragrafo.

**parallel** ['pærəlel] *a* parallelo(a) (fig) analogo(a) // *n* (line) parallela; (fig, GEO) parallelo.

**paralysis** [pə'rælɪsɪs] *n* paralisi *f inv.*

**paralyze** ['pærəlaɪz] *vt* paralizzare.

**paramount** ['pærəmaʊnt] *a*: **of ~ importance** di capitale importanza.

**paranoid** ['pærənɔɪd] *a* paranoico(a).

**paraphernalia** [pærəfə'neɪlɪə] *n* attrezzi *mpl*, roba.

**parasol** ['pærəsɔl] *n* parasole *m.*

**paratrooper** ['pærətru:pə*] *n* paracadutista *m* (soldato).

**parcel** ['pɑ:sl] *n* pacco, pacchetto // *vt* (also: ~ **up**) impaccare.

**parch** [pɑ:tʃ] *vt* riardere; ~**ed** *a* (person) assetato(a).

**parchment** ['pɑ:tʃmənt] *n* pergamena.

**pardon** ['pɑ:dn] *n* perdono; grazia // *vt* perdonare; (LAW) graziare; ~ **me!** mi scusi!; **I beg your ~!** scusi!; **I beg your ~?**, (US) ~ **me?** prego?

**parent** ['pεərənt] *n* genitore *m*; ~s *npl* genitori *mpl*; ~**al** [pə'rεntl] *a* dei genitori.

**parenthesis**, *pl* **parentheses** [pə'rεnθɪsɪs, -sɪːz] *n* parentesi *f inv.*

**Paris** ['pærɪs] *n* Parigi *f.*

**parish** ['pærɪʃ] *n* parrocchia; (civil) ≈ municipio // *a* parrocchiale.

**park** [pɑ:k] *n* parco // *vt*, *vi* parcheggiare.

**parka** ['pɑ:kə] *n* eskimo.

**parking** ['pɑ:kɪŋ] *n* parcheggio; "**no ~**" "sosta vietata"; ~ **lot** *n* (US) posteggio, parcheggio; ~ **meter** *n* parchimetro; ~ **ticket** *n* multa per sosta vietata.

**parlance** ['pɑ:ləns] *n* gergo.

**parliament** ['pɑ:ləmənt] *n* parlamento; ~**ary** [-'mεntərɪ] *a* parlamentare.

**parlour**, (US) **parlor** ['pɑ:lə*] *n* salotto.

**parochial** [pə'rəʊkɪəl] *a* parrocchiale; (pej) provinciale.

**parody** ['pærədɪ] *n* parodia.

**parole** [pə'rəʊl] *n*: **on ~** in libertà per buona condotta.

**parrot** ['pærət] *n* pappagallo.

**parry** ['pærɪ] *vt* parare.

**parsley** ['pɑ:slɪ] *n* prezzemolo.

**parsnip** ['pɑ:snɪp] *n* pastinaca.

**parson** ['pɑ:sn] *n* prete *m*; (Church of England) parroco.

**part** [pɑ:t] *n* parte *f*; (of machine) pezzo; (MUS) voce *f*; parte; (US: in hair) scriminatura // *a* in parte // *ad*

= **partly** // vt separare // vi (people) separarsi; (roads) dividersi; **to take ~ in** prendere parte a; **for my ~** per parte mia; **to take sth in good ~** prendere bene qc; **to take sb's ~** parteggiare per or prendere le parti di qn; **for the most ~** in generale; nella maggior parte dei casi; **to ~ with** vt fus separarsi da; rinunciare a; **~ exchange** n (Brit): **in ~ exchange** in pagamento parziale.

**partial** ['pɑ:ʃl] a parziale; **to be ~ to** avere un debole per.

**participate** [pɑ:'tɪsɪpeɪt] vi: **to ~ (in)** prendere parte (a), partecipare (a); **participation** [-'peɪʃən] n partecipazione f.

**participle** ['pɑ:tɪsɪpl] n participio.

**particle** ['pɑ:tɪkl] n particella.

**particular** [pə'tɪkjulə*] a particolare; speciale; (fussy) difficile; meticoloso(a); **~s** npl particolari mpl, dettagli mpl; (information) informazioni fpl; **in ~** in particolare, particolarmente; **~ly** ad particolarmente; in particolare.

**parting** ['pɑ:tɪŋ] n separazione f; (Brit: in hair) scriminatura // a d'addio.

**partisan** [pɑ:tɪ'zæn] n partigiano/a // a partigiano(a); di parte.

**partition** [pɑ:'tɪʃən] n (POL) partizione f; (wall) tramezzo.

**partly** ['pɑ:tlɪ] ad parzialmente; in parte.

**partner** ['pɑ:tnə*] n (COMM) socio/a; (SPORT) compagno/a; (at dance) cavaliere/dama; **~ship** n associazione f; (COMM) società f inv.

**partridge** ['pɑ:trɪdʒ] n pernice f.

**part-time** ['pɑ:t'taɪm] a, ad a orario ridotto.

**party** ['pɑ:tɪ] n (POL) partito; (team) squadra; gruppo; (LAW) parte f; (celebration) ricevimento; serata; festa // cpd (POL) del partito, di partito; (dress, finery) della festa; **~ line** n (TEL) duplex m inv.

**pass** [pɑ:s] vt (gen) passare; (place) passare davanti a; (exam) passare,

superare; (candidate) promuovere; (overtake, surpass) sorpassare, superare; (approve) approvare // vi passare // n (permit) lasciapassare m inv; permesso; (in mountains) passo, gola; (SPORT) passaggio; (SCOL: also: ~ mark) to get a ~ prendere la sufficienza; **to ~ sth through a hole** etc far passare qc attraverso un buco etc; **to make a ~ at sb** (col) fare delle proposte or delle avances a qn; **to ~ away** vi morire; **to ~ by** vi passare // vt trascurare; **to ~ on** vt passare; **to ~ out** vi svenire; **to ~ up** vt (opportunity) lasciarsi sfuggire, perdere; **~able** a (road) praticabile; (work) accettabile.

**passage** ['pæsɪdʒ] n (gen) passaggio; (also: **~way**) corridoio; (in book) brano, passo; (by boat) traversata.

**passbook** ['pɑ:sbuk] n libretto di risparmio.

**passenger** ['pæsɪndʒə*] n passeggero/a.

**passer-by** [pɑ:sə'baɪ] n passante m/f.

**passing** ['pɑ:sɪŋ] a (fig) fuggevole; **to mention sth in ~** accennare a qc di sfuggita; **~ place** n (AUT) piazzola f di sosta.

**passion** ['pæʃən] n passione f; amore m; **~ate** a appassionato(a).

**passive** ['pæsɪv] a (also LING) passivo(a).

**Passover** ['pɑ:səuvə*] n Pasqua ebraica.

**passport** ['pɑ:spɔ:t] n passaporto; **~ control** n controllo m passaporti inv.

**password** ['pɑ:swɔ:d] n parola d'ordine.

**past** [pɑ:st] prep (further than) oltre, di là di; dopo; (later than) dopo // a passato(a); (president etc) ex inv // n passato; **he's ~ forty** ha più di quarant'anni; **for the ~ few days** da qualche giorno; in questi ultimi giorni; **to run ~** passare di corsa.

**pasta** ['pæstə] n pasta.

**paste** [peɪst] n (glue) colla; (CULIN)

pâté m inv; pasta // vt collare.

**pastel** ['pæstl] a pastello inv.

**pasteurized** ['pæstəraızd] a pastorizzato(a).

**pastille** ['pæstl] n pastiglia.

**pastime** ['pɑːstaım] n passatempo.

**pastor** ['pɑːstə*] n pastore m.

**pastry** ['peıstrı] n pasta.

**pasture** ['pɑːstʃə*] n pascolo.

**pasty** n ['pæstı] pasticcio di carne // a ['peıstı] pastoso(a); (complexion) pallido(a).

**pat** [pæt] vt accarezzare, dare un colpetto (affettuoso) a.

**patch** [pætʃ] n (of material) toppa; (spot) macchia; (of land) pezzo // vt (clothes) rattoppare; (fig) to ~ up v or rappezzare; ~y a irregolare.

**pâté** ['pæteı] n pâté m inv.

**patent** ['peıtnt] n brevetto // vt brevettare // a patente, manifesto(a); ~ leather n cuoio verniciato.

**paternal** [pə'tə:nl] a paterno(a).

**path** [pɑːθ] n sentiero, viottolo; viale m; (fig) via, strada; (of planet, missile) traiettoria.

**pathetic** [pə'θetık] a (pitiful) patetico(a); (very bad) penoso(a).

**pathological** [pæθə'lɔdʒıkl] a patologico(a).

**patience** ['peıʃns] n pazienza; (Brit CARDS) solitario.

**patient** ['peıʃnt] n paziente m/f; malato/a // a paziente.

**patio** ['pætıəʊ] n terrazza.

**patriot** ['peıtrıət] n patriota m/f; ~ic [pætrı'ɔtık] a patriottico(a); ~ism n patriottismo.

**patrol** [pə'trəʊl] n pattuglia // vt pattugliare; ~ car n autoradio f inv (della polizia); ~man n (US) poliziotto.

**patron** ['peıtrən] n (in shop) cliente m/f; (of charity) benefattore/trice; ~ of the arts mecenate m/f; ~ize ['pætrənaız] vt essere cliente abituale di; (fig) trattare con condiscendenza.

**patter** ['pætə*] n picchiettio; (sales talk) propaganda di vendita.

**pattern** ['pætən] n modello; (design) disegno, motivo; (sample) campione m.

**paunch** [pɔ:ntʃ] n pancione m.

**pauper** ['pɔ:pə*] n indigente m/f.

**pause** [pɔ:z] n pausa // vi fare una pausa, arrestarsi.

**pave** [peıv] vt pavimentare; to ~ the way for aprire la via a.

**pavement** ['peıvmənt] n (Brit) marciapiede m.

**pavilion** [pə'vılıən] n padiglione m; tendone m.

**paving** ['peıvıŋ] n pavimentazione f; ~ stone n lastra di pietra.

**paw** [pɔ:] n zampa // vt dare una zampata a; (subj: person: pej) palpare.

**pawn** [pɔ:n] n pegno; (CHESS) pedone m; (fig) pedina // vt dare in pegno; ~broker n prestatore m su pegno; ~shop n monte m di pietà.

**pay** [peı] n stipendio, paga // vb (pt, pp paid) vt pagare // vi pagare; (be profitable) rendere; to ~ attention (to) fare attenzione (a); to ~ back vt rimborsare; to ~ for vt fus pagare; to ~ in vt versare; to ~ off vt (debt) saldare; (person) pagare; (employee) pagare e licenziare // vi (scheme, decision) dare dei frutti; to ~ up vt saldare; ~able a pagabile; ~ee n beneficiario/a; ~ envelope n (US) = ~ packet; ~ment n pagamento; versamento; saldamento; advance ~ment (part sum) anticipo, acconto; (total sum) pagamento anticipato; ~ packet n (Brit) busta f paga inv; ~ phone n cabina telefonica; ~roll n ruolo (organico); ~ slip n foglio m paga inv.

**PC** n abbr = **personal computer**.

**p.c.** abbr = **per cent.**

**pea** [pi:] n pisello.

**peace** [pi:s] n pace f; (calm) calma, tranquillità; ~able a pacifico(a); ~ful a pacifico(a), calmo(a).

**peach** [pi:tʃ] n pesca.

**peacock** ['pi:kɔk] n pavone m.

**peak** [pi:k] n (of mountain) cima, vetta; (mountain itself) picco; (fig) massimo; (: of career) acme f; ~ **hours** npl ore fpl di punta.

**peal** [pi:l] n (of bells) scampanio, carillon m inv; ~s of laughter scoppi mpl di risa.

**peanut** ['pi:nʌt] n arachide f, nocciolina americana.

**pear** [pɛə*] n pera.

**pearl** [pə:l] n perla.

**peasant** ['pɛznt] n contadino/a.

**peat** [pi:t] n torba.

**pebble** ['pɛbl] n ciottolo.

**peck** [pɛk] vt (also: ~ at) beccare; (food) mangiucchiare // n colpo di becco; (kiss) bacetto; ~**ing order** n ordine m gerarchico; ~**ish** a (Brit col): I feel ~**ish** ho un languorino.

**peculiar** [pɪ'kju:lɪə*] a strano(a), bizzarro(a); peculiare; ~ **to** peculiare di.

**pedal** ['pɛdl] n pedale m // vi pedalare.

**pedantic** [pɪ'dæntɪk] a pedantesco(a).

**peddler** ['pɛdlə*] n (US) = **pedlar.**

**pedestal** ['pɛdəstl] n piedestallo.

**pedestrian** [pɪ'dɛstrɪən] n pedone/a // a pedonale; (fig) prosaico(a), pedestre; ~ **crossing** n (Brit) passaggio pedonale.

**pediatrics** [pi:dɪ'ætrɪks] n (US) = **paediatrics.**

**pedigree** ['pɛdɪgri:] n stirpe f; (of animal) pedigree m inv // cpd (animal) di razza.

**pedlar** ['pɛdlə*] n venditore m ambulante.

**pee** [pi:] vi (col) pisciare.

**peek** [pi:k] vi guardare furtivamente.

**peel** [pi:l] n buccia; (of orange, lemon) scorza // vt sbucciare // vi (paint etc) staccarsi.

**peep** [pi:p] n (Brit: look) sguardo furtivo, sbirciata; (sound) pigolio // vi (Brit) guardare furtivamente; **to ~ out** vi mostrarsi furtivamente; ~**hole** n spioncino.

**peer** [pɪə*] vi: **to ~ at** scrutare // n (noble) pari m inv; (equal) pari m/f inv, uguale m/f; ~**age** n dignità di pari; pari mpl.

**peeved** [pi:vd] a stizzito(a).

**peevish** [pi:vɪʃ] a stizzoso(a).

**peg** [pɛg] n caviglia; (for coat etc) attaccapanni m inv; (Brit: also: **clothes** ~) molletta // vt (prices) fissare, stabilizzare.

**Peking** [pi:'kɪŋ] n Pechino f.

**pelican** ['pɛlɪkən] n pellicano; ~ **crossing** n (Brit AUT) attraversamento pedonale con semaforo a controllo manuale.

**pellet** ['pɛlɪt] n pallottola, pallina.

**pelmet** ['pɛlmɪt] n mantovana; cassonetto.

**pelt** [pɛlt] vt: **to ~ sb (with)** bombardare qn (con) // vi (rain) piovere a dirotto // n pelle f.

**pelvis** ['pɛlvɪs] n pelvi f inv, bacino.

**pen** [pɛn] n penna; (for sheep) recinto.

**penal** ['pi:nl] a penale; ~**ize** vt punire; (SPORT) penalizzare; (fig) svantaggiare.

**penalty** ['pɛnltɪ] n penalità f inv; sanzione f penale; (fine) ammenda; (SPORT) penalizzazione f; ~ **(kick)** n (FOOTBALL) calcio di rigore.

**penance** ['pɛnəns] n penitenza.

**pence** [pɛns] npl of **penny.**

**pencil** ['pɛnsl] n matita; ~ **case** n astuccio per matite; ~ **sharpener** n temperamatite m inv.

**pendant** ['pɛndnt] n pendaglio.

**pending** ['pɛndɪŋ] prep in attesa di // a in sospeso.

**pendulum** ['pɛndjuləm] n pendolo.

**penetrate** ['pɛnɪtreɪt] vt penetrare.

**penfriend** ['pɛnfrɛnd] n (Brit) corrispondente m/f.

**penguin** ['pɛŋgwɪn] n pinguino.

**penicillin** [pɛnɪ'sɪlɪn] n penicillina.

**peninsula** [pə'nɪnsjulə] n penisola.

**penis** ['pi:nɪs] n pene m.

**penitent** ['pɛnɪtnt] a penitente.

**penitentiary** [pɛnɪ'tɛnʃərɪ] n (US) carcere m.

**penknife** ['pɛnnaɪf] n temperino.

**pen name** n pseudonimo.

**penniless** ['pɛnɪlɪs] a senza un soldo.

**penny,** pl **pennies** or (Brit) **pence** ['pɛnɪ, 'pɛnɪz, pɛns] n penny m (pl pence); (US) centesimo.

**penpal** ['pɛnpəl] n corrispondente m/f.

**pension** ['pɛnʃən] n pensione f; **~er** n (Brit) pensionato/a.

**pensive** ['pɛnsɪv] a pensoso(a).

**penthouse** ['pɛnthaus] n appartamento (di lusso) nell'attico.

**pent-up** ['pɛntʌp] a (feelings) represso(a).

**people** ['piːpl] npl gente f; persone fpl; (citizens) popolo // n (nation, race) popolo // vt popolare; **4/several ~ came** 4/parecchie persone sono venute; **the room was full of ~** la stanza era piena di gente.

**pep** [pɛp] n (col) dinamismo; **to ~ up** vt vivacizzare; (food) rendere più gustoso(a).

**pepper** ['pɛpə*] n pepe m; (vegetable) peperone m // vt pepare; **~mint** n (plant) menta peperita; (sweet) pasticca di menta.

**peptalk** ['pɛptɔːk] n (col) discorso di incoraggiamento.

**per** [pəː*] prep per; a; **~ hour** all'ora; **~ kilo** etc il chilo etc; **~ day** al giorno; **~ annum** ad all'anno; **~ capita** a pro capite inv.

**perceive** [pə'siːv] vt (notice) accorgersi di.

**per cent** [pə'sɛnt] ad per cento.

**percentage** [pə'sɛntɪdʒ] n percentuale f.

**perception** [pə'sɛpʃən] n percezione f; sensibilità; perspicacia.

**perceptive** [pə'sɛptɪv] a percettivo(a); perspicace.

**perch** [pəːtʃ] n (fish) pesce m persico; (for bird) sostegno, ramo // vi appollaiarsi.

**percolator** ['pəːkəleɪtə*] n caffettiera a pressione; caffettiera elettrica.

**percussion** [pə'kʌʃən] n percussione

f; (MUS) strumenti mpl a percussione.

**peremptory** [pə'rɛmptərɪ] a perentorio(a).

**perennial** [pə'rɛnɪəl] a perenne // n pianta perenne.

**perfect** a, n ['pəːfɪkt] a perfetto(a) // n (also: **~ tense**) perfetto, passato prossimo // vt [pə'fɛkt] perfezionare; **mettere a punto; ~ly** ad perfettamente, alla perfezione.

**perforate** ['pəːfəreɪt] vt perforare; **perforation** [-'reɪʃən] n perforazione f; (line of holes) dentellatura.

**perform** [pə'fɔːm] vt (carry out) eseguire, fare; (symphony etc) suonare; (play, ballet) dare; (opera) fare // vi suonare; recitare; **~ance** n esecuzione f; (at theatre etc) rappresentazione f, spettacolo; (of an artist) interpretazione f; (of player etc) performance f; (of car, engine) prestazione f; **~er** n artista m/f; **~ing** a (animal) ammaestrato(a).

**perfume** ['pəːfjuːm] n profumo.

**perfunctory** [pə'fʌŋktərɪ] a superficiale, per la forma.

**perhaps** [pə'hæps] ad forse.

**peril** ['pɛrɪl] n pericolo.

**perimeter** [pə'rɪmɪtə*] n perimetro; **~ wall** n muro di cinta.

**period** ['pɪərɪəd] n periodo; (HISTORY) epoca; (SCOL) lezione f; (full stop) punto; (MED) mestruazioni fpl // a (costume, furniture) d'epoca; **~ic** [-'ɔdɪk] a periodico(a); **~ical** [-'ɔdɪkl] a periodico // n periodico.

**peripheral** [pə'rɪfərəl] a periferico(a) // n (COMPUT) unità f inv periferica.

**perish** ['pɛrɪʃ] vi perire, morire; (decay) deteriorarsi; **~able** a deperibile.

**perjury** ['pəːdʒərɪ] n spergiuro.

**perk** [pəːk] n vantaggio; **to ~ up** vi (cheer up) rianimarsi; **~y** a (cheerful) vivace, allegro(a).

**perm** [pəːm] n (for hair) permanente f.

**permanent** ['pəːmənənt] a permanente.

**permeate** ['pə:mieit] *vi* penetrare // *vt* permeare.

**permissible** [pə'misibl] *a* permissibile, ammissibile.

**permission** [pə'miʃən] *n* permesso.

**permissive** [pə'misiv] *a* tollerante; the ~ society la società permissiva.

**permit** *n* ['pə:mit] permesso // *vt* [pə'mit] permettere; to ~ sb to do permettere a qn di fare, dare il permesso a qn di fare.

**perpendicular** [pə:pən'dikjulə*] *a, n* perpendicolare (*f*).

**perplex** [pə'pleks] *vt* lasciare perplesso(a).

**persecute** ['pə:sikju:t] *vt* perseguitare.

**persevere** [pə:si'viə*] *vi* perseverare.

**Persian** ['pə:ʃən] *a* persiano(a) // *n* (*LING*) persiano; the (~) Gulf *n* il Golfo Persico.

**persist** [pə'sist] *vi*: to ~ (in doing) persistere (nel fare); ostinarsi (a fare); ~ent *a* persistente; ostinato(a).

**person** ['pə:sn] *n* persona; in ~ di or in persona, personalmente; ~able *a* di bell'aspetto; ~al *a* personale; individuale; ~al assistant (P.A.) *n* segretaria personale; ~al computer (PC) *n* personal computer *m inv*; ~ality [-'næliti] *n* personalità *f inv*; ~ally *ad* personalmente.

**personnel** [pə:sə'nel] *n* personale *m*.

**perspective** [pə'spektiv] *n* prospettiva.

**perspiration** [pə:spi'reiʃən] *n* traspirazione *f*, sudore *m*.

**persuade** [pə'sweid] *vt*: to ~ sb to do sth persuadere qn a fare qc.

**pert** [pə:t] *a* (*bold*) sfacciato(a), impertinente.

**pertaining** [pə:'teiniŋ]: ~ to *prep* che riguarda.

**perturb** [pə'tə:b] *vt* turbare.

**peruse** [pə'ru:z] *vt* leggere.

**pervade** [pə'veid] *vt* pervadere.

**perverse** [pə'və:s] *a* perverso(a).

**pervert** *n* [pə'və:t] pervertito/a // *vt* [pə'və:t] pervertire.

**pessimism** ['pesimizəm] *n* pessimismo.

**pessimist** ['pesimist] *n* pessimista *m/f*; ~ic [-'mistik] *a* pessimistico(a).

**pest** [pest] *n* animale *m* (*or* insetto) pestifero; (*fig*) peste *f*.

**pester** ['pestə*] *vt* tormentare, molestare.

**pet** [pet] *n* animale *m* domestico; (*favourite*) favorito/a // *vt* accarezzare // *vi* (*col*) fare il petting.

**petal** ['petl] *n* petalo.

**peter** ['pi:tə*]: to ~ out *vi* esaurirsi; estinguersi.

**petite** [pə'ti:t] *a* piccolo(a) e aggraziato(a).

**petition** [pə'tiʃən] *n* petizione *f*.

**petrified** ['petrifaid] *a* (*fig*) morto(a) di paura.

**petrol** ['petrəl] *n* (*Brit*) benzina; two/four-star ~ ≈ benzina normale/super; ~ **can** *n* tanica per benzina.

**petroleum** [pə'trəuliəm] *n* petrolio.

**petrol:** ~ **pump** *n* (*Brit*: in car, *garage*) pompa di benzina; ~ **station** *n* (*Brit*) stazione *f* di rifornimento; ~ **tank** *n* (*Brit*) serbatoio della benzina.

**petticoat** ['petikəut] *n* sottana.

**petty** ['peti] *a* (*mean*) meschino(a); (*unimportant*) insignificante; ~ **cash** *n* piccola cassa; ~ **officer** *n* sottufficiale *m* di marina.

**petulant** ['petjulənt] *a* irritabile.

**pew** [pju:] *n* panca (di chiesa).

**pewter** ['pju:tə*] *n* peltro.

**phallic** ['fælik] *a* fallico(a).

**phantom** ['fæntəm] *n* fantasma *m*.

**pharmaceutical** [fa:mə'sju:tikl] *a* farmaceutico(a).

**pharmacy** ['fa:məsi] *n* farmacia.

**phase** [feiz] *n* fase *f*, periodo // *vt*: to ~ sth in/out introdurre/eliminare qc progressivamente.

**Ph.D.** *n abbr* = **Doctor of Philosophy**.

**pheasant** ['feznt] *n* fagiano.

**phenomenon,** *pl* **phenomena** [fə'nɔminən, -nə] *n* fenomeno.

**philanthropist** [fɪ'lænθrəpɪst] *n* filantropo.

**philately** [fɪ'lætəlɪ] *n* filatelia.

**philosophical** [fɪlə'sɔfɪkl] *a* filosofico(a).

**philosophy** [fɪ'lɔsəfɪ] *n* filosofia.

**phlegmatic** [flɛg'mætɪk] *a* flemmatico(a).

**phobia** ['fəubjə] *n* fobia.

**phone** [fəun] *n* telefono // *vt* telefonare; **to be on the ~** avere il telefono; (*be calling*) essere al telefono; **to ~ back** *vt, vi* richiamare; **to ~ up** *vt* telefonare a // *vi* telefonare; **~ book** *n* guida del telefono, elenco telefonico; **~ box** *or* **booth** *n* cabina telefonica; **~ call** *n* telefonata; **~-in** *n* (*Brit* RADIO, TV) trasmissione *f* a filo diretto con gli ascoltatori.

**phonetics** [fə'nɛtɪks] *n* fonetica.

**phoney** ['fəunɪ] *a* falso(a), fasullo(a) // *n* (*person*) ciarlatano.

**phonograph** ['fəunəgraːf] *n* (*US*) giradischi *m inv*.

**phony** ['fəunɪ] *a* = **phoney**.

**phosphate** ['fɔsfeɪt] *n* fosfato.

**phosphorus** ['fɔsfərəs] *n* fosforo.

**photo** ['fəutəu] *n* foto *f inv*.

**photo...** ['fəutəu] *prefix*: **~copier** *n* fotocopiatrice *f*; **~copy** *n* fotocopia // *vt* fotocopiare; **~graph** *n* fotografia // *vt* fotografare; **~grapher** [fə'tɔgrəfə*] *n* fotografo; **~graphy** [fə'tɔgrəfɪ] *n* fotografia.

**phrase** [freɪz] *n* espressione *f*; (*LING*) locuzione *f*; (*MUS*) frase *f* // *vt* esprimere; **~ book** *n* vocabolarietto.

**physical** ['fɪzɪkl] *a* fisico(a); **~ education** *n* educazione *f* fisica; **~ly** *ad* fisicamente.

**physician** [fɪ'zɪʃən] *n* medico.

**physicist** ['fɪzɪsɪst] *n* fisico.

**physics** ['fɪzɪks] *n* fisica.

**physiology** [fɪzɪ'ɔlədʒɪ] *n* fisiologia.

**physique** [fɪ'ziːk] *n* fisico; costituzione *f*.

**pianist** ['pɪːənɪst] *n* pianista *m/f*.

**piano** [pɪ'ænəu] *n* pianoforte *m*.

**piccolo** ['pɪkələu] *n* ottavino.

**pick** [pɪk] *n* (*tool: also:* **~-axe**) piccone *m* // *vt* scegliere; (*gather*) cogliere; **take your ~** scelga; (*the ~* of il fior fiore di; **to ~ off** *vt* (*kill*) abbattere (uno dopo l'altro); **to ~ on** *vt fus* (*person*) avercela con; **to ~ out** *vt* scegliere; (*distinguish*) distinguere; **to ~ up** *vi* (*improve*) migliorarsi // *vt* raccogliere; (*collect*) passare a prendere; (*AUT: give lift to*) far salire; (*learn*) imparare; **to ~ up speed** acquistare velocità; **to ~ o.s. up** rialzarsi.

**picket** ['pɪkɪt] *n* (*in strike*) scioperante *m/f* che fa parte di un picchetto; picchetto // *vt* picchettare.

**pickle** ['pɪkl] *n* (*also:* **~s:** *as condiment*) sottaceti *mpl* // *vt* mettere sottaceto; mettere in salamoia.

**pickpocket** ['pɪkpɔkɪt] *n* borsaiolo.

**pickup** ['pɪkʌp] *n* (*Brit: on record player*) pick-up *m inv*; (*small truck*) camioncino.

**picnic** ['pɪknɪk] *n* picnic *m inv*.

**pictorial** [pɪk'tɔːrɪəl] *a* illustrato(a).

**picture** ['pɪktʃə*] *n* quadro; (*painting*) pittura; (*photograph*) foto(grafia); (*drawing*) disegno; (*film*) film *m inv* // *vt* raffigurarsi; **the ~s** (*Brit*) il cinema; **~ book** *n* libro illustrato.

**picturesque** [pɪktʃə'rɛsk] *a* pittoresco(a).

**pidgin English** ['pɪdʒɪn-] *n* inglese semplificato misto ad elementi indigeni.

**pie** [paɪ] *n* torta; (*of meat*) pasticcio.

**piece** [piːs] *n* pezzo; (*of land*) appezzamento; (*item*): **a ~ of furniture/advice** un mobile/consiglio // *vt*: **to ~ together** mettere insieme; **to take to ~s** smontare; **~meal** *ad* pezzo a pezzo, a spizzico; **~work** *n* (lavoro a) cottimo.

**pie chart** *n* grafico a torta.

**pier** [pɪə*] *n* molo; (*of bridge etc*)

pila.

**pierce** [pɪəs] *vt* forare; *(with arrow etc)* trafiggere.

**piercing** ['pɪəsɪŋ] *a (cry)* acuto(a).

**pig** [pɪg] *n* maiale *m*, porco.

**pigeon** ['pɪdʒən] *n* piccione *m*; ~**hole** *n* casella.

**piggy bank** ['pɪgɪ-] *n* salvadanaro.

**pigheaded** ['pɪg'hɛdɪd] *a* caparbio(a), cocciuto(a).

**piglet** ['pɪglɪt] *n* porcellino.

**pigskin** ['pɪgskɪn] *n* cinghiale *m*.

**pigsty** ['pɪgstaɪ] *n* porcile *m*.

**pigtail** ['pɪgteɪl] *n* treccia.

**pike** [paɪk] *n (spear)* picca; *(fish)* luccio.

**pilchard** ['pɪltʃəd] *n* specie di sardina.

**pile** [paɪl] *n (pillar, of books)* pila; *(heap)* mucchio; *(of carpet)* pelo // *vb (also:* ~ **up)** *vt* ammucchiare // *vi* ammucchiarsi; **to** ~ **into** *(car)* stiparsi *or* ammucchiarsi in.

**piles** [paɪlz] *npl* emorroidi *fpl*.

**pileup** ['paɪlʌp] *n (AUT)* tamponamento a catena.

**pilfering** ['pɪlfərɪŋ] *n* rubacchiare *m*.

**pilgrim** ['pɪlgrɪm] *n* pellegrino/a; ~**age** *n* pellegrinaggio.

**pill** [pɪl] *n* pillola; **the** ~ la pillola.

**pillage** ['pɪlɪdʒ] *vt* saccheggiare.

**pillar** ['pɪlə*] *n* colonna; ~ **box** *n (Brit)* cassetta postale.

**pillion** ['pɪljən] *n (of motor cycle)* sellino posteriore.

**pillory** ['pɪlərɪ] *vt* mettere alla berlina.

**pillow** ['pɪləu] *n* guanciale *m*; ~**case** *n* federa.

**pilot** ['paɪlət] *n* pilota *m/f* // *cpd (scheme etc)* pilota *inv* // *vt* pilotare; ~ **light** *n* fiamma pilota.

**pimp** [pɪmp] *n* mezzano.

**pimple** ['pɪmpl] *n* foruncolo.

**pin** [pɪn] *n* spillo; *(TECH)* perno // *vt* attaccare con uno spillo; ~**s and needles** formicolio; **to** ~ **sb down** *(fig)* obbligare qn a pronunciarsi; **to** ~ **sth on sb** *(fig)* addossare la colpa di qc a qn.

**pinafore** ['pɪnəfɔ:*] *n* grembiule *m (senza maniche).*

**pinball** ['pɪnbɔ:l] *n (also:* ~ **machine)** flipper *m inv*.

**pincers** ['pɪnsəz] *npl* pinzette *fpl*.

**pinch** [pɪntʃ] *n* pizzicotto, pizzico // *vt* pizzicare; *(col: steal)* grattare // *vi (shoe)* stringere; **at a** ~ in caso di bisogno.

**pincushion** ['pɪnkuʃən] *n* puntaspilli *m inv*.

**pine** [paɪn] *n (also:* ~ **tree)** pino // *vi:* **to** ~ **for** struggersi dal desiderio di; **to** ~ **away** *vi* languire.

**pineapple** ['paɪnæpl] *n* ananas *m inv*.

**ping** [pɪŋ] *n (noise)* tintinnio; ~-**pong** *n* ® ping-pong *m* ®.

**pink** [pɪŋk] *a* rosa *inv* // *n (colour)* rosa *m inv*; *(BOT)* garofano.

**pinpoint** ['pɪnpɔɪnt] *vt* indicare con precisione.

**pint** [paɪnt] *n* pinta *(Brit = 0.57l; US = 0.47l)*; *(Brit col)* ~ birra da mezzo.

**pioneer** [paɪə'nɪə*] *n* pioniere/a.

**pious** ['paɪəs] *a* pio(a).

**pip** [pɪp] *n (seed)* seme *m*; *(Brit: time signal on radio)* segnale *m* orario.

**pipe** [paɪp] *n* tubo; *(for smoking)* pipa; *(MUS)* piffero // *vt* portare per mezzo di tubazione; ~**s** *npl (also: bag~s)* cornamusa *(scozzese)*; **to** ~ **down** *vi (col)* calmarsi; ~ **cleaner** *n* scovolino; ~ **dream** *n* vana speranza; ~**line** *n* conduttura; *(for oil)* oleodotto; ~**r** *n* piffero; suonatore/trice di cornamusa.

**piping** ['paɪpɪŋ] *ad:* ~ **hot** caldo bollente.

**pique** [pi:k] *n* picca.

**pirate** ['paɪrət] *n* pirata *m*.

**Pisces** ['paɪsi:z] *n* Pesci *mpl*.

**piss** [pɪs] *vi (col)* pisciare; ~**ed** *a (col: drunk)* ubriaco(a fradicio(a).

**pistol** ['pɪstl] *n* pistola.

**piston** ['pɪstən] *n* pistone *m*.

**pit** [pɪt] *n* buca, fossa; *(also:* **coal** ~) miniera; *(also:* **orchestra** ~) orchestra // *vt:* **to** ~ **sb against sb**

opporre qn a qn; ~s npl (AUT) box m.

**pitch** [pɪtʃ] n (throw) lancia; (MUS) tono; (of voice) altezza; (Brit SPORT) campo; (NAUT) beccheggio; (tar) pece f // vt (throw) lanciare // vi (fall) cascare; (NAUT) beccheggiare; **to ~ a tent** piantare una tenda; **~ed battle** n battaglia campale.

**pitcher** ['pɪtʃə*] n brocca.

**pitchfork** ['pɪtʃfɔːk] n forcone m.

**piteous** ['pɪtɪəs] a pietoso(a).

**pitfall** ['pɪtfɔːl] n trappola.

**pith** [pɪθ] n (of plant) midollo; (of orange) parte f interna della scorza; (fig) essenza, succo; vigore m.

**pithy** ['pɪθɪ] a conciso(a), vigoroso(a).

**pitiful** ['pɪtɪful] a (touching) pietoso(a); (contemptible) miserabile.

**pitiless** ['pɪtɪlɪs] a spietato(a).

**pittance** ['pɪtns] n miseria, magro salario.

**pity** ['pɪtɪ] n pietà // vt aver pietà di; **what a ~!** che peccato!

**pivot** ['pɪvət] n perno.

**pizza** ['piːtsə] n pizza.

**placard** ['plækɑːd] n affisso.

**placate** [plə'keɪt] vt placare, calmare.

**place** [pleɪs] n posto, luogo; (proper position, rank, seat) posto; (house) casa, alloggio; (home): **at/to his ~** a casa sua // vt (object) posare, mettere; (identify) riconoscere, individuare; **to take ~** aver luogo, succedere; **to change ~s with sb** scambiare il posto con qn; **out of ~** (not suitable) inopportuno(a); **in the first ~** in primo luogo; **to ~ an order** dare un'ordinazione.

**placid** ['plæsɪd] a placido(a), calmo(a).

**plagiarism** ['pleɪdʒɪərɪzm] n plagio.

**plague** [pleɪg] n peste f // vt tormentare.

**plaice** [pleɪs] n (pl inv) pianuzza.

**plaid** [plæd] n plaid m inv.

**plain** [pleɪn] a (clear) chiaro(a), palese; (simple) semplice; (frank) franco(a), aperto(a); (not handsome) bruttino(a); (without seasoning etc) scondito(a); naturale; (in one colour) tinta unita inv // ad francamente, chiaramente // n pianura; ~ **chocolate** n cioccolato fondente; ~ **clothes** npl: **in ~ clothes** (police) in borghese; **~ly** ad chiaramente; (frankly) francamente.

**plaintiff** ['pleɪntɪf] n attore/trice.

**plaintive** ['pleɪntɪv] a (cry, voice) dolente, lamentoso(a).

**plait** [plæt] n treccia.

**plan** [plæn] n pianta; (scheme) progetto, piano // vt (think in advance) progettare; (prepare) organizzare // vi far piani or progetti.

**plane** [pleɪn] n (AVIAT) aereo; (tree) platano; (tool) pialla; (ART, MATH etc) piano // a piano(a), piatto(a) // vt (with tool) piallare.

**planet** ['plænɪt] n pianeta m.

**plank** [plæŋk] n tavola, asse f.

**planner** ['plænə*] n pianificatore/trice.

**planning** ['plænɪŋ] n progettazione f; **family ~** pianificazione f delle nascite; **~ permission** n permesso di costruzione.

**plant** [plɑːnt] n pianta; (machinery) impianto; (factory) fabbrica // vt piantare; (bomb) mettere.

**plantation** [plæn'teɪʃən] n piantagione f.

**plaque** [plæk] n placca.

**plaster** ['plɑːstə*] n intonaco; (also: ~ **of Paris**) gesso; (Brit: also: **sticking ~**) cerotto // vt intonacare; ingessare; (cover): **to ~ with** coprire di; **in ~** (leg etc) ingessato(a); **~ed** a (col) ubriaco(a) fradicio(a).

**plastic** ['plæstɪk] n plastica // a (made of plastic) di or in plastica; (flexible) plastico(a), malleabile; (art) plastico(a); ~ **bag** n sacchetto di plastica.

**plasticine** ['plæstɪsiːn] n ® plastilina ®.

**plastic surgery** n chirurgia plastica.

**plate** [pleɪt] n (dish) piatto; (sheet of metal) lamiera; (PHOT) lastra; (in book) tavola.

**plateau** [ˈplætəʊ] , ~s or ~x [ˈplætəʊ, -z] n altipiano.

**plate glass** n vetro piano.

**platform** [ˈplætfɔːm] n (stage, at meeting) palco; (RAIL) marciapiede m; (Brit: of bus) piattaforma; ~ ticket n (Brit) biglietto d'ingresso ai binari.

**platinum** [ˈplætɪnəm] n platino.

**platitude** [ˈplætɪtjuːd] n luogo comune.

**platoon** [pləˈtuːn] n plotone m.

**platter** [ˈplætə*] n piatto.

**plausible** [ˈplɔːzɪbl] a plausibile, credibile; (person) convincente.

**play** [pleɪ] n gioco; (THEATRE) commedia // vt (game) giocare a; (team, opponent) giocare contro; (instrument, piece of music) suonare; (play, part) interpretare // vi giocare; suonare; recitare; to ~ safe giocare sul sicuro; to ~ down vt minimizzare; to ~ up vi (cause trouble) fare i capricci; ~boy n playboy m inv; ~er n giocatore/trice; (THEATRE) attore/trice; (MUS) musicista m/f; ~ful a giocoso(a); ~ground n (in school) cortile m per la ricreazione; (in park) parco m giochi inv; ~group n giardino d'infanzia; ~ing card n carta da gioco; ~ing field n campo sportivo; ~mate n compagno/a di gioco; ~-off n (SPORT) bella; ~pen n box m inv; ~school n = ~group; ~thing n giocattolo; ~wright n drammaturgo/a.

**plc** abbr (= public limited company) società per azioni a responsabilità limitata quotata in borsa.

**plea** [pliː] n (request) preghiera, domanda; (excuse) scusa; (LAW) (argomento d) difesa.

**plead** [pliːd] vt patrocinare; (give as excuse) addurre a pretesto // vi (LAW) perorare la causa; (beg): to ~ with sb pregare qn.

**pleasant** [ˈplɛznt] a piacevole, gradevole; ~ries npl (polite remarks): to exchange ~ries scambiarsi i convenevoli.

**please** [pliːz] vt piacere a // vi (think fit): do as you ~ faccia come le pare; ~! per piacere!; ~ yourself! come ti (or le) pare!; ~d a: ~d (with) contento(a) (di); ~d to meet you! piacere!; **pleasing** a piacevole, che fa piacere.

**pleasure** [ˈplɛʒə*] n piacere m; "it's a ~" "prego".

**pleat** [pliːt] n piega.

**plectrum** [ˈplɛktrəm] n plettro.

**pledge** [plɛdʒ] n pegno; (promise) promessa // vi impegnare; promettere.

**plentiful** [ˈplɛntɪful] a abbondante, copioso(a).

**plenty** [ˈplɛntɪ] n abbondanza; ~ of tanto(a), molto(a); un'abbondanza di.

**pleurisy** [ˈpluərɪsɪ] n pleurite f.

**pliable** [ˈplaɪəbl] a flessibile; (person) malleabile.

**pliers** [ˈplaɪəz] npl pinza.

**plight** [plaɪt] n situazione f critica.

**plimsolls** [ˈplɪmsəlz] npl (Brit) scarpe fpl da tennis.

**plinth** [plɪnθ] n plinto; piedistallo.

**plod** [plɒd] vi camminare a stento; (fig) sgobbare; ~der n sgobbone m.

**plonk** [plɒŋk] (col) n (Brit: wine) vino da poco // vt: to ~ sth down buttare giù qc bruscamente.

**plot** [plɒt] n congiura, cospirazione f; (of story, play) trama; (of land) lotto // vt (mark out) fare la pianta di; rilevare; (: diagram etc) tracciare; (conspire) congiurare, cospirare // vi congiurare; ~ter n (instrument) plotter m inv.

**plough**, (US) **plow** [plau] n aratro // vt (earth) arare; to ~ back vt (COMM) reinvestire; to ~ through vt fus (snow etc) procedere a fatica in.

**ploy** [plɔɪ] n stratagemma m.

**pluck** [plʌk] vt (fruit) cogliere; (musical instrument) pizzicare; (bird) spennare // n coraggio, fegato; **to ~ up courage** farsi coraggio; **~y** a coraggioso(a).

**plug** [plʌg] n tappo; (ELEC) spina; (AUT: also: **spark(ing)** ~) candela // n (hole) tappare; (col: advertise) spingere; **to ~ in** vt (ELEC) attaccare a una presa.

**plum** [plʌm] n (fruit) susina // cpd: ~ **job** (col) impiego ottimo or favoloso.

**plumb** [plʌm] a verticale // n piombo // ad (exactly) esattamente // vt sondare.

**plumber** ['plʌmə*] n idraulico.

**plumbing** ['plʌmɪŋ] n (trade) lavoro di idraulico; (piping) tubature fpl.

**plume** [pluːm] n piuma, penna; (decorative) pennacchio.

**plummet** ['plʌmɪt] vi cadere a piombo.

**plump** [plʌmp] a grassoccio(a) // vt: **to ~ sth (down)** on lasciar cadere qc di peso su; **to ~ for** vt fus (col: choose) decidersi per.

**plunder** ['plʌndə*] n saccheggio // vt saccheggiare.

**plunge** [plʌndʒ] n tuffo // vt immergere // vi (fall) cadere, precipitare; **to take the ~** saltare il fosso; **~r** n sturalavandini m inv; **plunging** a (neckline) profondo(a).

**pluperfect** [pluː'pəːfɪkt] n piuccheperfetto.

**plural** ['pluərl] a, n plurale (m).

**plus** [plʌs] n (also: ~ **sign**) segno più // prep più; **ten/twenty** ~ più di dieci/venti.

**plush** [plʌʃ] a lussuoso(a).

**ply** [plaɪ] n (of wool) capo; (of wood) strato // vt (tool) maneggiare; (a trade) esercitare // vi (ship) fare il servizio; **to ~ sb with drink** dare di bere continuamente a qn; **~wood** n legno compensato.

**P.M.** n abbr = **prime minister**.

**p.m.** ad abbr (= post meridiem) del pomeriggio.

**pneumatic drill** [njuː'mætɪk-] n martello pneumatico.

**pneumonia** [njuː'məunɪə] n polmonite f.

**poach** [pəutʃ] vt (cook) affogare; (steal) cacciare (or pescare) di frodo // vi fare il bracconiere; **~er** n bracconiere m.

**P.O. Box** n abbr = **Post Office Box**.

**pocket** ['pɔkɪt] n tasca // vt intascare; **to be out of** ~ (Brit) rimetterci; **~book** n (wallet) portafoglio; (notebook) taccuino; ~ **knife** n temperino; ~ **money** n paghetta, settimana.

**pod** [pɔd] n guscio // vt sgusciare.

**podgy** ['pɔdʒɪ] a grassoccio(a).

**podiatrist** [pɔ'diːətrɪst] n (US) callista m/f, pedicure m/f.

**poem** ['pəuɪm] n poesia.

**poet** ['pəuɪt] n poeta/essa; **~ic** [-'ɛtɪk] a poetico(a); ~ **laureate** n poeta m laureato (nominato dalla Corte Reale); **~ry** n poesia.

**poignant** ['pɔɪnjənt] a struggente.

**point** [pɔɪnt] n (gen) punto; (tip: of needle etc) punta; (in time) punto, momento; (SCOL) voto; (main idea, important part) nocciolo; (also: **decimal** ~): **2 ~ 3 (2.3)** 2 virgola 3 (2,3) // vt (show) indicare; (gun etc): **to ~ sth at** puntare qc contro // vi mostrare a dito; **~s** npl (AUT) puntine fpl; (RAIL) scambio; **to be on the ~ of doing sth** essere sul punto di or stare per fare qc; **to make a ~** fare un'osservazione; **to get the ~** capire; **to come to the ~** venire al fatto; **there's no ~** (in doing) è inutile (fare); **to ~ out** vt far notare; **to ~ to** vt fus indicare; (fig) dimostrare; **~-blank** ad (also: **at ~-blank range**) a bruciapelo; (fig) categoricamente; **~ed** a (shape) aguzzo(a); (remark) specifico(a); **~edly** ad in maniera inequivocabile; **~er** n (stick) bacchetta; (needle) lancetta;

*(dog)* pointer *m*, cane *m* da punta; **~less** *a* inutile, vano(a); **~ of view** *n* punto di vista.

**poise** [pɔɪz] *n (balance)* equilibrio; *(of head, body)* portamento; *(calmness)* calma // *vt* tenere in equilibrio.

**poison** ['pɔɪzn] *n* veleno // *vt* avvelenare; **~ing** *n* avvelenamento; **~ous** *a* velenoso(a).

**poke** [pəʊk] *vt (fire)* attizzare; *(jab with finger, stick etc)* punzecchiare; *(put)*: **to ~ sth in(to)** spingere qc dentro; **to ~ about** *vi* frugare.

**poker** ['pəʊkə*] *n* attizzatoio; *(CARDS)* poker *m*; **~-faced** *a* dal viso impassibile.

**poky** ['pəʊkɪ] *a* piccolo(a) e stretto(a).

**Poland** ['pəʊlənd] *n* Polonia.

**polar** ['pəʊlə*] *a* polare; **~ bear** *n* orso bianco.

**Pole** [pəʊl] *n* polacco/a.

**pole** [pəʊl] *n (of wood)* palo; *(ELEC, GEO)* polo; **~ bean** *n (US: runner bean)* fagiolino; **~ vault** *n* salto con l'asta.

**police** [pə'li:s] *n* polizia // *vt* mantenere l'ordine in; **~ car** *n* macchina della polizia; **~man** *n* poliziotto, agente *m* di polizia; **~ station** *n* posto di polizia; **~woman** *n* donna *f* poliziotto *inv*.

**policy** ['pɒlɪsɪ] *n* politica; *(also: insurance ~)* polizza (d'assicurazione).

**polio** ['pəʊlɪəʊ] *n* polio *f*.

**Polish** ['pəʊlɪʃ] *n* polacco(a) // *n (LING)* polacco.

**polish** ['pɒlɪʃ] *n (for shoes)* lucido; *(for floor)* cera; *(for nails)* smalto; *(shine)* lucentezza, lustro; *(fig: refinement)* raffinatezza // *vt* lucidare; *(fig: improve)* raffinare; **to ~ off** *vt (work)* sbrigare; *(food)* mangiarsi; **~ed** *a (fig)* raffinato(a).

**polite** [pə'laɪt] *a* cortese; **~ness** *n* cortesia.

**politic** ['pɒlɪtɪk] *a* diplomatico(a); **~al** [pə'lɪtɪkl] *a* politico(a); **~ally**

*ad* politicamente; **~ian** [-'tɪʃən] *n* politico; **~s** *npl* politica.

**polka** ['pɒlkə] *n* polca; **~ dot** *n* pois *m inv*.

**poll** [pəʊl] *n* scrutinio; *(votes cast)* voti *mpl*; *(also: opinion ~)* sondaggio (d'opinioni) // *vt* ottenere.

**pollen** ['pɒlən] *n* polline *m*.

**pollination** [pɒlɪ'neɪʃən] *n* impollinazione *f*.

**polling** ['pəʊlɪŋ] *(Brit)*: **~ booth** *n* cabina elettorale; **~ day** *n* giorno delle elezioni; **~ station** *n* sezione *f* elettorale.

**pollute** [pə'lu:t] *vt* inquinare.

**pollution** [pə'lu:ʃən] *n* inquinamento.

**polo** ['pəʊləʊ] *n* polo; **~-neck** *a* a collo alto risvoltato.

**polyester** [pɒlɪ'estə*] *n* poliestere *m*.

**polystyrene** [pɒlɪ'staɪri:n] *n* polistirolo.

**polytechnic** [pɒlɪ'tɛknɪk] *n (college)* istituto superiore ad indirizzo tecnologico.

**polythene** ['pɒlɪθi:n] *n* politene *m*; **~ bag** *n* sacco di plastica.

**pomegranate** ['pɒmɪɡrænɪt] *n* melagrana.

**pomp** [pɒmp] *n* pompa, fasto.

**pompom** ['pɒmpɒm], **pompon** ['pɒmpɒn] *n* pompon *m inv*.

**pompous** ['pɒmpəs] *a* pomposo(a).

**pond** [pɒnd] *n* pozza; stagno.

**ponder** ['pɒndə*] *vt* ponderare, riflettere su; **~ous** *a* ponderoso(a), pesante.

**pong** [pɒŋ] *n (Brit col)* puzzo.

**pontiff** ['pɒntɪf] *n* pontefice *m*.

**pony** ['pəʊnɪ] *n inv* pony *m inv*; **~tail** *n* coda di cavallo; **~ trekking** *n (Brit)* escursione *f* a cavallo.

**poodle** ['pu:dl] *n* barboncino, barbone *m*.

**pool** [pu:l] *n (of rain)* pozza; *(pond)* stagno; *(artificial)* vasca; *(also: swimming ~)* piscina; *(sth shared)* fondo comune; *(billiards)* specie di biliardo a buca // *vt* mettere in comune; **typing ~** servizio comune di dattilografia; *(football)* **~s** ≈

totocalcio.

**poor** [puə*] a povero(a); (mediocre) mediocre, cattivo(a) // ad // npl: **the** ~ i poveri; ~**ly** ad poveramente; male // a indisposto(a), malato(a).

**pop** [pɔp] n (noise) schiocco; (MUS) musica pop; (US col: father) babbo // vt (put) mettere (in fretta) // vi scoppiare; (cork) schioccare; **to** ~ **in** vi passare; **to** ~ **out** vi fare un salto fuori; **to** ~ **up** vi apparire, sorgere; ~ **concert** n concerto m pop inv; ~**corn** n pop-corn m.

**pope** [pəup] n papa m.

**poplar** ['pɔplə*] n pioppo.

**poppy** ['pɔpɪ] n papavero.

**popsicle** ['pɔpsɪkl] n (US: ice lolly) ghiacciolo.

**popular** ['pɔpjulə*] a popolare; (fashionable) in voga; ~**ity** [-'lærɪtɪ] n popolarità; ~**ize** vt divulgare; (science) volgarizzare.

**population** [pɔpju'leɪʃən] n popolazione f.

**porcelain** ['pɔ:slɪn] n porcellana.

**porch** [pɔ:tʃ] n veranda.

**porcupine** ['pɔ:kjupaɪn] n porcospino.

**pore** [pɔ:*] n poro // vi: **to** ~ **over** essere immerso(a) in.

**pork** [pɔ:k] n carne f di maiale.

**pornographic** [pɔ:nə'græfɪk] a pornografico(a).

**pornography** [pɔ:'nɔgrəfɪ] n pornografia.

**porpoise** ['pɔ:pəs] n focena.

**porridge** ['pɔrɪdʒ] n porridge m.

**port** [pɔ:t] n porto; (opening in ship) portello; (NAUT: left side) babordo; (wine) porto; ~ **of call** (porto di) scalo.

**portable** ['pɔ:təbl] a portatile.

**portent** ['pɔ:tent] n presagio.

**porter** ['pɔ:tə*] n (for luggage) facchino, portabagagli m inv; (doorkeeper) portiere m, portinaio.

**portfolio** [pɔ:t'fəulɪəu] n (case) cartella; (POL, FINANCE) portafoglio; (of artist) raccolta dei propri lavori.

**porthole** ['pɔ:thəul] n oblò m inv.

**portion** ['pɔ:ʃən] n porzione f.

**portly** ['pɔ:tlɪ] a corpulento(a).

**portrait** ['pɔ:treɪt] n ritratto.

**portray** [pɔ:'treɪ] vt fare il ritratto di; (character on stage) rappresentare; (in writing) ritrarre.

**Portugal** [pɔ:tjugl] n Portogallo.

**Portuguese** [pɔ:tju'gi:z] a portoghese // n (pl inv) portoghese m/f; (LING) portoghese m.

**pose** [pəuz] n posa // vi posare; (pretend): **to** ~ **as** atteggiarsi a, posare a // vt porre.

**posh** [pɔʃ] a (col) elegante; (family) per bene.

**position** [pə'zɪʃən] n posizione f; (job) posto.

**positive** ['pɔzɪtɪv] a positivo(a); (certain) sicuro(a), certo(a); (definite) preciso(a); definitivo(a).

**posse** ['pɔsɪ] n (US) drappello.

**possess** [pə'zes] vt possedere; ~**ion** [pə'zeʃən] n possesso; (object) bene m; ~**ive** a possessivo(a).

**possibility** [pɔsɪ'bɪlɪtɪ] n possibilità f inv.

**possible** ['pɔsɪbl] a possibile; **as big as** ~ il più grande possibile.

**possibly** ['pɔsɪblɪ] ad (perhaps) forse; **if you** ~ **can** se Le è possibile; **I cannot** ~ **come** proprio non posso venire.

**post** [pəust] n (Brit) posta; (collection) levata; (job, situation) posto; (pole) palo // vt (Brit: send by post) impostare; (MIL) appostare; (notice) affiggere; (Brit: appoint): **to** ~ **to** assegnare a; ~**age** n affrancatura; ~**al order** n vaglia m inv postale; ~**box** n (Brit) cassetta postale; ~**card** n cartolina; ~**code** n (Brit) codice m (di avviamento) postale.

**poster** ['pəustə*] n manifesto, affisso.

**poste restante** [pəust'rɛstã:nt] n (Brit) fermo posta m.

**postgraduate** ['pəust'grædjuət] n laureato/a che continua gli studi.

**posthumous** ['pɔstjuməs] a postumo(a).

**postman** ['pəustmən] $n$ postino.

**postmark** ['pəustmɑːk] $n$ bollo $or$ timbro postale.

**postmaster** ['pəustmɑːstə*] $n$ direttore $m$ d'un ufficio postale.

**post-mortem** [pəust'mɔːtəm] $n$ autopsia.

**post office** $n$ (building) ufficio postale; (organization): **the Post Office** ≈ le Poste e Telecomunicazioni; **Post Office Box (P.O. Box)** $n$ casella postale (C.P.).

**postpone** [pəs'pəun] $vt$ rinviare.

**postscript** ['pəustskrɪpt] $n$ poscritto.

**posture** ['pɔstʃə*] $n$ portamento; (pose) posa, atteggiamento // $vi$ posare.

**postwar** ['pəust'wɔː*] $a$ del dopoguerra.

**posy** ['pəuzɪ] $n$ mazzetto di fiori.

**pot** [pɔt] $n$ (for cooking) pentola, casseruola; (for plants, jam) vaso; (col: marijuana) erba // $vt$ (plant) piantare in vaso; **to go to ~** (col: work, performance) andare in malora.

**potato**, **~es** [pə'teɪtəu] $n$ patata; **~ peeler** $n$ sbucciapatate $m$ inv.

**potent** ['pəutnt] $a$ potente, forte.

**potential** [pə'tɛnʃl] $a$ potenziale // $n$ possibilità $fpl$; **~ly** $ad$ potenzialmente.

**pothole** ['pɔthəul] $n$ (in road) buca; (Brit: underground) caverna; **potholing** $n$ (Brit): **to go potholing** fare la speleologia.

**potluck** [pɔt'lʌk] $n$: **to take ~** tentare la sorte.

**potshot** ['pɔtʃɔt] $n$: **to take ~s** $or$ $a$ **~ at** tirare a vanvera contro.

**potted** ['pɔtɪd] $a$ (food) in conserva; (plant) in vaso.

**potter** ['pɔtə*] $n$ vasaio // $vi$: **to ~ around**, **~ about** lavoracchiare; **~y** $n$ ceramiche $fpl$.

**potty** ['pɔtɪ] $a$ (col: mad) tocco(a) // $n$ (child's) vasino.

**pouch** [pautʃ] $n$ borsa; (ZOOL) marsupio.

**poultry** ['pəultrɪ] $n$ pollame $m$.

**pounce** [pauns] $vi$: **to ~ (on)** balzare addosso a, piombare su // $n$ balzo.

**pound** [paund] $n$ (weight) libbra; (money) (lira) sterlina; (for dogs) canile $m$ municipale // $vt$ (beat) battere; (crush) pestare, polverizzare // $vi$ (beat) battere, martellare.

**pour** [pɔː*] $vt$ versare // $vi$ riversarsi; (rain) piovere a dirotto; **to ~ away** $or$ **off** $vt$ vuotare; **to ~ in** $vi$ (people) entrare a flotti; **to ~ out** $vt$ vuotare; versare; (serve: a drink) mescere; **~ing** $a$: **~ing rain** pioggia torrenziale.

**pout** [paut] $vi$ sporgere le labbra; fare il broncio.

**poverty** ['pɔvətɪ] $n$ povertà, miseria; **~-stricken** $a$ molto povero(a), misero(a).

**powder** ['paudə*] $n$ polvere $f$ // $vt$ spolverizzare; (face) incipriare; **to ~ one's nose** incipriarsi il naso; **~ compact** $n$ portacipria $m$ inv; **~ed milk** $n$ latte $m$ in polvere; **~ puff** $n$ piumino della cipria; **~ room** $n$ toilette $f$ inv (per signore).

**power** ['pauə*] $n$ (strength) potenza, forza; (ability, POL: of party, leader) potere $m$; (MATH) potenza; (ELEC) corrente $f$ // $vt$ fornire di energia; **to be in ~** (POL etc) essere al potere; **~ cut** $n$ (Brit) interruzione $f$ or mancanza di corrente; **~ failure** $n$ interruzione $f$ della corrente elettrica; **~ful** $a$ potente, forte; **~less** $a$ impotente, senza potere; **~ point** $n$ (Brit) presa di corrente; **~ station** $n$ centrale $f$ elettrica.

**p.p.** abbr (= per procurationem): **~ J. Smith** per J. Smith.

**PR** abbr = **public relations**.

**practicable** ['præktɪkəbl] $a$ (scheme) praticabile.

**practical** ['præktɪkl] $a$ pratico(a); **~ity** [-'kælɪtɪ] $n$ (no pl) (of situation etc) lato pratico; **~ joke** $n$ beffa; **~ly** $ad$ (almost) quasi.

**practice** ['præktɪs] n pratica; (of profession) esercizio; (at football etc) allenamento; (business) gabinetto; clientela // vt, vi (US) = **practise**; **in** ~ (in reality) in pratica; **out of** ~ fuori esercizio.

**practise**, (US) **practice** ['præktɪs] vt (work at: piano, one's backhand etc) esercitarsi a; (train for: skiing, running etc) allenarsi a; (a sport, religion) praticare; (method) usare; (profession) esercitare // vi esercitarsi; (train) allenarsi; **practising** a (Christian etc) praticante; (lawyer) che esercita la professione.

**practitioner** [præk'tɪʃənə*] n professionista m/f.

**pragmatic** [præg'mætɪk] a prammatico(a).

**prairie** ['prɛərɪ] n prateria.

**praise** [preɪz] n elogio, lode f // vt elogiare, lodare; ~**worthy** a lodevole.

**pram** [præm] n (Brit) carrozzina.

**prance** [prɑːns] vi (horse) impennarsi.

**prank** [præŋk] n burla.

**prawn** [prɔːn] n gamberetto.

**pray** [preɪ] vi pregare.

**prayer** [prɛə*] n preghiera.

**preach** [priːtʃ] vt, vi predicare.

**precarious** [prɪ'kɛərɪəs] a precario(a).

**precaution** [prɪ'kɔːʃən] n precauzione f.

**precede** [prɪ'siːd] vt, vi precedere.

**precedence** ['presɪdəns] n precedenza.

**precedent** ['presɪdənt] n precedente m.

**precept** ['priːsept] n precetto.

**precinct** ['priːsɪŋkt] n (round cathedral) recinto; ~**s** npl (neighbourhood) dintorni mpl; vicinanze fpl; **pedestrian** ~ (Brit) zona pedonale.

**precious** ['preʃəs] a prezioso(a).

**precipitate** [prɪ'sɪpɪtt] a (hasty) precipitoso(a).

**précis**, pl **précis** ['preɪsiː, -z] n riassunto.

**precise** [prɪ'saɪs] a preciso(a); ~**ly** ad precisamente.

**preclude** [prɪ'kluːd] vt precludere, impedire.

**precocious** [prɪ'kəuʃəs] a precoce.

**precondition** [priːkən'dɪʃən] n condizione f necessaria.

**predecessor** ['priːdɪsesə*] n predecessore/a.

**predicament** [prɪ'dɪkəmənt] n situazione f difficile.

**predict** [prɪ'dɪkt] vt predire; ~**able** a prevedibile.

**predominantly** [prɪ'dɒmɪnəntlɪ] ad in maggior parte; soprattutto.

**predominate** [prɪ'dɒmɪnet] vi predominare.

**preen** [priːn] vt: **to** ~ **itself** (bird) lisciarsi le penne; **to** ~ **o.s.** agghindarsi.

**prefab** ['priːfæb] n casa prefabbricata.

**preface** ['prefəs] n prefazione f.

**prefect** ['priːfekt] n (Brit: in school) studente/essa con funzioni disciplinari; (in Italy) prefetto.

**prefer** [prɪ'fɜː*] vt preferire; ~**ably** ['prefrəblɪ] ad preferibilmente; ~**ence** ['prefərəns] n preferenza; ~**ential** [prefə'renʃəl] a preferenziale.

**prefix** ['priːfɪks] n prefisso.

**pregnancy** ['pregnənsɪ] n gravidanza.

**pregnant** ['pregnənt] a incinta af.

**prehistoric** ['priːhɪs'tɔrɪk] a preistorico(a).

**prejudice** ['predʒudɪs] n pregiudizio; (harm) torto, danno // vt pregiudicare, ledere; ~**d** a (person) pieno(a) di pregiudizi; (view) prevenuto(a).

**preliminary** [prɪ'lɪmɪnərɪ] a preliminare; **preliminaries** npl preliminari mpl.

**premarital** ['priː'mærɪtl] a prematrimoniale.

**premature** ['prɛmətʃuə*] a

prematuro(a).

**premier** ['prɛmɪə*] a primo(a) // n (POL) primo ministro.

**première** ['prɛmɪɛə*] n prima.

**premise** ['prɛmɪs] n premessa; ~s npl locale m; **on the** ~s sul posto.

**premium** ['priːmɪəm] n premio; **to be at a** ~ essere ricercatissimo; ~ **bond** n (Brit) obbligazione f a premio.

**premonition** [prɛmə'nɪʃən] n premonizione f.

**preoccupied** [priː'ɔkjupaɪd] a preoccupato(a).

**prep** [prɛp] n (SCOL: study) studio; ~ **school** n = **preparatory school.**

**prepaid** [priː'peɪd] a pagato(a) in anticipo.

**preparation** [prɛpə'reɪʃən] n preparazione f; ~s npl (for trip, war) preparativi mpl.

**preparatory** [prɪ'pærətərɪ] a preparatorio(a); ~ **school** n scuola elementare privata.

**prepare** [prɪ'pɛə*] vt preparare // vi: **to** ~ **for** prepararsi a; ~**d to** pronto(a) a.

**preposition** [prɛpə'zɪʃən] n preposizione f.

**preposterous** [prɪ'pɔstərəs] a assurdo(a).

**prerequisite** [priː'rɛkwɪzɪt] n requisito indispensabile.

**prescribe** [prɪ'skraɪb] vt prescrivere; (MED) ordinare.

**prescription** [prɪ'skrɪpʃən] n prescrizione f; (MED) ricetta.

**presence** ['prɛzns] n presenza; ~ **of mind** presenza di spirito.

**present** a ['prɛznt] a presente; (wife, residence, job) attuale // n regalo; (also: ~ **tense**) tempo presente // vt [prɪ'zɛnt] presentare; (give): **to** ~ **sb with sth** offrire qc a qn; **to give sb a** ~ fare un regalo a qn; **at** ~ al momento; ~**ation** [-'teɪʃən] n presentazione f; (gift) regalo, dono; (ceremony) consegna ufficiale; ~**day** a attuale, d'oggigiorno; ~**er** n

(RADIO, TV) presentatore/trice; ~**ly** ad (soon) fra poco, presto; (at present) al momento.

**preservative** [prɪ'zəːvətɪv] n conservante m.

**preserve** [prɪ'zəːv] vt (keep safe) preservare, proteggere; (maintain) conservare; (food) mettere in conserva // n (for game, fish) riserva; (often pl: jam) marmellata; (: fruit) frutta sciroppata.

**preside** [prɪ'zaɪd] vi presiedere.

**president** ['prɛzɪdənt] n presidente m; ~**ial** [-'dɛnʃl] a presidenziale.

**press** [prɛs] n (tool, machine) pressa; (for wine) torchio; (newspapers) stampa; (crowd) folla // vt (push) premere, pigiare; (squeeze) spremere; (: hand) stringere; (clothes: iron) stirare; (pursue) incalzare; (insist): **to** ~ **sth on sb** far accettare qc da qn // vi premere; accalcare; **we are** ~**ed for time** ci manca il tempo; **to** ~ **for sth** insistere per avere qc; **to** ~ **on** vi continuare; ~ **conference** n conferenza stampa; ~**ing** a urgente // n stiratura; ~ **stud** n (Brit) bottone m a pressione; ~**up** n (Brit) flessione f sulle braccia.

**pressure** ['prɛʃə*] n pressione f; ~ **cooker** n pentola a pressione; ~ **gauge** n manometro; ~ **group** n gruppo di pressione.

**prestige** [prɛs'tiːʒ] n prestigio.

**presumably** [prɪ'zjuːməblɪ] ad presumibilmente.

**presume** [prɪ'zjuːm] vt supporre; **to** ~ **to do** (dare) permettersi di fare.

**presumption** [prɪ'zʌmpʃən] n presunzione f; (boldness) audacia.

**presumptuous** [prɪ'zʌmpʃəs] a presuntuoso(a).

**pretence**, (US) **pretense** [prɪ'tɛns] n (claim) pretesa; **to make a** ~ **of doing** far finta di fare.

**pretend** [prɪ'tɛnd] vt (feign) fingere // vi (feign) far finta; (claim): **to** ~ **to sth** pretendere a qc; **to** ~ **to do** far finta di fare.

**pretense** [prɪ'tens] n (US) = **pretence**.

**pretension** [prɪ'tenʃən] n (claim) pretesa.

**pretentious** [prɪ'tenʃəs] a pretenzioso(a).

**pretext** ['pri:tekst] n pretesto.

**pretty** ['prɪtɪ] a grazioso(a), carino(a) // ad abbastanza, assai.

**prevail** [prɪ'veɪl] vi (win, be usual) prevalere; (persuade): to ~ (up)on sb to do persuadere qn a fare; **~ing** a dominante.

**prevalent** ['prevələnt] a (belief) predominante; (customs) diffuso(a); (fashion) corrente; (disease) comune.

**prevent** [prɪ'vent] vt prevenire; to ~ sb from doing impedire a qn di fare; **~ion** [-'venʃən] n prevenzione f; **~ive** a preventivo(a).

**preview** ['pri:vju:] n (of film) anteprima.

**previous** ['pri:vɪəs] a precedente; anteriore; **~ly** ad prima.

**prewar** ['pri:'wɔ:'] a anteguerra inv.

**prey** [preɪ] n preda // vi: to ~ on far preda di.

**price** [praɪs] n prezzo // vt (goods) fissare il prezzo di; valutare; **~less** a inapprezzabile; **~ list** listino (dei) prezzi.

**prick** [prɪk] n puntura // vt pungere; to ~ up one's ears drizzare gli orecchi.

**prickle** ['prɪkl] n (of plant) spina; (sensation) pizzicore m.

**prickly** ['prɪklɪ] a spinoso(a); (fig: person) permaloso(a); ~ **heat** n sudamina.

**pride** [praɪd] n orgoglio; superbia // vt: to ~ o.s. on essere orgoglioso(a) di; vantarsi di.

**priest** [pri:st] n prete m, sacerdote m; **~hood** n sacerdozio.

**prig** [prɪg] n: he's a ~ è compiaciuto di se stesso.

**prim** [prɪm] a pudico(a); contegnoso(a).

**primarily** ['praɪmərɪlɪ] ad

principalmente, essenzialmente.

**primary** ['praɪmərɪ] a primario(a); (first in importance) primo(a); ~ **school** n (Brit) scuola elementare.

**prime** [praɪm] a primario(a), fondamentale; (excellent) di prima qualità // vt (gun) innescare; (pump) adescare; (fig) mettere al corrente; **in the ~ of life** nel fior fiore della vita; **P~ Minister (P.M.)** n primo ministro.

**primer** ['praɪmə'] n (book) testo elementare.

**primeval** [praɪ'mi:vl] a primitivo(a).

**primitive** ['prɪmɪtɪv] a primitivo(a).

**primrose** ['prɪmrəuz] n primavera.

**primus (stove)** ['praɪməs(stəuv)] n ® (Brit) fornello a petrolio.

**prince** [prɪns] n principe m.

**princess** [prɪn'ses] n principessa.

**principal** ['prɪnsɪpl] a principale // n (headmaster) preside m.

**principle** ['prɪnsɪpl] n principio; **in ~** in linea di principio; **on ~** per principio.

**print** [prɪnt] n (mark) impronta; (letters) caratteri mpl; (fabric) tessuto stampato; (ART, PHOT) stampa // vt imprimere; (publish) stampare, pubblicare; (write in capitals) scrivere in stampatello; **out of ~** esaurito(a); **~ed matter** n stampe fpl; **~er** n tipografo; (machine) stampante f; **~ing** n stampa; **~out** n (COMPUT) tabulato.

**prior** ['praɪə'] a precedente // n priore m; ~ **to doing** prima di fare.

**priority** [praɪ'ɔrɪtɪ] n priorità f inv; precedenza.

**priory** ['praɪərɪ] n monastero.

**prise** [praɪz] vt: to ~ **open** forzare.

**prison** ['prɪzn] n prigione f // cpd (system) carcerario(a); (conditions, food) nelle or delle prigioni; **~er** n prigioniero(a).

**pristine** ['prɪstiːn] a immacolato(a).

**privacy** ['prɪvəsɪ] n solitudine f, intimità.

**private** ['praɪvɪt] a privato(a); personale // n soldato semplice; "~"

*(on envelope)* "riservata"; **in** ~ in privato; ~ **enterprise** *n* iniziativa privata; ~ **eye** *n* investigatore *m* privato; **~ly** *ad* in privato; *(within oneself)* dentro di sé; ~ **property** *n* proprietà privata; **privatize** *vt* privatizzare.

**privet** ['prɪvɪt] *n* ligustro.

**privilege** ['prɪvɪlɪdʒ] *n* privilegio.

**privy** ['prɪvɪ] *a*: **to be** ~ **to** essere al corrente di; ~ **council** *n* Consiglio della Corona.

**prize** [praɪz] *n* premio // *a (example, idiot)* perfetto(a); *(bull, novel)* premiato(a) // *vt* apprezzare, pregiare; ~ **giving** *n* premiazione *f*; **~winner** *n* premiato/a.

**pro** [prəu] *n (SPORT)* professionista *m/f*; **the ~s and cons** il pro e il contro.

**probability** [prɔbə'bɪlɪtɪ] *n* probabilità *f inv.*

**probable** ['prɔbəbl] *a* probabile; **probably** *ad* probabilmente.

**probation** [prə'beɪʃən] *n (in employment)* periodo di prova; *(LAW)* libertà vigilata; **on** ~ *(employee)* in prova; *(LAW)* in libertà vigilata.

**probe** [prəub] *n (MED, SPACE)* sonda; *(enquiry)* indagine *f*, investigazione *f* // *vt* sondare, esplorare; indagare.

**problem** ['prɔbləm] *n* problema *m.*

**procedure** [prə'si:dʒə*] *n (ADMIN, LAW)* procedura; *(method)* metodo, procedimento.

**proceed** [prə'si:d] *vi (go forward)* avanzare, andare avanti; *(go about it)* procedere; *(continue)*: **to** ~ **(with)** continuare; **to** ~ **to** andare a; passare a; **to** ~ **to do** mettersi a fare; **~ings** *npl* misure *fpl*; *(LAW)* procedimento; *(meeting)* riunione *f*; *(records)* rendiconti *mpl*; atti *mpl*; **~s** ['prəusi:dz] *npl* profitto, incasso.

**process** ['prəuses] *n* processo; *(method)* metodo, sistema *m* // *vt* trattare; *(information)* elaborare; **~ing** *n* trattamento; elaborazione *f.*

**procession** [prə'seʃən] *n* processione

*f*, corteo; **funeral** ~ corteo funebre.

**proclaim** [prə'kleɪm] *vt* proclamare, dichiarare.

**procrastinate** [prəu'kræstɪneɪt] *vi* procrastinare.

**prod** [prɔd] *vt* dare un colpetto a; pungolare.

**prodigal** ['prɔdɪgl] *a* prodigo(a).

**prodigy** ['prɔdɪdʒɪ] *n* prodigio.

**produce** *n* ['prɔdju:s] *(AGR)* prodotto, prodotti *mpl* // *vt* [prə'dju:s] produrre; *(to show)* esibire, mostrare; *(cause)* cagionare, causare; *(THEATRE)* mettere in scena; **~r** *n* *(THEATRE)* direttore/trice; *(AGR, CINEMA)* produttore *m.*

**product** ['prɔdʌkt] *n* prodotto.

**production** [prə'dʌkʃən] *n* produzione *f*; *(THEATRE)* messa in scena; ~ **line** *n* catena di lavorazione.

**productivity** [prɔdʌk'tɪvɪtɪ] *n* produttività.

**profane** [prə'feɪn] *a* profano(a); *(language)* empio(a).

**profession** [prə'feʃən] *n* professione *f*; **~al** *n* *(SPORT)* professionista *m/f* // *a* professionale; *(work)* da professionista; **~alism** *n* professionismo.

**professor** [prə'fɛsə*] *n* professore *m* *(titolare di una cattedra).*

**proficiency** [prə'fɪʃənsɪ] *n* competenza, abilità.

**profile** ['prəufaɪl] *n* profilo.

**profit** ['prɔfɪt] *n* profitto; beneficio *f* *vi*: **to** ~ **(by** *or* **from)** approfittare (di); **~ability** [-'bɪlɪtɪ] *n* redditività; **~able** *a* redditizio(a).

**profiteering** [prɔfɪ'tɪərɪŋ] *n (pej)* affarismo.

**profound** [prə'faund] *a* profondo(a).

**profusely** [prə'fju:slɪ] *ad* con grande effusione.

**progeny** ['prɔdʒɪnɪ] *n* progenie *f*; discendenti *mpl.*

**programme**, *(US)* **program** ['prəugræm] *n* programma *m* // *vt* programmare; **~r**, *(US)* **programer** *n* programmatore/trice.

**progress** n ['prəugres] progresso // vi [prə'gres] avanzare, procedere; **in ~** in corso; **to make ~** far progressi; **~ive** [-'gresɪv] a progressivo(a); (person) progressista m/f.

**prohibit** [prə'hɪbɪt] vt proibire, vietare; **~ion** [prəuɪ'bɪʃən] n (US) proibizionismo; **~ive** a (price etc) proibitivo(a).

**project** n ['prɔdʒekt] (plan) piano; (venture) progetto; (SCOL) studio // vb [prə'dʒekt] vt proiettare // vi (stick out) sporgere.

**projectile** [prə'dʒektaɪl] n proiettile m.

**projector** [prə'dʒektə*] n proiettore m.

**prolong** [prə'lɔŋ] vt prolungare.

**prom** [prɔm] n abbr = **promenade**; (US: ball) ballo studentesco.

**promenade** [prɔmə'nɑ:d] n (by sea) lungomare m; **~ concert** n concerto di musica classica.

**prominent** ['prɔmɪnənt] a (standing out) prominente; (important) importante.

**promiscuous** [prə'mɪskjuəs] a (sexually) di facili costumi.

**promise** ['prɔmɪs] n promessa // vt, vi promettere; promessa a promettersi.

**promote** [prə'məut] vt promuovere; (venture, event) organizzare; **~r** n (of sporting event) organizzatore/trice; **promotion** [-'məuʃən] n promozione f.

**prompt** [prɔmpt] a rapido(a), svelto(a); (punctual) puntuale; (reply) sollecito(a) // ad (punctually) in punto // n (COMPUT) prompt m // vt incitare; provocare; (THEATRE) suggerire a; **~ly** ad prontamente; puntualmente; **~ness** n prontezza; puntualità.

**prone** [prəun] a (lying) prono(a); **~ to** propenso(a) a, incline a.

**prong** [prɔŋ] n rebbio, punta.

**pronoun** ['prəunaun] n pronome m.

**pronounce** [prə'nauns] vt pronunziare // vi: **to ~ (up)on**

pronunziare su.

**pronunciation** [prənʌnsɪ'eɪʃən] n pronunzia.

**proof** [pru:f] n prova; (of book) bozza; (PHOT) provino; (of alcohol) grado // a: **~ against** a prova di.

**prop** [prɔp] n sostegno, appoggio // vt (also: **~ up**) sostenere, appoggiare; (lean): **to ~ sth against** appoggiare qc contro or a.

**propaganda** [prɔpə'gændə] n propaganda.

**propel** [prə'pel] vt spingere (in avanti), muovere; **~ler** n elica; **~ling pencil** n (Brit) matita a mina.

**propensity** [prə'pensɪtɪ] n tendenza.

**proper** ['prɔpə*] a (suited, right) adatto(a), appropriato(a); (seemly) decente; (authentic) vero(a); (col: real) noun + vero(a) e proprio(a); **~ly** ad (eat, study) bene; (behave) come si deve; **~ noun** n nome m proprio.

**property** ['prɔpətɪ] n (things owned) beni mpl; (land, building) proprietà f inv; (CHEM etc: quality) proprietà; **~ owner** n proprietario/a.

**prophecy** ['prɔfɪsɪ] n profezia.

**prophesy** ['prɔfɪsaɪ] vt predire.

**prophet** ['prɔfɪt] n profeta m.

**proportion** [prə'pɔ:ʃən] n proporzione f; (share) parte f // vt proporzionare, commisurare; **~al** a proporzionale; **~ate** a proporzionato(a).

**proposal** [prə'pəuzl] n proposta; (plan) progetto; (of marriage) proposta di matrimonio.

**propose** [prə'pəuz] vt proporre, suggerire // vi fare una proposta di matrimonio; **to ~ to do** proporsi di fare, aver l'intenzione di fare.

**proposition** [prɔpə'zɪʃən] n proposizione f.

**proprietor** [prə'praɪətə*] n proprietario/a.

**propriety** [prə'praɪətɪ] n (seemliness) decoro, rispetto delle convenienze sociali.

**prose** [prəuz] n prosa; (SCOL: translation) traduzione f dalla madrelingua.

**prosecute** ['prɔsɪkju:t] vt processare; **prosecution** [-'kju:ʃən] n processo; (accusing side) accusa; **prosecutor** n (also: **public prosecutor**) ≈ procuratore m della Repubblica.

**prospect** n ['prɔspekt] prospettiva; (hope) speranza // vb [prə'spekt] vt fare assaggi in // vi fare assaggi; ~s npl (for work etc) prospettive fpl; **prospective** [-'spektɪv] a possibile; futuro(a).

**prospectus** [prə'spektəs] n prospetto, programma m.

**prosperity** [prɔ'spɛrɪtɪ] n prosperità.

**prostitute** ['prɔstɪtju:t] n prostituta.

**protect** [prə'tɛkt] vt proteggere, salvaguardare; ~**ion** n protezione f; ~**ive** a protettivo(a).

**protégé** ['prəutəʒeɪ] n protetto; ~s n protetta.

**protein** ['prəuti:n] n proteina.

**protest** n ['prəutɛst] protesta // vt, vi [prə'tɛst] protestare.

**Protestant** ['prɔtɪstənt] a, n protestante (m/f).

**protester** [prə'tɛstə*] n dimostrante m/f.

**prototype** ['prəutətaɪp] n prototipo.

**protracted** [prə'træktɪd] a tirato(a) per le lunghe.

**protrude** [prə'tru:d] vi sporgere.

**protuberance** [prə'tju:bərəns] n sporgenza.

**proud** [praud] a fiero(a), orglioso(a); (pej) superbo(a).

**prove** [pru:v] vt provare, dimostrare // vi: to ~ **correct** etc risultare vero(a) etc; to ~ **o.s.** mostrare le proprie capacità.

**proverb** ['prɔvə:b] n proverbio.

**provide** [prə'vaɪd] vt fornire, provvedere; to ~ **sb with sth** fornire or provvedere qc a qn; to ~ **for** vt fus provvedere a; ~**d (that)** cj purché + sub, a condizione che + sub.

**providing** [prə'vaɪdɪŋ] cj purché + sub, a condizione che + sub.

**province** ['prɔvɪns] n provincia.

**provincial** [prə'vɪnʃəl] a provinciale.

**provision** [prə'vɪʒən] n (supply) riserva; (supplying) provvista; rifornimento; (stipulation) condizione f; ~s npl (food) provviste fpl; ~**al** a provvisorio(a).

**proviso** [prə'vaɪzəu] n condizione f.

**provocative** [prə'vɔkətɪv] a (aggressive) provocatorio(a); (thought-provoking) stimolante; (seductive) provocante.

**provoke** [prə'vəuk] vt provocare; incitare.

**prow** [prau] n prua.

**prowess** ['prauɪs] n prodezza.

**prowl** [praul] vi (also: ~ **about**, ~ **around**) aggirarsi; ~**er** n tipo sospetto (che s'aggira con l'intenzione di rubare, aggredire etc).

**proximity** [prɔk'sɪmɪtɪ] n prossimità.

**proxy** ['prɔksɪ] n procura.

**prudent** ['pru:dnt] a prudente.

**prudish** ['pru:dɪʃ] a puritano(a).

**prune** [pru:n] n prugna secca // vt potare.

**pry** [praɪ] vi: to ~ **into** ficcare il naso in.

**PS** abbr (= postscript) P.S.

**psalm** [sɑ:m] n salmo.

**pseudo-** ['sju:dəu] prefix pseudo...

**pseudonym** ['sju:dənɪm] n pseudonimo.

**psyche** ['saɪkɪ] n psiche f.

**psychiatric** [saɪkɪ'ætrɪk] a psichiatrico(a).

**psychiatrist** [saɪ'kaɪətrɪst] n psichiatra m/f.

**psychic** ['saɪkɪk] a (also: ~**al**) psichico(a); (person) dotato(a) di qualità telepatiche.

**psychoanalyst** [saɪkəu'ænəlɪst] n psicanalista m/f.

**psychological** [saɪkə'lɔdʒɪkl] a psicologico(a).

**psychologist** [saɪ'kɔlədʒɪst] n psicologo/a.

**psychology** [saɪ'kɔlədʒɪ] n psicologia.

**psychopath** ['saɪkəupæθ] n psicopatico/a.

**P.T.O.** abbr (= please turn over) v.r.

**pub** [pʌb] n abbr (= public house) pub m inv.

**pubic** ['pju:bɪk] a pubico(a), del pube.

**public** ['pʌblɪk] a pubblico(a) // n pubblico; **in** ~ in pubblico; ~ **address system (P.A.)** n impianto di amplificazione.

**publican** ['pʌblɪkən] n proprietario di un pub.

**publication** [pʌblɪ'keɪʃən] n pubblicazione f.

**public:** ~ **company** n società f inv per azioni (costituita tramite pubblica sottoscrizione); ~ **convenience** n (Brit) gabinetti mpl; ~ **holiday** n giorno festivo, festa nazionale; ~ **house** n (Brit) pub m inv.

**publicity** [pʌb'lɪsɪtɪ] n pubblicità.

**publicize** ['pʌblɪsaɪz] vt rendere pubblico(a).

**publicly** ['pʌblɪklɪ] ad pubblicamente.

**public:** ~ **opinion** n opinione f pubblica; ~ **relations (PR)** n pubbliche relazioni fpl; ~ **school** n (Brit) scuola privata; (US) scuola statale; ~-**spirited** a che ha senso civico; ~ **transport** n mezzi mpl pubblici.

**publish** ['pʌblɪʃ] vt pubblicare; ~**er** n editore m; ~**ing** n (industry) editoria; (of a book) pubblicazione f.

**puck** [pʌk] n (ICE HOCKEY) disco.

**pucker** ['pʌkə*] vt corrugare.

**pudding** ['pudɪŋ] n budino; (Brit: dessert) dolce m; **black** ~ sanguinaccio.

**puddle** ['pʌdl] n pozza, pozzanghera.

**puff** [pʌf] n sbuffo // vt: to ~ one's pipe tirare sboccate di fumo // vi uscire a sbuffi; (pant) ansare; to ~ **out smoke** mandar fuori sbuffi di fumo; ~**ed** a (col: out of breath) senza fiato; ~ **pastry** n pasta sfo-

glia; ~**y** a gonfio(a).

**pull** [pul] n (tug): to give sth a ~ tirare su qc; (fig) influenza // vt tirare; (muscle) strappare // vi tirare; to ~ **to pieces** fare a pezzi; to ~ **one's punches** (BOXING) risparmiare l'avversario; to ~ **one's weight** dare il proprio contributo; to ~ **o.s. together** ricomporsi, riprendersi; to ~ **sb's leg** prendere in giro qn; to ~ **apart** vt (break) fare a pezzi; to ~ **down** vt (house) demolire; (tree) abbattere; to ~ **in** vi (AUT: at the kerb) accostarsi; (RAIL) entrare in stazione; to ~ **off** vt (deal etc) portare a compimento; to ~ **out** vi partire; (AUT: come out of line) spostarsi sulla mezzeria // vt staccare; far uscire; (withdraw) ritirare; to ~ **over** vi (AUT) accostare; to ~ **through** vi farcela; to ~ **up** vi (stop) fermarsi // vt (uproot) sradicare; (stop) fermare.

**pulley** ['pulɪ] n puleggia, carrucola.

**pullover** ['puləuvə*] n pullover m inv.

**pulp** [pʌlp] n (of fruit) polpa; (for paper) pasta per carta.

**pulpit** ['pulpɪt] n pulpito.

**pulsate** [pʌl'seɪt] vi battere, palpitare.

**pulse** [pʌls] n polso.

**pummel** ['pʌml] vt dare pugni a.

**pump** [pʌmp] n pompa; (shoe) scarpetta // vt pompare; (fig: col) far parlare; to ~ **up** vt gonfiare.

**pumpkin** ['pʌmpkɪn] n zucca.

**pun** [pʌn] n gioco di parole.

**punch** [pʌntʃ] n (blow) pugno; (fig: force) forza; (tool) punzone m; (drink) ponce m // vt (hit): to ~ sb/ sth dare un pugno a qn/qc; to ~ a **hole** (in) fare un buco (in); ~ **line** n (of joke) battuta finale; ~-**up** n (Brit col) rissa.

**punctual** ['pʌŋktjuəl] a puntuale; ~**ity** [-'ælɪtɪ] n puntualità.

**punctuation** [pʌŋktju'eɪʃən] n interpunzione f, punteggiatura.

**puncture** ['pʌŋktʃə*] n foratura // vt

forare.

**pundit** ['pʌndɪt] n sapientone/a.

**pungent** ['pʌndʒənt] a piccante; (fig) mordace, caustico(a).

**punish** ['pʌnɪʃ] vt punire; **~ment** n punizione f.

**punk** [pʌŋk] n (also: ~ rocker) punk m/f inv; (also: ~ rock) musica punk, punk rock m; (US col: hoodlum) teppista m.

**punt** [pʌnt] n (boat) barchino; (FOOTBALL) colpo a volo.

**punter** ['pʌntə*] n (Brit: gambler) scommettitore/trice.

**puny** ['pjuːnɪ] a gracile.

**pup** [pʌp] n cucciolo/a.

**pupil** ['pjuːpl] n allievo/a; (ANAT) pupilla.

**puppet** ['pʌpɪt] n burattino.

**puppy** ['pʌpɪ] n cucciolo/a, cagnolino/a.

**purchase** ['pəːtʃɪs] n acquisto, compera // vt comprare; **~r** n compratore/trice.

**pure** [pjuə*] a puro(a).

**purely** ['pjuəlɪ] ad puramente.

**purge** [pəːdʒ] n (MED) purga; (POL) epurazione f // vt purgare; (fig) epurare.

**puritan** ['pjuərɪtən] a, n puritano(a).

**purl** [pəːl] n punto rovescio.

**purple** ['pəːpl] a di porpora; viola inv.

**purport** [pəː'pɔːt] vi: to ~ to be/do pretendere di essere/fare.

**purpose** ['pəːpəs] n intenzione f, scopo; on ~ apposta; **~ful** a deciso(a), risoluto(a).

**purr** [pəː*] vi fare le fusa.

**purse** [pəːs] n borsellino // vt contrarre.

**purser** ['pəːsə*] n (NAUT) commissario di bordo.

**pursue** [pə'sjuː] vt inseguire.

**pursuit** [pə'sjuːt] n inseguimento; (occupation) occupazione f, attività f inv.

**purveyor** [pə'veɪə*] n fornitore/trice.

**pus** [pʌs] n spinta; (effort) grande sforzo; (drive) energia // vt spingere;

(button) premere; (thrust): to ~ sth (into) ficcare qc (in); (fig) fare pubblicità a // vi spingere; premere; to ~ aside vt scostare; to ~ off vi (col) filare; to ~ on vi (continue) continuare; to ~ through vt (measure) far approvare; to ~ up vt (total, prices) far salire; **~chair** n (Brit) passeggino; **~er** n (drug ~er) spacciatore/trice; **~over** n (col): it's a ~over è un lavoro da bambini; **~up** n (US: press-up) flessione f sulle braccia; **~y** a (pej) opportunista.

**puss, pussy(-cat)** [pus, 'pusɪ(kæt)] n micio.

**put, pt, pp put** [put] vt mettere, porre; (say) dire, esprimere; (a question) fare; (estimate) stimare; to ~ about vi (NAUT) virare di bordo // vt (rumour) diffondere; to ~ across vt (ideas etc) comunicare; far capire; to ~ away vt (return) mettere a posto; to ~ back vt (replace) rimettere (a posto); (postpone) rinviare; (delay) ritardare; to ~ by vt (money) mettere da parte; to ~ down vt (parcel etc) posare, mettere giù; (pay) versare; (in writing) mettere per iscritto; (suppress: revolt etc) reprimere, sopprimere; (attribute) attribuire; to ~ forward vt (ideas) avanzare, proporre; (date) anticipare; to ~ in vt (application, complaint) presentare; to ~ off vt (postpone) rimandare, rinviare; (discourage) dissuadere; to ~ on vt (clothes, lipstick etc) mettere; (light etc) accendere; (play etc) mettere in scena; (food, meal) servire; (brake) mettere; to ~ on weight ingrassare; to ~ on airs darsi delle arie; to ~ out vt mettere fuori; (one's hand) porgere; (light etc) spegnere; (person: inconvenience) scomodare; to ~ up vt (raise) sollevare, alzare; (pin up) affiggere; (hang) appendere; (build) costruire, erigere; (increase) aumentare;

(*accommodate*) alloggiare; **to ~ up with** *vt fus* sopportare.

**putt** [pʌt] *vt* (*ball*) colpire leggermente // *n* colpo leggero; **~ing green** *n* green *m inv*; campo da putting.

**putty** ['pʌtɪ] *n* stucco.

**puzzle** ['pʌzl] *n* enigma *m*, mistero; (*jigsaw*) puzzle *m*; (*also:* **crossword ~**) parole *fpl* incrociate, cruciverba *m inv* // *vt* confondere, rendere perplesso(a) // *vi* scervellarsi.

**pyjamas** [pɪ'dʒɑ:məz] *npl* (*Brit*) pigiama *m*.

**pylon** ['paɪlən] *n* pilone *m*.

**pyramid** ['pɪrəmɪd] *n* piramide *f*.

**Pyrenees** [pɪrɪ'niːz] *npl*: **the ~** i Pirenei.

# Q

**quack** [kwæk] *n* (*of duck*) qua qua *m inv*; (*pej: doctor*) dottoruccio/a.

**quad** [kwɔd] *n abbr* = **quadrangle**, **quadruplet**.

**quadrangle** ['kwɔdræŋgl] *n* (*MATH*) quadrilatero; (*courtyard*) cortile *m*.

**quadruple** [kwɔ'drupl] *vt* quadruplicare // *vi* quadruplicarsi.

**quadruplet** [kwɔ'dru:plɪt] *n* uno/a di quattro gemelli.

**quagmire** ['kwægmaɪə*] *n* pantano.

**quail** [kweɪl] *n* (*ZOOL*) quaglia // *vi* (*person*) perdersi d'animo.

**quaint** [kweɪnt] *a* bizzarro(a); (*old-fashioned*) antiquato(a); grazioso(a), pittoresco(a).

**quake** [kweɪk] *vi* tremare // *n abbr* = **earthquake**.

**Quaker** ['kweɪkə*] *n* quacchero/a.

**qualification** [kwɔlɪfɪ'keɪʃən] *n* (*degree etc*) qualifica, titolo; (*ability*) competenza, qualificazione *f*; (*limitation*) riserva, restrizione *f*.

**qualified** ['kwɔlɪfaɪd] *a* qualificato(a); (*able*) competente, qualificato(a); (*limited*) condizionato(a).

**qualify** ['kwɔlɪfaɪ] *vt* abilitare;

(*limit*: *statement*) modificare, precisare // *vi*: **to ~ (as)** qualificarsi (come); **to ~ (for)** acquistare i requisiti necessari (per); (*SPORT*) qualificarsi (per *o* in).

**quality** ['kwɔlɪtɪ] *n* qualità *f inv*.

**qualm** [kwɑ:m] *n* dubbio; scrupolo.

**quandary** ['kwɔndrɪ] *n*: **in a ~** in un dilemma.

**quantity** ['kwɔntɪtɪ] *n* quantità *f inv*; **~ surveyor** *n* geometra *m* (*specializzato nel calcolare la quantità e il costo del materiale da costruzione*).

**quarantine** ['kwɔrnti:n] *n* quarantena.

**quarrel** ['kwɔrl] *n* lite *f*, disputa // *vi* litigare; **~some** *a* litigioso(a).

**quarry** ['kwɔrɪ] *n* (*for stone*) cava; (*animal*) preda // *vt* (*marble etc*) estrarre.

**quart** [kwɔ:t] *n* ≈ litro.

**quarter** ['kwɔ:tə*] *n* quarto; (*of year*) trimestre *m*; (*district*) quartiere *m* // *vt* dividere in quattro; (*MIL*) alloggiare; **~s** *npl* alloggio; (*MIL*) alloggi *mpl*, quadrato; **a ~ of an hour** un quarto d'ora; **~ final** *n* quarto di finale; **~ly** *a* trimestrale // *ad* trimestralmente; **~master** *n* (*MIL*) furiere *m*.

**quartet(te)** [kwɔ:'tet] *n* quartetto.

**quartz** [kwɔ:ts] *n* quarzo; **~ watch** *n* orologio al quarzo.

**quash** [kwɔʃ] *vt* (*verdict*) annullare.

**quaver** ['kweɪvə*] *n* (*Brit MUS*) croma // *vi* tremolare.

**quay** [ki:] *n* (*also:* **~side**) banchina.

**queasy** ['kwi:zɪ] *a* (*stomach*) delicato(a); **to feel ~** aver la nausea.

**queen** [kwi:n] *n* (*gen*) regina; (*CARDS etc*) regina, donna; **~ mother** *n* regina madre.

**queer** [kwɪə*] *a* strano(a), curioso(a); (*suspicious*) dubbio(a), sospetto(a); (*sick*): **I feel ~** mi sento poco bene // *n* (*col*) finocchio.

**quell** [kwɛl] *vt* domare.

**quench** [kwɛntʃ] *vt* (*flames*) spegnere; **to ~ one's thirst** dissetarsi.

**querulous** ['kwɛrʊləs] a querulo(a).

**query** ['kwɪərɪ] n domanda, questione f; (doubt) dubbio // vt mettere in questione.

**quest** [kwɛst] n cerca, ricerca.

**question** ['kwɛstʃən] n domanda, questione f // vt (person) interrogare; (plan, idea) mettere in questione or in dubbio; **it's a ~ of doing** si tratta di fare; **beyond ~** fuori di dubbio; **out of the ~** fuori discussione, impossibile; **~able** a discutibile; **~ mark** n punto interrogativo.

**questionnaire** [kwɛstʃəˈnɛə*] n questionario.

**queue** [kju:] (Brit) n coda, fila // vi fare la coda.

**quibble** ['kwɪbl] vi cavillare.

**quick** [kwɪk] a rapido(a), veloce; (reply) pronto(a); (mind) pronto(a), acuto(a) // ad rapidamente, presto // n: **cut to the ~** (fig) toccato(a) sul vivo; **be ~!** fa presto!; **~en** vt accelerare, affrettare; (rouse) animare, stimolare // vi accelerare, affrettarsi; **~ly** ad rapidamente, velocemente; **~sand** n sabbie fpl mobili; **~-witted** a pronto(a) d'ingegno.

**quid** [kwɪd] n (pl inv) (Brit col) sterlina.

**quiet** ['kwaɪət] a tranquillo(a), quieto(a); (ceremony) semplice; (colour) discreto(a) // n tranquillità, calma // vt, vi (US) = **~en; keep ~!** sta zitto!; **~en** (also: **~ down**) vi calmarsi, chetarsi // vt calmare, chetare; **~ly** ad tranquillamente, calmamente; sommessamente; discretamente.

**quilt** [kwɪlt] n trapunta; (continental ~) piumino.

**quin** [kwɪn] n abbr = **quintuplet**.

**quinine** [kwɪˈniːn] n chinino.

**quintuplet** [kwɪnˈtjuːplɪt] n uno/a di cinque gemelli.

**quip** [kwɪp] n frizzo.

**quirk** [kwə:k] n ghiribizzo.

**quit** [kwɪt], pt, pp **quit** or **quitted** [kwɪt] vt

lasciare, partire da // vi (give up) mollare; (resign) dimettersi; **notice to ~** preavviso (dato all'inquilino).

**quite** [kwaɪt] ad (rather) assai; (entirely) completamente, del tutto; **I ~ understand** capisco perfettamente; **~ a few of them** non pochi di loro; **~ (so)!** esatto!

**quits** [kwɪts] a: **~ (with)** pari (con); **let's call it ~** adesso siamo pari.

**quiver** ['kwɪvə*] vi tremare, fremere // n (for arrows) faretra.

**quiz** [kwɪz] n (game) quiz m inv; indovinello // vt interrogare; **~zical** a enigmatico(a).

**quota** ['kwəʊtə] n quota.

**quotation** [kwəʊˈteɪʃən] n citazione f; (of shares etc) quotazione f; (estimate) preventivo; **~ marks** npl virgolette fpl.

**quote** [kwəʊt] n citazione f // vt (sentence) citare; (price) dare, fissare; (shares) quotare // vi: **to ~ from** citare.

# R

**rabbi** ['ræbaɪ] n rabbino.

**rabbit** ['ræbɪt] n coniglio; **~ hutch** n conigliera.

**rabble** ['ræbl] n (pej) canaglia, plebaglia.

**rabies** ['reɪbiːz] n rabbia.

**RAC** n abbr (Brit) = Royal Automobile Club.

**race** [reɪs] n razza; (competition, rush) corsa // vt (person) gareggiare (in corsa) con; (horse) far correre; (engine) imballare // vi correre; **~ car** (US) = **racing car**; **~ car driver** n (US) = **racing driver**; **~course** n campo di corse, ippodromo; **~horse** n cavallo da corsa; **~ relations** npl rapporti mpl razziali; **~track** n pista.

**racial** ['reɪʃl] a razziale; **~ist** a, n razzista (m/f).

**racing** ['reɪsɪŋ] n corsa; **~ car** n (Brit) macchina da corsa; **~ driver**

*n* (*Brit*) corridore *m* automobilista.

**racism** ['reɪsɪzəm] *n* razzismo; **racist** *a*, *n* razzista (*m/f*).

**rack** [ræk] *n* rastrelliera; (*also:* **luggage** ~) rete *f*, portabagagli *m inv*; (*also:* **roof** ~) portabagagli *m* // *vt* torturare, tormentare; **to** ~ **one's brains** scervellarsi.

**racket** ['rækɪt] *n* (*for tennis*) racchetta; (*noise*) fracasso; baccano; (*swindle*) imbroglio, truffa; (*organized crime*) racket *m inv*.

**racquet** ['rækɪt] *n* racchetta.

**racy** ['reɪsɪ] *a* brioso(a); piccante.

**radar** ['reɪdɑ:*] *n* radar *m* // *cpd* radar *inv*.

**radial** ['reɪdɪəl] *a* (*also:* ~**ply**) radiale.

**radiant** ['reɪdɪənt] *a* raggiante; (*PHYSICS*) radiante.

**radiate** ['reɪdɪeɪt] *vt* (*heat*) irraggiare, irradiare // *vi* (*lines*) irradiarsi.

**radiation** [reɪdɪ'eɪʃən] *n* irradiamento; (*radioactive*) radiazione *f*.

**radiator** ['reɪdɪeɪtə*] *n* radiatore *m*.

**radical** ['rædɪkl] *a* radicale.

**radii** ['reɪdɪaɪ] *npl of* **radius**.

**radio** ['reɪdɪəu] *n* radio *f inv*; **on the** ~ alla radio.

**radioactive** [reɪdɪəu'æktɪv] *a* radioattivo(a).

**radio station** *n* stazione *f* radio *inv*.

**radish** ['rædɪʃ] *n* ravanello.

**radium** ['reɪdɪəm] *n* radio.

**radius** ['reɪdɪəs], *pl* **radii** *n* raggio; (*ANAT*) radio.

**RAF** *n abbr* = **Royal Air Force**.

**raffle** ['ræfl] *n* lotteria.

**raft** [rɑ:ft] *n* zattera; (*also:* **life** ~) zattera di salvataggio.

**rafter** ['rɑ:ftə*] *n* trave *f*.

**rag** [ræg] *n* straccio, cencio; (*pej: newspaper*) giornalaccio, bandiera; (*for charity*) iniziativa studentesca a scopo benefico // *vt* (*Brit*) prendere in giro; ~**s** *npl* stracci *mpl*, brandelli *mpl*; ~**-and-bone man** *n* (*Brit*) = **ragman**; ~ **doll** *n* bambola di

pezza.

**rage** [reɪdʒ] *n* (*fury*) collera, furia // *vi* (*person*) andare su tutte le furie; (*storm*) infuriare; **it's all the** ~ **fa** furore.

**ragged** ['rægɪd] *a* (*edge*) irregolare; (*cuff*) logoro(a); (*appearance*) pezzente.

**ragman** ['rægmæn] *n* straccivendolo.

**raid** [reɪd] *n* (*MIL*) incursione *f*; (*criminal*) rapina; (*by police*) irruzione *f* // *vt* fare un'incursione in; rapinare; fare irruzione in.

**rail** [reɪl] *n* (*on stair*) ringhiera; (*on bridge, balcony*) parapetto; (*of ship*) battagliola; (*for train*) rotaia; ~**s** *npl* binario, rotaie *fpl*; **by** ~ per ferrovia; ~**ing(s)** *n(pl)* ringhiere *fpl*; ~**road** *n* (*US*) = ~**way**; ~**way** *n* (*Brit*) ferrovia; ~**way line** *n* (*Brit*) linea ferroviaria; ~**wayman** *n* (*Brit*) ferroviere *m*; ~**way station** *n* (*Brit*) stazione *f* ferroviaria.

**rain** [reɪn] *n* pioggia // *vi* piovere; **in the** ~ sotto la pioggia; **it's** ~**ing** piove; ~**bow** *n* arcobaleno; ~**coat** *n* impermeabile *m*; ~**drop** *n* goccia di pioggia; ~**fall** *n* pioggia; (*measurement*) piovosità; ~**y** *a* piovoso(a).

**raise** [reɪz] *n* aumento // *vt* (*lift*) alzare; sollevare; (*build*) erigere; (*increase*) aumentare; (*a protest, doubt, question*) sollevare; (*cattle, family*) allevare; (*crop*) coltivare; (*army, funds*) raccogliere; (*loan*) ottenere; **to** ~ **one's voice** alzare la voce.

**raisin** ['reɪzn] *n* uva secca.

**rajah** ['rɑ:dʒə] *n* ragià *m inv*.

**rake** [reɪk] *n* (*tool*) rastrello; (*person*) libertino // *vt* (*garden*) rastrellare; (*with machine gun*) spazzare.

**rally** ['rælɪ] *n* (*POL etc*) riunione *f*; (*AUT*) rally *m inv*; (*TENNIS*) scambio // *vt* riunire, radunare // *vi* raccogliersi, radunarsi; (*sick person, Stock Exchange*) riprendersi; **to** ~

**round** *vt fus* raggrupparsi intorno a; venire in aiuto di.

**RAM** [ræm] *n abbr* (= *random access memory*) memoria ad accesso casuale.

**ram** [ræm] *n* montone *m*, ariete *m*; (*device*) ariete *m* // *vt* conficcare; (*crash into*) cozzare, sbattere contro; percuotere; speronare.

**ramble** ['ræmbl] *n* escursione *f* // *vi* (*pej*: *also*: ~ **on**) divagare; ~**r** *n* escursionista *m/f*; (*BOT*) rosa rampicante; **rambling** *a* (*speech*) sconnesso(a); (*BOT*) rampicante.

**ramp** [ræmp] *n* rampa; **on/off** ~ (*US AUT*) raccordo di entrata/uscita.

**rampage** [ræm'peɪdʒ] *n*: **to go on the** ~ scatenarsi in modo violento.

**rampant** ['ræmpənt] *a* (*disease etc*) che infierisce.

**rampart** ['ræmpɑːt] *n* bastione *m*.

**ramshackle** ['ræmʃækl] *a* (*house*) cadente; (*car etc*) sgangherato(a).

**ran** [ræn] *pt* of **run**.

**ranch** [rɑːntʃ] *n* ranch *m inv*; ~**er** *n* proprietario di un ranch; cowboy *m inv*.

**rancid** ['rænsɪd] *a* rancido(a).

**rancour**, (*US*) **rancor** ['ræŋkə*] *n* rancore *m*.

**random** ['rændəm] *a* fatto(a) or detto(a) per caso // *n*: **at** ~ a casaccio; ~ **access** *n* (*COMPUT*) accesso casuale.

**randy** ['rændɪ] *a* (*Brit col*) arrapato(a); lascivo(a).

**rang** [ræŋ] *pt* of **ring**.

**range** [reɪndʒ] *n* (*of mountains*) catena; (*of missile*, *voice*) portata; (*of products*) gamma; (*MIL*: *also*: **shooting** ~) campo di tiro; (*also*: **kitchen** ~) fornello, cucina economica // *vi*: **to** ~ **over** coprire; **to** ~ **from** ... **to** andare da ... a.

**ranger** ['reɪndʒə*] *n* guardia forestale.

**rank** [ræŋk] *n* fila; (*MIL*) grado; (*Brit*: *also*: **taxi** ~) posteggio di taxi // *vi*: **to** ~ **among** essere nel numero di // *a* puzzolente; vero(a) e pro-

prio(a); **the** ~**s** (*MIL*) la truppa; **the** ~ **and file** (*fig*) la gran massa.

**rankle** ['ræŋkl] *vi* bruciare.

**ransack** ['rænsæk] *vt* rovistare; (*plunder*) saccheggiare.

**ransom** ['rænsəm] *n* riscatto; **to hold sb to** ~ (*fig*) esercitare pressione su qn.

**rant** [rænt] *vi* vociare.

**rap** [ræp] *vt* bussare a; picchiare su.

**rape** [reɪp] *n* violenza carnale, stupro; (*BOT*) ravizzone *m* // *vt* violentare; ~**(seed) oil** *n* olio di ravizzone.

**rapid** ['ræpɪd] *a* rapido(a); ~**s** *npl* (*GEO*) rapida; ~**ly** *ad* rapidamente.

**rapist** ['reɪpɪst] *n* violentatore *m*.

**rapport** [ræ'pɔː*] *n* rapporto.

**rapture** ['ræptʃə*] *n* estasi *f inv*.

**rare** [rɛə*] *a* raro(a); (*CULIN*: *steak*) al sangue.

**rarefied** ['rɛərɪfaɪd] *a* (*air*, *atmosphere*) rarefatto(a).

**rarely** ['rɛəlɪ] *ad* raramente.

**raring** ['rɛərɪŋ] *a*: **to be** ~ **to go** (*col*) non veder l'ora di cominciare.

**rascal** ['rɑːskl] *n* mascalzone *m*.

**rash** [ræʃ] *a* imprudente, sconsiderato(a) // *n* (*MED*) eruzione *f*.

**rasher** ['ræʃə*] *n* fetta sottile (di lardo or prosciutto).

**raspberry** ['rɑːzbərɪ] *n* lampone *m*.

**rasping** ['rɑːspɪŋ] *a* stridulo(a).

**rat** [ræt] *n* ratto.

**rate** [reɪt] *n* (*proportion*) tasso, percentuale *f*; (*speed*) velocità *f inv*; (*price*) tariffa // *vt* giudicare; stimare; **to** ~ **sb/sth as** valutare qn/qc come; ~**s** *npl* (*Brit*) imposte *fpl* comunali; (*fees*) tariffe *fpl*; ~**able value** *n* (*Brit*) valore *m* imponibile or locativo (di una proprietà); ~**payer** *n* (*Brit*) contribuente *m/f* (che paga le imposte comunali).

**rather** ['rɑːðə*] *ad* piuttosto; **it's** ~ **expensive** è piuttosto caro; (*too much*) è un po' caro; **there's** ~ **a lot** ce n'è parecchio; **I would** or **I'd**

~ go preferirei andare.
**ratify** ['rætɪfaɪ] vt ratificare.
**rating** ['reɪtɪŋ] n classificazione f; punteggio di merito; (NAUT: category) classe f; (: Brit: sailor) marinaio semplice.
**ratio** ['reɪʃɪəu] n proporzione f.
**ration** ['ræʃən] n (gen pl) razioni fpl // vt razionare.
**rational** ['ræʃənl] a razionale, ragionevole; (solution, reasoning) logico(a); ~e [-'nɑːl] n fondamento logico; giustificazione f; ~ize vt razionalizzare.
**rat race** n carrierismo, corsa al successo.
**rattle** ['rætl] n tintinnio; (louder) strepito; (object: of baby) sonaglino; (: of sports fan) raganella // vi risuonare, tintinnare; fare un rumore di ferraglia // vt scuotere (con strepito); ~**snake** n serpente m a sonagli.
**raucous** ['rɔːkəs] a rauco(a).
**ravage** ['rævɪdʒ] vt devastare; ~**s** npl danni mpl.
**rave** [reɪv] vi (in anger) infuriarsi; (with enthusiasm) andare in estasi; (MED) delirare.
**raven** ['reɪvən] n corvo.
**ravenous** ['rævənəs] a affamato(a).
**ravine** [rə'viːn] n burrone m.
**raving** ['reɪvɪŋ] a: ~ **lunatic** pazzo(a) furioso(a).
**ravioli** [rævɪ'əʊlɪ] n ravioli mpl.
**ravishing** ['rævɪʃɪŋ] a incantevole.
**raw** [rɔː] a (uncooked) crudo(a); (not processed) greggio(a); (sore) vivo(a); (inexperienced) inesperto(a); ~ **deal** n (col) bidonata; ~ **material** n materia prima.
**ray** [reɪ] n raggio; a ~ of hope un barlume di speranza.
**rayon** ['reɪɔn] n raion m.
**raze** [reɪz] vt radere, distruggere.
**razor** ['reɪzə*] n rasoio; ~ **blade** n lama di rasoio.
**Rd** abbr = road.
**re** [riː] prep con riferimento a.
**reach** [riːtʃ] n portata; (of river etc)

tratto // vt raggiungere; arrivare a // vi stendersi; out of/within ~ fuori/a portata di mano; to ~ out vi: to ~ out for stendere la mano per prendere.
**react** [riː'ækt] vi reagire; ~**ion** [-'ækʃən] n reazione f.
**reactor** [riː'æktə*] n reattore m.
**read**, pt, pp read [riːd, rɛd] vi leggere // vt leggere; (understand) intendere, interpretare; (study) studiare; to ~ out vi leggere ad alta voce; ~**able** a (writing) leggibile; (book etc) che si legge volentieri; ~**er** n lettore/trice; (book) libro di lettura; (Brit: at university) professore con funzioni preminenti di ricerca; ~**ership** n (of paper etc) numero di lettori.
**readily** ['rɛdɪlɪ] ad volentieri; (easily) facilmente.
**readiness** ['rɛdɪnɪs] n prontezza; in ~ (prepared) pronto(a).
**reading** ['riːdɪŋ] n lettura; (understanding) interpretazione f; (on instrument) indicazione f.
**ready** ['rɛdɪ] a pronto(a); (willing) pronto(a), disposto(a); (quick) rapido(a); (available) disponibile // ad: ~-**cooked** già cotto(a) // n: at the ~ (MIL) pronto a sparare; (fig) tutto(a) pronto(a); to get ~ vi prepararsi // vt preparare; ~-**made** a prefabbricato(a); (clothes) confezionato(a); ~ **money** n denaro contante, contanti mpl; ~ **reckoner** n prontuario di calcolo; ~-**to-wear** a prêt-à-porter inv.
**real** [rɪəl] a reale; vero(a); in ~ terms in realtà; ~ **estate** n beni mpl immobili; ~**ism** n (also ART) realismo; ~**ist** n realista m/f; ~**istic** [-'lɪstɪk] a realistico(a).
**reality** [riː'ælɪtɪ] n realtà f inv.
**realization** [rɪəlaɪ'zeɪʃən] n presa di coscienza; realizzazione f.
**realize** ['rɪəlaɪz] vt (understand) rendersi conto di; (a project, COMM: asset) realizzare.
**really** ['rɪəlɪ] ad veramente, davvero.

**realm** [rɛlm] n reame m, regno.

**realtor** ['rɪəltɔ:*] n (US) agente m immobiliare.

**reap** [ri:p] vt mietere; (fig) raccogliere.

**reappear** [ri:ə'pɪə*] vi ricomparire, riapparire.

**rear** [rɪə*] a di dietro; (AUT: wheel etc) posteriore // n didietro, parte f posteriore // vt (cattle, family) allevare // vi (also: ~ up: animal) impennarsi.

**rearmament** [ri:'ɑ:məmənt] n riarmo.

**rearrange** [ri:ə'reɪndʒ] vt riordinare.

**rear-view mirror** ['rɪəvju:-] n (AUT) specchio retrovisore.

**reason** ['ri:zn] n ragione f; (cause, motive) ragione, motivo // vi: to ~ with sb far ragionare qn; to have ~ to think avere motivi per pensare; it stands to ~ that è ovvio che; ~able a ragionevole; (not bad) accettabile; ~ably ad ragionevolmente; ~ing n ragionamento.

**reassurance** [ri:ə'ʃuərəns] n rassicurazione f.

**reassure** [ri:ə'ʃuə*] vt rassicurare; to ~ sb of rassicurare qn di or su.

**rebate** ['ri:beɪt] n (on product) ribasso; (on tax etc) sgravio; (repayment) rimborso.

**rebel** n [rɛbl] ribelle m/f // vi [rɪ'bɛl] ribellarsi; ~lion n ribellione f; ~lious a ribelle.

**rebound** vi [rɪ'baund] (ball) rimbalzare // n [ri:baund] rimbalzo.

**rebuff** [rɪ'bʌf] n secco rifiuto.

**rebuke** [rɪ'bju:k] vt rimproverare.

**rebut** [rɪ'bʌt] vt rifiutare.

**recall** [rɪ'kɔ:l] vt richiamare; (remember) ricordare, richiamare alla mente // n richiamo.

**recant** [rɪ'kænt] vi ritrattarsi; (REL) fare abiura.

**recap** ['ri:kæp] vt ricapitolare // vi riassumere.

**recapitulate** [ri:kə'pɪtjuleɪt] vt, vi = recap.

**rec'd** abbr = received.

**recede** [rɪ'si:d] vi allontanarsi; ritirarsi; calare; **receding** a (forehead, chin) sfuggente; he's got a receding hairline sta stempiando.

**receipt** [rɪ'si:t] n (document) ricevuta; (act of receiving) ricevimento; ~s npl (COMM) introiti mpl.

**receive** [rɪ'si:v] vt ricevere; (guest) ricevere, accogliere.

**receiver** [rɪ'si:və*] n (TEL) ricevitore m; (of stolen goods) ricettatore/trice; (LAW) curatore m fallimentare.

**recent** ['ri:snt] a recente; ~ly ad recentemente.

**receptacle** [rɪ'sɛptɪkl] n recipiente m.

**reception** [rɪ'sɛpʃən] n ricevimento; (welcome) accoglienza; (TV etc) ricezione f; ~ desk n (in hotel) reception f inv; (in hospital, at doctor's) accettazione f; (in offices etc) portineria; ~ist n receptionist m/f inv.

**receptive** [rɪ'sɛptɪv] a ricettivo(a).

**recess** [rɪ'sɛs] n (in room) alcova; (POL etc: holiday) vacanze fpl; ~ion [rɪ'sɛʃən] n recessione f.

**recharge** [ri:'tʃɑ:dʒ] vt (battery) ricaricare.

**recipe** ['rɛsɪpɪ] n ricetta.

**recipient** [rɪ'sɪpɪənt] n beneficiario/a; (of letter) destinatario/a.

**recital** [rɪ'saɪtl] n recital m inv.

**recite** [rɪ'saɪt] vt (poem) recitare.

**reckless** ['rɛkləs] a (driver etc) spericolato(a).

**reckon** ['rɛkən] vt (count) calcolare; (consider) considerare, stimare; (think): I ~ that ... penso che ...; to ~ on vt fus contare su; ~ing n conto; stima.

**reclaim** [rɪ'kleɪm] vt (land) bonificare; (demand back) richiedere, reclamare.

**recline** [rɪ'klaɪn] vi stare sdraiato(a); **reclining** a (seat) ribaltabile.

**recluse** [rɪ'klu:s] n eremita m, appartato/a.

**recognition** [rɛkəg'nɪʃən] n riconoscimento; **to gain** ~ essere riconosciuto(a); **transformed beyond** ~ irriconoscibile.

**recognize** ['rɛkəgnaɪz] vt: **to** ~ **(by/as)** riconoscere (a or da/come).

**recoil** [rɪ'kɔɪl] vi (person): **to** ~ **(from)** indietreggiare (davanti a) // n (of gun) rinculo.

**recollect** [rɛkə'lɛkt] vt ricordare; **~ion** [-'lɛkʃən] n ricordo.

**recommend** [rɛkə'mɛnd] vt raccomandare; (advise) consigliare.

**reconcile** ['rɛkənsaɪl] vt (two people) riconciliare; (two facts) conciliare, quadrare; **to** ~ **o.s. to** rassegnarsi a.

**recondition** [ri:kən'dɪʃən] vt rimettere a nuovo.

**reconnaissance** [rɪ'kɔnɪsns] n (MIL) ricognizione f.

**reconnoitre, (US) reconnoiter** [rɛkə'nɔɪtə*] (MIL) vt fare una ricognizione di // vi fare una ricognizione.

**reconstruct** [ri:kən'strʌkt] vt ricostruire.

**record** n ['rɛkɔ:d] ricordo, documento; (of meeting etc) nota, verbale m; (register) registro; (file) pratica, dossier m inv; (also: police ~) fedina penale sporca; (MUS: disc) disco; (SPORT) record m inv, primato // vt [rɪ'kɔ:d] (set down) prendere nota di, registrare; (relate) raccontare; (MUS: song etc) registrare; **in** ~ **time** a tempo di record; **to keep a** ~ **of** tener nota di; **off the** ~ a ufficioso(a) // ad ufficiosamente; **~ card** n (in file) scheda; **~ed delivery** n (Brit POST): **~ed delivery letter** etc lettera etc raccomandata; **~er** n (LAW) avvocato che funge da giudice; (MUS) flauto diritto; **~ holder** n (SPORT) primatista m/f; **~ing** n (MUS) registrazione f; **~ player** n giradischi m inv.

**recount** [rɪ'kaunt] vt raccontare, narrare.

**re-count** n ['ri:kaunt] (POL: of votes) nuovo computo // vt [ri:'kaunt] ricontare.

**recoup** [rɪ'ku:p] vt ricuperare.

**recourse** [rɪ'kɔ:s] n ricorso; rimedio.

**recover** [rɪ'kʌvə*] vt ricuperare // vi (from illness) rimettersi (in salute), ristabilirsi; (country, person: from shock) riprendersi.

**recovery** [rɪ'kʌvərɪ] n ricupero; ristabilimento; ripresa.

**recreation** [rɛkrɪ'eɪʃən] n ricreazione f; svago; **~al** a ricreativo(a).

**recrimination** [rɪkrɪmɪ'neɪʃən] n recriminazione f.

**recruit** [rɪ'kru:t] n recluta // vt reclutare.

**rectangle** ['rɛktæŋgl] n rettangolo; **rectangular** [-'tæŋgjulə*] a rettangolare.

**rectify** ['rɛktɪfaɪ] vt (error) rettificare; (omission) riparare.

**rector** ['rɛktə*] n (REL) parroco (anglicano); **rectory** n presbiterio.

**recuperate** [rɪ'kju:pəreɪt] vi ristabilirsi.

**recur** [rɪ'kə:*] vi riaccadere; (idea, opportunity) riapparire; (symptoms) ripresentarsi; **~rent** a ricorrente, periodico(a).

**red** [rɛd] n rosso; (POL: pej) rosso/a // a rosso(a); **in the** ~ (account) scoperto; (business) in deficit; **~ carpet treatment** n cerimonia col gran pavese; **R~ Cross** n Croce f Rossa; **~currant** n ribes m inv; **~den** vt arrossare // vi arrossire; **~dish** a rossiccio(a).

**redeem** [rɪ'di:m] vt (debt) riscattare; (sth in pawn) ritirare; (fig, also REL) redimere; **~ing** a (feature) che salva.

**redeploy** [ri:dɪ'plɔɪ] vt (resources) riorganizzare.

**red-haired** [rɛd'hɛəd] a dai capelli rossi.

**red-handed** [rɛd'hændɪd] a: **to be caught** ~ essere preso(a) in flagrante or con le mani nel sacco.

**redhead** ['rɛdhɛd] n rosso/a.

**red herring** n (fig) falsa pista.

**red-hot** [rɛd'hɔt] a arroventato(a).

**redirect** [ri:daɪˈrɛkt] vt (mail) far seguire.

**redistribute** [ri:dɪˈstrɪbjuːt] vt ridistribuire.

**red light** n: to go through a ~ (AUT) passare col rosso; **red-light district** n quartiere m luce rossa inv.

**redo** [ri:ˈduː] vt irg rifare.

**redolent** [ˈrɛdələnt] a: ~ of che sa di; (fig) che ricorda.

**redouble** [ri:ˈdʌbl] vt: to ~ one's efforts raddoppiare gli sforzi.

**redress** [rɪˈdrɛs] n riparazione // vt riparare.

**Red Sea** n: the ~ il Mar Rosso.

**redskin** [ˈrɛdskɪn] n pellerossa m/f.

**red tape** n (fig) burocrazia.

**reduce** [rɪˈdjuːs] vt ridurre; (lower) ridurre, abbassare; "~ speed now" (AUT) "rallentare"; **reduction** [rɪˈdʌkʃən] n riduzione f; (of price) ribasso; (discount) sconto.

**redundancy** [rɪˈdʌndənsɪ] n licenziamento.

**redundant** [rɪˈdʌndnt] a (worker) licenziato(a); (detail, object) superfluo(a); **to be made** ~ essere licenziato (per eccesso di personale).

**reed** [ri:d] n (BOT) canna; (MUS: of clarinet etc) ancia.

**reef** [ri:f] n (at sea) scogliera.

**reek** [ri:k] vi: to ~ (of) puzzare (di).

**reel** [ri:l] n bobina, rocchetto; (TECH) aspo; (FISHING) mulinello; (CINEMA) rotolo // vt (TECH) annaspare; (also: ~ up) avvolgere // vi (sway) barcollare.

**ref** [rɛf] n abbr (col: = referee) arbitro.

**refectory** [rɪˈfɛktərɪ] n refettorio.

**refer** [rɪˈfɜː*] vt: to ~ sth to (dispute, decision) deferire qc a; to ~ sb to (inquirer: for information) indirizzare qn a; (reader: to text) rimandare qn a; **to** ~ **to** vt fus (allude to) accennare a; (apply to) riferire a; (consult) rivolgersi a.

trare.

**reference** [ˈrɛfrəns] n riferimento; (mention) menzione f, allusione f; (for job application: letter) referenza; lettera di raccomandazione; (: person) referenza; **with** ~ **to** riguardo a; (COMM: in letter) in o con riferimento a; ~ **book** n libro di consultazione; ~ **number** n numero di riferimento.

**referendum**, pl **referenda** [rɛfəˈrɛndəm, -də] n referendum m inv.

**refill** vt [ri:ˈfɪl] riempire di nuovo; (pen, lighter etc) ricaricare // n [ˈri:fɪl] (for pen etc) ricambio.

**refine** [rɪˈfaɪn] vt raffinare; ~**d** a (person, taste) raffinato(a).

**reflect** [rɪˈflɛkt] vt (light, image) riflettere; (fig) rispecchiare // vi (think) riflettere, considerare; to ~ **on** vt fus (discredit) rispecchiarsi su; ~**ion** [-ˈflɛkʃən] n riflessione f; (image) riflesso; (criticism): ~ion on giudizio su; attacco a; on ~ion pensandoci sopra.

**reflex** [ˈri:flɛks] a riflesso(a) // n riflesso; ~**ive** [rɪˈflɛksɪv] a (LING) riflessivo(a).

**reform** [rɪˈfɔːm] n riforma // vt riformare; **the R~ation** [rɛfəˈmeɪʃən] n la Riforma; ~**atory** n (US) riformatorio.

**refrain** [rɪˈfreɪn] vi: to ~ **from doing** trattenersi dal fare // n ritornello.

**refresh** [rɪˈfrɛʃ] vt rinfrescare; (subj: food, sleep) ristorare; ~**er course** n (Brit) corso di aggiornamento; ~**ing** a (drink) rinfrescante; (sleep) riposante, ristoratore(trice); ~**ments** npl rinfreschi mpl.

**refrigerator** [rɪˈfrɪdʒəreɪtə*] n frigorifero.

**refuel** [ri:ˈfjuəl] vi far rifornimento (di carburante).

**refuge** [ˈrɛfjuːdʒ] n rifugio; to take ~ **in** rifugiarsi in.

**refugee** [rɛfjuˈdʒiː] n rifugiato/a,

profugo/a.

**refund** n ['ri:fʌnd] rimborso // vt [rɪ'fʌnd] rimborsare.

**refurbish** [ri:'fɜ:bɪʃ] vt rimettere a nuovo.

**refusal** [rɪ'fju:zəl] n rifiuto; **to have first ~ on** avere il diritto d'opzione su.

**refuse** n ['refju:s] rifiuti mpl // vt, vi [rɪ'fju:z] rifiutare; **to ~ to do** rifiutare di fare; **~ collection** n raccolta di rifiuti.

**refute** [rɪ'fju:t] vt confutare.

**regain** [rɪ'geɪn] vt riguadagnare; riacquistare, ricuperare.

**regal** ['ri:gl] a regio(a); **~ia** [rɪ'geɪlɪə] n insegne fpl regie.

**regard** [rɪ'gɑ:d] n riguardo, stima // vt considerare, stimare; **to give one's ~s to** porgere i suoi saluti a; **"with kindest ~s"** "cordiali saluti"; **~ing, as ~s, with ~ to** riguardo a; **~less** ad lo stesso; **~less of** a dispetto di, nonostante.

**regenerate** [rɪ'dʒenəreɪt] vt rigenerare.

**régime** [reɪ'ʒi:m] n regime m.

**regiment** n ['redʒɪmənt] reggimento // vt ['redʒɪment] irreggimentare; **~al** [-'mentl] a reggimentale.

**region** ['ri:dʒən] n regione f; **in the ~ of** (fig) all'incirca di; **~al** a regionale.

**register** ['redʒɪstə*] n registro; (also: **electoral ~**) lista elettorale // vt registrare; (vehicle) immatricolare; (luggage) spedire assicurato(a); (letter) assicurare; (subj: instrument) segnare // vi iscriversi; (at hotel) firmare il registro; (make impression) entrare in testa; **~ed** a (design) depositato(a); (Brit: letter) assicurato(a); **~ed trademark** n marchio depositato.

**registrar** ['redʒɪstrɑ:*] n ufficiale m di stato civile; segretario.

**registration** [redʒɪs'treɪʃən] n (act) registrazione f; iscrizione f; (AUT: also: **~ number**) numero di targa.

**registry** ['redʒɪstrɪ] n ufficio del registro; **~ office** n (Brit) anagrafe f; **to get married in a ~ office** ≈ sposarsi in municipio.

**regret** [rɪ'gret] n rimpianto, rincrescimento // vt rimpiangere; **~fully** ad con rincrescimento; **~table** a deplorevole.

**regular** ['regjulə*] a regolare; (usual) abituale, normale; (soldier) dell'esercito regolare; (COMM: size) normale // n (client etc) cliente m/f abituale; **~ly** ad regolarmente.

**regulate** ['regjuleɪt] vt regolare; **regulation** [-'leɪʃən] n (rule) regola, regolamento; (adjustment) regolazione f.

**rehabilitation** ['ri:həbɪlɪ'teɪʃən] n (of offender) riabilitazione f; (of disabled) riadattamento.

**rehearsal** [rɪ'hɜ:səl] n prova.

**rehearse** [rɪ'hɜ:s] vt provare.

**reign** [reɪn] n regno // vi regnare.

**reimburse** [ri:ɪm'bɜ:s] vt rimborsare.

**rein** [reɪn] n (for horse) briglia.

**reindeer** ['reɪndɪə*] n (pl inv) renna.

**reinforce** [ri:ɪn'fɔ:s] vt rinforzare; **~d concrete** n cemento armato; **~ments** npl (MIL) rinforzi mpl.

**reinstate** [ri:ɪn'steɪt] vt reintegrare.

**reiterate** [ri:'ɪtəreɪt] vt reiterare, ripetere.

**reject** n ['ri:dʒekt] (COMM) scarto // vt [rɪ'dʒekt] rifiutare, respingere; (COMM: goods) scartare; **~ion** [rɪ'dʒekʃən] n rifiuto.

**rejoice** [rɪ'dʒɔɪs] vi: **to ~** (at or over) provare diletto in.

**rejuvenate** [rɪ'dʒu:vəneɪt] vt ringiovanire.

**relapse** [rɪ'læps] n (MED) ricaduta.

**relate** [rɪ'leɪt] vt (tell) raccontare; (connect) collegare // vi: **to ~ to** (connect) riferirsi a; (get on with) stabilire un rapporto con; **~d** a imparentato(a); collegato(a), connesso(a); **relating to** prep che riguarda, rispetto a.

**relation** [rɪ'leɪʃən] n (person) parente m/f; (link) rapporto, relazione f; ~**ship** n rapporto; (personal ties) rapporti mpl, relazioni fpl; (also: **family** ~**ship**) legami mpl di parentela.

**relative** ['rɛlətɪv] n parente m/f // a relativo(a); (respective) rispettivo(a).

**relax** [rɪ'læks] vi rilasciarsi; (person: unwind) rilassarsi // vt rilasciare; (mind, person) rilassare; ~**ation** [riːlæk'seɪʃən] n rilassamento; rilassamento; (entertainment) ricreazione f, svago; ~**ed** a rilasciato(a); rilassato(a); ~**ing** a rilassante.

**relay** ['riːleɪ] n (SPORT) corsa a staffetta // vt (message) trasmettere.

**release** [rɪ'liːs] n (from prison) rilascio; (from obligation) liberazione f; (of gas etc) emissione f; (of film etc) distribuzione f; (record) disco; (device) disinnesto // vt (prisoner) rilasciare; (from obligation, wreckage etc) liberare; (book, film) fare uscire; (news) rendere pubblico(a); (gas etc) emettere; (TECH: catch, spring etc) disinnestare; (let go) rilasciare; lasciar andare; sciogliere.

**relegate** ['rɛləgeɪt] vt relegare; (SPORT): **to be ~d** essere retrocesso(a).

**relent** [rɪ'lɛnt] vi cedere; ~**less** a implacabile.

**relevant** ['rɛləvənt] a pertinente; (chapter) in questione; ~ **to** pertinente a.

**reliability** [rɪlaɪə'bɪlɪtɪ] n (of person) serietà; (of machine) affidabilità.

**reliable** [rɪ'laɪəbl] a (person, firm) fidato(a), che dà affidamento; (method) sicuro(a); (machine) affidabile; **reliably** ad: **to be reliably informed** sapere da fonti sicure.

**reliance** [rɪ'laɪəns] n: ~ (**on**) fiducia (in); bisogno (di).

**relic** ['rɛlɪk] n (REL) reliquia; (of the past) resto.

**relief** [rɪ'liːf] n (from pain, anxiety)

sollievo; (help, supplies) soccorsi mpl; (of guard) cambio; (ART, GEO) rilievo.

**relieve** [rɪ'liːv] vt (pain, patient) sollevare; (bring help) soccorrere; (take over from: gen) sostituire; (: guard) rilevare; **to ~ sb of sth** (load) alleggerire qn di qc; **to ~ o.s.** fare i propri bisogni.

**religion** [rɪ'lɪdʒən] n religione f; **religious** a religioso(a).

**relinquish** [rɪ'lɪŋkwɪʃ] vt abbandonare; (plan, habit) rinunziare a.

**relish** ['rɛlɪʃ] n (CULIN) condimento; (enjoyment) gran piacere m // vt (food etc) godere; **to ~ doing** adorare fare.

**relocate** [riːləu'keɪt] vt trasferire // vi trasferirsi.

**reluctance** [rɪ'lʌktəns] n riluttanza.

**reluctant** [rɪ'lʌktənt] a riluttante, mal disposto(a); ~**ly** ad di mala voglia, a malincuore.

**rely** [rɪ'laɪ]: **to ~ on** vt fus contare su; (be dependent) dipendere da.

**remain** [rɪ'meɪn] vi restare, rimanere; ~**der** n resto; (COMM) rimanenza; ~**ing** a che rimane; ~**s** npl resti mpl.

**remand** [rɪ'mɑːnd] n: **on ~** in detenzione preventiva // vt: **to ~ in custody** rinviare in carcere; trattenere a disposizione della legge; ~ **home** n (Brit) riformatorio, casa di correzione.

**remark** [rɪ'mɑːk] n osservazione f // vt osservare, dire; (notice) notare; ~**able** a notevole; eccezionale.

**remedial** [rɪ'miːdɪəl] a (tuition, classes) di riparazione.

**remedy** ['rɛmədɪ] n: ~ (**for**) rimedio (per) // vt rimediare a.

**remember** [rɪ'mɛmbə*] vt ricordare, ricordarsi di; **remembrance** n memoria; ricordo.

**remind** [rɪ'maɪnd] vt: **to ~ sb of sth** ricordare qc a qn; **to ~ sb to do** ricordare a qn di fare; ~**er** n richiamo; (note etc) promemoria m *inv.*

**reminisce** [remɪ'nɪs] *vi*: to ~ (about) abbandonarsi ai ricordi (di).

**reminiscent** [remɪ'nɪsnt] *a*: ~ of che fa pensare a, che richiama.

**remiss** [rɪ'mɪs] *a* negligente.

**remission** [rɪ'mɪʃən] *n* remissione *f*; (*of fee*) esonero.

**remit** [rɪ'mɪt] *vt* (*send: money*) rimettere; ~**tance** *n* rimessa.

**remnant** ['remnant] *n* resto, avanzo; ~**s** *npl* (*COMM*) scampoli *mpl*; fine *f* serie.

**remorse** [rɪ'mɔ:s] *n* rimorso; ~**ful** *a* pieno(a) di rimorsi; ~**less** *a* (*fig*) spietato(a).

**remote** [rɪ'məut] *a* remoto(a), lontano(a); (*person*) distaccato(a); ~ **control** *n* telecomando; ~**ly** *ad* remotamente; (*slightly*) vagamente.

**remould** ['ri:məuld] *n* (*Brit: tyre*) gomma rivestita.

**removable** [rɪ'mu:vəbl] *a* (*detachable*) staccabile.

**removal** [rɪ'mu:vəl] *n* (*taking away*) rimozione *f*; soppressione *f*; (*Brit: from house*) trasloco; (*from office: dismissal*) destituzione *f*; (*MED*) ablazione *f*; ~ **van** *n* (*Brit*) furgone *m* per traslochi.

**remove** [rɪ'mu:v] *vt* togliere, rimuovere; (*employee*) destituire; (*stain*) far sparire; (*doubt, abuse*) sopprimere, eliminare; ~**rs** *npl* (*Brit: company*) ditta *or* impresa di traslochi.

**Renaissance** [rɪ'neɪsɑ:ns] *n*: the ~ il Rinascimento.

**render** ['rendə*] *vt* rendere; (*CULIN: fat*) struggere; ~**ing** *n* (*MUS etc*) interpretazione *f*.

**rendez-vous** ['rɔndɪvu:] *n* appuntamento; (*place*) luogo d'incontro; (*meeting*) incontro.

**renegade** ['renɪgeɪd] *n* rinnegato/a.

**renew** [rɪ'nju:] *vt* rinnovare; (*negotiations*) riprendere; ~**al** *n* rinnovamento; ripresa.

**renounce** [rɪ'nauns] *vt* rinunziare a; (*disown*) ripudiare.

**renovate** ['renəveɪt] *vt* rinnovare; (*art work*) restaurare; **renovation** [-'veɪʃən] *n* rinnovamento; restauro.

**renown** [rɪ'naun] *n* rinomanza; ~**ed** *a* rinomato(a).

**rent** [rent] *n* affitto // *vt* (*take for rent*) prendere in affitto; (*also: ~ out*) dare in affitto; ~**al** *n* (*for television, car*) fitto.

**renunciation** [rɪnʌnsɪ'eɪʃən] *n* rinnegamento; (*self-denial*) rinunzia.

**rep** [rep] *n abbr* (*COMM*: = *representative*) rappresentante *m/f*; (*THEATRE*: = *repertory*) teatro di repertorio.

**repair** [rɪ'pɛə*] *n* riparazione *f* // *vt* riparare; **in good/bad** ~ in buona/cattiva condizione; ~ **kit** *n* corredo per riparazioni; ~ **shop** *n* (*AUT etc*) officina.

**repartee** [repɑ:'ti:] *n* risposta pronta.

**repatriate** [ri:'pætrɪeɪt] *vt* rimpatriare.

**repay** [ri:'peɪ] *vt irg* (*money, creditor*) rimborsare, ripagare; (*sb's efforts*) ricompensare; ~**ment** *n* rimborsamento; ricompensa.

**repeal** [rɪ'pi:l] *n* (*of law*) abrogazione *f*; (*of sentence*) annullamento // *vt* abrogare; annullare.

**repeat** [rɪ'pi:t] *n* (*RADIO, TV*) replica // *vt* ripetere; (*pattern*) riprodurre; (*promise, attack, also COMM: order*) rinnovare // *vi* ripetere; ~**edly** *ad* ripetutamente, spesso.

**repel** [rɪ'pel] *vt* respingere; ~**lent** *a* repellente // *n*: **insect** ~**lent** prodotto *m* anti-insetti *inv*.

**repent** [rɪ'pent] *vi*: to ~ (of) pentirsi (di); ~**ance** *n* pentimento.

**repertoire** ['repətwɑ:*] *n* repertorio.

**repertory** ['repətəri] *n* (*also*: ~ *theatre*) teatro di repertorio.

**repetition** [repɪ'tɪʃən] *n* ripetizione *f*; (*COMM: of order etc*) rinnovo.

**repetitive** [rɪ'petɪtɪv] *a* (*movement*) che si ripete; (*work*) monotono(a); (*speech*) pieno(a) di ripetizioni.

**replace** [rɪ'pleɪs] *vt* (*put back*)

rimettere a posto; (take the place of) sostituire; ~**ment** n rimessa; sostituzione f; (person) sostituto/a.

**replay** ['ri:pleɪ] n (of match) partita ripetuta; (of tape, film) replay m inv.

**replenish** [rɪ'plenɪʃ] vt (glass) riempire; (stock etc) rifornire.

**replete** [rɪ'pli:t] a ripieno(a); (well-fed) sazio/a.

**replica** ['replɪkə] n replica, copia.

**reply** [rɪ'plaɪ] n risposta // vi rispondere; ~ **coupon** n buono di risposta.

**report** [rɪ'pɔ:t] n rapporto; (PRESS etc) cronaca; (Brit: also: school ~) pagella // vt riportare; (PRESS etc) fare una cronaca su; (bring to notice: occurrence) segnalare; (: person) denunciare // vi (make a report) fare un rapporto (or una cronaca); (present o.s.): to ~ (to sb) presentarsi (a qn); ~ **card** n (US, Scottish) pagella; ~**edly** ad stando a quanto si dice; he ~**edly told them to ...** avrebbe detto loro di ...; ~**er** n reporter m inv.

**repose** [rɪ'pəʊz] n: **in ~** (face, mouth) in riposo.

**reprehensible** [reprɪ'hensɪbl] a riprensibile.

**represent** [reprɪ'zent] vt rappresentare; ~**ation** [-'teɪʃən] n rappresentazione f; ~**ations** npl (protest) protesta; ~**ative** n rappresentativo/a; (US POL) deputato/a // a rappresentativo(a), caratteristico(a).

**repress** [rɪ'pres] vt reprimere; ~**ion** [-'preʃən] n repressione f.

**reprieve** [rɪ'pri:v] n (LAW) sospensione f dell'esecuzione della condanna; (fig) dilazione f.

**reprimand** ['reprɪmɑ:nd] n rimprovero // vt rimproverare.

**reprisal** [rɪ'praɪzl] n rappresaglia.

**reproach** [rɪ'prəʊtʃ] n rimprovero // vt: **to ~ sb with sth** rimproverare qn di qc; ~**ful** a di rimprovero.

**reproduce** [ri:prə'dju:s] vt riprodurre // vi riprodursi; **reproduc-**

**tion** [-'dʌkʃən] n riproduzione f.

**reproof** [rɪ'pru:f] n riprovazione f.

**reprove** [rɪ'pru:v] vt (action) disapprovare; (person): **to ~** (for) biasimare (per).

**reptile** ['reptaɪl] n rettile m.

**republic** [rɪ'pʌblɪk] n repubblica; ~**an** a, n repubblicano(a).

**repulse** [rɪ'pʌls] vt respingere.

**repulsive** [rɪ'pʌlsɪv] a ripugnante, ripulsivo(a).

**reputable** ['repjʊtəbl] a di buona reputazione; (occupation) rispettabile.

**reputation** [repjʊ'teɪʃən] n reputazione f.

**repute** [rɪ'pju:t] n reputazione f; ~**d** a reputato(a); ~**dly** ad secondo quanto si dice.

**request** [rɪ'kwest] n domanda; (formal) richiesta // vt: **to ~** (of or from sb) chiedere (a qn); ~ **stop** n (Brit: for bus) fermata facoltativa or a richiesta.

**require** [rɪ'kwaɪə*] vt (need: subj: person) aver bisogno di; (: thing, situation) richiedere; (want) volere; esigere; (order) obbligare; ~**ment** n esigenza; bisogno; requisito.

**requisite** ['rekwɪzɪt] n cosa necessaria // a necessario(a).

**requisition** [rekwɪ'zɪʃən] n: ~ (for) richiesta (di) // vt (MIL) requisire.

**rescue** ['reskju:] n salvataggio; (help) soccorso // vt salvare; ~ **party** n squadra di salvataggio; ~**r** n salvatore/trice.

**research** [rɪ'sɜ:tʃ] n ricerca, ricerche fpl // vt fare ricerche su.

**resemblance** [rɪ'zembləns] n somiglianza.

**resemble** [rɪ'zembl] vt assomigliare a.

**resent** [rɪ'zent] vt risentirsi di; ~**ful** a pieno(a) di risentimento; ~**ment** n risentimento.

**reservation** [rezə'veɪʃən] n (booking) prenotazione f; (doubt) dubbio; (protected area) riserva; (Brit: on road: also: **central ~**)

spartitraffico $m$ $inv$; **to make a ~ (in an hotel/a restaurant/on a plane)** prenotare (una camera/una tavola/un posto).

**reserve** [rɪ'zə:v] $n$ riserva // $vt$ ($seats$ $etc$) prenotare; **~s** $npl$ (MIL) riserve $fpl$; **in ~** in serbo; **~d** $a$ ($shy$) riservato(a); ($seat$) prenotato(a).

**reservoir** ['rezəvwa:*] $n$ serbatoio.

**reshuffle** [ri:'ʃʌfl] $n$: **Cabinet ~** (POL) rimpasto governativo.

**reside** [rɪ'zaɪd] $vi$ risiedere.

**residence** ['rezɪdəns] $n$ residenza; **~ permit** $n$ ($Brit$) permesso di soggiorno.

**resident** ['rezɪdənt] $n$ residente $m/f$; ($in$ $hotel$) cliente $m/f$ fisso(a) // $a$ residente; **~ial** [-'denʃəl] $a$ di residenza; ($area$) residenziale.

**residue** ['rezɪdju:] $n$ resto; ($CHEM$, $PHYSICS$) residuo.

**resign** [rɪ'zaɪn] $vt$ ($one's$ $post$) dimettersi da // $vi$ dimettersi; **to ~ o.s. to** rassegnarsi a; **~ation** [rezɪg'neɪʃən] $n$ dimissioni $fpl$; rassegnazione $f$; **~ed** $a$ rassegnato(a).

**resilience** [rɪ'zɪlɪəns] $n$ ($of$ $material$) elasticità, resilienza; ($of$ $person$) capacità di recupero.

**resilient** [rɪ'zɪlɪənt] $a$ ($person$) che si riprende facilmente.

**resin** ['rezɪn] $n$ resina.

**resist** [rɪ'zɪst] $vt$ resistere a; **~ance** $n$ resistenza.

**resolution** [rezə'lu:ʃən] $n$ risoluzione $f$.

**resolve** [rɪ'zɔlv] $n$ risoluzione $f$ // $vi$ ($decide$): **to ~ to do** decidere di fare // $vt$ ($problem$) risolvere.

**resort** [rɪ'zɔ:t] $n$ ($town$) stazione $f$; ($recourse$) ricorso // $vi$: **to ~ to** aver ricorso a; **as a last ~** come ultimo ricorso.

**resounding** [rɪ'zaundɪŋ] $a$ risonante; ($fig$) clamoroso(a).

**resource** [rɪ'sɔ:s] $n$ risorsa; **~s** $npl$ risorse $fpl$; **~ful** $a$ pieno(a) di risorse, intraprendente.

**respect** [rɪs'pekt] $n$ rispetto // $vt$ rispettare; **~s** $npl$ ossequi $mpl$; **with**

**~ to** rispetto a, riguardo a; **in this ~** per questo riguardo; **~able** $a$ rispettabile; **~ful** $a$ rispettoso(a).

**respective** [rɪs'pektɪv] $a$ rispettivo(a).

**respite** ['respaɪt] $n$ respiro, tregua.

**resplendent** [rɪs'plendənt] $a$ risplendente.

**respond** [rɪs'pɔnd] $vi$ rispondere.

**response** [rɪs'pɔns] $n$ risposta.

**responsibility** [rɪspɔnsɪ'bɪlɪtɪ] $n$ responsabilità $f$ $inv$.

**responsible** [rɪs'pɔnsɪbl] $a$ ($trustworthy$) fidato(a); ($job$) di (grande) responsabilità; ($liable$): **~ (for)** responsabile (di); **responsibly** $ad$ responsabilmente.

**responsive** [rɪs'pɔnsɪv] $a$ che reagisce.

**rest** [rest] $n$ riposo, ($stop$) sosta, pausa; ($MUS$) pausa; ($support$) appoggio, sostegno; ($remainder$) resto, avanzi $mpl$ // $vi$ riposarsi; ($remain$) rimanere, restare; ($be$ $supported$): **to ~ on** appoggiarsi su // $vt$ ($lean$): **to ~ sth on/against** appoggiare qc su/contro; **the ~ of them** gli altri; **it ~s with him to decide** sta a lui decidere.

**restaurant** ['restərɔŋ] $n$ ristorante $m$; **~ car** $n$ ($Brit$) vagone $m$ ristorante.

**restful** ['restful] $a$ riposante.

**rest home** $n$ casa di riposo.

**restitution** [restɪ'tju:ʃən] $n$ ($act$) restituzione $f$; ($reparation$) riparazione $f$.

**restive** ['restɪv] $a$ agitato(a), impaziente; ($horse$) restio(a).

**restless** ['restlɪs] $a$ agitato(a), irrequieto(a).

**restoration** [restə'reɪʃən] $n$ restauro; restituzione $f$.

**restore** [rɪ'stɔ:*] $vt$ ($building$) restaurare; ($sth$ $stolen$) restituire; ($peace$, $health$) ristorare.

**restrain** [rɪs'treɪn] $vt$ ($feeling$) contenere, frenare; ($person$): **to ~ (from doing)** trattenere (dal fare); **~ed** $a$ ($style$) contenuto(a), sobrio(a); (manner) riservato(a); ~t n (restriction) limitazione f; (moderation) ritegno.

**restrict** [rɪs'trɪkt] vt restringere, limitare; ~ion [-kʃən] n restrizione f, limitazione f.

**rest room** n (US) toletta.

**restructure** [ri:'strʌktʃə*] vt ristrutturare.

**result** [rɪ'zʌlt] n risultato // vi: to ~ in avere per risultato; as a ~ of in or di conseguenza a, in seguito a.

**resume** [rɪ'zju:m] vt, vi (work, journey) riprendere.

**résumé** ['reɪzjumeɪ] n riassunto.

**resumption** [rɪ'zʌmpʃən] n ripresa.

**resurgence** [rɪ'sə:dʒəns] n rinascita.

**resurrection** [rezə'rekʃən] n risurrezione f.

**resuscitate** [rɪ'sʌsɪteɪt] vt (MED) risuscitare; **resuscitation** [-'teɪʃən] n rianimazione f.

**retail** ['ri:teɪl] n (vendita al) minuto // cpd al minuto // vt vendere al minuto; ~er n commerciante m/f al minuto, dettagliante m/f; ~ price n prezzo al minuto.

**retain** [rɪ'teɪn] vt (keep) tenere, serbare; ~er n (servant) servitore m; (fee) onorario.

**retaliate** [rɪ'tælɪeɪt] vi: to ~ (against) vendicarsi (di); **retaliation** [-'eɪʃən] n rappresaglie fpl.

**retarded** [rɪ'tɑːdɪd] a ritardato(a); (also: **mentally** ~) tardo(a) (di mente).

**retch** [retʃ] vi aver conati di vomito.

**retire** [rɪ'taɪə*] vi (give up work) andare in pensione; (withdraw) ritirarsi, andarsene; (go to bed) andare a letto, ritirarsi; ~d a (person) pensionato(a); ~ment n pensione f; **retiring** a (person) riservato(a).

**retort** [rɪ'tɔːt] n (reply) rimbecco; (container) storta // vi rimbeccare.

**retrace** [ri:'treɪs] vt ricostruire; to ~ one's steps tornare sui passi.

**retract** [rɪ'trækt] vt (statement) trattare; (claws, undercarriage,

aerial) ritrarre, ritirare // vi ritrarsi.

**retrain** [ri:'treɪn] vt (worker) riaddestrare.

**retread** ['ri:tred] n (tyre) gomma rigenerata.

**retreat** [rɪ'tri:t] n ritirata; (place) rifugio // vi battere in ritirata; (flood) ritirarsi.

**retribution** [retrɪ'bju:ʃən] n castigo.

**retrieval** [rɪ'tri:vəl] n (see vb) ricupero; riparazione f.

**retrieve** [rɪ'tri:v] vt (sth lost) ricuperare, ritrovare; (situation, honour) salvare; (error, loss) riparare; (COMPUT) ricuperare; ~r n cane m da riporto.

**retrospect** ['retrəspekt] n: in ~ guardando indietro; ~**ive** [-'spektɪv] a retrospettivo(a); (law) retroattivo(a).

**return** [rɪ'tə:n] n (going or coming back) ritorno; (of sth stolen etc) restituzione f; (recompense) ricompensa; (FINANCE: from land, shares) profitto, reddito; (report) rapporto // cpd (journey, match) di ritorno; (Brit: ticket) di andata e ritorno // vi tornare, ritornare // vt rendere, restituire; (bring back) riportare; (send back) mandare indietro; (put back) rimettere; (POL: candidate) eleggere; ~s npl (COMM) incassi mpl; profitti mpl; in ~ (for) in cambio (di); by ~ of post a stretto giro di posta; many happy ~s (of the day)! auguri!, buon compleanno!

**reunion** [ri:'ju:nɪən] n riunione f.

**reunite** [ri:ju:'naɪt] vt riunire.

**rev** [rev] n abbr (= revolution: AUT) giro // vb (also: ~ up) vt imballare // vi imballarsi.

**revamp** [ri:'væmp] vt (house) rinnovare; (firm) riorganizzare.

**reveal** [rɪ'vi:l] vt (make known) rivelare, svelare; (display) rivelare, mostrare; ~**ing** a rivelatore(trice); (dress) scollato(a).

**reveille** [rɪ'vælɪ] n (MIL) sveglia.

**revel** ['revl] vi: to ~ in sth/in doing

dilettarsi di qc/a fare.

**revelation** [rɛvəˈleɪʃən] n rivelazione f.

**revelry** [ˈrɛvlrɪ] n baldoria.

**revenge** [rɪˈvɛndʒ] n vendetta; (in game etc) rivincita // vt vendicare; **to take ~** vendicarsi.

**revenue** [ˈrɛvənjuː] n reddito.

**reverberate** [rɪˈvɑːbəreɪt] vi (sound) rimbombare; (light) riverberarsi.

**reverence** [ˈrɛvərəns] n venerazione f, riverenza.

**Reverend** [ˈrɛvərənd] a (in titles) reverendo(a).

**reverie** [ˈrɛvərɪ] n fantasticheria.

**reversal** [rɪˈvɑːsl] n capovolgimento.

**reverse** [rɪˈvɑːs] n contrario, opposto; (back) rovescio; (AUT: also: ~ gear) marcia indietro // a (order, direction) contrario(a), opposto(a) // vt (turn) invertire, rivoltare; (change) capovolgere, rovesciare; (LAW: judgment) cassare // vi (Brit AUT) fare marcia indietro; **~d charge call** n (Brit TEL) telefonata con addebito al ricevente; **reversing lights** npl (Brit AUT) luci fpl per la retromarcia.

**revert** [rɪˈvɑːt] vi: **to ~ to** tornare a.

**review** [rɪˈvjuː] n rivista; (of book, film) recensione f // vt passare in rivista; fare la recensione di; **~er** n recensore/a.

**revile** [rɪˈvaɪl] vt insultare.

**revise** [rɪˈvaɪz] vt (manuscript) rivedere, correggere; (opinion) emendare, modificare; (study: subject, notes) ripassare; **revision** [rɪˈvɪʒən] n revisione f; ripasso.

**revitalize** [riːˈvaɪtəlaɪz] vt ravvivare.

**revival** [rɪˈvaɪvəl] n ripresa; ristabilimento; (of faith) risveglio.

**revive** [rɪˈvaɪv] vt (person) rianimare; (custom) far rivivere; (hope, courage) ravvivare; (play, fashion) riesumare // vi (person) rianimarsi; (hope) ravvivarsi; (activity) riprendersi.

**revolt** [rɪˈvəult] n rivolta, ribellione f // vi rivoltarsi, ribellarsi // vt (far)

rivoltare; **~ing** a ripugnante.

**revolution** [rɛvəˈluːʃən] n rivoluzione f; (of wheel etc) rivoluzione, giro; **~ary** a, n rivoluzionario(a).

**revolve** [rɪˈvɒlv] vi girare.

**revolver** [rɪˈvɒlvə*] n rivoltella.

**revolving** [rɪˈvɒlvɪŋ] a girevole.

**revue** [rɪˈvjuː] n (THEATRE) rivista.

**revulsion** [rɪˈvʌlʃən] n ripugnanza.

**reward** [rɪˈwɔːd] n ricompensa, premio // vt: **to ~** (for) ricompensare (per); **~ing** a (fig) soddisfacente.

**rewind** [riːˈwaɪnd] vt irg (watch) ricaricare; (ribbon etc) riavvolgere.

**rewire** [riːˈwaɪə*] vt (house) rifare l'impianto elettrico di.

**reword** [riːˈwɔːd] vt formulare or esprimere con altre parole.

**rheumatism** [ˈruːmətɪzəm] n reumatismo.

**Rhine** [raɪn] n: **the ~** il Reno.

**rhinoceros** [raɪˈnɔsərəs] n rinoceronte m.

**rhododendron** [rəudəˈdɛndrən] n rododendro.

**Rhone** [rəun] n: **the ~** il Rodano.

**rhubarb** [ˈruːbɑːb] n rabarbaro.

**rhyme** [raɪm] n rima; (verse) poesia.

**rhythm** [ˈrɪðm] n ritmo.

**rib** [rɪb] n (ANAT) costola // vt (tease) punzecchiare.

**ribald** [ˈrɪbəld] a licenzioso(a), volgare.

**ribbon** [ˈrɪbən] n nastro; **in ~s** (torn) a brandelli.

**rice** [raɪs] n riso.

**rich** [rɪtʃ] a ricco(a); (clothes) sontuoso(a); **the ~** npl i ricchi; **~es** npl ricchezze fpl; **~ly** ad riccamente; (dressed) sontuosamente; (deserved) pienamente; **~ness** n ricchezza.

**rickets** [ˈrɪkɪts] n rachitismo.

**rickety** [ˈrɪkɪtɪ] a zoppicante.

**rickshaw** [ˈrɪkʃɔː] n risciò m inv.

**ricochet** [ˈrɪkəʃeɪ] n rimbalzo // vi rimbalzare.

**rid**, pt, pp **rid** [rɪd] vt: **to ~** sb of

sbarazzare or liberare qn di; **to get ~ of** sbarazzarsi di.

**ridden** ['rɪdn] *pp of* **ride**.

**riddle** ['rɪdl] *n* (*puzzle*) indovinello // *vt*: **to be ~d with** essere crivellato(a) di.

**ride** [raɪd] *n* (*on horse*) cavalcata; (*outing*) passeggiata; (*distance covered*) cavalcata; corsa // *vb* (*pt* **rode**, *pp* **ridden**) *vi* (*as sport*) cavalcare; (*go somewhere: on horse, bicycle*) andare (a cavallo or in bicicletta *etc*); (*journey: on bicycle, motorcycle, bus*) andare, viaggiare // *vt* (*a horse*) montare, cavalcare; **to ~ a horse/bicycle/camel** montare a cavallo/in bicicletta/in groppa a un cammello; **to ~ at anchor** (*NAUT*) essere alla fonda; **to take sb for a ~** (*fig*) prendere in giro qn; fregare qn; **~r** *n* cavalcatore/trice; (*in race*) fantino; (*on bicycle*) ciclista *m/f*; (*on motorcycle*) motociclista *m/f*; (*in document*) clausola addizionale, aggiunta.

**ridge** [rɪdʒ] *n* (*of hill*) cresta; (*of roof*) colmo; (*of mountain*) giogo; (*on object*) riga (in rilievo).

**ridicule** ['rɪdɪkjuːl] *n* ridicolo; scherno // *vt* mettere in ridicolo.

**ridiculous** [rɪ'dɪkjuləs] *a* ridicolo(a).

**riding** ['raɪdɪŋ] *n* equitazione *f*; **~ school** *n* scuola di equitazione.

**rife** [raɪf] *a* diffuso(a); **to be ~ with** abbondare di.

**riffraff** ['rɪfræf] *n* canaglia.

**rifle** ['raɪfl] *n* carabina // *vt* vuotare; **~ range** *n* campo di tiro; (*at fair*) tiro a segno.

**rift** [rɪft] *n* fessura, crepatura; (*fig: disagreement*) incrinatura, disaccordo.

**rig** [rɪg] *n* (*also*: **oil ~**: *on land*) derrick *m inv*; (: *at sea*) piattaforma di trivellazione // *vt* (*election etc*) truccare; **to ~ out** *vt* (*Brit*) attrezzare; (*pej*) abbigliare, agghindare; **to ~ up** *vt* allestire; **~ging** *n* (*NAUT*) attrezzatura.

**right** [raɪt] *a* giusto(a); (*suitable*) ap-

propriato(a); (*not left*) destro(a) // *n* (*title, claim*) diritto; (*not left*) destra // *ad* (*answer*) correttamente; (*not on the left*) a destra // *vt* raddrizzare; (*fig*) riparare // *excl* bene!; **to be ~** (*person*) aver ragione; (*answer*) essere giusto(a) *or* corretto(a); **by ~s** di diritto; **on the ~** a destra; **to be in the ~** aver ragione, essere nel giusto; **~ now** proprio adesso; subito; **to ~ against the wall** proprio contro il muro; **~ ahead** sempre diritto; proprio davanti; **~ in the middle** proprio nel mezzo; **~ away** subito; **~ angle** *n* angolo retto; **~eous** ['raɪtʃəs] *a* retto(a), virtuoso(a); (*anger*) giusto(a), giustificato(a); **~ful** *a* (*heir*) legittimo(a); **~handed** *a* (*person*) che adopera la mano destra; **~hand man** *n* braccio destro; **~hand side** *n* lato destro; **~ly** *ad* bene, correttamente; (*with reason*) a ragione; **~ of way** *n* diritto di passaggio; (*AUT*) precedenza; **~wing** *a* (*POL*) di destra.

**rigid** ['rɪdʒɪd] *a* rigido(a); (*principle*) rigoroso(a).

**rigmarole** ['rɪgmərəul] *n* tiritera; commedia.

**rigorous** ['rɪgərəs] *a* rigoroso(a).

**rile** [raɪl] *vt* irritare, seccare.

**rim** [rɪm] *n* orlo; (*of spectacles*) montatura; (*of wheel*) cerchione *m*.

**rind** [raɪnd] *n* (*of bacon*) cotenna; (*of lemon etc*) scorza.

**ring** [rɪŋ] *n* anello; (*also*: **wedding ~**) fede *f*; (*of people, objects*) cerchio; (*of spies*) giro; (*of smoke etc*) spirale *m*; (*arena*) pista, arena; (*for boxing*) ring *m inv*; (*sound of bell*) scampanio; (*telephone call*) colpo di telefono // *vb* (*pt* **rang**, *pp* **rung**) *vi* (*person, bell, telephone*) suonare; (*also*: **~ out**: *voice, words*) risuonare; (*TEL*) telefonare // *vt* (*Brit TEL*: *also*: **~ up**) telefonare a; **to ~ the bell** suonare; **to ~ back** *vt, vi* (*TEL*) richiamare; **to ~ off** *vi* (*Brit TEL*) mettere giù, riattaccare;

~**ing** n (of bell) scampanio; (of telephone) squillo; (in ears) ronzio; ~**ing tone** n (Brit TEL) segnale m di libero; ~**leader** n (of gang) capobanda m.

**ringlets** ['rɪŋlɪts] npl boccoli mpl.

**ring road** n (Brit) raccordo anulare.

**rink** [rɪŋk] n (also: **ice** ~) pista di pattinaggio.

**rinse** [rɪns] n risciacquatura; (hair tint) cachet m inv // vt sciacquare.

**riot** ['raɪət] n sommossa, tumulto // vi tumultuare; **to run** ~ creare disordine; ~**ous** a tumultuoso(a); che fa crepare dal ridere.

**rip** [rɪp] n strappo // vt strappare // vi strapparsi; ~**cord** n cavo di sfilamento.

**ripe** [raɪp] a (fruit) maturo(a); (cheese) stagionato(a); ~**n** vt maturare // vi maturarsi; stagionarsi.

**rip-off** ['rɪpɔf] n (col): **it's a** ~! è un furto!

**ripple** ['rɪpl] n increspamento, ondulazione f; mormorio // vi incresparsi.

**rise** [raɪz] n (slope) salita, pendio; (hill) altura; (increase: in wages: Brit) aumento; (: in prices, temperature) rialzo, aumento; (fig: to power etc) ascesa // vi (pt **rose**, pp **risen** [rəuz, 'rɪzn]) alzarsi, levarsi; (prices) aumentare; (waters, river) crescere; (sun, wind, person: from chair, bed) levarsi; (also: ~ **up**: rebel) insorgere; ribellarsi; **to give** ~ **to** provocare, dare origine a; **to** ~ **to the occasion** essere all'altezza; **rising** a (increasing: number) sempre crescente; (: prices) in aumento; (tide) montante; (sun, moon) nascente, che sorge // n (uprising) sommossa.

**risk** [rɪsk] n rischio; pericolo // vt rischiare; **to take** or **run the** ~ **of doing** correre il rischio di fare; **at** ~ in pericolo; **at one's own** ~ a proprio rischio e pericolo; ~**y** a rischioso(a).

**risqué** ['riːskeɪ] a (joke) spinto(a).

**rissole** ['rɪsəul] n crocchetta.

**rite** [raɪt] n rito; **last** ~**s** l'estrema unzione.

**ritual** ['rɪtjuəl] a, n rituale (m).

**rival** ['raɪvl] n rivale m/f; (in business) concorrente m/f a rivale; che fa concorrenza // vt essere in concorrenza con; **to** ~ **sb/sth in** competere con qn/qc in; ~**ry** n rivalità; concorrenza.

**river** ['rɪvə*] n fiume m // cpd (port, traffic) fluviale; **up/down** ~ a monte/valle; ~**bank** n argine m.

**rivet** ['rɪvɪt] n ribattino, rivetto // vt ribadire; (fig) concentrare, fissare.

**Riviera** [rɪvɪ'ɛərə] n: **the (French)** ~ la Costa Azzurra; **the Italian** ~ la Riviera.

**road** [rəud] n strada; (small) cammino; (in town) via; **major/minor** ~ strada con/senza diritto di precedenza; ~**block** n blocco stradale; ~**hog** n guidatore m egoista e spericolato; ~**map** n carta stradale; ~**safety** n sicurezza sulle strade; ~**side** n margine m della strada; ~**sign** n cartello stradale; ~**way** n carreggiata; ~**works** npl lavori mpl stradali; ~**worthy** a in buono stato di marcia.

**roam** [rəum] vi errare, vagabondare // vt vagare per.

**roar** [rɔː*] n ruggito; (of crowd) tumulto; (of thunder, storm) muggito // vi ruggire; tumultuare; muggire; **to** ~ **with laughter** scoppiare dalle risa; **to do a** ~**ing trade** fare affari d'oro.

**roast** [rəust] n arrosto // vt (meat) arrostire; ~**beef** n arrosto di manzo.

**rob** [rɔb] vt (person) rubare; (bank) svaligiare; **to** ~ **sb of sth** derubare qn di qc; (fig: deprive) privare qn di qc; ~**ber** n ladro; (armed) rapinatore m; ~**bery** n furto; rapina.

**robe** [rəub] n (for ceremony etc) abito; (also: **bath** ~) accappatoio; (US: cover) coperta // vt vestire.

**robin** ['rɒbɪn] n pettirosso.

**robot** ['rəʊbɒt] n robot m inv.

**robust** [rəʊ'bʌst] a robusto(a); (material) solido(a).

**rock** [rɒk] n (substance) roccia; (boulder) masso; roccia; (in sea) scoglio; (Brit: sweet) zucchero candito // vt (swing gently: cradle) dondolare; (: child) cullare; (shake) scrollare, far tremare // vi dondolarsi; scrollarsi, tremare; **on the ~s** (drink) col ghiaccio; (ship) sugli scogli; (marriage etc) in crisi; **~ and roll** n rock and roll m; **~-bottom** a (fig) stremo // a bassissimo(a); **~ery** n giardino roccioso.

**rocket** ['rɒkɪt] n razzo; (MIL) razzo, missile m.

**rock fall** n caduta di massi.

**rocking** ['rɒkɪŋ]: **~ chair** n sedia a dondolo; **~ horse** n cavallo a dondolo.

**rocky** ['rɒkɪ] a (hill) roccioso(a); (path) sassoso(a); (unsteady: table) traballante.

**rod** [rɒd] n (metallic, TECH) asta; (wooden) bacchetta; (also: **fishing ~**) canna da pesca.

**rode** [rəʊd] pt of **ride**.

**rodent** ['rəʊdnt] n roditore m.

**rodeo** ['rəʊdɪəʊ] n rodeo.

**roe** [rəʊ] n (species: also: **~ deer**) capriolo; (of fish, also: **hard ~**) uova fpl di pesce; **soft ~** latte m di pesce.

**rogue** [rəʊg] n mascalzone m.

**role** [rəʊl] n ruolo.

**roll** [rəʊl] n rotolo; (of banknotes) mazzo; (also: **bread ~**) panino; (register) lista; (sound: of drums etc) rullo; (movement: of ship) rullio // vt rotolare; (also: **~ up: string**) aggomitolare; (also: **~ out: pastry**) stendere // vi rotolare; (wheel) girare; **to ~ about** or **around** vi rotolare qua e là; (person) rotolarsi; **to ~ by** vi (time) passare; **to ~ in** vi (mail, cash) arrivare a bizzeffe; **to ~ over** vi rivoltarsi; **to ~ up** vi (col: arrive) arrivare // vt (carpet)

arrotolare; **~ call** n appello; **~er** n rullo; (wheel) rotella; **~er coaster** n montagne fpl russe; **~er skates** npl pattini mpl a rotelle.

**rolling** ['rəʊlɪŋ] a (landscape) ondulato(a); **~ pin** n matterello; **~ stock** n (RAIL) materiale m rotabile.

**ROM** [rɒm] n abbr ( = read only memory) memoria di sola lettura.

**Roman** ['rəʊmən] a, n romano(a); **~ Catholic** a, n cattolico(a).

**romance** [rə'mæns] n storia (or avventura or film m inv) romantico(a); (charm) poesia; (love affair) idillio.

**Romania** [rəʊ'meɪnɪə] n = **Rumania**.

**Roman numeral** n numero romano.

**romantic** [rə'mæntɪk] a romantico(a); sentimentale.

**romanticism** [rə'mæntɪsɪzəm] n romanticismo.

**Rome** [rəʊm] n Roma.

**romp** [rɒmp] n gioco rumoroso // vi (also: **~ about**) far chiasso, giocare in un modo rumoroso.

**rompers** ['rɒmpəz] npl pagliaccetto.

**roof** [ru:f] n tetto; (of tunnel, cave) volta // vt coprire (con un tetto); **~ of the mouth** palato; **~ing** n materiale m per copertura; **~ rack** n (AUT) portabagagli m inv.

**rook** [rʊk] n (bird) corvo nero; (CHESS) torre f.

**room** [ru:m] n (in house) stanza; (also: **bed~**) camera; (in school etc) sala; (space) posto, spazio; **~s** npl (lodging) alloggio; **"~s to let"**, (US) **"~s for rent"** "si affittano camere"; **~ing house** n (US) casa in cui si affittano camere o appartamentini ammobiliati; **~mate** n compagno/a di stanza; **~ service** n servizio da camera; **~y** a spazioso(a); (garment) ampio(a).

**roost** [ru:st] n appollaiato // vi appollaiarsi.

**rooster** ['ru:stə*] n gallo.

**root** [ru:t] *n* radice *f* // *vt* (*plant*, *belief*) far radicare; **to ~ about** *vi* (*fig*) frugare; **to ~ for** *vi fus* fare il tifo per; **to ~ out** *vt* estirpare.

**rope** [rəup] *n* corda, fune *f*; (*NAUT*) cavo // *vt* (*box*) legare; (*climbers*) legare in cordata; **to ~ sb in** (*fig*) coinvolgere qn; **to know the ~s** (*fig*) conoscere i trucchi del mestiere.

**rosary** ['rəuzəri] *n* rosario; roseto.

**rose** [rəuz] *pt of* **rise** // *n* rosa; (*also:* ~ **bush**) rosaio; (*on watering can*) rosetta // *a* rosa *inv*.

**rosé** ['rəuzei] *n* vino rosato.

**rose-** ~**bud** *n* bocciolo di rosa; ~**bush** *n* rosaio.

**rosemary** ['rəuzməri] *n* rosmarino.

**rosette** [rəu'zet] *n* coccarda.

**roster** ['rɒstə*] *n*: **duty** ~ ruolino di servizio.

**rostrum** ['rɒstrəm] *n* tribuna.

**rosy** ['rəuzi] *a* roseo(a).

**rot** [rɒt] *n* (*decay*) putrefazione *f*; (*col: nonsense*) stupidaggini *fpl* // *vt*, *vi* imputridire, marcire.

**rota** ['rəutə] *n* tabella dei turni; **on a ~ basis** a turno.

**rotary** ['rəutəri] *a* rotante.

**rotate** [rəu'teit] *vt* (*revolve*) far girare; (*change round: crops*) avvicendare; (: *jobs*) fare a turno // *vi* (*revolve*) girare; **rotating** *a* (*movement*) rotante.

**rote** [rəut] *n*: **by** ~ (*by heart*) a memoria; (*mechanically*) meccanicamente.

**rotten** ['rɒtn] *a* (*decayed*) putrido(a), marcio(a); (*dishonest*) corrotto(a); (*col: bad*) brutto(a); (: *action*) vigliacco(a); **to feel** ~ (*ill*) sentirsi proprio male.

**rouge** [ru:ʒ] *n* belletto.

**rough** [rʌf] *a* aspro(a); (*person, manner: coarse*) rozzo(a), aspro(a); (: *violent*) brutale; (*district*) malfamato(a); (*weather*) cattivo(a); (*plan*) abbozzato(a); (*guess*) approssimativo(a) // *n* (*GOLF*) macchia; **to ~ it** far vita dura; **to sleep** ~ (*Brit*) dormire all'addiaccio; **to**

**feel** ~ sentirsi male; ~**age** *n* alimenti *mpl* ricchi in cellulosa; ~**and-ready** *a* rudimentale; ~**cast** *n* intonaco grezzo; ~ **copy**, ~ **draft** *n* brutta copia; ~**ly** *ad* (*handle*) rudemente, brutalmente; (*make*) grossolanamente; (*approximately*) approssimativamente.

**roulette** [ru:'let] *n* roulette *f*.

**Roumania** [ru:'meiniə] *n* = **Rumania**.

**round** [raund] *a* rotondo(a) // *n* tondo, cerchio; (*Brit: of toast*) fetta; (*duty: of policeman, milkman etc*) giro; (: *of doctor*) visite *fpl*; (*game: of cards, in competition*) partita; (*BOXING*) round *m inv*; (*of talks*) serie *f inv* // *vt* (*corner*) girare; (*bend*) prendere; (*cape*) doppiare // *prep* intorno a // *ad*: **all** ~ tutt'attorno; **to go the long way** ~ fare il giro più lungo; **all the year** ~ tutto l'anno; **it's just** ~ **the corner** (*also fig*) è dietro; l'angolo; ~ **the clock** *ad* ininterrottamente; **to go** ~ fare il giro; **to go** ~ **to sb's house** andare da qn; **go** ~ **the back** passi dietro; **to go** ~ **a house** visitare una casa; **enough to go** ~ abbastanza per tutti; **to go the** ~**s** (*story*) circolare; ~ **of ammunition** *n* cartuccia; ~ **of applause** *n* applausi *mpl*; ~ **of drinks** *n* giro di bibite; ~ **of sandwiches** *n* sandwich *m inv*; ~ **off** *vt* (*speech etc*) finire; **to** ~ **up** *vt* radunare; (*criminals*) fare una retata di; (*prices*) arrotondare; ~**about** *n* (*Brit AUT*) rotatoria; (: *at fair*) giostra // *a* (*route, means*) indiretto(a); ~**ers** *npl* (*game*) gioco simile al *baseball*; ~**ly** *ad* (*fig*) chiaro e tondo; ~**shouldered** *a* dalle spalle tonde; ~ **trip** *n* (*viaggio di*) andata e ritorno; ~**up** *n* raduno; (*of criminals*) retata.

**rouse** [rauz] *vt* (*wake up*) svegliare; (*stir up*) destare; provocare; risvegliare; **rousing** *a* (*speech, applause*) entusiastico(a).

**rout** [raut] *n* (*MIL*) rotta.

**route** [ruːt] *n* itinerario; (*of bus*) percorso; (*of trade, shipping*) rotta; ~ **map** *n* (*Brit: for journey*) cartina di itinerario.

**routine** [ruːˈtiːn] *a* (*work*) corrente, abituale; (*procedure*) solito(a) // *n* (*pej*) routine *f*, tran tran *m*; (*THEATRE*) numero; **daily** ~ orario quotidiano.

**roving** [ˈrəuviŋ] *a* (*life*) itinerante.

**row** [rəu] *n* (*line*) riga, fila; (*KNITTING*) ferro; (*behind one another: of cars, people*) fila; [rau] (*noise*) baccano, chiasso; (*dispute*) lite *f* // *vi* (*in boat*) remare; (*as sport*) vogare; [rau] litigare // *vt* (*boat*) manovrare a remi; **in a** ~ (*fig*) di fila; ~**boat** *n* (*US*) barca a remi.

**rowdy** [ˈraudɪ] *a* chiassoso(a); turbolento(a) // *n* teppista *m/f*.

**rowing** [ˈrəuiŋ] *n* canottaggio; ~ **boat** *n* (*Brit*) barca a remi.

**royal** [ˈrɔɪəl] *a* reale; **R**~ **Air Force (RAF)** *n* aeronautica militare britannica.

**royalty** [ˈrɔɪəltɪ] *n* (*royal persons*) (membri *mpl* della) famiglia reale; (*payment: to author*) diritti *mpl* d'autore; (*: to inventor*) diritti di brevetto.

**r.p.m.** *abbr* (= *revolutions per minute*) giri/min.

**R.S.V.P.** *abbr* (= *répondez s'il vous plaît*) R.S.V.P.

**Rt Hon.** *abbr* (*Brit: = Right Honourable*) = Onorevole.

**rub** [rʌb] *n* (*with cloth*) fregata, strofinata; (*on person*) frizione *f*, massaggio // *vt* fregare, strofinare; frizionare; **to** ~ **sb up** *or* (*US*) ~ **sb the wrong way** lisciare qn contro pelo; **to** ~ **off** *vi* andare via; **to** ~ **off on** *vt fus* lasciare una traccia su; **to** ~ **out** *vt* cancellare.

**rubber** [ˈrʌbə*] *n* gomma; ~ **band** *n* elastico; ~ **plant** *n* ficus *m inv*.

**rubbish** [ˈrʌbɪʃ] *n* (*from household*) immondizie *fpl*, rifiuti *mpl*; (*fig: pej*) cose *fpl* senza valore; robaccia; sciocchezze *fpl*; ~ **bin** *n* (*Brit*) pattumiera; ~ **dump** *n* (*in town*) immondezzaio.

**rubble** [ˈrʌbl] *n* macerie *fpl*; (*smaller*) pietrisco.

**ruby** [ˈruːbɪ] *n* rubino.

**rucksack** [ˈrʌksæk] *n* zaino.

**ructions** [ˈrʌkʃənz] *npl* putiferio, finimondo.

**rudder** [ˈrʌdə*] *n* timone *m*.

**ruddy** [ˈrʌdɪ] *a* (*face*) fresco(a); (*col: damned*) maledetto(a).

**rude** [ruːd] *a* (*impolite: person*) scortese, rozzo(a); (*: word, manners*) grossolano(a), rozzo(a); (*shocking*) indecente; ~**ness** *n* scortesia; grossolanità.

**rueful** [ˈruːful] *a* mesto(a), triste.

**ruffian** [ˈrʌfiən] *n* briccone *m*, furfante *m*.

**ruffle** [ˈrʌfl] *vt* (*hair*) scompigliare; (*clothes, water*) increspare; (*fig: person*) turbare.

**rug** [rʌg] *n* tappeto; (*Brit: for knees*) coperta.

**rugby** [ˈrʌgbɪ] *n* (*also:* ~ **football**) rugby *m*.

**rugged** [ˈrʌgɪd] *a* (*landscape*) aspro(a); (*features, determination*) duro(a); (*character*) brusco(a).

**rugger** [ˈrʌgə*] *n* (*Brit col*) rugby *m*.

**ruin** [ˈruːɪn] *n* rovina // *vt* rovinare; (*spoil: clothes*) sciupare; ~**s** *npl* rovine *fpl*, ruderi *mpl*; ~**ous** *a* rovinoso(a); (*expenditure*) inverosimile.

**rule** [ruːl] *n* regola; (*regulation*) regolamento, regola; (*government*) governo // *vt* (*country*) governare; (*person*) dominare; (*decide*) decidere // *vi* regnare; decidere; (*LAW*) decidere; **as a** ~ normalmente; **to** ~ **out** *vt* escludere; ~**d** *a* (*paper*) vergato(a); ~**r** *n* (*sovereign*) sovrano(a); (*leader*) capo (dello Stato); (*for measuring*) regolo, riga; **ruling** *a* (*party*) al potere; (*class*) dirigente // *n* (*LAW*) decisione *f*.

**rum** [rʌm] *n* rum *m* // *a* (*col*)

strano(a).

**Rumania** [ruːˈmeɪnɪə] n Romania.

**rumble** [ˈrʌmbl] n rimbombo; brontolio // vi rimbombare; (stomach, pipe) brontolare.

**rummage** [ˈrʌmɪdʒ] vi frugare.

**rumour**, (US) **rumor** [ˈruːməˈ] n voce f // vt: it is ~ed that corre voce che.

**rump** [rʌmp] n (of animal) groppa; ~ **steak** n bistecca di girello.

**rumpus** [ˈrʌmpəs] n (col) baccano; (: quarrel) rissa.

**run** [rʌn] n corsa; (outing) gita (in macchina); (distance travelled) percorso, tragitto; (series) serie f; (THEATRE) periodo di rappresentazione; (SKI) pista; (in tights, stockings) smagliatura // vb (pt ran, pp run) vt (operate: business) gestire, dirigere; (: competition, course) organizzare; (: hotel) gestire; (: house) governare; (COMPUT) eseguire; (water, bath) far scorrere; (force through: rope, pipe): to ~ sth through far passare qc attraverso; (to pass: hand, finger): to ~ sth over passare qc su // vi correre; (pass: road etc) passare; (work: machine, factory) funzionare, andare; (bus, train: operate) far servizio; (: travel) circolare; (continue: play, contract) durare; (slide: drawer; flow: river, bath) scorrere; (colours, washing) stemperarsi; (in election) presentarsi candidato; **there was a ~ on** ... c'era una corsa a ...; **in the long** ~ a lungo andare; **on the** ~ in fuga; **I'll** ~ **you to the station** la porto alla stazione; **to** ~ **a risk** correre un rischio; **to** ~ **about or around** vi (children) correre qua e là; **to** ~ **across** vt fus (find) trovare per caso; **to** ~ **away** vi fuggire; **to** ~ **down** vi (clock) scaricarsi // vt (production) ridurre gradualmente; (factory) rallentare l'attività di; (AUT) investire; (criticize) criticare; **to be** ~ **down** (person: tired) essere

esausto(a); **to** ~ **in** vt (Brit: car) rodare, fare il rodaggio di; **to** ~ **into** vt fus (meet: person) incontrare per caso; (: trouble) incontrare, trovare; (collide with) andare a sbattere contro; **to** ~ **off** vi fuggire // vt (copies) fare; **to** ~ **out** vi (person) uscire di corsa; (liquid) colare; (lease) scadere; (money) esaurirsi; **to** ~ **out of** vt fus rimanere a corto di; **to** ~ **over** vt (AUT) investire, mettere sotto // vt fus (revise) rivedere; **to** ~ **through** vt fus (instructions) dare una scorsa a; **to** ~ **up** vt (debt) lasciar accumulare; **to** ~ **up against** (difficulties) incontrare; ~**away** a (person) fuggiasco(a); (horse) in libertà; (truck) fuori controllo; (inflation) galoppante.

**rung** [rʌŋ] pp of **ring** // n (of ladder) piolo.

**runner** [ˈrʌnəˈ] n (in race) corridore m; (on sledge) pattino; (for drawer etc, carpet: in hall etc) guida; ~ **bean** n (Brit) fagiolo rampicante; ~**up** n secondo(a) arrivato(a).

**running** [ˈrʌnɪŋ] n corsa; direzione f; organizzazione f; funzionamento // a (water) corrente; (commentary) simultaneo(a); **to be in/out of the** ~ **for** sth essere/non essere più in lizza per qc; **6 days** ~ 6 giorni di seguito.

**runny** [ˈrʌnɪ] a che cola.

**run-of-the-mill** [ˈrʌnəvðəˈmɪl] a solito(a), banale.

**runt** [rʌnt] n (also pej) omuncolo; (ZOOL) animale m più piccolo del normale.

**run-through** [ˈrʌnθruː] n prova.

**run-up** [ˈrʌnʌp] n: ~ **to** (election etc) periodo che precede.

**runway** [ˈrʌnweɪ] n (AVIAT) pista (di decollo).

**rupee** [ruːˈpiː] n rupia.

**rupture** [ˈrʌptʃəˈ] n (MED) ernia.

**rural** [ˈruərl] a rurale.

**ruse** [ruːz] n trucco.

**rush** [rʌʃ] n corsa precipitosa; (of crowd) afflusso; (hurry) furia, fretta;

*(current)* flusso // *vt* mandare or spedire velocemente; *(attack: town etc)* prendere d'assalto // *vi* precipitarsi; **~es** *npl* (*BOT*) giunchi *mpl*; **~ hour** *n* ora di punta.

**rusk** [rʌsk] *n* biscotto.

**Russia** ['rʌʃə] *n* Russia; **~n** *a* russo(a) // *n* russo/a; (*LING*) russo.

**rust** [rʌst] *n* ruggine *f* // *vi* arrugginirsi.

**rustic** ['rʌstik] *a* rustico(a).

**rustle** ['rʌsl] *vi* frusciare // *vt* (*paper*) far frusciare; (*US: cattle*) rubare.

**rustproof** ['rʌstpruːf] *a* inossidabile.

**rusty** ['rʌsti] *a* arrugginito(a).

**rut** [rʌt] *n* solco; (*ZOOL*) fregola; to get into a ~ (*fig*) adagiarsi troppo.

**ruthless** ['ruːθlis] *a* spietato(a).

**rye** [rai] *n* segale *f*; ~ **bread** *n* pane *m* di segale.

# S

**Sabbath** ['sæbəθ] *n* (*Jewish*) sabato; (*Christian*) domenica.

**sabotage** ['sæbətɑːʒ] *n* sabotaggio // *vt* sabotare.

**saccharin(e)** ['sækərɪn] *n* saccarina.

**sachet** ['sæʃeɪ] *n* bustina.

**sack** [sæk] *n* (*bag*) sacco // *vt* (*dismiss*) licenziare, mandare a spasso; (*plunder*) saccheggiare; **to get the** ~ essere mandato a spasso; **~ing** *n* tela di sacco; (*dismissal*) licenziamento.

**sacrament** ['sækrəmənt] *n* sacramento.

**sacred** ['seɪkrɪd] *a* sacro(a).

**sacrifice** ['sækrɪfaɪs] *n* sacrificio // *vt* sacrificare.

**sad** [sæd] *a* triste.

**saddle** ['sædl] *n* sella // *vt* (*horse*) sellare; **to be ~d with sth** (*col*) avere qc sulle spalle; **~bag** *n* bisaccia; (*on bicycle*) borsa.

**sadistic** [sə'dɪstɪk] *a* sadico(a).

**sadness** ['sædnɪs] *n* tristezza.

**s.a.e.** *n abbr* = stamped addressed envelope.

**safe** [seɪf] *a* sicuro(a); (*out of danger*) salvo(a), al sicuro; (*cautious*) prudente // *n* cassaforte *f*; ~ **from** al sicuro da; ~ **and sound** sano(a) e salvo(a); (**just**) **to be on the** ~ **side** per non correre rischi; **~conduct** *n* salvacondotto; ~ **deposit** *n* (*vault*) caveau *m inv*; (*box*) cassetta di sicurezza; **~guard** *n* salvaguardia // *vt* salvaguardare; **~keeping** *n* custodia; **~ly** *ad* sicuramente; sano(a) e salvo(a); prudentemente.

**safety** ['seɪftɪ] *n* sicurezza; ~ **belt** *n* cintura di sicurezza; ~ **pin** *n* spilla di sicurezza; ~ **valve** *n* valvola di sicurezza.

**saffron** ['sæfrən] *n* zafferano.

**sag** [sæg] *vi* incurvarsi; afflosciarsi.

**sage** [seɪdʒ] *n* (*herb*) salvia; (*man*) saggio.

**Sagittarius** [sædʒɪ'tɛərɪəs] *n* Sagittario.

**Sahara** [sə'hɑːrə] *n*: **the** ~ (Desert) il (deserto del) Sahara.

**said** [sɛd] *pt, pp of* **say.**

**sail** [seɪl] *n* (*on boat*) vela; (*trip*): **to go for a** ~ fare un giro in barca a vela // *vi* (*boat*) condurre, governare // *vi* (*travel: ship*) navigare; (: *passenger*) viaggiare per mare; (*set off*) salpare; (*sport*) fare della vela; **they ~ed into Genoa** entrarono nel porto di Genova; **to ~ through** (*fig*) *vt fus* superare senza difficoltà // *vi* farcela senza difficoltà; ~**boat** *n* (*US*) barca a vela; ~**ing** *n* (*sport*) vela; **to go ~ing** fare della vela; ~**ing boat** *n* barca a vela; ~**ing ship** *n* veliero; ~**or** *n* marinaio.

**saint** [seɪnt] *n* santo/a.

**sake** [seɪk] *n*: **for the** ~ **of** per, per amore di.

**salad** ['sæləd] *n* insalata; ~ **bowl** *n* insalatiera; ~ **cream** *n* (*Brit*) (tipo di) maionese *f*; ~ **dressing** *n* condimento per insalata.

**salary** ['sælərɪ] *n* stipendio.

**sale** [seɪl] *n* vendita; (*at reduced prices*) svendita, liquidazione *f*; "for

~" "in vendita"; on ~ in vendita; on ~ or **return** da vendere o rimandare; **~room** n sala delle aste; **~s assistant**, (US) **~s clerk** n commesso/a; **~sman** n commesso; (representative) rappresentante m; **~swoman** n commessa.

**salient** ['seɪlɪənt] a saliente.

**sallow** ['sæləʊ] a giallastro(a).

**salmon** ['sæmən] n (pl inv) salmone m.

**saloon** [sə'luːn] n (US) saloon m inv, bar m inv; (Brit AUT) berlina; (ship's lounge) salone m.

**salt** [sɔlt] n sale m // vt salare // cpd di sale; (CULIN) salato(a); to ~ **away** vt (col: money) mettere via; ~ **cellar** n saliera; **~-water** a di mare; **~y** a salato(a).

**salute** [sə'luːt] n saluto // vt salutare.

**salvage** ['sælvɪdʒ] n (saving) salvataggio; (things saved) beni mpl salvati or recuperati // vt salvare, mettere in salvo.

**salvation** [sæl'veɪʃən] n salvezza; S~ **Army** n Esercito della Salvezza.

**same** [seɪm] a stesso(a), medesimo(a) // pronoun: the ~ lo(la) stesso(a), gli(le) stessi(e); the ~ book as lo stesso libro di (o che); at the ~ time allo stesso tempo; all or just the ~ tuttavia; to do the ~ fare la stessa cosa; to do the ~ as sb fare come qn; the ~ to you! altrettanto a te!

**sample** ['saːmpl] n campione m // vt (food) assaggiare; (wine) degustare.

**sanctimonious** [sæŋktɪ'məʊnɪəs] a bigotto(a), bacchettone(a).

**sanction** ['sæŋkʃən] n sanzione f // vt sancire, sanzionare.

**sanctity** ['sæŋktɪtɪ] n santità.

**sanctuary** ['sæŋktjʊərɪ] n (holy place) santuario; (refuge) rifugio; (for wildlife) riserva.

**sand** [sænd] n sabbia // vt cospargere di sabbia.

**sandal** ['sændl] n sandalo.

**sandbox** ['sændbɒks] n (US) =

**sandpit**.

**sandcastle** ['sændkaːsl] n castello di sabbia.

**sandpaper** ['sændpeɪpə*] n carta vetrata.

**sandpit** ['sændpɪt] n (for children) buca di sabbia.

**sandstone** ['sændstəʊn] n arenaria.

**sandwich** ['sændwɪtʃ] n tramezzino, panino, sandwich m inv // vt (also: in) infilare; **~ed between** incastrato(a) fra; **cheese/ham** sandwich al formaggio/prosciutto; ~ **course** n (Brit) corso di formazione professionale; ~ **man** n uomo m sandwich inv.

**sandy** ['sændɪ] a sabbioso(a); (colour) color sabbia inv, biondo(a) rossiccio(a).

**sane** [seɪn] a (person) sano(a) di mente; (outlook) sensato(a).

**sang** [sæŋ] pt of **sing**.

**sanitary** ['sænɪtərɪ] a (system, arrangements) sanitario(a); (clean) igienico(a); ~ **towel**, (US) ~ **napkin** n assorbente m (igienico).

**sanitation** [sænɪ'teɪʃən] n (in house) impianti mpl sanitari; (in town) fognature fpl; ~ **department** n (US) nettezza urbana.

**sanity** ['sænɪtɪ] n sanità mentale; (common sense) buon senso.

**sank** [sæŋk] pt of **sink**.

**Santa Claus** [sæntə'klɔːz] n Babbo Natale.

**sap** [sæp] n (of plants) linfa // vt (strength) fiaccare.

**sapling** ['sæplɪŋ] n alberello.

**sapphire** ['sæfaɪə*] n zaffiro.

**sarcasm** ['saːkæzm] n sarcasmo.

**sardine** [saː'diːn] n sardina.

**Sardinia** [saː'dɪnɪə] n Sardegna.

**sash** [sæʃ] n fascia; ~ **window** n finestra a ghigliottina.

**sat** [sæt] pt, pp of **sit**.

**Satan** ['seɪtən] n Satana m.

**satchel** ['sætʃl] n cartella.

**sated** ['seɪtɪd] a (appetite) soddisfatto(a); (person): ~ (with) sazio(a) di).

**satellite** ['sætəlaɪt] a, n satellite (m).

**satin** ['sætɪn] n raso // a di raso.

**satire** ['sætaɪə*] n satira.

**satisfaction** [sætɪs'fækʃən] n soddisfazione f.

**satisfactory** [sætɪs'fæktərɪ] a soddisfacente.

**satisfy** ['sætɪsfaɪ] vt soddisfare; (convince) convincere; **~ing** a soddisfacente.

**Saturday** ['sætədɪ] n sabato.

**sauce** [sɔːs] n salsa; (containing meat, fish) sugo; **~pan** n casseruola.

**saucer** ['sɔːsə*] n sottocoppa m, piattino.

**saucy** ['sɔːsɪ] a impertinente.

**Saudi** ['saʊdɪ]: **~ Arabia** n Arabia Saudita; **~ (Arabian)** a, n arabo(a) saudita.

**sauna** ['sɔːnə] n sauna.

**saunter** ['sɔːntə*] vi andare a zonzo, bighellonare.

**sausage** ['sɒsɪdʒ] n salsiccia; **~ roll** n rotolo di pasta sfoglia ripieno di salsiccia.

**savage** ['sævɪdʒ] a (cruel, fierce) selvaggio(a), feroce; (primitive) primitivo(a) // n selvaggio/a // vt attaccare selvaggiamente.

**save** [seɪv] vt (person, belongings, COMPUT) salvare; (money) risparmiare, mettere da parte; (time) risparmiare; (food) conservare; (avoid: trouble) evitare // vi (also: **~ up**) economizzare // n (SPORT) parata // prep salvo, a eccezione di.

**saving** ['seɪvɪŋ] n risparmio // a: the **~ grace** of l'unica cosa buona di; **~s** npl risparmi mpl; **~s bank** n cassa di risparmio.

**saviour**, (US) **savior** ['seɪvjə*] n salvatore m.

**savour**, (US) **savor** ['seɪvə*] n sapore m, gusto // vt gustare; **~y** a saporito(a); (dish: not sweet) salato(a).

**saw** [sɔː] pt of **see** // n (tool) sega // vt (pt **sawed**, pp **sawed** or **sawn** [sɔːn]) segare; **~dust** n segatura;

**~mill** n segheria; **~n-off shotgun** n fucile m a canne mozze.

**saxophone** ['sæksəfəʊn] n sassofono.

**say** [seɪ] n: to have one's **~** fare sentire il proprio parere; **to have a** or **some ~** avere voce in capitolo // vt (pt, pp **said**) dire; **could you ~ that again**? potrebbe ripeterlo?; **that goes without ~ing** va da sé; **~ing** n proverbio, detto.

**scab** [skæb] n crosta; (pej) crumiro/a.

**scaffold** ['skæfəʊld] n impalcatura; (gallows) patibolo; **~ing** n impalcatura.

**scald** [skɔːld] n scottatura // vt scottare.

**scale** [skeɪl] n scala; (of fish) squama // vt (mountain) scalare; **~s** npl bilancia; **on a large ~** su vasta scala; **~ of charges** tariffa; **to ~ down** vt ridurre (proporzionalmente); **~ model** n modello in scala.

**scallop** ['skɒləp] n pettine m.

**scalp** [skælp] n cuoio capelluto // vt scotennare.

**scalpel** ['skælpl] n bisturi m inv.

**scamper** ['skæmpə*] vi: to **~ away**, **~ off** darsela a gambe.

**scampi** ['skæmpɪ] npl scampi mpl.

**scan** [skæn] vt scrutare; (glance at quickly) scorrere, dare un'occhiata a; (poetry) scandire; (TV) analizzare; (RADAR) esplorare // n (MED) ecografia.

**scandal** ['skændl] n scandalo; (gossip) pettegolezzi mpl.

**Scandinavia** [skændɪ'neɪvɪə] n Scandinavia; **~n** a, n scandinavo(a).

**scant** [skænt] a scarso(a); **~y** a insufficiente; (swimsuit) ridotto(a).

**scapegoat** ['skeɪpgəʊt] n capro espiatorio.

**scar** [skɑː] n cicatrice f // vt sfregiare.

**scarce** [skɛəs] a scarso(a); (copy, edition) raro(a); **~ly** ad appena; **scarcity** n scarsità, mancanza.

**scare** [skɛə*] n spavento; panico // vt

spaventare, atterrire; **there was a bomb ~ at the bank** hanno evacuato la banca per paura di un attentato dinamitardo; **to ~ sb stiff** spaventare a morte qn; **~crow** n spaventapasseri m inv; **~d** a: **to be ~d** aver paura.

**scarf**, pl **scarves** [ska:f, ska:vz] n (long) sciarpa; (square) fazzoletto da testa, foulard m inv.

**scarlet** ['ska:lıt] a scarlatto(a).

**scathing** ['skeıðıŋ] a aspro(a).

**scatter** ['skætə*] vt spargere; (crowd) disperdere // vi disperdersi; **~brained** a scervellato(a), sbadato(a).

**scavenger** ['skævəndʒə*] n spazzino.

**scenario** [sı'nɑ:rıəu] n (THEATRE, CINEMA) copione m; (fig) situazione f.

**scene** [si:n] n (THEATRE, fig etc) scena; (of crime, accident) scena, luogo; (sight, view) vista, veduta; **~ry** n (THEATRE) scenario; (landscape) panorama m; **scenic** a scenico(a); panoramico(a).

**scent** [sεnt] n odore m, profumo; (sense of smell) olfatto, odorato; (fig: track) pista.

**sceptical**, (US) **skeptical** ['skεptıkəl] a scettico(a).

**sceptre**, (US) **scepter** ['sεptə*] n scettro.

**schedule** ['ʃεdju:l, (US) 'skεdju:l] n programma m, piano; (of trains) orario; (of prices etc) lista, tabella // vt fissare; **on ~** in orario; **to be ahead of/behind ~** essere in anticipo/ritardo sul previsto; **~d flight** n volo di linea.

**scheme** [ski:m] n piano, progetto; (method) sistema m; (dishonest plan, plot) intrigo, trama; (arrangement) disposizione f, sistemazione f; (pension ~ etc) programma m // vi fare progetti; (intrigue) complottare; **scheming** a intrigante // n intrighi mpl, macchinazioni fpl.

**schism** ['skızəm] n scisma m.

**scholar** ['skɔlə*] n erudito/a; **~ly** a

dotto(a), erudito(a); **~ship** n erudizione f; (grant) borsa di studio.

**school** [sku:l] n (in university) scuola, facoltà f inv // cpd scolare, scolastico(a) // vt (animal) addestrare; **~book** n libro scolastico; **~boy** n scolaro; **~children** npl scolari mpl; **~days** npl giorni mpl di scuola; **~girl** n scolara; **~ing** n istruzione f; **~master** n (primary) maestro; (secondary) insegnante m; **~mistress** n maestra; insegnante f; **~teacher** n insegnante m/f, docente m/f; (primary) maestro/a.

**sciatica** [saı'ætıkə] n sciatica.

**science** ['saıəns] n scienza; **~fiction** n fantascienza; **scientific** [-'tıfık] a scientifico(a); **scientist** n scienziato/a.

**scissors** ['sızəz] npl forbici fpl.

**scoff** [skɔf] vt (Brit col: eat) trangugiare, ingozzare // vi: **to ~ (at)** (mock) farsi beffe (di).

**scold** [skəuld] vt rimproverare.

**scone** [skɔn] n focaccina da tè.

**scoop** [sku:p] n mestolo; (for ice cream) cucchiaio dosatore; (PRESS) colpo giornalistico, notizia (in) esclusiva; **to ~ out** vt scavare; **to ~ up** vt tirare su, sollevare.

**scooter** ['sku:tə*] n (motor cycle) motoretta, scooter m inv; (toy) monopattino.

**scope** [skəup] n (capacity: of plan, undertaking) portata; (: of person) capacità fpl; (opportunity) possibilità fpl; **within the ~** of nei limiti di.

**scorch** [skɔ:tʃ] vt (clothes) strinare, bruciacchiare; (earth, grass) seccare, bruciare.

**score** [skɔ:*] n punti mpl, punteggio; (MUS) partitura, spartito; (twenty) venti // vt (goal, point) segnare, fare; (success) ottenere // vi segnare; (FOOTBALL) fare un goal; (keep score) segnare i punti; **on that ~** a questo riguardo; **to ~ 6 out of 10** prendere 6 su 10; **to ~ out** vt cancellare con un segno; **~board** n tabellone $m$ segnapunti.

**scorn** [skɔ:n] $n$ disprezzo // $vt$ disprezzare.

**Scorpio** ['skɔ:pɪəu] $n$ Scorpione $m$.

**scorpion** ['skɔ:pɪən] $n$ scorpione $m$.

**Scot** [skɔt] $n$ scozzese $m/f$.

**scotch** [skɔtʃ] $vt$ (rumour etc) soffocare; **S~** $n$ whisky $m$ scozzese, scotch $m$.

**scot-free** ['skɔt'fri:] $ad$: **to get off ~** farla franca.

**Scotland** ['skɔtlənd] $n$ Scozia.

**Scots** [skɔts] $a$ scozzese; **~man/ woman** $n$ scozzese $m/f$.

**Scottish** ['skɔtɪʃ] $a$ scozzese.

**scoundrel** ['skaundrl] $n$ farabutto/a, (child) furfantello/a.

**scour** ['skauə*] $vt$ (clean) pulire strofinando; raschiare via; ripulire; (search) battere, perlustrare.

**scourge** [skə:dʒ] $n$ flagello.

**scout** [skaut] $n$ (MIL) esploratore $m$; (also: **boy ~**) giovane esploratore, scout $m$ $inv$; **to ~ around** $vi$ cercare in giro.

**scowl** [skaul] $vi$ accigliarsi, aggrottare le sopracciglia; **to ~ at** guardare torvo.

**scrabble** ['skræbl] $vi$ (claw): **to ~ (at)** graffiare, grattare; (also: **~ around**: search) cercare a tentoni // $n$: **S~** ® Scarabeo ®.

**scraggy** ['skrægɪ] $a$ scarno(a), molto magro(a).

**scram** [skræm] $vi$ (col) filare via.

**scramble** ['skræmbl] $n$ arrampicata // $vi$ inerpicarsi; **to ~ out** etc uscire etc in fretta; **to ~ for** azzuffarsi per; **~d eggs** $npl$ uova $fpl$ strapazzate.

**scrap** [skræp] $n$ pezzo, pezzetto; (fight) zuffa; (also: **~ iron**) rottami $mpl$ di ferro, ferraglia // $vt$ demolire; (fig) scartare // $vi$: **to ~ (with** $qn$**)** fare a botte (con qn); **~s** $npl$ (waste) scarti $mpl$; **~book** $n$ album $m$ $inv$ di ritagli; **~ dealer** $n$ commerciante $m$ di ferraglia.

**scrape** [skreɪp] $vt$, $vi$ raschiare, grattare // $n$: **to get into a ~**

cacciarsi in un guaio; **to ~ through** $vi$ farcela per un pelo; **~r** $n$ raschietto.

**scrap:** **~ heap** $n$ mucchio di rottami; **~ merchant** $n$ (Brit) commerciante $m$ di ferraglia; **~ paper** $n$ cartaccia.

**scratch** [skrætʃ] $n$ graffio // $cpd$: **~ team** squadra raccogliticcia // $vt$ graffiare, rigare // $vi$ grattare, graffiare; **to start from ~** cominciare $or$ partire da zero; **to be up to ~** essere all'altezza.

**scrawl** [skrɔ:l] $n$ scarabocchio // $vi$ scarabocchiare.

**scrawny** ['skrɔ:nɪ] $a$ scarno(a), pelle e ossa $inv$.

**scream** [skri:m] $n$ grido, urlo // $vi$ urlare, gridare.

**scree** [skri:] $n$ ghiaione $m$.

**screech** [skri:tʃ] $n$ strido; (of tyres, brakes) stridore $m$ // $vi$ stridere.

**screen** [skri:n] $n$ schermo; (fig) muro, cortina, velo // $vt$ schermare, fare schermo a; (from the wind etc) riparare; (film) proiettare; (book) adattare per lo schermo; (candidates etc) selezionare; **~ing** $n$ (MED) dépistage $m$ $inv$; **~play** $n$ sceneggiatura.

**screw** [skru:] $n$ vite $f$; (propeller) elica // $vt$ avvitare; **to ~ up** $vt$ (paper etc) spiegazzare; (col: ruin) rovinare; **to ~ up one's eyes** strizzare gli occhi; **~driver** $n$ cacciavite $m$.

**scribble** ['skrɪbl] $n$ scarabocchio // $vt$ scribacchiare in fretta // $vi$ scarabocchiare.

**script** [skrɪpt] $n$ (CINEMA etc) copione $m$; (in exam) elaborato $or$ compito d'esame.

**Scripture** ['skrɪptʃə*] $n$ sacre Scritture $fpl$.

**scroll** [skrəul] $n$ rotolo di carta.

**scrounge** [skraundʒ] $vt$ (col): **to ~ sth (off** $or$ **from** $sb$**)** scroccare qc (a qn) // $vi$: **to ~ on** $sb$ vivere alle spalle di qn.

**scrub** [skrʌb] $n$ (clean) strofinata;

(*land*) boscaglia // *vt* pulire strofinando; (*reject*) annullare.

**scruff** [skrʌf] *n*: **by the ~ of the neck** per la collottola.

**scruffy** ['skrʌfɪ] *a* sciatto(a).

**scrum(mage)** ['skrʌm(ɪdʒ)] *n* mischia.

**scruple** ['skru:pl] *n* scrupolo.

**scrutiny** ['skru:tɪnɪ] *n* esame *m* accurato.

**scuff** [skʌf] *vt* (*shoes*) consumare strasciando.

**scuffle** ['skʌfl] *n* baruffa, tafferuglio.

**scullery** ['skʌlərɪ] *n* retrocucina *m or f*.

**sculptor** ['skʌlptə*] *n* scultore *m*.

**sculpture** ['skʌlptʃə*] *n* scultura.

**scum** [skʌm] *n* schiuma; (*pej: people*) feccia.

**scupper** ['skʌpə*] *vt* (*NAUT*) autoaffondare; (*fig*) far naufragare.

**scurrilous** ['skʌrɪləs] *a* scurrile, volgare.

**scurry** ['skʌrɪ] *vi* sgambare, affrettarsi; **to ~ off** andarsene a tutta velocità.

**scuttle** ['skʌtl] *n* (*NAUT*) portellino; (*also*: **coal ~**) secchio del carbone // *vt* (*ship*) autoaffondare // *vi* (*scamper*): **to ~ away, ~ off** darsela a gambe, scappare.

**scythe** [saɪð] *n* falce *f*.

**SDP** *n abbr* (*Brit*) = Social Democratic Party.

**sea** [si:] *n* mare *m* // *cpd* marino(a), del mare; (*ship, sailor, port*) marittimo(a), di mare; **by ~** (*travel*) per mare; **on the ~** (*boat*) in mare; (*town*) di mare; **to be all at ~** (*fig*) non sapere che pesci pigliare; **out to ~** al largo; (*out*) **at ~** in mare; **~board** *n* costa; **~food** *n* frutti *mpl* di mare; **~ front** *n* lungomare *m*; **~gull** *n* gabbiano.

**seal** [si:l] *n* (*animal*) foca; (*stamp*) sigillo; (*impression*) impronta del sigillo // *vt* sigillare; **to ~ off** *vt* (*close*) sigillare; (*forbid entry to*) bloccare l'accesso a.

**sea level** *n* livello del mare.

**seam** [si:m] *n* cucitura; (*of coal*) filone *m*.

**seaman** ['si:mən] *n* marinaio.

**seamy** ['si:mɪ] *a* orribile.

**seance** ['seɪɒns] *n* seduta spiritica.

**seaplane** ['si:pleɪn] *n* idrovolante *m*.

**search** [sə:tʃ] *n* (*for person, thing*) ricerca; (*of drawer, pockets*) esame *m* accurato; (*LAW: at sb's*) perquisizione *f* // *vt* perlustrare, frugare; (*examine*) esaminare minuziosamente // *vi*: **to ~ for** ricercare; **in ~ of** alla ricerca di; **to ~ through** *vt fus* frugare; **~ing** *a* minuzioso(a); penetrante; **~light** *n* proiettore *m*; **~ party** *n* squadra di soccorso; **~ warrant** *n* mandato di perquisizione.

**seashore** ['si:ʃɔ:*] *n* spiaggia.

**seasick** ['si:sɪk] *a* che soffre il mal di mare.

**seaside** ['si:saɪd] *n* spiaggia; **~ resort** *n* stazione *f* balneare.

**season** ['si:zn] *n* stagione *f* // *vt* condire, insaporire; **~al** *a* stagionale; **~ed** *a* (*fig*) con esperienza; **~ing** *n* condimento; **~ ticket** *n* abbonamento.

**seat** [si:t] *n* sedile *m*; (*in bus, train: place*) posto; (*PARLIAMENT*) seggio; (*buttocks*) didietro; (*of trousers*) fondo // *vt* far sedere; (*have room for*) avere or essere fornito(a) di posti a sedere per; **~ belt** *n* cintura di sicurezza.

**sea water** *n* acqua di mare.

**seaweed** ['si:wi:d] *n* alghe *fpl*.

**seaworthy** ['si:wə:ðɪ] *a* atto(a) alla navigazione.

**sec.** *abbr* = **second(s)**.

**secluded** [sɪ'klu:dɪd] *a* isolato(a), appartato(a).

**seclusion** [sɪ'klu:ʒən] *n* isolamento.

**second** ['sekənd] *num* secondo(a) // *ad* (*in race etc*) al secondo posto; (*RAIL*) in seconda // *n* (*unit of time*) secondo; (*in series, position*) secondo/a; (*AUT: also*: **~ gear**) seconda; (*COMM: imperfect*) scarto; (*Brit SCOL: degree*) laurea con *punteggio discreto* // *vt* (*motion*) appoggiare; ~**ary** *a* secondario(a); ~**ary school** *n* scuola secondaria; ~**class** *a* di seconda classe; ~**er** *n* sostenitore/trice; ~**hand** *a* di seconda mano, usato(a); ~ **hand** *n* (*on clock*) lancetta dei secondi; ~**ly** *ad* in secondo luogo; ~**ment** [sɪˈkɔndmənt] *n* (*Brit*) distaccamento; ~**rate** *a* scadente; ~ **thoughts** *npl* ripensamenti *mpl*; **on** ~ **thoughts** *or* (*US*) **thought** ripensandoci bene.

**secrecy** [ˈsiːkrəsɪ] *n* segretezza.

**secret** [ˈsiːkrɪt] *a* segreto(a) // *n* segreto; **in** ~ in segreto.

**secretariat** [sɛkrɪˈtɛərɪət] *n* segretariato.

**secretary** [ˈsɛkrətərɪ] *n* segretario/a; **S**~ **of State** (**for**) (*Brit POL*) ministro (di).

**secretive** [ˈsiːkrətɪv] *a* riservato(a).

**sect** [sɛkt] *n* setta; ~**arian** [-ˈtɛərɪən] *a* settario(a).

**section** [ˈsɛkʃən] *n* sezione *f*.

**sector** [ˈsɛktə*] *n* settore *m*.

**secure** [sɪˈkjuə*] *a* (*free from anxiety*) sicuro(a); (*firmly fixed*) assicurato(a), ben fermato(a); (*in safe place*) al sicuro // *vt* (*fix*) fissare, assicurare; (*get*) ottenere, assicurarsi.

**security** [sɪˈkjuərɪtɪ] *n* sicurezza; (*for loan*) garanzia.

**sedan** [sɪˈdæn] *n* (*US AUT*) berlina.

**sedate** [sɪˈdeɪt] *a* posato(a); calmo(a) // *vt* calmare.

**sedation** [sɪˈdeɪʃən] *n* (*MED*) l'effetto dei sedativi.

**sedative** [ˈsɛdɪtɪv] *n* sedativo, calmante *m*.

**seduce** [sɪˈdjuːs] *vt* sedurre; **seduction** [-ˈdʌkʃən] *n* seduzione *f*; **seductive** [-ˈdʌktɪv] *a* seducente.

**see** [siː] *vb* (*pt* **saw**, *pp* **seen**) *vt* vedere; (*accompany*): **to** ~ **sb to the door** accompagnare qn alla porta // *vi* vedere; (*understand*) capire // *n* sede *f* vescovile; **to** ~ **that** (*ensure*) badare che + *sub*, fare in modo che + *sub*; ~ **you soon!** *a*

presto!; **to** ~ **about** *vt fus* occuparsi di; **to** ~ **off** *vt* salutare alla partenza; **to** ~ **through** *vt* portare a termine // *vt fus* non lasciarsi ingannare da; **to** ~ **to** *vt fus* occuparsi di.

**seed** [siːd] *n* seme *m*; (*fig*) germe *m*; (*TENNIS*) testa di serie; **to go to** ~ fare seme; (*fig*) scadere; ~**ling** *n* piantina di semenzaio; ~**y** *a* (*shabby: person*) sciatto(a); (: *place*) cadente.

**seeing** [ˈsiːɪŋ] *cj*: ~ (**that**) visto che.

**seek** [siːk], *pt*, *pp* **sought** *vt* cercare.

**seem** [siːm] *vi* sembrare, parere; **there** ~**s to be** ... sembra che ci sia ...; ~**ingly** *ad* apparentemente.

**seen** [siːn] *pp* of **see**.

**seep** [siːp] *vi* filtrare, trapelare.

**seesaw** [ˈsiːsɔː] *n* altalena a bilico.

**seethe** [siːð] *vi* ribollire; **to** ~ **with** **anger** fremere di rabbia.

**see-through** [ˈsiːθruː] *a* trasparente.

**segregate** [ˈsɛgrɪgeɪt] *vt* segregare, isolare.

**seize** [siːz] *vt* (*grasp*) afferrare; (*take possession of*) impadronirsi di; (*LAW*) sequestrare; **to** ~ (**up**)**on** *vt fus* ricorrere a; **to** ~ **up** *vi* (*TECH*) grippare.

**seizure** [ˈsiːʒə*] *n* (*MED*) attacco; (*LAW*) confisca, sequestro.

**seldom** [ˈsɛldəm] *ad* raramente.

**select** [sɪˈlɛkt] *a* scelto(a) // *vt* scegliere, selezionare; ~**ion** [-ˈlɛkʃən] *n* selezione *f*, scelta.

**self** [sɛlf] *n* (*pl* **selves** [sɛlvz]): **the** ~ l'io *m* // *prefix* auto...; ~**catering** *a* (*Brit*) in cui ci si cucina da sé; ~**centred**, (*US*) ~**centered** *a* egocentrico(a); ~**coloured**, (*US*) ~**colored** *a* monocolore; ~**confidence** *n* sicurezza di sé; ~**conscious** *a* timido(a); ~**contained** *a* (*Brit: flat*) indipendente; ~**control** *n* autocontrollo; ~**defence**, (*US*) ~**defense** *n* autodifesa; (*LAW*) legittima difesa; ~**discipline** *n* autodisciplina; ~**employed** *a* che lavora in proprio;

~-**evident** $a$ evidente; ~-**governing** $a$ autonomo(a); ~-**indulgent** $a$ indulgente verso se stesso(a); ~-**interest** $n$ interesse $m$ personale; ~-**ish** $a$ egoista; ~-**ish-ness** $n$ egoismo; ~-**less** $a$ dimentico(a) di sé, altruista; ~-**pity** $n$ autocommiserazione $f$; ~-**portrait** $n$ autoritratto; ~-**possessed** $a$ controllato(a); ~-**preservation** $n$ istinto di conservazione; ~-**respect** $n$ rispetto di sé, amor proprio; ~-**righteous** $a$ soddisfatto(a) di sé; ~-**sacrifice** $n$ abnegazione $f$; ~-**satisfied** $a$ compiaciuto(a) di sé; ~-**service** $n$ autoservizio, self-service $m$; ~-**sufficient** $a$ autosufficiente; ~-**taught** $a$ autodidatta.

**sell** [sɛl], $pt$, $pp$ **sold** $vt$ vendere // $vi$ vendersi; **to ~** $at$ or $for$ **1000 lire** essere in vendita a 1000 lire; **to ~ off** $vt$ svendere, liquidare; **to ~ out** $vi$: **to ~ out** (to sb/sth) (COMM) vendere (tutto) (a qn/qc) // $vt$ esaurire; **the tickets are all sold out** i biglietti sono esauriti; ~-**by date** $n$ data di scadenza; ~**er** $n$ venditore/trice; ~-**ing price** $n$ prezzo di vendita.

**sellotape** ['sɛləuteɪp] $n$ ® (Brit) nastro adesivo, scotch $m$ ®.

**sellout** ['sɛlaut] $n$ tradimento; (of tickets): **it was a ~** registrò un tutto esaurito.

**selves** [sɛlvz] $npl$ of **self**.

**semblance** ['sɛmbləns] $n$ parvenza, apparenza.

**semen** ['si:mən] $n$ sperma $m$.

**semester** [sɪ'mɛstə*] $n$ (US) semestre $m$.

**semi...** ['sɛmɪ] $prefix$ semi...; ~**circle** $n$ semicerchio; ~**colon** $n$ punto e virgola; ~**detached (house)** $n$ (Brit) casa gemella; ~**final** $n$ semifinale $f$.

**seminar** ['sɛmɪnɑ:*] $n$ seminario.

**seminary** ['sɛmɪnərɪ] $n$ (REL) seminario.

**semiquaver** ['sɛmɪkweɪvə*] $n$ semi-

croma.

**semiskilled** ['sɛmɪ'skɪld] $a$ (worker) parzialmente qualificato(a); (work) che richiede una qualificazione parziale.

**senate** ['sɛnɪt] $n$ senato; **senator** $n$ senatore/trice.

**send** [sɛnd], $pt$, $pp$ **sent** $vt$ mandare; **to ~ away** $vt$ (letter, goods) spedire; (person) mandare via; **to ~ away for** $vt$ $fus$ richiedere per posta, farsi spedire; **to ~ back** $vt$ rimandare; **to ~ for** $vt$ $fus$ mandare a chiamare, far venire; **to ~ off** $vt$ (goods) spedire; (Brit SPORT: player) espellere; **to ~ out** $vt$ (invitation) diramare; **to ~ up** $vt$ (person, price) far salire; (Brit: parody) mettere in ridicolo; ~**er** $n$ mittente $m/f$; ~-**off** $n$: **to give sb a good ~off** festeggiare la partenza di qn.

**senior** ['si:nɪə*] $a$ (older) di più vecchio(a); (of higher rank) di grado più elevato // $n$ persona più anziana; (in service) persona con maggiore anzianità; ~ **citizen** $n$ persona anziana; ~**ity** [-'ɔrɪtɪ] $n$ anzianità.

**sensation** [sɛn'seɪʃən] $n$ sensazione $f$; **to create a ~** fare scalpore; ~**al** $a$ sensazionale; (marvellous) eccezionale.

**sense** [sɛns] $n$ senso; (feeling) sensazione $f$, senso; (meaning) senso, significato; (wisdom) buonsenso // $vt$ sentire, percepire; ~**s** $npl$ (sanity) ragione $f$; **it makes ~** ha senso; ~**less** $a$ sciocco(a); (unconscious) privo(a) di sensi.

**sensibility** [sɛnsɪ'bɪlɪtɪ] $n$ sensibilità; **sensibilities** $npl$ sensibilità $sg$.

**sensible** ['sɛnsɪbl] $a$ sensato(a), ragionevole.

**sensitive** ['sɛnsɪtɪv] $a$: ~ **(to)** sensibile (a).

**sensual** ['sɛnsjuəl] $a$ sensuale.

**sensuous** ['sɛnsjuəs] $a$ sensuale.

**sent** [sɛnt] $pt$, $pp$ of **send**.

**sentence** ['sɛntns] $n$ (LING) frase $f$; (LAW: judgment) sentenza; (:

*punishment*) condanna // *vt*: **to ~ sb to death/to 5 years** condannare qn a morte/a 5 anni.

**sentiment** ['sɛntɪmənt] *n* sentimento; (*opinion*) opinione *f*; **~al** [-'mɛntl] *a* sentimentale.

**sentry** ['sɛntrɪ] *n* sentinella.

**separate** *a* ['sɛprɪt] separato(a) // *vb* ['sɛpəreɪt] *vt* separare // *vi* separarsi; **~s** *npl* (*clothes*) coordinati *mpl*; **~ly** *ad* separatamente; **separation** [-'reɪʃən] *n* separazione *f*.

**September** [sɛp'tɛmbə*] *n* settembre *m*.

**septic** ['sɛptɪk] *a* settico(a); (*wound*) infettato(a); **~ tank** *n* fossa settica.

**sequel** ['si:kwl] *n* conseguenza; (*of story*) seguito.

**sequence** ['si:kwəns] *n* (*series*) serie *f*; (*order*) ordine *m*.

**sequin** ['si:kwɪn] *n* lustrino, paillette *f inv*.

**serene** [sə'ri:n] *a* sereno(a), calmo(a).

**sergeant** ['sɑ:dʒənt] *n* sergente *m*; (*POLICE*) brigadiere *m*.

**serial** ['sɪərɪəl] *n* (*PRESS*) romanzo a puntate; (*RADIO, TV*) trasmissione *f* a puntate // *a* (*number*) di serie; **~ number** *n* numero di serie.

**series** ['sɪərɪ:z] *n* (*pl inv*) serie *f inv*; (*PUBLISHING*) collana.

**serious** ['sɪərɪəs] *a* serio(a), grave; **~ly** *ad* seriamente.

**sermon** ['sə:mən] *n* sermone *m*.

**serrated** [sɪ'reɪtɪd] *a* seghettato(a).

**serum** ['sɪərəm] *n* siero.

**servant** ['sə:vənt] *n* domestico/a.

**serve** [sə:v] *vt* (*employer etc*) servire, essere a servizio di; (*purpose*) servire a; (*customer, food, meal*) servire; (*apprenticeship*) fare; (*prison term*) scontare // *vi* (*also TENNIS*) servire; (*be useful*): **to ~ as/for/to do** servire da/per/per fare // *n* (*TENNIS*) servizio; **it ~s him right** ben gli sta, se l'è meritata; **to ~ out, ~ up** *vt* (*food*) servire.

**service** ['sə:vɪs] *n* servizio; (*AUT: maintenance*) assistenza, revisione *f*

// *vt* (*car, washing machine*) revisionare; **the S~s** le forze armate; **to be of ~ to sb** essere d'aiuto a qn; **dinner ~** servizio da tavola; **~able** *a* pratico(a), utile; **~ charge** *n* (*Brit*) servizio; **~man** *n* militare *m*; **~ station** *n* stazione *f* di servizio.

**serviette** [sə:vɪ'ɛt] *n* (*Brit*) tovagliolo.

**session** ['sɛʃən] *n* (*sitting*) seduta, sessione *f*; (*SCOL*) anno scolastico (*or accademico*).

**set** [sɛt] *n* serie *f inv*; (*RADIO, TV*) apparecchio; (*TENNIS*) set *m inv*; (*group of people*) mondo, ambiente *m*; (*CINEMA*) scenario; (*THEATRE: stage*) scene *fpl*; (: *scenery*) scenario; (*MATH*) insieme *m*; (*HAIRDRESSING*) messa in piega // *a* (*fixed*) stabilito(a), determinato(a); (*ready*) pronto(a) // *vb* (*pt, pp* **set**) (*place*) posare, mettere; (*fix*) fissare; (*adjust*) regolare; (*decide: rules etc*) stabilire, fissare; (*TYP*) comporre // *vi* (*sun*) tramontare; (*jam, jelly*) rapprendersi; (*concrete*) fare presa; **to be ~ on doing** essere deciso a fare; **to ~ on music** mettere in musica; **to ~ on fire** dare fuoco a; **to ~ free** liberare; **to ~ sth going** mettere in moto qc; **to ~ sail** prendere il mare; **to ~ about** *vt fus* (*task*) intraprendere, mettersi a; **to ~ aside** *vt* mettere da parte; **to ~ back** (*in time*): **to ~ back (by)** mettere indietro (di); **to ~ off** *vi* partire // *vt* (*bomb*) fare scoppiare; (*cause to start*) mettere in moto; (*show up well*) dare risalto a; **to ~ out** *vi* partire; (*aim*): **to ~ out to do** proporsi di fare // *vt* (*arrange*) disporre; (*state*) esporre, presentare; **to ~ up** *vt* (*organization*) fondare, costituire; (*monument*) innalzare; **~back** *n* (*hitch*) intraccontrattempo, inconveniente *m*; **~ menu** *n* menù *m inv* fisso.

**settee** [sɛ'ti:] *n* divano, sofà *m inv*.

**setting** ['sɛtɪŋ] *n* ambiente *m*; (*of*

*jewel)* montatura.

**settle** ['sɛtl] *vt (argument, matter)* appianare; *(problem)* risolvere; *(MED: calm)* calmare // *vi (bird, dust etc)* posarsi; *(sediment)* depositarsi; *(also:* ~ **down)** sistemarsi, stabilirsi; calmarsi; to ~ **for** sth accontentarsi di qc; to ~ **on** sth decidersi per qc; to ~ **in** vi sistemarsi; to ~ **up** vi: to ~ **up with** sb regolare i conti con qn; ~**ment** *n (payment)* pagamento, saldo; *(agreement)* accordo; *(colony)* colonia; *(village etc)* villaggio, comunità *f inv;* ~**r** *n* colonizzatore/ trice.

**setup** ['sɛtʌp] *n (arrangement)* sistemazione *f; (situation)* situazione *f.*

**seven** ['sɛvn] *num* sette; ~**teen** *num* diciassette; ~**th** *num* settimo(a); ~**ty** *num* settanta.

**sever** ['sɛvə*] *vt* recidere, tagliare; *(relations)* troncare.

**several** ['sɛvərl] *a, pronoun* alcuni(e), diversi(e); ~ **of us** alcuni di noi.

**severance** ['sɛvərəns] *n (of relations)* rottura; ~ **pay** *n* indennità di licenziamento.

**severe** [sɪ'vɪə*] *a* severo(a); *(serious)* serio(a), grave; *(hard)* duro(a); *(plain)* semplice, sobrio(a); **severity** [sɪ'vɛrɪtɪ] *n* severità; gravità; *(of weather)* rigore m.

**sew** [səu], *pt* **sewed**, *pp* **sewn** *vt, vi* cucire; to ~ **up** *vt* ricucire.

**sewage** ['su:ɪdʒ] *n* acque *fpl* di scolo.

**sewer** ['su:ə*] *n* fogna.

**sewing** ['səuɪŋ] *n* cucitura; cucito; ~ **machine** *n* macchina da cucire.

**sewn** [səun] *pp of* **sew.**

**sex** [sɛks] *n* sesso; to have ~ **with** avere rapporti sessuali con; ~**ist** *a, n* sessista *(m/f).*

**sexual** ['sɛksjuəl] *a* sessuale.

**sexy** ['sɛksɪ] *a* provocante, sexy *inv.*

**shabby** ['ʃæbɪ] *a* malandato(a); *(behaviour)* vergognoso(a).

**shack** [ʃæk] *n* baracca, capanna.

**shackles** ['ʃæklz] *npl* ferri *mpl,* catene *fpl.*

**shade** [ʃeɪd] *n* ombra; *(for lamp)* paralume m; *(of colour)* tonalità *f inv; (small quantity):* a ~ **of** un po' or un'ombra di // *vt* ombreggiare, fare ombra a; **in the** ~ all'ombra; a ~ **smaller** un tantino più piccolo.

**shadow** ['ʃædəu] *n* ombra // *vt (follow)* pedinare; ~ **cabinet** *n (Brit POL)* governo *m* ombra *inv;* ~**y** *a* ombreggiato(a), ombroso(a); *(dim)* vago(a), indistinto(a).

**shady** ['ʃeɪdɪ] *a* ombroso(a); *(fig: dishonest)* losco(a), equivoco(a).

**shaft** [ʃɑ:ft] *n (of arrow, spear)* asta; *(AUT, TECH)* albero; *(of mine)* pozzo; *(of lift)* tromba; *(of light)* raggio.

**shaggy** ['ʃægɪ] *a* ispido(a).

**shake** [ʃeɪk] *vb (pt* **shook,** *pp* **shaken** [ʃuk, 'ʃeɪkn]) *vt* scuotere; *(bottle, cocktail)* agitare // *vi* tremare // *n* scossa; to ~ **one's head** *(in refusal, dismay)* scuotere la testa; to ~ **hands with** sb stringere or dare la mano a qn; to ~ **off** *vt* scrollare *(via); (fig)* sbarazzarsi di; to ~ **up** *vt* scuotere; **shaky** *a (hand, voice)* tremante; *(building)* traballante.

**shale** [ʃeɪl] *n* roccia scistosa.

**shall** [ʃæl] *auxiliary vb:* I ~ **go** andrò; ~ **I open the door?** apro io la porta?; I'll **get some,** ~ **I?** ne prendo un po', va bene?

**shallow** ['ʃæləu] *a* poco profondo(a); *(fig)* superficiale.

**sham** [ʃæm] *n* finzione *f,* messinscena; *(jewellery, furniture)* imitazione *f.*

**shambles** ['ʃæmblz] *n* confusione *f,* baraonda, scompiglio.

**shame** [ʃeɪm] *n* vergogna // *vt* far vergognare; **it is a** ~ **(that/to do)** è un peccato *(che +* sub/fare); **what a** ~! che peccato!; ~**faced** *a* vergognoso(a); ~**ful** *a* vergognoso(a); ~**less** *a* sfrontato(a); *(immodest)* spudorato(a).

**shampoo** [ʃæm'pu:] *n* shampoo *m*

*inv* // *vt* fare lo shampoo a; ~ **and set** *n* shampoo e messa in piega.

**shamrock** ['ʃæmrɔk] *n* trifoglio (*simbolo nazionale dell'Irlanda*).

**shandy** ['ʃændɪ] *n* birra con gassosa.

**shan't** [ʃɑ:nt] = **shall not.**

**shanty town** ['ʃæntɪ-] *n* bidonville *f inv.*

**shape** [ʃeɪp] *n* forma // *vt* formare; (*statement*) formulare; (*sb's ideas*) condizionare // *vi* (*also*: ~ **up**) (*events*) andare, mettersi; (*person*) cavarsela; **to take** ~ prendere forma; **-shaped** *suffix*: heart-shaped a forma di cuore; **~less** *a* senza forma, informe; **~ly** *a* ben proporzionato(a).

**share** [ʃɛə*] *n* (*thing received, contribution*) parte *f*; (*COMM*) azione *f* // *vt* dividere; (*have in common*) condividere, avere in comune; **to ~ out** (*among or between*) dividere (tra); **~holder** *n* azionista *m/f.*

**shark** [ʃɑ:k] *n* squalo, pescecane *m.*

**sharp** [ʃɑ:p] *a* (*razor, knife*) affilato(a); (*point*) acuto(a), acuminato(a); (*nose, chin*) aguzzo(a); (*outline*) netto(a); (*cold, pain*) pungente; (*voice*) stridulo(a); (*person: quick-witted*) sveglio(a); (: *unscrupulous*) disonesto(a); (*MUS*): C ~ do diesis // *n* (*MUS*) diesis *m inv* // *ad*: **at 2 o'clock** ~ alle due in punto; **~en** *vt* affilare; (*pencil*) fare la punta a; (*fig*) aguzzare; **~ener** *n* (*also*: pencil **~ener**) temperamatite *m inv*; **~eyed** *a* dalla vista acuta; **~ly** *ad* (*turn, stop*) bruscamente; (*stand out, contrast*) nettamente; (*criticize, retort*) duramente, aspramente.

**shatter** ['ʃætə*] *vt* mandare in frantumi, frantumare; (*fig: upset*) distruggere; (: *ruin*) rovinare // *vi* frantumarsi, andare in pezzi.

**shave** [ʃeɪv] *vt* radere, rasare // *vi* radersi, farsi la barba // *n*: **to have a** ~ farsi la barba; **~r** *n* (*also*: electric **~r**) rasoio elettrico.

**shaving** ['ʃeɪvɪŋ] *n* (*action*)

rasatura; **~s** *npl* (*of wood etc*) trucioli *mpl*; **~ brush** *n* pennello da barba; **~ cream** *n* crema da barba.

**shawl** [ʃɔ:l] *n* scialle *m.*

**she** [ʃi:] *pronoun* ella, lei; **~-cat** *n* gatta; **~-elephant** *n* elefantessa; *NB: for ships, countries follow the gender of your translation.*

**sheaf** [ʃi:f], *pl* **sheaves** *n* covone *m.*

**shear** [ʃɪə*] *vt* (*pt* **~ed**, *pp* **~ed** *or* **shorn**) (*sheep*) tosare; **to ~ off** *vt* spezzarsi; **~s** *npl* (*for hedge*) cesoie *fpl.*

**sheath** [ʃi:θ] *n* fodero, guaina; (*contraceptive*) preservativo.

**sheaves** [ʃi:vz] *npl of* **sheaf.**

**shed** [ʃed] *n* capannone *m* // *vt* (*pt, pp* **shed**) (*leaves, fur etc*) perdere; (*tears*) versare.

**she'd** [ʃi:d] = **she had, she would.**

**sheen** [ʃi:n] *n* lucentezza.

**sheep** [ʃi:p] *n* (*pl inv*) pecora; **~dog** *n* cane *m* da pastore; **~ish** *a* vergognoso(a), timido(a); **~skin** *n* pelle *f* di pecora.

**sheer** [ʃɪə*] *a* (*utter*) vero(a) *e* proprio(a); (*steep*) a picco, perpendicolare; (*almost transparent*) sottile // *ad* a picco.

**sheet** [ʃi:t] *n* (*on bed*) lenzuolo; (*of paper*) foglio; (*of glass*) lastra; (*of metal*) foglio, lamina; **~ lightning** *n* lampo diffuso.

**sheik(h)** [ʃeɪk] *n* sceicco.

**shelf** [ʃelf], *pl* **shelves** *n* scaffale *m*, mensola.

**shell** [ʃel] *n* (*on beach*) conchiglia; (*of egg, nut etc*) guscio; (*explosive*) granata; (*of building*) scheletro // *vt* (*peas*) sgranare; (*MIL*) bombardare, cannoneggiare.

**she'll** [ʃi:l] = **she will, she shall.**

**shellfish** ['ʃelfɪʃ] *n* (*pl inv*) (*crab etc*) crostaceo; (*scallop etc*) mollusco; (*pl: as food*) crostacei; molluschi.

**shelter** ['ʃeltə*] *n* riparo, rifugio // *vt* riparare, proteggere; (*give lodging to*) dare rifugio *or* asilo a // *vi* ripararsi, mettersi al riparo;

**shelve** [ʃɛlv] vt (fig) accantonare, rimandare; ~s npl of **shelf**.

**shepherd** [ʃɛpəd] n pastore m // vt (guide) guidare; ~'s **pie** n timballo di carne macinata e purè di patate.

**sheriff** [ʃɛrɪf] n sceriffo.

**sherry** [ʃɛrɪ] n sherry m inv.

**Shetland** [ʃɛtlənd] n (also: **the ~s, the ~ Isles**) le isole Shetland, la Shetland.

**shield** [ʃiːld] n scudo // vt: **to ~ (from)** riparare (da), proteggere (da or contro).

**shift** [ʃɪft] n (change) cambiamento; (of workers) turno // vt spostare, muovere; (remove) rimuovere // vi spostarsi, muoversi; ~**less** a: a ~less **person** un(a) fannullone(a); **~ work** n lavoro a squadre; ~**y** a ambiguo(a); (eyes) sfuggente.

**shilling** [ʃɪlɪŋ] n (Brit) scellino (= 12 old pence; 20 in a pound).

**shilly-shally** [ʃɪlɪʃælɪ] vi tentennare, esitare.

**shimmer** [ʃɪmə*] vi brillare, luccicare.

**shin** [ʃɪn] n tibia.

**shine** [ʃaɪn] n splendore m, lucentezza // vb (pt, pp **shone**) vi (ri)splendere, brillare // vt far brillare, far risplendere; (torch): **to ~ sth on** puntare qc verso.

**shingle** [ʃɪŋgl] n (on beach) ciottoli mpl; (on roof) assicella di copertura; ~**s** n (MED) herpes zoster m.

**shiny** [ʃaɪnɪ] a lucente, lucido(a).

**ship** [ʃɪp] n nave f // vt trasportare (via mare); (send) spedire (via mare); (load) imbarcare, caricare; **~building** n costruzione f navale; ~**ment** n carico; ~**ping** n (ships) naviglio; (traffic) navigazione f; ~**shape** a in perfetto ordine; ~**wreck** n relitto; (event) naufragio // vt: **to be ~wrecked** naufragare, fare naufragio; ~**yard** n cantiere m navale.

**shire** [ʃaɪə*] n (Brit) contea.

**shirk** [ʃəːk] vt sottrarsi a, evitare.

**shirt** [ʃəːt] n (man's) camicia; in ~

sleeves in maniche di camicia.

**shit** [ʃɪt] excl (col!) merda (!).

**shiver** [ʃɪvə*] n brivido // vi rabbrividire, tremare.

**shoal** [ʃəʊl] n (of fish) banco.

**shock** [ʃɔk] n (impact) urto, colpo; (ELEC) scossa; (emotional) colpo, shock m inv; (MED) shock // vt colpire, scioccare; scandalizzare; ~ **absorber** n ammortizzatore m; ~**ing** a scioccante, traumatizzante; scandaloso(a).

**shod** [ʃɔd] pt, pp of **shoe**.

**shoddy** [ʃɔdɪ] a scadente.

**shoe** [ʃuː] n scarpa; (also: **horse~**) ferro di cavallo // vt (pt, pp **shod**) (horse) ferrare; ~**horn** n calzante m; ~**lace** n stringa; ~ **polish** n lucido per scarpe; ~**shop** n calzoleria; ~**string** n (fig): **on a ~string** con quattro soldi.

**shone** [ʃɔn] pt, pp of **shine**.

**shoo** [ʃuː] excl sciò!, via!

**shook** [ʃʊk] pt of **shake**.

**shoot** [ʃuːt] n (on branch, seedling) germoglio // vb (pt, pp **shot**) vt (game) cacciare, andare a caccia di; (person) sparare a; (execute) fucilare; (film) girare // vi (with gun): **to ~ (at)** sparare (a), fare fuoco (su); (with bow): **to ~ (at)** tirare (su); (FOOTBALL) sparare, tirare (forte); **to ~ down** vt (plane) abbattere; **to ~ in/out** vi entrare/uscire come una freccia; **to ~ up** vi (fig) salire alle stelle; ~**ing** n (shots) sparatoria; (HUNTING) caccia; ~**ing star** n stella cadente.

**shop** [ʃɔp] n negozio; (workshop) officina // vi (also: **go ~ping**) fare spese; ~ **assistant** n (Brit) commesso/a; ~ **floor** n officina; (Brit fig) operai mpl, maestranze fpl; ~**keeper** n negoziante m/f, bottegaio/a; ~**lifting** n taccheggio; ~**per** n compratore/trice; ~**ping** n (goods) spesa, acquisti mpl; ~**ping bag** n borsa per la spesa; ~**ping centre**, (US) ~**ping center** n centro commerciale; ~-**soiled** a sciupato(a) a forza di stare in vetrina; ~ **steward** n (Brit INDUSTRY) rappresentante m sindacale; ~ **window** n vetrina.

**shore** [ʃɔː*] n (of sea) riva, spiaggia; (of lake) riva // vt: to ~ (up) puntellare.

**shorn** [ʃɔːn] pp of **shear**.

**short** [ʃɔːt] a (not long) corto(a); (soon finished) breve; (person) basso(a); (curt) brusco(a), secco(a); (insufficient) insufficiente // n (also: ~ **film**) cortometraggio; (a pair of) ~s (i) calzoncini; to be ~ of sth essere a corto di o mancare di qc; in ~ in breve; ~ of doing a meno che non si faccia; everything ~ of tutto fuorché; it is ~ for è l'abbreviazione or il diminutivo di; to cut ~ (speech, visit) accorciare, abbreviare; (person) interrompere; to fall ~ of venir meno a; non soddisfare; to stop ~ fermarsi di colpo; to stop ~ of non arrivare fino a; ~**age** n scarsezza, carenza; ~**bread** n biscotto di pasta frolla; ~**change** vt: to ~**change** sb imbrogliare qn sul resto; ~**circuit** n cortocircuito // vt cortocircuitare // vi fare cortocircuito; ~**coming** n difetto; ~**(crust) pastry** n (Brit) pasta frolla; ~**cut** n scorciatoia; ~**en** vt accorciare, ridurre; ~**fall** n deficit m; ~**hand** n (Brit) stenografia; ~**hand typist** n (Brit) stenodattilografo/a; ~**list** n (Brit: for job) rosa dei candidati; ~**ly** ad fra poco; ~**sighted** a (Brit) miope; ~**staffed** a a corto di personale; ~**story** n racconto, novella; ~**tempered** a irascibile; ~**term** a (effect) di or a breve durata; ~**wave** n (RADIO) onde fpl corte.

**shot** [ʃɔt] pt, pp of **shoot** // n sparo, colpo; (person) tiratore m; (try) prova; (injection) iniezione f; (PHOT) foto f inv; like a ~ come un razzo; (very readily) immediatamente; ~**gun** n fucile m da caccia.

**should** [ʃud] auxiliary vb: I ~ go now dovrei andare ora; he ~ be there now dovrebbe essere arrivato ora; I ~ go if I were you se fossi in te andrei; I ~ like to mi piacerebbe.

**shoulder** [ˈʃəuldə*] n spalla; (Brit: of road): **hard** ~ banchina // vt (fig) addossarsi, prendere sulle proprie spalle; ~ **bag** n borsa a tracolla; ~ **blade** n scapola; ~ **strap** n bretella, spallina.

**shouldn't** [ˈʃudnt] = should not.

**shout** [ʃaut] n urlo, grido // vt gridare // vi urlare, gridare; to ~ **down** vt zittire gridando; ~**ing** n urli mpl.

**shove** [ʃʌv] vt spingere; (col: put): to ~ sth in ficcare qc in; to ~ **off** vi (NAUT) scostarsi.

**shovel** [ˈʃʌvl] n pala // vt spalare.

**show** [ʃəu] n (of emotion) dimostrazione f, manifestazione f; (semblance) apparenza; (exhibition) mostra, esposizione f; (THEATRE, CINEMA) spettacolo // vb (pt ~**ed**, pp **shown**) vt far vedere, mostrare; (courage etc) dimostrare, dar prova di; (exhibit) esporre // vi vedersi, essere visibile; **on** ~ (exhibits etc) esposto(a); to ~ **in** vt (person) far entrare; to ~ **off** vi (pej) esibirsi, mettersi in mostra // vt (display) mettere in risalto; (pej) mettere in mostra; to ~ **out** vt (person) accompagnare alla porta; to ~ **up** vi (stand out) essere ben visibile; (col: turn up) farsi vedere // vt mettere in risalto; (unmask) smascherare; ~ **business** n industria dello spettacolo; ~**down** n prova di forza.

**shower** [ˈʃauə*] n (rain) acquazzone m; (of stones etc) pioggia; (also: ~**bath**) doccia // vi fare la doccia // vt: to ~ sb with (gifts, abuse etc) coprire qn di; (missiles) lanciare contro qn una pioggia di; ~**proof** a impermeabile.

**showing** [ˈʃəuiŋ] n (of film

proiezione f.
**show jumping** n concorso ippico (di salto ad ostacoli).
**shown** [ʃəun] pp of **show**.
**show-off** ['ʃəuɔf] n (col: person) esibizionista m/f.
**showroom** ['ʃəurum] n sala d'esposizione.
**shrank** [ʃræŋk] pt of **shrink**.
**shrapnel** ['ʃræpnl] n shrapnel m.
**shred** [ʃred] n (gen pl) brandello // vt fare a brandelli; (CULIN) sminuzzare, tagliuzzare; ~**der** n (vegetable ~der) grattugia; (document ~der) distruttore m di documenti.
**shrewd** [ʃruːd] a astuto(a), scaltro(a).
**shriek** [ʃriːk] n strillo // vt, vi strillare.
**shrill** [ʃrɪl] a acuto(a), stridulo(a), stridente.
**shrimp** [ʃrɪmp] n gamberetto.
**shrine** [ʃraɪn] n reliquario; (place) santuario.
**shrink** [ʃrɪŋk] vb (pt **shrank**, pp **shrunk**) vi restringersi; (fig) ridursi // vt (wool) far restringere // n (col: pej) psicanalista m/f; to ~ from doing sth rifuggire dal fare qc; ~**age** n restringimento; ~**wrap** vt confezionare con pellicola di plastica.
**shrivel** ['ʃrɪvl] (also: ~ up) vt raggrinzare, avvizzire // vi raggrinzirsi, avvizzire.
**shroud** [ʃraud] n sudario // vt: ~**ed in mystery** avvolto(a) nel mistero.
**Shrove Tuesday** ['ʃrəuv-] n martedì m grasso.
**shrub** [ʃrʌb] n arbusto; ~**bery** n arbusti mpl.
**shrug** [ʃrʌg] n scrollata di spalle // vt, vi: to ~ (one's shoulders) alzare le spalle, fare spallucce; to ~ off vt passare sopra a.
**shrunk** [ʃrʌŋk] pp of **shrink**.
**shudder** ['ʃʌdə*] n brivido // vi rabbrividire.
**shuffle** ['ʃʌfl] vt (cards) mescolare; to ~ (one's feet) strascicare i piedi.
**shun** [ʃʌn] vt sfuggire, evitare.

**shunt** [ʃʌnt] vt (RAIL: direct) smistare; (: divert) deviare.
**shut**, pt, pp **shut** [ʃʌt] vt chiudere // vi chiudersi, chiudere; to ~ **down** vt, vi chiudere definitivamente; to ~ **off** vt fermare, bloccare; to ~ **up** vi (col: keep quiet) stare zitto(a), fare silenzio // vt (close) chiudere; (silence) far tacere; ~**ter** n imposta; (PHOT) otturatore m.
**shuttle** ['ʃʌtl] n spola, navetta; (also: ~ **service**) servizio m navetta inv.
**shuttlecock** ['ʃʌtlkɔk] n volano.
**shy** [ʃaɪ] a timido(a).
**sibling** ['sɪblɪŋ] n fratello/sorella.
**Sicily** ['sɪsɪlɪ] n Sicilia.
**sick** [sɪk] a (ill) malato(a); (vomiting): to be ~ vomitare; (humour) macabro(a); to feel ~ avere la nausea; to be ~ of (fig) averne abbastanza di; ~ **bay** n infermeria; ~**en** vt nauseare // vi: to be ~**ening for sth** (cold etc) cavare qc.
**sickle** ['sɪkl] n falcetto.
**sick**: ~ **leave** n congedo per malattia; ~**ly** a malaticcio(a); (causing nausea) nauseante; ~**ness** n malattia; (vomiting) vomito; ~**pay** n sussidio per malattia.
**side** [saɪd] n lato; (of lake) riva // cpd (door, entrance) laterale // vi: to ~ **with sb** parteggiare per qn, prendere le parti di qn; by the ~ of a fianco di; (road) sul ciglio di; ~ by ~ fianco a fianco; to take ~s (with) schierarsi (con); ~**board** n credenza; ~**boards** (Brit), ~**burns** npl (whiskers) basette fpl; ~**effect** n (MED) effetto collaterale; ~**light** n (AUT) luce f di posizione; ~**line** n (SPORT) linea laterale; (fig) attività secondaria; ~**long** a obliquo(a); ~**saddle** ad all'amazzone; ~ **show** n attrazione f; ~**step** vt (question) eludere; (problem) scavalcare; ~**street** n traversa; ~**track** vt (fig) distrarre; ~**walk** n (US) marciapiede m; ~**ways** ad (move)

di lato, di fianco; (look) con la coda dell'occhio.

**siding** ['saɪdɪŋ] n (RAIL) binario di raccordo.

**sidle** ['saɪdl] vi: **to ~ up (to)** avvicinarsi furtivamente (a).

**siege** [si:dʒ] n assedio.

**sieve** [sɪv] n setaccio // vt setacciare.

**sift** [sɪft] vt passare al crivello; (fig) vagliare.

**sigh** [saɪ] n sospiro // vi sospirare.

**sight** [saɪt] n (faculty) vista; (spectacle) spettacolo; (on gun) mira // vt avvistare; **in ~** in vista; **out of ~** non visibile; **~seeing** n giro turistico; **to go ~seeing** visitare una località.

**sign** [saɪn] n segno; (with hand etc) segno, gesto; (notice) insegna, cartello // vt firmare; **to ~ on** vi (MIL) arruolarsi; (as unemployed) iscriversi sulla lista (dell'ufficio di collocamento) // vt (MIL) arruolare; (employee) assumere; **to ~ over** vt: **to ~ sth over to sb** cedere qc con scrittura legale a qn; **to ~ up** (MIL) vt arruolare // vi arruolarsi.

**signal** ['sɪgnl] n segnale m // vi (AUT) segnalare, mettere la freccia // vt (person) fare segno a; (message) comunicare per mezzo di segnali; **~man** n (RAIL) deviatore m.

**signature** ['sɪgnətʃə*] n firma; **~ tune** n sigla musicale.

**signet ring** ['sɪgnət-] n anello con sigillo.

**significance** [sɪg'nɪfɪkəns] n significato; importanza.

**significant** [sɪg'nɪfɪkənt] a significativo(a).

**signpost** ['saɪnpəust] n cartello indicatore.

**silence** ['saɪlns] n silenzio // vt far tacere, ridurre al silenzio; **~r** n (on gun, Brit AUT) silenziatore m.

**silent** ['saɪlnt] a silenzioso(a); (film) muto(a); **to remain ~** tacere, stare zitto; **~ partner** n (COMM) socio inattivo.

**silhouette** [sɪlu:'et] n silhouette f

inv.

**silicon chip** ['sɪlɪkən-] n piastrina di silicio.

**silk** [sɪlk] n seta // cpd di seta; **~y** a di seta.

**silly** ['sɪlɪ] a stupido(a), sciocco(a).

**silt** [sɪlt] n limo.

**silver** ['sɪlvə*] n argento; (money) monete da 5, 10 or 50 pence; (also: **~ware**) argenteria // cpd d'argento; **~ paper** n (Brit) carta argentata, (carta) stagnola; **~-plated** a argentato(a); **~smith** n argentiere m; **~y** a (colour) argenteo(a); (sound) argentino(a).

**similar** ['sɪmɪlə*] a: **~ (to)** simile (a); **~ly** ad allo stesso modo; così pure.

**simile** ['sɪmɪlɪ] n similitudine f.

**simmer** ['sɪmə*] vi cuocere a fuoco lento.

**simpering** ['sɪmpərɪŋ] a lezioso(a), smorfioso(a).

**simple** ['sɪmpl] a semplice; **simplicity** [-'plɪsɪtɪ] n semplicità.

**simultaneous** [sɪməl'teɪnɪəs] a simultaneo(a).

**sin** [sɪn] n peccato // vi peccare.

**since** [sɪns] ad da allora // prep da // cj (time) da quando; (because) poiché, dato che; **~ then** da allora.

**sincere** [sɪn'sɪə*] a sincero(a); **~ly** ad: **yours ~ly** (in letters) distinti saluti; **sincerity** [-'serɪtɪ] n sincerità.

**sinew** ['sɪnju:] n tendine m; **~s** npl (muscles) muscoli mpl.

**sinful** ['sɪnful] a peccaminoso(a).

**sing** [sɪŋ], pt **sang**, pp **sung** vt, vi cantare.

**singe** [sɪndʒ] vt bruciacchiare.

**singer** ['sɪŋə*] n cantante m/f.

**singing** ['sɪŋɪŋ] n canto.

**single** ['sɪŋgl] a solo(a), unico(a); (unmarried: man) celibe; (: woman) nubile; (not double) semplice // n (Brit: also: **~ ticket**) biglietto m (di sola) andata; (record) 45 giri m; **~s** npl (TENNIS) singolo; **to ~ out** vt scegliere; (distinguish) distinguere; **~ bed** n letto a una piazza;

**breasted** $a$ a un petto; ~ **file** $n$: in ~ **file** in fila indiana; ~-**handed** $ad$ senza aiuto, da solo(a); ~-**minded** $a$ tenace, risoluto(a); ~ **room** $n$ camera singola.

**singlet** ['sɪŋglɪt] $n$ canottiera.

**singly** ['sɪŋglɪ] $ad$ separatamente.

**singular** ['sɪŋgjulə*] $a$ (*exceptional*, *LING*) singolare; (*unusual*) strano(a) // $n$ (*LING*) singolare $m$.

**sinister** ['sɪnɪstə*] $a$ sinistro(a).

**sink** [sɪŋk] $n$ lavandino, acquaio // $vb$ (*pt* **sank**, *pp* **sunk**) $vt$ (*ship*) (far) affondare, colare a picco; (*foundations*) scavare; (*piles etc*): **to ~ sth into** conficcare qc in // $vi$ affondare, andare a fondo; (*ground etc*) cedere, avvallarsi; **to ~ in** $vi$ penetrare.

**sinner** ['sɪnə*] $n$ peccatore/trice.

**sinus** ['saɪnəs] $n$ (*ANAT*) seno.

**sip** [sɪp] $n$ sorso // $vt$ sorseggiare.

**siphon** ['saɪfən] $n$ sifone $m$; **to ~ off** $vt$ travasare (con un sifone).

**sir** [sə*] $n$ signore $m$; **S~ John Smith** Sir John Smith; **yes ~** sì, signore.

**siren** ['saɪərn] $n$ sirena.

**sirloin** ['sə:lɔɪn] $n$ controfiletto.

**sissy** ['sɪsɪ] $n$ (*col*) femminuccia.

**sister** ['sɪstə*] $n$ sorella; (*nun*) suora; (*Brit: nurse*) infermiera $f$ caposala $inv$; ~-**in-law** $n$ cognata.

**sit** [sɪt], *pt*, *pp* **sat** $vi$ sedere, sedersi; (*assembly*) essere in seduta // $vt$ (*exam*) sostenere, dare; **to ~ down** $vi$ sedersi; **to ~ in on** $vt$ fus assistere a; **to ~ up** $vi$ tirarsi su a sedere; (*not go to bed*) stare alzato(a) fino a tardi.

**sitcom** ['sɪtkɔm] $n$ *abbr* (= *situation comedy*) commedia di situazione.

**site** [saɪt] $n$ posto; (*also*: **building ~**) cantiere $m$ // $vt$ situare.

**sit-in** ['sɪtɪn] $n$ (*demonstration*) sit-in $m$ *inv*.

**sitting** ['sɪtɪŋ] $n$ (*of assembly etc*) seduta; (*in canteen*) turno; ~ **room** $n$ soggiorno.

**situated** ['sɪtjueɪtɪd] $a$ situato(a).

**situation** [sɪtju'eɪʃən] $n$ situazione $f$;

"~**s vacant**" (*Brit*) "offerte $fpl$ di impiego".

**six** [sɪks] $num$ sei; ~-**teen** $num$ sedici; ~-**th** $num$ sesto(a); ~-**ty** $num$ sessanta.

**size** [saɪz] $n$ dimensioni $fpl$; (*of clothing*) taglia, misura; (*of shoes*) numero; (*glue*) colla; **to ~ up** $vt$ giudicare, farsi un'idea di; ~-**able** $a$ considerevole.

**sizzle** ['sɪzl] $vi$ sfrigolare.

**skate** [skeɪt] $n$ pattino; (*fish*: *pl inv*) razza // $vi$ pattinare; ~-**board** $n$ skateboard $m$ *inv*; ~-**r** $n$ pattinatore/trice; **skating** $n$ pattinaggio; **skating rink** $n$ pista di pattinaggio.

**skeleton** ['skelɪtn] $n$ scheletro; ~ **key** $n$ passe-partout $m$ *inv*; ~ **staff** $n$ personale $m$ ridotto.

**skeptical** ['skeptɪkl] $a$ (*US*) = **sceptical**.

**sketch** [sketʃ] $n$ (*drawing*) schizzo, abbozzo; (*THEATRE*) scenetta comica, sketch $m$ *inv* // $vt$ abbozzare, schizzare; ~ **book** $n$ album $m$ *inv* per schizzi; ~-**y** $a$ incompleto(a), lacunoso(a).

**skewer** ['skju:ə*] $n$ spiedo.

**ski** [ski:] $n$ sci $m$ *inv* // $vi$ sciare; ~ **boot** $n$ scarpone $m$ da sci.

**skid** [skɪd] $n$ slittamento // $vi$ slittare.

**skier** ['ski:ə*] $n$ sciatore/trice.

**skiing** ['ski:ɪŋ] $n$ sci $m$.

**ski jump** $n$ (*ramp*) trampolino; (*event*) salto con gli sci.

**skilful** ['skɪlful] $a$ abile.

**ski lift** $n$ sciovia.

**skill** [skɪl] $n$ abilità $f$ *inv*, capacità $f$ *inv*; ~-**ed** $a$ esperto(a); (*worker*) qualificato(a), specializzato(a).

**skim** [skɪm] $vt$ (*milk*) scremare; (*soup*) schiumare; (*glide over*) sfiorare // $vi$: **to ~ through** (*fig*) scorrere, dare una scorsa a; ~-**med milk** $n$ latte $m$ scremato.

**skimp** [skɪmp] $vt$ (*work*) fare alla carlona; (*cloth etc*) lesinare; ~-**y** $a$ misero(a); striminzito(a); frugale.

**skin** [skɪn] $n$ pelle $f$ // $vt$ (*fruit etc*) sbucciare; (*animal*) scuoiare;

spellare; ~**-deep** a superficiale; ~ **diving** n nuoto subacqueo; ~**ny** a molto magro(a), pelle e ossa inv; ~**tight** a (dress etc) aderente.

**skip** [skɪp] n saltello, balzo; (container) benna // vi saltare; (with rope) saltare la corda // vt (pass over) saltare.

**ski:** ~ **pants** npl pantaloni mpl da sci; ~ **pole** n racchetta (da sci).

**skipper** [ˈskɪpə*] n (NAUT, SPORT) capitano.

**skipping rope** [ˈskɪpɪŋ-] n (Brit) corda per saltare.

**skirmish** [ˈskə:mɪʃ] n scaramuccia.

**skirt** [skə:t] n gonna, sottana // vt fiancheggiare, costeggiare; ~**ing board** n (Brit) zoccolo.

**ski suit** n tuta da sci.

**skit** [skɪt] n parodia; scenetta satirica.

**skittle** [ˈskɪtl] n birillo; ~**s** n (game) (gioco dei) birilli mpl.

**skive** [skaɪv] vi (Brit col) fare il lavatico.

**skulk** [skʌlk] vi muoversi furtivamente.

**skull** [skʌl] n cranio, teschio.

**skunk** [skʌŋk] n moffetta.

**sky** [skaɪ] n cielo; ~**light** n lucernario; ~**scraper** n grattacielo.

**slab** [slæb] n lastra.

**slack** [slæk] a (loose) allentato(a); (slow) lento(a); (careless) negligente // n (in rope etc) parte f non tesa; ~**s** npl pantaloni mpl; ~**en** (also: ~**en off**) vi rallentare, diminuire // vt allentare.

**slag** [slæg] n scorie fpl; ~ **heap** n ammasso di scorie.

**slain** [sleɪn] pp of slay.

**slam** [slæm] vt (door) sbattere; (throw) scaraventare; (criticize) stroncare // vi sbattere.

**slander** [ˈslɑːndə*] n calunnia; diffamazione f // vt calunniare; diffamare.

**slang** [slæŋ] n gergo, slang m.

**slant** [slɑːnt] n pendenza, inclinazione f; (fig) angolazione f, punto di vista;

~**ed** a tendenzioso(a); ~**ing** a in pendenza, inclinato(a).

**slap** [slæp] n manata, pacca; (on face) schiaffo // vt dare una manata a; schiaffeggiare // ad (directly) in pieno; ~**dash** a abborracciato(a); ~**stick** n (comedy) farsa grossolana; ~**-up** a: a ~**-up meal** (Brit) un pranzo (or una cena) coi fiocchi.

**slash** [slæʃ] vt squarciare; (face) sfregiare; (fig: prices) ridurre drasticamente, tagliare.

**slat** [slæt] n (of wood) stecca; (of plastic) lamina.

**slate** [sleɪt] n ardesia // vt (fig: criticize) stroncare, distruggere.

**slaughter** [ˈslɔːtə*] n strage f, massacro // vt (animal) macellare; (people) trucidare, massacrare.

**slave** [sleɪv] n schiavo/a // vi (also: ~ away) lavorare come uno schiavo; ~**ry** n schiavitù f.

**slay** [sleɪ], pt slew, pp slain vt (formal) uccidere.

**SLD** n abbr (Brit) = Social and Liberal Democrats.

**sleazy** [ˈsliːzɪ] a trasandato(a).

**sledge** [sledʒ] n slitta; ~**hammer** n mazza, martello da fabbro.

**sleek** [sliːk] a (hair, fur) lucido(a), lucente; (car, boat) slanciato(a), affusolato(a).

**sleep** [sliːp] n sonno // vi (pt, pp slept) dormire; **to go to** ~ addormentarsi; **to** ~ **in** vi (lie late) alzarsi tardi; (oversleep) dormire fino a tardi; ~**er** n (person) dormiente m/f; (Brit RAIL: on track) traversina; (: train) treno di vagoni letto; ~**ing bag** n sacco a pelo; ~**ing car** n vagone m letto inv, carrozza f letto inv; ~**ing pill** n sonnifero; ~**less** a: a ~**less night** una notte in bianco; ~**walker** n sonnambulo/a; ~**y** a assonnato(a), sonnolento(a); (fig) addormentato(a).

**sleet** [sliːt] n nevischio.

**sleeve** [sliːv] n manica.

**sleigh** [sleɪ] n slitta.

**sleight** [slaɪt] n: ~ of hand gioco di destrezza.

**slender** ['slɛndə*] a snello(a), sottile; (not enough) scarso(a), esiguo(a).

**slept** [slɛpt] pt, pp of **sleep**.

**slew** [slu:] vi girare // pt of **slay**.

**slice** [slaɪs] n fetta // vt affettare, tagliare a fette.

**slick** [slɪk] a (clever) brillante; (insincere) untuoso(a), falso(a) // n (also: oil ~) chiazza di petrolio.

**slide** [slaɪd] n (in playground) scivolo; (PHOT) diapositiva; (Brit: also: hair ~) fermaglio (per capelli); (in prices) caduta // vb (pt, pp slid [slɪd]) vt far scivolare // vi scivolare; ~ **rule** n regolo calcolatore; **sliding** a (door) scorrevole; **sliding scale** n scala mobile.

**slight** [slaɪt] a (slim) snello(a), sottile; (frail) delicato(a), fragile; (trivial) insignificante; (small) piccolo(a) // n offesa, affronto // vt (offend) offendere, fare un affronto a; **not in the** ~**est** affatto, neppure per sogno; ~**ly** ad lievemente, un po'.

**slim** [slɪm] a magro(a), snello(a) // vi dimagrire; fare (or seguire) una dieta dimagrante.

**slime** [slaɪm] n limo, melma; viscidume m.

**slimming** ['slɪmɪŋ] n (diet) dimagrante; (food) ipocalorico(a).

**sling** [slɪŋ] n (MED) benda al collo // vt (pt, pp slung) lanciare, tirare.

**slip** [slɪp] n scivolata, scivolone m; (mistake) errore m, sbaglio; (underskirt) sottoveste f; (of paper) striscia di carta; tagliando, scontrino // vt (slide) far scivolare // vi (slide) scivolare; (move smoothly): **to** ~ **into/out of** scivolare in/via da; (decline) declinare; **to** ~ **sth on/off** infilarsi/togliersi qc; **to give sb the** ~ sfuggire qn; **a** ~ **of the tongue** un lapsus linguae; **to** ~ **away** vi svignarsela; ~**ped disc** n spo-

stamento delle vertebre.

**slipper** ['slɪpə*] n pantofola.

**slippery** ['slɪpərɪ] a scivoloso(a).

**slip road** n (Brit: to motorway) rampa di accesso.

**slipshod** ['slɪpʃɔd] a sciatto(a), trasandato(a).

**slip-up** ['slɪpʌp] n granchio (fig).

**slipway** ['slɪpweɪ] n scalo di costruzione.

**slit** [slɪt] n fessura, fenditura; (cut) taglio; (tear) squarcio; strappo // vt (pt, pp slit) tagliare; (make a slit) squarciare; strappare.

**slither** ['slɪðə*] vi scivolare, sdrucciolare.

**sliver** ['slɪvə*] n (of glass, wood) scheggia; (of cheese etc) fettina.

**slob** [slɔb] n (col) sciattone(a).

**slog** [slɔg] (Brit) n faticata // vi lavorare con accanimento, sgobbare.

**slogan** ['sləugən] n motto, slogan m inv.

**slop** [slɔp] vi (also: ~ over) traboccare; versarsi // vt spandere; versare.

**slope** [sləup] n pendio; (side of mountain) versante m; (of roof) pendenza; (of floor) inclinazione f // vi: **to** ~ **down** declinare; **to** ~ **up** essere in salita.

**sloppy** ['slɔpɪ] a (work) tirato(a) via; (appearance) sciatto(a); (film etc) sdolcinato(a).

**slot** [slɔt] n fessura // vt: **to** ~ **sth into** infilare qc in // vi: **to** ~ **into** inserirsi in.

**sloth** [sləuθ] n (laziness) pigrizia, accidia.

**slot machine** n (Brit: vending machine) distributore m automatico; (for gambling) slot-machine f inv.

**slouch** [slautʃ] vi (when walking) camminare dinoccolato(a); **she was** ~**ing in a chair** era sprofondata in una poltrona; **to** ~ **about** vi (laze) oziare.

**slovenly** ['slʌvənlɪ] a sciatto(a), trasandato(a).

**slow** [sləu] a lento(a); (watch): **to**

be ~ essere indietro // ad lentamente // vt, vi (also: ~ **down**, ~ **up**) rallentare; "~" (road sign) "rallentare"; ~**ly** ad lentamente; // **motion** n: in ~ **motion** al rallentatore.

**sludge** [slʌdʒ] n fanghiglia.

**slug** [slʌg] n lumaca; (bullet) pallottola; ~**gish** a lento(a).

**sluice** [slu:s] n chiusa.

**slum** [slʌm] n catapecchia.

**slumber** ['slʌmbə*] n sonno.

**slump** [slʌmp] n crollo, caduta; (economic) depressione f, crisi f // vi crollare.

**slung** [slʌŋ] pt, pp of **sling**.

**slur** [slə:*] n pronuncia indistinta; (stigma) diffamazione f, calunnia; (smear): ~ **(on)** macchia (su); (MUS) legatura // vt pronunciare in modo indistinto.

**slush** [slʌʃ] n neve f mista a fango; ~ **fund** n fondi mpl neri.

**slut** [slʌt] n donna trasandata, sciattona.

**sly** [slaɪ] a furbo(a), scaltro(a).

**smack** [smæk] n (slap) pacca; (on face) schiaffo // vt schiaffeggiare; (child) picchiare // vi: to ~ of puzzare di.

**small** [smɔ:l] a piccolo(a); ~ **ads** npl (Brit) piccola pubblicità; ~ **change** n moneta, spiccioli mpl; ~ **holder** n piccolo proprietario; ~ **hours** npl: in the ~ hours alle ore piccole; ~**pox** n vaiolo; ~ **talk** n chiacchiere fpl.

**smart** [smɑ:t] a elegante; (clever) intelligente; (quick) sveglio(a) // vi bruciare; to ~**en up** vi farsi bello(a) // vt (people) fare bello(a); (things) abbellire.

**smash** [smæʃ] n (also: ~-up) scontro, collisione f // vt frantumare, fracassare; (opponent) annientare, schiacciare; (hopes) distruggere; (SPORT: record) battere // vi frantumarsi, andare in pezzi; ~**ing** a (col) favoloso(a), formidabile.

**smattering** ['smætərɪŋ] n: a ~ of

un'infarinatura di.

**smear** [smɪə*] n macchia; (MED) striscio // vt ungere; (fig) denigrare, diffamare.

**smell** [smɛl] n odore m; (sense) olfatto, odorato // vb (pt, pp smelt or smelled [smɛlt, smɛld]) vt sentire (l')odore di // vi (food etc): to ~ **(of)** avere odore (di); (pej) puzzare, avere un cattivo odore; it ~s good ha un buon odore; ~**y** a puzzolente.

**smile** [smaɪl] n sorriso // vi sorridere.

**smirk** [smə:k] n sorriso furbo; sorriso compiaciuto.

**smith** [smɪθ] n fabbro; ~**y** n fucina.

**smock** [smɔk] n grembiule m, camice m.

**smog** [smɔg] n smog m.

**smoke** [sməʊk] n fumo // vt, vi fumare; ~**d** a (bacon, glass) affumicato(a); ~**r** n (person) fumatore/trice; (RAIL) carrozza per fumatori; ~ **screen** n (MIL) cortina fumogena or di fumo; (fig) copertura; **smoking** n fumo; "no smoking" (sign) "vietato fumare"; **smoky** a fumoso(a); (surface) affumicato(a).

**smolder** ['sməʊldə*] vi (US) = **smoulder**.

**smooth** [smu:ð] a liscio(a); (sauce) omogeneo(a); (flavour, whisky) amabile; (movement) regolare; (person) mellifluo(a) // vt lisciare, spianare; (also: ~ **out**: difficulties) appianare.

**smother** ['smʌðə*] vt soffocare.

**smoulder**, (US) **smolder** ['sməʊldə*] vi covare sotto la cenere.

**smudge** [smʌdʒ] n macchia; sbavatura // vt imbrattare, sporcare.

**smug** [smʌg] a soddisfatto(a), compiaciuto(a).

**smuggle** ['smʌgl] vt contrabbandare; ~**r** n contrabbandiere/a; **smuggling** n contrabbando.

**smutty** ['smʌtɪ] a (fig) osceno(a), indecente.

**snack** [snæk] n spuntino; ~ **bar** n tavola calda, snack bar m inv.

**snag** [snæg] n intoppo, ostacolo imprevisto.

**snail** [sneɪl] n chiocciola.

**snake** [sneɪk] n serpente m.

**snap** [snæp] n (sound) schianto, colpo secco; (photograph) istantanea; (game) rubamazzo // a improvviso(a) // vt (far) schioccare; (break) spezzare di netto; (photograph) scattare un'istantanea di // vi spezzarsi con un rumore secco; to ~ **open/shut** aprirsi/chiudersi di scatto; **to ~ at** vt fus (subj: dog) cercare di mordere; **to ~ off** vt (break) schiantare; **to ~ up** vt afferrare; **~py** a (col: answer, slogan) d'effetto; **make it ~py!** (hurry up) sbrigati!, svelto!; **~shot** n istantanea.

**snare** [snɛə*] n trappola.

**snarl** [snɑːl] vi ringhiare.

**snatch** [snætʃ] n (fig) furto con strappo, scippo; (small amount): **~es** of frammenti mpl di // vt strappare (con violenza); (steal) rubare.

**sneak** [sniːk] vi: **to ~ in/out** entrare/uscire di nascosto; **~ers** npl scarpe fpl da ginnastica; **~y** a falso(a), disonesto(a).

**sneer** [snɪə*] vi ghignare, sogghignare.

**sneeze** [sniːz] vi starnutire.

**sniff** [snɪf] n fiutata, annusata // vi fiutare, annusare; tirare su col naso; (in contempt) arricciare il naso // vt fiutare, annusare.

**snigger** [ˈsnɪgə*] n riso represso // vi ridacchiare, ridere sotto i baffi.

**snip** [snɪp] n pezzetto; (bargain) (buon) affare m, occasione f // vt tagliare.

**sniper** [ˈsnaɪpə*] n (marksman) franco tiratore m, cecchino.

**snippet** [ˈsnɪpɪt] n frammento.

**snivelling** [ˈsnɪvlɪŋ] a (whimpering) piagnucoloso(a).

**snob** [snɔb] n snob m/f inv; **~bish** a snob inv.

**snooker** [ˈsnuːkə*] n tipo di gioco del biliardo.

**snoop** [snuːp] vi: **to ~ on sb** spiare qn; **to ~ about** curiosare.

**snooty** [ˈsnuːtɪ] a borioso(a), snob inv.

**snooze** [snuːz] n sonnellino, pisolino // vi fare un sonnellino.

**snore** [snɔː*] vi russare.

**snorkel** [ˈsnɔːkl] n (of swimmer) respiratore m a tubo.

**snort** [snɔːt] n sbuffo // vi sbuffare.

**snotty** [ˈsnɔtɪ] a moccioso(a).

**snout** [snaut] n muso.

**snow** [snəu] n neve f // vi nevicare; **~ball** n palla di neve; **~bound** a bloccato(a) dalla neve; **~drift** n cumulo di neve (ammucchiato dal vento); **~drop** n bucaneve m inv; **~fall** n nevicata; **~flake** n fiocco di neve; **~man** n pupazzo di neve; **~plough**, (US) **~plow** n spazzaneve m inv; **~shoe** n racchetta da neve; **~storm** n tormenta.

**snub** [snʌb] vt snobbare // n offesa, affronto; **~-nosed** a dal naso camuso.

**snuff** [snʌf] n tabacco da fiuto.

**snug** [snʌg] a comodo(a); (room, house) accogliente, comodo(a).

**snuggle** [ˈsnʌgl] vi: **to ~ up to sb** stringersi a qn.

**KEYWORD**

**so** [səu] ♦ ad **1** (thus, likewise) così; if ~ se è così, quand'è così; **I didn't do it — you did** ~! non l'ho fatto io — sì che l'hai fatto!; ~ **do I,** ~ **am I** ecc anch'io; **it's 5 o'clock —** ~ **it is!** sono le 5 — davvero!; **I hope** ~ lo spero; **I think** ~ penso di sì; ~ **far** finora, fin qui; (in past) fino ad allora

**2** (in comparisons etc: to such a degree) così; ~ **big (that)** così grande (che); **she's not** ~ **clever as her brother** lei non è (così) intelligente come suo fratello

**3**: ~ **much** a tanto(a) ♦ ad tanto; **I've got** ~ **much work/money** ho tanto lavoro/tanti soldi; **I love you** ~

much ti amo tanto; ~ **many** tanti(e)

**4** (*phrases*): **10 or** ~ circa 10; ~ **long!** (*col: goodbye*) ciao!, ci vediamo!

♦ *cj* **1** (*expressing purpose*): ~ **as to do** in modo *or* così da fare; **we hurried** ~ **as not to be late** ci affrettammo per non fare tardi; ~ (**that**) affinché + *sub*, perché + *sub* **2** (*expressing result*): **he didn't arrive ~ I left** non è venuto così me ne sono andata; ~ **you see, I could have gone** vedi, sarei potuto andare.

**soak** [səʊk] *vt* inzuppare; (*clothes*) mettere a mollo // *vi* inzupparsi; (*clothes*) essere a mollo; **to ~ in** *vi* penetrare; **to ~ up** *vt* assorbire.

**so-and-so** ['səʊəndsəʊ] *n* (*somebody*) un tale.

**soap** [səʊp] *n* sapone *m*; ~**flakes** *npl* sapone *m* in scaglie; ~ **opera** *n* soap opera *f inv*; ~ **powder** *n* detersivo; ~**y** *a* insaponato(a).

**soar** [sɔ:*] *vi* elevarsi in alto.

**sob** [sɔb] *n* singhiozzo // *vi* singhiozzare.

**sober** ['səʊbə*] *a* non ubriaco(a); (*sedate*) serio(a); (*moderate*) moderato(a); (*colour, style*) sobrio(a); **to ~ up** *vi* far passare la sbornia a *// vi* farsi passare la sbornia.

**so-called** ['səʊ'kɔ:ld] *a* cosiddetto(a).

**soccer** ['sɔkə*] *n* calcio.

**sociable** ['səʊʃəbl] *a* socievole.

**social** ['səʊʃl] *a* sociale // *n* festa, serata; ~ **club** *n* club *m inv* sociale; ~**ism** *n* socialismo; ~**ist** *a, n* socialista (*m/f*); ~**ize** *vi*: **to ~ize** (**with**) socializzare (con); ~ **security** *n* previdenza sociale; ~ **work** *n* servizio sociale; ~ **worker** *n* assistente *m/f* sociale.

**society** [sə'saɪətɪ] *n* società *f inv*; (*club*) società, associazione *f*; (*also*: **high** ~) alta società.

**sociology** [səʊsɪ'ɒlədʒɪ] *n* sociologia.

**sock** [sɔk] *n* calzino // *vt* (*hit*) dare un pugno a.

**socket** ['sɔkɪt] *n* cavità *f inv*; (*of eye*) orbita; (*Brit ELEC*: *also*: **wall** ~) presa di corrente; (: *for light bulb*) portalampada *m inv*.

**sod** [sɔd] *n* (*of earth*) zolla erbosa; (*Brit col!*) bastardo/a (!).

**soda** ['səʊdə] *n* (*CHEM*) soda; (*also*: ~ **water**) acqua di seltz; (*US: also*: ~ **pop**) gassosa.

**sodden** ['sɔdn] *a* fradicio(a).

**sodium** ['səʊdɪəm] *n* sodio.

**sofa** ['səʊfə] *n* sofà *m inv*.

**soft** [sɔft] *a* (*not rough*) morbido(a); (*not hard*) soffice; (*not loud*) sommesso(a); (*kind*) gentile; (*weak*) debole; (*stupid*) stupido(a); ~ **drink** *n* analcolico; ~**en** ['sɔfn] *vt* ammorbidire; addolcire; attenuare // *vi* ammorbidirsi; addolcirsi; attenuarsi; ~**ly** *ad* dolcemente, morbidamente // *vi* dolcezza; ~**ness** *n* dolcezza; morbidezza.

**software** ['sɔftwɛə*] *n* (*COMPUT*) software *m*.

**soggy** ['sɔgɪ] *a* inzuppato(a).

**soil** [sɔɪl] *n* (*earth*) terreno, suolo // *vt* sporcare; (*fig*) macchiare.

**solace** ['sɔlɪs] *n* consolazione *f*.

**solar** ['səʊlə*] *a* solare.

**sold** [səʊld] *pt, pp* of **sell**; ~ **out** *a* (*COMM*) esaurito(a).

**solder** ['səʊldə*] *vt* saldare // *n* saldatura.

**soldier** ['səʊldʒə*] *n* soldato, militare *m*.

**sole** [səʊl] *n* (*of foot*) pianta (del piede); (*of shoe*) suola; (*fish: pl inv*) sogliola // *a* solo(a), unico(a).

**solemn** ['sɔləm] *a* solenne; grave; serio(a).

**sole trader** *n* (*COMM*) commerciante *m* in proprio.

**solicit** [sə'lɪsɪt] *vt* (*request*) richiedere, sollecitare // *vi* (*prostitute*) adescare i passanti.

**solicitor** [sə'lɪsɪtə*] *n* (*Brit: for wills etc*) ~ notaio; (: *in court*) ~ avvocato.

**solid** ['sɔlɪd] *a* (*not hollow*) pieno(a);

(*strong, sound, reliable, not liquid*) solido(a); (*meal*) sostanzioso(a) // n solido.

**solidarity** [sɒlɪ'dærɪtɪ] n solidarietà.

**solitaire** [sɒlɪ'tɛə*] n (*games, gem*) solitario.

**solitary** ['sɒlɪtərɪ] a solitario(a); ~ **confinement** n (*LAW*): **in** ~ **confinement** in cella d'isolamento.

**solo** ['səʊləʊ] n assolo; ~**ist** n solista m/f.

**soluble** ['sɒljʊbl] a solubile.

**solution** [sə'lu:ʃən] n soluzione f.

**solve** [sɒlv] vt risolvere.

**solvent** ['sɒlvənt] a (*COMM*) solvibile // n (*CHEM*) solvente m.

**sombre**, (*US*) **somber** ['sɒmbə*] a scuro(a); (*mood, person*) triste.

| KEYWORD |

**some** [sʌm] ♦ a 1 (*a certain amount or number of*): ~ **tea/ water/cream** del tè/dell'acqua/della panna; ~ **children/apples** dei bambini/delle mele

2 (*certain: in contrasts*) certo(a); ~ **people say that ...** alcuni dicono che ..., certa gente dice che ...

3 (*unspecified*) un(a) certo(a), qualche; ~ **woman was asking for you** una tale chiedeva di lei; ~ **day** un giorno; ~ **day next week** un giorno della prossima settimana

♦ pronoun 1 (*a certain number*) alcuni(e), certi(e); **I've got** ~ (*books etc*) ne ho alcuni; ~ (**of them**) **have been sold** alcuni sono stati venduti

2 (*a certain amount*) un po'; **I've got** ~ (*money, milk*) ne ho un po'; **I've read** ~ **of the book** ho letto parte del libro

♦ ad: ~ **10 people** circa 10 persone.

**somebody** ['sʌmbədɪ] pronoun = **someone**.

**somehow** ['sʌmhaʊ] ad in un modo o nell'altro, in qualche modo; (*for some reason*) per qualche ragione.

**someone** ['sʌmwʌn] pronoun

qualcuno.

**someplace** ['sʌmpleɪs] ad (*US*) = **somewhere**.

**somersault** ['sʌməsɔːlt] n capriola; salto mortale // vi fare una capriola (*or* un salto mortale); (*car*) cappottare.

**something** ['sʌmθɪŋ] pronoun qualcosa, qualche cosa; ~ **nice** qualcosa di bello; ~ **to do** qualcosa da fare.

**sometime** ['sʌmtaɪm] ad (*in future*) una volta o l'altra; (*in past*): ~ **last month** durante il mese scorso.

**sometimes** ['sʌmtaɪmz] ad qualche volta.

**somewhat** ['sʌmwɒt] ad piuttosto.

**somewhere** ['sʌmwɛə*] ad in or da qualche parte.

**son** [sʌn] n figlio.

**song** [sɒŋ] n canzone f.

**sonic** ['sɒnɪk] a (*boom*) sonico(a).

**son-in-law** ['sʌnɪnlɔː] n genero.

**sonnet** ['sɒnɪt] n sonetto.

**sonny** ['sʌnɪ] n (*col*) ragazzo mio.

**soon** [su:n] ad presto, fra poco; (*early*) presto; ~ **afterwards** poco dopo; **as** ~ **as possible** prima possibile; **I'll do it as** ~ **as I can** lo farò appena posso; ~**er** ad (*time*) prima; (*preference*): **I would** ~**er do** preferirei fare; ~**er or later** prima o poi.

**soot** [sʊt] n fuliggine f.

**soothe** [su:ð] vt calmare.

**sophisticated** [sə'fɪstɪkeɪtɪd] a sofisticato(a); raffinato(a); complesso(a).

**sophomore** ['sɒfəmɔː*] n (*US*) studente/essa del secondo anno.

**sopping** ['sɒpɪŋ] a (*also*: ~ **wet**) bagnato(a) fradicio(a).

**soppy** ['sɒpɪ] a (*pej*) sentimentale.

**soprano** [sə'prɑːnəʊ] n (*voice*) soprano m; (*singer*) soprano m/f.

**sorcerer** ['sɔːsərə*] n stregone m, mago.

**sore** [sɔː*] a (*painful*) dolorante; (*col: offended*) offeso(a) // n piaga; ~**ly** ad (*tempted*) fortemente.

**sorrow** ['sɔrəu] n dolore m.

**sorry** ['sɔrɪ] a spiacente; (condition, excuse) misero(a); ~! scusa! (or scusi! or scusate!); to feel ~ for sb rincrescersi per qn.

**sort** [sɔ:t] n specie f, genere m // vt (also: ~ out: papers) classificare; ordinare; (: letters etc) smistare; (: problems) risolvere; ~ing office n ufficio m smistamento inv.

**SOS** n abbr (= save our souls) S.O.S. m inv.

**so-so** ['səusəu] ad così così.

**sought** [sɔ:t] pt, pp of **seek**.

**soul** [səul] n anima; ~-destroying a demoralizzante; ~ful a pieno(a) di sentimento.

**sound** [saund] a (healthy) sano(a); (safe, not damaged) solido(a), in buono stato; (reliable, not superficial) solido(a); (sensible) giudizioso(a), di buon senso // ad: ~ asleep profondamente addormentato // n (noise) suono; rumore m; (GEO) stretto // vt (alarm) suonare; (also: ~ out: opinions) sondare // vi suonare; (fig: seem) sembrare; to ~ like rassomigliare a; ~ barrier n muro del suono; ~ effects npl effetti sonori; ~ly ad (sleep) profondamente; (beat) duramente; ~proof vt insonorizzare, isolare acusticamente // a insonorizzato(a), isolato(a) acusticamente; ~track n (of film) colonna sonora.

**soup** [su:p] n minestra; brodo; zuppa; in the ~ (fig) nei guai; ~ plate n piatto fondo; ~spoon n cucchiaio da minestra.

**sour** ['sauə*] a aspro(a); (fruit) acerbo(a); (milk) acido(a), fermentato(a); (fig) arcigno(a); acido(a); it's ~ grapes è soltanto invidia.

**source** [sɔ:s] n fonte f, sorgente f; (fig) fonte.

**south** [sauθ] n sud m, meridione m, mezzogiorno // a del sud, sud inv, meridionale // ad verso sud; S~ Africa n Sudafrica m; S~ African a, n sudafricano(a); S~ America n

Sudamerica m, America del sud; S~ American a, n sudamericano(a); ~-east n sud-est m; ~erly ['saðəlɪ] a del sud; ~ern ['sʌðən] a del sud, meridionale; esposto(a) a sud; S~ Pole n Polo Sud; ~ward(s) ad verso sud; ~-west n sud-ovest m.

**souvenir** [su:və'nɪə*] n ricordo, souvenir m inv.

**sovereign** ['sɔvrɪn] a, n sovrano(a).

**soviet** ['səuvɪət] a sovietico(a); the S~ Union l'Unione f Sovietica.

**sow** n [sau] scrofa // vt [səu] (pt ~ed, pp sown) seminare.

**soya** ['sɔɪə], (US) **soy** [sɔɪ] n: ~ bean n seme m di soia; ~ sauce n salsa di soia.

**spa** [spɑ:] n (resort) stazione f termale; (US: also: health ~) centro di cure estetiche.

**space** [speɪs] n spazio; (room) spazio; (length of time) intervallo // cpd spaziale // vt (also: ~ out) distanziare; ~craft n (pl inv) veicolo spaziale; ~man/woman n astronauta m/f, cosmonauta m/f; ~ship n = ~craft; **spacing** n spaziatura.

**spacious** ['speɪʃəs] a spazioso(a), ampio(a).

**spade** [speɪd] n (tool) vanga; pala; (child's) paletta; ~s npl (CARDS) picche fpl.

**Spain** [speɪn] n Spagna.

**span** [spæn] pt of **spin** // n (of bird, plane) apertura alare; (of arch) campata; (in time) periodo; durata // vt attraversare; (fig) abbracciare.

**Spaniard** ['spænjəd] n spagnolo/a.

**spaniel** ['spænjəl] n spaniel m inv.

**Spanish** ['spænɪʃ] a spagnolo(a) // n (LING) spagnolo; the ~ npl gli Spagnoli.

**spank** [spæŋk] vt sculacciare.

**spanner** ['spænə*] n (Brit) chiave f inglese.

**spar** [spɑ:*] n asta, palo // vi (BOXING) allenarsi.

**spare** [speə*] a di riserva, di scorta; (surplus) in più, d'avanzo // n (part) pezzo di ricambio // vt (do without) fare a meno di; (afford to give) concedere; (refrain from hurting, using) risparmiare; to ~ (surplus) d'avanzo; ~ **part** n pezzo di ricambio; ~ **time** n tempo libero; ~ **wheel** n (AUT) ruota di scorta.

**sparing** ['spɛərɪŋ] a: to be ~ with sth risparmiare qc; ~**ly** ad moderatamente.

**spark** [spɑːk] n scintilla; ~**(ing) plug** n candela.

**sparkle** ['spɑːkl] n scintillio, sfavillio // vi scintillare, sfavillare; (bubble) spumeggiare, frizzare; **sparkling** a scintillante, sfavillante; (wine) spumante.

**sparrow** ['spærəu] n passero.

**sparse** [spɑːs] a sparso(a), rado(a).

**spartan** ['spɑːtən] a (fig) spartano(a).

**spasm** ['spæzəm] n (MED) spasmo; (fig) accesso, attacco; ~**odic** [spæz'mɔdɪk] a spasmodico(a); (fig) intermittente.

**spastic** ['spæstɪk] n spastico/a.

**spat** [spæt] pt, pp of **spit**.

**spate** [speɪt] n (fig): ~ **of** diluvio or fiume m di; **in** ~ (river) in piena.

**spatter** ['spætə*] vt, vi schizzare.

**spawn** [spɔːn] vt deporre // vi deporre le uova // n uova fpl.

**speak** [spiːk], pt **spoke**, pp **spoken** vt (language) parlare; (truth) dire // vi parlare; to ~ to sb/of or about sth parlare a qn/di qc; ~ **up!** parla più forte!; ~**er** n (in public) oratore/trice; (also: **loud**~**er**) altoparlante m; (POL): the S~**er** il presidente della Camera dei Comuni (Brit) or dei Rappresentanti (US).

**spear** [spɪə*] n lancia; ~**head** n (attack etc) condurre.

**spec** [spɛk] n (col): **on** ~ sperando bene.

**special** ['spɛʃl] a speciale; ~**ist** n specialista m/f; ~**ity** [spɛʃɪ'ælɪtɪ] n specialità f inv; ~**ize** vi: to ~**ize (in)** specializzarsi (in); ~**ly** ad specialmente, particolarmente.

**species** ['spiːʃiːz] n (pl inv) specie f inv.

**specific** [spə'sɪfɪk] a specifico(a); preciso(a); ~**ally** ad esplicitamente; (especially) appositamente.

**specimen** ['spɛsɪmən] n esemplare m, modello; (MED) campione m.

**speck** [spɛk] n puntino, macchiolina; (particle) granello.

**speckled** ['spɛkld] a macchiettato(a).

**specs** [spɛks] npl (col) occhiali mpl.

**spectacle** ['spɛktəkl] n spettacolo; ~**s** npl (glasses) occhiali mpl; **spectacular** [-'tækjulə*] a spettacolare // n (CINEMA etc) film m inv etc spettacolare.

**spectator** [spɛk'teɪtə*] n spettatore m.

**spectre**, (US) **specter** ['spɛktə*] n spettro.

**spectrum**, pl **spectra** ['spɛktrəm, -rə] n spettro; (fig) gamma.

**speculation** [spɛkju'leɪʃən] n speculazione f; congettura fpl.

**speech** [spiːtʃ] n (faculty) parola; (talk) discorso; (manner of speaking) parlata; (enunciation) elocuzione f; ~**less** a ammutolito(a), muto(a).

**speed** [spiːd] n velocità f inv; (promptness) prontezza; **at full** or top ~ a tutta velocità; to ~ **up** vi, vt accelerare; ~**boat** n motoscafo; ~**ily** ad velocemente, prontamente; ~**ing** n (AUT) eccesso di velocità; ~ **limit** n limite m di velocità; ~**ometer** [spɪ'dɔmɪtə*] n tachimetro; ~**way** n (SPORT) pista per motociclismo; (also: ~**way racing**) corsa motociclistica (su pista); ~**y** a veloce, rapido(a); pronto(a).

**spell** [spɛl] n (also: **magic** ~) incantesimo; (period of time) (breve) periodo // vt (pt, pp **spelt** (Brit) or ~**ed** [spɛlt, spɛld]) (in writing) scrivere lettera per lettera; (aloud) dire lettera per lettera; (fig) significare; to **cast a** ~ **on** sb fare un incantesimo a qn; **he can't** ~ fa errori di ortografia; ~**bound** a incantato(a); affascinato(a); ~**ing** n ortografia.

**spend**, pt, pp **spent** [spɛnd, spɛnt] vt (money) spendere; (time, life) passare; ~**thrift** n spendaccione/a.

**sperm** [spə:m] n sperma m.

**spew** [spju:] vt vomitare.

**sphere** [sfɪə*] n sfera.

**spice** [spaɪs] n spezia // vt aromatizzare.

**spick-and-span** ['spɪkən'spæn] a impeccabile.

**spicy** ['spaɪsɪ] a piccante.

**spider** ['spaɪdə*] n ragno.

**spike** [spaɪk] n punta.

**spill**, pt, pp **spilt** or ~**ed** [spɪl, -t, -d] vt versare, rovesciare // vi versare, rovesciarsi; **to ~ over** vi (liquid) versarsi; (crowd) riversarsi.

**spin** [spɪn] n (revolution of wheel) rotazione f; (AVIAT) avvitamento; (trip in car) giretto // vb (pt **spun**, **span**, pp **spun**) vt (wool etc) filare; (wheel) far girare // vi girare; **to ~ out** vt far durare.

**spinach** ['spɪnɪtʃ] n spinacio; (as food) spinaci mpl.

**spinal** ['spaɪnl] a spinale; ~ **cord** n midollo spinale.

**spindly** ['spɪndlɪ] a lungo(a) e sottile, filiforme.

**spin-dryer** [spɪn'draɪə*] n (Brit) centrifuga.

**spine** [spaɪn] n spina dorsale; (thorn) spina.

**spinning** ['spɪnɪŋ] n filatura; ~ **top** n trottola; ~ **wheel** n filatoio.

**spin-off** ['spɪnɔf] n applicazione f secondaria; (product) prodotto secondario.

**spinster** ['spɪnstə*] n nubile f; zitella.

**spiral** ['spaɪərl] n spirale f // a a spirale // vi (fig) salire a spirale; ~ **staircase** n scala a chiocciola.

**spire** [spaɪə*] n guglia.

**spirit** ['spɪrɪt] n (soul) spirito, anima; (ghost) spirito, fantasma m; (mood) stato d'animo, umore m; (courage)

coraggio; ~**s** npl (drink) alcolici mpl; **in good** ~**s** di buon umore; ~**ed** a vivace, vigoroso(a); (horse) focoso(a); ~ **level** n livella a bolla (d'aria).

**spiritual** ['spɪrɪtjuəl] a spirituale.

**spit** [spɪt] n (for roasting) spiedo // vi (pt, pp **spat**) sputare; (fire, fat) scoppiettare.

**spite** [spaɪt] n dispetto // vt contrariare, far dispetto a; **in ~ of** nonostante, malgrado; ~**ful** a dispettoso(a).

**spittle** ['spɪtl] n saliva; sputo.

**splash** [splæʃ] n spruzzo; (sound) ciac m inv; (of colour) schizzo // vt spruzzare // vi (also: ~ **about**) sguazzare.

**spleen** [spli:n] n (ANAT) milza.

**splendid** ['splɛndɪd] a splendido(a), magnifico(a).

**splint** [splɪnt] n (MED) stecca.

**splinter** ['splɪntə*] n scheggia // vi scheggiarsi.

**split** [splɪt] n spaccatura; (fig: division, quarrel) scissione f // vb (pt, pp **split**) vt spaccare; (party) dividere; (work, profits) spartire, ripartire // vi (divide) dividersi; **to ~ up** vi (couple) separarsi, rompere; (meeting) sciogliersi.

**splutter** ['splʌtə*] vi farfugliare; sputacchiare.

**spoil**, pt, pp **spoilt** or ~**ed** [spɔɪl, -t, -d] vt (damage) rovinare, guastare; (mar) sciupare; (child) viziare; ~**s** npl bottino; ~**sport** n guastafeste m/f inv.

**spoke** [spəuk] pt of **speak** // n raggio.

**spoken** ['spəukn] pp of **speak**.

**spokesman** ['spəuksmən], **spokeswoman** [-wumən] n portavoce m/f inv.

**sponge** [spʌndʒ] n spugna // vt spugnare, pulire con una spugna // vi: **to ~ off** or **on** scroccare a; ~ **bag** n (Brit) nécessaire m inv; ~ (**cake**) n pan m di Spagna.

**sponsor** ['spɔnsə*] n (RADIO, TV,

*SPORT etc)* finanziatore/trice (a scopo pubblicitario) // *vt* sostenere; patrocinare; **~ship** *n* finanziamento (a scopo pubblicitario); patrocinio.

**spontaneous** [spɔn'teɪnɪəs] *a* spontaneo(a).

**spooky** ['spu:kɪ] *a* che fa accapponare la pelle.

**spool** [spu:l] *n* bobina.

**spoon** [spu:n] *n* cucchiaio; **~feed** *vt* nutrire con il cucchiaio; *(fig)* imboccare; **~ful** *n* cucchiaiata.

**sport** [spɔ:t] *n* sport *m inv*; *(person)* persona di sport // *vt* sfoggiare; **~ing** *a* sportivo(a); to give sb a **~ing** chance dare a qn una possibilità (di vincere); **~ jacket** *n (US)* = **~s jacket**; **~s car** *n* automobile *f* sportiva; **~s jacket** *n* giacca sportiva; **~sman** *n* sportivo; **~smanship** *n* spirito sportivo; **~swear** *n* abiti *mpl* sportivi; **~swoman** *n* sportiva; **~y** *a* sportivo(a).

**spot** [spɔt] *n* punto; *(mark)* macchia; *(dot: on pattern)* pallino; *(pimple)* foruncolo; *(place)* posto; *(small amount):* a **~** of un po' di // *vt (notice)* individuare, distinguere; on the **~** sul posto; su due piedi; **~check** *n* controllo senza preavviso; **~less** *a* immacolato(a); **~light** *n* proiettore *m*; *(AUT)* faro ausiliario; **~ted** *a* macchiato(a); a puntini, a pallini; **~ty** *a (face)* foruncoloso(a).

**spouse** [spauz] *n* sposo/a.

**spout** [spaut] *n (of jug)* beccuccio; *(of liquid)* zampillo, getto // *vi* zampillare.

**sprain** [spreɪn] *n* storta, distorsione *f* // *vt:* to **~** one's ankle storcersi una caviglia.

**sprang** [spræŋ] *pt of* **spring.**

**sprawl** [sprɔ:l] *vi* sdraiarsi (in modo scomposto).

**spray** [spreɪ] *n* spruzzo; *(container)* nebulizzatore *m*, spray *m inv*; *(of flowers)* mazzetto // *vt* spruzzare; *(crops)* irrorare.

**spread** [spred] *n* diffusione *f*; *(dis-*

*tribution)* distribuzione *f*; *(CULIN)* pasta (da spalmare) // *vb (pt, pp* **spread)** *vt (cloth)* stendere, distendere; *(butter etc)* spalmare; *(disease, knowledge)* propagare, diffondere // *vi* stendersi, distendersi; spalmarsi; propagarsi, diffondersi; **~-eagled** ['spredɪ:gld] *a* a gambe e braccia aperte; **~sheet** *n (COMPUT)* foglio elettronico ad espansione.

**spree** [spri:] *n:* to go on a **~** fare baldoria.

**sprightly** ['spraɪtlɪ] *a* vivace.

**spring** [sprɪŋ] *n (leap)* salto, balzo; *(coiled metal)* molla; *(season)* primavera; *(of water)* sorgente *f* // *vi (pt* **sprang,** *pp* **sprung)** saltare, balzare; to **~** from provenire da; to **~** up *vi (problem)* presentarsi; **~board** *n* trampolino; **~clean** *n (also:* **~-cleaning)** grandi pulizie *fpl* di primavera; **~time** *n* primavera; **~y** *a* elastico(a).

**sprinkle** ['sprɪŋkl] *vt* spruzzare; spargere; to **~** water etc on, **~** with water etc spruzzare dell'acqua etc su; to **~** sugar etc on, **~** with sugar etc spolverizzare di zucchero etc; **~r** *n (for lawn)* irrigatore *m*; *(to put out fire)* sprinkler *m inv.*

**sprint** [sprɪnt] *n* scatto // *vi* scattare; **~er** *n (SPORT)* velocista *m/f.*

**sprout** [spraut] *vi* germogliare; **~s** *npl (also:* **Brussels ~)** cavolini *mpl* di Bruxelles.

**spruce** [spru:s] *n* abete *m* rosso // *a* lindo(a); azzimato(a).

**sprung** [sprʌŋ] *pp of* **spring.**

**spry** [spraɪ] *a* arzillo(a), sveglio(a).

**spun** [spʌn] *pt, pp of* **spin.**

**spur** [spə:*] *n* sperone *m*; *(fig)* sprone *m*, incentivo // *vt (also:* **~ on)** spronare; on the **~** of the moment lì per lì.

**spurious** ['spjʊərɪəs] *a* falso(a).

**spurn** [spə:n] *vt* rifiutare con disprezzo, sdegnare.

**spurt** [spə:t] *vi* sgorgare; zampillare.

**spy** [spaɪ] *n* spia // *vi:* to **~** on spiare

// vt (see) scorgere; ~ing n spionaggio.

**Sq.** abbr (in address) = **square**.

**sq.** abbr (MATH) = **square**.

**squabble** ['skwɔbl] vi bisticciarsi.

**squad** [skwɔd] n (MIL) plotone m; (POLICE) squadra.

**squadron** ['skwɔdrn] n (MIL) squadrone m; (AVIAT, NAUT) squadriglia.

**squalid** ['skwɔlɪd] a sordido(a).

**squall** [skwɔ:l] n raffica; burrasca.

**squalor** ['skwɔlə*] n squallore m.

**squander** ['skwɔndə*] vt dissipare.

**square** [skwɛə*] n quadrato; (in town) piazza; (instrument) squadra // a quadrato(a); (honest) onesto(a); (col: ideas, person) di vecchio stampo // vt (arrange) regolare; (MATH) elevare al quadrato // vi (agree) quadrare; **all** ~ pari; **a** ~ **meal** un pasto abbondante; **2 metres** ~ di 2 metri per 2; **1** ~ **metre** 1 metro quadrato; ~**ly** ad diritto; fermamente.

**squash** [skwɔʃ] n (SPORT) squash m; (Brit: drink): **lemon/orange** ~ sciroppo di limone/arancia // vt schiacciare.

**squat** [skwɔt] a tarchiato(a), tozzo(a) // vi accovacciarsi; ~**ter** n occupante m/f abusivo(a).

**squawk** [skwɔ:k] vi emettere strida rauche.

**squeak** [skwi:k] vi squittire.

**squeal** [skwi:l] vi strillare.

**squeamish** ['skwi:mɪʃ] a schizzinoso(a); disgustato(a).

**squeeze** [skwi:z] n pressione f; (also ECON) stretta // vt premere; (hand, arm) stringere; **to** ~ **out** vt spremere.

**squelch** [skwɛltʃ] vi fare ciac; sguazzare.

**squib** [skwɪb] n petardo.

**squid** [skwɪd] n calamaro.

**squiggle** ['skwɪgl] n ghirigoro.

**squint** [skwɪnt] vi essere strabico(a) // n: **he has a** ~ è strabico; **to** ~ **at sth** guardare qc di traverso;

(quickly) dare un'occhiata a qc.

**squire** ['skwaɪə*] n (Brit) proprietario terriero.

**squirm** [skwə:m] vi contorcersi.

**squirrel** ['skwɪrəl] n scoiattolo.

**squirt** [skwə:t] vi schizzare; zampillare.

**Sr** abbr = **senior**.

**St** abbr = **saint**, **street**.

**stab** [stæb] n (with knife etc) pugnalata; (col: try): **to have a** ~ **at (doing) sth** provare a fare qc // vt pugnalare.

**stable** ['steɪbl] n (for horses) scuderia; (for cattle) stalla // a stabile.

**stack** [stæk] n catasta, pila // vt accatastare, ammucchiare.

**stadium** ['steɪdɪəm] n stadio.

**staff** [stɑ:f] n (work force: gen) personale m; (: Brit SCOL) personale insegnante; (: servants) personale di servizio; (MIL) stato maggiore; (stick) bastone m // vt fornire di personale.

**stag** [stæg] n cervo.

**stage** [steɪdʒ] n palcoscenico; (profession): **the** ~ il teatro, la scena; (point) punto; (platform) palco // vt (play) allestire, mettere in scena; (demonstration) organizzare; (fig: perform: recovery etc) effettuare; **in** ~**s** per gradi; a tappe; ~**coach** n diligenza; ~ **door** n ingresso degli artisti; ~ **manager** n direttore m di scena.

**stagger** ['stægə*] vi barcollare // vt (person) sbalordire; (hours, holidays) scaglionare.

**stagnate** [stæg'neɪt] vi stagnare.

**stag party** n festa di addio al celibato.

**staid** [steɪd] a posato(a), serio(a).

**stain** [steɪn] n macchia; (colouring) colorante m // vt macchiare; (wood) tingere; ~**ed glass window** n vetrata; ~**less** a (steel) inossidabile; ~ **remover** n smacchiatore m.

**stair** [stɛə*] n (step) gradino; ~**s** npl (flight of ~s) scale fpl, scala; **on the**

~s sulle scale; ~**case**, ~**way** $n$ scale $fpl$, scala.

**stake** [steɪk] $n$ palo, piolo; (BETTING) puntata, scommessa // $vt$ (bet) scommettere; (risk) rischiare; to be at ~ essere in gioco.

**stale** [steɪl] $a$ (bread) raffermo(a), stantio(a); (beer) svaporato(a); (smell) di chiuso.

**stalemate** ['steɪlmeɪt] $n$ stallo; (fig) punto morto.

**stalk** [stɔːk] $n$ gambo, stelo // $vt$ inseguire // $vi$ camminare con sussiego.

**stall** [stɔːl] $n$ bancarella; (in stable) box $m$ inv di stalla // $vt$ (AUT) far spegnere // $vi$ (AUT) spegnersi, fermarsi; (fig) temporeggiare; ~s $npl$ (Brit: in cinema, theatre) platea.

**stallion** ['stælɪən] $n$ stallone $m$.

**stalwart** ['stɔːlwət] $n$ membro fidato.

**stamina** ['stæmɪnə] $n$ vigore $m$, resistenza.

**stammer** ['stæmə*] $n$ balbuzie $f$ // $vi$ balbettare.

**stamp** [stæmp] $n$ (postage ~) francobollo; (implement) timbro; (mark, also fig) marchio, impronta; (on document) bollo; timbro // $vi$ (also: ~ **one's foot**) battere il piede // $vt$ battere; (letter) affrancare; (mark with a ~) timbrare; ~ **album** $n$ album $m$ inv per francobolli; ~ **collecting** $n$ filatelia.

**stampede** [stæm'piːd] $n$ fuggi fuggi $m$ inv.

**stance** [stæns] $n$ posizione $f$.

**stand** [stænd] $n$ (position) posizione $f$; (MIL) resistenza; (structure) supporto, sostegno; (at exhibition) stand $m$ inv; (in shop) banco; (at market) bancarella; (booth) chiosco; (SPORT) tribuna // $vb$ (pt, pp **stood**) $vi$ stare in piedi; (rise) alzarsi in piedi; (be placed) trovarsi // $vt$ (place) mettere, porre; (tolerate, withstand) resistere, sopportare; to **make a ~** prendere posizione; to ~ **for parliament** (Brit) presentarsi come candidato (per il parlamento);

to ~ **by** $vi$ (be ready) tenersi pronto(a) // $vt$ fus (opinion) sostenere; to ~ **down** $vi$ (withdraw) ritirarsi; to ~ **for** $vt$ fus (signify) rappresentare, significare; (tolerate) sopportare, tollerare; to ~ **in for** $vt$ fus sostituire; to ~ **out** $vi$ (be prominent) spiccare; to ~ **up** $vi$ (rise) alzarsi in piedi; to ~ **up for** $vt$ fus difendere; to ~ **up to** $vt$ fus tener testa a, resistere a.

**standard** ['stændəd] $n$ modello, standard $m$ inv; (level) livello; (flag) stendardo // $a$ (size etc) normale, standard $inv$; ~s $npl$ (morals) principi $mpl$, valori $mpl$; ~ **lamp** $n$ (Brit) lampada a stelo; ~ **of living** $n$ livello di vita.

**stand-by** ['stændbaɪ] $n$ riserva, sostituto; **to be on** ~ (gen) tenersi pronto(a); (doctor) essere di guardia; ~ **ticket** $n$ (AVIAT) biglietto senza garanzia.

**stand-in** ['stændɪn] $n$ sostituto/a; (CINEMA) controfigura.

**standing** ['stændɪŋ] $a$ diritto(a), in piedi // $n$ rango, condizione $f$, posizione $f$; **of many years'** ~ che esiste da molti anni; ~ **order** $n$ (Brit: at bank) ordine $m$ di pagamento (permanente); ~ **orders** $npl$ (MIL) regolamento; ~ **room** $n$ posto all'impiedi.

**standoffish** [stænd'ɔfɪʃ] $a$ scostante, freddo(a).

**standpoint** ['stændpɔɪnt] $n$ punto di vista.

**standstill** ['stændstɪl] $n$: **at a** ~ fermo(a); (fig) a un punto morto; **to come to a** ~ fermarsi; giungere a un punto morto.

**stank** [stæŋk] $pt$ of **stink**.

**staple** ['steɪpl] $n$ (for papers) graffetta // $a$ (food etc) di base // $vt$ cucire; ~r $n$ cucitrice $f$.

**star** [stɑː*] $n$ stella; (celebrity) divo/a; (principal actor) vedette $f$ inv // $vi$: to ~ (**in**) essere il (or la) protagonista (di) // $vt$ (CINEMA) essere interpretato(a) da.

**starboard** [ˈstɑːbəd] n dritta.

**starch** [stɑːtʃ] n amido.

**stardom** [ˈstɑːdəm] n celebrità.

**stare** [steə*] n sguardo fisso // vi: to ~ at fissare.

**starfish** [ˈstɑːfɪʃ] n stella di mare.

**stark** [stɑːk] a (bleak) desolato(a) // ad: ~ **naked** completamente nudo(a).

**starling** [ˈstɑːlɪŋ] n storno.

**starry** [ˈstɑːrɪ] a stellato(a); **~-eyed** a (innocent) ingenuo(a).

**start** [stɑːt] n inizio; (of race) partenza; (sudden movement) sobbalzo // vt cominciare, iniziare // vi cominciare; (on journey) partire, mettersi in viaggio; (jump) sobbalzare; to ~ **doing** or **to do sth** (in)cominciare a fare qc; to ~ **off** vi cominciare; (leave) partire; to ~ **up** vi cominciare; (car) avviarsi // vt iniziare; (car) avviare; **~er** n (AUT) motorino d'avviamento; (SPORT: official) starter m inv; (: runner, horse) partente m/f; (Brit CULIN) primo piatto; **~ing point** n punto di partenza.

**startle** [ˈstɑːtl] vt far trasalire.

**starvation** [stɑːˈveɪʃən] n fame f, inedia.

**starve** [stɑːv] vi morire di fame; soffrire la fame // vt far morire di fame, affamare.

**state** [steɪt] n stato // vt dichiarare, affermare; annunciare; **the S~s** (USA) gli Stati Uniti; **to be in a ~** essere agitato(a); **~ly** a maestoso(a), imponente; **~ment** n dichiarazione f; (LAW) deposizione f; **~sman** n statista m.

**static** [ˈstætɪk] n (RADIO) scariche fpl // a statico(a).

**station** [ˈsteɪʃən] n stazione f; (rank) rango, condizione f // vt collocare, disporre.

**stationary** [ˈsteɪʃənərɪ] a fermo(a), immobile.

**stationer** [ˈsteɪʃənə*] n cartolaio/a; **~'s (shop)** n cartoleria; **~y** n articoli mpl di cancelleria.

**station master** n (RAIL) capostazione m.

**station wagon** n (US) giardinetta.

**statistic** [stəˈtɪstɪk] n statistica; **~s** n (science) statistica.

**statue** [ˈstætjuː] n statua.

**status** [ˈsteɪtəs] n posizione f, condizione f sociale; prestigio; stato; ~ **symbol** n simbolo di prestigio.

**statute** [ˈstætjuːt] n legge f; **~s** npl (of club etc) statuto; **statutory** a stabilito(a) dalla legge, statutario(a).

**staunch** [stɔːntʃ] a fido(a), leale.

**stave** [steɪv] n (MUS) rigo // vt: to ~ **off** (attack) respingere; (threat) evitare.

**stay** [steɪ] n (period of time) soggiorno, permanenza // vi rimanere; (reside) alloggiare, stare; (spend some time) trattenersi, soggiornare; to ~ **put** non muoversi; to ~ **with friends** stare presso amici; to ~ **the night** passare la notte; to ~ **behind** vi restare indietro; to ~ **in** vi (at home) stare in casa; to ~ **on** vi restare, rimanere; to ~ **out** vi (of house) rimanere fuori (di casa); to ~ **up** vi (at night) rimanere alzato(a); **~ing power** n capacità di resistenza.

**stead** [stɛd] n: in sb's ~ al posto di qn; to stand sb in good ~ essere utile a qn.

**steadfast** [ˈstɛdfɑːst] a fermo(a), risoluto(a).

**steadily** [ˈstɛdɪlɪ] ad continuamente, (walk) con passo sicuro.

**steady** [ˈstɛdɪ] a stabile, solido(a), fermo(a); (regular) costante; (person) calmo(a), tranquillo(a) // vt stabilizzare; calmare; to ~ **oneself** ritrovare l'equilibrio.

**steak** [steɪk] n (meat) bistecca; (fish) trancia.

**steal** [stiːl], pt **stole**, pp **stolen** vt, vi rubare.

**stealth** [stɛlθ] n: by ~ furtivamente; **~y** a furtivo(a).

**steam** [stiːm] n vapore m // vt trattare con vapore; (CULIN) cuocere a vapore // *vi* fumare; (*ship*): **to ~ along** filare; **~ engine** *n* macchina a vapore; (*RAIL*) locomotiva a vapore; **~er** *n* piroscafo, vapore *m*; **~roller** *n* rullo compressore; **~ship** *n* = **~er**; **~y** *a* (*room*) pieno(a) di vapore; (*window*) appannato(a).

**steel** [stiːl] *n* acciaio // *cpd* di acciaio; **~works** *n* acciaieria.

**steep** [stiːp] *a* ripido(a), scosceso(a); (*price*) eccessivo(a) // *vt* inzuppare; (*washing*) mettere a mollo.

**steeple** ['stiːpl] *n* campanile *m*.

**steer** [stɪə*] *n* manzo // *vt* (*ship*) governare; (*car*) guidare // *vi* (*NAUT: person*) governare; (: *ship*) rispondere al timone; (*car*) guidarsi; **~ing** *n* (*AUT*) sterzo; **~ing wheel** *n* volante *m*.

**stem** [stɛm] *n* (*of flower, plant*) stelo; (*of tree*) fusto; (*of glass*) gambo; (*of fruit, leaf*) picciolo // *vt* contenere, arginare; **to ~ from** *vt fus* provenire da, derivare da.

**stench** [stɛntʃ] *n* puzzo, fetore *m*.

**stencil** ['stɛnsl] *n* (*of metal, cardboard*) stampino, mascherina; (*in typing*) matrice *f*.

**stenographer** [stɛˈnɔgrəfə*] *n* (*US*) stenografo/a.

**step** [stɛp] *n* passo; (*stair*) gradino, scalino; (*action*) mossa, azione *f* // *vi*: **to ~ forward** fare un passo avanti; **~s** *npl* (*Brit*) = **stepladder**; **to be in/out of ~** (*with*) stare/non stare al passo (con); **to ~ down** *vi* (*fig*) ritirarsi; **to ~ off** *vt fus* scendere da; **to ~ up** *vt* aumentare; intensificare; **~brother** *n* fratellastro; **~daughter** *n* figliastra; **~father** *n* patrigno; **~ladder** *n* scala a libretto; **~mother** *n* matrigna; **~ping stone** *n* pietra di un guado; (*fig*) trampolino; **~sister** *n* sorellastra; **~son** *n* figliastro.

**stereo** ['stɛrɪəu] *n* (*system*) sistema *m* stereofonico; (*record player*) stereo *m inv* // *a* (*also*: **~phonic**) stereofonico(a).

**sterile** ['stɛraɪl] *a* sterile; **sterilize** ['stɛrɪlaɪz] *vt* sterilizzare.

**sterling** ['stəːlɪŋ] *a* (*gold, silver*) di buona lega; (*fig*) autentico(a), genuino(a) // *n* (*ECON*) (lira) sterlina; **a pound ~** una lira sterlina.

**stern** [stəːn] *a* severo(a) // *n* (*NAUT*) poppa.

**stew** [stjuː] *n* stufato // *vt, vi* cuocere in umido.

**steward** ['stjuːəd] *n* (*AVIAT, NAUT, RAIL*) steward *m inv*; (*in club etc*) dispensiere *m*; **~ess** *n* assistente *f* di volo, hostess *f inv*.

**stick** [stɪk] *n* bastone *m*; (*of rhubarb, celery*) gambo // *vb* (*pt, pp* **stuck**) *vt* (*glue*) attaccare; (*thrust*): **to ~ sth into** conficcare or piantare or infiggere qc in; (*col: put*) ficcare; (*col: tolerate*) sopportare // *vi* conficcarsi; tenere; (*remain*) restare, rimanere; **to ~ out, to ~ up** *vi* sporgere, spuntare; **to ~ up for** *vt fus* difendere; **~er** *n* cartellino adesivo; **~ing plaster** *n* cerotto adesivo.

**stickler** ['stɪklə*] *n*: **to be a ~ for** essere pignolo(a) su, tenere molto a.

**stick-up** ['stɪkʌp] *n* rapina a mano armata.

**sticky** ['stɪkɪ] *a* attaccaticcio(a), vischioso(a); (*label*) adesivo(a).

**stiff** [stɪf] *a* rigido(a), duro(a); (*muscle*) legato(a), indolenzito(a); (*difficult*) difficile, arduo(a); (*cold*) freddo(a), formale; (*strong*) forte; (*high: price*) molto alto(a); **~en** *vt* irrigidire; rinforzare // *vi* irrigidirsi; indurirsi; **~ neck** *n* torcicollo.

**stifle** ['staɪfl] *vt* soffocare.

**stigma** ['stɪgmə] *n* (*BOT, fig*) stigma *m*; **~ta** [stɪgˈmɑːtə] *npl* (*REL*) stigmate *fpl*.

**stile** [staɪl] *n* cavalcasiepe *m*; cavalcasteccato.

**stiletto** [stɪˈlɛtəu] *n* (*Brit: also*: **~ heel**) tacco a spillo.

**still** [stɪl] *a* fermo(a); silenzioso(a) // *ad* (*up to this time, even*) ancora;

(nonetheless) tuttavia, ciò nonostante; ~**born** a nato(a) morto(a); ~ **life** n natura morta.

**stilt** [stɪlt] n trampolo; (pile) palo.

**stilted** ['stɪltɪd] a formale; artificiale.

**stimulate** ['stɪmjuleɪt] vt stimolare.

**stimulus**, pl **stimuli** ['stɪmjuləs, 'stɪmjulaɪ] n stimolo.

**sting** [stɪŋ] n puntura; (organ) pungiglione m // vt (pt, pp **stung**) pungere.

**stingy** ['stɪndʒɪ] a spilorcio(a), tirchio(a).

**stink** [stɪŋk] n fetore m, puzzo // vi (pt **stank**, pp **stunk**) puzzare; ~**ing** a (fig: col): **a** ~**ing** ... uno schifo di ..., un(a) maledetto(a) ... .

**stint** [stɪnt] n lavoro, compito // vi: to ~ **on** lesinare su.

**stir** [stə:*] n agitazione f, clamore m // vt rimescolare; (move) smuovere, agitare // vi muoversi; **to** ~ **up** vt provocare, suscitare.

**stirrup** ['stɪrəp] n staffa.

**stitch** [stɪtʃ] n (SEWING) punto; (KNITTING) maglia; (MED) punto (di sutura); (pain) fitta // vt cucire, attaccare; suturare.

**stoat** [stəʊt] n ermellino.

**stock** [stɔk] n riserva, provvista; (COMM) giacenza, stock m inv; (AGR) bestiame m; (CULIN) brodo; (FINANCE) titoli mpl, azioni fpl // a (fig: reply etc) consueto(a); classico(a) // vt (have in stock) avere, vendere; **well-~ed** ben fornito(a); **in** ~ in magazzino; **out of** ~ esaurito(a); **to take** ~ **of** (fig) fare il punto di; ~**s and shares** valori mpl di borsa; **to** ~ **up** vi: to ~ **up** (**with**) fare provvista (di).

**stockbroker** ['stɔkbrəʊkə*] n agente m di cambio.

**stock cube** n (Brit) dado.

**stock exchange** n Borsa (valori).

**stocking** ['stɔkɪŋ] n calza.

**stockist** ['stɔkɪst] n (Brit) fornitore m.

**stock:** ~ **market** n Borsa, mercato

finanziario; ~ **phrase** n cliché m inv; ~**pile** n riserva // vt accumulare riserve di; ~**taking** n (Brit COMM) inventario.

**stocky** ['stɔkɪ] a tarchiato(a), tozzo(a).

**stodgy** ['stɔdʒɪ] a pesante, indigesto(a).

**stoke** [stəʊk] vt alimentare.

**stole** [stəʊl] pt of **steal** // n stola.

**stolen** ['stəʊln] pp of **steal**.

**stolid** ['stɔlɪd] a impassibile.

**stomach** ['stʌmək] n stomaco; (abdomen) ventre m // vt sopportare, digerire; ~ **ache** n mal m di stomaco.

**stone** [stəʊn] n pietra; (pebble) sasso, ciottolo; (in fruit) nocciolo; (MED) calcolo; (Brit: weight) = 6.348 kg.; 14 libbre // cpd di pietra // vt lapidare; ~**-cold** a gelido(a); ~**-deaf** a sordo(a) come una campana; ~**work** n muratura.

**stood** [stud] pt, pp of **stand**.

**stool** [stu:l] n sgabello.

**stoop** [stu:p] vi (also: **have a** ~) avere una curvatura; (bend) chinarsi, curvarsi.

**stop** [stɔp] n arresto; (stopping place) fermata; (in punctuation) punto // vt arrestare, fermare; (break off) interrompere; (also: **put a** ~ **to**) porre fine a // vi fermarsi; (rain, noise etc) cessare, finire; **to** ~ **doing** sth cessare o finire di fare qc; **to** ~ **dead** fermarsi di colpo; **to** ~ **off** vi sostare brevemente; **to** ~ **up** vt (hole) chiudere, turare; ~**gap** n (person) tappabuchi m/f inv; (measure) ripiego; ~**lights** npl (AUT) stop mpl; ~**over** n breve sosta; (AVIAT) scalo.

**stoppage** ['stɔpɪdʒ] n arresto, fermata; (of pay) trattenuta; (strike) interruzione f del lavoro.

**stopper** ['stɔpə*] n tappo.

**stop press** n ultimissime fpl.

**stopwatch** ['stɔpwɔtʃ] n cronometro.

**storage** ['stɔ:rɪdʒ] n immagazzinamento; (COMPUT)

memoria; ~ **heater** n radiatore m elettrico che accumula calore.

**store** [stɔː*] n provvista, riserva; (depot) deposito; (Brit: department ~) grande magazzino; (US: shop) negozio // vt immagazzinare; ~s npl (provisions) rifornimenti mpl, scorte fpl; **to ~ up** vt mettere in serbo, conservare; ~**room** n dispensa.

**storey**, (US) **story** ['stɔːrɪ] n piano.

**stork** [stɔːk] n cicogna.

**storm** [stɔːm] n tempesta, temporale m, burrasca; uragano // vi (fig) infuriarsi // vt prendere d'assalto; ~**y** a tempestoso(a), burrascoso(a).

**story** ['stɔːrɪ] n storia; favola; racconto; (US) = **storey**; ~**book** n libro di racconti.

**stout** [staut] a solido(a), robusto(a); (brave) coraggioso(a); (fat) corpulento(a), grasso(a) // n birra scura.

**stove** [stəuv] n (for cooking) fornello; (: small) fornelletto; (for heating) stufa.

**stow** [stəu] vt mettere via; ~**away** n passeggero(a) clandestino(a).

**straddle** ['strædl] vt stare a cavalcioni di.

**straggle** ['strægl] vi crescere (or estendersi) disordinatamente; trascinarsi; rimanere indietro; ~**r** n sbandato/a.

**straight** [streɪt] a dritto(a); (frank) onesto(a), franco(a) // ad dritto; (drink) liscio // n: **the ~** la linea retta; (RAIL) il rettilineo; (SPORT) la dirittura d'arrivo; **to put or get ~** mettere in ordine, mettere ordine in; ~ **away**, ~ **off** (at once) immediatamente; ~**en** vt (also: ~**en out**) raddrizzare; ~**-faced** a impassibile, imperturbabile; ~**-forward** a semplice; onesto(a), franco(a).

**strain** [streɪn] n (TECH) sollecitazione f; (physical) sforzo; (mental) tensione f; (MED) strappo; distorsione f; (streak, trace) tendenza; elemento // vt tendere;

(muscle) sforzare; (ankle) storcere; (friendship, marriage) mettere a dura prova; (filter) colare, filtrare // vi sforzarsi; ~**s** npl (MUS) note fpl; ~**ed** a (laugh etc) forzato(a); (relations) teso(a); ~**er** n passino, colino.

**strait** [streɪt] n (GEO) stretto; ~**jacket** n camicia di forza; ~**laced** a bacchettone(a).

**strand** [strænd] n (of thread) filo; ~**ed** a nei guai; senza mezzi di trasporto.

**strange** [streɪndʒ] a (not known) sconosciuto(a); (odd) strano(a), bizzarro(a); ~**r** n sconosciuto/a; estraneo/a.

**strangle** ['stræŋgl] vt strangolare; ~**hold** n (fig) stretta (mortale).

**strap** [stræp] n cinghia; (of slip, dress) spallina, bretella // vt legare con una cinghia; (child etc) punire (con una cinghia).

**strategic** [strə'tiːdʒɪk] a strategico(a).

**strategy** ['strætɪdʒɪ] n strategia.

**straw** [strɔː] n paglia; (drinking ~) cannuccia; **that's the last ~!** è la goccia che fa traboccare il vaso!

**strawberry** ['strɔːbərɪ] n fragola.

**stray** [streɪ] a (animal) randagio(a) // vi perdersi; ~ **bullet** n proiettile m vagante.

**streak** [striːk] n striscia; (fig: of madness etc) vena // vt striare, screziare // vi: **to ~ past** passare come un fulmine.

**stream** [striːm] n ruscello; corrente f; (of people) fiume m // vt (SCOL) dividere in livelli di rendimento // vi scorrere; **to ~ in/out** entrare/uscire a fiotti.

**streamer** ['striːmə*] n (of paper) stella filante.

**streamlined** ['striːmlaɪnd] a aerodinamico(a), affusolato(a); (fig) razionalizzato(a).

**street** [striːt] n strada, via // cpd stradale, di strada; ~**car** n (US) tram m inv; ~ **lamp** n lampione m;

~ **plan** n pianta (di una città); ~**wise** a (col) esperto(a) dei bassifondi.

**strength** [streŋθ] n forza; (of girder, knot etc) resistenza, solidità; ~**en** vt rinforzare; fortificare; consolidare.

**strenuous** ['strenjuəs] a vigoroso(a), energico(a); (tiring) duro(a), pesante.

**stress** [strɛs] n (force, pressure) pressione f; (mental strain) tensione f; (accent) accento f // vt insistere su, sottolineare.

**stretch** [strɛtʃ] n (of sand etc) distesa // vi stirarsi; (extend): to ~ to or as far as estendersi fino a // vt tendere, allungare; (spread) distendere; (fig) spingere (al massimo); to ~ out vi allungarsi, estendersi // vt (arm etc) allungare, tendere; (to spread) distendere.

**stretcher** ['strɛtʃə*] n barella, lettiga.

**strewn** [stru:n] a: ~ with cosparso(a) di.

**stricken** ['strɪkən] a (person) provato(a); (city, industry etc) colpito(a); ~ with (disease etc) colpito(a) da.

**strict** [strɪkt] a (severe) rigido(a), severo(a); (precise) preciso(a), stretto(a).

**stride** [straɪd] n passo lungo // vi (pt **strode**, pp **stridden** [straud, 'strɪdn]) camminare a grandi passi.

**strife** [straɪf] n conflitto; litigi mpl.

**strike** [straɪk] n sciopero; (of oil etc) scoperta; (attack) attacco // vb (pt, pp **struck**) vt colpire; (oil etc) scoprire, trovare // vi far sciopero, scioperare; (attack) attaccare; (clock) suonare; **on** ~ (workers) in sciopero; to ~ a match accendere un fiammifero; to ~ **down** vt (fig) atterrare; to ~ **out** vt depennare; to ~ **up** vt (MUS) attaccare; to ~ **up a friendship with** fare amicizia con; ~**r** n scioperante m/f; (SPORT) attaccante m; **striking** a che colpisce.

**string** [strɪŋ] n spago; (row) fila; sequenza; catena; (MUS) corda // vt (pt, pp **strung**): to ~ **out** disporre di fianco; to ~ **together** (words, ideas) mettere insieme; the ~s npl (MUS) gli archi; to **pull** ~s **for sb** (fig) raccomandare qn; to ~ **bean** n fagiolino; ~**(ed) instrument** n (MUS) strumento a corda.

**stringent** ['strɪndʒənt] a rigoroso(a); (reasons, arguments) stringente, impellente.

**strip** [strɪp] n striscia // vt spogliare; (also: ~ **down**: machine) smontare // vi spogliarsi; ~ **cartoon** n fumetto.

**stripe** [straɪp] n striscia, riga; ~**d** a a strisce or righe.

**strip lighting** n illuminazione f al neon.

**stripper** ['strɪpə*] n spogliarellista.

**striptease** ['strɪpti:z] n spogliarello.

**strive** [straɪv], pt **strove**, pp **striven** ['strɔuv, 'strɪvn] vi: to ~ **to do** sforzarsi di fare.

**strode** [straud] pt of **stride**.

**stroke** [strɔuk] n colpo; (MED) colpo apoplettico; (caress) carezza // vt accarezzare; **at a** ~ in un attimo.

**stroll** [strɔul] n giretto, passeggiatina // vi andare a spasso; ~**er** n (US) passeggino.

**strong** [strɔŋ] a (gen) forte; (sturdy: table, fabric etc) solido(a); **they are 50** ~ sono in 50; ~**box** n cassaforte f; ~**hold** n fortezza, roccaforte f; ~**ly** ad fortemente, con forza; energicamente, vivamente; ~**room** n camera di sicurezza.

**strove** [strɔuv] pt of **strive**.

**struck** [strʌk] pt, pp of **strike**.

**structural** ['strʌktʃərəl] a strutturale; (CONSTR) di struzione; di struttura.

**structure** ['strʌktʃə*] n struttura; (building) costruzione f, fabbricato.

**struggle** ['strʌgl] n lotta // vi lottare.

**strum** [strʌm] vt (guitar) strimpellare.

**strung** [strʌŋ] pt, pp of **string**.

**strut** [strʌt] n sostegno, supporto // vi pavoneggiarsi.

**stub** [stʌb] n mozzicone m; (of ticket etc) matrice f, talloncino m // vt: to ~ one's toe urtare or sbattere il dito del piede; **to ~ out** vt schiacciare.

**stubble** ['stʌbl] n stoppia; (on chin) barba ispida.

**stubborn** ['stʌbən] a testardo(a), ostinato(a).

**stuck** [stʌk] pt, pp of **stick** // a (jammed) bloccato(a); **~-up** a presuntuoso(a).

**stud** [stʌd] n bottoncino; borchia; (of horses) scuderia, allevamento di cavalli; (also: ~ horse) stallone m // vt (fig): **~ded with** tempestato(a) di.

**student** ['stjuːdənt] n studente/essa // cpd studentesco(a); universitario(a); degli studenti; **~ driver** n (US) conducente m/f principiante.

**studio** ['stjuːdɪəu] n studio; **~ flat**, (US) **~ apartment** n appartamento monolocale.

**studious** ['stjuːdɪəs] a studioso(a); (studied) studiato(a), voluto(a); **~ly** ad (carefully) deliberatamente, di proposito.

**study** ['stʌdɪ] n studio // vt studiare; esaminare // vi studiare.

**stuff** [stʌf] n cosa, roba; (belongings) cose fpl, roba; (substance) sostanza, materiale m // vt imbottire; (CULIN) farcire; **~ing** n imbottitura; (CULIN) ripieno; **~y** a (room) mal ventilato(a), senz'aria; (ideas) antiquato(a).

**stumble** ['stʌmbl] vi inciampare; **to ~ across** (fig) imbattersi in; **stumbling block** n ostacolo, scoglio.

**stump** [stʌmp] n ceppo; (of limb) moncone m // vt sconcertare, lasciare perplesso(a).

**stun** [stʌn] vt stordire; (amaze) sbalordire.

**stung** [stʌŋ] pt, pp of **sting**.

**stunk** [stʌŋk] pp of **stink**.

**stunt** [stʌnt] n bravata; trucco pub-

blicitario; (AVIAT) acrobazia // vt arrestare; **~ed** a stentato(a), rachitico(a); **~man** n cascatore m.

**stupefy** ['stjuːpɪfaɪ] vt stordire; intontire; (fig) stupire.

**stupendous** [stjuː'pɛndəs] a stupendo(a), meraviglioso(a).

**stupid** ['stjuːpɪd] a stupido(a); **~ity** [-'pɪdɪtɪ] n stupidità f inv, stupidaggine f.

**stupor** ['stjuːpə*] n torpore m.

**sturdy** ['stəːdɪ] a robusto(a), vigoroso(a); solido(a).

**sturgeon** ['stəːdʒən] n storione m.

**stutter** ['stʌtə*] n balbuzie f // vi balbettare.

**sty** [staɪ] n (of pigs) porcile m.

**stye** [staɪ] n (MED) orzaiolo.

**style** [staɪl] n stile m; (distinction) eleganza, classe f; **stylish** a elegante; **stylist** n (hair stylist) parrucchiere/a.

**stylus** ['staɪləs] n (of record player) puntina.

**suave** [swɑːv] a untuoso(a).

**sub...** [sʌb] prefix sub..., sotto...; **~conscious** a, n subcosciente (m); **~contract** vt subappaltare.

**subdue** [səb'djuː] vt sottomettere, soggiogare; **~d** a pacato(a), (light) attenuato(a); (person) poco esuberante.

**subject** n ['sʌbdʒɪkt] soggetto; (citizen etc) cittadino/a; (SCOL) materia // vt [səb'dʒɛkt]: **to ~ to** sottomettere a; esporre a; **to be ~ to** (law) essere sottomesso(a) a; (disease) essere soggetto(a) a; **~ive** [-'dʒɛktɪv] a soggettivo(a); **~ matter** n argomento; contenuto.

**subjunctive** [səb'dʒʌŋktɪv] a congiuntivo(a) // n congiuntivo.

**sublet** [sʌb'lɛt] vt subaffittare.

**submachine gun** ['sʌbmə'ʃiːn-] n mitra m inv.

**submarine** [sʌbmə'riːn] n sommergibile m.

**submerge** [səb'məːdʒ] vt sommergere; immergere // vi immergersi.

**submission** [səbˈmɪʃən] n sottomissione f.

**submissive** [səbˈmɪsɪv] a remissivo(a).

**submit** [səbˈmɪt] vt sottomettere // vi sottomettersi.

**subnormal** [sʌbˈnɔːməl] a subnormale(a).

**subordinate** [səˈbɔːdɪnət] a, n subordinato(a).

**subpoena** [səbˈpiːnə] n (LAW) citazione f, mandato di comparizione.

**subscribe** [səbˈskraɪb] vi contribuire; **to ~ to** (opinion) approvare, condividere; (fund) sottoscrivere; (newspaper) abbonarsi a; essere abbonato(a) a; **~r** n (to periodical, telephone) abbonato(a).

**subscription** [səbˈskrɪpʃən] n sottoscrizione f; abbonamento.

**subsequent** [ˈsʌbsɪkwənt] a successivo(a), seguente; conseguente; **~ly** ad in seguito, successivamente.

**subside** [səbˈsaɪd] vi cedere, abbassarsi; (flood) decrescere; (wind) calmarsi; **~nce** [-ˈsaɪdns] n cedimento, abbassamento.

**subsidiary** [səbˈsɪdɪərɪ] a sussidiario(a); accessorio(a) // n filiale f.

**subsidize** [ˈsʌbsɪdaɪz] vt sovvenzionare.

**subsidy** [ˈsʌbsɪdɪ] n sovvenzione f.

**subsistence** [səbˈsɪstəns] n esistenza; mezzi mpl di sostentamento.

**substance** [ˈsʌbstəns] n sostanza; (fig) essenza.

**substantial** [səbˈstænʃl] a solido(a); (amount, progress etc) notevole; (meal) sostanzioso(a).

**substantiate** [səbˈstænʃɪeɪt] vt comprovare.

**substitute** [ˈsʌbstɪtjuːt] n (person) sostituto(a); (thing) succedaneo, surrogato // vt: **to ~ sth/sb for** sostituire qc/qn a.

**subterfuge** [ˈsʌbtəfjuːdʒ] n sotterfugio.

**subterranean** [sʌbtəˈreɪnɪən] a sotterraneo(a).

**subtitle** [ˈsʌbtaɪtl] n (CINEMA) sottotitolo.

**subtle** [ˈsʌtl] a sottile.

**subtotal** [sʌbˈtəʊtl] n somma parziale.

**subtract** [səbˈtrækt] vt sottrarre; **~ion** [-ˈtrækʃən] n sottrazione f.

**suburb** [ˈsʌbəːb] n sobborgo; **the ~s** la periferia; **~an** [səˈbəːbən] a suburbano(a); **~ia** n periferia, sobborghi mpl.

**subversive** [səbˈvəːsɪv] a sovversivo(a).

**subway** [ˈsʌbweɪ] n (US: underground) metropolitana; (Brit: underpass) sottopassaggio.

**succeed** [səkˈsiːd] vi riuscire; aver successo // vt succedere a; **to ~ in doing** riuscire a fare; **~ing** a (following) successivo(a).

**success** [səkˈses] n successo; **~ful** a (venture) coronato(a) da successo, riuscito(a); **to be ~ful (in doing)** riuscire (a fare); **~fully** ad con successo.

**succession** [səkˈseʃən] n successione f.

**successive** [səkˈsesɪv] a successivo(a); consecutivo(a).

**succumb** [səˈkʌm] vi soccombere.

**such** [sʌtʃ] a tale; (of that kind): **~ a book** un tale libro, un libro del genere; **~ books** tali libri, libri del genere; (so much): **~ courage** tanto coraggio // ad talmente, così; **~ a long trip** un viaggio così lungo; **~ good books** libri così buoni; **~ a lot of** talmente or così tanto(a); **~ as** (like) come; **a noise ~ as** to un rumore tale da; **as ~** ad come or in quanto tale; **~-and-~** a tale (after noun).

**suck** [sʌk] vt succhiare; (breast, bottle) poppare; **~er** n (ZOOL, TECH) ventosa; (BOT) pollone m; (col) gonzo/a, babbeo/a.

**suction** [ˈsʌkʃən] n succhiamento; (TECH) aspirazione f.

**sudden** [ˈsʌdn] a improvviso(a); **all of a ~** improvvisamente, all'improvviso; **~ly** ad bruscamente, improvvisamente, di colpo.

**suds** [sʌdz] npl schiuma (di sapone).

**sue** [suː] vt citare in giudizio.

**suede** [sweɪd] n pelle f scamosciata // cpd scamosciato(a).

**suet** [suɪt] n grasso di rognone.

**suffer** ['sʌfə*] vt soffrire, patire; (bear) sopportare, tollerare // vi soffrire; **~er** n malato(a); **~ing** n sofferenza.

**suffice** [sə'faɪs] vi essere sufficiente, bastare.

**sufficient** [sə'fɪʃənt] a sufficiente; **~ money** abbastanza soldi; **~ly** ad sufficientemente, abbastanza.

**suffocate** ['sʌfəkeɪt] vi (have difficulty breathing) soffocare; (die through lack of air) asfissiare.

**suffused** [sə'fjuːzd] a: **~ with** (colour) tinto(a) di; **the room was ~ with light** nella stanza c'era una luce soffusa.

**sugar** ['ʃugə*] n zucchero // vt zuccherare; **~ beet** n barbabietola da zucchero; **~ cane** n canna da zucchero; **~y** a zuccherino(a), dolce; (fig) sdolcinato(a).

**suggest** [sə'dʒɛst] vt proporre, suggerire; indicare; **~ion** [-'dʒɛstʃən] n suggerimento, proposta.

**suicide** ['suɪsaɪd] n (person) suicida m/f; (act) suicidio.

**suit** [suːt] n (man's) vestito; (woman's) completo, tailleur m inv; (CARDS) seme m, colore m // vt andar bene a or per; essere adatto(a) a or per; (adapt): to **~ sth to** adattare qc a; **~able** a adatto(a); appropriato(a); **~ably** ad (dress) in modo adatto; (thank) adeguatamente.

**suitcase** ['suːtkeɪs] n valigia.

**suite** [swiːt] n (of rooms) appartamento; (MUS) suite f inv; (furniture): **bedroom/dining room ~** arredo or mobilia per la camera da letto/sala da pranzo.

**suitor** ['suːtə*] n corteggiatore m, spasimante m.

**sulfur** ['sʌlfə*] n (US) = sulphur.

**sulk** [sʌlk] vi fare il broncio; **~y** a imbronciato(a).

**sullen** ['sʌlən] a scontroso(a); cupo(a).

**sulphur,** (US) **sulfur** ['sʌlfə*] n zolfo.

**sultana** [sʌl'tɑːnə] n (fruit) uva (secca) sultanina.

**sultry** ['sʌltrɪ] a afoso(a).

**sum** [sʌm] n somma; (SCOL etc) addizione f; **to ~ up** vt, vi riassumere.

**summarize** ['sʌmaraɪz] vt riassumere, riepilogare.

**summary** ['sʌmərɪ] n riassunto // a (justice) sommario(a).

**summer** ['sʌmə*] n estate f // cpd d'estate, estivo(a); **~house** n (in garden) padiglione m; **~time** n (season) estate f; **~ time** n (by clock) ora legale (estiva).

**summit** ['sʌmɪt] n cima, sommità; (POL) vertice m.

**summon** ['sʌmən] vt chiamare, convocare; **to ~ up** vt raccogliere, fare appello a; **~s** n ordine m di comparizione // vt citare.

**sump** [sʌmp] n (Brit AUT) coppa dell'olio.

**sumptuous** ['sʌmptjuəs] a sontuoso(a).

**sun** [sʌn] n sole m; **in the ~** al sole; **~bathe** vi prendere un bagno di sole; **~burn** n abbronzatura; (painful) scottatura; **~ cream** n crema solare.

**Sunday** ['sʌndɪ] n domenica; **~ school** n ≈ scuola di catechismo.

**sundial** ['sʌndaɪəl] n meridiana.

**sundown** ['sʌndaun] n tramonto.

**sundry** ['sʌndrɪ] a vari(e), diversi(e); **all and ~** tutti quanti; **sundries** npl articoli diversi, cose diverse.

**sunflower** ['sʌnflauə*] n girasole m.

**sung** [sʌŋ] pp of **sing**.

**sunglasses** ['sʌŋglɑːsɪz] npl occhiali mpl da sole.

**sunk** [sʌŋk] pp of **sink**.

**sun:** ~**light** $n$ (luce $f$ del) sole $m$; ~**ny** $a$ assolato(a), soleggiato(a); (fig) allegro(a), felice; ~**rise** $n$ levata del sole, alba; ~ **roof** $n$ (AUT) tetto apribile; ~**set** $n$ tramonto; ~**shade** $n$ parasole $m$; ~**shine** $n$ (luce $f$ del) sole $m$; ~**stroke** $n$ insolazione $f$, colpo di sole; ~**tan** $n$ abbronzatura; ~**tan oil** $n$ olio solare.

**super** ['su:pə*] $a$ (col) fantastico(a).

**superannuation** [su:pərænju'eiʃən] $n$ contributi $mpl$ pensionistici; pensione $f$.

**superb** [su:'pə:b] $a$ magnifico(a).

**supercilious** [su:pə'siliəs] $a$ sprezzante, sdegnoso(a).

**superficial** [su:pə'fiʃəl] $a$ superficiale.

**superhuman** [su:pə'hju:mən] $a$ sovrumano(a).

**superimpose** ['su:pərim'pəuz] $vt$ sovrapporre.

**superintendent** [su:pərin'tendənt] $n$ direttore/trice; (POLICE) ≈ commissario (capo).

**superior** [su'piəriə*] $a$, $n$ superiore (m/f); ~**ity** [-'ɔriti] $n$ superiorità.

**superlative** [su'pə:lətiv] $a$ superlativo(a), supremo(a) // $n$ (LING) superlativo.

**superman** ['su:pəmæn] $n$ superuomo.

**supermarket** ['su:pəma:kit] $n$ supermercato.

**supernatural** [su:pə'nætʃərəl] $a$ soprannaturale.

**superpower** ['su:pəpauə*] $n$ (POL) superpotenza.

**supersede** [su:pə'si:d] $vt$ sostituire, soppiantare.

**superstitious** [su:pə'stiʃəs] $a$ superstizioso(a).

**supervise** ['su:pəvaiz] $vt$ (person etc) sorvegliare; (organization) soprintendere a; **supervision** [-'viʒən] $n$ sorveglianza; supervisione $f$; **supervisor** $n$ sorvegliante m/f; soprintendente m/f; (in shop) capocommesso/a.

**supine** ['su:pain] $a$ supino(a).

**supper** ['sapə*] $n$ cena.

**supplant** [sə'pla:nt] $vt$ (person, thing) soppiantare.

**supple** ['sapl] $a$ flessibile; agile.

**supplement** $n$ ['saplimənt] supplemento // $vt$ ['sapli'mɛnt] completare, integrare; ~**ary** [-'mɛntəri] $a$ supplementare.

**supplier** [sə'plaiə*] $n$ fornitore $m$.

**supply** [sə'plai] $vt$ (provide) fornire; (equip): **to** ~ (**with**) approvvigionare (di); attrezzare (con) // $n$ riserva, provvista; (supplying) approvvigionamento; (TECH) alimentazione $f$; **supplies** $npl$ (food) viveri $mpl$; (MIL) sussistenza; ~ **teacher** $n$ (Brit) supplente m/f.

**support** [sə'pɔ:t] $n$ (moral, financial etc) sostegno, appoggio; (TECH) supporto // $vt$ sostenere; (financially) mantenere; (uphold) sostenere, difendere; ~**er** $n$ (POL etc) sostenitore/trice, fautore/trice; (SPORT) tifoso/a.

**suppose** [sə'pəuz] $vt$, $vi$ supporre; immaginare; **to be** ~**d to do** essere tenuto(a) a fare; ~**dly** [sə'pauzidli] $ad$ presumibilmente; (seemingly) apparentemente; **supposing** $cj$ se, ammesso che + $sub$.

**suppress** [sə'pres] $vt$ reprimere; sopprimere; tenere segreto(a).

**supreme** [su'pri:m] $a$ supremo(a).

**surcharge** ['sə:tʃa:dʒ] $n$ supplemento; (extra tax) soprattassa.

**sure** [ʃuə*] $a$ sicuro(a); (definite, convinced) sicuro(a), certo(a); ~! (of course) senz'altro!, certo!; ~ **enough** infatti; **to make** ~ **of sth/that** assicurarsi di qc/che; ~**ly** $ad$ sicuramente; certamente.

**surety** ['ʃuərəti] $n$ garanzia.

**surf** [sə:f] $n$ (waves) cavalloni $mpl$; (foam) spuma.

**surface** ['sə:fis] $n$ superficie $f$ // $vt$ (road) asfaltare // $vi$ risalire alla superficie; (fig: person) venire a galla, farsi vivo(a); ~ **mail** $n$ posta ordinaria.

**surfboard** ['sɔːfbɔːd] n tavola per surfing.

**surfeit** ['sɔːfɪt] n: a ~ of un eccesso di; un'indigestione di.

**surfing** ['sɔːfɪŋ] n surfing m.

**surge** [sɔːdʒ] n (strong movement) ondata; (of feeling) impeto // vi (waves) gonfiarsi; (ELEC: power) aumentare improvvisamente; (people) riversarsi.

**surgeon** ['sɔːdʒən] n chirurgo.

**surgery** ['sɔːdʒərɪ] n chirurgia; (Brit: room) studio or gabinetto medico, ambulatorio; **to undergo** ~ subire un intervento chirurgico; ~ **hours** npl (Brit) orario delle visite or di consultazione.

**surgical** ['sɔːdʒɪkl] a chirurgico(a); ~ **spirit** n (Brit) alcool m denaturato.

**surly** ['sɔːlɪ] a scontroso(a), burbero(a).

**surname** ['sɔːneɪm] n cognome m.

**surpass** [sɔːˈpɑːs] vt superare.

**surplus** ['sɔːpləs] n eccedenza; (ECON) surplus m inv // a eccedente, d'avanzo.

**surprise** [səˈpraɪz] n sorpresa; (astonishment) stupore m // vt sorprendere; stupire; **surprising** a sorprendente, stupefacente; **surprisingly** ad (easy, helpful) sorprendentemente.

**surrender** [səˈrɛndə*] n resa, capitolazione f // vi arrendersi.

**surreptitious** [sʌrəpˈtɪʃəs] a furtivo(a).

**surrogate** [ˈsʌrəgɪt] n surrogato; ~ **mother** n madre f sostitutiva.

**surround** [səˈraʊnd] vt circondare; (MIL etc) accerchiare; ~**ing** a circostante; ~**ings** npl dintorni mpl; (fig) ambiente m.

**surveillance** [sɔːˈveɪləns] n sorveglianza, controllo.

**survey** [ˈsɔːveɪ] n quadro generale; (study) esame m; (in housebuying etc) perizia; (of land) rilevamento, rilievo topografico // vt [sɔːˈveɪ] osservare; esaminare; valutare;

rilevare; ~**or** n perito; geometra m; (of land) agrimensore m.

**survival** [səˈvaɪvl] n sopravvivenza; (relic) reliquia, vestigio.

**survive** [səˈvaɪv] vi sopravvivere // vt sopravvivere a; **survivor** n superstite m/f, sopravvissuto/a.

**susceptible** [səˈsɛptəbl] a: ~ (to) sensibile (a); (disease) predisposto(a) (a).

**suspect** a, n ['sʌspɛkt] sospetto(a) // n persona sospetta // vt [səsˈpɛkt] sospettare; (think likely) supporre; (doubt) dubitare.

**suspend** [səsˈpɛnd] vt sospendere; ~**ed sentence** n condanna con la condizionale; ~**er belt** n reggicalze m inv; ~**ers** npl (Brit) giarrettiere fpl; (US) bretelle fpl.

**suspense** [səsˈpɛns] n apprensione f; (in film etc) suspense m.

**suspension** [səsˈpɛnʃən] n (gen AUT) sospensione f; (of driving licence) ritiro temporaneo; ~ **bridge** n ponte m sospeso.

**suspicion** [səsˈpɪʃən] n sospetto.

**suspicious** [səsˈpɪʃəs] a (suspecting) sospettoso(a); (causing suspicion) sospetto(a).

**sustain** [səsˈteɪn] vt sostenere; sopportare; (LAW: charge) confermare; (suffer) subire; ~**ed** a (effort) prolungato(a).

**sustenance** [ˈsʌstɪnəns] n nutrimento; mezzi mpl di sostentamento.

**swab** [swɒb] n (MED) tampone m.

**swagger** [ˈswægə*] vi pavoneggiarsi.

**swallow** [ˈswɒləʊ] n (bird) rondine f // vt inghiottire; (fig: story) bere; **to** ~ **up** vt inghiottire.

**swam** [swæm] pt of **swim**.

**swamp** [swɒmp] n palude f // vt sommergere.

**swan** [swɒn] n cigno.

**swap** [swɒp] vt: **to** ~ (**for**) scambiare (con).

**swarm** [swɔːm] n sciame m // vi formicolare; (bees) sciamare.

**swarthy** [ˈswɔːðɪ] a di carnagione

scura.

**swastika** ['swɔstɪkə] n croce f uncinata, svastica.

**swat** [swɔt] vt schiacciare.

**sway** [sweɪ] vi (building) oscillare; (tree) ondeggiare; (person) barcollare // vt (influence) influenzare, dominare.

**swear** [sweə*], pt **swore**, pp **sworn** vi (witness etc) giurare; (curse) bestemmiare, imprecare; to ~ to sth giurare qc; ~**word** n parolaccia.

**sweat** [swet] n sudore m, traspirazione f // vi sudare.

**sweater** ['swetə*] n maglione m.

**sweatshirt** ['swetfə:t] n felpa.

**sweaty** ['swetɪ] a sudato(a); bagnato(a) di sudore.

**Swede** [swi:d] n svedese m/f.

**swede** [swi:d] n (Brit) rapa svedese.

**Sweden** ['swi:dn] n Svezia.

**Swedish** ['swi:dɪʃ] a svedese // n (LING) svedese m.

**sweep** [swi:p] n spazzata; (curve) curva; (expanse) distesa; (range) portata; (also: chimney ~) spazzacamino // vb (pt, pp **swept**) vt spazzare, scopare // vi camminare maestosamente; precipitarsi, lanciarsi; (extend) stendersi; to ~ **away** vt spazzare via; trascinare via; to ~ **past** vi sfrecciare accanto; passare accanto maestosamente; to ~ **up** vt, vi spazzare; ~**ing** a (gesture) largo(a); circolare; a ~**ing** statement un'affermazione generica.

**sweet** [swi:t] n (Brit: pudding) dolce m; (candy) caramella // a dolce; (fresh) fresco(a); (fig) piacevole; delicato(a), grazioso(a); gentile; ~**corn** n granturco dolce; ~**en** vt addolcire; zuccherare; ~**heart** n innamorato/a; ~**ness** n sapore m dolce; dolcezza; ~ **pea** n pisello odoroso.

**swell** [swel] n (of sea) mare m lungo // a (col: excellent) favoloso(a) // vb (pt ~**ed**, pp **swollen**, ~**ed**) vt gonfiare, ingrossare; aumentare // vi gonfiarsi, ingrossarsi; (sound) cre-

scere; (MED) gonfiarsi; ~**ing** n (MED) tumefazione f, gonfiore m.

**sweltering** ['sweltərɪŋ] a soffocante.

**swept** [swept] pt, pp of **sweep**.

**swerve** [swə:v] vi deviare; (driver) sterzare; (boxer) scartare.

**swift** [swɪft] n (bird) rondone m // a rapido(a), veloce.

**swig** [swɪg] n (col: drink) sorsata.

**swill** [swɪl] n broda // vt (also: ~ **out**, ~ **down**) risciacquare.

**swim** [swɪm] n: to go for a ~ andare a fare una nuotata // vb (pt **swam**, pp **swum**) vi nuotare; (SPORT) fare del nuoto; (head, room) girare // vt (river, channel) attraversare or percorrere a nuoto; (length) nuotare; ~**mer** n nuotatore/trice; ~**ming** n nuoto; ~**ming cap** n cuffia; ~**ming costume** n (Brit) costume m da bagno; ~**ming pool** n piscina; ~**suit** n costume m da bagno.

**swindle** ['swɪndl] n truffa // vt truffare.

**swine** [swaɪn] n (pl inv) maiale m, porco; (col!) porco(!).

**swing** [swɪŋ] n altalena; (movement) oscillazione f; (MUS) ritmo; swing m // vb (pt, pp **swung**) vt dondolare, far oscillare; (also: ~ **round**) far girare // vi oscillare, dondolare; (also: ~ **round**: object) roteare; (: person) girarsi, voltarsi; to be in full ~ (activity) essere in piena attività; (party etc) essere nel pieno; ~ **door**, (US) ~**ing door** n porta battente.

**swingeing** ['swɪndʒɪŋ] a (Brit: defeat) violento(a); (: price increase) enorme.

**swipe** [swaɪp] vt (hit) colpire con forza; dare uno schiaffo a; (col: steal) sgraffignare.

**swirl** [swə:l] vi turbinare, far mulinello.

**swish** [swɪʃ] a (col: smart) all'ultimo grido, alla moda // vi sibilare.

**Swiss** [swɪs] a, n (pl inv) svizzero(a).

**switch** [swɪtʃ] n (for light, radio etc) interruttore m; (change) cambiamento // vt (change) cambiare; scambiare; **to ~ off** vt spegnere; **to ~ on** vt accendere; (engine, machine) mettere in moto, avviare; **~board** n (TEL) centralino.

**Switzerland** ['swɪtsələnd] n Svizzera.

**swivel** ['swɪvl] vi (also: ~ round) girare.

**swollen** ['swəulən] pp of **swell**.

**swoon** [swu:n] vi svenire.

**swoop** [swu:p] vi (also: ~ down) scendere in picchiata, piombare.

**swop** [swɔp] n, vt = **swap**.

**sword** [sɔ:d] n spada; **~fish** n pesce m spada inv.

**swore** [swɔ:*] pt of **swear**.

**sworn** [swɔ:n] pp of **swear**.

**swot** [swɔt] vt sgobbare su // vi sgobbare.

**swum** [swʌm] pp of **swim**.

**swung** [swʌŋ] pt, pp of **swing**.

**syllable** ['sɪləbl] n sillaba.

**syllabus** ['sɪləbəs] n programma m.

**symbol** ['sɪmbl] n simbolo.

**symmetry** ['sɪmɪtrɪ] n simmetria.

**sympathetic** [sɪmpə'θɛtɪk] a (showing pity) compassionevole; (kind) comprensivo(a); ~ **towards** ben disposto(a) verso.

**sympathize** ['sɪmpəθaɪz] vi: **to ~ with sb** compatire qn; partecipare al dolore di qn; **~r** n (POL) simpatizzante m/f.

**sympathy** ['sɪmpəθɪ] n compassione f; in ~ with d'accordo con; (strike) per solidarietà con; **with our deepest ~** con le nostre più sincere condoglianze.

**symphony** ['sɪmfənɪ] n sinfonia.

**symptom** ['sɪmptəm] n sintomo, indizio.

**synagogue** ['sɪnəgɔg] n sinagoga.

**syndicate** ['sɪndɪkɪt] n sindacato.

**synonym** ['sɪnənɪm] n sinonimo.

**synopsis**, pl **synopses** [sɪ'nɔpsɪs, -si:z] n sommario, sinossi f inv.

**syntax** ['sɪntæks] n sintassi f inv.

**synthesis**, pl **syntheses** ['sɪnθəsɪs, -si:z] n sintesi f inv.

**synthetic** [sɪn'θɛtɪk] a sintetico(a).

**syphilis** ['sɪfɪlɪs] n sifilide f.

**syphon** ['saɪfən] n, vb = **siphon**.

**Syria** ['sɪrɪə] n Siria.

**syringe** [sɪ'rɪndʒ] n siringa.

**syrup** ['sɪrəp] n sciroppo; (also: golden ~) melassa raffinata.

**system** ['sɪstəm] n sistema m; (order) metodo; (ANAT) organismo; **~atic** [-'mætɪk] a sistematico(a); metodico(a); ~ **disk** n (COMPUT) disco del sistema; **~s analyst** n analista m programmatore.

# T

**ta** [ta:] excl (Brit col) grazie!

**tab** [tæb] n (loop on coat etc) laccetto; (label) etichetta; **to keep ~s on** (fig) tenere d'occhio.

**tabby** ['tæbɪ] n (also: ~ **cat**) (gatto) soriano, gatto tigrato.

**table** ['teɪbl] n tavolo, tavola // vt (Brit: motion etc) presentare; **to lay** or **set the ~** apparecchiare or preparare la tavola; **~cloth** n tovaglia; ~ **of contents** n indice m; **d'hôte** [ta:bl'dəut] a (meal) a prezzo fisso; ~ **lamp** n lampada da tavolo; **~mat** n sottopiatto; **~spoon** n cucchiaio da tavola; (also: **~spoonful**: as measurement) cucchiaiata.

**tablet** ['tæblɪt] n (MED) compressa; (: for sucking) pastiglia; (for writing) blocco; (of stone) targa.

**table**: ~ **tennis** n tennis m da tavolo, ping-pong m ®; ~ **wine** n vino da tavola.

**tabulate** ['tæbjuleɪt] vt (data, figures) tabulare, disporre in tabelle.

**tacit** ['tæsɪt] a tacito(a).

**tack** [tæk] n (nail) bulletta; (stitch) punto d'imbastitura; (NAUT) bordo, bordata // vt imbullettare; imbastire // vi bordeggiare.

**tackle** ['tækl] n attrezzatura, equipaggiamento; (for lifting) paranco; (RUGBY) placcaggio // vt (difficulty) affrontare; (RUGBY) placcare.

**tacky** ['tækɪ] a colloso(a), appiccicaticcio(a); ancora bagnato(a).

**tact** [tækt] n tatto; ~ful a delicato(a), discreto(a).

**tactical** ['tæktɪkl] a tattico(a).

**tactics** ['tæktɪks] n, npl tattica.

**tactless** ['tæktlɪs] a che manca di tatto.

**tadpole** ['tædpəul] n girino.

**taffy** ['tæfɪ] n (US) caramella f mou inv.

**tag** [tæg] n etichetta; **to ~ along** vi seguire.

**tail** [teɪl] n coda; (of shirt) falda // vt (follow) seguire, pedinare; **to ~ away**, **~ off** vi (in size, quality etc) diminuire gradatamente; **~back** n (Brit AUT) ingorgo; **~ coat** n marsina; **~ end** n (of train, procession etc) coda; (of meeting etc) fine f; **~gate** n (AUT) portellone m posteriore.

**tailor** ['teɪlə*] n sarto; **~ing** n (cut) stile m; **~-made** a (also fig) fatto(a) su misura.

**tailwind** ['teɪlwɪnd] n vento di coda.

**tainted** ['teɪntɪd] a (food) guasto(a); (water, air) infetto(a); (fig) corrotto(a).

**take**, pt **took**, pp **taken** [teɪk, tuk, 'teɪkn] vt prendere; (gain: prize) ottenere, vincere; (require: effort, courage) occorrere, volerci; (tolerate) accettare, sopportare; (hold: passengers etc) contenere; (accompany) accompagnare; (bring, carry) portare; (exam) sostenere, presentarsi a; **I ~ it** that suppongo che; **to ~ for a walk** (child, dog) portare a fare una passeggiata; **to ~ after** vt fus assomigliare a; **to ~ apart** vt smontare; **to ~ away** vt portare via; togliere; **to ~ back** vt (return) restituire; riportare; (one's words) ritirare; **to ~ down** vt (building) demolire; (letter etc)

scrivere; **to ~ in** vt (deceive) imbrogliare, abbindolare; (understand) capire; (include) comprendere, includere; (lodger) prendere, ospitare; **to ~ off** vi (AVIAT) decollare // vt (remove) togliere; (imitate) imitare; **to ~ on** vt (work) accettare, intraprendere; (employee) assumere; (opponent) sfidare, affrontare; **to ~ out** vt portare fuori; (remove) togliere; (licence) prendere, ottenere; **to ~ sth out of sth** (drawer, pocket etc) tirare qc fuori da qc; estrarre qc da qc; **to ~ over** vt (business) rilevare // vi: **to ~ over from sb** prendere le consegne or il controllo da qn; **to ~ to** vt fus (person) prendere in simpatia; (activity) prendere gusto a; **to ~ up** vt (one's story) riprendere; (dress) accorciare; (occupy: time, space) occupare; (engage in: hobby etc) mettersi a; **~away** a (food) da portar via; **~-home pay** n stipendio netto; **~off** n (AVIAT) decollo; **~out** a (US) = **~away**; **~over** n (COMM) assorbimento.

**takings** ['teɪkɪŋz] npl (COMM) incasso.

**talc** [tælk] n (also: **~um powder**) talco.

**tale** [teɪl] n racconto, storia; (pej) fandonia; **to tell ~s** (fig: to teacher, parent etc) fare la spia.

**talent** ['tælnt] n talento; **~ed** a di talento.

**talk** [tɔ:k] n discorso; (gossip) chiacchiere fpl; (conversation) conversazione f; (interview) discussione f // vi (chatter) chiacchierare; **~s** npl (POL etc) colloqui mpl; **to ~ about** parlare di; (converse) discorrere or conversare su; **to ~ sb out of/into doing** dissuadere qn da/convincere qn a fare; **to ~ shop** parlare del lavoro or degli affari; **·to ~ over** vt discutere; **~ative** a loquace, ciarliero(a); **~ show** n conversazione f televisiva, talk show

$m$ inv.

**tall** [tɔ:l] $a$ alto(a); **to be 6 feet ~** = essere alto 1 metro e 80; **~boy** $n$ (Brit) cassettone $m$ alto; **~ story** $n$ panzana, frottola.

**tally** ['tælɪ] $n$ conto, conteggio // vi: **to ~ (with)** corrispondere (a).

**talon** ['tælən] $n$ artiglio.

**tambourine** [tæmbə'ri:n] $n$ tamburello.

**tame** [teɪm] $a$ addomesticato(a); (fig: story, style) insipido(a), scialbo(a).

**tamper** ['tæmpə*] vi: **to ~ with** manomettere.

**tampon** ['tæmpɔn] $n$ tampone $m$.

**tan** [tæn] $n$ (also: **sun~**) abbronzatura // vt abbronzare // vi abbronzarsi // $a$ (colour) marrone rossiccio inv.

**tang** [tæŋ] $n$ odore $m$ penetrante; sapore $m$ piccante.

**tangent** ['tændʒənt] $n$ (MATH) tangente $f$; **to go off at a ~** (fig) partire per la tangente.

**tangerine** [tændʒə'ri:n] $n$ mandarino.

**tangle** ['tæŋgl] $n$ groviglio // vt aggrovigliare.

**tank** [tæŋk] $n$ serbatoio; (for processing) vasca; (for fish) acquario; (MIL) carro armato.

**tanker** ['tæŋkə*] $n$ (ship) nave $f$ cisterna inv; (truck) autobotte $f$, autocisterna.

**tantalizing** ['tæntəlaɪzɪŋ] $a$ allettante.

**tantamount** ['tæntəmaunt] $a$: **~ to** equivalente a.

**tantrum** ['tæntrəm] $n$ accesso di collera.

**tap** [tæp] $n$ (on sink etc) rubinetto; (gentle blow) colpetto // vt dare un colpetto a; (resources) sfruttare, utilizzare; (telephone) mettere sotto controllo; **on ~** (fig: resources) a disposizione; **~ dancing** $n$ tip tap $m$.

**tape** [teɪp] $n$ nastro; (also: **magnetic ~**) nastro (magnetico) // vt (record) registrare (su nastro); **~ measure** $n$ metro a nastro.

**taper** ['teɪpə*] $n$ candelina // vi assottigliarsi.

**tape recorder** $n$ registratore $m$ (a nastro).

**tapestry** ['tæpɪstrɪ] $n$ arazzo; tappezzeria.

**tar** [tɑ:*] $n$ catrame $m$.

**target** ['tɑ:gɪt] $n$ bersaglio; (fig: objective) obiettivo.

**tariff** ['tærɪf] $n$ (COMM) tariffa; (taxes) tariffe $fpl$ doganali.

**tarmac** ['tɑ:mæk] $n$ (Brit: on road) macadam $m$ al catrame; (AVIAT) pista di decollo.

**tarnish** ['tɑ:nɪʃ] vt offuscare, annerire; (fig) macchiare.

**tarpaulin** [tɑ:'pɔ:lɪn] $n$ tela incatramata.

**tarragon** ['tærəgən] $n$ dragoncello.

**tart** [tɑ:t] $n$ (CULIN) crostata; (Brit col: pej: woman) sgualdrina // $a$ (flavour) aspro(a), agro(a); **to ~ up** vt (col): **to ~ o.s. up** farsi bello(a); (pej) agghindarsi.

**tartan** ['tɑ:tn] $n$ tartan $m$ inv.

**tartar** ['tɑ:tə*] $n$ (on teeth) tartaro; **~ sauce** $n$ salsa tartara.

**task** [tɑ:sk] $n$ compito; **to take to ~** rimproverare; **~ force** $n$ (MIL, POLICE) unità operativa.

**tassel** ['tæsl] $n$ fiocco.

**taste** [teɪst] $n$ gusto; (flavour) sapore $m$, gusto; (fig: glimpse, idea) idea // vt gustare; (sample) assaggiare // vi: **to ~ of** (fish etc) sapere or avere sapore di; **it ~s like fish** sa di pesce; **can I have a ~ of this wine?** posso assaggiare un po' di questo vino?; **to have a ~ for** sth avere un'inclinazione per qc; **in good/bad ~** di buon/cattivo gusto; **~ful** $a$ di buon gusto; **~less** $a$ (food) insipido(a); (remark) di cattivo gusto; **tasty** $a$ saporito(a), gustoso(a).

**tatters** ['tætəz] npl: **in ~** (also: **tattered**) a brandelli, sbrindellato(a).

**tattoo** [tə'tu:] $n$ tatuaggio; (spectacle) parata militare // vt tatuare.

**taught** [tɔ:t] pt, pp of **teach**.

**taunt** [tɔ:nt] n scherno // vt schernire.

**Taurus** ['tɔ:rəs] n Toro.

**taut** [tɔ:t] a teso(a).

**tawdry** ['tɔ:drɪ] a pacchiano(a).

**tax** [tæks] n (on goods) imposta; (on services) tassa; (on income) imposte fpl, tasse fpl // vt tassare; (fig: strain: patience etc) mettere alla prova; ~**able** a (income) imponibile; ~**ation** [-'seɪʃən] n tassazione f; tasse fpl, imposte fpl; ~ **avoidance** n l'evitare legalmente il pagamento di imposte; ~ **collector** n esattore m delle imposte; ~ **disc** n (Brit AUT) ≈ bollo; ~ **evasion** n evasione f fiscale; ~**free** a esente da imposte.

**taxi** ['tæksɪ] n taxi m inv // vi (AVIAT) rullare; ~ **driver** n tassista m/f; ~ **rank** (Brit), ~ **stand** n posteggio dei taxi.

**tax:** ~ **payer** n contribuente m/f; ~ **relief** n agevolazioni fpl fiscali; ~ **return** n dichiarazione f dei redditi.

**TB** n abbr = **tuberculosis**.

**tea** [ti:] n tè m inv; (Brit: snack: for children) merenda; **high** ~ (Brit) cena leggera (presa nel tardo pomeriggio); ~ **bag** n bustina di tè; ~ **break** n (Brit) intervallo per il tè.

**teach** [ti:tʃ], pt, pp **taught** vt: **to** ~ **sb sth**, ~ **sth to sb** insegnare qc a qn // vi insegnare; ~**er** n insegnante m/f; (in secondary school) professore/essa; (in primary school) maestro/a; ~**ing** n insegnamento.

**tea cosy** n copriteiera m inv.

**teacup** ['ti:kʌp] n tazza da tè.

**teak** [ti:k] n teak m.

**team** [ti:m] n squadra; (of animals) tiro; ~**work** n lavoro di squadra.

**teapot** ['ti:pɔt] n teiera.

**tear** n [teə*] strappo; [tɪə*] lacrima // vb [teə*] (pt **tore**, pp **torn**) vt strappare // vi strapparsi; in ~s in lacrime; **to** ~ **along** vi (rush) correre all'impazzata; **to** ~ **up** vt (sheet of paper etc) strappare; ~**ful** a piangente, lacrimoso(a); ~ **gas** n gas m lacrimogeno.

**tearoom** ['ti:ru:m] n sala da tè.

**tease** [ti:z] vt canzonare; (unkindly) tormentare.

**tea set** n servizio da tè.

**teaspoon** ['ti:spu:n] n cucchiaino da tè; (also: ~**ful**: as measurement) cucchiaino.

**teat** [ti:t] n capezzolo.

**teatime** ['ti:taɪm] n ora del tè.

**tea towel** n (Brit) strofinaccio (per i piatti).

**technical** ['tɛknɪkl] a tecnico(a); ~**ity** [-'kælɪtɪ] n tecnicità; (detail) dettaglio tecnico.

**technician** [tɛk'nɪʃən] n tecnico/a.

**technique** [tɛk'ni:k] n tecnica.

**technological** [tɛknə'lɔdʒɪkl] a tecnologico(a).

**technology** [tɛk'nɔlədʒɪ] n tecnologia.

**teddy (bear)** ['tɛdɪ-] n orsacchiotto.

**tedious** ['ti:dɪəs] a noioso(a), tedioso(a).

**tee** [ti:] n (GOLF) tee m inv.

**teem** [ti:m] vi abbondare, brulicare; **to** ~ **with** brulicare di; **it is** ~**ing (with rain)** piove a dirotto.

**teenage** ['ti:neɪdʒ] a (fashions etc) per giovani, per adolescenti; ~**r** n adolescente m/f.

**teens** [ti:nz] npl: **to be in one's** ~ essere adolescente.

**tee-shirt** ['ti:ʃə:t] n = **T-shirt**.

**teeter** ['ti:tə*] vi barcollare, vacillare.

**teeth** [ti:θ] npl of **tooth**.

**teethe** [ti:ð] vi mettere i denti.

**teething** ['ti:ðɪŋ]: ~ **ring** n dentaruolo; ~ **troubles** npl (fig) difficoltà fpl iniziali.

**teetotal** ['ti:'təutl] a astemio(a).

**telegram** ['tɛlɪgræm] n telegramma m.

**telegraph** ['tɛlɪgrɑ:f] n telegrafo.

**telepathy** [tɪ'lɛpəθɪ] n telepatia.

**telephone** ['tɛlɪfəun] n telefono // vt (person) telefonare a; (message) telefonare; ~ **booth**, (Brit) ~ **box** n cabina telefonica; ~ **call** n telefonata; ~ **directory** n elenco telefonico; ~ **number** n numero di telefono; **telephonist** [tə'lefənɪst] n (Brit) telefonista m/f.

**telephoto** ['telɪ'fəʊtəʊ] a: ~ **lens** teleobiettivo.

**telescope** ['telɪskəʊp] n telescopio // vt incastrare a cannocchiale.

**televise** ['telɪvaɪz] vt teletrasmettere.

**television** ['telɪvɪʒən] n televisione f; ~ **set** n televisore m.

**telex** ['teleks] n telex m inv // vt, vi trasmettere per telex; **to** ~ **sb** contattare qn via telex.

**tell** [tel], pt, pp **told** vt dire; (relate: story) raccontare; (distinguish): **to** ~ **sth from** distinguere qc da // vi (talk): **to** ~ **(of)** parlare (di); (have effect) farsi sentire, avere effetto; **to** ~ **sb to do** dire a qn di fare; **to** ~ **off** vt rimproverare, sgridare; ~**er** n (in bank) cassiere/a; ~**ing** a (remark, detail) rivelatore(trice); ~**tale** a (sign) rivelatore(trice).

**telly** ['telɪ] n abbr (Brit col: = television) tivù f inv.

**temerity** [tə'merɪtɪ] n temerarietà.

**temp** [temp] n abbr (= temporary) segretaria temporanea.

**temper** ['tempə*] n (nature) carattere m; (mood) umore m; (fit of anger) collera // vt (moderate) temperare, moderare; **to be in a** ~ essere in collera; **to lose one's** ~ andare in collera.

**temperament** ['temprəmənt] n (nature) temperamento; ~**al** [-'mentl] a capriccioso(a).

**temperate** ['temprət] a moderato(a); (climate) temperato(a).

**temperature** ['temprətʃə*] n temperatura; **to have** or **run a** ~ avere la febbre.

**tempest** ['tempɪst] n tempesta.

**template** ['templɪt] n sagoma.

**temple** ['templ] n (building) tempio; (ANAT) tempia.

**temporary** ['tempərərɪ] a temporaneo(a); (job, worker) avventizio(a), temporaneo(a); ~ **secretary** n segretaria temporanea.

**tempt** [tempt] vt tentare; **to** ~ **sb into doing** indurre qn a fare; ~**ation** [-'teɪʃən] n tentazione f.

**ten** [ten] num dieci.

**tenable** ['tenəbl] a sostenibile.

**tenacity** [tə'næsɪtɪ] n tenacia.

**tenancy** ['tenənsɪ] n affitto; condizione f di inquilino.

**tenant** ['tenənt] n inquilino/a.

**tend** [tend] vt badare a, occuparsi di // vi: **to** ~ **to do** tendere a fare.

**tendency** ['tendənsɪ] n tendenza.

**tender** ['tendə*] a tenero(a); (delicate) fragile; (sore) dolorante; (affectionate) affettuoso(a) // n (COMM: offer) offerta // vt offrire.

**tendon** ['tendən] n tendine m.

**tenement** ['tenəmənt] n casamento.

**tenet** ['tenɪt] n principio.

**tennis** ['tenɪs] n tennis m; ~ **ball** n palla da tennis; ~ **court** n campo da tennis; ~ **player** n tennista m/f; ~ **racket** n racchetta da tennis; ~ **shoes** npl scarpe fpl da tennis.

**tenor** ['tenə*] n (MUS, of speech etc) tenore m.

**tense** [tens] a teso(a) // n (LING) tempo.

**tension** ['tenʃən] n tensione f.

**tent** [tent] n tenda.

**tentative** ['tentətɪv] a esitante, incerto(a); (conclusion) provvisorio(a).

**tenterhooks** ['tentəhuks] npl: **on** ~ sulle spine.

**tenth** [tenθ] num decimo(a).

**tent:** ~ **peg** n picchetto da tenda; ~ **pole** n palo da tenda, montante m.

**tenuous** ['tenjuəs] a tenue.

**tenure** ['tenjuə*] n (of property) possesso; (of job) permanenza; titolarità.

**tepid** ['tepɪd] a tiepido(a).

**term** [tə:m] n (limit) termine m; (word) vocabolo, termine; (SCOL) trimestre m; (LAW) sessione f // vt chiamare, definire; ~**s** npl (conditions) condizioni fpl; (COMM) prezzi mpl, tariffe fpl; ~ **of imprisonment** periodo di prigionia in the short/long ~ a breve/lunga scadenza; **to come to** ~s **with** (problem) affrontare.

**terminal** ['tə:mɪnl] a finale, terminale; (disease) nella fase terminale // n (ELEC) morsetto; (COMPUT) terminale m; (AVIAT, for oil, ore etc) terminal m inv; (Brit: also: **coach** ~) capolinea m.

**terminate** ['tə:mɪneɪt] vt mettere fine a // vi: **to** ~ **in** finire in or con.

**terminus**, pl **termini** ['tə:mɪnəs, 'tə:mɪnaɪ] n (for buses) capolinea m; (for trains) stazione f terminale.

**terrace** ['tɛrəs] n terrazza; (Brit: row of houses) fila di case a schiera; **the** ~s npl (Brit SPORT) le gradinate; ~d a (garden) a terrazze.

**terracotta** ['tɛrə'kɔtə] n terracotta.

**terrain** [tɛ'reɪn] n terreno.

**terrible** ['tɛrɪbl] a terribile; (weather) bruttissimo(a); (work) orribile; **terribly** ad terribilmente; (very badly) malissimo.

**terrier** ['tɛrɪə*] n terrier m inv.

**terrific** [tə'rɪfɪk] a incredibile, fantastico(a); (wonderful) formidabile, eccezionale.

**terrify** ['tɛrɪfaɪ] vt terrorizzare.

**territory** ['tɛrɪtərɪ] n territorio.

**terror** ['tɛrə*] n terrore m; ~**ism** n terrorismo; ~**ist** n terrorista m/f.

**terse** [tə:s] a (style) conciso(a); (reply) laconico(a).

**Terylene** ['tɛrɪli:n] n ® terital m ®, terilene m ®.

**test** [tɛst] n (trial, check, of courage etc) prova; (: of goods in factory) controllo, collaudo; (MED) esame m; (CHEM) analisi f inv; (exam: of intelligence etc) test m inv; (: in school) compito in classe; (also: **driving** ~) esame m di guida // vt provare; controllare, collaudare; esaminare; analizzare; sottoporre ad esame; **to** ~ **sb in history** esaminare qn in storia.

**testament** ['tɛstəmənt] n testamento; **the Old/New T~** il Vecchio/Nuovo testamento.

**testicle** ['tɛstɪkl] n testicolo.

**testify** ['tɛstɪfaɪ] vi (LAW) testimoniare, deporre; **to** ~ **to sth** (LAW) testimoniare qc; (gen) comprovare or dimostrare qc; (: be sign of) essere una prova di qc.

**testimony** ['tɛstɪmənɪ] n (LAW) testimonianza, deposizione f.

**test**: ~ **match** n (CRICKET, RUGBY) partita internazionale; ~ **pilot** n pilota m collaudatore; ~ **tube** n provetta.

**tetanus** ['tɛtənəs] n tetano.

**tether** ['tɛðə*] vt legare // n: **at the end of one's** ~ al limite (della pazienza).

**text** [tɛkst] n testo; ~**book** n libro di testo.

**textile** ['tɛkstaɪl] n tessile m.

**texture** ['tɛkstʃə*] n tessitura; (of skin, paper etc) struttura.

**Thames** [tɛmz] n: **the** ~ il Tamigi.

**than** [ðæn, ðən] cj (in comparisons) che; (with numerals, pronouns, proper names) di; **more** ~ 10/once più di 10/una volta; **I have more/less** ~ **you** ne ho più/meno di te; **I have more pens** ~ **pencils** ho più penne che matite; **she is older** ~ **you think** è più vecchia di quanto tu (non) pensi.

**thank** [θæŋk] vt ringraziare; ~ **you (very much)** grazie (tante); ~s npl ringraziamenti mpl, grazie fpl // excl grazie!; ~s **to** prep grazie a; ~**ful** a: ~**ful (for)** riconoscente (per); ~**less** a ingrato(a); **T~giving (Day)** n giorno del ringraziamento.

KEYWORD

**that** [ðæt] ♦ a (demonstrative: pl **those**) quel(quell', quello) m; quella(quell') f; ~ **man/woman/book** quell'uomo/quella donna/quel libro; (not "this") quell'uomo/quella donna/quel libro là; ~ **one** quello(a) là

♦ pronoun 1 (demonstrative: pl

**those**) ciò; (*not "this one"*) quello(a); **who's** ~? chi è?; **what's** ~? cos'è quello?; **is** ~ **you**? sei tu?; **I prefer this** ~ preferisco questo a quello; ~**'s what he said** questo è ciò che ha detto; **what happened after** ~? cosa è successo dopo?; ~ **is (to say)** cioè

**2** (*relative: direct*) che; (: *indirect*) cui; **the book** (~) **I read** il libro che ho letto; **the box** (~) **I put it in** la scatola in cui l'ho messo; **the people** (~) **I spoke to** le persone con cui o con le quali ho parlato

**3** (*relative: of time*) in cui; **the day** (~) **he came** il giorno in cui è venuto

◆ *cj* che; **he thought** ~ **I was ill** pensava che io fossi malato

◆ *ad* (*demonstrative*) così; **I can't work** ~ **much** non posso lavorare (così) tanto; ~ **high** così alto; **the wall's about** ~ **high and** ~ **thick** il muro è alto circa così e spesso circa così.

**thatched** [θætʃt] *a* (*roof*) di paglia; ~ **cottage** *n* cottage *m inv* col tetto di paglia.

**thaw** [θɔː] *n* disgelo // *vi* (*ice*) sciogliersi; (*food*) scongelarsi // *vt* (*food*) (fare) scongelare; **it's** ~**ing** (*weather*) sta sgelando.

**the** [ðiː, ðə] *definite article* **1** (*gen*) il(lo, l') *m*; la(l') *f*; i(gli) *mpl*; le *fpl*; ~ **boy/girl/ink** il ragazzo/la ragazza/l'inchiostro; ~ **books/pencils** i libri/le matite; ~ **history of** ~ **world** la storia del mondo; **give it to** ~ **postman** dallo al postino; **I haven't** ~ **time/money** non ho tempo/soldi; ~ **rich and** ~ **poor** i ricchi e i poveri

**2** (*in titles*): **Elizabeth** ~ **First** Elisabetta prima; **Peter** ~ **Great** Pietro il grande

**3** (*in comparisons*): ~ **more he works,** ~ **more he earns** più lavora

più guadagna.

**theatre,** (*US*) **theater** ['θɪətə*] *n* teatro; ~**-goer** *n* frequentatore/trice di teatri.

**theatrical** [θɪ'ætrɪkl] *a* teatrale.

**theft** [θɛft] *n* furto.

**their** [ðɛə*] *a* il(la) loro, *pl* i(le) loro; ~**s** *pronoun* il(la) loro, *pl* i(le) loro; *see also* **my, mine**.

**them** [ðɛm, ðəm] *pronoun* (*direct*) li(le); (*indirect*) gli, loro (*after vb*); (*stressed, after prep: people*) loro; (: *people, things*) essi(e); *see also* **me**.

**theme** [θiːm] *n* tema *m*; ~ **song** *n* tema musicale.

**themselves** [ðəm'sɛlvz] *pl pronoun* (*reflexive*) si; (*emphatic*) loro stessi(e); (*after prep*) se stessi(e); **between** ~ tra (di) loro; *see also* **oneself**.

**then** [ðɛn] *ad* (*at that time*) allora; (*next*) poi, dopo; (*and also*) e poi // *cj* (*therefore*) perciò, dunque, quindi // *a*: **the** ~ **president** il presidente di allora; **by** ~ allora; **from** ~ **on** da allora in poi.

**theologian** [θɪə'ləudʒən] *n* teologo/a.

**theology** [θɪ'ɔlədʒɪ] *n* teologia.

**theorem** ['θɪərəm] *n* teorema *m*.

**theoretical** [θɪə'rɛtɪkl] *a* teorico(a).

**theory** ['θɪərɪ] *n* teoria.

**therapeutic(al)** [θɛrə'pjuːtɪk(l)] *a* terapeutico(a).

**therapy** ['θɛrəpɪ] *n* terapia.

**there** [ðɛə*] *ad* **1**: ~ **is,** ~ **are** c'è, ci sono; ~ **are 3 of them** (*people*) sono in 3; (*things*) ce ne sono 3; ~ **is no-one here** non c'è nessuno qui; ~ **has been an accident** c'è stato un incidente

**2** (*referring to place*) là, lì; **up/in/down** ~ lassù/là dentro/laggiù; **he went** ~ **on Friday** c'è andato venerdì; **I want that book** ~ **voglio** quel libro là *or* lì; ~ **he is!** eccolo!

**3**: ~, ~ (*esp to child*) su, su.

**thereabouts** [ðɛərə'bauts] *ad* (*place*) nei pressi, da quelle parti; (*amount*) giù di lì, all'incirca.

**thereafter** [ðɛər'ɑ:ftə*] *ad* da allora in poi.

**thereby** [ðɛə'baɪ] *ad* con ciò.

**therefore** ['ðɛəfɔ:*] *ad* perciò, quindi.

**there's** [ðɛəz] = **there is**, **there has**.

**thermal** ['θə:ml] *a* termico(a).

**thermometer** [θə'mɔmɪtə*] *n* termometro.

**thermonuclear** ['θə:məu'nju:klɪə*] *a* termonucleare.

**Thermos** ['θə:məs] *n* ® (*also*: ~ **flask**) thermos *m inv* ®.

**thermostat** ['θə:məstæt] *n* termostato.

**thesaurus** [θɪ'sɔ:rəs] *n* dizionario dei sinonimi.

**these** [ði:z] *pl pronoun*, *a* questi(e).

**thesis**, *pl* **theses** ['θi:sɪs, 'θi:si:z] *n* tesi *f inv*.

**they** [ðeɪ] *pl pronoun* essi(esse); (*people only*) loro; ~ **say that** ... (*it is said that*) si dice che ...; ~**'d** = **they had**, **they would**; ~**'ll** = **they shall**, **they will**; ~**'re** = **they are**; ~**'ve** = **they have**.

**thick** [θɪk] *a* spesso(a); (*crowd*) compatto(a); (*stupid*) ottuso(a), lento(a) // *n*: **in the** ~ **of** nel folto di; **it's 20 cm** ~ ha uno spessore di 20 cm; ~**en** *vi* ispessire // *vt* (*sauce etc*) ispessire, rendere più denso(a); ~**ly** *ad* (*spread*) a strati spessi; (*cut*) a fette grosse; (*populated*) densamente; ~**ness** *n* spessore *m*; ~**set** *a* tarchiato(a), tozzo(a); ~**skinned** *a* (*fig*) insensibile.

**thief**, *pl* **thieves** [θi:f, θi:vz] *n* ladro/a.

**thigh** [θaɪ] *n* coscia.

**thimble** ['θɪmbl] *n* ditale *m*.

**thin** [θɪn] *a* sottile; (*person*) magro(a); (*soup*) poco denso(a); (*hair*, *crowd*) rado(a); (*fog*) leggero(a) // *vt* (*hair*) sfoltire; **to** ~ (**down**) (*sauce*, *paint*) diluire.

**thing** [θɪŋ] *n* cosa; (*object*) oggetto; (*contraption*) aggeggio; ~**s** *npl* (*belongings*) cose *fpl*; **for one** ~ tanto per cominciare; **the best** ~ **would be to** la cosa migliore sarebbe di; **how are** ~**s**? come va?

**think** [θɪŋk], *pt*, *pp* **thought** *vi* pensare, riflettere // *vt* pensare, credere; (*imagine*) immaginare; **to** ~ **of** pensare a; **what did you** ~ **of them**? cosa ne ha pensato?; **to** ~ **about sth/sb** pensare a qc/qn; **I'll** ~ **about it** ci penserò; **to** ~ **of doing** pensare di fare; **I** ~ **so/not** penso di sì/no; **to** ~ **well of** avere una buona opinione di; **to** ~ **out** *vt* (*plan*) elaborare; (*solution*) trovare; **to** ~ **over** *vt* riflettere su; **to** ~ **through** *vt* riflettere a fondo su; **to** ~ **up** *vt* ideare; ~ **tank** *n* commissione *f* di esperti.

**third** [θə:d] *num* terzo(a) // *n* terzo/a; (*fraction*) terzo, terza parte *f*; (*Brit SCOL: degree*) laurea col minimo dei voti; ~**ly** *ad* in terzo luogo; ~ **party insurance** *n* (*Brit*) assicurazione *f* contro terzi; ~**-rate** *a* di qualità scadente; **the T**~ **World** *n* il Terzo Mondo.

**thirst** [θə:st] *n* sete *f*; ~**y** *a* (*person*) assetato(a), che ha sete.

**thirteen** [θə:'ti:n] *num* tredici.

**thirty** ['θə:tɪ] *num* trenta.

---

KEYWORD

**this** [ðɪs] ◆ *a* (*demonstrative*: *pl* **these**) questo(a); ~ **man/woman/book** quest'uomo/questa donna/questo libro; (*not "that"*) quest'uomo/questa donna/questo libro qui; ~ **one** questo(a) qui

◆ *pronoun* (*demonstrative*: *pl* **these**) questo(a); (*not "that one"*) questo(a) qui; **who/what is** ~? chi è/che cos'è questo?; **I prefer** ~ **to that** preferisco questo a quello; ~ **is where I live** io abito qui; ~ **is what he said** questo è ciò che ha detto; ~ **is Mr Brown** (*in introductions*,.

*photo*) questo è il signor Brown; (*on telephone*) sono il signor Brown ♦ *ad* (*demonstrative*): ~ **high/long** *etc* alto/lungo *etc* così; **I didn't know things were** ~ **bad** non sapevo andasse così male.

**thistle** ['θɪsl] *n* cardo.

**thong** [θɔŋ] *n* cinghia.

**thorn** [θɔːn] *n* spina.

**thorough** ['θʌrə] *a* (*search*) minuzioso(a); (*knowledge, research*) approfondito(a), profondo(a); (*scienzioso*(a)); (*cleaning*) a fondo; ~**bred** *n* (*horse*) purosangue *m/f inv*; ~**fare** *n* strada transitabile; "**no** ~**fare**" "divieto di transito"; ~**ly** *ad* minuziosamente; in profondità; a fondo; **he** ~**ly agreed** fu completamente d'accordo.

**those** [ðəuz] *pl pronoun* quelli(e) // *pl a* quei(quegli) *mpl*; quelle *fpl*.

**though** [ðəu] *cj* benché, sebbene // *ad* comunque.

**thought** [θɔːt] *pt, pp of* **think** // *n* pensiero; (*opinion*) opinione *f*; (*intention*) intenzione *f*; ~**ful** *a* pensieroso(a), pensoso(a); (*considerate*) premuroso(a); ~**less** *a* sconsiderato(a); (*behaviour*) scortese.

**thousand** ['θauzənd] *num* mille; **one** ~ mille; ~**s of** migliaia di; ~**th** *num* millesimo(a).

**thrash** [θræʃ] *vt* picchiare; bastonare; (*defeat*) battere; **to** ~ **about** *vi* dibattersi; **to** ~ **out** *vi* dibattere.

**thread** [θrɛd] *n* filo; (*of screw*) filetto // *vt* (*needle*) infilare; ~**bare** *a* consumato(a), logoro(a).

**threat** [θrɛt] *n* minaccia; ~**en** *vi* (*storm*) minacciare // *vt*: **to** ~**en sb with sth/to do** minacciare qn con qc/di fare.

**three** [θriː] *num* tre; ~**dimensional** *a* tridimensionale; (*film*) stereoscopico(a); ~**-piece suit** *n* completo (con gilè); ~**-piece suite** *n* salotto comprendente un

divano *e* due poltrone; ~**-ply** *a* (*wood*) a tre strati; (*wool*) a tre fili.

**thresh** [θrɛʃ] *vt* (*AGR*) trebbiare.

**threshold** ['θrɛʃhəuld] *n* soglia.

**threw** [θruː] *pt of* **throw**.

**thrifty** ['θrɪftɪ] *a* economico(a).

**thrill** [θrɪl] *n* brivido // *vi* eccitarsi, tremare // *vt* (*audience*) elettrizzare; **to be** ~**ed** (*with gift etc*) essere commosso(a); ~**er** *n* film *m inv* (*or* dramma *m or* libro) del brivido; ~**ing** *a* (*book*) pieno(a) di suspense; (*news, discovery*) entusiasmante.

**thrive** [θraɪv], *pt* **thrived, throve** [θraɪv], *pp* **thrived, thriven** [θraɪv, 'θrɪvn] *vi* crescere *or* svilupparsi bene; (*business*) prosperare; **he** ~**s on it** gli fa bene, ne gode; **thriving** *a* fiorente.

**throat** [θrəut] *n* gola; **to have a sore** ~ avere (un *or* il) mal di gola.

**throb** [θrɔb] *vi* (*heart*) palpitare; (*engine*) vibrare; (*with pain*) pulsare.

**throes** [θrəuz] *npl*: **in the** ~ **of** alle prese con; in preda a.

**thrombosis** [θrɔm'bəusɪs] *n* trombosi *f*.

**throne** [θrəun] *n* trono.

**throng** [θrɔŋ] *n* moltitudine *f* // *vt* affollare.

**throttle** ['θrɔtl] *n* (*AUT*) valvola a farfalla // *vt* strangolare.

**through** [θruː] *prep* attraverso; (*time*) per, durante; (*by means of*) per mezzo di; (*owing to*) a causa di // *a* (*ticket, train, passage*) diretto(a) // *ad* attraverso; **to put sb** ~ **to sb** (*TEL*) passare qn a qn; **to be** ~ (*TEL*) ottenere la comunicazione; (*have finished*) avere finito; "**no** ~ **way**" (*Brit*) "strada senza sbocco"; ~**out** *prep* (*place*) dappertutto in; (*time*) per *or* durante tutto(a) // *ad* dappertutto; sempre.

**throve** [θrəuv] *pt of* **thrive**.

**throw** [θrəu] *n* tiro, getto; (*SPORT*) lancio // *vt* (*pt* **threw**, *pp* **thrown** [θruː, 'θrəun]) tirare, gettare; (*SPORT*) lanciare; (*rider*) disarcio-

nare; (fig) confondere; (pottery)
formare al tornio; to ~ a party
dare una festa; to ~ away vt
gettare or buttare via; to ~ off vt
sbarazzarsi di; to ~ out vt buttare
fuori; (reject) respingere; to ~ up
vi vomitare; ~away a da buttare;
~-in n (SPORT) rimessa in gioco.

**thru** [θru:] prep, a, ad (US) =
**through**.

**thrush** [θrʌʃ] n tordo.

**thrust** [θrʌst] n (TECH) spinta // vt
(pt, pp **thrust**) spingere con forza;
(push in) conficcare.

**thud** [θʌd] n tonfo.

**thug** [θʌg] n delinquente m.

**thumb** [θʌm] n (ANAT) pollice m //
vt (book) sfogliare; to ~ a lift fare
l'autostop; ~**tack** n (US) puntina da
disegno.

**thump** [θʌmp] n colpo forte; (sound)
tonfo // vt battere su // vi picchiare,
battere.

**thunder** ['θʌndə*] n tuono // vi
tuonare; (train etc): to ~ past
passare con un rombo; ~**bolt** n
fulmine m; ~**clap** n rombo di tuono;
~**ous** ['θʌndrəs] a fragoroso(a);
~**storm** n temporale m; ~**y** a
temporalesco(a).

**Thursday** ['θə:zdɪ] n giovedì m inv.

**thus** [δʌs] ad così.

**thwart** [θwɔ:t] vt contrastare.

**thyme** [taɪm] n timo.

**thyroid** ['θaɪrɔɪd] n tiroide f.

**tiara** [tɪ'ɑ:rə] n (woman's) diadema
m.

**Tiber** ['taɪbə*] n: the ~ il Tevere.

**tick** [tɪk] n (sound: of clock) tic tac m
inv; (mark) segno; spunta; (ZOOL)
zecca; (Brit col): in a ~ in un
attimo // vi fare tic tac // vt
spuntare; to ~ off vt spuntare;
(person) sgridare; to ~ over vi
(engine) andare al minimo; (fig)
andare avanti come al solito.

**ticket** ['tɪkɪt] n biglietto; (in shop: on
goods) etichetta; (: from cash register) scontrino; (for library) scheda;
~ **collector** n bigliettaio; ~ **office**

n biglietteria.

**tickle** ['tɪkl] n solletico // vt fare il
solletico a, solleticare; (fig)
stuzzicare; piacere a; far ridere.

**tidal** ['taɪdl] a di marea; ~ **wave** n
onda anomala.

**tidbit** ['tɪdbɪt] n (US) = **titbit**.

**tiddlywinks** ['tɪdlɪwɪŋks] n gioco
della pulce.

**tide** [taɪd] n marea; (fig: of events)
corso; to ~ **sb over** dare una mano
a qn; **high/low** ~ alta/bassa marea.

**tidy** ['taɪdɪ] a (room) ordinato(a),
lindo(a); (dress, work) curato(a), in
ordine; (person) ordinato(a) // vt
(also: ~ **up**) riordinare, mettere in
ordine; to ~ **o.s. up** rassettarsi.

**tie** [taɪ] n (string etc) legaccio; (Brit:
also: **neck~**) cravatta; (fig: link)
legame m; (SPORT: draw) pareggio
// vt (parcel) legare; (ribbon)
annodare // vi (SPORT) pareggiare;
to ~ **sth in a bow** annodare qc; to
~ **a knot in sth** fare un nodo a qc;
to ~ **down** vt fissare con una
corda; (fig): to ~ **sb down** to costringere qn a accettare; to ~ **up** vt
(parcel, dog) legare; (boat)
ormeggiare; (arrangements) concludere; to **be** ~**d up** (busy) essere
occupato or preso.

**tier** [tɪə*] n fila; (of cake) piano,
strato.

**tiff** [tɪf] n battibecco.

**tiger** ['taɪgə*] n tigre f.

**tight** [taɪt] a (rope) teso(a),
tirato(a); (clothes) stretto(a);
(budget, programme, bend)
stretto(a); (control) severo(a),
fermo(a); (col: drunk) sbronzo(a) //
ad (squeeze) fortemente; (shut)
ermeticamente; ~**s** npl (Brit) collant
m inv; ~**en** vt (rope) tendere;
(screw) stringere; (control)
rinforzare // vi tendersi; stringersi;
~-**fisted** a avaro(a); ~**ly** ad
(grasp) bene, saldamente; ~**rope** n
corda (da acrobata).

**tile** [taɪl] n (on roof) tegola; (on wall
or floor) piastrella, mattonella.

**till** [tɪl] n registratore m di cassa // vt (land) coltivare // prep, cj = **until**.

**tiller** ['tɪlə*] n (NAUT) barra del timone.

**tilt** [tɪlt] vt inclinare, far pendere // vi inclinarsi, pendere.

**timber** [tɪmbə*] n (material) legname m; (trees) alberi mpl da legname.

**time** [taɪm] n tempo; (epoch: often pl) epoca, tempo; (by clock) ora; (moment) momento; (occasion, also MATH) volta; (MUS) tempo // vt (race) cronometrare; (programme) calcolare la durata di; (remark etc) dire (or fare) al momento giusto; a long ~ molto tempo; for the ~ being per il momento; 4 at a ~ 4 per or alla volta; from ~ to ~ ogni tanto; in ~ (soon enough) in tempo; (after some time) col tempo; (MUS) a tempo; in a week's ~ fra una settimana; in no ~ in un attimo; any ~ in qualsiasi momento; on ~ puntualmente; 5 ~ 5 5 volte 5, 5 per 5; what ~ is it? che ora è?, che ore sono?; to have a good ~ divertirsi; ~'s up! è (l')ora!; ~ bomb n bomba a orologeria; ~ lag n intervallo, ritardo; (in travel) differenza di fuso orario; ~less a eterno(a); ~ly a opportuno(a); ~ off n tempo libero; ~r n (~ switch) temporizzatore m; (in kitchen) contaminuti m inv; ~ scale n periodo; ~ switch n (Brit) temporizzatore m; ~table n orario; ~ zone n fuso orario.

**timid** ['tɪmɪd] a timido(a); (easily scared) pauroso(a).

**timing** ['taɪmɪŋ] n sincronizzazione f; (fig) scelta del momento opportuno, tempismo; (SPORT) cronometraggio.

**timpani** ['tɪmpənɪ] npl timpani mpl.

**tin** [tɪn] n stagno; (also: ~ plate) latta; (Brit: can) barattolo (di latta), lattina, scatola; (for baking) teglia; ~foil n stagnola.

**tinge** [tɪndʒ] n sfumatura // vt: ~d with tinto(a) di.

**tingle** ['tɪŋgl] vi pizzicare.

**tinker** ['tɪŋkə*] n stagnino ambulante; (gipsy) zingaro/a; to ~ with vt fus armeggiare intorno a; cercare di riparare.

**tinkle** ['tɪŋkl] vi tintinnare.

**tinned** [tɪnd] a (Brit: food) in scatola.

**tin opener** ['-əupnə*] n (Brit) apriscatole m inv.

**tinsel** ['tɪnsl] n decorazioni fpl natalizie (argentate).

**tint** [tɪnt] n tinta; ~ed a (hair) tinto(a); (spectacles, glass) colorato(a).

**tiny** ['taɪnɪ] a minuscolo(a).

**tip** [tɪp] n (end) punta; (protective: on umbrella etc) puntale m; (gratuity) mancia; (for coal) discarica; (Brit: for rubbish) immondezzaio; (advice) suggerimento // vt (waiter) dare la mancia a; (tilt) inclinare; (overturn: also: ~ over) capovolgere; (empty: also: ~ out) scaricare; ~-off n (hint) soffiata; ~ped a (Brit: cigarette) col filtro.

**Tipp-Ex** ['tɪpeks] n ® correttore m.

**tipsy** ['tɪpsɪ] a brillo(a).

**tiptoe** ['tɪptəu] n: on ~ in punta di piedi.

**tiptop** ['tɪp'tɔp] a: in ~ condition in ottime condizioni.

**tire** ['taɪə*] n (US) = **tyre** // vt stancare // vi stancarsi; ~d a stanco(a); to be ~d of essere stanco or stufo di; ~some a noioso(a); **tiring** a faticoso(a).

**tissue** ['tɪʃu:] n tessuto; (paper handkerchief) fazzoletto di carta; ~ paper n carta velina.

**tit** [tɪt] n (bird) cinciallegra; to give ~ for tat rendere pan per focaccia.

**titbit** ['tɪtbɪt], (US) **tidbit** ['tɪdbɪt] n (food) leccornia; (news) notizia ghiotta.

**titivate** ['tɪtɪveɪt] vt agghindare.

**title** ['taɪtl] n titolo; ~ deed n (LAW) titolo di proprietà; ~ role n ruolo or parte f principale.

**titter** ['tɪtə*] *vi* ridere scioccamente.
**TM** *abbr* = **trademark**.

KEYWORD

**to** [tu:, tə] ♦ *prep* **1** (*direction*) a; to
go ~ France/London/school andare
in Francia/a Londra/a scuola; **to go
~ Paul's/the doctor's** andare da
Paul/dal dottore; **the road ~
Edinburgh** la strada per
Edimburgo; **~ the left/right** a
sinistra/destra
**2** (*as far as*) (fino) a; **from here ~
London** da qui a Londra; **to count
~ 10** contare fino a 10; **from 40 ~ 50
people** da 40 a 50 persone
**3** (*with expressions of time*): **a
quarter ~ 5** le 5 meno un quarto;
**it's twenty ~ 3** sono le 3 meno venti
**4** (*for, of*): **the key ~ the front
door** la chiave della porta d'ingresso; **a letter ~ his wife** una
lettera per la moglie
**5** (*expressing indirect object*) a; **to
give sth ~ sb** dare qc a qn; **to talk
~ sb** parlare a qn; **to be a danger
~ sb/sth** rappresentare un pericolo
per qn/qc
**6** (*in relation to*) a; **3 goals ~ 2** 3
goal a 2; **30 miles ~ the gallon** ~
11 chilometri con un litro
**7** (*purpose, result*): **to come ~ sb's
aid** venire in aiuto a qn; **to
sentence sb ~ death** condannare a
morte qn; **~ my surprise** con mia
sorpresa
♦ *with vb* **1** (*simple infinitive*): ~
**go/eat** *etc* andare/mangiare *etc*
**2** (*following another vb*): **to want/
try/start ~** do volere/cercare di/
cominciare a fare
**3** (*with vb omitted*): **I don't want ~**
non voglio (farlo); **you ought ~** devi
(farlo)
**4** (*purpose, result*) per; **I did it ~
help you** l'ho fatto per aiutarti
**5** (*equivalent to relative clause*): **I
have things ~ do** ho da fare; **the
main thing is ~ try** la cosa più
importante è provare

**6** (*after adjective etc*): **ready ~ go**
pronto a partire; **too old/young ~**
... troppo vecchio/giovane per ...
♦ *ad*: **to push the door ~** accostare la porta.

**toad** [təud] *n* rospo; **~stool** *n* fungo
(velenoso).
**toast** [təust] *n* (*CULIN*) toast *m*, pane
*m* abbrustolito; (*drink, speech*)
brindisi *m* // *vt* (*CULIN*) abbru-
stolire; (*drink to*) brindare a; **a
piece *or* slice of ~** una fetta di pane
abbrustolito; **~er** *n* tostapane *m inv*.
**tobacco** [tə'bækəu] *n* tabacco;
**~nist** *n* tabaccaio/a; **~nist's
(shop)** *n* tabaccheria.
**toboggan** [tə'bɒgən] *n* toboga *m
inv*; (*child's*) slitta.
**today** [tə'deɪ] *ad, n* (*also fig*) oggi
(*m*).
**toddler** ['tɒdlə*] *n* bambino/a che
impara a camminare.
**toddy** ['tɒdɪ] *n* grog *m inv*.
**to-do** [tə'du:] *n* (*fuss*) storie *fpl*.
**toe** [təu] *n* dito del piede; (*of shoe*)
punta; **to ~ the line** (*fig*) stare in
riga, conformarsi.
**toffee** ['tɒfɪ] *n* caramella.
**toga** ['təugə] *n* toga.
**together** [tə'geðə*] *ad* insieme; (*at
same time*) allo stesso tempo; **~
with** insieme a.
**toil** [tɔɪl] *n* travaglio, fatica // *vi*
affannarsi; sgobbare.
**toilet** ['tɔɪlət] *n* (*Brit: lavatory*)
gabinetto // *cpd* (*bag, soap etc*) da
toletta; **~ bowl** *n* vaso or tazza del
gabinetto; **~ paper** *n* carta
igienica; **~ries** *npl* articoli *mpl* da
toletta; **~ roll** *n* rotolo di carta
igienica; **~ water** *n* acqua di
colonia.
**token** ['təukən] *n* (*sign*) segno;
(*voucher*) buono; **book/record ~**
(*Brit*) buono-libro/disco.
**told** [təuld] *pt, pp of* **tell**.
**tolerable** ['tɒlərəbl] *a* (*bearable*)
tollerabile; (*fairly good*) passabile.
**tolerant** ['tɒlərnt] *a*: ~ (**of**)

tollerante (nei confronti di).

**tolerate** [ˈtɒləreɪt] vt sopportare; (MED, TECH) tollerare.

**toll** [təʊl] n (tax, charge) pedaggio // vi (bell) suonare; **the accident ~ on the roads** il numero delle vittime della strada.

**tomato,** ~es [təˈmɑːtəʊ] n pomodoro.

**tomb** [tuːm] n tomba.

**tomboy** [ˈtɒmbɔɪ] n maschiaccio.

**tombstone** [ˈtuːmstəʊn] n pietra tombale.

**tomcat** [ˈtɒmkæt] n gatto.

**tomorrow** [təˈmɒrəʊ] ad, n (also fig) domani (m inv); **the day after ~** dopodomani; **a week ~** domani a otto; **~ morning** domani mattina.

**ton** [tʌn] n tonnellata (Brit = 1016 kg; US = 907 kg; metric = 1000 kg); (NAUT: also: **register ~**) tonnellata di stazza (= 2.83 cu.m); **~s of** (col) un mucchio or sacco di.

**tone** [təʊn] n tono // vi intonarsi; **to ~ down** vt (colour, criticism, sound) attenuare; **to ~ up** vt (muscles) tonificare; **~-deaf** a che non ha orecchio (musicale).

**tongs** [tɒŋz] npl tenaglie fpl; (for coal) molle fpl; (for hair) arricciacapelli m inv.

**tongue** [tʌŋ] n lingua; **~ in cheek** ad ironicamente; **~-tied** a (fig) muto(a); **~-twister** n scioglilingua m inv.

**tonic** [ˈtɒnɪk] n (MED) tonico; (MUS) nota tonica; (also: **~ water**) (MED) acqua tonica.

**tonight** [təˈnaɪt] ad stanotte; (this evening) stasera // n questa notte; questa sera.

**tonnage** [ˈtʌnɪdʒ] n (NAUT) tonnellaggio, stazza.

**tonne** [tʌn] n (metric ton) tonnellata.

**tonsil** [ˈtɒnsl] n tonsilla; **~litis** [-ˈlaɪtɪs] n tonsillite f.

**too** [tuː] ad (excessively) troppo; (also) anche; **~ much** ad troppo // a troppo(a); **~ many** a troppi(e); **~ bad!** tanto peggio!, peggio così!

**took** [tʊk] pt of **take**.

**tool** [tuːl] n utensile m, attrezzo // vi lavorare con un attrezzo; **~ box/kit** n cassetta f portautensili/attrezzi inv.

**toot** [tuːt] vi suonare; (with car horn) suonare il clacson.

**tooth** [tuːθ], pl **teeth** (ANAT, TECH) dente m; **~ache** n mal m di denti; **~brush** n spazzolino da denti; **~paste** n dentifricio; **~pick** n stuzzicadenti m inv.

**top** [tɒp] n (of mountain, page, ladder) cima; (of box, cupboard, table) sopra m inv, parte f superiore; (lid: of box, jar) coperchio; (: of bottle) tappo; (toy) trottola // a più alto(a); (in rank) primo(a); (best) migliore // vt (exceed) superare; (be first in) essere in testa a; **on ~ of** sopra, in cima a; (in addition to) oltre a; **from ~ to bottom** da cima a fondo; **to ~ up,** (US) **~ off** vt riempire; **~ floor** n ultimo piano; **~ hat** n cilindro; **~-heavy** a (object) con la parte superiore troppo pesante.

**topic** [ˈtɒpɪk] n argomento; **~al** a d'attualità.

**top:** **~less** a (bather etc) col seno scoperto; **~-level** a (talks) ad alto livello; **~most** a il(la) più alto(a).

**topple** [ˈtɒpl] vt rovesciare, far cadere // vi cadere; traballare.

**top-secret** [ˈtɒpˈsiːkrɪt] a segretissimo(a).

**topsy-turvy** [ˈtɒpsɪˈtɜːvɪ] a, ad sottosopra (inv).

**torch** [tɔːtʃ] n torcia; (Brit: electric) lampadina tascabile.

**tore** [tɔː] pt of **tear**.

**torment** n [ˈtɔːment] tormento // vt [tɔːˈment] tormentare; (fig: annoy) infastidire.

**torn** [tɔːn] pp of **tear**.

**tornado,** ~es [tɔːˈneɪdəʊ] n tornado.

**torpedo,** ~es [tɔːˈpiːdəʊ] n siluro.

**torrent** [ˈtɒrnt] n torrente m.

**tortoise** [ˈtɔːtəs] n tartaruga; **~shell** [ˈtɔːtəʃel] a di tartaruga.

**torture** ['tɔ:tʃə*] *n* tortura // *vt* torturare.

**Tory** ['tɔ:rɪ] (*Brit POL*) *a* dei tories, conservatore(trice) // *n* tory *m/f inv*, conservatore/trice.

**toss** [tɔs] *vt* gettare, lanciare; (*pancake*) far saltare; (*head*) scuotere; **to ~ a coin** fare a testa o croce; **to ~ up for sth** fare a testa o croce per qc; **to ~ and turn** (*in bed*) girarsi e rigirarsi.

**tot** [tɔt] *n* (*Brit: drink*) bicchierino; (*child*) bimbo/a.

**total** ['tɔutl] *a* totale *m* // *n* totale *m* // *vt* (*add up*) sommare; (*amount to*) ammontare a.

**totally** ['tɔutəlɪ] *ad* completamente.

**totter** ['tɔtə*] *vi* barcollare.

**touch** [tʌtʃ] *n* tocco; (*sense*) tatto; (*contact*) contatto; (*FOOTBALL*) fuori gioco *m* // *vt* toccare; **a ~ of** (*fig*) un tocco di; un pizzico di; **in ~ with** in contatto con; **to get in ~ with** mettersi in contatto con; **to lose ~** (*friends*) perdersi di vista; **to ~ on** *vt fus* (*topic*) sfiorare, accennare a; **to ~ up** *vt* (*paint*) ritoccare; **~-and-go** *a* incerto(a); **~down** *n* atterraggio; (*on sea*) ammaraggio; (*US FOOTBALL*) meta; **~ed** *a* commosso(a); (*col*) tocco(a), toccato(a); **~ing** *a* commovente; **~line** *n* (*SPORT*) linea laterale; **~y** *a* (*person*) suscettibile.

**tough** [tʌf] *a* duro(a); (*resistant*) resistente; (*meat*) duro(a), tiglioso(a).

**toupee** ['tu:peɪ] *n* parrucchino.

**tour** ['tuə*] *n* viaggio; (*also: package ~*) viaggio organizzato or tutto compreso; (*of town, museum*) visita; (*by artist*) tournée *f inv* // *vt* visitare; **~ing** *n* turismo.

**tourism** ['tuərɪzəm] *n* turismo.

**tourist** ['tuərɪst] *n* turista *m/f* // *ad* (*travel*) in classe turistica // *cpd* turistico(a); **~ office** *n* pro loco *f inv*.

**tournament** ['tuənəmənt] *n* torneo.

**tousled** ['tauzld] *a* (*hair*) arruffato(a).

**tout** [taut] *vi*: **to ~ for** procacciare, raccogliere; cercare clienti per // *n* (*also: ticket ~*) bagarino.

**tow** [təu] *vt* rimorchiare; **"on ~"** (*US*) **"in ~"** (*AUT*) "veicolo rimorchiato".

**toward(s)** [tə'wɔ:d(z)] *prep* verso; (*of attitude*) nei confronti di; (*of purpose*) per.

**towel** ['tauəl] *n* asciugamano; (*also: tea ~*) strofinaccio; **~ing** *n* (*fabric*) spugna; **~ rail, ~ rack** (*US*) **~ rack** *n* portasciugamano.

**tower** ['tauə*] *n* torre *f*; **~ block** *n* (*Brit*) palazzone *m*; **~ing** *a* altissimo(a), imponente.

**town** [taun] *n* città *f inv*; **to go to ~** andare in città; (*fig*) mettercela tutta; **~ centre** *n* centro (città); **~ clerk** *n* segretario comunale; **~ council** *n* consiglio comunale; **~ hall** *n* = municipio; **~ plan** *n* pianta della città; **~ planning** *n* urbanistica.

**towrope** ['təurəup] *n* (cavo da) rimorchio.

**tow truck** *n* (*US*) carro *m* attrezzi *inv*.

**toxic** ['tɔksɪk] *a* tossico(a).

**toy** [tɔɪ] *n* giocattolo; **to ~ with** *vt fus* giocare con; (*idea*) accarezzare, trastullarsi con.

**trace** [treɪs] *n* traccia // *vt* (*draw*) tracciare; (*follow*) seguire; (*locate*) rintracciare; **tracing paper** *n* carta da ricalco.

**track** [træk] *n* (*of person, animal*) traccia; (*on tape, SPORT, path: gen*) pista; (: *of bullet etc*) traiettoria; (: *of suspect, animal*) pista, tracce *fpl*; (*RAIL*) binario, rotaie *fpl* // *vt* seguire le tracce di; **to keep ~ of** seguire; **to ~ down** *vt* (*prey*) scovare; snidare; (*sth lost*) rintracciare; **~suit** *n* tuta sportiva.

**tract** [trækt] *n* (*GEO*) tratto, estensione *f*; (*pamphlet*) opuscolo, libretto.

**tractor** ['træktə*] *n* trattore *m*.

**trade** [treɪd] *n* commercio; (*skill,*

*job*) mestiere *m* // *vi* commerciare; **to ~ with/in** commerciare con/in; **to ~ in** *vt* (*old car etc*) dare come pagamento parziale; **~ fair** *n* fiera commerciale; **~-in price** *n* prezzo di permuta; **~mark** *n* marchio di fabbrica; **~ name** *n* marca, nome *m* depositato; **~r** *n* commerciante *m/f*; **~sman** *n* fornitore *m*; (*shopkeeper*) negoziante *m*; **~ union** *n* sindacato; **~ unionist** sindacalista *m/f*; **trading** *n* commercio; **trading estate** *n* (*Brit*) zona industriale.

**tradition** [trə'dɪʃən] *n* tradizione *f*; **~al** *a* tradizionale.

**traffic** ['træfɪk] *n* traffico // *vi*: **to ~ in** (*pej*: *liquor, drugs*) trafficare in; **~ circle** *n* (*US*) isola rotatoria; **~ jam** *n* ingorgo (del traffico); **~ lights** *npl* semaforo; **~ warden** *n* addetto/a al controllo del traffico e del parcheggio.

**tragedy** ['trædʒədɪ] *n* tragedia.

**tragic** ['trædʒɪk] *a* tragico(a).

**trail** [treɪl] *n* (*tracks*) tracce *fpl*, pista; (*path*) sentiero; (*of smoke etc*) scia // *vt* trascinare, strascicare; (*follow*) seguire // *vi* essere al traino; (*dress etc*) strusciare; (*plant*) arrampicarsi; strisciare; **to ~ behind** *vi* essere al traino; **~er** *n* (*AUT*) rimorchio; (*US*) roulotte *f inv*; (*CINEMA*) prossimamente *m inv*; **~er truck** *n* (*US*: *articulated lorry*) autoarticolato.

**train** [treɪn] *n* treno; (*of dress*) coda, strascico // *vt* (*apprentice, doctor etc*) formare; (*sportsman*) allenare; (*dog*) addestrare; (*memory*) esercitare; (*point: gun etc*): **to ~ sth on** puntare qc contro // *vi* formarsi; allenarsi; **one's ~ of thought** il filo dei propri pensieri; **~ed** *a* qualificato(a); allenato(a); addestrato(a); **~ee** [treɪ'niː] *n* allievo/a; (*in trade*) apprendista *m/f*; **~er** *n* (*SPORT*) allenatore/trice; (*of dogs etc*) addestratore/trice; **~ing** *n* formazione *f*; allenamento; addestramento; **in ~ing** (*SPORT*)

allenamento; (*fit*) in forma; **~ing college** *n* istituto professionale; (*for teachers*) ≈ istituto magistrale; **~ing shoes** *npl* scarpe *fpl* da ginnastica.

**traipse** [treɪps] *vi* girovagare, andare a zonzo.

**trait** [treɪt] *n* tratto.

**traitor** ['treɪtə*] *n* traditore *m*.

**trajectory** [trə'dʒɛktərɪ] *n* traiettoria.

**tram** [træm] *n* (*Brit*: *also*: **~car**) tram *m inv*.

**tramp** [træmp] *n* (*person*) vagabondo/a; (*col*: *pej*: *woman*) sgualdrina // *vi* camminare con passo pesante // *vt* (*walk through*: *town, streets*) percorrere a piedi.

**trample** ['træmpl] *vt*: **to ~** (*under-foot*) calpestare.

**trampoline** ['træmpəliːn] *n* trampolino.

**tranquil** ['træŋkwɪl] *a* tranquillo(a); **~lizer** *n* (*MED*) tranquillante *m*.

**transact** [træn'zækt] *vt* (*business*) trattare; **~ion** [-'zækʃən] *n* transazione *f*; **~ions** *npl* (*minutes*) atti *mpl*.

**transatlantic** ['trænzət'læntɪk] *a* transatlantico(a).

**transcript** ['trænskrɪpt] *n* trascrizione *f*.

**transfer** *n* ['trænsfə*] (*gen, also SPORT*) trasferimento; (*POL*: *of power*) passaggio; (*picture, design*) decalcomania; (: *stick-on*) autoadesivo // *vt* [træns'fəː*] trasferire; passare; decalcare.

**transform** [træns'fɔːm] *vt* trasformare.

**transfusion** [træns'fjuːʒən] *n* trasfusione *f*.

**transient** ['trænzɪənt] *a* transitorio(a), fugace.

**transistor** [træn'zɪstə*] *n* (*ELEC*) transistor *m inv*; (*also*: **~ radio**) radio *f inv* a transistor.

**transit** ['trænzɪt] *n*: **in ~** in transito.

**transitive** ['trænzɪtɪv] *a* (*LING*) transitivo(a).

**translate** [træn'sleɪt] vt tradurre; **translation** [-'leɪʃən] n traduzione f; (SCOL: as opposed to prose) versione f; **translator** n traduttore/trice.

**transmission** [trænz'mɪʃən] n trasmissione f.

**transmit** [trænz'mɪt] vt trasmettere; **~ter** n trasmettitore m.

**transparency** [træns'pɛərnsɪ] n (Brit: PHOT) diapositiva.

**transparent** [træns'pærnt] a trasparente.

**transpire** [træn'spaɪə*] vi (happen) succedere; (turn out): it **~d** that si venne a sapere che.

**transplant** vt [træns'plɑ:nt] trapiantare // n ['trænsplɑ:nt] (MED) trapianto.

**transport** n ['trænspɔ:t] trasporto // vt [træns'pɔ:t] trasportare; **~ation** [-'teɪʃən] n (mezzo di) trasporto; (of prisoners) deportazione f; **~ café** n (Brit) trattoria per camionisti.

**trap** [træp] n (snare, trick) trappola; (carriage) calesse m // vt prendere in trappola, intrappolare; (immobilize) bloccare; (jam) chiudere, schiacciare; **~ door** n botola.

**trapeze** [trə'pi:z] n trapezio.

**trapper** ['træpə*] n cacciatore m di animali da pelliccia.

**trappings** ['træpɪŋz] npl ornamenti mpl; indoratura, sfarzo.

**trash** [træʃ] n (pej: goods) ciarpame m; (: nonsense) sciocchezze fpl; **~ can** n (US) secchio della spazzatura.

**trauma** ['trɔ:mə] n trauma m; **~tic** [-'mætɪk] a traumatico(a).

**travel** ['trævl] n viaggio; viaggi mpl // vi viaggiare; (move) andare, spostarsi // vt (distance) percorrere; **~ agency** n agenzia (di) viaggi; **~ agent** n agente m di viaggio; **~ler**, (US) **~er** n viaggiatore/trice; **~ler's cheque** n assegno turistico; **~ling**, (US) **~ing** n viaggi mpl // cpd (bag, clock) da viaggio; (expenses) di viaggio; **~ sickness** n mal m d'auto (or di mare or d'aria).

**travesty** ['trævəstɪ] n parodia.

**trawler** ['trɔ:lə*] n peschereccio (a strascico).

**tray** [treɪ] n (for carrying) vassoio; (on desk) vaschetta.

**treachery** ['trɛtʃərɪ] n tradimento.

**treacle** ['tri:kl] n melassa.

**tread** [trɛd] n passo; (sound) rumore m di passi; (of tyre) battistrada m inv // vi (pt trod, pp trodden) camminare; **to ~ on** vt fus calpestare.

**treason** ['tri:zn] n tradimento.

**treasure** ['trɛʒə*] n tesoro // vt (value) tenere in gran conto, apprezzare molto; (store) custodire gelosamente.

**treasurer** ['trɛʒərə*] n tesoriere/a.

**treasury** ['trɛʒərɪ] n tesoreria; the T~, (US) the T~ Department il ministero del Tesoro.

**treat** [tri:t] n regalo // vt trattare; (MED) curare; **to ~ sb to sth** offrire qc a qn.

**treatise** ['tri:tɪz] n trattato.

**treatment** ['tri:tmənt] n trattamento.

**treaty** ['tri:tɪ] n patto, trattato.

**treble** ['trɛbl] a triplo(a), triplice // vt triplicare // vi triplicarsi; **~ clef** n chiave f di violino.

**tree** [tri:] n albero.

**trek** [trɛk] n viaggio; camminata; (tiring walk) tirata a piedi // vi (as holiday) fare dell'escursionismo.

**trellis** ['trɛlɪs] n graticcio.

**tremble** ['trɛmbl] vi tremare; (machine) vibrare.

**tremendous** [trɪ'mɛndəs] a (enormous) enorme; (excellent) meraviglioso(a), formidabile.

**tremor** ['trɛmə*] n tremore m, tremito; (also: **earth ~**) scossa sismica.

**trench** [trɛntʃ] n trincea.

**trend** [trɛnd] n (tendency) tendenza; (of events) corso; (fashion) moda; **~y** a (idea) di moda; (clothes) all'ultima moda.

**trepidation** [trɛpɪ'deɪʃən] n trepidazione f, agitazione f.

**trespass** ['trɛspəs] vi: **to ~ on** entrare abusivamente in; *(fig)* abusare di; "no ~ing" "proprietà privata", "vietato l'accesso".

**trestle** ['tresl] *n* cavalletto; ~ **table** *n* tavolo su cavalletti.

**trial** ['traɪəl] *n* (*LAW*) processo; (*test: of machine etc*) collaudo; (*hardship*) prova, difficoltà *f inv*; (*worry*) cruccio; **by** ~ **and error** a tentoni.

**triangle** ['traɪæŋgl] *n* (*MATH, MUS*) triangolo.

**tribe** [traɪb] *n* tribù *f inv*.

**tribunal** [traɪ'bjuːnl] *n* tribunale *m*.

**tributary** ['trɪbjutəri] *n* (*river*) tributario, affluente *m*.

**tribute** ['trɪbjuːt] *n* tributo, omaggio; **to pay** ~ **to** rendere omaggio a.

**trice** [traɪs] *n*: **in a** ~ in un attimo.

**trick** [trɪk] *n* trucco; (*joke*) tiro; (*CARDS*) presa // *vt* imbrogliare, ingannare; **to play a** ~ **on sb** giocare un tiro a qn; **that should do the** ~ vedrai che funziona; ~**ery** *n* inganno.

**trickle** ['trɪkl] *n* (*of water etc*) rivolo; gocciolio // *vi* gocciolare.

**tricky** ['trɪkɪ] *a* difficile, delicato(a).

**tricycle** ['traɪsɪkl] *n* triciclo.

**trifle** ['traɪfl] *n* sciocchezza; (*Brit CULIN*) ≈ zuppa inglese // *ad*: **a** ~ **long** un po' lungo; **trifling** *a* insignificante.

**trigger** ['trɪgə*] *n* (*of gun*) grilletto; **to** ~ **off** *vt* dare l'avvio a.

**trim** [trɪm] *a* ordinato(a); (*house, garden*) ben tenuto(a); (*figure*) snello(a) // *n* (*haircut etc*) spuntata, regolata; (*embellishment*) finiture *fpl*; (*on car*) guarnizioni *fpl* // *vt* spuntare; (*decorate*): **to** ~ (**with**) decorare (con); (*NAUT: a sail*) orientare; ~**mings** *npl* decorazioni *fpl*; (*extras: gen CULIN*) guarnizione *f*.

**trinket** ['trɪŋkɪt] *n* gingillo; (*piece of jewellery*) ciondolo.

**trip** [trɪp] *n* viaggio; (*excursion*) gita, escursione *f*; (*stumble*) passo falso // *vi* inciampare; (*go lightly*) camminare con passo leggero; **on a**

~ **in viaggio; to** ~ **up** *vi* inciampare // *vt* fare lo sgambetto a.

**tripe** [traɪp] *n* (*CULIN*) trippa; (*pej: rubbish*) sciocchezze *fpl*, fesserie *fpl*.

**triple** ['trɪpl] *a* triplo(a).

**triplets** ['trɪplɪts] *npl* bambini(e) trigemini(e).

**tripod** ['traɪpɔd] *n* treppiede *m*.

**trite** [traɪt] *a* banale, trito(a).

**triumph** ['traɪʌmf] *n* trionfo // *vi*: **to** ~ (**over**) trionfare (su).

**trivia** ['trɪvɪə] *npl* banalità *fpl*.

**trivial** ['trɪvɪəl] *a* insignificante; (*commonplace*) banale.

**trod** [trɔd] *pt of* **tread**; ~**den** *pp of* **tread**.

**trolley** ['trɔlɪ] *n* carrello; ~ **bus** *n* filobus *m inv*.

**trombone** [trɔm'bəun] *n* trombone *m*.

**troop** [truːp] *n* gruppo; (*MIL*) squadrone *m*; ~**s** *npl* (*MIL*) truppe *fpl*; **to** ~ **in/out** *vi* entrare/uscire a frotte; ~**er** *n* (*MIL*) soldato di cavalleria; ~**ing the colour** *n* (*ceremony*) sfilata della bandiera.

**trophy** ['trəufɪ] *n* trofeo.

**tropic** ['trɔpɪk] *n* tropico; ~**al** *a* tropicale.

**trot** [trɔt] *n* trotto // *vi* trottare; **on the** ~ (*Brit: fig*) di fila, uno(a) dopo l'altro(a).

**trouble** ['trʌbl] *n* difficoltà *f inv*, problema *m*; difficoltà *fpl*, problemi; (*worry*) preoccupazione *f*; (*bother, effort*) sforzo; (*POL*) conflitti *mpl*, disordine *m*; (*MED*): **stomach etc** ~ disturbi *mpl* gastrici etc // *vt* disturbare; (*worry*) preoccupare // *vi*: **to** ~ **to do** disturbarsi a fare; ~**s** *npl* (*POL etc*) disordini *mpl*; **to be in** ~ avere dei problemi; **it's no** ~! di niente!; **what's the** ~? cosa c'è che non va?; ~**d** *a* (*person*) preoccupato(a), inquieto(a); (*epoch, life*) agitato(a), difficile; ~**maker** *n* elemento disturbatore, agitatore/trice; ~**shooter** *n* (*in conflict*) conciliatore *m*; ~**some** *a* fastidioso(a), seccante.

# trough 283 tuition

**trough** [trɔf] n (also: drinking ~) abbeveratoio; (also: feeding ~) trogolo, mangiatoia; (channel) canale m.

**trousers** ['trauzəz] npl pantaloni mpl, calzoni mpl; **short** ~ calzoncini mpl.

**trousseau**, pl ~x or ~s ['tru:səu, -z] n corredo da sposa.

**trout** [traut] n (pl inv) trota.

**trowel** ['trauəl] n cazzuola.

**truant** ['truənt] n: **to play** ~ (Brit) marinare la scuola.

**truce** [tru:s] n tregua.

**truck** [trʌk] n autocarro, camion m inv; (RAIL) carro merci aperto; (for luggage) carrello m portabagagli inv; ~ **driver** n camionista m/f; ~ **farm** n (US) orto industriale.

**truculent** ['trʌkjulənt] a aggressivo(a), brutale.

**trudge** [trʌdʒ] vi trascinarsi pesantemente.

**true** [tru:] a vero(a); (accurate) accurato(a), esatto(a); (genuine) reale; (faithful) fedele.

**truffle** ['trʌfl] n tartufo.

**truly** ['tru:lɪ] ad veramente; (truthfully) sinceramente; (faithfully) fedelmente.

**trump** [trʌmp] n atout m inv; ~**ed-up** n inventato(a).

**trumpet** ['trʌmpɪt] n tromba.

**truncheon** ['trʌntʃən] n sfollagente m inv.

**trundle** ['trʌndl] vt, vi: **to** ~ **along** rotolare rumorosamente.

**trunk** [trʌŋk] n (of tree, person) tronco; (of elephant) proboscide f; (case) baule m; (US AUT) bagagliaio; ~s npl (also: swimming ~s) calzoncini mpl da bagno.

**truss** [trʌs] n (MED) cinto erniario; **to** ~ **(up)** vt (CULIN) legare.

**trust** [trʌst] n fiducia; (LAW) amministrazione f fiduciaria; (COMM) trust m inv // vt (rely on) contare su; (entrust): **to** ~ **sth to sb** affidare qc a qn; ~**ed** a fidato(a); ~**ee** [trʌs'ti:] n (LAW) amministratore(trice) fiduciario(a); (of

school etc) amministratore/trice; ~**ful**, ~**ing** a fiducioso(a); ~**worthy** a fidato(a), degno(a) di fiducia.

**truth**, ~s [tru:θ, tru:ðz] n verità f inv; ~**ful** a (person) sincero(a); (description) veritiero(a), esatto(a).

**try** [traɪ] n prova, tentativo; (RUGBY) meta // vt (LAW) giudicare; (test: sth new) provare; (strain) mettere alla prova // vi provare; **to** ~ **to do** provare a fare; (seek) cercare di fare; **to** ~ **on** vt (clothes) provare; **to** ~ **out** vt provare, mettere alla prova; ~**ing** a (day, experience) logorante, pesante; (child) difficile, insopportabile.

**tsar** [za:*] n zar m inv.

**T-shirt** ['ti:ʃə:t] n maglietta.

**T-square** ['ti:skweə*] n riga a T.

**tub** [tʌb] n tinozza; mastello; (bath) bagno.

**tuba** ['tju:bə] n tuba.

**tubby** ['tʌbɪ] a grassoccio(a).

**tube** [tju:b] n tubo; (Brit: underground) metropolitana, metrò m inv; (for tyre) camera d'aria.

**tubing** ['tju:bɪŋ] n tubazione f; a piece of ~ un tubo.

**tubular** ['tju:bjulə*] a tubolare.

**TUC** n abbr (Brit: = Trades Union Congress) confederazione f dei sindacati britannici.

**tuck** [tʌk] n (SEWING) piega // vt (put) mettere; **to** ~ **away** vt riporre; **to** ~ **in** vt mettere dentro; (child) rimboccare // vi (eat) mangiare di buon appetito; abbuffarsi; **to** ~ **up** vt (child) rimboccare; ~ **shop** n negozio di pasticceria (in una scuola).

**Tuesday** ['tju:zdɪ] n martedì m inv.

**tuft** [tʌft] n ciuffo.

**tug** [tʌg] n (ship) rimorchiatore m // vt tirare con forza; ~**-of-war** n tiro alla fune.

**tuition** [tju:'ɪʃən] n (Brit) lezioni fpl; (: private ~) lezioni fpl private; (US: school fees) tasse fpl scolastiche.

**tulip** ['tju:lɪp] n tulipano.

**tumble** ['tʌmbl] n (fall) capitombolo // vi capitombolare, ruzzolare; (somersault) fare capriole; **to ~** to sth (col) realizzare qc; **~down** a cadente, diroccato(a); **~ dryer** n (Brit) asciugatrice f.

**tumbler** ['tʌmblə*] n bicchiere m (senza stelo); acrobata m/f.

**tummy** ['tʌmɪ] n (col) pancia.

**tumour**, (US) **tumor** ['tju:mə*] n tumore m.

**tuna** ['tju:nə] n (pl inv) (also: **~ fish**) tonno.

**tune** [tju:n] n (melody) melodia, aria // vt (MUS) accordare; (RADIO, TV, AUT) regolare, mettere a punto; **to be in/out of ~** (instrument) essere accordato(a)/scordato(a); (singer) essere intonato(a)/ stonato(a); **to ~ in** vi: **to ~ in** (to) (RADIO, TV) sintonizzarsi (su); **to ~ up** vi (musician) accordare lo strumento; **~ful** a melodioso(a).

**tunic** ['tju:nɪk] n tunica.

**tuning** ['tju:nɪŋ] n messa a punto; **~ fork** n diapason m inv.

**Tunisia** [tju:'nɪzɪə] n Tunisia.

**tunnel** ['tʌnl] n galleria // vi scavare una galleria.

**turban** ['tə:bən] n turbante m.

**turbot** ['tə:bət] n (pl inv) rombo gigante.

**turbulence** ['tə:bjuləns] n (AVIAT) turbolenza.

**tureen** [tə'ri:n] n zuppiera.

**turf** [tə:f] n terreno erboso; (clod) zolla // vt coprire di zolle erbose; **to ~ out** vt (col) buttar fuori.

**turgid** ['tə:dʒɪd] a (speech) ampolloso(a), pomposo(a).

**Turin** [tjuə'rɪn] n Torino f.

**Turk** [tə:k] n turco/a.

**Turkey** ['tə:kɪ] n Turchia.

**turkey** ['tə:kɪ] n tacchino.

**Turkish** ['tə:kɪʃ] a turco(a) // n (LING) turco.

**turmoil** ['tə:mɔɪl] n confusione f, tumulto.

**turn** [tə:n] n giro; (in road) curva;

(tendency: of mind, events) tendenza; (performance) numero; (MED) crisi f inv, attacco // vt girare, voltare; (milk) far andare a male; (change): **to ~ sth into** trasformare qc in // vi girare; (person: look back) girarsi, voltarsi; (reverse direction) girarsi indietro; (change) cambiare; (become) diventare; **to ~ into** trasformarsi in; **a good ~** un buon servizio; it gave me quite a ~ mi ha fatto prendere un bello spavento; "**no left ~**" (AUT) "divieto di svolta a sinistra"; **it's your ~** tocca a lei; **in ~** a sua volta; **a turno; to take ~s (at sth)** fare (qc) a turno; **to ~ away** vi girarsi (dall'altra parte); **to ~ back** vi ritornare, tornare indietro; **to ~ down** vt (refuse) rifiutare; (reduce) abbassare; (fold) ripiegare; **to ~ in** vi (col: go to bed) andare a letto // vt (fold) voltare in dentro; **to ~ off** vi (from road) girare, voltare // vt (light, radio, engine etc) spegnere; **to ~ on** vt (light, radio etc) accendere; (engine) avviare; **to ~ out** vt (light, gas) chiudere, spegnere // vi: **to ~ out to be ...** rivelarsi ..., risultare ...; **to ~ over** vi (person) girarsi // vt girare; **to ~ round** vi girare; (person) girarsi; **to ~ up** vi (person) arrivare, presentarsi; (lost object) saltar fuori // vt (collar, sound) alzare; **~ing** n (in road) curva; **~ing point** n (fig) svolta decisiva.

**turnip** ['tə:nɪp] n rapa.

**turnout** ['tə:naut] n presenza, affluenza.

**turnover** ['tə:nəuvə*] n (COMM) giro di affari.

**turnpike** ['tə:npaɪk] n (US) autostrada a pedaggio.

**turnstile** ['tə:nstaɪl] n tornella.

**turntable** ['tə:nteɪbl] n (on record player) piatto.

**turn-up** ['tə:nʌp] n (Brit: on trousers) risvolto.

**turpentine** ['tə:pəntaɪn] n (also:

turps) acqua ragia.

**turquoise** ['tɔ:kwɔɪz] n (stone) turchese m // a color turchese; di turchese.

**turret** ['tʌrɪt] n torretta.

**turtle** ['tɔ:tl] n testuggine f; **~neck (sweater)** n maglione m con il collo alto.

**tusk** [tʌsk] n zanna.

**tussle** ['tʌsl] n baruffa, mischia.

**tutor** ['tju:tə*] n (in college) docente m/f (responsabile di un gruppo di studenti); (private teacher) precettore m; **~ial** [-'tɔ:rɪəl] n (SCOL) lezione f con discussione (a un gruppo limitato).

**tuxedo** [tʌk'si:dəu] n (US) smoking m inv.

**TV** [ti:'vi:] n abbr (= television) tivù f inv.

**twang** [twæŋ] n (of instrument) suono vibrante; (of voice) accento nasale.

**tweed** [twi:d] n tweed m inv.

**tweezers** ['twi:zəz] npl pinzette fpl.

**twelfth** [twelfθ] num dodicesimo(a).

**twelve** [twelv] num dodici; at ~ (o'clock) alle dodici, a mezzogiorno; (midnight) a mezzanotte.

**twentieth** ['twentɪɪθ] num ventesimo(a).

**twenty** ['twentɪ] num venti.

**twice** [twaɪs] ad due volte; ~ as much due volte tanto.

**twiddle** ['twɪdl] vt, vi: to ~ (with) sth giocherellare con qc; to ~ one's thumbs (fig) girarsi i pollici.

**twig** [twɪg] n ramoscello // vt, vi (col) capire.

**twilight** ['twaɪlaɪt] n crepuscolo.

**twin** [twɪn] a, n gemello(a) // vt: to ~ one town with another fare il gemellaggio di una città con un'altra; **~-bedded room** n stanza con letti gemelli.

**twine** [twaɪn] n spago, cordicella // vi attorcigliarsi.

**twinge** [twɪndʒ] n (of pain) fitta; a ~ of conscience/regret un rimorso/rimpianto.

**twinkle** ['twɪŋkl] n scintillio // vi scintillare; (eyes) brillare.

**twirl** [twɔ:l] n piroetta // vt far roteare // vi roteare.

**twist** [twɪst] n torsione f; (in wire, flex) storta; (in story) colpo di scena // vt attorcigliare; (weave) intrecciare; (roll around) arrotolare; (fig) deformare // vi attorcigliarsi; arrotolarsi; (road) serpeggiare.

**twit** [twɪt] n (col) minchione/a.

**twitch** [twɪtʃ] n tiratina; (nervous) tic m inv // vi contrarsi; avere un tic.

**two** [tu:] num due; to put ~ and ~ **together** (fig) trarre le conclusioni; **~-door** a (AUT) a due porte; **~-faced** a (pej: person) falso(a); **~-fold** ad: to increase **~fold** aumentare del doppio; **~-piece (suit)** n due pezzi m inv; **~-piece (swimsuit)** n (costume m da bagno a) due pezzi m inv; **~-seater** n (plane) biposto; (car) macchina a due posti; **~some** n (people) coppia; **~-way** a (traffic) a due sensi.

**tycoon** [taɪ'ku:n] n: (business) ~ magnate m.

**type** [taɪp] n (category) genere m; (model) modello; (example) tipo; (TYP) tipo, carattere m // vt (letter etc) battere (a macchina), dattilografare; **~-cast** a (actor) a ruolo fisso; **~-face** n carattere m tipografico; **~-script** n dattiloscritto; **~-writer** n macchina da scrivere; **~-written** a dattiloscritto(a), battuto(a) a macchina.

**typhoid** ['taɪfɔɪd] n tifoidea.

**typhoon** [taɪ'fu:n] n tifone m.

**typhus** ['taɪfəs] n tifo.

**typical** ['tɪpɪkl] a tipico(a).

**typing** ['taɪpɪŋ] n dattilografia.

**typist** ['taɪpɪst] n dattilografo/a.

**tyrant** ['taɪərənt] n tiranno.

**tyre**, (US) **tire** ['taɪə*] n pneumatico, gomma; **~ pressure** n pressione f (delle gomme).

**tzar** [zɑ:*] n = **tsar**.

# U

**U-bend** ['ju:'bend] $n$ (*in pipe*) sifone $m$.

**udder** ['ʌdə*] $n$ mammella.

**UFO** ['ju:fəu] $n$ *abbr* (= *unidentified flying object*) UFO $m$ *inv*.

**ugh** [ə:h] *excl* puah!

**ugly** ['ʌglɪ] $a$ brutto(a).

**UK** $n$ *abbr* = **United Kingdom**.

**ulcer** ['ʌlsə*] $n$ ulcera; (*also*: mouth ~) afta.

**Ulster** ['ʌlstə*] $n$ Ulster $m$.

**ulterior** [ʌl'tɪərɪə*] $a$ ulteriore; ~ **motive** $n$ secondo fine $m$.

**ultimate** ['ʌltɪmət] $a$ ultimo(a), finale; (*authority*) massimo(a), supremo(a); ~**ly** $ad$ alla fine; in definitiva, in fin dei conti.

**ultrasound** ['ʌltrə'saund] $n$ (*MED*) ultrasuono.

**umbilical cord** [ʌmbɪ'laɪkl-] $n$ cordone $m$ ombelicale.

**umbrage** ['ʌmbrɪdʒ] $n$: **to take** ~ offendersi, impermalirsi.

**umbrella** [ʌm'brɛlə] $n$ ombrello.

**umpire** ['ʌmpaɪə*] $n$ arbitro.

**umpteen** ['ʌmp'ti:n] $a$ non so quanti(e); **for the** ~**th time** per l'ennesima volta.

**UN, UNO** $n$ *abbr* = **United Nations (Organization)**.

**unable** [ʌn'eɪbl] $a$: **to be** ~ **to** non potere, essere nell'impossibilità di; essere incapace di.

**unaccompanied** [ʌnə'kʌmpənɪd] $a$ (*child, lady*) non accompagnato(a).

**unaccountably** [ʌnə'kauntəblɪ] $ad$ inesplicabilmente.

**unaccustomed** [ʌnə'kʌstəmd] $a$ insolito(a); **to be** ~ **to** sth non essere abituato a qc.

**unanimous** [ju:'nænɪməs] $a$ unanime; ~**ly** $ad$ all'unanimità.

**unarmed** [ʌn'ɑ:md] $a$ (*without a weapon*) disarmato(a); (*combat*) senz'armi.

**unassuming** [ʌnə'sju:mɪŋ] $a$ mode-

sto(a), senza pretese.

**unattached** [ʌnə'tætʃt] $a$ senza legami, libero(a).

**unattended** [ʌnə'tɛndɪd] $a$ (*car, child, luggage*) incustodito(a).

**unauthorized** [ʌn'ɔ:θəraɪzd] $a$ non autorizzato(a).

**unavoidable** [ʌnə'vɔɪdəbl] $a$ inevitabile.

**unaware** [ʌnə'wɛə*] $a$: **to be** ~ **of** non sapere, ignorare; ~**s** $ad$ di sorpresa, alla sprovvista.

**unbalanced** [ʌn'bælənst] $a$ squilibrato(a).

**unbearable** [ʌn'bɛərəbl] $a$ insopportabile.

**unbeknown(st)** [ʌnbɪ'nəun(st)] $ad$: ~ **to** all'insaputa di.

**unbelievable** [ʌnbɪ'li:vəbl] $a$ incredibile.

**unbend** [ʌn'bɛnd] $vb$ (*irg*) $vi$ distendersi // $vt$ (*wire*) raddrizzare.

**unbias(s)ed** [ʌn'baɪəst] $a$ (*person, report*) obiettivo(a), imparziale.

**unborn** [ʌn'bɔ:n] $a$ non ancora nato(a).

**unbreakable** [ʌn'breɪkəbl] $a$ infrangibile.

**unbroken** [ʌn'brəukən] $a$ intero(a); continuo(a).

**unbutton** [ʌn'bʌtn] $vt$ sbottonare.

**uncalled-for** [ʌn'kɔ:ldfɔ:*] $a$ (*remark*) fuori luogo *inv*; (*action*) ingiustificato(a).

**uncanny** [ʌn'kænɪ] $a$ misterioso(a), strano(a).

**unceasing** [ʌn'si:sɪŋ] $a$ incessante.

**unceremonious** ['ʌnsɛrɪ'məunɪəs] $a$ (*abrupt, rude*) senza tante cerimonie.

**uncertain** [ʌn'sə:tn] $a$ incerto(a); dubbio(a); ~**ty** $n$ incertezza.

**unchecked** [ʌn'tʃɛkt] $a$ incontrollato(a).

**uncivilized** [ʌn'sɪvɪlaɪzd] $a$ (*gen*) selvaggio(a); (*fig*) incivile, barbaro(a).

**uncle** ['ʌŋkl] $n$ zio.

**uncomfortable** [ʌn'kʌmfətəbl] $a$ scomodo(a); (*uneasy*) a disagio, agitato(a); fastidioso(a).

**uncommon** [ʌn'kɔmən] a raro(a), insolito(a), non comune.

**uncompromising** [ʌn'kɔmprə-maizɪŋ] a intransigente, inflessibile.

**unconcerned** [ʌnkən'sə:nd] a: to be ~ (about) non preoccuparsi (di or per).

**unconditional** [ʌnkən'dɪʃənl] a incondizionato(a), senza condizioni.

**unconscious** [ʌn'kɔnʃəs] a privo(a) di sensi, svenuto(a); (unaware) inconsapevole, inconscio(a) // n: the ~ l'inconscio; ~ly ad inconsciamente.

**uncontrollable** [ʌnkən'trəuləbl] a incontrollabile; indisciplinato(a).

**unconventional** [ʌnkən'venʃənl] a poco convenzionale.

**uncouth** [ʌn'ku:θ] a maleducato(a), grossolano(a).

**uncover** [ʌn'kʌvə*] vt scoprire.

**undecided** [ʌndɪ'saɪdɪd] a indeciso(a).

**under** ['ʌndə*] prep sotto; (less than) meno di; al disotto di; (according to) secondo, in conformità a // ad (al) disotto; from ~ sth da sotto a or dal disotto di qc; ~ there là sotto; ~ repair in riparazione.

**under...** ['ʌndə*] prefix sotto..., sub...; ~ age a minorenne; ~carriage n (Brit) carrello (d'atterraggio); ~charge vt far pagare di meno a; ~coat n (paint) mano f di fondo; ~cover a segreto(a), clandestino(a); ~current n corrente f sottomarina; ~cut vt irg vendere a prezzo minore di; ~developed a sottosviluppato(a); ~dog n oppresso(a); ~done a (CULIN) al sangue; (pej) poco cotto(a); ~estimate vt sottovalutare; ~fed a denutrito(a); ~foot ad sotto i piedi; ~go vt irg subire; (treatment) sottoporsi a; ~graduate n studente(essa) universitario(a); ~ground n (Brit: railway) metropolitana; (POL) movimento clandestino // a sotterraneo(a); (fig) clandestino(a); ~growth n sottobo-

sco; ~hand(ed) a (fig) furtivo(a), subdolo(a); ~lie vt irg essere alla base di; ~line vt sottolineare; ~ling ['ʌndəlɪŋ] n (pej) subalterno/a, tirapiedi m/f inv; ~mine vt minare; ~neath [ʌndə'ni:θ] ad sotto, disotto // prep sotto, al di sotto di; ~paid a mal pagato(a); ~pants npl mutande fpl, slip m inv; ~pass n (Brit) sottopassaggio; ~privileged a non abbiente; meno favorito(a); ~rate vt sottovalutare; ~shirt n (US) maglietta; ~shorts npl (US) mutande fpl, slip m inv; ~side n disotto; ~skirt n (Brit) sottoveste f.

**understand** [ʌndə'stænd] vb (irg: like stand) vt, vi capire, comprendere; I ~ that ... sento che ...; credo di capire che ...; ~able a comprensibile; ~ing a comprensivo(a) // n comprensione f; (agreement) accordo.

**understatement** [ʌndə'steɪtmənt] n: that's an ~! a dire poco!

**understood** [ʌndə'stud] pt, pp of understand // a inteso(a); (implied) sottinteso(a).

**understudy** ['ʌndəstʌdɪ] n sostituto/a, attore/trice supplente.

**undertake** [ʌndə'teɪk] vt irg intraprendere; to ~ to do sth impegnarsi a fare qc.

**undertaker** ['ʌndəteɪkə*] n impresario di pompe funebri.

**undertaking** [ʌndə'teɪkɪŋ] n impresa; (promise) promessa.

**undertone** ['ʌndətəun] n: in an ~ a mezza voce, a voce bassa.

**underwater** [ʌndə'wɔ:tə*] ad sott'acqua // a subacqueo(a).

**underwear** ['ʌndəweə*] n biancheria intima.

**underworld** ['ʌndəwə:ld] n (of crime) malavita.

**underwriter** ['ʌndəraɪtə*] n (INSURANCE) sottoscrittore/trice.

**undies** ['ʌndɪz] npl (col) robina, biancheria intima da donna.

**undo** [ʌn'du:] vt irg disfare; ~ing n rovina, perdita.

**undoubted** [ʌn'daʊtɪd] a sicuro(a), certo(a); ~ly ad senza alcun dubbio.

**undress** [ʌn'dres] vi spogliarsi.

**undue** [ʌn'dju:] a eccessivo(a).

**undulating** ['ʌndjuleɪtɪŋ] a ondeggiante; ondulato(a).

**unduly** [ʌn'dju:lɪ] ad eccessivamente.

**unearth** [ʌn'ə:θ] vt dissotterrare; (fig) scoprire.

**unearthly** [ʌn'ə:θlɪ] a soprannaturale; (hour) impossibile.

**uneasy** [ʌn'i:zɪ] a a disagio; (worried) preoccupato(a).

**unemployed** [ʌnɪm'plɔɪd] a disoccupato(a) // npl: the ~ i disoccupati.

**unemployment** [ʌnɪm'plɔɪmənt] n disoccupazione f.

**unending** [ʌn'endɪŋ] a senza fine.

**unerring** [ʌn'ə:rɪŋ] a infallibile.

**uneven** [ʌn'i:vn] a ineguale; irregolare.

**unexpected** [ʌnɪk'spektɪd] a inatteso(a), imprevisto(a); ~ly ad inaspettatamente.

**unfailing** [ʌn'feɪlɪŋ] a (supply, energy) inesauribile; (remedy) infallibile.

**unfair** [ʌn'fɛə*] a: ~ (to) ingiusto(a) (nei confronti di).

**unfaithful** [ʌn'feɪθful] a infedele.

**unfamiliar** [ʌnfə'mɪlɪə*] a sconosciuto(a), strano(a).

**unfashionable** [ʌn'fæʃnəbl] a (clothes) fuori moda; (district) non alla moda.

**unfasten** [ʌn'fɑ:sn] vt slacciare; sciogliere.

**unfavourable,** (US) **unfavorable** [ʌn'feɪvərəbl] a sfavorevole.

**unfeeling** [ʌn'fi:lɪŋ] a insensibile, duro(a).

**unfit** [ʌn'fɪt] a inadatto(a); (ill) malato(a), in cattiva salute; (incompetent): ~ (for) incompetente (in); (: work, MIL) inabile (a).

**unfold** [ʌn'fəʊld] vt spiegare; (fig) rivelare // vi (view, countryside) distendersi; (story, plot) svelarsi.

**unforeseen** ['ʌnfɔ:'si:n] a imprevisto(a).

**unforgettable** [ʌnfə'getəbl] a indimenticabile.

**unfortunate** [ʌn'fɔ:tʃnət] a sfortunato(a); (event, remark) infelice; ~ly ad sfortunatamente, purtroppo.

**unfounded** [ʌn'faʊndɪd] a infondato(a).

**unfriendly** [ʌn'frendlɪ] a poco amichevole, freddo(a).

**ungainly** [ʌn'geɪnlɪ] a goffo(a), impacciato(a).

**ungodly** [ʌn'gɔdlɪ] a empio(a); at an ~ hour a un'ora impossibile.

**ungrateful** [ʌn'greɪtful] a ingrato(a).

**unhappiness** [ʌn'hæpɪnɪs] n infelicità.

**unhappy** [ʌn'hæpɪ] a infelice; ~ with (arrangements etc) insoddisfatto(a) di.

**unharmed** [ʌn'hɑ:md] a incolume, sano(a) e salvo(a).

**unhealthy** [ʌn'helθɪ] a (gen) malsano(a); (person) malaticcio(a).

**unheard-of** [ʌn'hə:dɔv] a inaudito(a), senza precedenti.

**uniform** ['ju:nɪfɔ:m] n uniforme f, divisa // a uniforme.

**uninhabited** [ʌnɪn'hæbɪtɪd] a disabitato(a).

**union** ['ju:njən] n unione f; (also: trade ~) sindacato // cpd sindacale, dei sindacati; U~ Jack n bandiera nazionale britannica.

**unique** [ju:'ni:k] a unico(a).

**unit** ['ju:nɪt] n unità f inv; (section: of furniture etc) elemento; (team, squad) reparto, squadra.

**unite** [ju:'naɪt] vt unire // vi unirsi; ~d a unito(a); unificato(a); (efforts) congiunto(a); U~d Kingdom (UK) n Regno Unito; U~d Nations (Organization) (UN, UNO) n (Organizzazione f delle) Nazioni Unite (O.N.U.); U~d States of America (US, USA) n Stati mpl Uniti (d'America) (USA).

**unit trust** n (Brit) fondo d'investimento.

**unity** [ˈjuːnɪtɪ] n unità.

**universal** [juːnɪˈvɜːsl] a universale.

**universe** [ˈjuːnɪvɜːs] n universo.

**university** [juːnɪˈvɜːsɪtɪ] n università f inv.

**unjust** [ʌnˈdʒʌst] a ingiusto(a).

**unkempt** [ʌnˈkempt] a trasandato(a); spettinato(a).

**unkind** [ʌnˈkaɪnd] a scortese; crudele.

**unknown** [ʌnˈnəʊn] a sconosciuto(a).

**unlawful** [ʌnˈlɔːful] a illecito(a), illegale.

**unleash** [ʌnˈliːʃ] vt sguinzagliare; (fig) scatenare.

**unless** [ʌnˈles] cj a meno che (non) + sub; ~ otherwise stated salvo indicazione contraria.

**unlike** [ʌnˈlaɪk] a diverso(a) // prep a differenza di, contrariamente a.

**unlikely** [ʌnˈlaɪklɪ] a improbabile; inverosimile.

**unlisted** [ʌnˈlɪstɪd] a (US TEL): to be ~ non essere sull'elenco.

**unload** [ʌnˈləʊd] vt scaricare.

**unlock** [ʌnˈlɔk] vt aprire.

**unlucky** [ʌnˈlʌkɪ] a sfortunato(a); (object, number) che porta sfortuna, di malaugurio; to be ~ essere sfortunato, non avere fortuna.

**unmarried** [ʌnˈmærɪd] a non sposato(a); (man only) scapolo, celibe; (woman only) nubile.

**unmistakable** [ʌnmɪsˈteɪkəbl] a indubbio(a); facilmente riconoscibile.

**unmitigated** [ʌnˈmɪtɪgeɪtɪd] a non mitigato(a), assoluto(a), vero(a) e proprio(a).

**unnatural** [ʌnˈnætʃrəl] a innaturale; contro natura.

**unnecessary** [ʌnˈnesəsərɪ] a inutile, superfluo(a).

**unnoticed** [ʌnˈnəʊtɪst] a: (to go) ~ (passare) inosservato(a).

**UNO** [ˈjuːnəʊ] n abbr = United Nations Organization.

**unobtainable** [ʌnəbˈteɪnəbl] a (TEL) non ottenibile.

**unobtrusive** [ʌnəbˈtruːsɪv] a di-

screto(a).

**unofficial** [ʌnəˈfɪʃl] a non ufficiale; (strike) non dichiarato(a) dal sindacato.

**unpack** [ʌnˈpæk] vi disfare la valigia (or le valigie).

**unpalatable** [ʌnˈpælətəbl] a (truth) sgradevole.

**unparalleled** [ʌnˈpærəleld] a incomparabile, impareggiabile.

**unpleasant** [ʌnˈpleznt] a spiacevole.

**unplug** [ʌnˈplʌg] vt staccare.

**unpopular** [ʌnˈpɔpjulə*] a impopolare.

**unprecedented** [ʌnˈpresɪdəntɪd] a senza precedenti.

**unpredictable** [ʌnprɪˈdɪktəbl] a imprevedibile.

**unprofessional** [ʌnprəˈfeʃənl] a: ~ conduct scorrettezza professionale.

**unqualified** [ʌnˈkwɔlɪfaɪd] a (teacher) non abilitato(a); (success) assoluto(a), senza riserve.

**unquestionably** [ʌnˈkwestʃənəblɪ] ad indiscutibilmente.

**unravel** [ʌnˈrævl] vt dipanare, districare.

**unreal** [ʌnˈrɪəl] a irreale.

**unrealistic** [ʌnrɪəˈlɪstɪk] a (idea) illusorio(a); (estimate) non realistico(a).

**unreasonable** [ʌnˈriːznəbl] a irragionevole.

**unrelated** [ʌnrɪˈleɪtɪd] a: ~ (to) senza rapporto (con); non imparentato(a) (con).

**unreliable** [ʌnrɪˈlaɪəbl] a (person, machine) che non dà affidamento; (news, source of information) inattendibile.

**unremitting** [ʌnrɪˈmɪtɪŋ] a incessante.

**unreservedly** [ʌnrɪˈzɜːvɪdlɪ] ad senza riserve.

**unrest** [ʌnˈrest] n agitazione f.

**unroll** [ʌnˈrəʊl] vt srotolare.

**unruly** [ʌnˈruːlɪ] a indisciplinato(a).

**unsafe** [ʌnˈseɪf] a pericoloso(a), rischioso(a).

**unsaid** [ʌnˈsed] a: to leave sth ~

passare qc sotto silenzio.

**unsatisfactory** [ˌʌnsætɪsˈfæktərɪ] a che lascia a desiderare, insufficiente.

**unsavoury**, (US) **unsavory** [ʌnˈseɪvərɪ] a (fig: person) losco(a); (: reputation, subject) disgustoso(a), ripugnante.

**unscathed** [ʌnˈskeɪðd] a incolume.

**unscrew** [ʌnˈskruː] vt svitare.

**unscrupulous** [ʌnˈskruːpjuləs] a senza scrupoli.

**unsettled** [ʌnˈsetld] a turbato(a); instabile; indeciso(a).

**unshaven** [ʌnˈʃeɪvn] a non rasato(a).

**unsightly** [ʌnˈsaɪtlɪ] a brutto(a), sgradevole a vedersi.

**unskilled** [ʌnˈskɪld] a: ~ worker manovale m.

**unspeakable** [ʌnˈspiːkəbl] a (awful) abominevole.

**unstable** [ʌnˈsteɪbl] a (gen) instabile; (mentally) squilibrato(a).

**unsteady** [ʌnˈstedɪ] a instabile, malsicuro(a).

**unstuck** [ʌnˈstʌk] a: to come ~ scollarsi; (fig) fare fiasco.

**unsuccessful** [ˌʌnsəkˈsesful] a (writer, proposal) che non ha successo; (marriage, attempt) mal riuscito(a), fallito(a); to be ~ (in attempting sth) non riuscire; (in attempting sth) non riuscire; (application) non essere considerato(a).

**unsuitable** [ʌnˈsuːtəbl] a inadatto(a); inopportuno(a); sconveniente.

**unsure** [ʌnˈʃuə*] a incerto(a); to be ~ of o.s. essere insicuro(a).

**unsympathetic** [ˌʌnsɪmpəˈθetɪk] a (person) antipatico(a); (attitude) poco incoraggiante.

**untapped** [ʌnˈtæpt] a (resources) non sfruttato(a).

**unthinkable** [ʌnˈθɪŋkəbl] a impensabile, inconcepibile.

**untidy** [ʌnˈtaɪdɪ] a (room) in disordine; (appearance, work) trascurato(a); (person, writing) disordinato(a).

**untie** [ʌnˈtaɪ] vt (knot, parcel) disfare; (prisoner, dog) slegare.

**until** [ʌnˈtɪl] prep fino a; (after negative) prima di // cj finché, fino a quando; (in past, after negative) prima che + sub, prima di + infinitive; ~ now finora; ~ then fino ad allora.

**untimely** [ʌnˈtaɪmlɪ] a intempestivo(a), inopportuno(a); (death) prematuro(a).

**untold** [ʌnˈtəuld] a incalcolabile, indescrivibile.

**untoward** [ˌʌntəˈwɔːd] a sfortunato(a), sconveniente.

**untranslatable** [ˌʌntrænzˈleɪtəbl] a intraducibile.

**unused** [ʌnˈjuːzd] a nuovo(a).

**unusual** [ʌnˈjuːʒuəl] a insolito(a), eccezionale, raro(a).

**unveil** [ʌnˈveɪl] vt scoprire; svelare.

**unwavering** [ʌnˈweɪvərɪŋ] a fermo(a), incrollabile.

**unwelcome** [ʌnˈwelkəm] a non gradito(a).

**unwell** [ʌnˈwel] a indisposto(a); to feel ~ non sentirsi bene.

**unwieldy** [ʌnˈwiːldɪ] a poco maneggevole.

**unwilling** [ʌnˈwɪlɪŋ] a: to be ~ to do non voler fare; ~ly ad malvolentieri.

**unwind** [ʌnˈwaɪnd] vb (irg) vt svolgere, srotolare // vi (relax) rilassarsi.

**unwise** [ʌnˈwaɪz] a poco saggio(a); (decision) avventato(a).

**unwitting** [ʌnˈwɪtɪŋ] a involontario(a).

**unworkable** [ʌnˈwɔːkəbl] a (plan) inattuabile.

**unworthy** [ʌnˈwɔːðɪ] a indegno(a).

**unwrap** [ʌnˈræp] vt disfare; aprire.

**unwritten** [ʌnˈrɪtn] a (agreement) tacito(a); (law) non scritto(a).

┌─────────────┐
│ KEYWORD │
└─────────────┘

**up** [ʌp] ◆ prep: he went ~ the stairs/the hill è salito su per le scale/sulla collina; the cat was ~ a tree il gatto era su un albero; **they live further ~ the street** vivono un po' più su nella stessa strada

◆ **ad 1** (*upwards, higher*) su, in alto; ~ **in the sky/the mountains** su nel cielo/in montagna; ~ **there** lassù; ~ **above** su in alto

**2: to be ~** (*out of bed*) essere alzato(a); ~ (*prices, level*) essere salito(a)

**3:** ~ **to** (*as far as*) fino a; ~ **to now** finora

**4: to be ~ to** (*depending on*): **it's ~ to you** sta a lei, dipende da lei; (*equal to*): **he's not ~ to it** (*job, task etc*) non ne è all'altezza; (*col: be doing*): **what is he ~ to?** cosa sta combinando?

◆ **n:** **~s and downs** alti e bassi *mpl*.

**up-and-coming** [ʌpənd'kʌmɪŋ] *a* pieno(a) di promesse, promettente.

**upbringing** ['ʌpbrɪŋɪŋ] *n* educazione *f*.

**update** [ʌp'deɪt] *vt* aggiornare.

**upheaval** [ʌp'hi:vl] *n* sconvolgimento; tumulto.

**uphill** [ʌp'hɪl] *a* in salita; (*fig: task*) difficile // *ad*: **to go ~** andare in salita, salire.

**uphold** [ʌp'həuld] *vt irg* approvare; sostenere.

**upholstery** [ʌp'həulstərɪ] *n* tappezzeria.

**upkeep** ['ʌpkiːp] *n* manutenzione *f*.

**upon** [ə'pɔn] *prep* su.

**upper** ['ʌpə*] *a* superiore // *n* (*of shoe*) tomaia; **~-class** *a* dell'alta borghesia; ~ **hand** *n*: **to have the ~ hand** avere il coltello dalla parte del manico; **~most** *a* il(la) più alto(a); predominante.

**upright** ['ʌpraɪt] *a* diritto(a); verticale; (*fig*) diritto(a), onesto(a) // *n* montante m.

**uprising** ['ʌpraɪzɪŋ] *n* insurrezione *f*, rivolta.

**uproar** ['ʌprɔ:*] *n* tumulto, clamore *m*.

**uproot** [ʌp'ru:t] *vt* sradicare.

**upset** *n* ['ʌpset] turbamento // *a* [ʌp'set] (*irg: like* set) (*glass etc*) rovesciare; (*plan, stomach*) scombussolare; (*person: offend*) contrariare; (: *grieve*) addolorare; sconvolgere // *a* [ʌp'set] contrariato(a); addolorato(a); (*stomach*) scombussolato(a), disturbato(a).

**upshot** ['ʌpʃɔt] *n* risultato.

**upside-down** ['ʌpsaɪd'daun] *ad* sottosopra.

**upstairs** [ʌp'stɛəz] *ad*, *a* di sopra, al piano superiore.

**upstart** ['ʌpstɑ:t] *n* parvenu m *inv*.

**upstream** [ʌp'stri:m] *ad* a monte.

**uptake** ['ʌptɛik] *n*: **he is quick/slow on the ~** è pronto/lento di comprendonio.

**uptight** [ʌp'taɪt] *a* (*col*) teso(a).

**up-to-date** ['ʌptə'deɪt] *a* moderno(a); aggiornato(a).

**upturn** ['ʌptə:n] *n* (*in luck*) svolta favorevole; (*COMM: in market*) rialzo.

**upward** ['ʌpwəd] *a* ascendente; verso l'alto; **~(s)** *ad* in su, verso l'alto.

**urban** ['ə:bən] *a* urbano(a).

**urbane** [ə:'beɪn] *a* civile, urbano(a), educato(a).

**urchin** ['ə:tʃɪn] *n* monello.

**urge** [ə:dʒ] *n* impulso; stimolo; forte desiderio // *vt*: **to ~ sb to do sth** esortare qn a fare, spingere qn a fare; raccomandare a qn di fare.

**urgency** ['ə:dʒənsɪ] *n* urgenza; (*of tone*) insistenza.

**urgent** ['ə:dʒənt] *a* urgente.

**urinate** ['juərineɪt] *vi* orinare.

**urine** ['juərɪn] *n* orina.

**urn** [ə:n] *n* urna; (*also:* **tea ~**) bollitore m per il tè.

**US, USA** *n abbr* = **United States (of America)**.

**us** [ʌs] *pronoun* ci; (*stressed, after prep*) noi; *see also* **me**.

**usage** ['ju:zɪdʒ] *n* uso.

**use** *n* [ju:s] uso; impiego, utilizzazione *f* // *vt* [ju:z] usare, utilizzare, servirsi di; **she** ~**d** to do it lo faceva (una volta), era solita farlo; **in** ~ in uso; **out of** ~ fuori uso; **to be of** ~ essere utile, servire; **it's no** ~ non serve, è inutile; **to be** ~**d to** avere l'abitudine di; **to** ~ **up** vt consumare; esaurire; ~**d** a (car) d'occasione; (re) a utile; ~**fulness** n utilità; ~**less** a inutile; ~**r** n utente m/f; ~**r-friendly** a (computer) di facile uso.

**usher** ['ʌʃə*] n usciere m; (in cinema) maschera; ~**ette** [-'rɛt] n (in cinema) maschera.

**USSR** n: **the** ~ l'URSS f.

**usual** ['juːʒuəl] a solito(a); **as** ~ come al solito, come d'abitudine; ~**ly** ad di solito.

**utensil** [juːˈtɛnsl] n utensile m; **kitchen** ~**s** utensili da cucina.

**uterus** ['juːtərəs] n utero.

**utility** [juːˈtɪlɪtɪ] n utilità; (also: public ~) servizio pubblico; ~ **room** n locale adibito alla stiratura dei panni etc.

**utmost** ['ʌtməust] a estremo(a) // n: **to do one's** ~ fare il possibile or di tutto.

**utter** ['ʌtə*] a assoluto(a), totale // vt pronunciare, proferire; emettere; ~**ance** n espressione f; parole fpl; ~**ly** ad completamente, del tutto.

**U-turn** ['juːˈtəːn] n inversione f a U.

## V

**v.** abbr = **verse, versus, volt;** (= vide) vedi, vedere.

**vacancy** ['veɪkənsɪ] n (Brit: job) posto libero; (room) stanza libera.

**vacant** ['veɪkənt] a (job, seat etc) libero(a); (expression) assente; ~ **lot** n (US) terreno non occupato; (: for sale) terreno in vendita.

**vacate** [vəˈkeɪt] vt lasciare libero(a).

**vacation** [vəˈkeɪʃən] n vacanze fpl.

**vaccinate** ['væksɪneɪt] vt vaccinare.

**vacuum** ['vækjum] n vuoto; ~ **bottle** n (US) = ~ **flask;** ~-

**cleaner** n aspirapolvere m inv; ~ **flask** n (Brit) thermos m inv ®; ~-**packed** a confezionato(a) sottovuoto.

**vagina** [vəˈdʒaɪnə] n vagina.

**vagrant** ['veɪɡrnt] n vagabondo/a.

**vague** [veɪɡ] a vago(a); (blurred: photo, memory) sfocato(a); ~**ly** ad vagamente.

**vain** [veɪn] a (useless) inutile, vano(a); (conceited) vanitoso(a); in ~ inutilmente, invano.

**valentine** ['væləntaɪn] n (also: ~ card) cartolina or biglietto di San Valentino.

**valet** ['væleɪ] n cameriere m personale.

**valiant** ['væliənt] a valoroso(a), coraggioso(a).

**valid** ['vælɪd] a valido(a), valevole; (excuse) valido(a).

**valley** ['vælɪ] n valle f.

**valour,** (US) **valor** ['vælə*] n valore m.

**valuable** ['væljuəbl] a (jewel) di (grande) valore; (time) prezioso(a); ~**s** npl oggetti mpl di valore.

**valuation** [væljuˈeɪʃən] n valutazione f, stima.

**value** ['væljuː] n valore m // vt (fix price) valutare, dare un prezzo a; (cherish) apprezzare, tenere a; ~ **added tax (VAT)** n (Brit) imposta sul valore aggiunto (I.V.A.); ~**d** a (appreciated) stimato(a), apprezzato(a).

**valve** [vælv] n valvola.

**van** [væn] n (AUT) furgone m; (Brit RAIL) vagone m.

**vandal** ['vændl] n vandalo/a; ~**ism** n vandalismo.

**vanilla** [vəˈnɪlə] n vaniglia // cpd (ice cream) alla vaniglia.

**vanish** ['vænɪʃ] vi svanire, scomparire.

**vanity** ['vænɪtɪ] n vanità; ~ **case** n valigetta per cosmetici.

**vantage** ['vɑːntɪdʒ] n: ~ **point** posizione f or punto di osservazione; (fig) posizione vantaggiosa.

**vapour,** (US) **vapor** ['veɪpə*] n

vapore m.

**variable** ['vɛəriəbl] a variabile; (mood) mutevole.

**variance** ['vɛəriəns] n: to be at ~ (with) essere in disaccordo (con); (facts) essere in contraddizione (con).

**varicose** ['værikəus] a: ~ veins varici fpl.

**varied** ['vɛərid] a vario(a), diverso(a).

**variety** [və'raiəti] n varietà f inv; (quantity) quantità, numero; ~ show n varietà m inv.

**various** ['vɛəriəs] a vario(a), diverso(a); (several) parecchie(i), molti(e).

**varnish** ['vɑ:niʃ] n vernice f // vt verniciare.

**vary** ['vɛəri] vt, vi variare, mutare.

**vase** [vɑ:z] n vaso.

**vaseline** ['væsili:n] n ® vaselina.

**vast** [vɑ:st] a vasto(a); (amount, success) enorme; ~ly ad enormemente.

**VAT** [væt] n abbr = value added tax.

**vat** [væt] n tino.

**Vatican** ['vætikən] n: the ~ il Vaticano.

**vault** [vɔ:lt] n (of roof) volta; (tomb) tomba; (in bank) camera blindata; (jump) salto // vt (also: ~ over) saltare (d'un balzo).

**vaunted** ['vɔ:ntid] a: much-~ tanto celebrato(a).

**VCR** n abbr = video cassette recorder.

**VD** n abbr = venereal disease.

**VDU** n abbr = visual display unit.

**veal** [vi:l] n vitello.

**veer** [viə*] vi girare; virare.

**vegetable** ['vɛdʒtəbl] n verdura, ortaggio // a vegetale.

**vegetarian** ['vɛdʒi'tɛəriən] a, n vegetariano(a).

**vehement** ['vi:imənt] a veemente, violento(a).

**vehicle** ['vi:ikl] n veicolo.

**veil** [veil] n velo // vt velare.

**vein** [vein] n vena; (on leaf) nervatura; (fig: mood) vena, umore m.

**velvet** ['vɛlvit] n velluto.

**vending machine** ['vɛndiŋ-] n distributore m automatico.

**veneer** [və'niə*] n impiallacciatura; (fig) vernice f.

**venereal** [vi'niəriəl] a: ~ disease (VD) malattia venerea.

**Venetian** [vi'ni:ʃən] a veneziano(a); ~ blind n (tenda alla) veneziana.

**vengeance** ['vɛndʒəns] n vendetta; with a ~ (fig) davvero; furiosamente.

**Venice** ['vɛnis] n Venezia.

**venison** ['vɛnisn] n carne f di cervo.

**venom** ['vɛnəm] n veleno.

**vent** [vɛnt] n foro, apertura; (in dress, jacket) spacco // vt (fig: one's feelings) sfogare, dare sfogo a.

**ventilate** ['vɛntileit] vt (room) dare aria a, arieggiare; **ventilator** n ventilatore m.

**ventriloquist** [vɛn'triləkwist] n ventriloquo/a.

**venture** ['vɛntʃə*] n impresa (rischiosa) // vt rischiare, azzardare // vi arrischiarsi, azzardarsi.

**venue** ['vɛnju:] n luogo di incontro; (SPORT) luogo (designato) per l'incontro.

**verb** [və:b] n verbo; ~al a verbale; (translation) letterale.

**verbatim** [və:'beitim] a, ad parola per parola.

**verdict** ['və:dikt] n verdetto.

**verge** [və:dʒ] n (Brit) bordo, orlo; on the ~ of doing sul punto di fare; to ~ on vi fus rasentare.

**verification** [vɛrifi'keiʃən] n verifica.

**veritable** ['vɛritəbl] a vero(a).

**vermin** ['və:min] npl animali mpl nocivi; (insects) insetti mpl parassiti.

**vermouth** ['və:məθ] n vermut m inv.

**versatile** ['və:sətail] a (person) versatile; (machine, tool etc) (che si presta a molti usi.

**verse** [və:s] n versi mpl; (stanza)

stanza, strofa; (in bible) versetto.
**version** ['vɜːʃən] n versione f.
**versus** ['vɜːsəs] prep contro.
**vertical** ['vɜːtɪkl] a, n verticale (m);
~**ly** ad verticalmente.
**vertigo** ['vɜːtɪgəu] n vertigine f.
**verve** [vɜːv] n brio; entusiasmo.
**very** ['vɛrɪ] ad molto // a: the ~ book
which proprio il libro che; at the ~
end proprio alla fine; the ~ last
proprio l'ultimo; at the ~ least
almeno; ~ **much** moltissimo.
**vessel** ['vɛsl] n (ANAT) vaso;
(NAUT) nave f; (container)
recipiente m.
**vest** [vɛst] n (Brit) maglia; (:
sleeveless) canottiera; (US:
waistcoat) gilè m inv; ~**ed inter-
ests** npl (COMM) diritti mpl
acquisiti.
**vestment** ['vɛstmənt] n (REL)
paramento liturgico.
**vestry** ['vɛstrɪ] n sagrestia.
**vet** [vɛt] n abbr (= veterinary
surgeon) veterinario // vt esaminare
minuziosamente; (text) rivedere.
**veteran** ['vɛtərn] n veterano; (also:
war ~) reduce m.
**veterinary** ['vɛtrɪnərɪ] a
veterinario(a); ~ **surgeon**, (US)
**veterinarian** n veterinario.
**veto** ['viːtəu] n, pl ~**es** veto // vt
opporre il veto a.
**vex** [vɛks] vt irritare, contrariare;
~**ed** a (question) controverso(a),
dibattuto(a).
**VHF** abbr (= very high frequency)
VHF, altissima frequenza.
**via** ['vaɪə] prep (by way of) via; (by
means of) tramite.
**viable** ['vaɪəbl] a attuabile; vitale.
**viaduct** ['vaɪədʌkt] n viadotto.
**vibrate** [vaɪ'breɪt] vi: to ~ (with)
vibrare di; (resound) risonare di.
**vicar** ['vɪkə*] n pastore m; ~**age** n
presbiterio.
**vicarious** [vɪ'kɛərɪəs] a indiretto(a).
**vice** [vaɪs] n (evil) vizio; (TECH)
morsa.
**vice-** [vaɪs] prefix vice....

**vice squad** n (squadra del) buon costume f.
**vice versa** ['vaɪsɪ'vɜːsə] ad
viceversa.
**vicinity** [vɪ'sɪnɪtɪ] n vicinanze fpl.
**vicious** ['vɪʃəs] a (remark) mali-
gno(a), cattivo(a); (blow) vio-
lento(a); ~ **circle** n circolo vizioso.
**victim** ['vɪktɪm] n vittima.
**victor** ['vɪktə*] n vincitore m.
**Victorian** [vɪk'tɔːrɪən] a
vittoriano(a).
**victory** ['vɪktərɪ] n vittoria.
**video** ['vɪdɪəu] cpd video... // n (~
film) video m inv; (also: ~
cassette) videocassetta; (also: ~
cassette recorder) videoregistratore
m; ~ **tape** n videotape m inv.
**vie** [vaɪ] vi: to ~ **with** competere
con, rivaleggiare con.
**Vienna** [vɪ'ɛnə] n Vienna.
**Vietnam** [vjɛt'næm] n Vietnam m;
~**ese** a, n (pl inv) vietnamita (m/f).
**view** [vjuː] n vista, veduta; (opinion)
opinione f // vt (situation)
considerare; (house) visitare; on ~
(in museum etc) esposto(a); in full
~ of sotto gli occhi di; in ~ of the
fact that considerato che; ~**er** n
(viewfinder) mirino; (small
projector) visore m; (TV)
telespettatore/trice; ~**finder** n
mirino; ~**point** n punto di vista.
**vigil** ['vɪdʒɪl] n veglia.
**vigorous** ['vɪgərəs] a vigoroso(a).
**vile** [vaɪl] a (action) vile; (smell)
disgustoso(a), nauseante; (temper)
pessimo(a).
**villa** ['vɪlə] n villa.
**village** ['vɪlɪdʒ] n villaggio; ~**r** n
abitante m/f di villaggio.
**villain** ['vɪlən] n (scoundrel) canaglia; (criminal) criminale m; (in
novel etc) cattivo.
**vindicate** ['vɪndɪkeɪt] vt comprovare; giustificare.
**vindictive** [vɪn'dɪktɪv] a
vendicativo(a).
**vine** [vaɪn] n vite f; (climbing plant)
rampicante m.

**vinegar** ['vɪnɪgə*] n aceto.

**vineyard** ['vɪnjɑːd] n vigna, vigneto.

**vintage** ['vɪntɪdʒ] n (year) annata, produzione f; ~ **wine** n vino d'annata.

**vinyl** ['vaɪnl] n vinile m.

**violate** ['vaɪəleɪt] vt violare.

**violence** ['vaɪələns] n violenza; (POL etc) incidenti mpl violenti.

**violent** ['vaɪələnt] a violento(a).

**violet** ['vaɪələt] a (colour) viola inv, violetto(a) // n (plant) violetta.

**violin** [vaɪə'lɪn] n violino; ~**ist** n violinista m/f.

**VIP** n abbr (= very important person) V.I.P. m/f inv.

**virgin** ['vəːdʒɪn] n vergine f // a vergine inv.

**Virgo** ['vəːgəu] n (sign) Vergine f.

**virile** ['vɪraɪl] a virile.

**virtually** ['vəːtjuəlɪ] ad (almost) praticamente.

**virtue** ['vəːtjuː] n virtù f inv; (advantage) pregio, vantaggio; **by** ~ **of** grazie a.

**virtuous** ['vəːtjuəs] a virtuoso(a).

**virus** ['vaɪərəs] n virus m inv.

**visa** ['viːzə] n visto.

**vis-à-vis** [viːzə'viː] prep rispetto a, nei riguardi di.

**visibility** [vɪzɪ'bɪlɪtɪ] n visibilità.

**visible** ['vɪzəbl] a visibile.

**vision** ['vɪʒən] n (sight) vista; (foresight, in dream) visione f.

**visit** ['vɪzɪt] n visita; (stay) soggiorno // vt (person) andare a trovare; (place) visitare; ~**ing hours** npl (in hospital etc) orario delle visite; ~**or** n visitatore/trice; (guest) ospite m/f; (in hotel) cliente m/f; ~**ors' book** n libro d'oro; (in hotel) registro.

**visor** ['vaɪzə*] n visiera.

**vista** ['vɪstə] n vista, prospettiva.

**visual** ['vɪzjuəl] a visivo(a); visuale; ottico(a); ~ **aid** n sussidio visivo; ~ **display unit (VDU)** n visualizzatore m.

**visualize** ['vɪzjuəlaɪz] vt immaginare, figurarsi; (foresee) prevedere.

**vital** ['vaɪtl] a vitale; ~**ly** ad estremamente; ~ **statistics** npl (fig) misure fpl.

**vitamin** ['vɪtəmɪn] n vitamina.

**vivacious** [vɪ'veɪʃəs] a vivace.

**vivid** ['vɪvɪd] a vivido(a); ~**ly** ad (describe) vividamente; (remember) con precisione.

**V-neck** ['viːnɛk] n maglione m con lo scollo a V.

**vocabulary** [vəu'kæbjulərɪ] n vocabolario.

**vocal** ['vəukl] a (MUS) vocale; (communication) verbale; ~ **chords** npl corde fpl vocali.

**vocation** [vəu'keɪʃən] n vocazione f; ~**al** a professionale.

**vociferous** [və'sɪfərəs] a rumoroso(a).

**vodka** ['vɔdkə] n vodka f inv.

**vogue** [vəug] n moda; (popularity) popolarità, voga.

**voice** [vɔɪs] n voce f // vt (opinion) esprimere.

**void** [vɔɪd] n vuoto // a (invalid) nullo(a); (empty) vuoto(a); ~ **of** privo(a) di.

**volatile** ['vɔlətaɪl] a volatile; (fig) volubile.

**volcano** [vɔl'keɪnəu] n, ~**es** n vulcano.

**volition** [və'lɪʃən] n: **of one's own** ~ di sua volontà.

**volley** ['vɔlɪ] n (of gunfire) salva; (of stones etc) raffica, gragnola; (TENNIS etc) volata; ~**ball** n pallavolo f.

**volt** [vəult] n volt m inv; ~**age** n tensione f, voltaggio.

**voluble** ['vɔljubl] a loquace, ciarliero(a).

**volume** ['vɔljuːm] n volume m; ~ **control** n (RADIO, TV) regolatore m or manopola del volume.

**voluntarily** ['vɔləntrɪlɪ] ad volontariamente; gratuitamente.

**voluntary** ['vɔləntərɪ] a volontario(a); (unpaid) gratuito(a), non retribuito(a).

**volunteer** [vɔlən'tɪə*] n volontario/a // vi (MIL) arruolarsi volontario; **to**

~ **to do** offrire (volontariamente) di fare.

**voluptuous** [və'lʌptjuəs] a voluttuoso(a).

**vomit** ['vɒmɪt] n vomito // vt, vi vomitare.

**vote** [vəut] n voto, suffragio; (cast) voto; (franchise) diritto di voto // vi votare; ~ **of thanks** discorso di ringraziamento; ~**r** n elettore/trice; **voting** n scrutinio.

**vouch** [vautʃ]: **to ~ for** vt fus farsi garante di.

**voucher** ['vautʃə*] n (for meal, petrol) buono; (receipt) ricevuta.

**vow** [vau] n voto, promessa solenne // vi giurare.

**vowel** ['vauəl] n vocale f.

**voyage** ['vɔɪdʒ] n viaggio per mare, traversata.

**vulgar** ['vʌlgə*] a volgare.

**vulnerable** ['vʌlnərəbl] a vulnerabile.

**vulture** ['vʌltʃə*] n avvoltoio.

# W

**wad** [wɒd] n (of cotton wool, paper) tampone m; (of banknotes etc) fascio.

**waddle** ['wɒdl] vi camminare come una papera.

**wade** [weɪd] vi: **to ~ through** camminare a stento in // vt guadare.

**wafer** ['weɪfə*] n (CULIN) cialda; (REL) ostia; (COMPUT) wafer m inv.

**waffle** ['wɒfl] n (CULIN) cialda; (col) ciance fpl; riempitivo // vi cianciare; parlare a vuoto.

**waft** [wɒft] vt portare // vi diffondersi.

**wag** [wæg] vt agitare, muovere // vi agitarsi.

**wage** [weɪdʒ] n (also: ~s) salario, paga // vt: **to ~ war** fare la guerra; ~ **packet** n busta f paga inv.

**wager** ['weɪdʒə*] n scommessa.

**waggle** ['wægl] vt dimenare, agitare

// vi dimenarsi, agitarsi.

**wag(g)on** ['wægən] n (horse-drawn) carro; (Brit RAIL) vagone m (merci).

**wail** [weɪl] n gemito; (of siren) urlo // vi gemere; urlare.

**waist** [weɪst] n vita, cintola; ~**coat** n (Brit) panciotto, gilè m inv; ~**line** n (giro di) vita.

**wait** [weɪt] n attesa // vi aspettare, attendere; **to lie in ~ for** stare in agguato a; **to ~ for** aspettare; **I can't ~ to** (fig) non vedo l'ora di; **to ~ behind** vi rimanere (ad aspettare); **to ~ on** vt fus servire; ~**er** n cameriere m; ~**ing** n: "**no ~ing**" (Brit AUT) "divieto di sosta"; ~**ing list** n lista di attesa; ~**ing room** n sala d'aspetto or d'attesa; ~**ress** n cameriera.

**waive** [weɪv] vt rinunciare a, abbandonare.

**wake** [weɪk] vb (pt **woke**, ~**d**, pp **woken**, ~**d**) vt (also: ~ **up**) svegliare // vi (also: ~ **up**) svegliarsi // n (for dead person) veglia funebre; (NAUT) scia; ~**n** vt, vi = **wake**.

**Wales** [weɪlz] n Galles m.

**walk** [wɔːk] n passeggiata; (short) giretto; (gait) passo, andatura; (path) sentiero; (in park etc) sentiero, vialetto // vi camminare; (for pleasure, exercise) passeggiare // vt (distance) fare or percorrere a piedi; (dog) accompagnare, portare a passeggiare; **10 minutes'** ~ **from** 10 minuti di cammino or a piedi da; **from all** ~**s of life** di tutte le condizioni sociali; **to ~ out on** vt fus (col) piantare in asso; ~**er** n (person) camminatore/trice; ~**ie-talkie** ['wɔːkɪ'tɔːkɪ] n walkie-talkie m inv; ~**ing** n camminare m; ~**ing stick** n bastone m da passeggio; ~**out** n (of workers) sciopero senza preavviso or a sorpresa; ~**over** n (col) vittoria facile, gioco da ragazzi; ~**way** n passaggio pedonale.

**wall** [wɔːl] n muro; (internal, of

*tunnel, cave*) parete *f*; ~**ed** *a* (*city*) fortificato(a).

**wallet** ['wɔlɪt] *n* portafoglio.

**wallflower** ['wɔːlflauə*] *n* violacciocca; **to be a** ~ (*fig*) fare da tappezzeria.

**wallop** ['wɔləp] *vt* (*col*) pestare.

**wallow** ['wɔləu] *vi* sguazzare, voltolarsi.

**wallpaper** ['wɔːlpeɪpə*] *n* carta da parati.

**wally** ['wɔlɪ] *n* (*col*) imbecille *m/f*.

**walnut** ['wɔːlnʌt] *n* noce *f*; (*tree*) noce *m*.

**walrus** *pl* ~ *or* ~**es** ['wɔːlrəs] *n* tricheco.

**waltz** [wɔːlts] *n* valzer *m inv* // *vi* ballare il valzer.

**wan** [wɔn] *a* pallido(a), smorto(a); triste.

**wand** [wɔnd] *n* (*also:* **magic** ~) bacchetta (magica).

**wander** ['wɔndə*] *vi* (*person*) girare senza meta, girovagare; (*thoughts*) vagare; (*river*) serpeggiare // *vt* girovagare per.

**wane** [weɪn] *vi* (*moon*) calare, (*reputation*) declinare.

**wangle** [wæŋgl] *vt* (*Brit col*): **to** ~ **sth** procurare qc con l'astuzia.

**want** [wɔnt] *vt* volere; (*need*) aver bisogno di; (*lack*) mancare di // *n*: **for** ~ **of** per mancanza di; ~**s** *npl* (*needs*) bisogni *mpl*; **to** ~ **to do** volere fare; **to** ~ **sb to do** volere che qn faccia; ~**ing** *a*: **to be found** ~**ing** non risultare all'altezza.

**wanton** ['wɔntn] *a* sfrenato(a); senza motivo.

**war** [wɔː*] *n* guerra; **to go to** ~ entrare in guerra.

**ward** [wɔːd] *n* (*in hospital: room*) corsia; (: *section*) reparto; (*POL*) circoscrizione *f*; (*LAW: child*) pupillo/a; **to** ~ **off** *vt* parare, schivare.

**warden** ['wɔːdn] *n* (*Brit: of institution*) direttore/trice; (*of park, game reserve*) guardiano/a; (*Brit: also:* **traffic** ~) addetto/a al controllo

del traffico e del parcheggio.

**warder** ['wɔːdə*] *n* (*Brit*) guardia carceraria.

**wardrobe** ['wɔːdrəub] *n* (*cupboard*) guardaroba *m inv*, armadio; (*clothes*) guardaroba; (*THEATRE*) costumi *mpl*.

**warehouse** ['wɛəhaus] *n* magazzino.

**wares** [wɛəz] *npl* merci *fpl*.

**warfare** ['wɔːfɛə*] *n* guerra.

**warhead** ['wɔːhed] *n* (*MIL*) testata.

**warily** ['wɛərɪlɪ] *ad* cautamente, con prudenza.

**warm** [wɔːm] *a* caldo(a); (*thanks, welcome, applause*) caloroso(a); **it's** ~ fa caldo; **I'm** ~ ho caldo; **to** ~ **up** *vi* scaldarsi, riscaldarsi; (*athlete, discussion*) riscaldarsi // *vt* scaldare, riscaldare; (*engine*) far scaldare; ~**-hearted** *a* affettuoso(a); ~**ly** *ad* caldamente; calorosamente; vivamente; ~**th** *n* calore *m*.

**warn** [wɔːn] *vt* avvertire, avvisare; ~**ing** *n* avvertimento; (*notice*) avviso; ~**ing light** *n* spia luminosa; ~**ing triangle** *n* (*AUT*) triangolo.

**warp** [wɔːp] *vi* deformarsi // *vt* deformare; (*fig*) corrompere.

**warrant** ['wɔrnt] *n* (*LAW: to arrest*) mandato di cattura; (: *to search*) mandato di perquisizione.

**warranty** ['wɔrəntɪ] *n* garanzia.

**warren** ['wɔrən] *n* (*of rabbits*) tana.

**warrior** ['wɔrɪə*] *n* guerriero/a.

**Warsaw** ['wɔːsɔː] *n* Varsavia.

**warship** ['wɔːʃɪp] *n* nave *f* da guerra.

**wart** [wɔːt] *n* verruca.

**wartime** ['wɔːtaɪm] *n*: **in** ~ in tempo di guerra.

**wary** ['wɛərɪ] *a* prudente.

**was** [wɔz] *pt of* **be**.

**wash** [wɔʃ] *vt* lavare // *vi* lavarsi // *n*: **to give sth a** ~ lavare qc, dare una lavata a qc; **to have a** ~ lavarsi; **to** ~ **away** *vt* (*stain*) togliere lavando; (*subj: river etc*) trascinare via; **to** ~ **off** *vi* andare via con il lavaggio; **to** ~ **up** *vi* (*Brit*) lavare i piatti; (*US*) darsi una lavata; ~**able** a lavabile; ~**basin,** (US) ~**bowl** n lavabo; ~**cloth** n (US: face cloth) pezzuola (per lavarsi); ~**er** n (TECH) rondella; ~**ing** n (linen etc) bucato; ~**ing machine** n lavatrice f; ~**ing powder** n (Brit) detersivo (in polvere); ~**ing-up** n rigovernatura, lavatura dei piatti; ~**ing-up liquid** n detersivo liquido (per stoviglie); ~**out** n (col) disastro; ~**room** n gabinetto.

**wasn't** ['wɔznt] = was not.

**wasp** [wɔsp] n vespa.

**wastage** ['weɪstɪdʒ] n spreco; (in manufacturing) scarti mpl; **natural** ~ diminuzione f di manodopera (per pensionamento, decesso etc).

**waste** [weɪst] n spreco; (of time) perdita; (rubbish) rifiuti mpl // a (material) di scarto; (food) avanzato(a) // vt sprecare (time, opportunity) perdere; ~s npl distesa desolata; **to lay** ~ (destroy) devastare; **to** ~ **away** vi deperire; ~ **disposal unit** n (Brit) eliminatore m di rifiuti; ~**ful** a sprecone(a); (process) dispendioso(a); ~ **ground** n (Brit) terreno incolto or abbandonato; ~**paper basket** n cestino per la carta straccia; ~**pipe** n tubo di scarico.

**watch** [wɔtʃ] n orologio; (act of watching) sorveglianza; (guard: MIL, NAUT) guardia; (NAUT: spell of duty) quarto // vt (look at) osservare; (: match, programme) guardare; (spy on, guard) sorvegliare, tenere d'occhio; (be careful of) fare attenzione a // vi osservare, guardare; (keep guard) fare or montare la guardia; **to** ~ **out** vi fare attenzione; ~**dog** n cane m da guardia; ~**ful** a attento(a), vigile; ~**maker** n orologiaio(a); ~**man** n guardiano; (also: **night** ~**man**) guardiano notturno; ~ **strap** n cinturino da orologio.

**water** ['wɔːtə*] n acqua // vt (plant) annaffiare // vi (eyes) lacrimare; **in**

British ~s nelle acque territoriali britanniche; **to** ~ **down** vt (milk) diluire; (fig: story) edulcorare; ~**colour** n acquerello; ~**colours** npl colori mpl per acquarello; ~**cress** n crescione m; ~**fall** n cascata; ~ **heater** n scaldabagno; ~ **lily** n ninfea; ~**line** n (NAUT) linea di galleggiamento; ~**logged** a saturo(a) d'acqua; imbevuto(a) d'acqua; (football pitch etc) allagato(a); ~ **main** n conduttura dell'acqua; ~**mark** n (on paper) filigrana; ~**melon** n anguria, cocomero; ~**proof** a impermeabile; ~**shed** n (GEO, fig) spartiacque m; ~**skiing** n sci m acquatico; ~**tight** a stagno(a); ~**way** n corso d'acqua navigabile; ~**works** npl impianto idrico; ~**y** a (colour) slavato(a); (coffee) acquoso(a).

**watt** [wɔt] n watt m inv.

**wave** [weɪv] n onda; (of hand) gesto, segno; (in hair) ondulazione f // vi fare un cenno con la mano; (flag) sventolare // vt (handkerchief) sventolare; (stick) brandire; ~**length** n lunghezza d'onda.

**waver** ['weɪvə*] vi vacillare; (voice) tremolare.

**wavy** ['weɪvɪ] a ondulato(a); ondeggiante.

**wax** [wæks] n cera // vt dare la cera a; (car) lucidare // vi (moon) crescere; ~**works** npl cere fpl; museo delle cere.

**way** [weɪ] n via, strada; (path, access) passaggio; (distance) distanza; (direction) parte f, direzione f; (manner) modo, stile m; (habit) abitudine f; (condition) condizione f; **which** ~? - **this** ~ da che parte or in quale direzione? - da questa parte or per di qua; **on the** ~ (en route) per strada; **to be on one's** ~ essere in cammino or sulla strada; **to be in the** ~ bloccare il passaggio; (fig) essere tra i piedi or d'impiccio; **to go out of one's** ~ **to do** (fig) mettercela tutta or fare di tutto per fare; **to lose one's ~** perdere la strada; **in a ~** in un certo senso; **in some ~s** sotto certi aspetti; **by the ~** ... a proposito ...; **"~ in"** (*Brit*) "entrata", "ingresso"; **"~ out"** (*Brit*) "uscita".

**waylay** [wer'ler] *vt irg* tendere un agguato a; attendere al passaggio.

**wayward** ['werwəd] *a* capriccioso(a); testardo(a).

**W.C.** ['dʌblju:'si:] *n* (*Brit*) W.C. *m inv*, gabinetto.

**we** [wi:] *pl pronoun* noi.

**weak** [wi:k] *a* debole; (*health*) precario(a); (*beam etc*) fragile; **~en** *vi* indebolirsi // *vt* indebolire; **~ling** ['wi:klɪŋ] *n* smidollato/a; debole *m/f*; **~ness** *n* debolezza; (*fault*) punto debole, difetto.

**wealth** [wɛlθ] *n* (*money, resources*) ricchezza, ricchezze *fpl*; (*of details*) abbondanza, profusione *f*; **~y** *a* ricco(a).

**wean** [wi:n] *vt* svezzare.

**weapon** ['wɛpən] *n* arma.

**wear** [wɛə*] *n* (*use*) uso; (*deterioration through use*) logorio, usura; (*clothing*): **sports/baby ~** abbigliamento sportivo/per neonati // *vb* (*pt* **wore**, *pp* **worn**) *vt* (*clothes*) portare; mettersi; (*damage: through use*) consumare // *vi* (*last*) durare; (*rub etc through*) consumarsi; evening **~** abiti *mpl* or tenuta da sera; **to ~ away** *vt* consumare; erodere // *vi* consumarsi; essere eroso(a); **to ~ down** *vt* consumare; (*strength*) esaurire; **to ~ off** *vi* sparire lentamente; **to ~ on** *vi* passare; **to ~ out** *vt* consumare; (*person, strength*) esaurire; **~ and tear** *n* usura, consumo.

**weary** ['wɪərɪ] *a* stanco(a); (*tiring*) faticoso(a).

**weasel** ['wi:zl] *n* (*ZOOL*) donnola.

**weather** ['wɛðə*] *n* tempo // *vt* (*wood*) stagionare; (*storm, crisis*) superare; **under the ~** (*fig: ill*) poco bene; **~-beaten** *a* (*person*) segnato(a) dalle intemperie; (*building*)

logorato(a) dalle intemperie; **~cock** *n* banderuola; **~ forecast** *n* previsioni *fpl* del tempo, bollettino meteorologico; **~ vane** *n = ~***cock**.

**weave** [wi:v], *pt* **wove**, *pp* **woven** *vt* (*cloth*) tessere; (*basket*) intrecciare; **~r** *n* tessitore/trice; **weaving** *n* tessitura.

**web** [wɛb] *n* (*of spider*) ragnatela; (*on foot*) palma; (*fabric, also fig*) tessuto.

**wed** [wɛd] *vt* (*pt, pp* **wedded**) sposare // *vi* sposarsi.

**we'd** [wi:d] *n* = **we had, we would**.

**wedding** ['wɛdɪŋ] *n* matrimonio; **silver/golden ~ anniversary** *n* nozze *fpl* d'argento/d'oro; **~ day** *n* giorno delle nozze *or* del matrimonio; **~ dress** *n* abito nuziale; **~ ring** *n* fede *f*.

**wedge** [wɛdʒ] *n* (*of wood etc*) cuneo; (*under door etc*) zeppa; (*of cake*) spicchio, fetta // *vt* (*fix*) fissare con zeppe; (*push*) incuneare.

**wedlock** ['wɛdlɔk] *n* vincolo matrimoniale.

**Wednesday** ['wɛdnzdɪ] *n* mercoledì *m inv*.

**wee** [wi:] *a* (*Scottish*) piccolo(a).

**weed** [wi:d] *n* erbaccia // *vt* diserbare; **~-killer** *n* diserbante *m*; **~y** *a* (*person*) allampanato/a.

**week** [wi:k] *n* settimana; **a ~ today/on Friday** oggi/venerdì a otto; **~day** *n* giorno feriale; (*COMM*) giornata lavorativa; **~-end** *n* fine settimana *m* or *f inv*, weekend *m inv*; **~ly** *ad* ogni settimana, settimanalmente // *a*, settimanale (*m*).

**weep** [wi:p], *pt, pp* **wept** *vi* (*person*) piangere; **~ing willow** *n* salice *m* piangente.

**weigh** [wer] *vt, vi* pesare; **to ~ down** *vt* (*branch*) piegare; (*fig: with worry*) opprimere, caricare; **to ~ up** *vt* valutare.

**weight** [wert] *n* peso; **to lose/put on ~** dimagrire/ingrassare; **~ing** *n* (*allowance*) indennità; **~ lifter**

pesista $m$; ~**y** $a$ pesante; *(fig)* importante, grave.

**weir** [wɪə*] $n$ diga.

**weird** [wɪəd] $a$ strano(a), bizzarro(a); *(eerie)* soprannaturale.

**welcome** ['wɛlkəm] $a$ benvenuto(a) // $n$ accoglienza, benvenuto // $vt$ accogliere cordialmente; *(also:* bid ~) dare il benvenuto a; *(be glad of)* rallegrarsi di; **to be** = essere il(la) benvenuto(a); **thank you - you're** ~**!** grazie - prego!

**weld** [wɛld] $n$ saldatura // $vt$ saldare.

**welfare** ['wɛlfɛə*] $n$ benessere $m$; ~ **state** $n$ stato assistenziale.

**well** [wɛl] $n$ pozzo // $ad$ bene // $a$: **to be** = essere bene // *excl* allora!; ma!; ebbene!; as = anche; as = as così come; oltre a; X as = as Y sia X che Y; **he did** as = as **he could** ha fatto come meglio poteva; ~ **done!** bravo(a)!; **get** ~ **soon!** guarisci presto!; **to be** ~ **in sth** riuscire in qc; **to** ~ **up** $vi$ sgorgare.

**we'll** [wi:l] = **we will, we shall.**

**well**: ~**behaved** $a$ ubbidiente; ~**being** $n$ benessere $m$; ~**built** $a$ *(person)* ben fatto(a); ~**dressed** $a$ ben vestito(a), vestito(a) bene; ~**heeled** $a$ *(col: wealthy)* agiato(a), facoltoso(a).

**wellingtons** ['wɛlɪŋtənz] $npl$ *(also:* wellington boots) stivali $mpl$ di gomma.

**well**: ~**known** $a$ noto(a), famoso(a); ~**mannered** $a$ ben educato(a); ~**meaning** $a$ ben intenzionato(a); ~**off** $a$ benestante, danaroso(a); ~**read** $a$ colto(a); ~**to-do** $a$ abbiente, benestante; ~**wisher** $n$ ammiratore/trice.

**Welsh** [wɛlʃ] $a$ gallese // $n$ *(LING)* gallese $m$; **the** ~ $npl$ i Gallesi; ~**man/woman** $n$ gallese $m/f$; ~ **rarebit** $n$ crostino al formaggio.

**went** [wɛnt] $pt$ *of* **go.**

**wept** [wɛpt] $pt$, $pp$ *of* **weep.**

**were** [wə:*] $pt$ *of* **be.**

**we're** [wɪə*] = **we are.**

**weren't** [wə:nt] = **were not.**

**west** [wɛst] $n$ ovest $m$, occidente $m$, ponente $m$ // $a$ (a) ovest $inv$, occidentale // $ad$ verso ovest; **the W**~ l'Occidente $m$; **the W**~ **Country** $n$ *(Brit)* il sud-ovest dell'Inghilterra; ~**erly** $a$ *(wind)* occidentale, da ovest; ~**ern** $a$ occidentale, dell'ovest // $n$ *(CINEMA)* western $m$ $inv$; **W**~ **Germany** $n$ Germania Occidentale // ~ **Indian** $a$ delle Indie Occidentali // $n$ abitante $m/f$ delle Indie Occidentali; **W**~ **Indies** $npl$ Indie $fpl$ Occidentali; ~**ward(s)** $ad$ verso ovest.

**wet** [wɛt] $a$ umido(a), bagnato(a); *(soaked)* fradicio(a); *(rainy)* piovoso(a); **to get** = bagnarsi; "~**paint**" "vernice fresca"; ~ **blanket** $n$ *(fig)* guastafeste $m/f$; ~ **suit** $n$ tuta da sub.

**we've** [wi:v] = **we have.**

**whack** [wæk] $vt$ picchiare, battere.

**whale** [weɪl] $n$ *(ZOOL)* balena.

**wharf**, $pl$ **wharves** [wɔ:f, wɔ:vz] $n$ banchina.

---

**KEYWORD**

**what** [wɔt] ◆ $ad$ **1** *(in direct/indirect questions)* che; quale; ~ **size is it?** che taglia è?; ~ **colour is it?** di che colore è?; ~ **books do you want?** quali or che libri vuole?

**2** *(in exclamations)* che; ~ **a mess!** che disordine!

◆ *pronoun* **1** *(interrogative)* che cosa, cosa, che; ~ **are you doing?** che or *(che)* cosa fai?; ~ **are you talking about?** di che cosa parli?; ~ **is it called?** come si chiama?; ~ **about me?** e io?; ~ **about doing ...?** e se facessimo ...?

**2** *(relative)* ciò che, quello che; **I saw** ~ **you did/was on the table** ho visto quello che hai fatto/quello che era sul tavolo

**3** *(indirect use)* (che) cosa; **he asked me** ~ **she had said** mi ha chiesto che cosa avesse detto; **tell me** ~ **you're thinking about** dimmi

a cosa stai pensando
♦ excl (disbelieving) cosa!, come!

**whatever** [wɔt'evə*] a: ~ book qualunque or qualsiasi libro + sub // pronoun: do ~ **is necessary/you want** faccia qualunque or qualsiasi cosa sia necessaria/lei voglia; ~ **happens** qualunque cosa accada; **no reason** or whatsoever nessuna ragione affatto or al mondo; **nothing** ~ proprio niente.
**whatsoever** [wɔtsəu'evə*] a see whatever.

**wheat** [wi:t] n grano, frumento.
**wheedle** ['wi:dl] vt: to ~ **sb into doing sth** convincere qn a fare qc (con lusinghe); to ~ **sth out of sb** ottenere qc da qn (con lusinghe).
**wheel** [wi:l] n ruota; (AUT: also: **steering** ~): **volante** m; (NAUT) (ruota del) timone m // vt spingere // vi (also: ~ **round**) girare; ~**barrow** n carriola; ~**chair** n sedia a rotelle; ~ **clamp** n (AUT) morsa che blocca la ruota di una vettura in sosta vietata.
**wheeze** [wi:z] vi ansimare.

*KEYWORD*

**when** [wen] ♦ ad quando; ~ **did it happen?** quando è successo?
♦ cj 1 (at, during, after the time that) quando; **she was reading ~ I came in** quando sono entrato lei leggeva; **that was ~ I needed you** era allora che avevo bisogno di te
2 (on, at which): **on the day ~ I met him** il giorno in cui l'ho incontrato; **one day ~ it was raining un** giorno che pioveva
3 (whereas) quando, mentre; **you said I was wrong ~ in fact I was right** mi hai detto che avevo torto, quando in realtà avevo ragione.
**whenever** [wen'evə*] ad quando mai // cj quando; (every time that) ogni volta che.
**where** [weə*] ad, cj dove; **this is ~**

è qui che; ~**abouts** ad dove // n: sb's ~**abouts** luogo dove qn si trova; ~**as** cj mentre; ~**by** pronoun per cui; ~**upon** cj al che; **wherever** [-'evə*] ad dove mai // cj dovunque + sub; ~**withal** n mezzi mpl.
**whet** [wet] vt (tool) affilare; (appetite etc) stimolare.
**whether** ['weðə*] cj se; **I don't know ~ to accept or not** non so se accettare o no; **it's doubtful ~** è poco probabile che; ~ **you go or not** che lei vada o no.

*KEYWORD*

**which** [witʃ] ♦ a 1 (interrogative: direct, indirect) quale; ~ **picture do you want?** quale quadro vuole?; ~ **one?** quale?; ~ **one of you did it?** chi di voi lo ha fatto?
2: **in** ~ **case** nel qual caso
♦ pronoun 1 (interrogative) quale; ~ (of these) **are yours?** quali di questi sono suoi?; ~ **of you are coming?** chi di voi viene?
2 (relative) che; (: indirect) cui, il (la) quale; **the apple ~ you ate/~ is on the table** la mela che hai mangiato/che è sul tavolo; **the chair on ~ you are sitting** la sedia sulla quale or su cui sei seduto; **he said he knew, ~ is true** ha detto che lo sapeva, il che è vero; **after ~** dopo di che.

**whichever** [witʃ'evə*] a: **take ~ book you prefer** prenda qualsiasi libro che preferisce; ~ **book you take** qualsiasi libro prenda.
**whiff** [wif] n soffio; sbuffo; odore m.
**while** [wail] n momento // cj mentre; (as long as) finché; (although) sebbene + sub; **for what** ~ per quanto + sub; **for a** ~ per un po'; **to** ~ **away** vt (time) far passare.
**whim** [wim] n capriccio.
**whimper** ['wimpə*] n piagnucolio // vi piagnucolare.
**whimsical** ['wimzikl] a (person) ca-

priccioso(a); (look) strano(a).

**whine** [waɪn] n gemito // vi gemere; uggiolare; piagnucolare.

**whip** [wɪp] n frusta; (for riding) frustino; (POL: person) capogruppo (che sovrintende alla disciplina dei colleghi di partito) // vt frustare; (snatch) sollevare (or estrarre) bruscamente; **~ped cream** n panna montata; **~-round** n (Brit) colletta.

**whirl** [wəːl] n turbine m // vt (far) girare rapidamente; (far) turbinare // vi turbinare; **~pool** n mulinello; **~wind** n turbine m.

**whirr** [wəː*] vi ronzare; rombare; frullare.

**whisk** [wɪsk] n (CULIN) frusta; frullino // vt sbattere, frullare; **to ~ sb away or off** portar via qn a tutta velocità.

**whiskers** ['wɪskəz] npl (of animal) baffi mpl; (of man) favoriti mpl.

**whisky**, (US, Ireland) **whiskey** ['wɪskɪ] n whisky m inv.

**whisper** ['wɪspə*] n sussurro; (rumour) voce f // vt, vi sussurrare.

**whistle** ['wɪsl] n (sound) fischio; (object) fischietto // vi fischiare.

**white** [waɪt] a bianco(a); (with fear) pallido(a) // n bianco; (person) bianco/a; **~ coffee** n (Brit) caffellatte m inv; **~-collar worker** n impiegato; **~ elephant** n (fig) oggetto (or progetto) costoso ma inutile; **~ lie** n bugia pietosa; **~ paper** n (POL) libro bianco; **~wash** n (paint) bianco di calce // vt imbiancare; (fig) coprire.

**whiting** ['waɪtɪŋ] n (pl inv) (fish) merlango.

**Whitsun** ['wɪtsn] n Pentecoste f.

**whittle** ['wɪtl] vt: **to ~ away**, **~ down** ridurre, tagliare.

**whizz** [wɪz] vi sfrecciare; **~ kid** n (col) prodigio.

*KEYWORD*

**who** [hu:] pronoun **1** (interrogative) chi; **~ is it?**, **~'s there?** chi è?

**2** (relative) che; **the man ~ spoke**

to me l'uomo che ha parlato con me; **those ~ can swim** quelli che sanno nuotare.

**whodunit** [hu:'dʌnɪt] n (col) giallo.

**whoever** [hu:'ɛvə*] pronoun: **~ finds it** chiunque lo trovi; **ask ~ you like** lo chieda a chiunque vuole; **~ she marries** chiunque sposerà, non importa chi sposerà; **~ told you that?** chi mai gliel'ha detto?

**whole** [həul] a (complete) tutto(a), completo(a); (not broken) intero(a), intatto(a) // n (total) totale m; (sth not broken) tutto; **the ~ of the time** tutto il tempo; **on the ~**, **as a ~** nel complesso, nell'insieme; **~hearted** a sincero(a); **~meal** a (bread, flour) integrale; **~sale** n commercio or vendita all'ingrosso // a all'ingrosso; (destruction) totale; **~saler** n grossista m/f; **~some** a sano(a); salutare; **~wheat** a = **~meal**; **wholly** ad completamente, del tutto.

*KEYWORD*

**whom** [hu:m] pronoun **1** (interrogative) chi; **~ did you see?** chi hai visto?; **to ~ did you give it?** a chi lo hai dato?

**2** (relative) che, prep + il (la) quale (check syntax of Italian verb used); **the man ~ I saw/to ~ I spoke** l'uomo che ho visto/al quale ho parlato.

**whooping cough** ['hu:pɪŋ-] n pertosse f.

**whore** [hɔː*] n (pej) puttana.

*KEYWORD*

**whose** [hu:z] ♦ a **1** (possessive: interrogative) di chi; **~ book is this?**, **~ is this book?** di chi è questo libro?; **~ daughter are you?** di chi sei figlia?

**2** (possessive: relative): **the man ~ son you rescued** l'uomo il cui figlio hai salvato; **the girl ~ sister you were speaking to** la ragazza alla

cui sorella stavi parlando
◆ *pronoun* di chi; ~ **is this?** di chi è questo?; **I know ~ it** is so di chi è.

**why** [waɪ] *ad, cj* perché // *excl* (*surprise*) ma guarda un po'!; (*remonstrating*) ma (via)!; (*explaining*) ebbene!; ~ **not?** perché no?; ~ **not do it now?** perché non farlo adesso?; **that's not ~ I'm here** non è questo il motivo per cui sono qui; **the reason ~** il motivo per cui; ~**ever** *ad* perché mai.

**wick** [wɪk] *n* lucignolo, stoppino.
**wicked** ['wɪkɪd] *a* cattivo(a), malvagio(a); maligno(a); perfido(a); (*mischievous*) malizioso(a).
**wicker** ['wɪkə*] *n* vimine *m*; (*also:* ~**work**) articoli *mpl* di vimini.
**wicket** ['wɪkɪt] *n* (*CRICKET*) porta; area tra le due porte.
**wide** [waɪd] *a* largo(a); (*area, knowledge*) vasto(a); (*choice*) ampio(a) // *ad*; **to open** ~ spalancare; **to shoot** ~ tirare a vuoto or fuori bersaglio; ~**-angle lens** *n* grandangolare *m*; ~**-awake** *a* completamente sveglio(a); ~**ly** *ad* (*differing*) molto, completamente; (*believed*) generalmente; ~**ly spaced** molto distanziati(e); ~**n** *vt* allargare, ampliare; ~ **open** *a* spalancato(a); ~**spread** *a* (*belief etc*) molto or assai diffuso(a).
**widow** ['wɪdəu] *n* vedova; ~**er** *n* vedovo.
**width** [wɪdθ] *n* larghezza.
**wield** [wi:ld] *vt* (*sword*) maneggiare; (*power*) esercitare.
**wife** [waɪf], *pl* **wives** *n* moglie *f*.
**wig** [wɪg] *n* parrucca.
**wiggle** ['wɪgl] *vt* dimenare, agitare.
**wild** [waɪld] *a* selvatico(a); selvaggio(a); (*sea*) tempestoso(a); (*idea, life*) folle; stravagante; ~**s** *npl* regione *f* selvaggia; ~**erness** ['wɪldənɪs] *n* deserto; ~ **goose chase** *n* (*fig*) pista falsa; ~**life** *n* natura; ~**ly** *ad* (*applaud*)

freneticamente; (*hit, guess*) a casaccio; (*happy*) follemente.
**wilful** ['wɪlful] *a* (*person*) testardo(a), ostinato(a); (*action*) intenzionale; (*crime*) premeditato(a).

**KEYWORD**

**will** [wɪl] ◆ *auxiliary vb* **1** (*forming future tense*): **I** ~ **finish it tomorrow** lo finirò domani; **I** ~ **have finished it by tomorrow** lo finirò entro domani; ~ **you do it?** - **yes I** ~/**no I won't** lo farai? - sì (lo farò)/no (non lo farò)

**2** (*in conjectures, predictions*): **he** *or* **he'll be there by** essere arrivato ora; **postman sarà** il [...]

**3** (*in comma* [...] you be quiet. [...] you come? vi [...] **help me?** mi [...] aiutare?; ~ [...] **tea?** vorrebbe una [...] won't put up wi[...] accettero?

◆ *vt* (*pt, pp* ~**ed**): t[...] volere che qn facci[...] **himself to go on** cont[...] un grande sforzo di volo[...] ~ **n** volontà; testamento.

**willing** ['wɪlɪŋ] *a* volont[...] **to do** disposto(a) a far[...] volontieri; ~**ness** *n* buona [...]
**willow** ['wɪləu] *n* salice *m*[...]
**will power** *n* forza di volo[...]
**willy-nilly** ['wɪlɪ'nɪlɪ] *ad* [...] nolente.
**wilt** [wɪlt] *vi* appassire.
**wily** ['waɪlɪ] *a* furbo(a).
**win** [wɪn] (*pt, pp* **won** *etc*) [...] *vb* (*pt, pp* **won** [wʌn]) *vt* [...] *prize*) vincere; (*money*) guad[...] (*popularity*) conquistare // *vi* v[...] **to** ~ **over**, (*Brit*) ~ **rou**[...] convincere.
**wince** [wɪns] *n* trasalimento, s[...] // *vi* trasalire.
**winch** [wɪntʃ] *n* verricello, arga[...]

**wind** $n$ [wɪnd] vento; (MED) flatulenza // $vb$ [waɪnd] (pt, pp **wound** [waʊnd]) $vt$ attorcigliare; (wrap) avvolgere; (clock, toy) caricare; (take breath away: inf) far restare senza fiato // $vi$ (road, river) serpeggiare; **to ~ up** $vt$ (clock) caricare; (debate) concludere; **~fall** $n$ colpo di fortuna; **~ing** ['waɪndɪŋ] $a$ (road) serpeggiante; (staircase) a chiocciola; **~ instrument** $n$ (MUS) strumento a fiato; **~mill** $n$ mulino a vento.

**window** ['wɪndəʊ] $n$ finestra; (in car, train) finestrino; (in shop etc) vetrina; (also: ~ **pane**) vetro; **~box** $n$ cassetta da fiori; **~ cleaner** (person) pulitore $m$ di finestre; **~ne** $n$ davanzale $m$; **~ pane** $n$ vetro; **~sill** $n$ davanzale $m$.

**...pe** ['wɪndpaɪp] $n$ trachea. **...een**, (US) **windshield** ['wɪnd.'wɪndʃiːld] $n$ parabrezza **~ washer** $n$ lavacristallo; **~** cristallo.

['wɪndswɛpt] $a$ ...al vento.

...spazzato dal vento. **windy** $a$ ventoso(a); **it's ~** c'è vento. **wine** $n$ vino; **~ cellar** $n$ cantina; **~ glass** $n$ bicchiere $m$ da vino; **~ list** $n$ lista dei vini; **~ tasting** $n$ gustazione $f$ dei vini; **~ waiter** melier $m$ inv.

**wing** [wɪŋ] $n$ ala; **~s** npl (THEA-TRE) quinte fpl; (SPORT) ala. **~er** ['wɪŋə*] $n$ (SPORT) ala. **wink** [wɪŋk] $n$ ammiccamento // $vi$ ammiccare, fare l'occhiolino.

**win...** $n$ (team) vincente; **~s** npl vincite ...a(a); **~s** npl vincite ...a guadagno. **...ttorio** ['wɪntə*] $n$ inverno; (battle) tttnt mpl invernali. **...agnare** $n$ invernale. **...incere**, **...d** $vt$ pulita, passata // $vt$ ...tinando); (dishes) ...insulto **~ off** $vt$ cancellare; ...o. ...che strofinando; **to ~** ...) pagare, liquidare;

---

(memory) cancellare; (destroy) annientare; **to ~ up** $vt$ asciugare.

**wire** ['waɪə*] $n$ filo; (ELEC) filo elettrico; (TEL) telegramma $m$ // $vt$ (house) fare l'impianto elettrico di; (also: ~ **up**) collegare, allacciare.

**wireless** ['waɪəlɪs] $n$ (Brit) telegrafia senza fili; (set) (apparecchio $m$) radio $f$ inv.

**wiring** ['waɪərɪŋ] $n$ impianto elettrico.

**wiry** ['waɪərɪ] $a$ magro(a) e nerboruto(a).

**wisdom** ['wɪzdəm] $n$ saggezza; (of action) prudenza; **~ tooth** $n$ dente $m$ del giudizio.

**wise** [waɪz] $a$ saggio(a); prudente; giudizioso(a).

**...wise** [waɪz] suffix: **time~** per quanto riguarda il tempo, in termini di tempo.

**wish** [wɪʃ] $n$ (desire) desiderio; (specific desire) richiesta // $vt$ desiderare, volere; **best ~es** (on birthday etc) i migliori auguri; **with best ~es** (in letter) cordiali saluti, con i migliori saluti; **to ~ sb good-bye** dire arrivederci a qn; **he ~ed me well** mi augurò di riuscire; **to ~ to do/sb to do** desiderare o volere fare/che qn faccia; **to ~ for** desiderare; **it's ~ful thinking** è prendere i desideri per realtà.

**wishy-washy** ['wɪʃɪ'wɒʃɪ] $a$ (col: colour) slavato(a); (: ideas, argument) insulso(a).

**wisp** [wɪsp] $n$ ciuffo, ciocca; (of smoke, straw) filo.

**wistful** ['wɪstful] $a$ malinconico(a).

**wit** [wɪt] $n$ (gen pl) intelligenza; presenza di spirito; (wittiness) spirito, arguzia; (person) bello spirito; **to be at one's ~s' end** (fig) non sapere più cosa fare; **to ~ ad** cioè.

**witch** [wɪtʃ] $n$ strega.

◇ KEYWORD

**with** [wɪð, wɪθ] prep **1** (in the company of) con; **I was ~ him** ero con lui; **we stayed ~ friends** siamo stati da amici; **I'll be ~ you in a minute** vengo subito

**2** (*descriptive*) con; **a room ~ a view** una stanza con vista sul mare (*or* sulle montagne *etc*); **the man ~ the grey hat/blue eyes** l'uomo con il cappello grigio/gli occhi blu

**3** (*indicating manner, means, cause*): **~ tears in her eyes** con le lacrime agli occhi; **red ~ anger** rosso dalla rabbia; **to shake ~ fear** tremare di paura

**4: I'm ~ you** (*I understand*) ti seguo; **to be ~ it** (*col: up-to-date*) essere alla moda; (*: alert*) essere sveglio(a).

**withdraw** [wɪθˈdrɔː] *vb* (*irg*) *vt* ritirare; (*money from bank*) ritirare; prelevare // *vi* ritirarsi; **~al** *n* ritiro; prelievo; (*of army*) ritirata; (*MED*) stato di privazione; **~n** *a* (*person*) distaccato(a).

**wither** [ˈwɪðə*] *vi* appassire.

**withhold** [wɪθˈhəuld] *vt irg* (*money*) trattenere; (*decision*) rimettere, rimandare; (*permission*): **to ~ (from)** rifiutare (a); (*information*): **to ~ (from)** nascondere (a).

**within** [wɪðˈɪn] *prep* all'interno; (*in time, distances*) entro // *ad* all'interno, dentro; **~ sight of** in vista di; **~ a mile of** entro un miglio da; **~ the week** prima della fine della settimana.

**without** [wɪðˈaut] *prep* senza.

**withstand** [wɪθˈstænd] *vt irg* resistere a.

**witness** [ˈwɪtnɪs] *n* (*person*) testimone *m/f* // *vt* (*event*) essere testimone di; (*document*) attestare l'autenticità di; **~ box**, (*US*) **~ stand** *n* banco dei testimoni.

**witticism** [ˈwɪtɪsɪzm] *n* spiritosaggine *f*.

**witty** [ˈwɪtɪ] *a* spiritoso(a).

**wives** [waɪvz] *npl of* **wife**.

**wizard** [ˈwɪzəd] *n* mago.

**wk** *abbr* = **week**.

**wobble** [ˈwɔbl] *vi* tremare; (*chair*) traballare.

**woe** [wəu] *n* dolore *m*; disgrazia.

**woke** [wəuk] *pt of* **wake**; **~n** *pp of* **wake**.

**wolf**, *pl* **wolves** [wulf, wulvz] *n* lupo.

**woman** [ˈwumən], *pl* **women** *n* donna; **~ doctor** *n* dottoressa; **women's lib** *n* (*col*) movimento femminista.

**womb** [wuːm] *n* (*ANAT*) utero.

**women** [ˈwɪmɪn] *npl of* **woman**.

**won** [wʌn] *pt, pp of* **win**.

**wonder** [ˈwʌndə*] *n* meraviglia // *vi*: **to ~ whether** domandarsi se; **to ~ at** essere sorpreso(a) di; meravigliarsi di; **to ~ about** domandarsi di; pensare a; **it's no ~ that** è poco *or* non c'è da meravigliarsi che **+ sub**; **~ful** *a* meraviglioso(a).

**won't** [wəunt] = **will not**.

**woo** [wuː] *vt* (*woman*) fare la corte a.

**wood** [wud] *n* legno; (*timber*) legname *m*; (*forest*) bosco; **~ carving** *n* scultura in legno, intaglio; **~ed** *a* boschivo(a); boscoso(a); **~en** *a* di legno; (*fig*) rigido(a); inespressivo(a); **~pecker** *n* picchio; **~wind** *npl* (*MUS*): **the ~wind** i legni; **~work** *n* parti *fpl* in legno; (*craft, subject*) falegnameria; **~worm** *n* tarlo del legno.

**wool** [wul] *n* lana; **to pull the ~ over sb's eyes** (*fig*) imbrogliare qn; **~len**, (*US*) **~en** *a* di lana; **~lens** *npl* indumenti *mpl* di lana; **~ly**, (*US*) **~y** *a* lanoso(a); (*fig*: *ideas*) confuso(a).

**word** [wəːd] *n* parola; (*news*) notizie *fpl* // *vt* esprimere, formulare; **in other ~s** in altre parole; **to break/ keep one's ~** non mantenere/ mantenere la propria parola; **~ing** *n* formulazione *f*; **~ processing** *n* elaborazione *f* di testi, word processing *m*; **~ processor** *n* word processor *m inv*; **~y** *a* verboso(a).

**wore** [wɔː*] *pt of* **wear**.

**work** [wə:k] n lavoro; (ART, LITERATURE) opera // vi lavorare; (mechanism, plan etc) funzionare; (medicine) essere efficace // vt (clay, wood etc) lavorare; (mine etc) sfruttare; (machine) far funzionare; **to be out of** ~ essere disoccupato(a); ~s n (Brit: factory) fabbrica // npl (of clock, machine) meccanismo; **to** ~ **loose** vi allentarsi; **to** ~ **on** vt fus lavorare a; (principle) basarsi su; **to** ~ **out** vi (plans etc) riuscire, andare bene // vt (problem) risolvere; (plan) elaborare; **it** ~s **out at £100 fa 100 sterline; to get** ~ed **up** andare su tutte le furie; eccitarsi; ~**able** a (solution) realizzabile; ~**aholic** n maniaco/a del lavoro; ~**er** n lavoratore/trice, operaio/a; ~**force** n forza lavoro; ~**ing class** n classe f operaia or lavoratrice; ~**ing-class** a operaio(a); ~**ing man** n lavoratore m; ~**ing order** n: **in** ~**ing order** funzionante; ~**man** n operaio; ~**manship** n abilità; lavoro; fattura; ~**sheet** n foglio col programma di lavoro; ~**shop** n officina; ~ **station** n stazione f di lavoro; ~**-to-rule** n (Brit) sciopero bianco.

**world** [wə:ld] n mondo // cpd (champion) del mondo; (power, war) mondiale; **to think the** ~ **of sb** (fig) pensare un gran bene di qn; ~**ly** a di questo mondo; ~**wide** a universale.

**worm** [wə:m] n verme m.

**worn** [wɔ:n] pp of **wear** // a usato(a); ~**out** a (object) consumato(a), logoro(a); (person) sfinito(a).

**worried** ['wʌrɪd] a preoccupato(a).

**worry** ['wʌrɪ] n preoccupazione f // vt preoccupare // vi preoccuparsi.

**worse** [wə:s] a peggiore // ad, n peggio; **a change for the** ~ un peggioramento; ~ **off** a in condizioni (economiche) peggiori; ~**n** vt, vi peggiorare.

**worship** ['wə:ʃɪp] n culto // vt (God)

adorare, venerare; (person) adorare; **Your W**~ (Brit: to mayor) signor sindaco; (: to judge) signor giudice.

**worst** [wə:st] a il(la) peggiore // ad, n peggio; **at** ~ al peggio, per male che vada.

**worsted** ['wustid] n: (wool) ~ lana pettinata.

**worth** [wə:θ] n valore m // a: **to be** ~ valere; **it's** ~ **it** ne vale la pena; **it is** ~ **one's while (to do)** vale la pena (fare); ~**less** a di nessun valore; ~**while** a (activity) utile; (cause) lodevole.

**worthy** ['wə:ðɪ] a (person) degno(a); (motive) lodevole; ~ **of** degno di.

┌─────────────────┐
│ *KEYWORD* │
└─────────────────┘

**would** [wud] auxiliary vb **1** (conditional tense): **if you asked him he** ~ **do it** se glielo chiedesse lo farebbe; **if you had asked him he** ~ **have done it** se glielo avesse chiesto lo avrebbe fatto

**2** (in offers, invitations, requests): **you like a biscuit?** vorrebbe or vuole un biscotto?; ~ **you ask him to come in?** lo faccia entrare, per cortesia; ~ **you open the window please?** apra la finestra, per favore

**3** (in indirect speech): **I said I** ~ **do it** ho detto che l'avrei fatto

**4** (emphatic): **it WOULD have to snow today!** doveva proprio nevicare oggi!

**5** (insistence): **she** ~**n't do it** non ha voluto farlo

**6** (conjecture): **it** ~ **have been midnight** sarà stato mezzanotte; **it** ~ **seem so** sembrerebbe proprio di sì

**7** (indicating habit): **he** ~ **go there on Mondays** andava lì ogni lunedì.

**would-be** ['wudbi:] a (pej) sedicente.

**wouldn't** ['wudnt] = **would not.**

**wound** vb [waund] pt, pp of **wind** // n, vt [wu:nd] n ferita // vt ferire.

**wove** [wəuv] *pt of* **weave**; ~**n** *pp of* **weave**.

**wrangle** ['ræŋgl] *n* litigio // *vi* litigare.

**wrap** [ræp] *n* (*stole*) scialle *m*; (*cape*) mantellina // *vt* (*also*: ~ **up**) avvolgere; (*parcel*) incartare; ~**per** *n* (*Brit: of book*) copertina; ~**ping paper** *n* carta da pacchi; (*for gift*) carta da regali.

**wrath** [rɔθ] *n* collera, ira.

**wreak** [ri:k] *vt* (*havoc*) portare, causare; to ~ **vengeance on** vendicarsi su.

**wreath** [ri:θ, ri:ðz] *n* corona.

**wreck** [rɛk] *n* (*sea disaster*) naufragio; (*ship*) relitto; (*pej: person*) rottame *m* // *vt* demolire; (*ship*) far naufragare; (*fig*) rovinare; ~**age** *n* rottami *mpl*; (*of building*) macerie *fpl*; (*of ship*) relitti *mpl*.

**wren** [rɛn] *n* (*ZOOL*) scricciolo.

**wrench** [rɛntʃ] *n* (*TECH*) chiave *f*; (*tug*) torsione *f* brusca; (*fig*) strazio // *vt* strappare; storcere; to ~ **sth from** strappare qc a or da.

**wrestle** ['rɛsl] *vi*: to ~ (**with sb**) lottare (con qn); to ~ **with** (*fig*) combattere or lottare contro; ~**r** *n* lottatore/trice; **wrestling** *n* lotta; (*also*: **all-in wrestling**) catch *m*, lotta libera.

**wretched** ['rɛtʃɪd] *a* disgraziato(a); (*col: weather, holiday*) orrendo(a), orribile; (: *child, dog*) pestifero(a).

**wriggle** ['rɪgl] *vi* dimenarsi; (*snake, worm*) serpeggiare, muoversi serpeggiando.

**wring** [rɪŋ], *pt, pp* **wrung** *vt* torcere; (*wet clothes*) strizzare; (*fig*): to ~ **sth out of** strappare qc a.

**wrinkle** ['rɪŋkl] *n* (*on skin*) ruga; (*on paper etc*) grinza // *vt* corrugare; raggrinzire // *vi* corrugarsi; raggrinzirsi.

**wrist** [rɪst] *n* polso; ~**watch** *n* orologio da polso.

**writ** [rɪt] *n* ordine *m*; mandato.

**write** [raɪt], *pt* **wrote**, *pp* **written**

*vt, vi* scrivere; to ~ **down** *vt* annotare; (*put in writing*) mettere per iscritto; to ~ **off** *vt* (*debt*) cancellare; (*depreciate*) deprezzare; to ~ **out** *vt* scrivere; (*copy*) ricopiare; to ~ **up** *vt* redigere; ~**off** *n* perdita completa; ~**r** *n* autore/trice, scrittore/trice.

**writhe** [raɪð] *vi* contorcersi.

**writing** ['raɪtɪŋ] *n* scrittura; (*of author*) scritto, opera; **in** ~ per iscritto; ~ **paper** *n* carta da scrivere.

**written** ['rɪtn] *pp of* **write**.

**wrong** [rɔŋ] *a* sbagliato(a); (*not suitable*) inadatto(a); (*wicked*) cattivo(a); (*unfair*) ingiusto(a) // *ad* in modo sbagliato, erroneamente // *n* (*evil*) male *m*; (*injustice*) torto // *vt* fare torto a; **you are ~ to do it** ha torto a farlo; **you are ~ about that**, **you've got it ~** si sbaglia; **to be in the ~** avere torto; **what's ~?** cosa c'è che non va?; to go ~ (*person*) sbagliarsi; (*plan*) fallire, non riuscire; (*machine*) guastarsi; **fare un** illegittimo(a); ingiusto(a); ~**ly** *ad* a torto.

**wrote** [rəut] *pt of* **write**.

**wrought** [rɔ:t] *a*: ~ **iron** ferro battuto.

**wrung** [rʌŋ] *pt, pp of* **wring**.

**wry** [raɪ] *a* storto(a).

**wt.** *abbr* = **weight**.

# X

**Xmas** ['eksməs] *n abbr* = **Christmas**.

**X-ray** ['eks'reɪ] *n* raggio X; (*photograph*) radiografia // *vt* radiografare.

**xylophone** ['zaɪləfəun] *n* xilofono.

# Y

**yacht** [jɔt] *n* panfilo, yacht *m inv*; ~**ing** *n* yachting *m*, sport *m* della vela.

**Yank** [jæŋk], **Yankee** ['jæŋkɪ] *n (pej)* yankee *m/f inv.*

**yap** [jæp] *vi (dog)* guaire.

**yard** [jɑːd] *n (of house etc)* cortile *m*; *(measure)* iarda *(= 914 mm; 3 feet)*; ~**stick** *n (fig)* misura, criterio.

**yarn** [jɑːn] *n* filato; *(tale)* lunga storia.

**yawn** [jɔːn] *vi* sbadiglio // *vi* sbadigliare; ~**ing** *a (gap)* spalancato(a).

**yd.** *abbr* = **yard(s).**

**yeah** [jɛə] *ad (col)* sì.

**year** [jɪəʳ] *n* anno; *(referring to harvest, wine etc)* annata; **he is 8 ~s old** ha 8 anni; **an eight-~-old child** un(a) bambino(a) di otto anni; ~**ly** *a* annuale // *ad* annualmente.

**yearn** [jəːn] *vi:* **to ~ for sth/to do** desiderare ardentemente qc/di fare; ~**ing** *n* desiderio intenso.

**yeast** [jiːst] *n* lievito.

**yell** [jɛl] *n* urlo // *vi* urlare.

**yellow** ['jɛləʊ] *a* giallo(a).

**yelp** [jɛlp] *vi* guaire, uggiolare.

**yeoman** ['jəʊmən] *n:* **Y~ of the Guard** guardiano della Torre di Londra.

**yes** [jɛs] *ad, n* sì *(m inv);* **to say/answer** ~ dire/rispondere di sì.

**yesterday** ['jɛstədɪ] *ad, n* ieri *(m inv);* ~ **morning/evening** ieri mattina/sera; **all day** ~ ieri per tutta la giornata.

**yet** [jɛt] *ad* ancora; già // *cj* ma, tuttavia; **it is not finished** ~ non è ancora finito; **the best** ~ finora il migliore; **as** ~ finora.

**yew** [juː] *n* tasso *(albero).*

**yield** [jiːld] *n* produzione *f*, resa; reddito // *vt* produrre, rendere; *(surrender)* cedere // *vi* cedere; *(US AUT)* dare la precedenza.

**YMCA** *n abbr ( = Young Men's Christian Association)* Y.M.C.A. *m.*

**yoga** ['jəʊgə] *n* yoga *m.*

**yog(h)ourt, yog(h)urt** ['jəʊgət] *n* iogurt *m inv.*

**yoke** [jəʊk] *n* giogo.

**yolk** [jəʊk] *n* tuorlo, rosso d'uovo.

**yonder** ['jɒndəʳ] *ad* là.

KEYWORD

**you** [juː] *pronoun* **1** *(subject)* tu; *(: polite form)* lei; *(: pl)* voi; *(: very formal)* loro; ~ **Italians enjoy your food** a voi Italiani piace mangiare bene; ~ **and I will go** tu ed io *or* lei ed io andiamo

**2** *(object: direct)* ti; la; vi; loro *(after vb);* *(: indirect)* ti; le; vi; loro *(after vb)*; **I know** ~ ti *or* la *or* vi conosco; **I gave it to** ~ te *or* l'ho dato; glie/l'ho dato; ve l'ho dato; l'ho dato loro

**3** *(stressed, after prep, in comparisons)* te; lei; voi; loro; **I told YOU to do it** ho detto a TE *(or* a LEI *etc)* di farlo; **she's younger than** ~ è più giovane di te *(or* lei *etc)*

**4** *(impersonal: one)* si; **fresh air does** ~ **good** l'aria fresca fa bene; ~ **never know** non si sa mai.

**you'd** [juːd] = **you had, you would.**

**you'll** [juːl] = **you will, you shall.**

**young** [jʌŋ] *a* giovane // *npl (of animal)* piccoli *mpl*; *(people):* **the** ~ i giovani, la gioventù; ~**ster** *n* giovanotto, ragazzo; *(child)* bambino/a.

**your** [jɔːʳ] *a* il(la) tuo(a), *pl* i(le) tuoi(tue); il(la) suo(a), *pl* i(le) suoi(sue); il(la) vostro(a), *pl* i(le) vostri(e); il(la) loro, *pl* i(le) loro *(etc); see also* **my.**

**you're** [juəʳ] = **you are.**

**yours** [jɔːz] *pronoun* il(la) tuo(a), *pl* i(le) tuoi(tue); *(polite form)* il(la) suo(a), *pl* i(le) suoi(sue); *(pl)* il(la) vostro(a), *pl* i(le) vostri(e); *(: very formal)* il(la) loro, *pl* i(le) loro *(etc);* ~ **sincerely/faithfully** cordiali/distinti saluti; *see also* **mine.**

**yourself** [jɔːˈsɛlf] *pronoun (reflexive)* ti; si; *(after prep)* te; sé; *(emphatic)* tu stesso(a); *(: pl)* lei stesso(a); **your-selves** *pl pronoun (reflexive)* vi; si; *(after prep)* voi; loro; *(emphatic)* voi stessi(e); loro stessi(e); *see also* oneself.

**youth** [ju:θ] n gioventù f; (young man: pl ~s [ju:ðz]) giovane m, ragazzo; ~**club** n centro giovanile; ~**ful** a giovane; da giovane; giovanile; ~ **hostel** n ostello della gioventù.

**you've** [ju:v] = **you have.**

**YTS** n abbr (Brit: = Youth Training Scheme) programma di addestramento professionale per giovani.

**Yugoslav** ['ju:gəu'slɑ:v] a, n jugoslavo(a).

**Yugoslavia** ['ju:gəu'slɑ:vɪə] n Jugoslavia.

**yuppie** ['jʌpɪ] n, a (col) yuppie (m/f inv).

**YWCA** n abbr (= Young Women's Christian Association) Y.W.C.A. m.

# Z

**zany** ['zeɪnɪ] a un po' pazzo(a).

**zap** [zæp] vt (COMPUT) cancellare.

**zeal** [zi:l] n zelo; entusiasmo.

**zebra** ['zi:brə] n zebra; ~

**crossing** n (Brit) (passaggio pedonale a) strisce fpl, zebre fpl.

**zero** ['zɪərəu] n zero.

**zest** [zɛst] n gusto; (CULIN) buccia.

**zigzag** ['zɪgzæg] n zigzag m inv // vi zigzagare.

**Zimbabwe** [zɪm'bɑ:bwɪ] n Zimbabwe m.

**zinc** [zɪŋk] n zinco.

**zip** [zɪp] n (also: ~ **fastener**, (US) ~**per**) chiusura f or cerniera f lampo inv // vt (also: ~ **up**) chiudere con una cerniera lampo; ~ **code** n (US) codice m di avviamento postale.

**zodiac** ['zəudiæk] n zodiaco.

**zombie** ['zɒmbɪ] n (fig): like a ~ come un morto che cammina.

**zone** [zəun] n zona; (subdivision of town) quartiere m.

**zoo** [zu:] n zoo m inv.

**zoology** [zu:'ɔlədʒɪ] n zoologia.

**zoom** [zu:m] vi: to ~ **past** sfrecciare; ~ **lens** n zoom m inv, obiettivo a focale variabile.

**zucchini** [zu:'ki:nɪ] npl (US: courgettes) zucchine fpl.

# ITALIAN VERBS

*1* Gerundio *2* Participio passato *3* Presente *4* Imperfetto *5* Passato remoto *6* Futuro *7* Condizionale *8* Congiuntivo presente *9* Congiuntivo passato *10* Imperativo

**andare** *3* vado, vai, va, andiamo, andate, vanno *6* andrò *etc 8* vada *10* va'!, vada!, andate!, vadano!

**apparire** *2* apparso *3* appaio, appari *o* apparisci, appare *o* apparisce, appaiono *o* appariscono *5* apparvi *o* apparsi, app_aristi, apparve *o* apparì *o* apparse, apparvero *o* apparirono *o* apparsero *8* appaia *o* apparisca

**aprire** *2* aperto *3* apro *5* aprii *o* apersi, apristi *8* apra

**AVERE** *3* ho, hai, ha, abbiamo, avete, hanno *5* ebbi, avesti, ebbe, avemmo, aveste, ebbero *6* avrò *etc 8* abbia *etc 10* abbi!, abbia!, abbiate!, abbiano!

**bere** *1* bevendo *2* bevuto *3* bevo *etc 4* bevevo *etc 8* beva *etc 9* bevessi *etc*

**cadere** *5* caddi, cadesti *6* cadrò *etc*

**cogliere** *2* colto *3* colgo, colgono *5* colsi, cogliesti *8* colga

**correre** *2* corso *5* corsi, corresti

**cuocere** *2* cotto *3* cuocio, cociamo, cuociono *5* cossi, cocesti

**dare** *3* do, dai, da, diamo, date, danno *5* diedi *o* detti, desti *6* darò *etc 8* dia *etc 9* dessi *etc 10* da'!, dia!, date!, diano!

**dire** *1* dicendo *2* detto *3* dico, dici, dice, diciamo, dite, dicono *4* dicevo *etc 5* dissi, dicesti

*6* dirò *etc 8* dica, diciamo, diciate, dicano *9* dicessi *etc 10* di'!, dica!, dite!, dicano!

**dolere** *3* dolgo, duoli, duole, dolgono *5* dolsi, dolesti *6* dorrò *etc 8* dolga

**dovere** *3* devo *o* debbo, devi, deve, dobbiamo, dovete, devono *o* debbono *6* dovrò *etc 8* debba, dobbiamo, dobbiate, devano *o* debbano

**ESSERE** *2* stato *3* sono, sei, è, siamo, siete, sono *4* ero, eri, era, eravamo, eravate, erano *5* fui, fosti, fu, fummo, foste, furono *6* sarò *etc 8* sia *etc 9* fossi, fossi, fosse, fossimo, foste, fossero *10* sii!, sia!, siate!, siano!

**fare** *1* facendo *2* fatto *3* faccio, fai, fa, facciamo, fate, fanno *4* facevo *etc 5* feci, facesti *6* farò *etc 8* faccia *etc 9* facessi *etc 10* fa'!, faccia!, fate!, facciano!

**FINIRE** *1* finendo *2* finito *3* finisco, finisci, finisce, finiamo, finite, finiscono *4* finivo, finivi, finiva, finivamo, finivate, finivano *5* finii, finisti, finì, finimmo, finiste, finirono *6* finirò, finirai, finirà, finiremo, finirete, finiranno *7* finirei, finiresti, finirebbe, finiremmo, finireste, finirebbero *8* finisca, finisca, finisca, finiamo, finiate, finiscano *9* finissi, finissi, finisse, finissimo, finiste, finissero *10*

311

finisci!, finisca!, finite!, finiscano!

**giungere** *2* giunto *5* giunsi, giungesti

**leggere** *2* letto *5* lessi, leggesti

**mettere** *2* messo *5* misi, mettesti

**morire** *2* morto *3* muoio, muori, muore, moriamo, morite, muoiono *6* morirò o morrò *etc 8* muoia

**muovere** *2* mosso *5* mossi, movesti

**nascere** *2* nato *5* nacqui, nascesti

**nuocere** *2* nuociuto *3* nuoccio, nuoci, nuoce, nociamo o nuociamo, nuocete, nuocciono *4* nuocevo *etc 5* nocqui, nuocesti *6* nuocerò *etc 7* nuoccia

**offrire** *2* offerto *3* offro *5* offersi o offrii, offristi *8* offra

**parere** *2* parso *3* paio, paiamo, paiono *5* parvi o parsi, paresti *6* parrò *etc 8* paia, paiamo, pariate, paiano

**PARLARE** *1* parlando *2* parlato *3* parlo, parli, parla, parliamo, parlate, parlano *4* parlavo, parlavi, parlava, parlavamo, parlavate, parlavano *5* parlai, parlasti, *parlò, parlammo, parlaste, parlarono *6* parlerò, parlerai, parlerà, parleremo, parlerete, parleranno *7* parlerei, parleresti, parlerebbe, parleremmo, parlereste, parlerebbero *8* parli, parli, parli, parliamo, parliate, parlino *9* parlassi, parlassi, parlasse, parlassimo, parlaste, parlassero *10* parla!, parli!, parlate!, parlino!

**piacere** *2* piaciuto *3* piaccio, piacciamo, piacciono *5* piac-

qui, piacesti *8* piaccia *etc*

**porre** *1* ponendo *2* posto *3* pongo, poni, pone, poniamo, ponete, pongono *4* ponevo *etc 5* posi, ponesti *6* porrò *etc 8* ponga, poniamo, poniate, pongano *9* ponessi *etc*

**potere** *3* posso, puoi, può, possiamo, potete, possono *6* potrò *etc 8* possa, possiamo, possiate, possano

**prendere** *2* preso *5* presi, prendesti

**ridurre** *1* riducendo *2* ridotto *3* riduco *etc 4* riducevo *etc 5* ridussi, riducesti *6* ridurrò *etc 8* riduca *etc 9* riducessi *etc*

**riempire** *1* riempiendo *3* riempio, riempi, riempie, riempiono

**rimanere** *2* rimasto *3* rimango, rimangono *5* rimasi, rimanesti *6* rimarrò *etc 8* rimanga

**rispondere** *2* risposto *5* risposi, rispondesti

**salire** *3* salgo, sali, salgono *8* salga

**sapere** *3* so, sai, sa, sappiamo, sapete, sanno *5* seppi, sapesti *6* saprò *etc 8* sappia *etc 10* sappi!, sappia!, sappiate!, sappiano!

**scrivere** *2* scritto *5* scrissi, scrivesti

**sedere** *3* siedo, siedi, siede, siedono *8* sieda

**spegnere** *3* spento *5* spengo, spengono *5* spensi, spegnesti *8* spenga

**stare** *2* stato *3* sto, stai, sta, stiamo, state, stanno *5* stetti, stesti *6* starò *etc 8* stia *etc 10* stessi *etc 10* sta'!, stia!, state!, stiano!

312

**tacere** *2* taciuto *3* taccio, tacciono *5* tacqui, tacesti *8* taccia

**tenere** *3* tengo, tieni, tiene, tengono *5* tenni, tenesti *6* terrò *etc* *8* tenga

**trarre** *1* traendo *2* tratto *3* traggo, trai, trae, traiamo, traete, traggono *4* traevo *etc* *5* trassi, traesti *6* trarrò *etc* *8* tragga *9* traessi *etc*

**udire** *3* odo, odi, ode, odono *8* oda

**uscire** *3* esco, esci, esce, escono *8* esca

**valere** *2* valso *3* valgo, valgono *5* valsi, valesti *6* varrò *etc* *8* valga

**vedere** *2* visto *o* veduto *5* vidi, vedesti *6* vedrò *etc*

**VENDERE** *1* vendendo *2* venduto *3* vendo, vendi, vende, vendiamo, vendete, vendono *4* vendevo, vendevi, vendeva, vendevamo, vendevate, vendevano *5* vendei *o* vendetti, vendesti, vendé *o* vendette, vendemmo, vendeste, venderono *o* vendettero *6* venderò, venderai, venderà, venderemo, venderete, venderanno *7* venderei, venderesti, venderebbe, venderemmo, vendereste, venderebbero *8* venda, venda, venda, vendiamo, vendiate, vendano *9* vendessi, vendessi, vendesse, vendessimo, vendeste, vendessero *10* vendi!, venda!, vendete!, vendano!

**venire** *2* venuto *3* vengo, vieni, viene, vengono *5* venni, venisti *6* verrò *etc* *8* venga

**vivere** *2* vissuto *5* vissi, vivesti

**volere** *3* voglio, vuoi, vuole, vogliamo, volete, vogliono *5* volli, volesti *6* vorrò *etc* *8* voglia *etc* *10* vogli!, voglia!, vogliate!, vogliano!

313

# VERBI INGLESI

| present | pt | pp | present | pt | pp |
|---------|-----|-----|---------|-----|-----|
| arise | arose | arisen | do (3rd | did | done |
| awake | awoke | awaked | person; | | |
| be (am, is, | was, were | been | he/she/it/ | | |
| are; | | | does) | | |
| being) | | | draw | drew | drawn |
| bear | bore | born(e) | dream | dreamed, | dreamed, |
| beat | beat | beaten | | dreamt | dreamt |
| become | became | become | drink | drank | drunk |
| begin | began | begun | drive | drove | driven |
| behold | beheld | beheld | dwell | dwelt | dwelt |
| bend | bent | bent | eat | ate | eaten |
| beseech | besought | besought | fall | fell | fallen |
| beset | beset | beset | feed | fed | fed |
| bet | bet, betted | bet, betted | feel | felt | felt |
| bid | bid, bade | bid, bidden | fight | fought | fought |
| bind | bound | bound | find | found | found |
| bite | bit | bitten | flee | fled | fled |
| bleed | bled | bled | fling | flung | flung |
| blow | blew | blown | fly | flew | flown |
| break | broke | broken | forbid | forbade | forbidden |
| breed | bred | bred | forego | forewent | foregone |
| bring | brought | brought | foresee | foresaw | foreseen |
| build | built | built | foretell | foretold | foretold |
| burn | burnt, | burnt, | forget | forgot | forgotten |
| | burned | burned | forgive | forgave | forgiven |
| burst | burst | burst | forsake | forsook | forsaken |
| buy | bought | bought | freeze | froze | frozen |
| can | could | (been | get | got | got, (US) |
| | | able) | | | gotten |
| cast | cast | cast | give | gave | given |
| catch | caught | caught | go (goes) | went | gone |
| choose | chose | chosen | grind | ground | ground |
| cling | clung | clung | grow | grew | grown |
| come | came | come | hang | hung, | hung, |
| cost | cost | cost | | hanged | hanged |
| creep | crept | crept | have | had | had |
| cut | cut | cut | hear | heard | heard |
| deal | dealt | dealt | hide | hid | hidden |
| dig | dug | dug | hit | hit | hit |

| present | pt | pp | present | pt | pp |
|---|---|---|---|---|---|
| hold | held | held | sell | sold | sold |
| hurt | hurt | hurt | send | sent | sent |
| keep | kept | kept | set | set | set |
| kneel | knelt, | knelt, | shake | shook | shaken |
| | kneeled | kneeled | shall | should | — |
| know | knew | known | shear | sheared | shorn, |
| lay | laid | laid | | | sheared |
| lead | led | led | shed | shed | shed |
| lean | leant, | leant, | shine | shone | shone |
| | leaned | leaned | shoot | shot | shot |
| leap | leapt, | leapt, | show | showed | shown |
| | leaped | leaped | shrink | shrank | shrunk |
| learn | learnt, | learnt, | shut | shut | shut |
| | learned | learned | sing | sang | sung |
| leave | left | left | sink | sank | sunk |
| lend | lent | lent | sit | sat | sat |
| let | let | let | slay | slew | slain |
| lie (lying) | lay | lain | sleep | slept | slept |
| light | lit, lighted | lit, lighted | slide | slid | slid |
| lose | lost | lost | sling | slung | slung |
| make | made | made | slit | slit | slit |
| may | might | — | smell | smelt, | smelt, |
| mean | meant | meant | | smelled | smelled |
| meet | met | met | sow | sowed | sown, |
| mistake | mistook | mistaken | | | sowed |
| mow | mowed | mown, | speak | spoke | spoken |
| | | mowed | speed | sped, | sped, |
| must | (had to) | (had to) | | speeded | speeded |
| pay | paid | paid | spell | spelt, | spelt, |
| put | put | put | | spelled | spelled |
| quit | quit, | quit, | spend | spent | spent |
| | quitted | quitted | spill | spilt, | spilt, |
| read | read | read | | spilled | spilled |
| rid | rid | rid | spin | spun | spun |
| ride | rode | ridden | spit | spat | spat |
| ring | rang | rung | split | split | split |
| rise | rose | risen | spoil | spoiled, | spoiled, |
| run | ran | run | | spoilt | spoilt |
| saw | sawed | sawn | spread | spread | spread |
| say | said | said | spring | sprang | sprung |
| see | saw | seen | stand | stood | stood |
| seek | sought | sought | steal | stole | stolen |

315

| present | pt | pp | present | pt | pp |
|---------|-----|-----|---------|-----|-----|
| stick | stuck | stuck | think | thought | thought |
| sting | stung | stung | throw | threw | thrown |
| stink | stank | stunk | thrust | thrust | thrust |
| stride | strode | strode | tread | trod | trodden |
| strike | struck | struck, stricken | wake | woke, waked | woken, waked |
| strive | strove | striven | waylay | waylaid | waylaid |
| swear | swore | sworn | wear | wore | worn |
| sweep | swept | swept | weave | wove, weaved | woven, weaved |
| swell | swelled | swollen, swelled | wed | wedded, wed | wedded, wed |
| swim | swam | swum | | | |
| swing | swung | swung | weep | wept | wept |
| take | took | taken | win | won | won |
| teach | taught | taught | wind | wound | wound |
| tear | tore | torn | wring | wrung | wrung |
| tell | told | told | write | wrote | written |

# I NUMERI

# NUMBERS

| | | |
|---|---|---|
| uno(a) | 1 | one |
| due | 2 | two |
| tre | 3 | three |
| quattro | 4 | four |
| cinque | 5 | five |
| sei | 6 | six |
| sette | 7 | seven |
| otto | 8 | eight |
| nove | 9 | nine |
| dieci | 10 | ten |
| undici | 11 | eleven |
| dodici | 12 | twelve |
| tredici | 13 | thirteen |
| quattordici | 14 | fourteen |
| quindici | 15 | fifteen |
| sedici | 16 | sixteen |
| diciassette | 17 | seventeen |
| diciotto | 18 | eighteen |
| diciannove | 19 | nineteen |
| venti | 20 | twenty |
| ventuno | 21 | twenty-one |
| ventidue | 22 | twenty-two |
| ventitré | 23 | twenty-three |
| ventotto | 28 | twenty-eight |
| trenta | 30 | thirty |
| quaranta | 40 | forty |
| cinquanta | 50 | fifty |
| sessanta | 60 | sixty |
| settanta | 70 | seventy |
| ottanta | 80 | eighty |
| novanta | 90 | ninety |
| cento | 100 | a hundred, one hundred |
| cento uno | 101 | a hundred and one |
| duecento | 200 | two hundred |
| mille | 1 000 | a thousand, one thousand |
| milleduecentodue | 1 202 | one thousand two hundred and two |
| cinquemila | 5 000 | five thousand |
| un milione | 1 000 000 | a million, one million |
| primo(a) | | first |
| secondo(a) | | second |
| terzo(a) | | third |
| quarto(a) | | fourth |
| quinto(a) | | fifth |
| sesto(a) | | sixth |

317

# I NUMERI

# NUMBERS

| | |
|---|---|
| settimo(a) | seventh |
| ottavo(a) | eighth |
| nono(a) | ninth |
| decimo(a) | tenth |
| undicesimo(a) | eleventh |
| dodicesimo(a) | twelfth |
| tredicesimo(a) | thirteenth |
| quattordicesimo(a) | fourteenth |
| quindicesimo(a) | fifteenth |
| sedicesimo(a) | sixteenth |
| diciassettesimo(a) | seventeenth |
| diciottesimo(a) | eighteenth |
| diciannovesimo(a) | nineteenth |
| ventesimo(a) | twentieth |
| ventunesimo(a) | twenty-first |
| ventiduesimo(a) | twenty-second |
| ventitreesimo(a) | twenty-third |
| ventottesimo(a) | twenty-eighth |
| trentesimo(a) | thirtieth |
| centesimo(a) | hundredth |
| centunesimo(a) | hundred-and-first |
| millesimo(a) | thousandth |
| milionesimo(a) | millionth |

### Frazioni etc

### Fractions etc

| | |
|---|---|
| mezzo | half |
| terzo | third |
| due terzi | two thirds |
| quarto | quarter |
| quinto | fifth |
| zero virgola cinque, 0,5 | (nought) point five, 0.5 |
| tre virgola quattro, 3,4 | three point four, 3.4 |
| dieci per cento | ten per cent |
| cento per cento | a hundred per cent |

### Esempi

### Examples

| | |
|---|---|
| abita al numero dieci | he lives at number 10 |
| si trova nel capitolo sette, a pagina sette | it's in chapter 7, on page 7 |
| abita al terzo piano | he lives on the 3rd floor |
| arrivò quarto | he came in 4th |
| scala uno a venticinquemila | scale 1:25,000 |

| **L'ORA** | **THE TIME** |
|---|---|
| *che ora è?, che ore sono?* | *what time is it?* |
| *è ..., sono ...* | *it is ...* |
| mezzanotte | midnight, twelve pm |
| l'una (della mattina) | one o'clock (in the morning), one (am) |
| l'una e cinque | five past one |
| l'una e dieci | ten past one |
| l'una e un quarto, l'una e quindici | a quarter past one, one fifteen |
| l'una e venticinque | twenty-five past one, one twenty-five |
| l'una e mezzo o mezza, l'una e trenta | half-past one, one thirty |
| le due meno venticinque, l'una e trentacinque | twenty-five to two, one thirty-five |
| le due meno venti, l'una e quaranta | twenty to two, one forty |
| le due meno un quarto, l'una e quarantacinque | a quarter to two, one forty-five |
| le due meno dieci, l'una e cinquanta | ten to two, one fifty |
| mezzogiorno | twelve o'clock, midday, noon |
| l'una, le tredici | one o'clock (in the afternoon), one (pm) |
| le sette (di sera), le diciannove | seven o'clock (in the evening), seven (pm) |
| *a che ora?* | *at what time?* |
| a mezzanotte | at midnight |
| all'una, alle tredici | at one o'clock |
| fra venti minuti | in twenty minutes |
| venti minuti fa | twenty minutes ago |

88-04-21688-3

90
1